Canary Citizens

Centenary Edition

The Official History of Norwich City F.C.

By Mike Davage, John Eastwood and Kevan Platt

JARROLD
publishing

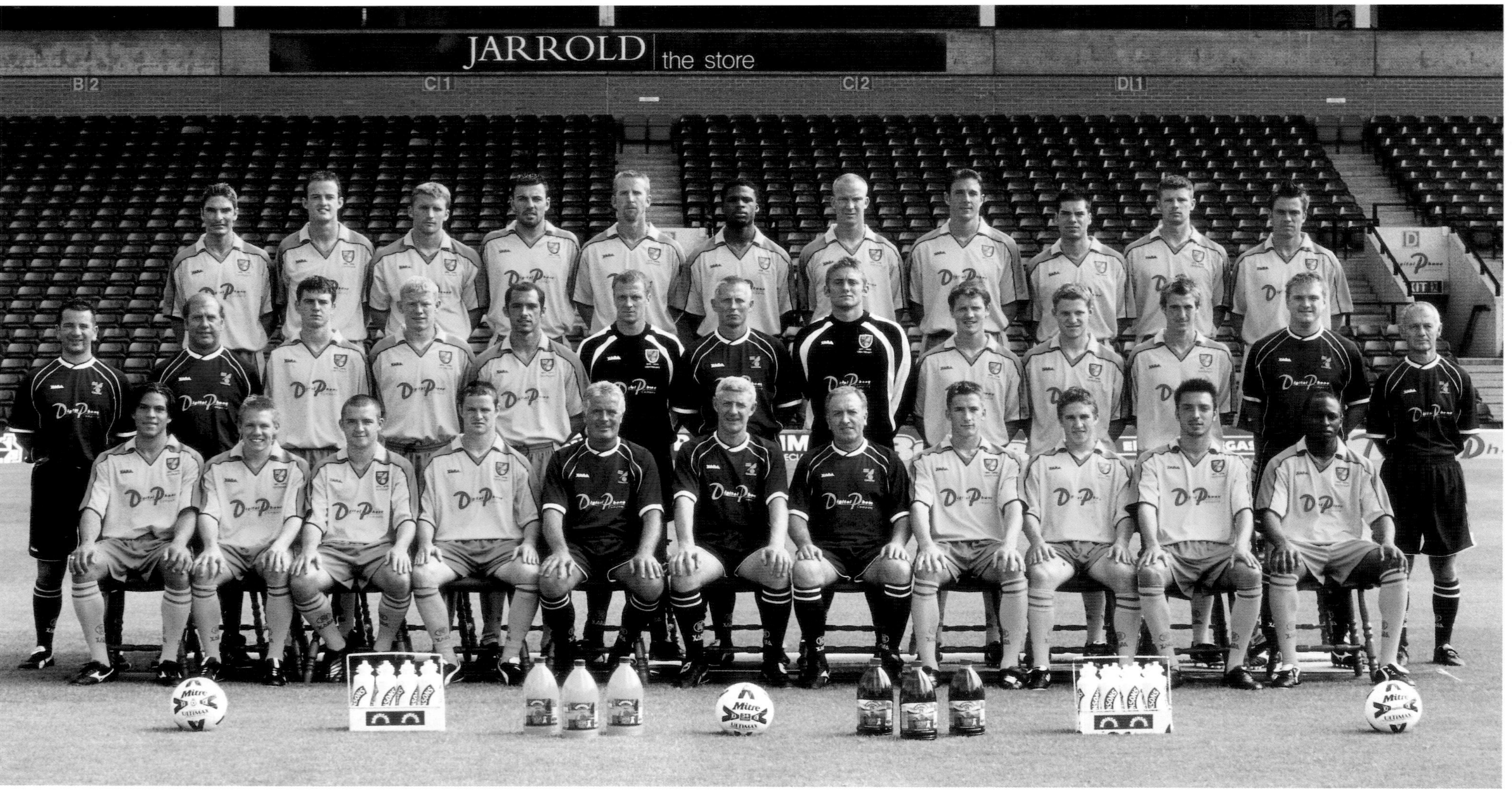

Norwich City 2001/2002

Back Row (left to right) Steen Nedergaard, Brian McGovern, Matt Jackson, Marc Libbra, Iwan Roberts, Zema Abbey, Neil Emblen, Malcolm Mackay, Gaetano Giallanza, Adrian Coote, Daryl Sutch

Middle Row (left to right) Dave Carolan (Sports Scientist), Terry Postle (Kit Manager), Chris Llewellyn, Gary Holt, Craig Fleming, Paul Crichton, Keith Webb (Reserve Team Coach), Robert Green, Mark Rivers, Lewis Blois, Paul Dalglish, Neal Reynolds (Physiotherapist), Keith Creamer (Assitant Physiotherapist)

Front Row (left to right) Darel Russell, Danny Bloomfield, Alex Notman, Philip Mulryne, Steve Foley (First Team Coach), Nigel Worthington (Manager), Doug Livermore (Assistant Manager), Adam Drury, Paul McVeigh, Clint Easton, Darren Kenton

Contents

"ON THE BALL, CITY!"

The Gentleman from Gillingham: "'Er, don't think I'm after your players."

The Canary: "No; but I don't doubt they'll be after you."

[Gillingham (the wooden spoonist of the Southern League) were at the Nest to-day.]

On the ball, City

In the days to call, which we have left behind,
Our boyhood's glorious game,
And our youthful vigour has declined
With its mirth and its lonesome end;
You will think of the time, the happy time,
Its memories fond recall
When in the bloom of your youthful prime
We've kept upon the ball

Kick off, throw it in, have a little scrimmage,
Keep it low, a splendid rush, bravo, win or die;
On the ball, City, never mind the danger,
Steady on, now's your chance,
Hurrah! We've scored a goal.

Let all tonight then drink with me
To the football game we love,
And wish it may successful be
As other games of old,
And in one grand united toast
Join player, game and song,
And fondly pledge your pride and toast,
Success to the City club.

Kick off, throw it in, have a little scrimmage,
Keep it low, a splendid rush, bravo, win or die;
On the ball, City, never mind the danger,
Steady on, now's your chance,
Hurrah! We've scored a goal.

The Norwich City FC anthem

Designed by Paul Westley, assisted by Don Friston

Project Management by Malcolm Crampton and
Sarah Letts for Jarrold Publishing

Edited by Mike Davage, John Eastwood, Kevan Platt and Tom Albrighton

Photographs supplied by Mike Davage, Eastern Counties Newspapers Group Limited, Jarrold Publishing, Dick Middleton, Norwich City Football Club Limited, Paul Stanley.

Printed and bound by Norwich Colour Print Limited
Reprographics by Anglia Colour Digital Origination

ISBN 0-7117-2020-7

Published by Jarrold Publishing, Whitefriars, Norwich NR3 1TR

Foreword

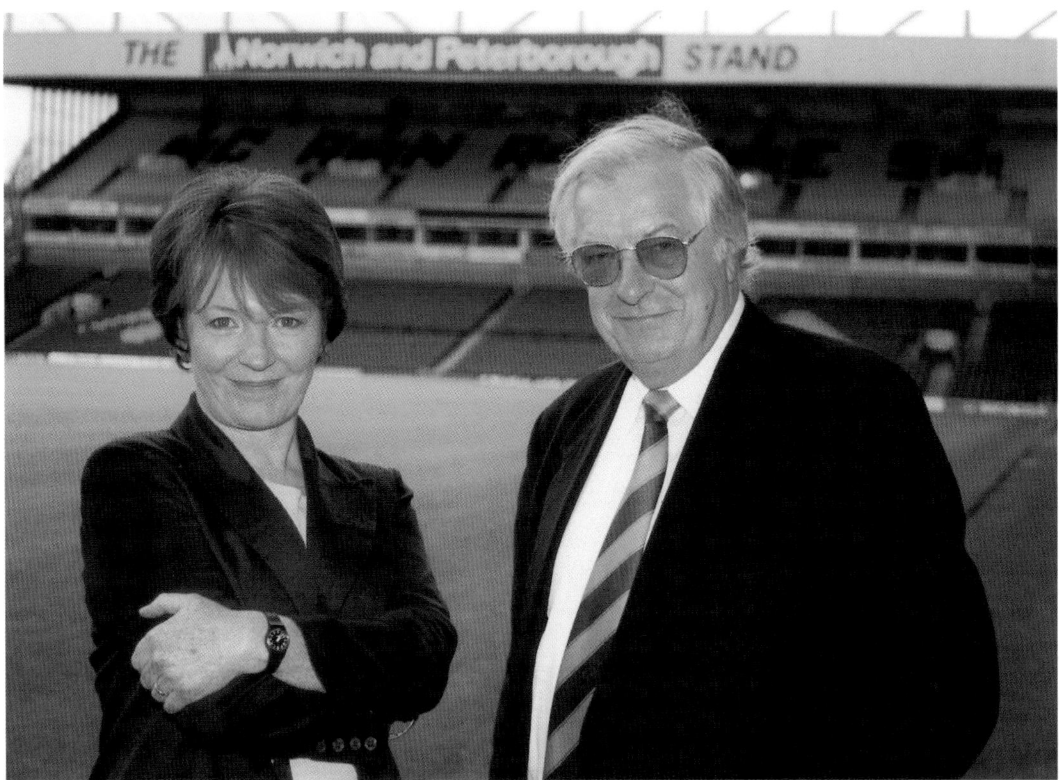

I have always envied those people who can reel off the names of, for instance, the Club's promotion-winning side of 1959/60 or can answer those fiendish quizzes (how many Norwich players have had names beginning with Y?) off the top of their heads. Somehow these 'Stattos' make me feel rather an inadequate supporter – and in one sense I am. How much attention have I been paying for the last fifty years? Yet I also have the irresistable urge to question their infallibility and prove them wrong! But I didn't have the means at my disposal.

Now I have. As a crib for becoming Norwich City quiz champion or taking the Canaries as your special subject on Mastermind, this updated edition of Canary Citizens is indispensable. It will also come in very handy when you bump into one of our Canary Legends during centenary year and want to break the ice. ('I see you started your career with Hamilton Academicals, that must have been interesting!')

But most important of all this book is an introduction to the family. All football clubs are extended families, and Norwich City is a particularly close-knit one. Canary Citizens is like a family tree – here are all those who have shared the same frustrations and triumphs, the same disappointments and joys over the past one hundred years and played their part in shaping events which have made our Club what it is today. They are part of us and we are part of them, if you want to know who they were, this book will tell you everything you could ever want to know.

Michael Wynn Jones

Preface and Acknowledgements

The acknowledgements pages of Canary Citizens and Glorious Canaries bore testimony to individuals and institutions who contributed to those sold out publications and my heartfelt thanks to all so mentioned therein. To all who subscribed and purchased the previous volumes you can take credit for my spending another decade of dedication, cross-referencing, and employment of technology not around previously. Added to historians, statisticians and supporters help; research in libraries, newspapers, football periodicals and club histories and census returns usage have been the welcome medium of CD Roms, Commonwealth War Graves and Ancestry sites, the World Wide Web, US Social Security records etc.

The 'Who's Who' segment alone has nearly a million characters when converted into a word document. There are only eight players and/or their families that I haven't spoken to yet, hence this is the only club history that traces careers back to the players' schooldays. Sadly we have lost 51 first eleven Football League players since 1990 – all of them reached a standard that the majority of supporters can only dream of.

Pride of place for assistance goes to Jim Creasy, my mentor and purveyor of wisdom. We have been jointly committed for nigh on 20 years for attempting to research, and therefore improve, football history. I am a massive baseball fan and I long for the day that one can quote stats as they do at almost a drop of a hat. John Eastwood is acknowledged because he wrote the original text, with pointers, as the co-author of Canary Citizens. I am thrilled to include the current Club Secretary Kevan Platt. He has been the driving force behind this book – completed in near record time. Do not, however, talk to him about line-up grids as he has seen at first hand the nightmare within. To my proofreaders Christina Bridger and Sophie Hubble – valued friends who both did well to read their segments, considering that they are not sports fans. Step forward James Woodrow for research that challenged the findings of the first Canary Citizens. I am always grateful for others' constructive views.

In addition to James' invaluable input I must also thank several other keen Canary fans who have granted their permission to reproduce the photographs which so enhance this revised edition: namely Paul Standley, Dick Middleton and Richard Bland. The Picture Library at Eastern Counties Newspapers Group Ltd allowed Kevan to raid their files and long-time club photographer, Roger Harris, for whom capturing the Canaries' greatest moments in the last twenty years has been a labour of love and we give them due accreditation. And finally, I must acknowledge Malcolm Crampton and Sarah Letts and all their staff at Jarrold for their hard work in producing and publishing this weighty volume in such a short time span – a truly tremendous effort!

Be proud of your club and respectful in rivalry towards the opposition's fans.

Mike Davage

31st August 2001

Introduction

Approach the ancient city of Norwich whichever way you will and one is constantly reminded that here is a very fine city indeed. Norwich stands on the river Wensum in the heartland of the county of Norfolk. Perched high above the colourful open market is the magnificently preserved Norman castle and nearby stands the equally handsome and ancient cathedral. The city derives its name from the Saxon North-Wic, the town or settlement in the north. It is said that Edward III brought the artisans of Bruges and Ghent to settle here. Their assistance was vital in the development of the woollen industry which brought great wealth to the city. Indeed in 1771 Norwich, with a population of 36,000, was the third greatest provincial centre in the land, surpassed only by Bristol and York. After the industrial revolution Norwich declined in power and had to find new industries to replace the faltering textile trade. The manufacture of boots and shoes gained in importance and it was a Norwich shopkeeper who hit upon the idea of stocking footwear in differing sizes. Jeremiah Colman moved his mustard processing works into the city in 1856 from nearby Stoke Holy Cross and Norwich soon became an important agricultural centre trading in grain and cattle. Another important, if slightly unusual, venture was the breeding and exporting of canaries. It was the Flemish immigrants who fostered the breeding of canaries and by the turn of the century over 30,000 were exported annually. Norfolk canaries were in great demand and it was estimated that there were between 2,000 and 3,000 breeders in the city by 1900. A working man might expect to cover the cost of his rent if he was fortunate enough to have a good stock. Later we shall see just how important this activity was but let us now turn our attention to the summer of 1902.

Below, the 1903-04 team

Right, an aerial view of the first match at Carrow Road, where Captain Doug Lochhead had the honour of scoring the first goal for City

The summer of 1902 was as eventful as it was wet and cold. On 31 May the Boer War ended and men from the Norfolk Regiment received a rapturous welcome at Thorpe Station as they returned home to their native county. On 26 June a Coronation Fete was held in Norwich, and it was estimated that the event attracted over 80,000 people. Edward VII became King after the death of his mother Queen Victoria on 22 January 1901 but his Coronation did not take place until the following year. In July Arthur James Balfour succeeded the 3rd Marquess of Salisbury as the Tory Prime Minister and late in the summer two American brothers commenced work on the first flying machine. The brothers were of course the Wright brothers, Orville and Wilber, and their prototype eventually took to the air on 17 December 1903 at Kitty Hawk, North Carolina. The Australian cricket team led by Joe Darling toured England that summer and had to face the worst of English weather. In the first Test at Birmingham, incidentally the first Test to be played in that city, the Australians were bowled out for only 36 in their first innings but rain prevented any play until 5.15pm on the third day and England were deprived of a possible victory. At Lord's in the second Test rain prevented any play on the second and third days (Test matches were restricted to three days in 1902), and only 105 minutes play had been possible on the first. Australia managed to win the third and fourth Tests, the latter by a margin of only 3 runs, and the final encounter at the Oval in August will always be remembered for the innings played by Gilbert Jessop on the last afternoon. When he came to the wicket England were 48 for 5, needing 215 more runs to win. He hit the ball all around the ground and reached his century in 75 minutes and when he was finally dismissed it was left to the legendary Hirst and Rhodes to complete a famous victory.

So then, in that summer of 1902, it was

Trumper and Jessop, Fry and MacLaren, and Hirst and Rhodes who figured prominently in the newspaper headlines. In the football world Sheffield United held the FA Cup and Sunderland the League Championship. In the Final of the FA Cup Sheffield United beat Southampton 2–1 after a replay. The first match finished 1–1 and the United goal was scored by Alf Common. Common was later transferred to Sunderland for the first £500 transfer fee, and in February 1905 he moved on to Middlesborough for the first £1,000 fee. In 1902 England regularly selected a centre forward from Derby County called Steve Bloomer who coincidentally also later moved to Middlesbrough. Despite all this activity the summer of 1902 will be remembered in Norfolk for a very different reason for on the evening of Tuesday 17 June 1902 the Norwich City Football Club, the most easterly of the 92 Football League teams, first saw the light of day.

Before we look in detail at that historic event we must briefly take a look at the very roots of football in Norfolk. The first recorded reference to football in the county appeared in the Norfolk Chronicle of Saturday 19 December 1868. The article was headed 'Norwich football Club' and continued ...

> *"We understand that a club bearing this name has just started in Norwich, and has already begun to play upon the Norfolk & Norwich cricket ground, where the members meet for practice on the Tuesday and Thursday of each week during the winter months. Mr Croker has been elected president and Edward J. Field secretary. The club already numbers upward of 30 members, but is still open to gentlemen who having been proposed by a member will send in their names to the secretary for the approval of the committee. We wish the club every success and hope to hear of some football matches before the close of the season."*

Later the paper went on to report some of the matches, and quite clearly these were not reports of association football as we know it today. Very often there were 13 or 14 players a side, 'touch downs' were obtained, and 'tries' were kicked. The club continued until about 1872 and we conclude that the venture was more related to the rugby code than to association and certainly cannot be regarded as important in the development of the latter.

By 1880 however there is evidence that

Canary fans at the FA Cup Semi-Final of 1958-59

association football was being played in Norfolk. Much credit for the popularisation and development of the game is due to Walter Edward Hansell. Hansell was born in Norfolk and attended Charterhouse School, a noted nursery of the association game. He gained an FA Cup winners medal with their old boy's team Old Carthusians in 1881. Old Carthusians beat Old Etonians 3–0 in the final at Kennington Oval on Saturday 9 April 1881. Just two months before this great match Hansell proposed that the time was ripe for the formation of a County Football Association in Norfolk. A meeting was held on 3 February 1881 at the Black Horse Hotel, King's Lynn and the Association was formed. A further meeting was held in Norwich on 24 February

Dave Watson lifts The 1985 Silver Jubilee Milk Cup (dubbed the 'Friendly Final', versus Sunderland) – the victory smiles could not be wider

1881 and attended by clubs from King's Lynn, Norwich, Downham Market and North Walsham. It was proposed that the Association should run a Challenge Cup competition the first Final of which was held at Lakenham on 11 March 1882. Over 1,000 spectators saw Norfolk & Norwich become the first holders of the trophy when they beat King's Lynn 3–1. Hansell, who was also a gifted musician, later became a solicitor in Norwich, and upon his death on Wednesday 25 May 1938 he was aptly described as the 'father' of Norfolk football.

It could not be said that association football was an instant success in Norfolk, indeed only 50 people attended the first County game between Norfolk and Suffolk and the editor of the local paper even wanted to charge 15s 0d (75p) to report the game. Gradually though the number of

Introduction

Efan Ekoku scores City's first ever goal in Europe

Chris Sutton, Jerry Goss, Rob Newman and Daryl Sutch celebrate that fantastic victory in Munich's Olympic Stadium

clubs increased and over the years some interesting and colourful characters emerged e.g. Henry Peter Hansell, younger brother of Walter, who kept goal for Norfolk County and Thorpe, a schoolmaster by profession he was for some years private tutor to the sons of King George V and Major Percy Wiltshire, who sometimes preferred to appear as 'V.E. Teran'. Occasionally a player would appear as 'O.N.E. More' or 'O.L.D. One' which surely shows more imagination than the current hackneyed standby 'A.N. Other'. One early newspaper report noted that 'surely the policy of having more than one half back is a doubtful tactic, the old formation of a goalkeeper, a full back, a single half back and eight forwards is much more reliable' – what would the modern coach make of that? One last quote from the Eastern Daily Press, Norfolk County had just suffered their heaviest defeat to date – an 11–0 reverse at Northampton. The following morning the paper explained the defeat in the following manner, –

> *"The sticky ground, the number of new hands in the side, the offside tactics of the Northampton defence and the very questionable nature of the goals (what all of them?), all told, more or less heavily, against the Norfolk Men. This when added to the very tiresome journey of over 5 hours and the unreliable play of the substitute goalkeeper Loomes makes it a very forgettable day."*

Loomes, may we add was loaned to Norfolk by Northampton.

Between 1880 and the turn of the century a number of new clubs sprang up all over Norfolk. Some just changed their name e.g. Norfolk & Norwich became Norwich Wanderers but most were entirely new concerns. On the east coast there were Yarmouth Town, Yarmouth Fearnoughts and Yarmouth Royal Artillery, there were Cromer and Sheringham in the north of the county and in the west there were Lynn Town and Lynn Alexandra. In Norwich there were Thorpe, Carrow Works, Swifans and Norwich Teachers, but most important of all was the Norwich Church of England Young Men's Society. Known locally as 'Church' or 'Initials' the Society was founded in April 1847 in order to promote and establish religious principles in the young men of the day. They moved in turn from St Clement's Schoolroom, to Rackham's Court, to Rampant Horse Street, to St Peters Street and in 1875 to Orford Place. As well as bible classes and mission work the Society encouraged the young men to indulge in athletic activity. Sadly the first attempt to form a cricket team failed in 1864 because the evening clashed with the bible class, but later all sorts of sporting activity took place including, on 22 August 1888, the creation of a football section. In August 1889 the Recreation Ground at Earlham Road was leased from the Church Commissioners at a yearly rental of £21. The section was an immediate success and the club were quickly established as the premier football club in the city of Norwich. Between 1897 and 1902 CEYMS won the Norfolk Senior Cup on four occasions and the club progressed from strength to strength. The captain and vice captain were respectively Robert Webster and Joseph Cowper Nutchey and it was Webster and Nutchey who issued a circular in that summer of 1902 inviting interested persons to join them in a new and very exciting adventure.

Carrow Road, August 2001

1902–1903

Notice appeared in the Eastern Daily Press (EDP from now on) of Saturday 14 June 1902 that a meeting was to be held at the Criterion Cafe in White Lion Street on Tuesday next at 8.30 in the evening. The purpose of the gathering was to form the Norwich City Football Club and the circulars dispatched to interested parties were duly signed by Webster and Nutchey. Both Robert Webster and Joseph Cowper Nutchey were schoolmasters in Norwich, but while Webster was a local man, Nutchey, marginally the younger of the two, was a native of Yorkshire. Robert Webster was born in Norwich in September 1858 and after attending Norman's School in the city trained to become a teacher at York Training College. He returned to Norwich a qualified teacher in 1880 and founded the Norfolk & Norwich Football Club. His involvement in local football quickly brought him into contact with Walter Hansell and both were deeply committed to the idea of starting a Norfolk County FA. In a long playing career Webster also represented Norwich Wanderers and Norwich Teachers and as we have seen was captain of the CEYMS during the 1901–02 season.

Joseph Nutchey was born in Tadcaster, Yorkshire in December 1864. Very soon his family moved to Scarborough and after playing a full and active part in the sporting life of that town Nutchey also decided to become a schoolmaster. After qualifying at Peterborough Training College he took a post in Norwich. He joined the CEYMS club and soon became friends with Webster, later, when they were captain and vice-captain Nutchey often used to joke that he never got a chance to toss the coin because Webster was never absent. Both men also enjoyed cricket, and Nutchey was said to have 'mastered the knack' of lawn tennis and billiards. Before the meeting on 17 June Webster and Nutchey enlisted the support of Arthur Turner, a Norfolk man who was well known in local football. Turner was born in Norwich in 1869 and had played for Thorpe Hamlet between 1885 and 1898, the last nine years as captain. At the time of the meeting he was secretary of Swifans FC a local junior side. The idea of forming a City team very much appealed to Turner and he soon became an enthusiastic member of the club. As in the course of our introduction we recognised Walter Hansell as the 'father' and spiritual guide of Norfolk football, so we must now look to Robert Webster, Joseph Nutchey and Arthur Turner as holding a similar position in the development of the Norwich City Football Club.

Left, Robert Webster and right, Joseph Cowper Nutchey. These two called the initial meeting, at the Criterion Cafe, to set up the Norwich club

A report of the meeting appeared in the EDP on the morning of Wednesday 18 June 1902 and it seems that a previous attempt had been made to form a City club. This was probably in the late 1890s but because of the lack of thought and organisation the venture was not a success. All through the meeting the relationship between the new club and the CEYMS was alluded to and it was Nutchey himself who said that he hoped that there would be enough room in the city for both clubs. Undoubtedly both Webster and Nutchey felt frustrated at the lack of ambition shown by their former club but there does not appear to be any really bad feeling abroad, at least not on the part of the promoters of Norwich City. The new City club had to find a ground on which to play and it was decided to approach the Norfolk County FA for permission to use Newmarket Road. The County FA leased the ground from Town Close Estates, but as they only used it for the Finals of the various County

Report of first meeting of the club, taken from the Eastern Daily Press – Wednesday 18 June 1902

FOOTBALL IN NORWICH

FORMATION OF A CITY CLUB.

A meeting was held at the Criterion Cafe last night, convened by the following circular:—"A meeting of those interested in football matters in the city will be held at the Criterion Cafe, White Lion Street, on Tuesday next, to consider the advisability of forming a Norwich City Club. You are cordially invited to attend.—J. C. Nutchey, R. Webster." There was no chairman, but among those present were Messrs. J. C. Nutchey, R. Webster, A. G. Arnold, W. R. Bond, James Howes, J. W. Howes, G. Starling, J. C. Ayers, E. Dunton, A. L. Wright, G. Burleigh, A. Amiss, — Nichols, Rev. H. Wimble, F. S. Culley (sec. N.C.F.A.), A. E. Chapman, H. and P. Robertson, A. Smith (sec. of the City League), W. Walton, — Underwood, J. Fiddament, S. R. B. Cowles, W. L. Burgess, E. Nicholson, F. E. Smith, R. W. Collinson, A. Turner, W. Sparks, F. Witham, T. Newell, E. Smith, Saunders, G. Wones, G. Yallop, A. E. Iversen (Catton F.C.), F. Adie, H. Duffin, A. Pout, &c.

Mr. Webster said for many years past there had been a great agitation in support of a Norwich City team. An attempt was made some time ago to form one, but it was abortive. He had been requested to see whether the time had not now come when such a club could be formed, unhampered by any restrictions or by any societies. Possessing as they did a population of 110,000 it was thought by many that Norwich ought, at least, to make a decent show in the football world. There were two things necessary for such a club—financial support and a team. As far as the first went, if he could judge aright, that was assured. Whether they could raise a team was another matter. They were present that night to discuss the probability of raising such a team.

Mr. J. C. Nutchey said there had been a demand for such a club as this in Norwich for some years, and it had been put very forcibly to him and to Mr. Webster that they would be doing a very good thing if they set such a club on its legs. They had been very closely connected with the Church of England Club for a number of years, and they had not a word to say against it. (Hear, hear.) He certainly hoped that this city club would work very amicably with the Church of England club. He had had a good deal to do with the Church club and he should be very sorry to see it go down. The question had been put to him, "Why try and ruin the Church Football Club?" He had no such wish, and he thought there was plenty of room for these two teams to run together. He had been to see Mr. Hansell, a gentleman for whom they had the very highest respect—[Hear, hear]—and Mr. Hansell thought with him that there was room for these two teams, and he did not see why they should overlap one another. As to players, the Church of England had had plenty of time in which to approach players, and he had not himself approached any player at all with regard to playing next year. He did not wish to upset any arrangement that the Church had made. The players of the Church of England who had received their circular had not been asked by him (Mr. Nutchey) to join the new club, and if they wished to remain with the Church they had a perfect right to do so. With regard to this city team three things were wanted. They wanted a ground, and there was a ground on the Newmarket Road, with the only football grand stand that there was in the city, capable of accommodating over 400 people, and he did not see why that ground should stand vacant, except on Easter Monday, if those present could fill it. The ground was certainly as well adapted for football as any ground in the county, and if they could get the County to let it to them at a reasonable rent, he thought the difficulty of the ground would be got over. Then as to the players, he had invited to this meeting the secretaries of the two junior football clubs in the city, the Swifans and Catton. A city team was an impossibility unless they could get the players, but they had left it altogether open to these gentlemen if they liked to join this City Club to do so. It did not cost very much to start a football club. As to there being room for another team, the one senior club in the city might be away for two or three Saturdays running. There was no reason because they were away that no other should play in the city.

The Rev. H. Wimble, who was loudly cheered, said he was very glad to hear that there was a likelihood of another team being formed in Norfolk. Let them have as many teams as possible all over the country. He (Mr. Wimble) wanted to brighten the life of the villages by forming football teams all over the country. In a great city like Norwich there certainly ought to be two teams. In all probability there would be keen rivalry between the two; of course it would be a good thing, for he was sure it would be a generous rivalry. (Hear, hear.) Mr. Nutchey had mentioned a point which had often struck him (Mr. Wimble). He had often come into Norwich on a Saturday, and naturally he had wanted to know whether there was a match. Again and again he had been told "No," the Church were out. If a good match could be found on the Newmarket Road it would be a boon to the city.

cup competitions and the odd County game it would be available for most of the season. The ground is still used as a sportsfield by Town Close House School and stands on the left of the Newmarket Road as you proceed out of the city, immediately after the intersection of Daniels Road. The original pavilion remained in place and comparatively intact until relatively recently when it was demolished after repeated attacks by vandals. The Norfolk County Cricket Club also used the ground in their early years, but of late have chosen to play at Lakenham and more recently at Horsford. The rent suggested by the County FA, and gratefully agreed to by Norwich City, was just £25 per annum.

The meeting went on to elect Robert Webster as the first chairman of Norwich City FC with Arthur Turner and John William Howes as joint secretaries. Arthur Turner was to be match secretary and look after the playing side while John Howes was to be in charge of administration. Joseph Nutchey was elected to become treasurer and Robert Whiteley Collinson was to be the first captain of the club. Sir Samuel Hoare, senior MP for the City of Norwich and evidently a rather colourful character, was elected president. He kicked off in the first game that City played and before he did so delivered an address to the assembled spectators. John Howes, like Webster and Nutchey, was also a schoolmaster and his association with Norwich City was to last until 1946. Collinson proved to be a most popular and able captain in those early years. He was born on 6 November 1875 at Halifax in Yorkshire and had already played for Yorkshire at cricket before he arrived in Norwich in the summer of 1900. He was a fine all round sportsman, as indeed were so many of his generation, and he regularly represented Norfolk at athletics and cricket. As well as converting the first competitive penalty for the club he also had the honour of scoring the first hat-trick. On 7 May 1904

Collinson married Blanche Hoover from Penn in the USA, the couple having met while they were travelling in Europe. Later in life Collinson worked as an analytical chemist for J & J Colman. He continued to watch Norwich City long after his retirement in 1938, and sadly passed away in a Norwich Nursing Home on 26 December 1963.

On 12 July 1902 Norwich City were elected to the Norfolk & Suffolk League and City's opponents that year would be Beccles Caxton, Kirkley, Lowestoft Town, Lynn Town, Norwich CEYMS, Ipswich Town and Yarmouth Town. The League was originally formed in the summer of 1897 and was the first of real stature in the Eastern Counties. The City Reserve team entered the North Norfolk & Norwich League, and a City Third team were set to participate in the Norwich City League. Arrangements were made to share Delf's Meadow in City Road with Swifans FC in order to fulfil the latter fixtures. You will have noted that we have not yet referred to Norwich City FC as the 'Canaries' and indeed at this stage in the club's history it would be wrong to do so. In 1902 they were the 'Citizens' or 'Cits' and they took to the field in blue and white halved shirts. Strangely, in early photographs the blue was sometimes on the left hand side of the shirt and sometimes on the right, and there were often mixed shirts in the same team. Among the players recruited from local clubs were skipper Collinson, William 'Dillo' Sparks, Tommy Newell and George Yallop from CEYMS, William Cracknell, Walter Crome, George Bardwell and Jack Yallop from Swifans, and Bertie Playford from Catton. William Sparks was the goalkeeper and his nickname 'Dillo' stemmed from the time he used to go about with an old hawker by that name. He was also the last survivor of that original team, passing away in Norwich on 29 July 1974 at the age of 93. Up until 1968 he used to visit Carrow Road regularly, but his health sadly failed him before the end.

Fine weather greeted the 'Citizens' as they ran out on to the lush Newmarket Road turf for their first ever encounter. About 2,000 spectators lined the ropes and the opposition in this friendly match were Harwich & Parkeston. The date was Saturday 6 September 1902 and the City team read William Sparks goalkeeper, George Bardwell and William Cracknell full backs, Walter Crome, George Yallop and Jack Yallop half backs, and Fred Witham, Bertie Playford, Bob Collinson, Jimmy Shields and Tommy Newell forwards. The EDP reported on the following Monday that –

> *"Shortly before half-past three Sir Samuel Hoare MP proceeded to the centre of the field, where in a loud clear voice he addressed those present. He explained that he had been asked to kick off. He could not refuse that kind request, although he felt he had very little ability to kick off a football. He thought that up to the age of 61 a man ought to be able to play football, and had he been asked on Monday he could not have acceded to the request, but as he was not 61 until tomorrow (Sunday) he felt able to play just one more game."*

Sir Samuel was probably more talented than he thought for later in the report we read that City almost scored straight from the kick off. Harwich took the lead in the first half but after the interval –

> *"Newell worked the leather down prettily, and chose the right moment to pass to*

Savoy Taylors Guild, currently occupying the site of the Criterion Café

Shields. The latter took aim, and had the satisfaction of seeing the ball get past the keeper. The keeper looked as if he could not understand how he had missed the ball. The spectators promptly shook hands with themselves (honest – that's what it says), and a prolonged cheer greeted the effort which once more placed the sides on a level footing."

So much for the first match that City ever played, a 1–1 draw in a friendly against Harwich & Parkeston at Newmarket Road.

Lowestoft Town were the strongest team in the Norfolk & Suffolk League at the turn of the century and it was no real surprise that City lost 0–5 when they met at Lowestoft on Saturday 20 September 1902. The game, being the Preliminary Round of the FA Cup, was City's first ever competitive match. The 'Citizens' fared little better when they returned to Lowestoft on Saturday 8 November 1902 to play the Second Qualifying Round of the Amateur Cup. They managed to score two goals but the home side scored four and Norwich City were now out of the running in both the cup competitions. The League fixtures however got off to a brighter start and the first ever competitive win was recorded on Saturday 27 September 1902 against Beccles Caxton. City won 4–2 after having led 4–1 at half time. On Saturday 15 November 1902 the first ever meeting between Norwich City and Ipswich Town took place at Norwich. The report of the match is typical of the times, it reads –

"A cold and dull afternoon, with just a suspicion of the vapoury element, did not prevent a large attendance, the visit of Ipswich Town having been looked forward to with a large amount of interest."

The first half was goalless but later we learn that Cornell in the Ipswich goal was beaten by a fine cross shot from Fred Witham. The game finished in fine style with both sides pressing hard but

Report of City's first ever match against Harwich & Parkeston played on Saturday 6 September 1902

SATURDAY'S MATCHES.

FIRST MATCH OF THE NEW CITY CLUB.

SPEECH BY SIR S. HOARE.

About 2000 persons witnessed the first match of the newly formed Norwich City Club at the Newmarket Road Ground, and were extremely pleased by the good show made by the team against the strong Essex players. With a less brilliant keeper than Kettle Harwich would have lost. As it was the game ended in a draw of one goal each. The players engaged were as follow:—

Norwich City—W. Sparks, goal; G. Bardwell and W. Cracknell, backs; W. Crome, G. Yallop, and J. Yallop, half-backs; F. Witham, B. Playford, R. W. Collinson, J. Shields, and T. Newell, forwards.

Harwich—F. Kettle, goal; Oswick and C. B. Wrigley, backs; Garland, Garton, and Hunt, half-backs; Snodgrass, Lyons, Harwood, Felgate, and Taylor, forwards.

Referee—G. L. Miller.

Shortly after half-past three Sir Samuel Hoare, Bart, M.P., proceeded to the centre of the field, where in a loud clear voice he addressed those present. He explained that he had been asked to kick off. He could not refuse the kind request, although he felt he had very little ability to kick off a football. He thought that up to the age of 61 a man ought to be able to play football, and had he been asked on Monday he could not have acceded to the request, but as he was not 61 till to-morrow (Sunday) he felt able to play one more game. (Laughter and applause.) His friend, Sir Harry Bullard, and himself were both extremely pleased to be present to see the match, and they wished the players all success. They hoped they would have one of those friendly, good, and honest tussles for which the game was celebrated. There was no game at present which excited more interest than the fine game of football. Twenty-five years ago they had very little football in the county of Norfolk, now every town and every little village had their football clubs. Might they long continue to succeed. There was no game where discipline was learned better, and pluck more admired. How many fine football fellows had been fighting for their country during the last two years, and had profited by the discipline learned and the experience gained in the football field in many ways. He was very pleased to see the club was engaged in a match with Harwich, because he was associated with that district in that one of his old friends of the cricket field represented the borough in the House of Commons at the present time. In conclusion, he wished that the Norwich club might prove worthy of the old City, and that the Harwich might give a good account of themselves too. Might the fine old game of football flourish for many many years, both in the county of Norfolk, in the neighbouring county of Suffolk, and in Essex, for it was not only good for those who played, but also for those who looked on.

Donning a blue and white cap, the colours of the City Club, the hon. member, on receiving the signal from George Miller, kicked the ball well ahead. Garton received it, but in less time than it takes to write Witham was able to send in a shot, which missed the goal by the merest shave. If it had been successful, one might almost have given Sir Samuel the credit of the goal, which would have followed so closely upon his kick-off. Harwich recovered from this sensational opening, and were soon bothering the ex-Swifan backs, but sooner than might have been expected the Cits had the ball in front of Kettle. Collinson seemed to miss an opening, but the ball was travelling across at a great pace, and one could hardly be surprised that the Yorkshireman failed to get in touch with it. Following upon this, Harwich were busy in the City half, and Sparks got one hand to a warm shot from Harwood. It was a clever save, but danger was not wholly removed. Several times the ball went over the gaol line near the posts, and once Sparkes ran out and missed, but the situation was saved by another defender. One passing movement was terminated with a nice cross shot from Snodgrass. Newell's efforts to get away were easily checked, and for several minutes the Cits were penned in their own half. Subsequently some play between Newell and J. Yallop resulted in the ball going towards the goal, and in a position that was favourable for a shot from Witham. The goalkeeper, however, intercepted the effort, but failed to get the ball away many yards, and the Cits made an unsuccessful attempt to drive their advantage home. Directly afterwards the Harwich goal was again in danger, and Kettle had all his work cut out to avoid a disaster. Playford and Shields figured prominently in the shooting, and with a little luck the Cits should have scored more than once. A warm shot from

Town could not score and City were left the 1–0 winners, the gate was 1,700 and takings just £20.

Kirkley were the visitors in the Norfolk & Suffolk League on Saturday 29 November 1902 and the kick off was delayed because some of the Kirkley players had been held up. The match eventually started about a quarter of an hour late and as it was a miserable day anyway it soon became clear that the later stages of the match would take place in very bad light. Nat Whitaker, the secretary of the Southern League, was the referee and after 78 minutes play it was impossible to see across the pitch and the match was abandoned with the score at 1–1. Sadly it was the last match that William Sparks ever played for the City, he dislocated his shoulder during the game and had to give up playing for good. A further victory over Ipswich Town, 2–1 at Ipswich on Saturday 13 December 1902, saw Norwich City go top of the league. On Boxing Day came the long awaited first competitive meeting between City and CEYMS. The two sides met at Earlham Road before a crowd of 4,500. Playford scored twice for City to give his side a 2–0 lead at the interval. Later Collinson, playing of course against his old club, scored two more, both were penalties – the first to be scored by City in a competitive match, and the 'Cits' won the first Norwich 'Derby' by 4–2.

The spring of 1903 brought varied results, CEYMS gained revenge in the return at Newmarket Road, winning by 2–1. City lost heavily at Kirkley and Lowestoft, and in the final league game of the season Norwich City needed to win by a hat full to overtake CEYMS in the league. The visitors on Thursday 30 April 1903 were Lynn Town and City soon built up a four goal lead. In the second half four further goals were added and when the calculations were done at the end of the match City had just manoeuvred themselves into third position in the league, above rivals CEYMS and only one point behind Ipswich Town. A local player who played the odd game for City was Ernie Campling, later we learned that he continued to play the game after he emigrated to America – an early disciple indeed. On the whole it was a good first season, with valuable experience being gained in competitive football. The Newmarket Road ground was as good as any to be found in the Norfolk & Suffolk League so would the 'Citizens' be content to sit back and take things easily? They certainly didn't for Arthur Turner had a very busy summer indeed, he scoured East Anglia looking for players to take City to the top of the league.

1903–1904

On Saturday 5 September 1903 the sports editor of the EDP reported that all was well with Norwich City FC. Although figures were not revealed the finances of the club were said to be in a very healthy state. Turner was reported as saying that Norwich City could not wait for fate to blow two or three Collinson's to their door, and the club openly advertised the fact that they would find suitable work in the city for 'footballers of stature'. Before the season started City had already signed Percy 'Putt' Gooch, Langford Baker and Alex Sutherland from Lowestoft Town and Edmund Chamberlin and the veteran goalkeeper Bill Cooks from Kirkley. They were soon joined by Bob Pointer and Horace King from Catton. Gooch in particular was well known in local football, and was called 'Putt' or 'Put' because that was the word he always screamed at his colleagues as he raced towards goal seeking a return pass. Langford Baker was another talented forward from Lowestoft, and both he and Horace 'Moosh' King knew where the net was. All three went on to join Football League clubs after they left City, Gooch played for Notts County and Birmingham, Baker with Grimsby Town, for whom he scored 16 goals in 59 appearances, and King briefly with Blackpool. In the close season of 1903 Arthur Turner travelled hundreds of miles looking for players, let no one doubt it – Norwich City FC were very ambitious indeed.

As we diligently searched among the advertisments for gout pills and laxative syrups we found that the City of Norwich had two very important and celebrated visitors in the late summer of 1903. The first week of August was Norwich Cricket Week and the captain of the London County team was none other than the old master himself – William Gilbert Grace. Although W.G. was now 55 years of age he was still a formidable opponent and it must have been a relief to the Norfolk bowlers when they dismissed him for a duck in the first innings. He reached only 31 in the second innings so it must be said that he hardly troubled the scorers at Lakenham that year. He did in fact make a return visit in 1904 and on that occasion scored 17 and 6. The other visitor of note to come to Norwich that summer was William Frederick Cody – better known as Buffalo Bill. After his exploits in the American West Cody became a travelling showman and toured the USA and Europe with his spectacular Wild West show. On the evening of Wednesday 9 September 1903 the show was in Lowestoft, by 6.00am the next morning it was on its way to Norwich by rail. It took four special trains to transport the props from venue to venue for it was reported that there were over 800 men and 500 horses to move on each occasion. The show set up on Dix's Land in Unthank Road, and over 8,000 people crowded into the afternoon performance. Unfortunately it rained heavily before the evening event took place and only 5,000 turned up. The tents were taken down that night and put on the trains bound for King's Lynn, Cody never returned to Norwich.

Alex Sutherland, a new signing for the 1903 season

The season will be remembered in particular for the unusual exit from the FA Cup. 1903–04 remains to this day the only season in which Norwich City have been undefeated in this competition, and it happened like this. Lowestoft Town, Yarmouth Town and Harwich & Parkeston were all beaten in the early stages of the competition and in the Third Qualifying Round City were paired with West Norwood. West Norwood had to travel to Norwich and the tie took place on Saturday 31 October 1903. The Londoners took an early lead thanks to an own goal by Rackham, the City full back, but Langford Baker soon equalised and the tie finished 1–1. It was agreed by the two sets of officials that City would travel to London for the replay on the following Thursday afternoon. On the following Saturday the Qualifying Rounds of the Amateur Cup were due to begin and during the week the Norwich committee decided to forgo the replay against West Norwood and scratch from the competition. Perhaps it was a good thing that City decided to concentrate on the Amateur Cup for they so nearly reached the Final. Again Lowestoft Town and Harwich & Parkeston, two of the strongest sides in East Anglia, were swept aside in the early rounds. The Second Round match with Ilford at Newmarket Road drew a crowd of 4,000 and after a drawn match at Ealing 5,000 turned out to witness the replay. Sadly the 'Cits' lost this important match 1–2 but they did have the

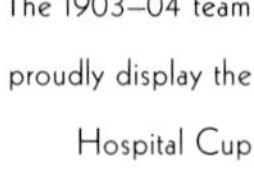

The 1903–04 team proudly display the Hospital Cup

satisfaction of playing a very sporting game. The match was completed without a serious foul and the paper reported that 'fouls were like angels' visits – few and far between'.

Lowestoft Town won the Norfolk & Suffolk League, their fourth win in a row, but City again finished in a respectable third position. Their heavy commitment in the various cup competitions probably didn't help their chances of winning the league. The season saw the inauguration of the Norfolk & Norwich Hospital Cup competition. Great rivals CEYMS were invited to compete in the first ever Final on Thursday 14 April 1904. It was evident that there was still some feeling between the two clubs for Norwich City officials protested to the competition secretary that CEYMS had not registered their players the required 28 days in advance. The row was eventually calmed by no less a figure than the Lord Mayor of Norwich and with some reluctance the match eventually got under way. The result was a 0–0 draw so a replay would have to be arranged. Exactly two weeks later the two sides met again in a more friendly atmosphere and City became the first holders of the Hospital Cup when they won the match 2–0. Every effort was made during the close season to improve upon the previous years work but no one could foresee the drama that lay ahead in the club's third full campaign.

1904–1905

The new season began with yet more new faces in the ranks. Arthur Turner had persuaded Henry Royal, a tall centre half from Lowestoft Town, Bob Baker, an inside forward from Fakenham, and Herbert Vigar from Redhill to join the club. Vigar in particular was an important capture for he finished top scorer in the season with 12 goals in his 14 competitive matches. Herbert Evelyn Vigar was born at Redhill on 29 November 1883 and between 1906 and 1911 played 15 matches for Surrey County Cricket Club as wicket-keeper. Bob Pointer took over the captaincy from Bob Collinson, who was now the vice-chairman of the club, and Percy 'Putt' Gooch was elected vice-captain. City now had an organised Supporters Club which met at the Public House kept by Arthur Turner, the Boar's Head in St Stephens, and everything was set well for a good season. Indeed the campaign could hardly have got off to a better start for the 'Cits' won their first five league games. Admittedly they were hurriedly dispatched from the FA Cup by Grays United in November after a replay, Grays travelling to Norwich on both occasions by arrangement, but the prize that year was the Amateur Cup and City officials believed that this was their year to secure the prodigious trophy. On 2 December 1904 an FA Commission sat at Lowestoft and examined the affairs of both Lowestoft Town and Kirkley FC, and on Thursday 8 December 1904 Arthur Turner received a letter from the FA requesting him to forward the books of Norwich City FC to FA headquarters. This all came as a severe blow to the ambitions of City, the affair was very serious indeed and news soon reached Norwich that the ruling body were not satisfied in matters relating to the amateur status of the club. Furthermore an official Commission of Enquiry was arranged to be held in Norwich on Saturday 17 December 1904.

Bob Collinson, all round sportsman and popular first captain of the 'Citizens'

The Commission required all the players and officials of the club to be present, and after the match against Lowestoft Town everyone connected with the club gathered at the Bell Hotel. The personnel of the Commission were exactly the same as had recently met at Lowestoft namely Messrs C.W. Alcock the chairman, G.S. Sherrington (Suffolk), R. Cook (Essex), E.L. Holland (Middlesex) and F.J. Wall the secretary. We let the EDP take up the story –

> *"From five o'clock onwards to 11pm, at which time the enquiry ended, the old-established hostelry was the scene of much bustle and excitement and the object of considerable attention from the football*

community. As the evening advanced troops of persons collected on the plain and discussed the situation in all its different aspects. Information as to the trend of affairs was eagerly sought after, and officials and players who had 'passed through the fire' of room No 10 were besieged with questions."

At the end of the long evening the gentlemen from the FA turned their attention to the ordering of their Sunday breakfasts pausing only briefly to tell the waiting reporters that the results of the enquiry would be announced in the middle of January.

In the event however City did not have so long to wait, for in the 'football edition' of the Evening News on Saturday 31 December 1904 it was revealed that the Commission had effectively found the Norwich City Football Club to be a professional organization. The date for the release of the findings was brought forward because City were due to meet Ilford in the First Round of the Amateur Cup on 7 January 1905 and as the Commission declared the club to be professional it was recommended that City be excluded from that competition. The main points raised by the Commission were as follows – Fees were paid for the use of a gymnasium and also for the training and massage of players. The sum of £8 was paid to a player when he left the club. Payments were made to players without a receipt being taken. The club advertised for players, and secretary Turner spent considerable sums of money in travelling to other towns in East Anglia. Complete outfits including shirts and boots were bought for players out of club funds. There was no adequate system for checking gate money, it often being left to just one man. Finally, travelling expenses were said to be excessive. In addition to the exclusion from the Amateur Cup competition the Commission also recommended that Messrs Webster, Nutchey and

Result of the FA Commission that investigated the affairs of Norwich City FC during the 1904–05 season

NORWICH CITY AND THE FOOTBALL ASSOCIATION.

RESULT OF THE COMMISSION

A DRASTIC REPORT.

CLUB DECLARED PROFESSIONAL.

THREE OFFICIALS SUSPENDED

The Football Association Commission appointed to inquire into the management of the Norwich City Club has issued its report. Stated briefly, the Commission have recommended, and their finding has been confirmed, that the club has forfeited its amateur status, and should be removed from the Amateur Cup Competition. The chairman, treasurer, and secretary are suspended from taking any part in football or football management until the 1st of next May. The players are granted relief, and not required to be registered as professionals.

Below will be found the report of the commission in full:—

"The commission, having taken evidence of the officials and players of the club, and inquired fully into its management, report as follows:

"The club was formed in the season of 1902-3 as an amateur club, in order to utilise the ground of the Norfolk County F.A., and, by providing employment in the city, obtained the services of several prominent players of other amateur clubs in the county and other districts. The club at once became a financial success (last season the home gate receipts alone were £751 13s. 4d.), and payments were made in violation of the rules of the Football Association, and other moneys were expended which, although not contrary to rule, the commission consider were an improper and undesirable expenditure for an amateur club.

"Fees were paid for the use of a gymnasium for the training of players, and also for massage treatment for players.

"A sum of £8 was paid to a player on his leaving the club, and considerable payments were also made for doctors' bills for players who, it was stated, were injured at football, without the consent of the Football Association, or the affiliated association, having been first obtained.

"Payments were also made to the players, for which receipts had not been taken, giving particulars, as required by the rules of the Football Association.

"The club advertised for amateur players, and it was also the practice of the secretary, at a considerable expense to the club, as was shown by the accounts, to visit various towns in East Anglia in the close season in search of players, and from the evidence it was proved that he had been successful in obtaining players upon the promise of obtaining employment for them at Norwich.

"Complete outfits, including shirts, knickerbockers, boots, stockings, belts, and material for training were provided out of the club funds for the use of the players.

"The commission is satisfied that there is not an adequate system of checking the gate receipts, it being left practically in the hands of one man only. The commission were unable to satisfy themselves that the entries shown in the book, which was produced, correctly represented the gate money received. It was, however, explained to the [illegible]

Turner be excluded from taking part in any football matters until the end of the season. As it was considered that the management of the club were at fault and not the players no recommendation was made to declare the players professional. Joe Nutchey was interviewed soon after the findings were made known and stated that the club had offended more against the 'spirit of amateurism' then the actual breaking of the rules. He hoped that the club would not be excluded from the Norfolk & Suffolk League.

No time was lost by City in their efforts to repair the damage and a meeting was called on Monday 2 January 1905 to decide what action should be taken. The club had also of course to replace the suspended officials. Bob Collinson took the chair after Bob Webster, Joe Nutchey and Arthur Turner had left the room amid rapturous applause. Wilfred Lawson Burgess became the new chairman, George Gibb became secretary and Percy Robertson the new treasurer. The meeting then debated the report in full and it was decided to forge ahead in the pursuit of professional football. Later in the month the Norfolk & Suffolk League met and thankfully agreed to allow City to continue their programme.

A grand public meeting of Norwich City FC was called on Friday 3 March 1905 at the Agricultural Hall. The room was densely crowded and many hundreds had to be turned away at the door. Wilfred Burgess, the new chairman, presided and was supported on the platform by the Mayor of Norwich Mr H.Z.T. Flowers, the Sheriff of Norwich Mr H.L. Clark, a leading Norwich businessman Mr George Chamberlin, Mr Nat Whitaker, the secretary of the Southern League and Mr Broadbridge, the chairman of Brighton & Hove Albion FC. After several rousing speeches a motion was proposed by Mr Chamberlin viz – 'That this meeting of citizens heartily endorses the action of the Norwich City Football Club in its determination to run a first class professional team, and also expresses its intention to do everything in its power to ensure the success of the proposed scheme'. Significantly the motion was seconded by Nat Whitaker, surely an indication that he at least was keen to see Norwich City admitted to the Southern League. Chelsea FC were formed in 1905 and had applied to join the Southern League, a move that was not popular with the existing London clubs. They were of course afraid that a new club would take spectators away from the established venues. Whitaker meanwhile was rather actively supporting Norwich City because he wanted the Southern League to spread its influence into the Eastern Counties. In passing we must add that Chelsea had the last laugh because they were elected straight into the Second Division of the Football League. Mr Chamberlin's motion was carried unanimously and the forms for the new shares were distributed immediately amid the greatest enthusiasm – Norwich City FC were on their way.

The board considered many applications for the post of secretary/manager and after much deliberation selected a young man from Queens Park Rangers for the job. John William Bowman was born in Middlesbrough on 23 April 1879 and was therefore in his 26th year in 1905. His career began at Port Vale in 1898 and after a year he moved on to near neighbours Stoke City. In 1901 he travelled south and joined Queens Park Rangers first as a player and later as secretary/manager. Bowman, as well as being a fine footballer, was a good all round athlete and it was reported that he had recently won races of 100 yards up to a distance of 10 miles. He was also a fine swimmer but not, surprisingly, a cricketer. Wilfred Burgess took great care in finding the right man and everyone connected with Southern League football gave Bowman a hearty recommendation. He was appointed on Wednesday 22 March 1905 but was not released by Rangers until Tuesday 28 March 1905. It was noted in the press that he was due to arrive in Norwich during the following week 'to run the rule over his new charges'.

Percy 'Putt' Gooch, a supreme goal scorer

A group of gentlemen, led by City chairman Wilfred Burgess, waited patiently at Norwich Station for the 1.18pm from London to arrive on Thursday 6 April 1905. The group showed some signs of anxiety as the train was delayed, but eventually drew to a halt a full seventeen minutes late. The deputation stepped forward to meet their new manager John Bowman and after exchanging a hand of welcome the party moved on to the Criterion Cafe for lunch. The EDP scribe wasted no time in securing his first interview with the new man, the result was a very fine piece of reporting –

> *"A few minutes of conversation revealed the secret of Bowman's popularity. Frankness seems stamped upon his agreeable features, and the expected touch of vanity, suggested by the trimly cut and pointed moustache, vanishes as the new manager talks easily and pleasantly, and with just the suspicion of an accent of a Midlander. Not every man glows with enthusiasm when the topic of conversation turns upon his daily work, but as the light kindles in John Bowman's bright grey eyes, it is easy to see that he loves the game and the sport none the less because it happens to be the medium of his weekly wage. One feels instinctively that Bowman has all that is best in the professional character; his forehead, from which the dark hair is brushed upwards, seems to indicate the brainy, intelligent player who makes for the good of the game."*

John Bowman proved a popular manager who would guide the team into professional status

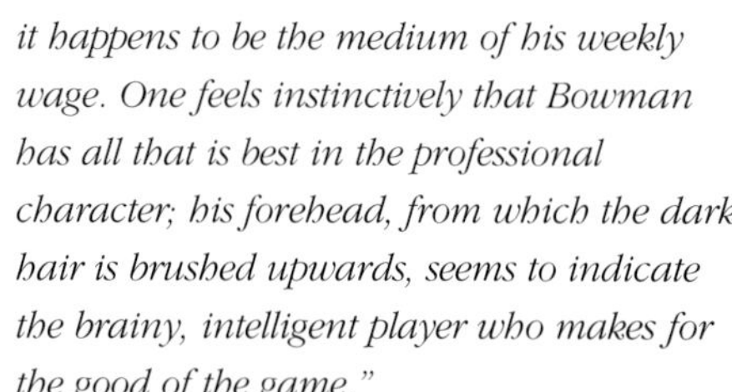

A glowing tribute indeed for one who was to shape the destinies of Norwich City FC and pilot them through the thorny paths of professionalism.

Later in the lengthy interview Bowman was asked if he had any previous knowledge of Norwich or its players. Bowman replied thus – 'Well, I knew of the City's existence, for in my schooldays geography was a favourite subject of mine, and I have since heard of the canaries'. This as far as we can tell is the first time that the popular pastime of the day ie the rearing and showing of canaries was linked with the Norwich City FC. Don't forget that the club still played in blue and white, and would continue to do so for another two seasons, but as time passed the association between the football club and the canaries grew stronger. Also note that 'canaries' in the quote does not have a capital 'c' which makes it even more likely that the reference was of a casual rather than a formal nature. After the interview Burgess informed the reporter that sufficient money had now been raised to start the club properly and by way of a celebration there would be a City contingent at the Hippodrome that very evening. Mr Albert Smith had promised to come along and sing 'On the ball, City' and the club had accepted a challenge from the Assam Baby Elephants for a football match on the 'Hippo' stage.

The song 'On the ball, City' is certainly older than the Norwich City FC and was probably written for Norwich Teachers or Caley's FC in the 1890s, it was of course 'On the ball, Teachers/Caley's in those days, and one version included the line 'On the ball, Teachers, Never mind your features'. A gentleman by the name of Albert Smith, who was on the staff of A. J. Caley & Son, used to tour the music halls and smoking concerts performing the song. As soon as City were formed in 1902 the song was immediately adopted as the clubs' anthem and there are many reports of it being vociferously sung at Newmarket Road. With the help of our intrepid reporter from the EDP let us return to that most popular venue of entertainment in Edwardian Norwich – the Hippodrome. The date is Thursday 6 April 1905 and the curtain is just rising on the second house.

> *"The enthusiasm of the audience was worked to a fine pitch by the singing of the popular war cry of the clubbers 'On the ball, City'. Mr Albert Smith led the company and the chorus was lustily sung by all. Each time the chorus was concluded there was an outburst of cheering and the song was sung over and over again."*

The singing eventually had to stop to allow the football match to take place. Unfortunately we are not told how many City players took part, but afterwards Gooch noted that some of the elephants were stronger defenders than some he had met in the Norfolk & Suffolk League. City won the tussle 4–2 thanks to two own goals by the elephant goalkeeper and after the match, which was enjoyed and applauded by all, the manager of the elephants took to the stage. In a solemn tone he explained that on the whole he was pleased with the performance of his 'men', the goalkeeper excepted, who it has to be said always experienced difficulty with the rule about changing over at half time. His chaps were not very proficient at the winter game you see, he went on, and actually I have to confess that they are not footballers at all – their true talent lies in the playing of the noble game of cricket. The packed audience loved it and John Bowman's first night in the City of Norwich was a great success.

City continued to do well in the Norfolk & Suffolk League and finished the season at the very top, 4 points ahead of Lowestoft Town. In order to get into shape for the forthcoming season several friendlies against superior opposition were arranged in the latter part of April. On Tuesday 25th April 1905 Derby County, including the England centre forward Steve Bloomer who scored a hat-trick, visited Newmarket Road and won 6–0. Two days later Woolwich Arsenal were the visitors and a deputation from the Southern League were among the very large crowd who saw City win 2–1. On Tuesday 30th May 1905 Norwich City FC were elected to the Southern League in place of Wellingborough. The meeting took place at the Holborn Restaurant in London and many months of hard work had reached a fruitful conclusion. In many ways these were the happiest days in the entire history of the club, the prospect of playing in the Southern League as a professional club was new to City and there is more than ample evidence to suggest that everyone connected with the venture enjoyed themselves enormously.

1905–1906

The 8.46am puffed noisily out of Norwich Thorpe Station on the morning of Friday 1 September 1905, on board the London bound train were the players and officials of the Norwich City FC. In front of them lay a long and tiring journey for City were off to Plymouth to play their first professional match in the Southern League. The morning was cold but bright and the passengers settled in their seats with their thoughts very much on the match that lay ahead. The train was due to arrive in Liverpool Street at 11.25am and was making good time until it suddenly shuddered to a halt a few hundred yards short of Witham Station. The train remained stationary for several minutes and the passengers grew increasingly impatient. Upon observing clouds of towering smoke rising from the direction of the station several passengers, including many of the City players, alighted and hurried along the track. An horrific sight met their eyes, the Norwich bound up train had careered into the platform and there was debris strewn everywhere. In all nine people lost their lives in the incident and many more were injured. Many of the City players joined in the rescue operation and they did not finally arrive in London until 4.00pm. The Great Eastern Railway had a good overall safety record but one of the worst disasters occurred in Norwich on 10 September 1874 when 26 people lost their lives. The Norwich party eventually reached Plymouth just after midnight, shocked and unnerved by the days events, hardly the ideal preparation for their important match against the Argyle.

During the summer John Bowman had made many new signings including that fine pair of full backs Arthur Archer and Jimmy McEwen. Archer was born in Ashby-de-la-Zouch in 1877 and had played for Burton Wanderers, Small Heath (later Birmingham City), New Brompton (later Gillingham) and Queens Park Rangers. Jimmy 'Punch' McEwen was made captain for the 1905–06 season and had previously been with Bury FC. In fact he played in the Bury FA Cup winning side of 1903, Bury beat Derby County 6–0, still the record win in an FA Cup Final. The regular half back line in 1905–06 was Livingstone, Bushell and Bemment. Archie Livingstone joined City from Brighton & Hove Albion, he was a tough, hard working Scot who later managed Peterborough City. Billy Bushell originally came from Wednesbury in the West Midlands and joined City after playing at Aston Villa amongst others. Left half Fred Bemment was a local lad from Lowestoft who later went on to play in the Football League with Notts. County and Chesterfield. When his playing days were over he became a miner, he died in March 1957 at the age of 73. The forward line was recruited from all over the British Isles, Robert Muir the outside right came from Notts County, but had previously been with Celtic, Bristol Rovers and his home town team Kilmarnock. Muir was an educated man and was an

Norwich, playing in blue and white halves take the field at Newmarket Road

influential member of the side. In later years he contributed a number of interesting articles to the Norwich City handbooks. On the other wing was George Graver Brown, known as 'Gee Gee' by his colleagues, and not only because of his initials either for he could move a bit and often won cups and medals in the local sports. At inside right was another Scot, Sam Graham who had spent 3 years at Newcastle United and had appeared in their First Division team.

Perhaps the best known members of the side were centre forward Duncan Ronaldson, his inside partner David Ross and goalkeeper Charlie Williams. Ronaldson was a much travelled Scot who had last been at Queens Park Rangers with Bowman. He was the ideal centre forward in that he was tall, had a good shot and was very brave. He formed a fine partnership with David Ross and between them they scored 27 competitive goals during the season. It was said that Ronaldson had a good voice but 'not in the least like a canary'. He later had another spell at Norwich during the 1909–10 season but, like a lot of players of his day, usually preferred to be on the move. David Ross was the brother of George Ross who had played for Bury for many years and had appeared in the FA Cup Finals of 1900 and 1903. The brothers were of Scots extraction, but were actually born in Lancashire. During the season Ross scored some wonderful goals and he quickly established himself as a favourite at Newmarket Road. Lastly we must mention the goalkeeper Charlie Williams. Williams started his career at Woolwich Arsenal in 1893 but after only one season left to go to Manchester City. While at Manchester City he shared a benefit match with Billy Meredith and it was reported that the sum raised was about £75. After his spell in the north he went back to London in 1902 and joined Spurs, he was of course known to John Bowman and it was he who persuaded Williams to come to Norwich. Later in life Williams left England to coach soccer in both Europe and South America. It was a fine side that John Bowman got together and a side that was to be a credit to Norwich City FC in their first season in the Southern League.

Centre forward Duncan Ronaldson, an ex QPR player

The suspended officials i.e. Bob Webster, Joe Nutchey and Arthur Turner all rejoined the club after their period of enforced retirement, and in 1905–06 the City board read thus – Wilfred Burgess chairman, and Tommy Delves, Bob Webster, Joe Nutchey, Bob Collinson, John Howes, Percy Robertson and 'On the ball, City' man Albert Smith directors. Joe Nutchey also served as secretary. The manager was of course John Bowman and Arthur Turner was assistant manager. The registered offices of the club were in Orford Place and the telephone number was Norwich 429. There was also a telephone up at Newmarket Road, the number was Norwich 861. In 1905–06 the Southern League consisted of 18 clubs, and with the exception of New Brompton all are familiar to us today. New Brompton by the way changed their name to Gillingham at the start of the 1912–13 season. The Southern League was started in the 1894–95 season, and from the outset was a professional league. Officials of Woolwich Arsenal had first tried to get a professional league going but met with great initial resistance from the old boy network of southern amateur clubs. In the end they gave up and joined the Football League, a professional organisation consisting in the main of clubs from the industrial north of England. Much credit for the formation of the Southern League must go to Millwall FC, they persisted where Arsenal had given up, and in the early days of professional football it is true to say there were two roughly equal organisations – the Football League in the north, and the Southern League in the south. Gradually the Football League edged ahead as the stronger southern teams changed their allegiance and by the outbreak of the First World War it could truly be said that the Football League was a national league. In 1905–06 though Tottenham Hotspur, West Ham United, Queen's Park Rangers and Southampton were all in the Southern League and all were scheduled to visit Newmarket Road and play Norwich City. Before we take a closer look at those epic matches we must mention a friendly match that took place on Thursday 28 September 1905. The visitors to Newmarket Road were Club Athletique Professionel Parisian from France. City, aided by six goals from David Ross, won the match 11–0 it being the first time that City had played opposition from overseas.

As we said before City had every reason to feel very pleased with their first years' work. The first ever Southern League match, at Plymouth on Saturday 2 September 1905 (the day after the train accident at Witham Station) was lost 0–2. The first point was secured in the 1–1 draw with Southampton at Newmarket Road the following week, the first City scorer being Freddy Wilkinson. Wilkinson soon left the club but returned for a spell between 1910–12. The first win in the league was against West Ham United, 1–0 at home, on Saturday 7 October 1905, and it must have given Bowman a great deal of pleasure to beat his old team Queens Park Rangers 4–0 in the very next home game. The first away win was recorded against Bristol

Norwich City FC 1905–06. Top row (left to right): Archer, McEwen, Bushell, Warnes. Second row: Miles (trainer), Bowman (manager), Childs, Cummings, Williams, Rose, Bemment, McQueen (assistant trainer). Seated: Muir, Graham, Wilkinson, Ronaldson, Ross, Brindley, Linward. Front: Vigar, Livingstone

Rovers, the previous season's champions, 1–0 on 28 October and this was followed later in the season by further away wins at Millwall, Northampton Town, Swindon Town and Brentford. There was a pleasing comment in the Athletic News after City's 1–1 draw with Watford on Saturday 23 September 1905 –

> *"Muir's arm was vigorously shaken by his pleased comrades and a tremendous shout went up from the crowd, 'Hurrah we've scored a goal' was rolled out and the sight presented by the waving hats would have made a splendid picture for the bioscope. Norwich City, the babes of the Southern League, did very well. There was any amount of enthusiasm at the cathedral city and the game has evidently caught on in East Anglia"*

When it was time to make a start on the annual quest for the FA Cup, City were comfortably placed in the middle of the table. They first had to travel to meet Sheppey United on Saturday 9 December 1905 and won quite easily 2–0 with goals from Ronaldson and Ross. Tunbridge Wells surprisingly held City to a 1–1 draw at Norwich in the next round but City easily won the replay 5–0 with David Ross scoring a hat-trick. It was in the Second Round proper on Saturday 3 February 1906 that City had to make the long journey north to play Manchester United. The match took place on a grassless pitch at Clayton in appalling weather but City were no match for United and lost 0–3. United were then in the Second Division and at the end of the season finished second to gain promotion to the First.

During the season an investment scheme was launched because shares had not sold as well as had been expected and the club was essentially undercapitalised. On Monday 5 February 1906 the details of the scheme were announced, and it was rather like buying your shares on the hire purchase. It was hoped that a further £1,500 could be raised in this way. We were never given any details as to how successful the scheme was but at the end of the season, a tremendously successful one on the playing side, it was announced that the club had lost £502 14s 7d. A total of £2577 9s 6d had been paid out in wages and the rent for Newmarket Road was £102 7s 1d. In order to give more financial stability to the club, Chairman Burgess asked George Chamberlin, a leading Norwich businessman, and his friend John Pyke to join the Board. Chamberlin you will remember proposed the motion that City should proceed with professional football at the meeting held on 3 March 1905, he was a regular City supporter and he accepted the challenge. He also arranged for some of his influential friends to guarantee loans from the bank. On Friday 8 June 1906 the club held an Annual Dinner at the Thatched Assembly Rooms. Speech after speech congratulated City on a fine first season and now with more financial backing it was thought that another fine season lay ahead.

1906–1907

City got back to work early on 3 August 1906 and by the end of the month had staged two public practice games. 4,000 people attended the first and reports said that even more came along to the second, all the proceeds went to charity. 9,000 turned up to watch the first match of the new campaign against Fulham, a 0–0 draw, but an exciting game nonetheless. The size of the attendance gives some indication of the depth of support that Norwich City could command, and serious consideration was given to further develop the Newmarket Road ground. On 21 June 1906 Norwich City FC had successfully applied for admission to the United League. In his address to the League committee Burgess claimed 'within a radius of 25 miles of Norwich there are 250,000 people – every one a Sportsman'. Well there were plenty who were keen to get along to Newmarket Road that is sure, but perhaps they were not all Sportsmen. The United League was a First team midweek league, and it was hoped that the extra interest would significantly increase the gate receipts. Again City held their own in the Southern League matches with Ronaldson and Ross doing the bulk of the goalscoring. The new City goalkeeper for 1906–07 was Fred Thompson another ex Bury FC player who played in the

1900 FA Cup Final. Yet another Bury FC player Willie Wood, he played in both their FA Cup Finals, joined City at the end of the previous season, he did remarkably well and became a great favourite with the crowd. Muir was suffering the recurrence of an old back injury and only played 11 games all season, he was replaced by George Lamberton. George, who had a brother James also on the staff that season, had joined the club from Luton Town. Surprise, surprise he joined Luton Town from Bury FC and after he finished at Norwich he went back to Bury.

On Saturday 12 January 1907 City met Hastings & St Leonards in the First Round of the FA Cup at Newmarket Road. City won 3–1 but the tie was remarkable in that Norwich were actually drawn to play the tie away from home. The two clubs got together and worked out a deal whereby Hastings were guaranteed £80 plus half the receipts over £160 if they consented to play the tie at Norwich. We must point out that there was nothing illegal about the arrangement, it sometimes happens today, but it is usually considered unfair to the supporters of the side originally drawn at home. In the next round City had to travel to Birmingham to meet West Bromwich Albion and a special week of preparation was undertaken at the Royal Hotel, Norwich. The City trainer was Charlie Miles who had been trainer at Queens Park Rangers and had come to Norwich with Bowman. Miles was born in Kent and in early life took a post as Gymnastic Instructor at Tunbridge Wells Grammar School. He later moved to New Brompton (Gillingham) FC and was trainer for three years before moving on to Queens Park Rangers. He trained the City players vigorously, but had the respect and affection of the entire staff. In their week of preparation he got them up at 7.30am, worked them hard, and made sure they were in bed by 10.00pm. There was a reference in the press that the players were receiving a special diet, including among other things raw eggs, no wonder they couldn't wait for the match! The great day dawned and two train loads of supporters left Norwich Thorpe early on the morning of Saturday 2 February 1907. The two trains met up at Bourne Station and the more boisterous of the party, which numbered about 1,000, alighted on to the platform and unfurled huge blue and white flags. There was much shouting and merry-making and of course the inevitable chorus of 'On the ball, City'

The great sportsman Charles Burgess Fry scribed the following words about the tie –

> *"As to West Bromwich v Norwich all this about a birdsinging contest is humbug. Birds do not sing with their boots, moreover, I have a Canary that, on the nail, will outsing any thrush – and any old cock pheasant into the bargain. Norwich play well away from home and will beat the Albion."*

Despite such praise from so worthy a practitioner as C.B. Fry, Norwich narrowly lost the tie. The game was played in fog, so thick at times that it was hard to see across the pitch, and the goal scored by Albion in the second minute was enough to decide the match. City played well and the national press were full of praise for their efforts. The loyal supporters had a night out in Birmingham and left by the midnight train. They arrived back in Norwich cold, hungry, and not too disappointed about five o'clock the next morning. It is interesting to note here that the nickname of the 'Canaries' is becoming more and more popular, certainly Bowman often referred to his team as such, and so did the national journalists.

City's free-scoring star forward David Ross, sold for a £650 fee to Manchester City

On the Saturday before the FA Cup tie at West Bromwich, City had beaten Tottenham Hotspur 5–0 at Newmarket Road and they should have been feeling on top of the world despite being knocked out of the Cup, but sadly a storm was brewing and there were changes in the air. Manchester City manager Mr Newbould travelled to Norwich on Thursday 7 February 1907 and agreed to pay City £650 for their star forward David Ross. Ross himself was in bed with a cold, but after talking with his family agreed to return to his native Lancashire. In addition to the transfer fee, which was in itself very large for the time and a record for a Southern League player, Manchester City agreed to play a friendly match and guarantee City a further £250. The move brought chaos to all connected with the club, the supporters demonstrated against the sale of their star forward – Ross that year had scored 28 goals in competitive matches, and the divisions within the boardroom were beginning to show. It all comes down in the end to pounds, shillings and pence, and City, despite their gates and their comparative success, were still losing money. The rift grew between Chairman Burgess and George Chamberlin the businessman, so much so that Burgess resigned on Thursday 21 February 1907. Within a week his place was taken by John Samuel Pyke, a local farmer and landowner and a friend of Chamberlin. The money obtained from the Ross transfer just about allowed City to break even on the years' trading but the Annual General Meeting held on Monday 17 June at the Municipal Secondary School was a stormy affair. Shortly after the meeting, on Thursday 20 June John Bowman resigned and on the following Saturday Wilfred Lawson Burgess resigned as a director. These were sad times for the City and the club which had finished eighth in the Southern League was now without a manager and a star forward. In the two years that John Bowman was manager the club exceeded all expectations and made a most solid start on their professional career. Where now would the road lead?

1907–1908

In addition to Burgess there were more resignations from the City board during the summer of 1907. Tommy Delves, Joe Nutchey, Percy Robertson and Albert Smith, all close friends of former Chairman Burgess, considered it appropriate to leave the club. Their places were filled by William Thomas Blyth, Arthur Edward Barham, Thomas Bury and Mark Nattrass. Blyth was the proprietor of the Great Eastern Hotel, in later years he retired to Kent and lived until he was 93 years of age. Barham was the youngest member of the board and was a leather merchant on Constitution Hill. Thomas Bury was a retired provisions merchant and he too lived until well into his 90s. The final member, Mark Nattrass, kept the cafe by Foundry Bridge for over 50 years. John Howes once again became secretary and Arthur Turner continued as assistant manager. After a lengthy discussion it was decided not to appoint a new manager from the many applications that were received, but to offer the job to Jimmy McEwen, the captain for the two previous seasons. At the same meeting it was also decided to change the club colours from blue and white to yellow and green, so for the coming season City would play in yellow shirts with green collars and cuffs. One paper produced the quote 'The Cits are dead but the Canaries are very much alive'. Norwich City FC first produced a handbook for the 1905–06 season, so by 1907–08 they were up to their third edition. We were lucky enough to have access, thanks to the Norwich City FC, to all the handbooks between 1906–07 and 1952–53, and the issue for 1907–08 contained an article by 'Tam' which was in effect a rallying cry to the faithful. In it he hoped that the supporters would back the new men in the battles that lay ahead.

Cyril Dunning, an England amateur international

Archer, Ronaldson and Wood also left the club at the end of the 1906–07 season. Archer and Ronaldson went to Brighton & Hove Albion and Wood joined Leyton. The new players included Tommy Allsopp, a goalscoring winger who had played cricket for Leicestershire and later played for Norfolk. Tommy joined City from Brighton & Hove Albion and gave four years splendid service. In 1916 he joined the Army and survived the war, but unfortunately caught flu on the way home and less than a week later he died at his

GREAT FOOTBALL MATCH

VISIT OF CUP-HOLDERS.

ENGLISH CUP-TIE.

NORWICH CITY

v.

SHEFFIELD WEDNESDAY.

SATURDAY, JAN. 11th.

Kick-off, 2.30 p.m.

PRICES OF ADMISSION:

Enclosure and Ring Seats (inclusive)........... 2s.
Ground and Ring Seats (inclusive) .... 1s.
Reserved and Numbered Seats in Centre of Grand Stand (including admission) .... 4s.

Remainder of Grand Stand will be Reserved if Seats are applied for before January 9th, 2s. (including admission).
Remittances must be sent with all orders for booking.

EXCURSION TRAINS are being run on day of match at following fares: From Yarmouth and Lowestoft 1s. 3d., Beccles, Bungay, Harleston, and Tivetshall 1s. 3d., Ipswich 2s. 3d., Stowmarket 1s. 9d., Diss 1s. 3d., Forncett 1s., Wells and Walsingham 2s. 3d., Fakenham and North Elmham 1s. 9d., Dereham 1s. 3d., Lynn 2s. 3d., Swaffham 1s. 9d., Cambridge and Ely 2s. 9d., Brandon 2s. 6d., Thetford 2s. 3d., Harling and Eccles Road 1s. 9d., Attleborough 1s. 3d., Wymondham 9d.
For time of trains see bills at stations or hoardings in various towns.

Notice of the FA Cup tie against Sheffield Wednesday

public house, the City Arms in Redwell Street. Another new arrival was James Rae Bauchop, an accomplished forward who scored over 200 goals in the Football League in a very long career. He was a Scot who started with his native Alloa in 1905 and was reported as playing for Lincoln City in 1924. New too were winger Ernie Coxhead, inside man John Flanagan who was known as 'Little Jack', Gerry Newlands a tough Scottish full back, Peter Roney the goalkeeper, Bobby Whiteman and James Young. Young was a friend of Robert Muir and was keen to team up with him again, the two had previously met at Bristol Rovers. Although the season was not as successful as the previous two had been, City managed to finish fairly comfortably in the Southern League, and created quite a ripple in the football world when they beat the holders of the FA Cup at Newmarket Road.

Every effort was made to accommodate as many spectators as possible at the Newmarket Road ground on Saturday 11 January 1908. During the week two temporary stands were erected and it was thought that 15,000 to 16,000 could be squeezed in on the day. All the seats were sold well in advance of the game and City again went into a week of special training (we hope there were not too many raw eggs this time round). The week had been very cold and there was some doubt as to whether or not the game would take place. A few minutes before 11.00am on the Saturday morning the excursionists from Sheffield pulled into Norwich Thorpe – the great day had arrived – Sheffield Wednesday the holders of the FA Cup were in Norwich ready to defend their treasured prize. The report on the arrival of the Sheffield supporters is again a classic. Sadly the newspaper (EDP) was not of good enough quality to reproduce in full but we quote the pick of the offering –

"Among the first batch of fans from Sheffield were a fair sprinkling of women. Nearly all were wearing blue and white rosettes, while a little band of individuals had brought with them an umbrella framed in the same colours. The utmost merriment prevailed among the whole party, and there was no doubt apparently on their part but that Sheffield were going to register yet another great victory. At 12.10 lusty cheering announced to all and sundry that the train conveying the second batch of supporters had struck 'the reet spot at last'. As the carriages disgorged their living freight it was seen that about 300 comprised the complement and from their appearance it is pretty clear that they had a very cold journey up. They danced to bring back the circulation and they yelled to let the natives know that they had 'coom up for th' match'. All wore their colours these 'Owls', blue all over even to the tip of their nose, for there was any amount of luminosity about them. From the pockets of many were to be seen peeping out suspicious looking bottles, many corked, but in the greater number of cases not so. One individual, obviously some kind of leader, bore as a badge of office a huge blue and white creation in the form of a tissue paper bouquet. Not among the whole motley crowd was there a man over 40, in fact the majority were from 16 to 30 years of age. After shouting and gyrating a little, the throng moved out of the station, and over

Foundry Bridge orderly and without a word to say. The crowd began to break up on its way up Prince of Wales Road and finally scattered to 'do the seets o' the city, before gooing to th' greaund."

We suspect that the reporter had not witnessed many football crowds, it was as though he was watching an invasion from outer space. As to the match itself the Canaries went ahead after 25 minutes on a treacherous frozen pitch. James Bauchop found himself free after his marker had slipped on the ice and 'quietly rounded the 'keeper and tipped the ball into the net'. After half time City went further ahead when Tommy Allsopp scored from 30 yards. At the end of the game there was much enthusiasm, in fact the EDP tells us 'There were wild scenes at the finish. The spectators, slipping and sliding all over the place, running in thousands across the ground. The majority of the City players were spared the trouble of walking to the pavilion'. The secret of City's fine win lay in the footwear they used, the Canaries played in rubber soled shoes but Wednesday used their normal football boots and paid the price. In the next round City accepted financial inducement to switch their tie to Fulham where they lost 1–2. Their guarantee was £650 and as over £670 had been taken at the Sheffield Wednesday match they should probably not have surrendered their home advantage.

John Pyke who masterminded the move to build a new City ground

As things turned out the Sheffield Wednesday match was the last FA Cup tie to be played at Newmarket Road. The Town Close Estate Charity wrote to the secretary of Norwich City FC early in January 1908 outlining the terms of any future lease that they might enter into. They stated that the Education Committee, who also used the Newmarket Road ground, would have the right to use the ground and facilities on each weekday except Saturdays when their rights would finish at noon. No matches would be allowed in the future to take place on Good Friday or Christmas Day and the Norwich City FC were to provide the necessary groundstaff and equipment for the upkeep of the playing surface. John Pyke, after reading the letter, made the following comment – 'It is rather like renting a shop, stocking it and preparing it for business, and someone else having the run of the place for five and a half days a week, no – it is obvious that we need a new ground'. It was John Pyke who had the idea of converting a disused chalk pit into a football ground, he first bought 'Ruymp's Hole' a disused chalk pit which was situated just off Rosary Road, then work began on levelling the site and making it suitable for football. There was much work to be done and thousands of tons of earth had to be moved but in the end all was ready for the new season. City still had money troubles, at the Annual General Meeting it was revealed that the club lost £1,206 during the 1907–08 season. Funds were urgently required to pay the summer wages and to move the stands from Newmarket Road to the new ground. Several schemes were put forward including a 6d ticket scheme, athletic sports, a cycle parade, a garden party, a guessing competition and there was even talk of holding promenade concerts on the new ground. It was also stated that Bowman had received a half years salary when he left the club – just over £120. John Howes, the secretary, when answering questions about expenses stated that he could not take another farthing off the outgoings of the club, a journey to London for the Reserves could not possibly be undertaken for less than 23s! Sadly Robert Webster who had acted as vice-chairman of the club for the past year resigned due to ill health. One last piece of business remained for the meeting to consider – a name for the new ground – and what else could you call the new home of the Canaries but the Nest. The curtain finally fell at Newmarket Road on the evening of Thursday 30 April 1908, the visitors were Chelsea in the Hospital Cup and the match finished 3–3. Thankfully it was a fine match and worthy of the occasion. City now had to leave behind their picturesque little ground and look forward to life in their new home at the Nest.

1908–1909

The stands at Newmarket Road were dismantled and transported to the Nest by horse and cart, a slow and arduous job, but one completed by the start of the 1908–09 season. Chairman John Pyke kicked off in the first match at the Nest, a friendly against Fulham on Tuesday 1 September 1908. The match commenced in pouring rain at 5.30pm before a crowd of just over 3,000. City won the match 2–1 despite missing a penalty, with new signing John Smith 'stirring the public pulse' by getting both the goals. Smith only played for the Canaries for the one season, he being a typical wandering soul who had already played for Wolverhampton Wanderers, Birmingham City and Bristol Rovers. He did however score 24 competitive goals during the season so it was a pity he didn't 'linger a little longer'. Norwich City FC again decided to enter the United League in addition to the Southern League. The United League was still a midweek affair, but the teams were now all recruited from the North and Midlands. City started very well in this the minor of the two league competitions and in fact only finished a single point behind the eventual winners Rotherham Town, but the gates were on the whole poor and not worthwhile. The move to the Nest certainly attracted more buyers of season tickets, sales were well up, and one could even purchase a 'Thursday Season' which allowed you to watch just the midweek fixtures. A bicycle park was provided on the new ground free of charge and the entrance fee was 1s at the Rosary Road end and 6d at the gates in Riverside Road and St Leonards Road.

The Southern League fixtures got off to a poor start, the first match being lost 0–4 at Luton and the second 2–10, yes 10, at Swindon. Apparently the match against Swindon Town was one of those games when everything went right for the home side, City were 1–6 down at the interval, and the final scoreline remains the heaviest defeat in their entire history. The first home game at the Nest in the Southern League took place on Saturday 12 September 1908. Portsmouth were the visitors and the match, which proved to be the last in a City shirt for Jimmy 'Punch' McEwen, finished in a 0–0 draw. McEwen was born in Liverpool in 1872 and had previously represented Luton Town, Glossop and of course Bury. He was a small man, he stood only 5ft 6ins, but was fearless on the field. Although the papers heralded him as manager in succession to John Bowman there is ample evidence that he did not have full managerial control. The team was often picked by Arthur Turner, the assistant manager, and it was not unknown for the directors to push their favourites forward when the teamsheet was being posted. After only 30 minutes play in the Portsmouth match McEwen badly injured his leg and left the pitch. He played 121 competitive games for the Canaries all as captain or 'manager'– what irony that his disablement should occur in the first Southern League game at the Nest. The 1994 book *Glorious Canaries* gives comprehensive details of his and everyone else's career.

New signing John Smith proved to be a 'shooting star' for City, lasting just the one season

City were drawn to play Reading in the FA Cup that season. The match was to have been at the Nest but Reading objected on the grounds that the pitch was not of the required size. The Football Association upheld the objection and Norwich were forced to play the tie at Stamford Bridge. A crowd of 15,732 witnessed a goalless draw and on the following Wednesday the two teams again drew, on this occasion 1–1 after

Preparing to build the Nest within the chalk pit site at Rosary Road

Further progress made in building the Nest

extra time at Reading. Yet again the two sides engaged in combat, this time at Villa Park, and it was left to 'Little Jack' Flanagan to score the winner in extra time. In the Second Round City were paired with First Division Liverpool and what is more they had to travel to Merseyside. Nobody of course gave City a chance of progressing through to the next round, but the gods that day were wearing yellow and green favours for City had three goal chances in the match and converted them all, the winner being scored in the last minute by John Smith. 32,000 watched the match in disbelief including the small band of City supporters who says the report – 'were swallowed up by the Liverpool hordes, they looked as insignificant as a Mersey ferry when compared with the Lusitania', which was at the time tied up by the Pier Head. Now what with disposing of Sheffield Wednesday in the 1907–08 competition and now First Division Liverpool the Canaries were gaining quite a reputation in the FA Cup, but sadly the bubble was burst at Bristol in the Third Round. The Canaries were no match for the Bristol City side that went on to reach the Final before being defeated 1–0 by Manchester United, a match watched incidentally by W.G. Grace who was supporting Bristol City.

A look at the list of City players about this time reveals an enormous amount of coming and going, top scorer John Smith was a good example for after just one season at the Nest he was off to Luton Town and later to Millwall. Walter James Rayner stayed for two seasons before also moving on to Luton Town. Later he managed Croydon Common in the Southern League and in 1920 became the first manager of Charlton Athletic in the Football League. Robert Hughes Beale, born in Maidstone early in 1884, joined City in the close season of 1908 from Brighton & Hove Albion and by the end of the season had replaced Peter Roney in the City goal. Beale was a fine goalkeeper and it was no surprise when, in the summer of 1912, Manchester United came for his services and as he had remained at Norwich for four years he was entitled to 35% of his transfer fee. When at Manchester United he represented the Football League against the Scottish League. After the First World War he returned to his native Kent and played one season with Gillingham, he passed away at Dymchurch on 5 October 1950. Charles Craig, a tall Scottish full back, stayed for two seasons joining City in November 1908 and leaving to join Southend United in readiness for the 1910–11 season. Top scorer for City in the Southern League in 1908–09 was Cyril Dunning an England Amateur International. Cyril scored his 15 Southern League goals in only 21 matches and found time to score a hat-trick in an England Amateur International against Germany on Saturday 13 March 1909. In all he won 5 Amateur caps and was a fine player but business and injury prevented him from substantially adding to his City appearances. He was born at Manor Farm, Colby on 20 February 1888 and died at Paston on 18 January 1962. One last point before we leave the players, it was noticeable that some players ages did not correspond with their career records and it appears that many of the players who drifted from club to club often shed a year or two while they were in their late 20s – no doubt it extended the career of many a man!

Probably the biggest mystery in the long history of the Canaries was the identity of the player who used the nom de plume 'A Canary' in three matches toward the end of the 1908–09 season. The author revealed his true idenitity in Norwich City's official handbook no.3.

When John Pyke stood up to present his report at the AGM at the end of the 1908–09 season there was a broad smile on his countenance. It appeared that the move across the city to the Nest had been a success, gates were up and the club even showed a small profit on the year's workings. In fact it was suggested by Pyke that if the club could have offered more accommodation under cover the profit would have been much higher. Unfortunately City finished third from the bottom of the Southern League, they had a very poor start to the season but they did manage to score 6 goals in each of the home matches against West Ham United, Brentford and Leyton, and one must not of course forget the famous FA Cup victory over Liverpool. During the season Robert Muir, who had now retired through injury, had a benefit match. The present City team played the men of the Past on Thursday 3 December 1908, Bowman played for the Past and scored a penalty. It was reported that he was a Sports Outfitter in Harrow Road, London, and he continued in the trade until his demise on 26 January 1943. Tucked just under the report of the 'Watton Rat and Sparrow Club', and what fun they had according to the account, was a note saying that the scheme for extending the Football League to include a Third Division was defeated at a meeting in Manchester on Friday 30 April 1909. We leave the Canaries in better financial shape after their initial season at their new home and look forward to Arthur Turner's first full campaign as the manager of Norwich City FC.

1909–1910

Louis Bleriot crossed the English Channel from Calais to Dover in an aeroplane on 25 July 1909 – he received the £1,000 prize from the Daily Mail for being the first man to perform the feat. On 1 January 1909 the first old age pension was paid out in Great Britain and Mr Ford stepped up the production of his famous Model T motor car. Later in the season on 19 February 1910 Old Trafford, the home of Manchester United FC was officially opened. Norwich City FC had a new secretary, Frank Kent, he took over from John Howes who remained a director of the club. Club captain for the season was the long serving Billy Bushell. It was decided not to enter the United League as the gates had not proved worthwhile. Percy 'Putt' Gooch was welcomed back to the club from Notts County, and in his first game of the season celebrated with a 28-minute hat-trick against Luton Town. Duncan Ronaldson was also welcomed back to the club, sadly minus his old partner David Ross, after a spell with Southend United. The man behind these reunions was of course City manager Arthur Turner but he also made some important new signings. William 'Billy' Hampson came to East Anglia from Bury FC, yet another to tread the familiar road. Billy was a fine full back born at Radcliffe (Lancs) on 26 August 1884. He stayed at Norwich until 1914 by which time he had chalked up 141 competitive First team appearances. After he left City he went to Newcastle United and remained there until 1927. He later became the first professional manager of Carlisle United, signing on Bill Shankly as a youngster, later still he became manager of Leeds United until 1947. He died at the Congleton War Memorial Hospital on 23 February 1966. Another new man was former England international centre half Sam Wolstenholme. Wolstenholme gained 3 England caps, one while at Everton and the other two

Billy Hampson

when he was at Blackburn Rovers. Turner also signed Percy Barnfather, a right winger from Croydon Common, Archie 'Ranji' Hubbard from Watford and later in the season inside forward William Rayner from Walthamstow.

Stan Wolstenhome, City's centre-half in 1909, and a former England international

Although not a very successful season, City finished sixth from the bottom of the Southern League, there was plenty of incident starting with the first fixture of the season. On Wednesday 1 September 1909 City visited Luton Town and travelled to the fixture by motor bus, it was the first time they had utilised this form of transport. On Saturday 18 September 1909 the visitors to the Nest were Bristol Rovers and their goalkeeper was former Canary Peter Roney. A large crowd gathered at the Nest on Monday 25 October 1909 to see City beat Crystal Palace 1–0, the attraction, as well as the football of course, was the visit of King Edward VII to Norwich (he did not actually attend the match). The Norwich City FC officials wished he would come to the city more often for the crowd of 12,078 was a new ground record at the Nest. City were plagued with bad luck, especially in their away games, for example in the fixture at Brighton & Hove Albion on Wednesday 1 December 1909 City were down to seven fit men at one stage and at one point there were only eight City men on the pitch. It came as no surprise that the home side won 5–0. On Tuesday 28 December 1909 City again felt the full force of the Swindon Town finishing, remember City had lost 2–10 the previous term, losing this time 1–7. In the FA Cup tie against Queen's Park Rangers at the Nest Archie Livingstone played for 70 minutes with a broken arm, at half time he received a pain killer and bravely carried on. The tie was drawn 0–0 but there was no FA Cup glory in 1909–10 for the replay was lost 0–3. The City Reserve centre half Honrie James Reed collapsed and died in a Second team fixture at Brighton on Saturday 5 February 1910. Reed was said to be a 27 year old blacksmith from London and at the start of the game was in perfect health. A benefit was played at Brighton on Saturday 19 February 1910 for his widow (see friendlies). City played the match at Southampton on Saturday 2 April with only 10 men because right half Swann did not put in an appearance. Swann lived in London and failed to meet the team at Waterloo Station, no explanation was ever given but he must have had a good excuse because he played two more matches later in the season. Despite the handicap City managed to draw the match 0–0.

On Wednesday 9 March 1910 the EDP informed its readers that Norwich City FC were to have a new manager. The notice, which was brief, simply said – 'We understand that a new manager of wide experience will shortly be

Below, a serious 1909–10 team pose with their board

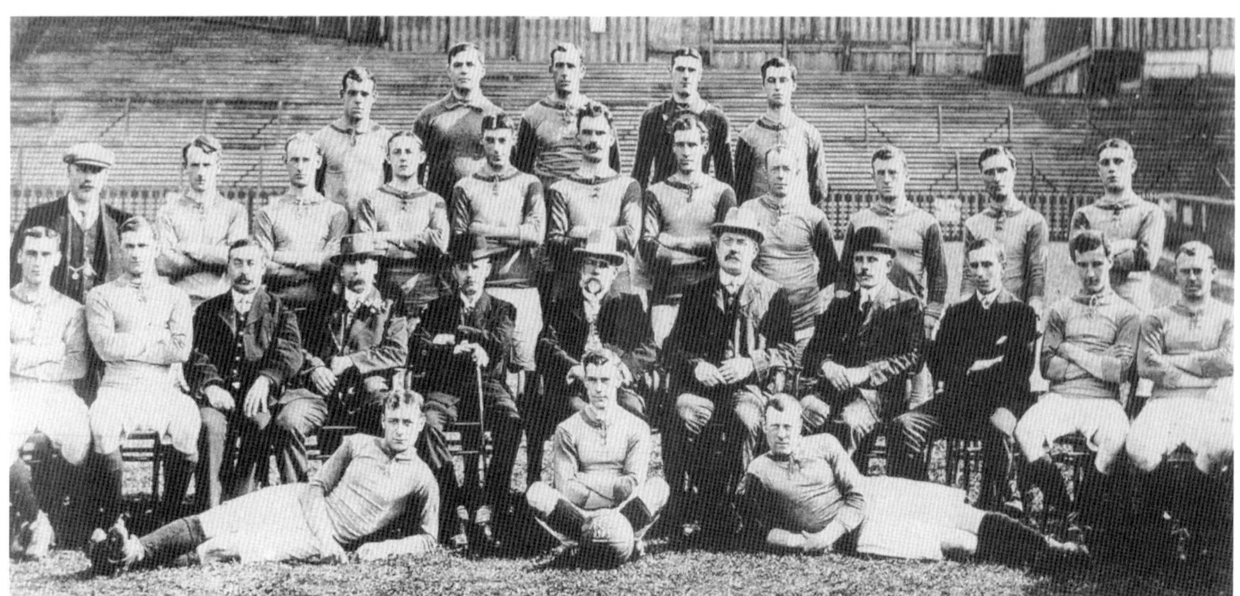

appointed to Norwich City FC'. On Friday the identity of the new man was made known, he was James Burton Stansfield. Stansfield, known as 'Bert', was a 35 year old married man who was a friend of the Football League official Mr Charles Sutcliffe. He was not to come to Norwich straight away but was expected in the city at the end of the month. On Good Friday 25 March 1910 Stansfield made his first public appearance when he sat next to Mr Pyke in the directors box at the Portsmouth match. He was a former secretary of Rossendale United FC and was later associated with Carlisle United FC. In his early days he had been a referee and it was said he possessed personal charm and integrity. Poor Arthur Turner was shown the door soon after the arrival of the new man, he had served the club well since their formation in 1902, and it was sad to see him go. What then would James Stansfield be able to achieve with the Canaries?

1910–1911

The club handbook of 1910–11 was a new format pocket-sized edition. It tells us that during the close season the playing surface at the Nest was completely overhauled. As soon as the 1909–10 season closed workmen moved in to plough up the pitch and put in new drains. They also made the playing area longer and there was now no question of not being able to stage FA Cup ties in Norwich. More terracing was added to the St Leonard's Road side and the Rosary Road end was also rebuilt. It was reckoned that the ground would now hold another 1,500 people. A cinder track was added for training purposes and the dressing room accommodation was doubled. What is needed now, said the handbook, is the support of the public to fill these improved spaces. In addition to the ground improvements City also had a new director Mr Charles Bolingbroke Leathes Prior, father of recent local Tory MP Mr James Prior, joined the board at the AGM. Several new men appeared as James Stansfield strove to find a winning combination. From Carlisle United came full back 'Jock' Mackenzie, born at Douglas, Lanarkshire in 1885, Mackenzie wore a City shirt until the outbreak of the First World War. In all he made 204 competitive appearances for the Canaries and was the first man to break the 200 barrier. William 'Billy' Ingham was signed from Stansfield's former club Rossendale United. Billy also went on to play for City for several seasons, he left to join Darlington in the summer of 1914, and twice represented the Southern League in October 1913. Other players who were known to Stansfield were Len Jobling who had been at Carlisle United but was born on Wearside and later attended the FA Cup tie between City and Sunderland in 1951, Eddie Whiteside who was formerly at Rossendale United and Arthur Stringfellow who came later in the season from Little Lever Lads.

The season started well with 7 wins and 2 draws in the first 12 games indeed after the 3–2 win over Luton Town on Saturday 22 October 1910 City were in third place in the league. The good start could not however be sustained and at the end of the season City had to be content with a mid-table position. Strangely Watford missed two penalties against City on Saturday 29 October 1910 and a fortnight later Plymouth Argyle did exactly the same thing, both matches were away from home and both were lost so it made no difference to the outcome. Later in the season Brentford had to play 30 minutes with ten men as one of their players missed his train, as in the incident at Southampton the previous season when City played the entire game a man short it makes one wonder why there was no travelling reserve. City lost in customary fashion at Swindon on Tuesday 27 December 1910 this time by I–5. We must point out though that Swindon Town were champions of the Southern League in 1910–11 and had a very fine side.

James B Stansfield, appointed manager in the 1910 season replacing the long-serving Arthur Turner

The excitement as usual was reserved for the FA Cup and mighty Sunderland were the visitors to the Nest on Saturday 14 January 1911. Billy

Above, Billy Ingham, a new forward signed by Stansfield

Hampson, usually of course a full back, was converted to centre forward for the day and scored two fine goals. In fact City shocked Sunderland by taking a 2 goal lead early in the game. The score at half time was 2–1 but City went further ahead after the interval and won 3–1. It was a fine scalp for the Canaries who were beginning to make quite a name for themselves in the FA Cup, for Sunderland finished third in the First Division that year. Another team who had a good season in their league, they finished fifth in the First Division with the same number of points as Sunderland, were Bradford City and they were City's opponents in the next round of the FA Cup. This time City had to travel and only narrowly lost by 1–2, Billy Ingham being the scorer. There is no doubt that these superb performances in the national soccer showpiece did City no harm at all, what was needed now was more consistency in the Southern League. Surprisingly the match against Sunderland did not attract a record crowd but the ground record was broken during the 1910–11 season in the Hospital Cup match against Newcastle United. United were the holders of the FA Cup and they brought it with them when they came to Norwich on Monday 19 September 1910. 13,473 forced their way into the Nest to snatch a glimpse of the glittering trophy, they were also treated to a fine match which ended in a 1–1 draw.

1911–1912

In 1911 British Members of Parliament were paid for the first time, a National Insurance scheme was introduced and on Thursday 14 December 1911 Roald Amundsen, the Norwegian explorer became the first man to reach the South Pole. On the night of 14/15 April 1912 the Titanic went down with great loss of life. Closer to home Norwich City FC were financially holding their head above water, but not it must be said, without difficulty. At the start of the season, in what was Stansfield's second full term, there were new faces at the Nest. Henry Woods, a

NORWICH CITY, 1911-12.
COMER, STRINGFELLOW, WOLSTENHOLME, HAMPSON, BEALE, MELLOR, HARTLEY, W. S. ALDEN, POTTS, PEARSON:
FELL, TAYLOR, (CAPTAIN) CURTIN, BIBBY, WILKINSON, MACKENZIE, KIRKMAN:
J.B. STANSFIELD. (MANAGER) JOBLING, INGHAM, POTTER, WOODS, BIRCHALL, C. MILES, (TRAINER).
(HAYWARD KIDD, PHOTO, BANK PLAIN, NORWICH.)

The team in 1911

Lancashire lad from St Helens, arrived and became joint top scorer of 4 for City in the Southern League. The problem that season was the lack of goals, only 40 in 38 Southern League games. Woods shared the dubious honour of top scoring with Billy Ingham, Dick Birchall and Cecil Potter, each man scored 7 goals. Henry Woods stayed with City until the war scoring in all 37 goals in competitive matches, later he played for Newcastle United, Arsenal and Luton Town. Cecil Bertram Potter meanwhile joined the club from Ipswich Town, then still an amateur club in the Southern Amateur League. Potter later returned to Norwich City as manager, but that was not until the mid 1920s. James William Peacock also played a few games for City that season, he was a friend of Potter and had also turned out for Ipswich Town.

In the first seven games of the season the same team did duty in every match – a club record. City eventually finished in 12th position despite the lack of goals and suffered only one bad reverse during a rather uneventful season.

On Saturday 28 October 1911 City travelled to Crystal Palace and lost 0–6. That great barometer of City's performances at this time, i.e. how the Canaries fared at Swindon, divulged no positive clue as to the future for Norwich lost 3–5 away and won 4–3 at the Nest. There was a swift exit from the FA Cup that year City having to travel to Blackburn where they lost 1–4. At the end of the season, which had begun in a heatwave, City said goodbye to two trusty servants, Robert Beale the goalkeeper went to Manchester United and Freddy Wilkinson, moved north to Darlington.

Fred Wilkinson

Sequel to FA Cup match at Blackburn. A cotton weaver tried to extort money from the City chairman by pretending to be the Blackburn Rovers goalkeeper.

1912–1913

Just before the season began the city of Norwich suffered greatly at the hands of a natural phenomenon – the great flood of 1912. It rained heavily all day on Monday 26 August 1912 and the deluge continued well into the following day. The Wensum rose to such a level that has never been seen before or since and that includes the terrible floods of 1953. In all, three people lost their lives and many more were flooded out and lost their possessions. Postcards and newspapers of the time vividly portray a very grim picture and the EDP informs us that seven and a half inches of rain fell in 24 hours. The Norwich Corporation quickly organised relief for stranded citizens and volunteers reached those in need with the aid of small boats. Another to suffer from the flood was the Norfolk County Cricket Club, they were leading the Minor Counties table but because of the weather were unable to play their final game. Earlier in the cricket season the Australian tourists played a match against an England XI at Lakenham and Michael Falcon became captain of the Norfolk CCC, a position he held until 1946.

Two more players who were known to manager Stansfield joined the club, left half Arthur Woodland from St Helens Town and right winger William Bauchop, brother of former Canary James Bauchop, came from Carlisle. City again had the old problem of lack of goals to contend with and this time managed one fewer than the previous seasons' total ie 39. Billy Ingham and Henry Woods were joint top scorers for City in the Southern League with 7 goals each. Only victories in the last 2 games prevented City from finishing in the bottom two,

'Jock' Mackenzie, an ever-present at full back in 1912–13

The team of 1912 included some fine players but could only achieve a mediocre season's performance

in fact they finished third from bottom. In the FA Cup City were drawn to play Leicester Fosse at Leicester (they changed their name to Leicester City after the First World War). The tie took place on Saturday 11 January 1913 and it snowed so much that the referee had to abandon the game after 65 minutes with the score at 0–0. On Thursday 18 January 1913 City again made the journey to the Midlands and were rewarded with a 4–1 victory. 1912–13 was not one of Leicester's better seasons, but they still managed to finish in the middle of the Second Division. 14,539 witnessed the Bristol Rovers v Norwich City match in the next round at Bristol, the final score was 1–1 and the replay at the Nest was fixed for Thursday 6 February 1913. The gates were locked before the kick off with 13,173 inside the ground. The decision to close the gates surprised us because you will remember that 13,473, exactly 300 more, had crowded in to see the Hospital Cup match on Monday 19 September 1910. Well whatever the reason the gates were closed and many more had to wait outside and listen to the crowd. Despite goals from Henry Woods and new boy Percy Sutcliffe, and a half hour period of extra time, the match finished in a 2–2 draw. City had the best of the exchanges but could not score the all important winner. The second replay took place at Stamford Bridge the following Monday and this time Rovers managed to secure a 1–0 victory. During the second half there was an unsavoury incident involving the City goalkeeper William Mellor, the referee made a subsequent report and Mellor was suspended for two weeks. On the whole then, the FA Cup matches aside, 1912–13 was another mediocre season enlivened though on Easter Monday 24 March 1913 when a flyer buzzed the patrons at the Nest during the game against Northampton Town.

On Monday 10 February 1913 Robert Webster, 'father', friend and mentor of Norwich City FC breathed his last breath. He had been troubled for some time with illness that had forced him to resign as a director of the club. His great friend and fellow founder of the club Joe Nutchey wrote a letter to the EDP simply headed – 'Bob Webster'

"Let the heading stand, Mr Editor, please. I know Mr Webster was headmaster of one of the largest boys' schools in Norwich, chairman of the Norfolk County FA, the Football Association representative, but Bob he will always be to me and a host of others. When I visited him a fortnight ago his spirits were low, and he was feeling the long struggle very bitterly. I tried to cheer him up by telling him he was playing a cup-tie, and he had never shirked it yet. For a moment his eyes brightened, and when I reminded him of some of our victories, he roused himself remarkably. The fighting force was there, but it had been weakened by many rough matches with disease, and when I visited him on Sunday I knew he was beaten, but he played the game gallantly through to the finish."

1913–1914

On Saturday 6 September 1913 Highbury Stadium was opened. 1913–14, the last full season before the outbreak of the First World War saw some improvement in City's position. They managed to increase the number of goals scored to 49 and moved up to 14th place in the Southern League. Top scorer in the latter competition was new signing Arthur Wolstenholme who joined the club from Gillingham. He managed to score 13 goals and Henry Woods was second with 10. Another new face that year belonged to Issac George 'Pompey' Martin, a centre half who was signed from Portsmouth. It was rather strange that he gained the cognomen 'Pompey' for he certainly didn't come from the south of England and he only played at Portsmouth for one season. He was in fact born at Gateshead in 1889 and joined Sunderland at the age of 19. After 3 years at Roker Park he moved to Portsmouth and in the summer of 1913 to Norwich City FC. He was a character, of that there is no doubt, and after the war he resumed his career with the Canaries and played until the end of the 1926–27 season for a long time as captain. He took the place of Sam Wolstenholme who had to give up the game because of injury, by the way Sam and Arthur Wolstenholme were not related. The high spot of another quite uninspiring season was the 6–0 victory over Southend United on Saturday 3 January 1914, Arthur Wolstenholme scored 4 goals and by all accounts City were unstoppable and should really have scored 6 more. Swindon Town won the championship that year and again achieved the double over the Canaries.

The FA Cup was organised on a different basis for the 1913–14 season; certain of the Southern League clubs were required to join the competition at the qualifying stage and on Saturday 29 November 1913 City met Walthamstow Grange in the 4th Qualifying Round at the Nest. It was not made clear if the London club were amateur or professional, but whichever they were no match for the Canaries. Henry Woods got a hat-trick and Arthur Wolstenholme a brace in the 6–0 win. Halifax Town were the next visitors to the Nest in December, it was their first visit to Norwich and not a very happy one because City won 2–0. On Saturday 10 January 1914 City travelled to London to play Crystal Palace in the First Round proper. The attendance was 8,888 and City were eliminated from the competition by the odd goal in three. After the match Newcastle United made a bid for City goalkeeper William Mellor, their offer of £765 was debated by the board and accepted. A week later Newcastle United came back for full back Billy Hampson and again they were successful. The fee it was said was the biggest that City had ever received, but the exact figure was not revealed. There was a new competition for Southern League clubs, the Southern Charity Cup, and City reached the Semi-final before being dispatched by Coventry City. The match took place at White Hart Lane and the final score was 0–3. At the end of a rather tranquil season it was difficult to foresee the upheaval that lay ahead – war clouds were gathering over the skies of Europe.

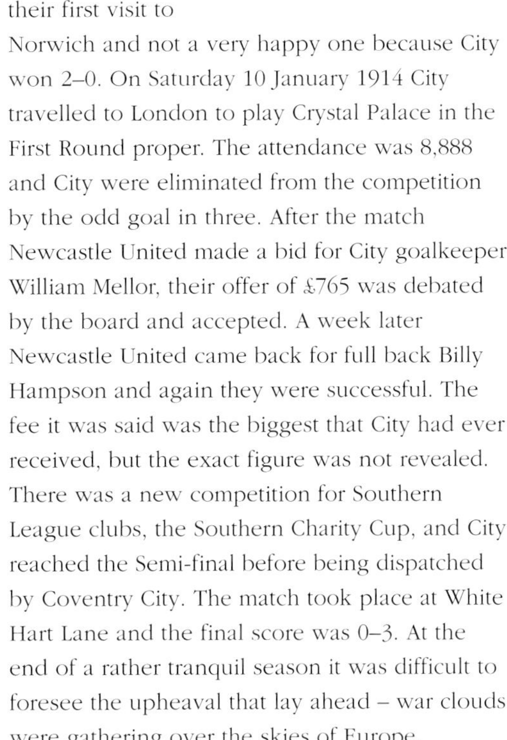

Arthur Wolstenholme, above, and George 'Pompey' Martin, left, were important new signings in this pre-war season

1914–1915

On Tuesday 4 August 1914 Great Britain declared war on Germany. As students of the period will know nothing much happened for the first few months so the football authorities decided to continue and a complete list of fixtures was played in both the Football League and the Southern League. The FA Cup was also played as normal in 1914–15, the trophy being won that year by Sheffield United who beat Chelsea 3–0. City showed a slight improvement over the previous season and finished in 13th position in the Southern League. 53 goals were scored in the competition with Cecil Potter and George Ritchie being joint top scorers with 11 goals each. Several new men were drafted into the team as others left to join the fighting forces.

The cup-tie played behind closed doors on 3 March 1915

A FAMOUS CUP-TIE.

BRADFORD THROUGH.

NORWICH MISS CHANCES

TWO GOALS IN LAST TEN MINUTES.

CROWD GAIN ADMISSION

The second re-play between the city teams of Norwich and Bradford took place yesterday on the ground of the Lincoln City Club, and produced another fine struggle. With the wind behind them Norwich had the best of matters in the first half, but Bradford's fine defence and the failure of the Norwich forwards to make the best use of some scoring opportunities, prevented them from getting the lead which the run of the play warranted. Bradford did better after the interval, but nothing vital happened till ten minutes from the end, when McDonald scored out of a scrimmage, and with the last kick of the match Bond scored a second goal from the penalty spot. Bradford thus qualified at the third attempt to meet Everton in the fourth round on Saturday. By order of the Football Association, no spectators were admitted, only the officials and the Press representatives being present, to the number of about 300. It was certainly a unique spectacle to see an F.A. Cup-tie minus the crowd, and to some it appeared that the opportunity for granting the proceeds of the "gate" to one of the deserving funds at the present juncture had been allowed to pass by. During the interval an attempt was made to force the main gate by several hundred people, and their attitude was so threatening that Mr. McKenna, the chairman of the Football League, ordered the gates to be opened, and the closing scenes of the historic match were witnessed by a fair company.

From Fulham came right half Arthur Collins; he had played at Fulham since 1905 and had been captain for four seasons. John 'Jock' Denoon, surely a fine name for a Scot, came from Chelsea and after the war played for Swansea Town for several seasons. The regular goalkeeper in 1914–15 was Joe Lansdale; born Little Lever, Lancashire 4 March 1894, Joe had been on the staff since July 1912, but had few opportunities of playing before the departure of Mellor. After the war Joe played for Millwall until 1930 and it was said he had a habit of hanging on to the net before he took his goalkicks. Joint top scorer George Ritchie joined the club the season before from Chester, but had previously played for Stansfield at Rossendale United. City even had a centre forward on the books called Arthur Turner, who as far as we know was no relation to the former City manager. As the war progressed and more men signed up in the armed forces a number of local men got to play, for example Walter Joseph Taylor born in Norwich in 1887. Taylor first played for City in 1906–07 as an amateur before leaving to join Doncaster Rovers for the 1908–09 season. He appeared in 31 games in 1914–15 his only season as a first choice Canary and scored 6 goals. Later in life he worked in the clicking room of W. Hurrell Ltd for over 30 years, many as foreman. He took over a newsagents business at 146, Magdalen Street from Hugh McQueen the old City trainer just after the Second World War and died in Norwich on 7 May 1961.

Other men to appear in 1914–15 were Thomas Valentine a Norwich teacher who played on 10 occasions and scored a goal, John Henry Allen from King's Lynn and Albert Frosdick. Allen was involved in an FA dispute after the war, it was said he received a silver cigarette case for playing as an amateur for the City Reserve side. He later became a fish merchant in his native King's Lynn. Frosdick was a local player for Carrow Works and carried on playing after the war making appearances in the Football League for City. A last local player was Charles William Christmas Abbs who made just one appearance as centre forward on Saturday 24 October 1914 against Millwall at the Nest. Abbs was a member of the fishmonger family of East Runton and he died there on 1 September 1956.

Crowds were down on the season which as we said was steady, but apart for another run in the FA Cup, never exciting. Jock Mackenzie created a new record on Tuesday 6 April 1915 when in an away fixture at Millwall he made his 200th City appearance, and the Canaries celebrated the occasion by winning 1–0. 'Pompey' Martin not yet the cool and dependable centre half that he was to become in his later years was sent off in the match against Swindon Town (a) on Saturday 3 October 1914, City lost 0–4 and Martin was later suspended for a month.

Despite the hostilities there was still some excitement in the FA Cup in 1914–15, City were drawn to play Nottingham Forest of the Second Division and before a crowd of 8,040 proceeded to march to victory by 4–1. Tottenham Hotspur, a First Division side, were visitors to the Nest in the next round and on Saturday 30 January 1915 the Canary bandwagon rolled on with a 3–2 victory. In the Third Round City had to travel to Bradford City and before a crowd of 20,877 held the First Division side to a 1–1 draw. After a further draw in the replay at the Nest the two sides met on neutral ground at Sincil Bank, Lincoln. The game took place on the afternoon of Wednesday 3 March 1915 and because it was thought that the game would distract the workers in the munition factory nearby the FA ordered the game to be played behind closed doors. Well, the workers knowing that the game was in progress tried to force their way into the ground and the Chairman of the Football League, Mr McKenna, who happened to be present ordered the gates to be opened on the grounds of public safety. About 1,000 were estimated to have eventually entered the ground, of course they paid nothing at all and no record of the actual attendance was ever kept. They proved to be bearers of bad luck for Norwich because the Northerners scored two goals in the last ten minutes to end City's interest in the FA Cup. City again entered the Southern Charity Cup and won their way through to the Second Round by beating Gillingham 4–1. Later because of the pressure of fixtures in the FA Cup City decided to withdraw undefeated from the competition. The hell of the trench warfare raged on the mainland of Europe and City waited for it all to end so that battle of a more sporting kind could continue at the Nest.

Cecil Potter, whose 11 goal tally made him joint top league scorer with George Ritchie in 1914–15

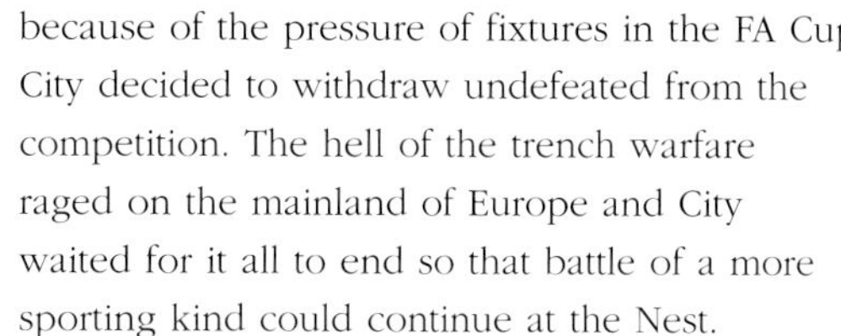

1915–1916

The football authorities held a meeting at the Winter Gardens, Blackpool on 5 July 1915 to decide the future of football. It came as no real surprise that it was agreed that in the best interests of the nation, and all those involved in the war effort, competitive football should close down until the war ended. It was left to individual clubs to decide if they wished to continue to play friendly matches or shut down completely. Norwich City FC chose the former option and arranged a series of friendlies mostly at the Nest. Nearly all were against Service sides (a full list appears in the statistical section) and included on Saturday 23 October 1915 a match against the 6th Norfolk Cyclists which City won 3–1. Of course by this time many regular players had left for active service and the gaps were filled either by local lads or servicemen stationed in Norfolk. One such local player to turn out regularly was Robert George Pilch, a grand nephew of the former England cricketer Fuller Pilch. He was born at Holt on 12 October 1877 and moved to Norwich in 1895 where he joined up with Webster and Nutchey at the CEYMS club. For 25 years he was the backbone of the club offering sterling service as centre forward, half back, full back and even on occasions goalkeeper. Add to that his work as president, chairman, secretary and committeeman and his proficiency at cricket, golf, hockey and squash and one gets some idea of his contribution to Norfolk sport. He twice turned out for Norwich City FC in the Southern League and even turned out against the Canaries on 30 April 1907 for Everton in the Hospital Cup Final at Newmarket Road. Jack Sharp the Everton and England outside right missed his train connection and George, who should have been the referee, agreed to turn out for the Liverpool club. Between 1923 and 1953 George served as a director of Norwich City FC and was vice chairman between 1930 and 1947. It was George who started the Norwich Sports Outfitters company of R.G. Pilch Ltd in 1906. He died on 1 November 1957 and must have been sad that City were at such a low ebb at the time.

Another local newcomer in 1915 was Arthur Robert Hawes known to all as 'Tricky'. Hawes was born at Swanton Morley on 20 October 1895 and like Pilch played his early football at Norwich CEYMS. In 1915, when he would have been 20 years old, he played in most of the City friendly fixtures and scored at least 34 goals (Norwich often scored so many in a match that the reporter lost count). 'Tricky' played for City in the 1919–20 season, their last in the Southern League, and then moved on to South Shields for a season. His next club was Sunderland for whom he played between 1921 and 1927, lastly he moved on to Bradford Park Avenue and stayed for a further 2 years. After his playing career in the north he returned to Norwich turning out for Frosts and later becoming the coach of Norwich Gothic. He died in Norwich on 11 October 1963. His father Arthur Thomas Hawes, and also known as 'Tricky', was assistant trainer at the Nest between 1915 and 1936. As we said, City scored a tremendous number of goals during the season, their record was – Played 40, Won 36, Drawn 1 and Lost 3. In all 220 goals were scored and only 40 conceded, on average City scored five and a half goals a game. It was reported that trainer Miles was also acting as groundsman at this time, a positive indication that money was in short supply. City had never had a lot of money and the situation was not getting any better.

Two local players – Robert George Pilch left, born in Holt, later to become a City Director and Arthur 'Tricky' Hawes, right, from Swanton Morley – featured in City's wartime team

1916–1917

Bennie Smith in his army service uniform

By 1916 it had dawned on most of the citizens of these Isles that Britain was involved in a very bloody and bitter struggle with Germany. Strange now to think that men had fought each other for a place in the joining up queue, just in case they were too late and would miss the action, and that young boys added years to their age in order to be accepted. At the Nest Norwich City continued to play their friendlies just as in the previous season. The record for the season read – played 33, won 28, drawn 2 and lost 3. 139 goals were scored and 40 conceded. Among those who played a few games were Henry Woods, 'Tricky' Hawes and Bennie Smith. 'Jock' Mackenzie, the former City full back, paid a visit to the Nest and would have played but he hadn't got his boots. He proudly wore two stripes upon his arm and we later heard he was promoted to sergeant, his regiment being the Royal Garrison Artillery. He returned to his unit in Egypt and when next in Norwich sported the Victory medal and the British War medal. One institution that was not allowed to disappear even in the depth of the war was the Norwich Hospital Cup. On Saturday 28 April 1917 Norwich City FC played the East Anglian Munitions League in the Final and won 4–1, the crowd was 1,260 and the receipts were £32.16s 6d.

1917–1918

It appears that only two matches took place during the 1917–18 season, the first a charity match on 27 October 1917 and the second the Norwich Hospital Cup match on 1 April 1918, City played the 193rd Infantry Brigade at the Nest and won 2–1 before a crowd of 3,959. There was however 'action' of a very different kind for on Monday 10 December 1917 a meeting was held at the Museum Cafe to wind up the Norwich City Football Club. It appears that the debts of Norwich City FC were more than had been feared and the only sensible thing to do was to call in the liquidator. The Mr C. Watling who had some words of comfort for the poor City directors was Charles Frederick Watling the father of City President Mr Geoffrey Watling. The affairs of the club were put on ice and the Nest was locked up to await the outcome of the whole sorry business, and on the mainland of Europe the terrible struggle continued.

NORWICH CITY F.C., LTD.

TO BE WOUND UP.

Norwich City Football Club, Ltd., after a plucky fight against adverse circumstances, has now to be wound up. This decision was made at the annual general meeting of shareholders held last evening at the Museum Cafe, the following resolution having been carried:—"That owing to the company being unable to meet its liabilities, it is hereby resolved that the same be wound up voluntarily, and that Mr. Robert Charles Spicer, of Queen Street, Norwich, incorporated accountant, be and is hereby appointed liquidator."

More than one of the shareholders expressed regret that this course was necessary, but it was generally accepted that there was no alternative. The resolution, in order to become really effective, will be submitted for confirmation to an extraordinary general meeting to be held at a later date. There is little likelihood of the resolution not receiving such confirmation.

The directors' report stated that the policy of "carrying on" during the war had further increased the indebtedness of the club by £309 16s. 4d., bringing the total accumulated losses up to £7328 19s. 7d.

According to the balance sheet the liabilities amount to £9294 8s. 6d., made up of the following items:—3292 shares at £1 each (less calls in arrears £51) £3241, loans and interest £3016 3s. 1d., balance due to bank £1981 10s. 7d., creditors £1055 14s. 10d. The assets are:—Estimated value of effects £400, goodwill £1500, sundry debtors £60 8s. 11d., South-Eastern League deposit £5.

Mr. W. T. Blyth, one of the directors, presided at the shareholders' meeting. "It is the first time I have been in the chair," he said, "and it looks as if it is going to be the last."

The financial statement and the directors' report were passed without comment.

The Chairman subsequently referred to the resolution that the club should go into liquidation, stating that it was unnecessary to go into the pros and cons of the case. It must, he said, be very evident to all of them that it was impossible for the club to continue. The bank were pressing for payment, and in the circumstances the directors had no option but to place the matter before the shareholders.

Mr. C. Watling moved the resolution, observing that to the shareholders it seemed that there was nothing else that could be done. Personally, he felt that the thanks of sportsmen in Norwich were due to the directors for having kept the old ship going as long as they have done. Some directors, Mr. Watling added, would have wound up the club long ago. "No one is more sorry than I am to see the club go into liquidation, but still we won't lose heart. There is really no reason why one of these days, when circumstances will become more favourable, the old club should not be started again and have a glorious future."

Mr. W. Kerry seconded the motion, which was carried unanimously.

Mr. Blyth, in acknowledging the friendliness of the comments, remarked that it showed that the shareholders agreed that the directors had really done their best to keep the old flag flying. Circumstances, however, had been so dead against them that it was impossible to go on. They had not been able to play any matches with any profit, and had accordingly only got further into difficulty. The course that had been taken had been forced upon them.

Mr. J. W. Howes (secretary pro. tem.) explained that should anything come forward between that date and the next extraordinary general meeting, for the salvation of the club, the resolution which had just been carried would not stand.

Acknowledging a vote of thanks, the Chairman spoke of his long association with the club, in which he said he had always been interested as a sportsman. The directors, who were a good body of men, had always worked amicably together, and if they could have seen their way they would have saved the club from such a fate. Perhaps some day it would revive, and if so he would be in it. (Applause)

In reply to a question as to whether there could be a match occasionally at the Nest, the Chairman said arrangements were being made to provide one on Christmas morning, but the club were not responsible for them.

1918–1919

The Great War finally ended on Monday 11 November 1918 and less than a week before that date, on Wednesday 6 November 1918, an extraordinary meeting of the Norwich City FC was held at the Norwich Social Club. City were of course in voluntary liquidation, but Mr Blyth who presided called upon the liquidator Robert Spicer to inform the meeting of the latest position. Spicer said that since the last meeting only £5 had been paid to the club, that being a deposit that had been forwarded to the South Eastern League, and had since been returned. There was no chance of any more debts of the club being paid for they were all outstanding from other football clubs, and they were as badly off as Norwich City. The net result therefore was that the total available assets realised was £5 and that sum was credited to the cost of the winding up expenses which it was estimated would amount to £47. This sum would be met by the directors who have from the start of the company thus lost the following sums. Loans and interest £3,016 3s 1d, guarantees for overdraft at bankers £1,900 and winding up expenses £42 the total of which is £4,958 3s 1d. The shareholders subscribed for 3,292 shares of which calls amounting to £51 were not paid. Every effort was made to collect this amount, but it was found impossible to collect anything from this source. It will be seen therefore that the creditors will obtain no dividend and that the shareholders capital has been entirely lost. Mr Blyth said that it was a very unsatisfactory statement, but added that it was the best that could be done. He went on to say that the winding up was disastrous and they had all lost a lot of money it was however best to do it and cut their losses. All present hoped that some day a new club might be formed, many in fact expressed a wish to do all they could to help a new club, but that was all in the future.

Above, chairman of the revived City club W Blyth and below, new manager Major Franklin Charles Buckley, also a very experienced player

The good people of Norwich did not have long to wait before proposals were afoot to restart a professional football club in the city, for on Saturday 15 February 1919 a meeting took place at the Great Eastern Hotel. At that meeting Mr Blyth read out a letter from the Southern League pointing out that Norwich City FC were still members of that body and at the conclusion of the meeting Blyth proposed that a company be formed with a nominal capital of £5,000 and Norwich City FC be reformed. The body of the meeting were unanimously in favour of the proposal and £1,800 was forthcoming that very evening. At a further meeting on Friday 7 March 1919 Chairman Blyth stated that another £750 had been pledged and it was decided to go ahead and get the Nest ready for the coming season. On Wednesday 19 March 1919 Major Franklin Charles Buckley was appointed the new Norwich City FC manager. Buckley was born in Manchester on 9 November 1883 and played as a centre half for Brighton & Hove Albion, Manchester United, Manchester City, Birmingham City, Derby County and Bradford City. He won one England cap on 14 February 1914 against Northern Ireland, England lost the match 0–3. During the war he joined the Middlesex 'footballers' battalion and was commissioned in January 1914. In March 1916 he was promoted to Captain and in less than a year became a Major. He was severely injured on the Somme and left the service on 9 November 1918. When appointed to the managers job at Norwich it was said he was a farmer at Redditch. He was 'six foot tall, an athlete down to his little toe and a gentleman into the bargain' said the local paper. He also mentioned that he would like to carry on playing but was not certain because of his injury.

City were lucky in their choice of manager and very soon the Nest was looking more like its old self. Some practice games were played in late April 1919 and Birmingham City journeyed to Norfolk for a friendly match on 3 May 1919. City won the match 2–1 with both goals being scored by Sam Jennings in the first half. City were glad to be back in business, the terror and destruction of the war was behind them, where now would the good Major Buckley lead his new team?

1919–1920

The newly sown grass at the Nest had, by the middle of August 1919, made good progress and work had also been carried out on new dressing rooms and bathrooms. There was a new recreation room for the players and improved accommodation for the directors. Major Buckley had been busy and signed a host of new players. Left winger Tom Batey had been with Bristol City before the war and was unlucky to break his leg in the match against Southampton on Saturday 15 November 1919, sadly he never played again. Batey had won medals for bravery in France and it was a nice gesture by Norwich City FC to organise a collection for him at the match with Gillingham on Saturday 29 November 1919, when over £90 was raised for him and his family. Inside forward Jimmy Broadhead had been with Rotherham County before the war, he later went on to South Shields and Nelson. Captain Harry Alban Dix played just three games and scored a goal for the Canaries during the season, Dix was stationed at Landguard Fort, Felixstowe and was the captain of Ipswich Town FC in the 1920–21 season. He didn't play many games though for his regiment and he was soon posted to Ireland. John Doran was a dashing centre forward, born in Belfast in 1896 John was top scorer in 1919–20 with 18 goals in the Southern League. 'Jack' Groves was a goalkeeper from the Midlands. Born in 1899 at Bulwell, 'Jack' was the 'keeper in the FA Cup tie at Darlington on 20 December 1919. City lost 0–5 and later Groves was suspended sine die by the Norwich City FC directors for his insubordination. It was pointed out at the time that the decision had nothing to do with his performance in the FA Cup tie. 1919–20 was George Gray's first season with the club, he played in all but one game and went on to play with distinction in the Football League.

Fretwell Hall was the youngest of 5 footballing brothers from the Sheffield area, he later played for Brighton & Hove Albion and Halifax Town. Philip Hope made his debut at left back and went on to play in the Football League. The Jennings brothers were also born at Bulwell, Nottinghamshire, Bill the older of the two by 7 years had played for Notts County before the war and was the father of Henry William Jennings who played for Ipswich Town FC in the late 40s. Sam Jennings

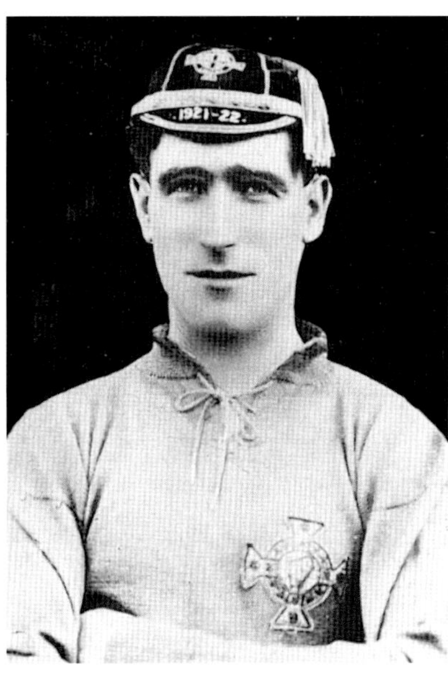

John Doran, top scoring centre forward from Belfast

The post-war team featured a host of Major Buckley's new signings

was transferred to Middlesbrough before the season ended and brought City a record fee of £2,250. Michael O'Brien played 10 games for the Canaries during the season, he later had a second spell at the club and later still became the first professional manager of Ipswich Town FC in 1936. Regular goalkeeper that year was Herbert Edward Skermer, a Midlander who went on to play in the Football League. Lastly we must mention Benjamin George Smith, a local full back who signed amateur forms and made 29 appearances during the season. City finished comfortably in the middle of the Southern League that season and had they have won any of their final 11 games they would have finished much higher. It was then a steady and fairly uneventful first campaign for Major Buckley, but it was also to be his last and the last that Norwich City FC played in the Southern League.

Edward Laxton, Norwich City's Brazilian-born player

On Monday 31 May 1920 the Football League held its Annual General Meeting in London. There was, before the assembly, a suggestion that the Football League form a Third Division consisting of a Southern and a Northern section. After debate it was agreed that subject to the consent of the Football Association the clubs that at present form Division One of the Southern League shall comprise the Third Division for 1920–21. In the following season the Football League formed the Northern section of the Third Division and they henceforth became known as Division 3 South and Division 3 North. City should have been overjoyed at the good news but back in Norwich there was again trouble brewing. Also on 31 May 1920 it was reported that Norwich City FC made a profit of £364 15s 8d on the years trading, the sale of Sam Jennings to Middlesbrough for £2,250 had been a major contributory factor, but nevertheless the figure was better than had been expected. In the very next column of the EDP it was revealed that William Blyth had resigned as chairman of the club though no reason for his action was proffered. We did not have very long to wait for an explanation however for at the AGM, held on Wednesday 9 June 1920 at the Nest, we learn that there had been much discord between members of the board for some months and in addition Major Buckley had also tendered his resignation. The City board consisted of twelve men, a large number for such a body and it was no real surprise to learn that they did not always see eye to eye. Major Buckley, who later managed Blackpool, Wolverhampton Wanderers, Notts County, Hull City, Leeds United and Walsall with such distinction, stated that there was often 'public house' talk at the board meetings and hardly a week went by without a major argument. In addition to losing the manager and half of the board City also lost most of their playing staff. Away went Mick O'Brien, Bill Jennings, top scorer John Doran, Joe Lansdale, James Broadhead and 'Tricky' Hawes. Hawes went to South Shields but an FA Commission later found that their approach had not been legal, they allowed the transfer to stand but fined South Shields £50. Arthur Latham, the former Derby County trainer who assisted Buckley during the 1919–20 season stated that 'things were not what they used to be. In my day it was cloak and dagger to be sure but now there was less of the cloak and more of the dagger'. In view of his excellent track record, especially at the Wolves, it was a pity that Major Buckley didn't stay longer but at least Norwich City FC provided him with his first job in football management – and the Canaries were now at the threshold of the Football League!

The Not so Roaring 20s

In 1920 Oxford University first allowed women to take degree courses. Vladimir Ilyich Ulyanov otherwise known as Lenin died at 6.50pm on 21 January 1924 at Gorki and a day later the first Labour government was formed in Great Britain by James Ramsay MacDonald. In the late spring of 1926 Britain was paralysed by the General Strike and only in 1928 did women gain full voting parity with men. An equally brief look at the football world reveals that in 1920 Joseph Lane became the first man to be transferred for a £3,000 fee. He moved from Blackpool to Birmingham City and kept over £1,000 of the fee for himself, the FA outlawed the practice shortly afterwards with the idea of preventing players from overtly shopping around for the best deal. By 1928 the transfer record had exceeded £10,000 when David Jack moved from Bolton Wanderers to Arsenal on 28 October. In 1921–22 Birmingham City forgot to enter for the FA Cup while in 1922–23 Bolton Wanderers were glad they did because they won the first FA Cup Final to be held at Wembley Stadium. They beat West Ham United 2–0 on 28 April 1923 before 126,047 fans and the pitch was reputed to have been cleared of spectators by a policeman on a white horse. On their way to the Final Bolton Wanderers beat the Canaries in the First Round at the Nest by 2–0. Billy Hampson, the former Canary, played for Newcastle United in the FA Cup Final of 1923–24 and is the oldest player to have appeared in an FA Cup Final. Huddersfield Town won the First Division championship in 1923–24, 1924–25 and 1925–26 and later Arsenal equalled the record in 1932–33, 1933–34 and 1934–35, Herbert Chapman was manager of both clubs during their periods of success. On 23 April 1927 Cardiff City became the first team to take the FA Cup out of England when they beat Arsenal 1–0 and a week later full back Sam Wynne became the first player to die during a Football League match. Playing for Bury against Sheffield United he collapsed after taking a free kick just before half time. Out of respect the match was abandoned and replayed the following week. It was reported that when Arsenal and Chelsea wore numbers on their shirts for the opening match of the 1928–29 season it was the first time it had occurred in the Football League. Note that they were not playing each other that day but had decided to participate in the same experiment, shirt numbering did not become compulsory until the 1939–40 season.

Ernest Henry Morse emerged as City chairman in succession to William Blyth at the AGM preceding the first season in the Football League. Morse was the founder of Eaton Nursery and in 1939 was said to have the largest stock of roses in the world. The other directors were John Pyke, Neville William Howlett who ran a shop selling musical instruments, William Hurrell the shoe manufacturer, it was Hurrell who first brought greyhound racing to Norwich at Boundary Park, William Henry Hyde Clarke who was also a shoe manufacturer, Charles Prior and John Howes the secretary. On 12 July 1920 Charles O'Hagan was appointed manager in succession to Major Buckley. O'Hagan was an Irish international, having represented his country on 11 occasions. He first played for Tottenham Hotspur and later moved on to Middlesbrough, Aberdeen and Greenock Morton. Born at Buncara, Co Donegal in 1882 he was said to approach the world with a smile on his face. He served in France for over 3 years with the Highland Light Infantry and Norwich City FC provided him with his first job in football management. George 'Pompey' Martin was appointed the captain for the season and he had under his control a whole crop of new men. Sam Austin who later gained an England cap and an FA Cup losers medal with Manchester City arrived with his friend Bob Dennison from Arnold St Mary's, also from the Midlands came wing half Harry Hopewell. George Travers, George Addy, George Dobson who came from Barnsley, Curtis Booth and Ernie Gadsden (see Who's Who for career details) also made their debuts in 1920–21. A young man who was to play a huge part in City's fortunes for many years to come made his debut against Newport County on Thursday 13 January 1921 – his name Joe Hannah. Joe played centre forward that day, but he was soon to settle down at full back, in all he made 427 appearances and scored 21 goals. Our favourite Hannah story is

Charles O'Hagan succeeded Major Buckley as manager in July 1920

about the time he was so disgruntled with his performance that he sentenced himself to walk all the way home to Sheringham – a 25-mile journey.

The first match that City played in the Football League was at Plymouth Argyle on Saturday 28 August 1920, strangely City had also travelled to Plymouth for their first Southern League match in 1905, but whereas they lost 0–2 in 1905 they drew 1–1 in 1920. The first City goal in the Football League was scored by Yorkshireman Vic Whitham after 67 minutes in the above match and exactly a week later Plymouth Argyle came to the Nest to play the first Football League match in Norwich, this ended in a 0–0 draw. About 12,000 people came along to the first game so interest in the city was high. Although the Canaries did not lose any of their first 4 games they didn't win any either and the poor fans had to wait until Saturday 6 November 1920, the 14th match of the season, for the first win in the Football League. This was in the away match at Reading and the very next week Reading came to Norwich and were again beaten this time by 2–0. Note here that fixtures in the first four seasons after the First World War were so arranged that the home and away matches were scheduled for successive weeks. Grimsby Town visited Norwich on Monday 27 December 1920 and attracted a record crowd of 14,610 and shortly afterwards Charles O'Hagan who had only been able to register 4 victories in 22 games resigned. He was replaced by Albert Arthur Gosnell the only other man to have been interviewed when O'Hagan was appointed in the previous July.

Vic Whitham who scored the first goal for Norwich as members of the Football League

Gosnell, born in Colchester 10 February 1880, gained one cap for England while he was playing for Newcastle United in 1906. His early career was in local football for Colchester Town and Essex County and he was working as a fitter when Charlie Miles the City trainer took him to New Brompton in 1902. In May 1904 he moved north to Newcastle United and played outside left in the losing FA Cup Final team of 1906. Gosnell was appointed after the FA Cup tie at Grimsby Town on Saturday 8 January 1921, it was not the happiest of days because City had just been beaten 0–1 with the winning goal coming from a penalty in the last few minutes, he took up his duties on 24 January 1921. City finished 16th in the league in that initial season of Football League competition and as they were quickly eliminated from the FA Cup it was not a memorable first term – never once did City score more than 3 goals in a match.

In Gosnell's first full season 1921–22 City changed their strip to yellow and green vertical stripes. Several new players arrived from far and near but could not help the Canaries to finish any higher than 15th position in the league. Sheffield Wednesday centre forward Joseph Armstrong was swapped for full back George Gray. Local boy Charles Bradbrook joined the Canaries from Yarmouth Town and left back James Hodge came from Millwall. Goalkeeper William O'Hagan, a cousin of former manager Charles O'Hagan, replaced Herbert Skermer in the latter part of the season. William had a receding hairline and looked much older than he actually was. Sid Scott a former Manchester City centre half had the misfortune to be involved in a clash with the Luton Town forward Turner in the first game of the campaign, Turner came off second best and broke his leg but his side managed to win 1–0 at the Nest. Jimmy Stoakes a speedy outside left came from Notts County, Stoakes had ran in an Olympic trial before the 1920 Antwerp Games and was only just beaten by Harold Abrahams. Just after the start of the match against Northampton Town at the Nest on Monday 17 April 1922, part of the barricade on the concrete wall snapped and sent about 60 people tumbling to the ground. Most were quickly on their feet but one lad received a badly cut head. The crowd that afternoon was over 14,000 and more than 8,000 had gone along to the Nest in the morning to see the Norfolk Senior Cup Final between Lynn and Gorleston. That game finished in a draw but Gorleston won the replay 1–0. In the FA Cup City travelled to the Old Kent Road in South London to play Metrogas in the 5th Qualifying Round, City won 2–1 with goals by Sam Austin and William Bertram. In the next round City had to visit

Oxford to play Oxford City and it needed a replay before they earned the right to meet Barnsley in the 1st Round Proper. City held out for a fine draw at Barnsley, who were a Second Division side in those days, but went down before another crowd of over 12,000 in the replay the following Thursday. During the season a player called 'Sandy' Higgins played 7 games for City and scored 2 goals, Higgins was a Scottish international as was his father, his real name was not Sandy – but Alex.

The Annual General Meeting which was held on 21 July 1922 heard that the finances of Norwich City FC were not in very good shape and there was 'nothing that the club could be proud of'. Despite the situation however the directors recommended that an increased rent should be paid to John Pyke. It was felt that because of Mr Pyke's enthusiasm he had not raised the rent as much as he should. It was also stated that the playing staff of the club had been increased by seven, but only £125 had been spent on transfer fees. Season ticket prices were slightly raised and it would now cost £3 5s 0d for reserved accommodation and £2 5s 0d for admission to the enclosure. A ground season ticket would cost £1 5s 0d. There had been an increased number of spectators visiting the Nest; 167,500 had watched the Football League matches, 54,247 had watched the Reserves in the Southern League, 16,585 the FA Cup matches and with the 10,129 in other games the total came to 248,461. Despite the guarded optimism though we have to report that City slipped during the 1922–23 season and finished in 18th place in the league. The league was won that year by Bristol City and two Welsh clubs occupied the final places Aberdare Athletic and Newport County.

During the season Charlie Dennington, the giant goalkeeper from Beccles and a very popular player with fans and management alike, made his debut in the home fixture against Queen's Park Rangers on Monday 28 August 1922 at the Nest. Charlie went on to make 209 competitive appearances for the Canaries before moving on to Bradford City in 1929. Stephen Wright, later to be trainer at Ipswich Town for a brief period, made his debut in the opening match of the season and Jack Peart, a bustling centre forward who was later to manage Fulham, was also a newcomer that season. The captain in 1922–23 was James Hodge and his regular partner at full back was Philip Hope. At the end of the long and at times frustrating campaign Joe Hannah made 11 appearances at centre forward and scored two goals in the match against Bristol Rovers on Monday 23 April 1923. In the FA Cup match at Southend on Saturday 2 December 1922 centre half 'Pompey' Martin was sent off along with Booth of the home side and was later suspended for 6 weeks. Charlton Athletic drew 13,005 spectators to the Nest on Boxing Day 1922 and that figure was exceeded when Bolton Wanderers visited the Nest in the First Round of the FA Cup on Saturday 13 January 1923. As we mentioned earlier they were on their way to the first ever Wembley Cup Final and beat the Canaries 2–0. Sadly City skipper James Hodge was sent off in the later stages of the match, but Norwich were no real match for the Division One side. Robert Dennison registered the first Canary hat-trick in the Football League when he scored all three in the 3–2 win over Millwall on Saturday 14 April 1923.

Above left, the hard working right back Philip Hope. Above right is Sam Austin, another ever-present, who supplied many goals in the early 20s

The popular, giant local goalkeeper, Charlie Dennington from Beccles

There were changes galore at the start of the 1923–24 season so let us look at them in order starting with the resignation of John Pyke from the board of directors. Mr Pyke had served Norwich City FC since 1906 mostly as chairman or vice-chairman. He was responsible for taking the club from Newmarket Road to the Nest, in fact he owned the Nest and it was his money that was instrumental in transposing the site from a disused chalk pit into the home of the Canaries. Mr Pyke was a farmer and he now felt it was time 'to hang up his cheque book and retire to the land'. After much discussion it was decided to ask that great Norfolk sportsman Robert George Pilch to take his place, an offer that he was glad to accept. It was also decided to change the club shirts for the forthcoming season to white with a Canary badge. Pressure was put on the City Council to provide the club with a new ground, it was thought that the venture would provide local employment in the city and the City Council would of course have a permanent source of revenue from the rental of the ground. Plans were drawn up but there was serious opposition from certain factions and the project never got off the ground. In passing it was also stated that Norwich lacked sports facilities for the youth of the day – a sorry state of affairs.

Above, Albert Gosnell, manager, signed several new names in the 1923–24 season including Albert Sturgess, below, England International and Norwich's oldest debutant

The playing strength was greatly increased when Gosnell secured the signatures of Albert Sturgess, James Jackson, Ernie Williamson and Jimmy Banks. Albert Sturgess was signed from Sheffield United and although now in the autumn of his long career he was a great influence both on and off the field. He had proudly represented England on two occasions, in 1911 versus Ireland and in 1914 against Scotland. He was immediately made captain of the side and was the oldest man to make his debut for the Canaries, a record that still stands. James Jackson was an old fashioned centre forward, he came from Derby County and finished top scorer that season with 15 goals in 35 games. Ernie Williamson the goalkeeper was also an England international, he too had played twice for his country the last time as recently as the previous season. He joined the club from Arsenal. Lastly there was Jimmy Banks who came from Tottenham Hotspur and his most treasured possession was an FA Cup winners medal secured in the 1921 Final. These new men helped City to rise to their highest position in the league to date – 11th.

In the two matches against Brentford, City had to face a famous England cricketer for 'Patsy' Hendren found time to take the inside forward berth in both games. Bennie Smith was suspended sine die by the FA for 'coupon betting' in late January 1924 and the 13,349 who attended the FA Cup tie against Bristol City went home sorely disappointed for the South Western team scored the only goal of the match with their last kick. In April a 'shilling fund' was launched it being hoped to raise 50,000 shillings or £2,500 for the summer wages. When all the contributions were counted in September 1924 it was found that the final total was 28,557 – the board was happy and very glad of the help.

Canaries come and Canaries go and 1924–25 was no exception to the rule. The most noteworthy outgoing before the new season began was Sam Austin, he left to join Manchester City for a fee of £2,000. Frank McCudden on the other hand joined City from Tottenham Hotspur and he was followed by Tom Coulthard from Newcastle United, Jack Duffus also from Tottenham Hotspur and Daniel McKinney an Irish international from Bradford City. Ernest North who also bowled for Middlesex County Cricket Club arrived from Gillingham and full back Archie Campbell, journeyed down from Derby County. Archie fondly recalled the coaching he received in his youth from the great England forward Steve Bloomer. In later life Archie served local firm Laurence & Scott for 40 years.

There was a slight change in the rules for the 1924–25 season it now being possible to score direct from a corner. 'Pompey' Martin once more became skipper of his beloved Canaries as Arthur

Above: The 1924–25 team who secured the Hospital Cup with a 6–1 victory over West Ham

Sturgess was troubled with a knee injury and only managed 17 games that term. Charlie Dennington became first choice 'keeper and only twice conceded more than three goals in a match that season. Joe Hannah, now converted to a half back had an especially fine season, but missed the latter stages of the season as he was selected to tour Australia with an England FA X1. While down under he met up with the old City player Jack Cutmore who sent his regards to all back home. Although City could only manage to finish in 12th position in the league they did delight a 13,000 Boxing Day crowd with a 5–0 victory over Queens Park Rangers. They did not however delight too many fans the following day for they undertook the long journey to Plymouth and lost 0–5 to the Argyle. Top scorer of the campaign was again James Jackson with 14 goals in the league. In the FA Cup City beat Folkestone Town, Rochdale and Doncaster Rovers before falling to Notts County 0–4 in the Second Round. A 20,161 crowd, which included about 2,000 from Norfolk, saw City finish with only nine men. Jimmy Banks and Charlie Bradbrook had left the field injured before the final whistle and Jimmy Stoakes and Ernest North were also injured but pluckily continued the fight. Manager Albert Gosnell had tried all he could to help City escape from the clutches of the Third Division but had failed, there were times when City built up a good head of steam but the elusive success just would not come. There was some relief in the Hospital Cup match, played at the Nest on 30 April 1925, when the Canaries beat the men from West Ham United 6–1 with both James Jackson and Frank McCudden scoring hat-tricks.

Hope, it is said springs eternal in the human breast and the same it appears issues freely from the pen of the editor of the Norwich City FC handbook for in the offering of 1925–26 we learn that this is going to be the year of the breakthrough. The year when the Canaries

Canary legend, above left, Joe Hannah and forward Jimmy Banks, right

march triumphantly into the Second Division, but sadly it was not to be and with his team struggling near the foot of the Third Division and his heart and spirit broken Albert Gosnell offered his resignation on Tuesday 9 February 1926. It was reluctantly accepted by a sympathetic board and the eighth manager of the Norwich City Football Club passed into obscurity. On 1 March 1926 James Burton Stansfield, the City manager in the period before

the Great War, was lured away from his Lowestoft Hotel to once again take on the task of managing the Canaries. He was by this time 57 years old and was 'rusty' after his long absence from football, he did his best but found the job very demanding. At the beginning of the campaign the City staff had been enriched by the arrival of Harry Wingham, Nick Walls and John Rogers, but they collectively failed to make their mark and it was a black day in the history of the club when Clapton, an amateur club, beat City in the FA Cup. The fateful day was Saturday 28 November 1925 and City lost 1–3. Earlier in the season Norwich City had taken part in the first sponsored match to be staged in East Anglia. On Thursday 22 October 1925 City beat Tottenham Hotspur 3–2 at Bury St Edmunds – the hosts were the Greene King Brewery. Off the pitch the Norwich City Supporters Club had been revived and their notes in the handbook included the following classic which remains so very true to this day – 'Come and be a Supporter not a spectator, the latter pays and expects but a Supporter pays and hopes'.

Left, retiring trainer Charlie Miles who served City almost continuously from 1905 to 27. Right, Joe McGrae signed from Tranmere Rovers

The optimism of the previous season was not repeated in the club handbook of 1926–27, the club had come of age, it being 21 years since professionalism had been embraced in that hectic summer of 1905. Reg Cropper, a goalscoring inside forward from Notts County, and Joe McGrae a Liverpool lad who had served five seasons with Everton but had been signed from Tranmere Rovers were the only players of note to join City that year. On Saturday 30 October 1926 City suffered their heaviest reverse to date in the Football League losing 1–7 at Crystal Palace and it came as no real surprise that Stansfield resigned on 19 November 1926. He returned to his hotel for a time and died in Newcastle on 5 January 1938. His place was taken by Cecil Bertram Potter who had been such a popular City player in the pre war days. In the interim he had managed Hartlepools United, Derby County and Huddersfield Town and his appointment was viewed with some enthusiasm by the City board. City had some success in the FA Cup competition beating Crystal Palace after a replay and Chatham before going out to Southampton 0–3 on Saturday 8 January 1927 but in the league it was the same sorry story. At the end of the season City said goodbye to trainer Charlie Miles, he had served the club with brief intermissions since 1905 and had richly earned his retirement.

All the world loves a hero, and a soccer crowd is no exception. During the 1927–28 campaign fate delivered to the regular followers at the Nest a hero to be proud of – Percy Seymour Varco – a goalscoring Cornishman. Varco arrived at Norwich via Torquay United, Aston Villa and Queens Park Rangers, Cecil Potter had seen him play late in the previous season and signed him on 11 July 1927 for a modest fee. He blasted 10 goals in the first 8 games and for a brief time City sat proudly at the top of the league for the first time in their history. Gradually though the early fire died away and by the end of the season City were once more to be found in the lower reaches of the division. There are still people in Norwich who remember the familiar cry of 'Give it to Varco', he brought relief, comfort and hope to the Nest when they were needed most. Injury prevented a repetition of the Varco legend, but in 1927–28 he scored 32 goals in 44 competitive games and in his brief City career he notched 47 goals in 65 games before moving on to Exeter City and Brighton & Hove Albion. He stood only 5 feet 9 inches but he weighed 13 stones and will be remembered not so much for the amount of goals that he scored, but for the way he scored them. In later life he went back to the little Cornish town of Fowey and twice was chosen to serve as Mayor. 1927–28 will also be remembered for the disastrous defeat by Luton Town in the FA Cup. The 0–6 reverse suffered on Saturday 10 December 1927 has thankfully only been equalled on one subsequent occasion – against Manchester City during the 1980–81 season. It was at the start of the extraordinary 1927–28 season that City changed their strip from white shirts with canary badge to yellow and green halves.

1928–29 was another rather poor season at the Nest in fact City spent several weeks at the very bottom of the league and only recovered in the final six games of the campaign. As we mentioned previously, Percy Varco was injured at the beginning of the season and did not turn out at all after 12 January 1929. The main burden of the goal scoring fell upon the slight shoulders of inside forward Francis (Frank) McKenna. McKenna was not a Scot, but a native of Tyne and Wear and had joined the club from Fulham during the close season. In his 44 games, he only stayed for the one season, he managed to find the net on 18 occasions. It looked for a time that there was to be another stirring run in the FA Cup for City beat Chatham Town 6–1 in the First Round and Newport County 6–0 in the Second Round. Percy Varco briefly came to the fore in these two games and scored 6 of the goals but it was not to last. The visitors to the Nest in the Third Round before a bumper crowd of 20,129 were the renowned Corinthians, an amateur side that contained the pick of the varsity men and who at one time were very close to joining the Football League. Despite losing their outside right R.G. Jenkins as early as the 11th minute they led City 2–0 at half time and after the interval increased their lead to 5–0. It was a shattering experience for both the club and Potter the manager, so much so that after defeat at the hands of Charlton Athletic the following week Potter resigned. He was not replaced immediately and for several weeks the club floundered at the foot of the table without a manager. At last it was announced that James Kerr, the manager of Walsall, was to be the next incumbent of the hot seat at the Nest. He was appointed on Thursday 4 April 1929 and soon got down to the mammoth task that lay before him. The first match under his control was lost 0–3 at Queens Park Rangers, but under his expert guidance City were undefeated in the remaining six games of the season and pulled clear of the bottom spot. Bob Young had replaced Charlie Miles as trainer and all was set well for a marked improvement in the campaign that lay ahead.

Left, Percy Varco who was sidelined by injury for most of 1929, a heavy blow for the Canaries.

Right, new manager James Kerr faced an uphill task on his appointment

The 1929 team who struggled hard to keep clear of the foot of the table

1929 saw the Wall Street crash and on 19 March 1932 Sydney Harbour Bridge was opened. Finally, in our very brief survey of the events of the period, it was on 30 January 1933 that Adolf Hitler was appointed Chancellor of Germany by Reich President Paul von Hindenburg.

During the close season of 1929 several of the senior City players went to do some coaching in South Africa, it proved to be a new and popular exercise. When they arrived back they discovered that manager Kerr had been very busy in the transfer market. City director Robert Pilch set the tone of the season when he wrote in the handbook – 'For too long we have tried the policy of 'safety first' now with our new management team we mean our policy to be "neck or nothing" in the future'. From Walsall came Mick O'Brien and from the same club came Doug Lochhead. O'Brien was in his second spell at the Nest and was immediately made club captain. He bought a newsagents shop in St Benedicts soon after his arrival and when, on 11 May 1930, he appeared for Ireland against Belgium at centre half he became the first City player to win an international cap whilst on the books of the club. Doug Lochhead needs little introduction to older supporters for, after a distinguished playing career, he eventually became manager of the club. He also scored the first City goal at Carrow Road. Another recruit from the Midlands was centre forward Tommy Hunt, he came from Wolverhampton Wanderers and when they saw he was scoring goals regularly they claimed he was only on loan to City. Fortunately City were able to clear up the situation to their advantage for in 29 First team outings he scored 25 goals. The new goalkeeper was John Jarvie, a Scot signed from Southend United, and a star performer at half back that season was another Scot, William Brown also from Wolverhampton Wanderers. William settled in Norwich after injury ended his career and lived near the old ground at the Nest. So with full backs Joe Hannah and Joe Richmond still in harness and Ernest Porter and Jacky Slicer providing accurate crosses from the wing City looked forward to a successful season.

Above, Thomas H Williams, inside left and right, William Hurrell, elected chairman in the 1931 season

A successful season indeed for City finished in 8th position, their highest to date, and on Saturday 15 March 1930 they recorded their biggest win ever in a First team competitive match. On Saturday 9 November 1929 City travelled to Coventry and were beaten 3–1, a not totally unexpected result for the Midlanders were one of the better sides in the division that year. The two teams were soon to meet again when they were paired in the First Round of the FA Cup, the tie to take place at the Nest on Saturday 30 November 1929. City led 3–2 until the dying minutes but Coventry scored a late equaliser and went on to win the replay 2–0. Whether or not City felt cheated by that late goal in the FA Cup tie we will never know, but when the two teams met in the return league game City had a surprise in reserve. 4–0 up at half time City tore into action in the second half and added a further 6 goals, Tommy Hunt scored 5, Coventry replied with 2 of their own and the final result was 10–2. This remains Norwich City's record win in a competitive game and the only time they have ever scored double figures. It must have been something special for the *Pink 'Un* headline simply read '1, 2, 3, 4, 5, 6, 7, 8, 9 and yes 10' – what a pity there were only 8,230 to witness the event.

We shall not dwell long on the 1930–31 season for Norwich City finished bottom of the Third Division (South) for the first time in their history. Tommy Hunt failed to score his expected number of goals, he managed only 7 that term, and the entire team could only

The 1931–32 team who finished a respectable 10th position in the league table

accumulate 47 between them. It was the season that City engaged a player called Francisco Enrique Gonsalez, but not surprisingly he changed his name before he started his Football League career and called himself Frank Peed. Sadly it was also the season in which the Norwich City Football Club lost one of its founder 'fathers'. Early on the morning of Sunday 15 February 1931 Joseph Cowper Nutchey died at his Norwich home. On the Saturday he was interested in the day's results and we are happy to record that City beat Bournemouth 2–1 at the Nest, only their 7th victory in the league to date. An enormous crowd attended the funeral at Norwich Cemetery on the following Thursday and included his friends from football, cricket, bowls and teaching. At the Annual General Meeting of the Football League in the summer of 1931 Norwich City FC were easily re-elected to the League topping the poll with 38 votes. The whole process of having to apply for re-election was a chastening experience for Norwich City FC and they made up their minds not to go through it all again. The recipe for future success lay in the purchase of more new players and an influx of new players were on view at the start of the 1931–32 season.

William Hurrell, the promoter of greyhound racing in Norfolk, was elected chairman during the 1931 close season and George Pilch was his vice-chairman. The move appeared to be successful as City finished the campaign in a respectable 10th position. New players included Norman Wharton, a goalkeeper from Sheffield United, Tom Williamson from Stoke City, Cecil Blakemore, an inside left from Brentford and Lionel 'Spud' Murphy, a left winger from Mansfield Town. Wharton was a 'keeper of considerable stature and it was said that no forward charged him twice. He was one of eight brothers, all of whom played football, the other seven it must be said followed the rugby code. Tom Williamson was a commanding centre half of the old school and had played at Stoke City when Stanley Matthews was a mere office boy. He was a Scot who could put over a very persuasive argument and after his playing days were over he remained in Norwich and kept the Rose Tavern. Blakemore had proved himself a useful goal scorer, but the star of the bunch was the left winger 'Spud' Murphy. Murphy had played for Derby County for seven seasons just after the First World War and had scored over 50 goals. A small man, he stood only 5ft 6ins, but his great asset was his speed and ability to cross the ball accurately. In the away match at Exeter

Left, new goalkeeper from Sheffield United, Norman Wharton. Right, Lionel 'Spud' Murphy a left winger newly signed from Mansfield Town

City on Saturday 2 April 1932 a young man made an impressive debut for City and he was to continue to play for the club until 12 March 1949, his name was Bernard Cecil Robinson. Robinson was born in Cambridge on 5 December 1911, but had spent much of his youth in King's Lynn. Those that remember him playing recall that he rarely if ever played a poor game and he was one of the first exponents of the long throw. He also had a very individual style when taking a penalty, from a short run he would turn and as often as not find the back of the net. He still lives in the Norwich area.

Above left, Robert Robinson, goalkeeper and right, Ken Burditt stylish inside forward

In the same game at Exeter, which incidentally the home side won 3–0. two of the goals were scored by the old City favourite Percy Varco. He was not the only former Canary to score against his old club that season, for in the match at Watford on Christmas Day, Mick O'Brien converted a penalty for his new club. Before the start of the season Mansfield Town were elected to the Football League after a long and successful career in the Midland League. There were some interesting notes in the club handbook that year for we learn that Sir Samuel Hill-Wood, the former chairman of Arsenal, regularly used to attend matches at Newmarket Road and was in fact a season ticket holder. John Bowman, City's first professional manager, visited the city during the summer and in a conversation with George Pilch stated that he was interested in the progress of the club and always looked out for their result on a Saturday. Billy Hampson, the old full back, and now manager of Carlisle United took a holiday in Norfolk and also found time to look up old friends. One last titbit from the handbook also came from George Pilch. Cricketers, he said, were often ruined by coaching, but footballers rarely got any coaching at all and could greatly benefit from 'talks on tactics'. We wonder if he would say the same today !

During the winter of 1932–33 the England cricketers under the captaincy of Douglas Robert Jardine undertook a controversial, but successful, tour of Australia. The Tests, which England won 4–1, were destined to become known as the 'Bodyline' series and to this very day the argument continues. City, perhaps inspired by the goings on down-under, had their most successful season to date. In late March they were top of the division and only a spell of three successive defeats in early April prevented them from topping the league. Before the start of the season Aldershot were elected to take the place of Thames in the Third Division (South), Mansfield Town moved over to the Third Division (North) to take the place of Wigan Borough and their place in the Southern Section was taken by Newport County. County had dropped out of the Football League at the end of the 1930–31 season, but were re-elected at the first time of asking. New players at the Nest included Stan Ramsay, Tom Scott and goalkeeper Robert Robinson. Stan Ramsay put through his own goal in the very first minute of his debut in the opening game of the season, but more than made amends with consistent displays in the rest of the matches. He joined the club from Blackpool and had previously played for Sunderland. City scored 88 goals in the league during the season and the leading marksmen were Oliver Brown and that most reliable of players Ken Burditt with 19 apiece. Close on their heels came Tom Scott with 17, Scott having joined the club from Preston North End.

The manager of Norwich City FC, and the chief architect of their success, James Kerr entered the Norfolk and Norwich hospital with bronchial pneumonia in January 1933. Up until the previous November he had never had a serious illness in his life. As the days rolled by his condition became worse and he finally expired on Thursday 18 February 1933, he was 51 years old. His early life had been spent in his native Scotland where he had assisted the Bathgate FC for many years. When he moved south he managed Coventry City and Walsall before coming to Norwich. The bearers at his funeral were City trainer Bob Young, Tom Williamson, Joe Hannah, Stan Ramsay, Doug

Lochhead and Jack Scott and on the Saturday after his death a minutes silence was observed on all the football fields of Norfolk. His replacement was Thomas Robert Parker, a former player at Southampton and Arsenal. Parker was a full back and had played for England against France in 1925 whilst on the books of Southampton. Parker was appointed on Tuesday 7 March 1933 and carried on where Kerr had left off. It was a pity that Kerr did not live to see the full fruits of his hard work and dedication.

It was reported in the club handbook that work had been carried out at the Nest during the close season of 1932. The area behind the Rosary Road goal had been re-terraced and there was also an extension to the main stand. The 'Chicken Run' opposite the main stand had been extended and it was thought that an extra 3,000 spectators could be comfortably accommodated. There was also a reference to 'the Programme Committee', not it was pointed out the same body as the Supporters Club, though the two were often confused. The Programme Committee were resposible for the advertising around the ground as well as producing and selling the club programme. The 'good old' Supporters Club meanwhile were increasing their membership season by season and it was reported that their annual outing would take them to Torquay on Whit Monday. Previously the happy throng had visited the likes of Brighton, Blackpool and the Lake District. One last snippet revealed that during the 1931–32 season, despite the recession, the ground record had been surpassed at no less than 19 Football League clubs.

Tom Parker told the football public of Norwich that he would do everything possible to secure Second Division football at the Nest in 1933–34 – he was true to his word and after a glorious campaign City sat proudly at the head of the Third Division (South) at the end of the season. 20,000 gallons of water had to be put on the turf of the Nest before the public practice game on Saturday 12 August 1933. The summer had been very hot and every drop of water was required to encourage the grass to grow. A huge quantity of soil had earlier been spread at the Rosary Road end in an effort to reduce the slope. All summer long there had been much talk in the city about moving the headquarters from the Nest to Boundary Park, but in the end the move was rejected. In his address to the supporters in the handbook manager Tom Parker appealed for 'team spirit on the terraces which is just as essential as team spirit on the field of play'. He had brought three new players of note to Norwich and allowed Oliver Brown to join West Ham United.

William Henry 'Billy' Warnes travelled up from Arsenal and his exciting wing play thrilled his new admirers. City had been short of a right winger for some time and now with Warnes on the right and Murphy on the left the forward line was complete. The new arrival at centre forward was Edward John 'Jack' Vinall and he finished joint top scorer in the league with Warnes, both scoring 21 goals.

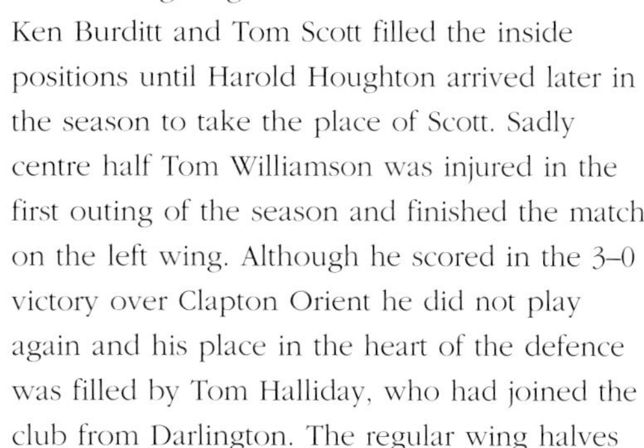

Ken Burditt and Tom Scott filled the inside positions until Harold Houghton arrived later in the season to take the place of Scott. Sadly centre half Tom Williamson was injured in the first outing of the season and finished the match on the left wing. Although he scored in the 3–0 victory over Clapton Orient he did not play again and his place in the heart of the defence was filled by Tom Halliday, who had joined the club from Darlington. The regular wing halves

Above, Thomas Robert Parker, was appointed manager in March 1933

Left, Stan Ramsay club captain 1933 and right, right winger WH 'Billy' Warnes

were Bernard Robinson and Doug Lochhead and the left back spot was occupied by club captain Stan Ramsay. Joe Hannah, obviously delighted with the success of the club, started the season at right back, but after sustaining an injury was replaced by Albert Thorpe. The last line of resistance was provided by Norman Wharton who managed to keep 16 clean sheets in the forty-two league matches.

City secured 9 points in the first 5 games and were top of the division for 28 out of the 34 weeks of the season. Only 5 away games were lost all season which was the least number by any of the 92 clubs in the Football League that season. 6 successive league wins were achieved between 21 October 1933 and 2 December 1933 and City suffered only 1 defeat in the last 20 league games. Enough then of statistics, it was a magnificent season which was greatly enjoyed and appreciated by the faithful City supporters. They had waited a long time for their success but had supported the club through thick and thin. 22,433 turned out to witness the home game against Newport County on Easter Monday 2 April 1934, a record crowd in a league game at the Nest and another 16,903 saw City make sure of promotion in the home match against Coventry City on Saturday 21 April 1934. There was no such glory in the FA Cup competition for City went out 0–3 at Crystal Palace in late November, but they did manage to reach the Semi-Final of the new Third Division (South) Cup before being beaten by Torquay United at Highbury. The Norfolk & Norwich Hospital Cup, the traditional finale to the season, was contested that year by Norwich City and Grimsby Town, the champions of the Second Division. The match took place on Monday 7 May 1934 before a crowd of 13,219. The happy crowd was in festive mood and went mad as City roared to a 7–2 victory. Five of the goals came from centre forward Jack Vinall and the remaining two were scored by a young former apprentice carpenter from Shouldham, a small village in west Norfolk. The same young man had earlier made his City debut on the right wing when Billy Warnes was injured. He was destined to later play for one of the leading club sides in the country and to represent his country in two sports – football and shooting – his name was Alfred John Kirchen.

Above right, Stan Ramsay with the Division 3 (South) shield at the Hospital Cup match; (right) free-scoring centre forward Edward 'Jack' Vinall

The Eighth Wonder of the World

The years between 1934 and 1946 were dominated either by the thoughts of war or by war itself. As usual we shall briefly review the world and national events starting on 7 June 1935 when Stanley Baldwin formed a Tory government. On 20 January 1936 Edward VIII became King and 325 days later he abdicated in favour of his brother the Duke of York. The Duke of York reigned as George VI and was the husband of the present Queen Mother. The 28 May 1937 saw a coalition government formed under Neville Chamberlain and at 11.00am on the morning of Sunday 3 September 1939 Britain was again at war with Germany, shortly afterwards Winston Churchill formed a National government on 11 May 1940. Between 27 May 1940 and 4 June 1940 Dunkirk was evacuated by a huge fleet of ships of all sizes. The first major battle of the war, the Battle of Britain, ended on 15 September 1940 with the RAF victorious. On 7 December 1941 the Japanese attacked Pearl Harbour and started war on a global scale. It was after the Battle of El Alamein on 23 October 1942 that the Allied offensive opened in North Africa. Mussolini, the Italian Dictator, was overthrown on 25 July 1943 and on 6 June 1944 the D-Day landings in Europe commenced. The war between Britain and Germany ended on 8 May 1945 and a new Labour government under Clement Attlee was elected on 26 July 1945. Two atomic bombs were dropped on Japan in early August 1945 (Hiroshima 6 August and Nagasaki 9 August) and they in effect ended the global conflict with peace coming on 2 September 1945 almost six years to the day after the initial declaration of war. On 20 November 1945 the trials of major war criminals opened in Nuremberg.

A brief look at the football world reveals there were some exceptional crowds recorded in Scotland during the late 1930s. At least 149,415 spectators watched the Scotland v England match at Hampden Park on Saturday 17 April 1937. The actual figure was variously recorded and it was thought that at least another 10,000 climbed over the wall. Just one week later Hampden Park had another full-house when 144,303 crowded in to watch the Scottish Cup Final between Celtic and Aberdeen, a match that Celtic won 2–1. On 2 January 1939 118,567 attended a Scottish League game between Rangers and Celtic at Ibrox Stadium. Parts of the 1937 FA Cup Final between Sunderland and Preston North End, Sunderland won 3–1, were televised and a year later the whole of the 1938 FA Cup Final was shown. Preston North End were again in the Final and they beat Huddersfield Town with a penalty in the last minute of extra time, incidentally the only goal of the match. There were Norwich City connections in that match for the referee who gave the penalty was James Jewell and early in 1939 he became the manager of Norwich City FC. By the way the first match to appear on British TV was probably a staged practice match involving the staff of Arsenal FC on Thursday 16 September 1937 (bet there were no action replays), Arsenal were probably picked not only for their popularity, but because they were close to the BBC studios at Alexandra Palace. Portsmouth FC have held the FA Cup for the greatest single span of time, it was they who

THE DUMPLING—"WELL, SOMETHING GOT TO BE DONE ABOUT IT, BOR!"
Now that the City have gained Second Division status, the question of finding alternative accommodation to the Nest is exercising the minds of all concerned.

The 1934–35 teams for the annual pre-season practise match

beat Wolverhampton Wanderers in the 1939 Final, 4–1 on Saturday 29 April 1939 and did not relinquish the trophy until Derby County won the 1946 Final on Saturday 27 April 1946. Another two days and Portsmouth would have held the FA Cup for seven years. The record pre-war transfer fee was paid for Welsh international Bryn Jones when he moved from Wolverhampton Wanderers to Arsenal in August 1938. The fee was £14,000 and again there were City connections for Bryn played for Norwich City during the 1949–50 season. Lastly we return to the 1934–35 season when City were starting out on their career in the Second Division – Arsenal completed a hat-trick of First Division titles that year and equalled the record set by Huddersfield Town in the 1920s.

Before the great new adventure of Second Division football was undertaken Tom Parker took a close look at his playing staff and decided there was no need for wholesale changes. He had received reports that neighbours Ipswich Town FC, still an amateur club in the Southern Amateur League, had a very good young goalkeeper in the side. After meeting the man in question, Harry Dukes, he persuaded him to sign professional forms for the City. Sam Bowen was signed from Aston Villa and eventually took over the left back spot from Stan Ramsay and another newcomer was Cecil 'Jack' Russell from Luton Town who replaced 'Spud' Murphy on the left wing. The first match in the higher grade was at Brentford on Saturday 25 August 1934 where City narrowly lost 1–2 and the first Second Division victory was recorded two days later when Bury FC visited the Nest. 18,821 watched City win 4–1 with goals from Ken Burditt (2), Billy Warnes and Jack Vinall. After a fair start five games in a row were lost during late September and early October but City managed to establish themselves and finished the season in 14th position. The highlight of the league season came on Saturday 17 November 1934 when Notts County were beaten 7–2 at the Nest. The gates remained pretty high all season and only fell below the 10,000 mark in the last few matches when City had been knocked out of the FA Cup and a mid-table position in the league was inevitable. Joe Hannah, the faithful full back, managed just one Second Division appearance in the away match against Plymouth Argyle on Wednesday 6 February 1935. The team must have tried especially hard that afternoon because they won 1–0 with a Cecil Russell goal in the second half. The promise and talent of Alf Kirchen was noted by Arsenal during the season and they made City a bid of £6,000, an offer that just could not be refused, and Kirchen left for London on Friday 1 March 1935. Alf did not let his new club down and played until injury ended his career during the war gaining three England caps in 1937.

There was excitement in the FA Cup that year when City managed to reach the Fifth Round. Bath City were beaten 2–0 at the Nest in the Third Round and the Canaries earned the right to play First Division Leeds United. The tie was played at home on Saturday 26 January 1935 and ended in an exciting 3–3 draw, Leeds United only securing the equaliser in the last minute. City had been 0–2 down at the interval, but two goals from Alf Kirchen and one by Jack Vinall put the home side in the lead. The replay took place on the following Wednesday and City defied all the odds by winning 2–1 before a crowd of 27,269. Once more into the hat went City for the Fifth Round draw and they again came out first against another Yorkshire First Division side. It was the turn of Sheffield Wednesday to visit the Nest and they did so before a record crowd of 25,037 on Saturday 16 February 1935. The game was never a classic, but exciting nevertheless, and it was the Wednesday who scored the only goal of the match thanks to their England international Ellis Rimmer. As things turned out it was the last FA Cup tie to be played at the Nest, fitting then that the game should have attracted a record crowd that would stand for all time. Before we leave the 1934–35 season to look at the dramatic events shortly to take place in the summer of 1935 let us turn our attention briefly to an article written by Tom Parker in the club handbook. It was headed 'Forward Policy' and appeared in a none too prominent spot towards the back of the publication. City had just reformed their 'A' team and Parker added –

"I would rather train young players to my own ideas than spend a fortune on buying new men who don't know how we play at Norwich. The venture will cost a considerable amount but when we see these men promoted to the Reserves and, in the course of time, to the First team, we shall find that the deficit has become a credit and we may then be able to afford the luxury of First Division football in Norwich."

Prophetic words indeed which need no further comment. During the season Wilfred Burgess, the chairman who guided the club to professionalism, died at his Norwich home as did Thomas Bury, a long standing former City director.

On 20 March 1935 plans and estimates were prepared to rebuild the main stand at the Nest, but the work was destined never to be undertaken. The directors of Norwich City FC were conscious that pressure would be applied to the club to improve the facilities offered at their ground. There were even thoughts of moving to a new ground and Boundary Park was the current favourite though surveys had been made of St James Hollow and Barrack Street. On Wednesday 15 May 1935 matters were brought to a head when the club received a letter from the Football Association stating that they were not satisfied that the Nest was suitable for housing large crowds. Norwich City FC were a particularly ambitious club at this time and they believed that their quest for First Division football would soon be forthcoming. Architects were urged to submit new plans that would transform the Nest and make it suitable for the higher grade of football, but no adequate scheme could be devised – there was nothing else for it the club would have to find a new home. On Monday 6 May mighty Arsenal had visited the Nest to play in the Hospital Cup and they beat City 1–0, it was the last game ever played on the Nest by Norwich City FC.

On 29 May a site adjoining the River Wensum was considered for the first time and had been offered to the club by J & J Colman Ltd. Many years later it was stated in the *Pink 'Un* that Tom Parker conducted the negotiations with one Mr Ryrie, the representative of J & J Colman. No director was present as they were divided over the Boundary Park affair. It was currently being used by the Boulton & Paul Sports Club and was sited at Carrow Road. The name 'Carrow' is taken from the ancient Carrow Abbey which stood on the south bank of the Wensum. Soon plans for the redevelopment of the site were placed before the City Council and work was commenced on the construction of the terraces by Messrs Harry Pointer Ltd at 3.45am on the morning of 11 June 1935. Boulton & Paul Ltd started work on the ferro-concrete piling on 28 June 1935 and soon after Messrs T. Gill & Son Ltd started building the dressing rooms and offices. It is said that the rubble used in the constuction of the River End bank came from the notorious Chicken Run at the Nest and that 45,000 tons of soil was carted in to complete the terraces. The largest construction job in the city since the building of Norwich Castle was miraculously completed in just 82 days and when City Officials visited the ground just before the opening of the season it was referred to as 'The eighth wonder of the world'.

Local farmer James Frederick Wright took over as Norwich City chairman in 1935

James Frederick Wright, a farmer from Aldeby near Beccles took over as chairman of Norwich City FC in the summer of 1935. William Hurrell had favoured the move to Boundary Park

Above, work in progress on the Carrow Road main stand in summer 1935 while the later picture below shows a curious public getting a sneak preview

and when his proposal was defeated he felt he should vacate the chair. Because of the great haste with which the project had been undertaken only the main stand was under cover, but new chairman James Wright promised the football followers of Norwich that it was the intention of the board to eventually cover all the terraces. West Ham United visited Norwich on Saturday 31 August 1935, and the largest crowd to that date ever to attend a football match in Norwich, 29,779, cheered wildly as the new stadium was officially opened by Mr Russell Colman, Lord-Lieutenant of Norfolk and President of Norwich City FC. The fans were

treated to a thrilling game suitable for the occasion which ended in a 4–3 victory for Norwich City and the honour of scoring the first goal at Carrow Road fell to City captain Doug Lochhead. Manager Tom Parker was rewarded for his sound work by being offered a new three year contract at the beginning of the season but after the initial victory over West Ham United, City lost their next seven games and were bottom of the league. Parker went into action and bought Frank Manders from Crystal Palace for a small fee plus full back Albert Thorpe. On 5 December 1935 the side was further strengthened by the signing of Peter Burke from Oldham Athletic and winger John Friar from Preston North End. Burke, a fine centre half, could consider himself very unlucky in that he had only missed playing for Eire because of injury. The slide towards the Third Division was quickly arrested and City finished the season in 11th place. Jack Vinall was top scorer with 24 goals proving he could continue to find the net in the more elevated company. Manchester United won the Second Division that year and they were managed by Mr A. Scott Duncan who later played such a large part in building the fortunes of Ipswich Town FC. Chelsea visited Norwich in the Third Round of the FA Cup on Saturday 11 January 1936 and attracted a record crowd of 32,378 the match was drawn 1–1 but City lost the replay the following Wednesday 1–3.

At the Annual General Meeting held at Carrow Road on Friday 3 July 1936 it was reported that a small loss of £179 6s 6d had been made on the previous season but the overdraft had risen to £13,232 and loans stood at £9,582 including £8,000 borrowed from the Football Association for the development of Carrow Road. It was further disclosed that the building of Carrow Road had cost the club £25,963. League gate receipts had advanced to £19,773 an increase of £4,448 over the previous season so it appeared that the move had been successful if only the debts could be kept under control. An amount of £3,773 15s 6d had been

Above, Mr Russell Colman, President of Norwich City FC performs the official opening on 31 August 1935 before the opening game against West Ham United

Below, an aerial view of the first match, and right, captain Doug Lochhead who had the honour of scoring the first ever goal at Carrow Road for City

paid to the Chancellor of the Exchequer by way of Entertainment Tax and, said Mr Howes the financial secretary, it is not surprising to find this matter the subject of earnest representation for amendment. A sum of £6,760 was spent on transfers and only £669 was received for players sold. No new players of note were signed on at the start of the new 1936–37 season because Tom Parker stated that he had faith in the available staff. However the strain of maintaining Second Division football proved difficult and the season only really came to life when the FA Cup trail began in January. City were drawn at home to First Division Liverpool in the Third Round and on Saturday 16 January 1937 a crowd of 26,856 saw City complete an historic 3–0 victory with Jack Vinall scoring two goals in the first five minutes. Matt Busby played for Liverpool that day, but could not prevent the emphatic City win. In the next round City were paired with Bolton Wanderers also of the First Division and a large band of Norwich supporters made the long trip north and were delighted with the 1–1 draw. 30,108 gathered at Carrow Road the following Thursday to witness the replay but were not so delighted this time round as Bolton secured a 2–1 victory in extra time.

Left, Frederick Hall, the 1936 keeper who stayed with City all through the war years. Billy Furness, right, a former England international, was bought from Leeds United in 1937

Within a fortnight of the replay manager Tom Parker asked to be released from his contract. He had been approached by Southampton, his home town club, to be their manager and his request was reluctantly granted on Tuesday 16 February 1937. When he left he took a young City reserve player with him, that player served his new club as player and manager for many years – his name was Ted Bates. The directors decided not to advertise the vacant managers job and on Monday 22 February 1937 the position was given to trainer Bob Young and former City skipper Doug Lochhead was named as his assistant and chief scout. On the Saturday preceding Young's appointment City had gained a couple of valuable points at Nottingham Forest in a 4–3 victory and Norwich needed all the points they could get to avoid relegation. One of the last decisions that Tom Parker made at Norwich was to bring Ernest 'Tim' Coleman to the club from Middlesbrough. Coleman, known as 'Tim' because of his tiny frame, had previously played for Arsenal and had won a championship medal while he was at Highbury. City managed to avoid the drop and finished in 17th place and in the penultimate game of the season a crowd of 25,052 were thrilled with the 5–1 victory over Aston Villa. Frank Manders was top scorer that season with 16 goals in the league and 1 in the FA Cup. The Reserves came second in the Southern League which was won that year by a club that had recently turned professional – Ipswich Town FC.

Owing to the generosity of Capt Evelyn Barclay, the vice-president of the club, the terrace at the Station end of the ground was covered and the work was completed ready for the opening of the 1937–38 season. To this day the stand which now houses the more vociferous of the home supporters is known as the Barclay Stand. 10,000 could be housed in the new enclosure bringing the total under cover to 17,500 and the capacity of the stadium up to 38,000. Because of the development of the ground, cash was still in short supply, but City were able to record a profit of £700 in the summer of 1937. In order to save money the 'A' team was abandoned for the 1937–38 season and Bury Town were adopted as a nursery club. Loyal servant Joe Hannah went to Bury St Edmunds to take control of the development and coaching. City however did allow themselves one luxury when they brought former England international Billy Furness to the club from Leeds United. City eventually finished the season in 14th position, but were never really free from the threat of relegation. There was an unsavory incident in the Boxing Day fixture when West Ham United visited Carrow Road, about 1,000 people rushed the turnstiles in the Barclay Stand and got in for nothing, we are glad to say that 27,475 were better behaved and were delighted with the 2–2 draw. On the following day City travelled to London for the return, the game should have been played on Christmas Day but was postponed because of fog, and included in the West Ham line up was Archie Macaulay who was later to become the City manager. 'Tim' Coleman captained Norwich City that year and he finished top scorer with 15 league goals. There was one sad note to the season when it was announced that former manager James 'Bert' Stansfield passed away on Wednesday 5 January 1938 just three days before the visit of Aston Villa in the FA Cup. A new record crowd of 33,346 saw City lose 2–3 to a Villa side that went on to win the Second Division, four points clear of Manchester United.

William Hurrell, the director and a previous chairman of the club, resigned from the board in the summer of 1938. At the same meeting it was reported that City had made a profit of £2,000 on the 1937–38 season and had invested £4,500, the highest fee they had ever paid, for the Wolverhampton Wanderers full back Jack Taylor and his team mate wing half Tom Smalley. The only other newcomer to the club was James Russell from Sunderland. The season kicked off with the Football League Jubilee match against Ipswich Town on Saturday 20 August 1938. Ipswich Town had been newly elected to the Football League and the encounter, which ended 1–1, was played to benefit the Football League fund for players who had fallen upon hard times. It also of course coincided with the celebration of 50 years of League football, the Football League having been formed in 1888. The first four games of the season were all lost and it soon became clear that City were unlikely to achieve their ambition of First Division football. Indeed after two successive away defeats, 0–7 at Sheffield Wednesday on 19 November and 0–6 at Blackburn Rovers a fortnight later City were dangerously near to the foot of the table. The month of January 1939 brought terrible weather and City were only able to play their FA Cup Third Round match with Manchester City after two postponements. The match was lost 0–5 at Carrow Road, the heaviest home defeat in the competition, and the board acted promptly by appointing James Jewell team manager on Saturday 21 January 1939. Jewell as we mentioned earlier had refereed the FA Cup Final of 1937–38 between Preston North End and Huddersfield Town. King George VI visited Norwich during late October 1938 and made an appearance at the City v Millwall match played on Saturday 29 October 1938. He only stayed for 15 minutes so we doubt he saw either of the two Millwall goals that secured them victory. It

Tom Smalley, left half, a former England International signed in 1938

HM King George VI during a short visit to the City v Millwall game on 29 October 1938

was the first time that a reigning monarch had attended a Second Division match.

The first positive action of the new manager was to buy centre forward Jack Acquroff and inside left Bill Graham from Bury FC on 3 February 1939. Acquroff was born in London of Scottish parents with Russian ancestry, a mixed pedigree indeed. Shortly full back John Milburn arrived from Leeds United, but City fell deeper and deeper into trouble. In the last game but

Above, full back John Milburn is welcomed to City by Bob Young in 1939

one, played on Wednesday 3 May 1939, City travelled to Plymouth desperate for points but there was to be no silver lining for they lost 0–1 and John Milburn missed a penalty. The final game was at home to fellow strugglers Nottingham Forest and City needed to win 4–0 to ensure that they remained in the Second Division – they could only manage a 1–0 victory with a second half goal by Harry Ware – their fate was sealed, they were back in the Third Division. They actually finished with the same number of points as Forest but were relegated on inferior goal average, the difference being just 0.048.

Relegation to the Third Division cost Norwich City dear and a large deficit was reported at the end of the 1938–39 season. James Jewell writing in the club handbook outlined at great length all the factors that precipitated the fall, but truth was that City would now have to rebuild and try again. Soon after the opening of the 1939–40 season war was declared and all his plans had to be abandoned. Three matches of the new season were played including the first meeting of Norwich City and Ipswich Town in a Football League encounter. The two sides met at Portman Road on Saturday 2 September 1939 and the result was a 1–1 draw. The Football League, on the advice of the government, decided to close down national competition for the duration of the war and the results of those early games were expunged from official records. Norwich City however decided to carry on playing and entered the regional competitions that had been hastily arranged. James Jewell soon left the club and Bob Young once more took charge at Carrow Road. For the duration of the war Bob Young worked endlessly for the club and did a magnificent job in preserving football in Norwich. We do not intend to look too closely at wartime football as all the details can be found under the heading of 'City at War' in the Statistical Section. There are however one or two items that we must briefly mention.

Guest players were allowed during the war and City soon made use of the talent that was available in the region. Ipswich Town closed down shortly after war was declared and several of their players travelled along the A140 to continue playing football. Goalkeeper Mick Burns, full backs Ossie Parry and Billy Dale, wing half Jimmy McLuckie and forwards Fred Chadwick, Ambrose Mulraney and Jackie Little all played a number of games for City. Nearly all of the Bolton Wanderers team which included several internationals was stationed in Norfolk between January 1941 and September 1942 and during this period Norwich City had a particularly strong team. Several of the 1938–39 side also served locally and played when they could especially Jack Acquroff, Billy Furness, Frank Manders, John Milburn, Harry Proctor, Bernie Robinson, Jack Taylor and Harry Ware. Sid Plunkett, was another who contributed much during the war years. Sid was a local lad who signed amateur forms for City in April 1938 before moving on to the Wolves in April 1939. After the outbreak of war he returned to Norwich and guested for City on numerous occasions. After the war he was permanently transferred back to the Canaries and appeared in the 1946–47 season. Another player to have his career so cruelly curtailed by the hostilities was Les Maskell. Les was born on the Isle of Wight on 30 November 1918 and as a young man moved to Norfolk and played for Frost's Athletic, then the City junior club. Mike Davage had computed that Les scored 232 goals for City at all levels, a staggering amount. After the war Les moved on to Lowestoft Town and Diss Town where he kept the Greyhound Inn for many years. He eventually became chairman of Diss Town and his sons played very successfully for the club. On Christmas Day 1940 City beat Brighton & Hove Albion 18–0, though it must be said that the Southerners did not have a very representative side out. Willie Thornton, the Rangers Scottish international played a number of games and Bill Shankly, disguised as 'A Newman', played in three matches.

As in the First World War, when City also continued to function throughout the hostilities, war football was not a paying proposition. City lost money throughout the period between 1939 and 1945 never managing to repay the debt incurred when the Carrow Road stadium was built. Players were paid £1 10s 0d per match with no win bonus and it cost a shilling to get into the ground and two shillings to sit in the stand. Because of its geographical position and munition factories Norwich was an easy target for enemy planes and the first of 44 major raids occurred on the night of 9 July 1940. City were also troubled by enemy action in some of their matches particularly on the occasion they travelled to London to play Queens Park Rangers on 9 November 1941. Just before the kick-off the alert was sounded and although the teams remained in the dressing rooms ready to play the game the all-clear was a long time coming. Eventually the referee decided to abandon the match and the City team returned to Norwich never having kicked a ball. Another nice story concerned the match against Reading on 9 March 1940. Mick Burns was in the City goal and Mapson was the Reading custodian. Burns had previously played for Preston North End and Mapson for Sunderland and they had played against each other in the FA Cup Final of 1936–37. Nottingham Forest were due to play at Carrow Road on 15 November 1941 and a crowd of 3,000 eagerly awaited the game, but the train which was scheduled to bring Forest to Norwich got diverted and Bob Young received a telegram from the Forest manager saying he was marooned with his team in the middle of Lincolnshire. It then being almost kick off time Young decided to play a seven-a-side exhibition game and most of the disappointed spectators stayed on and enjoyed the match. Such was life for a Football Club during the war, City continued to do what they could and provided the fans with some good sport, but as we mentioned before it only drove the club deeper in debt.

In August 1944 the end of the war was in sight and in readiness for the day when competitive football could be restarted City carried out extensive work on their ground. The pitch was levelled and returfed and the stand and dressing rooms were painted. The 1945–46 season was known as the transitional season and for the bulk of the matches guest players were still allowed. City played in the Division Three (South) – North Region for the first half of the season and did very well coming second to Queens Park Rangers. In the latter part of the season City played in the Division Three (South) – North Region Cup which was organised on a league table basis. City finished in fourth position after losing the first two games. The FA Cup was also brought out and brushed down, but City managed to lose both their games with Brighton & Hove Albion. For the only time in the long history of the competition the ties were played on a two leg basis so the 1945–46 season was the only time that City lost twice in the FA Cup in the same campaign. During the war City lost several good friends of the club. Former director Tommy Delves died soon after the commencement of the war and he was quickly followed by John Doran, the centre forward who made such an impression in the 1919–20 season. In the same year 'Jock' Mackenzie, the stalwart full back, passed away as did Horace 'Moosh' King on 4 February 1940. Mick O'Brien died in Uxbridge on 21 September 1940 aged only 47. William Hurrell, a former club chairman, died at his Norwich home on 14 December 1940 and 18 months later Jimmy 'Punch' McEwen the former City captain and manager passed away. Russell James Colman, the former City President who had opened Carrow Road, died at Crown Point on 22 March 1946 and shortly afterwards was followed by former chairman John Samuel Pyke. It was Pyke you will remember who took the club from Newmarket Road to the Nest.

Les Maskell, a gifted player with natural goalscoring abilities who's career was cut short by the war

Money is the root of all...

On I January 1947 the coal industry was nationalised, three months later on 1 April the school leaving age was raised to 15. On 20 November 1947 the Queen was married to the Duke of Edinburgh. 1 January 1948 saw the nationalisation of British Railways. On 30 January 1948 Mahatma Gandhi was assassinated in New Delhi. The State of Israel was proclaimed on 14 May 1948 and on 1 July of the same year the Berlin Airlift got under way. Bread rationing ended in the UK on 29 July 1948. Prince Charles was born on 14 November 1948. The North Atlantic Treaty Organisation (NATO) came into being on 24 August 1949 and petrol rationing finally ended on 26 May 1950, the year Princess Anne was born on 15 August. King George VI died at Sandringham on 6 February 1952 aged 56. On 20 January 1953 General Eisenhower became President of the USA and at the end of January 1953 there were great floods in Eastern England. Edmund Hillary and Sherpa Tenzing reached the top of Everest on 29 May 1953 and shortly afterwards, on 2 June 1953, London saw the Coronation of Queen Elizabeth II. Roger Bannister ran the first sub four minute mile on 6 May 1954 and Sir Anthony Eden replaced Sir Winston Churchill as Prime Minister on 6 April 1955. Independent TV began broadcasting on 22 September 1955 and on 14 December of the same year Hugh Gaitskell became leader of the Labour Party. The summer of 1956 saw the Suez crisis and Harold Macmillan replaced Eden as Prime Minister on 10 January 1957. The Common Market was formally begun on 25 March 1957 shortly before it was announced that National Service was to be abolished in 1960. The first Premium Bond draw was held on I June 1957.

Cyril Spiers, a rarity in being a former goalkeeper to become a manager

Football news in the period under review included the following – the players must have come back from the war intent on playing sporting football for no player was sent off in the Third Division (North) during the 1946–47 season. On 5 October 1946 Len Shackleton turned out for his new club Newcastle United and marked the occasion by scoring six goals in his sides 13–0 win over Newport County. He had recently been transferred from Bradford Park Avenue for a £13,000 fee and the fans must have thought it was money well spent. Neil McBain, the manager of New Brighton FC, had to play in goal for his side when they visited Hartlepool on 15 March 1947. At the time he was 52 years of age and is the oldest man to play in the Football League, he didn't have a very happy match for his side lost 3–0. On 17 January 1948 83,260 watched Manchester United play Arsenal, and strictly speaking the match was played on neutral ground. Old Trafford was bombed during the war and United played all their 'home' matches at Maine Road, the home of Manchester City. The huge attendance remains a record in the Football League. Jackie Sewell was transferred from Notts County to Sheffield Wednesday in 1951 for a fee of £34,500 and was the first player to be literally worth his weight in gold. Tosh Chamberlain, the Fulham player, scored with his first kick in the Football League on 20 November 1954 and when Carlisle United played Darlington in an FA Cup First Round second replay at St James Park, Newcastle on 28 November 1955 they became the first two Football League sides to play a competitive match under floodlights. The first Football League game to be played under floodlights was at Portsmouth on Wednesday 22 February 1956. Newcastle United were the visitors and won 2–0.

Doug Lochhead had taken over from Bob Young during the 1945–46 transitional season, but the City board felt that they needed an experienced hand to guide them into the battles that lay ahead and the man they chose for the job was Cyril Henry Spiers. Spiers was the manager of Cardiff City and had previously played as a goalkeeper for Aston Villa, Tottenham Hotspur and Wolverhampton Wanderers. He was born on 4 April 1902 and joined Villa during the First World War. He played his first game at the age of 17 before a huge crowd of 65,000. He played for the Midlanders until 1927 when he injured his leg and was told by the doctor that he would not play again. However after an operation he was as good as new and he moved south to join Spurs, playing in goal for them until 1933. He then broke his hand in a practice match and went to work with Major Frank Buckley, the former City manager, at the Wolves. Because of an injury crisis he was again pressed into service and resumed playing, carrying on his coaching duties at the same time. He was full of praise for Buckley and upon joining Norwich City stated that he had taught him all he knew. Among the players he coached as youths were Jack Taylor the City full back and Stan Cullis who had a long playing career at Wolves and later became manager. In 1939 Spiers went to manage Cardiff City who were as deeply in debt at the time as City were in 1946. He immediately instigated a youth policy and claimed he left the club in a healthy condition. There was some evidence that his claim was in fact true for Cardiff City were promoted to the Second Division at the end of the 1946–47 season, beating second placed Queens Park Rangers by nine points.

He arrived at Norwich on 12 June 1946 and immediately set to work. Several of the pre-war players remained on the staff and included John Church, Harry Dukes, Billy Furness, Fred Hall, Sid Plunkett, Harry Proctor, Bernie Robinson and Jack Taylor. New players included Ivan Armes, Derek Davis, Les Eyre who had played for Spiers at Cardiff, Ralph 'Ginger' Johnson, Sid Jones, Terry Ryder Jnr the son of the 1920s player, Maurice Tobin and Grenville Williams. In addition Spiers used his Welsh connections to secure Norman Low, a rugged centre half, from Newport County on 14 October 1946, Denis Morgan, a stylish full back, from Cardiff City on 7 October 1946 and winger George Morgan also from Cardiff City on 30 December 1946. At the end of the season centre forward Oscar Hold joined the club from Aldershot. With such a fine assortment of players it came as a shock to the Norwich public to see their team in 21st position at the end of the season, once again having to apply for re-election. The season had some high spots, for example Ralph Johnson scored the opening goal against Leyton Orient at Carrow Road on Saturday 19 October 1946 in only 10 seconds and Les Eyre scored five goals against Brighton & Hove Albion in the First Round of the FA Cup on Saturday 30 November 1946. The fixtures for the 1946–47 season were by the way exactly the same as would have been played in 1939–40 had not war intervened. 1946–47 was also the season noted for rather severe weather, but City were not too badly affected and managed to complete their fixtures by Saturday 17 May 1947, some were not so lucky and had to continue into June.

Despite the poor playing performances City still managed to show a profit on the season, £1,461 was the published figure, and, but for the debts, would probably have been able to buy themselves out of trouble. Spiers needed time for his young players to gain experience, but time as always was a commodity in short supply.

Les Eyre, a top-scoring striker in the post-war years

Mr Blenkinsop of Leeds United proposed that Norwich City FC should be re-elected to the Football League and happily his suggestion was accepted unanimously. James Hanly was elected to the board in 1946 and in the summer of 1947 became vice-chairman, taking the place of George Pilch. Another boardroom change was registered during 1946 when John William Howes, a founder director in 1905, stood down. On 4 August 1947 it was announced that William Clarke, a director in the 1930s, had died in Norwich. In addition to the chairman James Wright and vice-chairman James Hanly the board now consisted of George Pilch, Ernest Charles Bond, D.W.P. Cough, Charles Joice and Herbert George Sands. Cyril Spiers, writing in the handbook of 1947–48, praised the loyalty and patience of the City supporters and promised more effort in the future. He also made a remarkable statement about the previous season for he went on – 'here we were, competing in full league football, with only one player capable of playing the standard of football now required'. Later he went on to mention the 'Nursery' club, the Cardiff Nomads, in South

Victor Ralph 'Ginger' Johnson scored 123 goals in 107 wartime games for Norwich

Wales which ran three teams every Saturday. One for schoolboys between 14–16, a junior side for lads between 16–18 and a senior team for the over-18s. This he extrapolated was the way forward for the club.

Above, Noel Kinsey, skilful inside right and the poacher of many fine goals

Cyril Spiers did not stay to see the fruits of his youth policy for he returned to manage his old club Cardiff City on Monday 10 December 1947. There is no doubt that his thinking was right and the club was grateful for the fine legacy of young players that he brought to Norwich, but one is left with the impression that he did not handle his senior players too well. In the third match of the season against Watford at Carrow Road three players of note made their debuts, Noel Kinsey, Don Pickwick and Albert Foan. The first two matches had been lost and Spiers obviously decided it was time to give youth a chance. Noel Kinsey was another who had followed the familiar path from Cardiff City, playing for their Reserve side in 1946–47. He went on to make 243 appearances for City and scored 65 goals. He left for Birmingham City during the summer of 1953 and scored for his new club in the FA Cup Final of 1956. Don Pickwick, a diminutive wing half, was yet another Welshman and he contributed many gritty displays for City over the years. Albert Foan was just out of the Army and later moved back to his native London to join West Ham United in the summer of 1950. By the way City won the game against Watford 1–0 and Albert Foan scored the goal. When the Canaries travelled to Northampton on Saturday 27 September 1947 they took with them a young goalkeeper who was also to make a lasting impression at Carrow Road. In the two matches prior to the above match City had also used a young goalkeeper. His name was Don Edwards, another Welshman, this time from Wrexham. It has often been reported that Don was City's youngest ever Football League player, making his debut when only 16 years of age but as he was born on 2 August 1930 he was in fact 17 years and 46 days old when he played his first game on Wednesday 17 September 1947. His home debut the following Saturday was not a happy day for him as City lost 1–5 to Bristol Rovers. The name of the new 'keeper tried on 27 September was Kenneth Walter Samuel Nethercott, a 22 year old from Bristol. Among the long list of City goalkeepers, and there have been many fine custodians at Norwich, Ken stands with the very best. Powerful and brave he was blessed with uncanny anticipation often making the difficult save look easy and as we trip through the years we shall meet Ken time and time again. In all he made 416 competitive appearances for the Canaries including the early games of the great FA Cup run in 1958–59. His displays throughout the years of loyal service that he gave to the club are testimony of all that is good in the game of football.

Below, Norwich born James Laffan Hanly, who took over as chairman in 1948

Before we record the departure of Cyril Spiers there is one final card to be played, one last debutant to note, a living proof that his policy of giving youth a chance was right. On the very next Saturday after Nethercott's debut City called upon a young centre forward from Cambridgeshire to do his duty. The match was against Aldershot at Carrow Road and a crowd of 15,247 saw the Canaries go down 0–1, beaten by a surprise goal. The day will not be remembered for the football, but only as the foundation stone of an exceptional career – The City No 9 that afternoon was Ronald George Ashman. Because of his later reputation as a defender we tend to forget that Ron came to Norwich as a centre forward and we probably also forget that in addition to his record number of City appearances in the Football League he also scored 56 goals during his long and illustrious career. In overall competitive appearances his total of 662 was only surpassed by Kevin Keelan – and he was awarded an MBE! Exit then Cyril Spiers and welcome Doug Lochhead the new City manager.

During the rest of the season Doug Lochhead

had a rather difficult time, City were at the bottom of the league when he took over, but luckily there was plenty of enthusiasm around. The post war boom of watching football was at its peak, just look at the last three gates that City recorded that season. On Wednesday 21 April 1948 against Queens Park Rangers – 30,052, the following Saturday against Swansea Town – 25,435 and for the Notts County game four days later – 37,863 (still a City record in the Football League). Add them together and we see that 93,350 people passed through the Carrow Road turnstiles in a period of only eight days. Even more extraordinary was the fact that the Canaries were second from the bottom of the Third Division (South). In the first match against Queens Park Rangers Roy Hollis, a youngster from Great Yarmouth, scored a hat-trick in the first half hour of his debut, City won 5–2, he also scored against Swansea Town on the Saturday, but City lost 1–2 and on the following Wednesday Tommy Lawton scored the only goal of the match. Notts County had ambitiously signed Lawton from Chelsea in the previous November, but were attracting such large crowds wherever they played that they more than recouped their outlay. They were great days – a pity then that City would have to again seek re-election. To add flavour to the proceedings a journalist in a 'responsible' newspaper put about a story that the First and Second Division clubs wanted to see new blood in the competition – not a good time then to go cap in hand to the League.

As things turned out City had no problems in their quest for re-election, they and bottom club Brighton & Hove Albion received the great bulk of the votes. Colchester United were third in the poll and managed two votes, but no other club got more than one. In the club handbook Doug Lochhead paid tribute to former manager James Kerr and fondly recalled the day that he had been met on Norwich Thorpe Station by Kerr and Mick O'Brien in June 1929. During the summer of 1948 City had received approaches for at least two of their young players, but Lochhead like Spiers was committed to youth and refused to listen. The club had made a profit of £4,531 on the 1947–48 season and there was no need to sell the stars of the future. The 1948–49 season was not spectacular by any means, but City made progress and finished in 10th position with Ron Ashman ending the season as top scorer. In August 1948 City had a new chairman when James Laffan Hanly took over from James Wright. James Hanly was born in Norwich in 1905, the son of Bernard Hanly who had started the family shoe manufacturing business of James Southall & Co in 1891. There was one remarkable game on Saturday 15 January when City went to the West Country and beat Bristol City 6–1, Noel Kinsey completing a second half hat-trick. On the other occasion that the Canaries visited Bristol, the penultimate game of the season, a young Irish lad came in for his first game in a yellow and green shirt. He had arrived in Norwich on 9 August 1948 for a small fee from Limerick and he went on to play 338 games and score 132 goals in his long Carrow Road career – his name was John Thomas Gavin.

During the summer of 1949 Norwich City made a signing that made the soccer world sit up and look, from Arsenal they bought Welsh

Ron Ashman, began life as a centre forward and later took on many roles in his career. Arguably the most influential and longest serving member of Norwich City

Money is the root of all...

Goalkeeper Ken Nethercott was signed by Cyril Spiers for City in 1948 and gave sterling service

international Brynmor Jones. Though in the autumn of a long career Jones was still a name to be reckoned with and when he moved to Arsenal in 1938 he had cost £14,000. His career was one of many of the period that had been broken by the war, but he still managed to accumulate 17 International caps with his clever inside forward play. He was destined to only play 26 matches for City, but signing such an eminent player did the image of the club no harm at all. Lochhead remarked after the signing that it was 20 years to the day since he himself had come to Norwich. The club handbook was a lively number that year with Lochhead paying a warm tribute to trainers Harry Proctor and Billy Furness and secretary Peter Dash. Our attention was drawn by the foreword contributed by chairman James Hanly. He said that City would continue to play good and sporting football and never resort to the situation where players said 'I may not be able to play football, but I'll stop those who can'. He went on to pen the following –

> "I know that many years ago, when I used to save a few pence of my 'holiday money' at the end of the summer term to buy the Norwich City handbook, I used to read the Chairman's notes and visualise the Directors as a lot of old gentlemen wearing astrakhan collars and smoking cigars who, besides knowing sweet nothing about football, consistently robbed the club of what money came through the turnstiles.
>
> Of course I know now that it was not true then, any more than it is now."

Funny how the mind works when you are on the other side of the fence !

An Italian paper carried a story about British clubs adopting continental ideas and added –'Probably the only British club not to change its kit will be Norwich City FC – the most elegant team in England with their yellow silk shirts and green collars and cuffs'. It was also reported that the City attendances in 1948–49 showed a slight fall but just look at the Reserve gates – they were said to average 7,450. City continued their improvement in the autumn of 1949 and in November Doug Lochhead brought a Londoner to play at Carrow Road. He was full back Bill Lewis, although actually signed from Blackpool, Bill had played for West Ham United during the war and he went on to make 256 appearances for the Canaries.

Below, the 1949–50 squad

The City reputation in the FA Cup was badly in need of a boost and an excellent opportunity occurred when the Canaries were drawn to play Portsmouth in the Third Round at Fratton Park on Saturday 7 January 1950. Portsmouth were the current champions of the Football League when City made the trip to the south coast and against all the odds came away with a 1–1 draw. After the match it was revealed that Lindy Delaphena, the West Indian born Pompey winger, had handled the cross that gave the home team the lead at half time. Noel Kinsey replied for City after the interval and on the following Thursday 43,129 paid to see the replay at Carrow Road (then a ground record). Sadly City lost by 0–2 but managed to hold the very strong First Division side until after the interval. Doug Lochhead's health was shattered after an accident in August 1949 and after a period of illness it was announced that he would leave the club on Friday 3 March 1950. Norman Low, the City centre half, stepped up to become player-manager for the remainder of the season. City finished in 11th place at the end of the campaign and there was much speculation in Norwich as to who would become the next City boss. Tom Whittaker of Arsenal had been approached and it was said that City offered him a yearly salary of £2,500, a huge amount in those days, if he would come to Norfolk. In the end the rampant rumour came to nothing, many top names had been put forward, but City decided to appoint Norman Low to the post of manager. Low had fine leadership qualities and had been an exemplary player. In his first match as player-manager back on 4 March 1950 when City took on local rivals Ipswich Town at Carrow Road, he persuaded Ron Ashman, who had been struggling a bit at centre forward, to try his luck at wing half – it was an inspired decision and City were to reap the benefit for many years to come.

The summer of 1950 was long and hot and chairman Hanly predicted that few clubs would have a better playing surface than was to be seen at Carrow Road. Work had been carried out on the terracing and improvements made at the River End. The broadcasting system had also been overhauled and brought up to date. Norman Low had decided not to continue playing and his place at centre half was taken by Reg Foulkes, Low's first signing. Foulkes joined the club from Walsall and had usually proved to be a stumbling block when City had travelled to Fellows Park. Other imports were Tommy Docherty, a left winger from Lincoln City who seemed to reserve his best displays for the FA Cup, and Londoner Johnny Summers who while at Norwich scored 36 goals in 76 outings. After a 2–4 reverse at Nottingham Forest on the second Saturday of the season City did not suffer another defeat until the turn of the year. It was a fabulous start to the season and if Nottingham Forest, the eventual winners of the section that year, had not been such a strong side City would have got back into the Second Division. The run of 23 games without defeat still stands as a club record and the regular City side that season read Nethercott, Duffy and Lewis, Pickwick, Foulkes and Ashman, Gavin, Kinsey, Hollis, Eyre and Docherty. At the end of the very exciting season City occupied second place in the league, seven points clear of their nearest rivals, but as then only one side was promoted from the Third Division (South) they had to remain where they were and fight again.

Top, City centre half Norman Low took over at the start of the 50s as player-manager. Left, Reg Foulkes, one of the side which enjoyed a record run of 23 games without defeat during 1950. Right, Johnny Summers, another prolific scorer in the early 1950s

City also reached the Fifth Round of the FA Cup that year before being knocked out by Sunderland at Roker Park, 65,125 turning up to see the home side win 3–1. Earlier City had entertained Liverpool in the Third Round at Carrow Road and before another huge crowd of 34,693 Tommy Docherty scored twice in a 3–1 victory. Top scorer during the campaign was Johnny Gavin with 18 league and cup goals and close behind came Roy Hollis with 17 and Les Eyre with 16. An indication of how fortune smiled on the Canaries that season was seen on the trip to Newport County in late March where the home side built up a 5–1 lead on a terrible pitch. All through the game the rain continued to fall heavily and a bitter wind gusted to gale force. After 70 minutes conditions were so bad that the referee decided to abandon the match and when City returned on a much more tranquil day later in the season they managed to earn a 1–1 draw. It was a fine first season for Norman Low as manager, for the first time in years City had a really settled side and now they had to go all out to once more escape from the Third Division.

Above, Roy Hollis, and right, fearless left back William Albert 'Bill' Lewis, two more regular members of Norman Low's teams of the 1950s

A reference in the handbook of 1951–52 stated that Arthur Turner, one of the founders of the club, was still attending matches at Carrow Road and was as keen as ever. No doubt then he was eagerly awaiting the new campaign and hoping that City would top the league. On 26 January 1952 Neville Howlett, a City director in the 1930s, died at his Norwich home. Just before the start of the season Norman Low brought the Hull City centre forward Alf Ackerman to Norwich. Ackerman cost the club £9,500, a large fee in those days for a Third Division club, and equalled the club record set when Bill Lewis arrived from Blackpool in 1949. Paddy Sloan, reported to have been the first British player to go to Italy after the war, also arrived in Norfolk after a most complicated transfer (see Who's Who for details). Ken Oxford arrived from Chesterfield in July, but because of the fine form of Ken Nethercott would have to wait a long time for his chance. The first large win of the season was recorded on Wednesday 29 August 1951 when Colchester United were the visitors. City won 5–2 against the club that had joined the Football League during the 1950–51 campaign when the Third Division (South) was increased to 24 clubs. Later in the season Gillingham (H) 5–0, Bristol City (A) 5–2 and Torquay United (H) 7–0 were to suffer at the hands of the hungry City forward line, but worst hit of all were Walsall who were beaten 8–0 at Carrow Road on Saturday 29 December 1951. Centre forward Roy Hollis scored five in that game and with luck could have scored five more such was City's dominance. Johnny Gavin scored three hat-tricks during the season and Ron Ashman coverted six penalties, but still City could not get into the Second Division. Plymouth Argyle finished top of the league five points ahead of Reading and City.

Noel Kinsey was selected to represent Wales against Northern Ireland in Belfast on 7 March 1951 and later went on to make three more appearances for his country before leaving the club. Johnny Gavin meanwhile had first played for Eire against Finland in September 1949. He finished with a total of seven Eire caps five of which were gained while he was a Norwich City player. An inside forward who had joined Norwich from Reading during the close season made his debut against Exeter City on Wednesday 12 September 1951. The match, which was played at Carrow Road, was a rather tame 1–1 draw, but there was nothing tame about our debutant who went on to make 426 appearances for the club in a distinguished career before moving on to Colchester United – his name was Roy McCrohan. Arsenal knocked

Arsenal defeated the Canaries 5–0 on 12 January 1952 in front of 38,930 spectators at Carrow Road

City out of the FA Cup that year when they visited Carrow Road on Saturday 12 January 1952 in the Third Round. Another huge crowd of 38,930 gathered to witness the game, but must have been very disappointed with the result, for the Gunners won 5–0. At the end of the season City left for a tour of Holland, it being the first overseas excursion that the club had ever undertaken. The chairman and vice-chairman accompanied the 19 players and officials who left on the morning of Saturday 17 May 1952. The tour had been arranged by Mr M.J. Koolhaas the president of Dutch club Ajax Amsterdam and was successful both as a holiday and a playing exercise – City played four games and won them all (see friendlies section). When the happy band arrived back in Norfolk they were greeted by grim faced accountants – City had lost £6,052 on the season.

Perhaps the financial position was not as bad as it appeared for included in the reported loss were the transfer fees paid for winger Billy Coxon and centre forward Tom Johnston. Coxon came from Ilkeston Town and was noted for his rocket like shot. Johnston meanwhile came from Oldham Athletic and was later to repay a large slice of his transfer fee with two very important goals indeed. In fact the rugged Scot who always wore a bandage on his left wrist to protect an old injury got to work straight away and scored ten goals in his first nine outings, included among these were four against Shrewsbury Town on Saturday 13 September 1952. If the 13th is indeed unlucky for some it certainly was not so for Norwich City – the final score at Gay Meadow was 8–1 in favour of the Norfolk men. What is more City played with only ten men for most of the game, Don Pickwick unfortunately breaking his leg just before half time. The 8–1 scoreline still stands as a record away victory in

Above, the rugged Tom Johnston, a great centre forward

Left, City's record goal scorer, outside right John Thomas Gavin

Money is the root of all...

Alfred Ackerman, above, joint top scorer in 1952–53 matching Johnny Gavin's 20 goals

any competitive match for Norwich City. There was no FA Cup run in the 1952–53 season but City were in with a chance of promotion right until the end of the season and finally finished in fourth place. There were again many fine crowds at Carrow Road, Alf Ackerman and Johnny Gavin both scored 20 goals in the league as City recorded their highest total of goals achieved in a Football League season – 99.

Johnny Gavin was sent off in the game against Northampton Town on Saturday 13 December 1952, and was suspended for seven days. Tragically former chairman James Wright collapsed and died on the train as the team travelled back from a league match at Queens Park Rangers on Saturday 17 January 1953. Another former chairman, Ernest Morse, died on 9 November 1952 at the age of 80 and former City manager James Jewell died at his Brighton home on 21 October 1952, he was 54 years old.

At the start of the 1953–54 season there were 32 full time professionals on the City books including new men Bobby Brennan, who cost £15,000 from Fulham and Tony 'Darkie' Collins. The fee paid for Collins, who arrived from Watford, was £5,000. City made their best ever start to a season being undefeated in their first twelve games of which eight were won. City neighbours, Ipswich Town, also made an impressive start to the season and in late September the East Anglian clubs led the division. On Saturday 12 December 1953 Peter Gordon made his debut against Barnsley in the Second Round of the FA Cup. Peter had been on the staff since December 1949 and went on to make 176 appearances for the Canaries and scored 37 goals. On Christmas Day 1953 goalkeeper Ken Nethercott was dropped for the first time in his City career. His replacement was Ken Oxford who had had to wait over two years to make his debut. Later in the season, in the away match at Bournemouth, Nethercott, who had briefly regained his place was injured and Bobby Brennan donned the goalkeepers jersey for the whole of the second half and in what had been an eventful first season for the Northern Ireland international conceded two goals and City were beaten 0–2. Alan Woan who had joined the club from New Brighton FC in December made his debut on 19 April 1954 and scored in the third minute against Northampton Town, City went on to win the match convincingly by 4–1. Despite the early promise Norwich eventually finished in a disappointing 7th position and on 24 April 1954 Ron Ashman missed his first game since 4 March 1950 – a run of 192 consecutive games.

City had a typically exciting run in the FA Cup in 1953–54 confounding the football world by winning 2–1 in a breathtaking confrontation at Highbury. The two City goals were headed by centre forward Tom Johnston after a second minute penalty miss by Bobby Brennan. The game was marred in the 33rd minute when both Alex Forbes of the home side and Bobby Brennan were sent off for fighting. In the Fifth Round City were drawn at home to Leicester City but, after leading 1–0 at half time through a Brennan goal, eventually lost 1–2 to the side that won the Second Division championship that year. In the very next game at Carrow Road, played on the following Wednesday afternoon against Gillingham, City could only attract 6,697 spectators – the lowest ever crowd in a

A weary but jubilant group, below, after the 2–1 victory in the 1953–54 FA Cup win at Highbury

competitive First team match on the ground at the time. At the end of the season Alf Ackerman returned to Hull City for £5,000.

There was a sad start to the 1954–55 season when, just four days before the opening game, it was announced that John William Howes, for so many years a director and official of Norwich City FC, had died. Howes was born on 19 August 1864 and after training to become a teacher in London had returned to the city and taught at Norman's Endowed School, including 36 years as headmaster. In his youth Howes had played for Norwich Teachers as a goalkeeper and for many years was a keen club cricketer. Along with Webster, Nutchey and Turner, who of course were all close personal friends, Howes had attended the inaugural meeting of Norwich City FC on 17 June 1902. When, in 1905, the club turned professional he took on the role as secretary and continued to serve the club in an official capacity until 1946. When he died Howes was just two days short of his 90th birthday. During the season a young man from Billingford near Fakenham made an appearance in the Reserve team and scored a goal. He was later to find fame as a Norfolk, Middlesex and England batsman – his name was Peter Howard Parfitt. On 11 September 1954 full back Bill Lewis scored his only goal for the club with a fifty yard drive at Northampton and on Monday 27 December 1954, former City player Roy Hollis scored a hat-trick for Southend United in the 3–3 draw at Carrow Road. During the season Ken Nethercott made his 300th appearance for the club, Ron Ashman his 250th and Denis Morgan reached 200. The Reserve team reached the Final of the Combination Cup, but lost to Southampton 1–3 at the Dell.

In the FA Cup City entertained Headington United (later Oxford United) in the First Round at Carrow Road and won 4–2 but were beaten 5–1 by Brighton & Hove Albion after a replay at the next hurdle. Tony Collins missed a penalty in the first match against Brighton at Carrow Road and the game finished 0–0. Early in January 1955 manager Norman Low signed the Reading inside forward Sammy Chung and it proved to be the last major signing that he made. City finished the season in 12th position, their lowest placing since having to seek re-election at the end of the 1947–48 season, The board felt that it was time for a change and Low was relieved of his duties on Friday 22 April 1955. In his five years as manager of Norwich City FC the club had finished second, third, fourth, seventh and now twelfth in the Third Division (South). He had so nearly guided the club to a higher division and there were of course several momentous performances in the FA Cup to his credit, but major success had eluded him and he paid the price with his job. Later he managed Workington and Port Vale and carried out scouting duties for Liverpool. Although City made a modest profit during the 1954–55 season they were still deeply in debt. On Saturday 5 February 1955 Low had decided that a young centre half from Mulbarton was good enough to make his First team debut in the match at Watford. Time proved that the decision was a correct one for he went on to play 23 times for his country and when he was later transferred to Tottenham Hotspur for £17,250 the fee helped to clear some of City's debt – the name of the centre half was Maurice 'Monty' Norman.

Above, local talent emerged when young 'Monty' Norman from Mulbarton was signed in 1955

The man selected to replace Norman Low was Tom Parker, who had previously managed Norwich City in the mid 1930s. After leaving Norwich in February 1937 Parker returned to Southampton and continued as their manager until 1943. During the war he was involved in work for the Lloyds Register of Shipping and in 1946 he joined the Ministry of Transport (Marine Division). When he returned to Norwich on 2 May 1955 he was 57 years old. During the summer of 1955 Parker brought Ralph Hunt to Norwich from Bournemouth, a shrewd purchase indeed as he went on to score 33 goals during the season. It helped City to finish in 7th position though they were never really in the running for promotion. Part of the deal that took Maurice Norman to Tottenham Hotspur in November involved the return of Eire international Johnny

Above, Ralph Hunt got 33 goals in his first season, 1955–56, at Carrow Road

Gavin for his second spell with the Canaries. Soon after his return Gavin too was making a significant contribution to the City goalscoring, netting four in the 7–2 win over Southend United on Saturday 17 December 1955. The second half of City's match at Brentford on 3 September 1955 was broadcast by the BBC. The score was 1–1 at the interval, but City reserved their best play for the second period and eventually won 2–1. During the season England's Youth team played the Dutch Youth at Carrow Road and Norwich born Barry Bridges, later to star at Chelsea and other London clubs, scored four goals for City Boys against Barking Boys. In the FA Cup City beat Dorchester Town and Brighton & Hove Albion before being knocked out of the competition by Sunderland in the Third Round.

On Saturday 28 January 1956 the death was announced of Arthur Turner, a pioneer of football in Norwich. It was Turner you will remember who travelled throughout East Anglia looking for players in the old amateur days. After a spell as manager of the club in the early years of professionalism Turner faded from the scene but retained his interest in the club until his dying day. In addition to his love of local football he was well known in cricket circles and played for Thorpe Hamlet and Riverside Ramblers. He excelled too in the game of bowls and served as secretary of the Norfolk Bowling Association for over 50 years. In addition to his numerous business interests in Norwich he kept the Boars Head (St Stephens Street) and the King George IV (Ber Street) public houses and was said to be a fair conjuror and children's entertainer. He was 87 years old.

We come now to the events of the 1956–57 season – when City had to fight for their very existence. Let us examine in detail the extraordinary occurrences that temporarily brought the club to its knees and so nearly led to permanent closure. At the end of the 1955–56 season we left Norwich City FC in 7th place in Division Three (South). Tom Parker was in his second term as manager of the club but was no longer a young man and had spent some ten years away from the game working as a civil servant. Parker was committed to a policy of encouraging youth and during the summer of 1956 allowed Bobby Brennan to drift off to play for Great Yarmouth. He also sold Ron Hansell to Chester and Alan Woan to Northampton Town. The new season began encouragingly with City picking up ten points from the first six matches but they were then successful in only 1 of their next 28 league games. City were soon anchored at the bottom of the league and attendance's at Carrow Road fell steadily, only 8,481 saw the Boxing Day fixture against Colchester United. On Wednesday 17 October 1956 the new floodlights were switched on at Carrow Road with Sunderland providing the opposition. They beat the Canaries 3–0 that night, the new floodlit era had arrived but City could not really afford the new luxury for they cost the club in excess of £9,000. In the First Round of the FA Cup on Saturday 17 November 1956 the visitors were

The 1956–57 team faced an uncertain future at the foot of the table with falling attendances and Norwich City FC on the brink of disaster

Southern League Bedford Town and the Carrow Road crowd were stunned as City crashed to a 2–4 defeat. On the morning of Wednesday 12 December 1956 the club revealed that they were unable to find the cash to pay the £500 wages bill and Norwich City FC stood on the brink of disaster.

Fortunately the Norfolk News Company (now Eastern Counties Newspapers Group Ltd) lent the club sufficient money to carry on, but it was obvious that Norwich City FC faced a crisis of some magnitude. Several prominent businessmen under the chairmanship of the Lord Mayor of Norwich, Mr Arthur South, met together and formed an Appeal Committee. Messrs J.D. Alston, R.G. Carter, A. Ryrie and H. Robinson were delegated to compile a report on the affairs of the Norwich City FC and their 2,000 word statement was prepared for a meeting held on Monday 7 January 1957. We list below the broad content and recommendations of the report.

"At our request the auditors of the club have reported to us particularly on the question of expenses paid to the present directors and we have no criticism on this point for it appears that the directors have been very generous to the club. It is clear however that the club has already incurred substantial losses for the first half of the season. Gate receipts are well down and it is expected that the loss on the year will be at least £10,000. Although wages and salaries have been reduced the club will need a subsidy of £300 per week for the rest of the season. The present liabilities stand in excess of £20,000. We have looked into the question of liquidation but do not think it advisable. The loan to build the ground (£8,000 from the Football Association in 1935) has been paid back by instalments and the final payment is due next September. Despite recent results the spirit of the team is good and relations with the manager and training staff are quite satisfactory. We criticise the recent addition of floodlighting because it could not be afforded. We appreciate the contribution from the Supporters Club, but feel that it must be increased. There are discouraging signs for football clubs especially the credit squeeze, television and petrol rationing (because of the Suez crisis). A board of twelve people is too large and the new board should consist of not less than four and not more than six. The present board should resign right away. The Appeal Committee should aim to raise £25,000."

Lord Mayor of Norwich, Mr Arthur South, chaired the meeting to form an Appeal Committee to support Norwich City Football Club

An appeal was immediately started to raise the sum of £25,000. Meanwhile at least a dozen nominations were received for the new board including Messrs F.J. Andrews, George Fish, Geoffrey Fisher, Frederick C. Jex, James Hanly, Alfred Kirchen, Clifford Kowen, E.C. Page, George E. Pilch (Son of the former director R.G. Pilch), Henry Robinson, Leonard Votier and Geoffrey Watling. The shareholders of Norwich City FC met on the evening of Monday 4 February 1957 and after a lengthy ballot which finished at 12.50am the following were elected to form the new City board. Geoffrey Watling, James Hanly, George Fish, Henry Robinson and Frederick Jex. At the meeting Mr South forecast that £18,000 would be raised by the end of the month and £9,000 had already been promised. Later in the week the new board met and Geoffrey Watling was elected to become the new chairman of the club, George Fish was to be vice-chairman. Mr Watling said after the meeting that there were no plans to seek a new manager at present, but everything must be done to raise the £25,000 needed to put the club back on its feet. By Thursday 21 March 1957 only two more

Archie Macaulay faced an uphill task when taking on the manager's role in April 1957

matches had been won and manager Tom Parker's contract was terminated. Bobby Brennan was asked to rejoin the club and he played in the match at Swindon on Saturday 23 March 1957. On Monday 15 April 1957 a new manager was appointed and ended much speculation and rumour in the city as to who would secure the job. Despite the mammoth difficulties that any new manager would face there had been no shortage of applicants. The board were in full agreement that they had found the right man and in the fullness of time they would not be disappointed – the new man was a Scot and his name was Archibald Renwick Macaulay.

Archie Macaulay had in his career played for West Ham United, Brentford, Arsenal and Fulham and had represented Scotland on seven occasions. His first job in management was as player/manager of Guildford City, but he soon felt the desire to return north of the border and prior to his City appointment was trainer/coach at Dundee. He had a huge task ahead of him but with the full support of the board anything was possible. City finished the season at the very bottom of the Third Division (South) and once more had to seek re-election to the Football League. Before we close this most unfortunate chapter in the history of Norwich City FC we must pay tribute to the enthusiasm of the new board. The customers were soon flocking back to the terraces at Carrow Road, 28,783 attended the clash with Ipswich Town on Good Friday 1957, and things were gradually returning to normal. The citizens of Norwich, indeed Norfolk as a whole, rallied round the club in its hour of need and the target figure of £25,000 set by the Appeal Fund Committee was in sight by the end of the season – as a mark of their gratitude the club elected a new vice-president – the Lord Mayor of the City of Norwich, Mr Arthur South.

Enter Geoffrey Watling

The first satellite to orbit the earth was launched by the Russians on 4 October 1957. It weighed only 180lbs and was 23ins in diameter. On Christmas Day 1957 the Queen's Message was televised for the first time. Mr Khrushchev was elected prime minister of the USSR on 27 March 1958 and shortly afterwards General de Gaulle held a similar position in France. On 2 November 1959 the first section of the M1 was opened and Prince Andrew was born on 19 February 1960. Princess Margaret and Mr Anthony Armstrong-Jones were married on 6 May 1960, and later in the year the Olympic Games opened in Rome on 25 August 1960. President Kennedy was elected to office on 9 November 1960 shortly before the farthing ceased to be legal tender on the last day of 1960. Major Yuri Gagarin was the first man in space on 12 April 1961. On 5 August 1962 the actress Marilyn Monroe was found dead, she was 36 years old. The first buildings of the University of East Anglia were opened in Norwich on 29 September 1963 shortly before President Kennedy was assassinated on 22 November of the same year. In April of 1964 the Great Train Robbers were brought to trial and on 16 October 1964 Harold Wilson became Prime Minister. The death of Sir Winston Churchill was recorded on 24 January 1965 and on 30 July of the following year England won the World Cup at Wembley. The Aberfan disaster which killed 144 people including over 100 children occurred on 21 October 1966. On 4 January 1967 Donald Campbell was killed on Lake Coniston and on 1 July 1967 the BBC introduced colour programmes on BBC 2. Also in 1967, on 29 September, the liner Queen Elizabeth II was launched. During 1968 Dr Martin Luther King was assassinated on 4 April and on 5 June Senator Robert Kennedy suffered the same fate. Also in 1968 the 2 tier postal service was introduced on 19 September and President Nixon was elected to office on 5 November. Concorde made its maiden flight on 9 April 1969 and later in the same year saw the Investiture of Prince Charles at Caernarvon Castle. Edward Heath became Prime Minister on 18 June 1970 and on 15 February 1971 we all had to change to decimal currency.

Now then to our football events – the Third and Fourth Divisions were created instead of the North and South sections of Division Three at the start of the 1958–59 season. The bottom twelve clubs from each section formed the new Division Four. The Munich disaster on Thursday 6 February 1958 killed many of the Manchester United team and journalists who had reported the game. The aircraft flying the team home after a European Cup match crashed through the perimeter fence at Munich Airport in awful weather. During the 1960–61 season the Football League Cup was started and Norwich City FC were the second winners of the trophy. The highest crowd ever to witness a Fourth Division game was at Selhurst Park on 31 March 1961. Crystal Palace played Millwall and the attendance was 37,774. Accrington Stanley resigned from the Football League part way through the 1961–62 season and at the end of the season their place was taken by Oxford United. At the start of the 1965–66 season substitutes were allowed in the Football League for the first time. The first man to be so employed was Keith Peacock of Charlton Athletic in the opening game of the campaign on Saturday 21 August 1965. At the end of the 1967–68 season Peterborough United were fined by the Football League for offering illegal bonuses and were also relegated to the Fourth Division. In February 1970 Swansea Town changed their name to Swansea City and Cambridge United replaced Bradford Park Avenue in the Football League. 66 people were killed at Ibrox Stadium on 2 January 1971, Rangers were playing Celtic when the crowd surged back into the ground as the home side scored a late equaliser. Finally a look at the transfer fees at the start and end of our period of review. In September 1958 Albert Quixall cost £40,000 when he moved from Sheffield Wednesday to Manchester United and in March 1970 £200,000 changed hands when Martin Peters left West Ham United and signed for Tottenham Hotspur.

When the accounts for the 1956–57 season were released on 31 July 1957 it was seen that City had lost in excess of £11,000 in their times of trouble. However some of the cash from the Appeal Fund had been transferred to the Football Club and Archie Macaulay was busily getting a team together for the forthcoming campaign. He could of course still call upon his faithful senior professionals ie goalkeepers Ken Nethercott and Ken Oxford, full backs Ron Ashman and Roy McCrohan and forwards Bobby Brennan, Johnny Gavin, Peter Gordon and Ralph Hunt, but he was very short of quality

Enter Geoffrey Watling

Geoffrey Watling and Archie Macaulay secure Terry Allcock's signature for City

half backs. From Aberdeen he bought Bobby Wilson and from Dundee United came Eddie Stewart and Maurice Milne. Matt Crowe was signed from Partick Thistle and £5,000 secured the services of centre half Barry Butler from Sheffield Wednesday. When asked by Geoffrey Watling what he knew of Norwich City, Butler replied 'Only that they are bankrupt'. Thanks to the contributions of men like Butler and Crowe, City did not stay bankrupt for long and by the end of the season they had recovered to finish 8th in the league. The 1957–58 season saw the last of the Third Division (South) and City were glad to finish in the top half of the table and escape the ignominy of having to be one of the founder members of the new Fourth Division.

After a modest run in the FA Cup, City got to the Third Round before being eliminated by Darlington, manager Macaulay again moved into the transfer market. From Bolton Wanderers he bought Terry Allcock and from Blackpool he secured the services of Derrick Lythgoe. Allcock turned out to be a fine signing for the club and an important member of the team for many years. Known to his colleagues as 'The Count' because of his athletic frame and immaculate dress he had been the understudy to England centre forward Nat Lofthouse and while on the City books made 389 appearances and scored 127 goals. Don't run away with the idea that Macaulay was only looking to buy players, for in the summer of 1958 he allowed long serving Johnny Gavin and his inside partner Peter Gordon to move to Watford. Centre forward Ralph Hunt was another to be on the move – he left for Derby County in early August. In another busy summer City signed right winger Errol 'Cowboy' Crossan from Southend United and Jimmy Hill from Newcastle United. Jimmy Hill was an Irishman who later went on to play seven times for his country and when he arrived at Norwich he was an outside right. The 1958–59 season started quietly enough and up to Saturday 15 November 1958 City had played 19 games in the league, won 6, drawn 5 and lost 8. During the course of the season a new team was beginning to take shape – Roy McCrohan was moved up to right half and local lad Bryan Thurlow was drafted in to take his place. Another local lad, this time from Fincham, who had briefly been tried at centre forward during the 1956–57 season had again been given a chance. A chance that he grabbed with both hands for his name was Terry Bly. There was one last change that needed to be made and on Saturday 15 November 1958 when Ilford visited Norwich in the First Round of the FA Cup Jimmy Hill was brought in at inside left. They could never have known that day what drama was about to explode, City were losing 0–1 at the interval and made heavy weather of beating the amateur side. The FA Cup run that was to re-establish Norwich City as a force in the football world was about to begin.

At the end of a fabulous season City so nearly won promotion to the Second Division in addition to the long and glorious trail that led to the very threshold of Wembley. A booklet fittingly called 'Canary Crusade' was produced by the Norfolk News Company Ltd. at the end of the season to mark the momentous campaign and we are indebted to the company, now called Eastern Counties Newspapers Group Ltd. and the former Sports Editor Ted Bell for allowing us to reproduce sections from the publication. Ted Bell and his cameraman saw every goal scored and every ball kicked during that unforgettable winter it is only fitting that their work should live on in this publication.

CANARY CRUSADE

★ The men at the helm

Chairman
GEOFFREY WATLING

Manager:
ARCHIE MACAULAY

Golden road, but I can't forget the dark days

By "Nomad" of the "Eastern Evening News."

TWO years ago Norwich City were just emerging from a conflict that had threatened not only their prospects but their very existence. Today they stand re-established, prevented by the narrowest of margins from becoming the first club from the Third Division to reach the Cup Final; a club respected, admired and praised the world over.

Throughout these two years I have watched, at first hand, the rebirth of the club. It's been an exciting experience, quite the most exciting I have had in many years of football reporting. But in these times of happiness and prosperity I can't forget the dark days, two years ago, when the Canaries were headed irrevocably for re-election; when first-round defeat in the Cup (at home and by a non-League club, Bedford Town, at that) had so strained finances that the Norfolk News Company came to the rescue by footing a week's wage bill; when, to save the day, a tide of public sympathy landed an appeal fund of over £20,000 on the rocky beach on which City were stranded.

But for that public appeal—surely one of the greatest examples of loyalty in the history of football—Norwich City today might have been no more than an ex-League club on whose tombstone the misfortunes of post-war had written the letters "R.I.P."

The City Board (left to right): Messrs. J. L. Hanly, F. C. Jex, G. Watling, G. F. B. Fish, H. Robinson

Mr. Arthur South . . . 'superb control.'

Many thousands of football-lovers, both inside and outside East Anglia, still can't understand how a club with the support Norwich City have enjoyed since the war could have arrived at such a pass, for there is no doubt at all that the Norwich following deserves Second or even First Division soccer.

It was a story of football economics, a story that but for the rise of the supporters' club "pool," would by now have been repeated over and over again in the Football League. The post-war boom was allowed to come and go without sufficient provision being made for less sunny days; and when the blow eventually fell it was catastrophic.

It is a tribute to the Canaries' followers that, disappointed as they had been by their team's displays—and their dwindling numbers had precious little to cheer about a couple of seasons ago—they would not let the club go out of existence.

The thousands who this year have astonished the football world by the volume and voice of their support rallied magnificently to the cause. The life-saving capital was raised and in little more than a year the club had cleared their debts, wiped out their overdraft and were aiming at promotion.

It had not been a painless salvation. In the maelstrom of reorganisation and at a special meeting superbly controlled by the then Lord

2

Mayor, Mr. Arthur South, a new directorate came into being, including only one member of the old Board. And it was not long before manager Tom Parker made way for manager Archie Macaulay.

Since then, apart from one or two minor diversions, it has been a golden road. At one time last season the Second Division came tantalisingly into view, then vanished from sight; third round home defeat by Darlington ended hopes of Cup glory; but a great step forward had been taken in re-establishing Norwich City.

Under an enthusiastic Board, led by the most enthusiastic of chairmen; under the vigilant, pale blue-eyed watch of Archie Macaulay (whose own rise in managerial stature has been a schoolboy adventure story in itself) the Canaries have gone from strength to strength.

Yet even this season did not begin at all promisingly. There were injuries, and a series of unhappy performances, home as well as away, gave no inkling of what was to come.

But all along one had the feeling that given the right impulse the ball of success would start rolling. That jolt came from three shrewd managerial decisions that put Roy McCrohan, Jimmy Hill and Terry Bly in their key positions of right-half, inside-left and centre-forward; and from the news, after a Cup draw at Swindon, that the winners of that tie would entertain Manchester United.

From then onwards there was no holding either Norwich City or their supporters. The Babes came and went, to be followed, amid scenes of unparalleled excitement, by Cardiff City, Tottenham and Sheffield United. All four opponents drew maximum 38,000 crowds to Carrow Road and the flow of soccer gold that last December had dwindled to a nerve-wracking (for the directors) trickle became first a stream and then a flood.

Today Norwich City have stood, untroubled by financial anxiety, on the threshold of even greater glory. Luton Town, aided by good fortune, prevented them from writing soccer history; now the people who have made this such a memorable season—the Board, manager Macaulay, his players and the public—are looking forward to another day, the day for which East Anglia has waited far too long—when the Canaries return at long last to the higher division from which they were ejected just before the war.

Well, it didn't lead to Wembley—but it's been a golden road!

Highlighting Norwich City's history

1902—Norwich City F.C. founded.

1905—Professionalism adopted, club elected to Southern League.

1907—Beat Sheffield Wednesday (holders) in Cup. Last season at Newmarket Road.

1908—Reading objected to size of ground at the Nest for Cup-tie; match played at Stamford Bridge, City won second replay at Villa Park then beat Liverpool (away) before losing to Bristol City.

1915—Cup second replay, at Lincoln, with Bradford City, played behind closed gates by order of F.A. (first year of war) but crowd broke in, City lost 2-0.

1920—Founder-members of Division III (South).

1931—Finished bottom, re-elected.

1934—Promoted to Division II.

1935—Carrow Road ground opened.

1939—Relegated to Division III (South).

1947—Next to bottom, re-elected.

1948—Next to bottom, re-elected.

1951—Beat Liverpool in Cup (third round), lost at Sunderland in fifth. Runners-up, Division III (South).

1954—Beat Arsenal at Highbury in Cup (fourth round), lost to Leicester (home) in fifth.

1957—Financial crisis. Appeal fund saved club. New Board elected. Finished bottom, re-elected.

1958—Founder-members of new Third Division.

1959—Beat Manchester United, Cardiff, Tottenham, Sheffield United, to reach Cup semi-final. Lost to Luton in semi-final replay.

CUP CAMERA 1–*How it all began*

Above, first goal of the campaign as Ilford's Winch snaps the ball past Nethercott. Below, a sandwiched Nethercott punched this one away. Right, Allcock leapfrogs to get his head to a high one.

4

ROUND ONE

Norwich City 3 Ilford 1

NO one thought, on November 15th, 1958, that Norwich City were going to cut much ice in the season's F.A. Cup competition. They hadn't won a first team match at Carrow Road since September 20th—and they made heavy weather of the task of beating Isthmian League Ilford.

There was a nasty shock in store for them, in fact, before they made certain of appearing in the draw for Round Two. In the 27th minute, Castle hit an outswinging corner from the left, the ball was nodded forward to Winch—and the amateurs were a goal ahead!

They held on to their advantage, too, until five minutes after the interval when, from a Brennan pass, Hill hit the equaliser, off an upright, with a simple shot that sneaked through a ruck of players in the Ilford goalmouth.

Eight minutes later Hill returned the compliment for Brennan to put the Canaries ahead; and in the 83rd minute, after Groves had brilliantly saved a Crowe penalty, the left winger scored the third with a gentle lob, beautifully placed, that completely deceived the agile Ilford 'keeper. Not until then did the shadow of a replay entirely disappear.

City had to struggle, hard, to get over the first hurdle. Yet this match might well go down as the turning point of the season. It marked the abandonment of the "deep centre-forward" plan (Allcock moved forward to lead his line from the front); it saw a steadying of the defence generally; and it signalled the execution of a masterstroke by manager Archie Macaulay—the recall of Irish right-winger Jimmy Hill, at inside-left.

A not very distinguished display, altogether, but the shrewdness and quicksilver speed of Hill and the rapid understanding he struck up with Brennan stamped this as perhaps the match that started the Canaries on the road back.

NORWICH CITY — Nethercott; McCrohan, Thurlow; Hunt, Butler, Crowe; Crossan, Moran, Allcock, Hill, Brennan.

ILFORD—R. Groves; G. Simmons, E. Cross; J. Sharrod, A. Whittall, H. Dodkins; G. Saffrey, R. Winch, R. Birleson, A. Smith, S. Castle.

Referee—H. V. A. Stott (Boston). Attendance, 13,960 (£1727).

CUP CAMERA 2– *The draw at Swindon*

Above, Butler (left) stands ready for action as Thurlow (centre) and McCrohan go up for a heading duel. Below, it's 1-1 and nearly time—and an anxious moment for Butler and Nethercott as the ball rolls just wide of the City goal.

6

ROUND TWO

Swindon T. 1 Norwich City 1
Norwich City 1 Swindon T. 0

TWO days after Norwich City had drawn at Swindon on December 6th, they had the tremendous news that if they won the replay at Carrow Road the following Thursday, their third round Cup opponents would be Matt Busby's famous Manchester United "Babes."

The news was worth a goal start to the home team—and one goal was enough to give the Canaries victory. Swindon fought hard, but they never looked like checking City's progress and a single goal scarcely represented the difference between the sides. Yet it was a curious goal that did the damage; a Crossan shot that Burton looked for all the world to have turned for a corner. But it spun freakishly from the 'keeper's fingertips to curl into the top corner of the net.

This was the tie, however, that saw the Canaries turn the corner to confidence. It saw, at Swindon, the team which was to carry all before it in the following months. Bly was at centre-forward (he was replaced, because of injury, by Cleland in the replay), Allcock inside-right, McCrohan at right-half with Thurlow behind him.

Despite the encouragement of their picturesque " Moonraker " mascots, Swindon at the County Ground could only once pierce a Butler-inspired defence. That was in the 20th minute when Richards beat Nethercott with a header; and 18 minutes later Crossan laid on the pass for Hill to equalise.

So well did City play in the second half that Swindon looked glad to hear the final whistle—and in the replay they fought in hope, apparently, more than in confidence. Yet it was not until Nethercott left the field for treatment to a cut ear (Crowe replaced him temporarily) that the full fire and promise of City's play was revealed. Nethercott returned, and in the 59th minute Crossan put his side into the third round.

It was the Canaries' first and last sight of Third Division Cup opposition for the season, but it had served its purpose in shaping the side that was later to do so well. Matt Busby, who took the opportunity to get a preview, thought he had spotted the weaknesses, though he paid tribute to the quality of the Norwich football. A few weeks later the Canaries were to show him that they were even better than he thought.

SWINDON — Burton; Neal, Bingley (Lee); Morgan, Hudson, Owen (Fountain); Corbett, Richards, Kelly (Owen), Edwards, Davey.

NORWICH CITY — Nethercott; Thurlow, Ashman; McCrohan, Butler, Crowe; Crossan, Allcock, Bly (Cleland), Hill, Brennan. (Replay changes in parentheses.)

Referee—H. Haworth (Blackburn). Attendance, Swindon 14,758 (£1779), Norwich 12,235 (£1612).

CUP CAMERA 3–*Now for the "Babes"*

Matt Busby, of Manchester United, Geoffrey Watling, of Norwich City—and it's the Canaries chairman who looks the more confident after City's replay victory over Swindon. They had seen (below) a Swindon shot go past McCrohan, Thurlow, Nethercott—and the post; Burton (bottom left) tip the ball over in a spectacular save; Butler (bottom right) stop a Swindon attack with a fine sliding tackle.

8

'Where WERE you, Dad?' he'll ask– and I'll have my alibi!

(By Ian Wooldridge, of the "News Chronicle")

WHEN my son and heir is old and erudite enough to read this story, I'm going to have to think up a pretty good case for my own defence. For, between you and me, I think he's going to take a distinctly dim view of the fact that for the first three whole weeks of his life his dad saw him for only 20 fleeting minutes.

"Fine father you are," he's going to say. "Where WERE you all that time?"

He'll have a point, of course. But what's more, I'll have my alibi. "Listen son," I'm going to answer, "I'll tell you a story.

"Once upon a time there was a tiny football club called Norwich City. They had always been a friendly club, but unlike the big, bold Wolves or the mighty Busby Babes, they were neither rich nor famous. Well, one day they were drawn in the Third Round of the F.A. Cup against those very giants from Manchester United . . ."

Yes, that's how I'm going to start my explanation. And as my son sits back to hear the rest of this fairy tale from football, I'll tell him how his father was fortunate enough to get involved in it all.

On the afternoon of Friday, January 9th—which was the day before Norwich were due to meet Manchester United—his sports editor sent him up to Norfolk to write what is known in the newspaper world as a "prelim" of the game.

Now my little boy's father, believing himself an old hand at this business, decided that he would write *his* "prelim" on the train long before he *got* to Norwich.

After all, who could be crazy enough to suggest Norwich could win? So he wrote his article and ended it with the prediction: "Norwich City 0, Manchester United 5."

Then, feeling somewhat satisfied with himself, he disembarked from the train, strolled down to the Carrow Road ground to pay a courtesy call on Mr. Archie Macaulay.

It wasn't really an interview. For two hours Macaulay just talked . . . and talked . . . and talked. And again and again, in a low tone of absolute assurance, he repeated the words: "You know, we can BEAT Manchester United. I know their weak points. I know my boys are good enough to exploit them."

After 30 minutes my little boy's father was still saying "Yes Archie" out of politeness. After 60 minutes he was beginning to believe that Macaulay might possibly have a point. After 90 minutes he was convinced of it.

When the two hours were up, he rushed out of the Carrow Road stadium, jumped into a taxi, flew into his hotel room, whipped the already-written article out of his pocket, tore it into shreds and flung it out the window.

He then sat down at his typewriter, rolled in a clean sheet of paper and wrote: "Norwich City can cause the soccer sensation of the season tomorrow by beating Manchester United . . ."

That, then, is the story of how Archie Macaulay, the man who built the new Norwich City, talked ME into believing that a miracle was about to be performed.

It was a masterpiece of salesmanship. But more important, of course, was the fact that Macaulay had already sold the idea of success to his team. That was the whole secret behind Norwich City's fantastic assault on the F.A. Cup.

By this time my little boy will be bursting to ask one question. "It's all very interesting," he's going to say, "But you *still* haven't explained how I was more than three whole weeks old before you saw me for more than those 20 minutes . . .

"Mummy says that even then you rushed into the maternity home and rushed out again shouting 'Norwich for the Cup.' The midwives thought you were mad."

This, naturally, will be my cue to go on. "Well," I shall say, "Norwich City didn't end their sensation there. They went on and on and on.

"It was their job to make the news. And it was our job to write it. We had to live with the team, travel back and forth across Britain with them, tell the world everything about them.

"It was a tough but terrific assignment. And right bang in the middle of it all, you — our big, sturdy son—arrived in the world."

That's how my alibi will end.

Right now, I can't predict his reaction. But with a bit of luck he'll say:

"O.K., Dad, I'll believe you this time. And, by the way, that story was ten times better than 'Jack and the Beanstalk.'"

9

CUP CAMERA 4–*The rout of the "Babes"*

Matt Busby again, but not as happy this time as (below) Bly turns away after netting his first goal against Manchester United.

Victory smile from the "Terrible Twins"—Bly and Crossan—after they had scored the goals that beat United.

ROUND THREE

Norwich City 3 Manchester U. 0

THIS was the beginning of the big time; but for the majority of the 38,000 crowd who flocked to Carrow Road on that cold, icy afternoon of January 10th the match was the opportunity to watch the famous Babes in action rather than to roar a great team of giant killers to victory. What chance have we got, City supporters were saying, against the might of Manchester United, the glamour team who had just won eight successive First Division matches ?

There was a small group of people, however, who were confident of success. In the centre of it were the Canaries themselves. They, and manager Archie Macaulay, already had the " if it's impossible we can do it " spirit and they proceeded to show United that reputation meant nothing to them.

Macaulay had summed up the opposition to perfection. A quick-covering City defence, stepping sure-footed on an icebound surface, killed the menace of the Charlton-Viollet-Quixall personality trio—so efficiently that the Canaries could afterwards say that defensively this was the easiest game of the run.

And with the Babes held in a grip of steel the City forwards, with magnificent support from the wing-halves, tore United's own defence wide open. The " can opener " was wielded by Crossan and Brennan—and in the middle Bly established an overnight reputation as the new scourge of centre-halves and goalkeepers.

But it was Brennan whose calculating, experienced brain started the scoring. Allcock found him with a lobbed forward pass to the left of the Manchester goal in the 31st minute. With all the coolness in the world Brennan pulled the ball into the goalmouth and Bly, moving in, hammered it into the back of the net.

Crossan got the second in the 61st minute, though it needed a linesman to signal the goal after the winger had nodded the ball forward when Gregg failed to hold another power drive by Bly. But it was the third goal, two minutes from time, that set the seal on this great performance.

Bly cut in from the left, brushed off Cope's challenge as if he didn't exist, to crash in a drive that had even Gregg applauding. In 90 minutes City had, to the discerning, climbed from near-nonentity to become serious challengers in the 1958-59 Cup battle.

NORWICH CITY—Nethercott; Thurlow, Ashman; McCrohan, Butler, Crowe; Crossan, Allcock, Bly, Hill, Brennan.

MANCHESTER UNITED—Gregg; Foulkes, Carolan; Goodwin, Cope, McGuinness; Bradley, Quixall, Viollet, Charlton, Scanlon.

Referee—W. Clements (West Bromwich). Attendance 38,000 (£4500).

CUP CAMERA 5–"Bly, Bly Babes" (contd.)

Defence in depth—City outnumber their opponents two to one during a United attack.

This one from Bly brought a shower of snow from the Manchester crossbar.

Allcock shoots, Gregg dives in vain—but the ball goes just wide.

12

He found it wasn't a 'hot seat' after all!

That champagne cork has been a lucky one for Archie Macaulay

WHEN, in April, 1957, the Directors of Norwich City toasted Archie Macaulay's appointment as manager in a magnum of champagne, the first thing he did was to ask chairman Geoffrey Watling for the cork. It's one of a number in his possession, but it's the one that, right now, he must treasure the most. They say champagne corks are lucky. That one has certainly been so for Archie Macaulay.

He came to Norwich with plenty of ambition—but with no previous experience of League club management. He had spent a period as player-manager of Southern League Guildford and, of course, had seen plenty of League football. But coming into what was ominously described as the Norwich " hot seat " was something very different.

He had friends in Norfolk, for he was stationed at various points in East Anglia during the war. He has said, in fact, that he realised very quickly that, far from being a " hot seat," the managerial chair at Carrow Road carried with it tremendous possibilities for a man with ambition and the luck that is always part of the make-up of a successful manager.

It was not until after he arrived, for instance, that he could have appreciated the tremendous potential that Norwich commanded in the way of support. In all his football travelling, inside and outside the British Isles, he could never have come across an area where the public were prepared to give so freely in their love of football. If he needed encouragement in a difficult job he got it not only from his Board, but from the people of East Anglia as a whole.

It was a tough job to begin with . . . a club facing re-election and down in spirit because of it . . . precious little cash to play with and a considerable rebuilding task to do.

Maybe he was a little lucky. Almost all of the men whom he brought to Carrow Road in the early days—men who cost him little or nothing in the way of transfer fees—never let him down.

'THIS IS WHAT I WANT'

Macaulay believes in setting a personal example.

First " big " signing was Barry Butler—and he has proved worth every penny and ounce of energy Macaulay spent in getting him to Carrow Road.

Macaulay set about whipping his team into shape and spirit; and here he was right in his favourite territory. It soon became plain that City's new manager was also one of the game's best coaches and tacticians, and that he had the happy flair for getting his players solidly behind him in spirit and enthusiasm.

Look what happened. Admittedly with a new half-back line and with other positional changes, the team who had a few months earlier hit a post-war "low" went into the most gruelling of Third Division (South) campaigns with a completely revitalised outlook.

Fitness and hygiene. These were the first two factors that Macaulay insisted on having. His boast was that there would be no fitter team than the Canaries in the League—and he was right.

His side lacked the smooth confidence of the 1958-59 Cup fighters, but they had the same crusading spirit. Before long the thousands who had been driven from Carrow Road by the lacklustre displays of the previous season were swarming back to the fold.

The dreaded drop to the new Fourth Division was averted and for a time, in fact, City got their sights on promotion. The vision faded as the initial effort spent itself in the second half of the season. Injury to new boy, Jimmy Moran, didn't help; but one had the feeling all along that Macaulay would have been somewhat embarrassed had promotion arrived. He was by no means satisfied with first team strength, his reserve resources were slender, and he hadn't the cash to start buying as yet.

Just before the transfer deadline, however, he dipped into the purse—nearly drained it, in fact—for the transfer of Derrick Lythgoe and Terry Allcock. They were the start of the rebuilding programme, which continued during the summer with the acquisition of Ian Williamson, John Reid, Peter Cleland, Jimmy Hill, Morgan Hunt and Keith Ripley. The latter's stay was probably the shortest in the club's history, but in his case, as in others, Macaulay showed mature selling power, and City did not lose greatly in the deal.

Despite his building-up, however, Macaulay had to face a very sticky time in the early months of 1958-59. Try as he might, he couldn't find the recipe for success, and the following he and the team had built up began to dwindle again. Errol Crossan arrived from Southend at a big fee, but it was not until Ashman had fully recovered from injury and McCrohan, Bly, Allcock and Hill were shrewdly placed in the positions they have since held so well that the side suddenly sprang to life.

Since then it's been glory all the way. But City's phenomenal run of success, in both Cup and League, did not change the sober, cautious outlook of Macaulay, whose canny summing-up of the Cup opposition proved him the master of yet another branch of managerial life.

When Luton got the goal that ended the Wembley dream, Macaulay's comment was not of Luton luck. "That's football," he said—typical of a man who during his career has had to take the rough with the smooth of soccer.

Inevitably the managerial success of Macaulay—even more meteoric than in the days when his flame-coloured hair and personality play galvanised Scottish and English crowds—has brought rumours and reports of his imminent departure from Norwich.

Norwich and East Anglia sincerely hope he will not be tempted away from Carrow Road. In two short years the quiet Scot for whom Norwich was the key to League football managership, has learned fast and proved himself a "natural" for the job. In only his second year he has almost realised the ambition of all managers—the walk, with his team, on to the Wembley turf on Cup Final day. There seems no reason why that, and other dreams, should not still come true at Norwich.

'ANYTHING YOU CAN DO . . .'

14

'We should have been there, bor . . .'

Tale of two 'keepers

KEN NETHERCOTT: In years to come when other of Nethercott's exploits have faded from memory—and he has given Norwich supporters plenty of incident in his long service with the club — we shall always remember him as he was at Bramall Lane in February, 1959, when for the last vital half hour of the match he stood between the posts, his right arm helpless because of a dislocated shoulder, still keeping out what shots Sheffield United could get through a superb defence. Another player might have been aggrieved at losing his place in such an unlucky way. But not Nethercott. Always unselfish, ready to help others, he said after the replay: "I'm glad it was Sandy out there, not me; he's a much better 'keeper than I am.".

SANDY KENNON: We won't mention his real Christian names because he doesn't like them! But there's no doubt that in quick time he has established himself at Carrow Road in popularity. What an ordeal he had to face. He made his first-team debut for the Canaries in front of 38,000 pairs of highly critical eyes, in the electric atmosphere of the Cup replay with Sheffield United. But it was in the semi-final at White Hart Lane that the tall South African—who came from Huddersfield for practically nothing—endeared himself to Norwich supporters. And it's typical of him that when Wembley was so enticingly near he said: "Of course I'd like to play there; but let me have the glory; give Ken Nethercott the medal. He deserves it."

15

THE MEN WHO SO NEARL

RON ASHMAN: What a season it's been for the Norwich City skipper and left-back. The former Bevin Boy, who was born in Cambridgeshire, but is now as much a man of Norfolk as a native, has outstripped all other City players in the matter of first team appearances and has stayed on to see the day when, as leader of the Canaries, he has been able to cock a snook at the jibers who all but barracked him away from Carrow Road. Are his playing days coming to an end? There have been reports of him entering the managerial field; but, says Ashman, "I feel I still have a year or two of football left in me."

ROY McCROHAN: "Happy Wanderer" of the City side, McCrohan has played in more positions than most footballers since he came to Carrow Road from Reading (in a part exchange deal featuring Les Owens) as a keen young inside forward. The keenness is still there and has been directed by manager Archie Macaulay into a channel that obviously has suited "Roy Mac" down to the ground—that of a defensive-minded wing-half who can use his speed both in quick recovery and in the occasional spectacular burst upfield. Roy McCrohan's off-field passion is dancing; he hopes to start up in business in that line, with his wife, when his playing days are over.

BARRY BUTLER: "Best centre-half in the whole of the League" was the comment of a neutral onlooker after one of Butler's Cup games of 1958-59. He wasn't far wrong, either. When City persuaded Butler, just finishing his R.A.F. service, to join them from Sheffield Wednesday in the summer of 1957, they probably didn't realise themselves what a great stroke of business they had pulled off. Butler, with years of football still ahead of him, has an infectious spirit that shows best when things are going against his team. When in 1957-58 Southampton hammered the Canaries unmercifully at the Dell, the grim comment of the Stockton-on-Tees-born pivot was: "They won't do that at Norwich."

MATT CROWE: Like McCrohan, Crowe came to Norwich (for a small fee from Partick Thistle in the summer of 1957) as an inside forward. Like McCrohan, he has found at wing-half the consistency and freedom that eluded him in the forward line. "Dour Scot" is a good description of the man on the field; but there is nothing stolid about the service he provides for the men in front of him. He and McCrohan have acted as perfect foils for each other, and of Crowe himself nothing further need be said than that when Manchester United's Matt Busby came to run the rule over his club's Cup opponents the man he singled out for special mention was—Matt Crowe!

16

TOOK CITY TO WEMBLEY

ERROL CROSSAN: If the Canaries had got to Wembley it's a pound to a penny that the man who would have been busy keeping " Final nerves " at bay would have been " Cowboy " Errol Crossan. No soccer team is complete without its comedian, and in Canadian-born Crossan, City are extremely lucky in that respect. But opposing full-backs don't think there is anything funny about the devastating speed of the right winger, who has also had goalkeepers picking the ball out of the net so many times that he has qualified to join the ranks of a distinguished band of goalscoring Norwich outside-rights.

TERRY ALLCOCK: If ever a player qualified for the sub-title " A study in perpetual motion," that man is Terry Allcock. He came to Norwich, just before the 1957-58 transfer " deadline," carrying the label " Nat Lofthouse's deputy." It didn't suit him, for this tall, hard-working Yorkshireman, tough but friendly, is never more happy than when he is busy, with that deceptive, loping stride of his, grafting away in defence or attack. Since he gave up the leadership of the City attack he must have covered more miles than any of his colleagues. Hard work is his second nature; and he still finds time in the summer for that most arduous of cricket duties—wicket-keeping!

JIMMY HILL: Typical of football humorists, they nicknamed him " Tiger " Hill when he flashed into the Norwich City attacking picture towards the end of 1958 as an inside-left. Yet he joined them, from Newcastle some months earlier, as a right winger; and so dim were his prospects there, that he came within an ace of being transferred to Mansfield Town. Luck was with City when Mansfield didn't push their inquiries for the little Irishman. At inside forward he has shown the stamp of pure football genius. Don't be fooled by the frail-looking physique, Hill may not look like a tiger, but there are defenders who would sooner have been big game hunting than having to keep an eye on him.

BOBBY BRENNAN: There aren't many footballers who have " gone non-League " and made a successful return to League football. Brennan, former Irish International inside-forward, car salesman when he isn't playing soccer, is one of the exceptions. After a spell with Yarmouth he rejoined the Canaries, who had paid their record fee, £15,000, to Fulham for him, and a happy switch from inside-forward to outside-left, gave City the answer to a longstanding problem. Brennan says that if he had known how easy it is on the wing he would have made the move years ago! You only have to count the goals he has made, as well as those he has scored, to realise what an asset the "maestro" has been.

17

NORFOLK-BORN NORWICH HEROES

TERRY BLY: "Tearaway Terry," "Terry the Terror." Those are a couple of the nicknames Bly was given after scoring the golden goals that helped to account for such teams as Manchester United, Cardiff City, Spurs and Sheffield United. It's been a glory road for Bly. It was touch and go whether he was retained, after a couple of knee operations, at the end of 1957-58; and at the beginning of 1958-59 he was struggling so hard to regain his form that he played one Combination match at full-back! But since he found his touch it's been a wonderful time for the lad from Fincham. As one manager said after seeing him in goalscoring mood: "He didn't seem to do much; but he can shoot and he has the flair for being in the right place at the right time. And a lot of managers would pay a lot of money for a player like that."

BRYAN THURLOW: The other local (Loddon-born) boy who has made good in City's history-making team. He got his chance first when Ashman was injured at the start of the season, and he took it so well that when manager Macaulay decided to move McCrohan to right-half, it was Thurlow whom he chose for the vacant right-back berth. Whatever doubts there may have been about Thurlow's ability were soon dispelled. Maybe there were some over-enthusiastic tackles. Experience has reduced those in number; and when Thurlow goes into the tackle he has one object in view: to get the ball away from his opponent. Big-time, and R.A.F. service, haven't altered the outlook of this quiet Norfolk player. While others are celebrating he prefers to slip away, almost unnoticed. But he still goes down as one of the "finds" of 1958-59.

'Permanent Twelfth Man'

BOB WILSON: For fair-haired Wilson—free-transferred from Aberdeen soon after Archie Macaulay took over at Carrow Road, 1958-59 has been an unusual season. He has been with the Canaries at almost all of their Cup triumphs; but he hasn't played in one of them! In fact, he has earned the title of "permanent twelfth man." But he is a very useful twelfth man to have around, as he has shown on the occasions when he has been called into the League side. But for the brilliance of McCrohan and Crowe, he might himself have been numbered among the Cup heroes. And he's young enough to be making his colleagues fight for their places for some time to come.

He stands no nonsense

HARRY TOPPING: A football team can't be successful without a trainer who knows how to keep the players fit and on their toes. Harry Topping, chunky, tough and outspoken when there's need to be, has proved just the right man to carry out the precepts of the City manager. A survivor of the Tom Parker régime,

he was brought to Carrow Road from Aldershot, where he went after spending some time in Holland. Topping is a man who stands no nonsense—and his voice from the trainer's bench on match days is proof enough of how much he is wrapped up in the fortunes of the Canaries.

18

CUP CAMERA 6– *The conquest of Cardiff*

Something for the Welshmen to sing about—though not for long! Butler picks the ball out of the City net after Cardiff's first goal, scored by Hewitt (10) after avoiding a tackle by McCrohan, on the ground.

Another narrow escape for City. With Butler and Nethercott beaten Bonson, Cardiff's centre-forward, jumps for a high centre—and misses it!

19

ROUND FOUR

Norwich City 3 Cardiff City 2

CARDIFF CITY made a mistake when they came to Carrow Road on January 24th, 1959. They underestimated the skill and spirit of the Canaries—factors that were whipped to a peak again by the fervour of another all-ticket crowd. And they paid the penalty.

As a whole this was probably the toughest game of the campaign. Cardiff's chances were boosted by the first goal, scored by Hewitt in the 16th minute; and when Bonson hushed the terraces again in the 70th with the goal that made it 2-2 it looked odds on a replay at Ninian Park—and probably exit for Norwich.

But Cardiff reckoned without the fighting fanaticism that steeped Carrow Road in the early months of 1959—and they reckoned without the " killer spirit " of Bly and Crossan.

There were only three minutes to go when Crossan worried the ball away from a too-casual Stitfall, got it across the goalmouth and " Bly's Blockbuster " whistled through the narrow gap between Nicholls and the near post. It was a goal in a million—typical of the deadliness of City's fangs when they were up against it.

It was a tough, rugged battle, but throughout it the Canaries did not let it upset the smooth flow of their football. They didn't let themselves be upset by Cardiff's skilled opening, though there was depression in the ranks of their supporters when a slick movement left Hewitt with the opening from which the visitors took the lead. They held it, too, for the rest of the first half.

Only three minutes after the interval, however, Brennan " did it again." Beating Milne he shot over a low centre that Crossan slammed, unerringly, past Nicholls and into the net. Eight minutes later City were in the lead—and there was pandemonium around the ground. An Ashman free kick was nodded forward by Allcock, and Bly was there to steamroller the ball into the net.

In the 70th minute, with Allcock off the field and after the referee had told both skippers to keep their players' tempers under control, Bonson scored a fine equaliser. And there matters stood, with replay written all over the game, until the " Twins " put on their barnstorming, matchwinning act.

NORWICH CITY—Nethercott; Thurlow, Ashman; McCrohan, Butler, Crowe; Crossan, Allcock, Bly, Hill, Brennan.

CARDIFF CITY—Nicholls; Milne, Stitfall; Sullivan, Malloy, Baker; Walsh, Tapscott, Bonson, Hewitt, Reynolds.

Referee—J. Kelly (Chorley). Attendance 38,000 (£4550).

20

CUP CAMERA 7–*No Wembley for Wales*

The ball's in the back of the net, 'keeper Ron Nicholls is beaten all ends up. Bly's "blockbuster" has put Cardiff out of the Cup.

Close shave for Cardiff as this header from Allcock hits the crossbar and bounces over.

Victor's smile . . .

. . . and skipper Ron Ashman has good reason to look happy.

21

'Never shall I forget...'

Because Norwich MADE me believe in them

By John Bromley, of the "Daily Herald."

I HAVE had the privilege of reporting some of the great and memorable moments in sport. But none can touch the story I shall always label "Norwich—1959."

To me the fabulous Cup run of Norwich City had more drama and emotion than was ever dreamed up for a Hollywood production. Basically the story was of a littl'un beating a big'un, and hardened sports editors will tell you that there is no better ingredient for the hungry headlines of the world Press.

But this story had more to it than that. Norwich were doing something that the soccer world didn't believe possible—they were beating the top clubs on merit. By sheer class and sustained power they were making the big boys look as insignificant as bottom - of - the - bill comedians.

I ate, slept and dreamt Norwich City for a month. The myth that newspapermen are cold and cynical was shattered by the achievements of Archie Macaulay and his Marvels. I have never known so many of my colleagues to get so impregnated by Cup fever.

I remember so vividly after that unlucky semi-final defeat by Luton at Birmingham, Archie Macaulay turning to me and saying: "What are you looking so fed up about?"

The utter disappointment I felt must have shown through my mask of impartiality. I felt thoroughly deflated. This was the end of the road. For Norwich City. And for my story.

But memories of this great triumph that wrote such a glorious page in the history of soccer come flooding back to me . . .

Never shall I forget White Hart Lane on that sunny February afternoon. Over 20,000 Norwich supporters had packed into the vast stadium, and wherever you looked there was green and yellow.

And then, with the final seconds ticking away and the Norwich fans ready to roar a salute to their heroes, Cliff Jones equalised for Spurs. Crime writer Ian Fleming could not have thought up a greater moment of drama than this.

Never shall I forget the replay at Carrow Road. Thirty-eight thousand fans singing "On the ball, City" had more emotion in it for me than a Welsh crowd singing "Land of my fathers" on the final day of the Empire Games when they were told that Prince Charles was the new Prince of Wales.

On then to Sheffield . . . to the sensation of the injured Ken Nethercott . . . to the dazzling dribble by Bobby Brennan that took him past three men and produced the equaliser . . . and back that same evening to Norwich. To the cheering crowds at Thorpe Station . . . to the sight of Ron Ashman and his men being pushed along the platform on a porter's truck as if they had just returned from Wembley.

To the replay at Carrow Road . . . to feel again that tingling sensation generated by an emotional crowd . . . to write the triumph-over-tragedy story of goalkeeper Sandy Kennon . . . to marvel at the goal power of tearaway Terry Bly.

So to the final chapter. To White Hart Lane for the semi-final. To see Norwich play below form for the only time in their run . . . to cheer the "save-the-side" performance by Kennon . . . and to join in the praise for Brennan's wonder goal.

To Birmingham for the replay . . . to the game that wrote the end to "Norwich—1959."

I believed in Norwich City as I have never believed in a team before. Not because I had any reason at all to favour them but because Norwich, by their performances, MADE me believe in them.

And that, to me, was the measure of their greatness.

CUP CAMERA 8–*Agony of White Hart Lane*

The most poignant moment in the whole of the Cup run. Nethercott and Ashman on the ground, Butler, Allcock and McCrohan stand speechless as Cliff Jones nets Spurs' last-minute fifth-round equaliser.

A fine save by Nethercott —and in front of him, believe it or not, are rival centre-halves Norman and Butler.

23

ROUND FIVE

Tottenham 1 Norwich City 1
Norwich City 1 Tottenham 0

ELATION . . . heartache . . . and the "perfect goal" that was a mistake! These were the ingredients of Norwich City's fifth round Cup-ties with Tottenham Hotspur—at White Hart Lane on Saturday, February 14th and at Carrow Road the following Wednesday.

Elation . . . when in the seething atmosphere of the Tottenham cockpit more than 20,000 City supporters split the skies over London with the roar that told everyone within miles that the Canaries were in front. It was Allcock, slipping the ball past Hollowbread in the 64th minute, who was the hero then.

Heartache . . . when, with City victory almost in safe keeping, Cliff Jones netted the shattering last-minute equaliser that gave Spurs the chance to fight again. A lucky goal at that, deflected into the net off Butler after a wildly-sliced shot by Iley opened up the City defence as Spurs' orthodox attacking methods had failed to do.

The replay at Norwich, with the atmosphere created by another 38,000 spectators so electric that Carrow Road and its environments fairly cracked with tension.

And the dramatic 63rd minute, when a delicate "chip" by Ashman sent Bly running through to add yet another golden goal to his Cup tally.

The mistake? Not till now has Ashman disclosed that the "delicate chip" was, in fact, never intended! "I meant to put the ball out to Brennan on the left," is the story he tells, "but it bounced, hit my shin and went straight through the middle to Bly."

Not that City didn't deserve to win. They did, despite the tremendous efforts for Spurs of ex-Canary Monty Norman and skipper Bobby Smith. By now the stream of City's superb Cup-fighting football was in full flood. There was no danger of a last-minute equaliser this time. Spurs had neither the strength, nor the encouragement to stem the tide. Even the move that brought the much-discussed figure of Danny Blanchflower into their team for the replay, could not halt the Canaries' proud progress.

TOTTENHAM—Hollowbread; Baker, Hopkins; Dodge, Norman, Iley; Brooks (Medwin), Harmer (Blanchflower), Smith, Dunmore (Clayton), Jones. Replay changes in parentheses.

NORWICH CITY—Nethercott; Thurlow, Ashman; McCrohan, Butler, Crowe; Crossan, Allcock, Bly, Hill, Brennan.

Referee—J. W. Topliss (Grimsby). Attendances: White Hart Lane 67,633 (£9315); Carrow Road 38,000 (£6000).

CUP CAMERA 9–*No heartache this time!*

A picture that sums up the aggressive Cup spirit of the Canaries. Crossan and Bly converge on Hollowbread (hidden by full-backs Baker and Hopkins) during the replay against Tottenham at Carrow Road. On the extreme right is ex-Canary Maurice Norman; next to him Terry Allcock.

And out go Spurs

Hollowbread dives, but Bly's shot is on the way past him to put City into the sixth round.

What memories!

Tears and frustration to joy and fulfilment

By 'White Line' of the 'Eastern Daily Press'

THROUGH tears and frustration to joy and fulfilment. That has been the path of Norwich City's football progress this season. The turning point came with the Cup visit to Swindon on December 6th, when City desperately needed to avoid defeat to give them a chance of refurbishing their football reputation that had been tarnished so badly in September, October and November.

It was not a very bright or encouraging outlook that day, for there had been few indications that City were approaching those heights of understanding and confidence that are essential if eleven players are to become an effective and consistently successful team. In particular, great question marks still dominated the wing half and inside-forward positions, and when the strength there is in doubt there can be no expectations of victory—only hope.

So much rested that day upon the tall broad shoulders of Roy McCrohan, who was trying his hand again at wing half after a successful spell at full-back, and the slighter figure of Jimmy Hill, who was seeking a reputation at inside-left after disappointing at outside-right. That they succeeded beyond all that could have been dreamed is a fact written into the story of City's great Cup run.

Not only were McCrohan and Hill integral members of a team that got to the very threshold of Wembley, they were vital cogs in the machine. McCrohan was a towering figure of consistency and a perfect foil to the more aggressively minded Matt Crowe in the Canaries' defence, and Hill was the genius in attack and the ideal man to play alongside Terry Allcock, who, in the last three months, must have come as near as any footballer to personifying perpetual motion.

Those four provided the mainspring, and around them were deployed seven components so well matched that they became an outstanding Cup fighting machine. In attack there was the sheer strength of purpose of Terry Bly, the brilliantly exploited speed of Errol Crossan and the artistry and magic of Bobby Brennan, while the defence, built upon the rock of Barry Butler's perfection at centre-half, was blessed with the experience of Ron Ashman, the more youthful but no less determined enthusiasm of Bryan Thurlow, and, in goal, the only position where substitution, through injury, was necessary, there was first the rejuvenated dependability of Ken Nethercott and then the feline grace and agility of Sandy Kennon.

And what memories they created, from the near rout of Manchester United to those last desperate, but vain, efforts to secure right and proper justice against Luton at Birmingham. Out of cascading thought come the visions of Allcock stepping as certainly as a cat across the ice and snow while Manchester United floundered and were lost, the extraordinary scenes that followed Bly's unbelievable winner against Cardiff, and the agony of Tottenham's last-minute goal at White Hart Lane that postponed their death sentence for four days.

After Nethercott's injury at Sheffield there was the gnawing of fingers down to the bone . . . (flu made me sit that one out beside a radio receiver) and on to the elbow, as Sheffield United made their gallant but unavailing effort in the replay; the excitement of Bly's consistent opportunism, the goals Brennan laid on a plate and Kennon's heroic, "impossible" saves against Luton.

Above all, however, was the standard of football that promoted City from giant killers to giants long before the semi-final was reached . . . and behind it all were the echoes of Norfolk men and women in full song. While Ashman and company were carrying City to the highest pinnacles, their supporters were making "On the Ball, City," as famous a chorus as " The Blaydon Races," or " Sospen Fach." It was indeed a great crusade.

26

CUP CAMERA 10–*Tragedy at Bramall Lane*

Brennan's arms go up as he sees Crossan convert his centre for the equaliser at Sheffield.

Moment of tragedy—Nethercott falls at Hamilton's feet, plays on with a dislocated shoulder, but misses the rest of the Cup run.

A perfect study in marksmanship—but Brennan's shot was saved by Hodgkinson.

ROUND SIX

Sheffield Utd. 1 Norwich City 1
Norwich City 3 Sheffield Utd. 2

THIS was the tie that had everything! At Bramall Lane on February 28th, there was Sheffield United's second-minute shock goal, there was Brennan's brilliance that paved the way for the 75th-minute equaliser, and above all there was the bravery of Nethercott, who played out the last half-hour, superbly covered by his defence, with a dislocated shoulder.

In the thrill-soaked replay on March 4th there was the ordeal of Sandy Kennon, making his debut in City's first team, making mistakes, but making great saves as well.

At Bramall Lane they wouldn't let the City mascots on to the field and a ring of police kept a close watch on the crowd. But they couldn't stop City's "anthem" rolling over the ground, rolling over the sacred cricket square as well as the near-grassless pitch.

You could sense the drop in atmosphere when, with the game hardly started, Russell took a midfield pass, caught Nethercott in " no man's land " and coolly put United ahead. But City hadn't started yet. For most of the remainder of the game they gave Sheffield a lesson in smooth, attacking football. There were groans when Crossan netted, to be pulled up for offside (though he'll never agree with that decision to his dying day); and there was a roar of triumph when Brennan delicately beat man after man to lay on the equaliser for the right winger.

There had been groans again when Nethercott was hurt; cheer upon cheer as, with his left arm useless, he stopped what shots a tremendous defence couldn't prevent getting through.

So to the replay. City two up and apparently waltzing to victory, then easing just enough to give Sheffield the breathing space they needed. Kennon, cat-like in his work, fumbling a cross that gave Pace the chance to make it 2-1; Bly bringing the house down with the all-important third goal; United, still fighting, hammering back to 3-2 and, in the last phase giving Butler and his colleagues the toughest time they had in the whole of their Cup run. This, above all, was a tie to remember! Replay goal chart was Brennan (14th minute), Bly (31st), Pace (38th), Bly (71st), Summers (83rd).

SHEFFIELD UNITED—Hodgkinson; Coldwell, Shaw (G.); Hoyland, Shaw (J.), Summers; Lewis, Hamilton, Pace, Russell, Simpson.

NORWICH CITY—Nethercott (Kennon); Thurlow, Ashman; McCrohan, Butler, Crowe; Crossan, Allcock, Bly, Hill, Brennan.

Referee — J. Clough (Bolton). Attendance, Sheffield 57,000 (£7450), Norwich 38,000 (£6000).

28

CUP CAMERA 11–*Now for the semi-final*

That man Bly again—with a fine replay goal.

Sheffield hit back: Pace turns away after United's second goal.

Bly once more, with the goal that meant City were in the semi-final.

29

CUP CAMERA 12–*Still in the hunt*

Kennon and Baynham (above) watch the semi-final goals go in at White Hart Lane; Kennon (left and right) in confident action; Crossan (below) heads his disallowed "goal."

30

SEMI-FINAL

Norwich City 1 Luton Town 1
Norwich City 0 Luton Town 1

THIS was the end of the Cup journey; but never have a team earned more glory in defeat than did the Canaries at St. Andrew's on Wednesday, March 18th. When they went to Birmingham after a 1-1 semi-final draw at White Hart Lane the previous Saturday, City were playing their 11th game in the Cup. What an unlucky outing it proved to be.

For three parts of the game they hammered away at the Luton defence. Chances don't come often in a Cup semi-final, but twice in the first half, Bly was only a foot or so off target; Crossan had wretched luck with a lob that beat Baynham and went just wide; and on the stroke of the interval Hill sent the ball vertically from point blank range—after McNally had stuck out a foot to block the inside-left's header on the goal line.

It was in the 56th minute that disaster arrived. Brown worked the ball to the right corner flag and centred, there was a neat little backheel flick by Morton and Bingham jigged in delight as his shot whipped into the roof of the net. One somehow sensed then that it was all over; but never have a team gone down with their colours flying so defiantly as City.

For half an hour afterwards there were no dressing room visitors as the Canaries savoured the bitterness of this unlucky defeat; but their spirit was too buoyant to be subdued for long, and by the time they returned to a heroes' welcome at Norwich they were singing again.

Two men virtually put Luton into the Final. Bingham was never completely quelled and the veteran Owen held his defence together with the coolness and efficiency of one of the soccer greats.

But it seemed Luton had missed their chance when they failed to clinch matters at White Hart Lane. There they looked the better side and they had their due when Brown converted a Bingham centre (35th minute) to give them the lead. But this was Kennon's day, too. Some of his saves were uncanny and it was largely thanks to him that City lived to fight again.

It was Brennan, however, celebrating his 34th birthday against his former club, who, after Crossan had a goal disallowed, netted the equaliser in the 65th minute, snapping a first time shot, from a McCrohan pass, well wide of the diving Baynham.

The end of the trail, but it was by no means the end of the glory.

NORWICH CITY—Kennon; Thurlow, Ashman; McCrohan, Butler, Crowe; Crossan, Allcock, Bly, Hill, Brennan.

LUTON TOWN—Baynham; McNally, Hawkes; Groves, Owen, Pacey; Bingham, Brown, Morton, Cummins, Gregory.

Referee—W. Hickson (Wigan). Attendance: White Hart Lane 63,500 (£15,800); St. Andrew's 49,500.

31

CUP CAMERA 13–*The end of the trail*

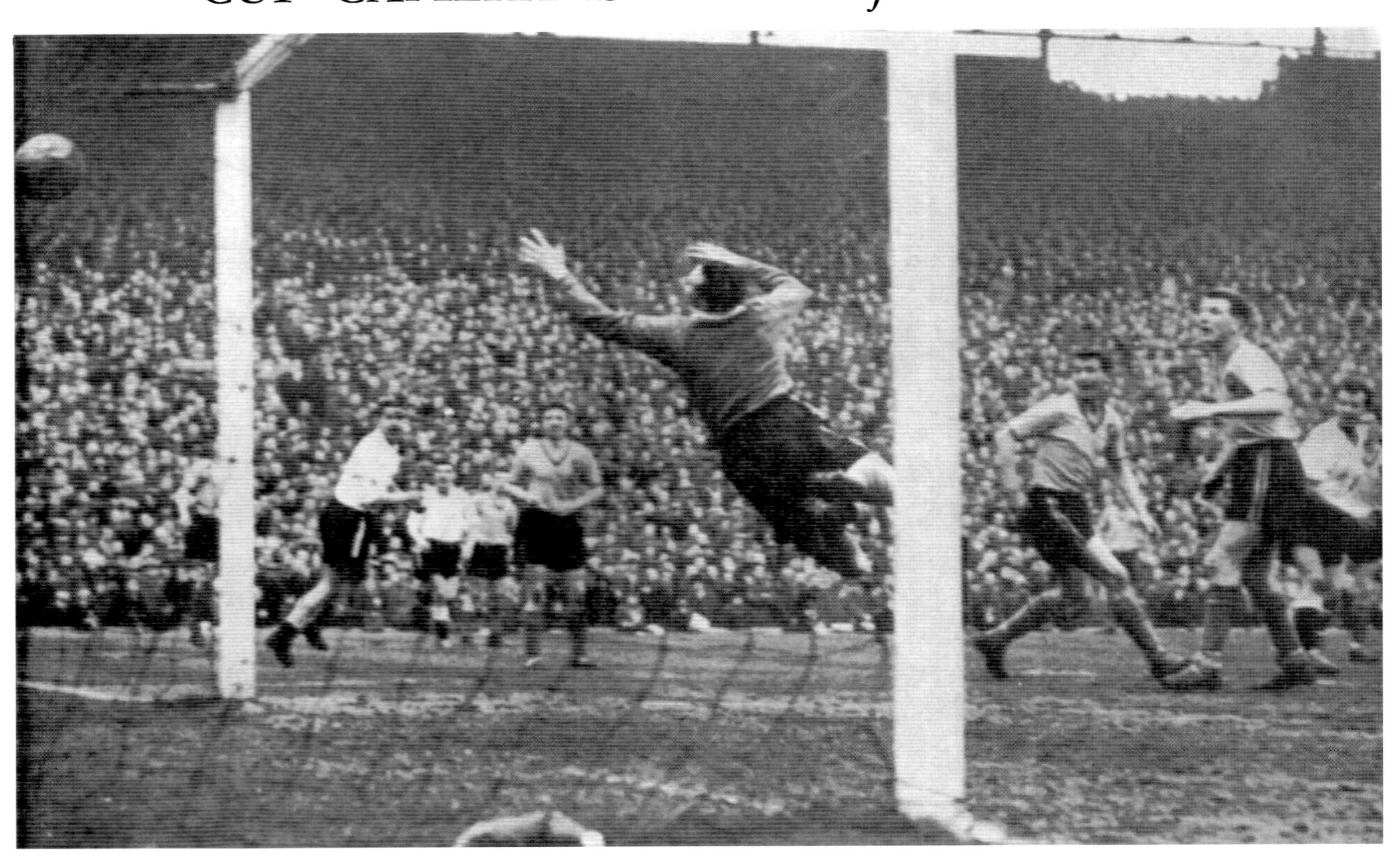

Kennon leaps, gets his fingertips to the ball, but Bingham's shot is in the net and for Norwich City the Cup dream is shattered—on the threshold of Wembley.

Top left, the City's 'secret weapon' in the Crusade revealed – traditional style PT and bags of fresh air

Centre left, City fans and players celebrate together at Norwich station

Centre right, City fans on song at Bramall Lane

Bottom left, it's semi-final day at White Hart Lane

Bottom right, the queue for 1959 Cup tickets outside Carrow Road

The 1959–60 team. Back row left to right: Thurlow, Allcock, McCrohan, Kennon, Butter, Bly, Crowe, Topping (Trainer). Front row left to right: Crossan, Hill, Whitehouse, Ashman, Larkin, Brennan, Punton

It is understandable that the 1959–60 season had an 'after the Lord Mayor's show' feeling about it but during the summer the new South stand was completed despite many difficulties. The soil had uneven bearing qualities and the limits of the site were restrictive. The steel structure was erected by Boulton & Paul Ltd and the main contractors were R.G. Carter Ltd. The only major signing before the season started was Bill Punton from Southend United and Macaulay saw him as an eventual replacement for Bobby Brennan. At his best Bill was one of the fastest and most direct wingers to play in the Football League and later after brief spells at Sheffield United and Scunthorpe United he returned to Norfolk to play for and manage Great Yarmouth. The Canaries carried on where they had left off the previous season and a crowd of 36,479 saw the home game against Barnsley on Wednesday 9 September 1959. When City lost at home to Bournemouth on Saturday 10 October 1959 it was their first reverse at Carrow Road since Hull City had won there 1–0 the week before the FA Cup run started. Sadly the Canaries did not proceed beyond the First Round of the FA Cup that year for they lost at the first hurdle to Reading after a replay, but if City were disappointed that the FA Cup glory could not be repeated they did not show it. Bunny Larkin and Brian Whitehouse were bought just before the transfer deadline in March 1960 and they helped City to finish second in the league and qualify for Second Division football.

Bill Punton in action against Southend

Ron Ashman, Barry Butler, Roy McCrohan and Bryan Thurlow played in every game that season and Matt Crowe, Sandy Kennon, Terry Allcock, Errol Crossan and Jimmy Hill missed only a handful between them when they were injured. Promotion was finally clinched when Southend United visited Carrow Road on Wednesday 27 April 1960 and the crowd of 34,905 were treated to an exciting 4–3 victory. 'On the ball, City' was sung throughout the entire match and after the final whistle thousands ran across the pitch in triumph. Norwich City FC were back in the Second Division after the near disaster of 1957. It was a magnificent achievement for all connected with the club. Once more there was money in the

Left, Bill Punton, centre, Jimmy Hill, right, goalkeeper Sandy Kennon

bank, over £10,000 profit had been made during the 1958–59 campaign and everyone looked forward to the day when First Division football would be on the menu at Carrow Road.

Manager Archie Macaulay felt that there was no need to strengthen his side for the Second Division and for the first time since most people could remember there were no new faces at Carrow Road at the start of the season. His confidence appeared to be justified because City soon settled to the task in hand and despite losing the services of Terry Allcock early in September City maintained a position in the top four until the turn of the year. It was in the match against Plymouth Argyle on Wednesday 7 September that Terry Allcock broke his leg after 30 minutes, but in less than 100 days he was once more wearing a City shirt, a fine recovery and typical of the spirit that flowed through the City dressing room at this period. Ipswich Town were also having a fine season, no doubt being inspired by their rivals from Norfolk, and for a time it looked as though both teams would march into the First Division, but come the end of the campaign City could only finish in fourth place. During the season George Waites had arrived at Carrow Road from Orient in a deal that saw Errol Crossan going in the

Carrow Road in 1961, local referee Tommy Dawes (with cap) inspecting the pitch with club secretary Bert Westwood (centre front) and groundsman Russell Allison (left)

NORWICH CITY
FOOTBALL CLUB
F.A. CUP SEMI-FINALISTS, SEASON 1958-59
No 42
FOOTBALL LEAGUE CUP FINAL (Second Leg)
TUESDAY, 1st MAY, 1962
Norwich City v. Rochdale
PRICE 4d. EACH

The programme from City's League Cup win over Rochdale, May 1962

promoted first time around. Another problem spot was at outside right and Gerry Mannion, who had twice been capped for England at Under 23 level, was bought from Wolverhampton Wanderers for £13,000. It proved to be Macaulay's last signing for after the 2–1 home win over Swansea Town on 14 October 1961 he announced he was leaving to manage West Bromwich Albion. When Archie Macaulay joined Norwich City FC they were at the foot of the Third Division (South) and to all practical purposes were bankrupt. He led the club to national prominence during the great FA Cup run and later to fourth place in the Second Division – a fine record.

Willie Reid was appointed to take up the managerial reins on Thursday 14 December 1961, and in the interim chairman Geoffrey Watling had himself handled the day to day running of the club. There were over 100 applicants for the job and out of the nine that were interviewed Reid was the only Scot. Willie Reid had been connected with St Mirren for over 17 years as player, trainer and latterly as manager and at the time of his Norwich City FC appointment was 44 years old. One player of the era told us that his broad Scottish accent was hard to understand, but he managed to get things done in his own quiet way. The Football League Cup competition which had started in the previous season provided City with a chance to again demonstrate their renown cup fighting qualities. In the early years not all the Football League teams bothered to enter the competition for there was no Wembley Final or automatic European qualification for the winners. The first match was played in September and City went on to beat Chesterfield, Lincoln City, Middlesbrough, Sunderland and Blackpool on their way to the two leg Final with Rochdale. Not only were Rochdale then in the Fourth Division but they only just finished in the top half of the table at the end of the season. The First Leg took place at Spotland on Thursday 26 April 1962 and City coasted to an easy 3–0 victory. 19,800 turned up at Carrow Road the following Tuesday to see City win 1–0 and lift their first national knock-out

other direction and later teenager Ollie Burton arrived fron Newport County for a reported fee of £11,000. The *Pink'Un* headline writers came up with some memorable offerings during the season our favourites being 'Huddersfelled' (1 October), 'Not Such a Bright Un' (8 October), 'Muddlesbrough' (15 October) and 'All at (Swan) Sea' (14 January). City had done well in their first season back in the higher grade and collected talent money at the end of the season – just £440.

Just after the 1960–61 season ended Archie Macaulay bought centre forward Jim Conway from Celtic for a £10,000 fee. Conway, who was usually seen with a crew cut, will be remembered for his dashing style and bullet like headers. He had not been able to break into the Celtic First team but had scored regularly for their Reserve side. The centre forward spot had been a problem for Macaulay ever since the departure of Terry Bly to Peterborough United in June 1960. Peterborough United were elected to the Fourth Division in readiness for the 1960–61 season, taking the place of Gateshead and thanks to the 52 goals scored by Bly were trophy. The victory was something of an anti-climax especially as City had won the First Leg so easily, but it must be remembered that Rochdale had accounted for Southampton and Blackburn Rovers in earlier rounds.

There was further excitement in the FA Cup when City were drawn against Ipswich Town, then on their way to winning the League championship, in the Fourth Round at Carrow Road. Another huge crowd of 39,890 saw the two teams draw 1–1 on Saturday 27 January 1962 and two Terry Allcock goals in the replay at Portman Road the following Tuesday saw City safely through to the next round. There must have beem memories of the 1958–59 Cup run in the minds of the team and the supporters as City travelled to meet Sheffield United on Saturday 17 February 1962. Sadly history did not repeat itself and City were beaten 1–3. At the end of the season Norwich had slipped to 17th in the league and Willie Reid decided to return to his native land. He had been City's 17th manager since 1905 and the fourth to come from over the Scottish border, he left the club on Wednesday 9 May 1962 only eight days after lifting the Football League Cup.

Again the search started for a new manager and the man chosen to replace Reid on Wednesday 23 May 1962 was the former Arsenal goalkeeper George Swindin. Swindin had played nearly 300 games for the famous London club making his debut in December 1936. Among his colleagues at Highbury were Archie Macaulay, Bryn Jones and Alf Kirchen. He made his last appearance for Arsenal in 1954 before being replaced in goal by Welsh international Jack Kelsey. He then went to manage Peterborough United and in 1958 returned to Highbury as manager until being replaced by Billy Wright at the end of the 1961–62 season. He arrived at Norwich in his car which bore the registration number AFC 100, but after comments by a local journalist stated that he would soon get it changed. We are not able to tell you if he did in fact get it changed, but we can tell you that after being in charge for only 20 games he left the club to go to Cardiff City on Saturday 10 November 1962. Yet again the board had to find a new manager and on this occasion they decided to look no further than club captain Ron Ashman. Ron was appointed acting manager on Monday 10 December 1962 and continued to play at centre half as well as being in charge of the team. Before George Swindin left he bought inside forward Tommy Bryceland from St Mirren for a club record fee of £20,000. Tommy played for St Mirren in two Scottish Cup Finals, they beat Aberdeen in the 1958–59 Final by 3–1 and he scored their opening goal and they lost to Rangers in the 1961–62 Final 0–2. In all Tommy made 281 appearances for Norwich City FC and scored 55 goals. Swindin had also brought Alistair Miller from St Mirren, Phil Kelly from Wolves, Jim Oliver from Falkirk, Jackie Bell from Newcastle United and Barry Staton from Doncaster Rovers to Carrow Road during the close season.

On Saturday 9 March 1963 Stoke City included Stanley Matthews in their line up at Carrow Road, but City still managed to win 6–0. A month later (13 April 1963) the Canaries travelled to Luton Town and lost 2–4. Ron Ashman, who was playing at centre half, could not have failed to have been impressed by the opposing centre forward as he scored all four of the Luton Town goals that day, he probably made a note of his name – it was Ronald Tudor Davies. City finished the season in an improved 11th position in the league and also reached the Fifth Round of the Football League Cup before

Ron Ashman, long-serving stalwart for Norwich played his last game for City on 19 October 1963 and later managed the side

Enter Geoffrey Watling

A all-time record crowd of 43,984 attended the FA Cup 6th round v Leicester City at Carrow Road on 30 March 1963

going out to Aston Villa 1–4 on Monday 3 December 1962. The main excitement of the season was reserved as usual for the FA Cup which, because of the very bad winter, did not get underway until March, the Third Round tie against Blackpool having itself being postponed 11 times. In only 26 days City progressed from the Third Round to the Sixth beating on the way Blackpool – after a replay, Newcastle United – Terry Allcock scoring four in the 5–0 victory and Manchester City 2–1 at Maine Road. It was beginning to feel like old times with Ron Ashman leading the team and Terry Allcock scoring the goals. In the Sixth Round City were drawn against Leicester City and a crowd of 43,984 crushed into Carrow Road on that bitter afternoon of Saturday 30 March 1963 hoping to again see the Canaries reach the Semi-Final stage, sadly they were disappointed and Norwich lost 0–2. The gate receipts were £8,182 7s 6d and the crowd was a record for any game at Carrow Road – and one that will never be surpassed.

Terry Allcock, a club record 37 goals in the 1962–63 season

There was again much activity in the transfer market in the summer of 1963 as Ron Ashman faced his first full season in control of Norwich City FC. Wing half Ken Hill arrived from Walsall and Freddie Sharpe was transferred from Tottenham Hotspur for £8,000. Another Hill, this time City favourite Jimmy Hill, left the club and moved north to Everton for a £25,000 fee. A goalkeeper was signed from Welsh club Wrexham for a modest £6,500 on 18 July 1963. The young man had been born in Calcutta, but had spent most of his boyhood days in the Midlands. He had already had spells at Aston Villa and Stockport County before moving to Wales and was to play a total of 673 games in the City goal. His name of course was Kevin Keelan and he proved to be the bargain of the century for City, saving them from defeat time and time again. City got off to a poor start and lost their first 4 league games – it was time for a gamble. Ron Ashman remembered the roasting he had received from Ron Davies the previous season and moved in with a £35,000 bid for the Welsh centre forward. The offer was accepted by Luton Town and chairman Geoffrey Watling famously stated 'if he fails his medical then sack the doctor'. Fortunately he had no need to take such drastic action and Ron Davies became a Norwich City player. On Saturday 19 October 1963 Ron Ashman played his last game for Norwich City FC against Southampton at Carrow Road and on Boxing Day 1963 was appointed manager of the club (he had been acting manager until this time). He first came to Norwich during the war and had played for the club in 17 league campaigns, captaining the side for the last ten. His total of 590 league games is a record for Norwich City as is his aggregate of 72 FA Cup games – perhaps to stand for all time. Of those that saw him few will forget his smiling, confident face, a ball tucked under his arm, leading his beloved Canaries out of the tunnel and on to the pitch at Carrow Road and if it hadn't been for one slip in the FA Cup Semi-Final at St Andrews he would have led the team out at Wembley.

Ron Davies scored in each of his first four games in a Canary shirt and finished the season with a total of 30 goals, proof that Ashman's bold step was fully justified. In March Gordon Bolland joined the club from Leyton Orient for another large fee but City could do no better than finish in 17th place, the last part of the season being disastrous. City won only 1 of their final 11 league games and at the end of the campaign it was reported that the club had lost £63,263 on the season. Expenses were up and gate receipts down. There was no run in the FA Cup that year, City lost to Bristol Rovers in the Third Round, and only a modest run in the Football League Cup. The Supporters Club had handed over £35,000 to the club during the season and also footed the bill of £6,500 for the new training ground at Trowse. During the season the deaths were recorded of Robert Collinson, the City skipper in the club's first ever match in 1902 and Mr Prior, a director of the club for many years.

The 1964–65 season got underway with only one major signing – Don Heath joining the club from Middlesbrough. Mal Lucas came from Leyton Orient in September and Terry Anderson the ex-Arsenal winger was signed in February 1965. A minutes silence was observed for Sir Winston Churchill before the home game against Swindon Town on Saturday 30 January 1965. Kevin Keelan was sent off in the match against Northampton Town on Saturday 20 March 1965 for allegedly striking an opposing forward, it was the first time that a City goalkeeper had been dismissed from the field. Sandy Kennon played his last game for the club on 4 November 1964. Sandy first played for City in the Sixth Round replay of the FA Cup when Sheffield United were the visitors and his final total of appearances came to 255. The season promised much and at one stage City managed to climb to 3rd place but another poor finish saw them drop to 6th. On Saturday 10 April 1965 a young man from Gorleston made his

Left, Ron Davies who scored 30 Canary goals in his first season

Right, Kevin Keelan who was to make 673 appearances for City

Above, Mal Lucas, a busy right half, joined in 1964

Left, the 1963–64 squad

An airborne Dave Stringer defends his goal

Right, Chairman, Geoffrey Watling hands the Barry Butler Memorial Trophy to first winner Terry Allcock in 1967

Canary debut at Coventry, City lost the match 0–3 but before he finally hung up his boots he was to have many more opportunities to make amends – his name was David Ronald Stringer.

At the opening of the 1965–66 season substitutes were introduced in Football League and FA Cup matches. The first Norwich City substitute was Gordon Bolland who came on for Terry Anderson who had strained a thigh muscle. The game was played on Tuesday 31 August against Bristol City at Ashton Gate, the substitution was timed at 70 minutes and the final result was a 0–0 draw. The league season was another of the 'win one lose one' variety, and although Ashman secured the services of Hugh Curran in early January it made no significant difference. Perhaps even more alarming than the inconsistent performances was the huge drop recorded in the Carrow Road attendance's, only 7,849 turned up to watch the match against Middlesbrough on Wednesday 27 April 1966. Earlier in the season City had won their way through to the Fifth Round of the FA Cup and they were drawn to play Blackburn Rovers at Carrow Road. It was announced some ten days before the tie that the admission prices would be doubled, although 30,751 turned up on the day, it could never be described as a popular decision. City managed to salvage a draw with almost the last kick of the game but on the following Wednesday were beaten 2–3 in the replay. Misfortune followed misfortune and on 9 April 1966 Barry Butler, the popular City centre half was killed in a tragic road accident. A memorial service was held in St Peter's Mancroft and there were queues several hundred yards long just to get near the church. As a mark of permanent respect the Norwich City FC 'Player of the Year' award was named the Barry Butler Memorial Trophy. Barry made 349 appearances for the club and was never found wanting in spirit or ability. A sad and unfortunate season

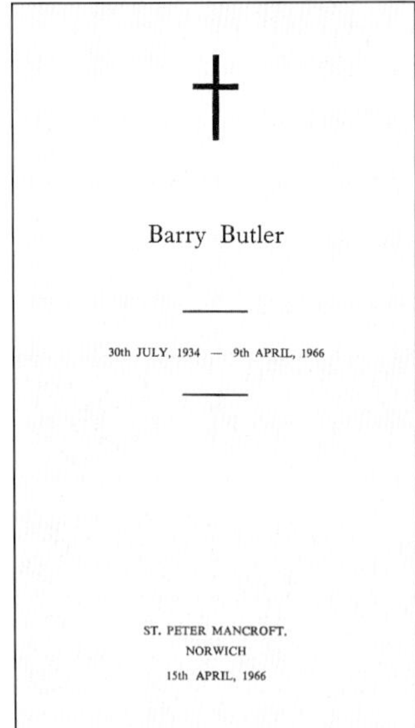

†

Barry Butler

30th JULY, 1934 – 9th APRIL, 1966

ST. PETER MANCROFT,
NORWICH
15th APRIL, 1966

Below, the death of popular centre half Barry Butler was marked by a minutes silence before a home match at Carrow Road

drew to a close and Ron Ashman severed his links with the club his replacement was already waiting to hang his coat in his office – his name was Laurence (Lol) Morgan.

Lol Morgan, a 35 year old Yorkshireman, had been a defender with Sheffield United, Huddersfield Town, Rotherham United and Darlington. In 1964 he became the manager of Darlington and led them to promotion from Division Four in his first year of management. There was uproar in Norwich when it was announced in early August that Ron Davies was to leave the club and go to Southampton. Certainly Ron had not been at his best at the end of the previous depressing season, but City fans felt cheated now that their goalscoring hero had been allowed to leave the club. In September Morgan made the first of a series of signings that he hoped would improve the playing strength of the club. He bought Scottish full back Alan Black from Sunderland for £9,000 and later in the month centre half Laurie Brown was transferred from Tottenham Hotspur for £25,000 to replace Barry Butler. In November the much travelled Laurie Sheffield was secured from Doncaster Rovers for £15,000 and in his debut against Derby County on 12 November 1966 he thrilled the crowd with a hat-trick in the 4–1 victory. Winger Mike Kenning was signed from Charlton Athletic in December for a reported fee of £25,000 and made his debut in the Boxing Day fixture at Millwall.

Once again City saved their best performances for the FA Cup and after beating Derby County 3–0 in the Third Round travelled to Old Trafford to take on Manchester United. At half time the teams were level at 1–1, but Gordon Bolland scored what proved to be the winner after the interval. Manchester United were at their height around this period, rarely finishing lower than fourth in the First Division and of course on 29 May 1968 they became the first English club to win the European Cup. The Final was played at Wembley and millions were glued to their TV screens as the match went into extra time. The final score was Manchester United 4 – Benfica 1 and the United goals were scored by Charlton 2, Best and Kidd. When Norwich City won at Old Trafford the United team included Bobby Charlton, Denis Law, George Best and Pat Crerand so you can see why the Canaries were given no chance of winning. The Fifth Round produced a home tie against Sheffield Wednesday and although a 41,000 capacity crowd gave the Canaries plenty of encouragement they could not prevent the First Division opposition winning 3–1. City finished just above the halfway point in the league, an improvement over the previous season, but could not find the consistency to challenge for promotion. Bill Punton played his last game for Norwich on 24 September 1966 in the 1–1 home draw with Preston North End and Kevin Keelan scored a penalty for the Reserves on 31 December 1966 against Birmingham City Reserves. When Norwich visited Coventry City on 14 January 1967 they trailed by the odd goal until the 88th minute. Laurie Sheffield then equalised and the crowd, thinking that the match would

When visited early in 1966 by Blackburn Rovers, Norwich played to a crowd of 30,751 in the 5th round of the FA Cup. Later that year Laurie Sheffield (below) was to join the Canaries

Left, Gordon Bolland, who had been City's first ever substitute, following the new FA and League ruling, scores the winning goal when Norwich overcame Manchester United at Old Trafford in February 1967

finish all square, began to leave the ground. It was not to be for an inside forward called Machin restored the home side's lead in the very last minute – we must point out that his name was Ernie Machin – Mel of course would never have done such a thing!

Morgan's second season at the helm, 1967–68, was relatively successful, City finished in 9th position. John Manning joined the club from Shrewsbury Town to replace the departing Laurie Sheffield, Ken Foggo came from West Bromwich Albion as did wing half Gerry Howshall. The latter was signed at the Annual Dinner of the Supporters Club for £25,000. As we mentioned earlier the Supporters Club did some sterling work in the 1960s and the signing of Howshall, of which much was expected, was a reward for all their efforts. Alas he made only 43 appearances in a City shirt. In January Charlie Crickmore came from Rotherham United to complete the signings for the season. This time you must remember was just after England's victory in the World Cup and the game was rapidly changing, twin centre halves, midfield men and all. Terry Allcock was moved back from his forward role to play in midfield and there were a host of other changes that could not always be fully understood by the spectators on the terraces. Players were also starting their careers earlier and during the season Neil O'Donnell, Nigel Cassidy and Trevor Howard were brought in for the odd game. Thankfully things did not quite reach the heights of eccentricity that was demonstrated in the United States of America. A concerted move was afoot to popularise the game in America, but the crowds could not understand why the play would suddenly cease only to start up again a few moments later. The reason was that the referee had instructions to stop the play during the advertisements and was warned of their approach by an electronic device that was strapped to his waist. Closer to home the death was reported during March 1968 of Edgar Henry Banger. Harry provided the 'Canary and Dumpling' cartoons that were enjoyed by the readers of the *Pink'Un* for many years.

Above, Ken Foggo, fast, and equally at home on either wing. Right, Duncan Forbes, a powerful centre half signed from Colchester

Duncan Forbes was signed from Colchester United in September 1968 for a £10,000 fee and made his debut on Wednesday 9 October 1968 against Crystal Palace. His signing was followed by that of Geoff Butler from Sunderland for £30,000 and Ken Mallender who came from Sheffield United for a then City record fee of £40,000. Morgan had been unable to produce a consistent team and was 'throwing a bit of

Below, The 1967–68 squad

Hat trick man, Hugh Curran in action in September 1968 as City beat Ipswich 4–2 at Portman Road in the Football League Cup

money' at the problem – always a dangerous thing to attempt. In January he splashed out another big fee on Albert Bennett from Newcastle United. Bennett had shown a lot of promise as a young player and had been rewarded with an England Under 23 cap while he was at his first professional club Rotherham United. To his credit Morgan had also been encouraging his younger players and two local lads to benefit were Max Briggs from Bramerton and Clive Payne from Aylsham. Max made his debut against Bury on Saturday 31 August 1968 and Clive came in for the very next match on the following Tuesday against Ipswich Town in the Football League Cup. The Ipswich match was particularly rewarding as City won 4–2 at Portman Road with Hugh Curran getting a hat-trick. Despite the big money signings City were not having a happy time and cushions were thrown on to the pitch in frustration after the 1–1 draw with Bristol City on Wednesday 26 March 1969. Morgan was finally asked to resign after the 1–4 defeat by Derby County at Carrow Road on Wednesday 16 April 1969. City finished the season in 13th position, which proved to be unlucky for manager Lol Morgan. The last time City had occupied 13th spot in the table was at the end of the 1965–66 season – and on that occasion it was Ron Ashman who suffered.

Earlier in the campaign Middlesbrough had visited Carrow Road and won 2–0 (Wednesday 14 August 1968), and they finished the game with only nine men. McMordie was sent off in the 55th minute and three minutes later he was joined by John Hickton. The final game of the season was played against Blackburn Rovers at Carrow Road and resulted in a 3–1 win for the Canaries. Terry Allcock had been brought back to help the youngsters – it was his 389th game in a Norwich City shirt – and it was also his last.

The new manager of Norwich City FC signed a four year contract just before the club's Annual General Meeting on Thursday 21 August 1969. Geoffrey Watling and his board had been delighted with their new manager, only the previous evening City had beaten Hull City at Carrow Road, their fourth match of the season,

Albert Bennett was signed by Lol Morgan for a substantial fee in January 1969

Enter Geoffrey Watling

New manager Ron Saunders and his enthusiastic Chairman Geoffrey Watling

and gone to the top of the division. Geoffrey Watling further stated that the new manager was one of the best paid in the Second Division – the man to receive such praise and backing from his board was Birkenhead born Ron Saunders. As a player Saunders had represented Everton, non league Tonbridge, Gillingham, Portsmouth, Watford and Charlton Athletic and in a career that stretched over 13 years had scored 201 goals in the Football League. Prior to joining Norwich City FC Saunders had been manager of Oxford United and before that was manager of Yeovil Town in the Southern League. He came to Norwich on 10 July 1969 after protracted negotiations with his previous club. His presence also appeared to unite the board and the shareholders for the only matter of concern at the AGM was the decision to change the colour of the players shorts from green to black, black shorts it was argued stayed smarter longer than green ones. The club had lost money on the previous season and there would be no fortunes for the new manager to spend, it was basically his job to get the best out of the players he already had at his disposal.

The only major signings during the season were Peter Silvester from Reading for £20,000 in September and Graham Paddon from Coventry City for £25,000 a month later. On Saturday 13 September 1969 at Carrow Road Charlton Athletic equalised with a very disputed penalty and cushions were hurled on to the pitch, an incident that led to the Football Association ordering warning notices to be posted at the ground. There was more drama when City visited the Valley for the return match on Saturday 13 December 1969 for Kevin Keelan fractured his arm while diving at Ray Treacy's feet and Clive Payne had to replace him in goal. On Saturday 21 February 1970 Dave Stringer scored his first goal for the club in the 1–1 draw at Huddersfield. Despite the early promise City had to be content with a mid-table position, but they did manage to beat Birmingham City 6–0 at Carrow Road in the penultimate game of the season. The 1969–70 season proved to be the last for Charlie Crickmore, Tommy Bryceland, Peter Vasper, Mal Lucas and Bryan Conlon. It was also the season in which El Salvador declared war on Honduras – after the two sides had met in a soccer match.

Below, Ron Saunders secures the signature of Graham Paddon in October 1969

The 1970–71 season was also a rather tame affair and at its conclusion City finished in 10th position. Doug Livermore had joined the club from Liverpool in November 1970 for a fee reported to have been £22,000. Joint top scorers in the league were Peter Silvester and Ken Foggo with 15 goals apiece, but collectively City could only manage to score 54 in the league – certainly not enough for promotion. Wolverhampton Wanderers, who were developing into something of a bogey side for City, dispatched the Canaries from the FA Cup in the Third Round. The two sides were level at half time, but contributions from McCalliog, Hibbitt and Gould 2 in the second period saw the Wolves build up a 5–1 lead and go through to the next round. At the end of the season City travelled to Portugal and won the Batista Trophy in face of competition from Atletico Lisbon, Sporting Lisbon and Dundee and while they were in Portugal they also played a friendly against Uniao. The result was a 1–1 draw and the City goal was headed by none other than Kevin Keelan who had come on as a substitute. Before the opening of the 1970–71 season City reported a loss of £34,122 which was accounted for by the fall in attendances and the lack of success in the Cup competitions. On 13 August 1970 it was reported that James Hanly had retired from the board after 23 years service, which included 7 years as chairman. He was elected president of the club and his place on the board was taken by Mr W M Young. At the same meeting it was announced that Billy Furness was to retire as physiotherapist and that he would be succeeded by Geoffrey Grainger who had held an appointment at a hospital in Hull. Roy Allison who had been responsible for the training ground at Trowse was also retiring and overall control of both Carrow Road and the training ground would now be undertaken by his brother Russell. Their father before them had been groundsman both at the Nest and Carrow Road and had once been gamekeeper on the Costessey Hall estate. To carry on the tradition Russell's son Russ joined his father at Carrow Road and over the years the Norwich City Football Club owes much to the dedicated work of the successive generations of the Allison family.

On 24 May 1971 it was reported that Boulton & Paul Ltd had bought 15 acres of land from Reckitt & Colman Food Division and included in the package was the 7 acres of land on which the Carrow Road ground is sited. The site had been secured by Reckitt & Colman in 1870 and the marshy ground used for the grazing of the horses owned by the company. Geoffrey Watling made no secret of the fact that the club would like to buy the Carrow Road site but was not worried in the near future as the lease had several years to run. In January 1972 it was announced that Norwich City FC had finally come to an agreement with Bolton & Paul Ltd and bought the ground, but no fee was disclosed.

When the 1971–72 season opened there was little to suggest that it would provide anything more than the previous two – a mid-table position in arguably the most competitive section of the Football League – the Second Division. City started well and by Saturday 25 September 1971, when they recorded a 1–0 victory over Bristol City at Ashton Gate, they were top of the league. By Saturday 16 October 1971 their unbeaten run in the league had extended to 13 games and by the half way point in the programme they had only suffered a single reverse. Main rivals for the two promotion spots that year were Birmingham City and Millwall, but all through the long and harrowing campaign City kept their sights firmly on the First Division. David Cross arrived from Rochdale for a club record fee of £40,000 in early October and later in the season he was joined by Phil Hubbard and Jimmy Bone. Skipper Duncan Forbes was injured on Saturday 30 October 1971 in the home match against Cardiff City and did not return until 11 March 1972, but Saunders managed to keep City rolling forward by utilising first Steve Govier, then Terry Anderson and finally loan player Bobby Bell as emergency centre halves. On Saturday 22 March 1972 City beat Swindon Town in a tense struggle at Carrow Road, big Duncan Forbes scored the only goal, and the Canaries required only two more points for promotion. Two days later, on Monday 24 April 1972, all roads led to Brisbane Road, Leyton, the home of Orient FC. Thousands travelled down from Norwich by car and rail and the stadium was a mass of yellow and green. A crowd of 15,530, most of whom came from Norfolk, loudly greeted the arrival of the players. All through the match the Norwich contingent kept up their cries of 'We are the champions' and 'Now you're gonna believe us', (there were

The successful 1971–72 squad brought First Division football to the city of Norwich

no reported renderings of 'On the ball, City', but we suspect that there were), and half time arrived with no goals recorded to either side. Ken Foggo opened the scoring after the resumption and Graham Paddon just for good measure added a penalty later on. Orient could only reply with a solitary goal in the last minute, it didn't matter, Norwich City FC were in the First Division for the first time in their history. The Norwich hordes swept across the pitch, hoarse, but baying for their champions. Ron Saunders appeared with a bottle of Champagne together with his triumphant players and they acknowledged the salute from their delighted fans. The public houses between Leyton and Norwich did a roaring trade as the excited fans reluctantly made their way home – for most of them it was a dream come true, after 70 long and gruelling years the Canaries had reached the highest perch in the Football League.

On the following Saturday the red-shirted (to avoid a colour clash with their hosts) Canaries ran out on to the pitch at Vicarage Road, Watford, needing a single point to ensure the championship of the Second Division. They led 1–0 at the interval but Watford, who were bottom of the league, equalised later in the game. It didn't matter because Norwich City FC were champions of the Second Division and fittingly it was Dave Stringer, that most reliable of performers, who scored the goal on so important an occasion. When asked by a local reporter if he thought that City would ever make the highest grade chairman Geoffrey Watling replied 'I've worked in the transport business during my life and I always hitch my waggon to a star'.

The next section is a reproduction of the 1972 Eastern Counties Newspapers publication *Canary Crusade*, published to document the Canaries' historic 1971–72 campaign.

We won't be found wanting

Geoffrey Watling

WHAT can I say that has not already been said? Over the years Norwich City have had many moments of glory – moments when we have said "It can't happen again." But it has.

There have been dark hours, too; hours when it has seemed that the tide would never turn in our favour. But it has.

There have been times, since I became Norwich City's chairman, when the critics have labelled me a super optimist. To them I would say: what's the use of being in the game of football unless you are an optimist?

Other critics have hinted that Norwich City have not wanted promotion; that they would prefer a near miss in the Second Division to a relegation fight in the First. To them I would say that Norwich City's aim has always been the top. Our efforts have always been geared with promotion in view.

Those efforts have now been rewarded and, for me, pride in achievement is coupled with gratitude to the manager, the players and everyone who has played a part in the success story. Not least to the officials and members of the Supporters' Club, to those who have travelled to away matches and to the elite band who have been to every game this season.

At the moment we are basking in the rare atmosphere that surrounds a club finding themselves in the First Division for the first time in their history. As the weeks go by the rosy glow will fade as we get down to the task of preparing for the biggest test Norwich City have yet faced.

But I shall not lose one degree of optimism. I have the greatest faith in manager Ron Saunders and the Norwich City players. I believe that, having won our way into the company of the greatest football teams in the country, we shall not be found wanting.

I look forward to every season with eagerness, but 1972–73 will have a very special meaning. It is one that will call for all-out effort, from chairman to youngest supporter. I am sure that effort will be forthcoming.

1

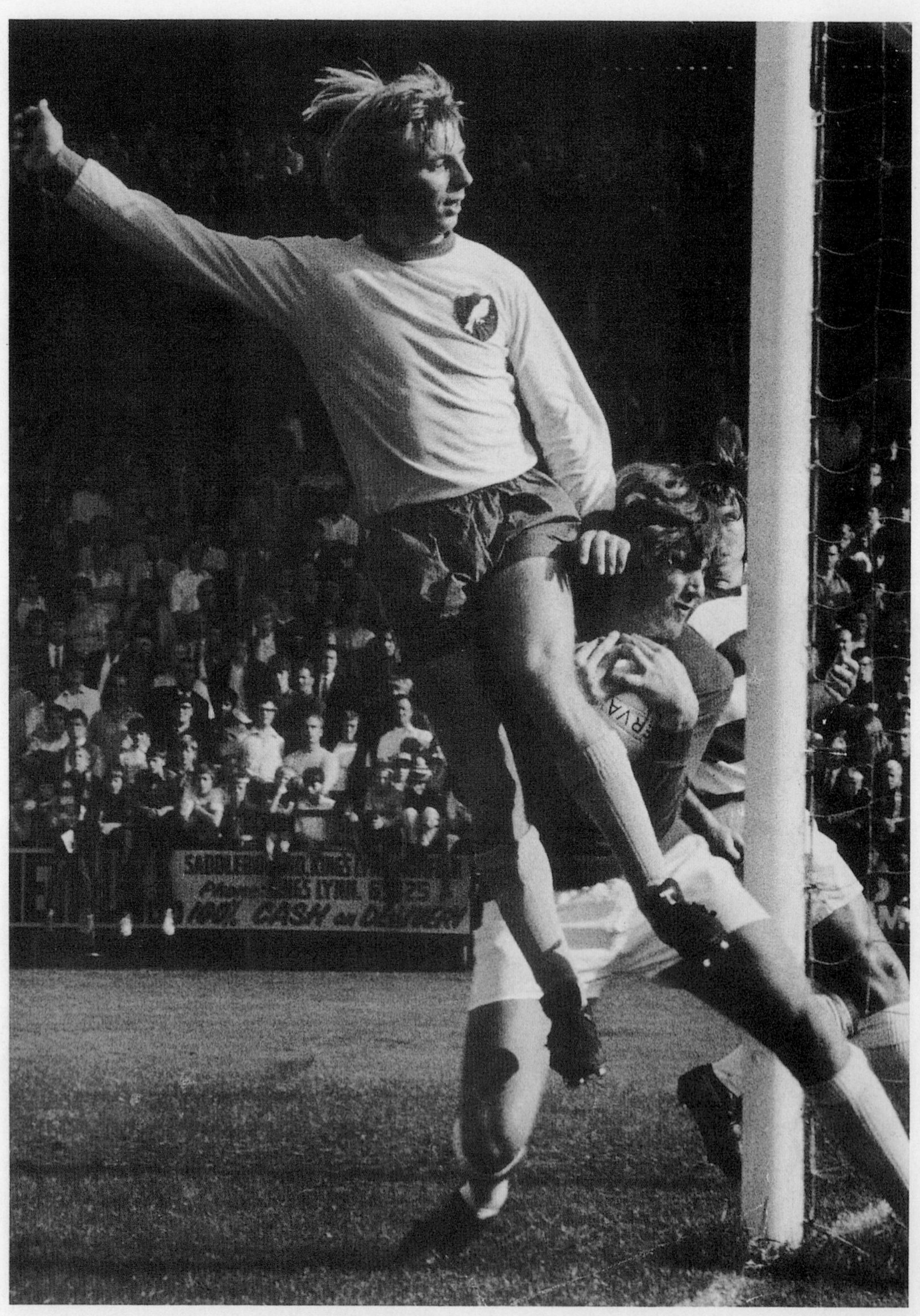

TREVOR HOWARD displays the sharpness in front of goal that brought him eight goals. Although relegated to substitute with the arrival of Cross, the King's Lynn boy has scored vital goals after coming on.

2

Profile of a season that led to glory

BY BRUCE ROBINSON

It can, of course, be argued with some justification that Norwich City's rise to prominence began the moment Ron Saunders took office, in July, 1969. It probably did. But for the purposes of this particular story it began only a year ago, as another dour season finally died.

City finished in 10th place in 1970/71, and it seemed about right. Much groundwork had been accomplished; the seeds of tactical efficiency had been sown, and the arrival of Doug Livermore had given the mid-field a degree of inventiveness they had not possessed since Lucas and Bryceland were at their peak.

But it was still not enough to turn the head of the man in the street. City's game was still based very largely on defensive strength, on rugged consistency and on a very strong and natural desire not to lose.

In short, City were difficult to beat, but they were dull with it.

It was not surprising to see, therefore, that while the League position had marginally improved, attendances had dropped considerably. The average was down to 13,259 – the lowest since the bankrupt years of 1956/57.

So much, we thought, for modern tactics, for 4–3–3, even for Saunders, who persisted in arguing that he was working on the right lines and making progress into the bargain. Clearly, few of us agreed with him.

Chairman Geoffrey Watling put the club's point of view at the annual meeting. He said: ". . . the bonuses are very substantial indeed, so that the directors have given the players every incentive to achieve a high position. It was considered that having satisfactory results in this way would be reflected in increased gates, which would enable these bonuses to be met, and it was somewhat disappointing to find that there was a fall in attendances."

And so it was that, with the side being beaten in their last three matches, the 1970/71 season came to a grinding end in an atmosphere of almost total indifference.

Apart from a very real lack of public interest in events at Carrow Road, and despite a prevalent feeling that City had been in Division Two too long, anyway, Saunders had other major problems. He was short of at least one forward, and with the luckless Bennett's knee still giving trouble it was Trevor Howard who was thrust into a striker's role.

And that, in a nutshell, was the situation when in May 1971, City left the unpredictable weather of East Anglia for the more reliable climate of Portugal.

Max Briggs, Norwich-born midfield dynamo who firmly established his place in the City line-up in the second half of the season.

In Lisbon, and in opulent surroundings, they promptly beat Atletico 2–1, Dundee 5–3 and Sporting Lisbon – on penalties, after a 1–1 draw – to become the unexpected holders of the Dr. Caecor Batista Trophy. It's size belied its importance. City fans remained largely unimpressed (being suspicious of foreign dealings) and the trophy broke in transit, anyway.

So we had to wait for the pre-season friendlies, and by the time the early training was completed with all the usual sweaty effort, publicity, verbal paraphernalia, promises, veiled hints and managerial

3

Graham Paddon, fair-haired midfield man from Coventry whose long throw has become an integral part of City's "set piece" strategy.

hocum, and by the time Ipswich were at Carrow Road on August 4th, the general situation had not really changed.

By this time, too, Albert Bennett was playing again alongside Silvester and Foggo, but the Ipswich game, and the succeeding friendly at Peterborough, proved merely that Bennett's physical problems were something he had not been able to overcome. Alas, he was not to appear in the senior side again.

But if the pre-season build-up had been uneventful and to a certain extent uninviting, the opening game at Luton was the opposite. Dour, yes, with Howard playing in attack and 70 minutes of defensive solidarity; but the thrills came in plenty in the closing 30 seconds. From a twice-taken penalty Paddon earned the side a 1–1 draw. It was as much as we could expect.

Next Portsmouth, and a 13,000 crowd at Carrow Road, this time with Malcolm Darling pitched in at the deep end. And this time a 3–1 victory kept the fans reasonably happy. But two goalless draws

Five games five goals: gates down to 11,000

against Fulham at Craven Cottage, and against Orient at Carrow Road, provided an apt reminder that still things were not as they should be.

By this time the burden of the front runners was being shared by Darling, Foggo and Silvester, but it was a low key formation short in height and penetration.

Against Carlisle, Silvester squeezed the winner, and against Brighton Livermore and Foggo scored the goals necessary to put the Canaries into the third round of the League Cup. But the writing was on the wall. They had scored only five goals in their first five League games. Gates were down to 11,000. It seemed an irrelevance that at this stage the top of the Second Division table read:

TERRY ANDERSON breaks into a smile as he watches his header pass the outstretched arm of Coventry 'keeper Bill Glazier during the friendly match with the Sky Blues. It was a mid-season tension easer.

	P	W	D	L	F	A	Pts
Blackpool	6	4	0	2	11	4	8
Bristol City	5	3	2	0	13	6	8
Norwich	**5**	**2**	**3**	**0**	**5**	**2**	**7**
Hull	5	3	1	1	4	2	7
Millwall	5	2	3	0	8	6	7
Q.P.R.	5	2	2	1	9	4	6

It was at this point that the reactionary handbills appeared, bemoaning City's lack of a striker and urging a boycott of the next home game against Oxford. Hoax or not – and the extent of their distribution was never successfully discovered – the bills nevertheless achieved their object of obtaining publicity. It is possible that knowledge of them stung the side to such an extent that they won their next four games – at Blackpool, against Oxford (the boycott call was a flop, for the 14,000 gate was above average), at Ashton Gate and at Deepdale, where two goals in the last 14 minutes gave the Canaries the points in another dour, hard match.

But Saunders, in any event, was ahead of the pack. His telephone had scarcely ceased ringing in his attempts to bring the search to fruition, and this time he at least had ammunition of a favourable sort to help in his persuasive discussions.

Nigel Cassidy, a former City player, had put Oxford ahead after only 20 seconds at Carrow Road, but City had recovered sufficiently from the blow to win 3–2 and go, for the first time, to the top of the table.

Then a goalless draw with Q.P.R. – which also attracted a 22,000 crowd – the biggest for four years – put them three points clear at the top. Goals or no, City were sitting pretty, and they were still unbeaten.

The fans' dilemma was obvious. They were uncertain of the side's ability, even disproving of the methods, but gradually they started to come back, and gradually the snowball of Canary fortune began to gather pace.

Carlisle were smashed 4–1 in the third round of the League Cup, three of the City goals coming in the last 32 minutes; it was the side's 12th successive unbeaten game (which equalled the 1953/54 record); and that same night, as that same match was in progress, they paid a club record fee of just over £40,000 to Rochdale for striker David Cross.

And from that point on the Canaries were on their way to Division One. The line-up by now was fairly settled: Keelan, as ever, was in goal; Payne, Forbes, the ultra-reliable Stringer and Butler were the back four; Anderson, Livermore and Paddon formed the mid-field trio, with Silvester, Foggo and Cross, taking over from Howard, in front.

They earned a 1–1 draw at Sunderland. Thirteen games undefeated. A new club record. And in the space of four days in October Burnley (a classic encounter, this) and Luton were both beaten in two splendid games at Carrow Road which yielded six goals for the Canaries and a combined gate of over 47,000.

There were three other significant facets to the Luton game. Before the kick-off, first the Supporters' Club handed over a cheque for £30,000, and then Saunders was presented with a gallon of whisky – his prize for having been selected Second Division Manager of the Month. The third facet was that, for the first time, perhaps, it began to dawn upon us that City might, after all, be in line for an unusually good season.

Cup-tie casualty: David Stringer is carried off against Chelsea

On October 16th the top of the table read:

	P	W	D	L	F	A	Pts
Norwich	**13**	**8**	**5**	**0**	**20**	**7**	**21**
Millwall	12	6	6	0	21	14	18
Bristol City ...	12	7	2	3	25	12	16
Burnley	13	7	2	4	24	14	16
Middlesbro'...	12	7	1	4	18	15	15
Sunderland ...	12	5	5	2	17	15	15
Q.P.R.	12	5	4	3	16	9	14
Birmingham ..	12	4	5	3	15	10	13
Luton	12	2	8	2	12	12	12
Oxford	13	3	6	4	13	13	12
Swindon......	12	4	4	4	9	9	12

Millwall had been trailing the Canaries for most of the season, and when the time came for the clash the general feeling was that a point from the Den would do. After all, City were three points ahead, they were the only unbeaten side in all four Divisions, and they also possessed the best defensive record in all four Divisions – a mere seven goals conceded in 13 outings.

Alas, reality was tougher than dreams in this instance. An own goal after five minutes by the luckless Stringer gave Millwall the whip hand, and although Silvester pulled one back, the Lions roared to a 2–1 victory. It was City's first defeat of the season.

Three days later City hung on by their fingernails to avoid defeat at Grimsby in the League Cup, in one of the most exciting and emotional matches of the season.

Then, four days after that, Cardiff were beaten 2–1 at Carrow Road in an inauspicious match notable only for the fact that Duncan Forbes damaged his hamstring in the 37th minute.

But it was to have the most serious repercussions.

It was perhaps the end of the first phase of City's promotion campaign. It was the point when City started to worry (Forbes was to miss the next 18 senior matches), and the point where the fans began to ask questions.

"Will the sports writers never give City credit?" asked one in the correspondence columns of the Pink Un of October 30th. "I could have heard a pin drop; where were all the fans at Millwall?" asked another.

It was a good question, and yet on November 11th, when Grimsby came for the League Cup replay, over 27,000 of them turned up to see the Mariners beaten 3–1 after a fine fight. Govier had been called in to replace Forbes, but the move lasted only three games.

Hull were beaten at Boothferry Park (it was Keelan's 300th appearance), and Birmingham held to a 2–2 draw at Carrow Road (Govier scoring, then conceding a penalty). But it was a close thing. Birmingham were allowed to look better, perhaps, than they should have done, and when mighty Chelsea came for their fifth round League Cup-tie Terry Anderson had been given the task of filling Forbes' role, Briggs coming in at left-half and Howard replacing the Cup-tied Cross.

The attendance (35,927) was Carrow Road's biggest since 1967. And the 1–0 reverse was the first home defeat of the season.

But at least the country was aware of the stirrings of muted excitement in East Anglia. Sheffield Wednesday were held 1–1 at Hillsborough in a continual snowstorm, and Middlesbrough were beaten 2–0 at Norwich, a result which put the Canaries a comforting and staggering six points clear of the third club.

On December 4th, Peter Silvester made his 100th appearance for the Canaries, and promptly celebrated by scoring the goal that beat Swindon at the County Ground. And the following week Graham Paddon, also making his 100th appearance, scored City's only goal against Watford.

The match, however, was a bitter disappointment. Watford were off form and bottom of the table and yet City, ostensibly the best in the Division, failed to stamp their authority on a match which eventually ended 1–1. There was not a great deal of surprise, therefore, when at Brunton Park on December 18th – a match attended, incidentally, by 72 fans who had flown in chartered D.C.3's from Norwich airport – the Canaries were turned inside out and tossed aside by a United side who were 2–0 ahead in 15 minutes.

The final score was 3–0, and City's campaign seemed to be grinding to a halt. Obviously, something had to be done.

Something was done, on Christmas Eve, and the new arrival was Phil Hubbard, a £20,000 signing from Lincoln, who stepped straight into the side for the Boxing Day game against Charlton.

City were unloved nationally and treated suspiciously locally, yet their position was such that they demanded attention. And so it was that 31,041 (the biggest League gate since 1961) came and cheered and watched Charlton being defeated, convincingly, and ironically by the same margin as City had lost at Carlisle nine days before.

It was a renewal of faith for the fans and a statement of intent by the club, and when City won 2–0 at Oxford and followed that with a 2–1 win over Fulham it seemed that the promotion chase was hotting up again – with City firmly established as favourites. Of course, we should have known better.

Payne at his post: ever-present

Clive graduated from youth teams

Hull came in the third round of the F.A. Cup on January 15th, and although the Canaries were reasonably confident – indeed, even torn between two loyalties, League and Cup – there was a feeling that defeat would not altogether be a bad thing; the worst thing would be a replay, an extra game.

But no one really forecast that Hull would win so decisively. It was Dave Stringer's 300th appearance, yet even he could not camouflage the fact that Norwich's game had gone off the boil, that they had become hesitant and uncertain just at a time when they might be expected to spread their wings. The Great Grey Period was with us, and it was to last, to all intents and purposes, for the next nine matches.

The root of the trouble, of course, was that City had been at the top for so long. The pressure was building up, and though Alan Black had replaced Butler at left-back, the side still lacked stability.

They clung to a point against Preston, lost disappointingly and testily at Burnley and – with loan player Bobby Bell, from Crystal Palace, at centre-half – fought a magnificent 2–2 draw with Millwall. A point at Ninian Park was followed by a shattering 4–0 defeat at Birmingham, even though Jim Bone (a £30,000 signing from Partick) had been brought in to sharpen a toothless attack.

The leading positions were:

	P	W	D	L	Ps
Millwall	31	14	14	3	42
Norwich	**30**	**15**	**11**	**4**	**41**
Sunderland	31	13	12	6	38
Birm'gham	30	12	13	5	37
Middlesbro'	30	16	4	10	36
Q.P.R.	30	13	9	8	35

Sunderland took another point in a 1–1 draw, and although the gloom was relieved by a 2–0 win over Hull, and although City were back on top of the table again, a 2–1 defeat at Fratton Park, in a miserably unattractive match, heralded in the crisis point and, indirectly, the final phase.

Saunders worked a miracle at Trowse that week. When City re-emerged they were cocky and confident, and from that point they never looked back. It was Division One all the way from then on.

Blackpool were swamped 5–1 (the average gate by this time had climbed to 21,900), and a frantic Easter brought four points from key games against Charlton, Rangers and Bristol City.

An 81st-minute goal from Forbes beat Sheffield Wednesday, and despite a check at Ayresome, where

Middlesbrough engineered City's sixth League defeat, victory over Swindon a week later steadied the ship and left East Anglia in a fever of belated excitement.

They needed two more points to clinch the matter, and at a conservative estimate 3,000 travelled to Brisbane Road the following Monday to see them clinch it. And they did. Goals from Foggo and Paddon sparked the celebrations.

And what celebrations they were! East Anglian reserve went by the board as the fans spilled on to the pitch, calling for their heroes and, no doubt, leaving Orient's own supporters recalling bitterly the days, not so very long ago, when they too had their moment of glory.

But although promotion had been clinched there still remained the championship issue. Anxious looks were still cast in the direction of Birmingham – and when it came to the last, key game of the season it seemed that practically the whole of City's following had decided to be at Watford to will their heroes to the title.

Vicarage Road must have seemed like home territory to the Canaries as they took the field in front of Watford's biggest attendance of the season. And in spite of the rain, in spite of a nailbiting second half in which doomed Watford threatened too much and too often for East Anglian peace of mind, the point needed for the championship was won.

Fittingly, it was Player of the Year Dave Stringer whose early goal did the trick. Watford's equaliser heightened the tension, taughtened the anticipation . . . and then it was all over, and the celebrations began again. The red shirts that the Canaries had worn to avoid a clash with Watford's colours were flung to a crowd saturated with emotion – and the glory trail that night led all the way back to Norwich.

City had achieved what nine months before had seemed the impossible; and that for much of the season without the inspiration of Forbes, without the striking power of Silvester who, injured in the home game with Preston in January, had to spend the rest of the campaign in the reflected glory of his colleagues.

All that remained was the pomp and ceremony befitting the champions – and a summer of anticipation.

PHIL HUBBARD, the fans' extra Christmas present when he was signed from Lincoln on Christmas Eve for £20,000. He has had to fight for a first team place and has also been troubled with injury.

Voice of the skipper! Duncan Forbes (above) gives vent to a captain's feelings while (below) his team show their own brand of enthusiasm to mark one of the goals that sank Blackpool at Carrow Road.

A FIRST DIVISION SMILE FROM

MISS CANARY

Looking champion, and no wonder! June Stangroom, 21-year-old assistant salesgirl from New Costessey, gives the camera a First Division smile after being voted Miss Canary, 1972. June became Norwich City's first Division One beauty queen in a contest at the Supporters' Social Club, winning the title from an entry of ten, with Gillian Tooke, 17, of Norwich second and 16-year-old Susan Mason of Taverham third.

10

Action from Peter Silvester, the striker from Reading who missed the last three months of the season through injury.

11

Before . . . and after. David Cross (above) steers the ball past Bryan King to give City a 2–1 lead against close rivals Millwall and (below) the celebration that followed. Right, newest Canary Jim Bone in full cry for goal.

WATNEYS PALE

What the other...

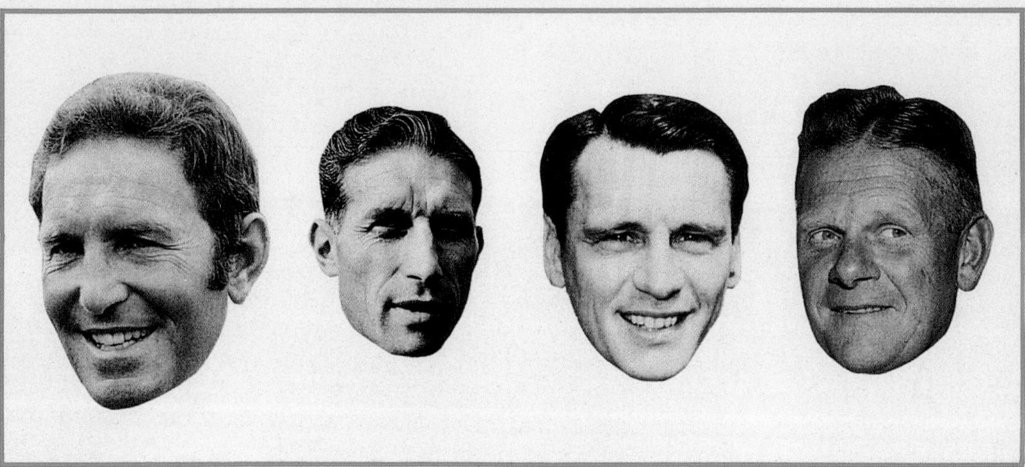

From the left: Dave Sexton, Ron Ashman, Bobby Robson and Alan Hardaker.

DAVE SEXTON, manager of Chelsea, was given a preview of Norwich City's First Division potential when Chelsea met the Canaries in a Football League Cup clash at Carrow Road.

Sexton says: "I consider our 1–0 win over Norwich was one of our best performances of the season. I am very proud of the way my team survived a hell of a lot of pressure.

"I was delighted because Norwich are such a good all-round side . . . a great credit to their manager, Ron Saunders. Even though they had a couple of injury problems, they threw everything at us.

"I prefer not to talk about individuals, but I think they will do well enough at Carrow Road to hold their own in the First Division. Norwich have similar qualities to Sheffield United who were promoted a season earlier. United made an impressive start because of their all-round effort – and I think City should manage to finish mid-way."

RON ASHMAN, the man who as player and manager saw the Canaries through so many eventful years, said from Scunthorpe, where he has added to East Anglian good humour by steering the Fourth Division club to promotion:

"It's a tremendous performance, by a team who haven't really been together for that long. If you can keep a team together for a couple of years you have a chance of getting there. This City team haven't been together for that time. They have done wonderfully well.

"When you think of the years gone by, of the managers who have tried to take City up and failed, it reflects great credit on the lads who have done it – and after all, that's where it is achieved, out there on the pitch.

"I know how it was at Scunthorpe in the last month. We didn't play well, because of the tension; but we fought, and won through.

"It must be a great feeling for everyone connected with City, especially after the Ipswich successes of recent years. But they're there at last!"

IPSWICH Town's manager **BOBBY ROBSON,** a man with more interest than most in the Canaries' promotion to the top flight says: "I am delighted for East Anglia that they have got promotion.

"Next season there will be a keen sense of rivalry between the two clubs and it should be very interesting. It has been missing from football in the area and will be good for the game here.

"I think that Ron Saunders has got 11 honest and genuine workers and if he can get these players going for him next season he could do well. He has a bit of skill in the right places and they have not conceded many goals – and this means confidence.

"There is hardly a bad side in the First Division, although two have to be relegated every year. I often compare the hard monthly programmes we have with the comparatively easy ones of the Second Division and that is one of the headaches Ron will have next year.

"All credit is due to him and he must take the bulk of the praise. Now we must see how he and his team do in the top flight. I wish both him and his

14

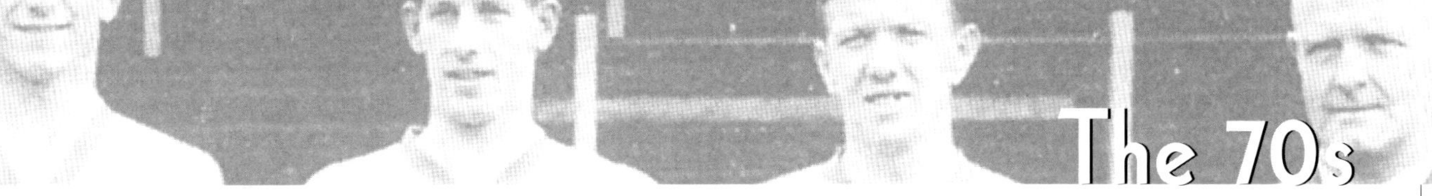

side all the luck in the world and am looking forward to meeting them."

FOOTBALL League Secretary **ALAN HARDAKER** was full of praise. "I think, first of all, I must congratulate the club, the players and the manager on a wonderful season. They have been front-runners for most of the season and it is a wonderful achievement to make their way to the First Division.

"Their promotion will be good for football and the Football League. It is going to spark interest in an area which has for a long time been starved of football, with Norwich joining Ipswich."

TED BATES, a native of Thetford who has gone on to become manager of Southampton – "CONGRATULATIONS! I am really delighted because no club deserves it more. You have had to work really hard and we can appreciate that from our own promotion days.

"Personally I am looking forward to coming to play Norwich next season. They have developed from a side who played it very tight last season, giving nothing away into a side that could win matches.

"I have tremendous admiration for any manager, player or chairman who can get promotion to Division One. Ron Saunders has done a tremendous job and I feel particular admiration for Geoffrey Watling who always stuck at the task of getting them out of Second Division football.

"Good luck and see you next season. . . ."

JIMMY BLOOMFIELD, manager of Leicester, who have had one season in the "big time" – "I am delighted for them that they have joined the exclusive band of clubs who have reached the First Division.

"But I would also like to add a word to the fans. . . . Be patient with them next year and give them all the encouragement they need.

"The biggest problem in the First Division and the big difference between that and the Second is that there are no bad sides. There is no let-up and if you do badly at home one week you face an even stiffer task away the following Saturday."

JOHN HARRIS, who took Sheffield United into the First Division last year and knows the elation and frustration of a first season says: "Norwich will do all right. They're strong in defence and that's important. They give nothing away.

"I think they'll hold their own in the First without setting the house on fire."

FOR IAN GREAVES at Huddersfield the boot is on the other foot. After two seasons in "a different world" he is on his way back into Division Two again.

"They'll need a lot of support and cash. The biggest problem is scoring goals. You can match teams for fitness and workrate but when you're up there you must have players who take their chances. But I think Norwich will be O.K."

...managers say

From the left: Ted Bates, Jimmy Bloomfield, John Harris and Ian Greaves.

Ron Saunders and

1. ....

1. Ron Saunders
2. Terry Anderson
3. Alan Black
4. Jim Bone
5. Max Briggs
6. Geoff Butler
7. David Cross
8. Ken Foggo
9. Duncan Forbes

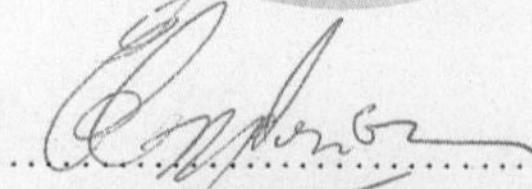

2. ....
3. ....

6. ....
7. ....
8. ....

12. ....
13. ....
14. ....

his crusading Canaries

Two pages for the autograph hunter

10. Trevor Howard
11. Phil Hubbard
12. Kevin Keelan
13. Doug Livermore
14. Graham Paddon
15. Clive Payne
16. Peter Silvester
17. David Stringer

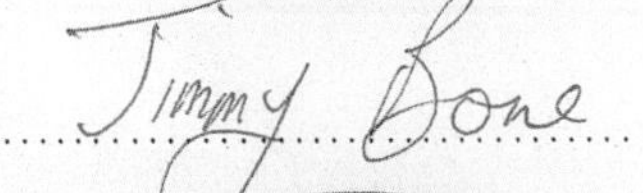

4\. ....

5\. ....

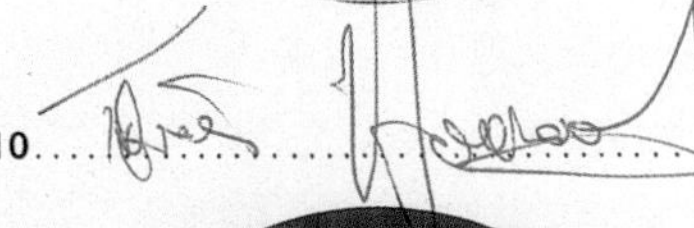

9\. ....

10\. ....

11\. ....

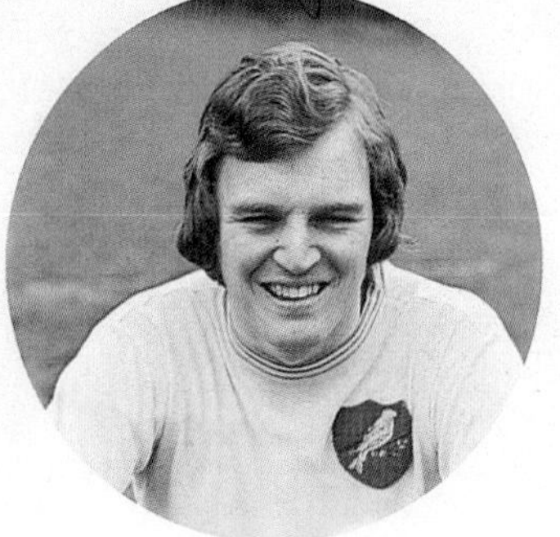

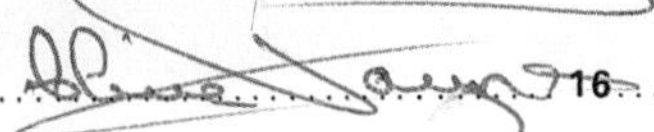

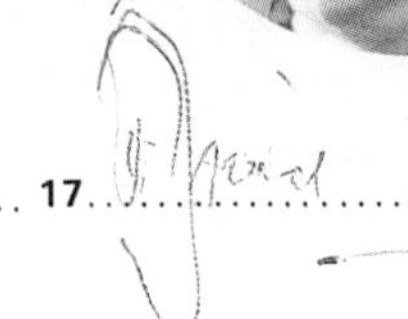

15\. ....

16\. ....

17\. ....

Ken Foggo (above) and Doug Livermore face the opposition.

the BIG twenty

THESE are the BIG Twenty; the football clubs already occupying the world's most elite soccer section – Division One of the Football League. And they are waiting for Norwich City and their promotion partners. Honours shown here exclude any the club might win this season.

ARSENAL: (manager Bertie Mee). Founded 1886; League champions eight times, F.A. Cup-winners four times. Ground, Highbury. Colours: red shirts with white sleeves, white shorts.

CHELSEA: (manager Dave Sexton). Founded 1905; League champions once, F.A. Cup-winners once. Ground, Stamford Bridge. Colours, Royal blue shirts, royal blue shorts with white stripe down seam.

COVENTRY CITY: (acting manager Bob Dennison). Founded 1883. Ground, Highfield Road. Colours, Sky blue shirts, dark blue neck and cuffs, sky blue shorts.

CRYSTAL PALACE: (manager Bert Head). Founded 1905. Ground, Selhurst Park. Colours, White shirts with broad claret and blue stripe down centre of chest and back, white shorts.

DERBY COUNTY: (manager Brian Clough). Founded 1884; F.A. Cup-winners once. Ground, Baseball Ground. Colours, White shirts, blue shorts.

EVERTON: (manager Harry Catterick). Founded 1878; League champions seven times, F.A. Cup-winners three times. Ground, Goodison Park. Colours, Royal blue shirts, white shorts.

IPSWICH TOWN: (manager Bobby Robson). Founded 1880. League champions once. Ground, Portman Road. Colours, Royal blue shirts, white shorts.

LEEDS UNITED: (manager Don Revie). Founded 1919. League champions once. Ground, Elland Road. Colours, White shirts, white shorts.

LEICESTER CITY: (manager Jimmy Bloomfield). Founded 1884. Ground, Filbert Street. Colours, Blue shirts, white shorts.

LIVERPOOL: (manager Bill Shankly). Founded 1892; League champions seven times, F.A. Cup-winners once. Ground, Anfield Road. Colours, Red shirts, red shorts.

MANCHESTER CITY: (general manager Joe Mercer, team manager Malcolm Allison). Founded 1887; League champions twice, F.A. Cup-winners four times. Ground, Maine Road. Colours, Sky blue shirts with white trimmings, white shorts.

MANCHESTER UNITED: (manager Frank O'Farrell). Founded 1880; League champions seven times, F.A. Cup-winners three times. Ground, Old Trafford. Colours, Red shirts with white trimmings, white shorts.

NEWCASTLE UNITED: (manager Joe Harvey). Founded 1882; League champions four times, F.A. Cup-winners six times. Ground, St. James' Park. Colours, black and white vertically-striped shirts, black shorts.

SHEFFIELD UNITED: (manager John Harris). Founded 1889; League champions once, F.A. Cup-winners four times. Ground, Bramall Lane. Colours, Red and white vertically-striped shirts, black shorts.

SOUTHAMPTON: (manager Ted Bates). Founded 1885. Ground, The Dell. Colours, Red and white vertically-striped shirts, black shorts.

STOKE CITY: (manager Tony Waddington). Founded 1863. Ground, Victoria Ground. Colours, Red and white vertically-striped shirts, white shorts.

TOTTENHAM HOTSPUR: (manager Bill Nicholson). Founded 1882; League champions twice, F.A. Cup-winners five times. Ground, White Hart Lane. Colours, White shirts, navy blue shorts.

WEST BROMWICH ALBION: (manager Don Howe). Founded 1879; League champions once, F.A. Cup-winners five times. Ground, The Hawthorns. Colours, Navy blue and white striped shirts, white shorts.

WEST HAM UNITED: (manager Ron Greenwood). Founded 1900; F.A. Cup-winners once. Ground, Upton Park. Colours, Claret shirts with blue sleeves and claret and blue facings, white shorts.

WOLVERHAMPTON WANDERERS: (manager Bill McGarry). Founded 1877 League champions three times, F.A. Cup-winners four times. Ground, Molineux. Colours, Old gold shirts with black ring round neck and cuffs, black shorts.

Where's the ball ..?
—RON SAUNDERS

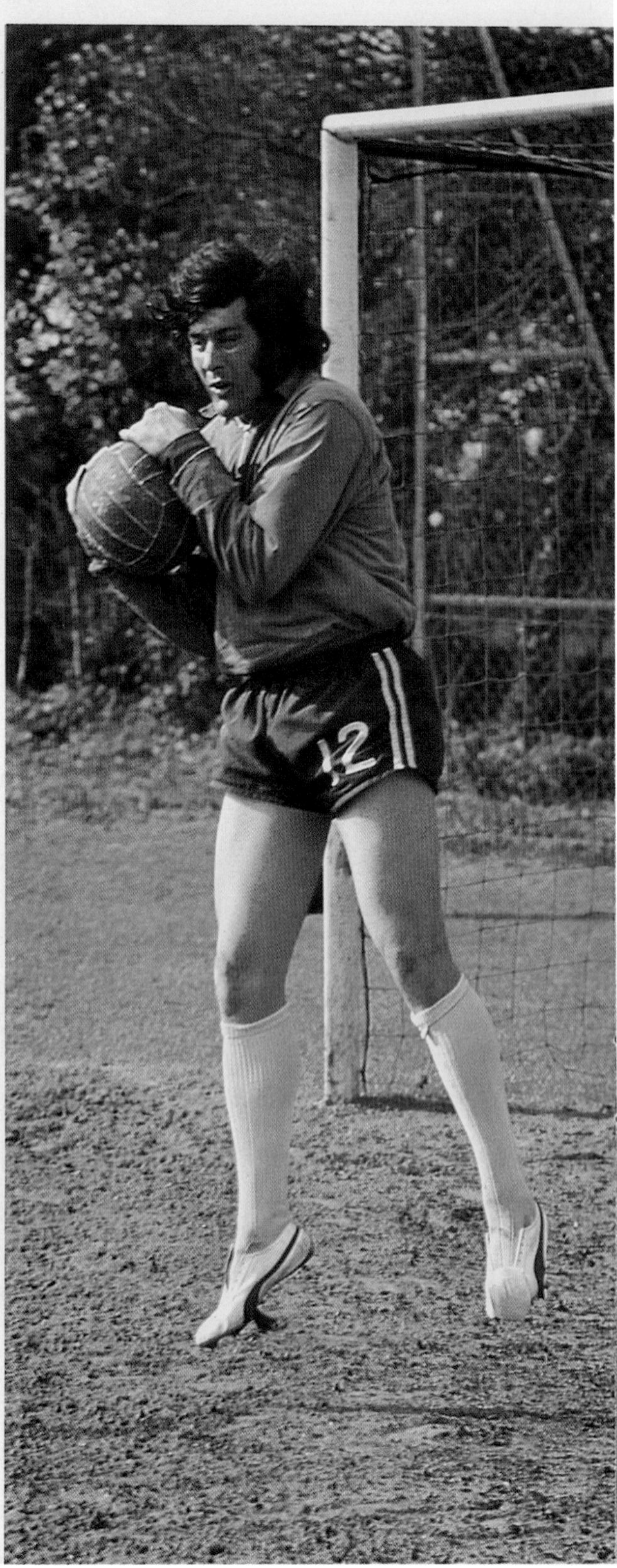

... I've got it!
—KEVIN KEELAN

The goal that eased the end-of-season tension. Duncan Forbes (above) heads the winner against Swindon. Below, the midfield partnership of Doug Livermore and Graham Paddon in typical action.

"It's about time – reckon we've been queueing long enough!"

Alan Black (left) and Geoff Butler (above), the two ex-Sunderland defenders who have shared the left-back berth in the City line-up.

22

Must rush, the other line is ringing....

KEITH SKIPPER
takes a flippant behind-the-scenes look at the First Division scene

"AND YOU can tell the company that giving away sock tabs to the fans is one thing, but dishing out plastic petrol pump attendants for every goal scored is quite another."

* * *

"Yes, Mr. Bremner and Mr. Sprake will be at the Happy Motoring Forecourt by 7.45. They'll want stamps, Mr. Mexaco. Thanks. Must rush, the other line is ringing. . . ."

* * *

"Hello, this is Dour Don the Pride of Yorksh . . . Revie speaking. Norwich? Where's that? Oh, didn't we meet your lot in the Fairs Cup on a night of sleet and raw emotion in one of those Low Countries in 1966? Sorry – you're obviously English.

* * *

"Turn right at King's Lynn, then take the . . . I know, I'll pop a map in the post. Must rush, the other line is ringing. . . ."

Carrots, Cornflakes

"And you can tell the company that after banning the boys from B.B.C. I'm not having Jimmy Hill's lot tainting the Baseball Ground with a penalty-kicking contest for donkeys. And I suppose we have to supply the carrots and a shovel.

* * *

"Look, I told Mr. Kellogg that teams like ours don't appear on the back of cornflake packets. Yes, Mr. Hector and Mr. Hinton will be at the Stars' Fancy Dress Ball. Must fly, the other line is buzzing. . . ."

"Hello, this is Breezy Brian the darling of Derb . . . Clough speaking. Norwich? I've heard of you and those Cup exploits of yesteryear. Well David – sorry, I call everyone that – welcome to the most exclusive club in the world. You'll be all right if you graft and pack a few thou. in every week.

* * *

"Turn right at Corpusty and ask for . . . I know, we'll send directions by post. Must fly, the other line is buzzing. . . . "

Touchline Band

"And you can tell the company that I don't like the idea of a Manchester pop group called the Touchline Band. I've told you before, it's not to make an outlandish impression that I wear these fluorescent shirts, but some of these grounds don't have top-grade floodlights.

* * *

"Yes, Mr. Bell and Mr. Lee will be available for the pantomime again. Must dash, the other line is ringing – and that's one line I am allowed near."

* * *

"Hello, this is Magnetic Malcolm, the Magician of Maine . . . Allison speaking. Norwich? Come on in, the water's fine. It's one hell of a sweat up here, and my task is that much harder since Joe took that syndicated column.

* * *

"Turn left at Torino, and you can get a cup of tea at Denis Laws's old digs . . . I know, I'll get literary Joe to slip a route in the post. Must dash, the other line is ringing – and that's one line I am allowed near."

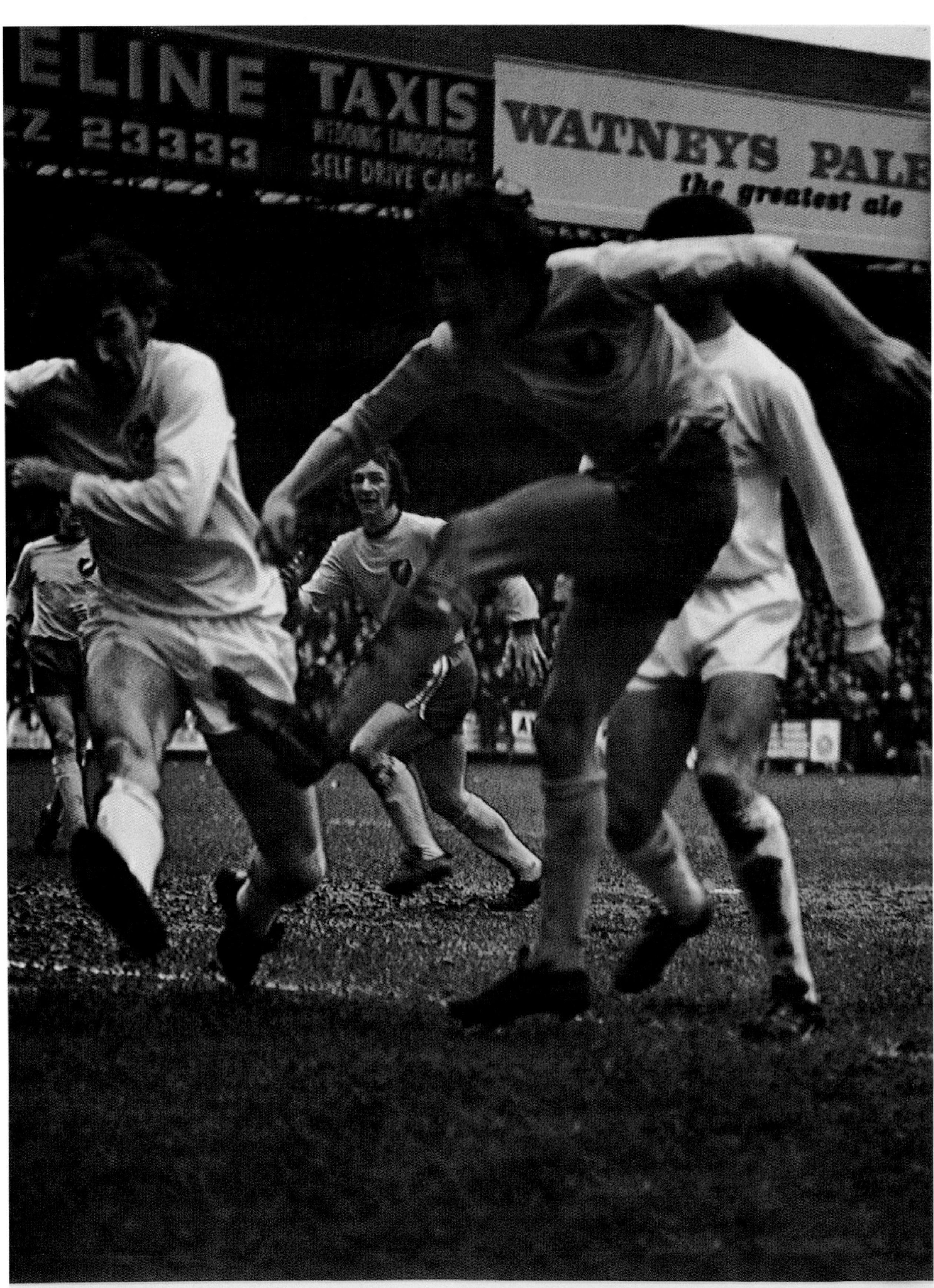

The Canaries' attack on the warpath. Ken Foggo is framed by David Cross' arm and leg as the City centre forward lashes the ball goalwards.

70 YEARS OF CANARIES

Picture that sums up the quaintness and atmosphere of City's former headquarters at the Nest, the former chalkpit that, in 1935, was classed by the F.A. as unsafe for large crowds.

by Ted Bell

It all started nearly 70 years ago, in the summer of 1902.

The spadework had been done by J. C. Nutchey and R. Webster, and on June 17th a general meeting was called at the Criterion Cafe, when a motion, "that the time has now arrived when it is desirable to form a Norwich City Football Club," was carried.

At that time the kings of Norwich soccer were C.E.Y.M.S., and there were many who wondered whether the city could support two clubs of such standing. "Why try and ruin the Church"? it was asked at the inaugural meeting. The question aroused stormy comment.

The new club was formed, however, and with players drawn from a number of local sides took the field for the first time at Newmarket Road on September 6th 1902, when a crowd of about 2,000 saw the President, Sir Samuel Hoare, kick off in a friendly against Harwich. City lined up: W. Sparks; G. Bardwell, W. Cracknell; W. Crome, G. Yallop, J. Yallop; F. Witham, B. Playford, R. W. Collinson, J. Shields, T. Newell.

Ron Davies sports his first Welsh 'cap', won during Carrow Road days

The match was drawn 1–1, to Shields going the honour of scoring Norwich City's first-ever goal.

The new club soon became firmly established. Elected to the Norfolk and Suffolk League they finished their first season in third place. The crusade had started.

Leading light in those early days was secretary Arthur Turner. Arthur's aim was simple: to make Norwich City the leading club in East Anglia. His quest for the best players in the area did nothing for his popularity among the players' clubs; but his skin was thick, his persistence was remarkable, and City steadily increased in strength.

In their second season, with Collinson as skipper, they had more than 500 members, gate receipts totalled over £750, and in the Amateur Cup, City reached the divisional semi-finals before losing to Ealing at Newmarket Road.

That season also produced another crisis in relations between City and C.E.Y.M.S. Chosen as the first teams to compete for the Norwich Hospital Cup, they played a goalless draw in a grim atmosphere tensioned by a City protest that the Church players were not eligible as their names had not been sent to the competition secretary 28 days before the match.

Feelings rose high and it was not until the Mayor intervened and called on the clubs' sporting instincts that the hatchet was buried and a second game played, City this time winning by two clear goals.

In the following season occurred the incident that changed the whole course of City's history and set them on the road by which they have travelled to the doorstep of Division One. In January 1905, three of the club's officials were suspended by the F.A. for the rest of the season following an inquiry into alleged payment of players. The club was declared professional and a meeting was called at the Agricultural Hall to discuss the possibility of forming, officially, a professional club in Norwich.

The chairman, Wilfrid Burgess, said that having been declared a professional club, Norwich City meant to take the F.A. at their word and see if good could not be produced out of evil. A limited liability company was formed; John Bowman of Queens Park Rangers was appointed manager and secretary and on May 30th Norwich City were elected to membership of the Southern League.

They were by no means an automatic choice. Other "hopefuls" included Leyton, Crystal Palace, Grays United and Clapton Orient, and Luton were seeking re-election. Orient, however, were voted into the Second Division and the result of the Southern League ballot was: Luton 31, Norwich City 21,

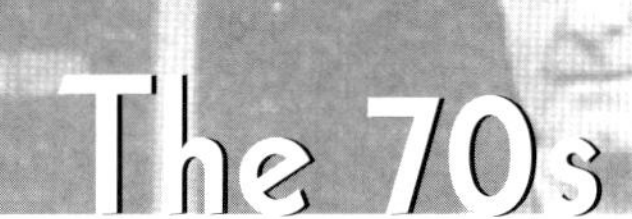

FACES FROM PAST

JOHN BOWMAN

CHARLIE WILLIAMS

DAVIE ROSS

Palace 18. No other votes were cast. City had used their persuasive powers to good effect.

Meanwhile, Bowman had been organising his forces. Even before the vital votes had been cast several attractive friendlies had been arranged. One was against Derby County – for whom the immortal Steve Bloomer netted three times in a 6–0 victory – and another against Woolwich Arsenal. In this game Bowman himself donned City's colours (blue and white at that time) and helped his side to a 2–1 success.

To cap a memorable season, City won the Norfolk and Suffolk League title by four clear points and added the Hospital Cup to their sideboard for the second successive season.

Throughout the following close season Bowman continued to add to his playing strength. Early signings included names such as Muir, Graham, Bushell, Ronaldson, Williams, Linward, Archer, McEwen, Cummings, Ross, Wilkinson and Vigar, and more were added as the club approached their first season in professional soccer.

The superstitious would say that they got off on the wrong foot. Their first match was at Plymouth, on September 2nd 1905, and it was reported: "The City's first Southern League encounter has been undertaken and decided amid circumstances of a most sensational character, and will ever be remembered by those players and officials who embarked on this most eventful journey".

The train in which the Norwich party were travelling was held up a few hundred yards from Witham, where ten people had been killed in a rail disaster. To add to this unnerving experience, and the consequent travel rearrangements, Bowman and Graham were injured in the match itself, Bowman so badly as to have to leave the field. A 2–0 defeat, therefore, was by no means an unsatisfactory result.

City's line-up that day (and there are still a few around who will remember it) was: Williams; McEwen, Archer; Bowman, Bushell, Cummings; Muir, Graham, Ronaldson, Ross, Linward.

Wilkinson took Graham's place in City's first home match, against Southampton, the following week, and it was he who netted the club's first goal in the Southern League. Despite bad weather, a crowd of nearly 7,000 paid £200 to watch the game. They had to be satisfied with a 1–1 draw and, in fact, City had to wait more than a month for their first Southern League victory. West Ham were the victims, and Ronaldson was the marksman whose only goal won the points.

City had settled, and when at the turn of the year a home victory over Plymouth took them into sixth place, hopes soared. As has so often happened, however, the season subsequently turned sour, and the side eventually did extremely well to finish seventh.

There were compensations. Punch McEwen proved himself an able and popular skipper. Davie Ross made a name for himself as a marksman – he topped the 1905–6 Southern League scoring list – and the Christmas Day fixture with Queens Park Rangers attracted a record 10,245 crowd. Receipts were £301! In the Cup, Ross netted three in a 5–0 away replay victory over Tunbridge Wells Rangers, before a visit to Manchester United ended in 3–0 defeat.

City fans, who in recent years have howled in rage at the departure of such players as Ron Davies

27

and Hugh Curran, can console themselves with the thought that such controversial transfers have not been unique in the club's history. There was an outcry when, in the 1906 close season, Charlie Williams – first in a long line of popular keepers – was not retained. And in February 1907 Ross, with 21 goals to his credit, was transferred to Manchester City.

The move netted City a fabulous £650 plus a £250 guarantee match that was played at Newmarket Road on Easter Tuesday with the Manchester club bringing their full League side and paying their own expenses.

The transfer came a week after a Cup defeat at West Bromwich and it had a disastrous effect on City's fortunes. Two was the most goals the team could muster in any game to the end of the season, and they finished in eighth place.

The next milestone in the club's history was the move from Newmarket Road to the Nest. After only three years of Southern League football it became obvious that new headquarters were needed, and thanks to the energy of chairman John Pyke the move was made to the ground that for nearly 30 years came to be regarded with affection by home supporters, with somewhat harder feelings by a number of visitors.

The Nest was originally a disused chalk pit. This was filled in to make a playing surface; a 50 ft.

JIMMY KERR

First of the Norwich City professional teams – the squad who spearheaded the club's venture into the old Southern League in 1905–6.

Nest–test of skull for unwary!

concrete retaining wall lined a cliff topped by a row of terraced houses and the final result was a compact, picturesque little ground that threatened imminent danger to those who watched play from its "kop", and one that was rated as worth a goal a match to the home team.

And it was by no means unknown for an unwary visiting player to test the quality of the concrete with his skull!

Change of ground did not bring any upsurge in playing fortunes. For the remainder of their spell in the Southern League, City were never higher than tenth in the table, and entry to the Third Division (South) in 1920 – they were one of the founder members – brought no immediate improvement.

The transfer to the Nest was not without its problems. In 1908 Reading objected that the ground was too small for a Cup-tie, and City played five away Cup games in succession, one of their victories being over Liverpool at Anfield. The Nest was subsequently enlarged, but space was still limited and for the last Cup-tie played there Sheffield Wednesday practised at Hillsborough on a roped-off area the size of the Norwich pitch.

For nine seasons the Canaries figured among the Third Division's mediocrities, their highest position being 11th in 1923–24. Then, in 1929, Jimmy Kerr was appointed manager. City climbed to eighth place in the table – and for the first time supporters were given visions of promotion.

They were quickly disillusioned! In a team-building gamble four of the forwards who had done so well were transferred and in 1930–31 the Canaries ended the season at the bottom of the table.

There were no re-election problems, however, and – not for the first time in their history – Norwich City proceeded to show their fighting qualities. The following year brought a climb to tenth position and in 1932–33 supporters at long last saw their team battling it out with the promotion challengers. Unhappily, Jimmy Kerr did not see the ultimate reward

Springbok-style save from Sandy Kennon

of his work, for at this critical stage he died, and in March 1933 Tom Parker was appointed his successor.

The season ended with City in third place, but Parker proved himself the right man for the job of building on what his predecessor had bequeathed him. He added players like Jack Vinall (from Sunderland), Billy Warnes (Arsenal) and Tommy Halliday (Darlington) to the playing strength, and when the end of the 1933–34 season arrived the Canaries had a clear seven-point lead over the nearest rivals, and Tom Parker had steered the club to the section championship in his first full year of office.

The new ground of the Second Division suited City at first. Without promising further promotion they established a comfortable position. But they lacked staying power.

The end came in 1938–39. It was an unhappy season, but right up to the end City had a chance to fight their way clear of the relegation pairing. With Tranmere certain to go down, the doubtful honour of accompanying them rested between the Canaries and Nottingham Forest.

In their next-to-last fixture the Canaries were at Plymouth, with a home game against Forest to come. A point at Home Park would have done the trick, but a missed penalty proved one of the costliest errors in the club's history. City were left needing to beat Forest by at least four clear goals, and the effort was too much for them. They won, but only by a single goal and so, after five seasons, back they went into Division Three.

Meantime, 1935 had produced another crisis. In May that year the Football Association issued a decree that made an immediate move from the Nest imperative. The rapidity of the events that followed can best be summed up in time-table form:

May 15th—The F.A. write to the club drawing attention to reports they had received of the unsuitability of the Nest for large crowds.

May 18th—City chairman William Hurrell announced "There is a grave possibility of the Nest being declared unsuitable".

June 1st—It was announced that arrangements had been made with J. & J. Colman Ltd. for the club to take over the Carrow Road ground on a 20-year lease. Tenders were invited the same day.

Carrow Road—a two-month building miracle

June 11th—Dumping material for the terraces began.

August 17th—Construction of terraces and stand was completed, except the extreme end of the river-end bank.

It was a remarkable achievement, even by modern standards. Between June 11th and August 16th the stands and practically all the terracing, capable of holding 35,000 spectators were rushed up, and all that remained to be done was the completion of the dressing rooms, offices and general headquarters beneath the main stand.

It can be said without question that the period since the last war has been the most memorable in City's history. The initial boom in public interest, climaxed by the record crowd of 43,129 who watched the F.A. Cup replay with Portsmouth at Carrow Road in January 1950, put the Canaries slap bang into the public eye, and ever since their progress has been marked with a flow of either adulation or criticism.

Any hopes City may have had of a quick return to Division Two were quickly shattered. The war had taken a heavy toll and it was a case of rebuilding almost from scratch. The job was assigned to Cyril Spiers, whose ability as a manager was a long-standing topic of argument.

Spiers, with an intricate filing system and his South Wales "nursery", had a remarkable flair for discovering young players. Whether, had he stayed, he would have been able to mould his material into a promotion side will never be answered, for in

Action in the early days at Newmarket Road.

THE CUP HEROES OF 1958-9

City's 1958–59 Cup team. Back row (left to right) Thurlow, Allcock, Bly, Kennon, Butler, McCrohan, Crowe. Seated: Crossan, Hill, Archie Macaulay (manager), Geoffrey Watling (chairman), Harry Topping (trainer), Ashman, Brennan.

December 1947, he and the club mutually agreed to part company to enable Spiers to return to Cardiff.

In 1947 and 1948 the Canaries had to make further re-election applications. Yet it was during those two seasons that attendances at Carrow Road rocketed to record figures – an enigma that made City one of the most envied of Football League clubs.

Spiers was followed as manager by Duggie Lochhead, who, as a tough, Scottish wing-half had netted the first goal ever scored at Carrow Road – against West Ham, beaten 4 3 in August 1935. Lochhead's leadership brought about a steady improvement, but midway through the 1949–50 season the club decided on another managerial change.

For the rest of the season Norman Low acted as player-manager, while the city hummed with rumours about a new appointment. One name that persisted for some time was that of Arsenal's Tom Whittaker; but the rumours faded and in May 1950 Low, centre-half whose career had taken in Liverpool, Newcastle and Newport, was officially appointed manager.

He promptly exploded the theory that a player cannot step straight into the manager's chair with the same club. In his five years of office the Canaries finished 2nd, 3rd, 4th, 7th and 11th, and their F.A. Cup exploits included the defeats of Liverpool at Carrow Road and Arsenal at Highbury.

The 1950–51 season was extraordinary. In any normal programme the Canaries' total of 65 points would have been more than enough for promotion. Unfortunately, the season also produced Nottingham Forest's "team of all the talents" (so far as Third Division soccer is concerned) and they swept into Division Two with a 70-point total.

Low's era ended in 1955 with the return to City's managerial chair of Tom Parker. But the latter's stay this time was destined to be far different from his first spell in office.

Parker's big signing was Ralph Hunt, from Bournemouth, who held the club's scoring record of 33 goals (in the 1955–56 season) until Terry Allcock smashed it with 37 in 1962–63. Hunt had edged in front of Percy Varco (of "Give it to Varco"! fame), whose record of 32 had stood since 1928.

But despite Hunt's efforts, despite a string of other, necessarily small-fee signings, Parker could not bring success, and in the spring of 1957 came the biggest crisis in City's history.

Faced with back-breaking debts they threw themselves on the mercy of the public – and the public responded magnificently. An appeal fund was launched; the cash to save the club was raised, and in the general upheaval a new board of directors came into being, Tom Parker's contract was terminated and, after a short, suspenseful spell, Archie Macaulay arrived as manager.

And that was the springboard from which Norwich City have leapt to their new-found eminence.

When Macaulay took over it was too late to save the Canaries from yet another cap-in-hand application for re-election. But, buying judiciously with what cash he had available, he set out to ensure that the club did not drop into the new Fourth Division – and he succeeded. He signed Barry Butler from Sheffield Wednesday to stiffen the defence, Terry Allcock from Bolton to boost the attack, and City finished eighth, to take their place in the new Third Division.

They never looked back. The 1958–59 season, with its never-to-be-forgotten Cup run, was unquestionably the club's most golden until 1971–72, and the team who took City to Wembley's threshhold were East Anglia's heroes. Even at this distance the line-up

Ashman's reign: new records in transfer market

flows almost automatically from the lips: Nethercott; Thurlow, Ashman; McCrohan, Butler, Crowe; Crossan, Allcock, Bly, Hill, Brennan.

Heroes, all of them. But it is impossible to avoid special mentionof Ken Nethercott, whose immaculate goalkeeping spanned the years from 1947 to 1959 and who would certainly have added to his 416 League and Cup appearances but for the tragedy at Bramall Lane where he played on despite a dislocated shoulder that, eventually, was to finish his career.

Alongside, and despite the Cup run, the Canaries battled almost to the end of the season to cap their efforts with promotion. They had to be content with third place. But further success was not far away. A nailbiting finish to 1959–60 saw them take second place to Southampton; but by now two clubs had the entree from Division Three to Division Two – and another milestone had been reached.

The impetus of success carried City to fourth place in their first season in the Second Division, but there followed an inevitable run-down. Gradually the giants of the Cup and promotion side disappeared from the Carrow Road scene and the Board, under the enthusiastic chairmanship of Geoffrey Watling, set about the re-building task.

Macaulay went, to be replaced for short spells by Scotman Willie Reid and George Swindin. Then for four years City pinned their faith in the leadership of Ron Ashman, most loyal of clubmen, who had come to Carrow Road soon after the end of the last war and, by the time he had finished playing in 1964, had totted up a remarkable 662 League and Cup appearances for the club.

Ashman's reign saw the Canaries set new records in the transfer market. Tommy Bryceland came from St. Mirren for £20,000; Ron Davies from Luton for £35,000. Other Ashman signings included Kevin Keelan, Gordon Bolland, Mal Lucas, Terry Anderson and Hugh Curran.

The crowd record soared to 43,984 for the visit of Leicester City in the Cup at the end March, 1963.

But the hoped-for assault on the Second Division's top placings never gained full momentum. City reached sixth place in 1964–65, and their Cup exploits included victories over Manchester City at Maine Road (acting-manager Ashman scored both the Canaries' goals there) and Blackpool at Bloomfield Road, and a narrow defeat by Forest at Nottingham. It wasn't enough, however, and in June 1966 Ashman went, to be replaced by Lol Morgan.

The last time a championship trophy was on display in Norwich . . . Stan Ramsay holds the Third (South) shield after City had won the title in 1934. With Ramsay is chairman "Billy" Hurrell, and the occasion was the Hospital Cup match against Grimsby (Division Two champions) at the Nest.

The team-building effort – sustained to a large extent by the magnificent work of the Supporters Club – continued with the arrival of players such as Alan Black (Sunderland), Laurie Brown (Spurs), Mike Kenning (£25,000 buy from Charlton), John Manning (Shrewsbury) and Ken Foggo (West Bromwich).

The climax to Morgan's efforts came in 1968–69 when the club paid £30,000 to Sunderland for Geoff Butler; £40,000 to Sheffield United for Ken Mallender and £25,000 to Newcastle for Albert Bennett. But still it wasn't enough.

The rest of the story is contemporary. Another managerial change, in July, 1969 brought Ron Saunders to Carrow Road – and the three-year "miracle" began.

32

Printed by The Soman-Wherry Press Ltd., Norwich

A Taste of the Big Time

As the years since 1972 are within the living memory of the majority of our readers we shall dispense with our regular events feature and get on with the story of Norwich City FC. Saturday 12 August 1972 will be remembered as the day that City first sampled First Division football. The visitors to Carrow Road were Everton who had reputedly spent over £200,000 to strengthen their side during the close season. City led 1–0 at half time through a goal scored by Jimmy Bone, but the crowd of 25,851 were disappointed as Everton equalised in the second period. Ron Saunders had made no major signings during the summer deciding that the men who had performed so well in the previous campaign should be given another chance. City started their away programme in style when they travelled to Portman Road and beat Ipswich Town 2–1 on Tuesday 15 August 1972. Nearly 30,000, including many from Norwich, witnessed the game. Jim Blair joined the club in September from St Mirren for an £18,000 fee, but his chances that season were to be very restricted. City recorded further notable victories over Arsenal, Tottenham Hotspur and Derby County before a disastrous spell of 19 league games without a win which began on Saturday 18 November 1972 forced them down into the relegation zone. Ken Foggo moved on to Portsmouth in January 1973 and Colin Suggett joined the club the following month. Jimmy Bone joined Sheffield United on 22 February 1973 and was part of the deal that brought the much-travelled Trevor Hockey to Carrow Road. Finally Saunders paid £65,000 for the services of winger Ian Mellor from Manchester City just before the transfer deadline. Despite the recent activity in the transfer market City still hadn't won another league game and it was not until Saturday 14 April 1973 that the tide turned. Chelsea were the visitors that day and City just scraped through with a goal from David Cross. Another victory in the next game at West Bromwich Albion, also by 1–0, and a further win, on an emotional evening, against Crystal Palace, just managed to preserve First Division football for another season.

When it came to the Cup competitions it was a very different story for City battled their way through to two Finals that season. In the Texaco Cup City reached the two legged Final against Ipswich Town by beating Dundee, Leicester City and Motherwell. Unfortunately City lost twice to their old rivals from Suffolk each time by 1–2 and three of the Ipswich goals were scored by players who would in time join Norwich. Peter Morris scored twice at Portman Road and Clive Woods scored one of the goals in the Carrow

Jimmy Bone puts City ahead v Everton at Carrow Road in the club's first ever Division One game on August 12 1972

Terry Anderson scores in City's first ever First Division victory, appropriately against local rivals Ipswich Town at Portman Road

Road leg. In the Football League Cup Norwich City achieved another ambition by winning their way through to a Wembley final, but first they had to suffer a fright at the Semi-Final stage. On Wednesday 13 December 1972 the Canaries visited Chelsea and won 2–0 and were leading 3–2 in the second leg at Carrow Road a week later when a blanket of fog descended. The fog was so dense that referee Gordon Hill abandoned the match with only five minutes of play remaining. After Christmas the fans, all 34,265 of them, gathered at Carrow Road for the second leg to begin again. This time the tie reached a happy conclusion and City were through to Wembley thanks to a goal from Steve Govier. The Final against Tottenham Hotspur was played on Saturday 3 March 1973, but apart from the preliminary antics of the huge Norwich contingent the day was a big disappointment. Substitute Ralph Coates scored the only goal of the match in the second half and it was Mike England and not Duncan Forbes who held the trophy aloft at the end of the game.

Duncan Forbes leading out Norwich City behind Ron Saunders at Wembley in March 1973

Two resignations dominated the 1973–74 season thereby setting the tone for a disastrous second term in the top division. Chairman Geoffrey Watling decided to stand down after nearly 17 years at the helm and he was succeeded on Thursday 30 August 1973 by Arthur South. A further boardroom change saw George Fish resign his vice-chairmanship through ill health to be replaced by Henry Robinson. Arthur South (knighted in June 1974) had been a club director since 1966 and had a proud record of civic service being the chairman of several committees. A forthright speaker with a passion for Norwich and its people he had, as mentioned previously, been instrumental in putting the club back on its feet in 1957 when as Lord Mayor he superbly masterminded the appeal fund. Ron Saunders preached discipline and endeavour and practised what he preached and consequently had his critics. He is rightly remembered in the club's annals as a man with two notable firsts – he took Norwich City to Division One and also to their first appearance at Wembley. Only two league wins in sixteen games culminated in a 1–3 defeat at home to Everton. After the game Saunders resigned following a bitter row in the boardroom. Without a manager team selection was in the hands of a small committee of board members together with trainer George Lee and coach Terry Allcock. The vacant manager's position was not filled until the 25 November 1973 and the new incumbent in the 'hot seat' at Carrow Road was the Colchester born ex West Ham United full back – John Frederick Bond. Upon leaving West Ham, after playing nearly 400 games, he joined Torquay United and played a further 129 games. He coached at Gillingham before moving on to become the manager of Bournemouth. Strangely enough some five years previously he had almost accepted a coaching position at Norwich under manager Lol Morgan. A man of flamboyance and ever ready with an opinion for the media he lavished both praise and controversy during his tenure in office.

His dealings in the transfer market brought such renowned figures as Ted MacDougall, Mel Machin, John Sissons and Phil Boyer to the club. Despite their introduction Bond could do little to arrest the slide into Division Two. There were however two useful runs in the Football League Cup and the Texaco Cup. In the Football League Cup City reached the Semi-final stage before being eliminated by their bogey side Wolverhampton Wanderers and in the Texaco Cup it was Burnley who dashed the Canaries hopes at the same stage. Eleven players made their debuts during a season of constant change, but the task of maintaining First Division status was just too much. John Bond would have to start his first full campaign rebuilding the clubs playing strength in the Second Division.

John Bond's editorial in the opening matchday programme summed up his mood and that of the Norwich public. He wrote "As you all know the last few weeks have been very busy ones and as a result of our efforts we have several new faces in our playing ranks. My aim will be to be among the promotion contenders right from the 'off' and I certainly do not think we have anything to fear from any team in the Second Division". The new arrivals included Peter Morris from Ipswich Town, Tony Powell from Bournemouth and Colin Sullivan from Plymouth Argyle. The unbeaten opening run of seven games augured well and two goals from Ted MacDougall against Manchester United on Wednesday 28 September helped City into second place. On Saturday 12 October 1974 City visited Nottingham Forest and trailed by a single goal at the interval. A second half revival led by Mel Machin, who scored his only hat-trick for the club, meant that City recorded a memorable 3–1 victory. After a disappointing spell midway through the season Bond again entered the transfer market and snapped up Mick McGuire from Coventry City. As the season drew to an exciting climax Bond, feeling that he needed a further experienced player to aid the final push to promotion played his master card. For a mere £50,000 Bond secured from Tottenham Hotspur a player who had represented his country on 67 occasions and was described by Sir Alf Ramsey as being years ahead of his time – he was of course the former England World Cup hero Martin Stanford Peters. The move was an immediate success and consecutive wins against Nottingham Forest and Portsmouth, both by 3–0, ensured that it was Norwich City who accompanied Manchester United and Aston Villa

Above, New striker Ted MacDougall and below, Phil Boyer were early signings by manager John Bond pictured (below left)

Duncan Forbes leads the Canaries out at Wembley to face Aston Villa in March 1975

back into Division One.

The marching display of the combined bands of the Royal Corp of Transport, the 5th Royal Enniskillin Dragoon Guards and the Queen's Own Hussars were said by many to be the highlight of the League Cup Final on Saturday 1 March 1975. The Canaries had embarked upon their annual quest for the Football League Cup on Tuesday 10 September 1974 when they visited Burnden Park, Bolton. The match against the Wanderers resulted in a 0–0 draw. A week later at Carrow Road City were victorious by 3–1, they went on to beat West Bromwich Albion, Sheffield United and Ipswich Town, each time needing a replay, before facing Manchester United at Old Trafford in the first leg of the Semi-Final. After a 2–2 draw City booked their Wembley ticket by overcoming United in the second leg at Carrow Road thanks to a solitary goal by Colin Suggett. Ron Saunders completed the unique hat-trick of taking three different sides to Wembley in successive years namely Norwich City, Manchester City and now Aston Villa. Sadly the game was an uninspiring affair decided by a Ray Graydon penalty rebound ten minutes from the end. The season ended with a fully deserved testimonial for Dave Stringer against the FA Cup holders West Ham United. In front of 13,247 fans a 65th minute Martin Peters goal was equalized by Frank Lampard a minute from time. On a more light-hearted note a statue of former West Ham United and England player Bobby Moore was withdrawn from Madame Tussaud's in London after three years and was melted down.

Club chairman Sir Arthur South was justifiably proud of the new South Stand seats that were added at the end of the 1974–75 season at a cost of £40,000. They were much debated and maligned before finally being accepted by the public. At that time over £100,000 was spent in making the Carrow Road stadium more comfortable and also to bring it into line with Football League and police requirements. New floodlighting had been installed and extra toilet facilities had been added. In addition much work had been undertaken at the Trowse training headquarters and the new complex was opened by the Bishop of Lynn Aubrey Aitken in December 1975. The season itself was greatly anticipated and all eyes were upon the club to see if they could establish themselves in the higher grade. Eventually City finished in 10th position and

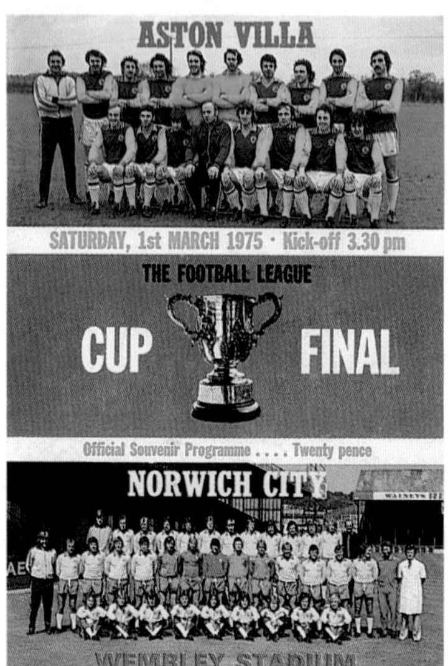

Right, the match programme from the Football League Cup Final against Aston Villa

Far right, Dave Stringer and Colin Suggett in action with Villa's Brian Little

Left, Martin Peters, Phil Boyer and Kevin McGuire celebrate promotion back to Division One in April 1975

Right, Kevin Reeves arrives from Bournemouth

managed to retain parity by recording 16 victories and 16 defeats. Doug Livermore moved on to Cardiff City at the start of the season and Bond managed to sign David Jones from Nottingham Forest in September 1975. The highlight of the campaign was the 3–1 win against eventual champions Liverpool at Anfield on Saturday 29 November 1975. When Liverpool visited Carrow Road on 20 March 1976 the match was sponsored by Dunlop Tyres, it was the first example of outside sponsorship at Norwich, but sadly for the 28,728 crowd Liverpool extracted their revenge and won 1–0. Ted MacDougall headed the list of goalscorers that year with 28 competitive goals and was well supported by Martin Peters with 13 and Phil Boyer with 11. John Bond must have been pleased that his team recorded the double over his old club West Ham United, both the wins were 1–0, and been very proud when his son Kevin came on to the field as an 85th minute substitute for Billy Steele on Saturday 10 April 1976 against Leicester City at Filbert Street.

There was little success in the Cup competitions that season for Manchester City knocked City out of the Football League Cup after two replays and although the Canaries reached the Fifth Round of the FA Cup they made hard work of beating Rochdale in the opening round and were eventually beaten by Bradford City of the Fourth Division 1–2 at Carrow Road. Before the season started the Football Association announced that any player accumulating more than twenty penalty points would automatically face a suspension. The warning obviously had an effect for the number of City bookings fell to 18, a dramatic improvement over the previous seasons total.

There was a rush of transfer activity at the start of the 1976–77 campaign. Peter Morris returned to Mansfield Town, his first Football League club, and took John Miller with him, Mervyn Cawston went to Gillingham and Steve Goodwin left for Southend United. John Ryan joined the club from Luton Town for £42,000. Early in September Ted MacDougall left the club

Colin Suggett, who's goal set the Canaries on the way to their 3–1 win at Anfield in November 1975, seen here with the Barry Butler Memorial Trophy

for Southampton, the fee being only £50,000 and shortly afterwards Dave Stringer left for Cambridge United. The transfer of MacDougall was a particularly bitter blow for the club as he had been the chief goalscorer for the past two seasons and while he was at Norwich he had played 7 times for Scotland. Bond immediately signed Viv Busby from Fulham and then persuaded Tottenham Hotspur to part with Jimmy Neighbour for £75,000. Injuries too played a part in a rather dismal season for Mick McGuire missed the entire campaign after

Manchester United fans on the rampage at Carrow Road in 1977

Below, John Ryan and, bottom right, Martin Peters is presented with a Player of the Month award by Chairman Geoffrey Watling

suffering achilles tendon damage while playing tennis, Graham Paddon broke his leg at Sunderland soon after his return from West Ham United and Phil Boyer missed most of the second half of the season. Peter Osgood had a month's loan in November, but failed to impress and was not retained. In February Kevin Reeves was signed from Bournemouth for £50,000 and another £5,000 was promised if he gained England Under 23 honours. Despite all the comings and goings City managed to maintain their First Division status, but there was no glory in either of the two Cup competitions as the Canaries were quickly eliminated in both. On Saturday 2 April 1977 City had the pleasure of beating Manchester United 2–1 at Carrow Road but the game is sadly more likely to be remembered for the very sorry display of hooliganism by the visiting followers – we can not bring ourselves to use the term fans or supporters.

The 1977–78 season started disappointingly with the sale of Phil Boyer to Southampton for £135,000. The only consolation was that the fee was only slightly less than that paid for him in February 1974. He was the first Canary to be capped by England at senior level when he played against Wales on 24 March 1976. Two goals by David Jones and another by John Ryan helped City to a 3–1 victory at West Ham on the opening day of the campaign, but sadly this was to be their only success on enemy territory all season. The City coach was parked next to a hall where a wedding reception was taking place and it was quickly surrounded by guests, bridesmaids and even the bride herself who posed for a photograph with Martin Peters. In December Viv Busby moved on to Stoke City for £50,000 and on 10 December came City's best result of the season when they beat Liverpool 2–1 at Carrow Road. On 27 December City travelled to Coventry City and lost 4–5 and it would have been 5–5 had not John Ryan missed

a last minute penalty.

When City made the long trip to Ashton Gate to meet Bristol City on Saturday 4 February 1978 Kevin Keelan played for 85 minutes with a broken right hand. Norwich lost 0–3 and Kevin did not play again all season. In the very next home league game on Saturday 25 February Nottingham Forest, who were to head the league at the end of the season, built up a three goal lead in only 24 minutes but City pulled back to level the match 3–3. The third City goal was scored by Keith Robson who had recently joined the club from Cardiff City for £25,000. In March Roger Gibbins was sold to New England Teamen for a fee reported to have been £60,000. The 1971–72 promotion team was re-assembled for Duncan Forbes' testimonial match – they beat the present side 3–0, and 18 days later Forbes, always a favourite at Carrow Road, was recalled to the First team against West Bromwich Albion. The fans went wild as big Duncan equalised for City in the last minute. City finished the season in 13th spot, 5 places higher than Ipswich Town, but it must be said that they did win the FA Cup that season. In the Cup competitions City fell at the first hurdle on both occasions, losing 1–3 to Burnley in the Football League Cup and 0–1 to Orient in the FA Cup after a replay. Orient surprised the football world that year by getting to the Semi-Final before being eliminated by Arsenal. 'Player of the Year' in 1977–78 was John Ryan who also finished top scorer with 16 goals.

The only major transfers at the start of the 1978–79 season were Martin Chivers from Swiss club Servette and central defender Phil Hoadley from Orient in August. In the case of the latter the fee was eventually fixed by a Football League tribunal. Also in August Colin Suggett returned to his native north east when he signed for Newcastle United for £60,000. The season opened brightly with a home victory over Southampton, the score was 3–1 and Chivers was delighted to score against his old club. Before the game with Birmingham City on Saturday 16 September Kevin Keelan received an award for being the best goalkeeper on view in the North American League that summer and also in September the former Aberdeen striker Davie Robb arrived from Tampa Bay Rowdies. 18,426 turned up to watch the testimonial match for Martin Peters against the England 1966 World Cup squad on 18 October 1978. Only Gordon Banks, George Cohen and Ray Wilson from the winning team failed to make an appearance and a good time was had by all. For the record City won 4–2. The lowest point of the season came on Saturday 6 January 1979 when Keith Weller, clad in tights to keep himself warm, inspired Leicester City to a 3–0 victory in the FA Cup at Filbert Street. The performance so incensed manager John Bond that he publicly accused certain of his senior players of not trying and the one to suffer most was Martin Chivers who was promptly dropped and put up for sale. His place in the next match was taken by teenager Justin Fashanu making his debut for the club and soon after Chivers moved on to Brighton & Hove Albion for £15,000. Chivers did in fact make one more appearance for Norwich in the 0–6 thrashing by Liverpool on Wednesday 21 February, a game in which Kevin Keelan broke his thumb in two places and again missed the rest of the season.

The skilful teenager Justin Fashanu made his debut in 1979

In the Football League Cup City accounted for Wrexham (a) 3–1 and Chester (a) 2–0 before going out to Manchester City 1–3 at Carrow Road. At the end of the campaign City finished in 16th place and did not record a single away

Above, Alan Taylor

victory all season. They also set a Football League record when they drew 23 of their games–and between 9 December 1978 and 10 February 1979 they drew seven league games in a row. On Tuesday 24 April 1979 work began on the new River End stand.

In readiness for the start of the 1979–80 season John Bond added central defender Roger Brown from Bournemouth and John McDowell and Alan Taylor from West Ham United to his squad. The latter pair cost in the region of £90,000 each. He also sold full back Ian Davies to Newcastle United for a sizeable fee and obtained the services of John Ryan and Kevin Keelan back on loan from their North American clubs. The opening match of the season was won 4–2 at Everton and it was City's first away win in the Football League for 42 games. The next two matches were at Carrow Road and after recording victories over Tottenham Hotspur and Leeds United City went top of the First Division for the first time in their history. Sadly the run did not continue and City lost the next match at Coventry 0–2. Before the start of the match the Coventry goalkeeper Jim Blyth injured his back during the warm up and had to be replaced by the Coventry City third choice goalkeeper Steve Murcott who was hurriedly called down from his seat in the stand. It turned out to be the only appearance that Murcott ever made in the Football League. In October Kevin Keelan broke Ron Ashman's long standing record of overall competitive appearances for the club, but fate saw to it that he was never to overtake either his total in the Football League or the FA Cup. On 22 November 1979 Kevin Reeves gained his first cap for England at senior level against Bulgaria at Wembley and finished on the winning side (England won 2–0) and on Saturday 24 November 1979 Mark Barham made his first appearance for Norwich City coming on as a 66th minute substitute for Justin Fashanu, it was not a happy debut for City lost the match 0–5. The following week Justin Fashanu was sent off in the home game against Aston Villa for alledgedly kicking Allan Evans. This provoked the much publicised coin throwing incident in which the Aston Villa goalkeeper Jimmy Rimmer was hit. Managers Bond and Saunders both appealed for calm and after five minutes play was able to resume. The episode was largely responsible for a protective fence being erected behind the Barclay goal. Billy Steele, whose career was sadly ended by a knee injury, had a testimonial match against an England Xl on 11 December 1979 and City finished on the wrong end of a 5–0 scoreline. An amazing match took place on Saturday 9 February against Liverpool at Carrow Road. Liverpool won the match 5–3, but Justin Fashanu netted the BBC's 'Goal of the Season'. It was also the end of the road for Kevin Keelan who played his last match for Norwich City. His final total was 673 competitive First team games and he later received an MBE in Her Majesty's Birthday Honours List in June 1980.

On Saturday 15 March 1980 Kevin Bond put through his own goal at Stoke and then converted a penalty and he did exactly the same thing in the very next match at home to West Bromwich Albion. Clive Woods – a lifelong City supporter – joined the club from Ipswich Town in March 1980 and soon afterwards Kevin Reeves left the club to go to Manchester City for £1,000,000. City finished another up and down season in 12th place and recorded only modest runs in the Cup competitions. Wolverhampton Wanderers defeated City in the Fourth round of the FA Cup and Liverpool quashed any plans that City may have had of once more going to Wembley in the Football League Cup. Kevin Bond was the City 'Player of the Year' and Justin Fashanu finished at the top of the goalscoring charts. In May Norwich City became only the second English club to tour China.

Below, Liverpool goalkeeper Ray Clemence looks on in disbelief after Justin Fashanu's superb strike at Carrow Road on 9 February 1980. It became the BBC's 'Goal of the Season'

The 1980–81 season saw an enormous number of changes at Carrow Road and also sadly saw the Canaries slip back into Division Two. Before we look at the major event of the season, the departure of manager John Bond to Manchester City, we must start at the beginning and register the activity in the close season. In July Alan Taylor signed for Vancouver Whitecaps for a large fee and soon afterwards Phil Lythgoe went to Oxford United for £15,000. David Jones was forced to retire through injury and Martin Peters left to become player/manager of Sheffield United. Joe Royle joined the club for a £60,000 fee in early August from Bristol City and in September John Bond signed Drazen Muzinic from Hadjuk Split in Yugoslavia for a record fee of £300,000. With Kevin Bond as skipper City easily overcame Stoke City 5–1 in the opening match, but they then lost their next four league games and everyone at the club knew that it was going to be a difficult season. John Bond moved on to Manchester City on 11 October 1980 and took John Benson and John Sainty with him. Bond's last match in control was the 1–1 draw with Wolverhampton Wanderers and this also proved to be the last match that Duncan Forbes played for the club. On 19 October it was announced that Ken Brown was to be the next manager of Norwich City and Mel Machin was named as his assistant. Tim Sheppard had become the Club's physiotherapist at the start of the season so it was a case of new men all round. Dave Stringer returned from Cambridge United and became Youth team coach and Doug Livermore returned from Cardiff City to look after the Reserves.

Dave Watson joined the club from Liverpool in late November and took a little time to settle in, but he made his debut in the match at Portman Road on Friday 26 December 1980. Amazingly there were still more changes to come and in February Kevin Bond left the club after losing the captaincy to Graham Paddon. Soon Tony Powell was also to leave for America and Martin O'Neill joined the Canaries from Nottingham Forest. City were now in trouble at the foot of the First Division and O'Neill insisted that he should be allowed to leave the club should Norwich City find themselves once more in the Second Division. City's confidence had been badly shaken when they travelled to Manchester City in the Fourth Round of the FA Cup on Saturday 24 January 1980 and were soundly beaten 0–6 by Bond's new team. Yet more new signings were registered when goalkeeper Chris Woods came from Queens Park Rangers on loan and Steve Walford was signed from Arsenal for £175,000.

Four straight wins around the Easter period looked as though it would be enough to keep City in the top flight, but the tension was maintained until the very last game of the campaign. Leicester City, already doomed to Second Division football, visited Norwich on Saturday 2 May 1981 and surprised the 24,675 crowd by winning 3–2. The rest of the teams at the foot of the table all won and left Norwich City stranded in the bottom three – once more City would have to sample football in the Second Division and only time would tell if they possessed the resilience to return at the first time of asking.

Ken Brown took over the manager's role from John Bond

Ken Brown embarked upon his first full season as manager in the summer of 1981 and even he could never have foretold what lay in store in the eventful 1981–82 campaign. Norwich City had first been promoted to Division One at the end of the 1971–72 season and after just two years in the top flight were back in the Second division for the 1974–75 campaign. They gained promotion at the end of that season and remained in the First Division until their drop in 1980–81. Could they possibly get back again at the first time of asking? Chris Woods signed permanently for Norwich before the season got underway for a £225,000 fee and Martin O'Neill left to go to Manchester City for £300,000. In August Brian Clough took young striker Justin Fashanu to Nottingham Forest for £1,000,000 and Keith Bertschin, on his 25th birthday, was bought from Birmingham City as his replacement. In September Keith Robson

Martin O'Neill joined the Canaries for his first spell in 1981

Above left, Keith Bertschin, who is also seen in action on the right scoring against Ipswich Town in the FA Cup 5th round on 14 February 1953

went to Leicester City and the former Scottish international full back Willie Donachie arrived from Portland Timbers for a reported £200,000 – the same fee that Norwich recouped when they sold him back to the same club in the following March. Also in September Shane and Wynton Rufer paid their own fares over from New Zealand for trials and although Norwich offered Wynton, later to star for his country in the World Cup, a contract the Home Office refused him a work permit. In November Roger Hansbury left for Eastern AA in Hong Kong for a nominal fee. John Deehan came on a months loan from West Bromwich Albion in December and on 6 January 1982 joined the Canaries permanently for £175,000, signing in public before a friendly against Aberdeen. In February Martin O'Neill was tempted back from Maine Road at a much reduced fee of £125,000. Also in February central defender Phil Hoadley went on a two month loan period to Eastern AA, Hong Kong, accompanied by (after a loan period at Millwall) Graham Paddon who had been dropped by City after the first few games of the season. Joe Royle played just two games that season before having to retire with a knee injury and almost immediately left the club to become manager of Oldham Athletic.

So much then for some of the many changes that took place that year. There were moderate runs in both Cup competitions in the middle of the season, Arsenal knocking City out of the Football League Cup in the Third Round and West Bromwich Albion ending the Canaries chances in the FA Cup in Round Five. In mid March City were in 13th spot in the Second Division, they had had their good games and some which they would rather forget. Suddenly it all seemed to come right for them and in the next 13 games, beginning on Saturday 13 March 1982, they won eleven, drew one and lost only one – promotion was after all a possibility. Thousands of Norwich City supporters flocked to Hillsborough for the final match of the season on Saturday 15 May 1982 and although Sheffield Wednesday were successful by two goals to one it didn't matter. Leicester City, the only side that could catch Norwich City, could only draw 0–0 with lowly placed Shrewsbury Town and the Canaries once more found themselves amongst the highest company in the First Division. Their late run had been remarkable, the goals from Bertschin, Deehan and Ross Jack suddenly started to flow, and it was enough to turn the tide. There was one last twist to the very unusual season – 1981–82 was the first time that clubs were awarded three points for a win instead of the two which had been in force since

Right, the match programme from City's match at Sheffield Wednesday on 15 May 1982 where promotion was won

the Football League began in 1888. Sheffield Wednesday won 20 of their games and drew 10 – a total of 70 points under the new system, Norwich City won 22 of their games and drew 5 – adding up to 71 points. Had the old system of two points for a win still been in vogue it would have been Wednesday and not City who would have gone into the First Division.

When the excitement of promotion had abated City began to prepare for the tough fight that lay ahead in the First Division. The homesick Drazen Muzinic was allowed to return home though not a single penny of his massive transfer fee was ever recouped. During the close season the World Cup Finals took place in Spain and Martin O'Neill led his Northern Irish team to the second stage surprisingly beating the host nation along the way. Greig Shepherd joined the mini exodus of City players to Hong Kong while former Forest full back Colin Smith reversed the trip, but only stayed for about two months. In September Dutchman Dennis Van Wijk joined the club from Ajax Amsterdam after previously walking in and asking for a trial and Jeremy Goss joined the staff through the government's Work Experience scheme. In October Eire international defender Mick Walsh spent a month's loan period at Norwich from Everton while Dave Watson was injured. City then took Norwegian international Aage Hareide on loan from Manchester City. Just before the end of the year Mick Channon leapt at the chance of once more playing in the top grade and joined the club from Bristol Rovers

The 1982–83 squad. Back row left to right: Sheppard (Physio) Bertschin, Bennett, Hareide, Woods Walford, Watson, Mendham, Brown (Manager), Machin (Coach). Front row left to right: McGuire, Haylock, Jack, Baker, Van Wijk, Deehan, O'Neill, Barham

Martin O'Neill received an MBE in the Queen's New Year Honours List for captaining his country in the World Cup Finals. At the end of the season Robert Chase and Jimmy Jones were elected on to the board. Also at the end of the season some figures were released demonstrating just where the money goes in football. During the 1982–83 season Norwich City FC paid £56,056.99 in VAT and the bill for the police presence at home games came to £42,678.2 l. The 1982–83 season was not an easy one for City, but a good run of results in April, including a ten match unbeaten run in the league (a record in the First Division for City), kept thoughts of relegation well away from Carrow Road. The season opened with the visit of John Bond's Manchester City. Both Kevin Reeves and Kevin Bond were in the Manchester City side and of course there was plenty of press interest in the game. The game itself was a rather scrappy affair which the Manchester team won 2–1. As City then settled down and got into their stride Downs, Mendham, Barham, Watson, Woods and Walford all completed 100 appearances each for the club and City completed doubles over Luton Town, Birmingham City (5–1 home & 4–0 away, the latter then being City's biggest away win in

Above,
Mick Channon

Left,
Chris Woods

Division One) and, more impressively, Liverpool. In the Football League Cup Liverpool extracted some revenge by eliminating City 2–0 in the Fourth Round at Anfield and a single controversial goal by Brighton's Jimmy Case prevented the Canaries from reaching the Semi-Final stage of the FA Cup. Our final comments must be reserved for the Norwich City Youth team for not only did they convincingly win the South East Counties League, but they also won the FA Youth Cup for the first time in their history, beating Southend United, Arsenal, Watford, Manchester United, Luton Town and Everton along the way.

Above, John Deehan, scorer of 70 goals for City and later to become manager

The only positive action on the transfer front during the summer of 1983 was the signing of Aage Hareide on a two year contract following his successful loan period. As the opening of the 1983–84 season approached however the activity increased when Greig Shepherd (back from Hong Kong) joined Southend United for £10,000 and Martin O'Neill, disappointed at not being offered an improved contract chose to join Notts County rather than Chelsea. During his two spells at Norwich O'Neill had gained 18 Northern Irish caps – a then record total for any player whilst on the books of the club. An interest was shown in Kevin Beattie, but Ipswich politely asked City not to pursue the matter in view of the compensation the player had been paid upon his retirement from the game. Ross Jack was sold to Lincoln City for £15,000 and then, after settling his contract differences with the club, Steve Walford returned to London in a surprise £165,000 deal with West Ham United. As a replacement Ken Brown bought Willie Young from Nottingham Forest for £40,000, but the deal unfortunately was not a success. Mark Farrington, who had impressed Norwich with his performance against them in the FA Youth Cup Final, was signed after being released by Everton. City's pre-season warm up took them to Kenya and Norway, something of a contrast in climate we suspect.

After rather mixed results at the start of the campaign proper City faced Manchester United at Carrow Road on Saturday 1 October 1983. After 56 minutes United had built up a three goal lead, but the Canaries, in true fighting spirit, managed to claw their way back into the match and level at 3–3. Louie Donowa, a young Ipswich born winger was playing his first full game in a yellow and green shirt, and it was he who scored the vital equaliser in the 89th minute of the game. In the same game Mike Pickering, on loan from Sheffield Wednesday, made a very brief substitute appearance (his only appearance for the club), but it was enough to be able to include him as one of the 639 Canaries who have worn a City shirt since Norwich City FC were elected to the Football League in 1920 up to 31 August 2001. The problem continued to be inconsistency, a good result was followed by a poor one, and in one of the latter against Queens Park Rangers at Carrow Road (City lost 0–3 on Saturday 29 October 1983) Mr Channon had exclusive use of the bathing facilities ie he was sent off. John Fashanu followed Ross Jack to Lincoln City on loan before signing permanently for £15,000, Mark Barham sustained a knee injury on Saturday 3 December against Tottenham Hotspur which was to keep him out of the game for a year and just before Christmas 1983 Robert Rosario was signed from Hillingdon Borough. Later in the season despite a 'get-away-from-it-all' break in Malta the only success worthy of note was the 6–1 thrashing of Watford on Saturday 7 April 1984 and the 1–1 draw at Anfield against the champions Liverpool. Tony Spearing broke his leg in the Liverpool match. City again finished the season in 14th place which because of the closeness at the foot of the division was not as comfortable as it sounds.

There were more good runs in the Cup matches, City reached the Fifth Round of the Milk Cup before surrendering 0–2 to Aston Villa at Carrow Road on Tuesday 17 January 1984 and in a rather disappointing game at Derby the Canaries ended their interest in the FA Cup at the same stage. Chris Woods and Greg Downs played in every game and the former was named 'Player of the Year'. Hareide asked to be released from his contract and returned to Norway, but he did add that if he had been younger (he was over 30 years old) he would have been pleased to stay at Norwich. Dave Watson and Chris Woods went on England's tour of South America in the summer, but while Watson played in all three games Chris

Woods had to watch from the bench.

The many arrivals and departures before and during the 1984–85 season are fully covered in the Who's Who section. We must mention one however, the arrival of defender Steve Bruce from Gillingham. In early July 1984 Steve travelled up from Kent and signed for City in a complicated transfer deal which cost Norwich City a total of around £135,000. In his very first game he put through his own goal in the 3–3 draw with Liverpool on Saturday 25 August 1984, but soon became a pillar of strength at the heart of the City defence. The season was dominated by three events – the fire, Wembley and relegation.

A fire broke out in the main stand at around 3.00am on the morning of Thursday 25 October 1984. Very soon a large contingent of firemen were on the scene, but they were not able to prevent extensive damage being done. The blaze completely destroyed the boardroom, the dressing rooms and a number of souvenirs that had been collected over the years. It was a sad event and it caused the club numerous problems in the staging of future matches at Carrow Road. By 21 February 1985 however plans were in hand to rebuild the stand, which were to contain excellent facilities for players, spectators and staff

Above, two views of the main stand, destroyed by fire in October 1984

Left, QPR players seen here leaving the Nest public house which served as a temporary changing room in the immediate aftermath of the fire

Right, Steve Bruce wheels away after scoring the decisive goal in City's 2–1 aggregate Milk Cup Semi-Final win over Ipswich Town

Below and bottom, celebrations following the 1985 Silver Jubilee Milk Cup Final, dubbed the 'friendly final', City versus Sunderland

alike. It was later renamed the Geoffrey Watling City Stand, in recognition of his fantastic contribution to the club.

The Silver Jubilee Milk Cup Final played at Wembley Stadium on Sunday 24 March 1985 will always be remembered as the 'friendly final'. Rural Norfolk and the harsher industrial landscape of Wearside are miles apart, but the supporters of Norwich City and Sunderland demonstrated that any obstacle can be overcome if the will is present. Wembley Stadium has hosted some great occasions including the 1948 Olympic Games, the 1966 World Cup Final and the 1982 Papal visit, but it is almost certain that it had never before seen a 60-a-side soccer match between rival supporters in the car park. The fans also mixed freely and swapped souvenirs and addresses – it left one hopeful for the future of our great national game. It was the first time that Norwich City had completed a competitive match on a Sunday and the first time that City had been involved in a live televised game. Asa Hartford created his own slice of history when he became the first player to appear in three League/Milk Cup Finals for three different clubs. He also got his name on the scoresheet when his shot was deflected past Turner a few seconds into the second half. City had to survive a penalty miss by Clive Walker later in the half but hung on to win by the odd goal. After a tour of the city in an open-topped bus the players were welcomed to a Civic

Reception by the Lord Mayor of Norwich and it was estimated that 20,000 people lined the route.

However, the last twelve league games produced just two victories and City found themselves sliding towards the dreaded Second Division. The final match which City won 2–1 on a waterlogged Stamford Bridge pitch appeared to have averted disaster as Coventry City now had to win their remaining three games, the last of which was against the champions Everton. The final events of the season are history now and we will say no more, Norwich City accompanied Stoke City and Sunderland into the Second Division, but time would prove that there is a silver lining to every cloud.

To add to their misery Norwich City FC along with the other English qualifiers found themselves excluded from European competition after the dreadful events of 29 May 1985 at the Heysel Stadium. Again we feel that here is not the place to discuss the problems of soccer hooliganism in depth suffice to say that it was a great pity that after all their hard work Norwich City were deprived of a place in the UEFA Cup competition of 1985–86.

Before we come to the footballing achievements of Norwich City FC in 1985–86 we must look very briefly at the boardroom unrest that occurred in the Autumn of 1985. Problems connected with the building of the new stand led to the resignation of the entire Norwich City FC board on Monday 25 November 1985. It was announced that a four man emergency committee consisting of James Alston CBE, Peter Sharman, Eric Abbs and Richard Parker would handle the affairs of the club until a new board could be formed. The new board when announced consisted of Robert Chase (chairman), J A Jones (vice chairman), E J Abbs, B W Lockwood, R J Munby, A Scholes and G A Paterson. On 8 November 1985 the death of James Laffan Hanly was announced. He was a

A celebration tour in an open-topped bus preceded a Civic Reception for the 1985–86 Second Divison Champions

Second Division Champions 1985–86. Back row left to right: Gordon, Williams, Clayton, Phelan, Woods, Bruce, Culverhouse, Brooke. Front row left to right: Van Wijk, Watson, Deehan, Drinkell

former chairman of the club and had been associated with Norwich City FC for over 40 years. He was 80 years old.

Ken Brown and Mel Machin must have been pleased that they were able to commence the 1985–86 season with a staff that was if anything stronger than that which had been relegated the previous term. During the summer Michael Phelan, from Burnley, Garry Brooke, who had played in the First Division with Tottenham Hotspur, David Williams, who had been player/manager of Bristol Rovers and Kevin Drinkell, a proven goalscorer with Grimsby Town, arrived at the club. Once the new season had started they were joined by Ian Culverhouse and Wayne Biggins. It was not the happiest of starts for the Canaries as only four points were collected from the first five games, but after they had found their bearings in the new company there was no stopping them. Between Saturday 12 October 1985 and Saturday 8 February 1986 City were undefeated in the league and included in that sequence was a run of ten straight league wins. Promotion was finally achieved on Saturday 12 March 1986 in the match against Bradford City. City won 2–0 with a goal in each half from Kevin Drinkell and Wayne Biggins. Because of the disastrous fire at Bradford the previous season the game was played at the Odsal Stadium, a rugby league/speedway venue – we pose the question – was it the first time that a Football League team won promotion in a rugby league stadium?

As we pick up the story of Norwich City's history where the original Canary Citizens book left it in the summer of 1986, the Club had just romped away with the Second Division Championship by seven clear points from their nearest rivals, Charlton Athletic.

The Chernobyl nuclear power station had just exploded, Chris De Burgh was top of the charts with 'Lady in Red' and that summer's World Cup brought equal measures of glory and infamy for the victorious Argentinians. Few could deny that they produced much of the best football on display in Mexico that summer, but the Diego Maradona 'Hand of God' goal against England at the Quarter-Final stage left a bitter taste as cheating became apparently acceptable.

In the City of Norwich, Canary fans were hoping for better things from their favourite club. Twice before, City had bounced back to the top flight of English football at the first time of asking, but their respective stays amongst the elite lasted just six and three years respectively.

The general air of optimism which surrounded Carrow Road was extended by the phoenix of the newly finished City Stand which had emerged from the ashes of the 1984 fire which destroyed the ground's original Main Stand. The new facility, which had been the cause of much boardroom unrest, provided excellent facilities for spectators, players and club officials alike, and was used for the first time as City turned on the style to beat Southampton 4–3 in the first home match of the campaign.

Manager Ken Brown had not rested on his laurels following his side's Championship

The 1986–87 squad

Rebuilding the main stand in 1984

winning success and the departure of Dave Watson, Chris Woods, John Deehan, Paul Haylock and Dennis Van Wijk. Former England Under-21 internationals David Hodgson and Shaun Elliott arrived from Sunderland; Trevor Putney formed part of the deal which took John Deehan to Ipswich Town; whilst the capture of Tottenham Reserve midfielder, Ian Crook proved to be an inspirational move as he proved to be the Canaries' playmaker for the next ten seasons or more.

In the course of the season, two more Canary stalwarts joined the ranks. Ian Butterworth was signed from Nottingham Forest and a young goalkeeper arrived from Aberdeen with a recommendation from Alex Ferguson no less. Bryan Gunn soon won a place in the City line-up and went on to record 477 appearances for Norwich and to twice claim the 'Player of the Season' trophy.

The 1986–87 campaign lived up to every fans' expectations as Norwich performed consistently throughout, topping the table in mid-October and seldom being outside of the top eight in the Division. Highlights included an away win against Manchester United and a thrilling home win against Liverpool, in which for the first time in a league match, Ian Rush scored for the Reds and ended up on a losing side. Unfortunately, a series of rather dull home draws prevented the Canaries from scaling even greater heights, although one of those draws, against Manchester City on February 14th 1987, was significant for the visit of the Duchess of

The Duchess of Kent officially opened the brand new main stand in February 1987

Kent who was at Carrow Road to officially open the City Stand.

The Canaries ended their season with a 2–1 win at Highbury, a result which saw them finish fifth in Division One, their highest ever league placing. Unfortunately City were denied a UEFA Cup place for the second time in three seasons as a result of the existing ban on English clubs competing in Europe as a consequence of the Heysel tragedy in 1985.

Above, bright young goalkeeper, Bryan Gunn, was signed from Aberdeen

Eventual champions Everton ended City's interest in the League Cup at the Fourth Round stage; a surprise defeat at Wigan ended any hopes of a glorious FA Cup run; but in the Full Members Cup, Norwich came within a whisker of reaching Wembley. Leading 1–0 at Selhurst Park against Charlton Athletic in the Semi-Final, courtesy of an 89th minute goal from Robert Rosario, Norwich contrived to concede a 90th minute equaliser from Paul Walsh, and then in extra-time an Ian Butterworth own goal decided the match in Charlton's favour.

It was a satisfying season for the management team of Ken Brown and Mel Machin and it gave great hope to Canary fans that the Club had really arrived amongst the country's top teams. If a couple more players could be added to the squad whilst retaining all the elements which had contributed to the relative success, who knows what the Club might achieve.

Unfortunately events didn't unfold in that way. An approach from Manchester City to lure Mel Machin away as Manager was not rejected. The Canaries' highly respected Coach left Carrow Road and, as often been the case in football, the remaining half of the management team found it difficult to maintain the momentum.

The departure of Mel Machin was the catalyst for almost unprecedented turmoil at the Club, which although it subsided from time to time, was to rumble on for ten years.

The summer of 1987 provided little indication of the changes that lay ahead for Norwich City. Ken Brown added Mark Bowen and Simon Ratcliffe, from Tottenham and Manchester United respectively, to his successful squad. David Williams and Dave Stringer were promoted to work with the senior squad following the departure of Mel Machin and expectations were high.

Three wins in the first fifteen league matches at the outset of the 1987–88 season was not as the doctor ordered. The team were playing with little confidence and unrest amongst supporters led to a mass of white handkerchiefs being waved, a sign of surrender, as City slipped to an ignominious defeat at Charlton on 7 November.

At an emotional press conference held two days later, it was announced that Ken Brown's tenure as Manager had come to an end and that Dave Stringer would take charge with Dave Williams as his assistant. Brown's departure brought about a furore amongst many Canary fans who felt that he was being harshly treated by City Chairman, Robert Chase.

On the field, Stringer and Williams were given the task of rescuing City's season and of avoiding relegation; off the field a bitter campaign against Robert Chase was launched, which eventually led to an Extraordinary General Meeting being held at St. Andrews Hall in February 1988 and with it a vote of no confidence in the Chairman. In the weeks leading up to the meeting there was a climate of conflict surrounding the Club, which thankfully did not spill over onto the pitch, as Stringer

Right, Dave Stringer promoted to work with the senior squad

marshalled his troops magnificently to guide them clear of the relegation zone.

The motion of no confidence was easily defeated and for the time being at least, all attentions returned to matters on the field.

Four wins in his first eight games in charge, including a hat-trick of wins over Christmas, plus the signings of Robert Fleck and John O'Neill, enabled Dave Stringer to gain the full support of the Canary faithful. Unfortunately for John O'Neill, and Norwich City Football Club, his Canary career lasted just 34 minutes of his debut at Wimbledon. A strong challenge from former Canary, John Fashanu, ended the Irishman's career. O'Neill later sued Fashanu, with the matter being settled out of court. Robert Fleck became the Canaries' record capture, at £580,000 from Glasgow Rangers and soon became a Carrow Road cult hero. His mischievous approach to the game endeared him to Norwich fans and made him 'a player to hate' for opposition fans, and his 84 goals, scored in two spells, took him to third place in the Club's all-time goalscoring charts.

Andy Linighan was signed in February from Oldham, to replace both the unfortunate O'Neill and the departed Steve Bruce, as Stringer gradually set about rebuilding his squad.

The season ended with relegation comfortably avoided, but in a run of six games without a win and with some players, seemingly out of favour, expressing their desire to leave Carrow Road. Stringer faced some difficult decisions with Kevin Drinkell, Wayne Biggins, Kenny Brown, Tony Spearing, Shaun Elliott and Graham Benstead all wanting to leave the club, and leave they did ahead of the 1988–89 season.

Few people could have predicted what the new season was to have in store for the Canaries. Dave Stringer was about to embark upon his first full season as Manager. The squad was numerically weaker than in any recent season, even with the summer arrivals of Paul Cook, Malcolm Allen and Andy Townsend and was without a proven goalscorer in top-flight football following the departure of Drinkell to Glasgow Rangers.

In fact, the season turned out to be one of the most memorable in the Club's entire history with many respected neutral observers talking about the Canaries winning the League/FA Cup Double as late as mid-April, with just six or seven matches of the season remaining.

The campaign got off to the best possible start with a 2–1 home success against Nottingham Forest. The result, and the free-flowing performance which earned it, seemed to give City's campaign real impetus. Three more league wins followed it and Norwich found themselves on top of Division One, a position they held, with the exception of one week, from mid-August until the New Year.

Away wins at Old Trafford and Anfield proved to the nation that Dave Stringer's side were competing for the title on merit. Praise rained in as City's passing game won them admirers from all quarters. A 2–1 home success against West Ham United on December 27th in their first ever league appearance on live television further cemented their league position and credibility amongst the pundits – Norwich were in for the long haul through to the season's end.

Robert Fleck signs to strengthen the forward line. Fleck was to become a cult hero

Arsenal emerged as City's greatest rivals for the league title and the two club's vied for the top spot through to early April.

In the meantime, Norwich had disposed of Port Vale, Sutton United, by an incredible 8–0 winning margin, Sheffield United and West Ham United, to take their place in the Semi-Final of the FA Cup for only the second time in the Club's history. Inflatable Canaries took their place in Club folk-lore as thousands of them flew to Upton Park and later Villa Park in support of their heroes.

As at April 1 1989, Norwich were lying second in Division One, three points behind Arsenal with a game in hand and with an FA Cup Semi-Final against struggling Everton, at Villa Park, to look forward to.

Four games and fifteen days later, City's hopes in both competitions laid in ruins, as did many people's love of the English game.

On April 1, City faced third placed Liverpool at Carrow Road. A win would have all but ended Liverpool's Championship hopes, but a Ronnie Whelan goal in the first-half, against a strangely

Malcolm Allen celebrates during the 8–0 FA Cup win over Sutton United

subdued Norwich, was enough to win the match. Four days later City lost 2–0 at Nottingham Forest and to complete a miserable week, the Canaries then lost 2–1 at Coventry. Three league defeats in eight days was not Championship winning form and Arsenal opened up a ten point advantage with Liverpool chasing hard.

April 15th 1989 will long be remembered by football fans everywhere. Unfortunately not for City's FA Cup Semi-Final against Everton, which ended in a 1–0 win for the Merseysiders, as Norwich produced another off-colour performance, but for the tragic events in the days other Semi-Final, at Hillsborough between Liverpool and Nottingham Forest. The events of that day in Sheffield are well chronicled as 95 Liverpool supporters lost their lives at what should have been a joyous sporting occasion. For those Norwich and Everton fans at Villa Park there was the surreal experience of learning of those events, via radio reports, as they unfolded and the realisation that victory or defeat on that particular day really didn't matter. Not that Norwich City and Everton didn't give their all in an attempt to reach the FA Cup Final, but the game unfolded in such a way that it seemed as if both sides were playing in full knowledge of the ongoing tragedy at Hillsborough. The majority of Norwich fans left Birmingham that afternoon not bemoaning their team's defeat in a cup semi-final, but stunned by the news from South Yorkshire.

Andy Townsend scores against West Ham, live on TV, on December 29 1988

Six points were gained from the last six league games of the season and City slipped down to fourth position in Division One, still their best ever league finish. Sadly there was still no reward of European football, the UEFA ban on English clubs was still in place, and the end of season slump in form did take some of the shine off what, in retrospect was a fantastic season for the Canaries.

Maybe Dave Stringer's side did freeze in those crucial end of season games, or maybe they were simply one or two players short in what is after all, 'not a sprint, but a marathon'. History should look back kindly on that great season as Norwich City had truly arrived amongst the big boys of English football – could they sustain it?

The summer of 1989 saw Club skipper Mike Phelan depart to Manchester United for a fee of £750,000, but the Canaries more than matched that income with the purchases of David Phillips, Tim Sherwood and Mark Walton for combined fees of £800,000.

Dave Stringer's outfit made an excellent start to the new campaign, remaining undefeated in their first eleven games, a run which included outstanding away wins at Sheffield Wednesday and Manchester United (for the second season in succession) as well as a thrilling 4–4 home draw with Southampton, a match highlighted by Robert Rosario's ITV 'Goal of the Season' volley at the Barclay End.

Danish Under-21 international striker Henrik Mortensen arrived from Aarhus for a fee of £360,000 as the Canaries sought to improve their squad from a position of strength and entering the Christmas sequence of games they held a very respectable fourth place in the table.

That, however, was to be the highpoint of the season. Despite some good performances, the team managed just five wins from the final nineteen league games of the campaign and eventually finished tenth in the table. Yet again Norwich City found themselves just short of finishing amongst the so called 'big-boys' of

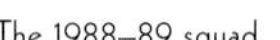

The 1988–89 squad

English football (seven points short of fifth position), and yet again they faced some difficult decisions – could they hold on to their highly-rated, emerging players? – could they build on their consistently good performances over three of the last four seasons? Time would tell.

Unfortunately for Dave Stringer his relatively successful squad began to fragment. Sizeable offers for his much admired players became difficult to resist and within a matter of weeks of the end of the 1989–90 season, Andy Townsend and Andy Linighan had been sold to Chelsea and Arsenal respectively, each for £1.2 million.

For some Canary fans they were indeed 'offers too good to refuse' and of course 'the Club couldn't stand in the way of players who wanted to play elsewhere', but for many it was the all too familiar pattern of the Club gaining success on the field, only to then 'balance the books' by cashing-in on its better players at the expense of further on the field progress.

Townsend and Linighan were replaced in the squad by John Polston, Paul Blades and Colin Woodthorpe, who arrived for a total of £1.175 million.

The Canaries continued to produce a brand of football which was pleasing to the eye, winning praise from many quarters, but there were early signs that some of the side's more durable qualities were on the wane.

A mid-season 4–0 home defeat at the hands of Wimbledon, with all four goals coming in the opening twenty minutes of the match, led to a sit-down protest in the Barclay (a sign of things to come perhaps) and that trauma was followed just three home games later by a 6–2 drubbing by Brian Clough's on-song Nottingham Forest outfit. There was to be no revenge for that particular result either, as City were thrashed 5–0 at the City Ground in the return fixture four months later. In truth it was an average season – City never seriously looked like mounting a charge for European football, which was now back on the agenda following the lifting of UEFA's ban on English clubs, and they were never in any serious trouble at the foot of the table. However, Norwich's standards had risen; the supporters were hoping for improvement – mid-table top-flight football was now not good enough. How times had changed!

David Phillips formed one part of a major £800,000 spending spree in the 1989–90 season

The season did have its bright spots though. Canary youngsters; Lee Power, Daryl Sutch, Robert Ullathorne and a certain Chris Sutton, all made their breakthrough into the senior ranks during 1990–91 and all went on to play regularly for the senior side with varying degrees of success.

There was also an excellent FA Cup run. Bristol City and Swindon Town were dispatched in rounds three and four at Carrow Road, which set up a live televised Fifth Round tie against Manchester United at Carrow Road. In a pulsating tie, Dale Gordon scored the winning goal to send Carrow Road wild and maintain the Canaries' excellent run of results against Alex

Above, FA Cup action from the 5th round match with Manchester United

Ferguson's men. That victory brought Nottingham Forest to Carrow Road and this Quarter-Final tie was everything that the Manchester United game wasn't. It was a dull encounter with few real chances, lacking in passion and atmosphere, played as it was on a Saturday afternoon (you can't beat a Carrow Road cup-tie under lights). The game was decided by a 61st minute strike from Roy Keane and Forest went on to lose the 'Gascoigne' Final to Tottenham at Wembley.

Dave Stringer's side of 1988–89 was beginning to break up. Before the end of the 1991–92 season, Dale Gordon, Robert Rosario and Tim Sherwood were all to leave the Club, bringing in another healthy sum of £2.5 million; whilst there were two new additions to the squad. Utility player Rob Newman arrived from Bristol City for £600,000 and the Canaries broke their transfer record by paying £925,000 for Port Vale striker Darren Beckford.

With only eleven league wins to their credit all season, the Canaries slumped from a relatively accomplished eighth place in Division One in late November, to finish the campaign in 18th place, flirting with relegation in the final weeks of the campaign, when a run of six successive defeats left everyone looking anxiously over their shoulders. Safety was finally achieved via a 1–1 home draw against Wimbledon. Robert Fleck scored the vital goal in that game, in front of the hoardings at the Barclay end of the ground, which masked the demolition work of the famous old terrace which had witnessed so much excitement in the previous 57 years.

League form was poor, but the FA Cup again brought the best out of Norwich, as they swept aside the challenge of Barnsley, Millwall and Notts. County to reach the Quarter-Final stage.

Below, City fans in full voice at the Hillsborough FA Cup Semi-Final

There they defeated Southampton after a replay (another great cup-tie under lights and the last in front of standing supporters at Carrow Road) to take them through to a Semi-Final clash with Second Division Sunderland at Hillsborough in a repeat of the 'Friendly' Milk Cup Final of 1985.

Optimism was high, boosted by the return, with the help of a specially rented recovery capsule, of Robert Fleck from injury. City were clear favourites, but the occasion again proved too much for the team. Sunderland scored with a suspiciously looking 'offside' goal and it wasn't until the game's closing fifteen minutes that the team displayed any urgency. A couple of chances came and went, the best of which fell to 18 year old Chris Sutton, and the Wembley dream was in tatters.

Norwich fans tried hard to be as gracious in defeat as the Sunderland fans had been at Wembley in March 1985, but it was difficult. Thousands left Hillsborough in a daze – unable to comprehend the feeling of utter despair brought on by such an indifferent performance on such a big day. Tears were shed by the bucketful as for the third time the Canaries fell at the penultimate hurdle in the FA Cup.

Former Norwich City Director Fred Kennedy died in March 1992 after a short illness. As mentioned earlier, the spring of 1992 was shaping up to be a time of great change at Norwich City Football Club. The old Barclay was, by late April, just a pile of rubble and just days after that relegation avoiding draw with Wimbledon came the shock news that Dave Stringer was resigning from his position as Manager of the Club.

Dave claimed that 'even if the Club had reached the FA Cup Final and won it, I would have still resigned. There is a time when every Manager reaches his sell-by date and I have reached mine'. Robert Chase was surprised by

FA Cup action from 1991–92

Left, Chris Sutton against Southampton

Far left, Robert Fleck against Sunderland

Left, Ruel Fox against Notts. County

Chris Sutton

the decision, but immediately seconded Dave's assistance in the search for his successor. Elsewhere the game, and events at Norwich City, moved on apace.

The Barclay Stand was demolished as City set about implementing the Taylor Report, which recommended the introduction of all-seater stadium in the aftermath of the 1989 Hillsborough tragedy. Chairman Robert Chase wasted no time in ensuring that Norwich City were at the forefront of such a revolution; taking advantage of every pound available through the Football Trust to reconstruct the Barclay and also install seating in the River End lower tier. At the outset of the 1992–93 season, only Norwich and near rivals, Ipswich Town, who had won promotion the previous season, had all-seater stadia for the onset of English football's other massive innovation – the Football Association Premier League.

In 1991 the top-flight Clubs had become more and more unhappy at having to share all the various commercial cakes with the other 70 clubs outside the First Division and so, plans were drawn up to form a breakaway league under the umbrella of the Football Association. After prolonged argument, and threats, the Football Association Premier League was formed (note that there was no sponsor at this time) to start in August 1992. With huge investment from BSkyB Television leading to large guaranteed pay-outs to all involved clubs, City's last gasp survival was even more gratefully received than it might normally have been.

A new era dawned for English club football, promising new riches beyond everyone's wildest dreams and down at Carrow Road, Norwich City were on the verge of another startling chapter in the Club's eventful history.

The summer of 1992 witnessed further change in Europe. Czechoslovakia was partitioned to form the new states of Slovakia and the Czech Republic; whilst in the war torn former Yugoslavia, the different religious, national and racial groups manoeuvred for independence.

On a brighter note, Disneyland Paris opened its doors for business and Denmark, who were only allowed to compete at the European Football Championships as a consequence of the war in Yugoslavia, surprised everyone by defeating Germany in the final courtesy of a blistering strike from John Jensen.

The Canaries preparations for the onslaught of the 'whole new ball game' that was to be the FA Premier League were far from smooth.

The appointment of a new Manager, to replace Dave Stringer, took several twists and turns before Reserve Team boss, Mike Walker was promoted into the Carrow Road hot-seat. It

Right, Gary Megson and, far right, Lee Power in action against Nottingham Forest

initially appeared that former England full-back, Phil Neal, was to be unveiled in the position, after he posed with Chairman Chase on the River End terrace, but following further talks, Walker emerged as the frontrunner and was eventually appointed. His first task was to bring in ex-Canary John Deehan as his coach and John Faulkner as his Reserve coach.

Then, on the eve of the season, fans' favourite Robert Fleck left for Chelsea for a fee of £2.1 million, to be replaced by Manchester United youngster Mark Robins, who cost £800,000; whilst the experienced Manchester City midfielder, Gary Megson arrived in Norwich on a free transfer.

Mike Walker's first forty-five minutes in charge of the Canaries gave little hint of the exciting nine months that lay ahead. Trailing 2–0 to Arsenal at Highbury, the Canaries looked out of contention, but the introduction of substitute Robins turned the game on its head. He netted twice with David Phillips and Ruel Fox also on the scoresheet as City's magnificent comeback took them to an unbelievable 4–2 success.

That remarkable turnaround in fortunes set City off on a fantastic journey which almost ended in an incredible, if unlikely, Premier League Championship victory. Seven of the first nine league games were won, including an emphatic 3–1 home success against Nottingham Forest on a balmy August Bank Holiday Monday evening, as Carrow Road experienced its first taste of BSkyB razzmatazz.

Mike Walker was promoted to manager following the resignation of Dave Stringer in 1992

Mike Walker's side, with Robins in tremendous early season form, hit the top of the Premier League in early September and remained in real contention for the league title until early April when successive defeats at the hands of Manchester United and Tottenham broke Canary hearts.

Pundits continually belittled Norwich's efforts and only begrudgingly gave praise, particularly in the first half of the campaign, but as it became clear that City were contesting the title with Manchester United and Aston Villa on

The 1992–93 squad

Efan Ekoku scores in the 3–3 draw at Middlesbrough in May 1993, helping to clinch City's UEFA Cup place

merit, several people were made to eat their words.

A 7–1 defeat at Blackburn in late October gave City's critics the perfect ammunition to write them off, but Mike Walker's side bounced back with four successive wins to open up an eight point lead at the top of the table after eighteen games. Then a run of five games without a goal over the Christmas period allowed United and Villa to draw level on points with the Canaries.

All three teams vied for top spot until late March when the fixture list provided the Canaries with successive home matches against their two nearest rivals. The first of those clashes was against Aston Villa and, on a most memorable evening, a second-half strike from John Polston, who just twenty four hours before became a father for the first time, together with an incredible miss from Villa's Garry Parker, gave City a vital 1–0 victory.

The top of the table now read:

	Pl	Pts
Norwich City	36	65
A. Villa	35	64
Man. U.	35	63

With just six games remaining City looked capable of pulling off a truly remarkable Championship success. A similar victory against Alex Ferguson's men would leave City five points clear of the men from Old Trafford, although United would still have a game in hand. As it transpired, United came to Carrow Road and in a blitzkrieg first-half, tore the City defence to shreds by virtue of their slick, explosive attacking play. United netted three times without reply and although Mark Robins pulled a goal back after the break, all was lost.

A 5–1 thrashing at Tottenham four days later showed how much that United defeat had taken out of the Canaries, but yet again they recovered brilliantly to take seven points from the final four games to finish in third place in the inaugural Premier League season.

That in itself was a fantastic achievement for a Club with such limited resources and the proverbial icing on the cake was to follow a couple of weeks after the end of the league season. This occurred when former Canary Andy Linighan scored the winning goal for Arsenal in the FA Cup Final replay victory against Sheffield Wednesday, a result which gave the Canaries qualification to the UEFA Cup for the first time in their history – a dream come true for City's loyal and committed supporters.

The draw for the UEFA Cup First Round paired City with Vitesse Arnhem from Holland and preparations began for a new adventure for all concerned with the Club. Fans checked their passports; City officials met with their counterparts from Holland and UEFA representatives; an exclusive deal with BBC to cover the European games was unveiled; and Mike Walker set about further strengthening his squad for the tests that lie ahead – not only in

Europe, but also at home as City looked to consolidate on the successes of 1992–93.

Towards the end of the previous season record signing Darren Beckford had been allowed to move to Oldham for a fee of £300,000, whilst Efan Ekoku was signed from AFC Bournemouth for £750,000, beating the transfer deadline by literally thirty seconds!

In the summer Spencer Prior arrived from Southend in a £300,000 deal whilst Scott Howie was signed from Clyde for £100,000. The only other change in the senior squad came with the departure of David Phillips to Nottingham Forest after he rejected the Canaries' offer of a new contract.

However, it was the developing young players, who had come through the ranks at Carrow Road that were to have the biggest impact during the exciting campaign ahead, as Darren Eadie, Ade Akinbiyi, Andy Johnson and Chris Sutton in particular, took the plaudits.

Despite losing at home to reigning Premier League Champions Manchester United on the opening day of the season, Norwich soon found their rhythm, winning their next three games; at Blackburn 3–2; at Leeds 4–0 with a blistering performance covered by the 'Match of the Day' cameras and including a fantastic volleyed 'Goal of the Month' by Jerry Goss; and then Ipswich at Carrow Road by 1–0, with Goss again on target.

By the time Vitesse Arnhem arrived at Carrow Road for the Canaries' first ever European tie, City were lying ninth in the Premiership table with their reputation for playing some of the best football in the country enhanced by those early season performances. Arnhem were an emerging force in Dutch football and included the likes of Raimond Van Der Gouw, Phillip Cocu, Glenn Helder, Roy Makaay and Willem Korsten in their squad.

Only 16,818 fans witnessed the historic moment when skipper for the day John Polston exchanged pennants with his Vitesse opposite number, but those inside Carrow Road that evening gained a foresight into the excitement yet to come. City gradually came to terms with their continental opponents to eventually run out comfortable 3–0 winners, with Efan Ekoku scoring his club's first ever European goal, before Goss and Polston completed the scoring.

A 5–1 thrashing of Everton at Goodison Park, with Efan Ekoku scoring four times, came before the UEFA Cup second-leg in Holland.

Approximately 1,500 City fans made the trip to Arnhem and behaved themselves impeccably, mixing with the locals and proving that not all English fans deserve the 'hooligan' tag which is so readily associated with English football supporters abroad. The Dutch stadium was a huge disappointment and was reminiscent of an English Third Division ground.

On the field City could, and should, have won comfortably. Efan Ekoku squandered three glorious chances to increase the aggregate scoreline, but on the day neither team could break the deadlock. The City fans celebrated and wondered where their European adventure would take them next – although one group of supporters were grateful their adventure was to continue at all. A plane carrying around 80 fans back from Holland ran off the end of the runway at Norwich Airport and only came to a standstill as it dug itself into the mud causing hundreds of other fans returning home by air to be diverted to Stansted.

Efan Ekoku scores City's first ever goal in Europe

A trip to the Olympic Stadium, Munich to face the mighty Bayern was the reward for City's win against Vitesse. It was a tremendous draw for the Club to face one of the greatest names in European football. It was reasonably accessible for City fans wishing to travel and, although no English club had ever beaten Bayern in Munich, the Germans were certainly not the force they were in years gone by. However, their squad still contained many familiar names; Jorghino, Thomas Helmer, Olaf Thon, Christian Ziege,

Canary fans in good voice in Europe at the Giuseppi Meazza Stadium, Milan

Right, Jeremy Goss nets the decisive goal against Bayern Muich at Carrow Road

Lothar Matthaus, Mehmet Scholl, Jan Wouters, and Adolfo Valencia amongst them.

Mike Walker's side went in to the away leg of the tie on the back of three successive victories and a second position in the Premiership table.

The Olympic Stadium was less than half full, but that didn't deter the Canaries, who stormed into a 2–0 lead with first-half goals from Jerrry Goss, another tremendous volley, and Mark Bowen. Nerlinger reduced the arrears before half-time, but City held on to their advantage with a superb rearguard action, highlighted by a brilliant Bryan Gunn save from point-blank range from Valencia.

It was a momentous victory for the Canaries and was rightly celebrated, by players and fans alike, as if the UEFA Cup itself had been won. If there was a danger that Norwich thought they already had the tie won those thoughts were soon dismissed in the return leg on an enthralling night at Carrow Road.

That home match against Bayern Munich will always remain as one of the greatest nights in Norwich City's history. The Germans arrived full of determination to put right the defeat on their home patch and when Valencia levelled the tie on aggregate after just three minutes it seemed as if the Canaries' audacity to actually win in Germany might be punished by the mightily experienced Bayern side. Again Norwich defended superbly and urged on by a fantastically noisy home crowd, City restored their advantage when Jerry Goss scored from close range early in the second-half. The remainder of the game passed incredibly slowly for City fans, but the final whistle was greeted with an enormous cheer as everyone took in the magnitude of the aggregate victory.

That two-legged cup-tie may well become an albatross for future City teams and Managers, just as the 1959 FA Cup run had been before that. However, it was still a fantastic achievement for Norwich City Football Club and anyone who was at either, or both, of those matches will never forget the atmosphere, the sense of history and the significance of that 2–1 aggregate victory. England's other UEFA Cup hopefuls had all been eliminated by the Third Round stage, leaving the nation to watch, and generally support, the Canaries' European efforts.

Mike Walker's team were on a bus heading north to Sheffield United when they heard who their Third Round opponents were to be – FC Internazionale Milano, or Inter Milan to you or me.

Yet again it was a fantastic draw against one of the truly great names of European football. The home leg was to come first against a multi-million pound squad which included many household names such as; Walter Zenga, Giuseppe Bergomi, Wim Jonk, Igor Shalimov, Dennis Bergkamp, Darko Pancev, Salvatore Schillaci and Ruben Sosa.

Mike Walker gets Manager of the Month recognition in 1993/94

The home leg against Inter brought another full-house to Carrow Road, with the new Thorpe extension to the City Stand in use for the first time. The crowd was in good voice, but this game was different to the previous two ties at Carrow Road. Inter came with the sole intention of sitting back, in true Italian style, and as a consequence the game lacked excitement. Another Jerry Goss volley almost opened the scoring, but the crossbar saved Walter Zenga's embarrassment and Ian Crook went close too, but in perfect 'smash and grab' style, the Italians broke away to earn a last minute penalty. Rob Newman was adjudged to have tripped Ruben

Chris Sutton, Jerry Goss, Rob Newman and Daryl Sutch celebrate that fantastic victory in Munich's Olympic Stadium

Mike Walker with City's 'Team Europe' from 1993–94

Sosa and Bergkamp coolly dispatched the resulting spot-kick. The feeling of anti-climax overwhelmed Carrow Road, but Mike Walker remained positive, knowing that his side had produced their best football so far this season away from their home.

That optimism appeared justified when City went blow for blow at Old Trafford against runaway Premiership leaders Manchester United. The game ended 2–2 and with Alex Ferguson heaping praise on City's performance.

Below, Ruel Fox tries to break down the Inter defence

Seven planes together with countless coaches transported approximately three thousand City fans to Milan for the second leg. The tie was played on a Wednesday afternoon, to appease various television schedulers in an eerie, foggy San Siro, or Giuseppe Meazza Stadium, in front of 30,000 fans. Unfortunately deprived of the services of the three Ians; Butterwoth, Crook and Culverhouse, through suspension, it was a strange looking Canary line-up that took the field.

To record the fact that City lost the second leg 1–0, also to a last minute Dennis Bergkamp strike, does not paint the picture of another gallant Canary performance. In the first-half City created, and unfortunately wasted, several good chances to level the tie on aggregate. Urged on by their impressive support Norwich continued to throw men forward and it was only in the game's dying moments, with Norwich now only using two defenders, that Bergkamp decided the tie.

The disappointment amongst players and fans alike was almost tangible. For the fans at least it lasted just a few minutes as they paid an amazing tribute to their heroes by embarking upon an unbelievable hour long chanting session which totally bemused the Italian supporters and police. They seemed to be expecting a near riot, if their numbers and demeanour were anything to go by. Everyone joined in and even if it was the end of an incredible adventure, it at least seemed a fitting end. The mist which surrounded the stadium and delayed some of the return flights to Norfolk, provided the perfect backdrop to this surreal scene. The Norwich players came back to pay their tribute to the fans and the Italian police picked the mood of the occasion to change their approach, making it a strangely happy occasion, despite the result.

So there it was. An European adventure lasting just three ties and six matches, but those stark facts cannot begin to account for the drama every Norwich fan felt during those heady weeks at the back end of 1993. At that time Norwich were at the heart of the English footballing nation and despite only reaching the Third Round of the UEFA Cup, the City and people of Norwich were justifiably proud of their team.

Whilst the team were preparing for that away match in Milan, with the national media in tow seeking stories each day, the first signs of a difference of opinion between Manager Mike Walker and Chairman Robert Chase began to emerge.

In an interview, Walker was quoted as saying that the Club might need to reward the players in line with their successes if they were to retain their services. Chase on the other hand commented that there should be no knee-jerk reaction to some degree of success and that loyalty couldn't be bought with higher salaries – players had to want to stay to be part of a successful side.

On the field City's form remained good with an away win at the Dell on New Years Day lifting them to sixth position in the table, but in the newspaper columns speculation mounted that all was not well at Carrow Road.

There was the inevitable speculation linking Mike Walker with each and every other managerial job as it became vacant and also concerning the underlying current of contrasting opinions regarding the 'next step' for Norwich City in view of their incredible eighteen months of success. Should they invest and try to move on up again or should they consolidate – that appeared to be the crux of the situation.

The December departure from Goodison Park of Manager Howard Kendall was the catalyst for the amazing events of early January 1994. Everton approached Robert Chase asking permission to talk to Mike Walker concerning their vacant Manager's job – Chase refused – Walker was disappointed by that refusal and eventually decided to walk out on the Club he had just steered to the most successful spell in their history. It was reported that Walker sought greater security than the one year roll-over contract he was on at Carrow Road, but in truth the full extent of the discussions between Walker and Chase have never come to light.

Therefore on the eve of the FA Cup Third Round tie at Wycombe, Robert Chase placed John Deehan in temporary charge of First Team affairs, a move which was soon made permanent, and the Club moved forward again.

Looking back at that turbulent period in the Club's history many people have observed that the day that Mike Walker packed his bags to join Everton coincided exactly with the onset of the Club's fall from its then particularly high perch. Football is seldom that simple and many other factors must be considered, but in hindsight Chase must wonder if Norwich City would have been better served by trying to build on their success rather than dismantling the successful formula which had lifted them to such dizzy heights.

Within four weeks of Walker's departure, Winger Ruel Fox was sold to Newcastle United for £2.2 million whilst Neil Adams was signed from Oldham as a direct replacement for just £250,000.

John Deehan's reign started with an incredible run of seven successive league draws, most of which should have been victories. The City fans were still being royally entertained by their team with twenty six goals coming in those seven draws and in general they were supportive of John Deehan. There was however, an increasing discontent with the Board over the departure of Walker and the subsequent sale of Ruel Fox – moves which they perceived to be to the detriment of the Club's future progress.

Another stunning drive from Mark Robins' left boot

The season petered out, although there were one or two high and low points still to be enjoyed or endured. On the plus side there was a satisfying 3–0 home win against Mike Walker's Everton outfit and a 1–0 win at Anfield (courtesy of yet another stunning strike from Jerry Goss) on the occasion of the last match to be played in front of the old Kop terrace. On the down side

Chris Sutton was eventually sold to Blackburn for a healthy £5 million fee

there were the 3–4 and 4–5 home defeats at the hands of struggling Queens Park Rangers and Southampton respectively. Norwich ended the campaign in 12th position and with speculation increasing about the future of 28 goal striker Chris Sutton. It looked as if it was going to be another interesting summer at Carrow Road.

The Chris Sutton saga certainly dominated the early summer headlines as far as Norwich City were concerned. At first it appeared that the Canaries were going to resist all bids, with Chairman Robert Chase going on the record with 'if Chris Sutton is not with this Club at the start of next season then neither shall I be'. However, the rate of speculation increased, culminating in a rather unseemly auction with Chase announcing that the player could after all leave the Club for the highest bid in excess of £5 million. Arsenal and Blackburn apparently led the race with Jack Walker's expanding empire eventually winning the day, with Sutton moving north to Blackburn for £5 million on July 13th 1994.

The move led to more criticism of the Club's lack of ambition and of its apparent reticence to move on from its consolidated position within the top-flight. The Club argued that Sutton was determined to move and that the £5 million was too good an offer to refuse, but the majority of fans remained unconvinced and worried for the future.

Gary Megson hung up his boots to concentrate on his newly defined coaching role alongside John Deehan, whilst Ian Culverhouse refused the offer of a new contract and spent the next six months confined to the Reserves until Swindon moved in for him. Ian Butterworth had also played his last game for the Canaries, but his demise came as a result of a water ski-ing accident which resulted in a career ending knee injury.

The other major event of the summer of 1994 was the move of City's training headquarters from Trowse to the state of the art Colney Training Centre. Colney, situated just off the new Norwich Southern by-pass provided top quality training facilities, including seven full-size pitches, a gym, fully equipped treatment room, a hydrotherapy pool, changing facilities, a dining area for the players and excellent office accommodation. Colney soon became recognised as one of the best of its kind anywhere in the country and received visits from many of the game's top figures to study its design and impressive facilities. It certainly became a major asset to Norwich City, particularly in attracting players to the club.

The Canaries were not slow to re-invest some of the Sutton money. Central defender Jon Newsome arrived from Leeds for a new Club record fee of £1,000,000 and he was joined by three other new signings; Carl Bradshaw from Sheffield United for £450,000; Mike Milligan from Oldham for £850,000; and early on in the campaign, Mike Sheron from Manchester City for £800,000.

The team made a steady start to the campaign and although they only lost one of

Right, Jon Newsome, signed from Leeds for a £1 million club record fee

their opening six league games, they only scored three goals in that time. However, in general, John Deehan's side were more than holding their own. A home win against Championship challengers Blackburn, despite Chris Sutton predictably opening the scoring against his former club, was soon followed by other good home wins against Leeds and Queens Park Rangers which maintained the momentum. Good progress was also being made in the Coca-Cola Cup as the Canaries reached the Quarter-Final stage with victories against Swansea, Tranmere and Notts. County.

In early December, which was to be a pivotal month in the Club's season and beyond, the Canaries splashed out again, following the £900,000 departure of Efan Ekoku to Wimbledon, when they signed Ashley Ward for £350,000 from Crewe Alexandra. His signing made an immediate impact as he scored decisive goals in each of his first two games helping to lift the Canaries into seventh place in the Premiership table after nineteen games.

A Boxing Day defeat at home to Tottenham was followed the next day by a televised clash at Nottingham Forest which City also lost, but which more importantly contained the defining moment of the Canaries season and Premiership future. In the seventh minute of the match, Canary goalkeeper Bryan Gunn made what appeared to be a routine save, but in doing so he broke his leg and sustained damaged ankle ligaments, an injury which was to rule him out of senior football until the start of next season. 19 year old Andy Marshall came off the bench to make his debut and in City's next game probably enjoyed one of the best ever home debuts by a Norwich player.

That came against high-flying Newcastle United when, after City had taken an early 2–0 lead, Marshall made several magnificent saves to ensure that City remained in seventh place, with twenty two of the seasons forty two games completed. Sheffield United keeper Simon Tracey was signed on loan as cover and everything appeared happy in the Canary camp.

Bryan Gunn suffered a broken leg and serious ligament damage right at a crucial time in the 1994–95 campaign

Less than two weeks later Canary fans were once again up in arms. City had lost their Coca-Cola Cup Quarter-Final at Bolton, but it was the sale of yet another striker, Mark Robins to Leicester for £1,000,000, which upset the supporters. A mini-protest took place at Carrow Road on the day of the Wimbledon match, which City ironically lost to a decisive goal from their former striker, Efan Ekoku and the tone was set for the rest of the season.

From New Years Day onwards, the Canaries won just one of their last twenty league games, the home match with Ipswich just prior to transfer deadline day. John Deehan tried manfully to bring in new faces as pressure mounted on him to strengthen the squad. A Fifth Round FA Cup humiliation at Everton, where City lost 5–0 further increased that pressure and supporters called for immediate action to head

The 1995–96 squad

off the Club's apparent free-fall out of the Premiership.

No new players arrived as transfer deadline day passed. Robert Chase insisted that there need be 'no panic' and that John Deehan's position was secure and that 'relegation was not an issue discussed at Carrow Road'. However, as the Club's position worsened and with fans venting their spleen on the Canaries' Boss , he launched a defensive broadside, stating that he felt the Club were 'a striker light following the sale of Mark Robins and that youngsters Jamie Cureton and Ade Akinbiyi could not be expected to shoulder the burden of a relegation fight on their own.'

On April 9th 1995 John Deehan resigned as the Club's Manager with his Assistant, Gary Megson, immediately being appointed Caretaker Manager. With five games of the season remaining, City realistically needed to take six points to ensure their safety – only one was forthcoming and City were relegated after nine successive seasons in the top flight.

Robert Chase welcomes former player Martin O'Neill to the manager's job at City in June 1995

The season was played out against a background of in-fighting. At each match there were loud and prolonged protests calling for Robert Chase to resign and for the last two home matches there was an imported sound system, allegedly brought in to boost the atmosphere, but the more cynical observers thought it was to drown out the protests. With the Premiership clubs renegotiating their original TV deal, the guaranteed income for member clubs was set to increase enormously. Despite the promise of two years worth of 'parachute payments' 1995 was a very bad year for Norwich City, or for the matter, any club to be relegated.

If City's European season of 1993–94 is remembered as the Club's most historic, then season 1995–96 will definitely be recalled as the single most traumatic campaign in Norwich City's long and colourful history.

The summer of 1995 began with Gary Megson still in the Carrow Road hot-seat, but the clamour for change was too great to resist and many names, including Ray Clemence, David Pleat and the most likely candidate, Jimmy Nicholl, were all linked with the Manager's job. Just as it seemed Nicholl was set to be appointed, the Canaries sprung a major, and most welcome, surprise on its supporters.

On June 13th, with very little speculation ahead of the announcement, former player, Martin O'Neill was unveiled as the Canaries' new Boss. O'Neill was received as something of a 'messiah' by Canary fans and Robert Chase won over many of his detractors with this appointment.

Martin O'Neill had built himself an excellent reputation at Wycombe Wanderers and the charismatic Irishman was seen by the majority of Norwich supporters as the right man for the job. Most people agreed that the Canaries best chance of regaining their Premiership status was at the first attempt and that O'Neill's arrival together with that of his lieutenants Steve Walford, John Robertson and Paul Franklin, would give them every chance of achieving just that.

The Canaries made just two other significant acquisitions during the summer of 1995. Matthew Rush was signed from West Ham United, but was to suffer a knee injury after just one appearance which all but ruined his Carrow Road career and Robert Chase purchased some land adjacent to the Carrow Road site which was the former home of Read's Flour Mill. The intention there was to increase car parking and allow for possible future development, with one idea being an indoor arena nicknamed the 'Chase Dome'. This particular business came in for heavy criticism from fans who wanted all the Club's efforts to be concentrated on winning promotion, after all 'what good is a flour mill?' That question was to be answered some six years later!

Martin O'Neill's side made a bright start to the campaign, winning three of their first five matches, by which time a certain Robert Fleck had been signed on loan from Chelsea, a move which became a permanent £650,000 deal soon after. Another potential transfer target, Hull City's Dean Windass, had been identified and the Canaries first bid was rejected.

Over the course of the next few weeks the name Windass was seldom far from the headlines as Norwich and Hull made claim and counter claim with regards to the status, or otherwise of the proposed transfer. Unfortunately the differing points of view were not just coming from Hull and Norwich. Martin O'Neill was becoming openly frustrated by Robert Chase's inability to conclude the deal to his satisfaction and the local media were delighted to convey the apparent disparity in the views of Manager and Chairman. O'Neill even went so far as to say that, 'he wanted to sign Windass, preferably before the end of the century!'

In early November talks of 'crisis meetings' between the two protagonists were carried in all the local media and to add to Robert Chase's problems, his long time Boardroom ally, Vice-Chairman Jimmy Jones, stepped down for 'health reasons' stating his desire to sell his 19% stakeholding in the Club.

Supporter discontent continued to grow and after each home match there were gatherings of approximately 100 fans calling for the Chairman to resign, or at least 'loosen the purse-strings' in support of the Manager.

Four successive league wins in November lifted the Canaries up to second place in the table, just one point behind Millwall, but all was not well at Carrow Road. O'Neill, with support from the fans and the local media continued in his campaign to sign Dean Windass. Conversely Chase was quoted as saying that 'a £3.5 million wage bill for 35 players and 8 staff was enough' and that if his critics could do any better then they should 'put up or shut up'.

On Friday December 1, Windass moved to Aberdeen for £600,000 and the following day City lost 1–0 at home to Stoke City. Five days later Mark McGhee walked out at Leicester City. City drew their next match, at home to Grimsby to go back to third place in the Division One table.

Mike Walker looked set to be announced as Leicester's new manager in time for the Canaries' live televised visit to Filbert Street on December 17th, but there was to be an incredible sequence of events which were to prevent that particular rumour coming true.

As thousands of Canary fans tuned into the live broadcast of the match at Leicester, they were greeted by the shock news that Martin O'Neill had resigned as Manager of Norwich City.

In the matter of a few short days, O'Neill usurped Mike Walker to be unveiled as the new Boss at Filbert Street (his season was to end in success as he guided the Foxes to Play-off victory), the Canaries progressed through to the Quarter-Finals of the Coca-Cola Cup with a penalty shoot-out win at Bolton and Gary Megson was brought back to Carrow Road as Norwich's new Manager.

Megson's first two games back in-charge both ended in 1–0 defeats, including an acrimonious Boxing Day home loss to Southend which was played out in an hostile atmosphere which could not have helped the players' performance. A crowd of nearly 1,000 gathered outside the Club's main entrance to protest and a 10,000 strong petition seeking Robert Chase's resignation was presented to the Club.

The Canaries' troubled season went from bad to worse as the Club were eliminated from both cup competitions in the space of eighteen days and former Vice-Chairman, Jimmy Jones, spoke out against the Chase regime. An away win at Sunderland followed soon after, but the team then entered into a long run without a win, dropping into the relegation zone in the process.

Gary Megson appointed Mick Wadsworth as his Assistant and former Canary favourite, Mick Phelan as his Reserve Coach, but the boardroom 'power-struggle' continued to dominate the news. Jimmy Jones launched an attempt to oust Chase via an EGM of shareholders, but apparently lacked the necessary 51% support, whilst rumours of a consortium buy-out of Chase's controlling interest continued to circulate.

In late February the Club published its accounts for period July 1994 to December 1995 and they showed that despite a profit on transfers of £4.3 million, the Club made a an overall profit of only £1.2 million, whilst at the same time increasing its loans by £2 million. In effect, the Club were in debt to the tune of £4.5 million, and Chase stated that 'Jon Newsome or someone is bound to leave', further infuriating the Canary faithful.

March 14th 1996 will go down as one of the saddest and most significant days in the Club's history. With the bank clamouring for a reduction in the Club's debts, the Canaries were forced to sell Jon Newsome to Sheffield Wednesday for £1.2 million and Ashley Ward to Derby County for £1 million. Manager Megson reacted angrily and accused the Board of undermining his position and the confidence of his squad. Perversely, two days later, the team then went out and won their first match in nine attempts, 3–0 at Reading, to ease the relegation worries.

Gordon Bennett became the Club's first Chief Executive after the buy-out of Robert Chase's shareholding by Geoffrey Watling

Seven days later, at the Club's AGM, Robert Chase revealed that he had found the 'right person with the right offer' to whom he might be prepared to sell his shares. It was soon disclosed that former Club Chairman, and then current President, Geoffrey Watling, was the prospective purchaser of Chase's shares and there was further speculation regarding a possible Carrow Road return for ex-boss, Mike Walker.

The Club's Youth Development Officer, Gordon Bennett, was seconded by Chase to takeover the running the Club's affairs, his previous experience as Chief Executive of Bristol Rovers and as Secretary of West Bromwich Albion was seen as invaluable at such a time. One of his first tasks was to assess the staffing levels at Carrow Road and Colney to make savings in the summer.

On May 2 Geoffrey Watling finally completed his purchase of Robert Chase's 34% shareholding in Norwich City Football Club. The announcement brought much rejoicing amongst the Carrow Road faithful who attended City's last game of the season, at Crystal Palace, in fancy dress to celebrate the dawning of a new era in the Club's colourful history.

• • •

The summer of 1996 was notable for the divorce of Charles and Di; the success of the Atlanta Olympics; and the arrival of Buzz Lightyear to our cinema screens in Disney's Toy Story.

The success of the Euro '96 tournament, staged in England, which almost saw 'the three lions' take the honours on home soil, lifted football's profile to even greater heights. The exploits of Shearer, Sheringham, Gascoigne, Seaman and Pearce captured the nation and undoubtedly sparked an even greater interest in domestic football. English football was on a high – could Norwich City capture that interest?

At Carrow Road the summer months were turbulent to say the least as the Club's financial plight became public knowledge and the post-Chase era began. It soon became apparent that Norwich City Football Club had come within a whisker of going out of business.

Gordon Bennett became the Club's first ever Chief Executive and he had several unenviable tasks ahead of him as he sought to bring some financial realism to a Club which, in the words of another club official, 'had the expenditure of Inter Milan and the income of Southend'.

With the Club's burden of debt reported to be 'greater than £5 million, but less than £8 million', with most of that sum payable on high interest overdraft facilities. Club officials spent much of the summer re-negotiating the repayment terms for the debt and emerged satisfied with their new arrangements which had restructured the debt in such a way that the Club could at least trade viably and move forward once again.

At Boardroom level, following Robert Chase's departure, former Director, Roger Munby rejoined the Board, whilst Geoffrey Watling's business partner, Keith Gregory was also seconded onto the Board, although his tenure was for a brief ten days as he decided to concentrate on his business affairs. Martin Armstrong, Chief Executive of Club sponsors, the Norwich and Peterborough Building Society, also joined the Board and played a significant part in restructuring the Club's debt. Barry Lockwood Trevor Nicholls and Gavin Paterson remained as Directors with Lockwood taking on the role of Acting Chairman.

Inevitably, at such a time of change, there were casualties. More than ten backroom staff at Carrow Road were made redundant, as Gordon Bennett sought to reduce expenditure in all areas. The Club's successful youth scouting programme was downgraded, a necessary but painful move, which had repercussions for several seasons beyond 1996, as the Canaries regular flow of exciting young talent dried to a trickle.

On the playing front, Canary stalwarts Mark Bowen, Jeremy Goss and Ian Crook, were among eleven players who left the Club during the summer, although Crook's situation developed into a real East Anglian drama. More of that later.

There were also several comings and goings amongst the coaching staff based at Colney. Long serving ex-player and Chief Scout, Duncan Forbes, was amongst that early round of redundancies, but like Ian Crook, he was to make a dramatic return to the fold only a few days after he eventually left. Then Mick Wadsworth left to become Scarborough's new boss as Gary Megson received an apparent 'vote of confidence' amidst mounting speculation that Mike Walker was set for a dramatic Carrow Road return.

Sure enough, Megson's 'vote of confidence' was followed by the sack, for the second summer in succession, just ten days later. The much heralded return of Walker followed on the same day, a move which received great support from City fans everywhere.

Walker soon appointed John Faulkner as his assistant and Steve Foley as his Reserve Coach. He also moved quickly to re-appoint Duncan Forbes as Chief Scout and to resolve the Ian Crook saga.

Having been made available on a free transfer Crook eventually agreed terms with local rivals Ipswich Town and was presented to Town fans at a press conference at almost the exact same time as Walker was holding his own press conference at Carrow Road announcing his return. Walker contacted Crook and asked him to reconsider his move, but Crook had already signed a contract with Ipswich for the forthcoming season. However, Crook's contract with Town was dated June 26th 1996 and technically he remained a Norwich player until June 30th. With Walker very keen to retain the services of his playmaker, Norwich exploited this loophole and re-signed the player, although Crook himself was later punished for signing a contract with Ipswich whilst already under contract to another club. The whole episode was greeted with great merriment in Norfolk, whilst south of the border the natives were far from impressed at Crook's u-turn.

Spencer Prior left for Leicester in a £600,000 deal whilst Robert Ullathorne became one of the first players to take advantage of the new Bosman Ruling, which allowed players to move internationally, without a transfer fee, at the end of their contracts. He moved to Spanish club, Osasuna, with the Canaries receiving not a penny for his services.

The atmosphere inside, and around, Carrow Road on August 17th 1996 was much changed to that of recent seasons. Gone were the protestors and anti-club chants and in their place were happy faces, the return of the boycotting fans and a renewed sense of optimism.

Despite an early season departure from the Coca-Cola Cup, Mike Walker's side, with Robert

Mike Walker returns as manager in June 1996

Darren Eadie

Fleck, Darren Eadie, Keith O'Neill and Andy Johnson all in outstanding form, were soon in their stride and a local derby win against Ipswich Town, on October 11th, lifted them to the top of Division One. Two more wins followed soon after and after fourteen matches City were lying in second in the league table, one point behind Bolton and six points clear of third placed Crystal Palace.

Injuries and suspensions, plus the sale of Jamie Cureton to Bristol Rovers for £250,000 were beginning to take their toll as, on occasions, Mike Walker found his resources stretched. A run of nine games without a win severely dented City's promotion ambitions. With successive 5–1 and 6–1 defeats at the hands of West Bromwich Albion and Port Vale, Walker was desperately in need of some extra defensive cover.

In the middle of that poor sequence of results and away from the action, on November 28th 1996, the Canaries unveiled their newly constituted Board of Directors. Trevor Nicholls stood down and four new Directors were co-opted on to the Board. The new Directors were Barry Skipper, Michael Foulger, Michael Wynn Jones and his wife, Authoress and TV Cook, Delia Smith. The new Directors were reported to be bringing in £2 million of fresh capital to further brighten the Club's financial position. Geoffrey Watling stated that he wished to 'retain his majority shareholding at this time'.

That newly found capital was not allowed to burn a hole in the Canaries' pocket as, on December 23rd, Mike Walker made his first signing in his second spell in charge, recruiting central defender Matt Jackson from Everton for a fee of £450,000.

Jackson's arrival, together with that of loan signings David Rocastle and Kevin Scott, coincided with a five game winning streak which lifted City back up into fifth place with realistic hopes of promotion. Unfortunately the Canaries were unable to sustain that level of performance and their Play-off challenge eventually ended at Ipswich in their third last game of the campaign.

There were other significant events in the final few weeks of the 1996–97 season.

Lee Marshall was signed from Enfield for £15,000 and Kevin Scott's £250,000 move from Tottenham was completed. Hot prospect Craig Bellamy was given his senior debut and he played his part in helping the Club's Youth team

The new Directors of Norwich City Football Club, left to right, Michael Foulger, Barry Skipper, Delia Smith and Michael Wynn Jones

claim the South East Counties League title for only the third time. There was also the very emotional parade, prior to the Stoke City home match on April 12th of Canary Legends – a gathering of ex-players which included Kevin Keelan, Martin Peters, Bernard Robinson and Johnny Gavin.

Overall though the season was seen as a massive step forward both on and off the field, where other brave new supporter based initiatives were launched. They included regular Supporter Forums and a Supporters Consultative Group, which was formed to improve communication between fans and the Board. Results on the field fell away at a crucial time, but there appeared to be genuine reason for optimism for the season ahead.

Having inherited a squad twelve months previously, with very few resources to strengthen it until the new Board was constituted in November, Mike Walker set about a rebuilding programme in the summer of 1997.

Ian Crook finally left Carrow Road to ply his trade in Japan, whilst his midfield partner, Andy Johnson, moved to Nottingham Forest for £2.25 million. The Club also received a £700,000 sell-on bonus as former player, Mike Sheron, moved from Stoke to Queens Park Rangers.

Armed with that income, Walker moved swiftly to bolster his resources. Defender Craig Fleming arrived from Oldham for £600,000, whilst striker Iwan Roberts was a £900,000 capture from Wolves. Spanish defender, Victor Segura was also signed and those three captures were soon joined, early on in the season by midfielder Peter Grant from Celtic and left-back Erik Fuglestad from Viking Stavanger.

City opened the campaign resplendent in their new all-yellow strip, designed by Delia Smith's friend, Bruce Oldfield, bearing the name of new shirt sponsors, Colman's.

The Canaries found themselves bottom of the table after just three matches and whilst relegation was always kept at bay, just, Mike Walker's injury ravaged squad never achieved a top ten place throughout the course of the season. Darren Eadie managed just nineteen league starts and Keith O'Neill six, as time and again the Canaries found themselves without vital, potential match-winning, players.

The first third of the campaign was also a very trying time for Mike Walker on a personal level. His wife Jacqui was losing her battle

Walker strengthened his team with left, Craig Fleming and right, Iwan Roberts

against cancer and in early November passed away. The supporters, who had clamoured for his return, were now calling for his head, despite another home derby success against Ipswich. And try as he might, he was never able to field his strongest side.

A rights issue of Club shares, underwritten by

Delia Smith introduced a new team strip designed by her old friend Bruce Oldfield (far left), but the yellow shorts were eventually to be given the thumbs down by fans

Delia Smith, brought in £2.6 million. Delia Smith and her husband, co-Director, Michael Wynn Jones, also bought Geoffrey Watling's majority shareholding to take their stake in the Club to 57%.

The continuing injury situation at the club led to the earlier than planned promotion to regular First Team football of youngsters such as Adrian Forbes, Craig Bellamy, Chris Llewellyn, Darren Kenton and Adrian Coote. However, these inexperienced youngsters found it difficult to bring consistency to the side and some poor performances; most notably at Ipswich (0–5),

Wolves (0–5) and at Oxford (0–3) increased the pressure on Walker.

With just four games of the season remaining and 'old favourites; Robert Fleck and Bryan Gunn' having flown the Canaries' nest, together with Danny Mills, who joined Charlton for £250,000, the Canaries were just three points above the relegation zone. City's form was poor – could they beat the drop?

A 5–0 win against Huddersfield at Carrow Road lifted some of the gloom, but a dismal 2–0 defeat at Stoke had City fans still looking over their shoulders. Remarkably, a second successive 5–0 home success, against Swindon, finally ensured the Club's safety.

Big money signing Iwan Roberts was at last delivering the goals he had been signed to score and his partnership with young Craig Bellamy was showing signs of developing into something very special. With Keith O'Neill and Darren Eadie to return, City fans left Carrow Road for the final time that season once again optimistic about the future.

Just five days later it was announced that Mike Walker was to leave Carrow Road for the second time and that he and the Club had 'agreed by mutual consent' to the decision. It was a shock move and led to yet another summer of debate and uncertainty.

Would it be Nigel Spackman, Dave Watson perhaps, or his ex-partner at the heart of the Canary rearguard, Steve Bruce? Maybe Bryan Hamilton, Nigel Worthington, Tony Pulis, Ian Atkins, or maybe Bruce Rioch?

Many newspaper column inches were filled with this latest round of Canary managerial speculation. Eventually, on June 11th, it was announced that Bruce Rioch and Bryan Hamilton were the Club's new managerial team. Rioch was named as First Team Manager, whilst Hamilton was designated as Director of Football, with responsibilities to include coaching the senior players as well as overseeing the Club's newly acquired Academy status.

Former Assistant Manager John Faulkner left the Club as did players John Polston and Rob Newman. At Boardroom level Gavin Paterson and Martin Armstrong vacated their positions whilst former Sainsbury's Director, Bob Cooper, joined the Board.

Once again there were causes for optimism.

Right, Craig Bellamy formed a prolific striking partnership with Iwan Roberts

The 1997–98 squad

Darren Eadie had signed a new contract and was fit for the start of the season, as was Keith O'Neill. The younger players were emerging and the new managerial duo possessed the necessary experience to lead the Canaries out of Division One.

Three straight league wins at the outset of the season took City to the top of Division One

and despite some mixed form they remained in fifth place going into the Christmas fixtures. Unfortunately, but not coincidentally, Darren Eadie and Keith O'Neill had both suffered long term injuries by this point in the season, soon to be followed by Craig Bellamy who was the 'victim' of a dreadful tackle by Wolves' Kevin Muscat at Molineux in mid-December. City's next league success came in late February and their next one after that came in early April – in fact they won just four games in the second half of the campaign.

O'Neill left in a £1 million deal to Middlesbrough, prior to him possibly walking out of Carrow Road for nothing in the summer and the Club received a £500,000 windfall from a sell-on clause relating to Tim Sherwood's move from Blackburn to Tottenham; whilst Malky Mackay was signed in September and Phil Mulryne, Cedric Anselin and Paul Dalglish were recruited in March to ensure there were no late season drop into the relegation zone.

It was another disappointing campaign, again highlighted by injuries to key players, the over-reliance on young players and general inconsistency of performance. The Iwan Roberts/ Craig Bellamy partnership contributed 36 league goals and was one of the Division's best, but City's next highest goalscorer was Neil Adams, with just three.

Other significant events during the course of the season included the succession of Barry Lockwood as Chairman by the Club's newest Director, Bob Cooper in December 1998. The Canaries' yellow shorts were given a massive thumbs down by the fans in a yellow card/green card vote – which would ensure a return to green shorts for 1999–2000.

Left, the new management team of Bruce Rioch and Bryan Hamilton

Former Club Sceretary Peter Dash died on 3rd April 1999. On April 17th 1999, the Club organised a 40 year reunion of the famous 1959 FA Cup Semi-Final squad. It was a fantastic day for everyone concerned with an emotional lap of honour ahead of the game against Tranmere and a commemorative dinner in the evening – many a tear was shed by player and spectator alike.

The summer of 1999 was relatively quiet, in Norwich City terms, although there was the usual spate of comings and goings.

On the managerial staff, Bryan Hamilton stepped aside from his First Team coaching duties to concentrate on the Club's extremely important Academy progress. Former player Doug Livermore was brought in as Bruce Rioch's Assistant.

Player wise the Club benefitted again from sell-on clauses, this time in respect of Danny Mills and Chris Sutton, to the tune of a total of £900,000. Neil Adams, Peter Grant, Kevin Scott and Victor Segura were all allowed to leave the

Below, Iwan Roberts receives the Barry Butler Trophy from Club President Geoffrey Watling

Club, whilst Jean Yves De Blasiis was signed on a Bosman free transfer and Pape Diop arrived on loan from Lens.

Pre-season optimism was shattered in the space of three cruel weeks as Rioch was deprived of three of his most creative players. First to be sidelined was Darren Eadie who suffered a recurrence of his knee injury whilst on tour in Sweden – he was to be out for ten weeks. Next to fall foul of the Club's continuing ill fortune was Craig Bellamy, who damaged his cruciate ligaments in a match at Southend – an injury which kept him out of action for nine months. Then, in the fourth league game of the campaign, Phil Mulryne suffered a double fracture of his right leg, sidelining him for seven months. It was a nightmare start to the campaign which, unsurprisingly, saw the Canaries take time to get into their stride.

Phil Mulryne's absence for a large part of 1999–2000 was a severe blow

City's first win came in league game number six, as Darren Eadie made his return to score the winning goal against Crewe and that was soon followed by a run of just one defeat in eleven games which lifted the Canaries into the top half of the table by early November.

At that same time Chief Executive Gordon Bennett announced his intention to leave the Club to join Aberdeen in a similar capacity. Chairman Bob Cooper took on the role of Chief Executive. Bennett's departure from Carrow Road was soon followed by that of one of his protegees. Darren Eadie, who Bennett had done so much to bring to Carrow Road as a schoolboy, was sold to Leicester City for £3 million, a move which angered the fans, who accused the Club of selling its ambition. The Club had only just announced that debts had risen to £7 million following a reported annual loss for the year to June 30th 1999 of £2.5 million.

Three league wins, either side of Eadie's departure lifted City into eighth place in the table on Boxing Day and only a last minute Barnsley equaliser prevented Rioch's team from moving into the Play-off zone in late January. Unfortunately Rioch's depleted troops were unable to sustain their Play-off challenge and the season began to ebb away.

On March 13 2000 Bruce Rioch announced his decision to leave the Club. His decision came as a great surprise to everyone, but the Board moved swiftly to instate Director of Football, Bryan Hamilton, in charge of First Team affairs. Chairman Cooper said, 'Rioch felt the financial resources of the Club were not sufficient for him to further his own plans for the Club, but he knew our resources were tight and that we tried to maximise them for him'.

Hamilton's first game in charge was away at the Club where he made his name as a player, high-flying Ipswich. In true 'Boys Own' fashion, the unfancied Canaries completely outplayed, and outfought, their Suffolk rivals to chalk up a 2–0 away win.

That result lifted everyone's spirits and Hamilton was soon promoted to the 'hot-seat' on a permanent basis and he set about injecting some fresh blood into the team. In a frantic pre-deadline day rush, Newcastle pair, Garry Brady and Des Hamilton arrived on loan, whilst Dutchmen Raymond De Waard and Fernando Derveld, together with Swiss Italian Gaetano Giallanza and Paul McVeigh joined the Club on contracts of varying lengths. Then there was the imminent return of Mulryne and Bellamy to look forward to. It all added up to an exciting last few weeks of the campaign.

Two wins, three draws and four defeats followed that Ipswich result, but the potential of the new players, together with the prospect of fit again Craig Bellamy and Phil Mulryne was there for all to see. City finished twelfth and set about preparing for the new campaign ahead.

Barry Lockwood retired from the Board after 14 years during the summer of 2000 to be replaced by local media executive, Russell Stuart. The Club also upgraded the catering and banqueting facilites in the Barclay Stand to provide the biggest such venue in Norfolk.

Nigel Worthington was brought in by Bryan Hamilton as joint Assistant Manager alongside Doug Livermore, whilst the only addition to those players who arrived in late March to bolster the squad was Dane Steen Nedergaard.

Making their exits from Carrow Road included Mike Milligan, Che Wilson, Shaun Carey and Erik Fuglestad, all of whom were released on free transfers.

A 1–0 opening day defeat at Barnsley set the scene for another traumatic week for the Canaries. Less than four days later, prize asset Craig Bellamy was on his way out of Carrow Road to join Coventry City in a £5 million deal. Again the Club came under fire for parting with their assets too cheaply, but with the possible dismantling of the transfer system on the horizon, it would have taken a brave Board to reject that kind of offer.

City once again got off to a bad start and found themselves bottom of the table after five games. Reinforcements were on their way and prior to game six, away at Stockport, Bryan Hamilton had brought in Jim Whitley and Garry Brady on loan, signed defender Brian McGovern from Arsenal and then lured experienced striker Tony Cottee from Leicester on a free transfer.

Cottee's arrival in particular seemed to give the Canaries a lift in their 3–1 win at Stockport and he was soon joined at Carrow Road by his former Leicester colleague, Steve Walsh. Despite some inconsistencies, by the time City had defeated Birmingham 1–0 at Carrow Road on November 7th they had improved to a respectable thirteenth position in the table.

Also by early November, Hamilton had sent Whitley and Brady back to Manchester City and Newcastle respectively; signed Danny Granville and Scott Parker on loan to replace them; lost Giallanza for the rest of the season, just as he was starting to impress, through a cruciate ligament injury; and most surprisingly of all allowed Tony Cottee to join Barnet as their new Player-Manager just two months after signing him from Leicester.

Despite the recent run of good results, and the recent signing of Scottish Under-21 international striker Alex Notman from Manchester United, the fans and local media were becoming critical of some of the Manager's decisions and when the team then lost five consecutive league games, Hamilton decided enough was enough and tendered his resignation to a surprised and disappointed Canary Board.

Above left, Bryan Hamilton resigned his post in December 2000

Above right, Gaetano Giallanza, who impressed City fans prior to his injury

It was certainly a difficult time for the Club, as it also had its application for planning permission for a new indoor Academy arena at Colney turned down and several key players were stalling on new contract talks.

Nigel Worthington was put in temporary charge on December 5th as speculation mounted about Hamilton's successor. Names such as David Jones, Steve Bruce, Kevin Drinkell, Ian Crook, Mel Machin and Jan Molby were all put in the frame. However, some impressive performances by the team throughout December and by Worthington himself in the media, led to the Board appointing Nigel Worthington as Manager on January 2 2001 to work alongside Doug Livermore and Steve Foley.

Within fourteen days of his appointment as Caretaker Boss, Worthington had completed the £350,000 signing of Zema Abbey from Cambridge; made it quite clear that Dutchmen De Waard and Derveld were surplus to his requirements by transfer listing them; and secured Craig Fleming on a new contract.

On the field, Worthington's first fourteen league games in-charge of the side brought twenty three points and just three defeats and

Nigel Worthington was appointed by the Norwich City Board to manager's position on 2 January 2001

there were more signs of his forthright approach paying dividends for the Club. Steve Walsh and Raymond De Waard were both ushered out of the Club, whilst Darren Kenton, Matt Jackson, Chris Llewellyn, Adrian Forbes and Adrian Coote were all to sign new contracts before the season's end.

Just as everything seemed to be 'going nicely', the Canaries almost pressed the 'self-destruct' button, losing five of their next six league games to induce fears of possible relegation to Division Two.

To avoid such a calamity there was the almost traditional pre-deadline activity. Lee Marshall completed a £600,000 move to Leicester, whilst City brought in Adam Drury from Peterborough for £275,000 and Gary Holt from Kilmarnock for £100,000. In the end City avoided the drop by six points, too close for comfort, and in the summer of 2001 everyone was once again looking forward.

What does the future hold for Norwich City Football Club as it embarks upon its 100th season?

On the field Nigel Worthington has some new faces in his squad, with Paul Crichton, Clint Easton, Neil Emblen, Marc Libbra and Mark Rivers all joining the Canaries in the summer of 2001. One or two familiar faces have departed the Carrow Road scene; Andy Marshall decided not to accept the offer of a new contract and signed for Ipswich Town, whilst Jean Yves De Blasiis was given a free transfer.

Worthington's rebuilding plans may well be influenced by the success or otherwise of the Club's redevelopment plans for their land adjacent to the River Wensum. The Club hopes to sell off the land, originally purchased by Robert Chase in 1995, to property developers and use the funds to rebuild the rapidly delapidating South Stand.

The financial gulf between the FA Premier League and the Football League continues to widen and Norwich City face that very difficult decision. Should they risk their financial stability in an attempt to reach the Premiership – with no guarantees – or should they continue to work within their means and move consistently forward in search of the winning formula and a return to the top-flight of English football.

The Club's fans have remained extremely patient since relegation in 1995 and deserve success. Their support, in terms of increasing season ticket holder numbers and other initiatives has been second to none.

The perfect conclusion to Norwich City's one hundred years of football would be a place back amongst the Manchester Uniteds and Liverpools of this world.

We recall the day so many years ago when Sir Samuel Hoare made a speech at the very first match, when Percy 'Putt' Gooch scored so many important goals and Sheffield Wednesday, the holders of the FA Cup, emerging from those very dressing rooms to be beaten by the infant Norwich City. In the approaching darkness it was easy to imagine those times of long ago and should you follow in our footsteps and fail to see the flickering ghosts of Canaries past – close your eyes – and on the wind no 'Son' of Norfolk can fail to hear the singing of the indelible anthem that has accompanied the footballers of the proud City of Norwich from the Norfolk & Suffolk League to the Premiership and Europe.

Who knows what season 2001–2002 will bring? If the Club's recent history is anything to go by it will be almost impossible to predict!

Who's Who

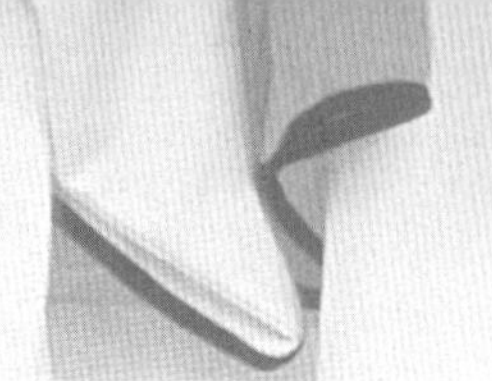

HOW DETAILS OF THE PLAYERS ARE RECORDED

NOMENCLATURE The players' full names, where known, are listed after checking with the player involved and their relatives, plus birth/death certificate; e.g. the 1930s goalkeeper told us his name was Dukes not Duke as has always been shown. In brackets, where appropriate, is shown the cognomen that the player more often than not used.

BIRTH/DEATH Births and deaths in England and Wales have been checked wherever possible against the records of the General Registry Office in London and may differ from previously published information. Birth dates and places have also been checked with the players involved and/or their families.

TRANSFER FEES Those quoted have generally been taken from press reports and other sporting or football publications, but are unlikely to be accurate all the time.

KEY TO INDIVIDUAL ENTRIES

(1997–1998) means debut year followed by the year of final appearance. If shown as **(1996–** , it means that the player is still signed for the club in the centenary year.

Denotes the positions in use at the time of a player's career (eg sadly, there are not too many out-and-out wingers these days). Modern terminology of defender, midfield etc. will only apply to present-day players.

Short resumé of the player's character and career moves, with notable events and achievements listed.

ABASCAL, Victor Segura

(1997–1998) **1997:** 6/1; 12/3
Defender **Career:** 28-5-0
Debut: 9 Aug 97 **Final:** 12 Dec 98 (sub)

Born: Zaragoza, Spain 30 Mar 1973

Career: Real Zaragoza 1989; Palamos 1993; CD. Logrones 1994; Union Esportiva Lleida 1995; NORWICH CITY 02.08.97–30.06.99; Getafe Jun 1999

A former Spanish Under-21 international, Victor joined City on a free transfer. With a good grounding in Spain of around 160 games, he was typically continental in his approach, with a range of passing skills, but more suited to a central defensive position. Took pride in his stamina and fitness levels. Known as Victor Segura in the UK.

First, the year information was recorded, followed by the player's height in ft/ins and weight in st/lbs (as originally listed).

Total number of games in career; substitutions; and goals scored up to **31 August 2001**.

Date of debut and final game. Detail in brackets records substitute appearance and if goal scored.

Player's earliest known signing through to latest known position. NORWICH CITY signing, in capitals, is followed by Football League ratified date of registration of the player for the club.

ABASCAL, Victor Segura

(1997–1998) **1997:** 6/1; 12/3
Defender **Career:** 28-5-0
Debut: 9 Aug 97 **Final:** 12 Dec 98 (sub)

Born: Zaragoza, Spain 30 Mar 1973

Career: Real Zaragoza 1989; Palamos 1993; CD. Logrones 1994; Union Esportiva Lleida 1995; NORWICH CITY 02.08.97–30.06.99; Getafe Jun 1999

A former Spanish Under-21 international, Victor joined City on a free transfer. With a good grounding in Spain of around 160 games, he was typically continental in his approach, with a range of passing skills, but more suited to a central defensive position. Took pride in his stamina and fitness levels. Known as Victor Segura in the UK.

ABBEY, Zema

(2000– **2000:** 6/2; 12/1
Forward **Career:** 16-9-1
Debut: 16 Dec 00 (sub)

Born: Luton 17 Apr 1977

Career: Ickneild Primary School; Ickneild Senior School; Ickneild Athletic; St Joseph's; Baldock Town 1994; Hitchin Town 1995; Cambridge United 11.02.2000; NORWICH CITY 15.12.2000

His father is from St Vincent, mother from St Kitts, and younger brother Nathan is a football league goalkeeper. Thirty-nine goals for Hitchin put Zema in the spotlight with his direct running at defences to the fore. His Canary goal was the winner over QPR in January 2001.

ACKERMAN, Alfred Arthur Eric

(1951–1953) **1951:** 5/10; 11/10
Centre/Inside Forward **Career:** 70-0-35
Debut: 18 Aug 51 (goal) **Final:** 10 Oct 53

Born: Daspoort nr Pretoria, S. Africa 5 Jan 1929
Died: Dunnottar, Transvaal 10 Jul 1988

Career: Pretoria Municipals; Clyde 10.07.47; Hull City 14.07.50; NORWICH CITY 16.08.51; Hull City 15.10.53; Derby County 16.03.55; Carlisle United 02.11.56; Millwall 29.01.59; Dartford player-manager July 1961; Gravesend & Northfleet manager Nov 1968–Feb 1974.

Originally a defender, he moved to the forward line where he became a feared marksman. He almost realised his ambition of scoring 200 Football League goals and was just outside the top 100 Football League goalscorers of all time. Netted four for Derby on 07.04.56 (h) Accrington. Later had a Newsagent/Tobacconist shop in Kent before returning to his native land.

Left: Alf Ackerman
Right: Zema Abbey

ACQUROFF, John (Jack)

(1939) **1939:** 5/10; 11/0
Centre Forward **Career:** 17-0-6
Debut: 2 Feb 39 **Final:** 6 May 39

Born: Chelsea 9 Sep 1911
Died: Launceston, Tasmania 14 Nov 1987

Career: Willesden Polytechnic (amat); Tottenham Hotspur 20.06.31 (amat), 15.08.31 (pro); Northfleet Jan 1932; Folkestone Jun 1934; Hull City 19.11.34; Bury 29.10.36; NORWICH CITY 03.02.39; Second World War guest for Birmingham, WBA, Wolves, Millwall, Fulham & Spurs. Additionally played for Norwich in Regional South games and reappeared after the war for City in two games in the 1945/6 transitional season; Metro (Australia) 1950; Tasmania (Australia); Caledonians Down Under (Australia) retiring 1960.

Born of Scottish parents with Russian ancestry, Jack was a sharp-shooting centre with plenty of dash and verve. He joined the RAF in September 1940, becoming a Sergeant and physical training instructor. Represented the RAF and London, Midland and Scottish Railways when employed as a clerk. In Aussie he played for Metro; captained Tasmania v China (lost 11–0) and Caledonians Down Under, retiring at 49. Incredibly scored a hat-trick for Telecom v Postal Institute at Launceston in 1983 at the age of 72.

ADAMS, Christopher James

(1952–1953) **1952:** 5/7; 10/7
Outside Left **Career:** 30-0-3
Debut: 13 Dec 52 **Final:** 5 Dec 53

Born: Hornchurch 6 Sep 1927

Career: Essex Schoolboys; Sutton's; Leytonstone; Romford; Army; Tottenham Hotspur 16.06.47 (amat), 26.11.48 (pro); NORWICH CITY 13.12.52; Watford 16.03.54; Dartford 22.11.56–1964.

Made only six League appearances for Spurs with a debut against Derby on 01.03.52. Never established himself at Carrow Road, with his 17 consecutive games from his debut being his best run. Also added 28 reserve appearances for six goals to his total. Chris spent eight years at Dartford making 216 appearances and scoring 21 goals before a troublesome knee injury ended his career. He now lives in Romford.

ADAMS, Neil James

(1994–1999)	**1994:** 5/8; 10/7
Winger	**Career:** 187-19-30
Debut: 19 Feb 94	**Final:** 6 Feb 99

Born: Stoke-on-Trent 23 Nov 1965

Neil Adams

Career: Moorland Road High School; Stoke-on-Trent Schoolboys; Johnson's Norcross; QM Rangers; Stoke City 01.07.85; Everton 07.07.86; Oldham Athletic (loan) 11.01.89, (signed) 16.08.89; NORWICH CITY 17.02.94; Oldham Athletic 06.07.99–released 08.05.2001.

After playing for his home town side Neil was pleased to sign for Joe Royle's team to quickly earn a Division Two championship medal. John Deehan, in making the England Under-21 international his first signing, said 'He is a quality player who can cross the ball. He doesn't have fancy frills and spectacular dribbles but he gets the ball into the danger area'. He returned to his former team but now works with Radio Norfolk and local media as well as being the Norwich City Academy Under-12 part-time coach.

ADDY, George William

(1920–1922)	**1920:** 5/11; 12/0
Left Half	**Career:** 33-0-6
Debut: 28 Aug 20	**Final:** 14 Jan 22

Born: Carlton, Barnsley 27 Apr 1891
Died: Ferry Fryston 18 Nov 1971

Career: Carlton Vics; During WW1 with Royal Welsh Fusiliers; Barnsley 01.05.19; NORWICH CITY 27.08.20–1922.

Won a medal in the Nelson league with Carlton and had one Division Two game with Barnsley. Played in City's first ever league game and the press report stated that he had a superb match. The Marvel *in 1921 said that he developed his ability in a school which turned out many fine middle men. Famous enough to appear on Pinnace card number 819.*

AITKEN, John Gordon

(1926–1927)	**1926:** 5/7; 10/8
Outside Left	**Career:** 46-0-8
Debut: 28 Aug 26	**Final:** 7 May 27

Born: Govan, Glasgow 17 Sep 1897
Died: Govan, Glasgow 1 Dec 1967

Career: John Watson's School; St Roch's 1920; Glasgow St Anthony's 1920; Clyde 1920; Bury 26.05.21; Southport 11.07.24; Crewe Alexandra 10.07.25; NORWICH CITY 23.08.26; Northampton Town 20.05.27; Kilmarnock 03.11.28; Alloa Athletic 17.10.32; St Mirren 04.09.33; Morton 09.02.34.

Played rugby at school and gained an engineering appointment before playing football. Very fast winger who was an ever-present in his one league season for City. Five clubs in six years was testimony to his wandering talent. In 14 games City had two Aitkens on the flanks – a reporter's nightmare! Scored in a Scottish Cup Final win and once netted five goals in a match versus Dundee United. A widower for 20 years, he was a retired shipyard storeman.

AITKEN, William John

(1926–1927)	**1926:** 5/9; 10/9
Outside Right	**Career:** 14-0-0
Debut: 18 Dec 26	**Final:** 7 May 27

Born: Peterhead 2 Feb 1894
Died: Gateshead 9 Aug 1973

Career: Kirkintilloch Rob Roy; Queens Park 26.09.17; Glasgow Rangers 18.08.18; Port Vale Aug 1919; Newcastle United 22.05.20; Preston North End 24.06.24; Chorley Sep 1926; NORWICH CITY 17.12.26; Bideford Town player coach 10.09.27; A.S.Cannes (France) 08.10.30; Stade de Reims (France) 05.07.34; Antibes FC (France) 1937/38.

As tricky and quick as his namesake, he scored hat-tricks against Airdrie and Falkirk for Queens Park but he was not a high scorer in English football. Played regularly in Division One in the 1920s and was good enough to play for the Anglo-Scots representative side in 1921. The Norwich City

secretary revealed in 1927 that he was on £4 per week. A winner of the Morpeth 100 in 1929, so it is a mystery why he did not aspire to greater heights on the football field.

AKINBIYI, Adeola Peter Oluwatoyin

(1993–1997) **1993:** 6/1; 11/10
Centre Forward **Career:** 24-34-5
Debut: 3 Nov 93 (sub) **Final:** 1 Jan 97 (sub)

Born: Hackney 10 Oct 1974

Career: Orchard Primary School; Hackney Free School; Inner London County Schools Under-11–16; Senrab Under-11–14; NORWICH CITY Mar 1989 (assoc), Jul 1991 (trainee), 01.02.93 (pro); Hereford United (loan) 21.01.94; Brighton & Hove Albion (loan) 24.11.94; Gillingham 06.01.97; Bristol City 28.05.98; Wolverhampton Wanderers 07.09.99; Leicester City 28.07.2000.

Of Nigerian parentage and an international, his fees for his last three clubs have all exceeded seven figures. A schools 100/200-metre champion, he made a City youth debut four days before his 16th birthday and netted three hat-tricks for the Canaries in youth /reserve games. Continues to thrill and exasperate in equal measure in the Premiership alongside Eadie and Marshall.

ALEXANDER, Philip James

(1982) **1982:** 6/0; 12/8
Left Half **Career:** 0-1-0
Debut/Final: 25 Sep 82 (sub)

Born: Slough 4 Sep 1962

Career: Waingeles Copse School; Reading Youth; Berkshire Under-19; England Under-18 and 19; Wokingham Town; NORWICH CITY 30.04.81; Gisborne City (New Zealand) player coach 1984; Wokingham Town 1987; Mirimar (New Zealand); Farnham Royals/Knights Jan 1989 (American Gridiron football); London Monarchs (American Gridiron football) Nov 1990; Kingstonian; Bracknell Town Oct 1992 general manager/player; Swindon Town Nov 1993 marketing controller; Crystal Palace Jun 1996 managing director.

Spotted while playing for England Under-18s and signed for a record Wokingham Town fee. Played in the Football League Trophy but his only League appearance for City was for just 19 minutes. A scale of payments was due if Phil played ten games and more if eventually for England. The book Glorious Canaries *gave an in-depth insight into Phil's diverse lifestyle after his Norwich City playing days.*

ALLCOCK, Terence

(1958–1969) **1964:** 5/11; 12/0
Inside Forward/Utility **Career:** 384-5-127
Debut: 15 Mar 58 **Final:** 23 Apr 69

Born: Leeds 10 Dec 1935

Career: St Anthony's School; Mount St Mary's School; Leeds Boys (three years); Yorkshire Schoolboys; National Schoolboy trials; Bolton Wanderers 13.12.52; NORWICH CITY 15.03.58, later youth team manager and chief coach; Manchester City coach/manager's assistant 1973.

'The Count' was a natural, confident goalscorer in netting 127 League/Cup goals to stand second highest in City's history. Considering that his last five seasons were spent at half back he would have undoubtedly have set the all time best had he stayed up front. A superb Clubman with his deceptive, loping stride – a study in perpetual motion. He recovered from a broken leg in 1960, playing again 100 days later. Talented wicket-keeper/batsman for Norfolk, from his debut 02.07.59 to his last 23.06.75 (47 matches; 1,513 runs; 91 victims). The first man to score hat-tricks in the FA Cup and League Cup in the same season. Terry had a spell with Dereham and some involvement with local village sides as well as over 20 years' service as the Norfolk County coach. A superb ambassador for the club, he is a matchday sponsor host at Carrow Road.

ALLEN, Malcolm

(1988–1990) **1989:** 5/8; 10/6
Centre Forward **Career:** 31-15-15
Debut: 27 Aug 88 **Final;** 10 Mar 90

Born: Deiniolen 21 Mar 1967

Career: Watford 19.07.83 (amat), 23.03.85 (pro); Aston Villa (loan) 03.09.87; NORWICH CITY 10.08.88; Millwall 20.03.90; Newcastle United 13.08.93; Aberystwyth Town; Gwynedd Council football development Jul 1996; Stevenage Borough Feb 1997 coaching and football in the community; Colney Heath Dec 1997; Molesey Dec 1999 assistant manager; Letchworth Youth Team Academy.

Malcolm won six Welsh youth caps,a 'B' international cap and three full ones prior to joining Norwich City for £175,000. A nimble striker and a good shielder of the ball, he netted four goals in our 8–0 FA Cup destruction of Sutton United. He gained full Welsh caps whilst with Watford, Norwich and Millwall. Eight knee operations proved insurmountable and after gaining a UEFA 'A' coaching qualification he is involved in EFCO schemes as well as being a BBC Wales soccer commentator.

ALLMAN, Leslie

(1926–1928)	**1927:** 5/11; 11/0
Goalkeeper	**Career:** 15-0-0
Debut: 6 Nov 26	**Final:** 17 Mar 28

Born: Burton-on-Trent 26 May 1902
Died: Leeds 21 Mar 1979

Career: First Northwich Boy Scouts; Marston Old Boys; Moulton Alexandra; Northwich Victoria Jul 1922; Llandudno Town; Ellesmere Port Town 1925; Lancaster Town; NORWICH CITY 26.08.26; Merthyr Town 24.07.28; Kettering Town 31.08.29; Shrewsbury Town Jun 1930.

Only on the winning side twice for City, making his debut in the week that manager Stansfield resigned. Centre of controversy in an abandoned Victory Cup game for the Reserves. He repeatedly kicked the ball off the spot when a penalty was awarded – then saved it when taken. Two minutes from time spectators made for him and he took to the centre of the field for refuge. The crowd were told to 'go home and take their opinion of the match with them'. Leslie was good enough though to win the Cheshire Amateur Cup with Moulton and to play for North Wales versus Scotland.

ANDERSON, George Russell

(1929–1930)	**1929:** 5/7; 10/10
Inside Left	**Career:** 30-0-12
Debut: 31 Aug 29	**Final:** 3 May 30

Born: Saltcotes, Strathclyde 29 Oct 1904
Died: Cambridge 9 Nov 1974

Career: Airdrieonians 03.06.25; Brentford 18.05.26; Chelsea 10.05.27; NORWICH CITY 20.05.29; Carlisle United 01.08.30; Gillingham (trial) Oct 1930; Cowdenbeath Oct 1930; Yeovil & Petters United Jul 1932; Bury 26.06.33; Huddersfield Town 29.11.34; Mansfield Town 1935; Newark Town Jun 1937.

George hit City's tenth league hat-trick but flitted from league to non-league with celerity. Never pretending to any footcraft, he enjoyed his best scoring run at Norwich in the company of Hunt and Thompson. City's interest in him was prompted by his scoring four goals in a London Combination game in November 1928. 'Hooso' in the Pink 'Un *in 1929 said that he was rather lacking in sporting knowledge – he had never heard of ups and downs and doubles!*

ANDERSON, Terence Keith

(1965–1973)	**1970:** 5/9; 11/4
Right Wing	**Career:** 258-21-19
Debut: 20 Feb 65	**Final:** 19 Dec 73

Born: Woking 11 Mar 1944
Died: Yarmouth Jan 1980 (between 24th–31st)

Career: Arsenal groundstaff Jul 1959, Aug 1960 (amat), 09.08.61 (pro); NORWICH CITY 18.02.65; Colchester United 07.02.74 (loan); Baltimore Comets (USA) May 1974–Aug 1974; Scunthorpe United 23.09.74; Bournemouth 09.01.75; Colchester United 21.08.75.

At Arsenal he won cups and leagues, gaining England Youth caps and an appearance in the UEFA Cup. 256 games at all levels for 128 goals was his remarkable record at Arsenal. He played in the first televised Match of the Day *game. His incisive wing play over a period of eight years for City culminated in a Divison Two championship medal and a League Cup runners up medal. Tragically found drowned after a training run.*

ANSELIN, Cedric

(1999–2000)	**1999:** 5/9; 11/4
Midfield	**Career:** 25-4-1
Debut: 5 Apr 99	**Final:** 22 Apr 00

Born: Lens, France 24 July 1977

Career: FC Girondins Bordeaux Juniors (France) 1992; Lille (France) (loan); FC Girondins Bordeaux First XI (France) 1995; Southampton (trial) Jan 1999; NORWICH CITY 25.03.99 (loan); 21.05.99 (signed)–28.06.2001; Notts County (trial) 29.08.2001

Cedric, Norwich City's first ever French player, was unable to speak fluent English when he joined the club following a loan stint but quickly endeared himself to the Carrow Road populace. At Bordeaux he played in a UEFA Cup Final with colleagues Dugarry, Lizarazu and Zidane – an impressive CV. An injection of 'inselin' (a press pun) at Southampton was rejected and City used him nominally as a wide right-sided midfield player.

ANSELL, George Thomas Leonard

(1936)	**1936:** 5/10; 11/10
Inside Forward	**Career:** 4-0-0
Debut: 22 Feb 36	**Final:** 14 Mar 36

Born: Worthing 28 Nov 1909
Died: Stafford 7 Oct 1988

Career: Steyning Grammar School, Worthing FC; Oxford University; Brighton & Hove Albion Jan 1929 (amat), 31.08.31 (pro); Corinthians; NORWICH CITY 17.02.36; Southampton 23.06.37; Kimbolton Town; Eynesbury Rovers.

Scored twice in a Sussex Senior Cup Final for Worthing and gained his Oxford Soccer Blue playing three years running (1928/9–30/1). Could play equally well in all three inside forward positions and was not on the losing side in his four first team games for Norwich. He left football to teach in Scarborough having graduated in classics from Jesus College. He made 22 appearances for 12 goals for the famed Corinthians. A master at Kimbolton School until his retirement in 1969.

ARMES, Ivan William

(1947–1950) **1947:** 5/7; 11/0
Left Half **Career:** 65-0-1
Debut: 29 Mar 47 **Final:** 11 Feb 50

Born: Lowestoft 6 Apr 1924

Career: Church Road Junior School; Brooke Marine; NORWICH CITY 20.06.45 (amat), 21.11.46 (pro); Exeter City 22.12.51; Lowestoft Town 20.08.53 to 23.04.59 player coach.

A strong tackler, quick in recovery, Ivan made his first team debut 13.10.45 in a D3S(N) game. Also made 110 reserve appearances, scoring four goals. Norwich alternated between Ivan and Grenville Williams, Len Dutton and Maurice Tobin for the left half position before Ron Ashman permanently claimed the shirt. Ivan became a newsagent upon retiring from football.

ARMSTRONG, Joseph Williams

(1921–1922) **1921:** 5/8; 12/4
Inside Left **Career:** 22-0-8
Debut: 10 Dec 21 **Final:** 6 May 22 (goal)

Born: Blaydon, Tyne & Wear 10 Oct 1892
Died: Cosham 14 May 1966

Career: Hedgefield; Scotswood May 1913; Portsmouth 24.12.13; Sheffield Wednesday 20.05.21; NORWICH CITY 29.11.21; Clapton (trial) 23.08.22; Bournemouth & Boscombe United 19.11.22; Portsmouth Tramways May 1924.

First senior appearance as a Portsmouth player on Boxing Day 1913 against South coast rivals Southampton. Hit 51 goals for them in 103 matches, making his post-War debut against Norwich. His weighty physique demanded respect but the Great War took its toll and he was less successful afterwards. One of six sons, with his unusual middle name being his mother's maiden name. He worked until retirement in 1950 for the Portsmouth Corporation Transport department.

ARNOLD, Eric Arthur

(1947–1952) **1949:** 5/8; 11/3
Left Back **Career:** 13-0-0
Debut: 4 Oct 47 **Final:** 19 Jan 52

Born: Lowestoft 13 Sep 1922

Career: Morton Road School; Lowestoft Corinthians; Brooke Marine; Lowestoft Town 28.12.46; NORWICH CITY 13.09.47; Yarmouth Town Jul 1952–08.05.54; Gorleston.

Served for five years in the Royal Marines. One of five Lowestoft-born men to play for City in the league post war. A cool, clean-kicking back who made an amazing 192 reserve appearances in his stay. His 102 games for Yarmouth Town put him at eleventh place in their charts of 35 ex-Canary first-teamers to play for the club. Given a benefit by Gorleston in May 1959, losing 6–1 to Ipswich Town.

Ron Ashman

ASHMAN, Ronald George

(1947–1963) **1950:** 5/11; 12/2
Left Half/Back **Career:** 662-0-56
Debut: 4 Oct 47 **Final:** 19 Oct 63

Born: Whittlesey, Cambridge 19 May 1926

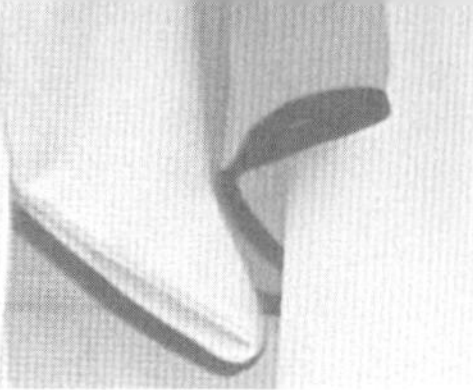

Career: Eastern Counties Air Training Corp; Whittlesey; Peterborough; NORWICH CITY 13.05.44, registered pro Football League 28.01.46. Later coach, acting manager 10.09.62 and Manager Dec 1963 to 23.06.66; Scunthorpe United 16.10.67 to Jun 1973 manager; Grimsby Town Jul 1973 to Feb 1975 manager; Scunthorpe United Jan 1976 to May 1981 manager.

One of the greatest names in City's roll call and rightly awarded an FA 20 year long service statuette. Long time skipper playing a record 590 league and 72 cup games; also made 71 reserve apps. for 20 goals. Shares with Keelan the fine record of playing in 17 successive seasons and Ron alone scored in 11 successive seasons-another record. Five times an ever present; also played at centre forward; took penalties and even played in goal. He of course captained Norwich in the 1959 cup campaign and when they won promotion the following season. His list of achievements and efforts for the club could fill a chapter and if his playing career was not enough he even signed Ron Davies. In an interview he said, 'I had a fantastic life with Norwich City and I never regretted spending my career there. I would do it all again'.

Left: Sidney Austin
Right: Jimmy Banks

ATKINSON, Walter

(1952) **1950:** 5/8; 11/3
Right Half **Career:** 1-0-0
Debut/Final: 2 Apr 52

Born: Ryton-on-Tyne, Gateshead 31 Aug 1920

Career: Hexham Hearts 1947; NORWICH CITY 20.01.49; Consett; Crawcrook Albion; Ashington; Crawcrook Albion retiring 1959.

Spotted by a local scout as an inside forward but adapted to wing half. Gave good service to the Reserves making 82 appearances scoring twice. An Army man (Royal Marine Commando's) he gave good service to Northern clubs for ten years. He retired after breaking an ankle and worked in a steel foundry and for the post office. Deafness and arthritis are crosses for him to bear sustained by visits to his daughter in Australia.

AUSTIN, Sidney William (Sam)

(1920–1924) **1920:** 5/8; 10/4
Outside Right **Career:** 164-0-39
Debut: 23 Oct 20 **Final:** 3 May 24 (goal)

Born: Arnold, Nottingham 29 Apr 1900
Died: Kidderminster 2 Apr 1979.

Career: Arnold United; Sheffield United (trial) 1919; Arnold St Mary's; NORWICH CITY 19.10.20; Manchester City 06.05.24; Chesterfield 09.12.31; Kidderminster Harriers Jun 1933; R.C. Roubaix (France) 1933/34.

Amazingly he started out as a goalkeeper but as an outfield player rapidly made a name for himself scoring and making goals. Arguably his greatest game was at Old Trafford in 1926 when in a stunning 6–1 win for the Blues he scored twice, hit the bar twice and the inside of a post once. Sam was fast, centred well and was the owner of a clinking shot. After leaving City he won a Division Two medal, played in the 1928 FA Cup final and gained an England cap. Scored regularly at the highest level (over 40 goals at Man City). Sam married a Norwich girl and his son Sam junior had a trial with Norwich in 1953. City made a healthy profit in selling him for £2,000 but one wonders what would have happened had he lingered at The Nest a while longer.

BACON, Ronald Alfred Sydney

(1955–1958) **1957:** 5/6; 10/7
Inside/Outside Right **Career:** 42-0-6
Debut: 24 Dec 55 (goal) **Final:** 25 Jan 58

Born: Fakenham 4 Mar 1935

Career: Holt Primary School; Holt United 1950; NORWICH CITY 13.12.55; Gillingham 07.05.58; King's Lynn Jul 1961–Apr 1968; Downham Town Sep 1970–1972.

Ron left the Army and trialled for Norwich City at Boundary Park. He scored on his first-team debut at Coventry. Took over Johnny Gavins' shirt, which was a hard act to follow. For the Reserves he scored 19 times in 63 games. City once rejected a £10,000 bid for him from Chelsea manager Ted Drake. He gave King's Lynn sterling service, making his 290th appearance for them on New Year's Eve 1966. An achilles heel injury and a bad knee

brought about his retirement, whereupon he became a self-employed master decorator.

BAKER, Clive Edward

(1978–1981) **1978:** 5/9; 11/0
Goalkeeper **Career:** 16-0-0
Debut: 26 Apr 78 **Final:** 31 Jan 81

Born: North Walsham 14 Mar 1959

Career: Paston School; Sheringham; NORWICH CITY (assoc), (juniors), 29.07.77 (pro); Barnsley 07.08.84; Coventry City 21.08.91; Ipswich Town 20.08.92–May 1996.

Played for England Under-19 cricket team and spent seven years as understudy to Kevin Keelan and Chris Woods, finally making only 14 League appearances. After 30 months without a League game he proceeded to keep 11 clean sheets in his first 14 games for Barnsley. He was their Player of the Year twice, making almost 300 appearances. After a second knee injury he was advised by his surgeon to give up the game to avoid problems in his later life. Possessor of a pure mathematics degree, he was studying for an HNC in business and finance. Now working in the insurance industry.

BALL, Stephen John

(1991–1992) **1991:** 6/0; 12/6
Inside Right **Career:** 0-4-0
Debut: 21 Sep 91 (sub) **Final:** 4 Mar 92 (sub)

Born: Colchester 2 Sep 1969

Career: Severals FC; Essex Schoolboys; Arsenal Schoolboys 1984, 29.09.87 (app); Ipswich Town (trial); Colchester United 29.12.89; NORWICH CITY 18.08.90; Colchester United 14.09.92; Sudbury Town Mar 1996–24.07.98; Hednesford Town; Stanway Rovers Oct 1998 player-manager.

Injuries have plagued Steve's career, from a serious ankle ligament problem whilst with Arsenal and hamstring trouble at Colchester to a tennis injury and a broken jaw. His FA Youth Cup winner's medal at Highbury was earned by playing alongside Miller, Hillier, Heaney and Campbell. For City he netted 11 goals in 64 reserve matches as an attacking midfielder. Disillusioned, he left professional football to join the non-league circuit.

BANKS, James Andrew

(1923–1927) **1923:** 5/8;11/12
Inside Forward/
Outside Right **Career:** 136-0-26
Debut: 6 Oct 23 **Final:** 30 Apr 27

Born: Wigan 28 Apr 1893
Died: Chelsea 25 Aug 1942

Career: Starcliffe Celtic; St Gregory's; Spennymoor United; All Saints FC Willington Athletic; Tottenham Hotspur Dec 1913; NORWICH CITY 29.09.23; Luton Town 31.08.27; London Public Omnibus Company player/coach to Oct 1930; Worthing Town Aug 1938 trainer/coach.

A strong resolute player who took hard knocks as a matter of course. Described as a scientific man not averse to making penalty claims by sliding into the area. For Spurs he hit 109 goals with five threes and one five, playing in the Charity Shield and a Cup Final. One admiring observer noted that 'He had verve, swerve and nerve'. That he could kick a ball goalwards as hard as most players was another press saying. He commanded attention and higher remuneration than his colleagues. Jimmy became a bus driver and was connected with a taxi-cab firm in Wood Green.

BANNISTER, Keith

(1956–1957) **1956:** 5/10: 11/8
Right Half **Career:** 7-0-0
Debut: 25 Dec 56 **Final:** 26 Jan 57

Born: Sheffield 13 Nov 1930

Career: Rawcliffe Boys; Sheffield & Haslam Boys; Oaks Fold; Sheffield United 26.05.48 from juniors; Birmingham City 20.07.50; King's Lynn Aug 1954; Wrexham 18.07.55; Chesterfield 13.12.55; NORWICH CITY 03.07.56; Peterborough United Jul 1957; King's Lynn Jul 1958.

Keith picked up an England Youth Cap while attached to Sheffield and Haslam in 1948. The 97th league debutant for the club after the War, and he did not pick up a win bonus in any of his seven games for Norwich. Also had 23 reserve games in City's colours, a total in keeping with his tally at his other clubs as he did not pass two dozen appearances at any of them. Ex-Royal Artillery, he also qualified as a bricklayer at night school.

BARHAM, Mark Francis

(1979–1987) **1984:** 5/7; 11/0
Winger **Career:** 213-10-25
Debut: 24 Nov 79 **Final:** 14 Feb 87

Born: Folkestone 12 Jul 1962

Career: NORWICH CITY 22.06.78 (app), 24.0.80 (pro); Huddersfield Town 03.07.87; Middlesbrough 29.10.88; Hythe Town Sep 1989; West Bromwich Albion (trial) 11.09.89; Brighton

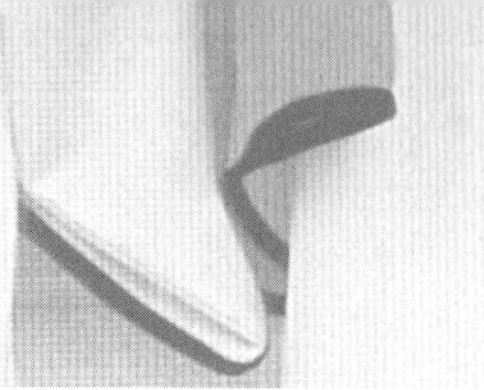

& Hove Albion 29.12.89; Shrewsbury Town 03.09.92; Kitchee (Hong Kong) Nov 1992; Southwick Feb 1993; Sittingbourne Aug 1993; Fakenham Town assistant manager, Apr 1996, Jul 1996–Dec 1997 manager; Mulbarton Feb 1998.

Mark Barham

Mark made his youth team debut in February 1978 and captained them to the South East Counties title in 1979/80. His twisting, speedy wing play won him full international honours for England, as a maker of goals rather than a personal scorer. He fulfilled an ambition of playing at Wembley, the occasion being City's Milk Cup win over Sunderland. Mark jokes that he had his own bed at BUPA, having endured 23 operations. Now involved with the corporate entertainment at Carrow Road he made a welcome 20-minute appearance at the end of physio Tim Sheppard's testimonial game against Glasgow Celtic in January 2001.

BARKAS, Edward (Ned)

(1920) **1920:** 5/8; 12/12
Centre Forward **Career:** 1-0-0
Debut/Final: 16 Oct 20

Born: Wardley Colliery, Northumberland 21 Nov 1901
Died: Little Bromwich, Birmingham 24 Apr 1962.

Career: St Hilda Old Boys; East Boldon; Hebburn Colliery; Bedlington United; South Shields; Wardley Colliery 1919; Hebburn Colliery Oct 1920; NORWICH CITY 16.10.20 (amat); Bedlington United; Huddersfield Town 27.01.21 (pro); Birmingham City 29.12.28; Chelsea 21.05.37; Solihull Town Jul 1939 player-manager; Willmott Breedon FC 1943; Nuffield Mechanisations FC

Ned was the one that got away. Joined City on trial after being spotted when scoring twice for Hebburn Colliery in the FA Cup. His Canary debut can be summed up as dashing at times with no support. Converted to full back, where he delighted in the good shoulder charge. He had a distinguished career at his next two clubs, gaining two League championship medals at Huddersfield and making two Wembley Cup Final appearances. Formerly a miner he had four footballing brothers: Sam (England international), who was in the car crash that finished the famed Eric Brook's career, Henry, Tom and James. He was also a cousin to England international William Felton.

BARNARD, Geoffrey

(1965–1966) **1966:** 5/11; 12/5
Goalkeeper **Career:** 6-0-0
Debut: 10 Apr 65 **Final:** 31 Dec 66

Born: Southend 23 Mar 1946

Career: Southend United (amat); NORWICH CITY 23.09.63; Scunthorpe United 03.07.68–1974; Scarborough Town 1974; Scunthorpe United 10.09.76–May 1977.

Geoff played 114 reserve matches in his five-year stay, once featuring in a 6–6 draw. Worked as an apprentice engineer at Southend Airport when joining City. Another keeper vying for the custodian's job with Kennon and Keelan. Conceded 11 goals in his six games before enjoying regular football at Scunthorpe alongside Nigel Cassidy, Bill Punton and Kevin Keegan.

BARNES, Charles Ronald (Ron)

(1963– 1964) **1964:** 5/11; 11/0
Outside Right **Career:** 25-0-1
Debut: 31 Aug 63 **Final:** 27 Mar 64

Born: Bolton 21 Feb 1936
Died: Darcy Lever 7 Dec 1991

Career: Juniors to Blackpool 06.05.54; Rochdale 02.06.59; Wrexham 18.07.61; NORWICH CITY 28.08.63; Peterborough United 25.06.64; Torquay United 27.01.66–1968; Cape Town City (South Africa) May 1969–Dec 1970.

Understudy to Stanley Matthews at Blackpool, which was a no-win situation. In competition for the right wing spot with Gerry Mannion when at Carrow Road. Netted twice in 15 reserve games for City but did best at Plainmoor where his scoring ratio was one in four expressed over 100 games. Alongside Brian Whitehouse for Wrexham's record win of 10–1 in 1962. He emigrated to South Africa where he worked in the printing trade for 20 years.

BARNSLEY, Geoffrey Robert

(1961–1962) **1961:** 5/10; 11/6
Goalkeeper **Career:** 8-0-0
Debut: 2 Dec 61 **Final:** 20 Jan 62

Born: Bilston 9 Dec 1935

Career: Bilston School; Erdington Albion; Wolverhampton Wanderers (trial); West Bromwich Albion 03.05.51; Plymouth Argyle 04.06.57; NORWICH CITY 12.05.61; Torquay United 03.12.62; Dudley Town Jul 1964; Hednesford Town; Bilston; Dudley Town; Darlaston retiring 1971.

City signed Geoff in preference to Bolton's Johnny Bollands and his eight games spread over just seven weeks saw City achieve a 5–4 win, a 5–4 loss, and a double loss against his former club. He was a popular regular at Plymouth, with a debut for them against Norwich and a last appearance against Ipswich at Plainmoor, as Home Park was closed by order of the FA after a bottle-throwing incident in a previous match. Geoff spent seven years on the non-league circuit and now lives in the West Midlands.

BAXTER, Laurence Raymond (Larry)

(1954–1955) **1955:** 5/11; 11/3
Inside Forward **Career:** 5-0-0
Debut: 27 Nov 54 **Final:** 12 Apr 55

Born: Leicester 24 Nov 1931

Career: Knarlborough Road School; Leicester Boys; Northampton Town 06.03.52; NORWICH CITY 05.11.54; Gillingham 24.10.55; Torquay United 06.09.57; Deal Town 1961; Margate 1962; Cheltenham Town Jul 1962; Deal Town Apr 1964 player-manager; Margate Dec 1965; Loughborough United Mar 1966; Newfoundpool WMC; Linwood Lane player-manager; Enderby Forest; GEC Leicester; Groby player-manager; Blaby Boys Club; St Andrew's to 1990.

Larry only played once at Carrow Road and was unfortunately on the losing side in all his five games. He felt that he deserved a longer run, and this is backed up by his strike rate for the City stiffs – 11 goals in 22 games. The value of speaking to every player where possible is evidenced by being able to record here Larry's remarkable 30-year career in non-league football.

BECKFORD, Darren Richard Lorenzo

(1991–1993) **1991:** 6/1; 11/11
Centre Forward **Career:** 40-9-13
Debut: 17 Aug 91 **Final:** 24 Jan 93

Born: Manchester 12 May 1967

Career: Abbott County Primary School; Burnage High School; Manchester Boys; Manchester City 13.11.81 (assoc), 18.04.84 (app), 21.08.84 (pro); Bury (loan) 10.10.85; Port Vale 26.03.87; NORWICH CITY 07.06.91; Oldham Athletic 25.03.93; Heart of Midlothian 14.08.96; Preston North End 10.01.97; Fulham 10.02.97; Walsall 25.03.97; Rushden & Diamonds (trial) 22.09.97; Southport 07.10.97; Total Network Solutions 07.11.97; Bury 08.12.97; Bacup Borough 20.12.98.

An England schoolboy and youth international, Darren spent six years at Maine Road. He joined the Canaries for a club record £925,000, fixed by a tribunal after Vale priced him at £1.5 million. A fine athlete with good pace, he had an unfortunate time at Carrow Road with his second season disrupted by injuries. In recent years he has moved from club to club on a regular basis.

BELL, John Russell (Jackie)

(1962–1964) **1957:** 5/8; 10/10
Left Half **Career:** 58-0-5
Debut: 18 Aug 62 **Final:** 30 Mar 64

Born: Evenwood, County Durham 17 Oct 1939
Died: Gainford, Darlington 22 Apr 1991

Career: Evenwood Town; Newcastle Utd 27.10.56; NORWICH CITY 16.07.62; Colchester United 29.05.65–30.06.66.

An attacking wing half who scored on his Football League debut (16.11.57). Overcame a knee injury and was later a subject of controversy when signed by City, as it was reckoned that the Geordies had not disclosed that Jackie was a diabetic. Good enough though to be an England Under-23 reserve. Sandy Kennon and Duncan Forbes played in the same Colchester side as Jackie. After football he worked in the building trade but following a work accident he had a leg amputated below the knee. Newcastle United played Evenwood Town in a testimonial match for him in 1990.

BELL, Robert Charles (Bobby)

(1972) **1971:** 6/0; 11/11
Centre Half **Career:** 3-0-0
Debut: 12 Feb 72 **Final:** 4 Mar 72

Born: Cambridge 26 Oct 1950

Career: Tottenham Hotspur 28.05.66 (app), 15.08.67 (amat); Ipswich Town 07.09.67 (amat), 07.01.68 (pro); Blackburn Rovers 11.09.71; Crystal Palace 23.09.71; NORWICH CITY 07.02.72 (a months loan); Hellenic (South Africa); York City 03.02.77; Fort Lauderdale Strikers (USA) Apr 1977–Jun 1977

Bobby could not displace Bill Baxter at Ipswich and he moved to Crystal Palace via Blackburn Rovers. Became City's first loan player with his last game resulting in City being displaced from the top of Division Two after a run of 23 weeks. Spells followed in South Africa and America before he returned to live in Suffolk.

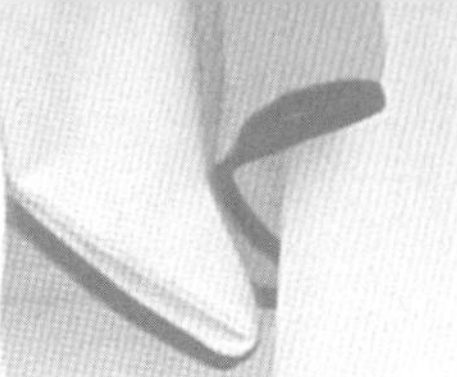

BELL, Samuel

(1930–1934) **1929:** 5/9; 10/6
Inside Right **Career:** 79-0-27
Debut: 6 Sep 30 (goal) **Final:** 21 Apr 34 (goal)

Born: Burnhope 6 Feb 1909
Died: Southend 6 Jan 1982

Career: Burnhope Institute; NORWICH CITY 28.04.30; Luton Town 30.04.34; Tottenham Hotspur 08.03.35; Southend United 07.05.37–1946; Chelmsford City Jul 1948; Tonbridge Jul 1949.

Sammy netted 117 goals in 281 career games. He 'had more brains and less brimstone and could take more than one berth in the attack'. Kept his wing man going with studied passes and packed a powerful shot, later traitorously used to score five times against Norwich. In charge of the Southend Greyhound Stadium after the War.

Left: Craig Bellamy
Right: Albert Bennett

BELL, Walter Charles

(1920) **1920:** 5/10; 12/0
Centre Forward/ Inside Left **Career:** 3-0-2
Debut: 16 Sep 20 (2 goals) **Final:** 16 Oct 20

Born: Norwich 26 Feb 1896
Died: Norwich 11 Dec 1982

Career: Old Meeting House School; Coslany United; St Gregory's; Technical Institute; Norwich Priory; Army; Norfolk County; NORWICH CITY 07.08.20; Norwich Priory; City Wanderers.

Wally had seven Southern League games for City scoring twice in addition to his football league stats above. He played for the RFA and scored 87 goals in one year for Coslany as well as over 30 goals for Norwich Priory. A most serviceable and popular forward recruited from local amateur circles. First Norwich City player to score two goals in a Football League match and all the more noteworthy as they came on the occasion of his debut. For 40 years he worked for a well-known local shoe factory.

BELLAMY, Craig Douglas

(1997–2000) **1997:** 5/9; 10/12
Forward **Career:** 78-13-34
Debut: 15 Mar 97 (sub) **Final:** 12 Aug 00

Born: St David's, Cardiff 13 Jul 1977

Career: Trowbridge Junior School; Rymney High School; Cardiff Schools; Caerstell YC; Bristol Rovers School of Excellence 1990; Canary Rangers; NORWICH CITY 13.07.93 (assoc), 02.08.95 (trainee), 20.01.97 (pro); Coventry City 17.07.2000; Newcastle United 26.06.2001.

Over 100 goals for his junior school and a City youth debut in October 1994 saw him net 59 goals at Under-First XI level. Plenty of self confidence and pace (his mother's maiden name) has seen Craig quite rightly capped at all levels for his country, both providing and scoring goals. Reached hero status at Carrow Road with his talented and determined efforts. A dreadful cruciate ligament injury ruled out almost an entire season but he recovered and joined Coventry linking up with his Welsh international colleague John Hartson. As we go to press he has signed for Newcastle, thereby maintaining his expressed wish of playing in the Premiership.

BENNETT, Albert

(1969–1971) **1970:** 5/11; 11/9
Forward **Career:** 59-1-16
Debut: 1 Mar 69 **Final:** 20 Feb 71

Born: Durham 16 Jul 1944

Career: Chester Moor Juniors 1961; Rotherham United 06.02.62; Newcastle United 22.07.65; NORWICH CITY 25.02.69 retired 30.03.71; Bury St Edmunds Jul 1972 player-manager; Sprowston Athletic (2 times); Thurlton; Yarmouth Town Oct 1979–May 1981; Sprowston; Carrow; Quebec Rovers; Sprowston Thursday; Taverners (Sunday).

Curly-haired and leggy, Albert was a good goalscorer but beset by injury. Gained England Youth & Under-23 caps, helping Newcastle into European soccer. He was Norwich's first signing after the sale of Hugh Curran and hit a fine hat-trick at Fratton Park in April 1970. At one time he was notable for his white boots. A colourful character off the field as well, he later worked at a variety of jobs: prison service, hotel catering, Lowestoft joke shop and local hostelries.

BENNETT, David Paul

(1979–1984) **1979:** 5/11; 11/7
Winger/later Midfield **Career:** 77-8-11
Debut: 10 Feb 79 **Final:** 31 Mar 84

Born: Oldham 26 Apr 1960

Career: Tameside Boys; Manchester City 15.07.76 (app); NORWICH CITY 03.08.78; Portland Timbers (USA) Jun 1982; MVV Maastricht (Holland); Volendam (Holland); Norwich Busmen.

Dave developed into a silky, technically brilliant player, unfortunately dogged by a stream of injuries. He took an insurance pay-out at the youthful age of 25. Returning from Holland he occasionally turned out in the Norwich Sunday league but by then he had had five knee operations. Quaintly he once had a bar in Ibiza called 'Confusion'. He was last spotted by the author at Dover when both were making a cross-channel ferry journey.

BENNETT, Edward Thomas

(1930) **1929:** 5/9; 11/10
Right Back **Career:** 11-0-0
Debut: 5 Apr 30 **Final:** 13 Sep 30

Born: Barton Regis 10 Aug 1904
Died: Bristol 1957

Career: Local Bristol football; Swansea Town 30.03.23; Wrexham 27.05.25; Manchester City 04.05.26; NORWICH CITY 10.05.29–May 1931.

Teamed up with Sam Austin at Maine Road but became disenchanted when he found senior opportunities limited. Fared little better at Norwich as City were well off for backs with Hannah and Richmond in occupancy. Edward refused the terms offered by City and his contract was cancelled for bad conduct, according to the Norwich City's secretary's report to Football League Headquarters. Latterly a barman, a publican and a council worker.

BENSON, John Harvey

(1973–1975) **1974:** 5/10; 11/10
Defender **Career:** 35-2-1
Debut: 15 Dec 73 **Final:** 11 Jan 75

Born: Arbroath 23 Dec 1942

Career: Stockport Boys; Manchester City 31.07.58 (amat), 03.07.61 (pro); Torquay United 15.06.64; Bournemouth 21.10.70; Exeter City (loan) 07.03.73; NORWICH CITY 12.12.73; Bournemouth & Boscombe Athletic 29.01.75 – Jan 1979 player-manager; Norwich City youth coach /scout; Manchester City Oct 1980 assistant manager, 08.02.83–06.06.83 manager; Burnley Aug 1984–May 1985 manager; coaching in Dubai; Al Nasa (Kuwait) 1987–1990 coach; Barnsley 1990–11.03.94 chief scout; NORWICH CITY 23.03.94 administration assistant, 09.04.95 assistant to G.Megson to 31.05.95; Wigan Athletic 02.11.95 assistant manager, Jun 1999–May 2000 manager, Apr 2001 youth development.

John was a development of Manchester City's junior teams and an early football Who's Who stated, 'He gets through his work in a quiet efficient manner with the minimum of frills'. Part of the Bond/Bournemouth dynasty, he followed John Bond on his many travels. He was in promotion-winning sides as a player and lost jobs after suffering relegation seasons. His club in season 1999/2000 had the longest unbeaten start to the campaign and his eventual replacement as manager was Bruce Rioch.

BENSTEAD, Graham Mark

(1985–1988) **1985:** 6/1; 12/11
Goalkeeper **Career:** 19-0-0
Debut: 6 Apr 85 **Final:** 6 Feb 88

Born: Aldershot 20 Aug 1963

Career: Mayford Athletic; Tudor Rovers; Wimbledon (amat); Queens Park Rangers 08.07.81; NORWICH CITY 28.03.85; Colchester United 10.08.87 (three month loan); Sheffield United (loan) 22.03.88, signed 19.07.88; Brentford 30.07.90; Kettering Town 24.09.93; Rushden & Diamonds Jul 1995; Kingstonian (loan) 25.02.97; Brentford Oct 1997–Jan 1998 player coach; Basingstoke Town; Chertsey Town Mar 1999.

Graham seemed destined to be a permanent understudy to Chris Woods until Woods' transfer afforded him the golden opportunity to establish himself in the first team. Among the managers of the personable Graham have been Tom Docherty and Terry Venables. His longest first-team spell was at Brentford with Garry Brooke and Simon Ratcliffe for company. Widely regarded as the best goalkeeper outside the Football League he represented his country at non-league level.

BERTRAM, William

(1921–1922) **1921:** 5/8; 11/4
Inside Right **Career:** 30-0-3
Debut: 27 Aug 21 **Final:** 6 May 22

Born: Langley Moor 31 Dec 1897
Died: Crossgate Hospital, Durham 27 Oct 1962

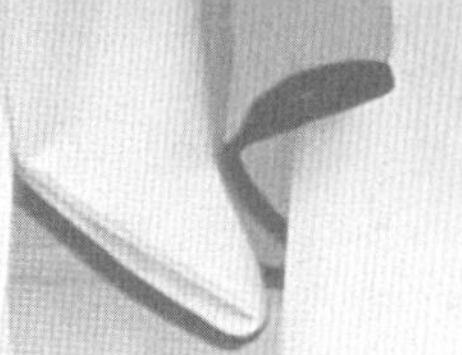

Career: Browney Colliery; Durham City (amat); Newcastle United 09.04.20; NORWICH CITY 18.05.21; Leadgate Park Aug 1922; Durham City 13.06.23; Rochdale 20.05.25; Accrington Stanley 09.10.31.

During the First World War William served in the Durham Light Infantry. A pocket dynamo of a player not unlike Trevor Hockey. City beat Derby and Glasgow Rangers to his signature and his three goals for the Canaries pales against his 104 career total. Became a noted player at Rochdale and upon retirement from the game he took on the role of publican but was latterly a coal miner stoneman.

BERTSCHIN, Keith Edwin

(1981–1984) **1982:** 6/1; 11/8
Striker **Career:** 136-2-38
Debut: 29 Aug 81 **Final:** 15 Sep 84

Born: Enfield 25 Aug 1956

Career: Mountgrace School; Barnet; Ipswich Town 01.10.73; Birmingham City 30.07.77; NORWICH CITY 25.08.81; Jacksonville Tea Men (USA) May 1982; Stoke City 15.11.84; Sunderland 25.03.87; Walsall 28.07.88; Chester City 22.11.90; Aldershot 03.09.91; Solihull Borough Mar 1992; Evesham United 1993; Barry Town 1994; Worcester City Aug 1994–16.03.95; Hednesford Town May 1995; Tamworth FC; Stafford Rangers 1996.

Famously scored with his first touch in the Football League and latterly recovered well from a broken leg in 1979. A likeable, whole-hearted, tireless worker with a Canary record not too dissimilar from that of Boyer. Brave and good in the air, his other sporting love is angling, being shown 'tight lines' by City's club photographer Roger Harris. He topped 100 league goals, including – remarkably – 29 for each of Birmingham, Norwich and Stoke. All his clubs benefited from Keith's effervescent ability until he hung up his boots in 1998. Has successively and successfully worked in insurance and as a salesman and is now a football agent with 19 players on his books.

BIGGINS, Wayne (Bertie)

(1985–1988) **1985:** 5/11; 11/0
Striker **Career:** 82-15-21
Debut: 23 Oct 85 **Final:** 7 May 88

Born: Sheffield 20 Nov 1961

Career: Lincoln City Feb 1977 (schoolboy), Jul 1978 (app), 11.11.79 (pro); Matlock Town Jun 1981; King's Lynn Aug 1981; Burnley 04.02.84; NORWICH CITY 14.10.85; Manchester City 29.06.88; Stoke City 10.08.89; Barnsley 02.10.92; Glasgow Celtic 25.11.93; Stoke City 24.03.94; Luton Town 20.01.95; Oxford United 06.07.95; Wigan Athletic 17.11.95–17.05.97; Leek Town Aug 1997; Stocksbridge Park Steels Aug 1998.

Bertie – a nickname held from the age of nine – was working as a hod carrier on a building site when he rejoined League football with Burnley – ironically replacing Kevin Reeves. He actually scored on his Football League debut and got a hat-trick in his fourth game for Burnley. Kevin Drinkell and Wayne Biggins scored many vital goals for the Canaries with the latter stating that he loved it at Norwich. Always enthusiastic, called 'Biggles' at Celtic (being good in the air) with a phenomenal workrate that made him popular with the fans. A Wembley appearance with Stoke was a particular highlight. He suffered superficial burns to his hands in a fire at his pallet business in 1998.

BILLINGTON, Charles Royston

(1956–1957) **1956:** 6/3; 13/7
Centre Half **Career:** 22-0-0
Debut: 28 Jan 56 **Final:** 1 May 57

Born: Chesterfield 8 Nov 1927
Died: Newbold 19 Nov 1985

Career: Chesterfield (amat); Aldershot Dec 1944, Jun 1947 (pro); NORWICH CITY 26.01.56; Watford 28.06.57; Mansfield Town 26.05.58; Burton Albion May 1959.

Admirably equipped physically for his position, he turned pro upon leaving the forces. A capable stopper topping over 200 appearances at Aldershot along with Ken Flint, Hedley Sheppard and John Jack. His Norwich spell was in a doleful season for City. He did no worse than anyone else but was eventually placed on the transfer list as being surplus to requirements. Latterly a core maker.

BIRCH, Clifford

(1950) **1950:** 5/6; 10/8
Outside Right **Career:** 5-0-3
Debut: 4 Feb 50 (goal) **Final:** 4 Mar 50

Born: Crumlin, Gwent 1 Sep 1928
Died: Norwich 28 Feb 1990

Career: Treowen Stars 1946; Cardiff City 1946 (amat); Ebbw Vale; NORWICH CITY 05.07.46 (app), 25.12.46 (pro); Newport County 12.10.50; Colchester United 03.06.54; Spalding Aug 1954; Yarmouth Town 11.07.55–31.03.56; Gorleston retiring 1958.

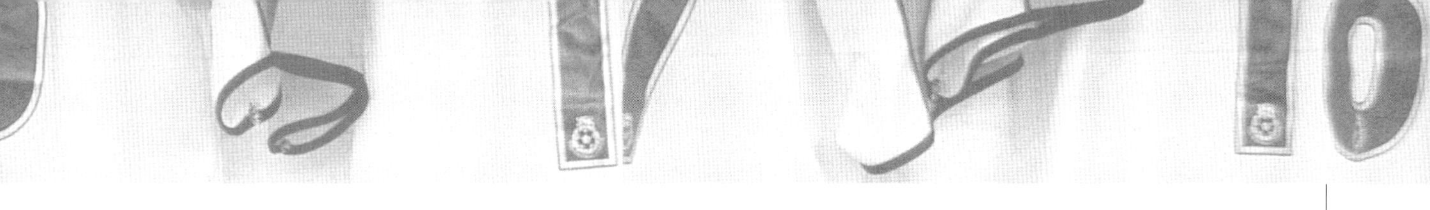

A lively winger whose Army service served to restrict his Canary appearances. Served his Welsh club with distinction for four years after being taken on a month's trial with a view to taking George Morgan's place. Played for the Welsh League in 1951. He married Daphne, a Norwich girl, on the morning of 25 March 1951 and scored against Norwich City in the afternoon. Scored 19 goals in 32 games for the 'Bloaters'. Cliff retired from the railways four years before his fatal heart attack.

BLACK, Alan Douglas

(1966–1973) **1970:** 6/0; 12/0
Left Back **Career:** 199-4-1
Debut: 6 Sep 66 **Final:** 10 Nov 73

Born: Alexandria, nr Dumbarton 4 Jun 1943

Career: Dumbartonshire Schools; Drumchapel Amateurs; Dumbarton 1961 (amat); Clydebank; Dumbarton May 1962; Sunderland 15.08.64; NORWICH CITY 06.09.66; Dumbarton 24.01.74–1975.

Alan captained his county schoolboy sides through to Under-18 and stayed an amateur in order to finish his apprenticeship as a toolmaker. Regular left back for six years, being Lol Morgan's first City signing. Not the demonstrative type of player, he proved a barrier to opposing marauders with sound and consistent displays. A knee injury precipitated his retirement and he undertook various occupations within the licensing trade followed by management of a hotel and a taxi firm business.

BLADES, Paul Andrew

(1990–1992) **1990:** 6/0; 11/0
Defender **Career:** 62-0-0
Debut: 25 Aug 90 **Final:** 2 May 92

Born: Peterborough 5 Jan 1965

Career: Gunthorpe Junior School; Walton Comprehensive School; Peterborough Boys; Cambridgshire County; Weston Star YC; Derby County 21.07.81 (app), 29.12.82 (pro); NORWICH CITY 03.07.90; Wolverhampton Wanderers 14.08.92; Rotherham United 18.07.95; Hednesford Town Jun 1997; Gresley Rovers Apr 1999–Aug 1999 player coach.

Paul won a TV penalty prize competition at Wembley when just thirteen. A pacy central defender with good aerial skills he joined City for a then-record fee of £700,000 – fixed by a tribunal. He became Rotherham's biggest signing and maintained his quality by making the FA XI squad – England's semi-pro team.

BLAIR, James

(1972–1973) **1973:** 6/0; 11/7
Inside Right **Career:** 6-5-1
Debut: 30 Sep 72 **Final:** 29 Dec 73

Born: Calderbank, nr Airdrie 13 Jan 1947

Career: Hibernian; St Mirren; NORWICH CITY 26.09.72; Mechelen (Belgium) Jun 1974 to 1978; Rotselaar (Belgium) Under-16 coach; FC Tremelo (Belgium) trainer; Sparta (Belgium) trainer; Haacht (Belgium) trainer

Rangy, willowy forward who left Scotland with a fine scoring record of 64 goals for Tommy Brycelands' St Mirren. Remarkable in that among his few Canary games were two Cup Final appearances. He successfully helped in the upturn of Mechelen and has resided in Belgium since 1974, where he works for the Belgium Aviation Authority.

BLAKEMORE, Cecil

(1931–1933) **1932:** 5/10; 11/6
Inside Left **Career:** 70-0-29
Debut: 29 Aug 31 **Final:** 14 Apr 33

Born: Stourbridge 8 Dec 1897
Died: Lutley 15 Sep 1963

Career: Redditch Town; Fairfield Villa; Stourbridge; Redditch Town; Aston Villa Oct 1921–May 1922 (amat); Crystal Palace 15.09.22; Bristol City 16.05.27; Brentford 02.05.29; NORWICH CITY 17.08.31; Swindon Town 30.06.33; Brierley Hill Alliance Jul 1934.

Norwich paid a good sum to capture Cecil and he continued to enhance his fine goalscoring reputation. In his first season with City he outscored Oliver Brown and Sam Bell and later hit a hat-trick against Coventry in February 1933. Won glowing praise in a wandering league career. Netted 140 goals in 347 league games including four hat-tricks. He was latterly a publican and hotelier.

de BLASIIS, Jean Yves

(1999–2001) **1999:** 5/9; 11/5
Midfield **Career:** 30-8-0
Debut: 7 Aug 99 **Final:** 10 Mar 01 (sub)

Born: Bordeaux, France 25 Sep 1973

Career: FC Girondis Bordeaux (France) 1988; Stade Malherbe Caen (France) 1996; Red Star 93 (France) 1997; NORWICH CITY 31.07.99–19.04.2001; FC Girondis Bordeaux (France), FC Istres Ville Nouvelle (France) Jul 2001.

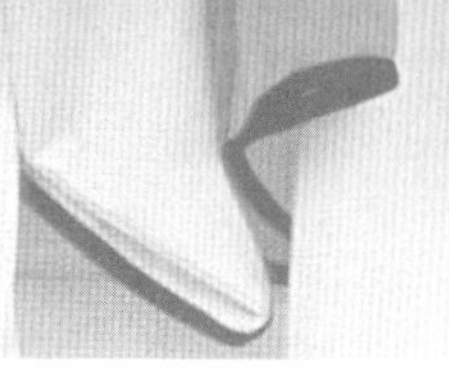

A stylish playmaker, Jean Yves was a free agent under the Bosman transfer ruling. He was signed to supplement City's beleagured team following the devastating injuries to Eadie and Bellamy. Thirteen caps at French youth level before becoming a contract player as an 'aspirant' and 'stagiaire'. His agent's fax to the club showed him playing 261 games in France. Sitting in front of the back four he performed admirably before suffering a cruciate ligament injury.

Left: Gordon Bolland
Right: Kevin Bond

BLY, Terrence Geoffrey

(1956–1960) **1964:** 6/0; 11/10
Centre forward **Career:** 67-0-38
Debut: 18 Aug 56 **Final:** 27 Feb 60

Born: Fincham, Norfolk 22 Oct 1935

Career: NORWICH CITY 'B'; RAF (Barnham); Bury St Edmunds: NORWICH CITY 13.08.56; Peterborough United 21.06.60; Coventry City 08.07.62; Notts County 14.08.63; Grantham Town 05.10.64 player-manager for 15 years.

One of the most famous names in Canary folklore needed two attempts to become a Norwich City player being initially watched by Tom Parker and Alf Kirchen. Came to prominence nationally during the 1958/9 Cup run but played surprisingly few games in a City shirt. A prolific scorer (205 league appearances – 141 goals), including a record 52 in Posh's first league season. Regularly returns for Old Boys reunions and is currently recovering from a hip operation in February 2001.

BOLLAND, Gordon Edward

(1964–1967) **1964:** 6/0; 11/4
Forward **Career:** 117-1-35
Debut: 17 Mar 64 **Final:** 11 Oct 67

Born: Boston, Lincolnshire 12 Aug 1943

Career: Kitwood Secondary Modern School; Lincolnshire County; Boston United (amat); Chelsea (groundstaff), Feb 1959 (amat), Aug 1960 (pro); Leyton Orient 03.03.62; NORWICH CITY 14.03.64; Charlton Athletic 27.11.67; Millwall 29.10.68; Boston United 01.06.75–1977 player-manager; Boston United Jan 1996 Director.

One scribe discerningly wrote, 'tall, long-striding with neat control and good shot'. He netted 112 Football League goals and among them were the third fastest home team goal at Carrow Road: against Swansea, just 30 seconds after the kick-off. Gordon holds the dubious honour of being the first ever used substitute in a league match by City. Latterly working for a tyre distributor in his home town.

BOND, Kevin John

(1976–1981) **1976:** 6/0; 12/0
Central Defender **Career:** 156-5-14
Debut: 10 Apr 76 **Final:** 21 Feb 81

Born: West Ham 22 Jun 1957

Career: Bournemouth 02.11.71 (assoc), 21.07.72 (app); NORWICH CITY 17.06.74 (app), 02.04.76 (pro); Seattle Sounders (USA) Feb 1981–Aug 1981; Manchester City 08.09.81; Southampton 25.08.84; Bournemouth 08.08.88; Exeter City 07.08.92; Sittingbourne 29.03.94; Dover Athletic Mar 1995; Manchester City Jul 1996 reserve coach; Stafford Rangers 17.10.97 player-manager; Portsmouth 06.05.98 coach, 09.12.99 assistant coach; Salisbury City Sep 2000; West Ham United scout.

Came as a bright young raw recruit, later attracting big transfer fees. Overcame the banter from the crowd that can be expected when the manager also happens to be your father. Moved up from full back and scored useful goals. He netted at both ends in successive games in March 1980. Rose to team captaincy, Player of the Year in 1979 and an England B cap. Kept meeting up with ex-Canaries – Barham (Sittingbourne), Ryan (Dover) and Bertschin and Butterworth at Stafford Rangers.

BONE, James

(1972–1973) **1973:** 5/9; 11/8
Striker **Career:** 47-0-13
Debut: 4 Mar 72 **Final:** 10 Feb 73

Born: Bridge of Allan, Stirlingshire 22 Sep 1949

Career: Stirling High School; Fallin Boys Brigade; Bannockburn; Airth Castle Rovers 1967; Partick Thistle 28.05.68; NORWICH CITY 29.02.72; Sheffield United 22.03.73; Glasgow Celtic 20.02.74; Arbroath 10.01.75; St Mirren

02.02.78; Toronto Blizzard (Canada) May 1979–Aug 1979; Hong Kong Rangers 08.06.81; Heart of Midlothian 03.08.83; Arbroath 21.02.85 player-manager; St Mirren 16.12.86–22.02.88 assistant manager; Dundee United 24.02.88 coaching staff; Airdrieonians 19.05.89–14.05.91 manager; Power Dynamoes (Zambia) 16.05.91 manager; St Mirren 26.05.92–14.08.96 manager; East Fife 05.10.96–10.12.97 manager; Dunfermline Athletic 07.01.98 coach; Dundee.

Bustling and aggressive and scorer of City's first ever Division One goal. Consistent scorer for the 'Jags', 'Red Lichties', 'Buddies' and 'Maroons' with his total o'er the border exceeding 100. His reckless bravery endeared him to the Carrow Road faithful. An illustrious coaching and management career in Scotland has him involved with the Scottish Football Association helping people become coaches.

BOOTH, Curtis (Tommy)

(1920–1923) **1921:** 5/9; 11/7
Inside Forward **Career:** 65-0-13
Debut: 2 Oct 20 **Final:** 5 May 23

Born: Gateshead 12 Oct 1891
Died: Amsterdam 29 Oct 1949

Career: Wallsend Elm Villa; Newcastle United 07.11.13; Leeds United Nov 1915–Mar 1916; NORWICH CITY 29.09.20; Accrington Stanley 28.06.23 player-manager; Erfurt FC (Germany) coach Jun 1925 for eight years; Turkey FA head coach; Racing Club de Paris (France) coach for three years; coaching in Egypt for one year.

After his Army service Norwich secured Tommy's signature in the face of competition from Manchester United and Middlesbrough. A contemporary wrote of him, 'Curtis enjoyed the cut and thrust of the game'. A fast, tricky, strong and able player, he became eminently successful coaching on the Continent, and his probated will saw him leave £1,318.7s.10d to his widow Margaret.

BOTTO, Lewis Anthony

(1929) **1929:** 5/8; 11/6
Goalkeeper **Career:** 2-0-0
Debut: 9 Mar 29 **Final:** 23 Mar 29

Born: Jarrow 12 Jul 1898
Died: Jarrow 4 Jun 1953

Career: Jarrow Rangers; Hebburn Colliery; Durham Aug 1923 (amat), 26.10.23 (pro); Shildon Athletic Aug 1925; Wolverhampton Wanderers 05.08.27; NORWICH CITY 15.10.28; Nelson 06.09.29; Jarrow Nov 1929 retiring May 1932.

Made his Canary debut in the Reserves as 'G.O. Alie', until the press were able to wrongly disclose that his name was L. Blotto. With a great deal of further research we have discovered his true identity. Lewis was a confident workmanlike custodian with a sturdy build, but it was stated that an inch or two added to his stature might have been an advantage. His probated will even referred to him as 'Louis, otherwise Lewis, otherwise Lewis Anthony'.

Mark Bowen

BOWEN, Mark Rosslyn

(1987–1996) **1988:** 5/8; 11/6
Defender **Career:** 394-5-27
Debut: 19 Aug 87 **Final:** 30 Mar 96 (sub)

Born: Neath 7 Dec 1963

Career: Afan Nedd Schools; Tottenham Hotspur Jun 1980 (app), 01.12.81 (pro); NORWICH CITY 10.07.87; West Ham United 04.07.96; Shimuzu S Pulse (Japan) Mar 1997; Charlton Athletic 15.09.97; Bristol City (trial) 20.07.99; Oxford United (trial) 27.07.99; Wigan Athletic 12.10.99; Reading 03.12.99; Crystal Palace Jun 2001 reserves manager

He has a full range of Welsh caps from schoolboy level to full international level. Called reverently 'Albert Tatlock' from being a renowned moaner, he was an essential part of

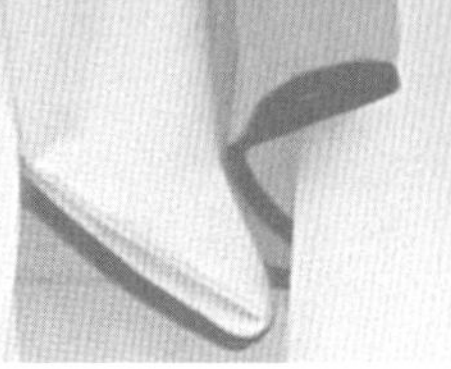

the Canary success with superb displays. A virtual ever-present for seven years with City he was the twelfth City player to reach 350 First XI games and he was left annoyingly one short of 400. Mark Hughes the Welsh national team manager has our Mark on board to assist with coaching and Steve Bruce has just hired him.

BOWEN, Samuel Edward

(1934–1938) **1935:** 5/9; 13/0
Left/Right Back **Career:** 139-0-2
Debut: 20 Oct 34 **Final:** 15 Jan 38

Born: Hednesford 17 Nov 1903
Died: Stafford 4 Mar 1981

Career: West Hill School; Hednesford Juniors; Hednesford Rovers; Hednesford Prims; Hednesford Congregationals; Rugeley; Hednesford Town Jul 1922; Aston Villa 25.04.23 (amat), 18.08.23 (pro); NORWICH CITY 18.10.34–1938.

Topical Times' Who's Who of 1933 *said, 'Although heavily built he was a dainty and gentle type of player'. A seasoned performer with over 200 Division One games, Sam had lost some pace when he joined City at almost 30 but was still highly efficient and canny. An ever-present in his third City season, which showed his staying power and durability. After World War Two he worked for his home town district social services department.*

BOYER, Philip John (Charlie)

(1974–1977) **1974:** 5/8; 10/4
Striker **Career:** 139-1-40
Debut: 9 Feb 74 **Final:** 11 Apr 77

Born: Nottingham 25 Jan 1949

'Charlie' Boyer

Career: Musters Road School; Rushcliffe; Derby County 18.08.65 (app), 29.11.66 (pro); York City 29.07.68; Bournemouth 24.12.70; NORWICH CITY 06.02.74; Southampton 09.08.77; Manchester City 28.11.80; Bulova (Hong Kong) (loan) Feb 1982; Grantham Town Jul 1983; Stamford; Shepshed Charterhouse Jul 1984; Grantham Town Dec 1985 as joint manager/coach to Feb 1987; Spalding United.

First Canary to be capped at senior England level while on the books of the club. A fine, neat, thoughtful attacker working in tandem with Ted MacDougall at four clubs. Became only the third player to appear 100 times in the Football League for four different clubs, achieving this landmark on 24.11.82. City bought Charlie for £145,000, a club record fee at the time. A fine goalscoring record at Southampton before Kevin Keegan's dramatic Dell arrival. Mike Channon often remarked that Charlie had no pace but was totally dedicated and loved training. Has subsequently scouted for Graham Carr at Northampton, Blackpool and Maidstone United.

BRADBROOK, Charles

(1921–1926) **1921:** 5/9; 10/9
Right Half/Left Back **Career:** 106-0-1
Debut: 2 May 21 **Final:** 1 May 26

Born: Overstrand, Norfolk 19 Jan 1902
Died: Gorleston, Norfolk 8 Aug 1982

Career: Cromer Council School; Yarmouth Town 06.09.19; NORWICH CITY 25.08.21 to May 1926; Yarmouth Town 28.08.26–01.05.39.

The Eastern Daily Press *report of his debut said, 'He tackled well, headed effectively and distributed the ball skilfully. His work was warmly commended'. Charles played for Norfolk County between 1919 and 1929 and was one of the finest amateurs in the area. In an interview he stressed the importance of training, enthusiasm and unity – don't you just love him? An outstanding Yarmouth Town career of 454 appearances for 119 goals before retiring at 37.*

BRADLEY, Cromwell Marland (Cecil)

(1928) **1928:** 5/8; 11/0
Outside Right **Career:** 4-0-1
Debut: 18 Feb 28 **Final:** 3 Nov 28

Born: Hemsworth, West Yorkshire 18 Nov 1904
Died: Redruth, Cornwall 10 May 1968

Career: Truro City; Cornwall; Falmouth; NORWICH CITY 01.09.27; Sheffield Wednesday 13.11.28; Margate Aug 1929; Truro City Jul 1932; Wadebridge Aug 1933; Falmouth Town Dec 1934; Helston Feb 1936.

Played cricket and football for Cornwall and he came to Norwich with good credentials. He netted in his third match – a 3–0 win over Torquay United. Under the stewardship of Alf Moule he helped his side win the Kent Senior Shield in February 1931. He joined the Falmouth family business and was latterly host of the Victoria Inn in Redruth.

BRADLEY, John (Jack)

(1951) **1939:** 5/10; 12/7
Inside Left **Career:** 6-0-0
Debut: 3 Mar 51 **Final:** 10 Nov 51

Born: Hemsworth, West Yorkshire 27 Nov 1916

Career: South Kirkby Colliery; Huddersfield Town 21.11.35 (amat); Swindon Town 26.08.36 (trial); Chelsea 05.06.38; Southampton 12.05.39; Bolton Wanderers 15.10.47; NORWICH CITY 25.11.50; Yarmouth Town player-manager from Jul 1952 to Jun 1955.

Described as big and strong with a powerful left foot shot and a workrate beyond cavil. Scored an FA Cup hat-trick in Nov 1937 against Gillingham and maintained a healthy scoring rate for Yarmouth in company with ex-City players Arnold, Plunkett and Rowlands. He guested for eight clubs during the Second World War, playing alongside such luminaries as Lofthouse, Mortenson, Matthews and Ramsey. Once netted in seven successive games for Southampton. His father Martin played for three Football League sides. A publican at The Jolly Farmers for 27 years.

BRADLEY, Ronald

(1964–1966) **1964:** 5/10; 12/2
Wing Half **Career:** 4-0-0
Debut: 26 Dec 64 **Final:** 2 Apr 66

Born: Wolverhampton 24 Apr 1939

Career: Harrison Primary School; Wolverhampton Schools; S.E. Staff Boys; West Bromwich Albion Apr 1954 (groundstaff), 09.06.56 (pro); NORWICH CITY 01.07.64; in Aug 1966 as FA coach helping Holt; Wolverhampton Wanderers Sep 1966 coach; Olympiakos Nicosia (Cyprus) 1970–1972 manager/coach; Scunthorpe United 1972 coach, Jun 1973–Nov 1974 manager; Libya national coach 1975; Scunthorpe United coach; Derby County coach; Wolverhampton Wanderers Oct 1982 coach.

Joined WBA groundstaff from school in 1954 and seemed destined to become a full back, but eventually gained a first team place at centre half. It's a strange fact of footballing life that schoolboy stars such as Ron often have moderate success at league level. Ron did however have 50 games for City Reserves in three years. He gained a deserved reputation as a coach being employed in England and abroad. He won the Cypriot championship for his side and Ron Ashman brought him back to Scunthorpe. He later ran soccer camps in America.

BRADSHAW, Carl

(1994–1997) **1995:** 6/0; 11/6
Defender **Career:** 63-11-3
Debut: 20 Aug 94 **Final:** 18 Apr 97

Born: Manor, Sheffield 2 Oct 1968

Career: City School; Manchester United (trial); Leeds United (trial); Manchester City (trial); Sheffield Wednesday 17.03.83 (assoc), 09.04.85 (app), 23.08.86 (pro); Barnsley (loan) 23.08.86; Manchester City 30.09.88; Sheffield United 07.09.89; NORWICH CITY 01.08.94; Wigan Athletic 06.10.97–21.05.2001; Scunthorpe United 11.07.2001.

Began his career as a striker with Sheffield Wednesday, finally settling into a defensive role with the Blades. Committed in his approach, he was a tough tackling player who captained Wigan to the Auto Windshields Trophy and narrowly missed promotion with his team last term.

BRADY, Garry

(2000) **1999:** 5/10; 11/10
Midfield **Career:** 10-0-0
Debut: 25 Mar 00 **Final:** 2 Oct 00

Born: Castlemilk, Glasgow 7 Sep 1976

Career: St Margaret Mary's School; Glasgow District & County Schools; Celtic Boys Club 1990; Tottenham Hotspur Jul 1992 (trainee), 09.09.93 (pro); Newcastle United 15.07.98; NORWICH CITY (loan) 22.03.2000; and 04.09.2000 (loan) Portsmouth (trial) Feb 2001, (signing) 01.03.2001.

A Scottish Under-18 international midfielder happiest on the right flank. A serious ankle injury impeded his progress at Newcastle, and after recovery he joined City with Des Hamilton, being taken on loan on two separate occasions by manager Bryan Hamilton. He later made the Portsmouth reserve goal against Norwich at Fratton Park.

BRAIN, Joseph

(1931) **1931:** 5/10; 11/7
Centre Forward **Career:** 13-0-5
Debut: 29 Aug 31 **Final:** 31 Oct 31

Born: Ebbw Vale, Gwent 28 Jan 1910
Died: Norwich 15 Mar 1981

Career: Ebbw Vale schoolboys; Ebbw Vale 1926; Sunderland 11.03.30; NORWICH CITY 07.05.31; Barrow 09.09.32; Preston North End 14.04.33; Swansea Town 13.08.34; Bristol City 01.06.37–Nov 1939; Second World War for Bristol City, Norwich and Watford.

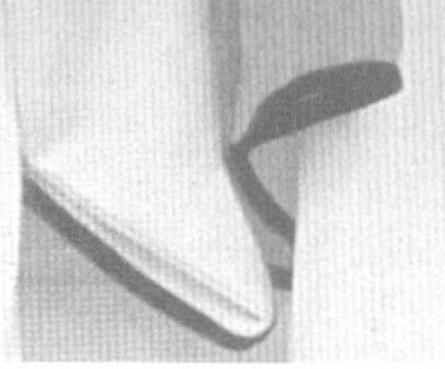

Scorer of over 50 goals in the Football League, fulfilling the promise shown when he once scored seven for City reserves on 16.1.32 (H) v. Bournemouth, including four in ten minutes. As a PTI in the Royal Artillery he played 21 matches for City in Second World War friendlies. Had a lifelong hobby of pigeon racing, played golf for Royal Norwich and ran a newsagent's shop on Foundry Bridge for over 30 years.

BRANNAN, Gerard Daniel

(1998) **1998:** 6/0; 12/3
Midfield **Career:** 11-1-1
Debut: 22 Aug 98 (sub) **Final**: 24 Oct 98

Born: Prescot 15 Jan 1972

Career: St Adens Primary School; St Thomas A'Beckett Comprehensive School; Merseyside; Coperas Villa FC; Liverpool Schoolboys; Tranmere Rovers 03.07.90; Manchester City 12.03.97; NORWICH CITY (loan) 18.08.98; Motherwell 26.10.98; Wigan Athletic 16.02.2001.

A two-month loan spell at City helped the club and drew praise from manager Bruce Rioch. The club got the player's enthusiasm back for the game and his goal was a diving header past the stocking clad Andy Goram. Veritable star performances for Motherwell saw him gain an international call up for the Cayman Islands that was subsequently scuppered by a FIFA row.

BRENNAN, Robert Anderson

(1953–1960) **1953:** 5/9; 10/11
Inside Forward **Career:** 250-0-52
Debut: 19 Aug 53 (goal) **Final:** 23 Apr 60

Born: Belfast 14 Mar 1925

'Bobby' Brennan

Career: Harland & Wolf Welders; Bloomfield United 1943; Distillery; Luton Town 20.10.47; Birmingham City 19.07.49; Fulham 16.06.50; NORWICH CITY 13.07.53; Yarmouth Town 30.07.56; NORWICH CITY 15.03.57; King's Lynn Jul 1961 coach.

Bobby used to play seven-a-side football with Danny Blanchflower for Bloomfield before they went their separate ways to Glentoran and Distillery. He played with and against the best players of the late 40s and 50s and did not suffer in comparison with any of them. His adept control and stratagems were a delight to savour as he gained Northern Ireland caps at three clubs. Released under Tom Parker's management but re-signed after the new City Board took over in February 1957. He continued to play until April 1960. Still lives locally and ex-City colleagues recall his name with reverence, stating he was a masterful player.

BRIGGS, Maxwell Francis

(1968–1974) **1971:** 5/8; 10/8
Right Winger **Career:** 160-10-2
Debut: 31 Aug 68 **Final:** 5 Feb 74

Born: Bramerton, Norfolk 9 Sep 1948

Career: Newton Flotman Primary School; Long Stratton Secondary School; South Norfolk Schools; Norfolk Schoolboy, Youth, County; NORWICH CITY from Juniors, 04.12.67 (pro); Oxford United 21.02.74–20.10.78.

Max was working for the Royal Exchange Insurance Company with no real ambitions to be a professional footballer until he was spotted by Ron Ashman. Started as a winger, later moving to wing half and turning in consistent performances. Home-grown player whose forceful, hard running style earned encomium. His first ever goal for City was against the club that he was later to join but his total of goals is a meagre return for someone who made so many appearances. Helped Norwich City gain promotion to Division One and the forthcoming reunion dinner should be a great success.

BROOKE, Garry James

(1985–1987) **1985:** 5/6; 10/5
Midfielder **Career:** 10-10-4
Debut: 17 Aug 85 **Final:** 3 Sep 87 (sub)

Born: Bethnal Green, London 24 Nov 1960

Career: Winns School; Sidney Choplin Junior High School; Waltham Forest District; McEntree Juniors; Essex County; Tottenham Hotspur 13.06.77 (app), 09.10.78 (pro); Gais Gothenburg

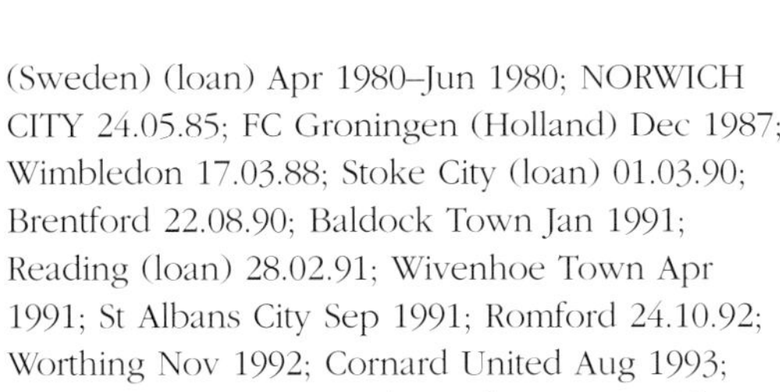

(Sweden) (loan) Apr 1980–Jun 1980; NORWICH CITY 24.05.85; FC Groningen (Holland) Dec 1987; Wimbledon 17.03.88; Stoke City (loan) 01.03.90; Brentford 22.08.90; Baldock Town Jan 1991; Reading (loan) 28.02.91; Wivenhoe Town Apr 1991; St Albans City Sep 1991; Romford 24.10.92; Worthing Nov 1992; Cornard United Aug 1993; Braintree Town Oct 1994; Worthing Sep 1996.

Garry had a go-ahead method, combining versatility with a powerful shot. At Spurs he won winner's medals in the FA Cup and UEFA Cup as well as playing in the Charity Shield before surviving a near-fatal car crash in February 1983. He extended his career a further ten years after City by playing for a succession of non-league clubs. Runs the Alexandra Park soccer school and was last seen playing for Spurs Veterans and in a five-a-side tournament in Mauritius.

BROUGHTON, Drewe Oliver

(1996–1997) **1996:** 6/3; 12/0
Forward **Career:** 3-6-1
Debut: 15 Mar 97 **Final:** 1 Nov 97 (sub)

Born: Hitchin 25 Oct 1978

Career: Hexton Junior Mixed Infants; Asprey Guise Lower School; Fullbrook Middle School; Woburn Lions; East Anglian Boys; Independent School; Milton Keynes & Border Counties Select XI; Canary Rangers; Bedford Public School; NORWICH CITY Schoolboy, 07.07.95 (trainee), 07.05.97 (pro); Wigan Athletic (loan) 15.08.97; Brentford 30.10.98; Peterborough United 17.11.98; Nuneaton Borough 04.02.2000–05.03.2000; Dagenham & Redbridge 21.09.2000; Kidderminster Harriers 21.02.2001.

A youth team hat-trick in August 1995 highlighted the start of a professional career full of potential. He nabbed 43 goals at Under-First XI level proving a handful as an athletic frontrunner with useful heading ability. A combination of injuries and loss of form restricted his appearances.

BROWN, Kenneth James

(1986–1987) **1986:** 5/8; 11/6
Full Back **Career:** 27-1-0
Debut: 29 Nov 86 (sub) **Final:** 28 Nov 87

Born: Barking 11 Jul 1967

Career: Hillside; NORWICH CITY 10.07.85; Plymouth Argyle 10.08.88; West Ham United 02.08.91; Huddersfield Town (loan) 07.09.95; Reading (loan) 27.10.95; Southend United (loan) 29.02.96; Crystal Palace (loan) 28.03.96; Reading (loan) 09.09.96; Birmingham City 27.12.96; Millwall 20.07.97; Gillingham 25.03.99; Colchester United (trial) Sep 1999; Kingstonian Dec 1999; Portadown 2000 and training with West Ham United; Barry Town 23.07.2000 player coach.

Despite his ability, Kenny was unable to displace Bowen and Culverhouse, who were both class acts. A good passer of the ball and comfortable on either flank, he left after his father's departure as manager. Helped Crystal Palace to the Division One play-off finals at Wembley and he was voted the Pilgrims Player of the Year in 1990/1. The West Ham supporters voted him as their 49th all-time favourite player and scorer of the 14th best ever goal scored by a WHU player.

BROWN, Laurence

(1966–1968) **1964:** 5/11; 12/5
Centre Half **Career:** 89-2-2
Debut: 27 Sep 66 **Final:** 28 Sep 68

Born: Shildon, Co. Durham 22 Aug 1937
Died: Aycliffe 30 Sep 1998

Career: Timothy Hackworth School; All Saints Secondary Modern School; Bishop Auckland Schools; Durham Schools; Shildon Workers; All Saints Rovers; Shildon Town; Woking Town; Fulham 07.05.51 (amat); Bishop Auckland (amat); Darlington 11.03.59; Northampton Town 18.10.60; Arsenal 18.08.61; Tottenham Hotspur 21.02.64; NORWICH CITY 27.09.66; Bradford Park Avenue 04.12.68 player-manager; King's Lynn Dec 1970 player-manager thence general manager; Altrincham player-manager; Stockton manager; Tow Law Town manager.

Laurie left school at 15 and worked as an apprentice cabinet maker before doing his national service as a PTI. Centre half for Great Britain in the Rome Olympics and a great success at centre forward for Northampton. Lol Morgan said 'Laurie was always a very enthusiastic and wholehearted player and was a good leader when given the captain's job'. He made over 300 appearances in the Football League spread amongst half a dozen clubs.

BROWN, Oliver Maurice

(1931–1933) **1932:** 5/10; 12/0
Centre Forward **Career:** 51-0-33
Debut: 19 Dec 31 **Final:** 6 May 33

Born: Burton-on-Trent 10 Oct 1908
Died: Royal Free Hospital, London 17 Jan 1953

Career: Broadway Central School; Trent Villa FC; Robirth Athletic; Burton Town; Nottingham

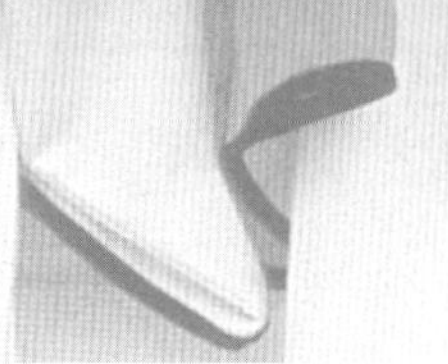

Forest 08.02.30; NORWICH CITY 19.12.31; West Ham United 15.6.33; Brighton & Hove Albion 16.03.34–retired 1937.

An exuberant character, he rejoiced in the nicknames 'Buster' and 'Bub'. Fared well in the days of telling tackles, scoring an amazing 76 goals in his short 118 league game career. Incredibly topped the 1933/34 list of scorers at Brighton – in just eight appearances. Four hat-tricks and a foursome were amongst his triumphs. Spent six years as a miner but found football far more dangerous: he sustained a torn ligament, a torn stomach muscle, a fractured skull, a broken jaw, a broken collarbone, a serious abdominal injury and a broken heart – his wife died in 1934, which not unnaturally affected his game and desire to play. Latterly he worked in the prison service. His brother Ambrose played for three league clubs without problems in the 1930s.

Left: Steve Bruce
Right: 'Ken' Burditt

BROWN, Roger William

(1979–1980) **1979:** 6/1; 11/10
Centre Half **Career:** 21-0-0
Debut: 1 Sep 79 **Final:** 23 Feb 80

Born: Tamworth, Staffordshire 12 Dec 1952

Career: Walsall 29.12.70 (amat); Paget Rangers; A.P. Leamington; Bournemouth 03.02.78; NORWICH CITY 13.07.79; Fulham 06.03.80; Bournemouth 03.12.83; Weymouth May 1987 player coach; Poole Town Oct 1987 manager; Colchester United manager 04.11.87–18.10.88; Bolehill Swifts Feb 1995 joint manager.

A short stay at Carrow Road replacing Hoadley before being transferred for a profit. Roger arrived with excellent credentials and, after a successful stay at Craven Cottage, returned to his first Football League club, helping them to win the Associate Members Cup. He netted 12 goals as a defender for Fulham in one season. He has worked as a production manager in a Leamington engineering firm and as an Insurance Agent in Colchester. Joined his brother Gary as joint manager of a Midland football alliance side.

BROWN, William

(1929–1931) **1930:** 6/0; 11/7
Right Half **Career:** 53-0-2
Debut: 31 Aug 29 **Final:** 17 Jan 31

Born: Hamilton 17 Nov 1902
Died: Norwich 16 Nov 1985

Career: Bellshill Athletic; Coventry City 18.06.25; Wolverhampton Wanderers 05.07.28; NORWICH CITY 10.05.29; Boulton & Paul (amat) May 1931–Apr 1932 and Dec 1934.

A programme summation of Bill: 'His reach is very helpful to him and his cleverness is manifest to everybody'. Bill related in an interview with the author that Spurs had made an offer for him but he joined Norwich and showed the solid virtues of high competence in forming a fine partnership with O'Brien and Lochhead. A loss to the game through early retirement at 29.

BRUCE, Stephen Roger

(1984–1987) **1985:** 6/0;12/6
Defender **Career:** 180-0-21
Debut: 25 Aug 84 **Final:** 5 Dec 87

Born: Corbridge 31 Dec 1960

Career: Walker Gate Primary School; Benfield Comprehensive School; Newcastle Boys Under-11–16; Wallsend Boys Club; Burnley (trial); Newcastle United (trial); Sunderland (trial); Derby County (trial); Sheffield Wednesday (trial); Bolton Wanderers (trial); Northumberland County; Southport (trial); Gillingham 09.07.77 (app), 27.10.78 (pro); NORWICH CITY 05.07.84; Manchester United 18.12.87; Birmingham City 22.05.96; Sheffield United 02.07.98 manager; Huddersfield Town May 1999 manager; Wigan Athletic 04.04.2001–29.05.2001 manager; Crystal Palace 31.05.2001 manager.

A former shipyard worker, Steve has richly confirmed the promise shown at Gillingham where he gained eight England youth caps and for three years running was selected as part of the PFA's Third Division representative team. His stunningly, powerful displays saw him confirmed as the supporters' Player of the Year in his first season with City, as well as obtaining the accolade of Man of the Match in the Milk Cup Final win at Wembley. He

captained all his sides including England 'B' and he won almost everything there was to win at Old Trafford, including two double-winning seasons. Norwich City can feel proud that they contributed to his football education.

BRYCELAND, Thomas (Tommy)

(1962–1969) **1963:** 5/7; 10/13
Inside Right **Career:** 281-3-55
Debut: 29 Sep 62 **Final:** 8 Nov 69 (goal)

Born: Greenock 1 Mar 1939

Career: Gourock Juniors; St Mirren 19.03.56; NORWICH CITY 27.09.62; Oldham Athletic 16.03.70; St Mirren 19.01.72 player-manager for two years.

A Scottish schoolboy international who scored 47 goals in 105 games for St Mirren, helping his side to a Scottish Cup Final win.
A diminutive craftsman, full of guile, his deft touches were allied to a goalscoring bent. Three times he finished City's second highest scorer in a season. Tommy turned down the chance to do some coaching for Ron Saunders and he left City when he was 31. His various occupations are detailed in Glorious Canaries *and he thoroughly enjoyed the 40-year reunion of the St Mirren 1958/59 side.*

BUCHANAN, Cameron Campbell

(1956) **1956:** 5/8; 10/12
Inside Right **Career:** 3-0-0
Debut: 3 Nov 56 **Final:** 24 Nov 56

Born: Chapelhall, Airdrie 31 Jul 1928

Career: Wolverhampton Wanderers 16.06.42 (amat), 04.05.46 (pro); Bournemouth 06.08.49–1954; coach for Province of Quebec Apr 1955; Hibernian player/coach (Team of sons of wartime refugees) in Montreal; NORWICH CITY 20.10.56; Barnstaple Jul 1957–May 1962 player-manager.

His main claim to fame is a Wolves debut on 26.09.42 v WBA at the tender age of 14 years 57 days. He even scored a wartime hat-trick for the Black and Golds in October 1945. His three City games did not provide a win bonus and he added just four reserve games to his total. Upon retirement he went into the laundry business.

BULLIMORE, Alwyn Arthur (Alan)

(1957) **1953:** 5/6; 10/12
Left Half **Career:** 1-0-0
Debut/Final: 23 Feb 57

Born: Norwich 22 Oct 1933

Career: Norwich Schoolboys 1947/48; March Town; NORWICH CITY 24.10.53; Gorleston until Mar 1965.

Scored both goals for Norwich Boys at Bath in March 1948. Principally a reserve Canary, waiting five years for his debut – and prefers not to be reminded of the score! Although pint sized and with opportunities at a premium he performed soundly in 41 reserve games alongside the likes of future England international Maurice Norman.

BURDITT, Frederick Charles Kendall (Ken)

(1931–1936) **1932:** 5/9; 11/3
Inside Forward **Career:** 173-0-61
Debut: 17 Jan 31 **Final:** 2 May 36

Born: Ibstock, Leicester 12 Nov 1906
Died: Ibstock, Leicester 27 Oct 1977

Career: Ibstock; Penistone Rovers; Gresley Rovers; NORWICH CITY 01.11.30; Millwall 07.08.36; Notts County 28.01.38; Colchester United May 1939; guesting for Leicester Second World War; Ibstock Colliery to 1959.

Scored a double hat-trick in an East Midlands League match for the Reserves and his sheer weight of goals precipitated his elevation to senior level. A forceful, quick player with a powerful, although sometimes wayward shot, he amply backed Tom Parkers' initial opinion of him – 'I am fully convinced that he has a bright future'. He is in the upper echelons of City goalscorers when one adds on his 80 reserve strikes. Reached FA Cup Semi-Final with Millwall and his younger brother George hit a hat-trick for Forest against City. At over 50 Ken was still playing for Ibstock Colliery.

BURKE, Peter Joseph

(1935–1939) **1936:** 6/1; 13/0
Centre Half **Career:** 119-0-0
Debut: 7 Dec 35 **Final:** 4 Mar 39

Born: Fazakerley 1 Feb 1912
Died: Walton, Liverpool 18 Nov 1979

Career: Blessed Sacrement School; Liverpool Schools; England Boys; Bootle JOC; Fazakerley ROF; Liverpool 05.10.29 (amat); Prescot Cables 01.05.31; Liverpool 13.06.31 (amat); Oldham Athletic 17.05.33 (pro); NORWICH CITY 05.12.35; Luton Town 14.6.39; Second World War guested for Brighton & Hove Albion; Southport 12.07.46; Prescot Cables Nov 1946.

Peter was one of seven children and represented England Boys v Scotland in 1925.

A car crash almost ended his career before it began. Always gave of his best and was a cogent force pre-war with Oldham scoring against City in Dec 1934. Bought to strengthen City's defence following promotion the season before. Missed playing for Irish Free State v Norway through being injured. Listed as a retired bricklayer upon his death. The cross on his mother's Aintree grave, where his ashes were scattered, is painted yellow and green.

BURLEY, Benjamin

(1935–1938) **1935:** 5/8; 11/0
Outside/Inside Left **Career:** 37-0-4
Debut: 7 Sep 35 **Final:** 23 Apr 38

Born: Sheffield 2 Nov 1912

Career: Darnall Road School; Sheffield & Yorkshire Boys; Netherhope Institute; Woodhouse Mill United; Sheffield United 05.11.31 (amat), 07.10.32 (pro); Southampton 09.09.33; Grimsby Town 28.06.34; NORWICH CITY 11.06.35; Darlington 17.05.38; Chelmsford City 05.06.39; Second World War guested for Southend, Millwall, Brighton, Q.P.R., Crystal Palace; Zwolle Boys (Holland) 1948 coach; Chelmsford City Jun 1951 secretary.

Had a penchant for changing clubs almost annually. A believer in direct methods and with his FA Coaching badge was coaching in Holland in the late 1940s. Ben played for and against us during the War and has kindly corrected his date of birth after we made contact with him. He now resides on the north Norfolk coast.

BURTON, Alwyn Derek (Ollie)

(1961–1963) **1964:** 5/11; 12/1
Right Half **Career:** 73-0-9
Debut: 4 Mar 61 **Final:** 21 May 63 (goal)

Born: Chepstow, Gwent 11 Nov 1941

Career: Portwall School; Bulwark Youth Club Sep 1957; Newport County 22.12.58; NORWICH CITY 03.03.61; Newcastle United 06.06.63–retired Oct 1972.

Began his career in 1958 on £9 per week, scoring a hat-trick for Newport in 1960 in a losing league cup tie. Ollie is remembered for his ginger hair and powerful shooting. Won Welsh caps at School, Under-23 and Full level, plus a League Cup medal in 1962 and a Fairs Cup medal in 1969. Could play anywhere in the intermediate line and good service at Newcastle earned him a testimonial. He went from Somerton Park to the San Siro by way of St James' and didn't take many prisoners along the way. Plagued by injuries – appendix and cartilage ops, both legs in plaster, and ankle trouble. A vibrant, cheerful character and a regular attendee at reunions.

BUSBY, Vivian Dennis

(1976–1977) **1977:** 6/0; 11/12
Striker **Career:** 23-0-11
Debut: 18 Sep 76 **Final:** 10 Sep 77

Born: Slough 19 Jun 1949

Career: Hatters Lane School; High Wycombe District; Buckinghamshire (trial); Terries FC; Wycombe Wanderers 1966; Luton Town 23.01.70; Newcastle United (loan) 19.12.71 to Feb 1972; Fulham 09.08.73; NORWICH CITY 16.09.76; Stoke City 10.11.77; Sheffield United (loan) 03.01.80 to Mar 1980; Tulsa Roughnecks (USA) Mar 1980; Blackburn Rovers 06.02.81; York City 2.08.82 player coach, manager 1984; Sunderland Mar 1987–Dec 1991 assistant manager; Manchester City Dec 1991 scout; Hartlepools United 15.02.93–23.11.93 manager; Southampton scout; West Bromwich Albion scout; Sheffield United 13.12.95 assistant coach; Everton Jun 1997 assistant manager; Fulham Nov 1999 reserve coach.

A useful, occasionally brilliant forward who had a turbulent career at Carrow Road but in a 'rolling stone' career proved to be a sought-after striker. Brother of Martin (QPR). Became the second ever City player to score a First Division hat-trick and left City with a good set of stats. Considered a 'Jonah' in some quarters in north-east footballing circles as Newcastle sold him after the Hereford defeat and Sunderland jettisoned him after a run of losses. His Stoke side were nicknamed 'Busby Babes 2'. Working on Metro Radio he has won his fight against leukaemia and became a father at 51.

BUTLER, Barry

(1957–1965) **1964:** 6/0; 13/2
Centre Half **Career:** 349-0-3
Debut: 24 Aug 57 **Final:** 9 Oct 65

Born: Stockton 30 Jul 1934
Died: Norwich 9 Apr 1966

Career: Richard Hind Secondary Modern School; Stockton Schoolboys; North Riding; Stockton West End; Billington Minors; South Bank Minors; South Bank; Middlesbrough (trial); Dundee (trial); Sheffield Wednesday 20.09.52; NORWICH CITY 21.08.57, briefly player-coach.

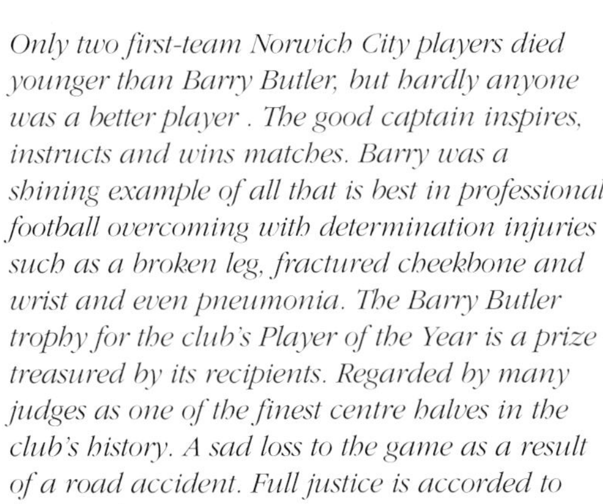

Only two first-team Norwich City players died younger than Barry Butler, but hardly anyone was a better player . The good captain inspires, instructs and wins matches. Barry was a shining example of all that is best in professional football overcoming with determination injuries such as a broken leg, fractured cheekbone and wrist and even pneumonia. The Barry Butler trophy for the club's Player of the Year is a prize treasured by its recipients. Regarded by many judges as one of the finest centre halves in the club's history. A sad loss to the game as a result of a road accident. Full justice is accorded to him in Glorious Canaries.

Left: Barry Butler
Right: Ian Butterworth

BUTLER, Geoffrey

(1968–1975) **1970:** 5/7; 11/0
Right/Left back **Career:** 192-4-1
Debut: 2 Nov 68 **Final:** 8 Nov 75

Born: Middlesbrough 29 Sep 1946

Career: Langbaurgh School; North Riding County; Middlesbrough 23.05.64; Chelsea 23.09.67; Sunderland 11.01.68; NORWICH CITY 30.10.68; Baltimore Comets (USA) 01.05.74; AFC Bournemouth 12.03.76 to 1981; Peterborough United 18.08.81 player coach; Trowbridge Town Jul 1982; Salisbury City Feb 1983 player-manager.

An accomplished defender outstanding for his reliability and good anticipation. His Football League debut came on 11.04.66 – a 6–0 defeat at Bolton was overcome, but real success did not come until he arrived at Carrow Road. Gained a Division Two championship medal and a losing Wembley appearance against Tottenham Hotspur. A remarkable 18 years as Salisbury's manager, and lately also managing director, was ended when he was sacked in a power struggle at the club. Geoff estimated that he had raised at least one million pounds for the club, and the team was in its highest ever position.

BUTTERWORTH, Ian Stuart

(1986–1994) **1986:** 6/1; 12/6
Defender **Career:** 286-7-4
Debut: 20 Sep 86 **Final:** 26 Mar 94

Born: Nantwich, Cheshire 25 Jan 1964

Career: Rudskin High School; Cheshire County; Coventry City Apr 1978 (assoc), 23.06.80 (app), 05.08.81 (pro); Nottingham Forest 03.06.85; NORWICH CITY 19.09.86 (temp), 29.11.86 (permanent); King's Lynn 28.11.95; Colorado Rapids (USA) player Feb 1996, to assistant manager; I.K.Brage (Sweden) 28.03.87, manager 30.08.97; Stafford Rangers Jan 1998; Darlington assistant manager to 02.08.2000; Cardiff City Oct 2000 head coach.

Ian represented his county at badminton, cricket and table tennis and gained eight England Under-21 caps. He joined City on loan before signing permanently for £165,000. A commanding central defender who rarely made mistakes and only missed matches through illness and injury. A retirement through a knee injury has seen him take his skills abroad before moving into management.

CAMPBELL, Archibald MacEachern

(1924–1928) **1924:** 5/10; 11/10
Full Back **Career:** 97-0-0
Debut: 30 Aug 24 **Final:** 6 Apr 28

Born: Johnstone, nr Paisley 21 Nov 1897
Died: Norwich 2 Feb 1987

Career: Kilbarchan Athletic 1918; Paisley Vulcan Nov 1920; Derby County 22.04.22; NORWICH CITY 19.06.24–Apr 1928; Gothic 11.10.29; Norwich CEYMS 07.12.31.

A dependable, two-footed regular full back and later captain of the reserves. Enjoyed Steve Bloomers' coaching at Derby but was unable to break into their senior team. His competition for the City first team was the redoubtable Joe Hannah. Archie worked for 40 years at Laurence Scott Electromotors, retiring as an assistant production manager.

CARBERRY, Robert (Bert)

(1953–1955) **1953:** 6/0; 11/11
Left Half **Career:** 5-0-0
Debut: 14 Nov 53 **Final:** 19 Feb 55

Born: Partick 16 Jan 1931

Career: St Peter's School; Avondale; NORWICH CITY 19.01.49; Bedford Town Jun 1955;

Gillingham 05.07.56; Port Vale 02.07.57; Exeter City 28.08.58; Burton Albion Jun 1959.

A promising Caledonian midfielder who waited almost five years for a league debut but was unable to command a regular spot, as is shown by his 127 reserve appearances for three goals. Bert is a retired engineer with a talented son who played for Jersey Scottish, as he now lives in his wife's birthplace of Jersey.

CAREY, Shaun Peter

(1995–2000) **1996:** 5/9; 10/6
Midfield **Career:** 56-20-0
Debut: 20 Sep 95 **Final:** 25 Mar 00

Born: Kettering 13 May 1976

Career: Our Lady's Roman Catholic Primary School; St Mary's; Thomas A'Beckett; Irthlingborough; Old Grammarians; Aston Villa School of Excellence; Northampton County; Arsenal (trial); NORWICH CITY 12.12.90 (assoc), 06.07.92 (trainee), 01.07.94 (pro)–26.04.2000; Gillingham (trial) Jul 2000; Bristol Rovers (trial) Jul 2000; Chesterfield (trial) Aug 2000; Rushden & Diamonds 07.09.2000.

At one point he was the youngest member of the City youth side, and devoted to the Canaries having been spotted when just 14. Had his ups and downs under a succession of managers, with a seemingly never-healing hamstring blighting his progress. Never managed a first team goal but hit the net 14 times in a combined youth/reserve total of 200 games.

CASSIDY, Francis Arthur Michael

(1937) **1937:** 6/2; 12/8
Inside Forward **Career:** 1-0-0
Debut/Final: 23 Oct 37

Born: Woodton, Norfolk 5 May 1917
Died: Oulton Broad, Suffolk 21 Nov 1983

Career: Brandeston School; Lowestoft Secondary School; Norfolk Juniors; Gorleston; Lowestoft Town 07.09.35; NORWICH CITY 08.04.36 (amat), 12.05.36 (pro); Lowestoft Town 1947–12.09.59.

Played for Suffolk County; his first-team debut arrived in the May 1937 Hospital Cup game. Scored 18 goals in 70 reserve games including a hat-trick against Tunbridge Wells. He scored goals alongside Ted Bates (the future Southampton Manager) and Geoff Edrich (a future Surrey cricketer). His brother played for Lowestoft and his son for Norwich post-war.

CASSIDY, Nigel

(1968) **1971:** 5/10; 12/6
Striker **Career:** 2-1-0
Debut: 8 May 68 **Final:** 30 Nov 68

Born: Sudbury, Suffolk 7 Dec 1945

Career: Lowestoft Grammar School; Suffolk Boys; Suffolk County; Norfolk Youth; Lowestoft Corinthians; Lowestoft Town Aug 1963; NORWICH CITY 08.07.67; Scunthorpe United 13.12.68; Oxford United 19.11.70; Cambridge United 13.03.74; Denver Dynamoes (USA) Apr 1975–Aug 1975; Bicester Town manager to 1979; Banbury Town Manager to 1982; Thame coach.

Nigel scored eleven goals in one game against Aldeby in October 1962 after scoring five in the morning for his school. Threes, fours and fives followed at regular intervals culminating in 112 goals for Lowestoft's first team. He powered home 24 reserve goals in his first City season. But he did not show artistic skills until playing in the lower Divisions, where he did well for his following three clubs.

CAWSTON, Mervyn William

(1971–1973) **1970:** 6/1; 11/6
Goalkeeper **Career:** 7-0-0
Debut: 9 Jan 71 **Final:** 3 Oct 73

Born: Diss, Norfolk 4 Feb 1952

Career: Old Buckenham Secondary Modern School; South Norfolk Schoolboys; Diss Aug 1966; NORWICH CITY 16.07.67 (amat), 16.07.69 (pro); Southend United (loan) 21.08.74–19.10.74; Chicago Stings (USA) Apr 1975–Aug 1975; Newport County (loan) Jan 1976; Gillingham 08.05.76–Apr 1977; Chicago Stings (USA) Apr 1978–Aug 1978; Southend United 18.08.78; Stoke City 22.03.84; Chelmsford City Jun 1984; Southend United 02.11.84; Cambridge United 1985 (non contract); Woodford Town Jul 1985–Sep 1985; Barking Town Sep 1985–Aug 1986; Heybridge Swifts Nov 1986–Dec 1986; Maidstone United Dec 1987–May 1989; Dartford (loan) Mar 1988–Apr 1988; Southend Manor (loan) Sep 1988–Apr 1989; Brighton & Hove Albion (loan) 01.11.88; Redbridge Forest Nov 1989–Jan 1992; Southend Manor Mar 1992–May 1992; Ford (Basildon) Sep 1992–Feb 1993; Chelmsford City Feb 1993.

Like many others he found Keelan in charge of the fortress, so much so that he had 169 reserve games. Dealt with high and low shots equally well and hit the headlines at Southend (80/1) keeping ten successive clean sheets at home and 25 clean in the season– both club

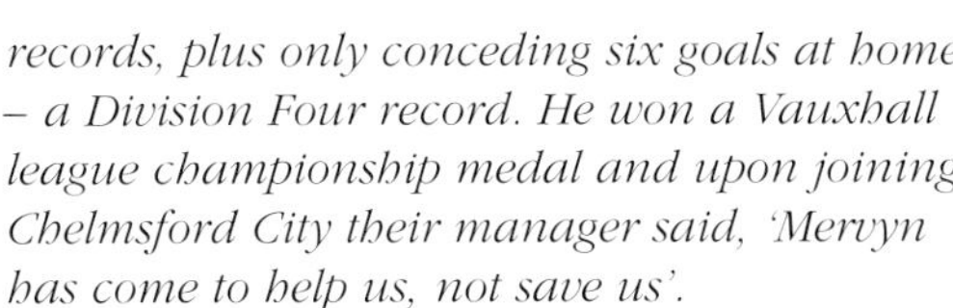

records, plus only conceding six goals at home – a Division Four record. He won a Vauxhall league championship medal and upon joining Chelmsford City their manager said, 'Mervyn has come to help us, not save us'.

CHANNON, Michael Roger

(1982–1985) **1983:** 6/0; 12/11
Striker **Career:** 108-4-25
Debut: 27 Dec 82 **Final:** 6 May 85

Born: Orcheston, Wiltshire 28 Nov 1948

Career: Shrewton; Amesbury Secondary Modern School; Salisbury & District Schools; Southampton 31.03.64 (app), 20.12.65 (pro); Manchester City 28.07.77; Southampton 11.09.79; Caroline Hills FC (Hong Kong) cs 1982; Newcastle United (loan) 08.09.82; Bristol Rovers 17.10.82; NORWICH CITY 21.12.82; Portsmouth 13.08.85; Finn Harps (Ireland) Oct 1986.

His testimonial programme of 1976 gives the best description of the man and player – 'sheer enjoyment'. He kept his charming village-green attitude of wanting to hit the back of the net for 21 years, from his reserve debut in September 1964, and has performed with silky ease for over 900 games and 300 goals. England caps and two Cup winning-medals for the lad signed after a visit from Tom Parker followed for a League registration fee plus a snack of scrambled eggs on toast in a café at school lunchtime. All his clubs welcomed his classy skills and infectious enthusiasm. Mick was used to playing at good places in football and he is determined to do the same in racing. His trainer's licence was gained in February 1990 and since then he has had astonishing success, even having the Arabs knocking at his door for his services. A kid from a two-up, two-down environment bought out HM the Queen's racing stable at West Ilsley. I wouldn't bet against Mick training a classic winner.

CHAPPELL, Archibald

(1929) **1929:** 5/9; 10/12
Inside Right **Career:** 10-0-2
Debut: 2 Feb 29 **Final:** 6 Apr 29

Born: Hucknall, Nottingham 14 Apr 1910
Died: Hucknall, Nottingham 23 Jun 1977

Career: Hucknall Boys; Hucknall Church 1924; Sunderland 01.03.27 (amat), 18.04.27 (pro); NORWICH CITY 14.06.28; Charlton Athletic 10.06.29; Mansfield Town May 1920; Guildford City Aug 1931; Walsall 13.08.32.

Left: Mick Channon

One of seven inside rights tried in a season of little success. No other league games elsewhere that we can find but he still played for Norwich with honest endeavour. His second City game saw all five forwards score – a fairly unique event. His Mansfield appearances were in the Midland League and again he notched up two goals.

CHEESLEY, Paul Martyn

(1971–1973) **1973:** 5/11; 11/4
Striker **Career:** 16-8-1
Debut: 17 Nov 71 (sub) **Final:** 22 Dec 73

Born: Bristol 20 Oct 1953

Career: Gordano School; Somerset Schools; Southwest of England Federation Boy's Club; Easton-in-Gordano FC; NORWICH CITY 17.04.70 (app), 04.10.71 (pro); Bristol City 28.12.73–07.05.77; Shepton Mallett 1 year; Frome Town 1 year; Odd Town 1 year, and manager for 3 months; Yeovil Town 1 year; Taylor Brothers manager 3 years; Beaufort player-manager to 1990 thence coach.

Reserve debut in November 1970, finishing with 74 reserve games for 35 goals. An alert, mobile and capable goalscorer whose first senior goal was wiped out through abandonment. Helped Bristol City back to Division One, netting a hat-trick amongst his 15 goals. Famously scored the club's first Division One goal for 65 years. Worked in Norwich for an insurance company and latterly a salesman for building materials and plastics.

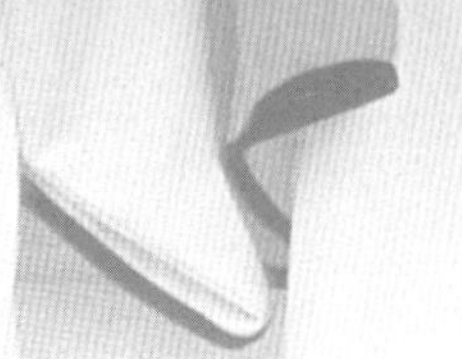

CHIVERS, Martin Harcourt

(1978–1979) **1979:** 6/1; 12/12
Centre forward **Career:** 13-0-4
Debut: 19 Aug 78 (goal) **Final:** 21 Feb 79

Born: Southampton 27 Apr 1945

Career: Foundry Lane Junior School; Taunton Grammar School; Hampshire Youth, Under-15's; CPC Sports May 1961; Southampton 06.09.62; Tottenham Hotspur 10.01.68; Servette (Switzerland) Jul 76; NORWICH CITY 01.07.78; Brighton & Hove Albion 20.03.79; Vard (Norway) for two years as player & trainer; Dorchester Town player-manager Aug 1980; Barnet Oct 1982 retiring after knee op Dec 1982.

Martin's mother was German and his father played in goal for Southampton Boys. He was a painter in an engineering works before embarking on an illustrious footballing career. Blessed with immense physique, he was one of the most feared England forwards for over a decade scoring 312 senior goals, encompassing 43 twos, nine threes and one four. At the height of his career he was voted the best centre forward in Great Britain by 20 of 22 football writers. Had the lot – heading and shooting power allied to speed and close control. He could never match that glory in spells with Norwich and Brighton. Combines working matchdays in the hospitality suites at White Hart Lane with a career as a sales and marketing manager with an asbestos removal firm.

CHRISTIE, Alexander Gray

(1923– 1924) **1923:** 5/9; 11/7
Half Back **Career:** 5-0-0
Debut: 25 Aug 23 **Final:** 26 Jan 24

Born: Broomlands 27 Jun 1896
Died: Reading 22 May 1981

Career: Royal Navy Barracks; Hamilton Academicals Aug 1914; Reading 1919; Walsall 14.06.21; Southampton 19.05.21; NORWICH CITY 11.07.23; Rochdale 24.07.24; Exeter City 26.05.28; Aldershot May 1929; H & G Simons Athletic Nov 1933.

Featured on 'Pinnace' card number 450 and while at Southampton was described as 'coolness personified'. He pushed the ball along the turf in the approved manner working his way from the Southern League through to the four divisions of the Football League. Teamed up with William Bertram at Rochdale. At Walsall he was described as being a distinct capture following 29 goals in 67 games for Reading.

CHUNG, Cyril (Sammy)

(1955–1957) **1964:** 5/9; 11/6
Inside Forward **Career:** 48-0-9
Debut: 8 Jan 55 (goal) **Final:** 1 May 57

Born: Abingdon 16 Jul 1932

Career: Abingdon Town; Headington United; Reading Aug 1949 (amat), 19.11.51 (pro); NORWICH CITY 10.01.55; Watford 18.06.57 to 1964; Ipswich Town assistant manager/chief coach Jul 1965; IFK Vasteras (Sweden) 1967 to 1972; Wolverhampton Wanderers assistant manager then manager Jun 1976 to Nov 1978; United Arab Emirates coach; Stoke City coach, Jun 1985–Oct 1989 assistant manager; Colchester United Jan 1990 assistant manager/coach; Doncaster Rovers School of Excellence 1990–Sep 1991; Blackburn Rovers chief scout; Coventry City scout; Oldswinford Sep 1991 manager; Tamworth Jan 1992–Jan 1993 manager; Doncaster Rovers Jul 1994–17 Aug 1996 manager.

Sammy's first eight Reading youth games saw him score 30 goals, including a record ten versus Aldershot. He was the son of a Chinese father and English mother; his nickname 'Sammy' was given to him by his brother. He was slightly built but effective, with a capacity to play in different positions (five different numbered shirts as a Canary). Recovered well from a badly broken leg in Nov 1955 which kept him out for 10 months. Gained the all important FA coaching badge while at Watford. For the last 30 years he has been coaching, scouting and managing a variety of sides.

CHURCH, John

(1938–1950) **1948:** 5/9; 10/4
Outside Right/Left **Career:** 114-0-16
Debut: 23 Apr 38 **Final:** 29 Apr 50

Born: Oulton Broad 17 Sep 1919

Career: Morton Road School; Lowestoft Town Schoolboys 1932; Lowestoft Town 1933; NORWICH CITY 27.07.36 (amat), 22.09.36 (pro); Colchester United 10.07.50 to 1953; Crittalls Athletic Jul 1954.

Immensely popular clubman who progressed through the 'A' team. Awarded the DSM with the Royal Marine Commandoes and he is one of the few men to play for City both sides of the war. John was a feared marksman in local amateur circles winning golden opinions. Hit three in three minutes versus Crystal Palace in the D3S(N) Cup. Served under five Norwich City

managers and he sadly lost six years' football to the War after a pre-War debut at age 18. He retired after 30 years as a UK representative in gold and silver for a London firm.

CLARE, Joseph

(1936–1937) **1936:** 5/11; 12/0
Outside Left **Career:** 22-0-5
Debut: 29 Aug 36 **Final:** 2 Jan 37

Born: Westhoughton, nr Wigan 4 Feb 1910
Died: Christchurch 23 Sep 1987

Career: Sacred Heart; Westhoughton; Westhoughton Town Oct 1929; Manchester City 08.08.30 (amat), 05.09.30 (pro); Wigan Borough 11.08.31; Westhoughton Town Oct 1931; Accrington Stanley 03.11.33; Arsenal 05.12.34; Margate (loan) 1935/6; NORWICH CITY 08.05.36; Lincoln City 30.06.37–05.05.45; Ruston Bucyrus Feb 1946; Bournemouth & Boscombe Athletic coach/trainer to 1960; Bournemouth & District Water Company trainer to 1968.

Scored twice for Margate against City's Reserves, an act that prompted his signing. As a winger of willowy build he excelled at Lincoln, playing until 1945 with over 200 games and 60 goals to his credit. His natural inward swerve and good pace held him in good stead in his one season with City and he ended with 45 First/Second XI games for 21 goals.

CLAYTON, Paul Spencer

(1983–1986) **1984:** 5/11; 11/3
Forward **Career:** 10-5-0
Debut: 17 Dec 83 **Final:** 3 May 86

Born: Dunstable 4 Jan 1965

Career: White Woman Lane Middle School; Sprowston High School; Norwich School Under-13–16; Norfolk County Under-19; NORWICH CITY schoolboy forms, app & pro Jan 1983; Summer spell in Finland cs 1984; Orebro Sport Club (Sweden) (loan) Jul 1986; Darlington 04.03.88; Crewe Alexandra 23.11.89; Macclesfield Town 1991; Stafford Rangers Jun 1992; Stalybridge Celtic 12.03.94; Northwich Victoria Jul 1995.

Paul scored eight goals in the FA Youth Cup success including two goals in the May 1983 Final win over Everton. A regular scorer for City at youth and reserve team level. Paul scored twice on his Darlington and Stafford debuts and top scored for the latter in one GM Vauxhall Conference season. He quit football in 1995 to train as a hospital theatre technician and was spotted playing in Dean Greygoose's (Crewe) testimonial match in May 1999.

CLEARY, William

(1953–1956) **1953:** 5/11; 11/0
Right Half **Career:** 21-0-0
Debut: 19 Dec 53 **Final:** 10 Mar 56

Born: Grangetown, nr Middlesbrough 20 Apr 1931
Died: Norwich 12 Mar 1991

Career: Southbank East End Juniors; Sunderland 28.05.49; NORWICH CITY 20.05.52; Wisbech Town Aug 1956; Port Vale 01.11.57; Boston 01.07.58; King's Lynn 1959–Apr 1961; Wisbech Town Aug 1961; King's Lynn 25.03.87 caretaker manager, Director 09.04.87–Apr 1988.

Spent four years as an understudy to the long-serving and ultra-consistent half back line of McCrohan, Foulkes and Ashman. His 109 reserve games for four goals proved that he would have done a solid job if given more chances. He became a key figure with King's Lynn as a player/caretaker manager and director.

CLELAND, Peter Melville

(1958) **1958:** 5/9; 11/4
Centre Forward **Career:** 4-0-0
Debut: 13 Dec 58 **Final:** 26 Dec 58

Born: Eaglesham, Renfrewshire 8 May 1932
Died: Bedford 23 Sep 1990

Career: Motherwell 08.03.51; Cheltenham Town 1954–1958; NORWICH CITY 11.08.58; Cheltenham Town Jan 1960; Bedford Town Sep 1960; Biggleswade Jul 1962.

His four games saw Gordon Banks in goal for Chesterfield; a waterlogged pitch; cup tickets on sale and a game in the 1958/59 cup run. Hit 38 goals in 48 games for Cheltenham in his last season before City signed him. His goals included hat-tricks versus Kidderminster and Merthyr as well as scoring in both legs of the 1957/8 Southern League Cup Final. To his chagrin at the time, the Rothmans publications had him listed as a Brummie from Worcester City with three Ls in his surname!

COLE, Michael Edward

(1956–1958) **1957:** 6/2; 13/0
Left Back **Career:** 3-0-0
Debut: 28 Apr 56 **Final:** 26 Apr 58

Born: Ilford 9 Jun 1937

Career: Downshall School; Ilford Boys; Essex & London Boys; Leyton Orient (reserves); Harwich (amat); NORWICH CITY 29.03.56 (amat),

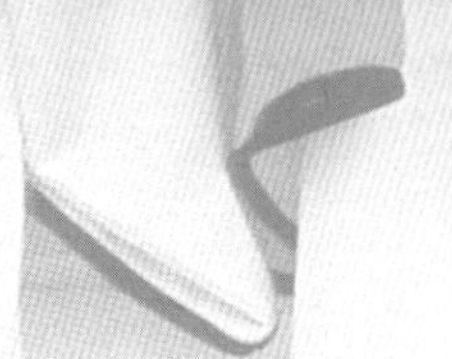

18.08.56 (pro); Chelmsford City Jan 1958; Biggleswade 1960; Lowestoft Town 18.08.62–09.05.63; Thetford Town Aug 1964.

Unique in that he had one game in each of three seasons, a record that does not help one in passing judgement. His up and down career on taking the professional ticket saw him make 38 reserve appearances. Still managed more games for City than Norman – his namesake. City's John Wilson joined him at Thetford, where reports said that Mike excelled as a centre half with his professional experience being obvious to all watchers.

COLE, Norman Philip

(1935) **1935**: 5/11; 12/4
Centre Forward **Career:** 1-0-0
Debut/Final: 28 Sep 35

Born: Woolston, Southampton 7 Nov 1913
Died: Southampton 29 Nov 1976

Career: Sholing School; Taunton Secondary Modern School; Itchen Sports; Thornycrofts; Newport (Isle of Wight); Hampshire County; Southampton 23.08.32 (amat), 20.10.32 (pro); NORWICH CITY 13.05.35 to Apr 1936.

Tall and powerful Norman played with Ted Drake and Ben Burley at the Dell joining City with a goalscoring reputation. No relation to Mike, he was plucky to a degree and took some stopping in his quest for goals. Norman was City's 200th Football League debutant. After football he was a Southampton Railways engineer; worked on cross channel ferries and for 35 years until retirement with Gnat Aircraft at Follands in Southampton.

COLEMAN, Ernest (Tim)

(1937– 1939) **1938:** 5/7; 11/2
Inside Right **Career:** 64-0-26
Debut: 13 Feb 37 **Final:** 6 May 39

Born: Blidworth, Nottingham 4 Jan 1908
Died: Nottingham 20 Jan 1984

Career: Hucknall Church Lads Brigade Boys Club; Hucknall Colliery; Nottingham Forest (trial) 26.03.26; Halifax Town 12.07.26; Grimsby Town 28.02.29; Arsenal 04.03.32; Middlesbrough 11.08.34; NORWICH CITY 13.02.37; coached a Pit team in Hucknall; Linby Colliery secretary/player/coach/manager (scoring Nov 52); Notts County manager Jul 1957–Oct 1957, in various capacities from 1958 to 1966 including managerships Nov 1961–Jul 1963 and Apr 1965–Mar 1966.

Nicknamed 'Tim' because of his tiny frame, he was a great capture for City, being able to play in all forward positions with equal facility. Even close marking couldn't dissipate his menace as he scored regularly at all his clubs. Still holds the Mariners' seasonal scoring record and was proud of his Championship medal gained when at Highbury where he netted 43 goals in 79 games. He continually dazzled the opposition and even had the temerity to play a game for Ipswich Town during wartime. He moved in illustrious company but was never overshadowed.

COLLINS, Anthony Norman (Darkie)

(1953–1955) **1955:** 5/11; 11/3
Outside Left **Career:** 31-0-2
Debut: 19 Aug 53 **Final:** 5 May 55

Born: Kensington 19 Mar 1926

Career: Brentford (amat); Acton United; Sheffield Wednesday 03.11.47; York City 19.07.49; Watford 05.08.50; NORWICH CITY 06.07.53; Torquay United 25.07.55; Watford 21.06.57; Crystal Palace 20.11.57; Rochdale 22.06.59, manager Jun 1960 to 1967; Bristol City chief scout Dec 1967, assistant manager 1976–1980, caretaker manager Sep 1980; Leeds United chief scout to Oct 1981; Manchester United chief scout Feb 1983–Jun 1988; Queens Park Rangers chief scout Feb 1989; Millwall scout.

Did marvellously at Spotland on a shoestring budget, being their manager when opposing Norwich in the League Cup Final. Gave good service to four clubs, totalling over 300 league appearances in his career. His 76 reserve games for Norwich saw him score ten times – mostly converted penalties. Had competition for the left wing position from Adams, Gavin and Gordon.

CONEY, Dean Henry

(1989–1990) **1989:** 6/0; 12/6
Forward **Career:** 12-5-1
Debut: 27 Mar 89 (sub) **Final:** 31 Mar 90 (sub)

Born: Dagenham 18 Sep 1963

Career: Valence Primary School; Erkenwald School; London & Essex Boys; Fulham 03.04.80 (app), 20.05.81 (pro); Queens Park Rangers 18.06.87; NORWICH CITY 16.03.89; Ernest Borell (Hong Kong); Farnborough Town Nov 91–96/7; Carshalton Athletic; Farnborough Town manager May 1998, first team coach.

He was in his own words, 'A half decent player and mad on the game taking a ball with me wherever I went'. Four England Under 21 caps gained. Norwich City signed him for a reported

£350,000 as he jumped at the chance of joining a footballing side. He was however handicapped by injuries, suffering from a hernia problem and a snapped cruciate ligament. Dean has since forged a fine career with Farnborough making 182 appearances before being forced to retire with a back injury.

CONLON, Bryan

(1968–1970)	**1970:** 6/1; 12/7
Centre forward	**Career:** 31-0-8
Debut: 26 Dec 68	**Final:** 7 Apr 70

Born: Shildon 14 Jan 1943
Died: Shildon 11 Oct 2000

Career: Shildon Morden Council School; Shildon Works Juniors; Durham County: Sheffield Wednesday (trial); Newcastle United May 22.05.61; South Shields May 1962; Darlington 22.08.64; Millwall 17.11.67; NORWICH CITY 20.12.68; Blackburn Rovers 22.05.70; Crewe Alexandra 18.01.72; Cambridge United 09.03.72; Hartlepool United 15.09.–Jun 1974; Shildon Athletic Jul 1974–Dec 1975.

A craggy player abetted by a powerful frame and whenever he scored for the first team they won the match. Given his chance on the sale of Manning and then vying for the no.9 shirt with Silvester. An undying memory of him was flinging his jersey to the ground when substituted against Blackburn Rovers. An exchange deal involving Malcolm Darling saw him move to Ewood Park.

CONWAY, James

(1961–1963)	**1962:** 5/10; 12/3
Centre Forward	**Career:** 50-0-15
Debut: 19 Aug 61	**Final:** 17 Sep 63

Born: Motherwell 27 Aug 1940

Career: Park Street Primary School; St Patrick's High School; Scottish Schoolboys; Coltness United 1956; Glasgow Celtic 23.08.56 (provisional), 27.08.57 (full); Glasgow Rangers (loan) 11.03.59; NORWICH CITY 03.05.61; Southend United 29.10.63; Partick Thistle 06.07.65; Portadown Aug 1966 player/assistant manager; Bolton Wanderers trainer 12.11.68, coach 1970–1981; Mansfield Town scout; Norwich City scout; Bolton Institute Higher Education Feb 1991 scout; Leigh RMI Apr 1996 coach.

An apprentice engine fitter who according to the Scottish press – 'had a great wallop in both feet'. Spotted scoring regularly for Celtic's reserve side and was captured in the face of competition from Blackburn, Blackpool, Derby and Sheffield Wednesday. A crew cut Scot he started with a purple patch scoring in 5 of his first 8 games. Netted 4 in one reserve match and his final reserve tally of 38 games and 20 goals showed that he was too good to languish in the seconds. Later played for the Irish League against Scottish League in Belfast in September 67. A Scot in an Irish team! Rated as one of the best coaches in the North West.

COOK, Paul Anthony

(1989–1990)	**1988:** 5/11; 11/10
Inside Right	**Career:** 4-4-0
Debut: 19 Apr 89 (sub)	**Final:** 9 Sep 90 (sub)

Born: Liverpool 22 Feb 1967

Career: Marine; Wigan 20.07.84; NORWICH CITY 12.05.88; Wolverhampton Wanderers 01.11.89; Coventry City 18.08.94; Tranmere Rovers (loan) 29.02.96, (signed) 28.03.96; Stockport County 23.10.97; Burnley (loan) 25.03.99, (signed) 08.07.99.

Norwich bought Paul for £73,000 as they were in need of a naturally gifted left-sided midfield player. He competed for a first team spot with the likes of Ruel Fox and Jeremy Goss. He filled the provider role for Wolves' prolific scorer Steve Bull and was much in demand, with fair-sized transfer fees paid for his services. He joined Gary Megson's Stockport before helping Burnley challenge for a play-off position last season.

COOKE, George Harry

(1923–1924)	**1923:** 5/6; 10/7
Outside Left	**Career:** 6-0-0
Debut: 25 Aug 23	**Final:** 8 Mar 24

Born: Clowne 20 Nov 1899
Died: Southsea 20 Sep 1977

Career: Cresswell White Star; Bolsover Town; Bolsover Colliery; Clowne Colliery; Chesterfield 06.02.22; Shirebrook Jul 1922; NORWICH CITY 14.05.23; Portsmouth 28.07.24; Southend United 14.05.25; Wigan Borough 13.08.26; Mansfield Town 01.05.28; Bradford Park Albion 09.05.29; Connah's Quay Aug 1930; Grantham Town Dec 1930.

One of six new debutants on the day for City. On the small side but sturdy, he was deemed to be a handful for the most vigilant of full backs. George was only able to displace Jimmy Stoakes from the first team half a dozen times. His brothers Fred (Sunderland, Swindon, Accrington) and Edwin (Mansfield, Barnsley, Brentford) were also league players in the 1920s.

COOTE, Adrian

(1997–	**1997:** 6/2; 12/0
Forward	**Career:** 21-40-3
Debut: 13 Sep 97 (sub)	

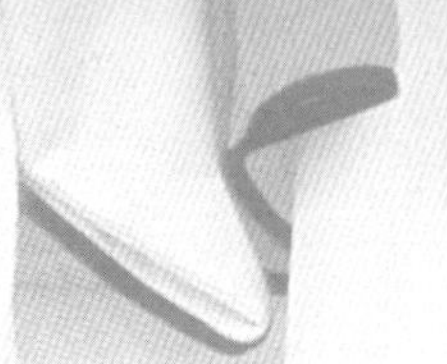

Born: Belton, nr Great Yarmouth 30 Sep 1978

Career: Belton First School; Waveney First School; Breydon Middle School; Cliff Park High School; B & B Tigers; NORWICH CITY Centre of Excellence; Shrublands; Great Yarmouth District & Norfolk County; NORWICH CITY 16.10.92 (assoc), 24.08.95 (trainee), 11.04.97 (pro); Roda (Holland) (trial) Oct 2000.

Adrian has risen from Fenland floodlit football to gain Northern Ireland international caps. His mother was born in Belfast and is a cousin of Bryan Hamilton. Has had to vie with Roberts and Llewellyn for a first team place and signed a new City contract in March 2001 with the club hoping he can transfer his prolific reserve scoring (57 goals) to the top level.

CORNWELL, Ralph Leslie

(1926) **1926:** 5/10; 11/12
Left Back **Career:** 2-0-0
Debut: 28 Aug 26 **Final:** 4 Sep 26

Born: Nottingham 7 Sep 1901
Died: Hoveringham 6 Mar 1988

Career: Sneinton Institute; Notts County 18.03.21 (amat), 18.11.21 (pro); NORWICH CITY 14.07.26; Sneinton Church Institute 02.01.30.

Tony Cottee

Spent five years at Notts County, playing in 42 Division One games. His Norwich City debut was in a sorry game result-wise, but it was said that Ralph had a capacity to play in either full back position, being admirably two-footed. A knee injury picked up at Notts County handicapped his mobility. During the Second World War he worked in a Royal Ordnance factory and he retired from the Ministry of Defence in 1965. He won many trophies at snooker and bowls and was latterly a master grocer.

CORRIGAN, Thomas Joseph

(1984) **1984:** 6/4; 15/9
Goalkeeper **Career:** 4-0-0
Debut: 29 Sep 84 **Final:** 13 Oct 84

Born: Manchester 18 Nov 1948

Career: Sale F.C.; Manchester City 24.09.66 (amat), 21.01.67 (pro); Seattle Sounders (USA) 25.03.83; Brighton & Hove Albion 15.09.83; NORWICH CITY (loan) 29.09.84; Stoke City (loan) 02.11.84 to May 1985; Liverpool goalkeeping coach 24.10.94.

Staggeringly, Joe's mother's maiden name was Keelan. Joe consistently guarded the Maine Road rigging with indomitable courage for a decade winning a ECWC medal. Deemed unlucky not to win more England caps principally being the third choice behind Clemence and Shilton. He was the only bearded City goalkeeper in memory at the time he played and won high praise for the way he stepped into the fray following an injury to Woods. Unfortunately he suffered a shoulder/neck injury while playing for Brighton's Reserves on QPR's artificial pitch. Latterly he ran a haulage business and has also coached goalkeepers at Celtic, Tranmere, Huddersfield and Stoke.

COTTEE, Antony Richard

(2000) **2000:** 5/9; 12/6
Forward **Career:** 6-3-2
Debut: 12 Sep 00 **Final:** 24 Oct 00

Born: West Ham 11 Jul 1965

Career: Warren Comprehensive School; Barking; Havering; Essex County; Chase Cross United; West Ham United 11.05.81 (app), 31.08.82 (pro); Everton 02.08.88; West Ham United 07.09.94; Selangor (Malaysia) 17.10.96–03.03.97; Leicester City 14.08.97; Birmingham City (loan) 14.11.97–24.12.97; NORWICH CITY 11.09.2000–31.10.2000; Barnet 01.11.2000–16.03.2001 player-manager; New England Revolution (USA) 17.03.2001–21.03.2001; Millwall 22.03.2001 to retirement 08.05.2001.

England caps; PFA young player of the year; club player of the year and almost 300 goals in a glittering career. He was once the most expensive player in Britain and doesn't boast about his achievements, although he is proud of them. Seemed an ideal signing for City but was allowed to move to Barnet after just seven weeks. The first player to play in the Premiership, First, Second and Third divisions in one season. Scored on his debut for his American side and had 23 clubs ring him prior to last years' transfer deadline. Began a coaching course in May 2001.

COULTHARD, Thomas DeArr

(1924–1926) **1924:** 5/9; 11/0
Full Back/Right Half **Career:** 42-0-1
Debut: 30 Aug 24 **Final:** 23 Jan 26 (goal)

Born: Cockerton 12 Feb 1900
Died: Newcastle 16 Sep 1971

Career: Darlington Forge Juniors; Darlington Railway Athletic; represented Third Army during First World War; Darlington; Newcastle United

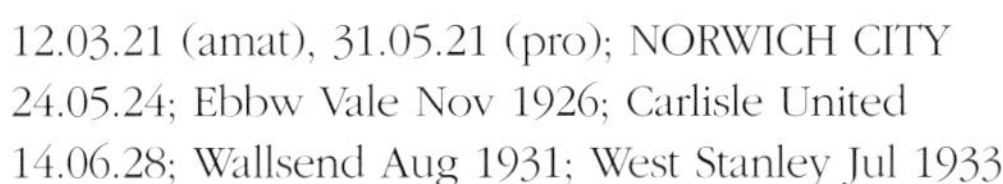

12.03.21 (amat), 31.05.21 (pro); NORWICH CITY 24.05.24; Ebbw Vale Nov 1926; Carlisle United 14.06.28; Wallsend Aug 1931; West Stanley Jul 1933.

Spent three years at Newcastle as an understudy to Irish international McCracken which helped give him a good grounding. Credited with two own goals against Charlton in October 1925 but nonetheless was a useful and steady performer. The Lancashire Daily Post Football Annual *gave his selling fee at most clubs as £250. His younger brother William made 120 appearances for Darlington.*

COUSINS, William Alfred

(1927–1928) **1927:** 5/10; 1 1/7
Outside Right **Career:** 26-0-0
Debut: 5 Feb 27 **Final:** 15 Sep 28

Born: Norwich 1 Dec 1902
Died: Wolverhampton 8 Apr 1983

Career: City of Norwich School; Boulton & Paul; City Wanderers 1922; Gorleston; NORWICH CITY 03.02.27 to 1928; Boulton & Paul; Gorleston Dec 1932 to 1933.

Scored three times for Norfolk County in six appearances between 1922 to 1927.
A prominent local amateur who was in competition with Porter for a first team place at a time when Norwich City were having poor results. His hat-trick against Lincolnshire showed what he was capable of but he sought reinstatement as an amateur in order to give more service to his former clubs when he left Norwich.

COXON, William George (Billy)

(1952–1958) **1953:** 5/8; 9/9
Outside Left **Career:** 105-0-26
Debut: 20 Dec 52 (goal) **Final:** 8 Mar 58

Born: Derby 28 Apr 1933

Career: Allerton Schoolboys; Derby Boys through Juniors, 10.05.50 (pro); Ilkeston Town 1951; NORWICH CITY 14.05.52; Lincoln City 14.03.58; Bournemouth 20.11.58–30.06.66; Poole Town Jul 1966; Parley Sports May 1967.

Billy had a good turn of speed and was ever-ready to shoot, as evidenced his debut goal after just 19 minutes. He exploded into the limelight in 1955/56 having scored 30 reserve goals, by then including a hat-trick over Watford. Played over 200 league games for Bournemouth joined at times by Crickmore and Spelman.

CRICKMORE, Charles Alfred

(1968–1969) **1964:** 5/9; 10/9
Left Wing **Career:** 62-2-10
Debut: 20 Jan 68 **Final:** 1 Nov 69

Born: Hull 11 Feb 1942

Career: Hull Schools; Hull 06.08.58 (amat), 11.02.59 (pro); Bournemouth 28.06.62; Gillingham 14.06.66; Rotherham United 03.11.67; NORWICH CITY 13.01.68; Notts County 14.03.70 retired Jun 1972 following a broken leg injury.

A speedy, down-the-line winger bought to replace Kenning and to provide aerial service for Manning. He was a needed 20 pounds heavier than his puny Hull days and excited the crowd with his dashing displays. Later played Rugby League for West Hull and ran a local marathon in 3 hrs 39 mins despite having kneecap trouble – a common problem with ex-footballers. Returned to Humberside and worked for the fire service for 23 years. Thereafter a caravan inspector and a driving instructor.

CROCKFORD, Harold Arthur

(1927) **1927:** 5/10; 12/4
Inside Forward **Career:** 2-0-0
Debut: 17 Sep 27 **Final:** 17 Dec 27

Born: Derby 25 Sep 1893
Died: Tunbridge Wells 15 Dec 1983

Career: Chatham Town; Vicar of Wakefield FC; Fulham Dec 1917–Feb 1919; Exeter City 23.05.22; Port Vale 23.05.23; Chesterfield 04.10.23; Gillingham 06.03.25; Accrington Stanley 26.05.25; Walsall 16.11.25; Darlington 31.05.26; NORWICH CITY 13.05.27; Bedford Town Sep 1928; Tunbridge Wells Rangers Dec 1929.

Harold was an energetic and industrious forward who netted goals at all his clubs prior to Norwich. Scorer of three hat-tricks, with the 1926 Athletic News *remarking he was proving a strong foundation for building up attacks. In the top ten of oldest City league debutants, so supporters did not see him at his best at the Nest. A retired turf accountant who beat all the odds to live to the marvellous age of 90.*

CROOK, Ian Stuart

(1986–1997) **1988:** 5/8; 10/6
Midfield **Career:** 380-38-24
Debut: 23 Aug 86 **Final:** 4 May 97

Born: Romford 18 Jan 1963

Career: Forest Lodge Comprehensive School; Great Danes; Havering Schools; Essex County

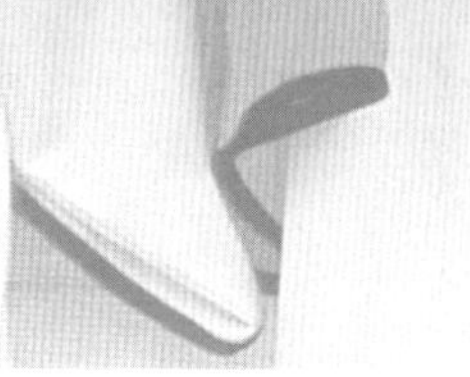

Ian Crook

(trials); Tottenham Hotspur 20.09.77 (assoc), 21.05.79 (app), 01.08.80 (pro); NORWICH CITY 13.06.86; Ipswich Town 21.06.96; NORWICH CITY 26.06.96; San Frecce Horoshima (Japan) Jun 1997; Northern Spirit (Australia) 1998, player coach Feb 2000 to assistant manager, head of youth development/First XI coach Oct 2000.

Spotted by Spurs while playing for a Brentwood Sunday league side. He played in 13 countries for Spurs including a UEFA cup semi-final. An England 'B' international and stylish midfielder whose creative talents and persistent industry were an integral part of City's renowned passing style of the time. His right leg being 8mm lower than his left did not affect his skills. One of City's ultimate bargain buys 'Chippy' is forging a respected career in Australia on the coaching and youth development front.

CROPPER, Arthur

(1928–1930)	**1929:** 5/9; 12/0
Centre Forward	**Career:** 23-0-3
Debut: 18 Feb 28	**Final:** 26 Apr 30

Born: Brimington 2 Jan 1906
Died: Norwich 25 Oct 1949

Career: Luton Town (trial); Matlock Town; Staveley Town; Alfreton Town; NORWICH CITY 28.12.27; Clapton Orient 20.10.30; Gillingham 29.07.32; Yarmouth Town 09.09.33 to 01.04.36.

In his early days at Norwich he had Percy Varco for competition, and later Thomas Hunt, so it was not surprising that he had limited opportunities to impress. His last game for City saw Swindon Town's Abe Morris score five at the Nest. Arthur showed that he was a cogent force, albeit on a lesser stage, by netting 35 goals in just 61 games for Yarmouth. Latterly the landlord of the East Suffolk Tavern in Yarmouth.

CROPPER, Reginald

(1926–1928)	**1926:** 5/8; 10/7
Inside Right/	
Centre Forward	**Career:** 53-0-18
Debut: 28 Aug 26	**Final:** 30 Apr 28

Born: Brimington 21 Jan 1902
Died: Chesterfield 25 May 1942

Career: Birmingham junior football; Staveley Town; Watford (trial) 29.08.24; Notts County 27.11.24; NORWICH CITY 14.07.26; Guildford City Sep 1928; Tranmere Rovers 21.08.29; Guildford City Jul 1930; Crystal Palace 25.09.31; Mansfield Town 26.08.32; Hollingwood Rangers Nov 1935.

His brother Arthur outscored him at other clubs but was no match for Reg at Norwich. A bustling, unselfish footballer who top-scored for City in the 1926/27 season. Fractured his right leg in a motorcycle accident and broke the left one in his second reserve match for Notts County. Reg grumbled that he was not a regular in City's team with a consequence being that he left the club. He died after an accident at work, employed as a railway fitter. The Croppers were certainly unfortunate to die in their 40s.

CROSS, David

(1971–1973)	**1971:** 5/11; 12/0
Centre Forward	**Career:** 105-1-30
Debut: 9 Oct 71	**Final:** 10 Nov 73

Born: Heywood, nr Bury 8 Dec 1950

Career: Heywood Grammar School; Heywood Boys; Rochdale 05.08.69; NORWICH CITY 07.10.71; Coventry City 14.11.73; West Bromwich

Arthur Cropper

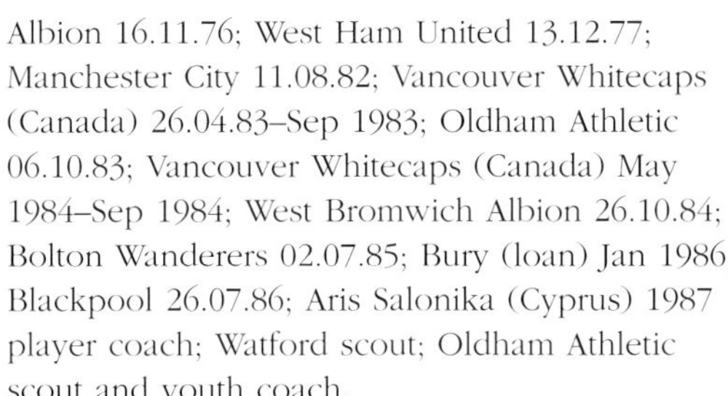

Albion 16.11.76; West Ham United 13.12.77; Manchester City 11.08.82; Vancouver Whitecaps (Canada) 26.04.83–Sep 1983; Oldham Athletic 06.10.83; Vancouver Whitecaps (Canada) May 1984–Sep 1984; West Bromwich Albion 26.10.84; Bolton Wanderers 02.07.85; Bury (loan) Jan 1986; Blackpool 26.07.86; Aris Salonika (Cyprus) 1987 player coach; Watford scout; Oldham Athletic scout and youth coach.

Have boots will travel – and they were utilised to telling effect, scoring over 250 career goals. City's signing of Dave was announced over the public address system after a League Cup tie. Helped take two of his sides to Division Two titles. FA Cup final appearance with West Ham and he aided Vancouver to their Western title. A distinguished career with four big money moves and a popular player with club fans. A believer that coaching is the next best thing after playing, he acknowledges the influences his many managers have had on him.

CROSSAN, Errol Gilmour

(1958–1960) **1958:** 5/6; 10/10
Outside Right **Career:** 116-0-32
Debut: 27 Sep 58 **Final:** 31 Dec 60

Born: Montreal, Canada 6 Oct 1930

Career: Murray Road School (Isle of Man); Gymnasium AFC; in Under-18 & Senior Amateur side & Junior Manx XI 1947/48; Westminster Royals; Manchester City 11.01.54; Gillingham 16.07.55; Southend United 27.07.57; NORWICH CITY 26.09.58; Orient 06.01.61; Toronto City (Canada) 1961.

Errol moved to the Isle of Man with the family in 1938. In 1949 the family moved back to Canada whilst Errol attempted to become a footballer. 'Cowboy' Crossan used his devastating speed to join the ranks of a distinguished band of goalscoring Norwich City right wingers. A rightful part of the total excitement that was the FA Cup crusade. A key member of the team that won promotion to Division Two. He returned home playing in the Canadian league which included stars such as Stanley Matthews and Johnny Haynes. Worked for 30 years as a supervisor for Canadian Forest Products and he was a star turn at the 59ers reunion. In May 2000 he was inducted into the Canadian Soccer Hall of Fame.

CROWE, Mark Anthony (Chic)

(1982) **1984:** 5/10; 10/10
Defender **Career:** 0-1-0
Debut/Final: 11 Dec 82 (sub)

Born: Southwold, Suffolk 21 Jan 1965

Career: Kirkley High School; Oulton Broad Eagles; Suffolk Under-14–16; NORWICH CITY 1980 (youth), 21.01.83 (pro); Torquay United 08.07.85; Cambridge United 24.12.86; Watton Jul 1989; Thetford Town Aug 1989; Wroxham Apr 1991; Lowestoft Town 1999 player coach.

His one appearance was made for City when Walford and Watson were both injured the previous week. The Youth team captain and their player of the year when they won the South East Counties League plus the FA Youth Cup (for the first time in the club's history). Also an unused substitute by City in four other first team games. At Watton with Mendham and with Wroxham he returned to Carrow Road to win the Norfolk Senior Cup. His joining Lowestoft Town was referred to the Football Association to decide who held his registration.

CROWE, Matthew Jackson

(1957–1962) **1964:** 5/8; 11/10
Left Half **Career:** 214-0-18
Debut: 2 Oct 57 (goal) **Final:** 20 Apr 62

Born: Bathgate, West Lothian 4 Jul 1932

Career: Bathgate Thistle; Partick Thistle; Bradford Park Avenue 04.07.49; Partick Thistle 05.01.54; NORWICH CITY 29.05.57; Brentford 04.07.62; Port Elizabeth City (South Africa) player-manager; Corinthians (Greek side in Johannesburg) manager 1968/69; Port Elizabeth City (South Africa) manager until folded 1974.

Matt suffered a broken leg at both Partick and Bradford. Signed as an inside forward but found consistency and freedom at wing half. A good provider for the forwards and a perfect foil for McCrohan. The catch of 1957 for £500, as he hardly missed a match. Won a Division Four medal with his next club as City sold him for five times the price they paid for him. He emigrated to South Africa and worked as a sales manager for a paint firm in Cape Province.

CULVERHOUSE, Ian Brett

(1985–1994) **1985:** 5/9; 11/1
Full Back **Career:** 368-1-2
Debut: 9 Oct 85 **Final:** 7 May 94

Born: Bishop's Stortford 22 Sep 1964

Career: Harlow District Boys; Essex County (trial) at Rugby; Hoddeston United; Tottenham Hotspur May 1981 (app), 24.09.82 (pro); NORWICH CITY 07.10.85; Swindon Town (loan) 09.12.94, (transfer) 30.12.94; Stevenage Borough (trial) Jul 1998; Kingstonian Jul 1998; Brighton & Hove Albion 08.07.99, Jul 2000 reserve manager; Barnet Jun 2001 youth team manager,

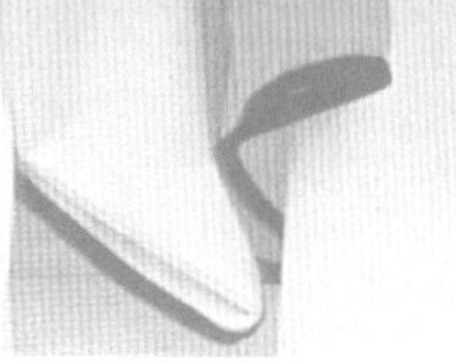

Ian Culverhouse

Opportunities were limited at Spurs but Ian was still able to win two England Youth caps plus a UEFA Cup winner's medal. Became a lucky charm at Norwich, setting a club record of not being on the losing side in his first 18 league games. In his years at Carrow Road he became the epitome of the model player being consistently reliable. He played for the team and not to the gallery. Player of the Year in 1990/1 and an integral part of the Norwich team that finished third in the Premiership and which enjoyed UEFA cup success. Since leaving City he has rejuvenated his career on the south coast.

CURETON, Jamie

(1994–1996)	**1994:** 5/10; 10/0
Striker	**Career:** 13-19-6
Debut: 5 Nov 94	**Final:** 5 May 96

Born: Bristol 28 Aug 1975

Career: St Nicholas; St Thomas More Comprehensive School; Bristol Schools; Avon Schools; Southampton Under-11–14; NORWICH CITY 09.05.90 (assoc), 28.08.91 (trainee), 05.02.93 (pro); Bournemouth (loan) 08.09.95; Bristol Rovers 20.09.96; Reading 21.08.2000.

Jamie's dad Chris was a prolific marksman in part time Western league soccer. Jamie was a phenomenal scorer at Carrow Road for the youth and reserve sides netting 135 goals in 187 games with seven hat-tricks, two fours, three fives and all six versus Leyton Orient in December 1992. Helped his last two sides reach the play offs topping his club and the league charts with his prolific goalscoring. With hindsight, a scorer of goals that Norwich City should have kept, but that's football.

CURRAN, Hugh Patrick

(1966–1969)	**1966:** 5/10; 11/3
Striker	**Career:** 124-0–53
Debut: 29 Jan 66 (goal)	**Final:** 18 Jan 69 (goal)

Born: Glasgow 28 Sep 1943

Career: Home Farm FC; Manchester United (app); Shamrock Rovers 1961; Third Lanark 11.09.62; Corby Town Jul 1963; Millwall 09.03.64; NORWICH CITY 13.01.66; Wolverhampton Wanderers 30.01.69; Oxford United 15.09.72; Bolton Wanderers 12.09.74; Oxford United 06.07.77; Banbury United Jul 1979 manager; Thames manager.

Hugh moved to Ireland when he was eleven and played all hurling and gaelic football. He played for five English clubs; gained five full Scottish caps and had five cartilage operations. Had undoubted attacking flair and a strong left-foot shot. Only six players reached 50 goals for City in fewer games than him. Ron Davies was the rapier and Hugh the scimitar as they tore into sides with great attacking flair.
A potent striker who continued to find the net at Wolves. His 100 goals for clubs after he left Carrow Road made one wish that manager Lol Morgan had retained his services.

DALGLISH, Paul Kenneth

(1999–2001)	**1999:** 5/10; 10/0
Forward	**Career:** 29-19-2
Debut: 3 Apr 99 (sub)	**Final:** 20 Feb 01 (sub)

Born: Glasgow 18 Feb 1977

Career: Merchant Secondary School; Preston North End Under-14; Blackburn Rovers May 1994; Glasgow Celtic from Juniors 20.07.95; Liverpool 14.08.96; Newcastle United 21.11.97; Bury (loan) 21.11.97; NORWICH CITY (loan) 25.03.99, (signed) 09.05.99, Wigan Athletic (loan) 22.03.01; NORWICH CITY (contract cancelled) 26.08.2001; Wigan Athletic (signed) 26.08.2001.

Son of Liverpool and Scotland legend Kenny and an Under-21 Scottish international.
He joined his father's teams up to and including Newcastle. Injuries at City hampered his progress but when switched to the right wing he used his pace to good effect. Sent off in consecutive Easter games for Wigan as his side, under first Rioch and then Bruce, failed to win promotion.

DARLING, Malcolm

(1970–1971) **1970:** 5/11; 10/0
Winger **Career:** 17-0-5
Debut: 5 Sep 70 **Final:** 4 Sep 71

Born: Arbroath 4 Jul 1947

Career: Luncarty Juniors; Blackburn Rovers 27.10.64; NORWICH CITY 22.05.70; Rochdale 06.10.71; Bolton Wanderers 25.09.73; Chesterfield 22.08.74; Stockport County (loan) 02.03.77; Sheffield Wednesday 24.08.77; Hartlepools United 22.09.77; Morecambe 23.10.77; Bury 04.03.78; Morecambe Apr 1978; California Sunshine (USA) May 1979; Darwen 1981 player-manager.

Utility player who, while at Carrow Road, wore four of the shirts that make up the conventional forward line which is usually a good guide that ones stay will be a short one. A consistent reserve scorer (29–12 goals) and for the Firsts he was substituted 7 times with 5 of them being made between 67 and 73 minutes. He extended his career by another ten years and retired with a record of 86 goals in 361 matches.

DARMODY, Aubrey

(1946) **1946:** 5/11; 12/0
Left Back **Career:** 2-0-0
Debut: 25 Dec 46 **Final:** 26 Dec 46

Born: Swansea 17 May 1921

Career: Townhill School; Swansea Boys; Welsh Juniors; Tower United; Army; NORWICH CITY 10.09.46 (amat), 07.10.46 (pro); Colchester United May 1947; Yarmouth Town 06.11.48–12.05.51.

Aubrey played in the same Tower United side as Jimmy Guy. A brief sampling of the senior game one Christmas and what a contrast. City had 10 men on the injured list as they beat Bournemouth but the next day they lost 6–1 at home to the same opposition. Aubrey added 16 reserve matches scoring three goals before playing 110 games for Yarmouth. Latterly a general storekeeper.

DAVIDS, Neil Graham

(1976) **1976:** 6/0; 11/3
Defender **Career:** 2-0-0
Debut: 31 Mar 76 **Final:** 2 Apr 76

Born: Bingley, West Yorkshire 2 Sep 1955

Career: Leeds United 24.08.73; NORWICH CITY 10.04.75; Northampton Town (loan) 14.09.75; Stockport County (loan) 28.01.76–27.02.76; Swansea Town 05.07.77; Wigan 22.07.78; Bromsgrove Jul 1981.

Won an England Youth Cap while at Leeds and had the misfortune to break his leg twice while at Wigan. Lost many appearances to the cold steel of Forbes and made his City appearances while said player was serving a suspension. His limited success on the football field is overshadowed by his business acumen away from the game. He owned jewellery shops in Lancashire and student halls of residence in Preston.

DAVIES, Glyndwr

(1934–1935) **1934:** 5/7; 10/8
Outside Left **Career:** 3-0-0
Debut: 22 Dec 34 **Final:** 4 May 35

Born: Aberaman 1 Oct 1908
Died: Carmarthen 6 Nov 1997

Career: Aberdare County School; Ystalyfera Grammar School; Welsh Schoolboys; Welsh Juniors; Swansea Town 05.05.26 (amat); Casuals; Bristol University; Swansea Town 25.06.30 (amat); Brentford (amat); NORWICH CITY 30.06.33 (amat); Cambridge; Kimbolton School 1933 coach.

Talent is one thing and good attitude is another. Glyn had a willingness to improve and the instinct to do the right thing. His representative honours are listed in Glorious Canaries. *Outside sport he gained a B.Sc. (Hons, Chemistry) and taught maths and physics, rising to Housemaster at Kimbolton School. He retired from the School Board of Governors in Pontadawe in 1981.*

DAVIES, Gordon Owen

(1926) **1926:** 5/10; 12/4
Right Half **Career:** 1-0-0
Debut/Final: 9 Jan 26

Born: Woolwich 26 Apr 1903
Died: Llandriddnod 25 Sep 1991

Career: Old Pastonian School; NORWICH CITY 24.08.23; Metropolitan Police Mar 1926; Waterlow's Jul 1927.

A strong robust player who took and gave a good shoulder charge. Short personal involvement came in an away draw at Eastville after almost three years in the Reserves. He was in good company in the stiffs, playing at times alongside Bradbrook, Murphy and Sturgess. His most memorable match for Norwich was the seven-goal thriller against West Ham United in the Norfolk and Norwich Hospital Cup.

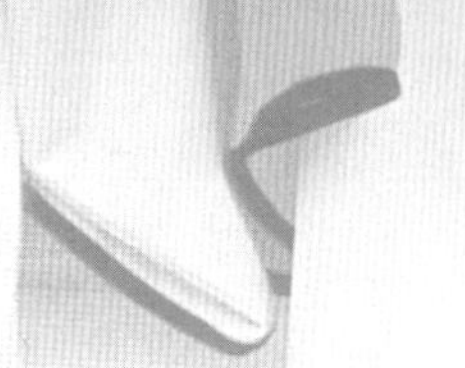

DAVIES, Ian Claude

(1974–1979) **1975:** 5/8; 10/8
Left Back **Career:** 31-3-2
Debut: 27 Apr 74 **Final:** 5 May 79

Born: Bristol 29 Mar 1957

Career: Fisons Sports; Clevedon Youth; NORWICH CITY 30.07.73 (amat), 03.04.75 (pro); Detroit Express (USA) (loan) 29.03.78–31.08.78; Newcastle United 26.06.79; Manchester City 01.08.82; Bury (loan) 04.11.82; Brentford (loan) 11.11.83; Cambridge United (loan) 05.02.84; Carlisle United 17.05.84; Exeter City 20.12.84; Bath City; Yeovil Town; Bury Town; Diss Town; Bristol Rovers 15.08.85; Swansea City 22.11.85–Feb 1986; Gloucester City Nov 1987.

A cultured defender with attacking flair, he reached Under-21 level for Wales and sat on the bench when England were well beaten in 1980. Voted player of the tournament in a European youth event involving Norwich City. A staggering list of clubs for someone under 30, and Ian did well to return to the league game, only to suffer a badly broken leg.

Chairman Geoffrey Watling presents Ron Davies with his full international cap won playing against Ireland in the 1963 season

DAVIES, Ronald Tudor

(1963–1966) **1964:** 6/0; 11/6
Centre Forward **Career:** 126-0-66
Debut: 7 Sep 63 (goal) **Final:** 7 May 66

Born: Holywell, Clwyd 25 May 1942

Career: Ysgol Inas Basim School; Holywell School; Flintshire Schools; Blackburn Rovers (trial); Chester 14.07.59; Luton Town 15.10.62; NORWICH CITY 05.09.63; Southampton 05.08.66; Portsmouth 27.04.73; Manchester United 28.11.74; Arcadia Shepherds (South Africa) Mar 1975; Millwall 11.11.75; Los Angeles Aztecs (USA) Apr 1976–Aug 1976; Dorchester Town Sep 1976; Tulsa Roughnecks (USA) Jul 1978; Seattle Sounders (USA) Apr 1979–Aug 1979; White Horse 1982; Totton Apr 1982; Winter Springs (USA) coaching director.

'If you fail your medical we'll sack the doctor', was Chairman Geoffrey Watling's comment, while Matt Busby described Ron as 'The greatest centre-forward in Europe' after another day when he terrorised the opposition defence. A Welsh international and one of the greatest post-war goalscorers, with heading ability that had to be seen to be believed. His four goals against Norwich City in one match alerted club officials to his obvious class. There was an outcry when City sold him for only £55,000. Another 152 goals were plundered elsewhere. His final total of 275 league goals confirms his greatness. He married an American dowager and has lived in the US for the last 20 years.

DAVIS, Derek Edgar Counsell

(1946–1948) **1948:** 5/11: 11/11
Goalkeeper **Career:** 28-0-0
Debut: 12 Sep 46 **Final:** 28 Feb 48

Born: Colwyn Bay 19 Jun 1922
Died: Manadon, Plymouth 7 Mar 1985

Career: Second World War for Plymouth Argyle; NORWICH CITY 13.09.45 (amat), 09.10.45 (pro); Torquay United 05.08.48; Bideford Town Jun 1952; Chippenham Town.

Reared not far from Argyle's Home Park and a Lochhead find in the 1945/46 transitional season, playing in friendlies, D3S(N) Cup and D3S(N) games. One of five keepers used in the 1946/47 season, coming in initially after an injury to Fred Hall. He was the pick of the defence against Ipswich Town in the Norfolk Jubilee Cup and would have won a bottle of champagne had they had Man of the Match awards. Latterly he worked in the dockyard and his son was a Plymouth player who had one league game for Southampton against Plymouth.

DEEHAN, John Matthew

(1981–1985) **1982:** 6/0; 11/3
Striker **Career:** 194-5-70
Debut: 28 Dec 81 (goal) **Final:** 6 May 85

Born: Solihull, nr Birmingham 6 Aug 1957

Career: St Peter's School; Birmingham Schools; Alton British Legion; Arsenal youth trial 1972; Aston Villa 09.08.73 (app), 01.04.75 (pro); West Bromwich Albion 21.09.79; NORWICH CITY

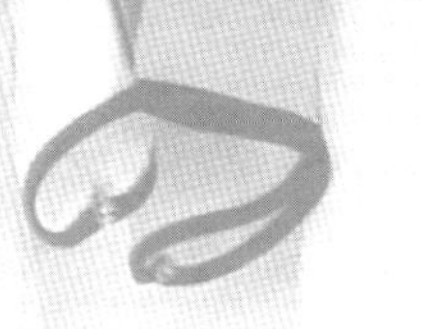

08.01.82; Ipswich Town 28.05.86; Manchester City May 1988 player coach, Nov 1989–15.12.89 caretaker manager; Barnsley player coach, Jan 1990 assistant manager; NORWICH CITY Jun 1992 assistant manager, Jan 1994–09.04.95 manager; Wroxham 12.08.95; Wigan 01.11.85 assistant manager; Sheffield United 03.07.98 First XI coach; Huddersfield Town May 1999 coaching staff; Aston Villa 20.07.2001 First XI coach.

John netted 70 goals for City and was consequently very popular with the players and supporters. Latterly used as a jack-of-all-trades and master-of-none, and with a striking position being denied to him, he made a shock move to Ipswich Town. Despite having an Irish father he chose to play for England and has seven youth and 11 Under-21 caps, and he was an England substitute versus Brazil. Also winner of a League Cup and Milk Cup medal before moving into management.

DEMPSEY, William Watson

(1925) **1925:** 5/10; 11/10
Left Back **Career:** 8-0-0
Debut: 19 Sep 25 **Final:** 31 Oct 25

Born: St German's, Cornwall 10 Sep 1896
Died: Dorset 7 Jan 1967

Career: Cawsand; Portland United; RAF; Wrexham 18.08.23 (amat); Arsenal 25.01.24 (amat); Ipswich Town Aug 1924; NORWICH CITY 12.03.25; London Prison O.S. Mar 1925; Queens Park Rangers Jul 1928; Tunbridge Wells Rangers Jun 1929; Grays Thurrock; Canterbury Waverley Aug 1931; Weymouth Jun 1933–May 1936.

Converted from centre forward, Bill broke his leg in a match at Exeter and gave up league football. An aircraftsman stationed at Felixstowe, he later joined the prison service. Played 113 games for Weymouth including gaining a Western league title. He was a retired electrician.

DENNINGTON, Charles

(1922–1929) **1924:** 6/1; 12/9
Goalkeeper **Career:** 209-0-0
Debut: 28 Aug 22 **Final:** 4 May 29

Born: Beccles, Suffolk 7 Oct 1899
Died: Beccles, Suffolk 25 Jan 1943

Career: Beccles Town; NORWICH CITY 19.08.22 (amat), 26.05.23 (pro); Bradford City 14.05.29; Kirkley (amat) Jun 1930; Beccles Town (amat) 11.11.31; Kirkley (amat) 08.07.33; Gorleston (amat) 29.07.35.

Right: John Deehan

An imposing sight in charge of the rigging as he was a custodian of considerable proportions. Not unnaturally he was adept at dealing with the high ball and became a favourite of the fans. Even missed a penalty, albeit in the benefit match for 'Pompey' Martin. He played in a Suffolk Senior Cup Final when 35 and was considered by eminent judges to be one of City's finest goalkeepers.

DENNIS, George Thomas

(1930) **1930:** 5/9; 11/10
Outside Left **Career:** 1-0-0
Debut/Final: 15 Feb 30

Born: Moira, Leicester 12 Sep 1897
Died: Burton-on-Trent 13 Oct 1969

Career: Stanton; Newhall Swifts Sep 1920; Coalville Swifts; Nottingham Forest 19.02.21; Luton Town 06.05.24; NORWICH CITY 16.05.29; Bristol Rovers 08.05.30–May 1931; Burton Town 1931/2.

He played for Leicester Fosse in 1918. He could play equally well at half back and knew how to control the ball on the move. Scorer of 50 goals elsewhere (including three for Rovers v City) and the papers of the day quoted that he scored with 22 successive penalties. He was a retired labourer (public works).

DENNISON, Robert

(1920–1924) **1920:** 5/8; 10/7
Inside Forward **Career:** 126-0-39
Debut: 11 Sep 20 **Final:** 21 Apr 24 (goal)

Born: Arnold, Nottingham 6 Oct 1900
Died: Norwich 24 Jun 1973

Career: Arnold St Mary's; NORWICH CITY 24.08.20; Brighton & Hove Albion 15.08.24; Manchester City 06.05.25; Clapton Orient 26.08.26; Chesterfield 08.07.29; Yarmouth Town 27.08.33–13.10.34.

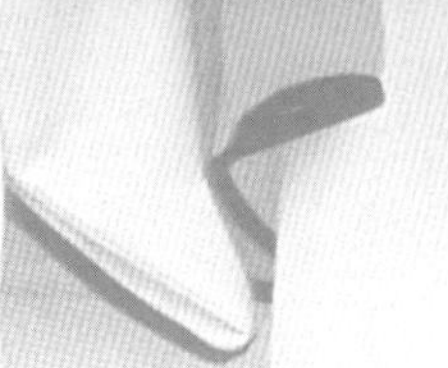

A Norwich City handbook said, 'young and likely to still improve'. How right they were, as he became an incisive scorer, playing in all four divisions. Scorer of City's first Football League hat-trick. He was at Brighton with Sam Jennings and Reg Wilkinson and at Manchester City with Sam Austin. 28 goals in 38 games for Yarmouth showed that he was still a talent.

DENT, Frederick

(1928–1929)	**1928:** 5/10; 11/10
Centre Forward	**Career:** 24-0-12
Debut: 25 Dec 28	**Final:** 4 May 29

Born: Sheffield 24 Jan 1896
Died: Leeds 11 Jan 1983

Career: St Cuthbert's; Vickers; Sheffield Wednesday 01.10.20; Halifax Town 11.06.21; Chesterfield 16.08.23; Mid Rhonnda Jul 1924; Bristol City May 1925; Exeter City 19.07.26; Merthyr Town 16.05.28; NORWICH CITY 24.12.28; Swindon Town 17.05.29; Luton Town 07.07.30; Sheffield Exchange Employment FC 07.12.31; Barnsley Ministry of Labour FC Feb 1935.

A nomad in football circles, he scored goals for eight of his nine league teams. A sprightly, bustling free scoring player and one of several Exeter men who migrated from Devonshire. A double hat-trick for Exeter City Reserves and a fabulous strike record for Norwich City.

DERVELD, Fernando Albert

(2000)	**2000:** 6/3; 12/9
Full Back	**Career:** 23-2-1
Debut: 15 Apr 00	**Final:** 2 Dec 00

Born: Vlissengen 22 Oct 1976

Career: Willem 11 1992 (Holland); FC Haarlem 1998 (Holland); NORWICH CITY Feb 2000, (contract) 26.04.2000; West Bromwich Albion (loan) 06.02.2001; Odense BK (Denmark) (trial) 06.06.2001–09.06.2001; NORWICH CITY released 15.06.2001; Odense BK (Denmark) 26.06.2001.

PLayed 69 games in Dutch football for one goal before scoring against Oxford United reserves for City as a triallist. Naturally left-sided, but he found it hard to adjust to the pace of the English game. An imposing physical presence who impressed Gary Megson enough to take him on loan, albeit briefly, before he moved to Denmark to relaunch his career.

DEVINE, John Anthony

(1983–1985)	**1984:** 5/10; 12/1
Defender	**Career:** 67-2-3
Debut: 27 Aug 83	**Final:** 16 Apr 85

Born: Dublin 11 Nov 1958

Career: St John Bosco Juniors; Arsenal Jan 1974 (amat), 13.11.74 (app), 11.10.76 (pro); NORWICH CITY 13.06.83; Stoke City 25.11.85; Kristiansand (Norway); Idretski Ubben Start (Norway) player coach; Shamrock Rovers (Ireland) Apr 1990; East Bengal Tigers (India); Shelbourne (Ireland) youth coach; Government Scheme of Excellence (Dublin) Nov 1995.

John, while still only 21, had played in European and Domestic Cup Finals as well as representing the Republic of Ireland at Youth, Under-21 and full level. He started as a full back before being converted to the midfield and by the time of his 95th league game had donned every shirt bar that of the goalkeeper. He suffered a broken leg at Stoke City. Married the 1981 Miss Universe runner-up and is a talented musician having recorded (but not released) a record entitled 'The Morning After the Night Before'.

DICKINSON, James

(1926–1927)	**1926:** 5/10; 12/0
Right/Left Half	**Career:** 16-0-0
Debut: 18 Sep 26	**Final:** 7 May 27

Born: Crawshaw Booth 11 Nov 1899
Died: Morecambe & Heysham, 11 Aug 1971

Career: Crawshaw Booth; Great Harwood; Rossendale United; Royal Navy; Plymouth Argyle May 1919 (amat), Nov 1919 (pro) to Nov 1924; Rossendale United Aug 1925; NORWICH CITY 26.08.26; Peterborough cs 1927; Guildford City Jun 1928.

Engaged in anti-sub operations during WW1 and was a regular at Plymouth (137 appearances), earning a benefit. A substantial fee was placed on him but removed during his period outside the football league. His first two games for Norwich produced 15 goals, happily ten of them for City.

DIOP, Pape Seydou

(1999)	**1999:** 5/9; 11/0
Wing Back	**Career:** 3-7-0
Debut: 14 Aug 99 (sub)	**Final:** 28 Dec 99

Born: Dakaar 12 Jan 1979

Career: CS Sedan–Ardennes (France) 1995; Valenciennes (France) (loan); Racing Club de Paris (France) 1998; NORWICH CITY (loan) 05.08.99; Racing Club de Paris (France) 29.12.99

Pape impressed Bruce Rioch in Daryl Sutch's testimonial match and in a reserve friendly

against Ipswich. He produced athleticism and pace at times that stunned the crowd. His Parisian wife found it hard to settle and the feeling is that City should have bought the Sengalese international Pape Malick Diop.

DOBSON, George Walter

(1920–1921)	**1920:** 5/6; 10/12
Outside Left	**Career:** 28-0-1
Debut: 28 Aug 20	**Final:** 7 May 21

Born: Kimberworth 14 Apr 1901
Died: Mexborough 6 Jan 1957

Career: Kimberworth Old Boys; Barnsley Feb 1919; Rawmarsh Athletic Mar 1920; NORWICH CITY 03.05.20; Rotherham County 14.08.21; Worksop Town Mar 1923; South Yorks Chemical Works Nov 1928.

Showed extreme pace in the public practice match prior to selection for City's first ever league game. Short in stature it was said that he tried to beat the defence by superior tactics. He beat several Brentford players to score his one goal for City!

DOCHERTY, Thomas

(1950–1953)	**1952:** 5/7; 10/12
Outside Left	**Career:** 92-0-7
Debut: 19 Aug 50	**Final:** 22 Apr 53

Born: Houghton-le-Spring 15 Apr 1924

Career: Sunderland Reserves (N. Eastern League); Army; Murton Colliery Welfare; Lincoln City 11.07.47; NORWICH CITY 28.06.50; Reading 15.07.53; Newport County 20.05.55; King's Lynn Jul 1958; March Town Jul 1960; Parson Drove Sep 1963; Wisbech Town 1965 reserve manager; March Town Jan 1967 trainer, 30.01.67–30.11.67 manager.

Fast and aggressive left footed player who especially rose to the occasion in cup ties. He crossed a string of tantalising centres and with Gavin on the opposite flank they created havoc. At Lincoln as a part time player whilst working as a plasterer. A darts and cribbage champion outside of football.

DOLDING, Desmond Leonard

(1948–1950)	**1948:** 5/9; 10/0
Right/Left Wing	**Career:** 12-0-1
Debut: 21 Aug 48	**Final:** 11 Apr 50

Born: Nundydroog, India 13 Dec 1922
Died: Wembley 23 Nov 1954

Career: Wealdstone; Second World War guested for Q.P.R.; Chelsea 25.07.45 (amat), 10.01.46 (pro); NORWICH CITY 03.07.48; Dover Town Jul 1951; Margate Aug 1953.

One of a dying breed, as he was a player of two sports being a cricketer with the MCC, Middlesex and a twelfth man for England. With forwards such as Church, Eyre, Gavin and Kinsey on the books his first team opportunities were limited. Appropriately living at Hooking Green when he was tragically killed in a car crash. The 1984 Who's Who of Cricketers *has his birthplace as Oordegem, Belgium but he left his home in India when aged seven.*

Thomas Docherty

DONACHIE, William (Willie)

(1981)	**1981:** 5/9; 11/5
Full Back	**Career:** 14-0-0
Debut: 3 Oct 81	**Final:** 5 Dec 81

Born: Castlemilk, Glasgow 5 Oct 1951

Career: Mitchell Hill School; King's Park School; Glasgow Amateurs; Glasgow United; Glasgow Celtic (groundstaff); Manchester City 22.10.68 (app), 12.12.68 (pro); Portland Timbers (USA) 19.03.80; NORWICH CITY 24.09.81; Portland Timbers (USA) 01.03.82; Burnley 19.11.82 to May 1984; Oldham Athletic 09.07.84 player coach, Jul 1985 assistant manager; Everton 10.11.94 assistant manager, Mar 1997 coach; Sheffield United May 1997 coach; Manchester City 1998 assistant manager, Oct 1998 caretaker manager (for one game); head coach.

A talented full back who excelled with his accurate distribution of the ball and powers of recovery when passed by the wingman. He only briefly displaced Downs despite having earned 35 full Scottish caps while at Maine Road to go with his two medals (win/loss) in the Football League Cup Final. Moved into coaching and assistant managerships suffering relegation from the Premiership with Joe Royle's team last season.

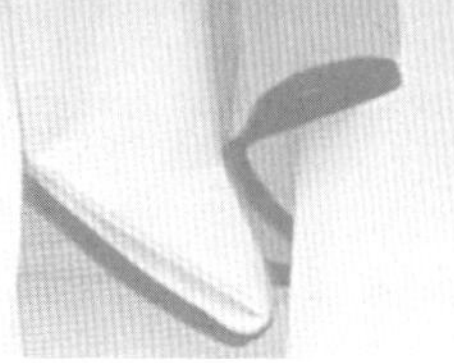

DONOWA, Brian Louie

(1982–1985) **1984:** 5/9; 11/0
Winger **Career:** 70-10-15
Debut: 24 Nov 82 (sub) **Final:** 31 Aug 85 (sub)

Born: Ipswich 24 Sep 1964

Career: Whitton; Ipswich Boys; Suffolk Schools; NORWICH CITY 1980 (youth), 28.09.82 (pro); Stoke City (loan) 23.12.85 for two months; Real Deportivo de la Coruna (Spain) (loan) 01.02.86 prior transfer; Willem 11 Tilburg (Holland) (trial) Jul 1989; Ipswich Town 14.08.89; Bristol Rovers 10.08.90; Birmingham City 30.08.91; Burnley (loan) 16.01.93; Crystal Palace (loan) 24.03.93; Shrewsbury Town (loan) 27.01.94; Birmingham City 24.02.94; Swansea City 28.02.96; Walsall 14.10.96; Peterborough United 29.11.96; Walsall 06.08.97–12.12.97; Ayr United; Cambridge United (trial) Jul 1998; Northampton Town (trial) 08.08.98; King's Lynn; TPS Turku (Finland); Boston United Mar 1999; Tamworth Mar 2000.

Louie bridged the considerable gap between the Youth team and the First Division remarkably well, with fine displays as an out-and-out winger. Had good control and benefitted from playing alongside the experienced Channon. He added a Milk Cup winner's medal to his F.A. Youth Cup medal and by the time he was transferred to Spain had played for England Under-21s, which confirms his rapid progress. After he left Norwich City he has been a nightmare to track down, playing every which place!

DOWNS, Gregory

(1977–1985) **1984:** 5/9; 10/7
Defender **Career:** 199-7-8
Debut: 30 Aug 77 **Final:** 14 May 85

Born: Carlton 13 Dec 1958

Right: Kevin Drinkell

Below: Greg Downs

Career: Weavers School; Raunds Town; NORWICH CITY 26.03.75 (app); 23.12.76 (pro); Connecticut Bi-Centennials (USA) (loan) 16.03.77–30.08.77; Torquay United (loan) 28.11.77–28.12.77; Coventry City 16.07.85; Birmingham City 27.07.90; Hereford United 22.06.92 player coach, 21.05.92 manager, 22.04.93–15.04.94 player-manager; Raunds Town 30.09.94; Redditch Town Oct 1994; Kettering Town 09.11.94; Merthyr Tydfil Dec 1994; Worcester City Mar 1995; Forest Green Rovers May 1995; Bridgnorth Town manager to Feb 1996; Malvern Town Mar 1996; Merthyr Tydfil Nov 1996; Yarmouth Town 30.09.97.

Converted from a striker to full back by the then reserve team coach Machin and became a reliable, attacking, overlapping full back. Greg played his first senior game against the England 1966 World Cup team in Martin Peters' benefit match. Ironically his first ever league game was for Torquay – and he scored. Suffered the disappointment of being dropped a few times yet recovered marvellously to scoop all the Player of the Year awards at the end of the 1981/82 season and was an FA Cup winner in 1987. Since then he has coached, played and managed in various leagues even playing at Carrow Road in 2001 in a losing Norfolk Senior Cup Final.

DRINKELL, Kevin Smith

(1985–1988) **1985:** 5/11; 12/6
Centre Forward **Career:** 150-0-57
Debut: 17 Aug 85 **Final:** 7 May 88

Born: Grimsby 18 Jun 1960

Career: Grimsby Schoolboys Jul 1976 (app), 20.06.78 (pro); NORWICH CITY 14.06.85; Glasgow Rangers 30.06.88; Coventry City 02.10.89; Birmingham City (loan) 19.10.91; Falkirk 24.07.92 player coach; Stirling Albion Mar 1994 coach, manager to 06.05.98; Montrose Oct 1998–11.10.2000 manager.

A Football League debutant at 16 and scorer of over 100 goals for Grimsby. Kevin surprised

the Norwich public with his aerial mastery and opportunistic scoring. He showed extreme bravery in reaching some of the crosses, deservedly winning the Barry Butler Memorial Trophy after a fine first season in the Canary colours. He moved into management in Scotland but is remembered fondly at Carrow Road as a goalscorer in the old fashioned mould.

DRIVER, Allenby

(1948–1949) **1955:** 5/11; 12/0
Inside Right/ Centre Forward **Career:** 49-0-19
Debut: 3 Jan 48 (goal) **Final:** 12 Nov 49

Born: Blackwell 29 Sep 1918
Died: Sheffield 31 Mar 1997

Career: Notts Boys; Mansfield Boys; Mansfield Shoe Company; Sheffield Wednesday 07.03.36 (amat), 02.04.36 (pro); Second World War guested for Millwall, Crystal Palace; Fulham & Watford; Luton Town 05.10.46; NORWICH CITY 05.01.48; Ipswich Town 16.01.50; Walsall 04.07.52; Frickley Athletic Aug 1954–1958.

Netted his first ever senior goal New Year's Day 1938. Served six years in the Royal Artillery and was a ball playing forward who improved the City attack when signed. Did especially well at Portman Road during his stay there.

DRURY, Adam James

(2001– **2001:** 5/10; 11/8
Full Back **Career:** 11-0-0
Debut: 31 Mar 01

Born: Cambridge 29 Aug 1978

Career: Cottenham Village College; Cottenham Hotspur; Girton Colts; NORWICH CITY 1989 (youth); East Anglia Boys; Cambridgeshire County; Peterborough United 1993 (youth), 01.08.95 (pro); NORWICH CITY 21.03.2001.

A homecoming for Adam in 2001 after being at Norwich from the age of ten. Remembers training at Trowse and he has since gained a good grounding at London Road after watching the likes of Mark Bowen at Norwich. He has already won approval for his performances with his former manager Barry Fry stating that Adam is one of the best defenders outside of the Premiership.

DUFFUS, John Murison Jack)

(1924–1927) **1925:** 5/8; 11/6
Right/Left half **Career:** 80-0-4
Debut: 30 Aug 24 **Final:** 7 May 27

Born: Aberdeen 10 May 1901
Died: Stockport 18 Sep 1975

Career: Aberdeen Richmond; Dumbarton 21.06.19; Boness (loan) Nov 1919; Dundee 1919; Scunthorpe United; Llanelly Jun 1921; Clapton Orient 18.10.22; Tottenham Hotspur 09.05.23; NORWICH CITY 27.05.24; Stockport County 08.07.27; Hyde United Aug 1928; Hurst Aug 1929.

A varied career playing in Scottish League, Midland League and the Welsh League, as well as the London Combination and the Football League. A thorough trier who kicked and headed most judiciously. Jack ran a nursery business in Stockport retiring in 1969 and was a churchwarden in Bramhall. His brother Bob also played for Dundee.

DUFFY, John

(1949–1954) **1952:** 5/9; 11/9
Right Back **Career:** 87-0-0
Debut: 31 Dec 49 **Final:** 1 May 54

Born: Plantation, Glasgow 24 Apr 1922
Died: Strathclyde 10 Apr 1996

Career: Stanley Celtic Juvenile School; Rutherglen Glencairn; Clyde 19.04.45; NORWICH CITY 21.03.49–30.06.54; Yarmouth Town 15.07.54–03.05.58.

Won a Glasgow Cup medal and toured South Africa with Clyde. Nicknamed 'Poker Face', as no hint of emotion showed on his countenance during a match. Unflurried and with sound positional sense, he had a continuous run as the City full back. He worked in shipyards before turning to gas pipe welding.

DUKES, Harry Parkinson

(1934–1946) **1936:** 5/10; 11/8
Goalkeeper **Career:** 124-0-0
Debut: 15 Sep 34 **Final:** 28 Dec 46

Born: Portsmouth 31 Mar 1912
Died: Cambridge 13 Aug 1988

Career: Sleaford 1930; Martlesham 1931; Melton 1932; Orwell Works 1933; Ipswich Town Jan 1934 (amat); NORWICH CITY 21.08.34; Bedford Town; Second World War guested for Brentford & Fulham; NORWICH CITY Aug 1945; Bedford Town; Guildford City Jul 1947; Newmarket Town player-manager 1949–Aug 1950.

An alert and mobile keeper who played Rugby at school and only took up soccer when he moved to Suffolk. Harry had 17 games for Ipswich, helping them to win the Southern

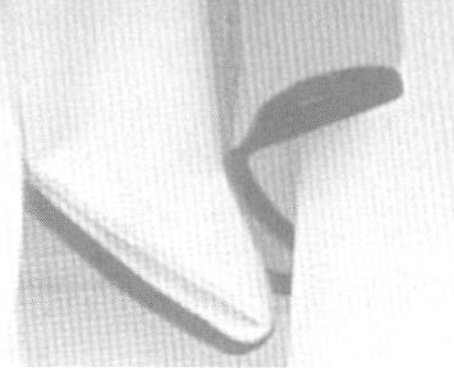

Amateur League. Kept in the last league match before the Second World War; the last game at the Nest and the first at Carrow Road. Another of the publicans. A cartoon of the day depicted Harry as 'Duke' and despite early protestations the name stuck.

DUNCAN, John Grant

(1920) **1920:** 5/8; 10/8
Outside Right **Career:** 4-0-0
Debut: 16 Sep 20 **Final:** 2 Oct 20

Born: Aberdeen 3 Feb 1898
Died: Aberdeen 19 Sep 1963

Career: Aberdeen Juniors; NORWICH CITY 08.09.20–06.11.20

The younger brother of Bill, his short stay also encompassed six reserve games for two goals. His four games were full of misfortune for City. His father was an Aberdeen cattle drover.

DUNCAN, William Wilson

(1920) **1920:** 5/10; 12/0
Centre Half **Career:** 2-0-0
Debut: 16 Sep 20 **Final:** 18 Sep 20

Born: Aberdeen 14 Jul 1895

Career: Aberdeen Juniors; NORWICH CITY 06.09.20; Montrose 18.05.21; Barrow 20.06.24; Peterhead 04.10.24.

Another migrator to England who supplemented his first team career by making 34 reserve appearances for three goals. Norwich City fixed a fee of £100 for his transfer but Montrose picked him up on a free. The DHSS dead letter office had an August 1988 tracing but no address. Can anyone help please to find Bill's whereabouts?

DUTHIE, John Flett

(1925–1927) **1925:** 5/8; 11/0
Inside Left **Career:** 27-0-4
Debut: 17 Jan 25 **Final:** 25 Apr 27

Born: Fraserburgh 7 Jan 1903
Died: Fraserburgh 30 Sep 1969

Career: Roselee FC; Fraserburgh Town; Hartlepools United 1922/23; Clydebank; Hartlepools United 05.09.23; NORWICH CITY 25.08.24; Fraserburgh Town; Queens Park Rangers 12.09.27; York City 09.08.28; Crystal Palace 03.05.29; York City 02.10.30; Crewe Alexandra 16.07.31; Aberdeen 1932; Cardiff City 09.05.33; Caerau Aug 1934; Peterborough & Fletton United May 1935.

A contemporary summed him up as 'a clever youngster who preferred ground passing to the airborne variety'. Rather inclined however to play the game too close. Had played in nearly every part of the country by the time he joined Cardiff. At Norwich he was the perpetual understudy to Jimmy Banks.

DUTTON, Leonard Lewis

(1946–1953) **1948:** 5/7; 10/7
Inside Forward/
Wing Half **Career:** 152-0-14
Debut: 12 Sep 46 **Final:** 17 Jan 53

Born: Cardiff 17 Jan 1922
Died: Norwich 19 Oct 1998

Career: Moorland Road School; Cardiff Corries; Welsh Schoolboys; Arsenal 17.06.38 (groundstaff), 1941 (pro); Army; NORWICH CITY 26.08.46; Wisbech Town 10.07.53.

Groomed by Arsenal for possible stardom but he lost good years to the war. The Pink 'Un *said of Len, 'A brainy player who could on his day rise to the heights'. A judicious feeder of the forwards and the maker of the famous ten-second goal for Johnson. He made 94 reserve appearances, scoring a dozen goals.*

EADIE, Darren Michael

(1993–1999) **1993:** 5/7; 9/12
Outside Left **Career:** 186-18-38
Debut: 15 Sep 93 (sub) **Final:** 4 Dec 99

Born: Chippenham 10 Jun 1975

Career: Corsham Comprehensive School; Corsham Boys Under-11–15; Biddleston Under-16; Mid Wilts District; Wiltshire County Under-13–15; England Under-15 (trial); NORWICH CITY Mar 1990 (assoc), Jul 1991 (trainee), 01.02.93 (pro); Leicester City 10.12.99.

Darren had special coaching at Southampton's Centre of Excellence from the age of eleven

Darren Eadie

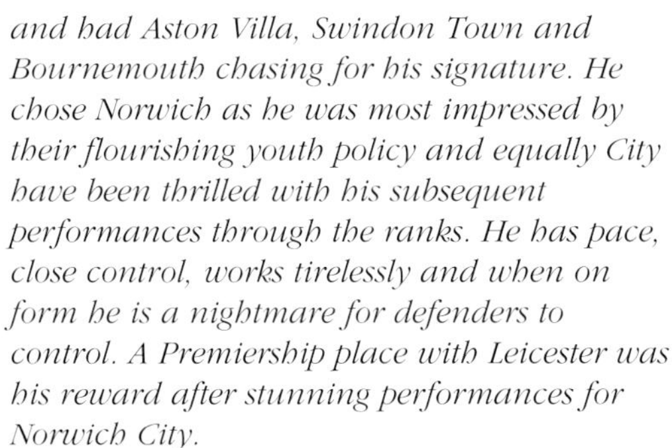

and had Aston Villa, Swindon Town and Bournemouth chasing for his signature. He chose Norwich as he was most impressed by their flourishing youth policy and equally City have been thrilled with his subsequent performances through the ranks. He has pace, close control, works tirelessly and when on form he is a nightmare for defenders to control. A Premiership place with Leicester was his reward after stunning performances for Norwich City.

EARL, Sidney Ernest

(1924–1926) **1925:** 5/8; 12/0
Left Half **Career:** 30-0-1
Debut: 9 Feb 24 (goal) **Final:** 13 Feb 26

Born: Norwich 25 Apr 1902
Died: Norwich 8 Nov 1992

Career: Norwich St Giles YMBC; Lamberts FC; NORWICH CITY 16.03.23 (amat), 15.10.23 (pro); Norfolk County 1923–27; City Wanderers; Norwich CEYMS retiring 1928.

Sid did well for the reserves and when promoted he was enthusiastic and a real sportsman. This was in the days when the tackling was robust to say the least. Sid's trade was as a cabinet maker, and he turned his hand to chimney sweeping in later years. He also boxed for the Lads' Club and was a good gymnast. He fondly recalled that Norwich paid him a maximum wage of £6 and with £2 paid for a win and £1 for a draw he earned £28 in bonuses.

EASTON, Clint Jude

(2001– **2001:** 5/11; 10/8
Midfield **Career:** 0-1-0
Debut: 11 AUG 01

Born: Barking 1 Oct 1977

Career: St Joseph's Primary School; All Saints Secondary School; Redbridge United; Barking & Dagenham District; Watford (assoc) 15.05.92, (trainee) 21.05.94, (pro) 05.07.96; Norwich City 15.06.2001.

Used at Watford as a left-side wide man showing enthusiasm and considerable strength allied to skill. 'Clint makes City's day' and 'Easton promise' were predictable local sportspages headlines upon his joining Norwich. A fistful of dollars secured his services and he quickly won over the City fans with impressive pre-season displays.

EDWARDS, Donald

(1947) **1948:** 5/9; 10/4
Goalkeeper **Career:** 2-0-0
Debut: 17 Sep 47 **Final:** 20 Sep 47

Born: Wrexham 2 Aug 1930
Died: Yarmouth 24 Mar 1995

Career: Brymbo Steelworks; Denbighshire County; Wrexham Victoria; Wrexham youth & reserves; NORWICH CITY 22.09.47–13.07.53; Gorleston Jul 1954; Holmes Athletic Mar 1965; Yarmouth Town Oct 1965; Red Star; Newtown Wanderers.

Don was at the time our youngest debutant being signed during the Spiers reign after he had played in a Welsh Junior Cup Final against City's South Wales nursery side. A cool and competent custodian with an unfortunate second appearance to his debit. His lengthy stay here was interspersed with 49 reserve games. Latterly a lorry driver.

EDWARDS, George Robert

(1936–1938) **1936:** 5/10; 11/6
Outside Right **Career:** 9-0-1
Debut: 11 Apr 36 **Final:** 7 May 38

Born: Great Yarmouth 1 Apr 1918
Died: Hockley Heath 21 Jan 1993

Career: Priory School; Northgate School; Yarmouth Town Boys 1932; Norfolk Boys; Yarmouth Caledonians; Norfolk County; NORWICH CITY 4.03.35 (amat), 01.04.36 (pro); Second World War guested for Aston Villa, Birmingham City, Nottingham Forest, Notts County, Walsall & Wrexham; Aston Villa 07.06.38–28.07.51; Bilston United 17.08.51; Yarmouth Town 20.08.55–29.09.55

Signed as an amateur when he was still only 16 just as Kirchen was moving to Highbury. He made just a few appearances for City before hostilities broke out. Assisted a number of Midland clubs during the War and he was a fine servant at Villa Park scoring an incredible 147 goals in total. A remarkable recovery since George was struck by tuberculosis and was in a sanatorium for a long time.

EDWARDS, James

(1937) **1937:** 5/9; 11/8
Left Half **Career:** 2-0-0
Debut: 6 Nov 37 **Final:** 13 Nov 37

Born: Tipton, West Bromwich 11 Dec 1905
Died: Tipton 4 April 1982

Career: Horseley Bridge Schools; Tipton Schools; Tipton Park; Newport Foundry;

Stourbridge; Great Bridge Celtic; West Bromwich Albion 12.05.26 (amat), 1927 (pro); NORWICH CITY 10.06.37 (pro); Bilston; Kingswinford; Dudley Town retiring 1944.

Nicknamed 'Iron' and hence as hard as nails, Jim had an illustrious career at West Bromwich playing over 200 First XI games including two FA Cup Final appearances. He kicked and tackled with equal power and judgement. His two City games were when Harry Proctor was unavailable.

EDWARDS, Robert Henry (Bob)

(1959) **1959:** 5/11; 11/7
Inside Left **Career:** 1-0-0
Debut/Final: 12 Dec 59

Born: Guildford, Surrey 22 May 1931

Career: Northmead School; Woking; Chelsea 19.11.51; Swindon Town 22.07.55; NORWICH CITY 14.12.59; Northampton Town 16.03.61; King's Lynn 30.06.62; Boston Town Oct 1965–1967.

Bob was an elegant inside forward who signed for Chelsea on his demobilization from the RAF and made his Football League debut on Boxing Day 1952 against Stoke City. Principally a reserve player at Chelsea and Norwich (36 apps – 10 goals) Bob had a fine goalscoring record at Swindon Town. His elder brother Leslie played for Bristol Rovers.

EKOKU, Efangwu Goziem

(1993–1994) **1994:** 6/1; 12/0
Centre Forward **Career:** 33-12-17
Debut: 5 Apr 93 (sub) **Final:** 1 Oct 94

Born: Cheetham Hill 8 Jun 1967

Efan Ekoku

Career: Sudley Junior School; Liverpool College; Merton; Sutton United Dec 1988; Charlton Athletic (trial); Bournemouth 11.05.90; NORWICH CITY 26.03.93; Wimbledon 14.10.94; Grasshoppers (Zurich) 25.08.99; Sheffield Wednesday (loan) 20.10.2000–May 2001, (signed) 31.07.2001.

Efan's lifelong cognomen of 'Gin' and present day admission of answering to 'The Chief' is highly acceptable as even the family surname has been truncated. He and his brothers have made their parents proud with their scholastic and sporting achievements. Impressive pace and skill led to big money moves and Nigerian international caps.

ELLIOTT, Shaun

(1986–1988) **1986:** 6/0; 11/6
Defender **Career:** 36-3-2
Debut: 23 Aug 86 **Final:** 20 Feb 88

Born: Haltwhistle 26 Jan 1957

Career: Haydon Bridge; Sunderland Jan 1974 (app), 10.01.75 (pro); Seattle Sounders (USA) May 1981–Aug 1981; NORWICH CITY 22.08.86; Blackpool 01.08.88; Colchester United Mar 1991; Gateshead Aug 1992; Bishop Auckland Aug 1993; Whitley Bay Mar 1995; Durham City.

Shaun is Sunderland's 11th highest league appearance maker and enjoyed a fine ten year career on Wearside. Alert and mobile he showed acute positional sense and won England 'B' recognition. He missed the League Cup final against Norwich through suspension. Extended his career by playing for top-quality northern non-league sides.

EMBLEN, Neil Robert

(2001– **2001:** 6/1; 13/11
Defender **Career:** 1-0-0
Debut: 11 Aug 01

Born: Bromley 19 Jun 1971

Career: Sussex Road County Primary School; Hayesbrook Secondary School; West Kent; North Tonbridge Boys Under-11-16; Tonbridge Rangers; Watford (trial) 1987; Sittingbourne Jul 1991; Millwall 08.11.93; Wolverhampton Wanderers 14.07.94; Crystal Palace 21.08.97; Wolverhampton Wanderers 26.03.98; NORWICH CITY 11.07.2001

A true utility player with both defensive and attacking qualities, he occupied every outfield role during his stay at Wolves. First linked to City in 1993, but with City riding high in the Premiership it was felt that Sittingbourne's boss John Ryan was asking for too much money. Has already endeared himself to the fans with superb pre-season displays and has been rewarded with the club captaincy for season 2001/2.

ENGLEFIELD, Grahame William Elwyn

(1956–1957) **1956:** 6/0; 12/2
Left Half **Career:** 22-0-0
Debut: 28 Apr 56 **Final:** 30 Mar 57

Born: Eltham, Greenwich 21 Sep 1931

Career: Charlton Athletic 18.01.49; NORWICH CITY 03.04.54; Dartford Jul 1957; Bexleyheath & Welling Apr 1961.

Grahame helped to end City's disastrous run of 26 league games without a win. He was one of four left halves (number six) to be used in a re-election season. Another regular reserve player, making 81 such appearances.

EPHGRAVE, George Arthur

(1949–1951) **1949:** 6/4; 13/0
Goalkeeper **Career:** 5-0-0
Debut: 3 Sep 49 **Final:** 17 Mar 51

Born: Reading 29 Apr 1918

Career: Guernsey Rangers; Tottenham Hotspur 16.10.35 (amat); Northfleet (loan); Aston Villa 08.10.36; Swindon Town 17.03.39; Southampton (trial) Apr 1946, 03.09.46 (pro); NORWICH CITY 03.07.48; Watford 14.08.51; Deal Town 01.08.52; March Town Aug 1953–05.06.54.

Originally spotted while playing for Guernsey against Jersey. George was captured on Crete in 1941 and was taken to Odessa. He was one of the tallest goalkeepers in the League and it was reckoned that on a sunny day the shadow from his cap covered half the field. His actual last appearance for Norwich was in the abandoned Newport match.

EVANS, David Douglas

(1977–1979) **1975:** 5/10; 11/10
Midfield **Career:** 15-4-1
Debut: 12 Feb 77 **Final:** 3 Nov 79

Born: Ystradgynlais, West Glamorgan 27 Sep 1956

Career: Maesydderwen Comprehensive School; NORWICH CITY 1972 (app), 06.08.74 (pro); Connecticut Bi-Centennials (USA) 11.05.77–30.08.77; Cambridge United 14.03.80; Tuen Wan (Hong Kong) for 18 months; Yarmouth Town 24.08.82; Lowestoft Town 20.08.83; Watton 1984; Bury Town 1986; Norwich United Jan 1988; Lakeford Rangers youth coach; Cambridge United coaching staff; Norwich City Academy Under-16 coach.

Doug had a varied career, with spells also in the USA and Hong Kong. He wore six different numbered shirts during his First XI appearances, being sent off in his penultimate game. Now in demand in local soccer circles and expressing himself in youth football. He has broadened his horizon through the establishment of his advanced soccer coaching school.

Les Eyre

EYRE, Ernest Leslie (Les)

(1946–1951) **1948:** 5/7; 10/2
Inside/Outside Left **Career:** 201-0-69
Debut: 26 Sep 46 **Final:** 15 Sep 51

Born: Ilkeston, Derby 7 Jan 1922
Died: Norwich 19 Nov 1991

Career: Bilsthorpe Colliery 1937; Cardiff City (amat); RAF; NORWICH CITY 09.07.47; Bournemouth 09.11.51; Chelmsford 03.07.53; Bilsthorpe Colliery 1953–1958.

Manager Spiers, with a pipeline to Cardiff, captured Les after keeping track of his dazzling displays for the RAF overseas. His great turn of speed and elusive swerve allied to a powerful shot has him now standing high in the club's annals of highest goalscorers. Unassuming and modest by temperament, Les qualified his nap hand against Brighton by saying, 'It was just my day, another 15 minutes and I would most likely have scored another three'. We tend to believe him. He worked at Colman's until his retirement.

FAIRCLOUGH, David

(1985) **1985:** 5/9; 11/0
Striker **Career:** 1-1-0
Debut: 9 Mar 85 **Final:** 20 Apr 85

Born: Liverpool 5 Jan 1957

Career: Liverpool 05.07.73 (app), 09.01.74 (pro); Toronto Blizzard (Canada) Apr 1982–Aug 1982; Lucerne FC (Switzerland) 04.07.83; Manchester City 12.02.85; NORWICH CITY 22.03.85; Oldham Athletic 15.08.85; Rochdale 01.07.86; KSK Beveren (Belgium) 18.08.86; Tranmere Rovers 21.06.89; Wigan Borough 21.09.90; Knowsley United to 1993.

Hates the title 'Supersub', but it is an apt description as he has scored in five different competitions coming off the bench. Including

reserve goals he netted over 100 times for the Reds and played in European and Domestic Cup Finals. Ironically he scored his first ever league goal and his only hat-trick against Norwich City. He played in three countries abroad and now works in local radio and for the PFA.

FARRINGTON, Mark Anthony

(1984–1985) **1984:** 5/10; 11/10
Centre Forward **Career:** 15-3-2
Debut: 12 May 84 **Final:** 2 Feb 85

Born: Garston, Liverpool 15 Jun 1965

Career: Hillfoot Hey School; Allerton Youth; Shrewsbury Town Schoolboy forms; Everton Sep 1982 (youth); NORWICH CITY 19.05.83 (pro); Cambridge United (loan) 28.03.85 to 11.05.85; Cardiff City 19.07.85; Portsmouth (trial) Aug 1988; Willem 11 Tilburg (Holland); Racing Genk (Belgium); Fortuna Sittard (Holland); Hertha BSC Berlin (Germany); Feyenoord (Holland) Jan 1991; Brighton & Hove Albion 25.03.91; Hereford United (loan) 07.10.94; Runcorn 11.11.95; Telford United Feb 1996.

Mark came to Norwich City's attention in the worst possible way by scoring four goals in the three games against City in the FA Youth Cup Final battle of 1983. In all he scored 11 goals during Everton's run to the Final and when released by Howard Kendall he was snapped up by Norwich. His energetic, bustling promise was somewhat spoiled by impetuosity. Pursued a career abroad before returning to England.

Left: John Fashanu
Right: Justin Fashanu

FASHANU, John

(1981–1982) **1982:** 6/1; 11/12
Striker **Career:** 6-1-1
Debut: 17 Oct 81 (sub) **Final:** 25 Sep 82

Born: Kensington 18 Sep 1963

Career: Attleborough High School; Cambridge United Feb 1979 (assoc); NORWICH CITY 23.10.79; Crystal Palace (loan) 14.08.83; Lincoln City (loan) 23.09.83, (signing) 08.11.83; Millwall 30.11.84; Wimbledon 27.03.86; Aston Villa 04.08.94–02.08.95.

One of five children, after a low-profile beginning he became a million-pound player and an England international. His all-action style provoked controversy at times and he enjoyed great success at Wimbledon. Charming and articulate off the field, he has a number of business interests, not least of which was his appointment as Nigeria's sports ambassador.

FASHANU, Justinus Soni

(1979–1981) **1979:** 6/1; 12/7
Centre Forward **Career:** 97-6-40
Debut: 13 Jan 79 **Final:** 2 May 81 (goal)

Born: Hackney 19 Feb 1961
Died: Shoreditch, London 2 May 1998

Career: Shropham; Attleborough High School; Peterborough United; NORWICH CITY 15.09.77 (app), 27.12.78 (pro); Adelaide City (Australia) summer 1980; Nottingham Forest 02.08.81; Southampton (loan) 26.08.82–Oct 1982; Notts County 13.12.82; Brighton & Hove Albion 14.06.85; Los Angeles Heat (USA) player-manager; Edmonton Brickmen (Canada) Jul 1988; Manchester City (trial) 10.10.89; West Ham United (trial) 20.11.89; Ipswich Town (trial) 07.02.90; Leyton Orient (trial) Feb 1990; Southall 09.03.91 player coach; Newcastle United (trial) 23.07.91; Leatherhead 11.11.91; Torquay United 05.12.91 player-manager, 02.06.92 assistant manager; Airdrieonians 05.02.93; Trelleborg (Sweden); Heart of Midlothian 09.07.93; Toronto Italia (Canada) to Jul 1994; Miramar Rangers (New Zealand) 31.10.96; Atlanta Ruckus (USA) 1997; Maryland Mania (USA) 1998 coach.

Justin lost the British Schoolboy Heavyweight Boxing Final in Blackpool in March 1977 when just 16 – which succinctly conveys the size, strength and power at his command.
He performed wonders at Norwich and among the many goals for the England Under-21 striker was the BBC's 1980 Goal of the Season against Liverpool. Knee surgery in the USA was expensive and sadly despite many attempts to resurrect his career both here and abroad it was not to be.

FEATHERBY, Walter Leonard

(1924–1926) **1924:** 5/8; 10/10
Outside Right **Career:** 26-0-3
Debut: 13 Sep 24 **Final:** 1 May 26

Born: King's Lynn 28 Jul 1905
Died: King's Lynn 22 Feb 1972

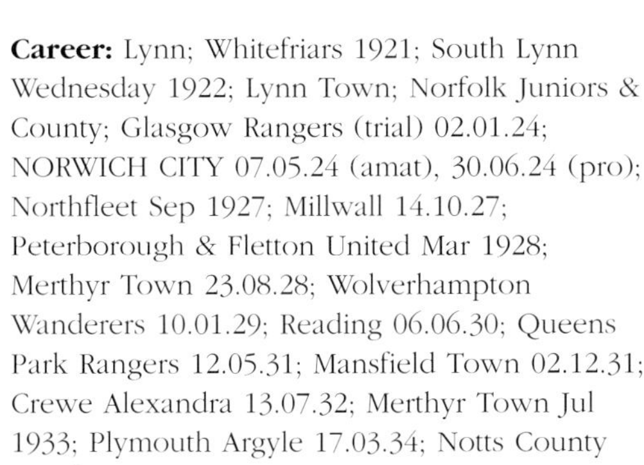

Career: Lynn; Whitefriars 1921; South Lynn Wednesday 1922; Lynn Town; Norfolk Juniors & County; Glasgow Rangers (trial) 02.01.24; NORWICH CITY 07.05.24 (amat), 30.06.24 (pro); Northfleet Sep 1927; Millwall 14.10.27; Peterborough & Fletton United Mar 1928; Merthyr Town 23.08.28; Wolverhampton Wanderers 10.01.29; Reading 06.06.30; Queens Park Rangers 12.05.31; Mansfield Town 02.12.31; Crewe Alexandra 13.07.32; Merthyr Town Jul 1933; Plymouth Argyle 17.03.34; Notts County 23.06.35; King's Lynn 1937–1939.

Len was a prominent local amateur who became a globetrotter. He turned down offers of coaching in the North and in Switzerland and after the War returned to Norfolk seeking employment as a groundsman. In September 1946 it was mooted that he might lend a hand to King's Lynn – sadly not to be, as he had given away his boots. An incredible number of clubs for a most likeable fellow.

FENN, Neale Michael Charles

(1998) **1998:** 5/10; 12/6
Forward **Career:** 6-1-1
Debut: 28 Mar 98 (sub) **Final:** 3 May 98

Born: Edmonton 18 Jan 1977

Career: Wilbury Way Junior School; Aylward School; Enfield District & Middlesex County; Tottenham Hotspur 06.07.93 (trainee), 01.07.95 (pro); Leyton Orient (loan) 30.01.98; NORWICH CITY (loan) 26.03.98; Swindon Town (loan) 13.11.98; Lincoln City (loan) 31.12.98; Peterborough United 03.05.2001, (signed) 06.07.2001.

Republic of Ireland caps at schoolboy, youth and Under-21 level as a result of his mother being from Cork. Hie 69 goals in 129 games for Spurs at all levels indicated his potential potency. Signed by Norwich City just seven minutes before the transfer deadline before moving on to play in the lower leagues.

FERRARI, Frederick Joseph

(1927–1928) **1927:** 5/8; 12/0
Centre Half/Left Back **Career:** 4-0-0
Debut: 17 Dec 27 **Final:** 7 Jan 28

Born: Stratford 22 May 1901
Died: Stratford 6 Aug 1976

Career: Barking Town; Leyton; Northampton Town 26.10.25; Sheffield Wednesday 23.06.26; Flint Town United (trial) Aug 1926; NORWICH CITY 22.12.27; Barrow 23.08.28; Nelson 06.06.29; Chesterfield (trial) 08.02.30; Burton Town Mar 1930; Bedouins Aug 1930; Mansfield Town Nov 1930; Queens Park Rangers Jan 1931; Hillsborough Old Boys Sep 1933; Darwin's Sports Oct 1936.

Our favourite name of all the Canaries. Fred was a timely replacement for the injured Chappell and Pembleton. With an Italian father Fred had a volatile nature at times which would explain some of the club's secretaries views on him in forms sent to the League. Scored hat-tricks for Barrow when converted to the forward line. A retired steelworks millhand was his last given occupation.

FIELD, Richard

(1923–1924) **1924:** 5/10; 12/7
Half Back **Career:** 29-0-0
Debut: 25 Aug 23 **Final:** 28 Apr 24

Born: Sunderland 2 Aug 1891
Died: Sunderland 15 Jul 1963

Career: Willington FC; Lambton Stars; Sunderland (Victory league); Barry FC cs 1914; Aberdare Athletic 08.12.22; NORWICH CITY 02.06.23; Grimsby Town 16.05.24; Accrington Stanley 20.06.25; Boston Town Jul 1927; West Stanley Aug 1928.

He rejoiced in the name 'Rusty' and he was a tenacious defender who often proved difficult to circumvent. His foraging style often drew appreciative applause from the spectators. Always full of humour and good spirits, and some would say that you had to be if you played for Norwich City in the 1920s.

FLACK, William Leonard Wallace

(1935–1947) **1936:** 5/8; 11/6
Wing Half/Full Back **Career:** 54-0-0
Debut: 30 Mar 35 **Final:** 22 Feb 47

Born: Cambridge 1 June 1916
Died: Bury St Edmunds 29 Mar 1995

Career: Higher Grade Central School; Cambridge Town; West Ham United 04.09.30 (amat); Arsenal 01.07.31 (amat); NORWICH CITY 08.05.33 (amat), 07.07.33 (pro); Southport Dec 1941 to 1944; Bury Town player/coach for 8 years and later vice president, Jul 1958 committee member.

The Pink 'Un *stated, 'He gives promise of developing into an exponent of the first rank as he has the touch of the artist'. As an amateur he captained the Midlands v South and South v North as well as playing for England against Scotland. He scored a hat-trick from half-back for Southport versus Rochdale on 18 Sep 1943. The War took vital years from his career and he latterly had a Local Authority job.*

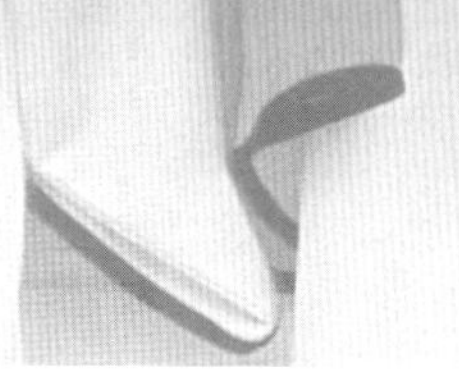

FLECK, Robert William

(1987–1992) & (1995–1998) **1988:** 5/7; 10/8
Striker **Career:** 271-28-84
Debut: 18 Dec 87 **Final:** 14 Mar 98

Born: Possil, Glasgow 11 Aug 1965

Career: Possil YM; Glasgow Rangers 22.07.83; Partick Thistle (loan) 05.11.83; NORWICH CITY 16.12.87; Chelsea 12.08.92; Bolton Wanderers (loan) 17.12.93; Bristol City (loan) 12.01.95; NORWICH CITY (loan) 29.08.95, (signed) 29.09.95; Reading 26.03.98; Gorleston 27.02.99 coaching, manager.

A man of his own vintage, being one of five children born and bred in the no-holds-barred Possilpark district. A medalled career at Ibrox saw him net 45 goals in 125 games in total with no less than five hat-tricks in one season. He joined Norwich for a club record fee of £580,000 and he happily ran himself ragged in the Canary cause with his name becoming synonymous with strength and power. He became the best known Canary outside Norwich. Has since led Gorleston to a Norfolk Senior Cup Final win in 2001 as well as a league runners-up position.

Left: Robert Fleck
Right: Craig Fleming

FLEETING, James

(1977–1978) **1977:** 6/1; 11/5
Half Back **Career:** 1-1-0
Debut: 12 Mar 77 (sub) **Final:** 16 Jan 78

Born: Glasgow 8 Apr 1955

Career: Knockentiber Amateurs; Kilbirnie Ladeside; NORWICH CITY (trial) 30.11.74–03.12.74, (signed) 24.04.75; Tampa Bay Rowdies (USA) (temp) 06.04.78–28.08.78; Ayr United 16.02.79; Irvine Meadow; Clyde 10.08.83; Morton 23.07.84; Airdrieonians coach, 1986 assistant manager; Stirling Albion Dec 1988–06.04.92 manager.

A rangy Caledonian defender who made his Canary debut in the Reserves on his 20th birthday. His two games for the firsts were both losses and his parting with the club came when he walked out in November 1978. He seemed happier back in his native land, moving eventually into management.

FLEMING, Craig

(1997– **1997:** 6/0; 11/7
Defender **Career:** 155-6-7
Debut: 9 Aug 97

Born: Calder 6 Oct 1971

Career: Ryburn Valley High School; Calderdale; West Yorkshire; Yorkshire Boys; Halifax Town 30.2.86 (assoc), 12.07.88 (trainee), 21.03.90 (pro); Oldham Athletic 15.08.91; NORWICH CITY 30.06.97.

A string of resolute displays at the heart of the Canaries rearguard has seen Craig become a crowd favourite. A strong tackler, he formed a bedrock with Matt Jackson in defence. He scored the first Carrow Road goal in the new millenium and he came close to winning the coveted Player of the Year award in 2000/1.

FOAN, Albert Thomas

(1947–1950) **1948:** 5/8; 10/1
Inside Right/Left **Career:** 18-0-4
Debut: 30 Aug 47 (goal) **Final:** 15 Apr 50

Born: Rotherhithe 30 Oct 1923

Career: Albion Street School; B.A.O.R; NORWICH CITY 19.07.46 (amat), 09.04.47 (pro); West Ham United 28.06.50; Margate 04.02.57; Lowestoft Town Jul 1962; Yarmouth Town 04.02.67–29.04.67; NORWICH CITY 'A' team trainer, 1969 coach; Norwich City All Stars XI.

Albert joined City when he had finished his Army career and he immediately showed that he possessed neat ball skills which, when added to his deceptive body swerve, made him a tricky opponent to contain. He played in the same West Ham teams as Ken Brown, John Bond and Fred Kearns.

FOGGO, Kenneth Taylor

(1967–1972) **1970:** 5/6; 10/8
Winger **Career:** 197-4-57
Debut: 7 Oct 67 **Final:** 30 Dec 72 (sub)

Born: Perth 7 Nov 1943

Career: Peebles High School; Peebleshire & Scotland Schools; Peebles YMCA; St Johnstone

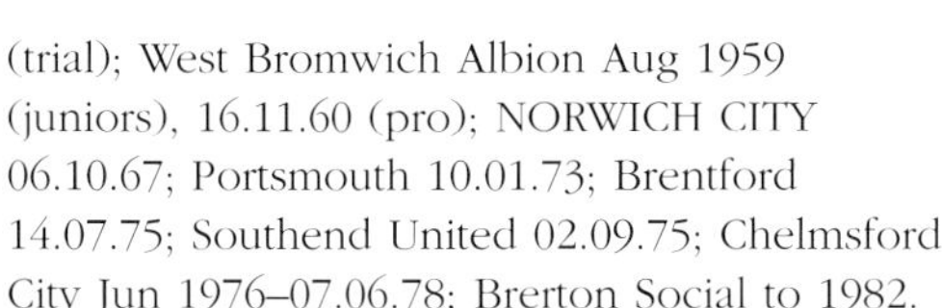

(trial); West Bromwich Albion Aug 1959 (juniors), 16.11.60 (pro); NORWICH CITY 06.10.67; Portsmouth 10.01.73; Brentford 14.07.75; Southend United 02.09.75; Chelmsford City Jun 1976–07.06.78; Brerton Social to 1982.

Ken was strong in all the facets of his craft being pacy, skilful and comfortable on both flanks. He was a fine servant and the usual City chant was, ' City one up through Foggo'. Two Player of the Year awards attested to his well-deserved popularity. Latterly he runs a dry cleaning and launderer's business in East London.

Left: Kenneth Foggo
Right: Reg Foulkes

FORBES, Adrian Emmanuel

(1996–2001) **1996:** 5/8; 11/4
Winger **Career:** 69-52-8
Debut: 31 Aug 96 (sub) **Final:** 16 Apr 01 (sub)

Born: Greenford, London 23 Jan 1979

Career: Brentside High School; Larkspur Rovers; West Middlesex County; Ealing District; Middlesex County Under-14–16; NORWICH CITY 25.01.93 (assoc), 10.07.95 (trainee), 21.01.97 (pro); Luton Town 16.07.2001.

Primarily a right winger, the former England youth cap rose through the City ranks with his all action approach and pacy style. At times he had to compete with Anselin and Dalglish for the right flank position, which helps to account for the record number of substitute apearances to his name.

FORBES, Duncan Scott

(1968–1980) **1970:** 5/11; 11/7
Centre Half **Career:** 350-7-12
Debut: 9 Oct 68 **Final:** 11 Oct 80

Born: Edinburgh 19 Jun 1941

Career: Craiglea Thistle; Musselburgh; Colchester United 04.09.61; NORWICH CITY 12.09.68; Torquay United (temp. transfer) 29.09.76–29.11.76; NORWICH CITY promotions, 1981 travel manager; Yarmouth Town 18.08.81; Diss Town 1981 coach; Unity Emeralds 1982 coach; NORWICH CITY 1981 continued, chief scout Mar 1988–retired May 2001.

The robbing of an opponent is a cardinal point in a centre half's football faith and when 'Big Dunc' comes at you – muscular, craggy and with a stentorian voice – you know that your days are numbered. Duncan led City by word and deed to two promotions and two Cup Finals forming a renowned partnership with Dave Stringer. A true fans favourite as he spent many hours travelling with them and more than any other player past or present has got to know them and appreciates their passion for the club. He rightly has a special niche in the club's folklore as a player, team and club captain and filled various club roles before he took a deserved retirement.

FORD, Alfred

(1924) **1924:** 5/8; 11/7
Outside Left **Career:** 1-0-0
Debut/Final: 3 May 24

Born: Newcastle-upon-Tyne 2 Aug 1901
Died: Peterborough 24 Mar 1976

Career: People's Hall FC; Spen Black & White; Seaton Delaval; Spen Black & White; Manchester City 14.05.21; Hyde Road Tramways Jul 1922; NORWICH CITY 11.06.23; Peterborough and Fletton United Sep 1924; Stamford Town; Peterborough Westwood Works.

Alf, from the north east production line, was a statistician's nightmare in that there were two A. Fords, both wingers, on Manchester City's books at the same time. Alf's solitary game for City was described by the pithy comment, 'Speedy, but he did not place his centres to advantage'. Worked later as a fitter/mechanical engineer.

FOULKES, Reginald Ernest

(1950–1956) **1953:** 6/0; 12/3
Centre Half **Career:** 238-0-8
Debut: 19 Aug 50 **Final:** 25 Apr 56

Born: Shrewsbury 23 Feb 1923

Career: Shrewsbury Town Boys; Manchester United (groundstaff); Second World War guested for Birmingham; Walsall 29.08.45; NORWICH CITY 17.05.50; Wisbech Town May 1956 player-manager; King's Lynn May 1957; Norwich CEYMS Aug 1960 coach.

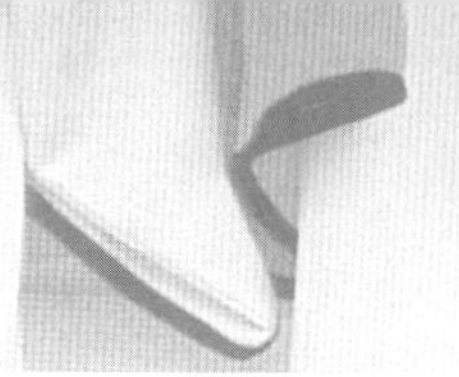

Reg was Norman Low's first signing and proved to be a bargain with his splendid generalship, resolute play and scrupulous method well to the fore. Joined after gaining FA representative honours while being Walsall's captain. Has since returned to live in his home town being a qualified accountant until his well earned retirement.

FOX, Ruel Adrian

(1986–1994) **1988:** 5/6; 10/0
Outside Right **Career:** 184-35-25
Debut: 4 Nov 86 **Final:** 24 Jan 94 (goal)

Born: Ipswich 14 Jan 1968

Ruel Fox

Career: Whitton 1980; Ipswich Town (trial); NORWICH CITY (assoc), 09.08.94 (app), 20.01.86 (pro); Newcastle United 02.02.94; Tottenham Hotspur 06.10.95; West Bromwich Albion 30.08.2000.

Ruel, Johnny Miller, Daryl Godbold, Louie Donowa and Adrian Pennock form a quintet of Ipswich born men who played in the football league for Norwich City. A tricky winger blessed with natural speed, he progressed through City's renowned youth scheme. The emergence of Dale Gordon gave the club a surfeit of riches and despite being an England 'B' international he made million pound moves to his next clubs. He helped West Brom reach the play-off zones where they faltered in their attempt to gain promotion.

FRIAR, John

(1935–1939) **1935:** 5/8; 11/8
Outside Right **Career:** 86-0-18
Debut: 7 Dec 35 **Final:** 15 Apr 39

Born: Cambusnethan 18 Jul 1911
Died: Bathgate 22 May 1979

Career: Carluke Juniors; Bradford City 04.09.29; Edinburgh Hibs Aug 1931; Portsmouth 22.04.32; Bournemouth 25.07.33; Port Vale 31.07.34; Preston North End 22.12.34; NORWICH CITY 05.12.35; Ipswich Town 09.06.39.

John was one of the nomads of the 30s, having served clubs in the Scottish league and English Division One, Two and Three (South). In a chequered career he did not suffer in comparison against the previous encumbent Alf Kirchen, and he later vied with Billy Warnes for the No. 7 shirt. He never played for Ipswich but one of his happiest days was when he scored a hat-trick against them in a benefit match. He worked in a Lanark pithead.

FROSDICK, Albert Walter

(1920–1921) **1920:** 5/7; 10/6
Outside Left **Career:** 5-0-0
Debut: 11 Sep 20 **Final:** 26 Nov 21

Born: Norwich 3 Oct 1893
Died: Norwich 11 Sep 1973

Career: Trowse 1908; Carrow Works FC 1910; NORWICH CITY 07.01.12 signing amateur forms 07.08.20.

A local amateur who excelled for Norfolk County between 1912 and 1923. He played for City on either side of the Great War and was part of the reserve side that won almost every medal and cup that they played for just before the advent of League football in Norwich. Enlisted in August 1915 serving with the RAMC and he was the proud owner of the Military Medal that he had won on the French front.

FUGLESTAD, Erik

(1997–2000) **1997:** 5/10; 11/4
Midfielder **Career:** 76-4-2
Debut: 18 Nov 97 **Final:** 1 Apr 00

Born; Stavanger, Norway 13 Aug 1974

Career: Randaberg (Norway) 1984; Viking Fotballklubb (Norway) 1991; NORWICH CITY 08.11.97–18.04.2000; Viking Fotballklubb (Norway) 19.04.2000.

Erik developed his defensive qualities to supplement his natural attacking flair. Well worth his free transfer 'Bosman style' and a former Norwegian Under-21 international. His thrilling runs and crosses made him one of the more successful City foreign imports before he returned to his homeland and started scoring goals in abundance.

FULTON, John

(1930) **1930:** 5/9; 11/12
Centre Half **Career:** 1-0-0
Debut/Final: 6 Dec 30

Born: Knockentiber 22 Dec 1903
Died: Luton 7 Oct 1963

Career: Kilbirnie Ladeside; Luton Town 10.03.27; NORWICH CITY 11.07.30; Vauxhall Motors 29.10.31.

He owed his unexpected debut to an injury sustained by Lochhead during one of City's blackest seasons. The Bristol Rovers scorers that day make interesting reading: Dix and Forbes (two). A car worker in later life, he left £1,471 in his will to his widow Elsie.

FURNESS, William Isaac

(1937–1946) **1938:** 5/9; 11/6
Inside Left **Career:** 96-0-21
Debut: 28 Aug 37 (2 goals) **Final:** 26 Dec 46

Born: New Washington, Co. Durham 8 Jun 1909
Died: Norwich 29 Aug 1980

Career: Washington Colliery; Usworth Colliery; Leeds United 12.08.28; NORWICH CITY 10.6.37 retired 1947, assistant trainer, & trainer until 1956, part time coaching Feb 1957, physio to Jun 1970.

Billy played for England alongside such legends as Bastin, Geldard, Hapgood and Hibbs and also toured with them to Czechoslovakia, Hungary and Switzerland. He was a fine player with a well-earned reputation as a taker of chances with his redoubtable shot. Equally able in defence or attack, his wartime games for City totalled an incredible 177 for 69 goals. With experience gained from war work in electrical engineering Billy set himself up in private practice post-war as an electrical masseur and returned to Carrow Road as a physiotherapist to complete 25 years' service in various capacities.

GADSDEN, Ernest

(1920–1921) **1921:** 5/11; 12/0
Left Back **Career:** 19-0-0
Debut: 28 Aug 20 **Final:** 26 Feb 21

Born: Bulwell, Nottingham 22 Dec 1895
Died: Nottingham 6 Jan 1966

Career: Bulwell St Albans 1914; Notts Sunday School league; Mansfield Town 1915; Nottingham Forest Jun 1916; Basford National Ordnance Factory; NORWICH CITY May 1919 (amat), 27.08.20 (pro); Shildon Athletic cs 1921; Portsmouth 23.05.22; Blackpool 23.08.23; Halifax Town 22.05.25.

A local scribe of flowery bent reckoned of Ernie, 'In his kicking he gets length without superfluous altitude and he can tackle to a purpose'. It was said that his play reminded one of Billy Hampson, which was praise indeed. He had an arduous time during WW1 alongside his brother Bert (a Stoke City goalkeeper).

Left: Erik Fuglestad
Right: William Furness

GALLEGO, Antonio

(1947) **1947:** 5/9; 11/0
Goalkeeper **Career:** 1-0-0
Debut/Final: 15 Mar 47

Born: San Sebastian, Spain 2 Jun 1924

Career: Cambridge YC; Cambridge City; Cambridge Town; NORWICH CITY 14.03.47; Abbey United 1948–1951; Cambridge United 1951; Canterbury; Margate; Biggleswade 1957.

Tony came to England as an evacuee from the Spanish Civil War with his three sisters and brother José – himself a pro with Brentford, Colchester and Southampton. Tony's one game was described thus, 'He did not set the Wensum on fire but he will develop with experience'. In December 1956 Sid Plunkett hit a five minute hat-trick past him for Yarmouth against Biggleswade when both brothers were playing for the latter side. He had been a salesman for Palmer & Harvey, wholesale tobacconist's and confectioner's, for 40 years.

GARDINER, John Graham

(1929) **1929:** 5/9; 11/3
Centre Half **Career:** 1-0-0
Debut/Final: 19 Jan 29

Born: Hamilton 14 Nov 1904
Died: Small Heath 12 Oct 1977

Career: Blantyre Victoria; Motherwell 10.09.25; Coventry 28.05.26; Wolverhampton Wanderers 12.06.28; NORWICH CITY 26.11.28; Kettering Town Jul 1929; Workington Jan 1930; Barrow 01.08.32; Lancaster Town Oct 1932.

He was signed on a month's trial with a reserve debut against Sheppey. It was said that he did well in his one game and he was engaged for the season without playing again. Described as being short in stature but combatative as most pivotal men should be to survive. Discovery of a

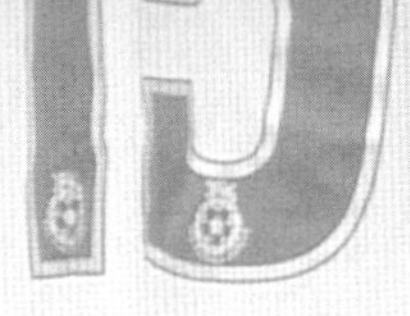

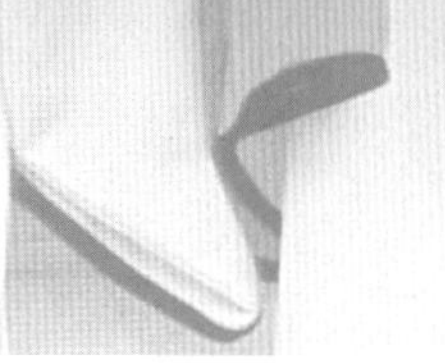

Scottish career helped me trace his family and add considerably to the career shown in Canary Citizens.

GAVIN, John Thomas

(1949–1958) **1949:** 5/9; 10/10
Outside Right **Career:** 338-0-132
Debut: 30 Apr 49 **Final:** 21 Apr 58

Born: Limerick 20 Apr 1928

Left: Johnny Gavin

Career: Jamesborough United; Limerick City; Irish Free State; NORWICH CITY 09.08.48; Tottenham Hotspur 14.10.54; NORWICH CITY 07.11.55; Watford 03.07.58; Crystal Palace 09.05.59; Cambridge City 01.07.61; Newmarket Town Aug 1962 player coach; Fulbourn Nov 1967.

Started out working as a painter on the railways and playing for Limerick City. Johnny is City's record holder for goalscoring and is likely to remain so for many years. Johnny had all the attributes of speed, toughness, positional sense and for City he hit 15 twos, four hat-tricks and a four. Returned for a second spell as part of the Maurice Norman exchange and continued to top-score for City. After being a publican for several years he turned his hand to painting and decorating. He underwent a hip replacement and endures osteoarthritis. The ultimate bargain, seeing that he was signed for just £1,500.

GIALLANZA, Gaetano Antonio

(2000– **2000:** 6/0; 11/7
Forward **Career:** 10-8-5
Debut: 15 Apr 00 (sub)

Born: Basle, Switzerland 6 Jun 1974

Career: Old Boys (Switzerland) 1991; Servette FC Geneva (Switzerland) 1993; BSC Young Boys Berne (Switzerland) 1994; FC Sion (Switzerland) 1995; FC Basel (Switzerland) 1996; FC de Nantes Atlantique (France) 1997; Bolton Wanderers (loan) 25.03.98–Jun 1998; FC Lugano (Switzerland) (loan) 1998 ; NORWICH CITY (loan) 29.03.2000, (signed) 03.07.2000.

Seemingly a natural goalscorer, he netted twice in a City friendly against Arsenal and was in line to be the ideal replacement for the departed Bellamy. Has scored goals for all of his clubs including double figures in a season for Young Boys and Basel and it is hoped he makes a full recovery from his unfortunate injury.

GIBBINS, Roger Graeme

(1976–1978) **1977:** 5/10; 11/12
Centre Forward **Career:** 51-1-13
Debut: 25 Aug 76 **Final:** 25 Feb 78

Born: Enfield 6 Sep 1955

Career: Enfield Schools; Middlesex & London Schoolboys; English Schools; Tottenham Hotspur (app), 27.05.71 (pro); Oxford United 15.08.75; NORWICH CITY 02.06.76; New England Tea Men (USA) Mar 1978–Aug 1978; Cambridge United 27.09.79; Cardiff City 01.08.82; Swansea City 10.10.85; Newport County 22.08.86, May 1987 player coach; Torquay United 24.03.88; Newport County 10.01.89; Cardiff City 01.03.89 to coaching; Cwmbran Town player coach; Merthyr Tydfil player coach; Weston-Super-Mare 1998; Merthyr Tydfil Apr 1999–Dec 1999 manager.

A product of school football, playing at this level for England and for Spurs in an FA Youth Cup Final. His father Eddie was also on Spurs' books in the 1950s. Roger performed admirably at the highest level (Division One) after Ted MacDougall had been sold. He settled and played in Wales, winning a Division Three championship medal and a Welsh Cup Final.

GILBERT, Noel Albert

(1956) **1956:** 5/11; 12/10
Outside Right **Career:** 1-0-0
Debut/Final: 28 Apr 56

Born: North Walsham, nr Norwich 25 Dec 1931

Career: North Walsham; NORWICH CITY 30.08.55; Holbeach United; Gorleston.

The Pink 'Un *football reporter commented, 'He is a reserve winger who is worth a run in the firsts'. For the Reserves he made 27 appearances scoring five times. A retired Police Inspector, he then part-owned a snooker centre in Norwich.*

GILGUN, Patrick

(1926–1927) **1926:** 5/8; 11/4
Forward **Career:** 12-0-4
Debut: 20 Nov 26 **Final:** 30 Apr 27

Born: Shotts 30 Dec 1901
Died: Carfin 26 Sep 1981

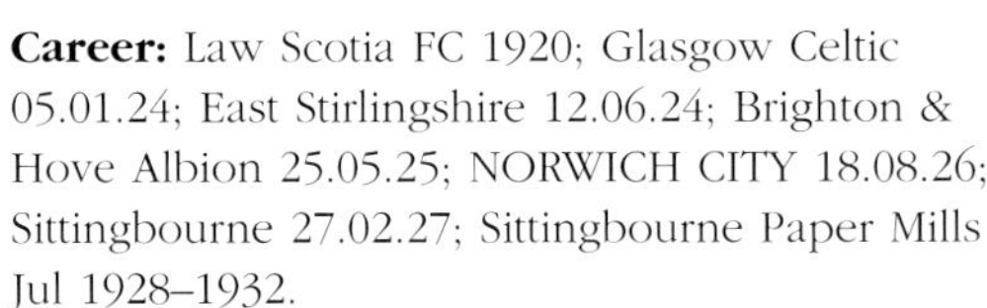

Career: Law Scotia FC 1920; Glasgow Celtic 05.01.24; East Stirlingshire 12.06.24; Brighton & Hove Albion 25.05.25; NORWICH CITY 18.08.26; Sittingbourne 27.02.27; Sittingbourne Paper Mills Jul 1928–1932.

A brief stay at City saw him score in three successive matches as well as playing in goal when keeper Dennington was injured during a match. Known as 'Scruffy' at Brighton he scored 23 goals in a season with forceful and thrustful play. He returned to Scotland to work as a steelworker.

GLADWIN, Robin

(1966–1967) **1966:** 5/11; 11/7
Left Back **Career:** 17-0-0
Debut: 12 Apr 66 **Final:** 6 Sep 67

Born: Harlow 12 Aug 1940

Career: Epping YC; Tottenham Hotspur Juniors; Leyton; Cambridge City (amat); Harlow Town (amat); Chelmsford City (amat), 1964 (pro); NORWICH CITY 07.01.66; Oxford United 02.07.68–30.06.70; Old Salasians coach; Garsington Boys coach.

Robin played in the days when Norwich were a middle of the table Division Two side and he alternated with Joe Mullett and Alan Black for the left back slot. He managed to play in 44 reserve games for City, being given a free transfer in May 1968. Later he coached his sons' side for many years.

GOBLE, Stephen Richard

(1979–1981) **1979:** 5/11; 10/6
Left Winger **Career:** 35-0-2
Debut: 20 Oct 79 **Final:** 20 Feb 81

Born: Erpingham, nr Aylsham 5 Sep 1960

Career: Alderman Peel School; NORWICH CITY Sep 1976 (youth), Dec 1976 (app); 01.06.77 (pro) to 1981; Gronigen (Holland) Aug 1981; NORWICH CITY 29.08.84; Volendam (Holland) (loan) Nov 1985; FC Utrecht (Holland) (loan); Cambridge United Feb 1988.

His youth team debut was on 11 Sep 1976 and on his turning pro Ken Brown said, 'If he works as hard as he has done as an apprentice he should have a good future'. His snappy footwork and nimble displays held him in good stead as he came to prominence following a good club tour of Australasia in 1979. It was deemed that he lacked consistency upon his return from Holland, but nonetheless City made a healthy profit selling a local lad.

GODBOLD, Daryl Martin

(1983–1984) **1984:** 5/11; 11/0
Full Back **Career:** 0-2-0
Debut: 3 Dec 83 (sub) **Final:** 21 Jan 84 (sub)

Born: Ipswich 5 Sep 1964

Career: Northgate Grammar School; Suffolk Under-14–16; NORWICH CITY (youth), 20.07.81 (app), 05.09.82 (pro); Colchester United Aug 1984; Wroxham 1986; Heartsease; Mackintosh; Wroxham Feb 1989; Coltishall HV Sep 1991; Sprowston Wanderers Oct 1991; Wroxham 1992; Old Catton Under-10s manager.

Another member of City's all-conquering youth team, he had but 87 minutes' play in the First Division before moving to Layer Road for nine games. He moved into non-league circles and is an accomplished all-rounder at cricket. Later dogged by a pelvic complaint, he has been a sales rep and latterly a financial advisor, still living locally.

GOFFEY, Herbert Henry

(1935–1937) **1936:** 5/9; 11/10
Inside Right **Career:** 35-0-9
Debut: 14 Sep 35 (goal) **Final:** 1 May 37

Born: Sundridge, Kent 9 May 1911
Died: Northampton 22 Sep 1991

Career: Spring Lane School; Northampton Boys; Higham Ferrers Town FC; Northampton Nomads FC; Sevenoaks FC; Northampton Town 24.12.30 (amat); Lotus FC; Northampton Nomads FC; Bristol Rovers 10.02.32 (amat); NORWICH CITY 10.12.34 (amat); 15.05.35 (pro); Brighton & Hove Albion 21.06.37 to 05.05.45.

He worked his way up through the reserves, winning a Norfolk Senior Cup medal. He scored his City goals against Midland and Southern teams but did better at Brighton where a goal from him meant that his side were not to lose the match. He was fortunate to survive evacuation from Dunkirk beaches and he was a retired railway guard. Bert was also the best man at Fred Hall's wedding.

GOODWIN, Stephen Alan

(1971–1974) **1974:** 5/9; 11/0
Utility **Career:** 7-1-2
Debut: 1 May 71 (sub) **Final:** 30 Nov 74

Born: Chadderton, Manchester 23 Feb 1954

Career: NORWICH CITY 30.05.70 (app), 28.02.72 (pro); Scunthorpe United (loan) 25.09.73; Southend United 12.06.75; Gjovik (Norway) May 1979.

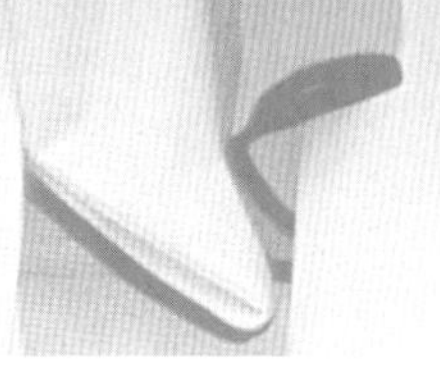

Steve would have been the youngest ever debutant if he had played from his unused substitute spot on 6 Mar 1971. He gave good service to the second team (141 apps–27 goals) in wearing eight different numbered shirts but did not make a league reappearance for three years until he was selected as the replacement for the suspended Phil Boyer. His greatest day for the Canaries was when he netted twice in his only League Cup tie for City. Found working in an Adidas factory in Norway.

Left: Dale Gordon
Right: Peter Gordon

GORDON, Dale Andrew

(1984–1991) **1984:** 5/10; 11/8
Winger **Career:** 248-13-43
Debut: 25 Aug 84 **Final:** 2 Nov 91

Born: Caister, Great Yarmouth 9 Jan 1967

Career: Caister; East Norfolk SFA; England Under-15; NORWICH CITY 1980 (youth), Jan 1981 (assoc), 16.05.83 (app), 17.01.84 (pro); Glasgow Rangers 04.11.91; West Ham United 08.07.93; Peterborough United (loan) 23.03.95; Millwall (loan) 21.03.96; Bournemouth player coach 18.07.96–Mar 1997; Yarmouth Town May 1997 general manager, 12.12.98 manager; Ipswich Town Football Academy (in Lowestoft) Apr 2000.

He turned down Manchester United and West Ham to join the Canaries as a youngster and was capped by England at Under-15–18 level. Although he supported Ipswich as a boy he showed a level headed attitude on taking the professional ticket. He won league and cup medals north of the border and at his best he produced scintillating displays. Netted West Ham United's first ever FA Carling Premiership goal before returning home to the East Coast.

GORDON, Peter John

(1953–1958) **1954:** 5/9; 11/5
Outside/Inside Right **Career:** 176-0-37
Debut: 12 Dec 53 **Final:** 26 Apr 58

Born: Northampton 21 May 1932
Died: Claydon 22 May 1990

Career: Northamptonshire County; NORWICH CITY 06.12.49; Watford 03.07.58; Exeter City 06.06.60; Newport County 26.06.62; Poole Town Jul 1963; followed by coaching spells at Hartlepools United, Southend United and Northampton Town to 1969.

His debut was in the FA Cup with a scoring debut a week later in the league – the 33rd player to achieve this feat for City. Once he was established Peter turned in consistent displays, regularly topping 30 appearances a season. In the 1955/56 season when Ralph Hunt became a City record breaker, Peter along with Billy Coxon was the main provider – still the pair of them shared 25 goals.

GOSS, Jeremy

(1984–1996) **1984:** 5/9; 10/9
Midfield **Career:** 198-40-23
Debut: 12 May 84 (sub) **Final:** 6 Apr 96 (sub)

Born: Dekalia, Cyprus 11 May 1965

Career: Crickhowell Primary School 1975; Brecon High School 1977; Kirkham Carr Hill Secondary Modern School Mar 1977–Sep 1977; Limvady Secondary Modern School Sep 1977–Feb 1979; Coleraine (trial); N.Ireland Schoolboys (trial); Edinburgh Secondary Modern School; Pent Valley Secondary Modern School Aug 1980–Aug 1982; Kent County Youth; Kent Schoolboys Under-16–19; England Under-18s (Kent SFA); Folkestone Town 1982; NORWICH CITY 23.03.83; Lulea (Sweden) (loan) Jul 1986; Charlton Athletic 18.07.96; Heart of Midlothian 29.07.96; Huddersfield Town Oct 1997; training with Colchester United 05.01.98; Gillingham (trial) Feb 1998; Guangzhou Apollo (China) for two weeks; Colchester United 25.03.98; Stevenage Borough (trial); King's Lynn 20.03.99–28.10.99; NORWICH CITY Academy fund raiser.

An unusual beginning as he joined City on a Manpower Work Experience Scheme doing well in the South East Counties League and scoring in the first leg of the 1983 FA Youth Cup Final. 1993 was his season with stunning televised goals against Leeds United and Bayern Munich. 'Mr Average' according to his own description, he won Welsh caps and is presently engaged in raising funds for Norwich City's Academy.

GOVIER, Stephen

(1971–1974) **1970:** 6/0; 12/0
Centre Half **Career:** 30-0-2
Debut: 16 Jan 71 **Final:** 1 Jan 74

Born: Watford 6 Apr 1952

Career: Oxhey Juniors; Bushey Rangers Under-14–16; Bushey Manor; Bushey Meads; Watford Boys; Hertfordshire (trial); NORWICH CITY 13.09.67 (amat), Aug 1968 (app), 11.07.69 (pro); Brighton & Hove Albion 29.04.74; Grimsby Town 19.12.74; Coltishall 28.07.90 manager; Wymondham Town 27.04.93 manager; Coltishall 18.05.94–23.06.95 manager; coach to Norfolk Police and Drayton Under-15s.

Mainly a reserve Canary, as can be seen from his mammoth total of 183 games for 11 goals at that level. He did well when replacing Duncan Forbes, whose ultra-consistent game served to limit his chances. A cruciate knee ligament injury whilst at Grimsby brought his career to an end. He had colourful managers in Bond, Taylor and Clough.

GRAHAM, Robert Currie

(1929–1931) **1929:** 5/9; 11/8
Left Back **Career:** 52-0-0
Debut: 9 Sep 29 **Final:** 2 May 31

Born: Muirkirk, nr Cumnock 25 Aug 1900
Died: Kilwinning 26 Oct 1965

Career: Muirkirk; Killwinning Rovers; Luton Town 15.06.21; NORWICH CITY 10.05.29; Thames 03.06.31; Bedford Town Oct 1932 player coach; Luton Davis Athletic Nov 1935.

A regular with Luton, playing 164 League games for them before being signed by City to bolster the defence after City had a poor season. Bob was an uncompromising, fearless tackler who employed a doughty kick. He remarkably left to join Thames who were an infinitely worse side than Norwich City.

GRAHAM, William

(1939) **1939:** 5/7; 10/4
Inside Left **Career:** 18-0-5
Debut: 2 Feb 39 **Final:** 29 Apr 39 (goal)

Born: Hetton-le-Hole, Durham 3 Oct 1914
Died: Chester 23 Sep 1996

Career: Eppleton School; Houghton Secondary School; Hetton Juniors; Burnley (trial) 1932; Blyth Spartans May 1932; Hetton; Burnley 24.09.32; Bury 05.05.35; NORWICH CITY 03.02.39; Barry Town Nov 1946; Holywell Town 1949 player/coach.

Bill was a fine goalscorer pre-war, when it was said that 'He had the secret of perpetual motion plus great positional awareness'. Formed a brief but productive partnership with Jack Acquroff at Bury. A war wound effectively finished his career and he kept fit with a few holes of golf every day in Clwyd, passing away just short of his 82nd birthday.

Jeremy Goss

GRANT, Peter

(1997–1999) **1997:** 5/9; 11/9
Midfield **Career:** 71-4-3
Debut: 23 Aug 97 **Final:** 13 Mar 99

Born: Glasgow 30 Aug 1965

Career: St Patrick's High School; St Aloysius Chapelhall; Glasgow Celtic Boys Club 1976; Glasgow Celtic 'S' form 1977, from Juniors 20.07.82; NORWICH CITY 22.08.97; Reading 20.08.99; AFC Bournemouth May 2000 player coach, 18.08.2000 assistant manager, head coach.

Peter was an immensely popular figure with the Celtic fans, where he won most of Scottish football's major honours including of course international caps. He showed absolute commitment to City's cause, being a fitness fanatic in the nicest sense. His organisational and motivational qualities have been carried forward into coaching and assisting with management.

GRANVILLE, Daniel Patrick

(2000) **2000:** 5/11; 12/5
Defender **Career:** 6-0-0
Debut: 4 Nov 00 **Final:** 25 Nov 00

Born: Islington 19 Jan 1975

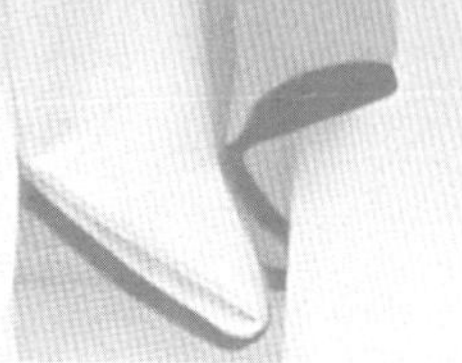

Career: Pakeman Primary School; St Aloysius Secondary Modern School; Chapel Market; Charlton Athletic Schoolboy forms; Tottenham Hotspur Under-17; Cambridge United 16.05.92 (trainee); 19.05.93 (pro); Chelsea 21.03.97; Leeds United 08.07.98; Manchester City 07.08.99; NORWICH CITY (loan) 27.10.2000.

Danny's father's cousin is the ex-Spurs player Jimmy Pearce – the latter a thorn to City in the past. A Premiership-class player, Danny did himself proud in City's colours during his all too brief stay. He liked the club and the spirit but he was recalled by Joe Royle for his club's unsuccessful relegation fight.

GRAPES, Steven Philip

(1971–1976) **1976:** 5/6; 9/0
Right Winger **Career:** 43-9-4
Debut: 23 Mar 71 (sub) **Final:** 18 Sep 76

Born: Norwich 25 Feb 1953

Career: Lakenham Secondary Modern School; NORWICH CITY 01.08.68 (app), 08.07.70 (pro); Bournemouth (loan) Mar 1976; Cardiff City 21.10.76; Torquay United 09.08.82; Bath City Jul 1983; Merthyr Tydfil Oct 1983; Llantwit Major AFC 1985–1988.

A diminutive winger who made the first of 173 reserve appearances on 21.12.68. His seasonal first team games were uneven until a foursome netted for the Reserves in Sep 1973 prompted his return to Division One. Experience gained while at City held him in good stead at his next club, where he was a regular selection for them. A split shin hastened his retirement and latterly he works for a manufacturer of fitness equipment.

GRAY, George Willie

(1920–1921) **1920:** 5/8; 12/2
Right Back **Career:** 51-0-0
Debut: 28 Aug 20 **Final:** 26 Nov 21

Born: Ecclesfield, nr Sheffield 27 Feb 1896
Died: Norwich 5 May 1962

Career: Eastwood Bible Class; Alfreton Juniors; Grimsby Town May 1919; NORWICH CITY 26.10.19 (amat), 27.08.20 (pro); Sheffield Wednesday 28.11.21 to 1923.

A Norwich City handbook described him as 'An honest journeyman with plenty of resource, with the length of his volleying being especially good'. Mind you, the same source gave his birthplace as Derby! George played for City in their Southern League days. He retired with knee trouble at just 27 and after football he became a publican and then a crane driver.

GREATREX, Edward John

(1958) **1954:** 5/10; 11/7
Goalkeeper **Career:** 1-0-0
Debut/Final: 26 Apr 58

Born: Nuneaton 18 Nov 1936

Career: Coventry City Schoolboy, 'A', 'B' teams; NORWICH CITY 16.05.53 (amat), 16.06.54 (pro); Cambridge City 1959; Chelmsford Aug 1960; Clacton 1962; Bury St Edmunds 1964; Yarmouth Town 02.09.66–Aug 1968.

His one Football League game that counted was a home defeat against Mansfield. Norwich were leading in his other game – the fogged-off match at Mansfield – so he has to be remembered for his 61 reserve games. A good cricketer, being attached to Warwickshire's Colts and Club & Ground side. Also a Yarmouth and Norfolk wicketkeeper. A retired Inland Revenue inspector.

GREEN, Robert Paul

(1999– **1999:** 6/2; 12/2
Goalkeeper **Career:** 14-1-0
Debut: 11 Apr 99

Born: Chertsey 18 Jan 1980

Career: Horsell Middle School; Woking District Schools; Bishop Reindorp School; West Surrey; Woking Boys; England Under-16–18; NORWICH CITY May 1996 (assoc), Jul 1996 (trainee), 24.05.97 (pro).

The highly rated City keeper gave a faultless display in keeping a clean sheet against Ipswich Town upon his debut in the first team. 120 games under his belt below first team level has started to prepare him for the rigours ahead. A

Robert Green

self confident and commanding keeper who pushed Andy Marshall to produce Player of the Year performances in order to retain his place.

GREENWELL, John Wilfred

(1928–1931) **1930:** 6/0; 11/7
Centre Half **Career:** 52-0-3
Debut: 27 Aug 28 **Final:** 24 Jan 31

Born: Hamsterley, nr Bishop Auckland 18 Feb 1901

Career: Stanhope; Crook Town; Ferryhill Athletic; Annfield Plain Jun 1927; NORWICH CITY 13.04.28 (amat), 06.08.28 (pro); Swindon Town 18.05.31; Bath City Oct 1932; Durham City; Western House Sep 1933.

A black-haired central defender who scored his first City goal against Swindon – the club he was later to join. He rejoiced in the nickname 'Sticks' and vied with Mick O'Brien for the pivotal role, but proved his versatility in the City reserves by scoring 17 goals, including a hat-trick from half back. The author alas is still unable to trace John and would be grateful for any help from readers.

GUNN, Bryan James

(1986–1998) **1986:** 6/2; 12/5
Goalkeeper **Career:** 477-0-0
Debut: 4 Nov 1986 **Final:** 31 Jan 98

Born: Thurso 22 Dec 1963

Career: Invergordon Boys Club; Invergordon Academy; Nairn County; Aberdeen (trial) 1978, 15.05.80 (pro); NORWICH CITY 15.10.86; Hibernian Feb 1998.

Bryan first played for the primary school side run by his father. He used to babysit Alex Ferguson's children while at Aberdeen. Norwich City's management decision to sign him for £100,000 paid off handsomely with Bryan turning in many brilliant performances in a dozen years. An excellent shot stopper with sharp reflexes, he took charge of his penalty area. A Scottish international, and the honour was well merited. He passed his Hibernian medical on crutches recovering from a broken leg. A superb ambassador for Norwich City, he is happily back at Carrow Road in the role of Sponsorship Sales Manager.

GURKIN, John

(1922–1923) **1922:** 5/9; 12/0
Left Half **Career:** 10-0-0
Debut: 27 Dec 22 **Final:** 28 Apr 23

Bryan Gunn

Born: Murton, Co. Durham 9 Sep 1895
Died: Sunderland 25 Feb 1976

Career: Dean Bank FC; South Hetton Royal Rovers; West Ham United 11.01.21; NORWICH CITY 05.06.22; Stalybridge Celtic Jul 1923; Durham City 04.09.24; Exeter City 29.05.29; Hyde United Aug 1930; Jarrow Aug 1932; Murton Colliery Welfare Nov 1932.

His Football League debut was on 27 August 1921 for West Ham United against Stoke City. Played principally for good class Northern sides apart from a productive spell at Exeter City joining Percy Varco.

GUY, Richard James

(1946–1948) **1946:** 5/10; 12/0
Left Half **Career:** 12-0-1
Debut: 31 Aug 46 **Final:** 20 Mar 48

Born: Swansea 29 Jan 1921
Died: Bradwell 22 Nov 1990

Career: RAF St Athan; Tower United; Wolverhampton Wanderers during Second World War; Swansea Town (amat); NORWICH CITY 30.07.46 (amat), 28.08.46 (pro); Yarmouth Town 21.08.48; Gorleston Jun 1950; Red Star manager in the 1960s.

Jim was signed by City immediately after a public practice match and scored in his second game from the centre forward spot. He was another player given different roles, none of which led to permanency. Scorer of 18 goals for Yarmouth and affectionately remembered by all who came in contact with him.

HALL, Bertie

(1932) **1932:** 5/10; 11/7
Right Half **Career:** 2-0-0
Debut: 12 Mar 32 **Final:** 19 Mar 32

Born: Newburn, nr Newcastle 18 Dec 1902
Died: Newcastle 25 Jan 1990

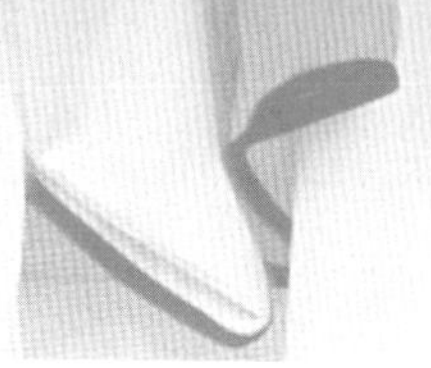

Career: Lemington Glass Works; Victoria Gatesfield; Newcastle United (trial) Apr 1925; Hartlepools United 10.09.26; Peterborough & Fletton United Sep 1929; NORWICH CITY 06.08.31; Bristol City 13.05.32.

Bert took Joe Joblings' place in the side but was displaced when Cecil Blakemore was temporarily moved to wing half. His elder brother Tom played for Sunderland, Newcastle and Gillingham before becoming a trainer. Indeed Tom scored one of the reputed finest goals ever seen at the Nest when he tricked several men and scored with a cross shot. Bertie was a retired factory labourer.

HALL, Frederick

(1936–1946) **1946:** 6/0; 12/10
Goalkeeper **Career:** 94-0-0
Debut: 18 Jan 36 **Final:** 7 Sep 46

Born: Drayton, nr Norwich 20 Oct 1914

Fred Hall

Career: Hellesdon Hospital FC; NORWICH CITY (trial) Dec 1933, 30.06.34 (amat), 26.09.34 (pro) and post war 17.05.46, later 'A' team trainer and scout.

The story goes that Fred walked into Tom Parker's office and asked for a trial. He was a custodian with a safe pair of hands and was in goal in the amazing wartime win over Brighton (18–0). His last game for City saw him collide with Jack Connor (Ipswich), which reduced him to hobbling along the left wing. A publican for many years and living locally after retirement from the Norwich Motor Company.

HALLIDAY, Thomas

(1933–1938) **1934:** 5/11; 11/8
Centre Half/Right Back **Career:** 203-0-0
Debut: 18 Aug 33 **Final:** 27 Dec 38

Born: Browney, Durham 11 Sep 1909
Died: Welwyn Garden City, Hertfordshire 18 Aug 1975

Career: Browney School; Deerness Valley Schools; England Under-15s; Durham Grammar School; Esh Winning Juniors; Meadowfield; Durham County; Sunderland 04.02.27; Darlington 02.09.28; NORWICH CITY 30.06.33; Exeter City 16.02.39.

Most centre forwards found his resolute play too much for them. He was described as being the great exponent of the one third back game and the Football Weekly Book of 650 Football Stars *added the comment, 'Former England Schoolboy star while studying chemistry at Durham Grammar School'. Like many of his predecessors and successors he became a publican.*

HALSEY, Mark Alan

(1978–1980) **1978:** 5/6; 10/10
Utility **Career:** 3-0-0
Debut: 26 Apr 78 **Final:** 1 Mar 80

Born: Romford 1 Dec 1959

Career: NORWICH CITY 20.10.76 (app), 19.04.78 (pro)–released Jul 1981; Yarmouth Town; Wroxham 1983; Sprowston Exiles; Newton Flotman; Mulbarton Feb 1998.

Mark was ignominiously sent off in his debut match, a feat later matched by Karl Simpson. His combativeness was evident in local football where he took few prisoners with his tough tackling. He can perform ably with the ball at his feet, evidenced his starring in an incredible 400 games for Wroxham.

HAMILTON, Derrik Vivian

(2000) **2000:** 5/11; 13/0
Midfield **Career:** 7-0-0
Debut: 25 Mar 00 **Final:** 29 Apr 00

Born: Bradford 15 Aug 1976

Career: Ryan Middle School; West Yorkshire Boys; Bradford City 01.06.94; Newcastle United 27.03.97; Sheffield United (loan) 16.10.98; Huddersfield Town (loan) 15.02.99; NORWICH CITY (loan) 22.03.2000; Bradford City (loan) Jul 2000; Tranmere Rovers (loan) 25.10.2000; Cardiff City 01.07.2001.

A powerfully built former England Under-21 player with an attacking bent. Neither Ruud Gullit or Bobby Robson picked him on a regular basis, hence his many loan spells. During his brief stay at Carrow Road he showed forceful tackling and impressed all with his professionalism and commitment.

HANNAH, James Henry (Joe)

(1921–1935) **1923:** 5/9; 11/7
Half Back **Career:** 427-0-22
Debut: 13 Jan 21 **Final:** 6 Feb 35

Born: Sheringham 30 Nov 1898
Died: Stepney, East London 1 Feb 1975

Career: Sheringham Teachers; Royal Engineers; Sheringham FC; NORWICH CITY 22.08.20 (amat), 16.06.21 (pro); Bury St Edmunds Jun 1937 coach; Observer Corps Second World War; NORWICH CITY 1945/46 assistant trainer.

A Canary legend, perched proudly in fifth spot in the all-time City appearance list. He had a fabulous career and for many years was regarded as the best back in the Division. Kept his eye on the ball and never gave an opponent room to manoeuvre. He was once so disgruntled with his display that he sentenced himself to walk home the 25 miles to Sheringham in the evening. From 1946 to December 1959 he was a Steward of the Morley Club in Sheringham thence moving to London. For eight years he was registered as 'Joe'. Manager Kerr sent a retained list showing him correctly as 'James Henry' to the Football League administration department, who then enquired whether he was a new player.

HANSBURY, Roger

(1974–1981)	**1974:** 5/11; 12/0
Goalkeeper	**Career:** 84-0-0
Debut: 21 Sep 74	**Final:** 28 Feb 81

Born: Barnsley 26 Jan 1955

Career: Worsborough High School; Worsborough Bridge; Barnsley Schoolboys; Yorkshire Youths; NORWICH CITY 27.08.71 (app), 23.01.73 (pro); Bolton Wanderers (loan); Cambridge United (loan) 04.11.77; Orient (loan) 15.12.78; Eastern Athletic (Hong Kong) Dec 1981; Burnley 02.08.83; Cambridge United 15.07.85; Birmingham City 27.03.86; Sheffield United (loan) 16.10.87, (signed) 16.11.87; Wolverhampton Wanderers (loan) 21.03.89; Colchester United (loan) 24.08.89; Cardiff City 23.12.89–07.05.92.

Roger had an unlucky time at Carrow Road in that he had to wait for the ageless Keelan to move to the USA before obtaining a deserved run in the firsts. He also broke a leg in training in July 1980 and suffered Yellow Jaundice prior to a move to Hong Kong. Scored with a drop kick for the Reserves v Yarwich in 1975. A roaming career, with his final game being a Welsh Cup Final win in 1992.

HANSELL, Ronald Arthur Robert

(1953–1955)	**1954:** 5/8; 10/0
Inside Right	**Career:** 36-0-10
Debut: 14 Nov 53 (goal)	**Final:** 21 Sep 55

Born: Norwich 3 Oct 1930

Left: 'Joe' Hannah
Right: Aage Hareide

Career: Wensum View YC; Norwich St Barnabas; Norfolk County; NORWICH CITY May 1949 (amat), 08.06.50 (pro); Chester 01.06.56; Lowestoft Town 1957; Yarmouth Town 24.08.58, Aug 1960 to 03.04.65 player coach; Old Duncanians.

A local amateur who had an almost indentical playing record at Chester to that gained at City. Coincidentally he scored most of his goals for City – be they for the Firsts or the Reserves – against London sides. Became a high scorer for Yarmouth playing alongside ex-City players Duffy, Rackham and Rowlands. Now lives on the East Coast.

HAREIDE, Aage Fridhjof

(1982–1984)	**1984:** 6/1; 12/4
Defender	**Career:** 52-2-3
Debut: 6 Nov 82	**Final:** 28 Apr 84 (goal)

Born: Hareide, an island N. West coast Norway 23 Sep 1953

Career: Hodd (Norway) 1969–1975; Army Service for 1 year; Molde F.K (Norway) 1976; Manchester City 03.09.81; NORWICH CITY 05.11.82 (loan) which extended to the end of the season, 24.08.83 on two-year contract; Molde F.K (Norway) part time player 1986, thence coach and manager resigning Oct 1997; Helsingborg IF (Sweden) Feb 1998 coach; Brondby (Norway) Jun 1999 manager.

A seasoned Norwegian international with Nordic good looks and humour: 'I think my family were named after the island and not the island after us'. He credits Mel Machin with improving him by 50% as a defender and his stay was only shortened because of a job opportunity in Norway running a kitchen and furniture manufacturers. There followed success in Norway and Sweden with Aage also coaching the Norwegian Youth team for two years.

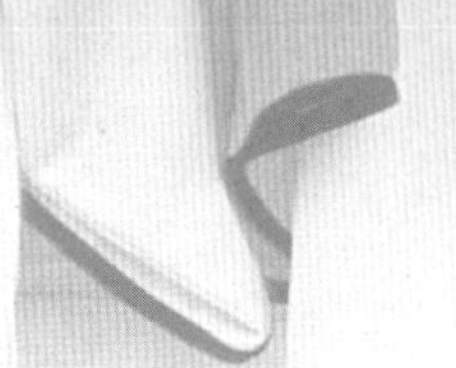

HARLEY, Alexander John

(1930) **1930:** 5/10; 12/0
Centre Forward **Career:** 1-0-0
Debut/Final: 20 Sep 30

Born: Edinburgh 17 Jul 1898
Died: Cardiff 9 Feb 1984

Career: Bonnyrigg Rose; Bathgate FC; Heart of Midlothian; Caernarfon Town Oct 1926; New Brighton 08.07.27; Millwall 25.06.28; Rhyl Athletic Sep 1929; Connah's Quay Jan 1930; NORWICH CITY 11.09.30–05.11.30.

Alex worked initially as a librarian in Edinburgh and came to City with a good goalscoring reputation, having hit 43 goals in one season at Caernarfon plus four in an FA Cup tie for New Brighton. The press report after his one appearance said that he 'did not rise to the occasion as well as had been expected'. A retired clerical officer in Cardiff.

HARRIS, Arthur

(1926) **1926:** 5/8; 11/0
Outside Right **Career:** 1-0-0
Debut/Final: 20 Sep 26

Born: Atherton, nr Bolton 15 Sep 1903
Died: Middleton 3 May 1970

Career: Hindley Green Colliery; Atherton; Atherton Collieries 1923; NORWICH CITY 23.08.26; Poole Town 1928; Bacup Borough Jul 1929.

Joined City with useful Lancashire Combination experience. Scored in the second Public Practice match on 21.08.26 in a 9–3 win for the Whites over the Colours. It was said that he impressed in this match trial, the game was described as 'the tuning of an orchestra'. As his only game resulted in a 6–1 City win it is difficult to comprehend why he never played again for Norwich City firsts.

HART, Andrew

(1981) **1981:** 5/8; 11/0
Defender **Career:** 0-1-0
Debut/Final: 19 Sep 81 (sub)

Born: Great Yarmouth 14 Jan 1963

Career: Oriel Grammar School; Yarmouth Boys; Norfolk County Under-15–16; NORWICH CITY 13.07.79 (app), 13.01.81 (pro); Gorleston 1983; Norwich United 1987–1991.

A nephew of Dave Stringer, Andrew replaced Mark Nightingale for 17 minutes of Division Two football, upon which performance it is impossible to give an assessment of his qualities. Did exceptionally well in a City Youth tour in Dusseldorf just prior to leaving City. Later struggled with a knee injury before recovering to win a Clubman of the Year award at Norwich United.

HARTFORD, Richard Asa

(1984–1985) **1985:** 5/7; 11/4
Inside Left/Midfield **Career:** 40-0-5
Debut: 10 Oct 84 (2 goals) **Final:** 14 May 85 (goal)

Born: Clydebank, Dumbartonshire 24 Oct 1950

Career: Fairfley Primary School; Clydebank High School; Dumbartonshire Schools; Drumchapel Amateurs; West Bromwich Albion 27.04.66 (ground staff), 28.05.66 (amat), 03.11.67 (pro); Manchester City 13.08.74; Nottingham Forest 22.06.79; Everton 30.08.79; Manchester City 01.10.81; Fort Lauderdale Sun (USA) 08.05.84; NORWICH CITY on a monthly contract, before signing 12.11.84; Coaching in Norway cs 1985; Bolton Wanderers 25.07.85 player coach; Stockport County 12.06.87 player coach; Oldham Athletic 23.03.89; Shrewsbury Town coach 15.07.89, caretaker manager 05.01.90, manager Jan 1990–17.01.91; Boston United Feb 1991–May 1991 player; Blackburn Rovers 1991 coaching staff, reserve manager 1992/3; Stoke City assistant manager 22.11.93, caretaker manager 08.09.94–29.09.94; Manchester City 08.07.95 assistant manager, Aug 1996 caretaker manager and later reserve team coach.

Besides possessing abundant skill he showed bravery, none more so than when, in November 1971, a proposed transfer to Leeds United fell through because of his hole-in-the-heart condition. Asa made a dream debut for City after being signed to lend authority to City's then youthful midfield. Always sought and distributed the ball well and was awarded the goal that beat Sunderland in the 1985 Milk Cup Final. Has since showed his mettle coaching and managing for a number of employers.

HAYLOCK, Paul

(1981–1985) **1981:** 5/8; 11/0
Full Back **Career:** 190-3-4
Debut: 28 Oct 81 **Final:** 6 May 85 (sub)

Born: Lowestoft 24 Mar 1963

Career: Kirkley Primary & High School; Lowestoft Town Boys; NORWICH CITY 13.07.79 (app), 13.01.81 (pro); Gillingham 18.08.86; Maidstone United 14.03.91; Woking; Shrewsbury Town 03.09.92; Sittingbourne Sep 1993; Barnet 30.09.93; Colchester United Jun 1994; Aylesbury

Aug 1994; Braintree Oct 1994; Sittingbourne Nov 1994 assistant manager to Jul 1999; Maidstone United.

A regular first-teamer for three seasons before being displaced by Ian Culverhouse in October 1985. A former schoolboy badminton star, Paul developed with the right coaching into a steady, honest defender of the first order. His career highlight was his 22nd birthday present of playing at Wembley. He continued to knuckle down and do his best at all times and was still performing into his late thirties.

Paul Haylock

HEATH, Donald

(1964–1967) **1965:** 5/11; 11/3
Right Winger **Career:** 88-3-18
Debut: 22 Aug 64 **Final:** 28 Aug 67

Born: Stockton 26 Dec 1944

Career: Stockton Schoolboys; Middlesbrough 08.08.60 (amat), 31.12.62 (pro); NORWICH CITY 22.07.64; Swindon Town 16.09.67; Oldham Athletic 06.07.70; Peterborough United 05.07.72; Hartlepools United 20.07.73; Gateshead 1974/75; Crook Town Jul 1975; Scouting for Portsmouth, Cardiff City, Swansea Town, Sunderland.

A hard working player who was at home on the wing or in an inside forward position. Played in the Don Rogers inspired League Cup Final win for Swindon Town and is chiefly remembered as a City player for scoring in the memorable FA Cup victory at Old Trafford in February 1967. An Anglo-Italian experience with Swindon Town was another highlight. Turned his hand to a number of occupations before becoming a materials controller for ICI.

HEFFER, Robert William

(1956–1957) **1956:** 6/0; 12/2
Outside Left **Career:** 2-0-1
Debut: 28 Nov 56 **Final:** 1 May 57 (goal)

Born: Eriswell, Suffolk 9 Nov 1935

Career: Mildenhall Secondary Modern School; Eriswell; Lakenheath; RAF Horsham St Faiths; NORWICH CITY 14.04.56; Weymouth Jul 1958; Tonbridge Jun 1959; King's Lynn Jul 1960; Bury St Edmunds 1963 retiring 1974.

As can be seen he scored in half of his First XI games. His reserve record of 54 games for 24 goals would indicate that he deserved more opportunities. In a desperate City season it was stated that with no funds available the club had to turn to untried youngsters. At King's Lynn he joined John Wilson and latterly he helped with coaching Costessey under-13s. At age 60 he was part of the team renovating the fire damaged Assembly House.

HEPPLE, Gordon

(1954–1955) **1954:** 5/10; 11/8
Left Back **Career:** 5-0-0
Debut: 21 Aug 54 **Final:** 5 May 55

Born: Sunderland 16 Sep 1925
Died: Kempston 25 Apr 1980

Career: North Sands; Middlesbrough 06.07.45; NORWICH CITY 14.06.54; Bedford Town Jul 1955.

Gordon took over from England international George Hardwick at his first club and was reputedly in the running for an England 'B' cap himself until he suffered a broken leg. A regular City reserve (45 games), but was unable to wrest the full back shirt from Bill Lewis, Denis Morgan and the converted full back Fred Kearns.

HETHERINGTON, Joseph

(1927) **1927:** 5/9; 11/4
Inside Right **Career:** 1-0-0
Debut/Final: 17 Dec 27

Born: Sunderland 11 Apr 1892
Died: Nottingham 6 Apr 1971

Career: Sunderland Royal Rovers; Southwick; South Shields 13.05.20 (amat), 15.09.20 (pro); Preston North End 23.06.24; Lincoln City 14.11.25; Durham City; NORWICH CITY 11.08.27; Guildford City Sep 1928; Walker Celtic 06.06.30; Sunderland Employment Exchange 27.11.30.

Scorer of 16 goals for South Shields, he is featured on Pinnace Card number 2037. Joe had just five games for Preston before breaking his leg, and his single City appearance proved to be his last ever in the Football League. Did better at Guildford, playing 61 games for them.

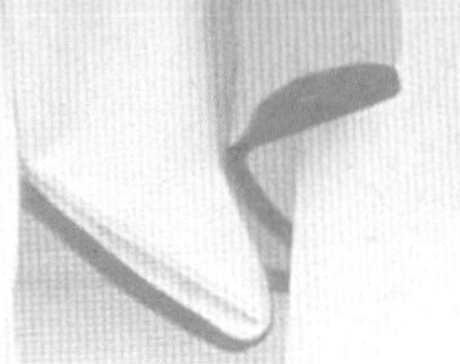

HEWITT, John Joseph

(1934–1935) **1934:** 5/11; 12/5
Inside Forward **Career:** 15-0-2
Debut: 8 Sep 34 **Final:** 28 Sep 35

Born: Evenwood, Durham 15 Jun 1911
Died: Dundee 7 Aug 1984

Career: Ruby United; Evenwood Town; Cockfield Aug 1929; Everton 03.09.29 (amat), 08.04.30 (pro); Hartlepools United 20.08.30; NORWICH CITY 16.05.34; Northampton Town 18.10.35 to 1938; Southport 04.07.39; Second World War Aldershot and Northampton Town.

Scorer of 56 goals for Hartlepools, including three hat-tricks, in one productive spell he netted in eight successive games. Formerly a miner, he showed distinct promise in the Reserves, netting three hat-tricks, but he did not rise to the heights in the firsts. His last game for City was his only League game at Carrow Road. An ex-Evenwood miner.

HIGGINS, Alexander (Sandy)

(1921–1922) **1921:** 5/9; 10/9
Inside Forward **Career:** 7-0-2
Debut: 10 Dec 21 **Final:** 6 May 22 (goal)

Born: Kilmarnock 4 Nov 1885
Died: Newcastle 15 Mar 1939

Career: Rugby XI; Belle Vue Juniors; Kilmarnock 1904; Newcastle United Jun 1905; Kilmarnock 01.08.19; Nottingham Forest 03.06.20; Jarrow Sep 1921 player-manager; NORWICH CITY 25.11.21; Wallsend Dec 1922; Workington Jun 1923; Berne (Switzerland) 1925 coach; Preston Colliery Jun 1926; Newcastle United coach.

One of six fathers and sons to have played football for Scotland. Known as 'Sandy' after his father, he also won Championship and Cup medals. His signing was regarded as a good stroke of business and even though he played so few games for City his press reviews adequately described his worthiness. They ranged from, 'Possessed a full compliment of tricks' to 'A purveyor of passes, he persuaded the ball to intended places with accomplished ease'. His occupations outside of football were shopkeeper, newspaper sportswriter and publican.

HILL, Kenneth

(1963–1966) **1964:** 5/10; 11/8
Right Half **Career:** 50-0-0
Debut: 3 Sep 63 **Final:** 8 Jan 66

Born: Walsall 28 Apr 1938

Career: North Walsall Boys; North Walsall Schools; Bescot United (amat); Oct 1954 (pro); Walsall 01.11.56; NORWICH CITY 26.07.63; Walsall 13.10.66; Nuneaton Borough Jul 1967; Stourbridge Jul 1969.

A career spent almost entirely with 'The Saddlers' rising from being the Boys centre half and the Schools right back to the captaincy of the Firsts. Played in three Divisions for them and after a half century of City appearances he rejoined, you guessed it – Walsall.

HILL, Matthew James

(1958–1963) **1963:** 5/8; 11/3
Inside Left **Career:** 195-0-66
Debut: 23 Aug 58 **Final:** 14 May 63

Born: Carrickfergus, Co. Antrim 31 Oct 1935

Career: Carrickfergus YMCA; Carrick Rangers; Linfield 1953; Newcastle United 13.06.57; NORWICH CITY 11.07.58; Everton 16.08.63; Port Vale 21.10.65; Derry City Feb 1968 player-manager; Linfield Aug 1971 manager; Carrick Rangers 05.11.88–May 1991 manager.

Jimmy Hill

Will-o'-the-wisp Jimmy – 'Tiger' to his colleagues – was a ball-playing luxury to some but a match-winner to the majority of supporters. Quick and clever, he represented the Irish League and won Northern Ireland caps at Schoolboy, Youth, Amateur, 'B' and Full level. Indeed 4 of his Full caps were gained whilst he was at Norwich. A measure of his talent is that he is equal to Ron Davies and Ted MacDougall in the all time City goalscoring chart. Jimmy says, 'Norwich was the best time of my career. I liked the people and the city.'

HINTON, William George

(1934) **1934:** 5/8; 11/4
Winger **Career:** 3-0-0
Debut: 13 Oct 34 **Final:** 25 Dec 34

Born: Sholing, Southampton 22 Jun 1913
Died: Southampton 17 Jul 1954

Career: Sholing; Salisbury City (amat); Southampton 28.01.33 (amat); Frost's Athletic; NORWICH CITY 15.08.33 amat), 24.11.33 (pro); Norfolk County 1934/5; Aldershot (trial) Jul 1935, (signed) 03.01.36; Bitterne Nomads Nov 1939.

Although he only made three appearances he showed ball skills and linked well with Alf Kirchen. A reserve hat-trick against Aldershot prompted their interest in him. The family building business in partnership with his brother Alfred – who himself was on Southampton's books. Coincidentally the author lived in the same street and my late mother tended him in hospital.

HOADLEY, Philip Frederick William

(1978–1981) **1979:** 5/11; 12/2
Defender **Career:** 86-3-1
Debut: 19 Aug 78 **Final:** 24 Oct 81

Born: Battersea, London 6 Feb 1952

Career: Surrey Schools; Southampton; South of England Schools; London Schoolboys; England Youth; Crystal Palace 1965 (assoc), 25.07.67 (amat), 25.06.69 (pro); Orient 04.10.71; NORWICH CITY 16.08.78; Eastern Athletic (Hong Kong) (loan) 29.02.82–May 1982; Loddon Grasshoppers Oct 1991 coach; Norwich United coach; Holt United 02.06.93 manager; Fakenham Town Sep 1996 assistant manager.

Phil played over 300 League games prior to joining City and he had a deserved reputation as a hard tackling, enthusiastic, scrupulously fair half back who always gave 100%. He retired after receiving an injury in a cup semi-final in Hong Kong – caused by colliding with the referee. He joined Norwich City as a community officer, moving from part-time to full-time.

HOCKEY, Trevor

(1973) **1973:** 5/7; 10/4
Midfield **Career:** 13-0-0
Debut: 24 Feb 73 **Final:** 28 Apr 73

Born: Keighley 1 May 1943
Died: Keighley 1 Apr 1987

Career: Eastwood School; Keighley Schools; West Riding; Keighley Central YC; Bradford City 19.05.58 (amat), May 1960 (pro); Nottingham Forest 21.11.61; Newcastle United 07.11.63; Birmingham City 19.11.65; Sheffield United 28.01.71; NORWICH CITY 22.02.73; Aston Villa 06.06.73; Bradford City 27.06.74; Athlone Town Mar 1976 player-manager; Stalybridge Celtic Aug 1977 manager; attempted to start soccer at Keighley Rugby Club in 1980; coaching the children of different units of the British Forces (Germany) and playing spells with San Diego Jaws (USA), San Jose Earthquakes USA) and Las Vegas Quicksilvers (USA).

Trevor arrived at Norwich as the 'Blade' without a razor. An ebullient personality, with long hair before the Beatles popularised it, and a piratical beard in keeping with his buccaneering, midfield generalship. He did a marvellous short term job in helping to keep City in Division One. Ever-colourful, at one time he ran the Trevor Hockey Quicksilver Lottery with 138 agents.

HODGE, James

(1922–1923) **1922:** 5/8; 11/4
Full Back **Career:** 55-0-1
Debut: 23 Feb 22 **Final:** 28 Apr 23

Born: Stenhousemuir 5 Jul 1891
Died: Chorlton-cum-Hardy, Manchester 2 Sep 1970

Career: Stenhousemuir; Manchester United May 1910; WW1 with the R.G.A; Millwall 26.12.19; NORWICH CITY 25.01.22; Southend United 01.09.23; Buxton Oct 1924; Buxton Medical Institution Apr 1933.

A wholehearted player who sought to place the ball advantageously. He gave many a vigorous display in the Canary cause and was rueful about being sent off in the Bolton FA Cup tie. Played in Millwall's very first Football League match; his younger brother John was also at Old Trafford.

HODGSON, David James

(1986–1987) **1986:** 5/10; 12/2
Striker **Career:** 6-3-4
Debut: 13 Sep 86 (sub) **Final:** 15 Nov 87

Born: Gateshead 6 Aug 1960

Career: Redleugh Boy's Club; Ipswich Town (trial); Bolton Wanderers (trial); Sheffield Wednesday (trial); Middlesbrough 06.08.76 (app), 19.08.78 (pro); Liverpool 12.08.82; Sunderland 24.08.84; NORWICH CITY 18.07.86; Middlesbrough (loan) 27.02.87; Jerez Club de Portivo (Spain) Jul 1987; Sheffield Wednesday 02.08.88; Mazda (Japan) 15.07.89; Metz (France); Swansea City 26.03.92; Mainz (Germany) (trial) 17.08.92; Rochdale 03.09.92; Darlington manager 24.05.95–02.12.95 and 12.11.96–02.08.2000.

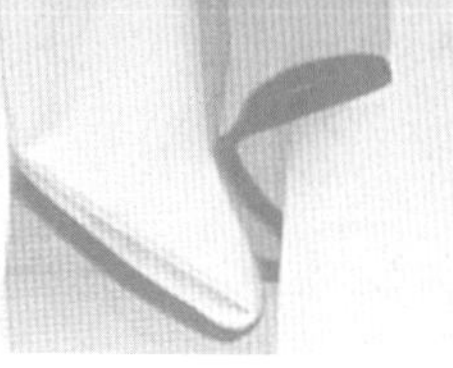

Right: Roy Hollis

An England Under-21 international, he won two Championship medals, a League Cup winners medal and he was on the bench for a European Cup Final. His City league goal was at Anfield (of all places) and his perfect league cup record for City was a hat-trick against Millwall. He later moved into management. A little-known fact is that he was Bryan Gunn's best man.

HOLD, Oscar

(1947–1948) **1948:** 5/9; 11/0
Centre Forward **Career:** 47-0-20
Debut: 1 Mar 47 **Final:** 9 Oct 48 (goal)

Born: Carlton, Barnsley 19 Oct 1918

Career: Regent Street Congregationals; Denaby United; Manchester United 'A'; Barnsley Aug 1937; Aldershot 01.04.39; Second World War guested for Aldershot, Barnsley, Bradford City, Burnley, Chelsea and Derby County; NORWICH CITY 01.03.46; Notts County 09.10.48; Chelmsford City Aug 1949; Everton 24.02.50; Queens Park Rangers 23.02.52; March Town Jul 1953 player-manager; Gainsborough Trinity manager; Wisbech Town Feb 1957 player-manager to Feb 1960; FA coach in Nigeria Jun 1960–Oct 1960; Cambridge City manager Mar 1961–Mar 1962; Doncaster Rovers Feb 1964 manager; Fenerbache (Turkey) Jan 1965; Ankara (Turkey) Feb 1966; National Sporting Club (Saudi Arabia) 1968; Apollon (Cyprus) 1972–1974; coaching in Kuwait to 1982; Apollon (Cyprus).

A much-travelled player and manager who has been working and living abroad for over 30 years. A somewhat basic description of him in the Pink 'Un *of 40 years ago said, 'He is a forceful type and can keep at it with rare zest'. Oscar had a remarkable debut for Notts County – four goals each from Lawton and Sewell and one from himself saw a 9–0 win over Exeter.*

HOLLIS, Roy Walter

(1948–1952) **1948:** 6/0; 11/5
Centre Forward **Career:** 107-0-59
Debut: 21 Apr 48 (3 goals) **Final:** 8 Mar 52 (goal)

Born: Great Yarmouth 24 Dec 1925
Died: Northgate 12 Nov 1998

Career: Yarmouth Town 31.08.46; RAF representative football; NORWICH CITY May 1947 (amat), 18.02.48 (pro); Tottenham Hotspur 23.12.52; Southend United 25.02.54; Chelmsford City 01.07.60; Yarmouth Town 21.10.61; Lowestoft Town Dec 1962–30.03.63.

The archetypal centre forward being a fast, powerful, persistent raider and a fine athlete. A startling City debut, a 20 minute hat-trick, was a prelude to goals galore. For the City firsts he hit one five, four threes and six twos, and still found time to net 54 reserve goals in only 88 games for them. He later managed to score over a century of goals for Southend including a threesome at Carrow Road on 27.12.54. Roy was a turf accountant for many years as well as working as an engineer and in haulage. His son Anthony related that Roy loved Frank Sinatra's music and that he was tipped to compete in the triple jump at the 1948 Olympic Games in London.

HOLMES, Bert Herbert Frank

(1949–1955) **1949:** 6/1; 12/0
Centre Half **Career:** 59-0-1
Debut: 30 Apr 49 **Final:** 29 Jan 55

Born: Norwich 27 Sept 1924

Career: Norman Old Boys; Royal Navy incl. v Eighth Army in Italy; Gothic; NORWICH CITY 25.08.47; Chelmsford City Jul 1955; Clacton Town Jul 1957; Gothic; Norman Old Boys; Norwich City All Stars.

A powerful player, with a style in keeping with his physique, who performed admirably in a career where his appearances were interestingly spaced. Among his 243 games for the Reserves was a Christmas Day match against Spurs when during the game he played at centre half, centre forward and in goal. He retired after 20 years at Jarrold's print works.

HOLT, Gary James

(2001– **2001:** 5/11; 11/3
Midfield **Career:** 8-1-0
Debut: 31 Mar 01

Born: Irvine 9 Mar 1973

Career: New Farm Loch Primary School; James Hamilton Academy; Loundon Academy; Army; B.A.O.R; Glasgow Celtic 1993; Stoke City 1994; Kilmarnock 18.08.95; NORWICH CITY 20.03.2001.

Scotland's manager Craig Brown described Scottish international Gary as a player who will put 90 minutes work into 15. Fearless and aggressive, he originally agreed to join Norwich on the day that Bryan Hamilton resigned. An ex-Army chef who was a fans' favourite at Kilmarnock, twice winning their Player of the Year award.

HOOPER, Charles

(1928) **1928:** 5/8; 10/5
Inside Right **Career:** 4-0-1
Debut: 10 Nov 28 **Final:** 1 Dec 28

Born: Darlington 23 Oct 1903
Died: Darlington 10 Aug 1972

Career: Darlington Railway Athletic; Crook Town; Lincoln City 10.03.25 (amat), 20.03.25 (pro); Sheffield Wednesday 07.06.26; NORWICH CITY 12.11.28 to Jan 1929; Darlington Wire Works.

Charlie's career saw three losses and a 6–1 Cup win before his papers were cancelled by City for, it was said, 'breaking discipline'. Of footballing stock with three brothers who played the game, Daniel, Frederick and Mark. Mark was the most famous of the four, being a 'regular box of tricks' and later the manager of Sheffield Public Tennis Courts. He was also the nephew of former Manchester United and England player Charlie Roberts.

HOPE, Philip

(1921–1924) **1922:** 6/0; 13/7
Right Back **Career:** 109-0-1
Debut: 17 Feb 21 **Final:** 3 May 24

Born: Kimblesworth 24 Apr 1897
Died: Durham 3 Jan 1969

Career: Northumberland Schools League; Washington Colliery; Durham City; Croxdale Colliery; Sunderland (trial); NORWICH CITY 1919, signing pro forms 29.08.20; Blackburn Rovers 19.5.24; Southend United 06.09.26; Clapton Orient 15.06.27; Washington Colliery Oct 1928; Rochdale 20.05.29–May 1930.

The 1923/24 City Handbook said of Phil, 'Tall and well-built with youth on his side, he should go far in the game'. He did indeed develop into a high-class back in partnership with either Hodge, Smith or Sturgess. He was well respected and fondly remembered. Outside of football he was a retired general labourer.

HOPEWELL, Thomas Henry (Harry)

(1920–1922) **1921:** 5/11; 11/6
Left Half **Career:** 27-0-0
Debut: 1 Sep 20 **Final:** 1 May 22

Born: Basford 12 Aug 1896
Died: Nottingham 24 Mar 1968

Career: Coventry Road School; Bagnall Rovers; Basford United; Nottingham Forest; WW1 captain of 29th Brigade Artillery; Bulwell Jun 1919; NORWICH CITY 27.08.20; Ilkeston United Aug 1922; Grantham Town; Loughborough Corinthians Aug 1925.

Harry was a perky and tenacious half back. He became the 12th Football League debutant for City despite missing three penalties for the Reserves in one season. Tracing him led us a merry dance as he was listed in the League records as Henry; had a first name of Thomas but was known universally as Harry.

HOUGHTON, Harold

(1934–1935) **1934:** 5/9; 10/10
Inside Left **Career:** 56-0-10
Debut: 10 Mar 34 **Final:** 19 Oct 35

Born: Liverpool 26 Aug 1906
Died: Liverpool 3 Feb 1986

Career: Anfield Social; England Under-15; Everton 26.01.22 (amat), 26.12.23 (pro); Exeter City 15.06.28; NORWICH CITY 09.03.34; Bristol Rovers 01.11.35; South Liverpool 24.09.37.

He played with Dixie Dean and Cliff Bastin, and Exeter once refused £3,000 for him as they were unwilling to split his great partnership with Percy Varco. 'Happy' was regarded as one of the best forwards in Division Two and had a final career total of over 300 games for 100 goals.

HOWARD, Trevor Edward

(1968–1974) **1970:** 5/7; 10/10
Utility **Career:** 111-45-19
Debut: 10 Feb 68 (sub) **Final:** 10 Aug 74

Born: King's Lynn 2 Jun 1949

Career: Gaywood Park Secondary Modern School; North End; Norfolk County; NORWICH CITY 28.05.65 (app), 15.07.67 (pro); Bournemouth 16.08.74; Cambridge United 03.07.76 to 1978.

His 45 substitute appearances for City plus being an unused Number 12 on 20 occasions is an indicator as to how he was 'used' while at Carrow Road. Scorer of the first goal by a City substitute, his reserve form (160 apps–28 goals) invariably meant that he was recalled to the seniors. A small frame housed a busy style and of the matches that he started he only failed to finish in ten of them, so proving to be a worthy player, a reputation to which he added at his next two clubs.

HOWELL, Henry Robert

(1926) **1926:** 5/4; 9/0
Outside Left **Career:** 4-0-0
Debut: 5 Apr 26 **Final:** 21 Apr 26

Born: Norwich 28 Jun 1895
Died: Norwich 15 Jan 1935

Career: Sherwood Foresters; Norwich City Supporters Club; NORWICH CITY 29.03.26; Sherwood Foresters.

Henry helped his previous club win the Norfolk Thursday Cup in March 1926 and scored for the reserves two days before his debut in the league. It was reported that 'He squared the ball accurately time after time and proved to be an acquisition to the team'. He was a sergeant home on leave from the Sherwood Foresters and he left for India with the Green Howards in September 1926. He was host at the Bishop Bridge Tavern, Norwich at the time of his demise.

HOWIE, Scott

(1994) **1993:** 6/1; 14/4
Goalkeeper **Career:** 1-1-0
Debut: 5 Feb 94 (sub) **Final:** 19 Feb 94

Born: Glasgow 4 Jan 1972

Career: Lenzie Youth Club; Dundee FC (trial); Dundee Boys Club Under-18; Lenzie Academy; Harestanes AFC 18–19; Clyde; NORWICH CITY 19.08.93; Motherwell Nov 1994; Coventry City (loan) Jan 1998; Reading 26.03.98–30.05.2001; Bristol Rovers Aug 2001.

Five Under-21 Scottish caps, but he spent most of his time at Norwich on the bench. His debut came as a result of Gunn's sending-off against Liverpool. He performed admirably at Motherwell, regularly appearing on Sky TV in their coverage of Scottish football. Has been back at Carrow Road playing for Reading's reserve side.

HOWSHALL, Gerald Thomas

(1968–1970) **1970:** 5/7; 11/2
Left Half **Career:** 37-6-0
Debut: 20 Jan 68 **Final:** 21 Nov 70

Born: Stoke 27 Oct 1944

Career: Thursham & Newton Abbott Schools; Torbay & Brixham Boys; Plymouth Argyle (amat); West Bromwich Albion 11.05.62; NORWICH CITY 04.11.67; Nuneaton Borough Jul 1971; Weymouth Jun 1973 retiring 1974.

Gerry was unusually signed at an Annual Supporters Club Dinner and he was unlucky in that his progress was halted by illness and injury. Added to his four season first-team career are 63 reserve games for five goals. His uncle John played for six league clubs in the 1930s.

HUBBARD, Philip John

(1971–1972) **1972:** 6/0; 12/2
Midfield **Career:** 6-4-1
Debut: 27 Dec 71 **Final:** 2 Sep 72 (sub)

Born: Lincoln 25 Jan 1949

Career: St Giles School; Lincoln Boys Under-11–15; Lincoln United 1963; Blanchard Sports 1964; Lincoln City Oct 1965 (app), 04.07.66 (pro); NORWICH CITY 27.12.71; Grimsby Town 25.10.72; Lincoln City 17.08.76; Columbus Magic (USA) Apr 1979–Sep 1979; Boston United Nov 1979; Skegness Town May 1982 player-manager; Ruston Sports Apr 1983.

Phil played over 400 games in his career, which showed his durability and was required to play. Tall, muscular and forceful in the tackle, he was signed by City to help stiffen the sinews of the senior squad, and he was unfortunate to have played just 34 minutes in Division One. He has the same birthdate as Phil Boyer.

HUGHES, John Paul

(1999) **1999:** 6/0; 12/6
Midfield **Career:** 2-2-1
Debut: 24 Mar 99 (sub) **Final:** 1 May 99 (goal)

Born: Hammersmith 19 Apr 1976

Career: Horsenden First & Middle School; Brentside High School; Bourne End Boys Club; Belmont Boys Club; Chelsea 11.07.94 (trainee),

07.03.97 (pro); NORWICH CITY (trial) 1998; Bristol City (loan) 10.10.98; Stockport County (loan) 17.12.98; NORWICH CITY (loan) 24.03.99; Crewe Alexandra (trial) 24.12.99; Southampton (loan) 23.02.2000, (signed) 01.10.2000; Luton Town 10.08.2001.

'A forward-thinking player who can pass the ball,' enthused manager Bruce Rioch. Once scorer of a Goal of the Season contender at Stamford Bridge, but like so many others at that club he was bypassed in favour of the Continental imports. Shin splints and a pelvic strain were overcome and he was at Carrow Road just long enough to score with a fine volley against Swindon Town.

HUNT, Morgan Marshall

(1958) **1958:** 5/11; 12/0
Right Half **Career:** 8-0-0
Debut: 25 Aug 58 **Final:** 22 Nov 58

Born: Bridgend 5 Mar 1931

Career: Askern Sutton Road School; Askern YC; Askern Welfare; Doncaster Rovers 27.02.52; NORWICH CITY 26.07.58; Port Vale 01.08.59; Boston United 1974; Askern Welfare 1976–1978 player-manager.

Joined City from Doncaster for a small fee after playing 50 league games for them. His actual last City appearance was in the abandoned match at Mansfield. To his total are added 21 reserve games for three goals. Noel Kinsey was with him at his last league club.

HUNT, Ralph Arthur Robert

(1955–1958) **1964:** 5/11; 12/0
Centre Forward **Career:** 132-0-72
Debut: 20 Aug 55 **Final:** 7 Apr 58

Born: Portsmouth 14 Aug 1933
Died: Grantham 17 Dec 1964

Career: Gloucester City 1949; Portsmouth (junior), 1950 (groundstaff), 18.08.50 (pro); Bournemouth 19.02.54; NORWICH CITY 07.07.55; Derby County 04.08.58; Grimsby Town 30.07.59; Swindon Town 23.06.61; Port Vale 08.12.61; Newport County 18.07.62; Chesterfield Jul 1964 to Dec 1964.

A dashing leader of the forward line with a marvellous scoring record at all his clubs, after hitting the headlines at Carrow Road. His first season club record total of 33 goals is likely to stand for many years. His brother Dennis made over 300 appearances for Gillingham. Ralph died in the Grantham and Kesteven Hospital from injuries sustained in a car crash.

Left: Ralph Hunt
Right: Thomas Hunt

HUNT, Thomas

(1929–1932) **1930:** 5/9; 11/8
Centre Forward **Career:** 51-0-33
Debut: 5 Oct 29 (goal) **Final:** 17 Sep 32

Born: West Bromwich 23 Jun 1908
Died: Hallam Hospital, West Bromwich 15 Jan 1975

Career: Wednesbury Town; Stourbridge; Birmingham (Central League); Wednesbury Town; Wolverhampton Wanderers 03.10.28; NORWICH CITY (loan) 10.05.29; Wolverhampton Wanderers 09.06.30; NORWICH CITY 27.11.30; Drumcondra Aug 1933; Watford 19.06.34; Oakengates Town (trial) Aug 1937.

After scoring five goals in his first home reserve game he burst onto the City scene in a sensational manner by netting in nine of his first ten league games. Wolves then reckoned that Tommy was only on loan to Norwich and they wanted him back. The City Directors and Supporters got together to buy him back but he did not reproduce his early brilliance. He later worked in the steel industry.

JACK, James Ross

(1980–1983) **1980:** 5/10; 11/2
Forward **Career:** 39-28-14
Debut: 23 Sep 80 **Final:** 2 May 83 (sub)

Born: Inverness 21 Mar 1959

Career: Ross County; Everton 08.02.77; Cardiff City (loan) 06.10.79; NORWICH CITY 28.12.79; Lincoln City 18.08.83; Dundee Jul 1985; Dunfermline 22.10.87; Kilmarnock 09.07.91; Sligo Rovers (loan) Jan 1993–Mar 1993; Montrose 24.03.93 player-manager; Ayr United 15.10.93.

An apprenticeship at Everton and a scoring League debut in his only game for them in March 1979. Converted to a midfielder with a brief to get forward, which he did to fine effect,

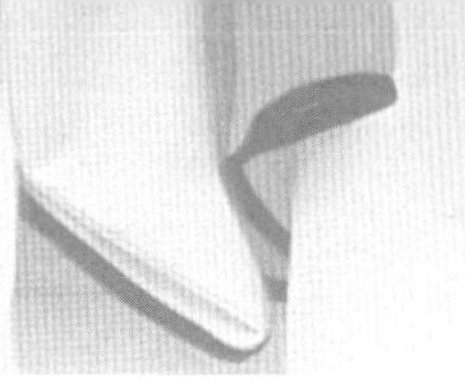

once netting in six successive League games for City. He showed the knack of getting into the right positions but was invariably used as a substitute as he was useful in a variety of roles. Presently an SFA Football Development Officer.

Left: James Jackson
Right: Matt Jackson

JACKSON, James Herbert

(1923–1927)	**1925:** 5/8; 11/12
Centre Forward	**Career:** 119-0-57
Debut: 27 Aug 23	**Final:** 24 Dec 27

Born: Bollington, Cheshire 27 Dec 1897
Died: Bollington 23 Dec 1964

Career: Lower House FC; Bollington Cross FC; Stockport County (trial); Macclesfield Town; Bollington Cross FC; Derby County 20.12.20 (amat), 06.01.21 (pro); NORWICH CITY 01.06.23 to 1927.

One of a fine succession of City centre forwards down the years who was not handicapped by his lack of height. The first player to top 20 goals in a season in the Football League for City, he regularly reached double figures in this regard until he broke his leg at Bristol City. Post-War he was working in a Bollington Mill and also in the building trade.

JACKSON, Matthew Alan

(1996–	**1996:** 6/1; 12/7
Defender	**Career:** 169-3-6
Debut: 26 Dec 96	

Born: Leeds 19 Oct 1971

Career: Sharnbrook Colts; Sharnbrook Upper School; Bedford & District; Bedfordshire: Riseley FC; Raunds Town Youth; Luton Town 13.11.86 (assoc); England Under-18–21; Luton Town 04.07.90 (pro); Preston North End (loan) 27.03.91; Everton 18.10.91; Charlton Athletic (loan) 27.03.96; Queens Park Rangers (loan) 20.08.96; Birmingham City (loan) 31.10.96; NORWICH CITY 23.12.96.

Former captain of England Under-18s and 21s and an FA Cup winner with Everton. He has given a string of high quality performances winning the Canaries' Player of the Year award in 1997/8. Not bad for a player who honed his skills at the Maardi International School playing barefoot Egyptian kids kicking a tin can.

JARVIE, John

(1929–1930)	**1929:** 5/9; 11/0
Goalkeeper	**Career:** 44-0-0
Debut: 31 Aug 29	**Final:** 3 May 30

Born: Old Monkland 19 Oct 1900
Died: Leicester 30 Jan 1985

Career: Bell's Hill Athletic Juniors; Bell's Hill Athletic; Third Lanark 13.06.23; Leicester City 13.05.25; Portsmouth 30.10.26; Southend United 13.03.28; Watford (trial) Jul 1929; NORWICH CITY 14.08.29; Chester Aug 1930; Shrewsbury Town Aug 1931; Solus FC Sep 1933.

He arrived at the Nest with wide experience having played in Division One with Leicester and Portsmouth. The Pink 'Un *said of him, 'Although lacking in inches for a custodian, he handled the ball cleanly. He pulls down the high ball in a very workmanlike manner'. A retired lorry driver.*

JOBLING, Joseph

(1929–1932)	**1930:** 5/10; 11/7
Right/Left Half	**Career:** 76-0-1
Debut: 9 Sep 29	**Final:** 5 Mar 32

Born: Annfield Plain, Co. Durham 29 Jul 1906
Died: Yarmouth 20 Jul 1969

Career: Sunderland Cooperatives; South Pontop Villa; Langley Park; Annfield Plain (trial) Aug 1925, (signed) Aug 1926; Gorleston Oct 1927; Norfolk County 1927–1929; NORWICH CITY 22.08.28 (amat), 10.05.29 (pro); Charlton Athletic 17.03.32 to May 1947, scout 1958–1962.

Formerly a miner, Joe was a strong, fearless player, with tackling and backing up the best features of his play. He played a gallant part in Charlton's rise to the top class, making over 200 appearances for them. In 1957/58 he was on Gorleston's committee and he was later the team manager. Subsequently in the catering trade; ran a fish shop and was in partnership in a turf accountants.

JOHNSON, Alexander

(1938–1939)	**1938:** 5/5 11/4
Right Back	**Career:** 5-0-0

Debut: 7 Sep 38 **Final:** 11 Feb 39

Born: Gateshead 5 Dec 1917
Died: South Arabian Coast 30 Aug 1944

Career: Birtley (amat); NORWICH CITY 08.10.37 (amat), 05.11.37 (pro); Second World War guested for Middlesbrough and Leeds United.

A Sport's Journalist opinion of him in his early days was, 'Has all the attributes of a good un'. As Corporal 905035 with the SAAF Squadron he met his death on active service and he is included in Jack Rollin's Roll of Honour in Soccer at War 1939–1945 at our request.

JOHNSON, Andrew James

(1992–1997) **1992:** 6/0; 12/0
Midfield **Career:** 64-11-15
Debut: 20 Apr 92 **Final:** 4 Mar 97

Born: Bristol 2 May 1974

Career: Brislington School; St Valier; Avon Athletic; Bristol Boys; Avon County; NORWICH CITY 16.12.88 (schoolboy), Dec 1989 (youth), 10.07.90 (pro); Nottingham Forest 02.07.97.

A Pink 'Un article early in Andy's career said, 'He has the dream of being a professional within his grasp. As the captain of City's youth team he has all the attributes to move to higher grade of football'. Recovering from a succession of injuries he was head and shoulders above his youth counterparts. He scored the goal that ultimately clinched third place for Norwich in the Premier league.

JOHNSON, Victor Ralph

(1946–1947) **1946:** 5/10; 11/0
Centre Forward **Career:** 23-0-10
Debut: 7 Sep 46 **Final:** 8 Mar 47

Born: Hethersett 15 Apr 1922

Career: Chesterfield (amat); NORWICH CITY 1942 signing league pro 17.05.46; Orient 24.04.47; Lowestoft Town 25.11.50–03.05.51.

During the Second World War he was invariably described as being brilliant near goal. In Wartime games for City he hammered 123 goals in 107 matches, including five threes, two fours, two fives and two sixes. Actually scored in 19 successive matches and in 24 of 25 with one spell of 13 goals in three games. His fleeting league career saw him have a spell in goal on his debut day for City, plus he netted the quickest goal from a kick-off at Carrow Road on 19.10.46.

Andy Johnson

JOHNSTON, Thomas Bourhill

(1952–1954) **1952:** 5/11; 11/7
Centre Forward **Career:** 67-0-33
Debut: 23 Aug 52 (goal) **Final:** 23 Sep 54

Born: Loanhead, Midlothian 18 Aug 1927

Career: Loanhead Mayflower; Peebles Rovers May 1949; Third Lanark (trial); Kilmarnock 30.11.49; Darlington 21.04.51; Oldham Athletic 01.03.52; NORWICH CITY 19.6.52; Newport County 16.10.54; Leyton Orient 24.02.56; Blackburn Rovers 07.03.58; Leyton Orient 14.02.59; Gillingham 20.09.61; Folkestone Town 06.07.62 player coach; Lytham St Annes Oct 1965; Lysaghts (Australia) coach.

Tom always wore a bandage on his left wrist as protection for an injury received in the pits. A rugged-looking Scot who had a career total to his name of just over 200 goals thereby failing in his personal ambition of surpassing the number reached by Hugh Gallacher. He emigrated to Australia in 1972.

JONES, Brynmor

(1949–1950) **1949:** 5/6; 10/0
Inside Forward **Career:** 26-0-2
Debut: 20 Aug 49 **Final:** 25 Feb 50

Born: Merthyr Tydfil 2 Feb 1912
Died: Wood Green 18 Oct 1985

Career: Queens Road School; Merthyr Amateurs; Plymouth United (amat); Southend United (trial); Swansea Town (trial); Glenavon 1932/3; Aberaman Aug 1933; Wolverhampton Wanderers 04.11.33; Arsenal 04.08.38; NORWICH CITY 23.06.49, Feb 1951 player coach.

This soccer immortal spent a few fleeting months as a Canary. A Welsh international who in 1938 was the games most expensive player. At his peak there were few men who

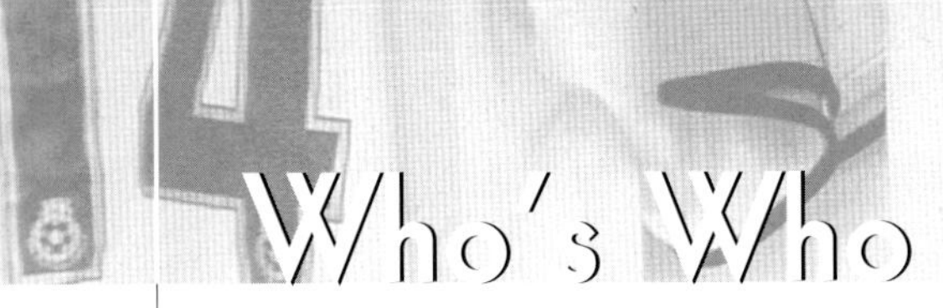

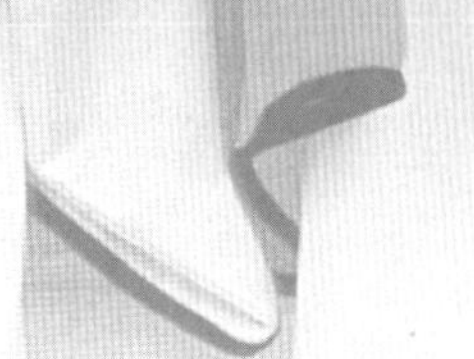

could bring the ball under control as quickly or as smoothly as Bryn. He had a newsagent's shop near Highbury and when he was asked for a treasured autograph in later life he was genuinely taken aback by the request – such was his shy, modest nature. (It was the author who asked him.)

JONES, David Edward

(1975–1980) **1976:** 6/1; 12/8
Centre Half **Career:** 128-4-5
Debut: 18 Oct 75 **Final:** 3 May 80

Born: Gosport 11 Feb 1952

Career: Portsmouth (assoc); Gosport Borough; Fareham Town; Bournemouth 28.01.70; Nottingham Forest 16.08.74; NORWICH CITY 26.09.75 April 1980; Wroxham Aug 1982–Oct 1985; Bournemouth part time coach; Lymington coach; New Milton coach.

A sound, powerful defender impressing all with his aerial dominance. A Welsh international who maintained his will-to-win attitude in his later successful Anglian Combination career. He will be remembered as the innocent party in the 'handball' clash with Joe Jordan (Scotland) that cost Wales a place in the 1978 World Cup Finals.

JONES, Denys John

(1951–1953) **1952:** 5/8; 9/9
Outside Right **Career:** 6-0-2
Debut: 29 Dec 51 (goal) **Final:** 24 Jan 53

Born: Aberdare 19 Oct 1930

Career: Cardiff City (groundstaff); Yarmouth Town 02.10.48; NORWICH CITY 23.04.51; Chelmsford City 1953; Wisbech Town 1955; Yarmouth Town 1957–26.04.58; Lowestoft Town 27.09.58–08.04.61; Gothic retiring 1969.

Couldn't have had a better start to his career – a goal in an 8–0 win over Walsall. He had been on the Carrow Road ground staff before and left because he was not offered terms. Denys showed confidence and poise and boldly attacked his back before returning to his regular place in the Reserves.

JONES, Eric Sidney

(1946–1948) **1946:** 5/8; 10/2
Outside Left **Career:** 48-0-10
Debut: 18 Sep 46 (goal) **Final:** 24 Jan 48

Born: Wrexham 10 Oct 1921
Died: Norwich 25 Apr 1981

Career: Bolton Wanderers 19.08.38; NORWICH CITY 21.12.45–01.05.48; March Town Aug 1948 player-manager; King's Lynn Sep 1951.

Sid fashioned many a chance from the wing after guesting for City during the Second World War. He was too young to join the Bolton team of Territorials in their en bloc call to the Middle East. Norwich signed him for just £500 and it was unfortunate that he lost productive years to the war. He was a café manager and passed away locally.

JONES, John Allan

(1962–1963) **1962:** 6/1; 12/7
Goalkeeper **Career:** 9-0-0
Debut: 15 Dec 62 **Final:** 21 Aug 63

Born: Cefn Mawr 12 Sep 1939

Career: Druids; Cardiff City Jun 1957 (amat), 09.05.58 (pro); Exeter City 14.07.59; NORWICH CITY 25.07.62; Wrexham 28.08.63; Worcester City Jul 1964; Witton Albion; Ellesmere Port Town; Sydney Club (Australia).

Managed the above appearances in the middle of Sandy Kennon's tenure. City swapped keepers with Wrexham and gained one Kevin Keelan. Emigrated to Australia, becoming a policeman and then working in a haulage company business.

JONES, Ormond Henry

(1935) **1935:** 6/0; 11/8
Goalkeeper **Career:** 10-0-0
Debut: 6 Feb 35 **Final:** 30 Mar 35

Born: Towyn, nr Abergele 24 August 1910
Died: Bilston 10 Apr 1972

Career: St Saviours School; Bilston Schoolboys; Hickman's Town; Towyn; Bilston United cs 1928; Wednesbury Town; Staffordshire County; Shrewsbury Town Apr 1930; Blackpool Mar 1932; Yeovil & Petters United Jun 1932; Port Vale 17.05.33; NORWICH CITY 01.06.34; Watford 01.02.35; Mansfield Town 31.07.36; Buxton; Winsford United (trial) Aug 1937; NORWICH CITY 08.09.37; Queen of the South Jul 1938; Yarmouth Town 22.10.38–01.05.39.

Teetotal and a non-smoker, he took the game seriously. A former Welsh Schoolboy international, he returned and played for Norwich City reserves in September 1937 following injury to the regular keeper. He moved annually in the professional game and later had a boarding house in Gorleston.

JORDAN, Hugh McNaughton

(1930–1931) **1930:** 5/9; 11/0
Inside Forward **Career:** 20-0-3
Debut: 8 Sep 30 **Final:** 25 Apr 31

Born: Musselburgh 24 Jul 1908

Career: Falkirk 18.06.28; NORWICH CITY 07.07.30 to 1931, Margate Oct 1934; Stade de Reims (France) 1935–1938; Dunkerque (France) 1937/8; Stade de Reims (France) 1938/9.

The Athletic News Annual *credited him with seven appearances for Falkirk. For City he was a forager and link man and one of eight casualties in the last month of a disastrous season. Fractured his arm in a midfield melee in Rotterdam while playing for Norwich City. Another traveller over Hadrian's Wall who has defied all attempts to trace him. Does any reader know of him?*

JOY, Harold Cuthbert

(1947) **1947:** 5/11; 11/7
Centre Forward **Career:** 8-0-4
Debut: 15 Mar 47 **Final:** 12 Apr 47

Born: Cardiff 8 Jan 1921
Died: Gwent 22 Feb 2000

Career: Spottland Schools; Cardiff Schools; Cardiff Corries; Margate; Lovell's Athletic; Pontllanfraith; NORWICH CITY 14.02.47; Ipswich Town 17.12.47; Newport County 08.01.48; Llanelly Aug 1948; Treharris; Chippenham Town; Pontllanfraith player-manager; Ebbw Vale District Schools coach

A 65-minute hat-trick for City in his second appearance and he had a brief stay at Portman Road without making the first team. Owner of an impish sense of humour. His weight according to him was '11 stone 7 pounds when it was raining'. A PTI in the RAF posted to East Anglia, which is why Ipswich and Norwich claimed his services. He later scouted most successfully for Newport County, Cardiff City, Spurs and Arsenal. A decorator; worked down the pits and in a steelworks.

KEARNS, Frederick Thomas

(1954–1955) **1954:** 5/10; 11/3
Centre Forward **Career:** 30-0-14
Debut: 26 Aug 54 (goal) **Final:** 26 Nov 55 (goal)

Born: Dublin 8 Jan 1927
Died: Margate 7 Jan 1987

Career: Shamrock Rovers; West Ham United 22.05.48; NORWICH CITY 09.06.54; Tonbridge Jul 1956; Margate Jul 1959; Deal Town; Margate Rangers Jan 1964 player coach.

An accomplished hurler before switching to soccer when 16. Made a Football League debut at full back on 08.10.49 before he was successfully switched to centre forward. Fred hit two 'Hammers' hat-tricks, and John Bond and Albert Foan were on his side when he scored his first trio against Bury on 03.01.53. He recovered from his first heart attack before succumbing one day short of his 60th birthday.

KEATING, Reginald

(1932) **1932:** 5/10; 12/2
Centre Forward **Career:** 3-0-0
Debut: 5 Sep 32 **Final:** 26 Nov 32

Born: Halton 14 May 1904
Died: North Walbottle 13 Oct 1961

Career: Halton Grange; Annfield Plain Nov 1925; Scotswood May 1926; Newcastle United 20.10.26; Lincoln City 08.07.27; Gainsborough Trinity Jun 1928; Scarborough Town May 1929; Stockport County 12.05.30; Birmingham City 04.06.31; NORWICH CITY 10.06.32; Cardiff City 15.06.33; North Shields (trial) Aug 1933; Bath City Dec 1933; Yeovil & Petters United; Cardiff City 08.01.34; Doncaster Rovers 20.06.36; Bournemouth 26.11.36; Carlisle United 06.07.37; Blyth Spartans Jun 1938.

A sprinter but overshadowed by his elder brother Albert, who was a fine goalscorer for four clubs. Reg though was able enough to notch nearly 50 career goals including threes v Aldershot & Millwall plus four v Exeter (all with Cardiff). His Nest opportunities were rare and the Cup defeat against Folkestone proved to be his last game for City. He died at a pithead baths.

KEELAN, Kevin Damien

(1963–1980) **1970:** 5/11; 12/10
Goalkeeper **Career:** 673-0-0
Debut: 24 Aug 63 **Final:** 9 Feb 80

Born: Calcutta, India 5 Jan 1941

Career: St Ambrose Roman Catholic School; Worcestershire Schools; Carpet Traders FC; Kidderminster Harriers; Aston Villa 1957 (junior), 05.07.58; Stockport County 04.04.61; Kidderminster Harriers; Wrexham 13.11.61; NORWICH CITY 18.07.63 to Feb 1980, although had spells with New England Tea Men (USA) Apr 1978–Aug 1980; Tampa Bay Rowdies (USA) May 1981–Sep 1981; Tampa Bay Rowdies coach in the 1990's plus University of Tampa soccer coach.

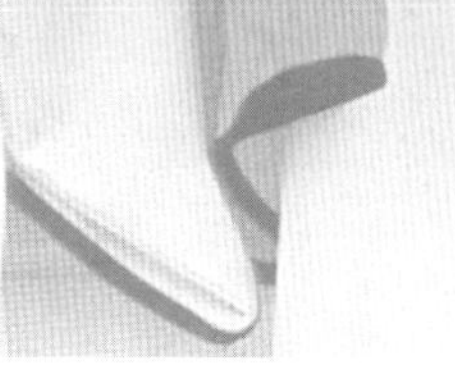

Kevin Keelan

Ron Ashman called him 'The bargain of the century'. Kevin – a spectacular, extrovert showman – overcame early hotheadedness and rashness (he was the first First XI keeper to be sent off) to consistently turn in 'blinders', twice winning the Player of the Year Award. Also voted the top Division One keeper by the Sunday People in 1978. Helped Norwich to the First Division twice; played in two League Cup Finals and he was a League ever-present in five seasons. An extrovert character who dealt with the goalframe falling on him in one game and had to face four penalties in another (only two were awarded –the first was retaken twice). His stage was the First Division and his daring, agility and dedication have surely ensured that he will remain as the longest serving City keeper of all time. He now lives in Florida and is a top salesman in contact lenses.

KEELING, Harold

(1932) **1932:** 5/9; 11/8
Inside Left **Career:** 5-0-1
Debut: 31 Aug 32 **Final:** 17 Sep 32

Born: Huthwaite, Nottingham 10 Feb 1906
Died: St Austell 24 Dec 1988

Career: Huthwaite CWS; Sutton Town; Gresley Rovers; Mansfield Town Feb 1926; Wolverhampton Wanderers 09.07.27; Notts County 18.08.28; Luton Town Feb 1929; Torquay United 09.09.29; Swindon Town 07.06.31; NORWICH CITY 20.05.32; Mansfield Town 10.07.33; Bath City Oct 1934; Sutton Town cs 1935; Hereford United cs 1936; Tamworth Town cs 1937; Brierley Hill Alliance cs 1938; Hereford United cs 1939.

Harry only made a career total of 54 Football League appearances, yet he scored 18 goals. Norwich City were alerted to his potential when he scored in both matches for Swindon Town against us in the previous season. When living in Weston-Super-Mare he related a tale of when he and a teammate were in the dressing room at half time: 'Ere, these b—s are better than us but we can stop them playing in the second half'. We think that the remark was made tongue-in-cheek.

KELL, Leonard William

(1954) **1954:** 5/9; 11/4
Inside Forward **Career:** 2-0-0
Debut: 25 Sep 54 **Final:** 29 Sep 54

Born: Billingham, nr Stockton-on-Tees 27 May 1932

Career: Chelsea 1948 (groundstaff), 23.02.50 (pro); Army; NORWICH CITY 09.06.54; Worcester City Jul 1955; Poole Town Jun 1956; Dorchester Town Jun 1959; Scarborough Town 1961; South Coast United 1963; Lowestoft Town 25.09.65–23.04.66.

A stockily built inside forward who joined Chelsea's ground staff in 1948 and had to wait until 08.09.53 before he made his Football League debut. His three First Division games against Arsenal, Huddersfield and Aston Villa exceeded the number that he played for City in the old Division Three South. Knee trouble brought about his retirement.

KELLOCK, William

(1973–1974) **1973:** 5/10; 10/11
Forward **Career:** 2-2-1
Debut: 4 Sep 73 (sub) **Final:** 13 Apr 74

Born: Glasgow 7 Feb 1954

Career: Glasgow Boys; Aston Villa Jun 1970; Cardiff City 12.07.71 (amat), 12.08.71 (app), 09.02.72 (pro); NORWICH CITY 22.05.73; Millwall 01.07.74; Chelmsford City 12.10.74; Kettering Town Feb 1976; Peterborough United 06.08.79; Luton Town 20.07.82; Wolverhampton Wanderers 09.03.83; Southend United 08.09.83; Port Vale 29.12.84; Halifax Town 02.07.86; Kettering Town Jul 1986.

Billy was another of the rolling-stone brigade and he had only a transient stay at Carrow Road. He was one of two City players sent off in an 'A' team game and he also played 34 reserve games for nine goals. Later scored on his debut for Peterborough and Wolves as he moved from club to club. Latterly the manager at the Barndale Country Club.

KELLY, James Philip Vincent

(1962–1966) **1964:** 5/9; 11/10
Right Back **Career:** 134-1-3
Debut: 12 Sep 62 **Final:** 10 Dec 66

Born: Dublin 10 Jul 1939

Career: Rosary School; Sparkhill Commercial School; Brookhill; Sheldon Town; Wolverhampton Wanderers 14.09.57; NORWICH CITY 09.08.62; Lowestoft Town May 1967 to Jun 1969 player coach; Newmarket Town; Thetford Town Nov 1971 player-manager; Reepham 1972; Thetford Town Jan 1975.

Once he was in the side Phil was a first-team regular and a consistent partner to Mullett, Thurlow and Staton until his forced retirement with a knee injury. He won five Eire caps while at Wolves and was signed by them in the West Bromwich Albion dressing room. He played in goal when Keelan was sent off against Northampton Town. He didn't let in a goal that day in a City side that had 1,414 appearances between them for the club.

KENNING, Michael John

(1966–1968) **1964:** 5/8; 10/12
Winger **Career:** 50-0-11
Debut: 26 Dec 66 **Final:** 10 Jan 68

Born: Birmingham 18 Aug 1940

Career: Slade Road School; Erdington & Birmingham District Schools; Brookhill; Aston Villa Jan 1957 (amat), 27.10.59 (pro); Shrewsbury Town 30.05.61; Charlton Athletic 02.11.62; NORWICH CITY 23.12.66; Wolverhampton Wanderers 12.01.68; Charlton Athletic 13.03.69; Queens Park Rangers May 1971; Watford 30.12.71; Atherstone Town Aug 1973; player-manager 4 years; Atherstone Town; Malvern Town; Germiston Dallies (South Africa); Durban United (South Africa) 1979 manager; Witts University (South Africa) part time manager.

Mike cost City a then-record fee for a winger of £25,000. He was a slim, raiding winger with a fierce shot who scored one goal for Wolves at Ipswich that earned cheers from Ipswich fans – rare praise indeed! 411 League games for 88 goals is testimony to a fine career. He now lives in South Africa working as a sales representative for a safety equipment company.

KENNON, Neil Sandilands (Sandy)

(1959–1964) **1964:** 6/1; 13/0
Goalkeeper **Career:** 255-0-0
Debut: 4 Mar 59 **Final:** 4 Nov 64

Sandy Kennon

Born: Regent's Park, nr Johannesburg, South Africa 26 Nov 1933

Career: Umbilo FC; Berea Park (Durban); Queen's Park (Bulawayo); Huddersfield Town 07.08.56; NORWICH CITY (trial) 05.02.59, (signed) 09.03.59; Colchester United 05.03.65 to May 1967; Lowestoft Town 19.08.67–10.04.70.

First spotted playing for Rhodesia against a touring FA XI, and from his Football League debut on 08.09.56 to his last appearance he was a credit to the game. Anyone who had a Dance Band called 'Sandy Kennon and the Blazers' has to be a character, and Sandy is rightly one of Norwich's favourite sons. Still living locally, he has had a varied career with bookmaker's interests and an executive role for a whiskey firm. I've always liked him!

KENT, Paul

(1974) **1974:** 5/8; 10/7
Full Back **Career:** 2-2-0
Debut: 6 Apr 74 (sub) **Final:** 10 Aug 74

Born: Rotherham 23 Feb 1954

Career: Roughwood Junior School; Whiston Junior School; Wickersley Secondary Modern School; Rotherham Boys; NORWICH CITY Jul 1970 (amat), 24.02.72 (pro); Halifax Town 14.08.76; Cambridge United 30.07.77; Norwich City All Stars; Unity Emeralds.

Had a first-team debut against Manchester United, coming on for Mel Machin in a relegation season but was unable to secure a regular place in the side. He gave good service to City though, with over 100 games for the Reserves starting with his debut for them on 15.8.70. Now runs his own local hairdressing business after suffering a dislocated knee that ended his career.

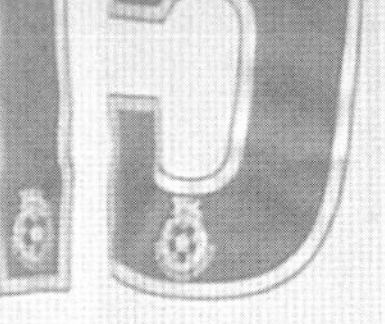
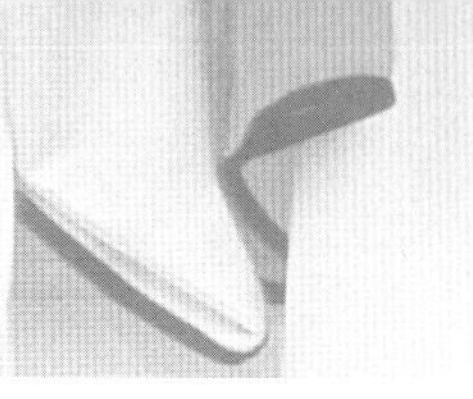

Left: Darren Kenton
Right: Noel Kinsey

KENTON, Darren Edward

(1997– **1997:** 5/10; 11/11
Defender **Career:** 88-15-4
Debut: 4 Oct 97

Born: Wandsworth 13 Sep 1978

Career: Leighton County Primary School; Walton School; Lofton United Under-11–13; Woodston Dynamoes; Peterborough Schools Under-13; NORWICH CITY Under-14–16, 07.07.95 (trainee), 11.04.97 (pro).

Darren was the youngest of three brothers; the family moved to Peterborough when Darren was aged one. A graduate of the championship-winning youth team of 1996/7, he has progressed to be a first-team regular with his well-timed tackles, aerial ability and pace being to the fore.

KIDGER, Edmund Alt

(1920) **1920:** 5/7; 11/0
Inside Right **Career:** 4-0-0
Debut: 28 Aug 20 **Final:** 8 Sep 20

Born: Derby 16 Jul 1892
Died: Sheffield 9 Oct 1976

Career: Kent Road School; Sheffield United 28.08.13; Worksop Town cs 1914; R.A.S.C.; NORWICH CITY 27.08.20; Peterborough & Fletton United Sep 1921.

All his appearances ended in draws and a scribe of the day stated, 'Proved a disappointment and his successor was the classier Dennison'. Surprising as he had won medals for football in the Midlands and in the Army, and he was a useful scorer for the Reserves with one hat-trick against Beccles being memorable.

KING, Alfred Page

(1921–1922) **1921:** 5/11; 11/0
Goalkeeper **Career:** 3-0-0
Debut: 31 Dec 21 **Final:** 11 Feb 22

Born: Swardeston, Norfolk 26 Nov 1895
Died: Swardeston, Norfolk 12 Jul 1975

Career: CEYMS Thursday; NORWICH CITY Sep 1915–Nov 1916 and Mar 1918, 08.09.20 (amat)–Dec 1925; Norfolk County 1919–1922.

A great servant to local football, patrolling the penalty area in Norfolk trials and ultimately County games. He played in 40 war friendlies for City, rising from private to corporal within the period. Attached to Norwich from their Southern League days, he earned his Football League games although they came in unfortunate circumstances as Herbert Skermer was sidelined through injury and a family bereavement.

KINSEY, Noel

(1947–1953) **1948:** 5/7; 10/4
Inside Right **Career:** 243-0-65
Debut: 30 Aug 47 **Final:** 2 May 53

Born: Treorchy, Glamorgan 24 Dec 1925

Career: Treorchy Amateurs 1938; Second World War for Cardiff City 04.03.41–04.05.46; NORWICH CITY 02.06.47; Birmingham City 16.06.53; Port Vale 25.02.58; Cheltenham Town Jul 1961; King's Lynn 11.04.62; Lowestoft Town 16.06.62–Aug 1966 player coach.

A Welsh international and a Birmingham Cup Final scorer, Noel changed from being a roving opportunist to that of a scheming craftsman, making openings for his colleagues with defence splitting passes. He still retained a penchant for the surprise shot at goal and he is 12th in the list of City all-time goalscorers. Now lives in retirement from his job at a local insurance company.

KIRCHEN, Alfred John

(1934–1935) **1935:** 5/10; 12/6
Outside Right **Career:** 18-0-10
Debut: 28 Apr 34 **Final:** 23 Feb 35 (goal)

Born: Shouldham, Norfolk 28 Apr 1913
Died: Norwich 17 Aug 1999

Career: Middleton School; King's Lynn Schools; King's Lynn Old Boys; Shouldham; NORWICH CITY 12.10.33 (amat), 02.11.33 (pro); Arsenal 01.03.35–11.09.43.

A former carpenter's apprentice whose contract of May 1934 earned him £2.12s.6d. per week from 07.05.34 to 20.08.34, rising to £4 per week for the playing season. He scored three hat-tricks for the Reserves and was given his chance at the end of City's Championship season. A speedy, dashing, forceful, sharpshooting eagle of the wing who later won England honours together with Championship and Cup medals. Alf was a double international, as he won the 1955 Clay Pigeon Championship of Great Britain and shot for England. Later a City director and an award-winning farmer.

KITCHENER, Raymond Alan

(1956–1957) **1956:** 5/9; 11/4
Inside Left **Career:** 19-0-0
Debut: 8 Sep 56 **Final:** 27 Apr 57

Born: Letchworth, Hertfordshire 31 Oct 1930

Career: Letchworth Boys Club; Letchworth Town 1946–1950 (amat); Hitchin Town 1952 (amat); Chelsea 10.07.54; NORWICH CITY 07.09.56; Biggleswade Town 01.07.57; Amesbury Rovers 1963; Stofold FC 1966–1969.

Ray played his one First Division game on 11 February 1956 at Maine Road. His other Chelsea games were friendlies against Baltimore Rockets, Borussia Dortmund, Lens (France), Dutch National XI, Rouen (France) and Aberdeen. For City he was a direct, unselfish inside forward who was equally at home on the left wing. Ray returned to his trade of Electrician and lives back in his home town.

KNOX, William

(1929) **1929:** 5/8; 10/11
Outside Right **Career:** 3-0-0
Debut: 9 Sep 29 **Final:** 16 Sep 29

Born: Old Cumnock 2 May 1904
Died: Renfrew 1985

Career: Kilbarchan Athletic; Kilbirnie Ladeside; Dundee 01.11.22; St Mirren 16.09.25; Third Lanark 09.11.26; Reading 01.06.27; NORWICH CITY 29.06.29; Carlisle United Jun 1930; Stenhousemuir Apr 1933.

Forty nine games in Scotland produced three goals before he tried his hand south of the border. His play in the practice matches showed him to be a speedy player but his three games passed without incident save for the fact that Mr Stanley Rous refereed his last one. His 11 reserve goals indicated that he was a proficient scorer but he was on his way to sign for Billy Hampson, the newly installed Carlisle United Manager.

LAMB, Joseph

(1927–1930) **1927:** 5/8; 10/13
Right Half **Career:** 86-0-2
Debut: 29 Aug 27 **Final:** 26 Apr 30

Born: Chilton, Ferryhill 28 Nov 1898
Died: Chelmsford 22 Nov 1982

Career: Chilton School 1911; Bishop Auckland; Northampton Town (trial) Apr 1923; Chilton Colliery; Bishop Auckland May 1924; Willington Athletic; Durham City 01.06.25 (amat), 22.08.25 (pro); Stockport County 09.06.26; NORWICH CITY 09.07.27; Walker Celtic 21.05.30; Jarrow 30.09.30; Crook Town 25.05.31; Lumley 6th Pit FC; North Shields 25.07.32; West Stanley Aug 1934; Lumley Colliery Welfare cs 1935; Hoffman Athletic Jan 1937 player/trainer/coach.

To play for Bishop Auckland in the 1920s was a good indicator of quality, and Joe confirmed this opinion by winning an England Amateur Cap. The Pink 'Un *took away one of his goals and gave it to Hannah after a half-time change of positions confused all present. He lived in Holland, but his wife did not want their two children to be brought up speaking Dutch so they returned to Chelmsford. He was a school caretaker up to his retirement.*

LARKIN, Bernard Patrick (Bunny)

(1960–1961) **1964:** 5/8; 11/4
Inside Forward **Career:** 48-0-16
Debut: 16 Mar 60 (2 goals) **Final:** 23 Sep 61

Born: Birmingham 11 Jan 1936

Career: Lea Hall YC 1952; Rockwood Albion; Birmingham City 01.07.54; NORWICH CITY 16.03.60; Doncaster Rovers 26.10.61; Watford 28.05.62; Lincoln City 06.10.64; Wisbech Jun 1966; Nuneaton Borough Jun 1968; King's Lynn Jul 1969; Stevenage Athletic Jun 1970; Attleborough Town 1975–1977 coach.

Bunny recovered from a broken leg received while playing for Birmingham's youth side to later score in an Inter Cities Fairs Cup Semi-Final. His European exploits are covered in more depth in Glorious Canaries*. He became the first man to score on his City debuts in the League, League Cup and FA Cup. Still useful enough in his thirties to score a hat-trick for Wisbech against Tonbridge.*

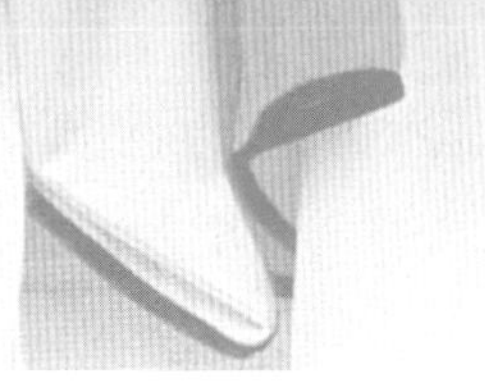

Left: Edward Laxton
Right: William Lewis

LASKEY, Russell George

(1957) **1957:** 5/8; 10/4
Inside Right **Career:** 4-0-2
Debut: 12 Jan 57 **Final:** 2 Feb 57

Born: Norwich 17 Mar 1937

Career: St Mark's School; Norwich Lads Club; Norfolk County Youth 1952; Gothic; NORWICH CITY 23.01.56; March Town; Gothic Aug 1962; Bury Town Aug 1963; Boulton & Paul Jul 1964.

Russell played for the National Association of Boys Clubs and collected his Norfolk County Youth Colours in 1952/53. He scored twice in two minutes for City in his third match as one of the youngsters used in 1957, when the economic climate at Carrow Road meant that money was not available to purchase 'stars'. The club were in jeopardy at the time that Russell was at the club.

LAW, Dudley George

(1938) **1938:** 5/10; 10/8
Centre Forward **Career:** 6-0-2
Debut: 7 May 38 **Final:** 1 Oct 38

Born: Earls Barton 12 May 1912
Died: Dover 2 Oct 1970

Career: Earls Barton School; Beau Ideal FC; Irchester FC; Wellingborough Town; Northampton Town 10.10.34; Rushden Town FC (loan) May 1936; NORWICH CITY 08.01.38; Colchester United 18.06.39; Lowestoft Town; Folkestone.

Had netted 38 goals for Rushden and after adding another 16 for City reserves in just two months he was elevated to the Firsts. His bustling, ever ready to have a go style pleased his followers. He was a Lowestoft lorry driver and died while on holiday in Kent.

LAXTON, Edward George

(1920–1921) **1920:** 5/9; 10/8
Outside Right **Career:** 16-0-0
Debut: 28 Aug 20 **Final:** 19 Mar 21

Born: Brazil circa 1896
Died: Nottingham 9 Aug 1961

Career: Queen's Walk Church School; Notts Boys; Netherfield Rangers; Nottingham Forest Reserves 1913; Grantham Town 1914; WW1 for Notts County; NORWICH CITY 09.12.19 (amat), 27.08.20 (pro); Shildon Athletic Aug 1921; Dublin Bohemians cs 1925; Heanor Town cs 1926.

The first 'Brazilian' to play in the Football League, being born there principally due to his father being engaged on an engineering project. A prolific medal winner as a schoolboy, he was the scorer of the last Southern League goal for City prior to our joining the Football League. My favourite match report of him reads, 'He was not deficient in making a game for his inside forwards'. Neither his death certificate nor his will gives his defined birthdate and Consular Births, the Brazilian Embassy and the Geneaological Sociteies in Sao Paulo have been unable to help.

LEWIS, William Albert

(1949–1955) **1952:** 5/9; 12/11
Left Back **Career:** 256-0-1
Debut: 12 Nov 49 **Final:** 17 Sep 55

Born: West Ham 23 Nov 1921
Died: Sprowston 27 Aug 1998

Career: South Hallsville Senior School; West Ham Boys; London & Essex Schoolboys; Leytonstone; West Ham United 11.05.38 (amat)–May 1945; Blackpool 25.07.45; NORWICH CITY 11.11.49–May 1956, later club coach and reserve team trainer.

From a family of nine, Bill gave many full-blooded City displays being absolutely fearless in the tackle. He had a rocket shot and it was a surprise that he only scored once – although many long distance efforts whistled just wide. He played over 40 games a season for four consecutive years and presently stands equal 28th in City's top appearance chart alongside Bill Punton and Dave Watson. City paid a club record fee for Bill and he gave unstinting service.

LIBBRA, Marc Sylvain-Rene

(2001– **2001:** 6/2: 13/6
Striker **Career:** 1-3-2
Debut: 18 Aug 01 (sub) (goal)

Born: Toulon, France 5 Aug 1972

Career: La Palasse YC (France); Le Pradet YC (France); FC Istres (France); Olympique Marseille (France) 1988; FC Istres Ville Nouvelle (France)

1992/3; En Avant Guingamp (France) (loan) 1998; AS Cannes (France) 1998; Toulouse (France) 1999; Hibernian (loan) Mar 2001; NORWICH CITY 26.07.2001

A stunning hat-trick against Fakenham (with a header and both feet) in the pre-season friendly had manager Worthington enthusing, 'The boy is a goalscorer'. Played against Celtic in the Scottish Cup Final and netted three times against them last season. Marc rejected Celtic's offer of employment by joining Norwich after a protracted affair involving his registration from his French club. On the field for 19 seconds with an actual playing time debut goal in eleven seconds - a club record. Magnifique! He handsomely beat the previous City record of just two minutes.

LINIGHAN, Andrew

(1988–1990) **1988:** 6/3; 12/6
Centre Half **Career:** 106-0-8
Debut: 5 Mar 88 **Final:** 5 May 90

Born: Hartlepool 18 Jun 1962

Career: Durham Boys; Smith's Boys Club; Smith's Docks FC; Hartlepools United 10.09.80; Leeds United 15.05.84; Oldham Athletic 17.01.86; NORWICH CITY 04.03.88; Arsenal 04.07.90; Crystal Palace 27.01.97; Queens Park Rangers (loan) 25.03.99; Oxford United 16.10.2000; St Albans City 27.06.2001.

Andy moved from being a plumber and playing part time for his home town club to 'Linighan-Boo' at Highbury until he won over their critical fans and headed Norwich City into Europe with an FA Cup Final goal. Dave Stringer said of him, 'He is good in the air, comfortable on the ball with both feet and for a big lad he is quite quick'. A good judge, was Mr Stringer. Andy's father, uncle and three brothers all are or were professional footballers.

LIVERMORE, Douglas Ernest

(1970–1975) **1971:** 5/81/2; 10/5
Winger/Midfield **Career:** 138-1-6
Debut: 28 Nov 70 **Final:** 8 Feb 75

Born: Huyton, Liverpool 27 Dec 1947

Career: Seal Road School; Huyton Schoolboys; Bolton Wanderers 27.05.63 (amat); Liverpool 13.11.65; NORWICH CITY 26.11.70; Bournemouth & Boscombe Athletic (loan) 15.03.75; Cardiff City 22.08.75; Chester 14.10.77; Cardiff City 1978–1980 coach; NORWICH CITY 03.11.80 coach; Swansea City Aug 1981–26.10.83 coach; Tottenham Hotspur 1984 coach, reserve team trainer, 31.10.87 caretaker manager for one month, Jun 1989 assistant manager, team manager/coach from May 1992; Wales National part time assistant manager for 8 years; Liverpool 20.07.94 coach; Nottingham Forest 14.04.99 coach; NORWICH CITY 07.06.99 coach, assistant manager.

Left: Andy Linighan
Right: Doug Livermore

Doug was a key midfield component in City's promotion winning side of 1971–72 and of course played in the first Division One game at Carrow Road. A shrewd reader of the game in tight situations he has toured the world with Wales and rejoined Norwich City with a fantastic CV, being highly regarded in the football world.

LLEWELLYN, Christopher Mark

(1998– **1998:** 5/11; 11/6
Forward **Career:** 108-31-18
Debut: 3 Jan 98 (sub)

Born: Merthyr Tydfil 29 Aug 1979

Career: St Mary's Primary School; St David's Primary School; Bishop Vaughan Comprehensive School; St Helen's Boys Club; Troedyrhiw Boy's Club; Gorfeinon Boy's Club; West Glamorgan Schools; Swansea Boys Under-14–15; Chepstow Centre of Excellence; NORWICH CITY 11.09.93 (assoc), Jul 1995 (trainee), 21.01.97 (pro).

Chris Llewellyn

He travelled from Wales with Craig Bellamy for training before they were teenagers. Naturally left-sided Chris can also play at wing back and has progressed from youth level to gaining full Welsh caps. The second highest City scorer with eight in 2000/1, he was consequently rewarded with a new contract in April 2001.

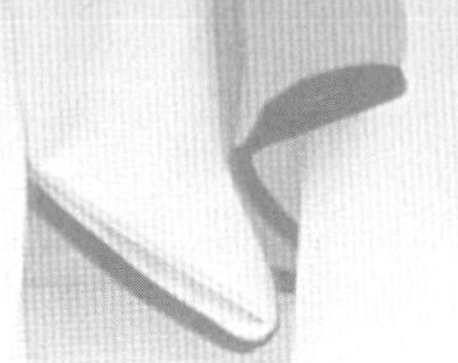

LOCHHEAD, Dougald

(1929–1935) **1931:** 5/11; 10/4
Left Half **Career:** 220-0-5
Debut: 31 Aug 29 **Final:** 16 Sep 35

Born: Partick 16 Dec 1904
Died: Leeds 29 Aug 1968

Career: St Peter's Boys Guild 1920; Eaglesham FC; Maryhill Juniors; St Anthony's; St Johnstone 20.06.25; Walsall 13.06.28; NORWICH CITY 24.06.29 to May 1935, 23.02.37 assistant manager, scouting, 1945–Jun 1946 interim manager, 10.12.47 to Mar 1950 manager; AFA Norfolk coach; Galatasary Sports Club (Istanbul) Oct 1950 to Oct 1952 chief scout; Almelo (Holland) Dec 1953 coaching; Merthyr Tydfil Jun 1956–1958 manager; Norwich City scout.

A great-hearted Canary legend, serving the club in various capacities for 20 years. Even made three wartime appearances – in each case helping out because of a player shortage. Scotland's loss (18 games for St. Johnstone) was East Anglia's gain, and of course Doug scored the first ever League goal at Carrow Road. Reports indicate that he had the ball from that first match – a collector's item if still around! In retrospect it could not be in better hands.

LOCKWOOD, Roy

(1956–1958) **1957:** 5/9; 11/6
Left Back **Career:** 37-0-0
Debut: 11 Feb 56 **Final:** 21 Apr 58

Born: Barnsley 20 Jun 1933

Career: Raley Secondary Modern School; New Lodge United 1950; Sheffield Wednesday 10.04.51 part time; NORWICH CITY 22.09.55; Kettering Town cs 1958; Rothwell Town 1959 retiring with a cartilage injury.

Roy was capped for England Youth in 1951 and 1952. He joined the club on trial and was taken on following consistent displays in the Reserves (66 games). His acute positional sense stood him in good stead. He has bowling green partners in Derrick Lythgoe and John Wilson and has now retired from Colman's after 29 years' service.

LONGDON, Samuel

(1920) **1920:** 5/9; 10/10
Outside Left **Career:** 3-0-0
Debut: 25 Sep 20 **Final:** 9 Oct 20

Born: Derby 22 Nov 1895
Died: Sydenham 2 Sep 1971

Career: Derby County Reserves; NORWICH CITY 24.09.20.

Sam came from Derby – the area that is, not the club. Did not bring City much luck as they failed to score in any of his games. He also played in our first reserve game upon reaching Football League status. He was a retired fireman at the time of his death.

LOW, Norman Harvey

(1946–1950) **1951:** 6/1; 11/10
Centre Half **Career:** 163-0-0
Debut: 12 Oct 46 **Final:** 6 May 50

Born: Newcastle 23 Mar 1914
Died: Toronto, Canada 21 May 1994

Career: Newcastle Schools; Rosehill Villa; Liverpool 30.10.33; Newport County 13.11.36; Second World War played for Liverpool, Swindon Town and Newport; Newport County 1946; NORWICH CITY 14.10.46 to 1950, 10.05.50–22.04.55 manager; Barry Town 1955/6 manager; Workington Jan 1956–Feb 1957 manager; Port Vale Feb 1957 manager; Cleveland Stokers (USA) coach; Liverpool Aug 1965–1967 chief scout; Witton Albion manager.

Norman Low

Cardiff outbid Norwich by £750 but Newport preferred him to play for City rather than their neighbours. How grateful City were, as Norman proved to be a skipper of granite. A superb reader of the game, and very difficult to beat in the air, he did the club a further service by bringing Reg Foulkes to Carrow Road. One of a famous footballing family with Uncle Harold (Sunderland), cousin Willie (Aberdeen) and his father Wilfred, a Scottish international, who sadly was killed in a 1933 road accident.

LUCAS, Peter Malcolm

(1964–1970) **1964:** 5/6; 11/0
Right Half **Career:** 201-3-10
Debut: 16 Sep 64 **Final:** 11 Mar 70

Born: Wrexham 7 Oct 1938

Career: Wrexham Youth; Bolton Wanderers (trial); Liverpool (trial); Bradley Rangers; Harrow Borough; Leyton Orient 08.09.58; NORWICH CITY 11.09.64; Torquay United 16.03.70 to 1973; Lowestoft Town Jun 1974 player-manager; Gorleston player-manager; Hoveton player-manager retiring 1982; Norwich City All Stars; Gorleston Dec 1998.

A Welsh international and one of the stalwarts of Orient's 1961 promotion side. A pocket dynamo of a player, he formed a fine partnership with fellow half backs Barry Butler and Terry Allcock. In recent years Mal has fallen outside City's top 50 all-time appearance charts. Latterly working for Brent Leisure Services Ltd.

LUMLEY, William Read

(1921–1922)	**1921:** 5/8; 11/4
Centre Forward	**Career:** 29-0-6
Debut: 19 Feb 21	**Final:** 1 May 22

Born: Swalwell 27 Dec 1898
Died: Whickham 11 Jun 1975

Career: Swalwell; County Durham Schoolboys; NORWICH CITY 09.02.21; Leadgate Park Jul 1922.

Manager Gosnell saw him get four goals in a match for Swalwell and promptly signed him for City. A hat-trick against the 11th Brigade Royal Field Artillery saw him promoted to the First's where he had a degree of success. Later worked as a colliery coal hewer.

LYTHGOE, Derrick

(1958–1962)	**1958:** 5/7; 10/10
Inside Forward	**Career:** 74-0-29
Debut: 22 Mar 58 (goal)	**Final:** 28 Apr 62

Born: Bolton 5 May 1933

Career: Whitecroft Road Secondary School; Bolton Lads Club; Bolton Boys; Lancashire & Cheshire Boys; Great Britain & England B.C.; Blackpool 18.05.50; NORWICH CITY 17.03.58; Bristol City 14.08.62; King's Lynn Jul 1963; Gothic Aug 1965 player coach; Lowestoft Town Jul 1970; Yarmouth Town 16.01.71; Hainford Jul 1971 player coach; Poringland coach; Unity Emeralds manager; Norwich United 1987 coach, Dec 1987 committee.

Afforded few opportunities at Blackpool but he became an opportunist scorer while at Norwich, as his record shows. Derrick scored on his City debut in three competitions and also has an impressive reserve tally of 77 games for 37 goals. Father of Philip (q.v.), he worked in local government.

Malcolm Lucas

LYTHGOE, John

(1922–1923)	**1922:** 5/8; 12/0
Inside Left	**Career:** 15-0-3
Debut: 26 Aug 22	**Final:** 10 Feb 23

Born: Dixon Fold 3 Apr 1892
Died: Little Hulton 5 Jun 1969

Career: Newbury FC; Walkden Central 1912; Bury 29.11.13; Nottingham Forest 07.09.18; Newport County 25.08.21; NORWICH CITY 03.06.22; Ebbw Vale Oct 1923; Eccles United Nov 1923; Chorley Mar 1924; Margate Aug 1925; Horwich RMI; Kearsley Celtic 29.10.31.

During the First World War he was in the Machine Gun Corps and the Tank Corps. Featured on Pinnace Card number 866, John was a powerful man with a good goal-getting reputation, as shown by his 69 strikes for Bury. However the advancing years had caught up with him by the time of his spell at the Nest. Like many footballers before and since he was a retired coal miner.

LYTHGOE, Philip

(1978–1979)	**1978:** 5/9; 11/0
Winger	**Career:** 9-3-1
Debut: 21 Jan 78	**Final:** 15 Dec 79 (sub)

Born: Norwich 18 Dec 1959

Career: Sprowston Junior School; Thorpe Grammar School; Bolton Wanderers (trial); Norwich Boys; Norfolk County; NORWICH CITY 03.05.75 (assoc), 07.08.76 (app), 23.12.77 (pro); Bristol Rovers (loan) 22.09.78; Oxford United 19.08.80–Apr 1982; Gorleston 1982; Lowestoft Town 1.09.83; Poringland 1985 (renamed Norwich United); Wroxham 04.01.92.

Phil was voted the best player in a 1977 Youth tournament in Holland but was used sparingly during City's First Division days in the late 1970s. Son of Derrick, he has turned

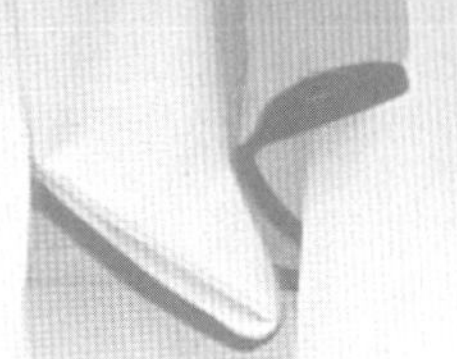

in dazzling performances for local sides and is usually a marked man. He helped Wroxham complete a treble in 1992/3 and in the mid 1990s he announced his intention to coach youngsters at two local schools.

McCOY, Peter Joseph

(1949) **1949:** 5/9; 11/6
Right Back **Career:** 6-0-0
Debut: 19 Mar 49 **Final:** 16 Apr 49

Born: Thornley 31 Jul 1923
Died: Peterlee 31 Jul 1986

Career: Shotton Juniors; 15th Hussars; Newcastle United 27.09.46; NORWICH CITY 09.02.49; Murton Colliery Welfare Oct 1950.

Peter was given the Number Two shirt for the first six games after Bernard Robinson's last appearance. His debut saw Swansea extend their home record to 17 straight wins and he bowed out on the winning side at Bournemouth, finally being released at the end of the 1949/50 season. Peter, a nightwatchman, died of heart failure at home on his 63rd birthday.

McCROHAN, Roy

(1951–1962) **1962:** 5/11; 12/4
Half Back **Career:** 426-0-23
Debut: 12 Sep 51 **Final:** 28 Apr 62

Born: Reading 22 Sep 1930

Career: Reading (Juniors), 17.01.49 (pro); NORWICH CITY 09.07.51; Colchester United 06.09.62; Bristol Rovers 03.08.64–19.04.65, coaching to 12.03.66; Crawley Town Jul 1966 player coach; Fulham 15.08.68 coach; Aldershot 1970 coach; Ipswich Town 1971 reserve trainer; Luton Town 1972 to assistant manager Dec 1977; Detroit Express (USA) 1978; Minnesota Kicks (USA) 1979; coaching in Florida and involved with the Warner international Soccer School (USA).

Roy McCrohan

Roy came to City as an inside forward, but he played in almost every position on the field in a fine career. Add 101 reserve games for 33 goals to his first-team total. His untiring enthusiasm and great half back play have ensured him a rightfully lofty place in Canary folklore. Latterly worked in a leisure centre and dabbled in photography; he then settled in Tallahasse and he has returned to Norwich City for reunions.

McCUDDEN, Joseph Francis

(1924–1926) **1925:** 5/9; 11/8
Inside Right **Career:** 41-0-14
Debut: 30 Aug 24 (goal) **Final:** 17 Apr 26

Born: Edmonton, London 17 Jan 1899
Died: Beckenham, Kent 14 Oct 1976

Career: Park Avondale; Gnome Athletic; Royal Field Artillery; Edmonton; Tottenham Hotspur Juniors; Clapton Orient 19.11.20 (amat); Tottenham Hotspur 16.03.22; NORWICH CITY 16.05.24; Clapton Orient 11.09.26; Grays Thurrock Nov 1926; Whitbreads Aug 1927.

'Frank' rejoiced in the description of 'a strong, rough and tumble sort'. He had his greatest City day when he scored a hat-trick in the 6–1 massacre of First Division West Ham United in the Hospital Cup. He was a local council foreman (retired) in later life.

McDONALD, Colin Barry

(1968) **1968:** 5/8; 9/7
Left Winger **Career:** 4-0-0
Debut: 20 Apr 68 **Final:** 8 May 68

Born: Norwich 15 May 1950

Career: Henderson Avenue School; Norfolk Boys; NORWICH CITY 03.09.65 (app), 08.07.67 (pro); Scunthorpe United 03.07.70; Brigg Town 1972; Ashby Institute 1974; Winterton Rangers 1976; Barton retiring 1979.

His Carrow Road career was mainly as an understudy, as can be seen from his reserve total of 115 games for 28 goals. At Scunthorpe he played in 20 league games with Kevin Keegan before playing for a number of non-league clubs and retiring from football at the early age of 29.

McDOWELL, John Alfred

(1979–1981) **1980:** 5/10; 12/4
Full Back **Career:** 44-1-1
Debut: 18 Aug 79 **Final:** 2 May 81

Born: East Ham 7 Sep 1951

Career: Essex Boys; West Ham United 24.07.67 (app), 28.08.69 (pro); NORWICH CITY 10.08.79, reserve team coach Aug 1981; Bristol Rovers 25.05.82 player coach; Mangotsfield United 1984.

John had the ability to apply his trade in virtually every defensive position. He won England Under-23 caps and an FA Cup winner's medal in a ten-year career at West Ham and was bought by John Bond to add experience to the side. The Upton Park

floodlights used to illuminate his bedroom. He became a publican, a grandfather in 1997 and moved into the advertising business.

McGOVERN, Brian Patrick

(2000– **2000:** 6/3; 12/7
Defender **Career:** 6-12-1
Debut: 22 Aug 00 (sub)

Born: Dublin 28 Apr 1980

Career: CBS Crumlin; Cherry Orchard; Dublin Schools; Arsenal from trainee 05.09.97; Queens Park Rangers (loan) 24.12.97; NORWICH CITY (loan) 22.07.2000, (signed) 22.08.2000.

A Republic of Ireland Under-21 international who was held back at Arsenal by having to compete with the vast array of imported 'superstars' at the club. A strong tackler he uses the ball well and has a desire to be a winner. Almost a permanent selection for City's reserves during their long unbeaten run in 2000/1 he has impressed immensely and looks destined for a regular first team place.

McGRAE, Joseph Russell

(1926–1929) **1927:** 5/10; 11/7
Centre/Left Half **Career:** 124-0-3
Debut: 28 Aug 26 **Final:** 4 May 29

Born: Kirkdale, Liverpool 24 Oct 1903
Died: Bootle, Liverpool 19 Nov 1975

Career: Liverpool Secondary School; Liverpool Boys; Liverpool City Schools; Liverpool Royal Albion; Everton Jun 1919; Tranmere Rovers 22.05.25; NORWICH CITY 23.08.26; Bradford City 14.05.29; Clapton Orient 27.07.30; Halifax Town 22.07.31; Macclesfield Town; Littlewoods FC Oct 1933; Hyde United Aug 1935.

Joe survived a disastrous team performance in his debut match to become a regular and consistent performer for City. It was said that he made opponents aware of his presence during a game. He rarely scored and when he did it failed to herald a victory for the side. He was later a food warehouse checker in Bootle.

McGUIRE, Michael James

(1975–1983) **1975**: 5/7; 10/6
Wing Half **Career:** 192-11-12
Debut: 18 Jan 75 **Final:** 12 Mar 83 (sub)

Born: Blackpool 4 Sep 1952

Career: Blackpool Grammar School; Coventry City 05.11.69 (app), Jul 1970 (pro); NORWICH CITY 16.01.75; Tampa Bay Rowdies (USA) 06.04.78; Barnsley 24.03.83; Oldham Athletic 05.01.85–May 1987; Blackpool 03.08.87–07.01.88; Grantham Town Mar 1988.

Mick played for England in the Little World Cup in Czechoslovakia and was on the verge of Under-23 honours when an achilles heel injury, received while playing tennis, caused him to miss all of the 1976/77 season. In his time at Carrow Road he had skippered the side, with his adaptability and versatility accounting for his wearing six different shirt numbers. He joined the PFA in June 1987 as YTS coordinator, since rising to assistant chief executive.

McKENNA, Francis Charles

(1928–1929) **1925:** 5/6; 10/7
Inside Left **Career:** 44-0-18
Debut: 25 Aug 28 **Final:** 4 May 29

Born: Wallsend, Tyne & Wear 9 Dec 1902
Died: Crook 8 Feb 1947

Career: Swan Hunter; Spennymoor United; Wallsend FC; Grimsby Town 17.05.22; Fulham 09.05.27; NORWICH CITY 11.07.28; Newport County 23.08.28; Walker Celtic Aug 1930; Wrexham 22.06.32; Walker Celtic Jun 1933.

A description of Francis: 'Slightly built yet a plucky performer displaying adroit footwork and a fair turn of speed'. His first ever Football League goals came on Christmas Day 1922 with a threesome against Accrington. He top-scored in his one season for City and he finally reached 68 career league/cup goals. A general labourer at the time of his demise.

McKINNEY, Daniel

(1924–1926) **1924:** 5/7; 10/7
Outside Right **Career:** 52-0-4
Debut: 1 Nov 24 **Final:** 13 Feb 26

Born: Belfast 9 Nov 1898
Died: Belfast 28 Feb 1956

Career: St Paul's Swifts; Belfast Celtic 1915; Hull City 09.10.20; Bradford City 30.07.23; NORWICH CITY 31.10.24 to Mar 1926.

An Irish international and Cup winner with Belfast Celtic before moving to England. Among his twelve goals for the 'Tigers' was a hat-trick on 04.03.22 against Leicester. He had good ball control and was clever in combination with his inside man. An early City programme rated him a popular member of the team and a typical Irish wit. He wasn't effectively replaced until Ernie Porter arrived in 1927.

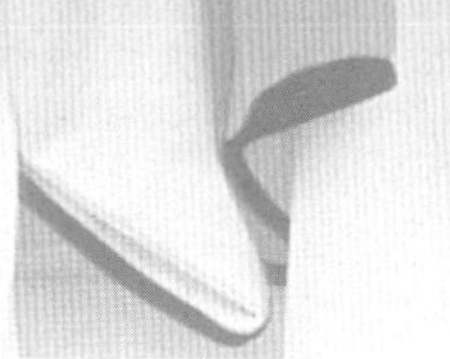

McLAVERTY, Bernard

(1928–1929) **1928:** 5/9; 10/7
Centre Half **Career:** 56-0-4
Debut: 14 Jan 28 **Final:** 2 May 29 (3 goals)

Born: Chester-le-Street, Durham 15 Mar 1898
Died: Duffield 24 Dec 1952

Career: Chester Moor FC; Leadgate Park; Durham City; Derby County 28.05.20; NORWICH CITY 14.01.28–02.05.29; Heanor Town; Offilers Brewery Jan 1933.

Bernard had over 100 games for Derby, scoring once for them on 23.10.26. He toured Holland, Germany, Denmark and Sweden with them and so was ripe in experience. His four City goals arrived in his last three matches for City from the inside right position with a spectacular finale. Like innumerable footballers before and since, Bernard became a licensed victualler, firstly at the local Locomotive and until his death at the New Inn in Duffield.

McMILLAN, Thomas

(1954–1955) **1954:** 5/6; 10/8
Outside Left **Career:** 19-0-2
Debut: 1 Sep 54 **Final:** 30 Apr 55

Born: Glasgow 12 Feb 1931
Died: Glasgow 4 Oct 1999

Career: Garrowhill Amateurs; Baillieston Juniors; Glasgow Celtic 06.11.52; NORWICH CITY 12.06.54; Albion Rovers (trial) 09.08.55; Workington 08.09.55; Albion Rovers (trial) 07.08.56; Cowdenbeath 28.08.56 retiring through injury.

A diminutive Scottish winger who had but a brief interlude at Carrow Road in competition with Martin Reagan for the Number 11 shirt. His two City goals came in one match, at Bournemouth. He had two games for Workington before returning to Scotland where he tore knee ligaments after just five minutes of his only game for Cowdenbeath.

McNEIL, Matthew Alex

(1956–1957) **1956:** 6/3; 12/5
Right Half **Career:** 44-0-2
Debut: 17 Mar 56 **Final:** 30 Mar 57

Born: Glasgow 28 Jul 1927
Died: Stobhill 23 Apr 1977

Career: Hibernian Apr 1947; Newcastle United 14.12.49; Barnsley 07.08.51; Brighton & Hove Albion 18.07.53; NORWICH CITY 15.03.56; Cambridge United 01.07.57.

A strong, defensive 'stopper' who through his height ensured that he was the master in the air. Matt was sent off in his second match just two minutes from the end – and the referee had to be escorted from the pitch. Did not aspire to great heights at any of his clubs, being especially unlucky to be at Newcastle when Scottish international Frank Brennan was in residence. He had a newsagent's business and was then a sales representative in Kirkintilloch.

McVEIGH, Paul Francis

(2000– **2000:** 5/8; 11/7
Forward **Career:** 9-8-3
Debut: 7 May 00 (sub)

Born: Belfast 6 Dec 1977

Career: St John Baptist Primary School; St Mary's School; Belfast Schools; Lisburn Youth; Tottenham Hotspur Mar 1992 (assoc), Jul 1994 (trainee), 10.07.96 (pro); Cambridge United Feb 2000 training; NORWICH CITY 23.03.2000.

Paul a Northern Ireland international striker knew Phil Mulryne and Adrian Coote from the international arena. In a short career he has already had a number of managers but despite this he showed stunning City reserve form by scoring 18 goals in 23 matches as the Canaries took the runners-up spot to Fulham in the Avon Insurance Combination League last season. He has started season 2001/2 in fine goal scoring form.

McWHIRR, James

(1926) **1926:** 5/9; 11/9
Outside Right **Career:** 4-0-2
Debut: 27 Nov 26 **Final:** 11 Dec 26 (goal)

Born: Partick 13 Jan 1905
Died: Oconomowac, Wisconsin, USA Nov 1976

Career: Glasgow Ashfield FC; Gillingham 27.05.25; NORWICH CITY 23.08.26; Merthyr Town 29.07.27; Portsmouth 02.12.27; Charlton Athletic 24.07.28–17.02.30.

A Scottish Junior international who had just six league games at Gillingham, one at Charlton and none at Portsmouth. He was unique in scoring in his only Canary league game and therefore played in more FA Cup ties than league matches for City. He had a short career at Merthyr too – 16 league games for 7 goals, with two goals in an 8–2 win over Swindon Town.

MACDOUGALL, Edward John (Ted)

(1973–1976) **1974:** 5/10; 11/11
Striker **Career:** 138-0-66
Debut: 8 Dec 73 **Final:** 11 Sep 76

Born: Inverness 8 Jan 1947

Career: Inverness High School; ICI Recs; Liverpool 1964 (amat), 15.01.66 (pro); York City 13.07.67; Bournemouth 21.07.69; Manchester United 30.09.72; West Ham United 01.03.73; NORWICH CITY 07.12.73; Southampton 16.09.76; Bournemouth 08.11.78; Detroit Express (USA) May 1979–Aug 1979; Blackpool 04.03.80 player coach, Oct 1980 assistant manager; Salisbury City Aug 1981; Poole Town Dec 1981; Totton Jan 1982; Gosport Borough Mar 1982; Athena (Australia) May 1982; Totton Oct 1982–Dec 1982; Athena (Australia); Andover Oct 1983–Dec 1983 coach; Vancouver 86ers (Canada) coaching; Portsmouth coaching, reserve manager to Dec 1999.

Ted was one of the greatest goalscorers that the Third and Fourth Divisions has ever known. In the FA Cup he scored six in one match and he still holds the all time record with nine (vs Margate 20.11.71). Not surprisingly all the 'big' clubs sought his talents, hence the large fees paid by a succession of clubs. A Scottish international, winning seven caps, he became the 15th post-War player to score 250 League goals. Truly a goal-scoring machine. He moved to Canada in 1985 but has since returned to help Portsmouth in a number of roles.

MACHIN, Melvyn

(1973–1977) **1974:** 5/10; 12/0
Defender **Career:** 113-4-4
Debut: 15 Dec 73 **Final:** 17 Sep 77

Born: Newcastle-under-Lyme, Staffs 16 Apr 1945

Career: Stoke-on-Trent Schoolboys, Juniors & Apprentice; Port Vale 1960 (app), 12.07.62 (pro); Gillingham 08.07.66; Bournemouth & Boscombe Athletic 03.12.70; Bournemouth College of Technology coach; NORWICH CITY 12.12.73; Seattle Sounders (USA) May 1977–Aug 1977; NORWICH CITY coaching capacities at Youth, reserve and First team level, 19.10.80 assistant manager, 18.10.81–18.05 87 chief coach; Manchester City 21.05.87–27.11.89 manager; Burnley 29.12.89–05.05.93 manager; Bournemouth 10.09.94 manager, Aug 2000 Director of football.

Mel started his career as a striker (indeed for City he has scored a first team and reserve team hat-trick) but adapted successfully to midfield and full back. A cultured player, appreciated more by fellow pros, he formed a highly effective and successful partnership with City manager Ken Brown. A proud day was leading Bournemouth to Wembley in the Auto Windscreens Shield Final.

Left: 'Ted' MacDougall
Right: Mel Machin

MACKAY, Malcolm George

(1998– **1998:** 6/1; 11/7
Defender **Career:** 86-13-3
Debut: 19 Sep 98 (sub)

Born: Bellshill 19 Feb 1972

Career: St Ambrose High School; Queens Park Youth; Bank of Scotland; Queens Park 1990; Glasgow Celtic 1994; NORWICH CITY (loan) 18.09.98, (signed) 21.09.98.

A centre back in the old fashioned mode, combining sheer physical power with strength in the air. Known affectionately by his fellow pros in the City dressing room as 'The Moaner'. He has already earned the respect and admiration of the Norwich crowd with his wholehearted displays in the Canary cause at the heart of the defence.

MACKRELL, James

(1937–1939) **1938:** 5/9; 11/8
Left Back **Career:** 39-0-0
Debut: 6 Mar 37 **Final:** 18 Feb 39

Born: New Monkland, nr Airdrie 13 Feb 1906
Died: Plains, nr Airdrie 3 Jan 1977

Career: Longriggend Rob Roy; Falkirk 10.07.28; Motherwell (trial) Aug 1931, (signed) Oct 1931; Portsmouth 08.08.33; NORWICH CITY 03.03.37.

The 1933 Topical Times Who's Who *had only the pithy comment, 'a steelworker'. He was in fact something of a penalty expert (scored such a goal versus City in February 1937) and the Norwich City handbook said of him, 'In his first season he gave a very good account of his*

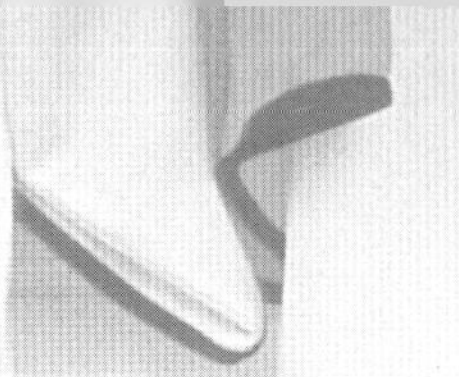

ability'. His City record was matched by his 39 games for Falkirk. His younger brother followed in his footsteps and joined Falkirk in June 1938. It would appear that Jim's father was illiterate, evidenced by our player's birth certificate listing his surname as 'McKrell' and the other two offspring as 'Mackell' and 'Macrell'!

MADDEN, Owen

(1936–1938) **1936:** 5/9; 11/10
Inside/Outside Left **Career:** 25-0-1
Debut: 29 Aug 36 **Final:** 1 Jan 38

Born: Cork 5 Dec 1916
Died: Cork 20 Jan 1991

Career: Cork High School; Cork Southern Rovers; Cork (Irish Free State); NORWICH CITY 11.05.36; Birmingham City 04.02.38; Cork City FC renamed Cork United Feb 1940; Cork Athletic 1948.

An illustrious career for Cork that saw him play twice for the Free State XI. Poaching of players is nothing new – 50 years ago Cork complained that City had made illegal overtures to Owen. Plain Stan Matthews (before the knighthood), was on his side in his Benefit match for Cork United versus Greenock Morton in February 1946. Owen won five championship medals and he had four FAI Cup Winner's medal to become a revered name in his home town.

MALLENDER, Kenneth

(1968–1970) **1970:** 5/9; 11/6
Defender **Career:** 48-0-1
Debut: 2 Nov 68 **Final:** 21 Oct 70

Born: Thrybergh, nr Rotherham 10 Dec 1943

Career: Dearne Boys; Sheffield United 08.08.60 (app), 25.02.61 (pro); NORWICH CITY 31.10.68; Hereford United Aug 1971; Telford United Jul 1974; Minehead Jun 1977; Gloucester City.

Ken made a First Division debut on 03.04.62 at Blackpool and became a regular Blade in front of England keeper Alan Hodgkinson. He scored two First Division goals against Northampton and Tottenham before joining City for a record fee (at the time). He coincidentally made 48 reserve appearances as well and still lives in Hereford, the club he joined from City.

MANDERS, Frank

(1935–1939) **1936:** 5/9; 11/0
Inside Forward **Career:** 137-0-43
Debut: 26 Oct 35 **Final:** 4 Mar 39

Born: Camberley 13 Jun 1914
Died: Sutton Coldfield Mar 1942

Career: Camberley & York Town; Aldershot 09.12.30 (amat); Crystal Palace 03.07.31; NORWICH CITY 26.10.35; Military Police; RAF.

Frank made his mark as a goalscoring 15 year old, and his weight of goals quickly earned him promotion to Palace's first team. The 1935 Football Weekly Who's Who *stated that he showed his prowess even earlier – at the age of nine. He played for us until April 1940 with his untimely demise being due to drowning.*

MANNING, John

(1967–1969) **1964:** 6/0; 12/2
Centre Forward **Career:** 67-0-22
Debut: 23 Sep 67 **Final:** 7 Mar 69 (goal)

Born: Liverpool 11 Dec 1940

Career: Liverpool (reserves); Tranmere Rovers 21.05.62; Shrewsbury Town 17.10.66; NORWICH CITY 23.09.67; Bolton Wanderers 13.03.69; Walsall 01.07.71; Tranmere Rovers 10.03.72; Crewe Alexandra 10.08.72; Barnsley 17.09.73; Crewe Alexandra 19.01.75, later trainer coach; Saudi Arabian National Under-19 coach; Merrick (Sudan) manager for 1 yr; scouting for Birmingham and Brighton; coaching in Kuwait; Middlesbrough scout.

John still remains as Tranmere's equal sixth highest league scorer of all time. An easy mover, predominantly right footed and a fine header of the ball. He left Norwich to be closer to his father-in-law who was ill back in Liverpool. John, after retiring from playing, had an overworked passport when he was 'signed up' by Jimmy Hill in the English exodus to Saudi Arabia. He visited Bangladesh, India, Iran, Iraq, France, Syria and the United Arab Emirates on tours. He is now a sales manager for a chemical company.

MANNION, Gerard Patrick

(1961–1967) **1964:** 5/9; 11/4
Winger **Career:** 119-0-21
Debut: 2 Sep 61 **Final:** 6 Sep 67

Born: Burtonwood 21 Dec 1939
Died: Warrington 14 Jun 1994

Career: Burtonwood Roman Catholic School; Newton Boys; Wolverhampton Wanderers 1955 (juniors), 27.11.57; NORWICH CITY 01.08.61; Chester 26.01.68; Kidderminster Harriers Jun 1969.

Gerry made his Wolves debut in the Charity Shield and he went on to earn England Under-

23 recognition. Signed by Archie Macaulay he made and took chances from the wing before suffering a broken leg in training in November 1965. He reappeared after a year out of the game to boost his reserve appearances to 59 for 15 goals. He played exactly 100 league games for City. When the crowd stood for a minute's silence in memory of Barry Butler he had his leg in plaster and was walking with the aid of crutches.

MANSFIELD, Frederick Charles Adam

(1947–1948) **1947:** 5/9; 11/4
Right Back **Career:** 37-0-0
Debut: 15 Feb 47 **Final:** 14 Feb 48

Born: Cambridge 9 Mar 1915
Died: Cambridge 1 Jan 1992

Career: St Phillip's Junior School; Central School; Cambridge Schoolboys; Railway Social FC; Cambridgeshire County; Abbey United 1937; Brentford; NORWICH CITY 17.02.47; Guildford City 1948; Abbey United 1949; Cambridge United 1951–1956; Gorleston Jul 1962–Sep 1962 trainer coach.

Pre-war Fred scored 42 goals for Abbey United and had Denis Morgan and Maurice Tobin for partners in his stay at Carrow Road. A post-war City handbook said of him, 'A dependable back, cool in an emergency and with a strong sense of the importance of correct positioning'. The 'Wanderer' in the local paper for season 1947/8 summed up the City team at the time as being guilty of 'Poor shooting, missed chances, gift goals and they crumbled again'. The local sports writers of the modern day seem quite benign in comparison!

MARSHALL, Andrew John

(1994–2001) **1994:** 6/2; 13/0
Goalkeeper **Career:** 217-2-0
Debut: 27 Dec 94 (sub) **Final:** 6 May 01

Born: Bury, Lancashire 14 Apr 1975

Career: Sawtry Village Junior School; Sawtry Village College Infants; Sawtry Archers; NORWICH CITY (trial) 1985; Sawtry FC; Huntingdon District; Cambridgeshire: NORWICH CITY 25.07.89 (schoolboy), 04.07.91 (trainee), 06.07.93 (pro); Bournemouth (loan) 09.09.96–08.11.96; Gillingham (loan) 21.11.96; Ipswich Town 02.07.2001.

A wealth of experience despite his relative youthfulness and he could have been a fireman if football wasn't his chosen career. He is regarded as one of the best young keepers in England and deservedly won the Barry Butler Memorial Trophy in season 2000/1. A just reward for twelve years' service to the club. With Norwich from the age of ten, spending three weeks in Finland for a tournament there. A superb shot-stopper with excellent reflexes, he is good enough to gain an international cap in the author's opinion, which he might achieve given his elevation to the Premiership and Europe.

Left: Gerard Mannion
Right: Andy Marshall

MARSHALL, Lee Keith

(1997–2001) **1997:** 6/0; 11/11
Midfielder **Career:** 100-23-13
Debut: 1 Nov 97 **Final:** 17 Mar 01

Born: Islington 21 Jan 1979

Career: Andrews Lane Primary School; Cheshunt Secondary School; Fairly House FC; Enfield; East Herts College; Hertfordshire County; Middlesex County; Luton Town School of Excellence; NORWICH CITY 27.03.97; Leicester City 21.03.2001.

Lee broke his ankle in only his second senior game for Norwich City. He was spotted by Dave Stringer playing against City's 'A' team and after adding fitness to his running engine he became a regular marauder from midfield. A bargain buy, he left after four years to join Premiership Leicester City to play alongside Akinbiyi and Eadie.

MARTIN, Isaac George (Pompey)

(1920–1927) **1922:** 5/8; 11/7
Centre Half **Career:** 243-0-1
Debut: 28 Aug 20 **Final:** 7 May 27

Born: Gateshead 25 May 1889
Died: Norwich 6 May 1962

Career: Gateshead Rodsley; Windy Nook FC; South Shields Parkside; Sunderland 19.02.08; Portsmouth 17.08.12; NORWICH CITY 12.07.13,

signing pro 29.8.20 to 1927; Boulton & Paul 08.09.28; Norwich CEYMS Oct 1928.

If ever £120 was well spent it was on the purchase of 'Pompey'. The nickname is surprising, since for Portsmouth he played only twelve Southern League, six Southern Alliance and one Pickford Benevolent Cup match. He deserved every accolade awarded to him in a great, whole-hearted Canary career. Towards the end of his career the obvious affection for him was shown in a match report that said, 'Although now silver-haired he has a young, vibrant heart and was much to the fore in a tremendous display'. His younger brother Frank played for Hull, Grimsby and Aberdare Athletic.

Left: 'Pompey' Martin
Right: Leslie Maskell

MASKELL, Leslie John

(1938)	**1938:** 5/7; 10/7
Centre Forward	**Career:** 7-0-2
Debut: 5 Feb 38	**Final:** 3 Sep 38

Born: Cowes, Isle of Wight 30 Nov 1918
Died: Diss 19 Nov 1995

Career: Isle of Wight Schoolboys; Hampshire Schoolboys; Cowes (Isle of Wight); Frost's Athletic; Norfolk County Junior & Senior; NORWICH CITY 26.10.33 (amat), pro 03.02.36; Lowestoft Town 30.11.46, May 1947 player coach; Diss Town 1950 player coach, later committee May 1958 and Chairman.

The career total of seven games above does an injustice to Les. A PTI in the Army, he found time to guest for Northampton, Aldershot and Ipswich as he effectively lost seven years of his career to the War. Added to his two league goals are another staggering 230 City goals as follows: First XI Friendlies 68, Reserves 84, 'A' Team 56, Transitional Season 10, War League Cup seven, and War League South five. Les was the Greyhound Inn licensee at Diss for 32 years and his four threes, two fours, four fives and one six would have made him a big star had his career not been so cruelly disrupted by the War. He was also a gentleman of the first order.

MASON, Arthur

(1927–1929)	**1927:** 5/11; 11/7
Right Back	**Career:** 8-0-0
Debut: 3 Dec 27	**Final:** 29 Mar 29

Born: Cornsay Colliery, nr Lanchester J/A/S 1895
Died: Clayton-le-Moors 22 Sep 1954

Career: Cornsay Colliery; Craghead United; West Stanley Jun 1925; Reading 26.08.25; NORWICH CITY 15.06.27; Hartlepools United 01.07.29; Crook Town Aug 1932; Annfield Plain Oct 1932; Cornsay Welfare Dec 1932; Thorne Colliery Oct 1933; Blackhall Welfare Aug 1934; Hesleden Rising Star Oct 1935.

Arthur helped Reading gain promotion to Division Two and therefore came to City with good credentials. Although a sturdy defender he only played 33 league games in his career. He joined John Hewitt at Hartlepools to finish an unremarkable career stats wise of only 33 games in six years.

MEGSON, Gary John

(1992–1995)	**1992:** 5/10; 11/6
Midfield	**Career:** 49-5-1
Debut: 15 Aug 92	**Final:** 5 Apr 95

Born: Manchester 2 May 1959

Career: Riding's High School; Frampton Rangers; Bristol Rovers Schoolboys; Parkway Juniors; Mangotsfield; Plymouth Argyle 19.08.75 (app), 09.05.77 (pro); Everton 13.02.80; Sheffield Wednesday 07.08.81; Nottingham Forset 20.08.84; Newcastle United 21.11.84; Sheffield Wednesday 20.12.85; Manchester City 12.01.89; NORWICH CITY 13.07.92, Jan 1994 player coach, 06.07.94 assistant manager, 09.04.95–05.07.95 caretaker manager; Lincoln City Jul 1995; Shrewsbury Town 08.09.95; Bradford City 29.11.95 coach; NORWICH CITY 22.12.95–21.06.96 manager; Blackpool 04.07.96 manager; Stockport County 01.07.97–25.06.99 manager; Stoke City 13.07.99–15.11.99 manager; West Bromwich Albion 09.03.2000 manager.

The son of Don, himself a former Sheffield Wednesday captain, Gary played with verve and an unquenchable spirit. The old head (called the General) on the young shoulders of Norwich with his steely combativeness ever to the fore. He has embarked on the roller coaster ride that is coaching and management, just failing to take his latest side up into the Premiership.

MELLON, David John Mead

(1921) **1921:** 5/8; 11/0
Outside Left **Career:** 1-0-0
Debut/Final: 26 Feb 21

Born: Felling-on-Tyne 6 May 1899
Died: Dudley 17 Sep 1981

Career: Woodskinners FC; NORWICH CITY 24.02.21–19.03.21 (amat); Felling Colliery; Aston Villa 03.05.22; Chesterfield 18.07.23.

Manager Gosnell beat Darlington to his signature, but he disappointed on his debut, with the Eastern Daily Press *saying of his display, 'At times he parted with the ball when he had a clear run'. He also had two reserve games before he parted company with City inside a month. David's occupation outside of football was brewery hand.*

MELLOR, Ian

(1973–1974) **1973:** 6/1; 10/12
Left Winger **Career:** 41-2-9
Debut: 10 Mar 73 **Final:** 12 Jan 74

Born: Sale, Manchester 19 Feb 1950

Career: Wythenshaw; Blackpool (amat); Bury (amat); Manchester City 13.11.67 (amat), 16.12.69 (pro); NORWICH CITY 08.03.73; Brighton & Hove Albion 06.05.74; Chester 24.02.78; Sheffield Wednesday 11.06.79; Bradford City 24.06.82; Tsun Wan (Hong Kong) Jan 1984; Worksop Town; Matlock Town; Gainsborough Trinity.

Ian, formerly a postman, joined City in their struggling Division One days. A tall, loose-limbed, ball playing winger he scored seven of his City goals in cup ties. Just over one third of his 300 league games were for Brighton. Nicknamed 'Spider' at Brighton, he has since joined the PFA in Manchester as a commercial manager.

MENDHAM, Peter Stanley

(1978–1986) **1978:** 5/10; 11/6
Midfield **Career:** 254-13-29
Debut: 30 Sep 78 (sub) **Final:** 19 Nov 86

Born: King's Lynn 9 Apr 1960

Career: St James' Infant School; St James' Park Juniors; Gaywood Park; West Norfolk & Norfolk Schoolboys Under-15 & Under-19; NORWICH CITY (schoolboy), (youth), 30.6.76 (app), Apr 1978 (pro); Mirimar (New Zealand) 1981 player coach; King's Lynn 01.06.87–Nov 1987 manager coach, 19.02.88 player; Hammarby (Sweden) (trial) Jun 1988; Watton United 21.06.88 player coach; NAC Breda (Holland) (trial) Nov 1989–Dec 1989; Diss Town 22.06.91; Wroxham 28.11.92; Diss Town Sep 1993; NORWICH CITY 'A' 15.10.94 (played one game)–10.03.96; North Walsham Town 11.11.94; Wroxham 07.10.95–06.04.98; Watton United 03.07.99; Attleborough Town 13.11.99; Red Roofs Oct 2000.

Left: Gary Megson
Right: Peter Mendham

Flame-haired Peter represented Norfolk at cross-country as a schoolboy and always turned in all-action, stamina-sapping displays. He overcame a number of injuries and reached double figures in goals in the triumphant march back to Division One in 1985/6. A long-standing pelvic injury meant that he could play but not train. He had a high profile role as Norwich City's Football in the Community Officer and he is now a full-time fund raiser for the East Anglian Ambulance Trust. He scored a Wembley winner for Diss Town to enable his side to pick up the FA Vase and he thoroughly deserved his testimonial match.

METCALF, Arthur

(1925) **1925:** 5/8; 11/5
Inside Forward **Career:** 2-0-0
Debut: 31 Aug 25 **Final:** 10 Oct 25

Born: Seaham Harbour 8 Apr 1889
Died: Liverpool 9 Feb 1936

Career: St George's FC; Herrington Swifts; Durham Schoolboys; Hebburn Argyle Aug 1908; North Shields Athletic; Newcastle United 05.04.09; Liverpool 25.05.12; Stockport County Aug 1918; Swindon Town 17.06.20; Accrington Stanley 21.06.22; Aberdare Athletic 01.06.23; NORWICH CITY 02.07.25.

Arthur played for Liverpool in the 1914 FA Cup Final, some four years after his Football League debut on 09.03.10. He therefore joined City after 15 years in the game so it is not surprising that his career at The Nest was of some brevity. Including wartime football he

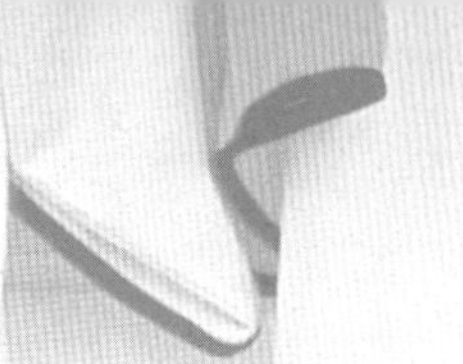

netted a career total of 118 goals with, it was said, 'A daring and determined style'. His brother George was a professional footballer with Sunderland and Huddersfield Town.

METCALF, Colin Christopher Anthony

(1962–1964) **1963:** 6/0; 12/7
Centre Half **Career:** 13-0-l
Debut: 5 Sep 62 **Final:** 27 Mar 64

Born: Norwich 3 Mar 1939

Career: Norman YC (amat); NORWICH CITY 11.7.60 part time, 29.01.62 (pro); Southend United 04.09.64; Wisbech Town Aug 1965; Lowestoft Town Jul 1971–23.04.74; Wymondham Town 1989 joint manager, 1990 manager.

Colin joined City from local amateur football and took until January 1962 before he signed as a full-time professional. He gave useful service to the club with 113 reserve games. At Southend he had just three league games with his last match being on 18.09.64 before being displaced by a centre half named Watson. His occupation outside football was that of an electrician.

METCALF, Mark Peter

(1982) **1984:** 5/10; 10/0
Midfield **Career:** 0-1-0
Debut/Final: 13 Nov 82 (sub)

Born: Norwich 25 Sep 1965

Career: Hewett School; Norfolk Under-15, 16, 18; England Under-18 squad; NORWICH CITY 1980 (youth), 02.07.82–25.09.83, 07.05.87 (pro); King's Lynn 25.06.87; Wroxham 24.01.88–May 1990; Lakeford United; Diss Town Oct 1991; Wymondham Town 1992.

At 21 Mark had experienced the highs and lows of the game. England Youth squads, an FA Youth Cup Winner's medal and a first team appearance at 17. Also suffered a broken leg in a Combination match and was later given a free transfer. He was then asked to help out because of a player shortage and did so well that he was re-engaged, scoring in the first reserve match of the 1986/87 campaign. Mark enjoyed most success with Wroxham, for whom he netted 29 goals in 88 matches.

MIDDLETON, John

(1937–1938) **1938:** 5/8; 10/6
Inside Right **Career:** 3-0-0
Debut: 6 Nov 37 **Final:** 19 Feb 38

Born: Mickley 15 Apr 1910
Died: Darlington 3 Aug 1971

Career: Mickley School; Mickley FC; Swansea Town 23.02.39; Walker Celtic Jul 1932; Darlington 27.06.33; Blackpool 02.04.35 NORWICH CITY 17.06.37; South Shields Jul 1938.

John was a useful goalscorer for Darlington (Division Three North) before stepping up to Division Two with Blackpool and Norwich. However, despite regular goals for the reserves, he found it difficult to displace Tim Coleman. He opposed his brother William in August 1939 in a match between South Shields and Darlington's reserves. He was a crane driver by occupation in later life.

MILBURN, John

(1939) **1939:** 5/11; 12/4
Left Back **Career:** 15-0-0
Debut: 25 Feb 39 **Final:** 6 May 39

Born: Ashington 18 Mar 1908
Died: Leeds 21 Aug 1979

Career: Seaton Hirst Corinthians; Spen Black & White; Bolton Wanderers (trial) Oct 1926; Leeds United 11.11.27; NORWICH CITY 24.02.39; Second World War guested for Bradford City, Darlington and Leeds; Bradford City 31.10.46 player coach, 1947–Jul 1948 manager, assistant manager to May 1949.

John, a former miner, was a player who believed that he was given his shoulders to use in a fair charge on an opponent. The Topical Times Annual *said of him, 'Steady and strong and never loses heart'. He was one of the Milburn brotherhood of Leeds. Remarkably his brothers, Jack, George and James hold the unique record of all having played as ever-presents in a season for Leeds.*

MILLER, James Alistair Williamson

(1962–1964) **1964:** 5/8; 10/12
Outside Left **Career:** 25-0-2
Debut: 18 Aug 62 **Final:** 1 Feb 64

Born: Glasgow 24 Jan 1936

Career: Glasgow Boys Brigade; Third Lanark 1954; St Mirren 23.07.57; Brighton & Hove Albion (trial) 28.04.62; NORWICH CITY 17.05.62; Berwick Rangers 06.07.64; Dumbarton 29.10.65; Hamilton Academicals 09.08.66.

Alistair scored over 50 goals for St Mirren, one of which came on 25.04.59 in a 3–1 Scottish Cup Final win over Aberdeen before 108,591

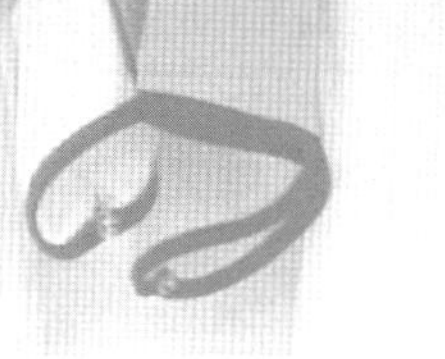
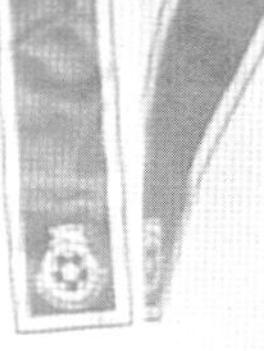

spectators. His English career did not reach those heady heights. A City goal against Southampton produced a Pink 'Un *headline of 'Merry Miller'. He extended his playing career by another four years by playing back in Scotland.*

MILLER, John Tony

(1974–1976) **1975:** 5/8; 10/9
Outside Right **Career:** 28-1-5
Debut: 26 Oct 74 **Final:** 6 Apr 76

Born: Ipswich 21 Sep 1950

Career: Whitton Infants; Whitton Juniors; Thurleston Secondary Modern School; Ipswich Boys; Suffolk Schoolboys; Ipswich Town 1966 (app), 15.07.68 (pro); NORWICH CITY 25.10.74; Mansfield Town 29.07.76; Port Vale 01.10.80; Oakham United 1983; Selston; Blidworth Welfare Mar 1993 assistant manager.

When Johnny scored twice at Portman Road for City in the League Cup Quarter Final match, Ipswich had not received the cash for his transfer, which had gone through some months earlier. Manager Peter Morris signed him for Mansfield. A specialist gave him the option to retire or face the possibility of walking with a stick in the future. Johnny latterly worked at the Watton Sports Centre.

MILLIGAN, Michael Joseph

(1994–2000) **1994:** 5/8; 11/0
Midfield **Career:** 130-12-5
Debut: 19 Sep 94 **Final:** 22 Mar 00

Born: Moss Side, Manchester 20 Feb 1967

Career: St Bedes Grammar School; Manchester County; Flixton Boys; Oldham Athletic Apr 1981 (app), 13.12.84 (YTS), 02.03.85 (pro); Everton 24.08.90; Oldham Athletic 17.07.91; NORWICH CITY 27.06.94; Blackpool 18.05.2000.

The 1996/97 Norwich City handbook's front cover pictures Mike with yours truly in the background crowd shot. A vastly experienced professional with the highest of pedigrees, he gave full value in a six year spell at Carrow Road with his tigerish, never-say-die attitude. Clubs need his like, with his non-stop talking and encouragement to players.

MILLS, Daniel John

(1995–1998) **1996:** 5/11; 11/9
Full Back **Career:** 51-22-1
Debut: 13 Aug 95 **Final:** 7 Mar 98 (sub)

Born: Norwich 18 May 1977

Danny Mills

Career: Garrick Green First School; Church Street Middle School; Sprowston High School; Sprowston Cubs; Old Catton Under-8–14; NORWICH CITY 19.05.91 (assoc), 05.07.93 (trainee), 07.11.94 (pro); Charlton Athletic 19.03.98; Leeds United 01.07.99.

Danny played in a variety of defensive roles for City, rising from a youth debut when 15 to a full England cap in 2001 under Sven-Goran Eriksson's leadership. Norwich-born, he is tenacious in the tackle and resolute in defence and was outstanding for Leeds United in their quest for European success last year. Life is a ball at the moment for Danny as he has just become a father for the second time.

MILLS, James Thompson

(1922–1923) **1922:** 5/8; 11/5
Inside Right **Career:** 6-0-3
Debut: 26 Aug 22 **Final:** 5 May 23

Born: Rochdale 15 Jan 1898
Died: Southport 27 Feb 1972

Career: Balderstone Parish Church; Rochdale All Saints; Rochdale Nov 1919; Bolton Wanderers 16.04.20; NORWICH CITY 17.06.22; Torquay Athletic Oct 1923; Chester; Rochdale Tradesmen (amat) May 1928; Bury Co-op (amat) Aug 1931.

James served in the Welsh Regiment in France and was later wounded at Gallipoli. Not unnaturally his League career was affected by this unfortunate event, and severe tonsilitis at Bolton meant that he never got to show his best while there. He did well at City in his half a dozen games and latterly was living in Southport as a retired salesman.

MILNE, Maurice

(1957–1958) **1957:** 5/9; 10/0
Outside Right **Career:** 5-0-0
Debut: 24 Aug 57 **Final:** 29 Mar 58

Born: Dundee 21 Oct 1932
Died: Tayport 10 Aug 1998

Career: St Joseph's Juniors; Tayport Amateurs; Dundee United (trial) 16.04.55, (signed) 20.04.55; NORWICH CITY 25.05.57; Gloucester City Jul 1958; Dunfermline Athletic 1959; Brechin City 25.09.59; Forfar Athletic (trial) 01.04.60.

Cardiff City had agreed to pay a considerably higher fee for his services than Norwich, but he preferred to join the Canaries. A brief stay at Carrow Road saw him score against Ipswich in a floodlight friendly and against Spurs in an East Anglian Cup game. There was annoyance that he never made ten appearances for the club, but a contract clause called for an additional payment to Dundee if this total was reached and the Norwich City Director's were mindful of the club finances.

MINETT, Jason Keith

(1990–1993) **1990:** 5/11; 10/7
Left Back **Career:** 0-3-0
Debut: 1 Sep 90 (sub) **Final:** 6 Mar 93 (sub)

Born: Peterborough 12 Aug 1971

Career: Sir Harry Smith Community College; Whittlesey Colts; Peterborough Rangers; Peterborough Boys; Huntingdonshire: PGL England; NORWICH CITY (junior), 1986 (assoc), Aug 1987 (YTS), 04.07.89 (pro); Exeter City 19.03.93; Lincoln City 10.07.95; Exeter City 17.01.97; Peterborough United (trial) Jul 1998; Kettering Town (trial) Jul 1998; Doncaster Rovers Aug 1998; Boston United 16.05.2000; King's Lynn 28.06.2001.

A Manchester United supporter as a boy who was invited to train with them after winning a Butlin's run competition for young footballers. Kit Carson brought three of his successful PGL team to Carrow Road: Jason, Lee Power and Robert Ullathorne. Described as 'Quiet, shy but aggressive in a subtle way with Ian Crook ability to pass and receive the return ball'. Eventually joined former colleague Tony Spearing under his tutorship at King's Lynn.

MOLBY, Jan

(1995–1996) **1995:** 6/1; 14/0
Midfield **Career:** 5-0-1
Debut: 30 Dec 95 **Final:** 24 Jan 96 (goal)

Born: Kolding, Denmark 4 Jul 1963

Career: Kolding IF (Denmark) Under-6–18; Ajax (Holland) 1982; Liverpool 24.08.84; Barnsley (loan) 22.09.95; NORWICH CITY (loan) 29.12.95–28.01.96; Swansea City 23.02.96–08.10.97 player-manager; Kidderminster Harriers 24.04.99 manager.

Danish international Jan (the surname is pronounced 'Molebu'), with his Scouse accent, faced grief about his waist size when playing but he ran Liverpool's midfield in a glittering career there. A playmaker from a sporting background – brother Torben is also a manager; sister Tytt is an international footballer and cousin Johnny a European championship winner with Denmark. He has experienced the ups and downs of managership, finally successfully leading his present side into the Football League.

MOORE, Neil

(1997) **1997:** 6/0; 12/9
Defender **Career:** 2-0-0
Debut: 25 Apr 97 **Final:** 4 May 97

Born: Walton, Liverpool 21 Sep 1972

Career: Walton High School; Liverpool Schoolboys; Merseyside Schoolboys; Jermingham FC; Everton 13.02.88 (assoc), 04.06.91 (pro); Blackpool (loan) 09.09.94; Oldham Athletic (loan) 16.02.95; Carlisle United (loan) 25.08.95; Rotherham United (loan) 20.03.96; NORWICH CITY (loan) 08.01.97; Burnley 29.08.97; Macclesfield Town 10.12.99; Telford United 24.03.2000.

Central defender Neil experienced a number of loan spells before manager Mike Walker brought him to City when the club was short of defensive cover. Neil's longest playing spell was at Burnley before he joined his ninth club, where the author witnessed him being sent off against Stevenage in September 2000.

MORAN, James

(1957–1959) **1962:** 5/7; 11/9
Inside Right **Career:** 40-0-18
Debut: 23 Nov 57 **Final:** 12 Dec 59 (goal)

Born: Cleland, nr Motherwell 6 Mar 1935

Career: Wishaw Juniors; Leicester City 10.12.55; NORWICH CITY 16.11.57; Northampton Town 26.01.61; Darlington 01.08.62; Workington 25.07.63 to 1965; Lowestoft Town Aug 1966–Aug 1967 player coach; Gothic Oct 1967; Yarmouth Town 01.11.67, Aug 1968–11.05.69 player-manager; Lowestoft Town Aug 1969–Feb 1971 player coach; Holt United manager; Gorleston manager; Coltishall HV 1986–Jul 1988 manager; Holt United Jul 1992 manager; Wymondhan Town Sep 1992 manager; Bury Town Oct 1992 coach.

His first appearance for City was in a friendly against Aberdeen playing under the nom de plume *'Johnstone'. He scored a hat-trick against Newport for City but was not a regular until he*

moved to Workington. He brought dicipline to his sides and improved their fortunes on the field. Two brothers also played league football.

MORGAN, George William

(1946–1950) **1948:** 5/7; 11/2
Outside Right/Left **Career:** 67-0-15
Debut: 28 Dec 46 **Final:** 11 Mar 50

Born: Cardiff 28 Mar 1923
Died: Norwich 3 Oct 1989

Career: Cardiff Nomads; Cardiff City 14.08.39 (amat); NORWICH CITY 30.12.46 to 1950; Newport County 10.06.50 retiring through injury.

George's transfer was ratified at the Football League on the 30th with his debut being made two days earlier in a torrid match against his home town team. One of two Welshman named Morgan on the books at the same time and it was difficult to decide which one was the fastest. He became a customs officer and lived in Wales for 30 years, but like so many former players with an affinity to Norfolk, he returned to reside in the area.

MORGAN, Richard Denis

(1946–1956) **1948:** 5/8; 11/6
Right Back **Career:** 250-0-3
Debut: 5 Oct 46 **Final:** 28 Jan 56

Born: Seven Sisters, Glamorgan 22 Sept 1925
Died: Aylesham, Kent 4 Jul 1980

Career: Briton Ferry; Cardiff City 17.08.42; NORWICH CITY 7.10.46 to 1956; Merthyr Jan 1957, later manager.

In the early 1950s Denis was widely tipped to gain Welsh recognition before a knee injury put him out of the game for a while. He was very fast and inclined to take risks but confident that he had the pace to recover any lost position. When he was on form he was a polished, classy performer. A railway porter (retired), he died tragically after developing gangrene (arterial) in the right leg and having a left mid-thigh amputation.

MORRIS, Peter John

(1974–1976) **1974:** 5/8; 11/3
Midfield **Career:** 86-0-1
Debut: 17 Aug 74 **Final:** 24 Apr 76

Born: New Houghton, Derbyshire 8 Nov 1943

Career: Longwith Boys Club; New Houghton Baptists; Ladybrook Celts; Mansfield Town 08.01.59 (app), 09.11.60 (pro); Ipswich Town 01.03.68; NORWICH CITY 13.06.74; Mansfield Town 09.07.76 player-manager; Newcastle United 23.02.78 assistant manager; Peterborough United Feb 1979 manager, Aug 1979–May 1982 non contract player; Crewe Alexandra Nov 1982–Jun 1983 manager; Southend United Jul 1983–Feb 1984 manager; Nuneaton Borough Jun 1985 manager; Aajar Sporting (Saudi Arabia) coach; Leicester City Jan 1987 coach, Dec 1987 caretaker manager, assistant manager, reserve coach; Kettering Town Jun 1988–27.05.92 manager; Boston United 02.06.92 manager; Northampton Town Sep 1993 manager, Dec 1994–Mar 1995 assistant manager, acting manager in Jan 1995; King's Lynn May 1995 manager; Kettering Town 02.05.98–Feb 2001 manager.

Denis Morgan

Peter's strength and non-stop running earned him the cognomen 'Diesel' in an admired career of over 600 league games. His accurate long passes helped Mansfield, Ipswich and Norwich win promotion. An amazing career in coaching and management makes him one of the most respected men in non-league circles and his services are always in demand.

MORRIS, Robert Arthur John

(1933–1938) **1934:** 5/11; 10/9
Left/Right Half **Career:** 46-0-0
Debut: 7 Oct 33 **Final:** 2 Apr 38

Born: Hatton, Bedfont 11 Mar 1913

Career: Slough; Leyton; Brentford; Southall; NORWICH CITY 08.05.33; Colchester United 21.7.38.

The Pink Un *originally referred to him as Roy. A 1936 comment: 'His reserve goals earned him transitory reappearances in the first team'. Robert had a long throw that almost rivalled that of Bernard Robinson. Including War friendlies he played 85 games for Colchester and he also guested for Southend United against Norwich City in wartime.*

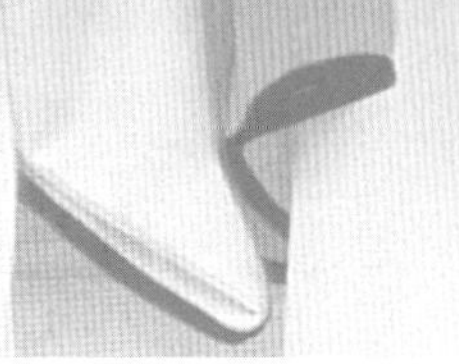

MORTENSEN, Henrik Egegod

(1989–1991) **1989:** 5/10; 11/3
Forward **Career:** 14-9-2
Debut: 29 Nov 89 (goal) **Final:** 23 Oct 91

Born: Odder, Denmark 12 Feb 1968

Career: Aarhus Gymnastik Forening (Denmark) 1974–1984; RSC Anderlecht (Belgium) Jul 1985; Aarhus Gymnastik Forening (Denmark) Apr 1988; NORWICH CITY 02.10.89–Dec 1991; Aarhus Gymnastik Forening (Denmark) 1992.

Henrik, the son of a lawyer, spoke English, Dutch and Danish and he was with Aarhus for ten years to the age of sixteen. An Under-21 Danish international having won a Young Player of the Year award in Denmark; a Belgian championship medal and made appearances in the quarter finals of the European Cup and ECWC. A twisting, darting forward who cost Norwich City 4.3 million Danish Crowns. Typically called 'The Great Dane' and 'Hooray Henryk' (a spelling mistake by the press) he returned home and helped his side win the Danish Cup in May 1996.

Left: Henrik Mortensen
Right: Philip Mulryne

MOULE, Alfred Samuel

(1927–1928) **1927:** 5/9; 11/7
Inside Left **Career:** 35-0-12
Debut: 27 Aug 27 (goal) **Final:** 21 Apr 28

Born: Canning Town 31 Jul 1894
Died: Sompting, Sussex 5 Feb 1973

Career: West Ham Corinthians; Catford South End; Leytonstone; Millwall Mar 1920 (amat), 19.05.21 (pro); NORWICH CITY 11.05.27; Watford 18.08.28; Margate Aug 1929, Aug 1930 player-manager.

Scored twice versus City for Millwall and increased his goal tally with each successive season. In 208 league games for the Lions he scored 64 goals including three hat-tricks. At Norwich he became the eighth player to score on his league debut. He was a brainy player with good ball control. Alf also excelled at cricket and played for Essex (1921–24), Falmouth and Devon. He coached in Cornwall and later at Lancing College and played against such cricketing legends as Fender, Rhodes, Sutcliffe and Tate.

MOUNTFORD, Peter

(1982) **1982:** 5/10; 10/10
Midfield **Career:** 1-3-0
Debut: 20 Feb 82 (sub) **Final:** 11 Dec 82

Born: Bucknall, Stoke-on-Trent 9 Apr 1960

Career: NORWICH CITY 22.04.78; Charlton Athletic 29.09.83; Orient 18.05.85; Fishers Athletic Jul 1987.

Peter was a midfield player but had his one full Canary game on the left flank. He was given a free transfer by both Norwich and Charlton and at times drew interest from Chester and Swansea before settling in London.

MULLETT, Joseph

(1959–1968) **1964:** 5/10; 11/0
Left Back **Career:** 246-2-5
Debut: 7 Mar 59 **Final:** 3 Feb 68 (sub)

Born: Blackheath, Birmingham 2 Oct 1936
Died: Sandwell, West Bromwich 3 Mar 1995

Career: Malt Hill United; Birmingham City 09.02.55 (amat), 06.07.55 (pro); NORWICH CITY 31.01.59; King's Lynn Jun 1968; Lowestoft Town Jul 1970; Yarmouth Town 13.10.71–01.01.72.

Joe, a fit young soldier, could not break into the St Andrews side and he found early life just as difficult at Carrow Road. Once established, however, he gave seven years of gold-star service, reaching 40 first team games a season regularly. His clinical accuracy with the ball, plus his power, made him a popular player with the fans. Joe became another of the myriad of ex-player landlords, keeping an inn in Cradley Heath before becoming a shopkeeper.

MULRYNE, Philip Patrick Stephen

(1999– **1999:** 5/8; 10/11
Midfield **Career:** 50-4-3
Debut: 3 Apr 99 (sub)

Born: Belfast 1 Jan 1978

Career: St Oliver Plunkett Primary School; De-la-Salle Boys Club; Manchester United from trainee, 17.03.95 (pro); NORWICH CITY 25.03.99.

Phil, possessor of a football brain, has great touch and vision. He is a full Northern Ireland

international but his 1999/2000 City campaign was wrecked by injury. A midfield general who bears the Old Trafford hallmark of class. With full fitness he is destined to gain the hero worship and respect attained by Martin Peters in the late 1970s at Carrow Road. We can praise him no higher.

MURPHY, John Edward

(1924–1926)	**1925:** 5/11; 11/6
Centre Half	**Career:** 36-0-0
Debut: 9 Feb 24	**Final:** 23 Jan 26

Born: Greenhead 3 Nov 1900
Died: Leicester 22 Nov 1973

Career: Bell's Close Wesleyan; Walker Celtic; South Shields 10.05.20; Walker Celtic Jun 1921; NORWICH CITY 09.06.23; Southend United 24.05.26; Scunthorpe United Jun 1927; Newark Town Mar 1928; Loughborough Corinthians; Bath City Aug 1931; Frost's Athletic Aug 1934.

Walker Celtic supplied many good players to first-class clubs and John was no exception to this rule. A City Handbook reckoned that with experience he was likely to develop into the best type of centre half. They had forgotten that 'Pompey' Martin had almost exclusive rights to this berth. A retired foreman painter.

MURPHY, Lionel (Spud)

(1931–1934)	**1932:** 5/6; 10/10
Outside Left	**Career:** 132-0-25
Debut: 29 Aug 31	**Final:** 22 Sep 34

Born: Hovingham, North Yorkshire 15 Sep 1895
Died: Derby 27 Oct 1968

Career: Melton Mowbray; Green Howards; Derby County 01.02.22; Bolton Wanderers 16.01.28; Mansfield Town Sep 1929; NORWICH CITY 11.05.31; Luton Town 24.10.34; British Celanese Aug 1935.

He was an expert at selling the dummy to a full back and an artist to his fingertips. Scorer of 50 goals at Derby with his deft balance and tricky swerve at speed proving to be disconcerting to all who faced him. A local Derby journalist wrote simply, 'Spud is a genius. A real terror for his size'. Even approaching 36 when joining Norwich City he gave three years' great service.

MUZINIC, Drazen

(1980–1981)	**1980:** 5/10; 11/10
Utility	**Career:** 17-6-0
Debut: 13 Sep 80	**Final:** 28 Dec 81

'Spud' Murphy

Born: Yugoslavia 25 Jan 1953

Career: Hadjuk Split (Yugoslavia); NORWICH CITY 12.09.80–cancelled contract 05.07.82.

When he was signed the local press said, 'Drazen Who-ic?'. He was a winner in his own country with 36 full international Caps, four League titles and five Cup Winner's medals to his name. That he had ball skills was not in doubt as Manager Bond bought him for the club record fee of £300,000. Bond faced two problems – where to play him and how to communicate – and did not solve either of them. An interpreter from the University of East Anglia was on the touchline for one game passing on instructions and by the time of Drazen's 19th game for City he had worn seven different numbered shirts. Latterly running a restaurant in Brac.

NEDERGAARD, Steen

(2000–	**2000:** 1.74m; 76kg
Defender	**Career:** 12-9-1
Debut: 5 Sep 00 (sub)	

Born: Alborg, Denmark 25 Feb 1970

Career: Vigerslev (Denmark) 1983; Odense Boldklub (Denmark) 1989; NORWICH CITY 03.07.2000.

Steen (his surname is pronounced 'Nurergore') has played in the three European competitions including a win at Real Madrid in the UEFA Cup – his most memorable game so far. He made 365 appearances for 39 goals for Odense and he also played three times for the Danish National league side. Right-sided, quick, athletic and versatile, with a handiness at taking free kicks, he is placed to make more City appearances than our two previous Danes put together.

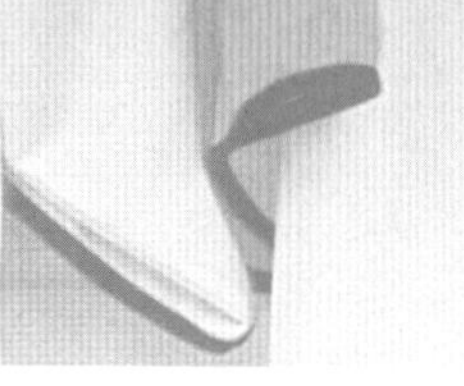

Left: Jimmy Neighbour
Right: Ken Nethercott

NEIGHBOUR, James Edward

(1976–1979) **1977:** 5/8; 11/10
Winger **Career:** 113-2-5
Debut: 2 Oct 76 **Final:** 8 Sep 79

Born: Chingford 15 Nov 1950

Career: Waltham Forest; Essex & London Boys; Tottenham Hotspur 16.04.66 (amat), 15.11.68 (pro); NORWICH CITY 30.09.76; Seattle Sounders (USA) 06.05.79 to 14.08.79; West Ham United 13.09.79; Bournemouth (loan) 13.01.83; Enfield Town Oct 1988 coach/trainer; West Ham United 10.10.90 youth development officer; Doncaster Rovers 30.09.94–21.12.94 First XI coach; Tottenham Hotspur youth development; St Albans City Feb 1997–Apr 1998 manager.

Jimmy played against City in a League Cup Final for Spurs and also picked up a UEFA Cup Winners medal. A provider rather than a scorer of goals with his twisting, darting runs being brought into play in over 300 career games, mostly at the top level. He knew the Clarence Park ground of St Albans as the Spurs reserve side play their home games there.

NETHERCOTT, Kenneth Walter Samuel

(1947–1959) **1952:** 5/11; 12/9
Goalkeeper **Career:** 416-0-0
Debut: 27 Sep 47 **Final:** 28 Feb 59

Born: Bristol 22 Jul 1925

Career: Board Plain Lads Club; Bristol & West of England Schoolboys; Bristol Boys 1936; Bristol City Colts; Cardiff City 1942 (amat); NORWICH CITY 09.04.47 (amat), 02.06.47 (pro) to 1959; Wisbech Jul 1959–1961; Gothic Oct 1965–1966.

Ken appeared at Carrow Road in February 1938 for Bristol Boys and was a grand signing by Cyril Spiers. A brilliant, fearless keeper who most undoubtedly deserved to win more than the one England 'B' cap that he gained in 1953. Powerfully built with uncanny anticipation he made his final Canary appearance in a Hospital Cup match. Still lives locally and he retains immense pride in being a Canary.

NEWMAN, Robert Nigel

(1991–1997) **1992:** 6/0; 13/0
Defender **Career:** 223-26-17
Debut: 17 Aug 91 **Final:** 3 Dec 97 (sub)

Born: Bradford-on-Avon 13 Dec 1963

Career: Heytesbury Primary School; Kingdown Comprehensive School; Mid Wiltshire Boys; Devizes Saints; Westown Harriers; Bristol City 20.10.79 (assoc), 27.06.80 (app), 05.10.81 (pro); NORWICH CITY 11.07.91–10.12.97; Motherwell (loan) 11.12.97; NORWICH CITY 10.03.98; Wigan (loan) 26.03.98; Southend United 28.07.98, player coach 1999, assistant manager.

Rob Newman

Rob, a wholehearted player, had a league debut under difficult circumstances as it followed immediately after the 'Ashton Gate Eight' episode. He topped City's scoring charts in his debut season, having one shot timed at 85mph. Despite admitting that he could not pass like Crook or run forever like Goss he continues to give value for money and has recently netted vital goals for Southend United. Also plays cricket occasionally for Swardeston.

NEWSOME, Jonathan

(1994–1996) **1994:** 6/2; 13/1
Centre Half **Career:** 75-1-8
Debut: 20 Aug 94 **Final:** 9 Mar 96

Born: Sheffield 6 Sep 1970

Career: Limpsfield Middle School; Hindy House Comprehensive School; Sheffield Boys Under-13–15; South Yorkshire Boys; Yorkshire; Sheffield Wednesday 07.06.85 (schoolboy), 01.07.87 (trainee), 01.07.89 (pro); Leeds United 11.06.91; NORWICH CITY 30.06.94; Sheffield Wednesday

15.03.96; Bolton Wanderers (loan) 18.11.98 retired 19.05.2000.

A club record million pound signing in 1994, he was immediately appointed captain. Powerfully built with the traditional centre-half's qualities of strength and aerial ability. A Player of the Year at Carrow Road as a reward for his great consistency and inspirational leadership.

NIGHTINGALE, Mark Barry Douglas

(1977–1981) **1978:** 5/10; 10/7
Midfield **Career:** 32-7-0
Debut: 30 Aug 77 **Final:** 10 Oct 81

Born: Salisbury 1 Feb 1957

Career: England Youth; Bournemouth 24.10.72 (app), 18.07.74 (pro); Crystal Palace 16.06.76; NORWICH CITY 08.07.77; Bulova (Hong Kong); Bournemouth 27.08.82; Peterborough United 04.08.86; Kettering Town Aug 1988; King's Lynn 28.07.90; Wisbech Town; Warboys Town; Bearings Direct FC.

Mark played in the same England Youth side as Peter Barnes and Ray Wilkins, both men of course winning full caps for their country. He was only a regular first teamer at Dean Court and he had passed 200 appearances for them by the end of the 1985/86 season. City used him to fill the gaps instead of finding him a permanent slot in the team. He joined Peter Morris at Kettering Town and gave excellent service to Warboys.

NIXON, William John

(1962) **1962:** 5/11; 11/7
Inside Right **Career:** 1-0-0
Debut/Final: 27 Feb 62

Born: Ballynahinch 28 Sep 1941

Career: Newtonards 1954; Distillery; NORWICH CITY 23.03.61; Shrewsbury Town 09.03.62; Newtonards Jun 1964–1976.

On the City staff have been a Reagan, Nixon and a Carter – with as far as we know no American ancestry. Bill was a Northern Ireland Schools international who netted seven reserve goals for City. His one Football League goal came at Bradford Park Avenue on 26.03.63 for Shrewsbury Town. He played over 500 games for Newtonards and he had a variety of roles with them. Latterly the Chairman and President of the Northern Ireland PFA.

NOBLE, Arthur

(1929) **1929:** 5/8; 11/7
Right Back **Career:** 1-0-0
Debut/Final: 2 Nov 29

Left: Jon Newsome
Right: 'Monty' Norman

Born: Norwich 15 Nov 1895
Died: Attleborough 29 Jul 1990

Career: Surrey Road School; Junior Institute 1910; Settlement House; St James 1911; First World War – Royal Field Artillery; Norfolk County; Norwich CEYMS 1919; City Wanderers FC 1920–1935; NORWICH CITY 29.08.29 (amat).

A modest man and a fine amateur player, helping his teams to win leagues and cups. He helped form the Wanderers Football Club, formed by old players from The Nest, and played for them until he was 39. In the Licensed trade at The Peacock, helping his parents, until he took over The Heartsease from 1932 to 1946.

NORMAN, Maurice (Monty)

(1955) **1964:** 6/1; 12/3
Centre Half **Career:** 35-0-0
Debut: 5 Feb 55 **Final:** 29 Oct 55

Born: Mulbarton, Norfolk 8 May 1934

Career: Norfolk Schools; Mulbarton FC; Wymondham Minors; NORWICH CITY, 1951 (amat), 30.09.52 (pro); Tottenham Hotspur 03.11.55 to 1965 – retiring after breaking his leg versus an Hungarian XI.

He was recommended to Norwich City by the late Neville Howlett and rivals Barkas (qv) as the one that got away. Cool, discriminate and unflappable, Monty was one of the finest pivots in the country when at Spurs. Represented England 23 times. An awesome and uncompromising tackler with a hairstyle that added inches to his frame. He was another player (see Hannah) given to walking home after a game if he was upset by the display. He used to clean the baths at Norwich and stood in ditches on the farm, so he was never changed by fame. Involved in a number of business enterprises until retirement in 1998 in order to spend more time with his grandchildren.

NORTH, Ernest Joseph

(1924–1926) **1925:** 5/9; 11/4
Inside Left **Career:** 60-0-20
Debut: 6 Sep 24 **Final:** 13 Mar 26

Born: Burton-on-Trent 23 Sept 1895
Died: Havant, Portsmouth 24 Aug 1955

Career: Tuxford School; Atlas & Norfolk Works; Sheffield Works football; Sheffield United (amat); Army; Arsenal 07.11.19 (amat), 17.12.19 (pro); Reading 12.05.22; Gillingham 16.07.23; NORWICH CITY 20.08.24; Watford 07.06.26; Northfleet Jul 1927; Camberley College coach.

The 1925/26 City handbook had the following description of him: 'Parts with the ball to advantage, and avoids hard knocks skilfully. Plucky and a good shot'. He played cricket for Middlesex – 24 games between 1923 and 1927. A more than useful bowler as he once made it into the top ten national bowling averages, dismissing the likes of Gunn and Woolley. At his peak it was said that the populace used to shout from the rooftops about his powers.

NOTMAN, Alexander McKeachie

(2000– **2000:** 5/8; 10/10
Forward **Career:** 10-7-1
Debut: 2 Dec 2000

Born: Edinburgh 10 Dec 1979

Career: East Houses Boys Club; Tynecastle Boys Club; Glasgow Rangers Youth; Manchester United from trainee 17.12.96; Sheffield United (loan) 20.01.2000; Aberdeen (loan) 11.02.2000; NORWICH CITY 28.11.2000.

At Old Trafford he netted 85 goals in 121 games from Under-17 to reserve level to outscore David Healy and Paul Scholes over the same period. A potentially lethal striker after coming to prominence by scoring three brilliant goals for Scotland Under-18s against Denmark and twice more in the Munich Testimonial match in August 1998. Breaking his City duck against Burnley in April 2001 should only lead to greater success.

O'BRIEN, Michael Terence

(1929–1931) **1930:** 6/1; 13/7
Centre Half **Career:** 65-0-5
Debut: 31 Aug 29 **Final:** 2 May 31

Born: Kilcock, Co. Dublin 10 Aug 1893
Died: Uxbridge 21 Sep 1940

Career: Walker Celtic; Wallsend; Blyth Spartans; Newcastle East End; Alloa Athletic (trial) Mar 1919; Brentford 03.05.19; NORWICH CITY Aug 1919; South Shields Dec 1919; Queens Park Rangers May 1920; Leicester City 16.03.22; Hull City 05.06.24; Brooklyn Wanderers (USA) May 1926; Derby County 13.12.26; Walsall 06.06.28; NORWICH CITY 17.05.29; Watford 08.06.31; Queens Park Rangers 01.05.33–10.10.35 manager; Brentford Nov 1935 assistant manager; Ipswich Town 29.05.36–11.08.37 manager.

A wandering Irishman whose managerships sadly ended in dispute following a 20-year playing career. You name it and he appeared to have done it. He served in the Army before the First World War and in the Navy and the Royal Flying Corp during it. A fine pivot and an Irish and Eire international, he had a local confectioner's and tobacconist's shop during his second spell at Norwich. Also an assistant groundsman – hardly anyone has packed more into 47 years.

O'DONNELL, Neil

(1967–1974) **1970:** 5/10; 11/8
Inside Right **Career:** 45-19-3
Debut: 19 Sep 67 **Final:** 16 Jan 74

Born: Glasgow 21 Dec 1949

Career: St Augustine's; Drumchapel Amateurs; NORWICH CITY (from Juniors), 30.12.66 (pro); Gillingham 08.07.74; Sheffield Wednesday 29.10.75 retiring Oct 1976 after breaking a bone in his back.

Neil, a Scottish Youth international, gave City excellent service as an adaptable player without being a regular first-teamer (178 reserve games for 25 goals). He was also an unused substitute on 25 occasions for City. Norwich were the opposition for him in his Testimonial Match in February 1977 in Sheffield, where he still resides and works for a finance company.

OGLE, Roger

(1931) **1931:** 5/9; 11/0
Left Back **Career:** 1-0-0
Debut/Final: 19 Sep 31

Born: Barrington 16 Sep 1904
Died: Clydach, Swansea 30 Aug 1991

Career: West Allotment Institute; Preston Colliery Jan 1924; Stakeford United; Barrington Colliery Welfare; Shildon Athletic; Bebside Gordon; Barnsley 07.09.29 (amat), Jan 1930 (pro); NORWICH CITY 22.05.31; Netherford United; Stakeford Albion Jul 1934; Bedlington District Pit Welfare Sep 1936.

Roger's one City game earned him a win bonus and there are not many players that have a 100% success record. He suffered from

injuries including a broken arm and cartilage trouble. In his time up north he remembered wet hot towels being put on his leg for a pulled muscle and iodine being administered for cuts. He fared little better at Barnsley where he had just eleven games. A retired colliery surface worker.

O'HAGAN, William

(1922–1923) **1922:** 6/1; 12/7
Goalkeeper **Career:** 57-0-0
Debut: 11 Mar 22 **Final:** 5 May 23

Born: Buncrana, Co. Donegal 8 Aug 1890
Died: Prescot 29 Jun 1972

Career: St Collumb's College; Londonderry Guild; Derry Celtic; Linfield; St Mirren Apr 1912–17.07.1919; First World War-Scottish Horse; Airdrieonians 14.05.21; NORWICH CITY 08.03.22; Fordson's Works Comnibation 1923; Aberdare Athletic 23.06.24; Fordson's Works Combination cs 1925.

Bill threw his weight around in his penalty area with fair abandon. He served in Gallipoli during the Great War after a fine career in Scotland. A tall Irish international keeper with receding hair and a terrific clearing punch who replaced Herbert Skermer in late 1922. The Marvel *in 1921 said of him, 'Lengthy too so that he can tip over the bar with ease some shots that others might have to jump for'. A near relative of former Norwich City manager Charles O'Hagan.*

OLIVER, James Robert

(1962–1965) **1964:** 5/9; 11/5
Forward **Career:** 47-0-17
Debut: 18 Aug 62 **Final:** 20 Feb 65

Born: Maddiston, nr Falkirk 3 Dec 1941

Career: Graham High School; Stirlingshire; Glasgow Schools; Woodburn Athletic; Linlithglow Rose; Falkirk 27.01.59; NORWICH CITY 10.08.62; Brighton & Hove Albion 06.03.65; Colchester United 23.02.68; King's Lynn 01.07.70; Lowestoft Town 13.07.71, Oct 1972 player coach; Gorleston; Sheringham player-manager; Corinthians; Post Office; City College Students manager for two years.

Jim, a Scottish Schoolboy international, was signed in Scotland and played for City in the Paisley Charity Cup match at St Mirren. His intense enthusiasm and quicksilver speed off the mark saw him add goal punch to the City attack. He twice recovered from a cracked bone in his leg and he was Brighton's first playing substitute in August 1966.

O'NEILL, John Patrick

(1987) **1987:** 6/0; 13/0
Centre Half **Career:** 1-0-0
Debut/Final 18 Dec 87

Born: Derry 11 Mar 1958

Career: Derry Athletic Boys Club; Leicester City 18.03.76 (non contract), 14.02.79 (pro); Queens Park Rangers 27.07.87; NORWICH CITY 16.12.87; Finn Harps Mar 1990–Mar 1992 manager; Derry City 24.08.92 committee/board for one year.

John, a Loughborough undergraduate at the same time as Sebastian Coe, gained degrees in economics and accountancy. He was a quality person and a quality footballer. Eleven years at Filbert Street for 345 games in an often relegation haunted side. A 34th minute collision with Wimbledon's John Fashanu ended his career with Norwich before it had started. A far happier day was the Testimonial Match granted to him in May 1989.

O'NEILL, Keith Padre Gerard

(1994–1999) **1994:** 6/1; 12/7
Winger **Career:** 65-22-10
Debut: 2 Nov 94 (sub) **Final:** 13 Mar 99

Born: Finglas, Dublin 16 Feb 1976

Career: Sacred Heart Boys Club; St Kevin's College Secondary School; Tolka Rovers 1982–1988; Home Farm 1989; NORWICH CITY School of Excellence 1990, 05.07.93 (trainee), 01.07.94 (pro); Middlesbrough 19.03.99; Coventry City 08.08.2001.

Keith O'Neill

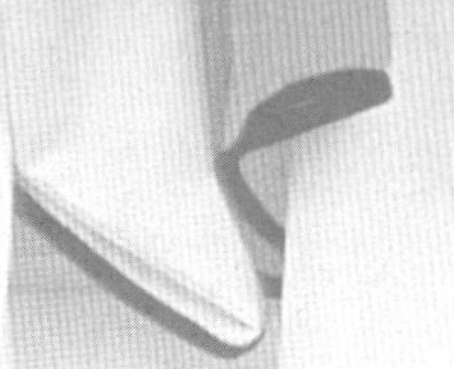

On his day Keith can be a matchwinner of the highest order. Possesses pace and a deceptive body swerve, and he does not lack confidence in his ability. Very tall for a wide player, he would have been more of an integral member of City sides but for a succession of injuries. He unfortunately continued in this same vein for his Premiership side and had to see a London specialist about his back injury.

O'NEILL, Martin Hugh Michael

(1981–1983) **1981:** 5/10; 11/3
Forward/Midfield **Career:** 74-1-13
Debut: 28 Feb 81 **Final:** 14 May 83

Born: Kilrea 1 Mar 1952

Career: St Collumb's College; St Malachy's College; Queens University; Distillery; Nottingham Forest 20.10.71; NORWICH CITY 26.02.81; Manchester City 25.06.81; NORWICH CITY 02.02.82; Notts County 26.08.83; Chesterfield 'A' 1984; Fulham Feb 1985; Grantham Town Aug 1987 manager; Shepshed Charterhouse Jul 1989 manager; Wycombe Wanderers Feb 1990 manager; NORWICH CITY 13.06.95–17.12.95 manager; Leicester City 21.12.95 manager; Glasgow Celtic 01.06.2000 manager.

Martin O'Neill

A gifted competitor who won almost every honour in the game: 64 full international Caps; Irish Cup medal; Championship; League Cup; Simod; Zenith Data; European Cup wins plus being involved in relegation and promotion struggles. His transfer deals at City make interesting reading. The first had an escape clause which meant that he could go if City were relegated. In the second, every penny was knocked off the money owed to Norwich by Man City for Kevin Reeves. The third went to a tribunal decision as County offered £15,000 and City wanted £100,000. He is doing just as well as a manager – FA Trophy, Bob Lord Trophy, Conference Championship, promotion, Coca-Cola Cup and a treble in his first season in Scotland.

O'REILLY, John (Jack)

(1936–1939) **1937:** 5/9; 11/9
Forward **Career:** 37-0-12
Debut: 5 Sep 36 (2 goals) **Final:** 11 Apr 39

Born: Cobh 7 May 1914

Career: Cobh Bohemians; Cobh Wanderers; Cobh Ramblers; Cork FC 1935; NORWICH CITY 13.05.36–05.05.39; Cork United 1940; Cork Athletic 1950.

He was a speedy winger in Ireland winning 8 Munster medals and a Cork County Rugby Cup medal. A threesome against Cheltenham and a foursome over Folkestone served to show that he was too good to languish in the Reserves. League of Ireland and Republic caps were secured and he scored seven goals in six F.A.I. Cup Finals. He emigrated to Canada and lives in Mississauga.

OSBORNE, Harold

(1924) **1924:** 5/9; 10/9
Outside Right **Career:** 1-0-0
Debut/Final: 27 Sep 24

Born: Wynberg, South Africa 2 Apr 1904
Died: Dulwich 9 Nov 1973

Career: Colchester Grammar School; Chelmsford Town (amat); NORWICH CITY 15.09.24 (amat).

Harold's father returning to England in 1911 was an RAMC Colonel with three sons who all became footballers. Harold the least successful made a winning appearance providing a perfect centre for the only goal of the match. His one game earned the pass mark, 'He did not attempt too much despite Banks promptings. His efforts were confined to the quick return of pass but there was marked accuracy in his centres'. Elder brother Frank won four caps for England and the middle son Reg played 240 games for Leicester City.

OSGOOD, Peter Leslie

(1976) **1976:** 6/1; 12/6
Centre Forward **Career:** 3-0-0
Debut: 10 Nov 76 **Final:** 27 Nov 76

Born: Windsor 20 Feb 1947

Career: Spital Old Boys; Windsor Corinthians; Windsor & Eton; Chelsea 19.02.64 (amat), 31.08.64 (pro); Southampton 16.03.74; NORWICH CITY 08.11.76 (temp. transfer); Philadelphia Fury (USA) Dec 1977–Aug 1978; Chelsea 13.12.78 to Sept 1979; coaching in the Far East & Gambia; Spitles & Aldwyk Bay Rowdies; Portsmouth Jun 1986–10.06.88 youth coach.

Peter learnt his football principally by kicking a ball against a wall until nine or ten at night. A brilliant individualist who graced the English football fields for a decade. His goal flair was most evident in cup finals, as he scored in Domestic and European games of this nature. His 150 goals for Chelsea included

twelve twos, three hat-tricks, a four and a five, and helped him win international honours. He is back at Chelsea looking after VIP guests as a Stamford Bridge matchday host.

OTTOSSON, Ulf Peter

(1997) **1997:** 5/10; 13/1
Centre Forward **Career:** 4-4-1
Debut: 18 Jan 97 (sub) **Final:** 25 Feb 97

Born: Degerfors, Sweden 2 Jul 1968

Career: Degerfors (Sweden) 1975; Degerfors Idrottsforening (Sweden) 1987; Locarno (Switzerland) (loan) 1991/2; Grupo Desportivo de Chaves (Portugal) 1995; Idrottsforening Kamraterna Norrkoping (Sweden) 1996; NORWICH CITY (loan) 13.01.97; Ljungskile (Sweden); Degerfors Idrottsforening (Sweden) 1997; Viterbese (Italy) Feb 2000; Degerfors Idrottsforening (Sweden) Jun 2000.

Swedish striker Ulf has travelled throughout Europe, playing in Sweden, Switzerland, Portugal, Italy and of course England. He started with his home town side when just seven, and by 1999 had made 270 appearances for them, scoring over 100 goals including over 20 goals in three separate seasons. He also scored a goal in a Swedish Cup Final triumph. Ulf scored twice on his City reserve debut and gleefully rammed home from eight yards against Sheffield United for a senior goal. Manager Mike Walker eventually chose not to offer him a full contact.

OWENS, Thomas Leslie

(1950–1951) **1950:** 5/10; 12/4
Centre Forward **Career:** 20-0-8
Debut: 18 Mar 50 (2 goals) **Final:** 5 May 51

Born: Monkwearmouth 17 Oct 1919
Died: Hellesdon 28 Mar 1974

Career: Grove Park School; Hylton Colliery Juniors; Sunderland Schools; Durham County; Ditchburn Social FC; Washington Chemical Works; Sunderland (trial); Charlton Athletic 16.09.37; Second World War-Coventry; Doncaster Rovers; Southport 29.12.47; Hartlepools United 20.07.49; NORWICH CITY 17.03.50; Reading 05.07.51; Brighton & Hove Albion 14.06.52; Dartford Aug 1953; Hellesdon 1960–1967 manager.

Les, at 18, scored his first Football League goal on 04.12.37 (h-Everton) in Division One. At only 19 he netted a hat-trick against Accrington for Doncaster. 'Exile' of the Pink 'Un *quoted his City joining fee as £2,000 but Les, despite showing thrustful play, was already 30 having lost many footballing years to the War. A distinguished Army career and his ingrained toughness meant that the breaking of several ribs and a fractured leg on the field were overcome. Also a prime organiser of the Norwich City All-Stars football team, who played throughout Norfolk raising considerable amounts for charities.*

Graham Paddon

OXFORD, Kenneth

(1953–1957) **1963:** 5/10; 11/5
Goalkeeper **Career:** 136-0-0
Debut: 25 Dec 53 **Final:** 9 Nov 57

Born: Oldham 14 Nov 1929
Died: Nottingham 6 Aug 1993

Career: Ardwick Lads Club; Manchester City 07.05.46 (amat), 05.11.47 (pro); Derby County 31.12.48; Chesterfield 08.06.50; NORWICH CITY 09.07.51; Derby County 12.12.57; Doncaster Rovers 01.07.64; Port Vale 16.03.65; Boston United Nov 1965 player coach; Boston FC Apr 1969 manager.

He had an unfortunate start to his career, as a permanent understudy to Frank Swift (Man City) and Ray Middleton (Chesterfield). His City debut arrived five years after his one previous league game. In 1957 Ken returned to the Baseball Ground and played over 150 games, almost eight years after being rejected by the club. He worked as a security guard and the Derby Evening Telegraph *paid him the fine tribute, 'Ken was a grand chap' – and I cannot improve on that.*

PADDON, Graham Charles

(1969–1973 & 1976–1981) **1970:** 5/7; 10/8
Forward **Career:** 338-2-37
Debut: 4 Oct 69 **Final:** 3 Oct 81

Born: Manchester 24 Aug 1950

Career: Coventry City 01.05.68; NORWICH CITY 02.10.69; West Ham United 06.12.73; NORWICH

CITY 11.11.76; Tampa Bay Rowdies (USA) Apr 1978–Aug 1978; Millwall 16.12.81; Hong Kong football cs 1982; Portsmouth Aug 1985 coaching, reserve coach, supervising youths; Stoke City 15.12.89 assistant manager, caretaker manager 23.02.91; Portsmouth 17.05.91 coaching staff, assistant manager, 07.02.95 reserves coach; scouting for Liverpool, Derby County and Leicester City.

A vital member of the City 1971/72 promotion team and the 1972/73 League Cup side. A marvellous competitor, with a powerful left foot shot his two spells at City were instrumental to the club's progress up the ladder. Graham enjoyed a successful spell with West Ham before rejoining City. After being a publican he ran the South Walsham Hall Country Club and squash courts. He has suffered the trials and tribulations of coaching and management at Stoke and Portsmouth.

PAINTER, Trevor Alfred

(1967) **1967:** 6/0; 12/10
Centre Half **Career:** 2-0-0
Debut: 25 Nov 67 **Final:** 2 Dec 67

Born: Norwich 2 Jul 1949

Career: Earlham Secondary Modern School; Norwich Boys; Norfolk Boys; Ipswich Town (trial); NORWICH CITY 28.05.66 (app), 08.07.67 (pro); Colchester United 05.05.70; King's Lynn for three years; Sir Thomas Moore's Under-12 Feb 1991 trainer.

Trevor made just two first-team appearances in three years as a professional at Norwich. He was selected to take the place of the suspended Laurie Brown and picked up two win bonuses. His 103 reserve games showed that he was good enough to deserve more first team chances. Still living locally and working for an insurance company.

PARKER, John Francis

(1920–1921) **1920:** 5/8; 12/7
Centre Forward **Career:** 12-0-2
Debut: 28 Aug 20 **Final:** 17 Feb 21

Born: Ellistown, Leicester 16 Jan 1896
Died: Newhall 2 Nov 1973

Career: Newhall UM; Midway Athletic; Newhall Swifts; Army (175th Brigade RFA); Leicester City (trial) Feb 1919, (signed) 06.05.19; NORWICH CITY 29.08.20; Gresley Rovers Feb 1921; Burton All Saints cs 1921; Gresley Rovers 1922; Newhall United; Burton Town (trial) Aug 1924; Newhall Swifts.

John averaged two goals per game for his Army unit. He was City's centre forward for the first league game and he continued to score well in friendlies and for the Reserves. He endured a suspension towards the end of the season for an unexplained incident in a reserve match. John was later a painter and decorator.

PARKER, Scott Mathew

(2000) **2000:** 5/9; 11/0
Midfield **Career:** 6-0-1
Debut: 4 Nov 00 **Final:** 25 Nov 00

Born: Lambeth 13 Oct 1980

Career: Haberdasher Askes Secondary Modern School; Lilleshall; Valley Valiants; Blackheath District; London County; Charlton Athletic 01.08.97 (trainee), 07.11.97 (pro); NORWICH CITY (loan) 31.10.2000.

Scott has recently signed a new Charlton contract (3 Apr 2001), so the talented young midfielder's impressive play at Carrow Road was beneficial to both sides. Has an excellent first touch coupled with impressive distribution, which hallmarks him as a genuine Premiership-class player. Capped at England Under-21 level, he endured promotion and relegation with his present side.

PARNELL, Denis Russel

(1961) **1961:** 5/10; 12/7
Outside Left **Career:** 2-0-0
Debut: 26 Aug 61 **Final:** 29 Aug 61

Born: Farnborough 17 Jan 1940

Career: St Mark's School; Aldershot & Farnborough Boys; Hampshire Boys; Aldershot 02.08.58; NORWICH CITY 08.07.61; Guildford City Jul 1962; Hillingdon Borough Jul 1965; Ashford Town Nov 1965; Farnborough Town Dec 1969–1972.

Unusual in that his two first team appearances were in away games – his debut described in the Sports Paper as 'a valley-nt draw'. Also made 17 reserve outings for five goals before moving around the non-league circuit where he had success at Guildford, winning the Southern League Cup Final with them. His occupation outside football was with an electronics company.

PAYNE, Clive Edward

(1968–1973) **1970:** 5/9; 11/4
Right Back **Career:** 147-3-3
Debut: 3 Sep 68 **Final:** 17 Nov 73

Born: Aylsham, nr Norwich 2 Mar 1950

Career: Aylsham Secondary Modern School; Aylsham Youth Club; Aylsham Wanderers; Norfolk Schoolboys; NORWICH CITY 11.09.65 (app), 11.03.68 (pro); Bournemouth 11.12.73 to

Apr 1976; Lowestoft Town 10.05.76 player coach; Aylsham FC player-manager; Aylsham Feathers Sep 1992 manager.

Clive was one of four graduates of the Youth team in the side on the day of his debut. By the time of his last match – the day Ron Saunders resigned – he was one of ten men on the books who had played 150 games or more in the First team. Once in the City side in this era, providing of course you were good enough, you stayed there. Strangely his three goals were scored in Cup ties. A good cricketer in local leagues, he has been in the windows industry for a number of years.

PEARCE, William

(1920–1923) **1922:** 5/10; 10/7
Utility Forward **Career:** 21-0-2
Debut: 23 Oct 20 **Final:** 13 Jan 23

Born: Ilkeston, Derby 24 Apr 1899
Died: Ilkeston, Derby 2 Mar 1984

Career: Trowell St Helen's School; Ilkeston United; Worksop Town; NORWICH CITY 10.07.20; Ilkeston United Oct 1923; Grantham Town; Loughborough Corinthians May 1932.

William moved to the full back position and was principally the vice captain of the Reserves. He was fearless and possessed attributes that forwards were prone to view somewhat askance. His one City reserve goal was supposedly a 65-yarder against Sheringham. Moving on he terrorised non-league attackers for a decade.

PEARSON, James

(1930–1931) **1930:** 5/7; 10/7
Outside Right **Career:** 20-0-3
Debut: 3 Sep 30 **Final:** 5 Dec 31

Born: Wardley 19 Oct 1906
Died: Wolverhampton 20 Jun 1992

Career: Washington Colliery 1926; NORWICH CITY 08.05.30; Aldershot Jun 1932; Wardley Colliery Welfare Jul 1933; Cromer Sep 1934.

He recovered from breaking his leg at City to score twice in his first team comeback. Jim also scored in his one appearance for Aldershot on 04.02.33, their 26th Football League game. Resourceful and resilient, with ripe experience. Latterly a painter and sensationally married to the same lady for 58 years.

PEART, John George (Jack)

(1922–1923) **1922:** 5/10; 12/3
Centre Forward **Career:** 24-0-8
Debut: 26 Aug 22 **Final:** 24 Feb 23

Clive Payne

Born: South Shields 3 Oct 1888
Died: Paddington 3 Sep 1948

Career: South Shields Adelaide 1905; Treharris (loan); Durham; Northumberland; Sheffield United 30.04.07; Stoke 06.06.11; Newcastle United 15.03.12; Notts County 11.02.13; Leeds City 19.02.16; Notts County 03.07.19; Birmingham 19.11.19; Derby County 23.01.20; Ebbw Vale Jul 1920 player-manager; Port Vale 20.01.22; NORWICH CITY 19.07.22; Rochdale 02.03.23 player-manager, retired playing May 1924; Bradford City Jul 1930–Mar 1935 manager; Fulham 23.05.35 manager until his death.

Jack was also good at cricket, golf and boxing although it is a wonder how he found time to play these sports given that he had a long football career. He played for the Southern League Representative side and had plenty of weight, height and experience. Up to 1952 he was the only player in history to negotiate his own transfer to a Football League club in his capacity as a manager (Ebbw Vale). Under his managership Fulham reached the Semi-Final of the FA Cup in 1937.

PEED, Francis Henry (Gonsalez, Francisco Enrique)

(1930–1931) **1930:** 5/9; 12/9
Centre/Inside Forward **Career:** 19-0-6
Debut: 25 Oct 30 **Final:** 6 Apr 31

Born: Vernado Tuerto, Argentine 27 Jul 1905
Died: Birmingham A/M/J 1969

Career: Corporation Road School; Orb Villa; Liswerry Church side; Brereton Social; Aston Villa 05.10.28 (amat), 19.10.28 (pro); Bournemouth 02.06.30; NORWICH CITY 25.10.30; Newport County 27.08.31; Barrow (trial) Nov 1933; Bath City Jul 1935.

'Frank' had a Wolverhampton mother who married an Argentinian and after the latter's demise he took his stepfather's surname.

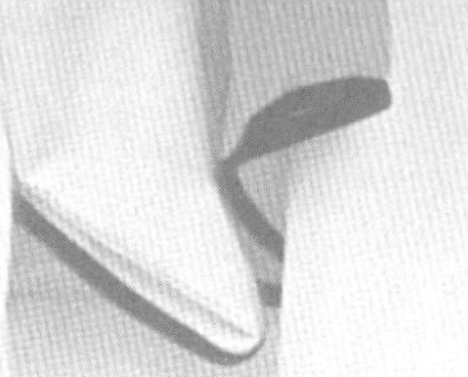

A useful scorer and another City player who was suspended by the club as a disciplinary measure. He featured in a Barrow versus Gateshead game on 05.05.34, scoring once in a 12–1 win. 'Frank' was later a checker at Swansea Docks.

PEGG, Frank Edward

(1932–1933) **1933:** 5/8; 10/12
Outside Right **Career:** 6-0-2
Debut: 10 Sep 32 **Final:** 25 Feb 33 (goal)

Born: Beeston, Nottingham 2 Aug 1902
Died: Bedford 9 Aug 1991

Career: Sawley United; Loughborough Corinthians; Blackpool (trial) 27.08.24; Nelson (trial) 24.12.24; Sunderland 12.05.25; Lincoln City 06.05.26; Bradford City 08.05.31; NORWICH CITY 15.06.32; New Brighton 11.08.33; Yarmouth Town 08.08.34–03.04.37.

He netted nine twos and a hat-trick for Lincoln in his four good seasons with them. In November 1934 he scored six goals for Yarmouth v Bury. Frank had Cropper and Dennison for teammates to make a strong Bloaters side, evidenced by his personal total of 47 goals in 75 games. He was finally traced residing in an old people's home.

PEMBERY, Gordon Dennis

(1947) **1947:** 5/8; 11/8
Outside Left **Career:** 1-0-0
Debut/Final: 25 Jan 47

Born: Cardiff 10 Oct 1926

Career: Cardiff Schools; Cardiff City Colts; Cardiff Nomads; Colchester Garrison; NORWICH CITY 23.09.46 (amat), 28.01.47 (pro); Cardiff City 12.08.48; Torquay United 20.06.50; Charlton Athletic 07.01.52; Swindon Town 18.06.56; Headington United Jul 1957; Merthyr Town Jul 1958; Nuneaton Borough 1960.

Gordon scored two goals on his reserve debut (12.10.46 (h) Reading) being brought in when A. Morris (Kingstonian) was unable to get to Norwich for his trial. He showed distinct promise before moving to his home town club where he again managed just one league game. He ran a fruiterer's and newsagent's shop in Wiltshire.

PEMBLETON, Arthur

(1927–1928) **1927:** 5/10; 11/8
Right/Centre Half **Career:** 21-0-0
Debut: 27 Aug 27 **Final:** 11 Feb 28

Born: Palterton, Derby 25 Jan 1895
Died: Luton 20 Feb 1976

Career: Woodhouse Exchange; Mansfield Mechanics; Notts County May 1919; Millwall 05.07.22; NORWICH CITY 11.05.27; Luton Town chief trainer.

'A diamond in the rough' said the 1919/20 Football Post. *Arthur had an inexhaustible supply of energy, described by 'Peeping Tom' in the* Football and Sports Favourite *as, 'Lean and lankily built on the lines of a colt'. He came to City after almost 200 League games spread over Division's 1, 2 and 3S.*

PENNOCK, Adrian Barry

(1990) **1989:** 6/0; 12/6
Defender **Career:** 1-0-0
Debut/Final: 17 Feb 90

Born: Ipswich 27 Mar 1971

Career: Sprites Lane Infants & Juniors; Chantry High School; Ipswich South; Suffolk County; Williem Browns-Jewson Juniors; NORWICH CITY Nov 1986 (assoc), Jan 1987 (trainee), 04.07.89 (pro); Molde Fotballklubb (Norway) (loan) 1990; Bournemouth 14.08.92; Gillingham 04.10.96

His City first team opportunity arrived when Butterworth and Sherwood were sidelined. He was in the same City South Eastern Counties team as Johnson, Sutch and Sutton. Adrian continued to produce quality performances at Bournemouth recovering after eight operations to reconstruct his knee. He appeared at Carrow Road for Gillingham in December 2000 after gaining an extension to his contract.

PERFECT, Frank Thomas

(1934) **1934:** 5/9; 12/2
Right Back **Career:** 1-0-0
Debut/Final: 28 Apr 34

Born: Gorleston 9 Mar 1915
Died: Guiseley, W. Yorkshire 17 Jul 1977

Career: Stradbroke Road School; Yarmouth Town Boys; Gorleston Juniors; Gorleston (amat); Norfolk County; NORWICH CITY 20.03.33 (amat); Mansfield Town 19.06.36; Wolverhampton Wanderers 17.12.36; Tranmere Rovers 02.02.38; Southampton 20.01.39.

Frank was Tom Parker's first signing as Norwich beat several league clubs to his signature. He placed a long pass with accuracy and he was given his chance the week after City were promoted. He won his county colours while a Gorleston player in season 1932/33.

PESCHISOLIDO, Paulo Pasquale (Paul)

(2001) **2001:** 5/7; 10/12
Forward **Career:** 3-2-0
Debut: 31 Mar 01 **Final:** 16 Apr 01 (sub)

Born: Scarborough, Ontario, 25 May 1971

Career: Toronto Blizzard (Canada); Birmingham City 11.11.92; Stoke City 01.08.94; Birmingham City 29.03.96; West Bromwich Albion 24.07.96; Fulham 24.10.97; Queens Park Rangers (loan) 03.11.2000; Sheffield United (loan) 18.01.2001; NORWICH CITY (loan) 22.03.2001; Sheffield United 10.07.2001.

A Canadian international striker with 40 caps and eleven goals who did not play football until he joined Toronto Blizzard. His transfer fees got progressively larger with each subsequent move. Of Italian parentage, Paul has worried many a defence with his pace and is approaching a century of goals in English football.

PETERS, Martin Stanford

(1975–1980) **1975:** 6/0; 11/10
Midfield **Career:** 231-1-50
Debut: 15 Mar 75 **Final:** 3 May 80

Born: Plaistow 8 Nov 1943

Career: Fanshawe Primary School; Dagenham, London, Essex & England Schoolboys; West Ham United 27.05.59 (app); 12.11.60 (pro); Baltimore Bays (USA); Tottenham Hotspur 16.03.70; NORWICH CITY 13.03.75; Sheffield United 01.08.80 player coach, later manager; Gorleston 1981/2; Tottenham Hotspur Aug 1998 non executive Director.

For five years he conducted a master class at Carrow Road and he was arguably Norwich City's most influential capture of modern times. Deserved to be in Championship winning sides in a 20 year League career. His elegant, blind side running was mastered to perfection and he will forever be remembered as one of the England 1966 World Cup winning side. Winner of Cup medals in the 1960s and 1970s plus 67 England caps and Norwich City captured him for a very modest outlay of £50,000. His autobigraphy was entitled Goals from Nowhere. *Those were the days.*

PHELAN, Michael Christopher

(1985–1989) **1985:** 5/10; 11/4
Midfield **Career:** 193-1-10
Debut: 17 Aug 85 **Final:** 13 May 89

Born: Nelson, Lancashire 24 Sep 1962

Left: Martin Peters
Right: Michael Phelan

Career: Barrowfield County Prmary School; Colne Park High School; Nelson & Colne Town; Lancashire Boys; Barrowfield Celtic Boys Club; Burnley Jul 1977 (assoc), Jul 1979 (app), 29.07.80 (pro); NORWICH CITY 30.05.85; Manchester United 08.06.89; West Bromwich Albion 11.07.94; NORWICH CITY Dec 1995 assistant manager, Feb 1996 reserve coach; Blackpool 25.03.97; Stockport County Jul 1997 assistant manager; Manchester United Jun 1999 Centre of Excellence; First team coach.

Michael, a former England Youth player, won a Third Division championship medal with Burnley. He showed himself to be a versatile performer as City stormed to the 1985/86 Division Two championship. Only injury kept him out of the City side, but a dream move to Manchester United saw him gain an England cap (versus Italy) plus an FA Cup winner's medal. The good players will always move from our lake to the ocean.

PHILIPSON, John

(1928) **1928:** 5/9; 12/0
Outside Left **Career:** 1-0-0
Debut/Final: 25 Aug 28

Born: Newburn 18 Nov 1905
Died: Newburn J/F/M 1984

Career: Willington Athletic; Bury 28.04.26 (amat), 10.05.26 (pro); Doncaster Rovers 30.07.27; NORWICH CITY 19.05.28; Throckley Welfare; Clara Vale United Sep 1932.

Scorer of sixteen goals in Bury's Central League side he was one of only two players to have made their one City appearance in the opening match of the season. The cutting press summation of his performance was that 'He did not fit in successfully with McKenna and some palpable misunderstandings occurred'. He only scored goals in the Football League for Doncaster where he notched four in their Division Three North days.

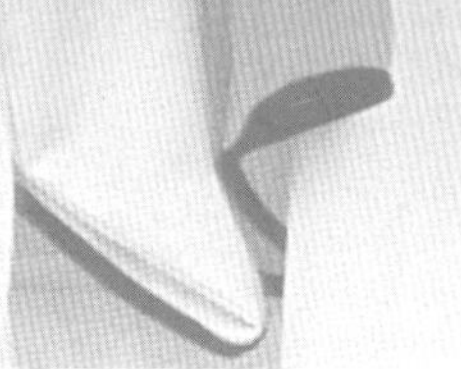

PHILLIPS, Alan Hedley

(1923–1924) **1923:** 5/9; 11/3
Inside left **Career:** 4-0-3
Debut: 27 Oct 23 **Final:** 22 Mar 24

Born: Oxford 13 Feb 1899
Died: Shrewsbury 2 May 1975

Career: Oxford High School; Jesus College (Oxford); RGA in France & Germany 1914–1918; Oxford City 1922; Corinthians 1920–1930; Sheringham 26.09.23; NORWICH CITY 04.10.23 (amat); Holt 06.03.24.

An Oxford Blue (1921–2–3) who scored for City in his second, third and fourth games. He also obtained Blues for Hockey and Cricket and he played the latter for Minor Counties in 1928. Alan was a master at Gresham School in 1923 and was at Shrewsbury School as Housemaster for 15 of his 38 years there, retiring in 1963.

Left: David Phillips
Right: John Polston

PHILLIPS, David Owen

(1989-1993) **1989:** 5/10; 11/2
Midfield **Career:** 186-0-20
Debut: 19 Aug 89 (goal) **Final:** 8 May 93

Born: Wegberg, W. Germany 29 Jul 1963

Career: Ascent School; Oranje Youth Club; Wadebridge Secondary Modern School; Wadebridge FC; Penweathers Secondary Modern School; Plymouth Argyle 20.08.79 (app), 03.08.81 (pro); Manchester City 23.08.84; Coventry City 05.06.86; NORWICH CITY 26.08.89; Nottingahm Forest 20.08.93; Huddersfield Town 04.11.97; Lincoln City 25.03.99; Stevenage Borough Oct 2000.

David had a fragmented education, being the son of a Caerphilly-born RAF father. He was educated at Brunssum and Cornwall and excelled at athletics, rugby and gymnastics, even being the Under-12 British Forces javelin champion. At the time he was the tenth Norwich City player to win a Welsh cap as he struck (especially in his early days) some long-range goals, and when on song he was a fine crosser of the ball from the wing. An FA Cup winner with Coventry and a part of Nottingham Forest's promotion-winning side.

PICKERING, Michael John

(1983) **1983:** 5/11; 12/6
Left Half **Career:** 0-1-0
Debut/Final: 1 Oct 83 (sub)

Born: Huddersfield 29 Sep 1956

Career: Heckmondwyke Grammar School; Spen Valley Boys; Barnsley 18.10.74; Southampton 11.06.77; Sheffield Wednesday 16.10.78; San Diego Sockers (USA) May 1981–Jul 1981; NORWICH CITY (loan) 30.09.83; Bradford City (loan) 04.11.83; Barnsley (loan) 1983/4; Rotherham United 20.01.84; York City 25.07.86; Stockport County 03.08.87; Hallam 1988; Goole Town 1989; Frickley Athletic Aug 1991.

Mike was a first-team Canary for just 16 minutes on the day we were losing 3–0 to Manchester United and pulled back to draw. A regular elsewhere, as can be seen by his record of over 100 league games for Barnsley, Sheffield Wednesday and Rotherham. He had an early ambition to be a physical education teacher and by the time he was 22 he had played in all four football league divisions.

PICKWICK, Donald Harry John

(1947–1956) **1952:** 5/6; 10/8
Right Half **Career:** 244-0-11
Debut: 30 Aug 47 **Final:** 28 Jan 56

Born: Pen-y-graig, Rhondda 7 Feb 1925

Career: Cardiff City 01.05.43 (amat); Bristol City (amat); Royal Welsh Fusiliers; NORWICH CITY 12.02.46 (amat), 25.08.47 (pro); Spalding United May 1956 player-manager; Lowestoft Town 22.08.59–Aug 1960.

Don scored against City Reserves in October 1945 and was attracting a good deal of attention. A Welsh Schoolboy Rugby international who was noticed by Cyril Spiers. A gritty but fair-playing wing half with consistency being a keynote of his displays. Remembered for sustaining a broken leg during the 8–1 win at Shrewsbury in 1952. He has lived for many years in Australia.

PIGGIN, Albert

(1920) **1920:** 5/9; 11/4
Centre Forward **Career:** 2-0-0
Debut: 11 Sep 20 **Final:** 16 Sep 20

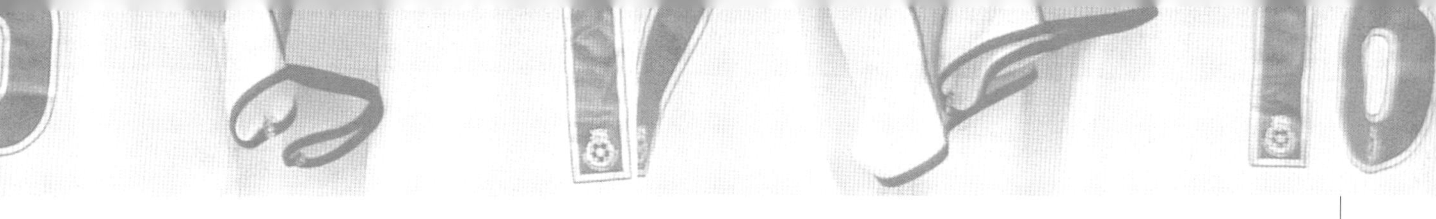

Born: Norwich 29 Dec 1894
Died: Norwich 26 May 1967

Career: Junior Institute; Norwich CEYMS; NORWICH CITY Jun 1919 signing league forms 07.08.20 (amat); Norfolk County 1920/1.

A prolific scorer for the Reserves in 1919/20, helping them to win six cups by scoring over 50 goals in the season. The Athletic News revealed that he was one of seven amateurs signed in readiness for the new campaign. City's equal 13th Football League debutant.

PIKE, Theophilus (Theo)

(1933–1935) **1934:** 5/10; 11/4
Inside Left **Career:** 21-0-7
Debut: 6 Sep 33 **Final:** 2 Mar 35

Born: Sunderland 25 Mar 1907
Died: Bury St Edmunds 26 Oct 1967

Career: Sunderland Co-op Wednesday; Southend United 21.04.25 (amat); Fulham 20.07.25; Bournemouth 23.06.27; Birmingham 03.02.28; Southend United 21.06.30; NORWICH CITY 02.06.33; Bury Town 29.07.35, May 1937 trainer/coach; Norfolk & Suffolk SFA 1938/39 coach.

A sportswriter of the day penned the following in respect of Theo: 'He can kill the ball in a manner that is the hallmark of a fine player'. His last four league goals were netted in successive matches. A former shop assistant, he made 120 Football League appearances in his roving career. Latterly a publican.

PLUNKETT, Sidney Ernest

(1938–1947) **1946:** 5/9; 10/3
Outside Right **Career:** 36-0-7
Debut: 5 Nov 38 **Final:** 19 Apr 47

Born: Norwich 2 Oct 1920
Died: Norwich 26 Jun 1986

Career: Esdelle Shoe Works; Norwich YMCA (amat); NORWICH CITY 20.04.38 (amat); 05.05.38 (pro); Wolverhampton Wanderers 22.04.39; re-transferred to NORWICH CITY 14.12.45 (pro) to 1947, (retiring from a fractured skull injury caused when he was knocked off his bicycle); Chelmsford City; Yarmouth Town 23.08.52; Gorleston 20.11.54; Yarmouth Town Aug 1956–07.05.57.

Sid, another player whose career was shortened by the war, made 165 City appearances in all and netted 85 goals. He set scoring records at Chelmsford (42 goals in one season) and at Yarmouth (164 games for 110 goals). With him at various times at Yarmouth were Messrs Arnold, Bradley, Brennan, Rackham and Rowlands. He became a publican and then worked for the Courtauld Weaving Company in Norwich.

POINTER, Reginald Ernest

(1956–1957) **1956:** 6/0; 11/7
Centre Half **Career:** 12-0-0
Debut: 10 Sep 56 **Final:** 12 Jan 57

Born: Norwich 28 Jan 1935

Career: City of Norwich School; CNSOBU; NORWICH CITY 07.06.56; Norfolk County Sep 1956; CNSOBU; Mulbarton; Farnsfield White Post.

A City of Norwich Schoolboy who struck up a good impression in the Reserves with Ken Smith. Reg was credited with an own goal in his last City appearance. He was only the second CNSOBU player to be awarded county colours and he netted with a header in the 1970 Norfolk Senior Cup win over St Andrews.

POLSTON, John David

(1990–1998) **1990:** 5/11; 11/0
Defender **Career:** 246-17-12
Debut: 25 Aug 90 **Final:** 3 May 98 (sub)

Born: Walthamstow 10 Jun 1968

Career: Waltham Forest Schools; Essex Schools; London Schools; Tottenham Hotspur 21.06.84 (app), 16.07.85 (pro); NORWICH CITY 20.07.90; Reading 21.05.98–30.05.2001 retirement.

He excelled at football, cricket and basketball at school. In March 1990 he and his brother Andy became the first brothers to jointly play for Spurs since 1912. Signed for £300,000 after a tribunal fixation manager Dave Stringer said, 'He's versatile and can play as a central defender or as a full back'. John was hardly ever found wanting as his assured play bolstered and stiffened the Canary defence. A knee injury failed to respond to two operations and he intends to go for a 'B' license in order to become involved in Academy work.

PORTER, Ernest Wesley

(1927–1931) **1929:** 5/8; 11/0
Outside Right **Career:** 139-0-31
Debut: 27 Aug 27 **Final:** 2 May 31

Born: Annfield Plain J/F/M 1901

Career: Ouston Rovers 1922; Birtley 1923; Sheffield United 17.04.23; Boston Town Aug 1925; Reading 07.07.26; NORWICH CITY 02.06.27; Boston Town Sep 1931.

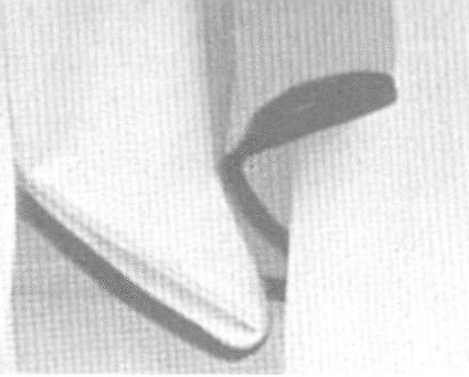

Reading, with Ernie in sparkling form, reached the FA Cup semi-finals. A provider of crosses from the wing with Jacky Slicer, which helped Percy Varco to a tremendous first season with the club. He found time to score regularly himself and he was the club's equal 100th Football League debutant. An out-and-out winger who scored goals regularly – his like are worth a fortune in today's transfer market. I am still unable to trace Ernie having recently discounted a Cleethorpes death in 1956.

POWELL, Anthony

(1974–1981) **1975:** 5/11; 11/1
Left Half **Career:** 273-2-5
Debut: 17 Aug 74 (goal) **Final:** 14 Feb 81

Born: Bristol 11 Jun 1947

Career: Lawrence Weston Boys; National Smelting FC; Bath City; Bournemouth 27.04.68; NORWICH CITY 16.08.74; San Jose Earthquakes (USA) Mar 1981–Aug 1982; Seattle Sounders (USA) May 1983–Aug 1983.

'Tony' Powell

Tony was 'Mr Dependable' and very rarely had an off day in a Canary shirt. He was a league ever-present for the three seasons in the middle of his City career, finally taking his consecutive run of such games to 140. He played more than 200 games for both his league clubs, scoring on his debut for both teams. Former City Manager John Bond made reference to Tony in a long interview for the local Norwich paper recently and despite his updated news I have been unable to find Tony in his home in America. His UK family do not know where he is either.

POWER, Lee Michael

(1990–1994) **1990:** 6/1; 11/4
Striker **Career:** 29-19-10
Debut: 28 Apr 90 **Final:** 13 Feb 94 (sub)

Born: Lewisham 30 Jun 1972

Career: Crofton Park School; Blackheath; South London; PGL England; NORWICH CITY Nov 1986 (assoc), Jul 1988 (trainee), 10.07.90 (pro); Charlton Athletic (loan) 04.12.92; Sunderland (loan) 13.08.93; Portsmouth (loan) 15.10.93; Bradford City (loan) 08.03.94; Millwall (loan) 01.01.95; Peterborough United 27.07.95; Heart of Midlothian Oct 1996; Dundee Dec 1996; Hibernians 20.03.97; Ayr United Apr 1998; Carlisle United (trial) Jul 1998; Plymouth Argyle 04.08.98; Halifax Town 11.12.98, 14.01.99 (permanent); Boston 06.11.99.

Lee's early promise culminated in playing for PGL England. He is the youngest Canary to score twice in a first division (now the Premiership) match. He has been loaned, loathed and loved in a very topsy-turvy career. Eighty-one goals in 162 appearances for City to include all levels highlighted the talent he possessed. He announced in 2000 that he was a player's agent.

PRICE, Eric

(1926–1927) **1926:** 5/9; 11/0
Inside Left **Career:** 16-0-6
Debut: 28 Aug 26 **Final:** 15 Apr 27

Born: Kinsley 3 Sep 1905
Died: Crewe 6 Feb 1976

Career: Stockport Secondary School; Morley FC; Wilmslow; Sandbach Ramblers 1923; Manchester City 24.10.24 (amat), 16.11.24 (pro); NORWICH CITY 23.08.26; Northampton Town 28.05.27; Torquay United 15.06.28–18.02.29.

A Lancashire cup win with Manchester was a highlight for Eric but he could not displace Horace Barnes from their first team. Eric was a forward with a powerful left foot shot. He figured in City's heaviest first game of the season defeat but on the plus side he notched a Canary hat-trick in his sixth game. He had a surprisingly short stay at the Nest and outside football was a retired chief clerk who passed away after a long illness.

PRICE, Raymond

(1964) **1964:** 5/10; 11/7
Left Back **Career:** 1-0-0
Debut/Final: 29 Feb 64

Born: Durham 18 May 1944
Died: Grimsby 18 Nov 1990

Career: NORWICH CITY 1962 (groundstaff), 08.07.63 (pro); Colchester United 01.07.64 to 1966.

His only game for City came as a result of Joe Mullett being incapacitated with tonsilitis. The Eastern Daily Press *remarked of his appearance, 'A lack of experience in his play'. His full back partner for his Colchester debut on 6.2.65 (A) Oldham was Duncan Forbes. They played alongside each other for 11 league games before Ray's final Football League appearance on 15.01.66 (H) Doncaster. He was a fine badminton player and a retired insurance salesman.*

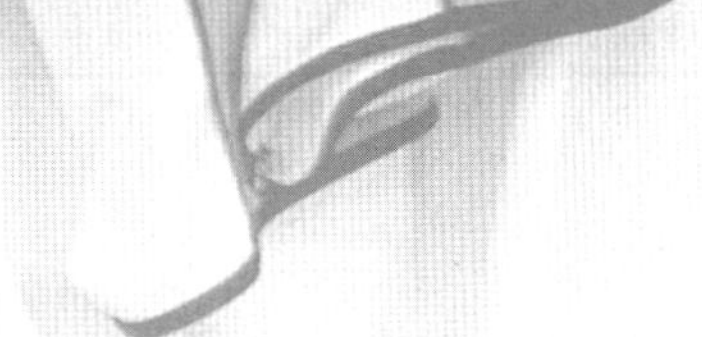
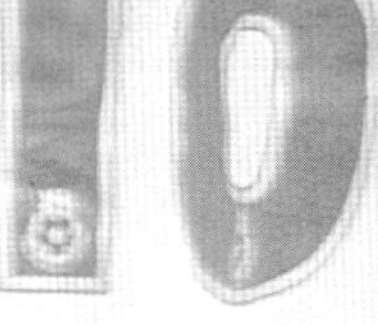

PRIOR, Spencer Justin

(1993–1996) **1993:** 6/3; 12/10
Defender **Career:** 79-10-2
Debut: 1 Sep 1993 **Final:** 5 May 1996

Born: Rochford, Essex 22 Apr 1971

Career: Greensword Secondary Modern School; South East Essex; Southend United Apr 1987 (assoc), 20.07.87 (trainee), 22.05.89 (pro); NORWICH CITY 17.06.93; Leicester City 17.08.96; Derby County 22.08.98; Manchester City 23.03.2000; Cardiff City 28.06.2001.

Spencer was Norwich's first signing of the 1993 close season and he was hailed as Chris Sutton's long lost brother – given the facial resemblance. He was blooded by the Shrimpers at 17, spearheading Southend's almost seasonal promotion and/or play-off fight. Never overawed by a player's pedigree, he constantly proved to be at least their equal. Later he teamed up with Martin O'Neill (at Leicester), Joe Royle (at Manchester City) and Ian Butterworth (at Cardiff City).

PROCTOR, David

(1953–1954) **1953:** 6/0; 12/2
Right Back **Career:** 17-0-0
Debut: 31 Jan 53 **Final:** 20 Mar 54

Born: Belfast 10 Oct 1929

Career: Portadown; Grimsby Town 11.01.49; Blackpool 06.08.49; NORWICH CITY 19.01.53; Northwich Victoria cs 1954; Barrow 16.10.54; Wrexham 25.08.59–May 1960.

Principally a reserve to Denis Morgan, David made his appearances when City were a top six side in their Division Three (South) days. He went on to give Barrow good service for four seasons and has since returned to his homeland.

PROCTOR, Michael Henry (Harry)

(1934–1946) **1934:** 5/10; 11/8
Left Half **Career:** 116-0-3
Debut: 3 Nov 34 **Final:** 28 Dec 46

Born: Ushaw Moor 7 Jul 1912
Died: Eaton, Norwich 6 Feb 1984

Career: Ushaw Moor Junior School; Johnson's Technical School, Durham County; Esh Winning Juniors; Washington Colliery Welfare; Newcastle United (trial); Portsmouth 23.10.31 (amat); Hartlepools United 05.07.32; NORWICH CITY 16.05.34 (pro); Second World War–Army & Eastern Command; NORWICH CITY to 1946, later coach/trainer to 18.08.56; Gorleston 1957 committee, trainer coach to Mar 1958.

'Harry' Proctor

Harry was a tough, strong-tackling half back who never shirked the issue and gave 90 minutes' endeavour in every match. Among his 14 goals for Hartlepools was a hat-trick on 17.03.34 (H) Barrow. He played 304 City games in total and as a corporal appeared against City Reserves for No. 2 ITC. Stanley Matthews ran the line for his testimonial match in 1954. Harry was a publican and hotelier for many years.

PROPHETT, Colin George

(1973–1974) **1973:** 5/11; 12/2
Defender **Career:** 47-1-0
Debut: 25 Aug 73 **Final:** 10 Aug 74

Born: Crewe 8 Mar 1947

Career: Crewe Junior football; Sheffield Wednesday Aug 1967 (app), 06.06.68 (pro); NORWICH CITY 31.05.73; Swindon Town 02.10.74; Chesterfield 15.09.78; Crewe Alexandra 18.10.79; Cardiff City 1981/2 reserve coach; Matlock Town Aug 1982; Heanor Town; Alfreton Town Jun 1983; Scouting for Reading, Crystal Palace and Southampton.

Colin made his Football League debut on 06.09.69 (A) Arsenal for Sheffield Wednesday and ultimately gave good service to all his teams, finally playing over 400 career games. He was handily proportioned for a defender, although City hinted that his stay for them would be short by fielding him in six different numbered shirts. He retired from his woodworking tool manufacturer's in 1997.

PROUDLOVE, Andrew George

(1976) **1976:** 5/10; 11/9
Left Winger **Career:** 0-2-0
Debut: 21 Sep 76 (sub) **Final:** 25 Sep 76 (sub)

Born: Buxton, Derby 15 Jan 1955

Career: Reading 30.09.70 (app); Buxton Town Jul 1972; Sheffield Wednesday 12.09.75 (pro);

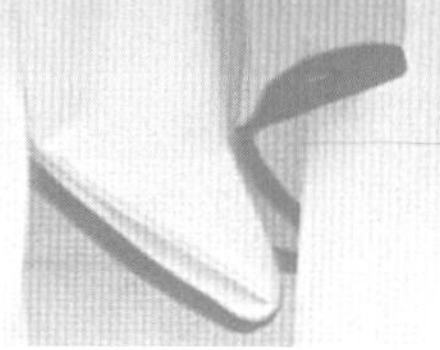

NORWICH CITY 05.02.76; Hereford United 13.05.77; Port Vale 02.11.78; Buxton Town 1981.

Andy's brief encounter with City saw him replace Colin Suggett and Mel Machin in a non winning side. One deprecating critic wrote in the City programme, 'He lost his place and looked set for lower grade football'. Fifty-two minutes' first team football for City was supplemented by 51 reserve games.

PUNTON, William Hamilton

(1959–1966) | **1964:** 5/8; 11/8
Left Winger | **Career:** 256-0-29
Debut: 17 Oct 59 | **Final:** 24 Sep 66

Born: Glenkindrie, East Lothian 9 May 1934

Career: Bredalbane; Portadown Oct 1952; Newcastle United 26.02.54; Southend United 26.06.58; NORWICH CITY 10.07.59; Sheffield United 18.11.66; Scunthorpe United 26.01.68; Yarmouth Town Jun 1969 player-manager, player to 21.05.74, manager to 05.05.90; Norfolk County 1988–26.05.94 manager; Diss Town May 1990–May 1997 manager.

Bill Punton

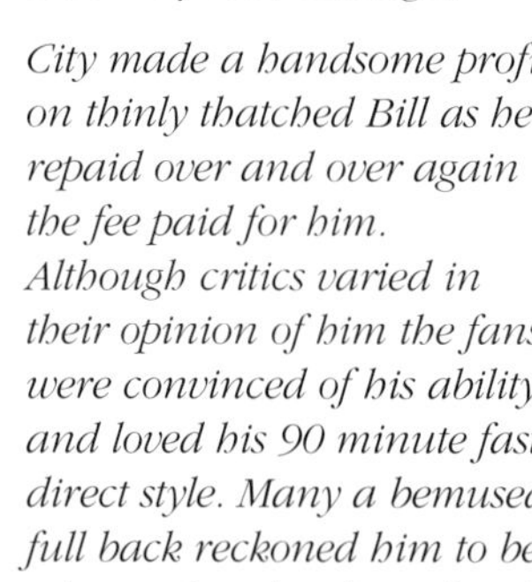

City made a handsome profit on thinly thatched Bill as he repaid over and over again the fee paid for him. Although critics varied in their opinion of him the fans were convinced of his ability and loved his 90 minute fast, direct style. Many a bemused full back reckoned him to be one of the quickest wingers that they have faced. A tremendous record in leading Yarmouth and Diss, and he can be regularly heard as a football pundit on local radio. Currently working at Carrow Road on match days.

PURDY, Arthur

(1930) | **1930:** 5/10; 11/6
Goalkeeper | **Career:** 12-0-0
Debut: 30 Aug 30 | **Final:** 6 Dec 30

Born: Evenwood, Durham 23 Jul 1904
Died: Thirsk, Yorkshire 25 Oct 1970

Career: Cockfield St. Mary's; Evenwood Juniors; Coundon United; Tottenham Hotspur 10.04.23 (amat), 25.04.23 (pro); Luton Town 08.05.25; Southend United 27.05.26; Durham City 11.07.27; Blackpool 09.02.28; Colwyn Bay United Aug 1929; NORWICH CITY 16.06.30; Fleetwood Sep 1933; Throckley Welfare May 1939; Evenwood Town Sep 1957 committee.

Arthur played two games for the Welsh League but he had a poor time at The Nest, letting in 27 goals, and only keeping a clean sheet on two occasions. He had 31 Division Two games for Blackpool and he managed 25 such matches for Luton Town. His elder brother Albert played for three league clubs and was the Fulham groundsman for four decades.

PUTNEY, Trevor Anthony

(1986–1989) | **1986:** 5/9; 11/2
Midfield | **Career:** 94-6-10
Debut: 23 Aug 86 | **Final:** 6 May 89 (sub)

Born: Harold Hill, Romford 9 Apr 1960

Career: Havering Boys; Brentwood Town; Ipswich Town 01.06.80; NORWICH CITY 13.06.86; Middlesbrough 14.08.89; Watford 16.08.91; Leyton Orient 29.07.93; Colchester United (loan) 26.08.94; Leyton Orient 01.12.94–Dec 1994.

Trevor earned a fine reputation as a quick tackling and tenacious midfield player. He suffered injuries in abundance mainly it seems because if the ball was there to be won he went for it no matter what the consequences. A £300,000 move to Middlesbrough was going well until a Gordon Cowans tackle broke his leg. He had the ability to play wide on either flank and outside of football he had a go at currency dealing.

RACKHAM, Derrick Richard

(1951–1952) | **1952:** 5/8; 10/5
Outside Left | **Career:** 10-0-2
Debut: 8 Dec 51 (goal) | **Final:** 19 Jan 52

Born: Norwich 14 Jun 1928
Died: Drayton 24 Mar 1996

Career: Norman Youth Club; Norfolk County Youth; NORWICH CITY 15.05.46 (amat), 24.11.49 (pro); Yarmouth Town 22.08.53 player, Aug 1964–04.05.67 manager.

Derrick was slightly built, yet deployed a strong shot in either foot in winning his Norfolk County Youth colours. A less succinct writer called him, 'A slick mover with plenty of ideas'. He made 266 appearances for Yarmouth Town scoring 41 goals. A trained printer who ended his career as an ECN compositor, retiring in 1993.

RAMSAY, Stanley Hunter

(1932–1934) | **1933:** 5/10; 11/10
Wing Half | **Career:** 83-0-1
Debut: 27 Aug 32 | **Final:** 6 Oct 34

Born: Ryton-upon-Tyne 10 Aug 1904
Died: Chipping Sodbury 19 Jul 1989

Career: Ryton FC; Sunderland 07.05.24; Blackpool 29.02.28; NORWICH CITY 01.07.32; Shrewsbury Town Jun 1935 player-manager; Dereham Town Aug 1936.

Stan and Steve Bruce share the unwanted record of being credited with scoring an own goal within a minute of the start of their first City game. Stan was described as a mature player who had been taught the value of constructive as well as destructive play. He was the club captain in the 1933/34 Championship side and among his rave press reviews was the comment, 'Opponents were requested to get out of the way when he was going for the ball'. He retired from his job as secretary of an old people's home in 1973.

RATCLIFFE, Simon

(1987)	**1987:** 5/11; 11/9
Defender	**Career:** 8-3-0
Debut: 1 Sep 87 (sub)	**Final:** 7 Nov 87

Born: Davyhulme 8 Feb 1967

Career: St Patrick's High School; St Patrick's Roman Catholic School; Eccles; City of Salford Schools; Salford Lads Club; Salford; Greater Manchester; England Boys; England Youth; Manchester United 13.02.85; NORWICH CITY 01.06.87; Brentford 13.01.89; Gillingham 04.08.95, youth development officer.

Simon was the England schoolboys captain and in his last match versus Scotland was carried off to have his spleen removed. City paid £40,000 for the 20-year-old England Youth international who was decribed as a utility player. He played over a century of games for his next two clubs.

RATTRAY, Peter Kerr

(1952–1953)	**1952:** 6/1; 11/11
Inside left	**Career:** 27-0-5
Debut: 23 Aug 52 (goal)	**Final:** 3 Oct 53

Born: Bannock Burn 7 Nov 1925

Career: Rutherglen Glencairn; Stirling Schoolboys; Dundee 22.08.45; Plymouth Argyle 31.08.50; NORWICH CITY 30.06.52; Stirling Albion 16.10.53; St. Johnstone 14.11.56.

Peter made his Football League debut for Plymouth on 02.09.50 against Port Vale and played his last match for them versus Norwich on 30.04.52. City bought him for nearly five figures, with our chairman saying 'The deal has emptied our till'. Every time he scored for City they won. He returned to Scotland and lives in Alloa.

REAGAN, Charles Martin

(1954–1956)	**1954:** 5/7; 10/8
Outside Left	**Career:** 36-0-4
Debut: 21 Aug 54 (goal)	**Final:** 3 Mar 56

Born: Scotswood, Newcastle 12 May 1924

Career: St Wilfreds; St George's; English Martyrs & York Schools; York City 11.09.41; York Railway Institute; York City Sep 1946 (amat); Hull City 30.05.47; Middlesbrough 12.02.48; Shrewsbury Town 01.08.51; Portsmouth 24.12.52; NORWICH CITY 05.07.54; March Town Jun 1956 player-manager; Goole Town Jul 1957– 1959; Manager of England's Womens' Football Team Oct 1979–Mar 1991; FA appointment covering the district from York to Scarborough in addition to being Chairman of his local Youth Leagues.

Martin's exceptional speed and clinical shooting made him a popular winger at all his clubs. Only 18 league goals in his 142 games was a poor reward for his ability, which was never better illustrated than with his City debut goal – typically at full speed and hit first time. He took the England Women's team to the first UEFA Cup Final and has travelled all over Europe with the side. Martin has a busy home life with six children and was a self-employed sales agent.

REAY, Albert Frederick

(1923–1924)	**1923:** 5/9; 11/8
Left Back	**Career:** 2-0-0
Debut: 29 Sep 23	**Final:** 26 Apr 24

Born: West Derby 15 Sep 1901
Died: Rainhill 31 Dec 1962

Career: Gnome Athletic; Brentford 10.08.20; Gillingham 17.08.22; NORWICH CITY 18.05.23; Guildford City Sep 1924; Sheppey United cs 1925.

He started with East London junior club Gnome Athletic and later managed to play 15 games for Gillingham. He gave promising displays in the public practice trials but not unnaturally he found it impossible to displace the former England international Albert Sturgess. Later a general labourer.

REEVES, Kevin Philip

(1977–1980)	**1977:** 5/10; 11/2
Striker	**Career:** 132-1-42
Debut: 15 Jan 77	**Final:** 8 Mar 80 (goal)

Born: Burley 20 Oct 1957

Career: Twynham; Wessex Schools; Bournemouth Colts, Youth, 04.06.74 (app), 04.07.75 (pro); NORWICH CITY 11.02.77; Manchester City 11.03.80; Burnley 20.08.83, retired from playing and to the coaching staff; Boston Town; Barrow 09.11.85; Yeovil Town; Birmingham City Feb 1986–29.05.87 youth coach; PFA Crewe Community Officer; Wrexham 23.11.89 assistant manager.

Left: Kevin Reeves
Right: Leonard Reilly

Kevin, who won two full England caps, became one of Britain's costliest players when City sold him for £1 million. In Manager John Bond's words, 'He was magic and did the business for Norwich'. At the majority of his Football League clubs his manager was John Bond. Kevin is one of the few City connected players to have scored in an FA Cup Final and he was thrilled with the reception he received when he returned to Carrow Road for John O'Neill's testimonial match.

REID, Ernest James

(1946)	**1946:** 5/7; 11/0
Right Back	**Career:** 7-0-0
Debut: 5 Jan 46	**Final:** 26 Sep 46

Born: Pentrebach, Merthyr Tydfil 25 Mar 1914

Career: Troedyrhiw; Plymouth United; Swansea Town (trial) 18.07.32; Chelsea 30.20.37 (amat), 15.05.40 (pro); Brighton & Hove Albion Sep 1942–Aug 1945; NORWICH CITY 01.05.43, 01.06.45 (Football League); Bedford Town Oct 1947.

A terrier-like tackler he deputised for Sam Weaver (Chelsea) in his Football League debut on 05.11.38 (A) Grimsby. As a Norwich City registered player he guested for Brighton in seventy three war games. He retired to live in Kent and sadly will be unable to attend the club's planned centenary dinner.

REILLY, Leonard Harold

(1937–1946)	**1938:** 5/11; 11/8
Centre Half	**Career:** 30-0-0
Debut: 18 Dec 37	**Final:** 28 Sep 46

Born: Rotherhithe 31 Jan 1917
Died: Queensand, Australia 26 Jun 1998

Career: Diss Stanley School; Diss Town; Norfolk County Junior & Senior Colours; NORWICH CITY 28.02.35 (amat), 05.02.36 (pro); RAF; Chelmsford City 1947; Gorleston 1948 player coach.

Len had a daunting debut, being given the task of marking former City hero Vinall. He played regularly for the Reserves and had 19 wartime matches for City firsts. He was good enough to play for the FA against Cambridge University in November 1935. In Jan 1959 he left England and worked as a teacher for the New South Wales Education Department.

RICHARDS, John Barrington

(1959–1960)	**1959:** 5/11; 12/4
Centre Forward	**Career:** 5-0-2
Debut: 12 Dec 59	**Final:** 5 Mar 60 (2 goals)

Born: West Bromwich 14 Jun 1931

Career: Royal Orphanage; Bristol University; Gloucestershire; English Universities; Combined University; Reading; Wiltshire; Swindon Town 27.08.56; NORWICH CITY 14.12.59; Aldershot 14.10.60; Corby Town Jul 1962; Stevenage Town Jul 1963–1964.

His league games/goals record at each club, namely Swindon (104–37), Norwich (above) and Aldershot (19–8); showed that his strong, bustling play brought a healthy reward in a short career. John followed a fine last City game by scoring in his first match for the 'Shots'. Outside of football he was involved with personnel and industrial relations.

RICHMOND, Joseph

(1926–1930)	**1927:** 5/11; 12/0
Utility	**Career:** 130-0-9
Debut: 28 Aug 26 (goal)	**Final:** 1 Mar 30

Born: Leasingthorne 26 Feb 1897
Died: Norwich 6 Mar 1953

Career: Leeholme School; Durham Schoolboys; Sittingbourne; RAF; Shildon Athletic; Leeds United 07.12.22; Barnsley 03.02.26; NORWICH CITY 19.07.26 retiring cs 1930; Letchworth Town 1947 player coach.

As a Flight Sergeant in the RAF he was awarded the French Medal Militaire, and as a

footballer he also had a rewarding experience – winning a Division Two medal with Leeds. His 'utility' description was brought about by his being able to play in defence and attack with like facility. Indeed he netted a hat-trick for Leeds (29.09.23) and he later scored one for Norwich. Post-War he was Licensee of the Quebec Tavern and later the Beaufort Arms, where he died after a long illness.

RIGBY, Jonathan Kendall

(1984–1985) **1984:** 6/1; 11/2
Forward **Career:** 7-3-0
Debut: 14 Feb 84 (sub) **Final:** 11 May 85 (sub)

Born: Bury St Edmunds 31 Jan 1965

Career: George White Middle School; Blyth Jex School; Norfolk Under-13–16; England Youth trials 1979; NORWICH CITY (schoolboy), 30.06.81 (app), 11.05.84 (pro); Kuopion Pallosuera (Finland) 1983–1987; Aldershot 20.03.86; Cambridge United 07.10.86; Thetford Town Sep 1988; Wroxham 21.01.89.

Jon was a vital part of the City Youth treble winning side (1980) and FA Youth Cup winners (1983) and had netted hat-tricks for City Youths, Reserves and in Kenya on tour with the Firsts. He also netted goals for Cambridge before a pelvic injury ended his league career. An amazing goalscorer for Wroxham, usually at least 30 in a season, with a host of medals to his name as a result of his exploits.

RIPLEY, Stanley Keith

(1958) **1964:** 6/1; 12/6
Centre Forward **Career:** 12-0-6
Debut: 3 Sep 58 **Final:** 11 Oct 58 (goal)

Born: Normanton 29 Mar 1935

Career: Normanton Secondary School; Altofts YMCA; Leeds United Juniors, 04.04.52 (pro); NORWICH CITY 09.08.58; Mansfield Town 07.11.58; Peterborough United 15.07.60; Doncaster Rovers 07.08.62–30.06.66.

His impressive physique enabled him to brush aside most challenges. Keith was at Leeds when Jack Charlton was starting his career and they both helped take the side to the First Division. Also in Peterborough's promotion side in the year that Terry Bly went goal crazy. He left Norwich because his wife couldn't settle in the area and his three month stay here was followed by lengthier spells at his next three clubs, culminating in his final Football League appearance on 09.04.66 (H) Chester.

ROBB, David Thomson (Davie)

(1978–1979) **1978:** 5/10; 12/4
Forward **Career:** 5-1-1
Debut: 30 Sep 78 (goal) **Final:** 10 Feb 79

Born: Broughty Ferry, Angus 15 Dec 1947

Career: Chelsea groundstaff; Newburgh Juniors; Aberdeen 31.07.65; Tampa Bay Rowdies (USA) May 1977–Aug 1978; NORWICH CITY 20.09.78 to Feb 1979; Philadelphia Fury (USA) 16.03.79; Vancouver Whitecaps (Canada) Mar 1981–Jul 1981; Tulsa Roughnecks (USA) Aug 1981 for 4 months before retiring.

Davie was an all-action, willing grafter of a forward who revelled in pressurising defenders. He had a brief flirtation with City after invaluable service at Pittodrie where he won Cup Winners medals. Scorer of many goals for Aberdeen including the winner in the 1977 League Cup Final. Latterly a drilling engineer in the Abu Dhabi oilfields.

Iwan Roberts receives the Barry Butler Memorial Trophy from Club President Geoffrey Watling as Norwich City's player of the season for 1999/2000.

ROBERTS, Iwan Wyn

(1997– **1997:** 6/3; 14/2
Centre Forward **Career:** 178-10-68
Debut: 9 Aug 97

Born: Bangor 26 Jun 1968

Career: Ysgor Ardudwy Secondary Modern School; Harlech Town; Gwynedd County; North Wales; Caernarvon Town Feb 1985; Watford 28.05.85 (trainee), 04.07.86 (pro); Huddersfield Town 02.08.90; Leicester City 25.11.93; Wolverhampton Wanderers 15.07.96; NORWICH CITY 07.07.97.

Iwan just missed out on a three-peat (as the Yanks say) of City Player of the Year awards, as he once again led the Norwich scoring

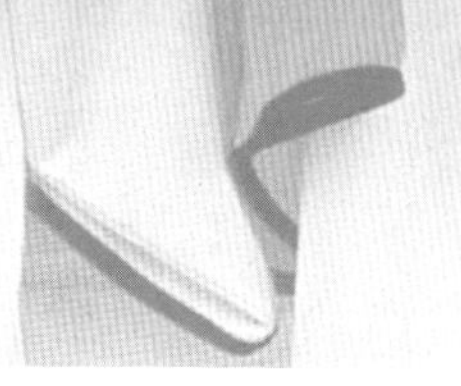

charts by a wide margin. He gives City the one thing that makes a difference for a mid table side: goals. He will battle all day in the air for the team, and he is no slouch with groundwork either. A current Welsh international who is adored by the Carrow Road faithful – they are hoping for at least one more good season from Iwan.

Left: Mark Robins
Right: Bernard Robinson

ROBINS, Mark Gordon

(1992–1995) **1992:** 5/7; 10/4
Forward **Career:** 64-14-21
Debut: 15 Aug 92 (sub) (2 goals) **Final:** 26 Dec 95

Born: Ashton-under-Lyme 22 Dec 1969

Career: North Chadderton Comprehensive School; Boundary Park Juniors; Oldham Boys; Greater Manchester Co FA; Lilleshall School of Excellence; England Youth; England Under-21; Manchester United 02.02.84 (assoc), 28.07.86 (trainee), 23.12.86 (pro); NORWICH CITY 14.08.92; Leicester City 16.01.95; Copenhagen (Denmark) 18.10.96; CD Orense (Spain) 1997; Reading (loan) 29.08.97; Panionios (Greece) Aug 1998; Manchester City (loan) 25.03.99; Walsall 05.08.99; Rotherham United 25.06.2000.

A former England Under-21 international, reckoned by many judges to have saved Alex Ferguson from losing his Manchester United job by scoring some crucial goals for the team. On his day he is one of the best penalty-box predators around, with the uncoachable asset of awareness in front of goal. An unselfish support player, he has had a stunning 2000/1 season with Rotherham, netting from all angles and distances.

ROBINSON, Bernard Cecil

(1932–1949) **1948:** 5/11; 11/3
Right Half **Career:** 380-0-14
Debut: 2 Apr 32 **Final:** 12 Mar 49

Born: Cambridge 5 Dec 1911

Career: King's Lynn School; Lynn Boys; Gaywood Boys; King's Lynn; Norfolk County 1931/2; NORWICH CITY 01.12.31 to 09.11.49.

'Robbo' was one of the finest wing halves in the game and virtually carried City in the pre-war and difficult War years. There would be a frantic dash to sign him if he were around today: a long throw specialist and supreme penalty taker with barely an indifferent game to his name. Indeed the majority of his outings were described as outstanding. Add a phenomenal 160 games during the War and it is apparent why he is regarded as one of the club's finest servants. A licensed victualler for many years, he now lives in retirement in Sprowston near Norwich.

ROBINSON, Joseph

(1946) **1938:** 5/7; 10/6
Left Half **Career:** 2-0-0
Debut: 31 Aug 46 **Final:** 4 Sep 46

Born: East Stanley 14 Nov 1918
Died: Hitchin Oct 1988

Career: Ouston United; NORWICH CITY 07.10.37 (amat), 13.11.37 (pro); Letchworth Town; Tabulator Club.

Joe made his City debut in the Reserves during the 1937/38 season and scored his first goals for them on 26.02.38 (H) Folkestone. Also made a pre-War appearance in the May 1939 Hospital Cup game and turned in some trojan displays in wartime City friendlies in 1943/44. An exceptional bowls player winning many titles and having an England trial in 1977.

ROBINSON, Leslie St John

(1927–1928) **1927:** 5/8; 11/8
Inside Right **Career:** 34-0-12
Debut: 27 Aug 27 **Final:** 5 May 28

Born: Barking 2 May 1898
Died: Barking 10 Oct 1965

Career: Stirling Athletic 1919–21 (amat); WWI Essex Regiment; Barking; London League v London Combination; West Ham United 08.04.20 (amat), 09.04.20 (pro); Northampton Town 22.05.25; NORWICH CITY 02.06.27; Thames Athletic Sep 1928; Torquay United 08.07.29.

Spasmodic appearances for the Hammers (scoring 23.04.21 (H) Port Vale) led to a 30 goal season for the Cobblers. For the latter he hit three hat-tricks, including one against City on 03.10.25. City's equal 100th League debutant Les did especially well in Cup ties. He was a retired storekeeper for Barking Borough Council.

ROBINSON, Robert

(1932–1934) **1932:** 5/10; 11/3
Goalkeeper **Career:** 37-0-0
Debut: 5 Sep 32 **Final:** 11 Apr 34

Born: Willington 27 Mar 1910
Died: Crosshills 22 Jan 1989

Career: West Rainton School; Lambton & Hetton; South Hylton FC; South Hetton Colliery Welfare; Hebburn Colliery Welfare; Durham County; Sunderland 14.05.26; Guildford City 28.07.31; NORWICH CITY 18.05.32; Barrow 09.07.34; Scarborough Town Jun 1937; Post-War Gainsborough Trinity.

He was spotted while playing against City's Reserves and signed within a week. Brought with him the experience of 34 Division One games for Sunderland and showed great style and resourcefulness, vying with Wharton for the custodian's spot. He held for over 50 years the record unbeaten City league run from a debut: 15 games. The Northern Echo, *reporting his demise, said that he died of a heart attack.*

ROBSON, Keith

(1978–1981) **1978:** 5/10; 10/4
Forward **Career:** 66-5-14
Debut: 25 Feb 78 (goal) **Final:** 21 Mar 81

Born: Hetton-le-Hole, Durham 15 Nov 1953

Career: Newcastle United 24.05.71; West Ham United 05.09.74; Team Hawaii (USA) May 1977–Aug 1977; Cardiff City 26.08.77; NORWICH CITY 09.02.78; Leicester City Sep 11.09.81; Carlisle United Mar 1983 (loan); Hong Kong football Sep 1983; Norwich Busmen; Corinthians; Mackintosh coach; Wroxham Aug 1988, assistant manager 1993/4.

Keith had to compete with Tyneside hero Malcolm MacDonald at Newcastle so his chances were limited, but he proved a capable deputy when called upon. His longest spell was at Norwich as he became widely travelled in pursuit of his profession. A Daily Telegraph *sportswriter's opinion of Keith was, 'He does not always prefer the cerebral approach'. A fine servant to Wroxham, he is now a machine operator in Norwich.*

ROCASTLE, David Carlyle

(1997) **1997:** 5/9; 11/0
Midfield **Career:** 11-0-0
Debut: 18 Jan 97 **Final:** 8 Mar 97

Born: Lewisham 2 May 1967
Died: Slough 31 Mar 2001

Career: Turnham Primary School; Roger Manwood Secondary Modern School; Lewisham

Robert Robinson

Way; South London Schoolboys; Vista FC; Arsenal 29.05.82 (schoolboy), 04.08.83 (app), 31.12.84 (pro); Leeds United 04.08.92; Manchester City 22.12.93; Chelsea 12.08.94; NORWICH CITY 09.01.97 (temp); Hull City 09.10.97 (temp); Sabah (Malaysia) Jun 1998.

Rocky played fourteen times for England during a glittering bemedalled career at Arsenal. A classy, silky player with outrageous dummies amongst his repertoire who was a crowd favourite to an extent that Mike Walker's success in securing his services for a second month was dubbed 'Rocky 2'. A tragic early death through cancer saw Arsenal invite his son Ryan to be the club's mascot for the first FA Cup final at the Millenium Stadium.

ROGERS, John

(1925–1926) **1923:** 5/9; 11/5
Inside Forward **Career:** 13-0-4
Debut: 24 Oct 25 **Final:** 27 Feb 26

Born: Helston, Cornwall 20 Jun 1895
Died: Helston, Cornwall 21 Mar 1977

Career: Aberdare Athletic 22.06.21; Sunderland 07.05.23; NORWICH CITY 15.10.25; Newquay 30.09.26; Helston British Legion 19.07.28.

Had a tremendous introduction to the game playing alongside such greats as Buchan, Cresswell and Clunas while at Roker Park. John was deemed to be a clever and assertive player, but as he was 30 when he joined City it was felt that his stamina was not superior to those men already in the side. He later gained an amateur permit in order to play in south-west non-league football.

ROLLINGS, Andrew Nicholas

(1972–1974) **1973:** 6/0; 11/8
Centre Half **Career:** 7-0-0
Debut: 13 Sep 72 **Final:** 1 Jan 74

Born: Portishead, Avon 14 Dec 1954

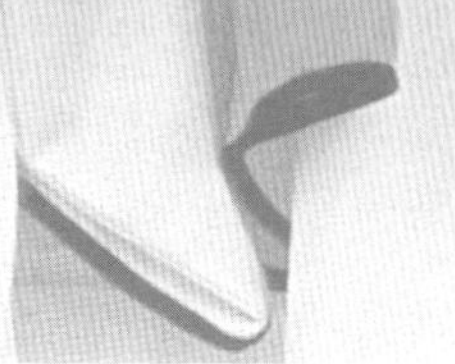

Career: Easton-in-Gordano; Bristol Boys; NORWICH CITY 15.08.70 (app), 21.12.72 (pro); Brighton & Hove Albion 29.04.74; Swindon Town 17.05.80; Portsmouth 05.08.81; Torquay United 02.09.83; Brentford Nov 1983; Aldershot 18.02.84; Maidstone United 1984; Littlehampton Town 1985; Steyning Town 1986; Brighton & Hove Albion 1986-May 1987; Southwick Aug 1987; Peacehaven & Telscombe; Newhaven Dec 1992; Shoreham.

Andy was given his City league debut because Duncan Forbes was serving a suspension – during his reign as pivot it was the only way that you got into the side! He gained enough experience in the Reserves (110 games) to hold him in good stead with Brighton at Division One level. Has returned to the South Coast where he owns a café.

RONSON, Brian

(1959) **1959:** 5/11; 12/7
Goalkeeper **Career:** 1-0-0
Debut/Final: 7 Nov 59

Born: Durham 7 Aug 1935

Career: Bear Park School; Langley Park Juniors; Willington Athletic; Fulham 10.03.53; Southend United 14.08.56; NORWICH CITY 08.08.59; Peterborough United 03.07.61 to 1962; Spalding United player–coach, player-manager to 1967.

Brian played in the one league game that Sandy Kennon missed in the promotion season of 1959/60. His Posh debut was against Grimsby on 16.09.61 with Keith Ripley and Terry Bly as team mates. He was nearly always signed as cover for goalkeepers already in residence. His coaching stint was terminated after a change of employment meant shift work.

Above: Robert Rosario

ROSARIO, Robert Michael Edward

(1984–1991) **1984:** 6/3; 12/1
Striker **Career:** 147-14-29
Debut: 7 Apr 84 **Final:** 2 Jan 91

Born: Hammersmith 4 Mar 1966

Career: Harrow Borough; Hillingdon Borough Aug 1983; NORWICH CITY 23.12.83; Wolverhampton Wanderers (loan) 13.12.85; Coventry City 22.03.91; Nottingham Forest 02.03.93; Greensboro Dynamos (USA) (loan) 1995 (club became Carolina Dynamos); Charleston Battery (USA) Apr 1998; Carolina Dynamos (USA) assistant coach.

Robert had a trial with Spurs and spent two months with Watford before City were alerted to his potential. He had the attributes of size and power and the national press, in anticipation of his City debut, said 'He steps out of class (an 'A' level student) and into the First Division'. He netted the ITV Goal of the Season in 1989 and gained four England Under-21 caps before his Forest appointment led to coaching positions in the States.

ROWE, George William

(1927) **1927:** 5/10; 12/3
Left Back **Career:** 3-0-0
Debut: 22 Oct 27 **Final:** 5 Nov 27

Born: Boosbeck 22 May 1899
Died: Derby 8 Nov 1966

Career: Loftus Albion (amat); North Riding; Middlesbrough 10.12.19 (amat); Hartlepools United 06.12.21 (amat); Derby County 15.06.23; NORWICH CITY 16.05.27; Chesterfield 30.07.28; Coleraine 19.09.28; Loughborough Corinthians Feb 1929; Chester Jan 1930; Trent Motors Feb 1930.

George added to his learning of the game by also playing in Inter-county matches for the North Riding FA. 27 league games for Hartlepools were followed by one Division Two appearance for Derby on 13.02.26 (A) Swansea, with McLaverty and Murphy being fellow Rams. His City debut came following injury to Archie Campbell but the boisterous play that was the order of the day was not to his liking.

ROWELL, Gary

(1985) **1985:** 5/10; 11/3
Striker **Career:** 2-4-1
Debut: 9 Mar 85 (sub) (goal) **Final:** 20 Apr 85 (sub)

Born: Seaham 6 Jun 1957

Career: Seaham Northlee Comprehensive School; Seaham Juniors; Sunderland Aug 1972 (app), 01.07.74 (pro); NORWICH CITY 24.08.84; Middlesbrough 16.07.85; Brighton & Hove Albion 30.08.86; Dundee United (trial) 29.02.88; Carlisle United 23.03.88; Burnley 02.08.88–20.05.89.

A modern day Roker Park hero with almost 300 games and 99 goals, including 24 penalties. Gary was a regular scorer against City and he was signed to strengthen our squad. He scored on his reserve debut and limped off – which sadly summed up his injury-beset stay at Carrow Road. Gary's

father John was a professional footballer with Bournemouth, Wrexham and Aldershot.

ROWELL, Joseph Peter

(1922) **1922:** 5/7; 11/4
Outside Right **Career:** 1-0-0
Debut/Final: 9 Dec 22

Born: Norwich 19 Oct 1901
Died: Norwich 19 Dec 1985

Career: Norwich CEYMS; NORWICH CITY 07.07.22 (amat), 28.08.22 (pro); Millwall 25.05.23; Gorleston 18.08.27; Norwich CEYMS Aug 1928; Sexton, Son & Everard's 21.07.29.

Thirty-five reserve games for three goals, and he did well to make one first team appearance as he was the understudy to Austin. Joe was one of three unrelated Rowells to appear on the books of Norwich City. Joe, the son of a gymnastic instructor, and a more than useful amateur boxer, was at Millwall with Lansdale, Moule and Lamberton.

ROWLANDS, Trevor Ivor

(1947–1949) **1948:** 5/9; 11/2
Left Half **Career:** 11-0-2
Debut: 1 Sep 47 **Final:** 26 Dec 49

Born: Wallston 2 Feb 1922
Died: Norwich 22 Jul 1973

Career: Cardiff Nomads; Cardiff City 1945/6; NORWICH CITY 16.08.46; Colchester United 20.07.50; Lovell's Athletic Jul 1953; Yarmouth Town 22.08.53–03.05.58.

A Welsh schoolboy international and one of the myriad of Welshmen at the club in the 1940s. His performances for the Reserves were the centre of much discussion and prompted his promotions to the firsts. One description of the period portrays him as, 'Hearty and one in whom City must place great trust this term'.
It would appear that his 103 reserve games for 11 goals was not a proper reflection of his worth. He went on to give tremendous service to Yarmouth, making 194 appearances for them.

ROY, John Robin

(1934–1935) **1934:** 5/10; 11/10
Outside Left **Career:** 10-0-1
Debut: 25 Jan 34 **Final:** 21 Sep 35

Born: Southampton 23 Mar 1914
Died: Bournemouth 24 Nov 1980

Career: Sholing (amat); NORWICH CITY 24.07.33 (amat), 25.08.33 (pro); Mansfield Town 16.04.36; Sheffield Wednesday 09.02.37; Notts County 17.03.38; Tranmere Rovers 16.12.38; Yeovil & Petters United May 1939; Aberaman Athletic; Southampton 24.12.39; Ipswich Town 07.02.46; Gravesend Jun 1947.

He was a lively winger and crowd pleaser who worked his way through the City 'A's and Reserves to the Firsts. He scored 56 goals for the lower XIs, including three threes, and was known as 'Wroxham' owing to the association of his name with a local store. He only failed to score for Notts County but his goal tally of eight at senior level for all his clubs showed that he rarely troubled the rigging. A retired engineering inspector.

ROYLE, Joseph

(1980–1981) **1981:** 6/1; 13/8
Centre Forward **Career:** 44-3-10
Debut: 16 Aug 80 **Final:** 5 Dec 81

Born: Norris Green, Liverpool 8 Apr 1949

Career: Quarry Bank High School; Liverpool Boys; Liverpool Schools; Everton 29.07.64 (app), 22.08.66 (pro); Manchester City 24.12.74; Bristol City (loan) 25.11.77; NORWICH CITY 05.08.80; Oldham Athletic 14.07.82 manager; England Under-21 11.09.90 manager (one game); Oldham Athletic continuous from 1982; Everton 10.11.94 manager; Manchester City 18.02.98–21.05.2001 manager.

A skilful, goalscoring target-man who was held in high esteem by his fellow professionals. Winner of Football League, England Youth, Under-23 and Full Caps and he was involved in trophy-chasing with Everton and Manchester City and in relegation battles with Bristol City, Manchester City and Norwich. Incidentally his son Darren is starring in defence for non-league clubs.

RULE, Alan Harry

(1956–1957) **1956:** 5/10; 11/6
Right Half **Career:** 8-0-0
Debut: 20 Oct 56 **Final:** 23 Feb 57

Born: Southampton 10 Jan 1930

Career: Swaythling Youth Club; Pirelli General; Thornycrofts; Basingstoke Town; Winchester City; Chelsea 01.11.52; NORWICH CITY 26.09.56; Bournemouth 12.06.57–30.06.59; Swaythling Athletic coach

Alan spent four years at Stamford Bridge and played in three first-team friendlies.
A Coronation match on 04.05.53 versus Fulham and two games on an American tour in May 1954. A fee of £2,000 was set for joining City, but this was subsequently reduced on appeal to nil. Alan was not on the winning side in any of

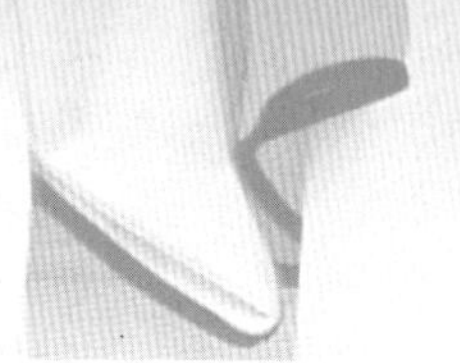

his eight games but his outings did come in the middle of a 20 game sequence when City did not win at all and when they tried five different players in the Number Four shirt. He returned to the South Coast and now lives in his home town. He coached the author at his last club.

RUSH, Matthew James

(1995–1997) **1995:** 5/11; 12/0
Midfield **Career:** 0-3-0
Debut: 19 Aug 95 (sub) **Final:** 15 Mar 97 (sub)

Born: Hackney 6 Aug 1971

Career: Deptford Park Primary School; Deptford Park Junior School; Addey & Stanhope FC; Vista FC; River Cray FC; London Schools; West Ham United 10.10.85 (assoc), 11.07.88 (trainee), 24.03.90 (pro); Cambridge United (loan) 12.03.93; Swansea Town (loan) 10.01.94; NORWICH CITY 18.08.95; Northampton Town (loan) 28.10.96; Oldham Athletic 27.03.97; Dulwich Hamlet 1999; Dagenham & Redbridge Nov 1999.

Matthew was Martin O'Neill's first City signing but he immediately suffered a knee injury that sidelined him. For the Hammers he earned a reputation as a utility man with good pace, difficult to knock off the ball. He was principally a reserve there, though with 135 such games for a dozen goals. His latter career was also injury prone and he duly left league football in September 1998. He has the ambition of being a PE teacher.

RUSSELL, Cecil John (Jack)

(1934–1936) **1934:** 5/10; 11/0
Outside Left **Career:** 61-0-23
Debut: 6 Oct 34 **Final:** 18 Apr 36

Born: Northfield, Birmingham 19 Jun 1904
Died: Blackwell, nr Bromsgrove 10 Dec 1995

Career: King's Norton Council School; Northfield; Bourneville; Bromsgrove Rovers cs 1923; Birmingham 05.02.24; Bristol Rovers 14.06.27; Worcester City Jul 1928; Bournemouth 17.05.30; Luton Town 15.06.34; NORWICH CITY 05.10.34; Worcester City 06.05.36; Shirley Town Aug 1937, player coach/manager, 1939 committee; Solihull Town Jun 1939 committee.

Jack once scored an incredible 48 goals in 11 school matches. He later did especially well at Bournemouth in netting 46 goals including two fours in January 1933 against Clapton Orient and Bristol City. In March 1933 he broke his collarbone in a collision with City's Stan Ramsay with no blame apportioned to either player. In an interview with the author he proudly remembered the opening match at Carrow Road.

RUSSELL, Darel Francis Roy George

(1998– **1998:** 5/11; 11/9
Midfield **Career:** 82-20-9
Debut: 3 May 98

Born: Mile End 22 Oct 1980

Career: St Augustine Primary School; Trinity Catholic School; Redbridge District; Essex County; Sarvic FC; NORWICH CITY 20.03.95 (assoc), 14.07.97 (trainee), 28.11.97 (pro).

Darel trained at the club's Centre of Excellence at Clearview and thankfully joined City after two weeks' work experience. With a style not dissimilar to that of England international Paul Ince, he is highly rated in the game and rightly so. Strong, aggressive and a powerful non stop runner, which is not surprising considering that he represented England as a teenager at the pentathlon and heptathlon. A first team regular at 21 and destined to go on to greater things.

RUSSELL, James Walker

(1938–1946) **1938:** 5/9; 11/7
Inside Right **Career:** 14-0-2
Debut: 1 Sep 38 **Final:** 28 Sep 46 (goal)

Born: Edinburgh 14 Sep 1916
Died: Naples, Florida, USA 17 Aug 1994

Career: Craiglockhart–Merchiston Schools; Craigmer Juveniles; Murrayfield Amateurs; Carrickmuir Juniors; Scotland Schoolboys; Queens Park (trial); Heart of Midlothian (trial); Sunderland 09.06.34; NORWICH CITY 18.05.38; Crystal Palace 02.12.46; New Brighton 16.07.48; Fleetwood 31.07.49.

James Russell

Ball control and swinging cross-field passes were James' calling cards. The Sunderland Manager Mr Cochrane described James as, 'A top-notcher in the making', but the brilliance of Raich Carter restricted him to just five league games for the Rokerites. Secured by City for £1,500; he soon displayed exceptional close dribbling skills. He returned to play for City from September

1945 after working in a Shipyard and playing for Carlisle during the War. I enjoyed my visit to see him as he had a fund of entertaining stories.

RYAN, John Gilbert

(1976–1980) **1977:** 5/11; 11/8
Wing Half **Career:** 128-4-29
Debut: 21 Aug 76 **Final:** 9 Feb 80

Born: Lewisham 20 Jul 1947

Career: Tonbridge; Maidstone United; Arsenal 15.10.64; Fulham 02.07.65; Luton Town 04.07.69; NORWICH CITY 19.08.76 to 05.03.79; Seattle Sounders (USA) Mar 1979–Aug 1979; Sheffield United 24.09.80; Manchester City Aug 1982 player/youth coach; Stockport County 28.08.83 player coach; Chester City 28.09.83 player coach; Cambridge United 20.01.84 player-manager; Maidstone United 1985 player coach, 1986 assistant manager; Sittingbourne Sep 1991 manager; Dover Athletic Feb 1995–Nov 1995 manager; Dulwich Hamlet manager.

John had a fine career of over 500 league games, including a sensational scoring season for City in 1977/78. His long passes and superb opportunism made him a valued and popular member of the side in the 70s. To quote John, 'I did all the running and Martin Peters did all the playing'. He took up working in the family haulage business while managing at non-league level.

RYDER, Isaac Terence (Terry snr)

(1925–1926) **1925:** 5/8; 10/12
Centre Forward **Career:** 3-0-0
Debut: 7 Mar 25 **Final:** 17 Apr 26

Born: Norwich 4 Sep 1904
Died: Norwich 3 Oct 1977

Career: Heigham YMCA; City Wanderers; Norfolk County 1923–1928; NORWICH CITY 14.01.24; Gorleston 18.08.27; Norwich CEYMS Sep 1927; Boulton & Paul 11.10.29.

Terry's first City appearance was in the May 1924 Hospital Cup game against West Ham United. His three competitive games resulted in three losses – a sequence that did not help to further his career. A heavy reserve team scorer with a goal every two games on average. Father of the post-war Terry Ryder.

RYDER, Terence Roy (Terry jnr)

(1946–1950) **1948:** 5/5; 9/10
Outside Right **Career:** 51-0-12
Debut: 14 Sep 46 **Final:** 6 May 50

Born: Norwich 3 Jun 1928

Career: Norwich St Mark's; Norfolk County Youth colours 1944/45; NORWICH CITY 08.11.45 (groundstaff), 15.05.46 (amat), 05.09.46 (pro); Portsmouth 30.10.50; Swindon Town 10.07.52; King's Lynn 22.08.53 to 1957 player-manager; Newmarket Town 13.10.62.

Regarded as the brains of the Norfolk Minors attack in the FA Youth competition. A phenomenal scorer at reserve level and equally proficient in the senior ranks. For Swindon against Norwich he scored three goals in the two matches of the 1952/53 season. He lives locally.

SARGEANT, Charles

(1930–1931) **1930:** 5/9; 11/4
Outside Left **Career:** 13-0-1
Debut: 2 Oct 30 **Final:** 14 Mar 31

Born: Cornsay Colliery 2 Feb 1909
Died: Sedgefield 11 Sep 1988

Career: Cornsay Park Albion; Esh Winning Juniors; Washington Colliery; Cornsay Colliery; Bishop Auckland Aug 1928; Tow Law Town Dec 1928; White-le-head Rangers; Ushaw Moor; NORWICH CITY 20.03.30; Bristol City 19.06.31; Hull City 26.05.32; Chester 15.03.34; Stockport County 16.03.38; Plymouth Argyle 18.05.39; Post War for Blackhall Colliery Welfare; Cornsay Park Albion Sep 1949.

He took a number of years to reach league level and then had a measure of success winning a Division Three North medal with Hull. Also twice a Welsh Cup finalist with Chester. One City enthusiast wrote, 'He was judicious with his centres'. He additionally found time to score over 100 goals in his career including ten twos, three hat-tricks and a four. His father played for Esh Winning and West Stanley.

SARGENT, Gary Stewart

(1971) **1971:** 5/8; 10/2
Forward **Career:** 0-1-0
Debut/Final: 28 Aug 71 (sub)

Born: Turvey, nr Bedford 11 Sept 1952

Career: NORWICH CITY 15.07.68 (app), 05.09.70 (pro); Scunthorpe United 01.07.72; Bedford Town; Peterborough United 25.06.77; Northampton Town 11.06.79; Irthlingborough; Irthlingborough Diamonds; Northampton Spencer 1987 player, Feb 1988 player-manager, 1990 manager.

Gary possessed a fine junior and reserve record but he was given little chance to impress in senior company. His 30 minutes for City in Division Two was followed by a roving

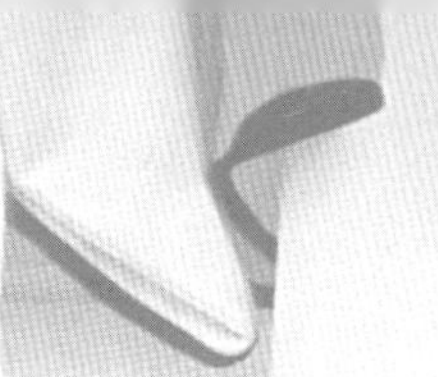

career in the lower divisions. He was Steve Grapes' best man and now works in newspaper advertising.

SAVINO, Raymond John

(1957–1962) **1958:** 5/7; 10/2
Right Winger **Career:** 27-0-4
Debut: 20 Feb 57 **Final:** 28 Apr 62

Born: Norwich 16 Nov 1938

Career: Thorpe Village; Heatrae Reserves; Norwich Boys; NORWICH CITY 1955/56 (groundstaff), 11.2.57 (pro); Bristol City 06.07.62; King's Lynn Mar 1968–Apr 1970; Lowestoft Town Jul 1970–1973; Wisbech Town; Yarmouth Town 14.09.76; Norfolk County 1977; St Andrews Old Boys player-manager; St Andrews 29.04.89 manager for one year.

'Small in stature but not a shirker', was the succinct comment of one newspaper columnist. A local lad who in seven years with City achieved a reserve tally of 89 games for 16 goals. Ray was a regular right winger for Bristol, where his centres were aimed at the prolific scorer John Atyeo. True to form, like so many ex-City men he returned to reside in Norfolk.

SCOTT, John McRae

(1929–1930) **1929:** 5/9; 11/7
Inside Left **Career:** 10-0-4
Debut: 2 Sep 29 **Final:** 22 Apr 30

Born: Sanquhar, Dumfries 3 Nov 1906
Died: Kirkconnel 18 Sep 1981

Career: Euchan Thistle cs 1922; Kello Rovers cs 1926; Nithsdale Wanderers (trial) 1926; Luton Town 08.06.28; Loughborough Corinthians Oct 1928; NORWICH CITY 10.05.29; Bristol Rovers 07.05.30; Walsall 21.07.31; York City 20.05.33; Southport 16.07.34; Workington cs 1935.

John left school to work down the mines with his dad, so he took the game of football up later. A roving Scot (no pun intended) who in only his third game for us scored twice in City's record Football League win. He had a particularly strong left foot shot but he lasted less than a year as a Canary. He returned to the mines having an arm crushed by a huge stone and suffering with a gangrenous foot. Us Southerners have had it easy!

SCOTT, John Redvers (Jack)

(1932–1937) **1937:** 5/10; 12/0
Centre Half **Career:** 45-0-1
Debut: 23 Jan 32 **Final:** 13 Mar 37

Born: Grimethorpe, Barnsley 4 Dec 1905
Died: Shirley, Southampton 9 Mar 1976

Career: Hull Rugby League football; Featherstone Rovers (also Rugby League); Pilkington's Recreational; Doncaster Rovers 15.03.29 (amat), 02.09.29 (pro); NORWICH CITY 03.07.31; Southampton 25.03.37 player coach & assistant trainer; Nicholas FC coach.

Jack sampled two codes of first class football, having also played rugby for Featherstone Rovers. Not unnaturally he was a fine athlete and not one for shamming – when injured he was invariably on his feet before the trainer reached him. O that more of the players of the current era would follow his example! His brother was a Bournemouth player and rather curiously considering that Jack was never friendly towards an opponent, he worked quietly at Southampton's City Library. Unbeknownst to me at the time he helped me with some of my early research into football.

SCOTT, Keith

(1995–1997) **1995:** 6/3; 13/4
Striker **Career:** 10-19-5
Debut: 21 Nov 95 (goal) **Final:** 15 Mar 97

Born: Westminster, London 10 Jun 1967

Career: Hinckley Athletic 1984; Bedworth United 1987/88; Hinckley United cs 1988; Leicester United cs 1989; Aston Villa Reserves; Leicester City (trial) 19.02.90; Lincoln City 22.03.90; Gateshead (loan) Oct 1990; Boston United (loan) Feb 1991; Wycombe Wanderers (loan) Mar 1991, (permanent) Mar 1991; Swindon Town 18.11.93; Stoke City 30.12.94; NORWICH CITY 11.11.95; Bournemouth (loan) 16.12.96; Watford (temp) 07.02.97; Wycombe Wanderers 27.03.97; Reading 24.02.99; Colchester United (loan) 13 Oct 2000, (signed) 19.03.2001-06.06.2001; Dover Athletic Aug 2001.

An unusual career in the modern age in that he drifted into non-league football before regaining his rightful place as a league player. He was with Martin O'Neill at Wycombe where his bustling, traditionally English-style centre forward play reaped rewards. A great start in a Canary shirt, but later competition from Fleck and Ward saw him mostly start from the bench. In August 2000 he scored against City's reserves at Carrow Road.

SCOTT, Kevin Watson

(1997–1998) **1996:** 6/3; 14/5
Defender **Career:** 33-3-0
Debut: 22 Jan 97 **Final:** 11 Aug 98 (sub)

Born: Easington 17 Dec 1966

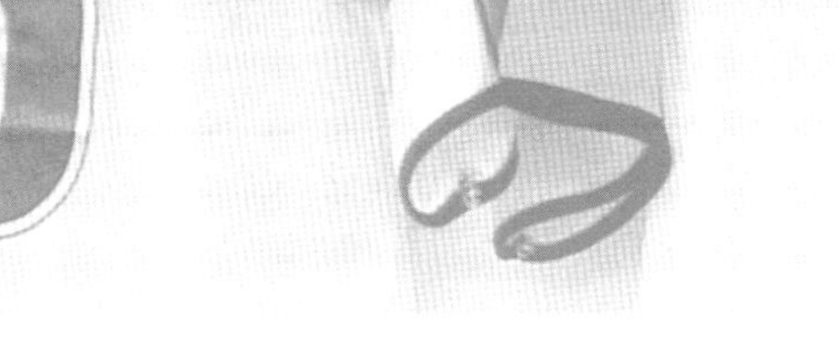

Career: South Hetton Junior School; Hetton Comprehensive School; Durham County; Eppleton Colliery Welfare; Easington Juniors; Middlesbrough 30.06.83; Leicester City (trial); Sherburn 1984; Newcastle United 19.12.84; Tottenham Hotspur 01.02.94; Port Vale (loan) 13.01.95; Charlton Athletic (temp) 20.12.96; NORWICH CITY 21.01.97; Darlington 29.01.99–11.05.99 retired Aug 1999.

A solid and reliable defender, particularly effective in the air. He was spotted by Jack Charlton in an FA Youth Cup match before moving to Spurs for £800,000. Not afraid of hard work as he was employed in a lumber yard, a paper mill and at one point passed the medical to join the Army. His last league club was David Hodgson's Darlington. He has bought a greyhound and has a car valeting business.

SCOTT, Richard Sydney Arthur (Dick)

(1961–1963)	**1962:** 5/10; 11/7
Right Half	**Career:** 36-0-3
Debut: 3 Apr 61	**Final:** 20 Mar 63

Born: Thetford, Norfolk 26 Oct 1941

Career: Thetford Town; NORWICH CITY 03.11.58; Cardiff City 07.07.63; Scunthorpe United 29.09.64; Lincoln City 01.07.66; King's Lynn 23.03.67–Apr 1968; Lowestoft Town 19.08.68; Thetford Sep 1969 player, 1970 player coach, manager to 1983.

Dick graduated to City's first team through Groundstaff, 'B' and reserve sides. He also played in a forward position – once netting a threesome for City Reserves versus Mansfield on 03.03.62. An interesting debut at Cardiff alongside John and Mel Charles on 24.08.63 against Norwich City.

SCOTT, Sidney

(1921–1922)	**1921:** 5/10; 12/5
Centre Half	**Career:** 26-0-1
Debut: 27 Aug 21	**Final:** 18 Apr 22

Born: Macclesfield 11 Feb 1892
Died: Northwich 7 Mar 1947

Career: Macclesfield Town; Castle Primitives; Northwich Victoria Sep 1911; Manchester City 02.05.13; Tranmere Rovers May 1916; NORWICH CITY 17.06.21; New Brighton 25.10.22; Stafford Rangers 1923/24; Altrincham cs 1924.

Sid could not displace Max Woosnam at Manchester City and won a Cheshire County Cup medal with Tranmere. His Canary debut was notable for a collision with Luton's Parker, which incident sadly broke the latter player's leg. Durable, big, strong and capable – Norwich City spent £500 securing his services.

SCOTT, Thomas

(1932–1934)	**1932:** 5/10; 11/12
Inside Right	**Career:** 55-0-26
Debut: 1 Oct 32	**Final:** 6 Oct 34

Born: Newcastle-on-Tyne 6 Apr 1904
Died: Bootle 24 Dec 1979

Career: Swifts FC; Pandon Temperance Colliery; Sunderland 05.12.22; Darlington 04.06.24; Liverpool 13.02.25; Bristol City 26.10.28; Preston North End 19.06.30; NORWICH CITY 24.06.32; Exeter City 11.10.34; Hartlepools United Jun 1936; Bangor City Aug 1937; Blyth Spartans Jun 1938.

Tom was regarded as the brains of any side that he played for, stretching from the day he scored his first ever league goal on 28.03.25 to his last one on 17.10.36. One discerning local judge said of him, 'He is the cleverest Norwich City forward since Banks'. He scored 76 football league goals in a career total of 204 games to reaffirm the high opinions of him. He was a Liverpool licensee outside of football.

SEAGRAVES, Mark

(1986)	**1986:** 6/1; 12/10
Left Back	**Career:** 3-0-0
Debut: 22 Nov 86	**Final:** 6 Dec 86

Born: Bootle 22 Oct 1966

Career: Salesian High School; Bootle & District Schools FA; Merseyside Co SFA; Liverpool 04.11.83; NORWICH CITY (loan) 21.11.86–06.12.86; Manchester City 22.09.87; Bolton Wanderers 24.09.90; Swindon Town 06.06.95–29.05.98; Barrow to Mar 1999; Runcorn Apr 1999; Blackpool assistant manager.

Mark, an England schoolboy and Youth international, was signed by City on a month's loan with the help of Liverpool's manager Kenny Dalglish. He deputised for Tony Spearing until his own suspension curtailed his stay. Ian Butterworth's arrival meant that his services were no longer needed and he has since plied his trade with a number of clubs. Whilst at Anfield his brother Chris cleaned Dalglish's boots while Mark did the came for Ian Rush.

SELF, Glenn Walter

(1970–1972)	**1971:** 5/9; 11/3
Forward	**Career:** 5-1-2
Debut: 13 Oct 70	**Final:** 26 Aug 72 (sub)

Born: Norwich 4 Feb 1953

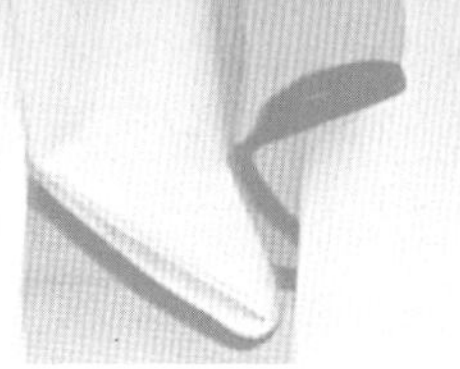

Career: Framingham Earl Secondary Modern School; NORWICH CITY Aug 1968 (app), 05.09.70 (pro); Torquay United (loan) 09.03.73 to Aug 1973; Lowestoft Town 06.10.73–06.11.73.

A good reserve scorer, he owed his debut principally due to the fact that Briggs, Foggo, Silvester and Stringer were all injured. He played 21 minutes in Division One after getting a hat-trick the week before for the Reserves. The arrival of David Cross rendered him superflous in the management's eyes and he retired from the game altogether within the year. His son Danny is now on City's Academy books.

SHARPE, Frederick Charles (Freddie)

(1963–1968) **1964:** 5/10; 11/6
Centre/Left Half **Career:** 122-4-0
Debut: 24 Aug 63 **Final:** 26 Oct 68

Born: Greenwich, London 11 Nov 1937

Career: Stanley Street School; London Boys; Tottenham Hotspur Jun 1954 (amat), 09.05.56 (pro); NORWICH CITY 24.07.63; Reading 01.07.69 to 30.06.71.

Freddie Sharpe

Freddie scored the only goal of the game on his Spurs debut against Nottingham Forest on 17 September 1958. For nine years he was a regular member of their Combination side but he was unable to break the Blanchflower and Mackay midfield stranglehold. He was a shrewd and seasoned player who performed admirably as a Canary for five seasons. He later coached in schools as well as for Finchampstead Under-12s.

SHAW, Colin Michael

(1964) **1964:** 5/7; 10/6
Centre Forward **Career:** 4-0-0
Debut: 30 Mar 64 **Final:** 7 Nov 64

Born: St Albans 19 Jun 1943

Career: Chelsea 08.08.59 (juniors), 15.05.60 (pro); NORWICH CITY 24.08.63; Leyton Orient 16.3.65; Natal (South Africa) 1966.

Colin was a prodigious scorer of goals in Chelsea's junior and reserve sides. He got seven versus Fulham in one FA Youth Cup tie and three versus Hounslow in a first team friendly. Surprising to see, therefore, that he had only one Football League game for the Pensioners namely, 03.02.62 (H) West Ham United. His City reserve tally was 53 games for 23 goals so it would appear that he deserved more first team opportunities. He now lives in Transvaal.

SHEFFIELD, Jonathan

(1989) **1989:** 5/11; 11/7
Goalkeeper **Career:** 1-0-0
Debut/Final: 2 Apr 89

Born: Bulkington, nr Coventry 1 Feb 1969

Career: Nuneaton Borough; PGL England; NORWICH CITY 06.08.85 (app), 16.02.87 (pro); Aldershot (loan) 22.09.89 –11.11.89; Ipswich Town (loan) 21.03.90; Aldershot (loan) 25.08.90–10.11.90; Cambridge United 18.03.91–31.07.91; Swindon Town (loan) 28.01.94; Colchester United 23.12.93 (temp); Hereford United (loan) 15.09.94; Cambridge United 13.11.94; Peterborough United 24.07.95; Watford (temp) 21.03.97; Oldham Athletic (temp) 27.03.97; Plymouth Argyle 28.07.97–04.05.2001; Yeovil Town 10.07.2001.

An agile goalkeeper with a good temperament, he starred in games in Sweden, Denmark, Iceland and France for the PGL side. He was the last apprentice signed before the introduction of the YTS scheme and his one City first team game came as a result of Bryan Gunn's suspension. A remakable travelling career since has seen him play a further 300 games.

SHEFFIELD, Lawrence Joseph

(1966–1967) **1964:** 5/9; 11/10
Centre Forward **Career:** 29-0-16
Debut: 12 Nov 66 (3 goals) **Final:** 23 Aug 67

Born: Swansea 27 Apr 1939

Career: Swansea Boys; Welsh Schoolboys; Bristol Rovers 11.07.56; Royal Welsh Fusiliers; Barry Town (loan) Jan 1959; Newport County 24.04.62; Doncaster Rovers 05.08.65; NORWICH CITY 10.11.66; Rotherham United 25.08.67; Oldham Athletic 12.12.67; Luton Town 20.07.68; Doncaster Rovers 29.10.69; Peterborough United 12.08.70–30.06.72; Doncaster Rovers youth coach for 7 years.

The Norwich City Supporters Club handed a cheque for £15,000 to the club and chairman Geoffrey Watling revealed that the club were negotiating for a very good player. He started with a hat-trick and continued his record of scoring on average a goal every other game. A season at each club was the norm for Lawrie, and his greatest feat when coaching was the discovery of Ian Snodin. Remarried after the death of his first wife, he coaches youngsters at a local (to him) leisure centre.

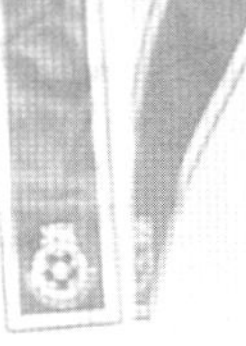

SHEPHERD, Jamie Greig

(1980–1982) **1979:** 6/1; 12/0
Forward **Career:** 15-4-2
Debut: 26 Jan 80 (sub) **Final:** 20 Mar 82

Born: Edinburgh 29 Sep 1960

Career: Musselburgh Windsor; Glasgow Rangers (schoolboy); Hibernian (trial); Heart of Midlothian (trial); NORWICH CITY 26.03.79; Eastern Athletic (Hong Kong) (loan) Aug 1982; Southend United 13.08.83; Peterborough United 14.12.84; King's Lynn Feb 1987; Unity Emeralds Mar 1987; Wroxham May 1987–Sep 1990; Eynesbury Rovers Oct 1992.

Greig's City League debut ostensibly occurred because Justin Fashanu had been dropped and fined following his dangerous play in the previous game. He was one of seven players to wear the Number Eight shirt in the 1981/82 season following the departure of Fashanu to Forest. He scored regularly with Peterborough but had his greatest success at Wroxham where he netted an amazing 84 goals in just 93 games. He now works for the Cambridgeshire Constabularly and has been seen in the Moys End enclosure at London Road keeping an eye on the away fans.

SHERON, Michael Nigel

(1994–1995) **1994:** 5/9; 11/3
Striker **Career:** 29-9-7
Debut: 31 Aug 94 **Final:** 7 Oct 95 (sub)

Born: Liverpool 11 Jan 1972

Career: Starting Gate FC; Pen Lake Juniors; Manchester City Apr 1986 (assoc), 04.07.88 (trainee), 05.07.90 (pro); Bury (loan) 28.03.91; NORWICH CITY 26.08.94; Stoke City 13.11.95; Queens Park Rangers 02.07.97; Barnsley Jan 1999.

96 goals in just 99 starts for Manchester City's youths/reserves is a staggering haul. On his day a gifted striker capable of netting stunning goals and skilful in linking with his colleagues. A hat-trick over Swindon Town reserves held promise of great things at Carrow Road, but he had greater success at Stoke before big-money moves to his next two clubs.

SHERWOOD, Timothy Alan

(1989–1991) **1989:** 6/1; 11/7
Midfield **Career:** 82-6-13
Debut: 26 Aug 89 **Final:** 28 Dec 91

Born: St Albans 6 Feb 1969

Career: Herts Schools Under-16s; Forest United; Watford May 1985 (trainee), Feb 1988 (app), 07.02.87 (pro); NORWICH CITY 11.07.89; Blackburn Rovers 12.02.92; Tottenham Hotspur 04.02.99.

Tim Sherwood

Tim supported Arsenal as a boy, but ironically won his England caps as a Spurs player. He had a roller-coaster ride at Carrow Road, with bookings and injuries laced with fine displays that enhanced his reputation weekly before Blackburn's bid for him proved too tempting to resist. A Championship medal as the Rovers' midfield leader saw him fulfil his obvious potential.

SHORT, James

(1923) **1923:** 5/8; 11/3
Inside Left **Career:** 11-0-3
Debut: 25 Aug 23 **Final:** 24 Nov 23

Born: Hucknall

Career: Arnold St Mary's; South Notts Hussars Yeomanry; Lincoln City 1916; Notts County Dec 1917; Birmingham Mar 1919; Watford May 1920, 20.08.20 (signing league forms); Ilkeston United Aug 1922; NORWICH CITY 12.05.23; Newark Town Sep 1924; Grantham Town; Lewison 16.09.27.

Gained his reputation at Notts County where among his goals were two hat-tricks: 28.09.18 (H) Sheffield United and 25.01.19. (A) Bradford City. Another promising career lost to the War, from which he did not emerge unscathed. He helped Ilkeston win the Derbyshire Cup and returned to non-league football after his brief stay at the Nest. I and many other eminent researchers are struggling to find James' birth and death. Can anyone help please?

SILVERTHORNE, James

(1921–1924) **1921:** 5/8; 12/7
Centre Forward **Career:** 22-0-8
Debut: 10 Dec 21 **Final:** 12 Jan 24

Born: Bedminster 3 Aug 1894
Died: Harwich 13 Nov 1962

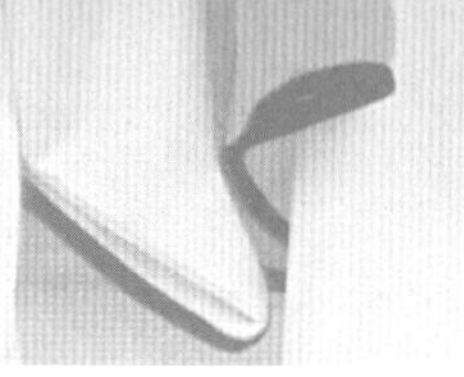

Career: Royal Navy Barracks; Harwich & Parkeston; Gorleston; Manchester City (amat); NORWICH CITY 28.11.21 (amat); Gorleston cs 1922; Norfolk County 1922/3; NORWICH CITY 18.06.23 (pro); Weymouth Sep 1924; Bristol City (trial) Oct 1924; Parkeston Railway Aug 1928; Harwich & Parkeston Aug 1928 player/trainer.

A keen, bustling Navy player who was attached to HMS Pangbourne. *He netted five for City Reserves versus Gorleston thus earning a First XI spot. James could not buy himself out of the service and turn professional with City until a year had elapsed, so he rejoined Gorleston until he was given FA clearance. A complete change to his details here after discovering that James was ten years older than previously thought.*

Left: James Silverthorne
Right: Peter Silvester

SILVESTER, Peter Dennis

(1969–1974) **1970:** 5/11: 11/8
Forward **Career:** 112-1-37
Debut: 16 Sep 69 **Final:** 2 Feb 74

Born: Wokingham 19 Feb 1948

Career: Earley Primary School; Presentation College; Reading Boys; Berkshire Boys; Reading 02.12.64 (app), 19.02.66 (pro); NORWICH CITY 13.09.69; Colchester United (loan) 04.10.73; Southend United 15.02.74; Baltimore Comets (USA) May 1974–Aug 1974; Reading (loan) 15.03.75; Baltimore Comets (USA) May 1975–Aug 1975; San Diego Jaws (USA) May 1976–Jul 1976; Vancouver Whitecaps (Canada) Jul 1976–Aug 1976; Blackburn Rovers (loan) 07.10.76; Washington Diplomats (USA) Apr 1977–Aug 1977; Cambridge United 10.08.77; Maidstone United Aug 1978; Lakeford Rangers coach, assistant manager.

Peter was a fine header of the ball, whether glancing, diving or with power, and always needed watching. He had three cartilage operations while he was at City and was sold after the arrival of Phil Boyer and Ted MacDougall. He played in all four divisions of the Football League and abroad for Baltimore Comets, Vancouver Whitecaps, San Diego Jaws and Washington Diplomats. At Lakeford his coaching strategem is based on keeping up both fitness and fun for his amateur charges.

SIMONS, Henry Thomas

(1920) **1920:** 5/8; 11/4
Inside Right **Career:** 3-0-0
Debut: 25 Sep 20 **Final:** 9 Oct 20

Born: Hackney 6 Oct 1887
Died: Stoke Newington 26 Aug 1956

Career: Peel Insitute; Leyton Mar 1906; Tufnell Park; Middlesex County; Sheffield United 07.07.07; Merthyr Tydfil Aug 1912; Brentford Aug 1913; Dalston; WWI-assisted Fulham, Tottenham Hotspur & Queens Park Rangers; NORWICH CITY 24.09.20; Margate Nov 1920.

He scored in his first and last games for Spurs and also represented Middlesex. The local press said of his City debut, 'He amply justified his inclusion and with better acquaintance with the team will be an asset'. Norwich City were under the impression that he was 28 when they signed him. He was one of several footballing brothers, being the son of a one-time groundsman of Clapton Orient.

SIMPSON, Karl Edward

(1995–1997) **1995:** 5/11; 11/9
Midfield **Career:** 5-6-0
Debut: 20 Sep 95 **Final:** 8 Nov 97 (sub)

Born: Newmarket 14 Oct 1976

Career: South Wootton Junior School & First School; South Wootton; King Edward V11 School; Lea Valley District; Ressley FC; NORWICH CITY School of Excellence 1988, 09.12.90 (assoc), 16.05.92 (trainee), 04.07.95 (pro); Witney Town; Hendon May 1999; Worthing Nov 1999.

A right-sided midfielder who had speed and was well balanced in his movement. Spotted as a 12-year-old, he rose from 167 games for 19 goals at non-first XI level to a first-team sending-off after 77 minutes of his debut in a 6–1 cup tie win over Torquay United. Injuries and the form of Neil Adams led to his release into non-league football.

SISSONS, John Leslie

(1974–1975) **1974:** 5/7; 10/8
Left Winger **Career:** 20-1-3
Debut: 1 Jan 74 **Final:** 6 Aug 75

Born: Hayes, Middlesex 30 Sep 1945

Career: Hayes School; Hayes SFA; Middlesex & England Schoolboys (4 goals on debut); West Ham United 25.07.61 (app), 02.10.62 (pro); Sheffield Wednesday 01.08.70; NORWICH CITY 29.12.73; Chelsea 15.08.74; Tampa Bay Rowdies (USA) Apr 1975–Aug 1975; Cape Town (South Africa) May 1976–1983.

Ron Greenwood's autobiography said, 'Sissons had rare gifts, including a left foot that was a miracle'. Blonde and baby-faced John won Youth and Under-23 caps, plus Domestic and European medals as well as scoring in an FA Cup Final when just 18. He now lives in Cape Town and is a director of a motor products and warranty company.

SKERMER, Herbert Edward

(1920–1922) **1920:** 5/11; 11/6
Goalkeeper **Career:** 73-0-0
Debut: 28 Aug 20 **Final:** 4 Mar 22

Born: Selston, Nottingham 19 Feb 1896
Died: Norwich 25 Nov 1954

Career: Selston St Helen's; Selston Colliery; Hartshay Colliery; NORWICH CITY 23.12.19 (amat), 28.8.20 (pro); Ramsgate Town Aug 1922; Coalville Swifts Nov 1922; Loughborough Corinthians 1924/25.

City's goalkeeper in their first ever league game joined us with good credentials, having won medals in the Mansfield Church League, Eastwood District League and Derbyshire Senior League. A contemporary journalist said of him, 'His movements came of purpose and were backed by uncanny anticipation'. Latterly a licensed victualler.

SLACK, William

(1930–1931) **1930:** 5/8; 12/7
Outside Left **Career:** 31-0-2
Debut: 30 Aug 30 **Final:** 2 May 31

Born: Sutton-in-Ashfield 20 Jan 1906
Died: Sutton-in-Ashfield 9 Aug 1989

Career: Sutton Junction cs 1924; Shirebrook Jan 1927; Sutton Junction Mar 1927; Blackpool 19.05.27; Nelson 16.03.28; Portsmouth Aug 1928; Merthyr 14.09.29; NORWICH CITY 13.05.30; Mansfield Town 15.8.32; Sutton Town cs 1936; Ripley Town Feb 1937.

Bill started on the wing and moved to inside left and thence to left half. A useful cricketer, playing principally for New Hucknall Colliery, he became a regular at Mansfield, playing in 98 League games for them. Bill was later a local authority employee in Mansfield.

SLICER, Jacky

(1927–1930) **1928:** 5/8; 10/1
Outside Left **Career:** 133-0-14
Debut: 27 Aug 27 (goal) **Final:** 3 May 30

Born: Bramley, nr Leeds 24 Nov 1902
Died: Huddersfield 13 Aug 1979

Career: Bullercroft Colliery; Chesterfield Apr 1923 (amat); Doncaster Rovers 05.09.23; Mexborough Athletic May 1924; Huddersfield Town 25.03.25; NORWICH CITY 19.05.27; Luton Town 10.07.30; Ashton National Aug 1932; York City 28.09.33; Bury Aug 1934.

A jinky winger in the style of Ruel Fox, Jacky played seven Division One matches for Huddersfield, scoring twice on 02.10.26 (H) against Leicester. He was the first Canary to complete successive seasons without missing a game and in three years at the club only missed one league game. On 29.03.32 he showed his allegiance by scoring twice for Luton against Norwich in a 7–1 win.

SLOAN, Joshua Walter (Paddy)

(1952) **1952:** 5/9; 11/6
Centre Forward **Career:** 6-0-0
Debut: 16 Jan 52 **Final:** 19 Apr 52

Born: Lurgan 30 Apr 1920
Died: Victoria, Australia 7 Jan 1993

Career: Glenavon; Manchester United 31.08.37; Tranmere Rovers 24.05.39; Arsenal 23.05.46; Sheffield United 23.02.48; Brescia (Italy) Aug 1948; Torino (Italy) Aug 1949; Udinese (Italy) Aug 1950; Brescia (Italy) Aug 1951; NORWICH CITY 19.12.51 (7 million Lira = £4,000); Peterborough United 1952; Rabat Ajax FC (Malta) Jul 1954 player coach; Bath City Jul 1955; Hastings United Sep 1955 player coach; Lockheed Leamington Spa Jan 1956 player-manager; Bath City Aug 1956 player coach; Woodford Town 1962 coach; South Melbourne Hellas (Australia) Feb 1964 coach; N.S.C.A. (Australia) Chairman.

Transfer talks were held in a Paris Hotel. The sellers (Italian) spoke Italian, German and French but no English. The buyers (English) spoke only English plus the Italian colloquialism of Paddy (Irish). The Bank Manager (French) spoke French, English and Spanish but no Italian. The Interpreter spoke French and Italian but no English. It seems a shame that Paddy made only six appearances after all that effort to secure him. A sports teacher in Australia, his ashes were buried with permission at Highbury.

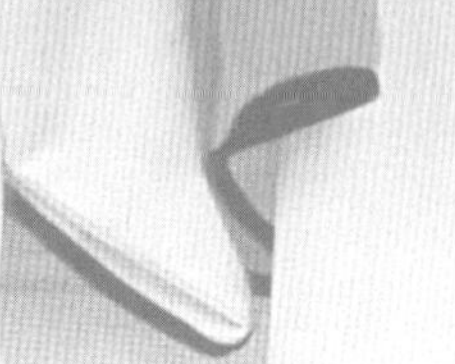

SMALLEY, Tom

(1938–1939) **1938:** 5/8; 11/10
Left Half **Career:** 43-0-1
Debut: 27 Aug 38 **Final:** 6 May 39

Born: Kinsley, nr Hemsworth 13 Jan 1912
Died: Wolverhampton 1 Apr 1984

Career: Hemsworth Colliery; South Kirkby Colliery; Barnsley (trial); Wolverhampton Wanderers 08.05.31; NORWICH CITY 10.08.38; Northampton Town 07.10.41–31.07.51; Lower Gornal Jul 1951–May 1953 player coach.

Tom joined City after having played 177 of his 179 games for Wolves in the First Division, gaining an England cap in 1937. A class wing half who displayed a propensity for hard work. He retired from playing aged 39, after making 200 post-War appearances for the Cobblers. He received a Football League benefit settlement in February 1951 of £367.17s.5d. – a small reward for a dedicated professional.

SMITH, Benjamin George

(1920–1924) **1920:** 5/8; 12/0
Left back **Career:** 81-0-0
Debut: 2 Oct 20 **Final:** 12 Jan 24

Born: Norwich 21 Sep 1892
Died: Norwich 3 Jul 1972

Career: Crooks Place School; New City FC; Norwich CEYMS; Norfolk County 1912; NORWICH CITY 16.04.15, 07.08.20 (Football League amat) – 19.03.24

Benjamin Smith

Bennie was fearless, a keen tackler and always a trier. He won 19 County caps and was suspended by an FA Commission for coupon betting (the equivalent of doing the pools). One of the men to have played in the Southern League and the Football League for Norwich City with his very first appearance in a 1915 wartime friendly. Latterly in the boot and shoe trade.

SMITH, Colin Richard

(1982) **1982:** 6/0; 12/10
Defender **Career:** 3-2-0
Debut: 31 Aug 82 **Final:** 6 Oct 82

Born: Ruddington, Nottingham 3 Nov 1958

Career: Rushcliffe Comprehensive School; England Boys Club; Northumberland County Schools SFA; Notts County 1973 (schoolboy); Nottingham Forest 01.04.76 (assoc), 01.06.77 (app), Feb 1981 (pro); Caroline Hill (Hong Kong) Feb 1982–Jun 1982; Huddersfield Town (trial); NORWICH CITY 26.08.82; See Bee (Hong Kong); Shepshed Charterhouse Jul 1983–Oct 1983; Cardiff City 01.10.83; Aldershot 30.12.84; Wokingham Town Jul 1990–Oct 1991.

Colin was signed on a non-contract basis and was then offered a month's contract, but was released after six weeks. A strong, solidly built defender who became more of a regular at his next two clubs. He represented Hong Kong twice during his stays out there and he is now a games master.

SMITH, David Christopher

(1990–1994) **1989:** 5/9; 11/12
Midfield **Career:** 16-7-0
Debut: 21 Apr 90 **Final:** 16 Apr 94

Born: Liverpool 26 Dec 1970

Career: Campion High School; Cammel Lairds; Arch Royal; NORWICH CITY Nov 1987 (trainee), 04.07.89 (pro); Oxford United 21.06.94; Stockport County 03.02.99.

Born on Boxing Day, he played for his father's Sunday League team Arch Royal. When unemployed he showed initiative by writing to clubs for a trial. A product of the famed 1988/89 youth team, he was only on the fringes of the City first team despite giving wholehearted, committed displays in the Canary cause. Oxford United expended £100,000 for him before he teamed up with Gary Megson at Stockport.

SMITH, James McQueen Anderson

(1930–1931) **1930:** 5/11; 12/0
Goalkeeper **Career:** 32-0-0
Debut: 18 Oct 30 **Final:** 2 May 31

Born: Leith 28 Nov 1901
Died: Kirkcaldy 5 Apr 1991

Career: Rosyth Juniors; Rosyth Recreation; East Fife; Tottenham Hotspur 04.06.25; St Johnstone Nov 1928; NORWICH CITY 16.05.30; Ayr United 17.09.31.

He made his Football League debut on 31 October 1925 for Spurs against Leicester. He had three games for St Johnstone before joining City and subsequently returned to Scotland thereby showing that Chris Woods was not the first Canary keeper to move north of the border.

SMITH, Kenneth George

(1956–57) **1956:** 6/1; 11/7
Centre Half **Career:** 10-0-0
Debut: 14 Jan 56 **Final:** 27 Apr 57

Born: Norwich 22 Apr 1936

Career: York Athletic; NORWICH CITY 20.09.55; Gothic Nov 1961–Apr 1969; Corinthians.

Ken made his debut in the absence, through injury, of Foulkes and had a testing debut coping with Maurice Cook (Watford). The Eastern Football News *said of his performance, 'He looked out of touch at times but he stuck well to his task'. It has to be noted that Cook scored over 150 league goals so he was no slouch. He was virtually a permanent reserve (76 apps) during his five year stay. Ken was one of 10 men of the 1957/58 staff of 35 to be in the forces.*

SMITH, Samuel James

(1935) **1935:** 6/0; 12/0
Inside Right **Career:** 1-0-0
Debut/Final: 16 Sep 35

Born: Pelsall, nr Walsall 7 Sep 1909
Died: Walsall 19 Nov 1994

Career: Pleck Old Boys; Walsall (trial) cs 1926; Darlaston; Cannock Town 07.07.26; Walsall L.M.S; Birmingham City 24.12.30 (pro); Chelsea 15.06.34; NORWICH CITY 25.05.35; Walsall 18.01.36; Stourbridge Aug 1936..

A thrustful player who showed clever touches, he scored five goals on his Birmingham debut versus Atherstone in a Combination match, followed by a brace on 21.11.31 in his Division One debut. He scored 13 goals in the top league but after Chelsea (no games) and City (one game) it took a move to his home town side to restart his scoring touch. He was a retired bricklayer.

SMITH, Sydney Joseph

(1923) **1923:** 5/9; 11/10
Inside Left **Career:** 3-0-0
Debut: 27 Aug 23 **Final:** 29 Dec 23

Born: Aston, Birmingham 11 Jul 1895

Career: Aston Manor; Aston Rangers; Stourbridge; Cradley Heath & St Lukes; Derby County 08.06.21 (amat), 11.08.21 (pro); NORWICH CITY 26.06.23; Gillingham 14.07.24.

A Football League debut for the Rams on 30.09.22 (H) Barnsley was his only appearance for them. The Canary connection was evident as Cecil Potter was his Manager at Derby, and among his team mates that day were McLaverty and Murphy. The City handbook said, 'Has the weight and build for a successful inside forward'. I do dislike searching for Smiths!

SMITH, Thomas Gable

(1930) **1930:** 5/8; 11/11
Inside Right **Career:** 1-0-0
Debut/Final: 30 Aug 30

Born: Whitburn 18 Oct 1900.
Died: Whitburn 22 Feb 1934

Career: Marsden Villa 1918; Whitburn FC; South Shields May 1919; Leicester City 05.12.19 (amat); Manchester United 11.01.24; Northampton Town 06.06.27; NORWICH CITY 13.05.30; Whitburn 28.02.31.

Tom and his six footballing brothers graced the game. Our man had a great enthusiasm and keeness for the game. Had a good career at Northampton with 112 league games bringing him 22 goals including two in the club's record win on 05.11.27 (H) over Walsall. The Smith brothers made 1,573 appearances for 183 goals. It may be a common surname but they were an uncommonly talented set of footballers.

SMITH, William Harris

(1931–1934) **1932:** 5/9; 11/7
Left Back **Career:** 102-0-1
Debut: 10 Jan 31 **Final:** 25 Jan 34

Born: Kelvin, Glasgow 23 Mar 1906
Died: Glasgow 26 Mar 1979

Career: Old Kilpatrick; Burnbank Athletic; NORWICH CITY 19.06.30; Exeter City 09.03.34; Stenhousemuir 01.10.35.

Bill gained three Scottish junior caps against England, Wales and Ireland. His only City goal came when he was tried at centre forward against Luton Town. A steady performer and an unsung hero in partnership with Joe Hannah at full back. As an RAF Corporal aged 38 he played for a totally outclassed service side against Norwich City in September 1944.

SPEARING, Anthony

(1984–1988) **1984:** 5/9; 10/12
Left Back **Career:** 80-2-0
Debut: 5 May 84 **Final:** 7 May 88

Born: Romford 7 Oct 1964

Career: Kirkley High School; Oulton Broad Eagles; England Youth; NORWICH CITY 27.05.81

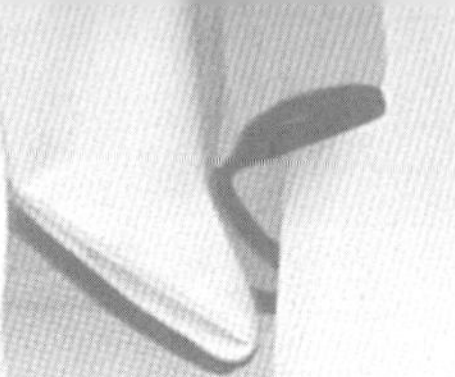

(app), 11.10.82 (pro); Stoke City (loan) 01.11.84 to 16.1.85 , Oxford United (loan) 01.02.85 to March 1985; Leicester City 12.07.88; Plymouth Argyle 01.07.91; Peterborough United 21.01.93–May 1997; King's Lynn 24.07.97 player coach, manager May 1998–Sep 1998, reverting to a player role, caretaker manager, 15.08.2000 manager.

An England Youth team captain and possessor of an FA Youth cup-winner's medal with Norwich. Tony gained valuable experience on loan to Stoke and Oxford and was pursued by Lincoln, Gillingham and Plymouth but returned to Carrow Road, fulfilling his obvious potential. A speedy and tenacious defender, he extended his career to a dozen years beyond his City days. He has just managed King's Lynn into third place in their league in season 2000/1.

SPELMAN, Ronald Edward

(1958–1960) **1964:** 5/9; 11/9
Right Winger **Career:** 3-0-1
Debut: 26 Apr 58 **Final:** 19 Nov 60

Born: Blofield, Norfolk 22 May 1938

Career: City of Norwich School; CNSOBU; Norfolk County Schools; NORWICH CITY 28.07.56; Northampton Town 24.11.60; Bournemouth 02.03.62; Watford 06.09.63; Oxford United 24.05.65; Wisbech Town Aug 1966; Gothic Nov 1968.

Ron had but three senior outings in his five-year Canary career. He was not idle while at Carrow Road as he netted 21 goals in his 92 reserve matches. He was a team-mate of Edwards and Moran at the County Ground and he was on the opposite flank to Crickmore at Dean Court. He had a varied civvy life outside of football.

SPINKS, Henry Charles

(1946–1947) **1946:** 5/10; 11/5
Centre forward **Career:** 2-0-1
Debut: 28 Dec 46 (goal) **Final:** 4 Jan 47

Born: Norwich 1 Feb 1920

Career: Norwich St Pauls Juniors; Wolverhampton Wanderers 1935; Norfolk County; Norwich CEYMS; Second World War-Aberavon; NORWICH CITY 20.10.46 (amat); Yarmouth Town 08.10.48; Lowestoft Town 17.09.49–17.03.51.

Henry marked his City reserve and First Team debuts with goals. He had a 'goalden' career as a local amateur. As an example, for CEYMS he hit a double hat-trick at Fakenham and he followed this with nine more goals in his next five games. Henry continued to find the net with regularity at Yarmouth and Lowestoft, and he still lives locally having just recovered from a heart attack.

STATON, Barry

(1962–1963) **1962:** 6/0; 11/10
Left Back **Career:** 31-0-1
Debut: 18 Aug 62 **Final:** 4 May 63 (goal)

Born: Doncaster 9 Sep 1938

Career: Sheffield & Hallam SFA; Doncaster SFA; Doncaster Rovers (juniors), 28.05.56 (pro); NORWICH CITY 11.07.62 to 21.12.63; Thetford Town Jan 1964.

Barry won England Youth caps while at Sheffield & Hallam and Doncaster, and confirmed this potential when he turned professional. His last game for Rovers saw Bunny Larkin score twice as they lost at Colchester on 30.04.62. His calm, cool and collected style was to the fore before an injury ended his career. Almost 10,000 fans turned out for his testimonial match against an international XI. Barry was occupied outside of football with his own wholesale meat company in Hertfordshire.

STEELE, William McCallum

(1973–1977) **1974:** 5/9; 10/8
Winger **Career:** 63-13-3
Debut: 26 Dec 73 **Final:** 23 Apr 77

Born: Kirkmuirhill, Lanark 16 Jun 1955

Career: Sandon Rangers; NORWICH CITY 05.07.71 (app), 20.06.73 (pro); Bournemouth (loan) 15.01.76–Apr 1977.

Billy was a busy little player whose career was plagued by injury – he had four operations and seven manipulations. He had begun to make his mark as a midfield player of distinction and was granted a Testimonial Match against an England XI. After leaving the game he worked in sports shops and in business partnerships locally at the Ironmongers Arms and the Shirehall. A loss to the game through a knee injury and he reckoned that football was the best job in the world – being paid to get fit. He now lives in Canada.

STENNER, Arthur William John

(1956) **1956:** 5/8; 11/0
Left Winger **Career:** 6-0-0
Debut: 18 Aug 56 **Final:** 8 Sep 56

Born: Yeovil 7 Jan 1934

Career: Yeovil Town; Bristol City 25.08.54; Plymouth Argyle 25.07.55; NORWICH CITY 18.08.56; Exeter City 06.12.56; Oldham Athletic 13.04.57; Yeovil Aug 1957; Chard Town Jul 1959 player coach; Trowbridge Town Sep 1960; Poole Town Nov 1960; Weymouth; Bridport Town

His Football League debut was against Leicester City on 24 September 1955 with his ninth (and last) appearance for Argyle being on 7 April 1956 versus Bury. Four wins and a draw in his City appearances were an amazing statistic considering that the Canaries had a dire season. 30% of his spasmodic league appearances were at Norwich. On retirement from football he had his own furniture removal business.

STEPHENSON, John

(1928–1929) | **1928:** 5/7; 12/0
Inside Forward | **Career:** 21-0-2
Debut: 25 Aug 28 | **Final:** 1 Apr 29

Born: Crawcrook 1 Jun 1899
Died: Crawcrook 30 Dec 1969

Career: Crawcrook Amateurs; Prudhoe Castle; Craghead United; Durham City Jun 1924; NORWICH CITY 14.06.28; Hartlepools United Jun 1929; Grantham Town Dec 1930; Crawcrook Albion Aug 1931–Nov 1931; Cork FC May 1932; Wallsend Town Sep 1932; West Stanley Aug 1934.

In his Durham days he partnered such well-known players as Camsell, Elliott and Crooks. Also in the team were Lewis Botto and Joseph Lamb, who were to join him in the City side. His career covered 160 league games for 11 goals so he could not be considered a scoring forward. A no-nonsense Northerner who added steel and backbone to the side.

STEWART, Edward McDonald

(1957) | **1957:** 5/9; 11/0
Left Half | **Career:** 13-0-0
Debut: 24 Aug 57 | **Final:** 19 Oct 57

Born: Dundee 15 Nov 1934

Career: Stobswell Secondary School; Ashdale Amateurs; Dundee Osborne; Dundee United 22.09.54; NORWICH CITY 16.07.57; Dundee United; Arbroath 04.03.59; Leeds United (trial) Mar 1959; St Johnstone Jul 1959–Oct 1959; Nairn County 1960.

Eddie was the first of four Scots brought in by Archie Macauley within a fortnight. He was stationed at Aldershot and he was on loan until his demobilization in December 1957. Matt Crowe took over the left half position afterwards and became a permanent choice. Eddie returned to live in Dundee and worked in the building trade.

STEWART, Robert Whyte

(1922–1923) | **1922:** 5/9; 11/0
Inside Left | **Career:** 15-0-0
Debut: 7 Oct 22 | **Final:** 7 Apr 23

Born: Paisley 19 Dec 1899
Died: Paisley 17 Sep 1950

Career: St Mirren 1918; NORWICH CITY 30.06.22 until registration cancelled by the club 26.5.23.

A prolific scorer for St Mirren who was highly spoken of by William O'Hagan, a former team mate of his. He was featured on Pinnace Card number 1730 as a City player. At Norwich he was overshadowed by Austin and Stoakes in the days when City vied for the wooden spoon on a regular basis.

STOAKES, James Henry

(1921–1925) | **1923:** 5/9; 11/9
Outside Left | **Career:** 150-0-6
Debut: 8 Sep 21 | **Final:** 12 Dec 25

Born: Newark, Nottingham 17 Dec 1895
Died: Newark, Nottingham 5 Feb 1979

Career: Newark Athletic; Army for North Staffordshires; Notts County Reserves May 1919 (amat); NORWICH CITY 27.04.21 (amat), 12.05.21 (pro); Newark Town Sep 1926; Ransome & Marles 07.01.28.

A flyer with very few equals for speed. He won trophies galore in Brigade and Battalion Athletic meets at sprints and hurdles events. James took part in England Olympic trials and was just beaten by the famed Abrahams. Not a goalscorer, but it was said that he centred with fine judgement for his inside men. He was reputedly a fine singer as well.

Above: Dave Stringer

STRINGER, David Ronald

(1965–1976) | **1970:** 5/10; 11/6
Defender | **Career:** 497-2-22
Debut: 10 Apr 65 | **Final:** 21 Aug 76

Born: Southtown, Gt.Yarmouth 15 Oct 1944

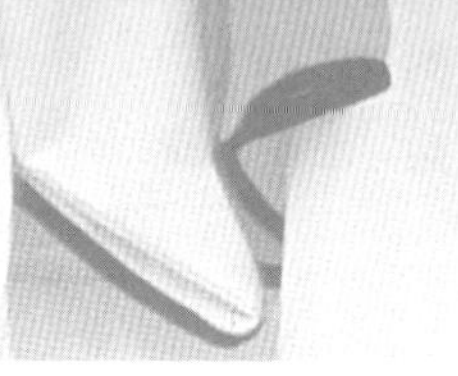

Career: Edward Worlledge School; Alderman Leach School; Arsenal (3 apps in S.E. Counties Lge); Crystal Palace (trial); Chelmsford City Feb 1961; Gorleston Minors Apr 1961; NORWICH CITY 13.02.62 'B', 23.05.63 (pro); Cambridge United 30.09.76; NORWICH CITY 1980 youth team manager, assistant manager 22.05.87, acting manager 09.11.87, 30.12.87–01.05.92 manager, 1994/95 played Norwich 'A', Assistant Academy Director to retirement July 2001.

Left: Albert Sturgess
Right: Colin Suggett

A valuable club servant on and off the field. From gaining an England Youth Cap in 1963 to his final league appearance on 11 October 1980 he was a credit to the game. A superbly balanced style that dovetailed perfectly in harness with Duncan Forbes. A favourite quote on the two was 'tight at the back'. Dave is a former City Player of the Year and stands third among the Canaries with most appearances in competitive games. The youthful reserve side finished third under his guidance in 1985/86 as a prelude to his taking on more and more demanding roles. Glorious Canaries *does him far better justice than I can in the space available here.*

STURGESS, Albert

(1923–1925)	**1923:** 5/11; 11/10
Full Back	**Career:** 52-0-0
Debut: 25 Aug 23	**Final:** 14 Feb 25

Born: Etruria, Stoke-on-Trent 21 Oct 1882
Died: Sheffield 16 Jul 1957

Career: Hathersage 1897; Tunstall Crosswells 1901; Stoke City 25.10.01; Sheffield United 17.06.08; NORWICH CITY 21.7.23 to 14.02.25 and retirement.

The oldest Football League debutant for Norwich City. Albert had 125 League games for Stoke and 336 for Sheffield in a fabulous career, winning an FA Cup medal in 1914/15 and two Full England Caps. He had clever anticipation and it was said that he took a cold shower even on a freezing day. Upon retirement from the game he ran a crockery shop in Eccleshall. His son Arthur played for Rotherham.

SUGGETT, Colin

(1973–1978)	**1973:** 5/9; 10/12
Inside Left	**Career:** 240-3-29
Debut: 24 Feb 73	**Final:** 29 Apr 78

Born: Chester-le-Street 30 Dec 1948

Career: Washington Grammar School; Chester-le-Street School; Chester-le-Street Co SFA; Durham; Sunderland 24.08.64 (app), 09.01.66 (pro); West Bromwich Albion Jul 1969; NORWICH CITY 16.02.73; Newcastle United 21.08.78 , Jun 1981 youth coach, caretaker manager 11.10.88, youth coach 05.02.94; Portsmouth scout; Ipswich Town 13.03.95 Director of coaching, chief scout Jul 1998.

Colin was a former England Schools and Youth player who twice won FA Youth Cup winner's medals (1966, 1967). He was the first north-eastern player to be transferred for a six-figure fee. He started as a striker, being quick and a useful goalscorer, but was converted to midfield by John Bond. Had good, close control and was an exponent of the through ball. He started his coaching career at Newcastle and he is in his sixth year at Ipswich.

SULLIVAN, Colin John

(1974–1978)	**1975:** 5/7; 10/11
Full Back	**Career:** 179-3-3
Debut: 17 Aug 74	**Final:** 14 Oct 78

Born: Saltash, Cornwall 24 Jun 1951

Career: Cornwall Schools; Plymouth Argyle Schoolboys; Saltash United; Plymouth Argyle 10.08.67 (app), 01.07.68 (pro); NORWICH CITY 19.06.74; Cardiff City 29.01.79; Hereford United

Colin Sullivan

14.11.81; Portsmouth 26.02.82; Swansea City 26.03.85; Locksheath Jul 1986 player/trainer; Warsash Under-15 and 16 trainer.

Colin made his Football League debut on 19.03.68 against Rotherham, to become the youngest ever Argyle player in the first team. He won England Youth and Under-23 honours and he was a calming influence to the Argyle and City defences. The mark of a good player is the number of years he plays after reaching the age of 30 – Colin, with over 600 career games to his credit, was proof of this adage. He was a postman for a while and latterly a landscape gardener.

SUMMERS, John Henry

(1951–1954) **1952:** 5/10; 11/9
Forward **Career:** 76-0-36
Debut: 17 Mar 51 (goal) **Final:** 1 May 54 (goal)

Born: Shepherds Bush 10 Sep 1927
Died: Bloomsbury, London 2 Jun 1962

Career: Hexham; RAMC; Fulham 05.02.44 (amat), 07.02.47 (pro); NORWICH CITY 22.06.50; Millwall 07.05.54; Charlton Athletic 16.11.56 to 1961

A compelling performer, being a whole-hearted, penetrating winger and difficult to quell. Added to his senior City goals were a reserve haul of 73 games (41 goals); Millwall 92 league (41 goals) and Charlton 171 league (100 goals). It's very clear, therefore, that he was a constant source of danger near the opposition's penalty area. He twice scored five in a game for Charlton (on 21.12.57 and 01.10.60) with the first occasion being five second half goals in a famous 7–6 win over Huddersfield. His perfect Summers' day saw them overturn a 5–1 defecit and the opposing goalkeeper was none other than Sandy Kennon. A noted Cockney wit, he observed, 'I once played in a town so small that they had to shoot someone to start a cemetery'. It was a tragic quip considering that he passed away at such an early age in the University College Hospital.

SUTCH, Daryl

(1990– **1990:** 6/0; 12/0
Utility **Career:** 284-46-9
Debut: 9 Oct 90 (sub)

Born: Lowestoft 11 Sep 1971

Career: Benjamin Britten High School; Waveney Youth; Lowestoft Town; North Suffolk; Norfolk County; NORWICH CITY Jan 1986 (assoc), Jul 1988 (trainee), 06.07.90 (pro).

Left: Daryl Sutch
Right: Chris Sutton

As a football trainee Daryl looked after Culverhouse, Fleck and Fox, and he was given a good grounding at youth and reserve level where it is essential to get games under your belt. He even scored a hat-trick against Rushden Town in the Eastern Junior Cup, outscoring Chris Sutton that day. He gained England Youth and Under-21 honours and he exudes an unflappable temperament and fine technique that flourished after the departure of Dale Gordon. Over 300 games in a Canary shirt, and we forgive him his green boots against Ipswich Town in one game.

SUTTON, Christopher Roy

(1991–1994) **1991:** 6/0; 11/12
Striker **Career:** 113-13-43
Debut: 4 May 91 (sub) **Final:** 7 May 94

Born: Nottingham 10 Mar 1973

Career: Horsford First & Middle School; Hellesdon High School; Norfolk County Under-14s; Norwich Schools; Carrow Under-16s; Horsford Boys; NORWICH CITY Apr 1989 (youth), 27.07.89 (trainee), 29.06.91 (pro); Blackburn Rovers 14.07.94; Chelsea 16.07.99; Glasgow Celtic 11.07.00.

Chris was a talented cricketer before following his father's footsteps into football. Forty goals for the youths/reserves and success for the firsts quite rightly thrust him into the national spotlight. He has an old head on young shoulders and enjoyed tremendous success at Blackburn, winning a chamionship medal in partnership with Alan Shearer (their partnership was known as the 'SAS' – Sutton and Shearer). Chelsea broke their transfer record to secure him, but in retrospect the club's patient, probing chess-like style didn't suit his more robust play. Triple success with Celtic should kickstart the England international's career.

SUTTON, Michael John

(1963–1966) **1964:** 5/10; 11/10
Utility **Career:** 49-5-3
Debut: 14 May 63 **Final:** 5 Nov 66

Born: Norwich 5 Oct 1944

Career: Hellesdon Secondary Modern School; Norwich Boys; Norfolk County; NORWICH CITY Sep 1960 (groundstaff), 06.05.61 (amat), 07.09.62 (pro); Chester 12.05.67; Carlisle United 01.06.70 to 1971; Gorleston 1978; Yarmouth Town 30.09.78–03.02.87; Norwich City All Stars; NORWICH CITY 1990 coaching Under-15s, 1992 coaching Under-14s.

Mike was a local product on the groundstaff who graduated to the professional ranks. 107 City reserve games for 30 goals were also played before he left for Chester aged 22. His adaptability was never more evident than in a 17-game spell at Sealand Road when he donned all the shirts from number five to number twelve. Three of his 'less famous' children were county standard sports players, with the youngest, John, being on Tottenham's books.

SYMONDS, Richard

(1978–1983) **1979:** 6/1; 11/5
Utility **Career:** 63-5-0
Debut: 28 Oct 78 **Final:** 12 Mar 83

Born: Langham, Norfolk 21 Nov 1959

Career: Langham Primary School; Langham Secondary Modern School; Litcham YC; Dereham; NORWICH CITY 03.05.75 (assoc), 07.08.76 (app), 03.08.78 (pro); Poringland 1983; Watton; Dereham Hobbies; Thetford Town Apr 1990 assistant manager/coach; Dereham Hobbies Oct 1990–May 1992 manager.

By the end of his second season he had worn ten different shirts and with his penultimate game (at number five) he needed only to wear the keeper's jersey to complete the set. After just a handful of games Bobby Robson (Ipswich manager) offered £50,000 for him. Richard was a specialist man-to-man marker and he was invariably called upon when it was felt by management that such a task needed performing. Richard was an FA Sunday Cup winner in non-league circles.

TANNER, Nicholas

(1990) **1989:** 6/2; 13/10
Defender **Career:** 6-0-0
Debut: 3 Mar 90 **Final:** 31 Mar 90

Born: Kingswood, Bristol 24 May 1965

Career: Mangotsfield; Bristol Rovers 19.04.85; Liverpool 08.07.88; NORWICH CITY (loan) 01.03.90; Swindon Town (loan) 28.09.90; Liverpool retired injured on 01.03.94; Bath City Jul 1994; Yeovil Town; Mangotsfield United Feb 1997 manager

A former machine shop apprentice for British Aerospace who was nicknamed 'Whoosh' at Bristol. In May 1985 he came on as a sub in the Gloucestershire Cup Final (against rivals City) and he scored with a 45 yarder. Progressing from the Western league he was a strong central defender with good control. He missed out on a championship medal at Liverpool through not playing enough games to qualify. He had an uneventful time at Norwich apart from only being on the losing side once. He expressed an interest while at Bath in owning and training racehorses.

TAYLOR, Alan David

(1979–1980 & (1988–1989) **1980:** 5/9; 10/6
Forward **Career:** 25-9-8
Debut: 18 Aug 79 (sub) **Final:** 7 Jan 89

Born: Hinckley, nr Leicester 14 Nov 1953

Career: Mount Grace Comprehensive School; Carnforth Secondary School; Lancaster Boy's Club; Preston North End Oct 1969 (app); Lancaster City; Morecambe 1972; Rochdale 15.05.73; West Ham United 26.11.74; NORWICH CITY 16.08.79; Vancouver Whitecaps (Canada) 10.07.80–Sep 1980; Cambridge United 21.10.80–Feb 1981; Vancouver Whitecaps (Canada) May 1981–Aug 1981, Mar 1982–Aug 1982, Apr 1983–Jul 1983; Hull City Dec 1983; Burnley 03.08.84: Bury 14.07.86; NORWICH CITY Aug 1988, Oct 1988 (monthly contract) registered 23.11.88, club cancelled 25.07.89; Bury Town Jul 1989; Thetford Town 10.09.89, Jul 1990 player & assistant manager, manager to 25.07.81; Dereham 27.01.90 (guest).

Alan, a former apprentice mechanic, worked with a refreshing directness and is remembered for his two opportunist FA Cup Final goals for West Ham against Fulham in 1976. Very speedy, and fast too in moving round the soccer circuit, playing for seven league clubs. An amazing City comeback nine years down the line and he rattled in reserve goals including three over Wortwell. Winner of a Norfolk Senior Cup medal with Thetford. Alan is now a local newsagent having previously been a milkman.

TAYLOR, Geoffrey Arthur

(1946) **1946:** 5/8; 10/0
Left Wing **Career:** 1-0-0
Debut/Final: 14 Sep 46

Born: Henstead, nr Kessingland 22 Jan 1923

Career: City of Norwich & Bungay Grammar Schoolboy; CNSOBU; RAF; NORWICH CITY 02.08.46 (amat), 23.08.46 (pro); Reading 10.03.47; Lincoln City 11.08.47; Boston United Mar 1948–Apr 1948; Brighton & Hove Albion 25.08.48; Stade Rennais (France) Dec 1949 player coach; Bristol Rovers 27.09.51; S.C.Bruhl (Switzerland) May 1952 player coach; Queens Park Rangers 14.11.53; VFR 07 Kirn (Germany) May 1955 player coach; FC Sobernheim (Germany) 1958 player coach; FC Idar Oberstein (Germany) 1964 player coach; VFL Weierbach (Germany) 1965 player coach; SV Bergen (Germany) 1967 player coach; FSV Schwarzerden (Germany) 1975 player coach; SV Bundenbach (Germany) 1980–1984 player coach.

Geoff served 66 months in the Middle East and was given his first team chance after showing, 'Nice perception of accurate positioning in the pre-season trial'. An overall record of ten League games for his six clubs spread over seven years must surely constitute a record? There followed an amazing career in France, Switzerland and Germany and I am so glad that he wrote detailing his coaching career as the spellings were a nightmare to deal with over the phone.

TAYLOR, John (Jack)

(1938–1946) | **1938:** 5/9; 11/4
Full Back | **Career:** 56-0-0
Debut: 24 Sep 38 | **Final:** 21 Dec 46

Born: Barnsley 15 Feb 1914
Died: Barnsley 22 Feb 1978

Career: Barnsley Grammar School; Worsborough Bridge FC; Worsborough Bridge Old Boys; Wolverhampton Wanderers Jun 1931 (groundstaff), 15.12.33 (amat), 18.01.34 (pro); NORWICH CITY 04.06.38; Hull City 23.07.47; Weymouth May 1950 player-manager; Queens Park Rangers 24.06.52 manager; Leeds United May 1959 to 13.03.61 manager.

Jack was a capture who gave great satisfaction to City's supporters, being a defender built on classic lines. Another player who had his best footballing years taken by the War – 215 war games for City is evidence of the unfortunate timing. Jack's post-war play was summed thus: 'He still covered his territory quickly, an asset being a capacity to run backwards at speed'. His elder brother Frank (Wolves) was an England international, and they played together for Norwich just eight days after Pearl Harbour.

TAYLOR, Walter Joseph

(1921–1922) | **1921:** 5/7; 10/8
Centre Forward | **Career:** 2-0-0
Debut: 26 Nov 21 | **Final:** 26 Dec 22

Jack Taylor

Born: Norwich 6 June 1887
Died: Norwich 7 May 1961

Career: Bull Close School; Junior Institute; Norwich St James; Norfolk County; NORWICH CITY Oct 1906; Doncaster Rovers 30.12.08; NORWICH CITY 03.10.10 to 1915 (amat), 11.10.20 (pro); Phoenix Works Jul 1924.

Wally was a distinct credit to himself and the game, a pre-war City amateur who had a total of 49 games for seven goals in the Southern League days. For those who know of the Nest it was richly said of him, 'He shoots as if he wants to knock the concrete wall away'. He even hit a hat-trick for Manchester City against King's Lynn in a exhibition match. For 30 years, many of them as foreman, he worked in the clicking room of a shoe factory. On retiring, he took over a tobacco and confectionery business from the former City trainer Hugh McQueen.

TAYLOR, William

(1931–1932) | **1931:** 5/8; 10/10
Outside Right | **Career:** 14-0-2
Debut: 29 Aug 31 | **Final:** 12 Dec 32

Born: Langley Green, 5 Jun 1898
Died: Northfield 22 Aug 1965

Career: Langley Green Zion; West Bromwich Albion Colts; West Bromwich Albion 23.10.20 (amat), 30.11.20 (pro); Redditch; Stourbridge 1922; Cardiff City 08.01.23; Aberdare Athletic 08.02.25; Hull City 12.06.26; NORWICH CITY 11.6.30; Llanelly Aug 1932; Aldershot 28.08.33–May 1934.

A league career of 204 games for 25 goals was a fine record for a seasoned two-footed player player with wide vision and good dribbling skills. The City handbook listed his age as 28 from Langley (Worcestershire) upon joining the Canary ranks. Other sources make him five years older than this and as we go to press I have just read that in the local Norwich

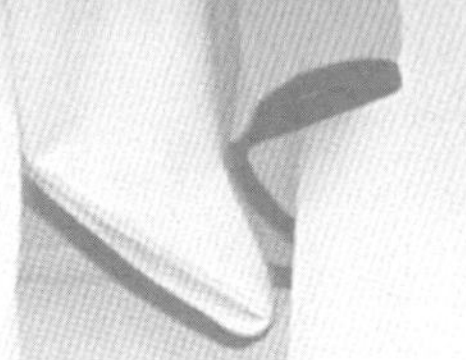

paper that he was age 23 on the 14th June 1926. More investigation is needed. In Bartholomew's Gazetteer of Britain *(First Edition) there are 15 Langleys and four Langley Greens.*

TENNANT, William

(1930) **1930:** 5/10; 12/6
Forward **Career:** 12-0-1
Debut: 30 Aug 30 **Final:** 13 Dec 30

Born: Kirkfieldbank 13 Sep 1904

Career: Motherwell 1924; NORWICH CITY 4.08.30.

In 88 Scottish League games for Motherwell he scored 45 goals to prove himself a marksman of note. He was featured on Pinnace Card number 2079 in Motherwell colours. Unfortunately he suffered from injuries during his spell at the Nest and at the end of the season he was placed on the available for transfer list with six other players.

THOMPSON, Andrew

(1931–1932) **1931:** 5/9; 11/6
Inside Forward **Career:** 14-0-3
Debut: 5 Dec 31 **Final:** 29 Mar 32 (goal)

Born: Newcastle-under-Lyne 21 Jan 1899
Died: London E.10, 1 Jan 1970

Career: Newburn; Whickham Park Villa; Tottenham Hotspur 09.11.20; NORWICH CITY 16.11.31; Chester 16.07.32; Clapton Orient 11.10.32; Northfleet cs 1933 player coach; Chelsea coach; Tottenham Hotspur staff; Ashford Mar 1934.

Sixty-six games (22 goals) for Spurs in eleven seasons from a debut on 26.03.21 against Sunderland to a last appearance on 24.01.31 at West Bromwich Albion. Andy undertook three long tours with Spurs with Malta, Switzerland and Holland included in his peregrinations. He was a good finisher with no nerves and returned to Spurs in a backroom capacity. A coal miner in later life.

THOMPSON, James William

(1929–1930) **1929:** 5/9; 12/5
Centre Forward **Career:** 30-0-17
Debut: 31 Aug 29 **Final:** 3 May 30

Born: Plaistow 19 Apr 1898
Died: Epsom 27 Aug 1984

Career: West Ham Schoolboys; Custom House Aug 1919; Charlton Athletic Aug 1921 (amat); Wimbledon Sep 1921; Millwall Athletic 10.12.21 (pro); Coventry 21.05.23; Clapton Orient 29.08.24; Luton Town 12.07.25; Chelsea 24.05.27; NORWICH CITY 10.05.29; Sunderland 16.05.30; Fulham 01.11.30; Hull City 03.10.31; Tunbridge Wells Rangers Dec 1931; Tranmere Rovers Jul 1932; Sittingbourne Oct 1932; Peterborough United Aug 1934; Belfast Linfield Jul 1935; Aldershot Aug 1935; Lucerne (Switzerland) Sep 1935; Enfield trainer; Letchworth Town Jun 1937 trainer coach; Territorial Army Sports Board coach; Dartford Jul 1939–1960 manager; post war a Scout for Chelsea and Southampton.

James Thompson

A thrusting, robust centre forward who had 150 career games scoring 97 goals. A powerful left foot was employed to score fifteen twos, three threes and a four. Jimmy was a character who insisted on having a free transfer in his pocket. He had a dislike of new boots and for years and years he would have the same pair stitched, soled and attended. A star maker extraordinaire, he discovered Jimmy Greaves, Terry Venables and Bobby Tambling amongst many others. You must read the Jimmy Greaves national tabloid press article of the 16th April 1994 that covers Jimmy Thompson and Scott Parker – it is a fabulous read.

THOMSON, Norman Shaw

(1929–1930) **1929:** 5/9; 11/7
Inside Forward **Career:** 16-0-0
Debut: 31 Aug 29 **Final:** 8 Feb 30

Born: Glasgow 20 Feb 1901
Died: Ferring, West Sussex 6 Jun 1984

Career: Glasgow St Anthony's; Dumbarton 23.03.22; Hibernian 14.06.24; Luton Town 08.08.25; Clapton Orient 15.01.27; Brighton & Hove Albion 15.05.27; Walsall 12.05.28; NORWICH CITY 24.07.29; Brentford 15.08.30; Swindon Town 01.08.32; Folkestone Aug 1933.

City's equal 125th League debutant and it was said that he had a pleasing style. The Pink 'Un

of August 1929 described him thus: 'He played the typically Scotch style of football, and his cleverness is allied with finish'. His career total of 102 league games brought him 25 goals. He had a motor business near West Ham's ground, his wife was the sister of Brighton's Alf Edmonds and his son played cricket for Sussex and England.

THORPE, Albert Edward

(1932–1935) **1933:** 5/10; 10/8
Right Back **Career:** 62-0-0
Debut: 17 Sep 32 **Final:** 12 Oct 35

Born: Pilsey, Derbyshire 14 Jul 1910
Died: Langwith. Nottingham 3 Jan 1971

Career: Langwith Colliery; E. Derbyshire Schoolboys; Shirebrook 1926; Coventry (trial) Apr 1928; Wolverhampton Wanderers 12.05.28; Mansfield Town May 1929; Notts County 10.09.30; NORWICH CITY 21.05.32; Crystal Palace 25.10.35; Scunthorpe & Lindsey United; Hereford United Sep 1939.

His first encounter with Norwich was when he was in the side that lost to Norwich Boys in the English Schools Shield. Described in 1935 by the local press as being the most stylish back at Norwich since the days of Hampson – praise indeed. Albert placed the ball beautifully and he worked well in tandem with Joe Hannah. In his free time he was a passionate sea angler.

THURLOW, Bryan Alfred

(1955–1964) **1964:** 5/9; 11/6
Right Back **Career:** 224-0-1
Debut: 31 Dec 55 **Final:** 18 Apr 64

Born: Loddon 6 Jun 1936

Career: Loddon Reserves; Norton Minors; Bungay Minors; Bungay Town; NORWICH CITY 02.08.54; Bristol City 21.07.64; Lowestoft Town Jul 1965–06.02.71.

One of the few locals in the famed Cup side of 1958/59. Bryan performed with artistry and consistency being part of the City back six that appeared in almost every league game for two years without change. One would consider him to be a first team fixture so it is surprising to find that he played in 112 City reserve matches. Still lives locally.

TOBIN, Maurice

(1946–1950) **1948:** 5/8; 11/0
Left Back **Career:** 105-0-0
Debut: 7 Sep 46 **Final:** 13 Sep 50

Born: Longriggend; Airdrie 30 Jul 1920

Left: Bryan Thurlow
Right: Andy Townsend

Career: Boy's Guild; Longriggend; NORWICH CITY 19.09.38 & 28.05.46, later on coaching staff; Norwich Electricity coach.

A pre-war wing half whose career was interrupted by the War. A 1940s City handbook had the following description of Maurice: 'Showed great promise and bids fair to develop into a most serviceable player.' He gave good service to the stiffs, with 80 appearances. Today he resides locally.

TOWNSEND, Andrew David

(1988–1990) **1989:** 5/11; 127
Midfield **Career:** 82-6-10
Debut: 23 Sep 88 (sub) **Final:** 28 Apr 90

Born: Maidstone 23 Jul 1963

Career: Welling United Aug 1980; Weymouth Mar 1984; Southampton 15.01.85; NORWICH CITY 25.08.88; Chelsea 05.07.90; Aston Villa 26.07.93; Middlesbrough 29.08.97–30.06.99; West Bromwich Albion 17.09.99–Jul 2000.

'Mr nearly man' finally and deliriously lost this self-imposed title when he collected his Coca-Cola Cup winners medal in 1994. Recovering from a broken leg whilst playing for Southampton, he blossomed into a constructive and penetrative performer. Five Carrow Road players pulled on an international shirt at one stage, namely Allen, Bowen, Gunn, Phillips and our cockney Irishman. Big-money transfers followed and he enhanced the play of all his sides before becoming a football TV pundit.

TRACEY, Simon Peter

(1995) **1994:** 6/0; 13/0
Goalkeeper **Career:** 3-0-0
Debut: 25 Jan 95 **Final:** 28 Jan 95

Born: Woolwich 9 Dec 1967

Career: Pickadee Comprehensive School; Villa Court Rovers; Kent County; Chelsea (trial);

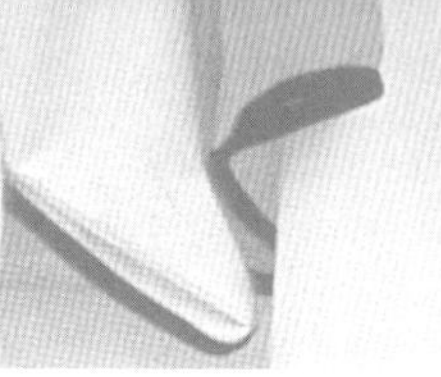

Wimbledon 17.08.85 (YTS), 03.02.86 (pro); Sheffield United 19.10.88; Manchester City (loan) 28.10.94; NORWICH CITY (loan) 31.12.94; Wimbledon (loan) 01.11.95; Sheffield United 27.02.95.

Simon came to Norwich on loan as cover to Andy Marshall following an injury to Bryan Gunn. His spell at Carrow Road was not a happy one, with an embarrassing lapse against Coventry and being stretchered off injured in an FA Cup tie. He was however still a keeper in demand before re-establishing himself as Sheffield United's first team goalkeeper.

TRAVERS, George Edward

(1920–1921) **1920:** 5/8; 11/10
Forward **Career:** 30-0-14
Debut: 23 Oct 20 **Final:** 7 May 21

Born: Bow 19 Aug 1901
Died: Bromley J/F/M 1965

Career: Swindon Town 1919/20; Millwall Jun 1920; NORWICH CITY 22.10.20; Gillingham 14.06.21; Nuneaton Town Sep 1921; Cradley Heath Nov 1922; Bilston United 1929–May 1931.

George was in Millwall's first ever league side and he is also in the record books as the scorer of the only goal in City's first ever league win. I trust the august Athletic News *when all is said and done, and they stated that George was a Londoner, not a Midlander, hence the new birth and death detail. A chance finding of a court case hearing in Gillingham was extremely helpful. In his one Canary season George topped the goalscoring charts.*

TURNER, David William

(1930–1931) **1930:** 5/8; 11/0
Right Half **Career:** 3-0-0
Debut: 27 Dec 30 **Final:** 10 Jan 31

Born: Wallsend 12 May 1905
Died: Newcastle-upon-Tyne 25 Feb 1978

Career: Burnhope Institute; Spennymoor United; Burnhope Institute; NORWICH CITY 28.04.30 (amat); Horden Colliery Welfare 12.11.32; Crook Town cs 1934; Hexham 1936/7.

David was a clubmate of Sam Bell at Burnhope Institute. He played just three senior games for City – all losses. The verdict on his debut was, 'He has not got the physical advantages of Bill Brown but he is a resourceful and tenacious defender'. His wife refused to move to Norwich and he returned to work in the coal mines after his non-league activity. His two daughters in Canada have written and faxed me with some marvellous memories of their beloved father.

ULLATHORNE, Robert

(1991–1996) **1991:** 5/8; 10/7
Utility **Career:** 104-11-8
Debut: 24 Apr 91 **Final:** 5 May 96

Born: Wakefield 11 Oct 1971

Career: Goole Grammar School; England Under-18; NORWICH CITY Oct 1986 (assoc), 08.07.88 (trainee), 01.07.90 (pro); Club Atletico Osasuna (Spain) 17.09.96; Leicester City 17.02.97; Huddersfield Town Oct 1999 training; Real Zaragoza (Spain) (trial); Tenerife (Spain) (trial); Newcastle United Sep 2000 (trial); Sheffield United 09.12.2000.

Robert Ullathorne

Robert gained two Under-18 caps versus Denmark and Czechoslovakia, expressing a desire to work hard in training and do well in City's reserves at the outset. Norwich City were strong on their left flank in the 1990s so he had to show strength of character to fight for recognition – made more admirable by his overcoming injuries. Principally left-footed, his career took a downturn and became a broken dream when he broke his leg after just 11 minutes of his Leicester debut in the first leg of the Coca Cola semi-final against Wimbledon. He then broke his other leg and was out of contract, being forced to continue his rehabiliation without pay or an insurance payout.

VAN WIJK, Dennis Johannes

(1982–1986) **1984:** 6/0; 11/4
Utility/Defender **Career:** 145-10-4
Debut: 18 Sep 82 (sub) **Final:** 6 May 86

Born: Oostzaan, Holland 16 Dec 1962

Career: Ajax (Holland); NORWICH CITY 17.09.82 (non contract), 28.10.82; Club Brugge KV (Belgium) 18.08.86; PAS Yanniana (Greece) 1990; KSV Cercle Brugge (Belgium) (loan); Club Brugge KV (Belgium); Knokke (Belgium) youth coach; KV Oostende (Belgium) coach; Cercle Brugge (Belgium) technical director.

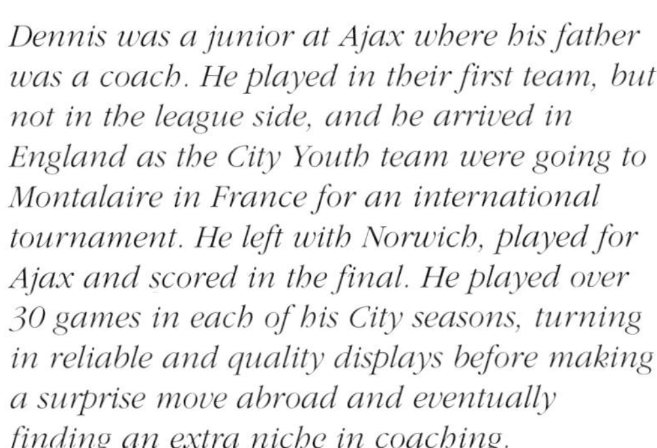

Dennis was a junior at Ajax where his father was a coach. He played in their first team, but not in the league side, and he arrived in England as the City Youth team were going to Montalaire in France for an international tournament. He left with Norwich, played for Ajax and scored in the final. He played over 30 games in each of his City seasons, turning in reliable and quality displays before making a surprise move abroad and eventually finding an extra niche in coaching.

VARCO, Percy Seymour

(1927–1929) **1928:** 5/9; 13/0
Centre Forward **Career:** 65-0-47
Debut: 27 Aug 27 (goal) **Final:** 26 Dec 29 (goal)

Born: Fowey, Cornwall 17 Apr 1904
Died: Fowey, Cornwall 29 Jan 1982

Career: Fowey Schools; Torquay United Aug 1923; Aston Villa 20.12.23; Queens Park Rangers 12.06.26; NORWICH CITY 11.07.27; Exeter City 03.02.30; Brighton & Hove Albion 02.06.32; St Austell 1933; St Blazey Oct 1933; AFA Cornwall 1938/9 coach.

Powerfully built and difficult to knock off the ball, he became a City legend, scoring in seven of his first eight games. The press said, 'He loses no time with the ball, fearless in attack and has a kick that sometimes makes one gasp. Goes for goal like a bull at a gatepost'. Percy had 164 career league games for 82 goals including fifteen twos, three hat-tricks and a four, and is forever remembered for the crowd chant of 'Give it to Varco', which remains a surprise considering how short his Canary career was – just over two years. He became a fish merchant, running two aquariums, and served for two spells as the Mayor of Fowey.

VASPER, Peter John

(1968–1970) **1970:** 6/0; 12/0
Goalkeeper **Career:** 32-0-0
Debut: 2 Mar 68 **Final:** 21 Feb 70

Born: Bromley 3 Sep 1945

Career: Orient 04.11.63; Guildford City Aug 1964; NORWICH CITY 14.02.68; Cambridge United 24.09.70; Dartford Jul 1974; St Ives Town manager; Bluntisham.

Manager Lol Morgan, on signing Peter, said of him, 'He is a very reliable keeper and has a good chance of making the grade'. His debut, courtesy of an incapacity to Kevin Keelan, saw him handle cleanly as the side recorded their first league win for three months. He earned rave reviews in his second game for fearlessly diving at Kevin Hector's feet three times. A three-year first choice at Cambridge, playing 136 league games, he latterly worked in insurance.

Left: Dennis Van Wijk
Right: Percy Varco

VINALL, Edward John (Jack)

(1933–1937) **1934:** 5/10; 11/4
Centre Forward **Career:** 181-0-80
Debut: 26 Aug 33 **Final:** 6 Sep 37

Born: Witton, Birmingham 16 Dec 1910
Died: Worcester 26 May 1997

Career: Allan & Everitt's FC; Ellisons; Birmingham City 27.08.29 (amat); Folkestone Sep 1930 (amat); Sunderland 26.10.31 (pro); NORWICH CITY 27.06.33; Luton Town 14.10.37; Second World War–Coventry & Walsall until 1946/47; Worcester City Jan 1948 to Nov 1950 manager; Aston Villa scout.

Jack would have been a legend in any lifetime for he was a dashing, free-scoring pre-war centre forward with powerful finishing, ball control and excellent distribution. How sad that none of his 174 career goals have been preserved on celluloid. Jack's younger brother Albert (a triallist at City) was a useful defender for Aston Villa and Walsall until a broken leg ended his career. He is not remembered like the charasmatic Varco, which is surprising because Jack scored more goals for City than Percy, with a more refined style in four memorable years. Jack lived in Worcester in retirement and celebrated 65 years of marriage.

'Jack' Vinall

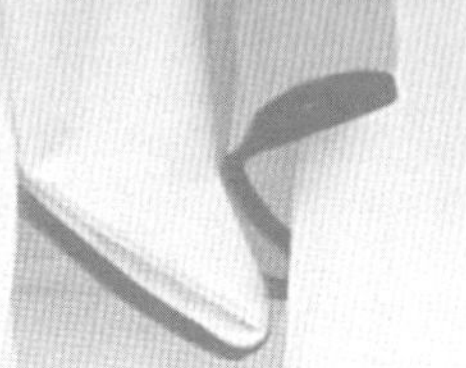

de WAARD, Raymond Marienus

(2000) **2000:** 6/3; 12/5
Winger **Career:** 5-8-0
Debut: 25 Mar 00 **Final:** 21 Nov 00 (sub)

Born: Rotterdam, Holland 27 Mar 1973

Career: Feyenoord Youth (Holland) 1989; L.M.O (Holland) 1994; Excelsior (Holland) 1997; Cambuur Leewarden (Holland) 14.07.99; NORWICH CITY 22.03.2000; AZ Alkmaar (Holland) Mar 2001.

Raymond enjoyed a good grounding in football and life with Feyenoord for five years. 138 games for 11 goals in Dutch football was a prelude to him being signed by Bryan Hamilton on a two-year contract. He failed to live up to early promise that saw him whip in dangerous centres at pace from his wide position. Raymond's contract was terminated and he made a losing debut against de Graafschap back in Holland for his new team.

WAITES, George Edward

(1961–1962) **1961:** 5/8; 11/7
Winger **Career:** 40-0-11
Debut: 14 Jan 61 **Final:** 24 Mar 62

Born: Stepney 12 Mar 1938
Died: Watford 24 Aug 2000

Career: Army; Harwich 1957; Orient Sep 1958 (amat), 01.12.58 (pro); NORWICH CITY 12.01.61; Orient 18.07.62; Brighton & Hove Albion 30.11.62; Millwall 13.04.65; Gravesend & Northfleet Sep 1965–May 1968.

George was the first 'big' City signing after they won promotion to Division Two. A clever ball player who performed consistently in the firsts and the seconds (15 games, five goals). As his wife could not settle away from London, George moved back to Orient for two games in Division One, playing with Mal Lucas and Gordon Bolland. Retirement from football due to the onset of arthritis in his knee saw him standing for most of the day as a greengrocer.

WALFORD, Stephen James

(1981–1983) **1981:** 6/1; 11/7
Defender **Career:** 108-0-2
Debut: 14 Mar 81 **Final:** 14 May 83

Born: Highgate 5 Jan 1958

Career: Holloway School; Islington Schools; Tottenham Hotspur 24.04.74 (app), 08.04.75 (pro); England Youth 1976; Arsenal 01.08.77; NORWICH CITY 12.03.81; West Ham United 23.08.83; Huddersfield Town (loan) 26.10.87; West Ham United 10.12.87; Gillingham (loan) 07.12.88; West Bromwich Albion (loan); Lai Sun (Hong Kong) Aug 1989; Turkish football 1990; Wycombe Wanderers Oct 1990; Wealdstone Mar 1992; Wycombe Wanderers youth coach; NORWICH CITY 04.07.95 reserve manager, caretaker manager for one game; Leicester City Dec 1995 assistant manager; Glasgow Celtic Jun 2000 assistant manager.

Steve Walford

Upgraded from apprentice to professional at Spurs but he had only two games there against Liverpool and Ipswich before moving with manager Terry Neill to Highbury. He made an FA Cup Final appearance while there and is a good reader of situations with an excellent left peg. He rarely missed a match at Norwich City and performed most capably. Steve enjoyed a successful spell at his third London club before joining Martin O'Neill's staff.

WALKER, Cyril John

(1946) **1946:** 5/10; 12/0
Inside Right **Career:** 3-0-2
Debut: 31 Aug 46 (goal) **Final:** 12 Sep 46 (goal)

Born: Pirton 24 Feb 1914

Career: Hitchin Town; Watford Sep 1935 (amat); Leavesden Mental Hospital Oct 1935; Watford Nov 1935 (pro); Gillingham May 1937; Sheffield Wednesday 23.10.37; Chelmsford Aug 1938; Shorts Sports 08.07.39; RAF; Second World War guested for Sheffield Wednesday, Crystal Palace, Watford & Gillingham; NORWICH CITY 23.08.46; Dartford Aug 1947; Chatham Aug 1949 coach; Snowdon Colliery Welfare coach; Dartford Nov 1952 coach.

Cyril played 34 war friendlies for City scoring 37 goals, including a three, a four and a five. He was regarded as the brains of the attack and scored many goals with fine trickery. Also had the temerity to play for the RAF against Norwich and but for the intervention of war he would undoubtedly have had a long Football League career. An amusing story, only after the event, was his being left behind in a Northampton hospital after fearing that he had

broken his leg. He asked to have the plaster removed later when he found that he could move his leg. We are talking of 63 years ago when technology was not as it is today.

WALLBANKS, James

(1931–1932) **1931:** 5/9; 11/10
Wing Half **Career:** 3-0-0
Debut: 14 Nov 31 **Final:** 23 Apr 32

Born: Platt Bridge, nr Wigan 12 Sep 1909
Died: Reading 28 Oct 1979

Career: Chopwell Rangers; Annfield Plain Jul 1928; Barnsley 01.04.29 (amat), Oct 1930 (pro); NORWICH CITY 11.05.31; Northampton Town 09.08.32; Annfield Plain Aug 1933; Wigan Athletic Feb 1934; Millwall 29.06.34; Reading Oct 1937; Second World War guested for Wrexham, Fulham, Sunderland; Ramsgate cs 1947 player-manager; Carlisle United trainer; Millwall Sep 1950 assistant trainer/coach; Reading 1951 trainer cs 1951; Millwall 1952–1970s physio.

'A typical Barnsley tackler' was how one pundit described this fair-haired, hard-working player. He did not mind where he played as long as he got a game. Came from a remarkable family of footballing brothers who, between the five of them, played all over the country as follows: Fred: Bury, Chesterfield, Scarborough, Bradford City, West Ham United & Forest; Horace: Aberdeen, Grimsby & Luton; Harold: Fulham, Southend & Workington; John: Barnsley, Chester & Bradford City.

WALLS, Nicholas

(1925–1927) **1925:** 5/7; 10/11
Wing Half **Career:** 31-0-2
Debut: 10 Oct 25 (goal) **Final:** 8 Jan 27

Born: Chester-le-Street 22 Jan 1901
Died: Chester-le-Street 16 Jul 1957

Career: Ouston Park Rangers; Consett; Durham County; England Schoolboys; Birtley; Annfield Plain; Chester-le-Street Jul 1924; NORWICH CITY 25.06.25; Annfield Plain Jun 1927; Jarrow Nov 1929; Crook Town 25.05.31; Jarrow Jun 1933; Spennymoor United 1937; Horden Colliery Welfare Dec 1938;

As a schoolboy Nick was reputed to have scored 142 goals in one season. He had a varied stay at City with a scoring debut; a sending off in another match and a fractured thigh in another after colliding with a goalpost. Nonetheless he was a useful player who returned to the non-league northern circuit after his City spell. He left £962.13s.4d in his administered will to his widow Hannah.

WALSH, Michael Thomas

(1982) **1982:** 6/0; 12/1
Defender **Career:** 5-0-0
Debut: 2 Oct 82 **Final:** 30 Oct 82

Born: Blackley, Manchester 20 Jun 1956

Career: Bolton Wanderers 25.07.74; Everton 10.08.81; NORWICH CITY (loan) 02.10.82; Burnley (loan) 24.12.82; Fort Lauderdale Strikers (USA) Jul 1983–Aug 1983; Manchester City 14.10.83; Blackpool 03.02.84; Bury 1990–Sep 1995 manager; Swindon Town assistant manager

An Eire international who played only for Northern League sides apart from his one month sojourn to East Anglia. He was taken on as cover for Dave Watson, who had sustained a cracked cheekbone. His own City debut was eventful as he needed stitches to a head wound. Fine service to the 'Tangerines' and appearing on SKY TV he stated that he was a player's representative.

WALSH, Steven

(2000) **2000:** 6/3; 14/6
Defender **Career:** 2-3-0
Debut: 19 Sep 00 **Final:** 7 Nov 00 (sub)

Born: Fulwood, Preston 3 Nov 1964

Career: Savick Primary School; London Road Labour Club; YMCA (Lytham) Sep 1976; Ashton-on-Ribble High School; Preston Schoolboys; Blackpool Under-16's; Lancashire SFA; Blackpool 23.11.78 (assoc); Fulwood Athletic; Preston North End (trial); Wigan Athletic 11.09.82; Leicester City 24.06.86; NORWICH CITY 18.09.2000–26.01.2001; Loughborough FC Aug 2001 Director of Football.

Brian Little reckoned that Steve's name was the first one to go on the team sheet. His aerial presence and tremendous spirit carried him through 600 games. Fourteen years and 14 dismissals at Leicester with regular trips to Wembley for play-off games and Cup finals. 'Steve Walsh has got a broken leg. Really? Whose is it?' was a one-time terrace chant. A veteran who knew his way around the block being an experienced Premiership player, but he played for only 129 minutes for City at a considerable cost to the club.

WALTON, Mark Andrew

(1990–1992) **1989:** 6/3; 13/3
Goalkeeper **Career:** 28-0-0
Debut: 28 Apr 90 **Final:** 7 Oct 92

Born: Merthyr Tydfil 1 Jun 1969

Career: Swansea City 1985 (app); Luton Town 21.02.87; Colchester United 25.08.87; NORWICH CITY 15.08.89; Wrexham (loan) 27.08.93; Dundee

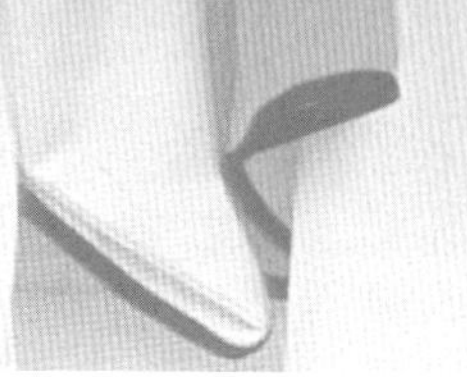

United (loan) 27.01.94; St. Johnstone (trial) Feb 1994; West Ham United (trial) Feb 1994; Wroxham 09.09.94; Merthyr Tydfil Nov 1994; Barry Town 23.06.95; Fakenham Town 03.07.96; Fulham 12.08.96; Gillingham 06.02.98; NORWICH CITY (loan) 26.03.98; Brighton & Hove Albion 08.07.98; Cardiff City 01.07.2000

An all-action goalkeeper who always issued instructions loud and long to his defence. Assistant Manager Dave Williams said, 'Mark has the right temperament', with Bryan Gunn commenting, 'He looks cool under pressure. I envy his length of kicking'. Had 114 reserve games at Norwich City and an incredible number of moves in the 1990s before settling back in his homeland. Mark is also a talented cricketer, having represented Wales and returning to Norfolk to play in the local leagues.

WARD, Ashley Stuart

(1994–1996) **1994:** 6/1; 12/4
Centre Forward **Career:** 60-0-21
Debut: 10 Dec 94 (2 goals) **Final:** 9 Mar 96

Born: Crumpsall, Manchester 24 Nov 1970

Career: William Hulmes Grammar School; Cheadle Town; Manchester City School of Excellence, 01.07.87 (trainee), 09.08.89 (pro); Wrexham (loan) 10.01.91; Leicester City 30.07.91; Blackpool (loan) 21.11.92; Crewe Alexandra 01.12.92; NORWICH CITY 08.12.94; Derby County 16.03.96; Barnsley 03.09.97; Blackburn Rovers 29.12.98; Bradford City 18.08.2000.

Score two goals on your debut and you are on your way to being accepted by the supporters. A tremendously willing worker with excellent control for a target man. Defenders are given a testing time by Ashley, and clubs paid successively higher fees for him, culminating in Blackburn's reported outlay of £4.5 million. Despite his best efforts he could not save Bradford City from relegation last season.

Ashley Ward

WARE, Harry

(1937–1946) **1938:** 5/11; 11/8
Centre Forward **Career:** 45-0-14
Debut: 13 Nov 37 (goal) **Final:** 9 Jan 46 (goal)

Born: Birmingham 22 Oct 1911
Died: Stoke-on-Trent 28 Oct 1970

Career: Stoke St. Peter's School; Hanley St Lukes; Corbridge Celtic; North Staffs Boys; Stoke City Dec 1927 (amat), 17.12.29 (pro); Newcastle United 24.09.35; Sheffield Wednesday 07.05.37; NORWICH CITY 12.11.37; Northwich Victoria Sep 1946 manager; Haarlem (Holland) Aug 1948 trainer/coach; Northwich Victoria 1950 manager; Port Vale 1956 coach; Crewe Alexandra Jun 1958–May 1960 manager; Stoke City 1960 assistant trainer and Scout until his demise.

He followed the vocation of a potter and he was at Stoke City with Stanley Matthews. Indeed he scored in the first match that Stan did and was regarded as a schemer who could get goals. His club record was: Stoke (53 games, 16 goals); Newcastle (44 games, nine goals); Sheffield Wed (12 games, one goal). He reappered for City in the transitional season of 1945/6 but a chest wound sustained in Normandy proved trouble-some so he retired from league football. For the cost of £11–£12,000 City could field a forward line of Friar, Coleman, Ware, Furness and Manders – a formidable collection of characters.

WARNES, William Henry

(1933–1937) **1934:** 5/7; 10/8
Outside Right **Career:** 118-0-49
Debut: 26 Aug 33 (goal) **Final:** 6 Feb 37

Born: Rotherhithe 14 Nov 1907

Career: Cambridge University Mission; Nunhead; West Norwood 1925; Woking (amat); Surrey

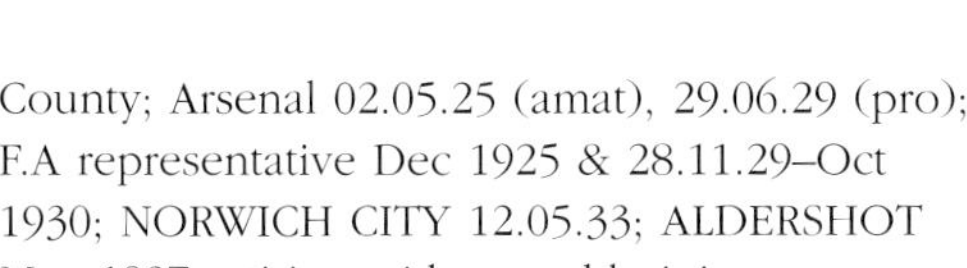

County; Arsenal 02.05.25 (amat), 29.06.29 (pro); F.A representative Dec 1925 & 28.11.29–Oct 1930; NORWICH CITY 12.05.33; ALDERSHOT May 1937 retiring with an ankle injury.

Billy's great grandfather and grandfather were from Long Stratton. Billy won three England Amateur caps while with Woking, and such was his fast, elusive, clever wing play that he thrilled spectators at the Nest for four years. He once scored in six of seven successive league games for City including his only hat-trick (H) Charlton on 18.11.33. He played cricket for Catford and he came from a sporting family with his father being R.C. Warnes, the celebrated amateur middleweight boxing champion and later a leading ring referee. Billy later ran the family business – a tobacconist and confectioners.

WATSON, David

(1980–1986) **1981:** 5/11: 11/12
Defender **Career:** 256-0-15
Debut: 26 Dec 80 **Final:** 6 May 86

Born: Liverpool 20 Nov 1961

Career: Liverpool Schools; Liverpool 25.05.79; NORWICH CITY 29.11.80; Everton 21.08.86 , First team player coach, 02.04.97 caretaker manager , Jul 1997 coaching; Tranmere Rovers 04.05.2001 manager.

Dave played for Liverpool 'A' while a sheet metal worker at the docks. City spotted him playing at Villa Park in a reserves game. A pillar of strength for just over five years with the gift of leadership. Mel Machin said of him on is signing, 'He has the good habits one associates with Liverpool. A strict discipline and authorative'. A former Player of the Year with Ken Brown's summation being, 'Our jewel in the crown'. Dave's move back home made the Canaries a £1 million profit and he left City as the man to earn the most England caps as a Norwich player. He also played against England for a Hong Kong Golden Select XI and we wish him well as he embarks on a managerial career.

WATT, Michael George

(1998–1999) **1998:** 6/1; 11/10
Goalkeeper **Career:** 8-1-0
Debut: 8 Sep 98 (sub) **Final:** 9 Jan 99

Born: Aberdeen 27 Nov 1970

Career: Robert Gordon's College; Inn at the Park Dons Under-15s; Cove Rangers; Aberdeen 1989; Blackburn Rovers 09.08.97; NORWICH CITY (trial), (contract)11.09.98; York City (trial) Jul 1999; Kilmarnock Aug 1999.

Left: Dave Watson
Right: Clarence Wharton

The former Scottish Under-21 international left Aberdeen for two unused Premier League substitute appearances and two Central league games for Blackburn, whereupon he had his jaw broken in a collision. He joined City stating that he was here to work hard and provide competition for the goalkeeper's jersey. Michael's debut was as a replacement for Marshall in the game where City changed shorts from blue to yellow at half time. Eight successive games with two win bonuses before Marshall ousted him for good.

WEIR, James

(1930–1931) **1930:** 5/7; 11/5
Inside Right **Career:** 9-0-0
Debut: 3 Sep 30 **Final:** 14 Mar 31

Born: Glasgow 12 Jun 1901
Died: Glasgow 21 April 1984

Career: Kilsyth Rangers; Kilmarnock 02.05.24; Hamilton Academicals 27.02.28; Queen of the South Feb 1930; NORWICH CITY 08.07.30; Armadale 10.11.31; Dunfermline Athletic Aug 1932; Dundee United 13.10.33

A renowned Scottish forward of the 1920s who scored 43 goals in 81 Scottish League games prior to joining Norwich. He netted a double hat-trick in a cup tie in January 1930. The club believed that he was 25 when he joined hence the original estimate of birth in Canary Citizens. *He never achieved the same heights in England and moved back to Scotland to ply his trade.*

WHARTON, Clarence Norman

(1931–1935) **1932:** 6/1; 12/3
Goalkeeper **Career:** 109-0-0
Debut: 29 Aug 31 **Final:** 2 Feb 35

Born: Askam in Furness 28 Jul 1903
Died: Askam in Furness 13 Jul 1961

Career: Askam; Barrow 18.05.22; Preston North End 27.08.25; Barrow 29.09.27; Sheffield United

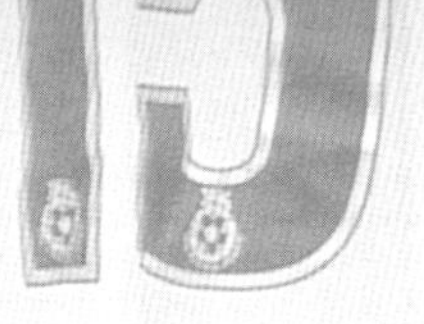
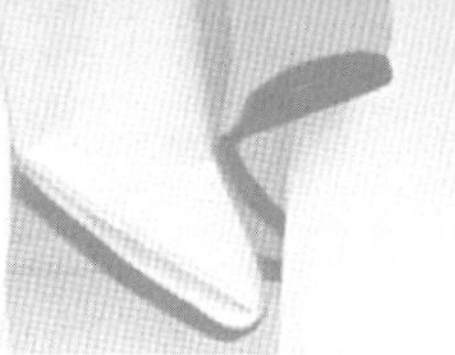

10.05.28; NORWICH CITY 23.07.31; Doncaster Rovers 28.05.35; York City 25.05.36; Leeds United 29.08.39.

Norman was an agile and safe keeper who made exactly 350 Football League appearances in a career that saw him play with distinction in all four divisions (One, Two, Three South and Three North). He had seven football-playing brothers who all preferred the Rugby code. His great joy was to meet a forward who did not know him and who tried to rush through to goal. It was said that no forward tried it twice. He retired during the Second World War and he was an Electrician by vocation, installing, among many jobs, the warning bells at Doncaster for the referee, players and directors.

WHING, John Thomas Anderson

(1921) **1921:** 5/10; 11/5
Centre Forward **Career:** 7-0-0
Debut: 27 Aug 21 **Final:** 26 Nov 21

Born: Percy Main 23 Apr 1895
Died: Gateshead 17 Jan 1972

Career: local Gateshead football; Gordon Villa; Teamby United; Whitburn Park Villa; NORWICH CITY 11.05.21; West Stanley Jul 1922; Chester-le-Street; Marley Hill United; Watergate Colliery 30.10.29; Bensham St Hilda's Nov 1930, Jun 1933 committee.

He joined City from the East Tyne League and was one of four new debutants for the first game of the 1921 season. He scored in a friendly against Cambridge University for City but only appeared intermittently, and in three different positions, for the firsts. He needed to play as he bizarrely maintained that he never got fit through just training. He prolonged his career by a decade by playing back in the Durham area.

WHITEHOUSE, Brian

(1960–1962) **1960:** 5/10; 11/8
Centre Forward **Career:** 49-0-18
Debut: 12 Mar 60 **Final:** 10 Mar 62

Born: West Bromwich 8 Sep 1935

Career: George Salter School; Vono Sports; West Bromwich Albion Apr 1950 (amat), 20.10.52 (pro); NORWICH CITY 10.03.60; Wrexham 16.03.62; Crystal Palace 19.11.63; Charlton Athletic 11.03.66; Orient 27.06.66; Luton Town Jun 1968 coach; Arsenal Aug 1969 youth coach; West Bromwich Albion Jul 1971 coaching staff, Apr 1975 temporary manager, Jul 1975–1980 assistant manager; Manchester United 1980 coaching staff; Aston Villa 1993 chief scout; Coventry City Jan 2000 scout.

If Brian scored, City usually won – in fact they lost just one of the 14 games in which he scored. He has the honour of netting the club's first ever League Cup goal and he had a career average of scoring in every third game. His coaching career has lasted longer than his playing career and he has been over 50 years in the game.

WHITHAM, Victor

(1920–1921) **1920:** 5/6; 10/4
Inside Left **Career:** 10-0-3
Debut: 28 Aug 20 (goal) **Final:** 26 Feb 21 (goal)

Born: Burnley 12 Feb 1894
Died: Rotherham 8 Nov 1962

Career: Park Street School; Kimberworth Parish Church; Kimberworth Congregationals; Rotherham County; Kimberworth Old Boys; Barnsley Feb 1919; NORWICH CITY 28.08.20; Scunthorpe United Jun 1921; Southend United 09.05.23; Boston Town Jul 1924; Scunthorpe & Lindsey United May 1925.

The scorer of City's first ever Football League goal after 67 minutes of the first game. His initial league goal was on 01.03.1919 (A) Coventry with his last, ironically against City, for Southend on 19.01.24. Again the periodicals of the time were misleading as to his age. They stated that he was 23 upon joining City. These old-timers were apt to be much older than stated. A retired checker in a steelworks.

WHITLEY, Jim

(2000) **2000:** 5/9; 11/0
Midfield **Career:** 7-1-1
Debut: 28 Aug 00 **Final:** 17 Oct 00

Born: Ndola, Zambia 14 Apr 1975

Career: Ysgol Rryn Alyn Comprehensive School; Brickfield Rangers; Bradley YC; Loreto College; Llay United; Manchester City 01.08.94; Blackpool (loan) 20.08.99; NORWICH CITY (loan) 25.08.2000–25.10.2000; Swindon Town (loan) 15.12.2000; Northampton Town (loan) 27.02.2001; Nottingham Forest (loan) 30.03.2001; Wrexham 03.08.2001.

The elder of the two Whitley brothers at Manchester City. Their dad was from Belfast and came to England when he was eleven. A skilful midfielder, he helped the 'Blues' win the Pontin's League title to kick-start his career. Recommended to City by Joe Royle as a very good team player who will add steel to the midfield. Bryan Hamilton, commenting on the loan spell, said that Jim did a great job for us and we wish him well.

WIGG, Percival Frederick

(1926) **1926:** 5/8; 10/7
Outside Right **Career:** 9-0-3
Debut: 28 Aug 26 **Final:** 13 Nov 26

Born: Oulton Broad 5 Oct 1899
Died: Lowestoft 18 Mar 1985

Career: Roman Hill School 1910: Lowestoft Boys 1912; Pakefield Harriers 1913; Vickers Works; Lowestoft Town Mar 1921; NORWICH CITY 29.03.26 (amat); Lowestoft Town 16.08.27, 10.08.31–29.06.32 trainer's assistant.

Percy was a product of the Norfolk and Suffolk League, being born and bred in the region. He captained Lowestoft Boys and when he later rejoined them he helped his team to lift the Suffolk Senior Cup. He was only on the winning side for the firsts' twice – the two games in which he scored. He later netted 49 goals for Lowestoft in a fine extension to his career.

WILKINSON, Reginald George

(1920–1923) **1920:** 5/10; 10/6
Wing Half **Career:** 107-0-9
Debut: 28 Aug 20 **Final:** 5 May 23

Born: Norwich 26 Mar 1899
Died: Norwich 14 Sep 1946

Career: Thorpe Hamlet School; Norwich CEYMS; Army King's R.R. Battalion; NORWICH CITY 1919; Sunderland 02.06.23; Brighton & Hove Albion 15.05.24; Frost's Athletic Aug 1934; Norwich Electricity Works Sep 1936.

He gained his first medal in 1912/13 (Bury Boys Cup) and he was regarded as deadly at free kicks. Had played for City prior to their joining the Football League and was a great servant to Brighton for ten years. Reg tragically collapsed and subsequently died while playing for Norwich Electricity against CEYMS.

WILLIAMS, Alan Clifford

(1947) **1947:** 5/8; 10/8
Right Half **Career:** 1-0-0
Debut/Final: 8 Feb 47

Born: Abernant 4 Dec 1923

Career: Cardiff Nomads; NORWICH CITY 15.01.47; Barry AFC, later Board of Directors 1962–1967.

Alan played for Fulham during the War while working in London repairing bombed bridges. He had 16 reserve games and was regarded as one of the most promising of the younger lads on the books. The local sports' reporters opinion of his debut: 'He did well and with added experience is likely to be knocking hard at the door for a position in the Third Division side'. The needed experience was not forthcoming as he was later given a free transfer. He was later the Barry captain as his side won the Welsh FA Cup.

David Williams

WILLIAMS, David Michael

(1985–1988) **1985:** 5/10; 11/8
Utility **Career:** 70-4-12
Debut: 17 Aug 85 **Final:** 4 Apr 88

Born: Cardiff 11 Mar 1955

Career: Mostyn High School; Howardian High School; Clifton Athletic; South Wales Youth; Bristol Rovers 11.12 75; NORWICH CITY 30.05.85, 22.05.87 player coach, 20.08.88 assistant manager. AFC Bournemouth 07.07.92 assistant manager, 23.07.93 registered non contract player; Everton 24.01.94 assistant manager; Leeds United Jul 1995 coach; Manchester United youth coach.

A stylish midfielder with a footballing brain. He distributed the ball sagaciously and with calmness and he was rewarded with the club captaincy for season 1986/87. He gave up the player managership of the Rovers for a further try to reach top level. He achieved a full complement of Welsh caps having represented them at Schoolboy, Amateur, Youth, Under-21, Under-23, and Full level and he also had a spell as the Welsh 'B' manager. Not surprising given his pedigree that he moved equally successfully into coaching, being part of Manchester United's continuing success.

WILLIAMS, Grenville Rees

(1946–1947) **1947:** 5/10; 12/0
Left Half **Career:** 43-0-0
Debut: 7 Sep 46 **Final:** 1 Nov 47

Born: Swansea 30 Jun 1921

Career: Arsenal (groundstaff), 09.05.38 (amat); Canterbury Waverley; NORWICH CITY 27.06.46;

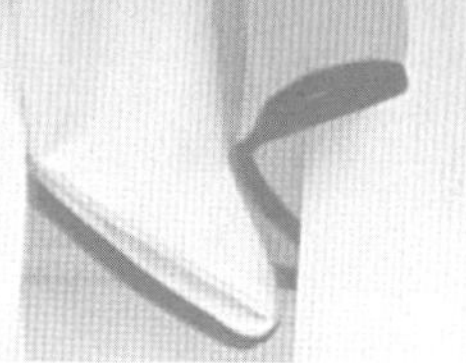

Newport County 16.05.49; King's Lynn; Yarmouth Town 19.08.50; Lowestoft Town 28.09.57-25.04.59; Stowmarket.

One of the discoveries of Cyril Spiers' regime at Carrow Road. He displayed great form during City's disastrous 1946/47 season. A Welsh Schoolboy international who was spoken of as a 'coming full Welsh cap' before injuries took their toll. He extended his career after City by a dozen years by playing in non-league football.

WILLIAMS, Roderick

(1933–1936) **1934:** 5/10; 11/5
Centre forward **Career:** 20-0-12
Debut: 25 Dec 33 (goal) **Final:** 15 Feb 36

Born: Bedwelty 2 Dec 1909
Died: East Dereham 14 Aug 1987

Career: Sutton United; Epsom Town; Uxbridge Town; Athenian League representative; Middlesex County; Crystal Palace (amat); NORWICH CITY 08.05.33; Exeter City 06.05.36; Reading 26.06.37; West Ham United 13.11.37; Clapton Orient 24.09.38.

Rod took a long time to trace in view of misleading information in the journals of the day. The City handbook said that he was born in Wandsworth, while Sutton United's Club History listed him as Rodney – a local junior doing well. A prolific reserve scorer with 106 goals in three years including eight threes, three fours and a five. He continued his high scoring endeavours at all his subsequent clubs, for example he scored 36 for Exeter in 1936/37 season. Rod, who was deaf, was too self-effacing to bring it to anyone's attention.

Left: Thomas Williams
Right: Ernest Williamson

WILLIAMS, Thomas Hutchinson

(1930–1932) **1930:** 5/9; 12/0
Inside Left **Career:** 28-0-13
Debut: 30 Aug 30 **Final:** 2 Apr 32

Born: Easington 23 May 1899
Died: Easington 14 Dec 1960

Career: Ryhope Colliery; Huddersfield Town (trial); Clapton Orient 27.08.21; Charlton Athletic 22.08.23; Gillingham 14.02.24; Ashington 02.08.24; Mid Rhondda 1925; Bristol Rovers 21.01.26; Bristol City 19.06.28; Merthyr Town 05.02.29; NORWICH CITY 08.05.30; Easington Colliery Welfare Oct 1933; Frost's Athletic Aug 1934.

Tom netted almost 100 goals in a career that took him to the four points of the compass. He arrived unheralded at his tenth club and performed well and with vigour. He scored three or more in a game for Gillingham, Bristol Rovers, Merthyr and Norwich against Brentford, Millwall, Crystal Palace and Gillingham respectively. He won several sprinting handicaps on northern playing fields and tragically for the families Tom died within five days of his brother Owen, a former England international.

WILLIAMSON, Ernest Clarke (Tim)

(1923–1925) **1923:** 5/10; 12/12
Goalkeeper **Career:** 47-0-0
Debut: 25 Aug 23 **Final:** 2 May 25

Born: Murton Colliery, Co. Durham 24 May 1890
Died: Norwich 30 Apr 1964

Career: Murton Red Star; Wingate Albion; Croydon Common Jun 1913; Arsenal 1916; Tottenham Hotspur 10.04.17; Footballers' Battalion; RASC; NORWICH CITY 29.06.23 to 1925

A great goalkeeper and a favourite with the crowd. A man of confidence and agility who was purportedly known as 'Tim' after Williamson the Middlesbrough net minder. An England international he played twice for the Army in the Bull Dog Cup and he won a Combination medal with Arsenal. A useful cricketer and for many years a publican.

WILLIAMSON, John Ian

(1958–1959) **1958:** 5/7;11/2
Left Winger **Career:** 10-0-1
Debut: 3 Sep 58 **Final:** 7 Mar 59 (goal)

Born: Larbert, nr Falkirk 14 Apr 1939

Career: Falkirk 28.02.56; NORWICH CITY 31.05.58; Bradford Park Avenue 01.06.62; King's Lynn 1963; Wisbech Aug 1965; King's Lynn; Boston.

Ian vied for the Number 11 shirt with Bobby Brennan in his first season but he was mainly a reserve with 104 games for 13 goals. His winning last appearance was the occasion of Sandy Kennon's City league debut. He played 16 of his 17 Bradford league games at left half (Number Six) before making a final appearance on 16 February 1963 at Bristol

City. A company director in Kings Lynn besides being a County golfer of long standing. Also a qualified electrician with a talented golfer son, Neil, who once beat Ernie Els in the British Amateur Championship and himself has won the Norfolk Amateur Golf Championship on a number of occasions.

WILLIAMSON, Thomas Robertson

(1931–1933) **1932:** 5/9; 11/6
Centre Half **Career:** 85-0-4
Debut: 29 Aug 31 **Final:** 26 Aug 33 (goal)

Born: Dalmuir, Glasgow 8 Feb 1901
Died: Norwich 1 Apr 1988

Career: Kilbowie Ross Dhu; Kirkintilloch Rob Roy Dec 1920; Blackburn Rovers 17.05.21; Third Lanark 30.06.24; Stoke City 08.11.26; NORWICH CITY 09.07.31; Frost's Atheltic 09.07.34.

In Tom's days at Stoke the legendary Stan Matthews was the office boy. An inspiring captain and richly described as a past pluperfect prestissimo player of the game. Formerly a ship's plater on the Clyde, he went on to play over 150 games for Stoke. He was a determined fighter in trying to improve players wages and conditions before retiring through injury. For a while he managed the Rose Tavern in Norwich.

WILLIS, Graham

(1965) **1965:** 5/10; 10/0
Full Back **Career:** 1-0-0
Debut/Final: 19 Apr 65

Born: Bradwell, Gt Yarmouth 20 Oct 1946

Career: Alderman Leach School; Gorleston Minors Nov 1961; Arsenal (groundstaff); NORWICH CITY 27.10.64–31.03.66; Oxford United 09.04.66; Bedford Town May 1966; Lowestoft Town Jul 1967–23.08.69; Town Hall

Graham should have played more than once for the City first team. He was in a pre-season friendly at Colchester on 18.08.64 and he was twice in the First's squad but was not selected to face the redoubtable wingers Terry Paine and Mike Summerbee. Of minimal weight (under 10 St when training) he also made 44 reserve appearances. An electrician, he proudly recalls having worked on the River End lights at Carrow Road.

WILSON, Che Christian Aaron Clay

(1998–2000) **1998:** 5/9; 11/3
Defender **Career:** 19-6-0
Debut: 5 Dec 98 **Final:** 19 Feb 00 (sub)

Born: Ely 17 Jan 1979

Career: Little Thetford Primary School; Impington Village College; Girton Colts; Sawston Colts; Cambridge Colts; East Anglian Rep. Colts; East Anglian Boys; Cambridge Schools; Cambridgeshire County; NORWICH CITY 1993 (assoc), 07.07.95 (trainee); 11.04.97 (pro) – 29.04.2000; Bristol Rovers 06.07.2000.

Che was a member of the 1996/7 championship-winning City youth squad. He reads the game well and has the prime requirement of being comfortable in possession. An unused substitute on 12 occasions in his last City season, as he was predominantly seen as a jack-of-all-trades and not a master of one position. He apparently is named after the political revolutionary who was assasinated by CIA backed forces in Bolivia.

WILSON, Gordon Gill

(1932–1933) **1932:** 5/10; 11/10
Left Back **Career:** 3-0-0
Debut: 24 Sep 32 **Final:** 21 Oct 33

Born: West Auckland, Co. Durham 19 Jun 1904
Died: Newcastle-upon-Tyne 15 Oct 1947

Career: St Helens School; Tindale Crescent Juniors; Evenwood Juniors; Middlesbrough (trial) 1921; Evenwood Town; Bishop Auckland; Scotswood; Hull City 15.04.26; Luton Town 04.06.31; NORWICH CITY 16.05.32; Barrow 18.06.34.

A capable and steady defender well able to play in both full back positions with equal facility. He had only 29 league games in five years at Hull, being unable to displace Bell and Gibson. His two-footed ability was very evident in his play so just three senior City games is a surprisingly low figure. Son of a former Bishop Auckland player and a brother to Tucker and Moses, both prominent in north-eastern football.

WILSON, John Christopher

(1953–1958) **1954:** 5/10; 11/3
Right Back **Career:** 48-0-0
Debut: 25 Dec 53 **Final:** 17 Sep 58

Born: Norwich 28 Oct 1934

Career: George White School; Alderman Jex School; City College; Johnson & Pearce; Norwich Schoolboys & Youth; NORWICH CITY Feb 1951 (amat), 06.08.53 (pro); Lowestoft Town 08.11.58; Chesterfield 02.07.59; King's Lynn Jul 1960; Lowestoft Town Jul 1962; Thetford Aug 1964; Hellesdon; Nestle FC.

John played for a Norwich City XI against Yarmouth in the County's first floodlit match on 27.02.53. His only Canary goal was at Portman Road in the Combination Cup on 11.04.53. His 98 reserve games represent good service to the club before he joined the local football circuit. At Lowestoft it was like an old boys reunion with Messrs Cole, Foan and Kinsey also on their staff. John successfully ran and jumped for Norfolk and Eastern Counties and lives locally, as do so many ex-Canaries.

WILSON, Joseph

(1924–1926) **1925:** 5/8; 11/4
Outside Left **Career:** 41-0-4
Debut: 3 Sep 24 **Final:** 1 May 26

Born: Southwick, Sunderland circa 1901

Career: Southwick; Manchester United 15.09.20 (amat); Leadgate Park; Durham City Mar 1921; Sheffleld Wednesday 20.06.22; NORWICH CITY 18.06.24

The first of seven Wilsons to have played for City in the Football League, and the only forward among them. Learnt his trade in the Wearside leagues and he did well to play so many games in competition for the flanker's berth with Stoakes. He was a regular in Sheffield Wednesdays' Second Division side prior to linking with the Canaries. If he died in Oldham in 1973 he has a birth of 1 April 1901 but if he died East Cleveland in 1974 he had a birthday of 12th May 1901 – there is still research needed on my part.

WILSON, Leslie John

(1973) **1973:** 5/8; 10/11
Full Back **Career:** 11-0-0
Debut: 22 Sep 73 **Final:** 12 Dec 73

Born: Manchester 10 Jul 1947

Career: Wolverhampton Wanderers 1963 (juniors), 23.09.64 (pro); Bristol City 10.03.71; NORWICH CITY 08.09.73; Vancouver Whitecaps (Canada) May 1974–1983 player/coach/manager.

A Football League debut on 30.03.65 (H) Fulham being the first of 100 Division One games for Wolves. He netted the first of his eight career goals at Everton on 02.09.67 after coming on as a substitute and he confirmed his latent scoring ability when he was moved to the forward line alongside Hugh Curran. He was nicknamed 'the Reverend' by Derek Dougan when at Wolves. Now employed by the Canadian Football Association as the Manager/Administrator of their National Football teams.

WILSON, Paul Andrew

(1975) **1975:** 5/10; 12/0
Half Back **Career:** 0-1-0
Debut/Final: 22 Nov 75 (sub)

Born: Norwich 19 Jun 1956

Career: NORWICH CITY 26.07.74 to 1976; Gorleston; Lowestoft Town; IL Hodd (Norway) manager

Paul was the second man to achieve this dubious distinction of making his only first team appearance as a substitute. Son of former reserve Canary 'Tug' Wilson, who played from 1945 to 1950, Paul played about 10 more City reserve games and scored more goals than his father. His side in Norway played Norwich United at Plantation Park in 1992 as part of the part-timers pre-season preparations. A knee injury ended his playing career when age 35 and Paul has won a coach and man of the year award in the Telemark region.

WILSON, Robert Smail Whitelaw

(1957–1959) **1958:** 5/10; 11/7
Wing Half **Career:** 66-0-0
Debut: 24 Aug 57 **Final:** 8 Apr 59

Born: Musselburgh 29 Jun 1934

Career: Musselburgh; Aberdeen Nov 1954; NORWICH CITY 27.05.57; Gillingham 13.06.60; Accrington Stanley 22.07.61; Chester 23.04.62; GKN Sankey player/coach/ manager

Bobby won a Scottish League Cup winners medal with Aberdeen (beat St Mirren) being in a side packed with full internationals, namely Pat Buckley, Archie Glen, Graham Leggatt, Fred Martin and Henry Yorston. Balanced against this was the experience of having 33 Football League games expunged from his career. He was the skipper of Accrington when they folded in 1962 and the appearances of that season do not count. An unflappable fair-haired wing half he played with Ron Davies at Chester with his final league game arriving on 20.10.62 at Oxford. He became a buyer for Joseph Sankey & Sons Ltd and managed his works' side into the bargain.

WINGHAM, Harry Charles

(1925–1926) **1925:** 5/11; 11/10
Full Back **Career:** 44-0-1
Debut: 19 Sep 25 **Final:** 27 Dec 26

Born: Selsey, Sussex 25 Jun 1895
Died: Cowes, Isle of Wight 24 Apr 1969

Career: Woolston; Royal Engineers; Thorneycrofts; Bournemouth 22.06.23; Clapton Orient 23.05.24;

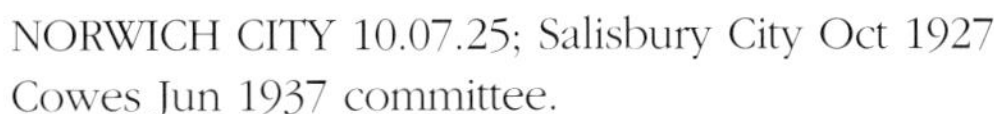

NORWICH CITY 10.07.25; Salisbury City Oct 1927; Cowes Jun 1937 committee.

A Southerner who impressed when he played for Bournemouth against City, Harry was a regular in Clapton's London Combination side. He signed for City at over 30 and had a useful run before returning to the South Coast. His son Ashley was a respectable centre forward for Newport (IOW) in the 1950s and 1960s. Harry, if truth were known looked like a ghost, with his saucer eyes, black swept-back hair and gaunt face.

WISEMAN, George

(1946–1947) **1946:** 6/0; 12/7
Goalkeeper **Career:** 8-0-0
Debut: 25 Dec 46 **Final:** 15 Feb 47

Born: East Dereham 23 May 1921

Career: Church School; Dereham Secondary School; Dereham Town; Notts County 20.02.45; RAF; NORWICH CITY 05.09.46; Metropolitan Police Feb 1948–1952.

George played against the British Army and at Notts County alongside Jesse Pye and John Sewell of England fame. He was one of five keepers used by City in the first post-war football league season. In eight games he faced five penalties and only two were scored. Seventeen reserve appearances were added to his total before he joined the Metropolitan Police. Now retired after serving with the Norfolk Constabulary for 35 years.

WOAN, Alan Esplin

(1954–1956) **1954:** 5/8; 10/8
Inside Left **Career:** 23-0-8
Debut: 19 Apr 54 (goal) **Final:** 31 Mar 56

Born: Liverpool 8 Feb 1931

Career: Anfield Road School; Bootle; New Brighton; NORWICH CITY 07.12.53; Northampton Town 03.07.56; Crystal Palace 29.10.59; Aldershot 17.02.61; Chertsey Town Jun 1964; New Brighton.

Almost a gross of league goals in 289 games showed that his style was an amalgam of opportunity and penetration. Alan scored after three minutes of his City debut against Northampton and for the latter side he scored in a minute on 23 August 1958 – the first ever Fourth Division goal. He was constantly in the right place at the right time, as was shown by his 43 reserve goals in 77 City games. He is fiercely proud of his son Ian, who made his debut against Norwich City in 1991.

WOODFORD, George Arthur

(1936–1937) **1936:** 5/10; 11/8
Left Back **Career:** 10-0-0
Debut: 4 Apr 36 **Final:** 27 Feb 37

Born: Lymington 22 Apr 1915
Died: Lymington 21 Apr 1966

Career: Lymington; NORWICH CITY 10.10.34 (amat), 04.09.35 (pro); Southampton Dec 1937; Lymington cs 1939.

George did well to play ten games for City considering that the regular full backs were the redoubtable Bowen and Halliday. A Southampton onlooker described one of his performances thus, 'The outstanding traits of his game are industry and mobility' as he followed Tom Parker to the Dell to become a deputy again this time behind Albert Roberts and Charlie Sillett. He returned home to live and tragically died the day before his 51st birthday.

WOODHOUSE, Christopher Henry (Charlie)

(1921–1922) **1921:** 5/10: 11/0
Outside Left **Career:** 18-0-5
Debut: 27 Aug 21 **Final:** 16 Mar 22

Born: Sheringham, Norfolk 5 Feb 1902
Died: North Walsham 14 Aug 1978

Career: Sheringham; NORWICH CITY 16.06.20; Sheringham May 1923.

Charlie signed professional forms with City along with Joe Hannah. His City debut was in the 1920/21 Hospital Cup game and he played with an unyielding adherence. A fine local who had a buoyant and enthusiastic style of play. His wife Maud died just 26 days after Charlie and at the same age of 76.

WOODS, Christopher Charles Eric

(1981–1986) **1982:** 6/1; 12/8
Goalkeeper **Career:** 267-0-0
Debut: 14 Mar 81 **Final:** 6 May 86

Born: Swineshead, Lincolnshire 14 Nov 1959

Career: Swineshead Sunday League; Priory Celtic; Lincolnshire; Nottingham Forest 19.09.75 (assoc), 08.06.76 (app), 01.12.76 (pro); Queens Park Rangers 04.07.79; NORWICH CITY 12.03.81 (after a month's loan); Glasgow Rangers 01.07.86; Sheffield Wenesday 15.08.91; Reading (loan) 27.10.95; Colorado Rapids (USA); Southampton 31.10.96; Sunderland 26.03.97; Kansas City Wizards (USA); Burnley 17.07.97; Birmingham City 29.07.98 goalkeeping coach; Everton goalkeeping coach.

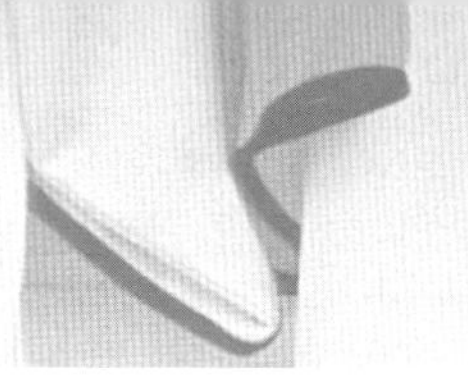

A competent executant in all aspects of the goalkeeper's craft. Possessed lightning reflexes and a propensity to work as hard as his hero, Peter Shilton. Has won League Cup, European Cup, Charity Shield and Milk Cup medals. Unusually he played in a Cup Final at Wembley before he had made his league debut. Chris, an England international, has followed the same path as the great Scottish international Willie Thornton who moved to Ibrox from Norwich after playing brilliantly for City (during the Second World War). He broke his left leg in a collision with Blackburn's Hendrie while at the Dell. Chris' final tally of caps was 43 and he holds the British record of going 1,196 minutes without conceding a goal.

Chris Woods

WOODS, Clive Richard

(1980–1981) **1980:** 5/9; 10/10
Winger **Career:** 34-3-4
Debut: 15 Mar 80 **Final:** 24 Oct 81

Born: Norwich 18 Dec 1947

Career: St Augustine's Junior School; Ipswich Town (trial) 14.07.66; Wisbech Aug 1966; Gothic; Chelmsford City (trial) Nov 1967; Wolverhampton Wanderers (trial) Dec 1967; Scunthorpe United (trial) Jan 1968; Ipswich Town 21.06.69 (pro); NORWICH CITY 13.03.80; City Supporters; Newton Flotman Apr 1982 player & later player/joint manager; Watton Town; Saxlingham; Wroxham Apr 1990; Mulbarton Reserves 1997; Diss Town Reserves.

Clive, a local lad, had a Combination game for Ipswich as an amateur when 17 but was not taken on. He could, on his day, baffle the best defences with his tantalising, close skills and in ten years appeared regularly in Europe with Town. He rose to the heights in the 1978 Cup Final when he was voted Man of the Match. Equally adept in midfield he had 338 games for Ipswich. Clive has retired at least six times to the author's knowledge since playing non-league football missing out on a testimonial match each time.

WOODTHORPE, Colin John

(1991–1994) **1990:** 5/11; 11/9
Full Back **Career:** 43-10-1
Debut: 11 May 91 **Final:** 9 Apr 94 (sub)

Born: Walton, Liverpool 13 Jan 1969

Career: Stanney Grange Junior School; Ellesmere Port Schoolboys; Stanney Comprehensive School; Cheshire Schoolboys; Birkett Rovers; Brombro Boys; Chester City Sep 1985 (assoc), 03.09.86 (pro); NORWICH CITY 10.07.90; Aberdeen 17.07.94; Stockport County 29.07.97.

A regular at Sealand Road, where his displays warranted a higher grade of football. Norwich from Chester was like going from secondary modern to university, and Colin expressed the wish to graduate with honours. Adaptable and versatile, his strong tackling and defensive attributes were to the fore, but mostly in City's reserves, where he played 94 times. One infamous day at Pittordie was when in a reserve game he was shown two yellow cards and proceeded to throw away the brandished red card.

WOOLLEY, Robert George

(1923–1925) **1923:** 5/8; 11/0
Full Back **Career:** 3-0-0
Debut: 5 May 23 **Final:** 26 Apr 25

Born: Medway 22 Jan 1899
Died: Lowestoft 28 Jul 1970

Career: Lowestoft Town 24.09.21; NORWICH CITY 19.07.22 (amat), 18.08.22 (pro); Lowestoft Town 1924 to 17.02.34.

Bob was the seventh local player signed in three seasons, but unfortunately for him, Albert Sturgess barred his way to a First team place. A diligent, thick-set player, he was in the combined Lowestoft/Yarmouth/Kirkley side that lost 9–4 to Norwich City at Crown Meadow in October 1926. A marvellous servant to Lowestoft with a final tally of 236 games for eleven goals.

WOOLMER, Anthony John

(1966–1968) **1966:** 5/10; 11/0
Centre Forward **Career:** 4-1-1
Debut: 29 Oct 66 (sub) **Final:** 20 Apr 68

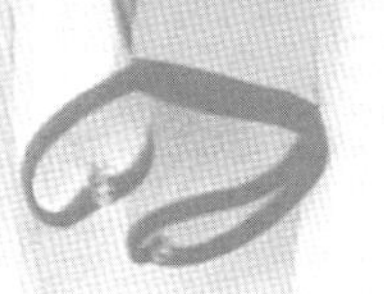

Born: Swardeston, Norfolk 25 Mar 1946

Career: NORWICH CITY 1963 (amat), 20.12.65 (pro); Bradford Park Avenue 16.10.69; Scunthorpe United 05.11.70; King's Lynn Jun 1972.

104 reserve games for 34 goals with a strike rate of one every other game in the 1968/69 season prompted a recall to the Firsts. However he played most of his football in the Fourth Division and he was among old friends at Scunthorpe. Fellow team mates were Geoff Barnard, Nigel Cassidy, Stephen Deere and Colin McDonald, with a certain Kevin Keegan embarking on a useful career! Tony's final league appearance came at Newport on 01.05.72.

WORRELL, Colin Harvey

(1962–1964) **1962:** 5/8; 11/0
Full Back **Career:** 10-0-0
Debut: 3 Nov 62 **Final:** 2 Sep 64

Born: Yarmouth 29 Aug 1943

Career: NORWICH CITY 06.05.61 (amat), 06.11.61; Orient 08.09.64; Charlton Athletic 01.07.66–09.08.66; Crescent Athletic Nov 1967.

Colin was another of the promising local youngsters who hopefully and loyally wait for First team opportunities. His chances came at Orient where at Numbers Three and Four were Worrell and Sorrell. A debut for the Londoners against Ipswich on 28.11.64 with three non-winning games against City before a final league outing on 30.04.66 (A) Bristol City. He now lives in Romford.

WORTON, Alfred James

(1934–1937) **1935:** 5/10; 11/0
Left Back **Career:** 23-0-0
Debut: 13 Oct 34 **Final:** 11 Dec 37

Born: Wolverhampton 4 Apr 1914
Died: Stourbridge 9 Dec 2000

Career: St Saviour's School; Priestfield Albion; Ettingshall Westley; Bilston United; Walsall Aug 1933; NORWICH CITY 09.06.34; Colchester United Jul 1938

City signed him in the face of competition from Blackpool, Arsenal and Birmingham. A regular and popular reserve who did not let the side down when promoted to the Firsts. The outbreak of war interrupted his career before it had really begun, and Alf had a legion of footballing stories that warm the cockles of one's heart on a cold winter's night.

WREN, Thomas James

(1932) **1932:** 5/9; 11/0
Right Back **Career:** 2-0-0
Debut: 29 Mar 32 **Final:** 2 Apr 32

Born: Rossington 4 Mar 1907
Died: Tunbridge Wells 16 May 1973

Career: Rossington; Huddesfield Town 15.10.26; Bradford City 31.12.28; Portsmouth Jun 1930; NORWICH CITY 21.08.31; Bristol City 13.05.32; Tunbridge Wells Rangers Jun 1933–1938.

Tom was one of ten players to finish their City careers in the 1931/32 season. His two games saw a 7–1 loss at Luton and a 3–0 loss at Exeter. This last game was the start of B.C. Robinson's lengthy career. He even missed by less than a year Tunbridge Wells Rangers winning the Southern Midweek league and the Kent Senior Cup.

WRIGHT, Jonathan

(1994–1997) **1994:** 5/8; 10/9
Full Back **Career:** 5-2-0
Debut: 15 Oct 94 (sub) **Final:** 21 Dec 97
Born: East Belfast 24 Nov 1975

Career: Strand Town Primary School; Orangefield High School; Bloomfield; St Andrew's (Belfast); N.Ireland Under-16; NORWICH CITY 05.03.89 (schoolboy), 06.07.92 (trainee), 01.07.94 (pro); Gillingham (trial) Jul 1997; Wroxham 25.09.97; Glenavon Nov 1997; Ards Aug 1998.

He shares a common bond with the legendary George Best in that they both attended the same high school. Jon's goals helped the Northern Ireland team reach the Under-16 European Championship Finals in Cyprus. A competitive and exciting defensive prospect but mainly a City reserve, evidenced by his 75 games at that level.

WRIGHT, Stephen

(1922–1923) **1922:** 5/7; 11/3
Left Half **Career:** 40-0-1
Debut: 26 Aug 22 **Final:** 5 May 23

Born: Leicester 24 Dec 1882
Died: Leicester 15 Oct 1959

Career: Belvoir Street School; Belvoir Street Sunday School; Leicestershire; Dublin Bohemians; 4th Leicesters & RAMC; Bolton Wanderers 01.05.19; NORWICH CITY 22.07.22; Brighton & Hove Albion 16.08.23; Lincoln City 1934 trainer; Ipswich Town Jul 1938 trainer; Dundalk manager for 7 years.

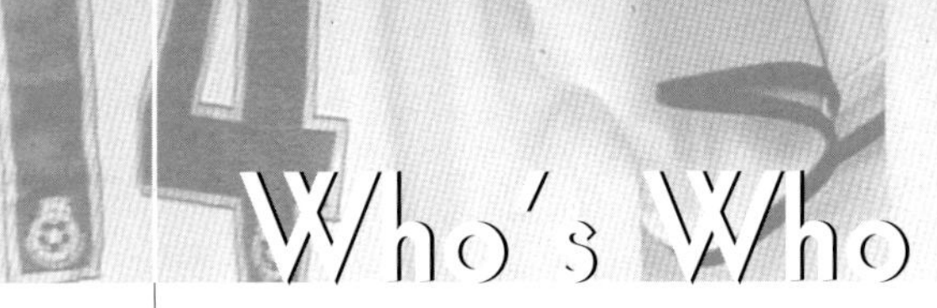

Stephen was the son of Edmund, a shoe finisher, and Maria Hope – and what a fine Xmas present the couple received on Christmas Eve! He had ten First Division games with Bolton, who fixed a £750 fee on him. His City debut was against the side he was to join after an unsuccessful application to become player/manager of a club in Chatham. He is featured as a Norwich City player on Pinnace Card number 1728. After leaving Brighton he managed Dundalk for seven years.

YOUNG, William David

(1983) **1983:** 6/3; 14/3
Centre Half **Career:** 6-1-0
Debut: 27 Aug 83 **Final:** 24 Sep 83 (sub)

Born: Edinburgh 25 Nov 1951

Career: Penraitland Primary School; Tranent Secondary School; Seton Athletic; Falkirk (trial); Aberdeen 1969; Tottenham Hotspur 08.09.75; Arsenal 02.03.77; Nottingham Forest 09.12.81; NORWICH CITY 25.08.83; Brighton & Hove Albion 08.12.83; Darlington 17.09.84 to 06.11.84.

Willie was a craggy, fearless stopper who frequently made opposing centre forwards jump. It was generally reckoned that if his distribution had been on par with his aggressive tackling he would have won Full Scottish caps to go with his Under-23 honours. He played in Domestic and European Cup Finals doing especially well at Aberdeen and Arsenal. You should never ask him, 'Do you remember that tackle?'. It refers to the 1980 FA Cup Final. After running a horseriding school with his wife he bought the Bramcote Manor pub and became a genial host. His wife represented Scotland at showjumping with son Steve a Junior European showjumping champion and his other two children having ridden for England.

Statistical Section

Notes

Shirt Numbers

These did not actually come into compulsory use until 1939–40. All numbers shown prior to that season are 'presumed' as from newspaper line-ups and usual positions, e.g. right-back usually denoted as number 2

Attendances

After the Second World War we have shown the Home Attendances as submitted to the Football League by Norwich City FC.

1939–40 Season

The three matches played in Division Three (South) at the start of the season are not included but appear in the 'Canaries at War' section

2001–02 Season

The first four matches of this season are included in the players' individual and Club total records, but the line-ups are not included herein

Symbols

4' Player scored a goal

4■ Player was captain

(4) Player was substituted

(4)˙& 19˙ Player 4 was substituted by player 19

(4)∴ Player 4 came on as a substitute and was later substituted

1902–03 NORFOLK & SUFFOLK LEAGUE

NO.		DATE	OPPONENTS	V.	H-T	F-T	Sparks W.	Bardwell G.	Cracknell W.	Crome W.	Yallop G.	Yallop J.	Witham A.	Playford B.	Collinson R.W.	Shields J.	Newell T.H.	Steele T.	Horton W.	Jeffries W.	Palmer R.M.	Wallace W.	Desborough R.	Clarke A.J.	Sidwell W.T.	Harris E.	Butcher H.	Hook J.	Kelf J.	Miller G.	Tidman A.	Campling E.	Schmidt E.	Pointer R.G.	Green A.	Own Goals	ATTD.
1	S	27 Sept 1902	Beccles Caxton	A	4-1	4-2	1	2	3	4	5	6	7	8^{1}	9^{1}	10^{2}	11																				–
2	S	15 Nov 1902	Ipswich Town	H	0-0	1-0	1	4	3		5	6	7^{1}	9	10		11	2	8																		1,700
3	S	13 Dec 1902	Ipswich Town	A	2-1	2-1		4	3			6	7^{1}	8	5		11	2	9^{1}	1	10																GOOD
4	F	26 " 1902	Norwich C.E.Y.M.S.	A	2-0	4-2		4	3			6	7	8^{2}	5^{2}		11		9		10	1	2														4,500
5	S	3 Jan 1903	Kirkley	A	0-4	0-7		4	3			6	7	8	5		11				10	1	2	9													GOOD
6	S	10 " 1903	Yarmouth Town	H	1-0	1-0		4	3			6	7	8	5		11		9		10	1	2													$-^{1}$	2,000
7	S	17 " 1903	Beccles Caxton	H	2-0	4-1		4	3		5	6	7	8^{1}	2^{1}		11				10	1			9^{2}												1,100
8	S	31 " 1903	Norwich C.E.Y.M.S.	H	0-1	1-2		6	3		5		7	10	9^{1}		11	2	8			1			4												3,000
9	S	7 Feb 1903	Yarmouth Town	A	0-0	1-2		4	3				7	10	5		11	2	8			1			9^{1}	6											GOOD
10	S	14 " 1903	Kirkley	H	0-0	0-1		4	3				7	10	5		11	2				1		8	9	6											2,000
11	W	8 Apr 1903	Lynn Town	A	1-2	4-5		3					8^{1}	9^{3}			10									6	1	2	4	5	7	11					–
12	Tu	14 " 1903	Lowestoft Town	H	0-0	2-0					5		7	8	10^{2}		11	2					9		4	6							1	3			3,000
13	Th	23 " 1903	Lowestoft Town	A	1-4	2-9		5					7	8^{2}			11	2					9		4	6							1	3	10		–
14	Th	30 " 1903	Lynn Town	H	4-1	8-1							7^{3}	10^{1}			11^{2}	2						9^{2}		6				5	8		1	3	4		GOOD

F.A. CUP

NO.		DATE	OPPONENTS	V.	H-T	F-T	Sparks W.	Bardwell G.	Cracknell W.	Crome W.	Yallop G.	Yallop J.	Witham A.	Playford B.	Collinson R.W.	Shields J.	Newell T.H.	Own Goals	ATTD.
1	S	20 Sept 1902	Lowestoft Town (Prelim Round)	A	0-2	0-5	1	2	3	4	5	6	7	8	9	10	11		1,500

F.A. AMATEUR CUP

NO.		DATE	OPPONENTS	V.	H-T	F-T	Sparks W.	Bardwell G.	Cracknell W.	Yallop G.	Yallop J.	Witham A.	Playford B.	Collinson R.W.	Newell T.H.	Steele T.	Horton W.	Palmer R.M.	Own Goals	ATTD.
1	S	11 Oct 1902	Lynn Town (1st Qual. Round)	H	2-0	5-0	1	4	3	5	6	7^{2}	8	9^{1}	11	2		10^{1}	$-^{1}$	700
2	S	8 Nov 1902	Lowestoft Town (2nd Qual. Round)	A	2-0	2-4	1	4	3	5	6	7^{2}	8	10	11	2	9			AVG

NORFOLK SENIOR CUP

NO.		DATE	OPPONENTS	V.	H-T	F-T	Bardwell G.	Cracknell W.	Yallop G.	Yallop J.	Witham A.	Playford B.	Collinson R.W.	Newell T.H.	Steele T.	Wallace W.	Sidwell W.T.	Own Goals	ATTD.
1	S	24 Jan 1903	Lynn Town (1st Round)	A	1-0	1-2	4	3	5	6	7	10	9	11	2	1	8	$-^{1}$	1,200

1902–03 APPEARANCES & GOALS

	N. & S. LGE APPR.	N. & S. LGE GLS	F.A. CUP APPR.	F.A. CUP GLS	AMATEUR CUP APPR.	AMATEUR CUP GLS	NORFOLK SEN. CUP APPR.	NORFOLK SEN. CUP GLS
Newell T.H.	14	2	1	–	2	–	1	–
Playford B.	14	10	1	–	2	–	1	–
Witham A.	14	6	1	–	2	4	1	–
Bardwell G.	12	–	1	–	2	–	1	–
Collinson R.W.	11	7	1	–	2	1	1	–
Cracknell W.	10	–	1	–	2	–	1	–
Steele T.	8	–			2	–	1	–
Wallace W.	7	–					1	–
Yallop J.	7	–	1	–	2	–	1	–
Harris E.	6	–						
Horton W.	6	1			1	–		
Sidwell W.T.	6	3					1	–
Desborough R.	5	–						
Palmer R.M.	5	–			1	1		
Yallop G.	5	–	1	–	2	–	1	–
Clarke A.J.	3	2						
Pointer R.G.	3	–						
Schmidt E.	3	–						
Green A.	2	–						
Miller G.	2	–						
Sparks W.	2	–	1	–	2	–		
Tidman A.	2	–						
Butcher H.	1	–						
Campling E.	1	–						
Crome W.	1	–	1	–				
Hook J.	1	–						
Jeffries W.	1	–						
Kelf J.	1	–						
Shields J.	1	2	1	–				
Own Goals		1				1		1

NORFOLK & SUFFOLK LEAGUE

1902–03	P	W	D	L	F	A	PTS
Lowestoft Town	14	11	1	2	54	15	23
Ipswich Town	14	8	1	5	34	24	17
Norwich City	**14**	**8**	**0**	**6**	**34**	**33**	**16**
Norwich C.E.Y.M.S.	14	7	2	5	28	28	16
Yarmouth Town	14	7	1	6	25	21	15
Lynn Town	14	5	3	6	36	36	13
Kirkley	14	4	3	7	18	18	11
Beccles Caxton	14	0	1	13	11	65	1

1903–04 NORFOLK & SUFFOLK LEAGUE

NO.		DATE	OPPONENTS	V.	H-T	F-T	Cooks W.	Sidwell W.T.	Desborough R.	Sutherland A.	Chamberlin E.	Harris E.	Playford B.	Baker L.	Gooch P.G.	Collinson R.W.	King H.H.	Rackham F.H.	Pointer R.G.	Newell T.H.	Palmer J.	Hook J.	Green A.	Sayer H.J.	Campling E.	Cutmore J.	Palmer R.M.	Mitchell L.	Bardwell G.	Ellis H.	Snelling C.	Dunning C.E.	Brown A.	Witham A.	ATTD.
1	S	10 Oct 1903	Cromer	H	2-1	5-1	1	2	3	4	5	6	7	8^{2}	9^{1}	10^{1}	11^{1}																		1,700
2	S	28 Nov 1903	Lowestoft Town	A	0-2	2-2	1	7		4	5	6		8^{1}	9	10^{1}	11	2	3																2,000
3	S	19 Dec 1903	Cromer	A	1-0	1-0	1	7		4	5	6	9	8		3	10^{1}	2		11															–
4	S	26 " 1903	Kirkley	H	2-0	5-0	1			4^{1}	5	6		8^{1}	9^{2}		10	2^{1}	3	11	7														4,000
5	S	2 Jan 1904	Lowestoft Town	H	0-2	1-2	1			4	5	6		8^{1}	9	10	11	2	3		7														3,600
6	S	9 " 1904	Yarmouth Town	A	0-1	0-1	1			4	5	6		8	10		9	2	3	11	7														LARGE
7	S	30 " 1904	Norwich C.E.Y.M.S.	H	2-2	3-3	1		9^{1}	4^{1}	5	6	10	8				2	3	11	7														2,000
8	S	6 Feb 1904	Kirkley	A	0-1	0-5	1				5	6		8					3		7	2	4	9	10	11									SMALL
9	S	12 Mar 1904	Lynn Town	A	0-0	1-2	1			4	5	6		8	9^{1}			2	3	11	7						10								GOOD
10	S	19 " 1904	Yarmouth Town	H	0-1	1-1				4	5	6		8	9^{1}				3	11	7	2					10	1							2,000
11	S	26 " 1904	Ipswich Town	A	4-1	6-1	1			4	5	6		10	8^{2}		9^{2}		3	11^{2}	7								2						700
12	Tu	5 Apr 1904	Ipswich Town	H	1-1	1-1				4		6			5		10		3	11	9^{1}							1		2	7	8			–
13	Th	21 " 1904	Lynn Town	H	3-0	5-0	1		6		5				8^{2}		9^{2}		3	11	7^{1}			4	10					2					POOR
14	s	23 " 1904	Norwich C.E.Y.M.S.	A	1-1	1-1	1				5	6			8		9	2	3	11	7^{1}			4		10									3,000

F.A. CUP

NO.		DATE	OPPONENTS		V.	H-T	F-T	Cooks W.	Sidwell W.T.	Desborough R.	Sutherland A.	Chamberlin E.	Harris E.	Playford B.	Baker L.	Gooch P.G.	Collinson R.W.	King H.H.	Rackham F.H.	Pointer R.G.	Newell T.H.	Palmer J.	Hook J.	Green A.	Sayer H.J.	Campling E.	Cutmore J.	Palmer R.M.	Mitchell L.	Bardwell G.	Ellis H.	Snelling C.	Dunning C.E.	Brown A.	Witham A.	ATTD.
1	S	19 Sept 1903	Lowestoft Town	(Prelim. Round)	H	1-0	4-1	1			4	5	6		8	9^{3}	10^{1}			3	11													2	7	4,000
2	S	3 Oct 1903	Yarmouth Town	(1st Qual Round)	A	1-0	2-1	1	7	3	4	5	6	8	9^{1}		10^{1}	11	2																	3,000
3	S	17 " 1903	Harwich & Parkeston	(2nd Qual Round)	A	1-0	4-2	1	6		4	5		7	8^{1}		9^{3}	10	2	3	11															GOOD
4	S	31 " 1903	West Norwood	(3rd Qual Round)	H	1-1	1-1	1	6		4	5		7	8^{1}	9	10		2	3	11															3,000

F.A. AMATEUR CUP

NO.		DATE	OPPONENTS		V.	H-T	F-T	Cooks W.	Sidwell W.T.	Desborough R.	Sutherland A.	Chamberlin E.	Harris E.	Playford B.	Baker L.	Gooch P.G.	Collinson R.W.	King H.H.	Rackham F.H.	Pointer R.G.	Newell T.H.	Palmer J.	Hook J.	Green A.	Sayer H.J.	Campling E.	Cutmore J.	Palmer R.M.	Mitchell L.	Bardwell G.	Ellis H.	Snelling C.	Dunning C.E.	Brown A.	Witham A.	ATTD.
1	S	7 Nov 1903	Harwich & Parkeston	(2nd Qual Round)	H	3-1	5-1	1	6		4	5		7	8^{1}	9^{2}	10^{2}		2	3	11															2,350
2	S	21 " 1903	Leiston	(3rd Qual Round)	H	3-0	5-1	1	7		4	5	6		8^{1}	9^{2}	10^{2}	11	2	3																1,627
3	S	12 Dec 1903	Kirkley	(4th Qual Round)	A	1-0	2-0	1	7		4	5	6		8	9^{1}	3	10^{1}	2		11															1,500
4	S	23 Jan 1904	Lowestoft Town	(1st Round)	H	0-0	3-0	1	6		4	5			8^{1}	10	9^{2}		2	3	11	7														4,160
5	S	13 Feb 1904	Ilford	(2nd Round)	H	1-0	3-1	1	6		4	5			8	10	9		2^{1}	3	11^{1}	7^{1}														4,000
6	S	27 " 1904	Ealing	(3rd Round)	A	0-0	0-0	1	6		4	5			8	10	9		2	3	11	7														2,000
7	S	5 May 1904	Ealing	(Replay)	H	0-1	1-2	1	6		4	5			8	10	9		2^{1}	3	11	7														5,000

NORFOLK SENIOR CUP

NO.		DATE	OPPONENTS		V.	H-T	F-T	Cooks W.	Sidwell W.T.	Desborough R.	Sutherland A.	Chamberlin E.	Harris E.	Playford B.	Baker L.	Gooch P.G.	Collinson R.W.	King H.H.	Rackham F.H.	Pointer R.G.	Newell T.H.	Palmer J.	Hook J.	Green A.	Sayer H.J.	Campling E.	Cutmore J.	Palmer R.M.	Mitchell L.	Bardwell G.	Ellis H.	Snelling C.	Dunning C.E.	Brown A.	Witham A.	ATTD.
1	S	20 Feb 1904	Lynn Town	(1st Round)	A	0-4	2-5	1			4	5			8	9^{1}		10^{1}	2	3	11			6											7	1,800

1903–04 APPEARANCES & GOALS

	N. & S. LGE APPR.	N. & S. LGE GLS	F.A. CUP APPR.	F.A. CUP GLS	AMATEUR CUP APPR.	AMATEUR CUP GLS	NOR. SEN. CUP APPR.	NOR. SEN. CUP GLS
Chamberlin E.	13	–	4	–	7	–	1	–
Harris E.	13	–	2	–	2	–		
Cooks W.	12	–	4	–	7	–	1	–
Pointer R.G.	12	–	3	–	6	–	1	–
Baker L.	11	5	4	3	7	3	1	–
Gooch P.G.	11	9	2	3	7	5	1	1
Palmer J.	11	3			4	1		
Sutherland A.	11	2	4	–	7	–	1	–
King H.H.	10	6	2	–	2	1	1	1
Newell T.H.	10	3	3	–	6	1	1	–
Rackham F.H.	8	1	3	–	7	2	1	–
Collinson R.W.	4	2	4	5	7	6		
Desborough R.	3	1	1	–				
Playford B.	3	–	3	–	1	–		
Sayer H.J.	3	–						
Sidwell W.T.	3	–	3	–	7	–		
Campling E.	2	–						
Cutmore J.	2	–						
Ellis H.	2	–						
Hook J.	2	–						
Mitchell L.	2	–						
Palmer R.M.	2	–						
Bardwell G.	1	–						
Dunning C.E.	1	–						
Green A.	1	–					1	–
Snelling C.	1	–						
Brown A			1	–				
Witham A.			1	–			1	–

NORFOLK & SUFFOLK LEAGUE

1903–04	P	W	D	L	F	A	PTS
Lowestoft Town	14	9	3	2	34	18	21
Kirkley	14	7	2	5	33	18	16
Norwich City	**14**	**5**	**5**	**4**	**32**	**20**	**15**
Lynn Town	14	6	3	5	26	27	15
Norwich C.E.Y.M.S.	14	5	2	7	23	28	12
Ipswich Town	14	4	3	7	28	37	11
Yarmouth Town	14	4	3	7	17	23	11
Cromer	14	5	1	8	19	41	11

1904–05 NORFOLK & SUFFOLK LEAGUE

NO.		DATE	OPPONENTS	V.	H-T	F-T	Cooks W.	Ellis H.	Pointer R.G.	Kelf J.	Royal H.	Harris E.	Cutmore J.	Snelling C.	Gooch P.G.	King H.H.	Baker R.W.	Collinson R.W.	Chamberlin E.	Vigar H.	Rackham F.H.	Desborough R.	Newell T.H.	Lathan T.	Playford B.	Kay A.	MacIntyre R.	Bardwell G.	ATTD.
1	S	24 Sept 1904	Beccles Caxton	A	0-0	1-0	1	2	3	4	5	6	7	8	9	10^{1}	11												GOOD
2	S	15 Oct 1904	Cromer	A	1-0	1-0	1	6	3		5	4	7	9	8	10^{1}	11	2											V.GOOD
3	S	12 Nov 1904	Kirkley	H	2-0	3-0	1		3		5^{1}	6	7		8^{1}	10	11	2	4	9^{1}									2,500
4	S	19 " 1904	Beccles Caxton	H	2-0	3-0	1		3		5	6	7		8	10^{2}	11	2	4^{1}	9									2,000
5	S	26 " 1904	Cromer	H	0-2	4-2	1		3		5	6		7	8	10^{1}	11	2^{1}	4	9^{2}									V.GOOD
6	S	17 Dec 1904	Lowestoft Town	H	1-1	1-1	1		3		5	6	7		8	10	11	2^{1}	4	9									3,500
7	M	26 " 1904	Yarmouth Town	H	0-0	0-0	1		3		5	6	7	8		10	11		4	9	2								5,000
8	S	14 Jan 1905	Ipswich Town	H	2-0	2-0	1		3		5	6			7	8^{1}	11^{1}	10	4	9	2								2,000
9	S	11 Feb 1905	Lowestoft Town	A	2-1	3-1	1				5	6			7	8	11	10^{1}	4	9^{2}	2	3							3,500
10	S	25 " 1905	Kirkley	A	3-1	4-2	1		3		5	6			7	8		10^{1}	4	9^{3}	2		11						GOOD
11	S	18 Mar 1905	Norwich C.E.Y.M.S.	A	1-0	2-1	1		3		5	6			7	8	11	10	4	9^{2}	2								4,000
12	S	25 " 1905	Lynn Town	A	0-3	3-4	1		3		5	6			7	8	11^{1}	10^{1}	4	9^{1}	2								1,400
13	S	1 Apr 1905	Lynn Town	H	1-1	2-2	1		3		5	6			7^{1}	8	11	10		9^{1}	2			4					5,000
14	S	8 " 1905	Norwich C.E.Y.M.S.	H	1-0	3-1	1		3		5	6	7		8^{1}	10	11	9^{2}	4		2								5,000
15	F	21 " 1905	Yarmouth Town	A	0-1	1-1	1		3		5	6				8		9	4		2				7	10^{1}	11		4,000
16	S	29 " 1905	Ipswich Town	A	0-0	0-1	1		3	7					8	10	11	5		9	2	4						6	2,000

F.A. CUP

NO.		DATE	OPPONENTS	V.	H-T	F-T	Cooks W.	Ellis H.	Pointer R.G.	Kelf J.	Royal H.	Harris E.	Cutmore J.	Snelling C.	Gooch P.G.	King H.H.	Baker R.W.	Collinson R.W.	Chamberlin E.	Vigar H.	ATTD.
1	S	29 Oct 1904	Grays United (3rd Qual. Round)	H	0-0	0-0	1		3		5	6	7		8	10	11	2	4	9	3,000
2	Th	3 Nov 1904	Grays United (Replay)	H	1-0	2-3	1		3		5	6	7		8^{1}	10	11^{1}	2	4	9	GOOD

1904–05 APPEARANCES & GOALS

	N. & S. LGE APPR.	N. & S. LGE GLS	F.A. CUP APPR.	F.A. CUP GLS
Cooks W.	16	–	2	–
King H.H.	16	6	2	–
Harris E.	15	–	2	–
Pointer R.G.	15	–	2	–
Royal H.	15	1	2	–
Baker R.W.	14	2	2	1
Collinson R.W.	14	7	2	–
Gooch P.G.	14	3	2	1
Chamberlin E.	12	1	2	–
Vigar H.	12	12	2	–
Rackham F.H.	10	–		
Cutmore J.	7	–	2	–
Snelling C.	4	–		
Desborough R.	2	–		
Ellis H.	2	–		
Kelf J.	2	–		
Bardwell G.	1	–		
Kay A.	1	1		
Lathan T.	1	–		
MacIntyre R.	1	–		
Newell T.H.	1	–		
Playford B.	1	–		

NORFOLK & SUFFOLK LEAGUE

1904–05	P	W	D	L	F	A	PTS
Norwich City	**16**	**10**	**4**	**2**	**33**	**16**	**24**
Lowestoft Town	16	9	2	5	34	26	20
Norwich C.E.Y.M.S.	16	9	1	6	37	24	19
Yarmouth Town	16	8	3	5	28	25	19
Ipswich Town	16	9	0	7	34	21	18
Lynn Town	16	7	3	6	41	31	17
Kirkley	16	5	1	10	21	40	11
Cromer	16	3	2	11	21	39	8
Beccles Caxton	16	4	0	12	17	44	8

1905–06 SOUTHERN LEAGUE

NO.		DATE	OPPONENTS	V.	H-T	F-T	Williams Charlie	McEwen Jimmy	Archer Arthur	Bowman John	Bushell William	Cummings William	Muir Robert	Graham Samuel	Ronaldson Duncan	Ross David	Linward William	Bemment Fred	Wilkinson Freddy	Brindley Horace	King Horace	Livingstone Archie	Childs William	Rose Fred	Vigar Herbert	Brown George	Wilcox Thomas	Wood William	Gooch Percy	ATTD.
1	S	2 Sept 1905	Plymouth Argyle	A	0-1	0-2	1	2	3	4	5	6	7	8	9	10	11													8,000
2	S	9 " 1905	Southampton	H	0-0	1-1	1	3	2		5	4	7		9	10		6	8^{1}	11										7,000
3	S	16 " 1905	Reading	A	1-2	1-3	1	3	2		5	4	7		9^{1}	8		6		11	10									6,000
4	S	23 " 1905	Watford	H	0-0	1-1	1	3			5		7^{1}		9	10	11	6	8			2	4							7,000
5	S	30 " 1905	Brighton & Hove Albion	A	0-1	1-2	1	3	2		5		7		9	10^{1}	11	6						4	8					5,000
6	S	7 Oct 1905	West Ham United	H	1-0	1-0	1	3	2	4	5		7	8	9^{1}	10		6		11										6,000
7	S	14 " 1905	Fulham	A	0-1	1-2	1	3	2		5	4	7	8	9	10^{1}		6		11										17,000
8	S	21 " 1905	Queens Park Rangers	H	4-0	4-0	1	3	2		5		7^{1}	8^{1}	9	10^{2}		6				4				11				7,000
9	S	28 " 1905	Bristol Rovers	A	1-0	1-0	1	3	2		5		7	8^{1}	9	10		6				4				11				7,000
10	S	4 Nov 1905	New Brompton	H	2-0	4-1	1	3	2^{1}		5		7^{2}	8	9	10^{1}		6				4				11				6,000
11	S	11 " 1905	Portsmouth	A	1-1	1-2	1	3	2		5		7	8	9	10		6				4				11^{1}				5,000
12	S	25 " 1905	Millwall Athletic	A	0-0	1-0	1	3	2		5		7	8^{1}	9	10		6				4				11				8,000
13	S	2 Dec 1905	Luton Town	H	0-1	1-1	1	3	2^{1}		5		7	8	9	10		6				4				11				8,000
14	S	16 " 1905	Brentford	H	0-0	1-1	1	3	2		5		7	8	9	10^{1}		6				4				11				5,000
15	S	23 " 1905	Northampton Town	A	2-0	2-0		3	2^{1}		5		7	8	9	10^{1}		6				4				11	1			4,000
16	M	25 " 1905	Swindon Town	H	0-0	1-0		3	2		5		7	8	9	10^{1}		6				4				11	1			10,245
17	S	30 " 1905	Plymouth Argyle	H	1-1	2-1		3	2		5		7^{1}		9^{1}	10		6			8	4				11	1			5,500
18	S	6 Jan 1906	Southampton	A	0-1	1-2		3	2^{1}		5		7	8	9	10		6				4				11	1			5,000
19	S	20 " 1906	Reading	H	0-1	2-3		3			5		7	8	9	10^{2}		6				4		2		11	1			5,000
20	S	27 " 1906	Watford	A	0-0	0-1	1	3		4	5			8	9	10		6				2	7			11				3,500
21	S	10 Feb 1906	West Ham United	A	1-1	1-6	1	3	2	4			7	8	9	10^{1}		6				5				11				6,000
22	S	17 " 1906	Fulham	H	0-0	0-0	1	3	2		5		7	8	9	10		6				4				11				8,000
23	S	24 " 1906	Queens Park Rangers	A	0-0	0-0	1	3	2		5		7	8	9	10		6				4				11				10,000
24	S	3 Mar 1906	Bristol Rovers	H	0-0	0-0	1	3	2		5		7	8	9	10		6				4				11				8,000
25	S	10 " 1906	New Brompton	A	0-0	0-0	1	3	2	4	5		7	8	9	10						6				11				4,000
26	S	17 " 1906	Portsmouth	H	0-0	1-1	1	3	2	4	5			7^{1}	9	10						6				11		8		9,000
27	S	24 " 1906	Swindon Town	A	0-1	3-1	1	3		4	5		7	8^{2}	9	10^{1}		6		11		2								3,000
28	S	31 " 1906	Millwall Athletic	H	1-1	1-1	1	3	2^{1}		5		7	8	9	10		6		11		4								8,000
29	Th	5 Apr 1906	Brighton & Hove Albion	H	0-0	2-0		3	2		5	6	7			10^{1}				11		4					1	8	9^{1}	5,000
30	S	7 " 1906	Luton Town	A	0-1	1-2	1	3	2		5		7		9	10^{1}		6		11		4						8		8,000
31	S	14 " 1906	Tottenham Hotspur	H	2-1	4-1	1	3	2^{1}		5		7		9^{1}	10^{2}		6		11		4						8		11,500
32	Tu	17 " 1906	Tottenham Hotspur	A	0-3	0-3		3	2			5	7		9	10		6		11		4					1	8		9,000
33	S	21 " 1906	Brentford	A	1-0	2-0	1	3	2		5		7	8	9			6		11		4						10^{2}		6,000
34	S	28 " 1906	Northampton Town	H	3-0	4-0	1	3	2		5		7		9^{1}	10^{1}		6^{1}		11		4						8^{1}		5,000

F.A. CUP

NO.		DATE	OPPONENTS	V.	H-T	F-T	Williams Charlie	McEwen Jimmy	Archer Arthur	Bowman John	Bushell William	Cummings William	Muir Robert	Graham Samuel	Ronaldson Duncan	Ross David	Linward William	Bemment Fred	Wilkinson Freddy	Brindley Horace	King Horace	Livingstone Archie	Childs William	Rose Fred	Vigar Herbert	Brown George	Wilcox Thomas	Wood William	Gooch Percy	ATTD.
1	S	9 Dec 1905	Sheppey United (4th Qual. Round)	A	1-0	2-0	1	3	2		5		7	8	9^{1}	10^{1}		6		11		4								3,000
2	S	13 Jan 1906	Tunbridge Wells Rangers (1st Round)	H	0-0	1-1		3	2		5^{1}		7	8	9	10		6		11		4					1			3,919
3	W	17 " 1906	Tunbridge Wells Rangers (Replay)	A	2-0	5-0		3		4	5			8^{2}	9	10^{3}		6		11		2	7				1			4,000
4	S	3 Feb 1906	Manchester United (2nd Round)	A	0-1	0-3	1	3	2		5		7	8	9	10		6		11		4								11,000

1905–06 APPEARANCES & GOALS

	SOUTHERN LGE APPR.	SOUTHERN LGE GLS	F.A. CUP APPR.	F.A. CUP GLS
McEwen Jimmy	34	–	4	–
Ronaldson Duncan	33	5	4	1
Ross David	33	17	4	4
Bushell William	32	–	4	1
Muir Robert	32	5	3	–
Archer Arthur	30	6	3	–
Bemment Fred	30	1	4	–
Livingstone Archie	28	–	4	–
Williams Charlie	27	–	2	–
Graham Samuel	24	6	4	2
Brown George	19	1		
Brindley Horace	12	–	4	–
Bowman John	7	–	1	–
Wilcox Thomas	7	–	2	–
Wood William	7	3		
Cummings William	6	–		
Linward William	3	–		
Childs William	2	–	1	–
King Horace	2	–		
Rose Fred	2	–		
Wilkinson Freddy	2	1		
Gooch Percy	1	1		
Vigar Herbert	1	–		

SOUTHERN LEAGUE

1905–06	P	W	D	L	F	A	PTS
Fulham	34	19	12	3	44	15	50
Southampton	34	19	7	8	58	39	45
Portsmouth	34	17	9	8	61	35	43
Luton Town	34	17	7	10	64	40	41
Tottenham Hotspur	34	16	7	11	46	29	39
Plymouth Argyle	34	16	7	11	52	33	39
Norwich City	**34**	**13**	**10**	**11**	**46**	**38**	**36**
Bristol Rovers	34	15	5	14	56	56	35
Brentford	34	14	7	13	43	52	35
Reading	34	12	9	13	53	46	33
West Ham United	34	14	5	15	42	39	33
Millwall Athletic	34	11	11	12	38	41	33
Queens Park Rangers	34	12	7	15	58	44	31
Watford	34	8	10	16	38	57	26
Swindon Town	34	8	9	17	31	52	25
Brighton & Hove Albion	34	9	7	18	30	55	25
New Brompton	34	7	8	19	20	62	22
Northampton Town	34	8	5	21	32	79	21

1906–07 SOUTHERN LEAGUE

NO.		DATE	OPPONENTS	V.	H-T	F-T	Thompson Fred	Archer Arthur	McEwen Jimmy	Livingstone Archie	Bushell William	Bemment Fred	Muir Robert	Wood Willie	Ronaldson Duncan	Ross David	Chalmers James	Birnie Alexander	Liddell Alexander	Lamberton George	Byrne John	Brindley Horace	King Horace	Gooch Percy	Baker Langford	Lamberton James	McLarney Patrick	Jex William	Bugg Walter	Taylor Wally	Martin George	Cannon John	Fitchie Tom	Fiske William	Own Goals	ATTD.
1	S	1 Sept 1906	Fulham	H	0-0	0-0	1	2	3	4	5	6	7	8	9	10	11																			9,000
2	S	8 " 1906	Southampton	A	1-1	2-2	1	2	3	4	5	6		8	9^{1}	10^{1}	11	7																		5,000
3	S	15 " 1906	West Ham United	H	3-1	3-2	1	2^{1}	3	4	5	6		8	9	10^{2}	11	7																		9,000
4	S	22 " 1906	Tottenham Hotspur	A	2-1	2-2	1	2	3	4	5	6	7	8	9^{1}	10^{1}	11																			18,000
5	S	29 " 1906	Swindon Town	H	0-1	1-1	1	2	3	4	5	6		8	9^{1}	10	11	7																		8,000
6	S	6 Oct 1906	Bristol Rovers	A	0-1	1-3	1	2	3	4	5	6		8	9	10^{1}	11	7																		6,000
7	S	13 " 1906	Luton Town	A	0-0	3-1	1		3	2	5	6		8^{1}	9	10^{2}	11		4	7																5,000
8	S	20 " 1906	Crystal Palace	H	3-2	4-2	1	2	3	4	5	6		8^{1}	9	10^{2}	11			7^{1}																9,000
9	S	27 " 1906	Brentford	A	0-0	1-2	1	2	3	4	5	6		8	9	10	11			7^{1}																7,000
10	S	3 Nov 1906	Millwall Athletic	H	1-0	3-0	1	2	3	4	5	6		8	9^{1}	10^{1}	11^{1}			7																5,500
11	S	10 " 1906	Leyton	A	0-1	1-1	1	2	3	4	5	6		8	9	10^{1}	11			7																9,000
12	S	17 " 1906	Portsmouth	H	1-2	1-3	1	2	3	4	5	6		8^{1}	9	10	11			7																7,000
13	S	24 " 1906	New Brompton	A	1-0	1-0	1	2	3	4	5	6		8	9	10	11			7^{1}																5,000
14	S	1 Dec 1906	Plymouth Argyle	H	0-1	0-1	1	2	3	4	5				9	10		7		8	6	11														6,000
15	S	8 " 1906	Brighton & Hove Albion	A	2-0	2-0	1	2	3	4	5	6		8	9^{1}	10				7^{1}			11													6,000
16	S	15 " 1906	Reading	H	2-1	4-2	1	2	3	4	5	6		8^{2}	9	10^{2}				7			11													6,000
17	S	22 " 1906	Watford	H	0-0	2-0	1	2	3	4	5	6		8^{1}	9	10^{1}				7			11													4,500
18	Tu	25 " 1906	Northampton Town	H	3-1	3-1	1	2	3	4	5	6		8	9^{1}	10^{2}				7			11													10,000
19	W	26 " 1906	Queens Park Rangers	A	0-1	1-1	1	2^{1}	3	4	5	6		8	9	10				7			11													6,000
20	Th	27 " 1906	Northampton Town	A	1-1	1-1	1	2	3	4	5	6		8	9	10^{1}				7			11													3,000
21	S	29 " 1906	Fulham	A	1-1	1-1	1	2^{1}	3	4	5	6		8	9	10				7			11													12,000
22	S	5 Jan 1907	Southampton	H	1-0	1-1	1	2	3	4	5	6^{1}		8	9	10				7			11													8,000
23	S	19 " 1907	West Ham United	A	1-2	1-3	1	2	3	4	5	6	7	8	9	10^{1}							11													7,000
24	S	26 " 1907	Tottenham Hotspur	H	1-0	5-0	1	2	3	4	5^{1}	6		8^{1}	9^{1}	10^{1}	11^{1}							7												5,000
25	S	16 Feb 1907	Luton Town	H	0-0	0-1	1	2	3	4	5	6		10	8					9			11	7												5,000
26	S	23 " 1907	Swindon Town	A	1-1	1-3	1	2	3	4	5	6		8^{1}	9					7		11			10											6,000
27	S	2 Mar 1907	Brentford	H	1-0	1-1	1	2	3	4	5	6		8^{1}	9					7		11			10											6,000
28	Th	7 " 1907	Bristol Rovers	H	0-0	1-0	1	2^{1}			5	6		8	9				4	7		11	10			3										3,500
29	S	9 " 1907	Millwall Athletic	A	1-0	2-1	1	2		4	5	6	7	8^{1}	9							11	10^{1}				3									5,000
30	S	16 " 1907	Leyton	H	0-1	1-1	1	2	3	4	5	6	7	8	9					10^{1}		11														5,000
31	S	23 " 1907	Portsmouth	A	0-0	0-1	1	2	3	4	5	6	7	8	9				4	10		11														12,000
32	F	29 " 1907	Queens Park Rangers	H	0-0	1-0	1	2	3	4		6	7	8	9				5	10^{1}								11								9,000
33	S	30 " 1907	New Brompton	H	1-1	2-2	1	2		5		6	7	8^{2}	9				4	10		11					3									4,500
34	S	6 Apr 1907	Plymouth Argyle	A	0-0	0-2	1	2		5		6		8	9			7	4	10		11					3									4,000
35	S	13 " 1907	Brighton & Hove Albion	H	0-1	1-2	1	2	3	4^{1}		6	7	9						10		11							5	8						2,500
36	S	20 " 1907	Reading	A	0-2	0-3	1	2	3			6	7	9	4					10		11							5	8						4,000
37	W	24 " 1907	Crystal Palace	A	1-0	1-0	1	2	3			6	7	8	9^{1}				4	5		11	10													2,000
38	S	27 " 1907	Watford	H	0-1	2-1	1	2	3	4	5	6		8	10					7			11								9^{2}					3,000

UNITED LEAGUE

NO.		DATE	OPPONENTS	V.	H-T	F-T	Thompson Fred	Archer Arthur	McEwen Jimmy	Livingstone Archie	Bushell William	Bemment Fred	Muir Robert	Wood Willie	Ronaldson Duncan	Ross David	Chalmers James	Birnie Alexander	Liddell Alexander	Lamberton George	Byrne John	Brindley Horace	King Horace	Gooch Percy	Baker Langford	Lamberton James	McLarney Patrick	Jex William	Bugg Walter	Taylor Wally	Martin George	Cannon John	Fitchie Tom	Fiske William	Own Goals	ATTD.
1	M	3 Sept 1906	Leyton	A	2-0	4-2	1	2	3	4		6		8^{2}	9^{1}	10	11	7^{1}	5																	–
2	M	10 " 1906	New Brompton	A	0-1	3-1	1	2	3	4	5	6		8	9^{1}	10^{2}	11	7																		–
3	W	26 " 1906	Watford	A	1-1	1-1	1	2	3	4	5			8	9	10	11^{1}	7			6															–
4	Th	4 Oct 1906	New Brompton	H	4-0	7-0	1	2	3		5^{1}	6			9^{1}	10^{2}	11	7	4	8^{2}															$–^{1}$	3,500
5	Th	11 " 1906	Brighton & Hove Albion	H	0-1	1-1	1			2^{1}	5	6		8		10	11		3	7	4			9												4,000
6	W	17 " 1906	Brighton & Hove Albion	A	3-2	3-4			3	2		5		8	9^{1}	10^{1}	11		4	7^{1}	6											1				2,000
7	Th	25 " 1906	Watford	H	2-0	3-0	1	2	3	4	5	6		8	9^{1}					7		11	10^{2}													2,000
8	Th	1 Nov 1906	Luton Town	H	2-0	4-0	1	2	3	4	5	6			9^{2}	10^{1}	11^{1}			7													8			3,000
9	M	12 " 1906	Luton Town	A	0-2	1-5	1	2	3	4	5	6		8	9^{1}		11			7			10													SMALL
10	W	28 " 1906	Crystal Palace	A	0-0	2-2	1	2		4	5	6		9		10^{1}	11	7					8^{1}			3										2,000
11	W	20 Feb 1907	Hastings & St. Leonards	A	0-2	1-3	1	2		5		6		10	8		11		4	7				9^{1}		3										2,000
12	Th	11 Apr 1907	Crystal Palace	H	0-0	0-2	1	2	3	6				8	9			7		10		11				4			5							FEW
13	M	15 " 1907	Leyton	H	0-0	0-0	1		3			6	7	9	4					10		11				2			5	8						FEW
14	Th	18 " 1907	Hastings & St. Leonards	H	4-0	4-1		2				6	7		9^{3}							11	10			3	4		5	8^{1}				1		SMALL

F.A. CUP

NO.		DATE	OPPONENTS	V.	H-T	F-T	Thompson Fred	Archer Arthur	McEwen Jimmy	Livingstone Archie	Bushell William	Bemment Fred	Muir Robert	Wood Willie	Ronaldson Duncan	Ross David	Chalmers James	Birnie Alexander	Liddell Alexander	Lamberton George	Byrne John	Brindley Horace	King Horace	Gooch Percy	Baker Langford	Lamberton James	McLarney Patrick	Jex William	Bugg Walter	Taylor Wally	Martin George	Cannon John	Fitchie Tom	Fiske William	Own Goals	ATTD.
1	S	12 Jan 1907	Hastings & St. Leonards (1st Round)	H	1-0	3-1	1	2^{1}	3	4	5	6		8	9	10^{2}				7			11													4,387
2	S	2 Feb 1907	West Bromwich Albion (2nd Round)	A	0-1	0-1	1	2	3	4	5	6		8	9	10	11							7												25,400

1906–07 APPEARANCES & GOALS

	SOUTHERN LGE APPR.	SOUTHERN LGE GLS	UNITED LEAGUE APPR.	UNITED LEAGUE GLS	F.A. CUP APPR.	F.A. CUP GLS
Thompson Fred	38	–	12	–	2	–
Archer Arthur	37	4	11	–	2	1
Bemment Fred	37	1	12	–	2	–
Ronaldson Duncan	37	8	12	11	2	–
Wood Willie	37	12	11	2	2	–
Livingstone Archie	34	1	11	1	2	–
McEwen Jimmy	34	–	10	–	2	–
Bushell William	32	1	8	1	2	–
Lamberton George	29	6	9	3	1	–
Ross David	24	19	8	7	2	2
Chalmers James	14	2	10	2	1	–
King Horace	14	1	4	3	1	–
Brindley Horace	12	–	4	–		
Muir Robert	11	–	2	–		
Liddell Alexander	7	–	5	–		
Birnie Alexander	6	–	6	1		
McLarney Patrick	3	–	1	–		
Baker Langford	2	–				
Bugg Walter	2	–	3	–		
Gooch Percy	2	–	2	1	1	–
Taylor Wally	2	–	2	1		
Byrne John	1	–	3	–		
Jex William	1	–				
Lamberton James	1	–	5	–		
Martin George	1	2				
Cannon John			1	–		
Fitchie Tom			1	–		
Fiske William			1	–		
Own Goals				1		

SOUTHERN LEAGUE

1906–07	P	W	D	L	F	A	PTS
Fulham	38	20	13	5	58	32	53
Portsmouth	38	22	7	9	64	36	51
Brighton & Hove Albion	38	18	9	11	53	43	45
Luton Town	38	18	9	11	52	52	45
West Ham United	38	15	14	9	60	41	44
Tottenham Hotspur	38	17	9	12	63	45	43
Millwall Athletic	38	18	6	14	71	50	42
Norwich City	**38**	**15**	**12**	**11**	**57**	**48**	**42**
Watford	38	13	16	9	46	43	42
Brentford	38	17	8	13	57	56	42
Southampton	38	13	9	16	49	56	35
Reading	38	14	6	18	57	47	34
Leyton	38	11	12	15	38	60	34
Bristol Rovers	38	12	9	17	55	54	33
Plymouth Argyle	38	10	13	15	43	50	33
New Brompton	38	12	9	17	47	59	33
Swindon Town	38	11	11	16	43	54	33
Queens Park Rangers	38	11	10	17	47	55	32
Crystal Palace	38	8	9	21	46	66	25
Northampton Town	38	5	9	24	29	88	19

UNITED LEAGUE

1906–07	P	W	D	L	F	A	PTS
Crystal Palace	14	8	5	1	39	20	21
Brighton & Hove Albion	14	6	6	2	33	26	18
Luton Town	14	8	1	5	23	27	17
Norwich City	**14**	**6**	**4**	**4**	**34**	**22**	**16**
Hastings & St. Leonards	14	6	2	6	27	24	14
Leyton	14	3	4	7	24	27	10
New Brompton	14	3	3	8	24	35	9
Watford	14	3	1	10	15	38	7

1907–08 SOUTHERN LEAGUE

NO.		DATE	OPPONENTS	V.	H-T	F-T	Thompson Fred	Jones Albert	McEwan Jimmy	Hutchison Harry	Bushell William	Livingstone Archie	Muir Robert	Young James	Bauchop James	Smith Wally	Allsopp Tommy	Newlands Gerry	Roney Peter	Whiteman Bobby	Lamberton George	Divine Alex	Jex William	Coxhead Ernie	Pegg Joe	Simpson Vivian	Cutmore Jack	Taylor Wally	Rayner Walter	Martin George	Flanagan John	Bellamy James	Randall Theo	Dunning Cyril	ATTD.
1	M	2 Sept 1907	Portsmouth	H	2-0	4-0	1	2	3	4	5	6	7	8[1]	9[1]	10[1]	11[1]																		6,000
2	S	7 " 1907	Brighton & Hove Albion	H	1-1	1-2	1	2	3	4	5	6	7	8	9[1]	10	11																		9,000
3	S	14 " 1907	Portsmouth	A	0-0	1-1	1		3	4	5	6	7	8[1]	9	10	11	2																	8,000
4	S	21 " 1907	Bradford Park Avenue	H	1-0	2-0	1		3	4	5	6	7	8	9[1]	10	11[1]	2																	9,000
5	S	28 " 1907	Millwall Athletic	A	1-2	1-6	1		3	4	5	6	7	8	9[1]	10	11	2																	8,000
6	S	5 Oct 1907	Brentford	H	1-1	3-2			3	5		4	7	8	10[1]		11[1]	2	1	6	9[1]														7,000
7	S	12 " 1907	Bristol Rovers	A	2-1	2-2			3	5		4	7	8	9	10[2]	11	2	1	6															7,000
8	S	19 " 1907	Leyton	H	0-0	1-1			3	5		4	7	8[1]	9	10	11	2	1	6															5,000
9	S	26 " 1907	Reading	A	0-0	1-2			3	5		4	7	8[1]			11	2	1	6		9	10												6,500
10	S	2 Nov 1907	Watford	H	2-0	2-0			3	5		4	7	8			11	2	1	6		9[1]	10[1]												4,500
11	S	9 " 1907	New Brompton	A	0-1	1-2			3	5			4	8			9	2	1	6			10[1]	7	11										7,000
12	S	16 " 1907	Northampton Town	A	0-0	1-0			3	4	5			8[1]	11		9	2	1	6			10	7											5,000
13	S	23 " 1907	Southampton	H	0-1	0-1			3	4	5		9	8			11	2	1	6				7		10									5,000
14	S	30 " 1907	Plymouth Argyle	A	0-1	0-1			3	4	5			8	9			2	1	6			10	7	11										10,000
15	S	7 Dec 1907	West Ham United	H	1-1	1-1			3	5		4		8[1]	9		11	2	1	6				7			10								5,000
16	S	14 " 1907	Queens Park Rangers	A	1-2	1-3			3	6	5	4		8	9[1]		11	2	1					7			10								6,000
17	S	21 " 1907	Tottenham Hotspur	H	1-0	2-1			3	6	5	4	7		9[2]		11	2	1								10	8							5,000
18	W	25 " 1907	Crystal Palace	H	0-1	0-1			3	6	5		7	8	9		11	2	1	4							10								9,143
19	Th	26 " 1907	Luton Town	A	0-0	0-0			3	6	5		7	9		10	11	2	1	4								8							7,000
20	S	28 " 1907	Swindon Town	A	1-0	1-1			3	6	5		7	9		10	11	2	1	4								8[1]							4,000
21	S	4 Jan 1908	Brighton & Hove Albion	A	0-0	0-1	1			5		4	7	9			11	2		6			10					8	3						5,000
22	S	18 " 1908	Bradford Park Avenue	H	1-1	1-1			3	6	5		7	9	10[1]		11	2	1	4	8														10,000
23	S	25 " 1908	Millwall Athletic	H	0-1	0-1				6	5	2	7	9	10		11	2	1	6								8							3,500
24	S	8 Feb 1908	Bristol Rovers	H	0-0	0-0			3		5	4	7	8	10		11	2	1	6										9					3,500
25	S	15 " 1908	Leyton	A	0-1	0-2			3		5	4	7	8				2	1	6			10		11					9					3,000
26	S	22 " 1908	Reading	H	0-0	0-0	1		3	4	5				9		11	2		6	8			7							10				3,000
27	S	29 " 1908	Watford	A	0-1	0-1	1			4	5	2			9		11	2		6	8			7							10				3,000
28	S	7 Mar 1908	New Brompton	H	1-1	2-1	1		3		5	4			10[1]		11	2		6	9			7							8[1]				3,000
29	M	9 " 1908	Brentford	A	0-2	1-2			3		5	4			9		11	2	1	6			10[1]	7							8				3,000
30	S	14 " 1908	Northampton Town	H	1-0	2-1	1		3		5	4			9[1]		11	2		6				7							10	8[1]			4,000
31	S	21 " 1908	Southampton	A	0-0	3-0	1		3		5	4					11[2]	2		6				7							10	8[1]	9		4,000
32	S	28 " 1908	Plymouth Argyle	H	1-0	2-1	1		3		5	4					9[1]	2		6				7	11						10	8[1]			6,000
33	S	4 Apr 1908	West Ham United	A	0-1	0-3	1		3		5	4					9	2		6				7	11						10	8			7,000
34	S	11 " 1908	Queens Park Rangers	H	0-1	0-1		3			5	4					11	2	1	6				7							10	8		9	6,000
35	S	18 " 1908	Tottenham Hotspur	A	0-2	0-3	1		3	5		4				10	11	2		6				7								8		9	10,000
36	M	20 " 1908	Crystal Palace	A	0-2	1-2	1	2		5		6				8		3		4	11[1]				7								9	10	14,000
37	Tu	21 " 1908	Luton Town	H	6-0	6-1		3		4	5[1]	2					11		1	6[1]	9[2]		10	7										8[2]	5,000
38	S	25 " 1908	Swindon Town	H	0-1	3-1		2	3		5	4					11[1]		1	6	9[1]			7							10			8[1]	4,000

F.A. CUP

NO.		DATE	OPPONENTS	V.	H-T	F-T	Thompson Fred	Jones Albert	McEwan Jimmy	Hutchison Harry	Bushell William	Livingstone Archie	Muir Robert	Young James	Bauchop James	Smith Wally	Allsopp Tommy	Newlands Gerry	Roney Peter	Whiteman Bobby	Lamberton George	Divine Alex	Jex William	Coxhead Ernie	Pegg Joe	Simpson Vivian	Cutmore Jack	Taylor Wally	Rayner Walter	Martin George	Flanagan John	Bellamy James	Randall Theo	Dunning Cyril	ATTD.
1	S	11 Jan 1908	The Wednesday (1st Round)	H	1-0	2-0			3	6	5	4	7	9	10[1]		11[1]	2	1									8							10,366
2	S	1 Feb 1908	Fulham (2nd Round)	A	0-2	1-2			3		5	4	7	9	10		11[1]	2	1	6			8												20,000

1907–08 APPEARANCES & GOALS

	SOUTHERN LGE APPR.	SOUTHERN LGE GLS	F.A. CUP APPR.	F.A. CUP GLS
Allsopp Tommy	35	7	2	2
Newlands Gerry	34	–	2	–
McEwan Jimmy	32	–	2	–
Whiteman Bobby	31	1	1	–
Livingstone Archie	29	–	2	–
Bushell William	28	1	2	–
Hutchison Harry	28	–	1	–
Young James	24	6	2	–
Roney Peter	23	–	2	–
Bauchop James	22	11	2	1
Muir Robert	21	–	2	–
Coxhead Ernie	18	–		
Thompson Fred	15	–		
Smith Wally	11	3		
Flanagan John	10	1		
Jex William	9	3	1	–
Lamberton George	8	5		
Bellamy James	6	3		
Jones Albert	6	–		
Pegg Joe	6	–		
Dunning Cyril	5	3		
Taylor Wally	5	1	1	–
Cutmore Jack	4	–		
Divine Alex	2	1		
Martin George	2	–		
Randall Theo	2	–		
Rayner Walter	1	–		
Simpson Vivian	1	–		

SOUTHERN LEAGUE

1907–08	P	W	D	L	F	A	PTS
Queens Park Rangers	38	21	9	8	82	57	51
Plymouth Argyle	38	19	11	8	50	31	49
Millwall Athletic	38	19	8	11	49	32	46
Crystal Palace	38	17	10	11	54	51	44
Swindon Town	38	16	10	12	55	40	42
Bristol Rovers	38	16	10	12	59	56	42
Tottenham Hotspur	38	17	7	14	59	48	41
Northampton Town	38	15	11	12	50	41	41
Portsmouth	38	17	6	15	63	52	40
West Ham United	38	15	10	13	47	48	40
Southampton	38	16	6	16	51	60	38
Reading	38	15	6	17	55	50	36
Bradford Park Avenue	38	12	12	14	53	54	36
Watford	38	12	10	16	47	59	34
Brentford	38	14	5	19	49	52	33
Norwich City	**38**	**12**	**9**	**17**	**46**	**49**	**33**
Brighton & Hove Albion	38	12	8	18	46	59	32
Luton Town	38	12	6	20	33	56	30
Leyton	38	8	11	19	51	73	27
New Brompton	38	9	7	22	44	75	25

1908–09 SOUTHERN LEAGUE

NO.		DATE	OPPONENTS	V.	H-T	F-T	Roney Peter	Newlands Gerry	McEwan Jimmy	Tomlinson James	Wagstaffe Teddy	Whiteman Bobby	Coxhead Ernie	Flanagan John	Smith John	Silor William	Allsopp Tommy	Livingstone Archie	Rayner Walter	Porter George	Dunning Cyril	Swann Charles	Druce Walter	Church Walter	Beale Robert	Martin George	Pegg Joe	Craig Charles	French Charlie	Reynolds Walter	Bushell William	Divine Alex	Long Tommy	Gunton Sam	Bacon Sam	Milnes Fred	Hunt Ernest	Sims George	Randall Theo	Cutmore Jack	Brooks Arthur	McQueen Hugh	Chambers Horace		Own Goals	ATTD.
1	W	2 Sept 1908	Luton Town	A	0-0	0-4	1	2	3	4	5	6	7	8	9	10	11																												4,000
2	S	5 " 1908	Swindon Town	A	1-6	2-10	1	2	3	4	5	6	7^1	8	9	10^1	11																												5,000
3	S	12 " 1908	Portsmouth	H	0-0	0-0	1	2	3	5		6	7	8	9	10	11	4																											6,700
4	S	19 " 1908	Exeter City	A	1-3	2-3	1	2		5		6	7	8		10^2	11	4	3	9																									6,000
5	S	26 " 1908	Northampton Town	H	1-0	1-0	1	2		5		6	7		9	10	11	4	3		8^1																								6,095
6	W	30 " 1908	Crystal Palace	A	0-2	0-4	1	2		5		6	7		9	10	11	4	3		8																								4,900
7	S	3 Oct 1908	New Brompton	A	0-1	0-2	1	2		5		6	7		9	10	11		3		8	4																							6,000
8	S	10 " 1908	Millwall Athletic	H	0-1	2-2	1			4	5	6	7	10	9		11^1		3		8^1		2																						6,000
9	Th	15 " 1908	Crystal Palace	H	1-0	2-0	1	2		4	5	6		7	9^1	10	11		3		8^1																								5,000
10	S	24 " 1908	Coventry City	H	2-0	2-0	1	2		4	5	6		7	9^1	10	11		3		8^1																								5,000
11	S	31 " 1908	Bristol Rovers	A	0-2	0-2	1	2		4	5	6		7	9		11		3		8			10																					10,000
12	S	7 Nov 1908	Watford	H	1-1	2-2	1	2		4	5	6		7	9	10	11		3		8^2																								5,000
13	S	14 " 1908	Plymouth Argyle	H	0-0	0-0		2		4	5	6		7		10	11		3		8				1	9																			5,000
14	S	21 " 1908	Reading	A	1-1	1-7		2		4	5	6	7	8	9^1	10			3						1		11																		9,000
15	S	28 " 1908	Southampton	H	2-1	2-2		2		4	5	6	7		11^1	10	9^1				8				1			3																	7,100
16	S	5 Dec 1908	Leyton	A	0-2	0-2		2		4	5	6	7		9	10	11				8				1			3																	6,000
17	S	12 " 1908	West Ham United	H	1-3	6-3	1	2		4^1	5			7^1	10^1		11^1				8^2							3	6	9															4,000
18	S	19 " 1908	Brighton & Hove Albion	A	0-3	0-3	1			9	4			7	10		11				8							3	6	2	5														3,000
19	F	25 " 1908	Queens Park Rangers	A	1-1	2-2	1			9	5	6	7^1	10			11											3	4^1	2		8													20,000
20	S	26 " 1908	Brentford	H	1-0	6-1	1			9^1	5	6	7	10			11^1				8^3							3	4	2															$-^1$	9,104
21	M	28 " 1908	Luton Town	H	2-1	3-2	1	4		9^1		6	7	10			11				8^2							3	5	2																6,431
22	S	2 Jan 1909	Swindon Town	H	0-0	0-0	1	4		9	5	6		10			11				8							3		2		7													6,437
23	S	9 " 1909	Portsmouth	A	0-0	1-1	1	4		9^1	5	6		10			11							8				3	2			7													8,000
24	S	23 " 1909	Exeter City	H	2-0	2-0	1	4		9^1		6			10^1		11	5			8							3	2				7												5,830
25	S	30 " 1909	Northampton Town	A	1-1	2-1	1	4				6		8	9^2	10		5					2				11		3				7												7,000
26	S	13 Feb 1909	Millwall Athletic	A	0-2	1-2	1	4			5	6		8	9	10	11^1						2						3				7												5,000
27	S	27 " 1909	Coventry City	A	0-1	0-2	1	4			5	6			9	10	11	3						8					2				7												5,000
28	S	6 Mar 1909	Bristol Rovers	H	2-0	4-1	1	4								10^1				7	8^1					9	11	3^1	6^1	2	5														4,000
29	S	13 " 1909	Watford	A	0-0	1-1	1	4			5			8		10				7						9^1	11	3	6	2															3,000
30	S	20 " 1909	Plymouth Argyle	A	0-1	1-2	1	4^1			5			8	9	10											11	3	6	2			7												6,000
31	S	27 " 1909	Reading	H	0-0	0-1	1	4			5		7		10		11				8					9		3	6	2															7,500
32	W	31 " 1909	Southend United	A	0-2	0-3	1	4		9	5			8	10		11			7								3	6	2															2,000
33	S	3 Apr 1909	Southampton	A	0-1	0-1	1	4			5			8	10		11			7						9		3	6	2															5,000
34	F	9 " 1909	Brentford	A	1-0	1-3	1			9^1	5				8	10	11	4		7								3	6	2															10,000
35	S	10 " 1909	Leyton	H	1-1	6-1		4					7^1		8^2	10^3	11			9			2		1				6	3	5														5,100
36	M	12 " 1909	Queens Park Rangers	H	3-0	3-2		4					7		9^3	10	11			8			2		1				6	3	5														9,300
37	S	17 " 1909	West Ham United	A	0-2	1-2		4					7^1		9	10				8					1		11	3	6	2	5														5,000
38	Th	22 " 1909	Southend United	H	0-0	2-0		4								10	11	6			8^1		2	7	1					3	5			9											$-^1$	3,000
39	S	24 " 1909	Brighton & Hove Albion	H	1-0	1-1		4					7		9^1	10	11	6							1			3		2	5				8											5,000
40	M	26 " 1909	New Brompton	H	0-0	0-0		4					7			11	9	6			8				1			3		2	5				10											2,400

UNITED LEAGUE

NO.		DATE	OPPONENTS	V.	H-T	F-T	Roney Peter	Newlands Gerry	McEwan Jimmy	Tomlinson James	Wagstaffe Teddy	Whiteman Bobby	Coxhead Ernie	Flanagan John	Smith John	Silor William	Allsopp Tommy	Livingstone Archie	Rayner Walter	Porter George	Dunning Cyril	Swann Charles	Druce Walter	Church Walter	Beale Robert	Martin George	Pegg Joe	Craig Charles	French Charlie	Reynolds Walter	Bushell William	Divine Alex	Long Tommy	Gunton Sam	Bacon Sam	Milnes Fred	Hunt Ernest	Sims George	Randall Theo	Cutmore Jack	Brooks Arthur	McQueen Hugh	Chambers Horace		Own Goals	ATTD.
1	W	9 Sept 1908	Lincoln City	A	1-0	1-0	1			4	5	6	7		9^1	10	11		3		8															2										FEW
2	Th	17 " 1908	Lincoln City	H	0-0	1-0	1	2		5		6	7		9^1	10	11	4	3		8																								2,000
3	Th	24 " 1908	Coventry City	A	2-0	5-2	1	2		5^1		6		8^1	9^2	10^1	11	4															7			3										MOD
4	M	9 Nov 1908	Walsall	A	1-1	1-2	1	2			5	6		8	9^1	10	11		3														7	4													POOR
5	Th	10 Dec 1908	Rotherham Town	H	3-0	4-0	1			9		6		7	10^2		11^1				8^1							3	4	2	5														–
6	Th	17 " 1908	Peterborough City	A	0-0	4-0	1	5			4				10^1	8	9^1		3								11^1		6	2			7^1												1,000
7	Th	21 Jan 1909	Walsall	H	2-2	3-3										10^2		5				4	2	8	1		11			3			7	6			9^1									1,500
8	Th	4 Feb 1909	Peterborough City	H	2-1	2-4															8^1		2		1		11				5			4			10	3	6	7	9^1					2,000
9	M	15 Mar 1909	Rotherham Town	A	1-2	1-6	1	4		5					9^1	10													3	6	2			7		8							11				1,500
10	Th	1 Apr 1909	Coventry City	H	2-1	3-1	1					6					11^1				8	4^1	2	9									7	5	10^1								3			2,000
11	Th	8 " 1909	Grantham Avenue	A	0-0	1-1	1					6		8		10	11^1	4					3	7		9				2	5														–
12	Th	29 " 1909	Grantham Avenue	H	5-0	7-0		4								10^1		6						7	1		11	3		2	5			9^5	8^1											SMALL

F.A. CUP

NO.		DATE	OPPONENTS	V.	H-T	F-T	Roney Peter	Newlands Gerry	McEwan Jimmy	Tomlinson James	Wagstaffe Teddy	Whiteman Bobby	Coxhead Ernie	Flanagan John	Smith John	Silor William	Allsopp Tommy	Livingstone Archie	Rayner Walter	Porter George	Dunning Cyril	Swann Charles	Druce Walter	Church Walter	Beale Robert	Martin George	Pegg Joe	Craig Charles	French Charlie	Reynolds Walter	Bushell William	Divine Alex	Long Tommy	Gunton Sam	Bacon Sam	Milnes Fred	Hunt Ernest	Sims George	Randall Theo	Cutmore Jack	Brooks Arthur	McQueen Hugh	Chambers Horace		Own Goals	ATTD.
1	S	16 Jan 1909	Reading (1st Round)	S	0-0	0-0	1	4		9	5	6		7	10		11				8							3	2																	15,732
2	W	20 " 1909	Reading (Replay)	A	0-0	1-1	1	4		9	5	6	7	8	10		11^1											3	2																	8,393
3	M	25 " 1909	Reading a.e.t (2nd Replay)	V	1-0	3-2	1	4		9^1	5	6	7	8^1	10		11^1											3	2																	6,000
4	S	6 Feb 1909	Liverpool (2nd Round)	A	1-0	3-2	1	4		9^1	5	6		8	10		11^1											3	2				7												32,000
5	S	20 " 1909	Bristol City (3rd Round)	A	0-1	0-2	1	4		9	5	6		8	10		11											3	2				7												24,008

S – PLAYED AT STAMFORD BRIDGE V – PLAYED AT VILLA PARK

1908–09 APPEARANCES & GOALS

	SOUTHERN LGE APPR.	SOUTHERN LGE GLS	UNITED LGE APPR.	UNITED LGE GLS	F.A. CUP APPR.	F.A. CUP GLS
Newlands Gerry	35	1	6	–	5	–
Allsopp Tommy	34	5	8	4	5	3
Roney Peter	30	–	9	–	5	–
Smith John	29	14	7	9	5	1
Silor William	27	7	9	4		
Tomlinson James	26	6	5	1	5	2
Wagstaffe Teddy	25	–	3	–	5	–
Whiteman Bobby	25	–	7	–	5	–
Flanagan John	24	1	4	1	5	1
Dunning Cyril	21	15	5	2	1	–
Craig Charles	20	1	3	–	5	–
French Charlie	20	2	3	–	5	–
Coxhead Ernie	20	4	2	–	2	–
Reynolds Walter	19	–	6	–		
Livingstone Archie	11	–	5	–		
Rayner Walter	11	–	4	–		
Beale Robert	10	–	3	–		
Porter George	9	–				
Bushell William	8	–	4	–		
Druce Walter	6	–	4	–		

	SOUTHERN LGE APPR.	SOUTHERN LGE GLS	UNITED LGE APPR.	UNITED LGE GLS	F.A. CUP APPR.	F.A. CUP GLS
Pegg Joe	6	–	4	1		
Long Tommy	5	–	6	1	2	–
Martin George	5	1	1	–		
Church Walter	4	–	4	–		
Divine Alex	3	–				
McEwan Jimmy	3	–				
Bacon Sam	2	–	3	2		
Gunton Sam	1	–	5	5		
Swann Charles	1	–	2	1		
Brooks Arthur			1	1		
Chambers Horace			1	–		
Cutmore Jack			1	–		
Hunt Ernest			2	1		
McQueen Hugh			1	–		
Milnes Fred			2	–		
Randall Theo			1	–		
Sims George			1	–		
Own Goals		2				

SOUTHERN LEAGUE

1908–09	P	W	D	L	F	A	PTS
Northampton Town	40	25	5	10	90	45	55
Swindon Town	40	22	5	13	96	55	49
Southampton	40	19	10	11	67	58	48
Portsmouth	40	18	10	12	68	60	46
Bristol Rovers	40	17	9	14	60	63	43
Exeter City	40	18	6	16	56	65	42
New Brompton	40	17	7	16	48	59	41
Reading	40	11	18	11	60	57	40
Luton Town	40	17	6	17	59	60	40
Plymouth Argyle	40	15	10	15	46	47	40
Millwall Athletic	40	16	6	18	59	61	38
Southend United	40	14	10	16	52	54	38
Leyton	40	15	8	17	52	55	38
Watford	40	14	9	17	51	64	37
Queens Park Rangers	40	12	12	16	52	50	36
Crystal Palace	40	12	12	16	62	62	36
West Ham United	40	16	4	20	56	60	36
Brighton & Hove Albion	40	14	7	19	60	61	35
Norwich City	**40**	**12**	**11**	**17**	**59**	**75**	**35**
Coventry City	40	15	4	21	64	91	34
Brentford	40	13	7	20	59	74	33

UNITED LEAGUE

1908–09	P	W	D	L	F	A	PTS
Rotherham Town	12	8	1	3	39	16	17
Lincoln City	12	7	2	3	32	18	16
Norwich City	**12**	**7**	**2**	**3**	**33**	**19**	**16**
Walsall	12	5	2	5	23	25	12
Coventry City	12	5	1	6	27	31	11
Peterborough City	12	4	1	7	18	34	9
Grantham Avenue	12	1	1	10	12	41	3

1909–10 SOUTHERN LEAGUE

NO.	DAY	DATE	OPPONENTS	V.	H-T	F-T	Beale Robert	Hampson Billy	Reynolds Walter	Wolstenholme Sam	Bushell William	French Charlie	Barnfather Percy	Dunning Cyril	Ronaldson Duncan	Hubbard Arthur	Allsopp Tommy	Cooch George	Craig Charles	Newlands Gerry	Gooch Percy	Livingstone Archie	Chick John	Bacon Sam	Riddell Fred	Druce Walter	Rayner William	Chambers Horace	Baker Bob	Gunton Sam	Fielding Arthur	Swann Charles	Taylor Wally	ATTD.
1	W	1 Sept 1909	Luton Town	A	0-1	1-1	1	2	3	4	5	6	7	8^1	9	10	11																	4,000
2	S	4 " 1909	West Ham United	H	0-1	1-3	1	2	3	4	5	6	7^1	8	9	10	11																	8,000
3	Th	9 " 1909	Luton Town	H	1-0	6-0		2		4	5		7	8^1	10^1		11^1	1	3	6	9^3													4,000
4	S	11 " 1909	Portsmouth	A	1-1	1-2		2		4	5		7	8	10		11	1		6	9^1	3												8,000
5	S	18 " 1909	Bristol Rovers	H	1-0	1-1		2		4	5	3	7	8	10	9^1	11	1		6														7,500
6	S	25 " 1909	Exeter City	A	1-1	2-2		2		4		3	7	8^1		10^1	11	1		5	9		6											8,000
7	S	2 Oct 1909	Brentford	A	0-0	1-0	1	2		4	5		7	8		10	11^1		3		9	6												7,000
8	Th	7 " 1909	Brighton & Hove Albion	H	0-0	1-1	1	2		4	5		7	8		10	11		3		9^1	6												3,554
9	S	9 " 1909	Coventry City	H	0-1	0-1	1			4	5	3	7	8	9		11		2	6				10										6,199
10	W	13 " 1909	Crystal Palace	A	0-2	0-4	1		3	4	5		11		9	10			2	6			8		7									5,000
11	S	16 " 1909	Watford	A	0-1	1-1	1			4	5		11^1	8		10			2	3	9		6		7									4,000
12	S	23 " 1909	Reading	H	2-1	4-2	1			4	5		7	8^1		10	11		3	2	9^3		6											4,536
13	M	25 " 1909	Crystal Palace	H	0-0	1-0	1			4	5		7	8^1		10	11		3	2	9		6											12,078
14	S	30 " 1909	Southend United	A	2-2	5-2	1			4^1	5		7	8^2		10	11^1		3	2	9^1		6											5,000
15	S	13 Nov 1909	Plymouth Argyle	A	0-1	0-1	1			4	5		7		8	10	11		3	2	9		6											7,000
16	S	20 " 1909	Southampton	H	0-2	0-3	1			4	5		7	10	8		11		3	2	9		6											5,736
17	S	27 " 1909	Croydon Common	A	0-1	0-2	1			4	5		7	9	8		11			3		6		8		2								4,500
18	W	1 Dec 1909	Brighton & Hove Albion	A	0-1	0-5	1			4	5		7			10			3			6				2	8	9	11					2,000
19	S	4 " 1909	Millwall Athletic	H	3-1	4-1				4	5		7			8	11	1	3		9^1	2					10^3	6						4,000
20	S	11 " 1909	New Brompton	A	1-3	2-5				4	5		7			8	11	1		2	9	3					10^2	6						6,000
21	S	25 " 1909	Queens Park Rangers	A	0-1	0-1		2		5			7	8			11	1	3	4	9						10	6						20,000
22	M	27 " 1909	Leyton	H	1-1	1-1		2		5			7	8			11	1	3	4	9						10^1	6						10,150
23	Tu	28 " 1909	Swindon Town	A	0-3	1-7		2		5			7		8		11	1	3	4	9^1						10	6						7,000
24	S	8 Jan 1910	West Ham United	A	0-3	0-5		2		4	5		7		8		11	1	3	4	9						10							6,000
25	S	29 " 1910	Bristol Rovers	A	0-0	0-1				4	5		7		8	10		1		3	9		6			2				11				3,000
26	S	5 Feb 1910	Exeter City	H	0-0	1-0				4	5		7			8	11			3	10^1		6			2	9				1			2,851
27	S	12 " 1910	Brentford	H	2-1	5-1				4	5		7^1			9^1	11^1			3			6	8^1		2	10^1				1			5,000
28	S	26 " 1910	Watford	H	2-1	2-2				4	5		7^1			9	11	1		3			6	8		2	10^1							3,856
29	S	5 Mar 1910	Reading	A	0-2	0-3	1			4	5					9				3	11		6	8	7	2	10							–
30	S	12 " 1910	Southend United	H	1-0	3-0	1			5						9^1	11		3	2			6	8^1	7		10^1					4		3,033
31	S	19 " 1910	Leyton	A	1-1	1-2	1			5						9	11		3	2			6	8^1			10					4	7	–
32	F	25 " 1910	Portsmouth	H	1-0	2-1	1			5						9	11		3	2			6	8^1	7^1		10					4		7,223
33	S	26 " 1910	Plymouth Argyle	H	0-2	2-4	1				5		7			9^1	11						6	8		2	10^1	3				4		4,800
34	M	28 " 1910	Queens Park Rangers	H	0-0	0-0	1			5	4				9		11		3	2			6		7		10						8	9,826
35	Tu	29 " 1910	Swindon Town	H	0-2	1-3	1			5	4				9		11^1		3				6			2	10			7			8	5,000
36	S	2 Apr 1910	Southampton ‡	A	0-0	0-0	1			5						8	11		3				6	7		2	9			4				3,000
37	S	9 " 1910	Croydon Common	H	1-0	4-2	1			5	4					9^1	11		3				6	8		2	10^2			7^1				3,000
38	M	11 " 1910	Coventry City	A	1-0	1-2	1			5	4					9	11		3				6	8^1			10	2		7				2,000
39	Th	14 " 1910	Northampton Town	H	0-0	2-0	1	2		5	4				10^1		11^1		3				6	8	7		9							3,000
40	S	16 " 1910	Millwall Athletic	A	0-3	0-3	1			5			11		9	10							6	8	7	2		3				4		4,000
41	S	23 " 1910	New Brompton	H	1-0	1-0	1	2		5	4		7		9		11		3				6	8			10^1							3,500
42	S	30 " 1910	Northampton Town	H	0-1	1-3	1	2		5			7		9		11		3				6^1				10					4	8	7,000

F.A. CUP

NO.	DAY	DATE	OPPONENTS	V.	H-T	F-T	Beale Robert	Hampson Billy	Reynolds Walter	Wolstenholme Sam	Bushell William	French Charlie	Barnfather Percy	Dunning Cyril	Ronaldson Duncan	Hubbard Arthur	Allsopp Tommy	Cooch George	Craig Charles	Newlands Gerry	Gooch Percy	Livingstone Archie	Chick John	Bacon Sam	Riddell Fred	Druce Walter	Rayner William	Chambers Horace	Baker Bob	Gunton Sam	Fielding Arthur	Swann Charles	Taylor Wally	ATTD.
1	S	15 Jan 1910	Queens Park Rangers (1st Round)	H	0-0	0-0				4	5		7		8		11	1	3	2	9	6								10				9,295
2	W	19 " 1910	Queens Park Rangers (Replay)	A	0-1	0-3				4	5		7		8	10	11	1	3	2	9							6						6,000

‡ CITY HAD ONLY 10 MEN

1909–10 APPEARANCES & GOALS

	SOUTHERN LGE APPR.	SOUTHERN LGE GLS	F.A. CUP APPR.	F.A. CUP GLS
Wolstenholme Sam	41	1	2	–
Allsopp Tommy	36	6	2	–
Barnfather Percy	32	4	2	–
Bushell William	32	–	2	–
Beale Robert	28	–		
Craig Charles	28	–	2	–
Hubbard Arthur	28	6	1	–
Newlands Gerry	27	–	2	–
Chick John	26	1		
Rayner William	23	13		
Gooch Percy	20	12	2	–
Ronaldson Duncan	19	2	2	–
Dunning Cyril	17	7		
Bacon Sam	15	5		
Hampson Billy	15	–		
Cooch George	12	–	2	–
Druce Walter	12	–		
Chambers Horace	9	–	1	–
Riddell Fred	8	1		
Livingstone Archie	7	–	1	–
Swann Charles	6	–		
French Charlie	5	–		
Gunton Sam	5	1	1	–
Taylor Wally	4	–		
Reynolds Walter	3	–		
Fielding Arthur	2	–		
Baker Bob	1	–		

SOUTHERN LEAGUE

1909–10	P	W	D	L	F	A	PTS
Brighton & Hove Albion	42	23	13	6	69	28	59
Swindon Town	42	22	10	10	92	46	54
Queens Park Rangers	42	19	13	10	56	47	51
Northampton Town	42	22	4	16	90	44	48
Southampton	42	16	16	10	64	55	48
Portsmouth	42	20	7	15	70	63	47
Crystal Palace	42	20	6	16	69	50	46
Coventry City	42	19	8	15	71	60	46
West Ham United	42	15	15	12	69	56	45
Leyton	42	16	11	15	60	46	43
Plymouth Argyle	42	16	11	15	61	54	43
New Brompton	42	19	5	18	76	74	43
Bristol Rovers	42	16	10	16	37	48	42
Brentford	42	16	9	17	50	58	41
Luton Town	42	15	11	16	72	92	41
Millwall Athletic	42	15	7	20	45	59	37
Norwich City	**42**	**13**	**9**	**20**	**59**	**78**	**35**
Exeter City	42	14	6	22	60	69	34
Watford	42	10	13	19	51	76	33
Southend United	42	12	9	21	51	90	33
Croydon Common	42	13	5	24	52	96	31
Reading	42	7	10	25	38	73	24

1910–11 SOUTHERN LEAGUE

NO.		DATE	OPPONENTS	V.	H-T	F-T	Beale Robert	Hampson Billy	Mackenzie Jock	Wilkinson Fred	Wolstenholme Sam	Chick William	Jobling Len	Ingham William	Makin Tommy	Whiteside Eddie	Allsopp Tommy	Levi Harold	Askew Leslie	Rayner William	McCall John	Bibby Ralph	Hemnell Russell	Kirkman Albert	Taylor Wally	Mosley Fred	Donnelly George	Stringfellow Arthur	Holt Henry	Mellor William	Own Goals	ATTD.
1	S	3 Sept 1910	Bristol Rovers	A	0-0	1-0	1	2	3	4	5	6	7	8[1]	9	10	11															6,000
2	S	10 " 1910	Millwall Athletic	H	0-0	1-1	1	2	3	4	5	6	7	8[1]	9	10		11														8,000
3	S	17 " 1910	Crystal Palace	A	2-0	3-0	1	2	3	4	5[1]	6	7	8[1]	9	10		11[1]														6,000
4	S	24 " 1910	Queens Park Rangers	H	0-0	0-0	1	2	3	4	5	6	7	8	9	10		11														9,000
5	S	1 Oct 1910	Berntford	A	0-2	0-2	1	2	3	4		6	7	8	9	10		11	5													10,000
6	S	8 " 1910	West Ham United	H	0-0	2-0	1	2	3	4[1]	5	6	7	8		10		11		9[1]												8,000
7	S	15 " 1910	Leyton	A	1-0	2-0	1	2	3	4	5	6	7	8[1]		10		11		9[1]												5,000
8	S	22 " 1910	Luton Town	H	1-1	3-2	1	2	3	4	5	6	7	8[1]		10[1]		11		9[1]												9,000
9	S	29 " 1910	Watford	A	0-1	0-3	1	2	3	4	5	6	7	8		10		11		9												3,000
10	S	5 Nov 1910	Portsmouth	H	2-0	2-0	1	2	3	4	5[1]	6	7	8[1]		10		11		9												8,000
11	S	12 " 1910	Plymouth Argyle	A	0-1	0-1	1	2	3	4	5		7	8		6		11		10	9											4,000
12	S	19 " 1910	Northampton Town	H	0-0	1-0	1	2	3	4[1]	5	6	7	8		10		11		9												4,802
13	S	26 " 1910	Southampton	A	0-2	1-2	1	2	3	4			7	8[1]	9	10		11	5			6										6,000
14	S	3 Dec 1910	Brighton & Hove Albion	H	1-1	1-1	1	2	3	4	5		7	8	9[1]	10		11				6										4,737
15	S	10 " 1910	Southend United	A	0-0	0-1	1	2	3	4	5		7	8	9			11		10		6										2,000
16	S	17 " 1910	Exeter City	A	1-3	1-3	1	2	3	4	5		9	8[1]		10		11				6	7									4,000
17	S	24 " 1910	Coventry City	H	1-0	5-2	1	2	3	4	5	6	9[2]	8[1]		10		11[1]					7								–[1]	3,261
18	M	26 " 1910	Swindon Town	H	1-2	1-2	1	2	3	4	5[1]	6	9	8		10		11					7									12,500
19	Tu	27 " 1910	Swindon Town	A	1-3	1-5	1	2	3	4		6	9	8[1]		10		11	5				7									8,000
20	S	31 " 1910	Bristol Rovers	H	0-0	1-0	1	2	3	4	5	6	7	8		10[1]				9	11											4,000
21	S	7 Jan 1911	Millwall Athletic	A	0-1	0-1	1		3	4		6	7	8	9	10		11	5					2								10,000
22	S	21 " 1911	Crystal Palace	H	0-1	0-1	1		3	4		6	7	8		10		11	5	9				2								4,000
23	S	28 " 1911	Queens Park Rangers	A	0-1	1-1	1	2[1]	3	4		6	7	8		10			5		11				9							6,000
24	S	11 Feb 1911	West Ham United	A	1-1	1-2	1	2	3	4		6	7	8		10		11	5	9[1]												12,000
25	S	18 " 1911	Leyton	H	0-0	0-0	1	2	3	4		6	7	8	10	11			5							9						5,006
26	S	25 " 1911	Luton Town	A	1-2	1-3	1	2	3	4[1]		6	7	8				11	5	10						9						6,000
27	S	4 Mar 1911	Watford	H	1-0	5-1	1	2	3[1]	4			7	8[1]		10[1]	11		5			6				9[2]						4,500
28	S	11 " 1911	Portsmouth	A	0-0	1-1	1	2	3	4	5		7	8		10	11					6				9[1]						5,000
29	S	18 " 1911	Plymouth Argyle	H	2-1	3-1	1	2	3	4	5		7	8[1]		10[1]	11					6				9[1]						5,000
30	S	25 " 1911	Northampton Town	A	0-2	0-4	1	2	3	4	5		7	8		10	11					6				9						10,000
31	S	1 Apr 1911	Southampton	H	1-0	2-1	1	2	3	4	5[1]		7	8[1]	9	10	11					6										5,009
32	S	8 " 1911	Brighton & Hove Albion	A	0-1	0-2	1	2	3	4	5		7	8		10	11					6				9						5,000
33	F	14 " 1911	New Brompton	A	0-1	1-1	1	2	3	4	5		7	8		10[1]	11					6				9						7,000
34	S	15 " 1911	Southend United	H	0-0	1-0	1	2	3	4	5		7	8		10	11					6				9[1]						5,500
35	M	17 " 1911	New Brompton	H	1-0	2-1	1	2	3	4	5		7	8[1]		10[1]	11										6	9				11,000
36	Tu	18 " 1911	Brentford	H	1-0	1-0	1	2	3[1]	4	5		11	8		10						6						9	7			3,500
37	S	22 " 1911	Exeter City	H	0-0	0-0	1	2	3	4	5		11	8		10						6						9	7			4,000
38	S	29 " 1911	Coventry City	A	0-2	1-3		2[1]	3	4	5		7	8		10					11	6						9		1		8,000

F.A. CUP

NO.		DATE	OPPONENTS	V.	H-T	F-T	Beale Robert	Hampson Billy	Mackenzie Jock	Wilkinson Fred	Wolstenholme Sam	Chick William	Jobling Len	Ingham William	Makin Tommy	Whiteside Eddie	Allsopp Tommy	Levi Harold	Askew Leslie	Rayner William	McCall John	Bibby Ralph	Hemnell Russell	Kirkman Albert	Taylor Wally	Mosley Fred	Donnelly George	Stringfellow Arthur	Holt Henry	Mellor William	Own Goals	ATTD.
1	S	14 Jan 1911	Sunderland (1st Round)	H	2-1	3-1	1	9[2]	3	4		6	7	8		10[1]			5		11			2								11,426
2	S	4 Feb 1911	Bradford City (2nd Round)	A	0-1	1-2	1	9	3	5		6	7	8[1]		10			4			11		2								23,288

1910–11 APPEARANCES & GOALS

	SOUTHERN LGE APPR.	SOUTHERN LGE GLS	F.A. CUP APPR.	F.A. CUP GLS
Ingham William	38	14	2	1
Jobling Leonard	38	2	2	–
Mackenzie Jock	38	2	2	–
Wilkinson Fred	38	3	2	–
Beale Robert	37	–	2	–
Hampson Billy	36	2	2	2
Whiteside Eddie	36	6	2	1
Wolstenholme Sam	28	4		
Levi Harrold	22	2		
Chick William	21	–	2	–
Bibby Ralph	15	–	1	–
Rayner William	12	4		
Makin Tommy	11	1		
Allsopp Tommy	10	–		
Askew Leslie	10	–	2	–
Mosley Fred	9	5		
Hemnell Russell	4	–		
McCall John	4	–	1	–
Strinfgellow Arthur	4	–		
Holt Henry	2	–		
Kirkman Albert	2	–	2	–
Donnelly George	1	–		
Mellor William	1	–		
Taylor Wally	1	–		
Own Goals		1		

SOUTHERN LEAGUE

1910–11	P	W	D	L	F	A	PTS
Swindon Town	38	24	5	9	80	31	53
Northampton Town	38	18	12	8	54	27	48
Brighton & Hove Albion	38	20	8	10	58	36	48
Crystal Palace	38	17	13	8	55	48	47
West Ham United	38	17	11	10	63	46	45
Queens Park Rangers	38	13	14	11	52	41	40
Leyton	38	16	8	14	57	52	40
Plymouth Argyle	38	15	9	14	54	55	39
Luton Town	38	15	8	15	67	63	38
Norwich City	**38**	**15**	**8**	**15**	**46**	**48**	**38**
Coventry City	38	16	6	16	65	68	38
Brentford	38	14	9	15	41	42	37
Exeter City	38	14	9	15	51	53	37
Watford	38	13	9	16	49	65	35
Millwall Athletic	38	11	9	18	42	54	31
Bristol Rovers	38	10	10	18	42	55	30
Southampton	38	11	8	19	42	67	30
New Brompton	38	11	8	19	34	65	30
Southend United	38	10	9	19	47	64	29
Portsmouth	38	8	11	19	34	53	27

1911–12 SOUTHERN LEAGUE

NO.		DATE	OPPONENTS	V.	H-T	F-T	Beale Robert	Hampson Billy	Mackenzie Jock	Wilkinson Freddy	Wolstenholme Sam	Donnelly George	Jobling Leonard	Ingham William	Potter Cecil	Woods Harry	Birchall Dick	Pilch George	Bibby Ralph	Peacock James	Stringfellow Arthur	Potts John	Pearson James	Taylor Wally	Mellor William	Valiant James	Curtin Charles	Cutmore Jack	Turner Walter	ATTD.
1	S	2 Sept 1911	Bristol Rovers	H	0-0	0-0	1	2	3	4	5	6	7	8	9	10	11													8,000
2	S	9 " 1911	Swindon Town	A	1-3	3-5	1	2	3	4	5	6	7	8	9^{1}	10^{1}	11^{1}													8,000
3	W	13 " 1911	Reading	A	0-0	1-2	1	2	3	4	5	6	7	8	9^{1}	10	11													2,000
4	S	16 " 1911	Northampton Town	H	1-0	1-0	1	2	3	4	5	6	7	8	9	10^{1}	11													6,000
5	S	23 " 1911	Brighton & Hove Albion	A	0-0	1-1	1	2	3	4	5	6	7	8	9^{1}	10	11													8,000
6	S	30 " 1911	Stoke	H	1-0	2-1	1	2	3	4^{1}	5	6	7	8	9	10^{1}	11													4,400
7	S	7 Oct 1911	Coventry City	A	0-2	0-3	1	2	3	4	5	6	7	8	9	10	11													9,000
8	S	14 " 1911	Leyton	H	2-0	2-0	1	2	3		5		7	8	9^{2}	10	11	4	6											5,000
9	S	21 " 1911	Luton Town	A	0-0	1-0	1	2	3	4	5	6	7	8^{1}	9	10	11													5,000
10	S	28 " 1911	Crystal Palace	A	0-1	0-6	1	2	3	4	5	6	7	8	9	10	11													5,000
11	S	4 Nov 1911	Southampton	H	0-0	0-0	1	2	3	4	5		7	8	9	10			6	11										5,000
12	S	11 " 1911	Plymouth Argyle	A	0-0	0-3	1	2	3	4	5		7	8		19			6	11	9									3,000
13	S	25 " 1911	Watford	A	1-2	1-3	1	2			5		7	8		10^{1}			6	11	9	3	4							5,000
14	S	2 Dec 1911	New Brompton	H	0-0	1-0	1	2^{1}			5		7	8	9	10			6		11	3	4							5,000
15	S	9 " 1911	Exeter City	A	0-0	0-1	1	2	3		5		7	8		10	11		4		9		6							2,000
16	S	16 " 1911	Brentford	H	1-0	2-0	1	2	3		5		7	8^{1}	9	10			6		11^{1}		4							5,000
17	S	23 " 1911	Queens Park Rangers	A	1-1	2-1	1	2	3		5		7^{1}	8	11^{1}	10			6		9		4							8,000
18	M	25 " 1911	Millwall Athletic	H	0-1	0-2	1	2	3		5		7	8	11	10			6		9		4							8,000
19	Tu	26 " 1911	Millwall Athletic	A	0-0	0-0		2	3	7	5			8		10	11		6				4	9	1					6,000
20	S	30 " 1911	Bristol Rovers	A	1-2	1-4		2	3					8^{1}	9	10	11		6				4		1	5	7			6,000
21	S	6 Jan 1912	Swindon Town	H	1-2	4-3	1	2	3		5			8^{1}		10^{1}	9^{1}		6		11		4^{1}				7			5,000
22	S	20 " 1912	Northampton Town	A	0-0	0-1	1	2	3		5		7	8		10	9		6		11		4							5,000
23	S	27 " 1912	Brighton & Hove Albion	H	1-0	2-0	1	2	3	4	5		7	8		10	9^{1}		6		11^{1}									5,000
24	S	3 Feb 1912	Stoke	A	0-0	1-1	1	2	3	4	5		7	8		10^{1}	9		6		11									6,000
25	S	10 " 1912	Coventry City	H	0-0	1-1	1	2	3	4	5		7	8		10	9		6		11^{1}									5,200
26	S	17 " 1912	Leyton	A	0-0	0-1	1	2	3	4	5			8		10	9		6		11						7			5,000
27	S	24 " 1912	Luton Town	H	1-1	2-2	1	2^{1}	3	4	5			8		10	9^{1}		6		11						7			4,500
28	S	2 Mar 1912	Crystal Palace	A	0-0	1-1	1	2	3	4	5			8^{1}	11	10	9		6									7		6,300
29	S	9 " 1912	Southampton	A	1-1	1-1	1	2	3	4				8	11	10	9^{1}		6				5					7		4,000
30	S	16 " 1912	Plymouth Argyle	H	0-1	1-1	1	2	3	4	5			8^{1}	11	10	9		6										7	6,000
31	S	23 " 1912	Reading	H	0-0	3-1	1	2	3	4	5			8	11	10	9^{2}		6								7^{1}			4,000
32	S	30 " 1912	Watford	H	0-0	1-1	1	2	3	4	5			8^{1}	11	10	9		6								7			4,000
33	F	5 Apr 1912	West Ham United	A	0-1	0-4		2	3	4	5			8	11	10	9		6						1		7			10,000
34	S	6 " 1912	New Brompton	A	0-1	1-3		2	3	4	5			8	11	10	9		6						1		7^{1}			7,000
35	M	8 " 1912	West Ham United	H	2-2	2-2		2	3	4	5			8	11^{1}	10	9		6						1		7^{1}			11,000
36	S	13 " 1912	Exeter City	H	0-1	1-1		2	3	4^{1}	5			8	11	10	9	6							1		7			4,000
37	S	20 " 1912	Brentford	A	0-2	0-3		2	3	4	5			8	11	10	9		6						1		7			4,000
38	S	27 " 1912	Queens Park Rangers	H	1-0	1-1		2	3	4	5			8	11	10^{1}			6		9				1		7			6,000

F.A. CUP

NO.		DATE	OPPONENTS	V.	H-T	F-T	Beale Robert	Hampson Billy	Mackenzie Jock	Wilkinson Freddy	Wolstenholme Sam	Donnelly George	Jobling Leonard	Ingham William	Potter Cecil	Woods Harry	Birchall Dick	Pilch George	Bibby Ralph	Peacock James	Stringfellow Arthur	Potts John	Pearson James	Taylor Wally	Mellor William	Valiant James	Curtin Charles	Cutmore Jack	Turner Walter	ATTD.
1	S	13 Jan 1912	Blackburn Rovers (1st Round)	A	1-2	1-4	1	2	3		5			8		10	9^{1}		6		11		4				7			22,947

1911–12 APPEARANCES & GOALS

	SOUTHERN LGE APPR.	SOUTHERN LGE GLS	F.A. CUP APPR.	F.A. CUP GLS
Hampson Billy	38	2	1	–
Ingham William	38	7	1	–
Woods Harry	38	7	1	–
Mackenzie Jock	36	–	1	–
Wolstenholme Sam	36	–	1	–
Beale Robert	30	–	1	–
Birchall Dick	30	7	1	1
Bibby Ralph	28	–	1	–
Wilkinson Fred	28	2		
Potter Cecil	27	7		
Jobling Leonard	22	1		
Stringfellow Arthur	15	3	1	–
Curtin Charles	12	3	1	–
Pearson James	11	1	1	–
Donnelly George	9	–		
Mellor William	8	–		
Peacock James	3	–		
Cutmore Jack	2	–		
Pilch George	2	–		
Potts John	2	–		
Taylor Wally	1	–		
Turner Walter	1	–		
Valiant James	1	–		

SOUTHERN LEAGUE

1911–12	P	W	D	L	F	A	PTS
Queens Park Rangers	38	21	11	6	59	35	53
Plymouth Argyle	38	23	6	9	63	31	52
Northampton Town	38	22	7	9	82	41	51
Swindon Town	38	21	6	11	82	50	48
Brighton & Hove Albion	38	19	9	10	73	35	47
Coventry City	38	17	8	13	66	54	42
Crystal Palace	38	15	10	13	70	46	40
Millwall Athletic	38	15	10	13	60	57	40
Watford	38	13	10	15	56	68	36
Stoke	38	13	10	15	51	63	36
Reading	38	11	14	13	43	59	36
Norwich City	**38**	**10**	**14**	**14**	**40**	**60**	**34**
West Ham United	38	13	7	18	64	69	33
Brentford	38	12	9	17	60	65	33
Exeter City	38	11	11	16	48	62	33
Southampton	38	10	11	17	46	63	31
Bristol Rovers	38	9	13	16	41	62	31
New Brompton	38	11	9	18	35	72	31
Luton Town	38	9	10	19	49	61	28
Leyton	38	7	11	20	27	62	25

1912–13 SOUTHERN LEAGUE

NO.		DATE	OPPONENTS	V.	H-T	F-T	Mellor William	Hampson Billy	Mackenzie Jock	Pearson James	Wolstenholme Sam	Woodlands Arthur	Bauchop Will	Ingham William	Hughes William	Woods Harry	Petter Cecil	Houghton Jack	Turner Walter	Valient James	Travis Aaron	Beevers Tom	Osborne Alf	Sutcliffe Percy	Taylor Wally	Hall William	Lansdale Joe	Curtin Charles	ATTD.
1	M	2 Sept 1912	Stoke	A	1-0	1-0	1	2	3	4	5	6	7	8^{1}	9	10	11												7,000
2	Th	5 " 1912	Stoke	H	1-0	1-0	1	2	3	4	5	6	7	8^{1}	9	10	11												4,000
3	S	7 " 1912	Queens Park Rangers	A	0-1	0-1	1	2	3	4	5	6	7	8	9	10	11												12,000
4	S	14 " 1912	Brentford	H	1-0	2-0	1	2	3	4	5^{1}	6	7	8	9	10^{1}	11												5,000
5	S	21 " 1912	Millwall Athletic	A	0-1	0-1	1	2	3	4	5	6	7	8	9	10	11												25,000
6	S	28 " 1912	Bristol Rovers	H	1-1	1-1	1		3	4	5	6		8^{1}	9	10	11	2	7										6,000
7	S	5 Oct 1912	Swindon Town	A	0-1	0-3	1		3	4	5	6	7	8	9	10	11	2											6,000
8	S	12 " 1912	Portsmouth	H	0-0	0-0	1	2	3		5	6	7	8		10	11			4	9								5,500
9	S	19 " 1912	Exeter City	A	0-1	0-1	1	2	3	4	5	6	7	8		10	11				9								5,000
10	S	26 " 1912	West Ham United	H	1-0	2-0	1	2	3	4	5	6	11	8^{1}	9^{1}	10	7												7,000
11	S	2 Nov 1912	Brighton & Hove Albion	A	0-1	2-2	1	2	3	4	5	6	11	8^{1}	9^{1}	10	7												5,000
12	S	9 " 1912	Coventry City	H	0-1	0-3	1	2	3	4	5	6	11	8	9	10	7												5,000
13	S	16 " 1912	Watford	A	0-1	0-2	1	2	3	4	5	6	11		9	10	7					8							4,500
14	S	23 " 1912	Merthyr Town	H	0-0	0-0	1	2	3	4	5	6	11	8	9	10	7												5,000
15	S	30 " 1912	Crystal Palace	A	0-1	0-1	1	2	3	4	5	6	11	8	9	10	7												5,000
16	S	7 Dec 1912	Plymouth Argyle	H	0-2	0-3	1	2	3	4	5	6	11	8	9	10	7												4,000
17	S	14 " 1912	Southampton	A	0-1	0-1	1		3	4	5	6	11	8	7	10	9	2											6,000
18	S	21 " 1912	Reading	H	1-1	3-1	1		3		5	6	11		9^{1}	10	8^{1}	2					7^{1}	4					4,000
19	W	25 " 1912	Gillingham	A	0-0	0-1	1		3		5	6	11		7	10	8	2					9	4					4,000
20	Th	26 " 1912	Gillingham	H	3-0	4-0	1		3		5^{1}	6	11		7	10^{1}	8	2					9^{2}	4					6,200
21	S	28 " 1912	Queens Park Rangers	H	1-0	2-0	1		3		5	6	11^{1}		8	10^{1}	7	2					9	4					6,000
22	S	4 Jan 1913	Brentford	A	0-0	0-1	1		3		5	6	11		8	10	7	2					9	4					3,000
23	S	18 " 1913	Millwall Athletic	H	1-0	2-0	1		3		5	6	11		8	10	7^{1}	2			9^{1}			4					5,800
24	S	25 " 1913	Bristol Rovers	A	1-1	1-2	1		3		5	6	11		8^{1}	10	7	2			9			4					7,000
25	S	8 Feb 1913	Swindon Town	H	0-1	0-2	1		3	5		6	11	8		10	7	2			9			4					6,000
26	S	15 " 1913	Portsmouth	A	0-1	0-2	1		3		5	6	11	8	9	10	7	2						4					8,000
27	S	22 " 1913	Exeter City	H	0-1	1-1	1		3		5	6	11		9^{1}	10	7	2			8			4					4,000
28	S	1 Mar 1913	West Ham United	A	1-2	1-2	1	2	3		5	6				10	7				9^{1}			4	8	11			8,000
29	S	8 " 1913	Brighton & Hove Albion	H	0-1	0-1		2	3		5	6				10	7				9			4	8	11	1		4,000
30	S	15 " 1913	Coventry City	A	0-1	0-3		2	3		5	6	11	8		10	9							4			1	7	5,000
31	S	22 " 1913	Watford	H	0-1	1-1	1	2	3		5	6	11	8		10	9^{1}							4				7	4,000
32	M	24 " 1913	Northampton Town	H	1-0	2-2	1	2^{1}	3		5	6	11	8		10	9							4				7^{1}	5,000
33	Tu	25 " 1913	Northampton Town	A	0-1	0-3	1	2	3			6	11	8	9	10		5						4				7	9,000
34	S	29 " 1913	Merthyr Town	A	1-0	2-2	1	2	3		5	6		8		10	9^{1}							4^{1}		11		7	3,000
35	S	5 Apr 1913	Crystal Palace	H	2-2	2-2	1	2	3		5	6		8		10^{2}	9							4		11		7	5,000
36	S	12 " 1913	Plymouth Argyle	A	0-0	1-3	1		3			6	11	8		10^{1}	9	2		5				4				7	9,000
37	S	19 " 1913	Southampton	H	1-0	3-0	1	9^{2}	3			6		8		10^{1}	11	2		5				4				7	5,000
38	S	26 " 1913	Reading	A	2-1	5-2	1	2	3			6	11	8^{2}		10	9^{2}			5^{1}				4				7	–

F.A. CUP

NO.		DATE	OPPONENTS		V.	H-T	F-T	Mellor William	Hampson Billy	Mackenzie Jock	Pearson James	Wolstenholme Sam	Woodlands Arthur	Bauchop Will	Ingham William	Hughes William	Woods Harry	Petter Cecil	Houghton Jack	Turner Walter	Valient James	Travis Aaron	Beevers Tom	Osborne Alf	Sutcliffe Percy	Taylor Wally	Hall William	Lansdale Joe	Curtin Charles	ATTD.
1	S	11 Jan 1913	Leicester Fosse	(1st Round)	A	0-0	0-0	ABANDONED AFTER 65 MINS. BECAUSE OF SNOWSTORM. SCORE WAS 0-0																						10,000
2	Th	16 " 1913	Leicester Fosse	(1st Round)	A	2-0	4-1	1		3		5^{1}	6^{1}	11		8^{1}	10	7	2					9^{1}	4					8,600
3	S	1 Feb 1913	Bristol Rovers	(2nd Round)	A	0-1	1-1	1		3		5	6	11		8	10^{1}		2			7		9	4					14,539
4	Th	6 " 1913	Bristol Rovers	a.e.t. (Replay)	H	0-1	2-2	1		3		5	6	11		8	10^{1}	7	2			9			4^{1}					13,173
5	M	10 " 1913	Bristol Rovers	(2nd Replay)	S	0-1	0-1	1		3		5	6	11		8	10		2					9	4				7	16,706

S – STAMFORD BRIDGE

1912–13 APPEARANCES & GOALS

	SOUTHERN LGE APPR.	SOUTHERN LGE GLS	F.A. CUP APPR.	F.A. CUP GLS
Mackenzie Jock	38	–	4	–
Woodland Arthur	38	–	4	1
Woods Harry	38	7	4	2
Potter Cecil	37	6	2	–
Mellor William	36	–	4	–
Wolstenholme Sam	33	2	4	1
Bauchop Will	32	1	4	–
Ingham William	27	7		
Hughes William	25	5	4	1
Hampson Billy	24	3		
Sutcliffe Percy	21	1	4	1
Pearson James	17	–		
Houghton Jack	16	–	4	–
Curtin Charles	9	1	1	–
Travis Aaron	8	2	2	–
Osborne Alf	5	3	3	1
Hall William	4	–		
Valiant James	4	1		
Lansdale Joe	2	–		
Taylor Wally	2	–		
Beevers Tom	1	–		
Turner Walter	1	–		

SOUTHERN LEAGUE

1912–13	P	W	D	L	F	A	PTS
Plymouth Argyle	38	22	6	10	77	36	50
Swindon Town	38	20	8	10	66	41	48
West Ham United	38	18	12	8	66	46	48
Queens Park Rangers	38	18	10	10	46	35	46
Crystal Palace	38	17	11	10	55	36	45
Millwall Athletic	38	19	7	12	62	43	45
Exeter City	38	18	8	12	48	44	44
Reading	38	17	8	13	59	55	42
Brighton & Hove Albion	38	13	12	13	48	47	38
Northampton Town	38	12	12	14	61	48	36
Portsmouth	38	14	8	16	41	49	36
Merthyr Town	38	12	12	14	42	60	36
Coventry City	38	13	8	17	53	59	34
Watford	38	12	10	16	43	50	34
Gillingham	38	12	10	16	36	53	34
Bristol Rovers	38	12	9	17	55	64	33
Southampton	38	10	11	17	40	72	31
Norwich City	**38**	**10**	**9**	**19**	**39**	**50**	**29**
Brentford	38	11	5	22	42	55	27
Stoke	38	10	4	24	39	75	24

1913–14 SOUTHERN LEAGUE

NO.		DATE	OPPONENTS	V.	H-T	F-T	Mellor William	Hampson Billy	Mackenzie Jock	Hill Frank	Kennedy James	Woodland Arthur	MacDonald George	Ingham William	Wolstenholme Arthur	Woods Harry	Potter Cecil	Sutcliffe Percy	Martin 'Pompey'	Bell George	Wilson Danny	Valiant James	Valentine Tommy	Osborne Alf	Landsdale Joe	Houghton Jack	Curtin Charles	Popham Reg	Ritchie George	Own Goals	ATTD.
1	Th	4 Sept 1913	Watford	H	1-1	3-1	1	2	3	4	5	6	7	8^1	9	10^1	11													$-^1$	6,000
2	S	6 " 1913	Northampton Town	H	1-1	1-1	1	2	3	4	5	6	7	8	9^1	10	11														7,000
3	W	10 " 1913	Watford	A	0-1	0-2	1	2	3	4	5	6	7	8	9	10	11														3,000
4	S	13 " 1913	Southend United	A	1-2	2-2	1	2	3			6	7	8	9^1	10^1	11	4	5												6,000
5	S	20 " 1913	Brighton & Hove Albion	H	0-1	1-1	1	2	3			6	7	8	10	9^1	11	4	5												7,000
6	S	27 " 1913	Portsmouth	A	0-1	0-1	1	2	3				7	8	10	9		4	5	6	11										12,000
7	S	4 Oct 1913	Millwall Athletic	H	0-0	2-2	1	2	3				7	8	10	9^1		4		6^1	11	5									6,000
8	S	11 " 1913	Exeter City	A	0-0	1-0	1	2^1	3				7		9	8	11	4		6	10	5									5,000
9	S	18 " 1913	Cardiff City	H	2-2	2-2	1	2	3				7		9	8^1	11^1	4		6	10	5									5,000
10	S	25 " 1913	Swindon Town	A	0-2	0-2	1	2	3				7		9	8	11	4		6		5	10								7,000
11	S	1 Nov 1913	Bristol Rovers	H	1-0	1-1	1	2	3		5		7		9^1	8	11	4		6	10										6,000
12	S	8 " 1913	Merthyr Town	A	0-0	0-0	1	2	3				7	8	9		11	4		6	10	5									5,000
13	S	15 " 1913	West Ham United	H	0-0	1-0	1	2	3				7	8^1	9		11	4		6	10	5									7,000
14	S	22 " 1913	Plymouth Argyle	A	0-1	0-2	1	2	3				7		9	8	11	4		6	10	5									8,000
15	S	6 Dec 1913	Reading	A	0-2	2-3	1	2	3				7^1		9	8	11^1	4		6	10	5									3,000
16	S	20 " 1913	Coventry City	A	0-1	2-1	1	2	3			6	7		9	8^1	11	4			10^1	5									5,000
17	Th	25 " 1913	Queens Park Rangers	A	0-1	1-1	1	2	3			6	7^1		10	8	11	4			9	5									20,000
18	F	26 " 1913	Queens Park Rangers	H	1-2	2-3	1	2	3			6	7		10	8	11^1	4			9^1	5									12,000
19	S	27 " 1913	Northampton Town	A	1-0	1-1	1	2	3			6	7	8	9	10		4			11^1	5									9,000
20	S	3 Jan 1914	Southend United	H	1-0	6-0	1	2	3			6	7^1		10^4	8	11	4	5					9^1							6,000
21	S	17 " 1914	Brighton & Hove Albion	A	0-1	2-4		2							10^1	8	11	4	5	6				9^1	1	3	7				5,000
22	S	24 " 1914	Portsmouth	H	0-0	0-0			3						10	8	7	4	5	6	11			9	1	2					4,500
23	S	31 " 1914	Southampton	H	2-1	2-1			3				7^1	8^1	10			4	5	6	11			9	1	2					5,000
24	S	7 Feb 1914	Millwall Athletic	A	1-1	2-2			3				7	8	9^2	10		4	5	6	11				1	2					15,000
25	S	14 " 1914	Exeter City	H	2-1	3-1			3				7	8		10^2	9	4	5	6	11				1	2				$-^1$	5,000
26	S	21 " 1914	Cardiff City	A	0-1	0-3			3				7	8	9	10			5	6	11				1	2		4			15,000
27	S	28 " 1914	Swindon Town	H	1-0	1-2			3				7	8		10^1		4	5	6	11				1	2			9		10,000
28	S	7 Mar 1914	Bristol Rovers	A	0-2	1-2							7	8	9	10		4^1	5	6	11				1	3		2			7,000
29	S	14 " 1914	Merthyr Town	H	2-1	5-2			3				7	8	9^2	10		4	5	6	11^3				1	2					4,000
30	S	21 " 1914	West Ham United	A	1-1	1-1			3				7	8	9^1	10		4	5	6	11				1	2					6,000
31	S	28 " 1914	Plymouth Argyle	H	1-0	1-1			3				7	8	9	10		4^1	5	6	11				1	2					6,000
32	Th	2 Apr 1914	Crystal Palace	H	0-0	0-0			3				7	8	9	10		4	5	6	11				1	2					5,000
33	S	4 " 1914	Southampton	A	0-1	0-2			3				7	8	9	10		4	5	6	11				1	2					5,000
34	F	10 " 1914	Gillingham	A	0-0	0-0			3	4			7	8		10			5	6	11		9		1	2					7,000
35	S	11 " 1914	Reading	H	0-0	0-0			3	4			7	8		10			5	6	11		9		1	2					6,000
36	M	13 " 1914	Gillingham	H	0-0	2-0			3					8		10	7		5	6	11		9^2		1	2		4			12,000
37	S	18 " 1914	Crystal Palace	A	0-0	0-3			3						10	8	7		5	6	11		9		1	2		4			9,000
38	S	25 " 1914	Coventry City	H	0-1	1-1			3					8		10^1	7	4	5	6	11		9		1	2					5,000

F.A. CUP

NO.		DATE	OPPONENTS	V.	H-T	F-T	Mellor William	Hampson Billy	Mackenzie Jock	Hill Frank	Kennedy James	Woodland Arthur	MacDonald George	Ingham William	Wolstenholme Arthur	Woods Harry	Potter Cecil	Sutcliffe Percy	Martin 'Pompey'	Bell George	Wilson Danny	Valiant James	Valentine Tommy	Osborne Alf	Landsdale Joe	Houghton Jack	Curtin Charles	Popham Reg	Ritchie George	Own Goals	ATTD.
1	S	29 Nov 1913	Walthamstow Grange (4th Qual Round)	H	2-0	6-0	1	2	3				7		9^2	8^3	11^1	4		6	10	5									5,500
2	S	13 Dec 1913	Halifax Town (5th Qual Round)	H	1-0	2-0	1	2	3				7			8	11^1	4	9	6	10^1	5									6,284
3	S	10 Jan 1914	Crystal Palace (1st Round)	A	0-1	1-2	1	2	3			6	7^1		10	8	11	4	5					9							8,888

SOUTHERN CHARITY CUP

NO.		DATE	OPPONENTS	V.	H-T	F-T	Mellor William	Hampson Billy	Mackenzie Jock	Hill Frank	Kennedy James	Woodland Arthur	MacDonald George	Ingham William	Wolstenholme Arthur	Woods Harry	Potter Cecil	Sutcliffe Percy	Martin 'Pompey'	Bell George	Wilson Danny	Valiant James	Valentine Tommy	Osborne Alf	Landsdale Joe	Houghton Jack	Curtin Charles	Popham Reg	Ritchie George	Own Goals	ATTD.
1	Th	20 Nov 1913	Gillingham (1st Round)	H	1-0	1-0	1	2	3		5		7	8^1	9		11	4		6	10										–
2	Th	19 Feb 1914	Queens Park Rangers (2nd Round)	H	2-0	3-0			3					8		10	9^2	4	5	6	11^1				1	2	7				2,035
3	M	16 Mar 1914	Coventry City (Semi Final)	W	0-1	0-3			3				7	8		10		4	5	6	11		9		1	2					–

W – AT WHITE HART LANE

1913–14 APPEARANCES & GOALS

	SOUTHERN LGE APPR.	SOUTHERN LGE GLS	F.A. CUP APPR.	F.A. CUP GLS	SOUTHERN CHARITY CUP APPR.	SOUTHERN CHARITY CUP GLS
Mackenzie Jock	36	–	3	–	3	–
Woods Harry	35	10	3	3	2	–
Macdonald George	33	4	3	1	2	–
Wolstenholme Arthur	32	13	2	2	2	–
Sutcliffe Percy	30	2	3	–	3	–
Wilson Danny	30	6	2	1	3	1
Bell George	28	1	2	–	3	–
Ingham William	25	3			3	1
Potter Cecil	23	3	3	2	2	2
Martin 'Pompey'	22	–	2	–	2	–
Hampson Billy	21	1	3	–	1	–
Mellor William	20	–	3	–	1	–
Houghton Jack	18	–			2	–
Landsale Joe	18	–			2	–
Valiant James	12	–	2	–		
Woodland Arthur	10	–	1	–		
Valentine Tommy	6	2				
Hill Frank	5	–				
Kennedy James	4	–			1	–
Osborne Alf	4	2	1	–		
Popham Reg	4	–				
Curtin Charles	1	–			1	–
Ritchie George	1	–				
Own Goals		2				

SOUTHERN LEAGUE

1913–14	P	W	D	L	F	A	PTS
Swindon Town	38	21	8	9	81	41	50
Crystal Palace	38	17	16	5	60	32	50
Northampton Town	38	14	19	5	50	37	47
Reading	38	17	10	11	43	36	44
Plymouth Argyle	38	15	13	10	46	42	43
West Ham United	38	15	12	11	61	60	42
Brighton & Hove Albion	38	15	12	11	43	45	42
Queens Park Rangers	38	16	9	13	45	43	41
Portsmouth	38	14	12	12	57	48	40
Cardiff City	38	13	12	13	46	42	38
Southampton	38	15	7	16	55	54	37
Exeter City	38	10	16	12	39	38	36
Gillingham	38	13	9	16	48	49	35
Norwich City	**38**	**9**	**17**	**12**	**49**	**51**	**35**
Millwall Athletic	38	11	12	15	51	56	34
Southend United	38	10	12	16	41	66	32
Bristol Rovers	38	10	11	17	46	67	31
Watford	38	10	9	19	50	56	29
Merthyr Town	38	9	10	19	38	61	28
Coventry City	38	6	14	18	43	68	26

1914–15 SOUTHERN LEAGUE

NO.		DATE	OPPONENTS	V.	H-T	F-T	Lansdale Joe	Houghton Jack	Mackenzie Jock	Collins Arthur	Martin 'Pompey'	Bell George	Valentine Tommy	Woods Harry	Potter Cecil	Ritchie George	Wilson Danny	Denoon John	Turner Arthur	Allen John	Woodland Arthur	Thompson George	Taylor Wally	Abbs Charles	Molyneux William	Humphreys Percy	Crossley Arthur	Frosdick Albert	Peacock James	Own Goals	ATTD.
1	S	5 Sept 1914	Cardiff City	A	0-0	0-1	1	2	3	4	5	6	7	8	9	10	11														5,000
2	W	9 " 1914	Crystal Palace	H	2-0	2-1	1	2	3	4	5	6	7	8	9	10[2]	11														2,000
3	S	12 " 1914	Exeter City	H	3-1	3-1		2	3	4	5	6	9[1]	8[2]	7	19	11	1													3,000
4	S	19 " 1914	Luton Town	A	1-1	1-1		2	3	4	5	6		8	7	10	11	1	9[1]												5,000
5	S	26 " 1914	Portsmouth	H	0-0	0-0		2	3	4	5	6		8	7	10	11	1	9												5,000
6	S	3 Oct 1914	Swindon Town	A	0-2	0-4			3	4	5		7	8		10	11	1	9	2	6										5,000
7	S	10 " 1914	Southend United	H	0-1	1-1		2	3	4	5	6	7	8		10	11	1	9[1]												5,000
8	S	17 " 1914	Queens Park Rangers	A	0-1	1-1		2	3	4			7	10	8[1]		11	1	9		6	5									6,000
9	S	24 " 1914	Millwall Athletic	H	0-2	1-3		2	3	4				10	8[1]		11	1			6	5	7	9							5,000
10	S	31 " 1914	Bristol Rovers	A	1-2	2-4			3	5			7	10[2]	11	8		1	9		6		2		4						6,000
11	S	7 Nov 1914	Croydon Common	H	1-1	1-1	1		3	4			7	10	8		11		9[1]	2	5				6						4,000
12	S	14 " 1914	Reading	A	0-0	0-1	1		3	4	8		7	10	9		11			2	5				6						5,000
13	S	21 " 1914	Southampton	H	0-0	0-0	1		3		5		7	10		8	11			2	6				4	9					4,000
14	S	28 " 1914	Northampton Town	A	0-1	1-4	1		3		5			10	7	8[1]	11		9	2	6				4						4,000
15	S	5 Dec 1914	Watford	H	1-0	2-0	1		3	4					7[1]	10[1]	11			2	5		8		6	9					3,000
16	S	12 " 1914	Plymouth Argyle	A	1-1	2-2	1		3	4					7[1]	10	11			2	5		8		6	9[1]					1,000
17	S	19 " 1914	West Ham United	H	0-0	0-0	1		3	4					7	10	11		9	2	5		8		6						4,000
18	F	25 " 1914	Gillingham	A	1-2	3-3	1		3	4					7[1]	10[1]	9[1]			2	5		8		6		11				2,000
19	S	26 " 1914	Gillingham	H	3-0	4-0	1		3	4					7	10	9[2]			2	5		8		6		11[2]				3,000
20	M	28 " 1914	Crystal Palace	A	0-1	1-2	1		3		4					10	9[1]		7	2	5		8		6		11				1,000
21	S	2 Jan 1915	Cardiff City	H	0-1	2-1	1		3	4					7	10	9[2]			2	5		8		6		11				4,000
22	S	16 " 1915	Exeter City	A	0-2	0-2	1		3	4				11	7	10	9			2	5		8		6						2,000
23	S	23 " 1915	Luton Town	H	4-1	5-1	1		3	4				9[2]	7	10[1]				2	5		8[2]		6			11			3,000
24	S	6 Feb 1915	Swindon Town	H	1-0	1-1	1		3		6				7[1]	10	9			2	5		8		4			11			4,000
25	S	13 " 1915	Southend United	A	1-2	1-4	1		3	4					7	10	9[1]			2	5		8		6			11			2,500
26	S	6 Mar 1915	Bristol Rovers	H	1-1	5-1	1		3	4	6				7[1]	10[1]	9[2]			2	5		8[1]					11			2,000
27	S	13 " 1915	Croydon Common	A	0-1	1-4	1		3	4	6			8	7	10	9[1]			2	5							11			5,000
28	S	20 " 1915	Reading	H	0-1	0-2	1		3	4	6			11	7	10	9			2	5		8								4,000
29	W	24 " 1915	Queens Park Rangers	H	1-0	2-1	1	4	3		5			8	7[1]	10[1]	11			2			9		6						2,000
30	S	27 " 1915	Southampton	A	0-1	2-2	1		3	4	6			11	7	10	9			2	5[1]		8							–[1]	5,000
31	F	2 Apr 1915	Brighton & Hove Albion	A	0-1	2-2	1		3	4	6			11	7[1]	10[1]			9	2	5		8								5,000
32	S	3 " 1915	Northampton Town	H	0-0	0-1	1		3	4	6				7	10			9	2	5		8					11			4,000
33	M	5 " 1915	Brighton & Hove Albion	H	1-1	2-1	1		3	4[1]	6				7[1]	10			9	2	5		8						11		6,000
34	Tu	6 " 1915	Millwall Athletic	A	1-0	1-0	1		3		6				7	10			9	2	5		8		4			11		–[1]	3,000
35	S	10 " 1915	Watford	A	0-1	1-2	1		3		6			11	7	10			9	2	5		8[1]		4						–
36	S	17 " 1915	Plymouth Argyle	H	1-0	2-0	1		3		6			11	7[1]	10[1]			9	2	5		8		4						4,000
37	S	24 " 1915	West Ham United	A	0-1	1-1	1		3		6			11	7	10[1]			9	2	5		8		4						7,000
38	S	1 May 1915	Portsmouth	A	0-0	0-0	1		3		6			11	7	10			9	2	5		8		4						–

F.A. CUP

NO.		DATE	OPPONENTS	V.	H-T	F-T	Lansdale Joe	Houghton Jack	Mackenzie Jock	Collins Arthur	Martin 'Pompey'	Bell George	Valentine Tommy	Woods Harry	Potter Cecil	Ritchie George	Wilson Danny	Denoon John	Turner Arthur	Allen John	Woodland Arthur	Thompson George	Taylor Wally	Abbs Charles	Molyneux William	Humphreys Percy	Crossley Arthur	Frosdick Albert	Peacock James	Own Goals	ATTD.
1	S	9 Jan 1915	Nottingham Forest (1st Round)	A	2-1	4-1	1		3	4	6			11	7[1]	10[1]	9[1]			2	5		8[1]								8,040
2	S	30 " 1915	Tottenham Hotspur (2nd Round)	H	2-2	3-2	1	4	3		6			11	7	10	9[2]			2	5		8[1]								9,758
3	S	20 Feb 1915	Bradford City (3rd Round)	A	0-0	1-1	1	4	3		6			11	7[1]	19	9			2	5		8								20,877
4	S	27 " 1915	Bradford City (Replay)	H	0-0	0-0	1	4	3		6			11	7	10	9			2	5		8								8,043
5	W	3 Mar 1915	Bradford City (2nd Replay)	S	0-0	0-2	1	4	3		6				7	10	9			2	5		8					11			1,000

S – PLAYED AT SINCILBANK, LINCOLN

SOUTHERN CHARITY CUP

NO.		DATE	OPPONENTS	V.	H-T	F-T	Lansdale Joe	Houghton Jack	Mackenzie Jock	Collins Arthur	Martin 'Pompey'	Bell George	Valentine Tommy	Woods Harry	Potter Cecil	Ritchie George	Wilson Danny	Denoon John	Turner Arthur	Allen John	Woodland Arthur	Thompson George	Taylor Wally	Abbs Charles	Molyneux William	Humphreys Percy	Crossley Arthur	Frosdick Albert	Peacock James	Own Goals	ATTD.
1	W	18 Nov 1914	Gillingham (1st Round)	A	3-1	4-1	1	3			5			10[2]		8	11		9[2]	2	6		7		4						SMALL

1914–15 APPEARANCES & GOALS

	SOUTHERN LGE APPR.	SOUTHERN LGE GLS	F.A. CUP APPR.	F.A. CUP GLS	SOUTHERN CHARITY CUP APPR.	SOUTHERN CHARITY CUP GLS
Mackenzie Jock	38	–	5	–		
Potter Cecil	34	11	5	2		
Ritchie George	34	11	5	1	1	–
Woodland Arthur	31	1	5	–	1	–
Lansdale Joe	30	–	5	–	1	–
Allen John	29	–	5	–	1	–
Collins Arthur	28	1	1	–		
Wilson Danny	28	10	5	3	1	–
Martin 'Pompey'	25	–	5	–	1	–
Taylor Wally	25	4	5	2	1	–
Woods Harry	25	6	4	–	1	2
Molyneux William	22	–			1	–
Turner Arthur	18	3			1	2
Valentine Tommy	10	1				
Houghton Jack	9	–	4	–	1	–
Denoon John	8	–				
Frosdick Albert	7	–	1	–		
Bell George	6	–				
Crossley Arthur	4	2				
Humphreys Percy	3	1				
Thompson George	2	–				
Abbs Charles	1	–				
Peacock James	1	–				
Own Goals		2				

SOUTHERN LEAGUE

1914–15	P	W	D	L	F	A	PTS
Watford	38	22	8	8	68	46	52
Reading	38	21	7	10	68	43	49
Cardiff City	38	22	4	12	72	38	48
West Ham United	38	18	9	11	58	47	45
Northampton Town	38	16	11	11	56	51	43
Southampton	38	19	5	14	78	74	43
Portsmouth	38	16	10	12	54	42	42
Millwall Athletic	38	16	10	12	50	51	42
Swindon Town	38	15	11	12	77	59	41
Brighton & Hove Albion	38	16	7	15	46	47	39
Exeter City	38	15	8	15	50	41	38
Queens Park Rangers	38	13	12	13	55	57	38
Norwich City	**38**	**11**	**14**	**13**	**53**	**56**	**36**
Luton Town	38	13	8	17	61	73	34
Crystal Palace	38	13	8	17	47	61	34
Bristol Rovers	38	14	3	21	53	75	31
Plymouth Argyle	38	8	14	16	51	61	30
Southend United	38	10	8	20	44	64	28
Croydon Common	38	9	9	20	47	63	27
Gillingham	38	6	8	24	43	82	20

1919–20 SOUTHERN LEAGUE

NO.		DATE	OPPONENTS	V.	H-T	F-T	Lansdale Joe	Gray George	Smith Ben	Jennings William	Martin 'Pompey'	O'Brien Mick	Herbert Joe	Jennings Sam	Doran John	Hawes Arthur	Batey Tom	Hall Fretwell	Broadhead James	Buckley Frank	Groves Jack	Barclay Bill	Frosdick A.W.	Glazebrook	Kirk Walter	Skermer Herbert	Taylor Wally	Popham Reg	Laxton Ted	Brown Thomas	Hope Philip	Dix Harry	King Alfred	Astill William	Dexter George	Wilkinson Reg	Bell Walter	Poole William	Lacey William	Bacon Arthur	King Charles	Thompson George	Paling George	Gadsden Ernie	Cullum Charles	Lamang Richard	ATTD.
1	S	30 Aug 1919	Newport County	H	1-1	4-1	1	2	3	4	5	6[1]	7	8	9[2]	10[1]	11																														7,000
2	W	3 Sept 1919	Brighton & Hove Albion	A	1-1	2-2	1	2	3	4	5	6	7	8[2]	9	10	11																														5,341
3	S	6 " 1919	Portsmouth	A	0-0	0-3	1	2	3	4	5	6	7	8	9	10	11																														12,000
4	S	13 " 1919	Northampton Town	H	3-1	3-1	1	2		3	5	6	7[1]		9[2]	10	11	4	8																												8,000
5	S	20 " 1919	Crystal Palace	A	1-0	1-3	1	2			3	6	7	10	9[1]		11	4	8	5																											10,000
6	S	4 Oct 1919	Watford	A	0-0	1-0	1	2	3	5		6	7	10	9		11[1]	4	8																												5,000
7	S	11 " 1919	Brentford	A	0-1	1-1	1	2	3	5		6	7		9	10	11	4	8[1]																												8,000
8	Th	16 " 1919	Brighton & Hove Albion	H	2-0	2-0	1	2	3	5		6	7		9[2]	10	11	4	8																												4,500
9	S	18 " 1919	Merthyr Town	H	2-0	4-0	1	2	3	5[1]	4	6	7		9[2]	10[1]	11		8																												8,500
10	S	25 " 1919	Plymouth Argyle	A	0-0	0-4	1	2	3	5	4		7		9	10	11	6	8																												12,000
11	S	1 Nov 1919	Bristol Rovers	H	2-0	5-1		2	3	5	6		7		9[3]	10[2]	11	4	8		1																										7,000
12	S	8 " 1919	Reading	A	1-1	2-3		2	3	5	6			8	9[1]	10	11[1]		7		1	4																									10,000
13	S	15 " 1919	Southampton	H	2-1	2-1		2	3	5	6	4	7	10[1]	9		11		8[1]		1																										8,000
14	S	22 " 1919	Luton Town	A	0-0	1-1		2	3	5	6		7[1]	8		10		4	9		1		11																								6,000
15	S	29 " 1919	Gillingham	H	1-0	5-0		2	3	5	6		7[1]	10[1]	9	11[1]		4	8[2]		1																										6,000
16	S	6 Dec 1919	Swansea Town	A	0-2	0-2		2	3	5	6			10	9	11		4	8		1			7																							12,000
17	S	13 " 1919	Exeter City	H	0-0	0-0	1	2	3	5	6		7		9	10		4	8						11																						8,000
18	Th	25 " 1919	Swindon Town	A	0-0	1-0		2	3	5	6		7		9[1]			4	8						11	1	10																				8,000
19	S	27 " 1919	Queens Park Rangers	H	1-0	3-1		2	3	5	6			8[2]	9	11[1]										1	10	4	7																		12,500
20	Th	1 Jan 1920	Cardiff City	A	0-0	0-1		2	3	5	6			8	9	10		4								1			7	11																	14,000
21	S	3 " 1920	Newport County	A	1-4	2-5		2	3	5	6			8	9[2]	10		4								1			7	11																	8,000
22	S	24 " 1920	Northampton Town	A	0-0	0-0	1	2	3	5	6			8	9	11		4									10		7																		5,000
23	S	31 " 1920	Crystal Palace	H	2-0	2-0		2	3	5	6			8[1]	9[1]	11		4								1	10		7																		10,000
24	S	7 Feb 1920	Southend United	H	1-1	1-1		2		5	6			8[1]	9	11		4								1	10		7		3																9,000
25	S	14 " 1920	Watford	H	1-0	1-0		2	3	5	6			10[1]	9	11		4	8							1			7																		9,000
26	S	21 " 1920	Brentford	H	0-1	1-1		2	3	5	6			8	9[1]	11		4								1	10					7															9,000
27	S	28 " 1920	Merthyr Town	A	1-0	2-0		2		5	6			10[1]		11		4	9[1]							1			7		3	8															9,000
28	S	6 Mar 1920	Plymouth Argyle	H	1-0	2-3		2		5	6			8[1]		10		4	9												3	7[1]	1	11													10,000
29	S	13 " 1920	Bristol Rovers	A	2-3	3-5*			2	5						11		4	8[2]						10				7				1		3	6	9										6,000
30	S	20 " 1920	Reading	H	1-0	2-0		2	3	5	6			10[2]		11		4	8							1			7								9										9,000
31	Th	25 " 1920	Swindon Town	H	1-1	4-1		2	3		6			10[2]		11		4								1			7								9[1]	8[1]	5								9,000
32	S	27 " 1920	Southampton	A	0-1	0-3		2		4	6			10					8							1			7								9		5	3	11						10,000
33	F	2 Apr 1920	Millwall Athletic	A	0-1	0-1		2		5	6		7	10				4	8							1			11		3						9										25,000
34	S	3 " 1920	Luton Town	H	1-1	1-1		2	3	5[1]	6			10		11		4	8							1			7								9										10,000
35	M	5 " 1920	Millwall Athletic	H	0-1	1-2		2		5	6			10		11		4	8							1			7		3						9[1]										13,000
36	Th	8 " 1920	Portsmouth	H	0-1	1-1		2	3	5	6					11		4	9			10			8[1]	1			7																		4,500
37	S	10 " 1920	Gillingham	A	0-1	0-1		2			6					11			9			8				1			7		3					4						5	10				7,000
38	W	14 " 1920	Southend United	A	1-1	1-2		2								10		6	9[1]				11		8	1			7		3					4						5					3,000
39	S	17 " 1920	Swansea Town	H	1-1	1-1		2		8	6					10[1]			9				11			1			7							4						5		3			7,000
40	S	24 " 1920	Exeter City	A	1-0	1-2		3		5	6					10[1]			9				11			1			7		2					4									8		7,000
41	Th	29 " 1920	Cardiff City	H	0-1	1-1		2		5	6					10		4	9				11			1			7[1]		3														8		6,000
42	S	1 May 1920	Queens Park Rangers	A	0-0	0-1		2		5						10						6	11			1			7							4								3	8	9	10,000

F.A. CUP

* OWN GOAL SCORED IN THIS MATCH

NO.		DATE	OPPONENTS	V.	H-T	F-T	Lansdale Joe	Gray George	Smith Ben	Jennings William	Martin 'Pompey'	O'Brien Mick	Herbert Joe	Jennings Sam	Doran John	Hawes Arthur	Batey Tom	Hall Fretwell	Broadhead James	Buckley Frank	Groves Jack	ATTD.
1	S	20 Dec 1919	Darlington (6th Qual. Rd.)	A	0-3	0-5		2	3	5	6		7	10	9	11		4	8		1	9,919

1919–20 APPEARANCES & GOALS

	SOUTHERN LGE APPR.	SOUTHERN LGE GLS	F.A. CUP APPR.	F.A. CUP GLS
Gray George	41	–	1	–
Jennings William	38	2	1	–
Hawes Arthur	36	8	1	–
Martin 'Pompey'	36	–	1	–
Broadhead James	30	8	1	–
Hall Fretwell	30	–	1	–
Smith Ben	28	–	1	–
Jennings Sam	26	15	1	–
Doran John	25	18	1	–
Laxton Ted	22	1		
Skermer Herbert	22	–		
Herbert Joe	17	3	1	–
Batey Tom	13	2		
Lansdale Joe	12	–		
O'Brien Mick	10	1		
Hope Philip	9	–		
Bell Walter	7	2		
Frosdick Albert	6	–		
Groves Jack	6	–	1	–
Taylor Wally	6	–		
Wilkinson Reg	6	–		
Kirk Walter	5	1		
Barclay Bill	4	–		
Cullum Charles	3	–		
Dix Harry	3	1		
Thompson George	3	–		
Brown Thomas	2	–		
Gadsden Ernie	2	–		
King Alfred	2	–		
Lacey William	2	–		
Astill William	1	–		
Bacon Arthur	1	–		
Buckley Frank	1	–		
Dexter George	1	–		
Glazebrook Harold	1	–		
King Charles	1	–		
Lamang Richard	1	–		
Paling George	1	–		
Popham Reg	1	–		
Poole William	1	1		
Own Goals		1		

SOUTHERN LEAGUE

1919–20	P	W	D	L	F	A	PTS
Portsmouth	42	23	12	7	73	27	58
Watford	42	26	6	10	69	42	58
Crystal Palace	42	22	12	8	69	43	56
Cardiff City	42	18	17	7	70	43	53
Plymouth Argyle	42	20	10	12	57	29	50
Queens Park Rangers	42	18	10	14	62	50	46
Reading	42	16	13	13	51	43	45
Southampton	42	18	8	16	72	63	44
Swansea Town	42	16	11	15	53	45	43
Exeter City	42	17	9	16	57	51	43
Southend United	42	13	17	12	46	48	43
Norwich City	**42**	**15**	**11**	**16**	**64**	**57**	**41**
Swindon Town	42	17	7	18	65	68	41
Millwall Athletic	42	14	12	16	52	55	40
Brentford	42	15	10	17	52	59	40
Brighton & Hove Albion	42	14	8	20	60	72	36
Bristol Rovers	42	11	13	18	61	78	35
Newport County	42	13	7	22	45	70	33
Northampton Town	42	12	9	21	64	103	33
Luton Town	42	10	10	22	51	76	30
Merthyr Town	42	9	11	22	47	78	29
Gillingham	42	10	7	25	34	74	27

1920–21 DIVISION 3

NO.		DATE	OPPONENTS	V.	H-T	F-T	Skermer Herbert	Gray George	Gadsden Ernie	Wilkinson Reg	Addy George	Martin 'Pompey'	Laxton Edward	Kidger Edward	Parker John	Whitham Vic	Dobson George	Hopewell Harry	Dennison Robert	Piggin Albert	Frosdick Albert	Duncan William	Duncan John	Bell Wally	Simons Henry	Longdon Samuel	Smith Ben	Booth Curtis	Barkas Edward	Austin Sam	Travers George	Pearce William	Hannah Joe	Hope Philip	Lumley William	Mellon David	Bradbrook Charles	ATTD.
1	S	28 Aug 1920	Plymouth Argyle	A	0-1	1-1	1	2	3	4	5	6	7	8	9	10^{1}	11																					14,000
2	W	1 Sept 1920	Exeter City	A	0-0	1-1	1	2	3	4	5		7	8	9^{1}	10	11	6																				5,000
3	S	4 " 1920	Plymouth Argyle	H	0-0	0-0	1	2	3	4	5		7	8	9	10	11	6																				12,000
4	W	8 " 1920	Exeter City	H	0-0	0-0	1	2	3	4	5		7	8	9	10	11	6																				7,000
5	S	11 " 1920	Crystal Palace	H	0-0	0-1	1	2	3	4	5		7			10		6	8	9	11																	11,000
6	Th	16 " 1920	Swansea Town	A	2-2	2-5	1	2	3		4							6	8	10	11	5	7	9^{2}														10,000
7	S	18 " 1920	Crystal Palace	A	0-0	0-1	1	2	3		4		7					6	9		11	5	8	10														10,000
8	S	25 " 1920	Southampton	H	0-0	0-1	1	2	3	4		5				10		6	9				7		8	11												9,000
9	S	2 Oct 1920	Southampton	A	0-0	0-1	1	2		4		5						6	9				7		8	11	3	10										15,000
10	S	9 " 1920	Brentford	H	0-0	0-0	1	2		8	4	5	7					6							9	11	3	10										9,000
11	S	16 " 1920	Brentford	A	0-2	1-3	1	2	3	4		6	7				11^{1}	5	8					10					9									9,000
12	S	23 " 1920	Bristol Rovers	A	0-0	2-2	1	2	3	4		5					11	6	10^{2}											7	8	9						12,000
13	S	30 " 1920	Bristol Rovers	H	0-0	1-1	1	2	3	4		5					11	6	9^{1}									10		7	8							10,000
14	S	6 Nov 1920	Reading	A	1-0	1-0	1	2		4		5					11	6	9								3	10		7	8^{1}							8,000
15	S	13 " 1920	Reading	H	1-0	2-0	1	2		4		5					11	6	9^{1}								3	10^{1}		7	8							9,000
16	S	20 " 1920	Luton Town	A	0-2	0-4	1	2		4		5					11	6	9								3	10		7	8							7,000
17	S	27 " 1920	Luton Town	H	1-0	3-0	1	2		4	6^{1}	5					11		8								3	10		7	9^{2}							10,000
18	S	4 Dec 1920	Millwall Athletic	H	2-0	2-0	1	2		4	6	5					11		8								3	10		7	9^{2}							5,000
19	S	11 " 1920	Millwall Athletic	A	0-0	0-2	1	2	3	4	6	5					11		8									10		7	9							15,000
20	S	25 " 1920	Grimsby Town	A	0-0	1-1	1	2		4	6	5			7	9^{1}	11										3	10			8							10,000
21	M	27 " 1920	Grimsby Town	H	0-0	0-0	1	2		4	6	5					11		8								3	10		7	9							14,610
22	S	1 Jan 1921	Swansea Town	H	1-1	1-1	1	2		4	6	5			7	9	11		10^{1}								3			8								7,000
23	Th	13 " 1921	Newport County	A	0-1	0-2	1	2	3	4	5				10			6			11									7	8		9					3,000
24	S	22 " 1921	Newport County	H	2-0	3-0	1	2	3	4	6	5	11		9													10^{1}		7^{2}	8							5,000
25	S	5 Feb 1921	Queens Park Rangers	H	1-0	2-0	1	2	3	4	6	5	11		9^{1}													10		7^{1}	8							9,000
26	S	12 " 1921	Gillingham	A	0-0	0-0	1	2	3	4	6	5	11		9				10											7	8							7,000
27	Th	17 " 1921	Queens Park Rangers	A	0-0	0-2	1	2	3		4		7		9		11	6	10												8			5				6,000
28	S	19 " 1921	Gillingham	H	2-0	2-1	1	2	3	4		5	11					6	10											7^{1}	9^{1}				8			8,000
29	S	26 " 1921	Swindon Town	A	2-2	2-4	1	2	3	4	6	5				10^{1}														7	8^{1}				9	11		12,000
30	S	5 Mar 1921	Swindon Town	H	2-0	3-2	1	2		4	6	5	11															10^{1}		7	8^{1}	3			9^{1}			10,000
31	S	12 " 1921	Portsmouth	A	1-0	1-2	1	2		4	6^{1}	5	11															10		7	8	3			9			12,000
32	S	19 " 1921	Portsmouth	H	1-1	2-2	1	2		4	6^{1}	5	11															10^{1}		7	8	3			9			9,000
33	F	25 " 1921	Brighton & Hove Albion	A	0-1	0-2	1	2		4	6	5					11		9									10		7		3			8			14,500
34	S	26 " 1921	Watford	H	1-0	1-1	1	2		4	6^{1}	5					11		10								3			7	8				9			8,000
35	M	28 " 1921	Brighton & Hove Albion	H	3-0	3-0	1	2		4	6^{1}	5					11		10								3			7	8^{2}				9			14,000
36	S	2 Apr 1921	Watford	A	0-0	0-2	1	2		4	6	5					11		10								3			7	8				9			5,000
37	S	9 " 1921	Northampton Town	H	0-2	3-3	1	2		4		5					11	6	10^{1}								3			7	8^{1}				9^{1}			5,000
38	S	16 " 1921	Northampton Town	A	0-1	0-1	1	2		4		5					11	6	9								3	10		7	8							7,000
39	S	23 " 1921	Southend United	H	2-0	3-1	1	2		4		5					11	6									3	10		7	8^{2}				9^{1}			5,000
40	S	30 " 1921	Southend United	A	1-1	1-3	1	2		4		5					11	6									3	10		7	8^{1}				9			6,000
41	M	2 May 1921	Merthyr Town	H	0-0	0-0	1	2		6		5					11										3	10		7	8				9		4	5,000
42	S	7 " 1921	Merthyr Town	A	0-0	0-0	1	2		4		5					11	6									3	10		7	8				9			2,500

F.A. CUP

NO.		DATE	OPPONENTS	V.	H-T	F-T	Skermer Herbert	Gray George	Gadsden Ernie	Wilkinson Reg	Addy George	Martin 'Pompey'	Laxton Edward	Kidger Edward	Parker John	Whitham Vic	Dobson George	Hopewell Harry	Dennison Robert	Piggin Albert	Frosdick Albert	Duncan William	Duncan John	Bell Wally	Simons Henry	Longdon Samuel	Smith Ben	Booth Curtis	Barkas Edward	Austin Sam	Travers George	Pearce William	Hannah Joe	Hope Philip	Lumley William	Mellon David	Bradbrook Charles	ATTD.
1	S	8 Jan 1921	Grimsby Town (1st Round)	A	0-0	0-1	1	2		4	6	5			7	10	11		8								3				9							12,000

1920–21 APPEARANCES & GOALS

	FOOTBALL LGE APPR.	FOOTBALL LGE GLS	F.A. CUP APPR.	F.A. CUP GLS
Gray George	42	–	1	–
Skermer Herbert	42	–	1	–
Wilkinson Reg	39	–	1	–
Martin 'Pompey'	34	–	1	–
Austin Sam	29	4		
Travers George	29	14	1	–
Addy George	27	5	1	–
Dobson George	27	1	1	–
Dennison Robert	25	6	1	–
Hopewell Harry	23	–		
Booth Curtis	22	4		
Gadsden Ernie	19	–		
Smith Ben	19	–	1	–
Laxton Edward	16	–		
Lumley William	14	3		
Parker John	11	2	1	–
Whitham Vic	9	3	1	–
Pearce William	5	–		
Duncan John	4	–		
Frosdick Albert	4	–		
Kidger Edward	4	–		
Bell Walter	3	2		
Longdon Samuel	3	–		
Simons Henry	3	–		
Duncan William	2	–		
Piggin Albert	2	–		
Barkas Edward	1	–		
Bradbrook Charles	1	–		
Hannah Joe	1	–		
Hope Philip	1	–		
Mellon David	1	–		

DIVISION 3

1920–21	P	W	D	L	F	A	PTS
Crystal Palace	42	24	11	7	70	34	59
Southampton	42	19	16	7	64	28	54
Queens Park Rangers	42	22	9	11	61	32	53
Swindon Town	42	21	10	11	73	49	52
Swansea Town	42	18	15	9	56	45	51
Watford	42	20	8	14	59	44	48
Millwall Athletic	42	18	11	13	42	30	47
Merthyr Town	42	15	15	12	60	49	45
Luton Town	42	16	12	14	61	56	44
Bristol Rovers	42	18	7	17	68	57	43
Plymouth Argyle	42	11	21	10	35	34	43
Portsmouth	42	12	15	15	46	48	39
Grimsby Town	42	15	9	18	49	59	39
Northampton Town	42	15	8	19	59	75	38
Newport County	42	14	9	19	43	64	37
Norwich City	**42**	**10**	**16**	**16**	**44**	**53**	**36**
Southend United	42	14	8	20	44	61	36
Brighton & Hove Albion	42	14	8	20	42	61	36
Exeter City	42	10	15	17	39	54	35
Reading	42	12	7	23	42	59	31
Brentford	42	9	12	21	42	67	30
Gillingham	42	8	12	22	34	74	28

1921–22 DIVISION 3 SOUTH

NO.		DATE	OPPONENTS	V.	H-T	F-T	Skermer Herbert	Hope Philip	Smith Ben	Wilkinson Reg	Scott Sidney	Martin 'Pompey'	Austin Sam	Bertram William	Whing John	Booth Curtis	Woodhouse Chris	Pearce William	Lumley William	Stoakes James	Dennison Bob	Hopewell Harry	Gray George	Bradbrook Charles	Addy George	Hannah Joe	Taylor William	Frosdick Albert	Higgins Alex	Silverthorne James	Armstrong James	King Alfred	Hodge James	O'Hagan William	Own Goals	ATTD.
1	S	27 Aug 1921	Luton Town	H	0-0	0-1	1	2	3	4	5	6	7	8	9	10	11																			11,000
2	M	29 " 1921	Plymouth Argyle	A	1-1	1-1	1		3	6	5	4	7	8[1]	9	10	11	2																		12,000
3	S	3 Sept 1921	Luton Town	A	0-2	1-2	1		3	4	5	6	7	8		10	11	2	9[1]																	11,000
4	Th	8 " 1921	Plymouth Argyle	H	1-1	1-1	1		3	4	5	6	7	8		10[1]		2	9	11																7,000
5	S	10 " 1921	Queens Park Rangers	H	0-0	0-0	1		3	4	5	6	7	8				2	9	11	10															8,000
6	S	17 " 1921	Queens Park Rangers	A	0-2	0-2	1		3		5	6	7	8	9			2		11	10	4														10,000
7	S	24 " 1921	Newport County	H	1-0	2-2	1		3		5	6	7[1]	8		10[1]		2		11	9	4														8,000
8	S	1 Oct 1921	Newport County	A	0-0	0-1	1		3		5	6	7		4	10			8	11	9		2													8,000
9	S	8 " 1921	Southampton	H	0-1	2-2	1		3		5	6	7	10	9					11	8[2]		2	4												8,000
10	S	15 " 1921	Southampton	A	0-1	0-2	1	2	3		5	6	7	10	9					11	8			4												12,000
11	S	22 " 1921	Reading	A	0-1	1-2	1		3			5	7	10		9				11	8[1]		2	4	6											10,000
12	S	29 " 1921	Reading	H	2-0	4-1	1		3			5	7	10		9[2]				11[1]	8		2	4	6[1]											7,500
13	S	5 Nov 1921	Bristol Rovers	H	0-0	0-1	1		3			5	7	10		9				11	8		2	4	6											8,000
14	S	12 " 1921	Bristol Rovers	A	0-3	2-4	1		3	6		5	7[1]			10			8	11			2	4		9[1]										16,000
15	S	19 " 1921	Brentford	H	0-0	0-0	1		3	4	5	6	7	11		10					8		2	9												6,000
16	S	26 " 1921	Brentford	A	1-1	1-2	1		3	4	5	6		10	7				8[1]				2				9	11								6,000
17	S	10 Dec 1921	Aberdare Athletic	H	0-0	0-0	1	2	3		5	6	7				11							4					8	9	10					9,000
18	S	24 " 1921	Brighton & Hove Albion	A	0-0	2-0	1	2	3		5	6	7[1]	8			11							4						9[1]	10					7,000
19	M	26 " 1921	Charlton Athletic	A	0-2	1-2	1	2	3		5	6	7	8			11							4						9	10[1]					14,000
20	Tu	27 " 1921	Charlton Athletic	H	1-0	2-0	1	2	3		5	6	7[2]	8		11								4					10	9						14,000
21	S	31 " 1921	Watford	H	1-1	1-1		2	3		5	6	7	8						11				4						9[1]	10	1				9,000
22	S	14 Jan 1922	Watford	A	1-2	2-4	1	2	3	4		5	7			10	11[1]								6				8	9[1]						6,000
23	S	21 " 1922	Swindon Town	H	0-2	1-2	1	2	3		5	6	7	8			11							4					10		9				–[1]	3,500
24	S	4 Feb 1922	Gillingham	H	0-0	2-0		2	3		5	6	7			10								4					11[1]	9[1]	8	1				4,500
25	S	11 " 1922	Gillingham	A	0-3	2-5		2	3		5	6	7[2]			10								4					11	9	8	1				7,000
26	Th	23 " 1922	Millwall Athletic	H	1-0	3-1	1	2		6		5	7[1]	8		10[1]	11				9[1]			4									3			5,000
27	S	25 " 1922	Millwall Athletic	A	1-0	2-2	1	2		6		5	7	8		10	11[2]				9			4									3			18,000
28	S	4 Mar 1922	Exeter City	H	0-0	0-0	1	2		6		5	7	8		10	11				9			4									3			6,000
29	S	11 " 1922	Exeter City	A	0-1	0-2		2		6		5	7			10	11				8			4						9			3	1		6,000
30	Th	16 " 1922	Aberdare Athletic	A	1-0	2-1		2		6		5	7				11				8[1]			4						9	10[1]		3	1		7,000
31	S	18 " 1922	Swansea Town	A	0-1	1-1		2		6		5	7							11	8			4						9[1]	10		3	1		10,000
32	S	25 " 1922	Swansea Town	H	2-0	3-2		2		6		5	7							11	8[1]			4[1]						9	10[1]		3	1		8,000
33	S	1 Apr 1922	Southend United	A	1-0	1-0		2		6		5	7					3		11	8			4						9[1]	10			1		4,000
34	Th	6 " 1922	Brighton & Hove Albion	H	0-1	1-1		2		6		5	7					3		11	8			4						9	10[1]			1		8,000
35	S	8 " 1922	Southend United	H	0-1	1-1		2		6		5	7							11	8			4						9	10		3	1	–[1]	7,000
36	S	15 " 1922	Portsmouth	A	1-0	1-0		2		6		5	7	8						11	9[1]			4							10		3	1		16,000
37	M	17 " 1922	Northampton Town	H	1-0	2-0		2		6		5	7	8[1]						11	9			4							10[1]		3	1		14,000
38	Tu	18 " 1922	Northampton Town	A	0-0	0-3		2		4	5		7						8	11	9			6							10		3	1		6,000
39	S	22 " 1922	Portsmouth	H	0-0	2-1		2		6		5	7[1]						8	11	9			4							10[1]		3	1		10,000
40	S	29 " 1922	Merthyr Town	A	0-1	0-3						5	7			10		3	8	11	9	6		4									2	1		5,000
41	M	1 May 1922	Swindon Town	A	1-3	1-6						5	7			10		2	8[1]	11	9	6		4									3	1		3,000
42	S	6 " 1922	Merthyr Town	H	0-0	2-0		2	3			5	7	8						11				4					10[1]		9[1]		6	1		6,000

F.A. CUP

NO.		DATE	OPPONENTS	V.	H-T	F-T	Skermer Herbert	Hope Philip	Smith Ben	Wilkinson Reg	Scott Sidney	Martin 'Pompey'	Austin Sam	Bertram William	Whing John	Booth Curtis	Woodhouse Chris	Pearce William	Lumley William	Stoakes James	Dennison Bob	Hopewell Harry	Gray George	Bradbrook Charles	Addy George	Hannah Joe	Taylor William	Frosdick Albert	Higgins Alex	Silverthorne James	Armstrong James	King Alfred	Hodge James	O'Hagan William	Own Goals	ATTD.
1	S	3 Dec 1921	Metrogas (London) (5th Qual. Round)	A	1-1	2-1	1	2	3		5	6	7[1]	10[1]			11		9		8				4											4,00
2	S	17 " 1921	Oxford City (6th Qual. Round)	A	0-1	1-1	1	2	3		5	6	7	10			11		9					4							8[1]					6,12
3	Th	22 " 1921	Oxford City (Replay)	H	1-0	3-0	1	2	3		5[1]	6	7[1]	8			11[1]		9					4							10					4,57
4	S	7 Jan 1922	Barnsley (1st Round)	A	1-1	1-1	1	2	3		5	6	7	8			11[1]		9					4							10					17,12
5	Th	12 " 1922	Barnsley (Replay)	H	0-0	1-2	1	2	3		5	6	7[1]	8			11		9					4							10					12,00

1921–22 APPEARANCES & GOALS

	FOOTBALL LGE APPR.	FOOTBALL LGE GLS	F.A. CUP APPR.	F.A. CUP GLS
Austin Sam	41	9	5	3
Martin 'Pompey'	41	–	5	–
Bradbrook Charles	32	1	4	–
Dennison Bob	26	7	1	–
Hope Philip	26	–	5	–
Smith Ben	26	–	5	–
Bertram William	25	2	5	1
Skermer Herbert	25	–	5	–
Stoakes James	24	1		
Wilkinson Reg	23	–		
Booth Curtis	21	5		
Scott Sidney	21	–	5	1
Armstrong James	18	7	4	1
Hodge James	15	–		
Silverthorne James	15	6		
O'Hagan William	14	–		
Woodhouse Chris	13	3	5	2
Lumley William	10	3	5	–
Pearce William	10	–		
Gray George	8	–		
Higgins Alex	7	2		
Whing John	7	–		
Addy George	4	1	1	–
Hopewell Harry	4	–		
King Alfred	3	–		
Frosdick Albert	1	–		
Hannah Joe	1	1		
Taylor Walter	1	–		
Own Goals		2		

DIVISION 3 SOUTH

1921–22	P	W	D	L	F	A	PTS
Southampton	42	23	15	4	68	21	61
Plymouth Argyle	42	25	11	6	63	24	61
Portsmouth	42	18	17	7	62	39	53
Luton Town	42	22	8	12	64	35	52
Queens Park Rangers	42	18	13	11	53	44	49
Swindon Town	42	16	13	13	72	60	45
Aberdare Athletic	42	17	10	15	57	51	44
Watford	42	13	18	11	54	48	44
Brentford	42	16	11	15	52	43	43
Swansea Town	42	13	15	14	50	47	41
Merthyr Town	42	17	6	19	45	56	40
Millwall Athletic	42	10	18	14	38	42	38
Reading	42	14	10	18	40	47	38
Bristol Rovers	42	14	10	18	52	67	38
Norwich City	**42**	**12**	**13**	**17**	**50**	**62**	**37**
Charlton Athletic	42	13	11	18	43	56	37
Northampton Town	42	13	11	18	47	71	37
Gillingham	42	14	8	20	47	60	36
Brighton & Hove Albion	42	13	9	20	45	51	35
Newport County	42	11	12	19	44	61	34
Exeter City	42	11	12	19	38	59	34
Southend United	42	8	11	23	34	74	27

1922–23 DIVISION 3 SOUTH

NO.		DATE		OPPONENTS	V.	H-T	F-T	O'Hagan William	Hope Philip	Hodge James	Wilkinson Reg	Martin 'Pompey'	Wright Stephen	Austin Sam	Mills James	Peart Jack	Lythgoe John	Stoakes James	Dennington Charlie	Dennison Bob	Smith Ben	Stewart Bob	Booth Curtis	Pearce William	Rowell Joe	Bradbrook Charles	Taylor Walter	Gurkin John	Hannah Joe	Woolley Robert	Own Goals	ATTD.
1	S	26 Aug	1922	Brighton & Hove Albion	A	0-0	0-0	1	2	3	4	5	6	7	8	9	10	11														12,000
2	M	28 "	1922	Queens Park Rangers	H	0-1	1-1		2	3	4	5	6	7		9^1	10	11	1	8												10,823
3	S	2 Sept	1922	Brighton & Hove Albion	H	1-0	1-0	1	2	3	4	5	6	7		9	10	11		8^1												10,506
4	M	4 "	1922	Queens Park Rangers	A	0-0	0-2	1	2	3	4	5	6	7		9	10	11		8												5,000
5	S	9 "	1922	Brentford	H	0-2	0-2	1	2	3	4	5	6	7		9	10	11		8												8,597
6	S	16 "	1922	Brentford	A	3-0	4-1	1	2	3	4	5	6	7^1		9^1	10^1	11		8^1												9,000
7	S	23 "	1922	Southend United	H	0-0	2-1	1	2	3	4^1	5	6	7		9	10^1	11		8												9,704
8	S	30 "	1922	Southend United	A	0-2	1-3	1	2		4	5	6	7		9	10	11		8^1	3											10,000
9	S	7 Oct	1922	Northampton Town	H	1-0	1-0	1	2	3	4	5	6	7^1		9		11		8		10										8,659
10	S	14 "	1922	Northampton Town	A	0-1	1-1	1	2	3	4	5	6	7^1		9		11		8		10										8,000
11	S	21 "	1922	Swindon Town	A	2-0	2-1	1	2	3	4	5	6	7		9^1		11		8^1		10										9,000
12	S	28 "	1922	Swindon Town	H	0-0	0-0	1	2	3	4	5	6	7				11		8		10	9									9,504
13	S	4 Nov	1922	Exeter City	A	0-0	0-2	1	2	3	4	5	6	7			10	11		9		8										6,000
14	S	11 "	1922	Exeter City	H	4-0	6-0	1	2	3	4	5	6^1	7^2			10^1	11		8				9^2								6,955
15	S	18 "	1922	Merthyr Town	A	1-0	1-0	1	2	3	4	5	6	7			10	11^1		8				9								5,000
16	S	25 "	1922	Merthyr Town	H	1-1	1-1	1	2	3	4	5	6	7		9^1	10	11		8												8,600
17	S	9 Dec	1922	Reading	A	1-2	1-4	1		2	4	5	6			9		11		8^1	3		10		7							4,000
18	S	23 "	1922	Gillingham	H	1-1	1-1	1	2	6	4		5	7		9		11		8^1			10	3								6,429
19	M	25 "	1922	Charlton Athletic	A	0-1	0-3	1		2	4		5	7		9		11		8			10	3		6						9,000
20	Tu	26 "	1922	Charlton Athletic	H	2-2	2-3	1		2	4^1		5	7				11		8	3	10	9^1				6					13,005
21	W	27 "	1922	Reading	H	2-0	2-0	1		2	4			7^1				11		8	3	10	9^1			5		6				5,934
22	S	6 Jan	1923	Bristol Rovers	H	0-0	0-0	1	2	3	4		6	7				11		8		10	9			5						6,700
23	S	20 "	1923	Plymouth Argyle	A	1-1	1-1	1	2	5			6	7^1		9		11		8	3		10			4						9,000
24	S	27 "	1923	Plymouth Argyle	H	0-0	1-0	1	2		4		6	7^1		9		11		8	3		10					5				7,130
25	S	3 Feb	1923	Aberdare Athletic	A	2-0	2-0	1	2		4	5	6	7		9^1	10	11		8^1	3											6,000
26	S	10 "	1923	Aberdare Athletic	H	1-1	1-4	1	2		4	5	6	7		9^1	10	11		8	3											7,108
27	S	17 "	1923	Swansea Town	A	1-2	1-3	1	2		4		6	7		9		11		8^1	3	10						5				20,000
28	S	24 "	1923	Swansea Town	H	0-3	1-4	1	2	3	4^1	5		7		9		11		8		10						6				6,452
29	S	3 Mar	1923	Newport County	H	0-1	1-1	1		3	4^1	5	6	7				11		8		10	9					2				4,563
30	S	10 "	1923	Newport County	A	2-1	3-1		2	9^1	4^1	5	6	7				11	1	8^1			10						3			7,000
31	S	17 "	1923	Bristol City	H	1-2	2-2		2	9	4^1	5	6	7				11	1	8	3		10								$-^1$	8,000
32	S	24 "	1923	Bristol City	A	0-2	0-4	1	2	9	4	5	6	7	8			11			3		10									15,000
33	F	30 "	1923	Watford	A	1-1	1-2	1	2	3	4^1	5		7				11		8		10						6	9			10,000
34	S	31 "	1923	Portsmouth	A	1-0	1-2	1	2	3	4	5		7	8^1			11				10						6	9			8,000
35	M	2 Apr	1923	Watford	H	1-0	2-0	1		2	4	5		7	8^2			11			3	10						6	9			11,600
36	S	7 "	1923	Portsmouth	H	0-2	0-2	1		2	4	5		7	8			11			3	10						6	9			6,435
37	S	14 "	1923	Millwall	H	2-2	3-2	1	2	3	4	5	6	7				11		8^3			10						9			6,000
38	S	21 "	1923	Millwall	A	0-2	0-3	1	2	3	4	5	6	7				11		8			10						9			12,000
39	M	23 "	1923	Bristol Rovers	A	1-1	2-3	1	2	3	4	5	6	7				11		8			10						9^2			4,000
40	W	25 "	1923	Gillingham	A	0-1	0-5	1	2	3		5	6	7				11		8			10			4			9			2,000
41	S	28 "	1923	Luton Town	H	0-1	1-2	1	2	3	4		6	7^1				11		8			10					5	9			5,000
42	S	5 May	1923	Luton Town	A	0-2	0-4	1	2		4	5	6		7			11		8			10						9	3		7,000

F.A. CUP

NO.		DATE		OPPONENTS		V.	H-T	F-T	O'Hagan William	Hope Philip	Hodge James	Wilkinson Reg	Martin 'Pompey'	Wright Stephen	Austin Sam	Mills James	Peart Jack	Lythgoe John	Stoakes James	Dennington Charlie	Dennison Bob	Smith Ben	Stewart Bob	Booth Curtis	Pearce William	Rowell Joe	Bradbrook Charles	Own Goals	ATTD.
1	S	2 Dec	1922	Southend United	(5th Qual. Round)	A	1-1	2-2	1	2	3	4	5	6	7		9	10	11		8^2								8,541
2	Th	7 "	1922	Southend United	(Replay)	H	2-0	2-1	1		3	4	5	6	7		9		11		8			10^1	2			$-^1$	10,113
3	S	16 "	1922	Ilford	(6th Qual. Round)	H	3-1	5-1	1	2	3	4^2	5	6	7		9^2		11		8			10^1					9,153
4	S	13 Jan	1923	Bolton Wanderers	(1st Round)	H	0-1	0-2	1	2	3	4		6	7				11		8			10	9		5		15,286

1922–23 APPEARANCES & GOALS

	FOOTBALL LGE APPR.	FOOTBALL LGE GLS	F.A. CUP APPR.	F.A. CUP GLS
Stoakes James	42	1	4	–
Austin Sam	40	9	4	–
Wilkinson Reg	40	7	4	2
O'Hagan William	39	–	4	–
Dennison Bob	37	13	4	2
Hodge James	36	1	4	–
Wright Stephen	36	1	4	–
Hope Philip	35	–	3	–
Martin 'Pompey'	33	–	3	–
Peart Jack	21	6	3	2
Booth Curtis	19	2	3	2
Stewart Robert	15	–		
Lythgoe John	14	3		
Smith Ben	13	–		
Hannah Joe	11	2		
Gurkin John	10	–		
Mills James	6	3		
Bradbrook Charles	5	–	1	–
Pearce William	4	2	2	–
Dennington Charlie	3	–		
Rowell Joe	1	–		
Taylor Walter	1	–		
Woolley Robert	1	–		
Own Goals		1		1

DIVISION 3 SOUTH

1922–23	P	W	D	L	F	A	PTS
Bristol City	42	24	11	7	66	40	59
Plymouth Argyle	42	23	7	12	61	29	53
Swansea Town	42	22	9	11	78	45	53
Brighton & Hove Albion	42	20	11	11	52	34	51
Luton Town	42	21	7	14	68	49	49
Portsmouth	42	19	8	15	58	52	46
Millwall	42	14	18	10	45	40	46
Swindon Town	42	17	11	14	62	56	45
Northampton Town	42	17	11	14	54	44	45
Watford	42	17	10	15	57	54	44
Queens Park Rangers	42	16	10	16	54	49	42
Charlton Athletic	42	14	14	14	55	51	42
Bristol Rovers	42	13	16	13	35	36	42
Brentford	42	13	12	17	41	51	38
Southend United	42	12	13	17	49	54	37
Gillingham	42	15	7	20	51	59	37
Merthyr Town	42	11	14	17	39	48	36
Norwich City	**42**	**13**	**10**	**19**	**50**	**71**	**36**
Reading	42	10	14	18	36	55	34
Exeter City	42	13	7	22	47	84	33
Aberdare Athletic	42	9	11	22	42	69	29
Newport County	42	8	11	23	40	70	27

1923–24 DIVISION 3 SOUTH

NO.		DATE	OPPONENTS	V.	H-T	F-T	Williamson Ernest	Sturgess Albert	Smith Ben	Christie Alex	Martin 'Pompey'	Field Richard	Austin Sam	Dennison Bob	Silverthorne James	Short James	Cooke George	Hope Philip	Hannah Joe	Jackson James	Smith Syd	Stoakes James	Reay Archie	Banks James	Phillips Alan	Woolley Robert	Bradbrook Charles	Murphy John	Earl Sidney	Dennington Charlie	Ford Alf	Own Goals	ATTD
1	S	25 Aug 1923	Millwall	H	1-0	1-1	1	2	3	4	5	6	7	8^{1}	9	10	11																12,110
2	M	27 " 1923	Aberdare Athletic	A	0-0	0-0	1	3		4		5	7	8				2	6	9	10	11											6,000
3	S	1 Sept 1923	Millwall	A	1-1	1-2	1	3		4		5	7^{1}	8				2	6	9	10	11											22,000
4	M	3 " 1923	Aberdare Athletic	H	1-0	5-0	1	3			5	6	7	8^{1}		10		2	4	9^{3}		11^{1}											7,730
5	S	8 " 1923	Plymouth Argyle	H	0-1	0-1	1		3		5	6	7	8		10		2	4	9		11											11,291
6	M	10 " 1923	Watford	H	0-0	0-0	1		3		5	6	7	8		10		2	4	9		11											7,474
7	S	15 " 1923	Plymouth Argyle	A	0-0	0-2	1		3		5	6	7	8		10		2	4	9		11											9,000
8	S	22 " 1923	Merthyr Town	H	0-0	2-0	1		3		5	6	7^{1}	10		8^{1}		2	4	9		11											7,812
9	S	29 " 1923	Merthyr Town	A	0-2	3-2	1				5	6	7^{1}	8		10^{1}		2	4	9^{1}		11	3										7,000
10	S	6 Oct 1923	Bournemouth	H	0-1	1-1	1		3		5	6	7	9^{1}		10		2	4			11		8									9,129
11	S	13 " 1923	Bournemouth	A	1-0	2-1	1		3		5	6	7			10^{1}		2	4	9		11		8								$–^{1}$	8,000
12	S	20 " 1923	Charlton Athletic	A	0-0	0-0	1		3		5	6	7			10		2	4	9		11		8									9,000
13	S	27 " 1923	Charlton Athletic	H	2-1	2-2	1		3		5	6	7^{1}					2	4	9^{1}		11		8	10								8,400
14	S	3 Nov 1923	Newport County	A	0-0	0-1	1	3			5	6	7	8				2	4	9		11		10									7,000
15	S	10 " 1923	Newport County	H	1-0	3-1	1	3			5	6	7^{1}	8	9			2	4			11		10^{2}									6,843
16	S	17 " 1923	Swindon Town	H	2-0	2-0	1	3			5	6	7	8^{1}	9			2	4			11		10^{1}									6,944
17	S	24 " 1923	Swindon Town	A	1-0	2-4	1	3			5	6	7	8^{1}	9^{1}	10		2	4			11											5,000
18	S	8 Dec 1923	Watford	A	0-0	0-0	1	6	3		5		7	8	9			2	4			11		10									5,000
19	S	22 " 1923	Swansea Town	A	0-0	0-1	1	6	3		5		7	8				2	4	9		11		10									14,000
20	Tu	25 " 1923	Gillingham	A	1-2	1-3	1	6	3		5		7	8^{1}						9		11		10		2	4						8,000
21	W	26 " 1923	Gillingham	H	1-0	1-0	1	6	3		5		7	8				2	4	9^{1}		11		10									8,212
22	S	29 " 1923	Northampton Town	A	0-0	0-1	1	6	3		5		7					2	4	9	8	11		10									9,000
23	S	5 Jan 1924	Northampton Town	H	1-1	1-4	1	6	3		5		7	8^{1}				2	4	9		11		10									7,268
24	S	19 " 1924	Southend United	H	1-0	3-1	1	3		4	5	6	7^{2}	10			11	2	9^{1}					8									5,268
25	S	26 " 1924	Southend United	A	1-1	1-3	1	3		4	5	6	7				11	2	9^{1}	10				8									6,000
26	S	9 Feb 1924	Exeter City	A	0-1	2-1	1	3					7					2	9	10^{1}		11		8			4	5	6^{1}				5,000
27	Th	14 " 1924	Exeter City	H	2-0	4-0	1	3					7					2	9^{2}	10^{2}		11		8			4	5	6				2,962
28	S	16 " 1924	Portsmouth	H	1-0	3-1	1	3					7^{1}						2	10^{1}		11		8	9^{1}		4	5	6				10,000
29	S	23 " 1924	Portsmouth	A	0-1	0-4	1	3					7					2	9	10		11		8			4	5	6				8,000
30	S	1 Mar 1924	Brentford	H	1-2	2-3	1	3					7					2	4	10		11		8^{1}	9^{1}			5	6				7,000
31	S	8 " 1924	Brentford	A	0-2	0-3	1	3					7	8			11		2	9				10			4	5	6				7,000
32	S	15 " 1924	Bristol Rovers	A	1-2	1-3	1	3			5	6	7	8				2	4	10^{1}		11		9									7,000
33	S	22 " 1924	Bristol Rovers	H	2-0	3-1	1	3			5	6	7^{2}	8				2	4			11		9	10^{1}								6,000
34	S	29 " 1924	Brighton & Hove Albion	A	0-1	0-3	1	3			5	6	7	8				2	4	9		11		10									6,000
35	S	5 Apr 1924	Brighton & Hove Albion	H	1-0	1-0	1	3			5	6	7	8				2	4^{1}	9		11		10									10,000
36	S	12 " 1924	Luton Town	A	0-2	1-2		3			5	6	7	8^{1}				2	4	9		11		10						1			4,000
37	F	18 " 1924	Queens Park Rangers	A	0-1	1-2	1	3			5	6	7	8				2	4	9^{1}		11		10									7,000
38	S	19 " 1924	Luton Town	H	1-0	2-0	1	3			5	6	7^{1}	8				2	4	9^{1}		11							10				7,000
39	M	21 " 1924	Queens Park Rangers	H	2-0	5-0	1	3			5		7	8^{1}				2^{1}	4	9^{2}		11		10^{1}					6				12,000
40	S	26 " 1924	Reading	A	0-2	0-3	1				5	6	7						4	9		11	3	10		2			8				5,000
41	M	28 " 1924	Swansea Town	H	0-0	2-0	1	3			5	6	7^{1}						2	9		11		8^{1}			4		10				6,000
42	S	3 May 1924	Reading	H	0-0	2-2	1	3			5		7^{1}					2	4	9				8^{1}			6		10		11		6,000

F.A. CUP

NO.		DATE	OPPONENTS		V.	H-T	F-T	Williamson Ernest	Sturgess Albert	Smith Ben	Christie Alex	Martin 'Pompey'	Field Richard	Austin Sam	Dennison Bob	Silverthorne James	Short James	Cooke George	Hope Philip	Hannah Joe	Jackson James	Smith Syd	Stoakes James	Reay Archie	Banks James	ATTD
1	S	1 Dec 1923	Folkestone Town	(5th Qual. Round)	A	2-1	3-2	1	3			5	6	7^{1}	8^{1}	9^{1}		11	2	4					10	4,20
2	S	15 " 1923	Stockport County	(6th Qual. Round)	H	1-0	2-0	1	6	3		5		7	8^{1}				2	4	9		11		10^{1}	11,57
3	S	12 Jan 1924	Bristol City	(1st Round)	H	0-0	0-1	1	6	3		5		7	8	9		11	2	4					10	11,33

1923–24 APPEARANCES & GOALS

	FOOTBALL LGE APPR.	GLS	F.A. CUP APPR.	GLS
Austin Sam	42	13	3	1
Williamson Ernest	41	–	3	–
Hannah Joe	40	5	3	–
Stoakes James	37	1	1	–
Hope Philip	36	1	3	–
Jackson James	34	15	1	–
Martin 'Pompey'	34	–	3	–
Sturgess Albert	32	–	3	–
Banks James	31	7	3	1
Dennison Bob	29	9	3	2
Field Richard	28	–	1	–
Smith Ben	15	–	2	–
Earl Sidney	11	1		
Short James	11	3		
Bradbrook Charles	8	–		
Murphy John	6	–		
Christie Alex	5	–		
Silverthorne James	5	1	2	1
Cooke George	4	–	2	–
Phillips Alan	4	3		
Smith Syd	3	–		
Reay Archie	2	–		
Woolley Robert	2	–		
Dennington Charlie	1	–		
Ford Alf	1	–		
Own Goals		1		

DIVISION 3 SOUTH

1923–24	P	W	D	L	F	A	PTS
Portsmouth	42	24	11	7	87	30	59
Plymouth Argyle	42	23	9	10	70	34	55
Millwall	42	22	10	10	64	38	54
Swansea Town	42	22	8	12	60	48	52
Brighton & Hove Albion	42	21	9	12	68	37	51
Swindon Town	42	17	13	12	58	44	47
Luton Town	42	16	14	12	50	44	46
Northampton Town	42	17	11	14	64	47	45
Bristol Rovers	42	15	13	14	52	46	43
Newport County	42	17	9	16	56	64	43
Norwich City	**42**	**16**	**8**	**18**	**60**	**59**	**40**
Aberdare Athletic	42	12	14	16	45	58	38
Merthyr Town	42	11	16	15	45	65	38
Charlton Athletic	42	11	15	16	38	45	37
Gillingham	42	12	13	17	43	58	37
Exeter City	42	15	7	20	37	52	37
Brentford	42	14	8	20	54	71	36
Reading	42	13	9	20	51	57	35
Southend United	42	12	10	20	53	84	34
Watford	42	9	15	18	45	54	33
Bournemouth	42	11	11	20	40	65	33
Queens Park Rangers	42	11	9	22	37	77	31

1924–25 DIVISION 3 SOUTH

NO.		DATE	OPPONENTS	V.	H-T	F-T	Dennington Charlie	Coulthard Tom	Campbell Archie	Hannah Joe	Martin 'Pompey'	Sturgess Albert	Banks James	McCudden Frank	Jackson James	Duffus Jack	Stoakes James	Wilson Joseph	North Ernest	Bradbrook Charles	Earl Sidney	Featherby Les	Osborne Harold	McKinney Daniel	Murphy John	Duthie John	Williamson Ernest	Ryder Terry	Own Goals	ATTD.
1	S	30 Aug 1924	Plymouth Argyle	H	0-0	1-1	1	2	3	4	5	6	7	8^1	9	10	11													10,000
2	W	3 Sept 1924	Bournemouth	A	0-0	0-0	1	2		6	5	3	10	8	9	4	7	11												6,000
3	S	6 " 1924	Bristol City	A	0-0	0-2	1	2		6	5	3	8		9	4	7	11	10											12,000
4	M	8 " 1924	Brighton & Hove Albion	H	2-1	2-2	1	2		7	5	3	8		9^2		11		10	4	6									6,000
5	S	13 " 1924	Swindon Town	H	1-0	4-0	1	2		4	5	3	8^1		9		11		10^2		6	7							$-^1$	8,000
6	S	20 " 1924	Aberdare Athletic	A	0-1	1-2	1	2		4	5	3	8		9		11		10^1		6	7								3,000
7	S	27 " 1924	Merthyr Town	H	1-0	1-0	1	2	3		5		8		9^1	4	11		10		6		7							9,000
8	S	4 Oct 1924	Brentford	H	1-0	3-0	1	2	3	4^1	5		8^1		9		11		10^1		6	7								8,000
9	Th	9 " 1924	Bournemouth	H	4-0	6-3	1	2	3	4^1	5^1		8^1		9^2		11		10^1		6	7								4,500
10	S	11 " 1924	Millwall	A	0-0	0-0	1	2	3	4	5		8		9		11		10		6	7								15,000
11	S	18 " 1924	Luton Town	H	0-1	1-1	1	2	3	4	5		8		9^1		11		10		6	7								9,000
12	S	25 " 1924	Reading	A	0-1	0-2	1		3	4	5	2	8		9		11		10		6	7								8,000
13	S	1 Nov 1924	Swansea Town	H	1-0	2-0	1	2	3	4	5		8		9		11		10^2		6			7						8,000
14	S	8 " 1924	Exeter City	A	0-1	0-1	1	2	3	4	5		8		9	6	11		10					7						6,000
15	S	15 " 1924	Bristol Rovers	H	1-1	1-1	1	2	3	4	5		8		9	6		11^1	10					7						7,000
16	S	22 " 1924	Newport County	A	0-1	0-3	1	2	3	4			8		9			11	10		6			7	5					8,000
17	S	6 Dec 1924	Watford	H	1-1	2-1	1	2	3	4	5		10	8^1			11		9^1	6				7						6,000
18	S	20 " 1924	Charlton Athletic	A	2-2	2-3	1	2	3	4	5			8	10			11	9^1	6		7^1								5,000
19	Th	25 " 1924	Queens Park Rangers	A	2-1	2-1	1		2	4	5	6	10^1	8^1				11	9	3				7						16,000
20	F	26 " 1924	Queens Park Rangers	H	2-0	5-0	1		2	4	5	6	10^1	8^1			11^1		9	3				7					$-^1$	13,000
21	S	27 " 1924	Plymouth Argyle	A	0-3	0-5	1		2	4	5	6	10	8			11		9	3				7						9,000
22	S	3 Jan 1925	Bristol City	H	0-0	0-0	1		2	4	5	6	10	8			11		9	3				7						7,000
23	S	17 " 1925	Swindon Town	A	0-1	0-1	1		2	4	5	6		8			11		9	3				7		10				6,000
24	S	24 " 1925	Aberdare Athletic	H	0-0	1-1	1		2	4	5	6	10	8^1			11		9	3				7						5,000
25	S	7 Feb 1925	Brentford	A	0-0	1-1			2	4	5	6		8^1			11		9	3				7		10	1			8,000
26	S	14 " 1925	Millwall	H	0-1	2-2	1		2	4	5	6	10	8^1			11		9^1	3				7						8,000
27	S	21 " 1925	Luton Town	A	0-0	0-0	1	3	2	4	5		8	9		6	11		10					7						5,000
28	S	28 " 1925	Reading	H	0-1	0-2	1		2	4	5		6	8	9		11		10	3				7						7,000
29	S	7 Mar 1925	Swansea Town	A	0-1	0-2	1	2		4	5		10	8			11		6	3				7				9		15,000
30	S	14 " 1925	Exeter City	H	0-0	0-1	1	2		4	5		10	8			11			3	6			7				9		6,000
31	S	21 " 1925	Bristol Rovers	A	0-1	0-3	1		2	6	5			8	10	4		11	9	3				7						7,000
32	M	23 " 1925	Merthyr Town	A	0-0	2-0	1		2	6^1	5			8	9^1	4		11	10	3				7						2,000
33	S	28 " 1925	Newport County	H	2-1	2-1	1		2	6	5		7	8	9^1	4		11	10^1	3										5,000
34	S	4 Apr 1925	Southend Unived	A	0-0	1-0	1		2		6		7	8^1	9	4		11	10	3					5					7,000
35	F	10 " 1925	Gillingham	A	1-0	1-3	1		2		6		7	8	9^1	4		11	10	3					5					7,000
36	S	11 " 1925	Watford	A	1-0	2-0	1		2		6		7	8	9^2	4		11	10	3					5					6,000
37	M	13 " 1925	Gillingham	H	0-0	0-0	1		2		6		10	8	9	4		11		3				7	5					12,000
38	Tu	14 " 1925	Southend United	H	0-1	0-1	1		2		6		7	8	9	4		11		3					5	10				6,000
39	S	18 " 1925	Northampton Town	A	1-1	1-1	1		2		6		7	10	9^1	4		11		3				8	5					7,000
40	Th	23 " 1925	Northampton Town	H	1-0	4-0	1		2		6		10	8^2	9^1	4		11^1		3				7	5					5,500
41	S	25 " 1925	Charlton Athletic	H	1-1	2-1	1		2		6		10	8	9^1	4		11		3				7^1	5					7,000
42	S	2 May 1925	Brighton & Hove Albion	A	0-2	1-3			2				10	8^1	9	4	11			3	6			7	5		1			6,000

F.A. CUP

NO.		DATE	OPPONENTS		V.	H-T	F-T	Dennington Charlie	Coulthard Tom	Campbell Archie	Hannah Joe	Martin 'Pompey'	Sturgess Albert	Banks James	McCudden Frank	Jackson James	Duffus Jack	Stoakes James	Wilson Joseph	North Ernest	Bradbrook Charles	Earl Sidney	Featherby Les	Osborne Harold	McKinney Daniel	Murphy John	Duthie John	Williamson Ernest	Ryder Terry	Own Goals	ATTD.
1	S	29 Nov 1924	Folkestone Town	(5th Qual. Round)	H	1-0	2-0	1	2	3	4	5		7	8	9		11^1		10^1	6										6,866
2	S	13 Dec 1924	Rochdale	(6th Qual. Round)	H	0-0	1-0	1	2	3	4^1	5		10	8			11		9	6				7						10,241
3	S	10 Jan 1925	Doncaster Rovers	(1st Round)	A	1-0	2-1	1		2	4	5	6	10^2		8		11		9	3				7						13,042
4	S	31 " 1925	Notts. County	(2nd Round)	A	0-1	0-4			2	4	5	6	10	8			11		9	3				7			1			20,161

1924–25 APPEARANCES & GOALS

	FOOTBALL LGE APPR.	FOOTBALL LGE GLS	F.A. CUP APPR.	F.A. CUP GLS
Dennington Charlie	40	–	3	–
Martin 'Pompey'	40	1	4	–
Banks James	37	5	4	2
Campbell Archie	35	–	4	–
North Ernest	33	11	4	1
Hannah Joe	32	3	4	1
Jackson James	30	14	2	–
McCudden Frank	28	12	3	–
Stoakes James	27	1	4	1
Bradbrook Charles	26	–	4	–
McKinney Daniel	24	1	3	–
Coulthard Tom	20	–	2	–
Duffus Jack	19	–		
Wilson Joseph	17	2		
Sturgess Albert	15	–	2	–
Earl Sidney	13	–		
Murphy John	10	–		
Featherby Les	8	1		
Duthie John	3	–		
Ryder Terry	2	–		
Williamson Ernest	2	–	1	–
Osborne Harold	1	–		
Own Goals		2		

DIVISION 3 SOUTH

1924–25	P	W	D	L	F	A	PTS
Swansea Town	42	23	11	8	68	35	57
Plymouth Argyle	42	23	10	9	77	38	56
Bristol City	42	22	9	11	60	41	53
Swindon Town	42	20	11	11	66	38	51
Millwall	42	18	13	11	58	38	49
Newport County	42	20	9	13	62	42	49
Exeter City	42	19	9	14	59	48	47
Brighton & Hove Albion	42	19	8	15	59	45	46
Northampton Town	42	20	6	16	51	44	46
Southend United	42	19	5	18	51	61	43
Watford	42	17	9	16	38	47	43
Norwich City	**42**	**14**	**13**	**15**	**53**	**51**	**41**
Gillingham	42	13	14	15	35	44	40
Reading	42	14	10	18	37	38	38
Charlton Athletic	42	13	12	17	46	48	38
Luton Town	42	10	17	15	49	57	37
Bristol Rovers	42	12	13	17	42	49	37
Aberdare Athletic	42	14	9	19	54	67	37
Queens Park Rangers	42	14	8	20	42	63	36
Bournemouth	42	13	8	21	40	58	34
Brentford	42	9	7	26	38	91	25
Merthyr Town	42	8	5	29	35	77	21

1925–26 DIVISION 3 SOUTH

NO.	DATE	OPPONENTS	V.	H-T	F-T	Dennington Charlie	Campbell Archie	Bradbrook Charles	Coulthard Tom	Murphy John	Martin 'Pompey'	McKinney Daniel	McCudden Frank	Jackson James	Banks Jimmy	Stoakes James	Duffus Jack	Metcalf Arthur	Hannah Joe	North Ernest	Wilson Joseph	Wingham Harry	Dempsey William	Walls Nick	Featherby Les	Rogers John	Earl Sidney	Davies Gordon	Duthie John	Howell Henry	Ryder Terry	Own Goals	ATTD.
1	S 29 Aug 1925	Bristol City	A	0-0	1-0	1	2	3	4	5	6	7	8	9	10	11[1]																	17,517
2	M 31 " 1925	Watford	H	1-0	1-1	1	2	3	4	5		7		9[1]	10	11	6	8															9,660
3	S 5 Sept 1925	Plymouth Argyle	H	0-2	0-3	1	2	3	4	5		7		9	8	11			6	10													11,936
4	W 9 " 1925	Watford	A	0-1	1-3	1	2	3	4	5		7		9	8		6			10[1]	11												5,603
5	S 12 " 1925	Southend United	A	1-0	1-0	1	2	3	4	5		7		9[1]	8		6			10	11												8,764
6	M 14 " 1925	Brighton & Hove Albion	H	1-1	1-2	1	2	3	4	5		7		9[1]	8		6			10	11												7,381
7	S 19 " 1925	Bournemouth	H	2-1	3-1	1			4	5		7	8	9[1]			6			10[1]	11[1]	2	3										7,366
8	S 26 " 1925	Millwall	H	1-0	1-0	1			4	5		7	8	9[1]			6			10	11	2	3										8,994
9	S 3 Oct 1925	Northampton Town	A	2-2	2-3	1			4	5		7[1]	8	9			6[1]			10	11	2	3										10,805
10	S 10 " 1925	Aberdare Athletic	H	0-2	2-3	1				5		7				11	6	10	4[1]	9		2	3	8[1]									7,604
11	S 17 " 1925	Charlton Athletic	A	0-1	0-3	1			4		5		8		10		6			9	11	2	3		7								9,720
12	S 24 " 1925	Gillingham	H	1-0	1-0	1			4		5	7		9	8[1]		6				11	2	3			10							6,942
13	W 28 " 1925	Brighton & Hove Albion	A	1-1	1-1	1				5	6	7[1]		9	8	11	4					2	3			10							5,171
14	S 31 " 1925	Exeter City	A	0-0	1-0	1				5		7		9[1]	10	11	6		4			2	3			8							6,036
15	S 7 Nov 1925	Reading	H	3-0	3-1	1		4		5		7		9[1]	10[1]	11	6		2			3				8						–[1]	6,053
16	S 14 " 1925	Luton Town	A	0-3	2-3	1		4		5		7		9[2]	10	11	6		2			3				8							6,380
17	S 21 " 1925	Queens Park Rangers	H	0-1	1-1	1		4		5		7		9[1]	10	11			2			3				8	6						6,258
18	S 5 Dec 1925	Swindon Town	H	1-1	2-2	1		11	4		5	7		9[1]			6		2	10		3				8[1]							5,405
19	S 12 " 1925	Merthyr Town	A	0-3	1-3	1		3	4		5	7		9	10	11			2							8[1]	6						4,387
20	S 19 " 1925	Newport County	H	0-0	0-0	1	2	3	4		5	7	8	9	10					11							6						4,660
21	F 25 " 1925	Crystal Palace	H	2-2	4-3	1	2	3	4		5	7		9			6			10[3]	11					8[1]							8,166
22	S 26 " 1925	Crystal Palace	A	0-2	0-2	1	2	3	4		5	7		9	8		6			10	11												20,208
23	S 2 Jan 1926	Bristol City	H	0-3	1-3	1	2	3	4		5	7		9			6			10	11					8[1]							6,086
24	S 9 " 1926	Bristol Rovers	A	2-2	2-2	1		3	2	5				9	8		6[1]			10[1]	11				7			4					6,397
25	S 16 " 1926	Plymouth Argyle	A	1-2	3-6	1		3	4	5				9[1]	8[1]		6		2	10[1]	11				7								9,205
26	S 23 " 1926	Southend United	H	0-0	1-2	1		3	4[1]	5				9	8		6		2	10	11				7								5,248
27	S 6 Feb 1926	Millwall	A	0-1	1-3	1	3	11			5	7[1]	8						2	10				4		9	6						17,468
28	S 13 " 1926	Northampton Town	H	2-0	2-1	1		6			5	7	8[2]		9				2	10		3		4			11						6,032
29	S 20 " 1926	Aberdare Athletic	A	1-1	1-3	1		6			5		8		9				2	10	11[1]	3		4	7								5,053
30	S 27 " 1926	Charlton Athletic	H	2-0	3-0	1					5				8		6		2	9[1]	11	3[1]		4	7[1]	10							5,964
31	S 6 Mar 1926	Gillingham	A	0-0	0-2	1					5				8		6		2	9	11	3		4	7				10				5,962
32	S 13 " 1926	Exeter City	H	2-1	3-1	1					5			9[2]	8[1]		4		2	10	11	3		6	7								5,788
33	S 20 " 1926	Reading	A	0-2	0-2	1				5				9	8		4		2		11	3		6	7				10				12,963
34	S 27 " 1926	Luton Town	H	0-0	2-0	1					6			9	8[2]		4		2		11	3		5	7				10				5,763
35	F 2 Apr 1926	Brentford	A	0-2	1-5	1					5			9	8		6		2		11	3		4[1]	7				10				11,463
36	S 3 " 1926	Queens Park Rangers	A	0-0	1-0	1					5			9[1]	8		4		2		11	3		6	7				10				6,006
37	M 5 " 1926	Brentford	H	1-0	1-0	1					5			9[1]	8		6		2			3		4	7				10	11			11,694
38	S 10 " 1926	Bristol Rovers	H	1-0	1-0	1					5			9[1]	8		6		2			3		4	7				10	11			5,597
39	S 17 " 1926	Swindon Town	A	1-1	1-3	1					5		8				6		2			3		4	7[1]				10	11	9		3,930
40	W 21 " 1926	Bournemouth	A	1-1	2-2	1		6			5			9[1]	8				2			3		4	7				10[1]	11			4,128
41	S 24 " 1926	Merthyr Town	H	1-0	2-2	1		6			5			9[1]	8[1]				2		11	3		4	7				10				5,160
42	S 1 May 1926	Newport County	A	1-0	1-1	1		6			5			9[1]	8				2		11	3		4	7				10				3,284

F.A. CUP

NO.	DATE	OPPONENTS	V.	H-T	F-T	Dennington Charlie	Campbell Archie	Bradbrook Charles	Coulthard Tom	Murphy John	Martin 'Pompey'	McKinney Daniel	McCudden Frank	Jackson James	Banks Jimmy	Stoakes James	Duffus Jack	Metcalf Arthur	Hannah Joe	North Ernest	Wilson Joseph	Wingham Harry	Dempsey William	Walls Nick	Featherby Les	Rogers John	Earl Sidney	Davies Gordon	Duthie John	Howell Henry	Ryder Terry	Own Goals	ATTD.
1	S 28 Nov 1925	Clapton (1st Round)	A	0-0	1-3	1		4		5		7		9[1]	10	11			2			3				8	6						3,543

1925–26 APPEARANCES & GOALS

	FOOTBALL LGE APPR.	FOOTBALL LGE GLS	F.A. CUP APPR.	F.A. CUP GLS
Dennington Charlie	42	–	1	–
Jackson James	34	20	1	1
Banks Jimmy	33	7	1	–
Duffus Jack	27	1		–
Wingham Harry	31	1	1	–
Hannah Joe	26	–	1	–
Martin 'Pompey'	25	–		
Bradbrook Charles	24	–	1	–
McKinney Daniel	24	3	1	–
Wilson Joseph	24	2		
North Ernest	23	8		
Coulthard Tom	20	1		
Murphy John	19	–	1	–
Featherby Les	18	2		
Walls Nick	17	2		
Rogers John	12	4	1	–
Campbell Archie	11	–		
Duthie John	11	1		
McCudden Frank	10	2		
Stoakes James	10	1	1	–
Dempsey William	8	–		
Earl Sidney	5	–	1	–
Howell Henry	4	–		
Metcalf Arthur	2	–		
Davies Gordon	1	–		
Ryder Terry	1	–		
Own Goals		1		

DIVISION 3 SOUTH

1925–26	P	W	D	L	F	A	PTS
Reading	42	23	11	8	77	52	57
Plymouth Argyle	42	24	8	10	107	67	56
Millwall	42	21	11	10	73	39	53
Bristol City	42	21	9	12	72	51	51
Brighton & Hove Albion	42	19	9	14	84	73	47
Swindon Town	42	20	6	16	69	64	46
Luton Town	42	18	7	17	80	75	43
Bournemouth	42	17	9	16	75	91	43
Aberdare Athletic	42	17	8	17	74	66	42
Gillingham	42	17	8	17	53	49	42
Southend United	42	19	4	19	78	73	42
Northampton Town	42	17	7	18	82	80	41
Crystal Palace	42	19	3	20	75	79	41
Merthyr Town	42	14	11	17	69	75	39
Watford	42	15	9	18	73	89	39
Norwich City	**42**	**15**	**9**	**18**	**58**	**73**	**39**
Newport County	42	14	10	18	64	74	38
Brentford	42	16	6	20	69	94	38
Bristol Rovers	42	15	6	21	66	69	36
Exeter City	42	15	5	22	72	70	35
Charlton Athletic	42	11	13	18	48	68	35
Queens Park Rangers	42	6	9	27	37	84	21

1926–27 DIVISION 3 SOUTH

NO.		DATE		OPPONENTS	V.	H-T	F-T	Dennington Charlie	Hannah Joe	Cornwell Ralph	Walls Nick	Martin 'Pompey'	McGrae Joe	Wigg Percy	Cropper Reg	Richmond Joe	Price Eric	Aitken John	Wingham Harry	Duffus Jack	Banks Jimmy	Jackson James	Dickinson James	Harris Arthur	Duthie John	Allman Leslie	Campbell Archie	Gilgun Patrick	McWhirr James	Aitken William	Cousins William	Own Goals	ATTD.
1	S	28 Aug	1926	Millwall	A	0-1	1-6	1	2	3	4	5	6	7	8	9[1]	10	11															19,732
2	S	4 Sept	1926	Bristol Rovers	H	1-0	2-0	1		3	4	5	6	7[1]	8[1]	9	10	11	2														8,725
3	M	6 "	1926	Northampton Town	A	0-0	0-3	1	2		4	5	6	7	8	9	10	11	3														4,491
4	S	11 "	1926	Swindon Town	A	2-1	2-3		2				5	7	4	9	10[2]	11	3	6	8												8,042
5	S	18 "	1926	Exeter City	H	2-3	4-4	1	2				5		9[2]		10	11[1]	3	6	8	7[1]	4										8,089
6	M	20 "	1926	Northampton Town	H	5-0	6-1	1	2				5		9[2]		10[3]	11	3	6	8[1]		4	7									5,123
7	S	25 "	1926	Merthyr Town	A	1-1	1-1	1	2		4		5	7	9[1]		10	11	3		8		6										3,422
8	S	2 Oct	1926	Southend United	H	1-0	1-1	1	2		4		5	7	9		10	11[1]	3		8		6										8,980
9	W	6 "	1926	Brighton & Hove Albion	A	0-1	2-3	1	2		4		5	7	8[1]	9	10	11[1]	3				6										5,479
10	S	9 "	1926	Luton Town	A	1-2	2-2	1	2		4		5		8[1]	9	10[1]	11	3		7		6										8,775
11	S	16 "	1926	Aberdare Athletic	A	0-0	2-1	1	2		4		5		8	9[2]	10	11	3		7		6										2,478
12	S	23 "	1926	Gillingham	H	0-0	0-0	1	2		4		5		8	9	10	11	3		7		6										7,796
13	Th	28 "	1926	Brighton & Hove Albion	H	0-0	0-2	1	2		4		5		8	9	10	11	3		7		6										3,893
14	S	30 "	1926	Crystal Palace	A	1-4	1-7	1	2		4		5		8	9		10	3			7	6		10[1]								12,184
15	S	6 Nov	1926	Coventry City	H	2-0	3-0		2		4		5	7[2]	9	10		11	3		8[1]		6			1							6,427
16	S	13 "	1926	Queens Park Rangers	A	0-0	0-4		2		4		5	7	9	10		11			8		6			1	3						6,954
17	S	20 "	1926	Charlton Athletic	H	1-3	2-3		2				4		10	5		11[1]		6	8[1]	9				1	3	7					4,712
18	S	4 Dec	1926	Bournemouth	H	2-1	4-1	1	2			5	6		8[1]			11		4	10	9[2]					3		7[1]				5,619
19	S	18 "	1926	Newport County	H	0-0	1-0	1				5	6		8			11	2	4[1]	10	9					3			7			6,667
20	S	25 "	1926	Brentford	H	1-0	2-1	1	2			5	6		8[1]			11		4	10	9[1]					3			7			10,743
21	M	27 "	1926	Brentford	A	0-2	0-3	1	2			5	6		8			11	3	4	10	9								7			17,002
22	S	15 Jan	1927	Millwall	H	0-0	0-2	1	2			5	6				10	11		4	8	9					3			7			7,928
23	S	22 "	1927	Bristol Rovers	A	0-0	0-1	1	2				6		8	5		11		4		9			10		3			7			4,878
24	S	29 "	1927	Swindon Town	H	1-0	2-1	1	2				6		8	5		11[1]		4		9[1]			10		3			7			6,423
25	S	5 Feb	1927	Exeter City	A	0-1	0-1	1	2				6		8	5		11		4		9			10		3				7		4,987
26	W	9 "	1927	Bristol City	A	0-0	1-1	1	2				6[1]		8	5		11		4		9			10		3				7		9,121
27	S	12 "	1927	Merthyr Town	H	0-0	4-0	1	2				6		8[1]	5		11		4					10[1]		3	9[2]			7		6,335
28	S	19 "	1927	Southend United	A	1-1	3-3	1	2				6		8	5		11[1]		4					10[1]		3	9[1]			7		6,517
29	S	26 "	1927	Luton Town	H	1-0	3-2	1	2				6		8	5		11[1]		4[1]					10		3	9[1]			7		7,270
30	S	5 Mar	1927	Aberdare Athletic	H	1-1	2-2	1	2				6[1]		8[1]	5		11		4					10		3	9			7		5,942
31	S	12 "	1927	Gillingham	A	0-1	0-1	1	2				6		8	5		11		4					10		3	9			7		4,448
32	S	19 "	1927	Crystal Palace	H	0-1	0-1	1	2				6		9	5		11		4	8						3	10			7		7,087
33	S	26 "	1927	Coventry City	A	0-1	0-1	1	2				6		10	5		11		4	8		3					9			7		8,968
34	S	2 Apr	1927	Queens Park Rangers	H	0-1	0-1		2				6		8	5		11		4	10					1	3	9			7		10,973
35	S	9 "	1927	Charlton Athletic	A	0-1	0-2	1	2			5	6			9	10	11					4		8		3			7			3,300
36	F	15 "	1927	Watford	A	0-0	1-1	1	2			5	6		8	9	10	11[1]					4				3			7			7,785
37	S	16 "	1927	Bristol City	H	1-0	1-1	1	2			5	6		8[1]	9		11		4	10						3			7			8,578
38	M	18 "	1927	Watford	H	2-0	4-0	1	2			5	6		8	9[3]		11		4	10						3			7		–[1]	11,371
39	S	23 "	1927	Bournemouth	A	1-0	1-0	1	2			5	6			9[1]		11		4					10		3	8		7			4,253
40	M	25 "	1927	Plymouth Argyle	A	0-2	1-2	1	2			5	6			9[1]		11		4					10		3	8		7			5,273
41	S	30 "	1927	Plymouth Argyle	H	0-1	0-2	1	2			5	6			9		11		4	10						3	8		7			7,943
42	S	7 May	1927	Newport Country	A	0-0	0-0		2			5	6		8	9		11		10			4			1	3			7			2,425

F.A. CUP

NO.		DATE		OPPONENTS		V.	H-T	F-T	Dennington Charlie	Hannah Joe	Cornwell Ralph	Walls Nick	Martin 'Pompey'	McGrae Joe	Wigg Percy	Cropper Reg	Richmond Joe	Price Eric	Aitken John	Wingham Harry	Duffus Jack	Banks Jimmy	Jackson James	Dickinson James	Harris Arthur	Duthie John	Allman Leslie	Campbell Archie	Gilgun Patrick	McWhirr James	Aitken William	Cousins William	Own Goals	ATTD.
1	S	27 Nov	1926	Crystal Palace	(1st Round)	A	0-0	0-0	1	2			5	6		8			11		4	10	9					3		7				15,000
2	Th	2 Dec	1926	Crystal Palace	(Replay)	H	1-0	1-0	1	2			5	6		8			11		4	10[1]	9					3		7				9,821
3	S	11 "	1926	Chatham	(2nd Round)	H	3-0	5-0	1	2			5	6		8[2]			11		4	10	9[2]					3		7[1]				12,052
4	S	8 Jan	1927	Southampton	(3rd Round)	A	0-1	0-3	1	2		4	5	6		8	7		11			10	9					3						15,587

1926–27 APPEARANCES & GOALS

	FOOTBALL LGE APPR.	FOOTBALL LGE GLS	F.A. CUP APPR.	F.A. CUP GLS
itken John	42	8	4	–
cGrae Joe	42	2	4	–
annah Joe	40	–	4	–
ropper Reg	37	13	4	2
ennington Charlie	37	–	4	–
chmond Joe	33	8	1	–
uffus Jack	27	2	3	–
ampbell Archie	25	–	4	–
anks Jimmy	23	3	4	1
ickinson James	16	–		
artin 'Pompey'	16	–	4	–
ice Eric	16	6		
ingham Harry	16	–		
tken William	14	–		
uthie John	13	3		
alls Nick	13	–	1	–
lgun Patrick	12	4		
ckson James	12	5	4	2
ousins William	10	–		
gg Percy	9	3		
man Leslie	5	–		
ornwell Ralph	2	–		
arris Arthur	1	–		
cWhirr James	1	1	3	1
wn Goals		1		

DIVISION 3 SOUTH

1926–27	P	W	D	L	F	A	PTS
Bristol City	42	27	8	7	104	54	62
Plymouth Argyle	42	25	10	7	95	61	60
Millwall	42	23	10	9	89	51	56
Brighton & Hove Albion	42	21	11	10	79	50	53
Swindon Town	42	21	9	12	100	85	51
Crystal Palace	42	18	9	15	84	81	45
Bournemouth	42	18	8	16	78	66	44
Luton Town	42	15	14	13	68	66	44
Newport County	42	19	6	17	57	71	44
Bristol Rovers	42	16	9	17	78	80	41
Brentford	42	13	14	15	70	61	40
Exeter City	42	15	10	17	76	73	40
Charlton Athletic	42	16	8	18	60	61	40
Queens Park Rangers	42	15	9	18	65	71	39
Coventry City	42	15	7	20	71	86	37
Norwich City	**42**	**12**	**11**	**19**	**59**	**71**	**35**
Merthyr Town	42	13	9	20	63	80	35
Northampton Town	42	15	5	22	59	87	35
Southend United	42	14	6	22	64	77	34
Gillingham	42	11	10	21	54	72	32
Watford	42	12	8	22	57	87	32
Aberdare Athletic	42	9	7	26	62	101	25

1927–28 DIVISION 3 SOUTH

NO.		DATE	OPPONENTS	V.	H-T	F-T	Dennington Charlie	Hannah Joe	Campbell Archie	Pembleton Arthur	Richmond Joe	McGrae Joe	Porter Ernest	Robinson Les	Verco Percy	Moule Alf	Slicer Jacky	Lamb Joseph	Crockford Harold	Cropper Reg	Rowe George	Mason Arthur	Allman Leslie	Ferrari Fred	Hetherington Joe	Cousins William	Jackson James	Mclaverty Bernard	Bradley Cecil	Cropper Arthur	Own Goals	ATTD.
1	S	27 Aug 1927	Crystal Palace	H	2-1	4-1	1	2^1	3	4	5	6	7	8	9^1	10^1	11^1															13,140
2	M	29 " 1927	Luton Town	A	2-0	3-1	1	2	3	5		6	7	8	9^2	10^1	11	4														9,157
3	S	3 Sept 1927	Exeter City	A	0-0	2-2	1	2	3	5		6	7	8	9^1	10	11	4													$-^1$	7,567
4	M	5 " 1927	Luton Town	H	2-0	3-0	1	2	3	5		6	7	8^1	9^1	10^1	11	4														13,640
5	S	10 " 1927	Torquay United	H	2-0	4-0	1	2	3	5		6	7	8^1	9^2	10^1	11	4														12,887
6	S	17 " 1927	Walsall	A	0-0	1-1	1	2	3	5		6	7	8		9^1	11	4	10													12,412
7	S	24 " 1927	Northampton Town	A	1-2	2-4	1	2	3	5		6	7	8	9^2	10	11	4														13,921
8	S	1 Oct 1927	Southend United	H	2-0	2-1	1	2	3	5		6	7^1	8	9^1	10	11	4														9,079
9	S	8 " 1927	Brighton & Hove Albion	A	0-0	0-1	1	2	3	5		6	7	8	9	10	11	4														9,286
10	S	15 " 1927	Bournemouth	H	2-1	3-3	1	2	3	4	5	6	7		9	8^2	11			10^1												9,675
11	S	22 " 1927	Bristol Rovers	H	3-2	4-2	1	2		5		6	7^1		9^1	8^1	11	4		10^1	3											10,946
12	S	29 " 1927	Plymouth Argyle	A	2-2	2-4	1	2		5		6	7		9^2	8	11	4		10	3											10,912
13	S	5 Nov 1927	Merthyr Town	H	4-0	4-0	1	2^1		5		6	7		9^2	8	11	4^1		10	3											7,967
14	S	12 " 1927	Charlton Athletic	A	1-1	2-3	1	2	3	5		6	7		9^1	8^1	11	4		10												10,530
15	S	19 " 1927	Watford	H	1-0	1-1	1	2	3	5		6	7	8^1	9		11	4		10												6,049
16	S	3 Dec 1927	Swindon Town	H	0-2	1-3	1	2			5	6	7	8^1	9	10	11	4				3										7,479
17	S	17 " 1927	Coventry City	H	0-2	0-2		2			3	6	7		9		11	4	10				1	5	8							5,358
18	S	24 " 1927	Gillingham	A	0-2	0-3		2			3	5	7	8	10		11	4					1			6	9					4,078
19	Tu	27 " 1927	Millwall	A	1-1	1-2	1	2			5	6		8^1	9	10	11	4						3		7						16,550
20	S	31 " 1927	Crystal Palace	A	0-1	1-2	1	2			5	6		8	9^1	10	11	4						3		7						7,446
21	S	7 Jan 1928	Exeter City	H	1-2	2-2	1	2			5	6		8	9^1	10	11	4^1						3		7						6,706
22	S	14 " 1928	Newport County	A	0-2	2-2	1	2^1	3			6		8	9^1	10	11	4								7		5				2,875
23	S	21 " 1928	Torquay United	A	1-2	2-4	1	2	3			6^1		8	9	10	11^1	4								7		5				3,336
24	S	28 " 1928	Walsall	H	1-2	1-4		2	3	5			7		9	10^1	11	8					1			4		6				5,730
25	S	4 Feb 1928	Northampton Town	H	1-1	3-4		2		4	3	6	7	10^1	9^2	8	11						1					5				6,760
26	S	11 " 1928	Southend United	A	0-1	1-1		2		4	3	6	7	10^1	9	8	11						1					5				4,671
27	S	18 " 1928	Brighton & Hove Albion	H	0-0	0-0		2			3	6			8		11	4		10			1					5	7	9		8,131
28	S	25 " 1928	Bournemouth	A	1-1	1-2		2			3	6		10	9^1	8	11	4					1					5	7			6,04
29	S	3 Mar 1928	Bristol Rovers	A	0-1	0-3		2			3	6	7	10	9	8	11	4					1					5				7,03
30	S	10 " 1928	Plymouth Argyle	H	2-0	2-0		2^1			3	6	7	10	9	8^1	11	4					1					5				7,21
31	S	17 " 1928	Merthyr Town	A	1-1	1-1		2			3	6	7		9^1	8	11	4		10			1					5				2,31
32	S	24 " 1928	Charlton Athletic	H	0-0	0-0	1	2			3	6		10	9	8	11	4								7		5				7,25
33	S	31 " 1928	Watford	A	0-1	0-2	1	2			3	6		10	8		11	4								7		5		9		9,88
34	F	6 Apr 1928	Brentford	A	0-1	1-3	1	2	3		5		7	10	9^1		11	4										6		8		11,814
35	S	7 " 1928	Newport County	H	0-1	1-1	1	2			3	6	7^1	8	9	10	11	4										5				7,64
36	M	9 " 1928	Brentford	H	1-1	1-1	1	2			3	6	7	8^1	9	10	11	4										5				10,84
37	S	14 " 1928	Swindon Town	A	1-0	1-1	1				3	6			9	10	11	4		8^1		2				7		5				4,98
38	S	21 " 1928	Queens Park Rangers	H	2-1	3-1	1				3	6	7		9^3	10	11			8		2				4		5				4,86
39	S	28 " 1928	Coventry City	A	2-1	2-2	1	2			3	6	7	10^2	9		11	4		8								5				9,10
40	M	30 " 1928	Millwall	H	1-0	2-0	1	2			3	6	7	10	9^2		11	4		8								5				8,97
41	Th	3 May 1928	Queens Park Rangers	A	0-0	0-0	1	2			3	6	7	8	9		11									4		5		10		4,69
42	S	5 " 1928	Gillingham	H	0-0	0-0	1	2			3	6	7	8	9		11									4		5		10		6,55

F.A. CUP

NO.		DATE	OPPONENTS		V.	H-T	F-T	Dennington Charlie	Hannah Joe	Campbell Archie	Pembleton Arthur	Richmond Joe	McGrae Joe	Porter Ernest	Robinson Les	Verco Percy	Moule Alf	Slicer Jacky	Lamb Joseph	Crockford Harold	Cropper Reg	Rowe George	Mason Arthur	ATTD.
1	S	26 Nov 1927	Poole Town	(1st Round)	A	0-1	1-1	1	2	3	5		6	7	10^1	9	8	11	4					4,49
2	Th	1 Dec 1927	Poole Town	(Replay)	H	4-0	5-0	1	2	3	5		6	7	8^1	9^3	10^1	11	4					5,95
3	S	10 " 1927	Luton Town	(2nd Round)	A	0-5	0-6	1	2		5		6	7	8	9	10	11	4				3	10,75

1927–28 APPEARANCES & GOALS

	FOOTBALL LGE APPR.	GLS	F.A. CUP APPR.	GLS
Slicer Jacky	42	2	3	–
Verco Percy	41	29	3	3
Hannah Joe	40	4	3	–
McGrae Joe	40	1	3	–
Lamb Joseph	35	2	3	–
Dennington Charlie	32	–	3	–
Moule Alf	32	11	3	1
Porter Ernest	32	3	3	–
Robinson Les	31	10	3	2
Richmond Joe	26	–		
McLaverty Bernard	21	–		
Pembleton Arthur	18	–	3	–
Campbell Archie	16	–	2	–
Cousins William	13	–		
Cropper Reg	12	3		
Allman Leslie	10	–		
Cropper Arthur	5	–		
Ferrari Fred	4	–		
Mason Arthur	3	–	1	–
Rowe George	3	–		
Bradley Cecil	2	–		
Crockford Harold	2	–		
Hetherington Joe	1	–		
Jackson James	1	–		
Own Goals		1		

DIVISION 3 SOUTH

1927–28	P	W	D	L	F	A	PTS
Millwall	42	30	5	7	127	50	65
Northampton Town	42	23	9	10	102	64	55
Plymouth Argyle	42	23	7	12	85	54	53
Brighton & Hove Albion	42	19	10	13	81	69	48
Crystal Palace	42	18	12	12	79	72	48
Swindon Town	42	19	9	14	90	69	47
Exeter City	42	17	12	13	70	60	46
Southend United	42	20	6	16	80	64	46
Newport County	42	18	9	15	81	84	45
Queens Park Rangers	42	17	9	16	72	71	43
Charlton Athletic	42	15	13	14	60	70	43
Brentford	42	16	8	18	76	74	40
Luton Town	42	16	7	19	94	87	39
Bournemouth	42	13	12	17	72	79	38
Watford	42	14	10	18	68	78	38
Gillingham	42	13	11	18	62	81	37
Norwich City	**42**	**10**	**16**	**16**	**66**	**70**	**36**
Walsall	42	12	9	21	75	101	33
Bristol Rovers	42	14	4	24	67	93	32
Coventry City	42	11	9	22	67	96	31
Merthyr Town	42	9	13	20	53	91	31
Torquay United	42	8	14	20	53	103	30

1928–29 DIVISION 3 SOUTH

No.		Date	Opponents	V.	H-T	F-T	Dennington Charlie	Hannah Joe	Richmond Joe	Lamb Joseph	McLaverty Bernard	McGrae Joe	Slicer Jacky	Stephenson John	Varco Percy	McKenna Frank	Philipson James	Greenwell Wilf	Porter Ernest	Cropper Arthur	Cousins William	Mason Arthur	Bradley Cecil	Hooper Charlie	Dent Fred	Gardiner John	Chappell Archie	Botto Lewis	Own Goals	ATTD.
1	S	25 Aug 1928	Coventry City	A	0-3	0-3	1	2	3	4	5	6	7	8	9	10	11													16,011
2	M	27 " 1928	Bournemouth	H	3-0	5-1	1	2	3	4	6		11^{1}	8	9^{2}	10^{2}		5	7											8,060
3	S	1 Sept 1928	Northampton Town	H	1-0	1-1	1	2	3	4	6		11^{1}	8		10		5	7	9										11,120
4	W	5 " 1928	Bournemouth	A	0-1	0-2	1	2	3	4	6		11	8		10		5		9	7									3,902
5	S	8 " 1928	Charlton Athletic	A	0-1	0-1	1	2	3	4	6		11	8		10		5		9	7									10,190
6	S	15 " 1928	Crystal Palace	H	0-1	0-1	1	2	3	4	6		11	8	9	10		5			7									9,892
7	S	22 " 1928	Brighton & Hove Albion	H	3-1	3-1	1	2	3		6	4	11	8	9	10^{1}		5	7^{1}										–^{1}	7,425
8	S	29 " 1928	Exeter City	A	1-1	1-3	1	2	3		6	4	11		9	10^{1}		5	7	8										6,416
9	S	6 Oct 1928	Southend United	H	1-1	2-5	1	2	3		6	4	11		9	10^{2}		5	7	8										7,472
10	S	13 " 1928	Merthyr Town	A	0-2	1-2	1	4^{1}	3	8		6	11			10		5	7	9		2								4,231
11	S	20 " 1928	Swindon Town	A	1-0	2-1	1	2	3	4		6	11	8	9	10^{1}		5^{1}	7											6,403
12	S	27 " 1928	Torquay United	H	1-0	3-0	1	2	3	4		6	11	8	9	10^{1}		5					7^{1}						–^{1}	6,975
13	S	3 Nov 1928	Gillingham	A	0-1	0-4	1	2	3	4		6	11	8		10		5		9			7							4,356
14	S	10 " 1928	Plymouth Argyle	H	0-2	0-3	1	2	3	4	5	6	11		9	10			7					8						7,790
15	S	17 " 1928	Fulham	A	1-0	1-2	1	2	3	4	5	6	11		9^{1}	10			7					8						15,050
16	S	1 Dec 1928	Bristol Rovers	A	0-2	0-2	1	2	3	4		6	11			10		5	7			9		8						6,652
17	S	15 " 1928	Walsall	A	2-1	3-3	1	2	3	4		6	11	8	9^{1}	10		5	7^{2}											3,696
18	S	22 " 1928	Newport County	H	2-1	3-1	1	2	3	4		6	11	8	9^{1}	10^{1}		5	7^{1}											4,824
19	Tu	25 " 1928	Luton Town	A	0-0	1-2	1	2	3	4	6		11	8		10^{1}		5	7						9					14,146
20	W	26 " 1928	Luton Town	H	2-0	3-0	1	2	3	4	6		11	8^{1}		10^{1}		5	7						9^{1}					12,418
21	S	29 " 1928	Coventry City	H	1-0	3-0	1	2	3	4	6		11	8		10^{1}		5	7^{1}						9^{1}					7,632
22	S	5 Jan 1929	Northampton Town	A	0-1	0-2	1	2	3	4	6		11	8				5	7	10					9					7,057
23	S	19 " 1929	Charlton Athletic	H	0-0	0-1	1	2	3		6	4	11			8		5	7						9	10				3,690
24	S	2 Feb 1929	Brighton & Hove Albion	A	0-1	0-3	1	2	3	4	5	6	11			10			7						9		8			2,093
25	S	9 " 1929	Exeter City	H	0-0	5-0	1	2	3	4	5	6	11^{1}			10^{1}			7^{1}						9^{1}		8^{1}			4,615
26	S	16 " 1929	Southend United	A	0-1	3-5	1	2	3	4	5	6	11			10^{1}			7						9^{2}		8			3,459
27	S	23 " 1929	Merthyr Town	H	3-1	3-1	1	2	3	4	5	6	11			10^{1}			7						9^{2}		8			4,111
28	S	2 Mar 1929	Swindon Town	H	1-0	1-1	1	2	3	4	5	6	11			10^{1}			7						9		8			6,363
29	W	6 " 1929	Crystal Palace	A	0-2	1-2	1	2	3	4	5	6	11			10			7^{1}						9		8			9,171
30	S	9 " 1929	Torquay United	A	2-0	3-0		2	3	4	5	6	11			10			7						9^{2}		8^{1}	1		8,324
31	S	16 " 1929	Gillingham	H	1-1	1-2	1	2	3	4	5	6	11			10^{1}			7						9		8			5,385
32	S	23 " 1929	Plymouth Argyle	A	0-1	0-4			3	4	5	6	11			10			7			2			9		8	1		7,093
33	F	29 " 1929	Brentford	A	0-0	0-4	1		3	4	5	6	11	8		10			7			2			9					10,049
34	S	30 " 1929	Fulham	H	2-1	2-2	1	2	3	4	5	6	11	8^{1}		10^{1}			7						9					7,737
35	M	1 Apr 1929	Brentford	H	1-3	2-4	1	2	3	4	5	6	11	8		10			7^{1}						9^{1}					9,713
36	S	6 " 1929	Queens Park Rangers	A	0-0	0-3	1	2	3	4	6		11			10		5	7						9		8			12,961
37	S	13 " 1929	Bristol Rovers	H	1-0	2-1	1	2	3	4	8	6	11			10		5	7^{2}						9					4,363
38	S	20 " 1929	Watford	A	0-2	2-2	1	2	3	4	8	6	11^{1}			10		5	7^{1}						9					9,405
39	M	22 " 1929	Queens Park Rangers	H	3-0	3-1	1	2	3	4	8^{1}	6	11^{1}			10		5	7						9^{1}					7,670
40	S	27 " 1929	Walsall	H	1-1	2-1	1	2	3	4	8	6	11			10		5	7^{1}						9^{1}					6,161
41	Th	2 May 1929	Watford	H	3-1	5-2	1	2	3^{1}	4	8^{3}	6	11			10		5	7						9				–^{1}	6,732
42	S	4 " 1929	Newport County	A	0-2	2-2	1	2	3	4		6	11			10		5	7^{2}	8					9					2,117

F.A. CUP

No.		Date	Opponents		V.	H-T	F-T	Dennington Charlie	Hannah Joe	Richmond Joe	Lamb Joseph	McLaverty Bernard	McGrae Joe	Slicer Jacky	Stephenson John	Varco Percy	McKenna Frank	Philipson James	Greenwell Wilf	Porter Ernest	Cropper Arthur	Cousins William	Mason Arthur	Bradley Cecil	Hooper Charlie	Own Goals	ATTD.
1	S	24 Nov 1928	Chatham Town	(1st Round)	H	2-0	6-1	1	2^{1}	3	4	5	6	11		9^{2}	10			7^{1}					8^{1}	–^{1}	6,368
2	S	8 Dec 1928	Newport County	(2nd Round)	H	2-0	6-0	1	2^{1}	3	4		6	11^{1}	8	9^{4}	10		5	7							9,072
3	S	12 Jan 1929	Corinthians	(3rd Round)	H	0-2	0-5	1	2	3	4		6	11	8	9	10		5	7							20,129

1928–29 APPEARANCES & GOALS

	FOOTBALL LGE APPR.	FOOTBALL LGE GLS	F.A. CUP APPR.	F.A. CUP GLS
Richmond Joe	42	1	3	–
Slicer Jacky	42	5	3	1
McKenna Frank	41	18	3	–
Dennington Charlie	40	–	3	–
Hannah Joe	40	1	3	2
Lamb Joseph	38	–	3	–
Porter Ernest	36	14	3	1
McLaverty Bernard	34	4	1	–
McGrae Joe	32	–	3	–
Greenwell Wilf	27	1	2	–
Dent Fred	24	12		
Stephenson John	19	2	2	–
Varco Percy	12	5	3	6
Chappell Archie	10	2		
Cropper Arthur	9	–		
Mason Arthur	4	–		
Cousins William	3	–		
Hooper Charlie	3	–	1	1
Botto Lewis	2	–		
Bradley Cecil	2	1		
Gardiner John	1	–		
Philipson James	1	–		
Own Goals		3		1

DIVISION 3 SOUTH

1928–29	P	W	D	L	F	A	PTS
Charlton Athletic	42	23	8	11	86	60	54
Crystal Palace	42	23	8	11	81	67	54
Northampton Town	42	20	12	10	96	57	52
Plymouth Argyle	42	20	12	10	83	51	52
Fulham	42	21	10	11	101	71	52
Queens Park Rangers	42	19	14	9	82	61	52
Luton Town	42	19	11	12	89	73	49
Watford	42	19	10	13	79	74	48
Bournemouth	42	19	9	14	84	77	47
Swindon Town	42	15	13	14	75	72	43
Coventry City	42	14	14	14	62	57	42
Southend United	42	15	11	16	80	75	41
Brentford	42	14	10	18	56	60	38
Walsall	42	13	12	17	73	79	38
Brighton & Hove Albion	42	16	6	20	58	76	38
Newport County	42	13	9	20	69	86	35
Norwich City	**42**	**14**	**6**	**22**	**69**	**81**	**34**
Torquay United	42	14	6	22	66	84	34
Bristol Rovers	42	13	7	22	60	79	33
Merthyr Town	42	11	8	23	55	103	30
Exeter City	42	9	11	22	67	88	29
Gillingham	42	10	9	23	43	83	29

1929–30 DIVISION 3 SOUTH

NO.		DATE	OPPONENTS	V.	H-T	F-T	Jarvie John	Hannah Joe	Richmond Joe	Brown William	O'Brien Mick	Lochhead Doug	Porter Ernest	Thomson Norman	Thompson James	Anderson George	Slicer Jacky	Scott John	Graham Robert	Jobling Joe	Knox William	Cropper Arthur	Lamb Joseph	Greenwell Wilf	Hunt Thomas	Noble Arthur	Varco Percy	Dennis George	Bennett Edward	Own Goals	ATTD.
1	S	31 Aug 1929	Fulham	H	0-3	0-4	1	2	3	4	5	6	7	8	9	10	11														15,778
2	M	2 Sept 1929	Luton Town	A	0-0	1-1	1	2	3	4	5	6	7	8	9^1		11	10													11,097
3	S	7 " 1929	Brighton & Hove Albion	A	0-3	3-6	1	2	3	4	5	6	7	8	9^3		11	10													7,546
4	M	9 " 1929	Luton Town	H	0-1	1-1	1	2			5	6		10	9	8^1	11		3	4	7										9,086
5	S	14 " 1929	Crystal Palace	A	1-1	2-3	1	2		4	5	6		10	9^1	8	11^1		3		7										14,067
6	M	16 " 1929	Walsall	H	3-0	3-0	1	2		4	5^1	6		8	9	10^2	11		3		7										7,927
7	S	21 " 1929	Gillingham	H	2-0	2-0	1	2		4	5	6	7^2	8	9	10	11		3												9,981
8	S	28 " 1929	Northampton Town	A	0-2	0-4	1	2		4	5	6	7		9	10	11		3			8									12,302
9	S	5 Oct 1929	Exeter City	H	1-1	3-1	1	2	3			6	7		10^1	8^1	11						4	5	9^1						9,914
10	S	12 " 1929	Southend United	A	1-0	1-1	1	2	3				7		10	8	11			6			4	5	9^1						8,981
11	S	19 " 1929	Bristol Rovers	H	1-1	4-2	1		3				7^1		10^1	8^1	11		2	6			4	5	9^1						9,088
12	S	26 " 1929	Brentford	A	0-0	0-3	1		3				7		10	8	11		2	6			4	5	9						11,052
13	S	2 Nov 1929	Clapton Orient	H	0-0	1-0	1						7		10	8	11		3	6			4	5	9^1	2					9,344
14	S	9 " 1929	Coventry City	A	0-2	1-3	1	2				8	7		10^1	9	11		3	6			4	5							10,104
15	S	16 " 1929	Watford	H	2-0	3-1	1	2	3	4			7	8	10^1	9^1	11			6				5^1							5,555
16	S	23 " 1929	Newport County	A	1-0	4-4	1	2	3	4			7		10^3	8	11			6				5			9^1				2,541
17	S	7 Dec 1929	Merthyr Town	A	3-1	5-1	1	2	3		5	6	7		10^2	8^1	11^1			4							9^1				1,115
18	S	21 " 1929	Swindon Town	A	0-0	1-2	1	2	3		5	6	7^1		10	8	11			4							9				4,524
19	W	25 " 1929	Queens Park Rangers	H	2-0	3-0	1	2	3		5	6	7	8	10^1		11			4					9^2						11,163
20	Th	26 " 1929	Queens Park Rangers	A	1-1	2-3	1	2	3	4	5	6	7	10			11								9^1		8^1				13,530
21	S	28 " 1929	Fulham	A	1-1	3-3	1	2	3	4	5	6	7		8^1		11					10^1			9^1						12,410
22	S	4 Jan 1930	Brighton & Hove Albion	H	0-0	2-0	1	2	3	4	5	6	7^1	10	8		11								9^1						9,654
23	S	11 " 1930	Torquay United	H	0-0	2-0	1	2^1	3	4	5	6	7	10	8		11								9^1						8,864
24	S	18 " 1930	Crystal Palace	H	1-1	2-2	1	2	3	4	5^1	6	7^1	10	8		11								9						10,348
25	S	25 " 1930	Gillingham	A	2-1	2-1	1	2	3	4	5	6	7		10		11					8			9^1						3,24
26	S	1 Feb 1930	Northampton Town	H	2-1	4-3	1	2	3	4^1	5	6	7	10			11					8^1			9^2						11,68
27	S	8 " 1930	Exeter City	A	0-3	0-3	1	2	3	4	5	6	7	10			11					8			9						5,03
28	S	15 " 1930	Southend United	H	1-0	1-1	1	2	3	4	5	6	7		10							8^1			9			11			9,81
29	S	22 " 1930	Bristol Rovers	A	0-0	1-0	1	2	3	4	5	6	7		10^1		11					8			9						5,82
30	S	1 Mar 1930	Brentford	H	1-1	2-2	1	2	3	4	5	6	7^1		10		11^1					8			9						14,08
31	S	8 " 1930	Clapton Orient	A	0-0	0-0	1	2		4	5	6	7		10	8	11		3						9						9,85
32	S	15 " 1930	Coventry City	H	4-0	10-2	1	2		4	5	6^1	7^1			8	11^1	10^2	3						9^5						8,23
33	S	22 " 1930	Watford	A	1-0	1-2	1	2		4	5	6	7			8	11	10	3						9					$–^1$	6,88
34	S	29 " 1930	Newport County	H	2-1	4-1	1	2		4	5^2	6	7			8	11	10^1	3						9^1						8,47
35	S	5 Apr 1930	Torquay United	A	2-0	2-2	1			4	5	6	7			8	11	10^1	3						9^1				2		3,92
36	S	12 " 1930	Merthyr Town	H	0-1	5-1	1			4	5	6	7			8^3	11	10	3						9^2				2		7,24
37	S	19 " 1930	Plymouth Argyle	A	0-1	1-4	1			4	5	6	7			8	11^1	10	3						9				2		19,89
38	M	21 " 1930	Bournemouth	A	3-1	3-2	1			4	5	6	7^1			8	11	10	3						9^2				2		6,57
39	Tu	22 " 1930	Bournemouth	H	0-0	1-0	1			4	5	6^1	7			8	11	10	3						9				2		10,43
40	S	26 " 1930	Swindon Town	H	0-2	1-5	1				5	6	7			8^1	11		3			10	4		9				2		7,59
41	M	28 " 1930	Plymouth Argyle	H	1-0	1-2	1	2		4		6	7			8^1	11		3					5	9				10		13,73
42	S	3 May 1930	Walsall	A	0-0	0-1	1	2		4			7		10	8	11		3	6				5	9						2,84

F.A. CUP

NO.		DATE	OPPONENTS	V.	H-T	F-T	Jarvie John	Hannah Joe	Richmond Joe	Brown William	O'Brien Mick	Lochhead Doug	Porter Ernest	Thomson Norman	Thompson James	Anderson George	Slicer Jacky	Scott John	Graham Robert	Jobling Joe	Knox William	Cropper Arthur	Lamb Joseph	Greenwell Wilf	Hunt Thomas	Noble Arthur	Varco Percy	Dennis George	Bennett Edward	Own Goals	ATTD.
1	S	30 Nov 1929	Coventry City (1st Round)	H	3-2	3-3	1	2	3	4			7		10	8	11^1			6				5^1			9^1				12,47
2	Th	5 Dec 1929	Coventry City (Replay)	A	0-2	0-2	1	2	3		5	6	7		10	8	11			4							9				7,70

1929–30 APPEARANCES & GOALS

	FOOTBALL LGE APPR.	FOOTBALL LGE GLS	F.A. CUP APPR.	F.A. CUP GLS
Jarvie John	42	–	2	–
Slicer Jacky	41	5	2	1
Porter Ernest	39	9	2	–
Lochhead Doug	35	2	1	–
Hannah Joe	33	1	2	–
O'Brien Mick	32	4	1	–
Brown Wiliam	31	1	1	–
Hunt Thomas	29	25		
Thompson James	29	17	2	–
Anderson George	28	12	2	–
Richmond Joe	23	–	2	–
Graham Robert	21	–		
Thomson Norman	15	–		
Jobling Joe	12	–	2	–
Greenwell Wilf	10	1	1	1
Scott John	10	4		
Cropper Arthur	9	3		
Bennett Edward	7	–		
Lamb Joseph	7	–		
Varco Percy	4	3	2	1
Knox William	3	–		
Dennis George	1	–		
Noble Arthur	1	–		
Own Goals		1		

DIVISION 3 SOUTH

1929–30	P	W	D	L	F	A	PTS
Plymouth Argyle	42	30	8	4	98	38	68
Brentford	42	28	5	9	94	44	61
Queens Park Rangers	42	21	9	12	80	68	51
Northampton Town	42	21	8	13	82	58	50
Brighton & Hove Albion	42	21	8	13	87	63	50
Coventry City	42	19	9	14	88	73	47
Fulham	42	18	11	13	87	83	47
Norwich City	**42**	**18**	**10**	**14**	**88**	**77**	**46**
Crystal Palace	42	17	12	13	81	74	46
Bournemouth	42	15	13	14	72	61	43
Southend United	42	15	13	14	69	59	43
Clapton Orient	42	14	13	15	55	62	41
Luton Town	42	14	12	16	64	78	40
Swindon Town	42	13	12	17	73	83	38
Watford	42	15	8	19	60	73	38
Exeter City	42	12	11	19	67	73	35
Walsall	42	13	8	21	71	78	34
Newport County	42	12	10	20	74	85	34
Torquay United	42	10	11	21	64	94	31
Bristol Rovers	42	11	8	23	67	93	30
Gillingham	42	11	8	23	51	80	30
Merthyr Town	42	6	9	27	60	135	21

1930–31 DIVISION 3 SOUTH

O.		DATE		OPPONENTS	V.	H-T	F-T	Purdy Arthur	Hannah Joe	Graham Robert	Brown William	O'Brien Mike	Lochhead Doug	Porter Ernest	Smith Tom	Tennant William	Williams Thomas	Slack William	Bennett Edward	Pearson James	Weir James	Bell Sam	Jordan Hugh	Jobling Joe	Harley Alex	Sargeant Charles	Smith James	Peed Frank	Greenwell Wilf	Hunt Thomas	Fulton John	Turner David	Smith William	Burditt Ken	ATTD.
1	S	30 Aug	1930	Exeter City	A	0-1	0-1	1	2	3	4	5	6	7	8	9	10	11																	5,914
2	W	3 Sept	1930	Watford	A	2-2	2-2	1		3	4[1]	5	6			9[1]	10	11	2	7	8														7,217
3	S	6 "	1930	Queens Park Rangers	H	1-0	1-1	1		3	4	5	6			9	10	11	2	7		8[1]													12,472
4	M	8 "	1930	Notts. County	H	1-1	2-2	1		3	4	5	6					11[1]	2	7	9	8[1]	10												10,985
5	S	13 "	1930	Walsall	A	0-5	0-7	1		3	4	5	6					11	2	7	9	8	10												5,251
6	S	20 "	1930	Coventry City	H	2-1	2-2	1	2	3		5	6	7			10[1]	11[1]					8	4	9										8,488
7	S	27 "	1930	Fulham	A	0-0	0-1	1	2	3		5	6	7		9	10	11					8	4											13,663
8	Th	2 Oct	1930	Notts. County	A	0-1	0-4	1	2	3		5	6			9	8			7	10			4		11									6,987
9	S	4 "	1930	Swindon Town	H	0-0	2-0	1	2	3	4	5	10				8[1]			7		9[1]		6		11									8,714
10	S	11 "	1930	Bournemouth	A	1-0	1-4	1	2	3	4	5	10				9[1]			7		8		6		11									6,044
11	S	18 "	1930	Brighton & Hove Albion	A	0-0	0-1		2	3	4	5	6	7		9		11			10		8				1								8,641
12	S	25 "	1930	Torquay United	H	1-0	3-0		2	3	4	5	6	7			10[1]	11					8[2]				1	9							9,012
13	S	1 Nov	1930	Northampton Town	A	1-1	1-3		2	3	4	5	6	7			10	11					8				1	9[1]							9,393
14	S	8 "	1930	Brentford	H	0-0	3-0		2	3	4	5	6	7[1]		10		11					8[1]				1	9[1]							9,172
15	S	15 "	1930	Crystal Palace	A	0-0	1-2		2	3	4	5		7		10		11					8	6			1	9[1]							10,415
16	S	22 "	1930	Southend United	H	0-1	0-1		2	3	4	5	6	7		10		11					8				1	9							7,485
17	S	6 Dec	1930	Bristol Rovers	H	1-1	1-3	1	2	3	4			7		10		11										8	5	9[1]	6				8,495
18	Th	18 "	1930	Newport County	A	0-1	0-3		2	3	4							11		7			10	6			1	8	5	9					1,116
19	S	20 "	1930	Gillingham	H	2-0	4-0		2	3	4						10[3]	11		7	8			6			1		5	9[1]					6,061
20	Th	25 "	1930	Clapton Orient	H	2-0	2-0		2	3	4						10[1]	11		7			8	6			1		5	9[1]					9,701
21	F	26 "	1930	Clapton Orient	A	0-1	0-2		2	3	4						10	11		7			8	6			1		5	9					3,359
22	S	27 "	1930	Exeter City	H	1-1	1-2		2	3							10	11		7[1]		8		6			1		5	9		4			10,480
23	S	3 Jan	1931	Queens Park Rangers	A	0-0	1-3		2	3							10			7	8			6		11[1]	1	9	5			4			6,553
24	S	10 "	1931	Luton Town	A	0-0	0-1		2								10			7	8			6		11	1	9	5			4	3		5,032
25	S	17 "	1931	Walsall	H	2-1	3-1		2		4		6							7		8[1]				11	1		5	9[2]			3	10	5,251
26	S	24 "	1931	Coventry City	A	0-1	0-3		2				6									8	7	4		11	1		5	9			3	10	7,458
27	S	31 "	1931	Fulham	H	0-1	1-1		2			5	6	7[1]								8		4		11	1			9			3	10	8,496
28	S	7 Feb	1931	Swindon Town	A	0-2	2-5		2			5	6	7			10[2]	11				8		4			1	9					3		4,543
29	S	14 "	1931	Bournemouth	H	0-0	2-1		2			5	6	7			10					8[1]		4		11	1	9[1]					3		5,347
30	S	21 "	1931	Brighton & Hove Albion	H	1-1	2-2		2			5	6	7[1]			10[1]					8		4		11	1	9					3		7,570
31	S	28 "	1931	Torquay United	A	0-1	0-2		2			5	6	7			10					8		4		11	1						3	9	3,282
32	S	7 Mar	1931	Northampton Town	H	0-1	1-1		2			5	6	7			10[1]						8	4		11	1			9			3		6,033
33	S	14 "	1931	Brentford	A	1-0	1-3		2			5	6	7							8		10	4		11	1			9[1]			3		9,013
34	S	21 "	1931	Crystal Palace	H	2-0	2-1		2			5	6	7[1]				11						4			1	8		9			3	10[1]	7,756
35	S	28 "	1931	Southend United	A	0-2	0-2		2			5	6	7				11						4			1	8		9			3	10	5,638
36	F	3 Apr	1931	Thames	A	0-0	0-2		2			5	6					11				7	8	4			1	9					3	10	1,231
37	S	4 "	1931	Luton Town	H	1-0	1-0		2	3		5	6					11				7		4			1	8					9[1]	10	7,903
38	M	6 "	1931	Thames	H	0-0	0-0		9	2		5	6					11				7		4			1	8					3	10	13,485
39	S	11 "	1931	Bristol Rovers	A	0-2	0-3		2	3		5	6	7				11				8		4			1			9				10	5,345
40	S	18 "	1931	Newport County	H	2-1	4-1		2	3		5[1]	6	7				11				8[1]		4			1			9[1]				10[1]	4,563
41	S	25 "	1931	Gillingham	A	1-1	1-2		2	3		5	6	7				11				8	10	4			1							9[1]	2,693
42	S	2 May	1931	Watford	H	0-0	0-1		2	3		5	6	7				11				8		4			1			9				10	5,394

F.A. CUP

		DATE		OPPONENTS	V.	H-T	F-T	Purdy Arthur	Hannah Joe	Graham Robert	Brown William	O'Brien Mike	Lochhead Doug	Porter Ernest	Smith Tom	Tennant William	Williams Thomas	Slack William	Bennett Edward	Pearson James	Weir James	Bell Sam	Jordan Hugh	Jobling Joe	Harley Alex	Sargeant Charles	Smith James	Peed Frank	Greenwell Wilf	Hunt Thomas	Fulton John	Turner David	Smith William	Burditt Ken	ATTD.
1	S	29 Nov	1930	Swindon Town (1st Round)	H	1-0	2-0	1	2	3	4		6	7		10		11					8					9[2]	5						11,800
2	S	13 Dec	1930	Brentford (2nd Round)	A	0-1	0-1		2	3	4		6			10		11					8				1	9	5	7					12,000

1930–31 APPEARANCES & GOALS

	FOOTBALL LGE APPR.	FOOTBALL LGE GLS	F.A. CUP APPR.	F.A. CUP GLS
annah Joe	38	–	2	–
ochhead Doug	33	–	2	–
' Brien Mike	32	1		
mith James	31	–	1	–
obling Joe	30	–		
raham Robert	29	–	2	–
ack William	29	2	2	–
orter Ernest	23	4	1	–
illiams Thomas	21	12		
ell Sam	20	6		
rown William	19	1	2	–
ordan Hugh	18	3	2	–
eed Frank	17	4	2	2
unt Thomas	16	7	1	–
earson James	15	1		
mith William	15	1		
urditt Ken	13	3		
argeant Charles	13	1		
urdy Aurthur	11	–	1	–
reenwill Wilf	10	–	2	–
ennant William	10	1	2	–
eir James	9	–		
ennett Edward	4	–		
urner David	3	–		
ulton John	1	–		
arley Alex	1	–		
mith Tom	1	–		

DIVISION 3 SOUTH

1930–31	P	W	D	L	F	A	PTS
Notts. County	42	24	11	7	97	46	59
Crystal Palace	42	22	7	13	107	71	51
Brentford	42	22	6	14	90	64	50
Southend United	42	22	5	15	76	60	49
Brighton & Hove Albion	42	17	15	10	68	53	49
Northampton Town	42	18	12	12	77	59	48
Luton Town	42	19	8	15	76	51	46
Queens Park Rangers	42	20	3	19	82	75	43
Fulham	42	18	7	17	77	75	43
Bournemouth	42	15	13	14	72	73	43
Torquay United	42	17	9	16	80	84	43
Swindon Town	42	18	6	18	89	94	42
Exeter City	42	17	8	17	84	90	42
Coventry City	42	16	9	17	75	65	41
Bristol Rovers	42	16	8	18	75	92	40
Gillingham	42	14	10	18	61	76	38
Walsall	42	14	9	19	78	95	37
Watford	42	14	7	21	72	75	35
Clapton Orient	42	14	7	21	63	91	35
Thames	42	13	8	21	54	93	34
Newport County	42	11	6	25	69	111	28
Norwich City	**42**	**10**	**8**	**24**	**47**	**76**	**28**

1931–32 DIVISION 3 SOUTH

NO.		DATE		OPPONENTS	V.	H-T	F-T	Wharton Norman	Hannah Joe	Smith William	Jobling Joe	Williamson Tom	Lochhead Doug	Taylor William	Williams Thomas	Brain Joe	Blakemore Cecil	Murphy Lionel	Bell Sam	Ogle Roger	Burditt Ken	Pearson James	Walbanks James	Thompson Andrew	Brown Oliver	Scott Jack	Hall Bert	Hunt Thomas	Wren Thomas	Robinson Bernard	Own Goals	ATTD
1	S	29 Aug	1931	Brighton & Hove Albion	A	1-1	1-2	1	2	3	4	5	6	7	8^{1}	9	10	11														10,19
2	M	31 "	1931	Mansfield Town	H	1-0	1-1	1	2	3	4	5^{1}	6	7	8	9	10	11														13,91
3	S	5 Sep	1931	Northampton Town	H	0-0	0-0	1	2	3	4	5	6	7	8	9	10	11														12,45
4	W	9 "	1931	Bournemouth	A	0-1	0-1	1	2	3	4	5	6	7	8	9	10	11														6,18
5	S	12 "	1931	Swindon Town	H	2-1	4-2	1	2^{1}	3	4	5	6	7	8	9^{2}	10^{1}	11														9,75
6	M	14 "	1931	Bournemouth	H	0-2	1-2	1	2	3	4	5	6	7		9	10^{1}	11	8													8,73
7	S	19 "	1931	Clapton Orient	A	1-0	3-1	1	2		4	5	6	7^{1}		9^{1}	10^{1}	11	8	3												10,19
8	S	26 "	1931	Torquay United	H	2-0	2-0	1	2	3	4	5	6	7		9^{2}	10	11	8													10,58
9	S	3 Oct	1931	Bristol Rovers	A	1-0	1-0	1	2	3	4	5	6	7		9	10	11	8													8,51
10	S	10 "	1931	Queens Park Rangers	H	2-1	2-1	1	2	3	4	5	6	7^{1}		9	10	11	8^{1}													13,16
11	S	17 "	1931	Reading	A	1-1	1-1	1	2	3	4	5	6	7		9	10	11	8^{1}													10,25
12	S	24 "	1931	Southend United	H	0-0	1-1	1	2	3	4	5	6	7		9	10	11	8													16,76
13	S	31 "	1931	Fulham	A	0-2	0-4	1	2	3	4	5	6	7		9		11	8		10											16,41
14	S	7 Nov	1931	Thames	H	4-0	7-0	1	2	3	4	5	6^{1}				10	11^{1}	8^{1}		9^{2}	7^{2}										9,18
15	S	14 "	1931	Brentford	A	1-0	1-0	1	2	3	4	5					10	11	8^{1}		9	7	6									11,48
16	S	21 "	1931	Exeter City	H	0-0	0-1	1	2	3	4	5	6				10	11	8		9	7										12,82
17	S	5 Dec	1931	Gillingham	H	1-1	1-1	1	2	3	4	5	6					11	8		9^{1}	7		10								7,72
18	S	19 "	1931	Cardiff City	H	0-0	2-0	1	2	3	5		6				10^{1}	11			7^{1}		4	8	9							7,90
19	F	25 "	1931	Watford	A	1-1	1-1	1	2	3	4	5	6				10	11			7			8	9						$-^{1}$	10,00
20	S	26 "	1931	Watford	H	1-0	4-1	1	2	3	4	5	6				10^{1}	11			7			8	9^{3}							17,16
21	S	2 Jan	1932	Brighton & Hove Albion	H	0-1	2-1	1	2	3	4	5^{1}	6				10	11			7			8	9^{1}							9,08
22	S	9 "	1932	Coventry City	A	0-3	0-3	1	2	3	4	5	6				10	11			7			8	9							13,49
23	S	16 "	1932	Northampton Town	A	2-1	2-2	1	2	3	4	5	6				10	11			8			7	9^{1}							4,90
24	S	23 "	1932	Swindon Town	A	0-0	0-2	1	2	3	4		6				10	11			8			7	9	5						5,07
25	S	30 "	1932	Clapton Orient	H	2-2	3-2	1	2	3	4	5	6				10^{1}	11^{1}	8^{1}		7				9							8,58
26	S	6 Feb	1932	Torwquay United	A	2-1	4-2	1	2	3	4^{1}	5	6				10	11	8		7^{1}				9^{2}							3,05
27	S	13 "	1932	Bristol Rovers	H	1-0	6-0	1	2	3	4	5	6				10^{2}	11	8^{2}		7				9							7,53
28	S	20 "	1932	Queens Park Rangers	A	2-2	2-2	1	2	3	4	5	6				10	11^{2}	8		7				9							9,63
29	S	27 "	1932	Reading	H	0-0	0-0	1	2	3	4	5	6				10	11	8		7				9							12,51
30	S	5 Mar	1932	Southend United	A	0-2	0-2	1	2	3	4	5	6				10	11	8		7				9							7,26
31	S	12 "	1932	Fulham	H	2-1	2-2	1	2	3		5	6				10	11^{1}	8		7						4	9^{1}				11,75
32	S	19 "	1932	Thames	A	0-0	0-1	1	2	3		5	6				10	11	8		7						4	9				1,14
33	F	25 "	1932	Crystal Palace	A	0-3	1-3	1	2	3		5	6				4	11	7		8^{1}			10	9							18,97
34	S	26 "	1932	Brentford	H	0-0	1-0	1	2	3		5	6				4	11	8		7			10	9^{1}							10,42
35	M	28 "	1932	Crystal Palace	H	3-2	3-2	1	2	3		5	6				4	11	8^{1}		7			10^{1}	9^{1}							16,41
36	Tu	29 "	1932	Luton Town	A	0-5	1-7	1		3		5	6				4	11	8		7			10^{1}	9				2			2,61
37	S	2 Apr	1932	Exeter City	A	0-2	0-3	1		3		5			10		6	11	8		7				9				2	4		5,27
38	S	9 "	1932	Coventry City	H	2-1	6-2	1	2	3		5	6				10^{1}	11^{1}	8^{1}		7^{1}				9^{2}					4		6,01
39	S	16 "	1932	Gillingham	A	1-1	3-3	1	2	3		5	6				10^{2}	11	8^{1}		7				9					4		2,04
40	S	23 "	1932	Luton Town	H	3-1	3-3	1	2	3		5	6				10^{2}	11	8		7		4					9			$-^{1}$	6,24
41	S	30 "	1932	Cardiff City	A	2-0	2-0	1	2	3		5	6				10^{1}	11	8		7^{1}							9		4		6,48
42	S	7 May	1932	Mansfield Town	A	0-3	2-5	1	2	3		5	6				10	11	8^{2}		7				9					4		4,10

F.A. CUP

NO.		DATE		OPPONENTS	V.	H-T	F-T	Wharton Norman	Hannah Joe	Smith William	Jobling Joe	Williamson Tom	Lochhead Doug	Taylor William	Williams Thomas	Brain Joe	Blakemore Cecil	Murphy Lionel	Bell Sam	Ogle Roger	Burditt Ken	Pearson James	Walbanks James	Thompson Andrew	Brown Oliver	Scott Jack	Hall Bert	Hunt Thomas	Wren Thomas	Robinson Bernard	Own Goals	ATTD
1	S	28 Nov	1931	Wimbledon (1st Round)	A	1-0	3-1	1	2	3	4	5	6					11^{1}	8		9^{1}	7		10^{1}								12,8
2	S	12 Dec	1931	Brentford (2nd Round)	A	0-1	1-4	1	2	3	4	5	6	7	10			11			9^{1}			8								17,0

1931–32 APPEARANCES & GOALS

	FOOTBALL LGE APPR.	FOOTBALL LGE GLS	F.A. CUP APPR.	F.A. CUP GLS
Murphy Lionel	42	6	2	1
Wharton Norman	42	–	2	–
Smith William	41	–	2	–
Blakemore Cecil	40	16		
Hannah Joe	40	1	2	–
Lochhead Doug	40	1	2	–
Williamson Tom	40	2	2	–
Bell Sam	30	12	1	–
Burditt Ken	30	8	2	2
Jobling Joe	30	1	2	–
Brown Oliver	21	14		
Brain Joe	13	5		
Taylor William	13	2	1	–
Thompson Andrew	12	2	2	1
Williams Thomas	6	1	1	–
Robinson Bernard	5	–		
Hunt Thomas	4	1		
Pearson James	4	2	1	–
Wallbanks James	3	–		
Hall Bert	2	–		
Wren Thomas	2	–		
Ogle Roger	1	–		
Scott Jack	1	–		
Own Goals		2		

DIVISION 3 SOUTH

1931–32	P	W	D	L	F	A	PTS
Fulham	42	24	9	9	111	62	57
Reading	42	23	9	10	97	67	55
Southend United	42	21	11	10	77	53	53
Crystal Palace	42	20	11	11	74	63	51
Brentford	42	19	10	13	68	52	48
Luton Town	42	20	7	15	95	70	47
Exeter City	42	20	7	15	77	62	47
Brighton & Hove Albion	42	17	12	13	73	58	46
Cardiff City	42	19	8	15	87	73	46
Norwich City	**42**	**17**	**12**	**13**	**76**	**67**	**46**
Watford	42	19	8	15	81	79	46
Coventry City	42	18	8	16	108	97	44
Queens Park Rangers	42	15	12	15	79	73	42
Northampton Town	42	16	7	19	69	69	39
Bournemouth	42	13	12	17	70	78	38
Clapton Orient	42	12	11	19	77	90	35
Swindon Town	42	14	6	22	70	84	34
Bristol Rovers	42	13	8	21	65	92	34
Torquay United	42	12	9	21	72	106	33
Mansfield Town	42	11	10	21	75	108	32
Gillingham	42	10	8	24	40	82	28
Thames	42	7	9	26	53	109	23

1932–33 DIVISION 3 SOUTH

NO.		DATE	OPPONENTS	V.	H-T	F-T	Wharton Norman	Hannah Joe	Smith William	Ramsay Stan	Williamson Tom	Lochhead Doug	Burditt Ken	Bell Sam	Brown Oliver	Blakemore Cecil	Murphy Lionel	Robinson Bernard	Keeling Harry	Robinson Robert	Keating Reg	Pegg Frank	Thorpe Albert	Hunt Thomas	Wilson Gordon	Scott Thomas	Scott Jack	ATTD.
1	S	27 Aug 1932	Watford	H	1-1	1-2	1	2	3	4	5	6	7	8	9	10	11^{1}											13,477
2	W	31 " 1932	Gillingham	A	1-0	2-0	1	2	3	8	5	6	7		9^{2}		11	4	10									6,824
3	S	3 Sep 1932	Cardiff City	A	0-2	2-4	1	2	3	8^{1}	5	6	7^{1}		9		11	4	10									9,767
4	M	5 " 1932	Gillingham	H	0-0	2-0		2	3	8	5	6	7^{2}				11	4	10	1	9							8,583
5	S	10 " 1932	Reading	H	1-1	2-2		2	3	8	5	6	9^{1}				11	4	10^{1}	1		7						11,557
6	S	17 " 1932	Clapton Orient	A	0-0	0-0			3	8	5	6	7				11	4	10	1			2	9				9,633
7	S	24 " 1932	Brighton & Hove Albion	A	0-1	1-1				8	5	6	9			10	11	4		1		7^{1}	2		3			5,486
8	S	1 Oct 1932	Bristol Rovers	H	0-1	1-1				3	5	6	9			10	11^{1}	4		1		7	2			8		8,731
9	S	8 " 1932	Aldershot	A	2-0	3-1			3		5	6	9^{2}			10^{1}	11	4		1		7	2			8		5,079
10	S	15 " 1932	Queens Park Rangers	H	3-1	3-2			3	7	5	6	9^{2}			10	11	4		1			2			8^{1}		9,457
11	S	22 " 1932	Swindon Town	H	2-1	5-2			3	7	5	6	9^{1}			10^{1}	11	4		1			2			8^{3}		9,292
12	S	29 " 1932	Bournemouth	A	0-1	1-1			3	9	5	6		7		10	11	4		1			2			8^{1}		3,823
13	S	5 Nov 1932	Newport County	H	1-0	3-1			3	7	5	6	9^{2}			10^{1}	11	4		1			2			8		9,913
14	S	12 " 1932	Luton Town	A	1-0	1-1			3	7	5	6	9^{1}	10			11	4		1			2			8		5,501
15	S	19 " 1932	Exeter City	H	0-0	0-0			3	7		6	9				11	4		1	8		2			10	5	10,697
16	S	3 Dec 1932	Brentford	H	1-0	3-0			3		5	6	7		9^{2}	10	11	4		1			2			8^{1}		14,180
17	S	17 " 1932	Bristol City	H	0-0	3-0			3		5^{1}	6	7		9	10^{1}	11	4		1			2			8^{1}		8,875
18	S	24 " 1932	Northampton Town	A	1-1	2-2			3		5	6	7^{1}		9^{1}	10	11	4		1			2			8		6,237
19	M	26 " 1932	Southend United	A	1-1	1-2		2	3		5	6	7		9^{1}	10	11	4		1						8		8,342
20	Tu	27 " 1932	Southend United	H	0-0	1-0		2	3		5	6	7		9	10^{1}	11	4		1						8		17,161
21	S	31 " 1932	Watford	A	1-1	2-1		2	3		5	6	7		9	10	11^{1}	4		1						8^{1}		6,975
22	S	7 Jan 1933	Cardiff City	H	0-0	3-1		2	3		5	6	7^{1}		9^{2}	10	11	4		1						8		9,486
23	S	14 " 1933	Torquay United	A	1-1	2-2		2	3	6	5		7^{1}		9	10^{1}	11	4		1						8		4,396
24	S	21 " 1933	Reading	A	0-2	2-3		2	3		5	6	7		9	10	11	4		1						8^{2}		8,388
25	S	28 " 1933	Clapton Orient	H	1-0	2-0		2		3	5	6	8^{1}	7	9	10	11^{1}	4		1								6,899
26	Th	2 Feb 1933	Coventry City	A	2-2	5-3		2		3	5	6	7		9	10^{3}	11^{2}	4		1						8		6,016
27	S	4 " 1933	Brighton & Hove Albion	H	1-0	1-0		2		3	5	6	7		9^{1}	10	11	4		1						8		10,385
28	S	11 " 1933	Bristol Rovers	A	0-0	1-1		2		3	5	6	7^{1}		9	10	11	4		1						8		7,771
29	Th	23 " 1933	Aldershot	H	1-2	3-2		2		3	5	6			9^{2}	10^{1}	11	4		1		7				8		5,512
30	S	25 " 1933	Queens Park Rangers	A	1-2	2-2		2		3	5	6		8^{1}	9	10	11	4		1		7^{1}						4,586
31	S	4 Mar 1933	Swindon Town	A	1-2	4-2		2		3	5	6		7	9^{2}	10	11^{1}	4		1						8^{1}		5,150
32	S	11 " 1933	Bournemouth	H	3-0	6-0		2		3	5	6		7^{1}	9^{4}	10^{1}	11	4		1						8		11,955
33	S	18 " 1933	Newport County	A	3-2	4-3		2		3	5	6		7^{1}	9^{1}	10^{1}	11^{1}	4		1						8		4,490
34	S	25 " 1933	Luton Town	H	1-0	2-1		2	3	6	5			7	9	10^{1}	11	4		1						8^{1}		14,098
35	S	1 Apr 1933	Exeter City	A	1-0	1-2		2	3	6	5			7^{1}	9	10	11	4		1						8		14,849
36	S	8 " 1933	Torquay United	H	0-2	1-2		2	3	6	5			7	9	10	11	4		1						8^{1}		11,467
37	F	14 " 1933	Crystal Palace	A	0-2	0-4		2	3		5	6	7		9	10	11	4		1						8		18,365
38	S	15 " 1933	Brentford	A	1-2	2-2	1	2	3	6	5		10^{1}	7	9		11^{1}	4								8		20,693
39	M	17 " 1933	Crystal Palace	H	1-0	3-0	1	2	3	6	5		10	7^{1}	9^{1}		11	4								8^{1}		20,540
40	S	22 " 1933	Coventry City	H	2-1	2-1	1	2	3	6	5		10	7	9		11^{1}	4								8^{1}		9,351
41	S	29 " 1933	Bristol City	A	1-1	1-1	1	2	3	6	5		10^{1}	7	9		11	4								8		6,423
42	S	6 May 1933	Northampton Town	H	1-0	2-0	1	2	3	6	5		10	7	9		11	4								8^{2}		7,913

F.A. CUP

NO.		DATE	OPPONENTS		V.	H-T	F-T	Wharton Norman	Hannah Joe	Smith William	Ramsay Stan	Williamson Tom	Lochhead Doug	Burditt Ken	Bell Sam	Brown Oliver	Blakemore Cecil	Murphy Lionel	Robinson Bernard	Keeling Harry	Robinson Robert	Keating Reg	Pegg Frank	Thorpe Albert	Hunt Thomas	Wilson Gordon	Scott Thomas	Scott Jack	ATTD.
1	S	26 Nov 1932	Folkestone	(1st Round)	A	0-1	0-1			3	7	5	6	9				11	4		1	8		2			10		5,199

1932–33 APPEARANCES & GOALS

	FOOTBALL LGE APPR.	GLS	F.A. CUP APPR.	GLS
Murphy Lionel	42	10	1	–
Robinson Bernard	41	–	1	–
Williamson Tom	41	1	1	–
Robinson Robert	34	–	1	–
Lochhead Doug	33	–	1	–
Burditt Ken	33	19	1	–
Scott Thomas	33	17	1	–
Ramsay Stan	32	1	1	–
Smith William	31	–	1	–
Blakemore Cecil	30	13		
Brown Oliver	30	19		
Hannah Joe	29	–		
Bell Sam	16	5		
Thorpe Albert	13	–	1	–
Wharton Norman	8	–		
Pegg Frank	6	2		
Keeling Harry	5	1		
Keating Reg	2	–	1	–
Hunt Thomas	1	–		
Scott Jack	1	–		
Wilson Gordon	1	–		

DIVISION 3 SOUTH

1932–33	P	W	D	L	F	A	PTS
Brentford	42	26	10	6	90	49	62
Exeter City	42	24	10	8	88	48	58
Norwich City	**42**	**22**	**13**	**7**	**88**	**55**	**57**
Reading	42	19	13	10	103	71	51
Crystal Palace	42	19	8	15	78	64	46
Coventry City	42	19	6	17	106	77	44
Gillingham	42	18	8	16	72	61	44
Northampton Town	42	18	8	16	76	66	44
Bristol Rovers	42	15	14	13	61	56	44
Torquay United	42	16	12	14	72	67	44
Watford	42	16	12	14	66	63	44
Brighton & Hove Albion	42	17	8	17	66	65	42
Southend United	42	15	11	16	65	82	41
Luton Town	42	13	13	16	78	78	39
Bristol City	42	12	13	17	83	90	37
Queens Park Rangers	42	13	11	18	72	87	37
Aldershot	42	13	10	19	61	72	36
Bournemouth	42	12	12	18	60	81	36
Cardiff City	42	12	7	23	69	99	31
Clapton Orient	42	8	13	21	59	93	29
Newport County	42	11	7	24	61	105	29
Swindon Town	42	9	11	22	60	105	29

1933–34 DIVISION 3 SOUTH

NO.		DATE	OPPONENTS	V.	H-T	F-T	Wharton Norman	Hannah Joe	Smith William	Robinson Bernard	Williamson Tom	Ramsay Stan	Warnes Billy	Scott Thomas	Vinall Jack	Burditt Ken	Murphy Lionel	Halliday Tom	Pike Theo	Morris Robert	Wilson Gordon	Lochhead Doug	Bell Sam	Thorpe Albert	Kirchen Alf	Williams Rod	Houghton Harold	Perfect Frank	Robinson Robert	Scott Jack	Roy John	ATTD
1	S	26 Aug 1933	Clapton Orient	H	1-0	3-0	1	2	3	4	5^1	6	7^1	8^1	9	10	11															14,54
2	M	28 " 1933	Bristol City	H	2-0	7-2	1	2	3	4		6	7^1	8^1	9^4	10	11^1	5														11,35
3	S	2 Sept 1933	Swindon Town	A	0-0	0-0	1	2	3	4		6	7	8	9	10	11	5														11,83
4	W	6 " 1933	Bristol City	A	1-0	1-0	1	2	3	4		6	7	8	9	10^1		5	11													7,79
5	S	9 " 1933	Brighton & Hove Albion	H	3-1	4-3	1	2	3	4		6	7^1	8^1	9	10^1	11^1	5														14,93
6	S	16 " 1933	Aldershot	A	1-1	1-2	1	2	3	4		6	7	8^1	9	10	11	5														8,02
7	S	23 " 1933	Luton Town	H	2-0	4-0	1	2	3	4		6	7^1	8	9^1	10^2	11	5														12,59
8	S	30 " 1933	Northampton Town	A	1-1	2-2	1	2	3	4		6	7	8^1	9^1	10	11	5														7,60
9	S	7 Oct 1933	Torquay United	H	0-2	0-2	1	2	3	4		5	7	8	9	10	11			6												12,33
10	S	14 " 1933	Queens Park Rangers	A	1-3	2-5	1	2	3			6	7^1	8	10	9^1	11	5		4												8,57
11	S	21 " 1933	Gillingham	H	2-0	4-1	1	2				4	7^1	8	9^2	10	11^1	5			3	6										9,38
12	S	28 " 1933	Exeter City	A	1-1	4-3	1	2		4		3	7^1	8	9^3		11	5				6	10									6,62
13	S	4 Nov 1933	Cardiff City	H	1-0	2-0	1	2		4		3	7^1	8	9		11	5				6	10^1									10,69
14	S	11 " 1933	Bournemouth	A	1-2	4-2	1	2		4		3	7	8^2	9^2		11	5				6	10									8,24
15	S	18 " 1933	Charlton Athletic	H	1-0	3-0	1	2		4		3	7^3		9	10	11	5				6	8									16,36
16	S	2 Dec 1933	Reading	H	1-1	3-2	1	2		4		3	7^1	8^2	9		11	5				6	10									10,94
17	Th	14 " 1933	Coventry City	A	0-0	0-0	1	2		4		3	7		9	10	11	5				6	8									6,80
18	S	16 " 1933	Southend United	H	0-0	0-0	1	2		4		3	7		9	10	11	5				6	8									9,13
19	S	23 " 1933	Bristol Rovers	A	0-2	0-3	1	2		4		3	7	8	9	10	11	5				6										12,09
20	M	25 " 1933	Crystal Palace	A	1-0	1-0	1			4		3	7	8	11	10		5				6		2		9^1						22,12
21	Tu	26 " 1933	Crystal Palace	H	2-0	2-0	1			4		3	7		8^1	10	11	5				6		2		9^1						16,38
22	S	30 " 1933	Clapton Orient	A	1-3	2-3	1			4		3	7^1		8	10	11	5				6^1		2		9						10,52
23	S	6 Jan 1934	Swindon Town	H	0-1	3-2	1			4		3	7^1		8	10^1	11	5				6		2		9^1						9,33
24	S	13 " 1934	Watford	A	3-1	3-1	1		3	4			7		9	8^1	11	5	10^2			6		2								7,20
25	S	20 " 1934	Brighton & Hove Albion	A	1-1	1-1	1			4		3	7		9	8^1	11	5	10			6		2								8,89
26	S	27 " 1933	Aldershot	H	0-0	2-2	1			4		3	7^2		9	8	11	5	10			6		2								11,72
27	S	3 Feb 1934	Luton Town	A	1-0	3-2	1	2		4			7^1		9	8		5	11^1			6	10^1	3								7,65
28	S	10 " 1934	Northampton Town	H	0-0	2-0	1	2		4			7		10	8	11	5				6		3		9^2						13,17
29	S	17 " 1934	Torquay United	A	1-0	2-1	1	2		4			7		10	8	11^2	5				6		3		9						3,88
30	S	24 " 1934	Queens Park Rangers	H	1-0	1-0	1	2		4		3	7^1		9	8	11	5	10			6										20,39
31	S	3 Mar 1934	Gillingham	A	1-1	2-1	1	2		4		3	7		10^1	8	11	5				6				9^1						7,48
32	S	10 " 1934	Exeter City	H	0-0	1-1	1			4		3	7		9	8^1	11	5				6		2			10					14,18
33	S	17 " 1934	Cardiff City	A	2-0	2-0	1			4		3	7		9	8	11^1	5				6		2			10^1					8,63
34	S	24 " 1934	Bournemouth	H	1-1	6-1	1			4		3	7^2		9^2	8^2	11	5				6		2			10					11,85
35	F	30 " 1934	Newport County	A	0-0	0-0	1			4		3	7		9	8	11	5				6		2			10					8,96
36	S	31 " 1934	Charlton Athletic	A	1-2	3-3	1	2				4	7		9	8^1	11^1	5				6		3			10^1					20,65
37	M	2 Apr 1934	Newport County	H	1-1	2-1	1	2				4	7		9^1	8^1	11	5				6		3			10					22,43
38	S	7 " 1934	Watford	H	2-0	3-1	1					3	7^1		9^2	8	11	5		4		6		2			10					12,09
39	S	14 " 1934	Reading	A	0-0	0-1	1					3			8		11	5		4		6	7	2		9	10					12,48
40	S	21 " 1934	Coventry City	H	2-1	3-1	1					3			9^1	8^1	11	5		4		6	7^1	2			10					16,90
41	S	28 " 1934	Southend United	A	0-0	0-0	1					3			9	8	11	5	6	4					7		10	2				4,70
42	S	5 May 1934	Bristol Rovers	H	0-0	0-0	1					3	7		9	8	11	5	4			6		2			10					14,61

F.A. CUP

NO.		DATE	OPPONENTS	V.	H-T	F-T	Wharton Norman	Hannah Joe	Smith William	Robinson Bernard	Williamson Tom	Ramsay Stan	Warnes Billy	Scott Thomas	Vinall Jack	Burditt Ken	Murphy Lionel	Halliday Tom	Pike Theo	Morris Robert	Wilson Gordon	Lochhead Doug	Bell Sam	Thorpe Albert	Kirchen Alf	Williams Rod	Houghton Harold	Perfect Frank	Robinson Robert	Scott Jack	Roy John	ATTD
1	S	25 Nov 1933	Crystal Palace (1st Round)	A	0-1	0-3	1	2		4		3	7	8	9	10	11	5				6										22,09

DIVISION 3 SOUTH CUP

NO.		DATE	OPPONENTS	V.	H-T	F-T	Wharton Norman	Hannah Joe	Smith William	Robinson Bernard	Williamson Tom	Ramsay Stan	Warnes Billy	Scott Thomas	Vinall Jack	Burditt Ken	Murphy Lionel	Halliday Tom	Pike Theo	Morris Robert	Wilson Gordon	Lochhead Doug	Bell Sam	Thorpe Albert	Kirchen Alf	Williams Rod	Houghton Harold	Perfect Frank	Robinson Robert	Scott Jack	Roy John	ATTD
1	Th	25 Jan 1934	Gillingham (1st Round)	H	0-0	4-0	1	2	3	4			7^2		9^1	8				6			10^1							5	11	2,76
2	Th	8 Feb 1934	Clapton Orient (2nd Round)	H	1-0	3-0	1	2		4		3	7^1		9^2	8				6			10							5	11	2,56
3	W	21 Mar 1934	Northampton Town (3rd Round)	H	3-1	3-2		2		4			7		10	8				6	3					9^3			1	5	11	2,73
4	W	11 Apr 1934	Torquay United (Semi-final)	N	0-2	1-4		2				3	7		9	8		4	10	6									1	5	11^1	3,72

N – PLAYED AT HIGHBURY

1933–34 APPEARANCES & GOALS

	FOOTBALL LGE APPR.	FOOTBALL LGE GLS	F.A. CUP APPR.	F.A. CUP GLS	DIV 3 (S) CUP APPR.	DIV 3 (S) CUP GLS
Vinall Jack	42	21	1	–	4	3
Wharton Norman	42	–	1	–	2	–
Halliday Tom	40	–	1	–	1	–
Murphy Lionel	39	7	1	–		
Warnes Billy	39	21	1	–	4	3
Ramsay Stan	38	–	1	–	2	–
Burditt Ken	37	14	1	–	4	–
Robinson Bernard	33	–	1	–	3	–
Lochhead Doug	31	1	1	–		
Hannah Joe	26	–	1	–	4	–
Thrope Albert	20	–				
Scott Thomas	17	9	1	–		
Houghton Harold	11	2				
Smith William	11	–			1	–
Bell Sam	10	3			2	1
Pike Theo	8	3			1	–
Williams Rod	8	6			1	3
Morris Robert	6	–			4	–
Kirchen Alf	1	–				
Perfect Frank	1	–				
Williamson Tom	1	1				
Wilson Gordon	1	–			1	–
Scott Jack					4	–
Roy John					4	1
Robinson Robert					2	–

DIVISION 3 SOUTH

1933–34	P	W	D	L	F	A	PTS
Norwich City	**42**	**25**	**11**	**6**	**88**	**49**	**61**
Coventry City	42	21	12	9	100	54	54
Reading	42	21	12	9	82	50	54
Queens Park Rangers	42	24	6	12	70	51	54
Charlton Athletic	42	22	8	12	83	56	52
Luton Town	42	21	10	11	83	61	52
Bristol Rovers	42	20	11	11	77	47	51
Swindon Town	42	17	11	14	64	68	45
Exeter City	42	16	11	15	68	57	43
Brighton & Hove Albion	42	15	13	14	68	60	43
Clapton Orient	42	16	10	16	75	69	42
Crystal Palace	42	16	9	17	71	67	41
Northampton Town	42	14	12	16	71	78	40
Aldershot	42	13	12	17	52	71	38
Watford	42	15	7	20	71	63	37
Southend United	42	12	10	20	51	74	34
Gillingham	42	11	11	20	75	96	33
Newport County	42	8	17	17	49	70	33
Bristol City	42	10	13	19	58	85	33
Torquay United	42	13	7	22	53	93	33
Bournemouth	42	9	9	24	60	102	27
Cardiff City	42	9	6	27	57	105	24

1934–35 DIVISION 2

NO.		DATE	OPPONENTS	V.	H-T	F-T	Wharton Norman	Thorpe Albert	Ramsay Stan	Robinson Bernard	Halliday Tom	Lochhead Doug	Warnes Billy	Burditt Ken	Vinall Jack	Houghton Harold	Pike Theo	Murphy Lionel	Hewitt John	Dukes Harry	Kirchen Alf	Scott Thomas	Roy John	Russell Cecil	Worton Alfred	Hinton William	Bowen Sam	Proctor Harry	Morris Robert	Williams Rod	Davies Glyn	Scott Jack	Jones Ormond	Hannah Joe	Flack Len	ATTD.
1	S	25 Aug 1934	Brentford	A	0-1	1-2	1	2	3	4	5	6	7	8^{1}	9	10	11																			24,000
2	M	27 " 1934	Bury	H	2-0	4-1	1	2	3	4	5	6	7^{1}	8^{2}	9^{1}	10		11																		18,643
3	S	1 Sep 1934	Fulham	H	0-0	0-0	1	2	3	4	5	6	7	8	9	10		11																		19,502
4	S	8 " 1934	Bradford Park Avenue	A	0-0	1-1	1	2	3	4	5	6		9^{1}	7	10		11	8																	9,573
5	S	15 " 1934	Plymouth Arglye	H	2-0	3-0		2	3	4	5	6		9^{2}	7	10		11^{1}	8	1																17,436
6	M	17 " 1934	Bury	A	0-0	0-1		2	3	4	5	6		9	11	10			8	1	7															6,371
7	S	22 " 1934	Manchester United	A	0-3	0-5		2	3	4	5	6		9	7	10		11		1		8														13,000
8	S	29 " 1934	Newcastle United	A	0-0	0-2		2	3	4	5	6		7	9	10				1		8	11													20,000
9	S	6 Oct 1934	West Ham United	H	1-0	1-2		2	3	4	5	6		7^{1}	9		10			1		8		11												16,314
10	S	13 " 1934	Blackpool	A	0-2	1-2		2		4	5	6		8	9		10			1				11^{1}	3	7										15,000
11	S	20 " 1934	Port Vale	H	0-0	0-0		2		4	5	6		8	9		10			1				11		7	3									14,195
12	S	27 " 1934	Barnsley	A	0-1	1-2		2		4	5	6			9	10	8^{1}			1	7			11			3									5,700
13	S	3 Nov 1934	Sheffield United	H	2-0	3-1		2		4	5		7^{1}	8	9^{1}		10^{1}			1				11			3	6								14,245
14	S	10 " 1934	Bradford City	A	0-0	1-1		2		4	5		7	8	9		10^{1}			1				11			3	6								9,070
15	S	17 " 1934	Notts. County	H	4-1	7-2		2		4	5		7^{2}	8	9^{3}		10^{1}			1				11^{1}			3	6								11,297
16	S	24 " 1934	Southampton	A	2-0	4-1		2		4	5		7^{2}	8	9^{1}		10			1				11^{1}			3	6								11,930
17	S	1 Dec 1934	Bolton Wanderers	H	0-1	2-3		2		4	5		7	8^{1}	9^{1}		10			1				11			3	6								21,371
18	S	8 " 1934	Oldham Athletic	A	1-2	2-4		2		4	5		7	8	9	10^{1}				1				11			3	6^{1}								5,730
19	S	15 " 1934	Burnley	H	0-3	2-3		2		4	5	6	7		9^{1}		10			1				11^{1}			3		8							10,634
20	S	22 " 1934	Swansea Town	A	0-0	1-1		2		4	5	6			8					1	7^{1}			10			3			9	11					2,000
21	Tu	25 " 1934	Nottingham Forest	A	1-2	2-5				4	2	6			8					1	7^{1}			10		11	3			9^{1}		5				22,000
22	W	26 " 1934	Nottingham Forest	H	0-2	3-3	1			4	2	6			9	10^{1}			8		7			11^{2}			3					5				16,903
23	S	29 " 1934	Brentford	H	1-0	2-1	1			4	2	6			9	10^{1}			8^{1}		7			11			3					5				13,365
24	S	5 Jan 1935	Fulham	A	2-0	3-1	1			4	2	6			9^{1}	10			8		7^{2}			11			3					5				16,000
25	S	19 " 1935	Bradford Park Avenue	H	0-0	3-0	1			4	2	6			9^{1}	10			8		7^{1}			11^{1}			3					5				10,388
26	S	2 Feb 1935	Manchester United	H	2-2	3-2	1			4	2	6		8	9^{1}	10					7^{1}			11^{1}			3					5				14,260
27	W	6 " 1935	Plymouth Argly	A	0-0	1-0				4				8	9	10					7			11^{1}			3	6				5	1	2		7,000
28	S	9 " 1935	Newcastle United	H	0-0	2-0				4	2	6		8^{1}	9^{1}	10					7			11			3					5	1			16,128
29	M	18 " 1935	West Ham United	A	0-0	0-1				4	2			8	9	10					7		11				3	6				5	1			13,700
30	S	23 " 1935	Blackpool	H	1-1	1-1				4	2	6		8	9	10					7^{1}						3				11	5	1			11,290
31	S	2 Mar 1935	Port Vale	A	1-0	1-1				4	2	6	7	8	9^{1}	10	11										3					5	1			9,000
32	S	9 " 1935	Barnsley	H	0-1	0-1				4	2	6	7	8	9	10								11			3					5	1			9,128
33	S	16 " 1935	Sheffield United	A	0-1	1-1				4	2	6	7		8	10^{1}			9				11				3					5	1			17,473
34	S	23 " 1935	Bradford City	H	1-1	6-1				4	2	6	7^{2}		8^{1}	10^{1}							11				3			9^{2}		5	1			7,438
35	S	30 " 1935	Notts. County	A	0-1	0-1					2	6	7		8	10							11				3			9		5	1		4	6,000
36	S	6 Apr 1935	Southampton	H	3-0	4-0				4	2	6	7	9	8^{2}	10^{2}				1							3			11		5				8,414
37	S	13 " 1935	Bolton Wanderers	A	0-2	0-4				4	2	6	7	9	8	10				1							3			11		5				12,000
38	F	19 " 1935	Hull City	H	1-0	3-0				4	2	6	7		8	10^{1}			9^{1}	1				11			3^{1}					5				11,927
39	S	20 " 1935	Oldham Athletic	H	0-0	0-0				4	2	6	7		8	10			9	1				11			3					5				10,815
40	M	22 " 1935	Hull City	A	0-1	0-1				4	2		7		8	10				1				11			3	6		9		5				7,000
41	S	27 " 1935	Burnley	A	0-1	0-1				4	2		7		8	10			9	1				11			3	6				5				3,000
42	S	4 May 1935	Swansea Town	H	0-1	2-2				4	2	6	7^{1}	8^{1}	9	10				1							3				11	5				7,415

F.A. CUP

NO.		DATE	OPPONENTS	V.	H-T	F-T	Wharton Norman	Thorpe Albert	Ramsay Stan	Robinson Bernard	Halliday Tom	Lochhead Doug	Warnes Billy	Burditt Ken	Vinall Jack	Houghton Harold	Pike Theo	Murphy Lionel	Hewitt John	Dukes Harry	Kirchen Alf	Scott Thomas	Roy John	Russell Cecil	Worton Alfred	Hinton William	Bowen Sam	Proctor Harry	Morris Robert	Williams Rod	Davies Glyn	Scott Jack	Jones Ormond	Hannah Joe	Flack Len	ATTD.
1	S	12 Jan 1935	Bath City (3rd Round)	H	1-0	2-0	1			4	2	6			9^{1}	10			8		7^{1}			11			3					5				12,879
2	S	26 " 1935	Leeds United (4th Round)	H	0-2	3-3	1			4	2	6			9^{1}	10			8		7^{2}			11			3					5				13,710
3	W	30 " 1935	Leeds United (Replay)	A	1-1	2-1	1			4	2	6		8^{1}	9^{1}	10					7			11			3					5				27,269
4	S	16 Feb 1935	Sheffield Wednesday (5th Round)	H	0-0	0-1				4	2	6		8	9	10					7			11			3					5	1			25,037

1934–35 APPEARANCES & GOALS

	FOOTBALL LGE APPR.	GLS	F.A. CUP APPR.	GLS
Vinall Jack	42	16	4	3
Halliday Tom	41	–	4	–
Robinson Bernard	41	–	4	–
Bowen Sam	32	1	4	–
Lochhead Doug	32	–	4	–
Houghton Harold	31	8	4	–
Burditt Ken	27	10	2	1
Russell Cecil	25	9	4	–
Dukes Harry	24	–		
Scott Jack	22	–	4	–
Warnes Billy	22	9		
Thorpe Albert	20	–		
Kirchen Alf	13	7	4	3
Pike Theo	12	4		
Hewitt John	11	2	2	–
Proctor Harry	10	1		
Jones Ormond	9	–	1	–
Ramsay Stan	9	–		
Wharton Norman	9	–	3	–
Williams Rod	7	3		
Murphy Lionel	5	1		
Roy John	5	–		
Davis Glyn	3	–		
Hinton William	3	–		
Scott Thomas	3	–		
Flack Len	1	–		
Hannah Joe	1	–		
Morris Robert	1	–		
Worton Alfred	1	–		

DIVISION 2

1934–35	P	W	D	L	F	A	PTS
Brentford	42	26	9	7	93	48	61
Bolton Wanderers	42	26	4	12	96	48	56
West Ham United	42	26	4	12	80	63	56
Blackpool	42	21	11	10	79	57	53
Manchester United	42	23	4	15	76	55	50
Newcastle United	42	22	4	16	89	68	48
Fulham	42	17	12	13	76	56	46
Plymouth Arglye	42	19	8	15	75	64	46
Nottingham Forest	42	17	8	17	76	70	42
Bury	42	19	4	19	62	73	42
Sheffield United	42	16	9	17	79	70	41
Burnley	42	16	9	17	63	73	41
Hull City	42	16	8	18	63	74	40
Norwich City	**42**	**14**	**11**	**17**	**71**	**61**	**39**
Bradford Park Avenue	42	11	16	15	55	63	38
Barnsley	42	13	12	17	60	83	38
Swansea Town	42	14	8	20	56	67	36
Port Vale	42	11	12	19	55	74	34
Southampton	42	11	12	19	46	75	34
Bradford City	42	12	8	22	50	68	32
Oldham Athletic	42	10	6	26	56	95	26
Notts. County	42	9	7	26	46	97	25

1935–36 DIVISION 2

NO.		DATE	OPPONENTS	V.	H-T	F-T	Dukes Harry	Halliday Tom	Bowen Sam	Robinson Bernard	Scott Jack	Lochhead Doug	Warnes Billy	Burditt Ken	Vinall Jack	Houghton Harold	Russel Cecil	Thorpe Albert	Proctor Harry	Hewitt John	Burley Ben	Goffey Herbert	Smith Sam	Worton Alfred	Roy John	Cole Norman	Manders Frank	Friar John	Burke Peter	Hall Fred	Williams Rod	Ansell George	Woodford George	Flack Len	Edwards George			Own Goals	ATTD.
1	S	31 Aug 1935	West Ham United	H	3-2	4-3	1	2	3	4	5	6^{1}	7^{1}	8	9^{2}	10	11																						29,779
2	W	4 Sept 1935	Blackpool	A	1-1	1-2	1	2	3	4	5	6	7	8	9	10	11																						19,259
3	S	7 " 1935	Swansea Town	A	2-1	3-4	1	5	3	4			7		9^{3}	10		2	6	8	11																		12,988
4	W	11 " 1935	Blackpool	H	0-0	0-1	1	5	3	4		6	7	8	9	10	11	2																					22,337
5	S	14 " 1935	Leicester City	H	1-0	1-2	1	5	3	4		6	7		9	10		2			11	8^{1}																	20,554
6	M	16 " 1935	Doncaster Rovers	A	0-2	0-3	1	5	3	4		6	7		9			2			11	8	10																10,000
7	S	21 " 1935	Bradford Park Avenue	A	0-1	0-1	1	5		4					9	10		2	6		11	8		3	7														10,719
8	S	28 " 1935	Sheffield United	H	0-1	0-1	1	5		4					7	10	11	2	6	8				3		9													18,322
9	S	5 Oct 1935	Southampton	A	0-1	1-1	1	5		4			7	8	9^{1}	10	11	2	6					3															15,073
10	S	12 " 1935	Port Vale	H	2-1	4-2	1	5		4			7^{2}	8	9^{2}	10	11	2	6					3															16,324
11	S	19 " 1935	Fulham	A	1-0	1-1	1	5	2	4			7	8^{1}	9	10	11		6					3															17,034
12	S	26 " 1935	Burnley	H	1-0	2-0	1	5	2	4			7^{1}	10	9		11^{1}		6					3			8												18,030
13	S	2 Nov 1935	Charlton Athletic	A	1-2	1-4	1	5	2	4			7	10^{1}	9		11		6					3			8												18,377
14	S	9 " 1935	Hull City	H	1-0	3-0	1	5	2	4			7	10^{1}	9		11^{2}		6					3			8												11,906
15	S	16 " 1935	Barnsley	A	0-1	3-2	1	5	2	4^{1}			7	10	9^{1}		11		6					3			8^{1}												6,957
16	S	23 " 1935	Manchester United	H	2-2	3-5	1	5	2	4^{1}			7	10	9		11^{1}		6					3			8^{1}												17,266
17	S	30 " 1935	Bradford City	A	1-0	1-0	1	2	3	4	5		7		9		11		6			8					10^{1}												7,688
18	S	7 Dec 1935	Newcastle United	H	0-0	1-0	1	2	3	4					9		11		6			8					10^{1}	7	5										11,995
19	S	14 " 1935	Tottenham Hotspur	A	1-1	1-2	1	2	3	4					9		11		6			8^{1}					10	7	5										29,204
20	S	21 " 1935	Plymouth Argyle	H	0-0	0-0	1	2	3	4					9		11		6			8					10	7	5										12,867
21	W	25 " 1935	Bury	A	1-0	1-0	1	2	3	4					9		11^{1}		6			8					10	7	5										11,215
22	Th	26 " 1935	Bury	H	3-0	5-3	1	2	3	4				8	9^{2}		11^{1}		6								10	7^{2}	5										18,537
23	S	28 " 1935	West Ham United	A	0-2	2-3	1	2	3	4					9^{1}		11^{1}		6			8					10	7	5										24,438
24	S	4 Jan 1936	Swansea Town	H	0-1	0-1	1	2	3	4					9		11		6			8					10	7	5										13,148
25	S	18 " 1936	Leicester City	A	1-0	1-1		2		4			11		9^{1}				6			8					10	7	5	1	3								13,236
26	S	1 Feb 1936	Sheffield United	A	1-1	2-3		2		4			11^{1}		9				6			8					10	7	5	1	3							–^{1}	27,661
27	S	8 " 1936	Southampton	H	1-0	5-1		2		4			11^{1}		9^{3}		10		6								8^{1}	7	5	1	3								12,982
28	S	15 " 1936	Port Vale	A	1-3	1-3		2		4			11		9^{1}		10		6								8	7	5	1	3								6,129
29	S	22 " 1936	Fulham	H	1-0	1-0			2	4			7		9		11^{1}		6					3			10		5	1		8							11,362
30	S	29 " 1936	Newcastle United	A	1-1	1-1			2	4			7		9		11^{1}		6					3			10		5	1		8							3,964
31	S	7 Mar 1936	Barnsley	H	1-0	3-1			2	4			7		9		11^{2}		6					3			10^{1}		5	1		8							12,652
32	S	14 " 1936	Hull City	A	0-0	0-0			2	4			7		9		11		6					3			10		5	1		8							3,759
33	S	21 " 1936	Charlton Athletic	H	0-1	3-1			2	4^{1}			7	8	9^{1}		11		6					3			10		5	1									19,385
34	S	28 " 1936	Manchester United	A	0-1	1-2			2	4			11	8^{1}	9				6					3			10	7	5	1									31,596
35	S	4 Apr 1936	Bradford City	H	0-1	1-1			2	4			7	8	9		11^{1}		6								10		5	1			3						11,032
36	F	10 " 1936	Nottingham Forest	A	2-1	2-2		5	2	4^{1}			7	8	9^{1}		11		6								10			1			3						10,870
37	S	11 " 1936	Burnley	A	1-0	1-1		5	2	4				8	9^{1}						11						10			1			3	6	7				10,651
38	M	13 " 1936	Nottingham Forest	H	2-0	4-0		5	2	4			7^{2}	8	9		11^{1}										10^{1}			1			3	6					24,645
39	S	18 " 1936	Tottenham Hotspur	H	0-0	1-0		5	2	4			7	8	9^{1}		11										10			1			3	6					23,952
40	S	25 " 1936	Plymouth Argyle	A	0-2	1-5		5	2	4			7	8	9						11^{1}						10			1			3	6					6,601
41	Th	30 " 1936	Bradford Park Avenue	H	1-0	4-1		5	2	4			7^{1}	8	9^{1}						11^{1}			3			10^{1}		6	1									9,263
42	S	2 May 1936	Doncaster Rovers	H	1-0	2-1		5	2	4			7^{1}	8	9^{1}						11			3			10		6	1									12,464

F.A. CUP

NO.		DATE	OPPONENTS	V.	H-T	F-T	Dukes Harry	Halliday Tom	Bowen Sam	Robinson Bernard	Scott Jack	Lochhead Doug	Warnes Billy	Burditt Ken	Vinall Jack	Houghton Harold	Russel Cecil	Thorpe Albert	Proctor Harry	Hewitt John	Burley Ben	Goffey Herbert	Smith Sam	Worton Alfred	Roy John	Cole Norman	Manders Frank	Friar John	Burke Peter	Hall Fred	Williams Rod	Ansell George	Woodford George	Flack Len	Edwards George			Own Goals	ATTD.
1	S	11 Jan 1936	Chelsea (3rd Round)	H	0-0	1-1	1	2	3	4	5				9		11		6			8					10^{1}	7											32,37
2	W	15 " 1936	Chelsea (Replay)	A	1-2	1-3	1	2	3	4	5		11^{1}	8	9				6								10	7											31,73

1935–36 APPEARANCES & GOALS

	FOOTBALL LGE APPR.	FOOTBALL LGE GLS	F.A. CUP APPR.	F.A. CUP GLS
Robinson Bernard	42	4	2	–
Vinall Jack	42	24	2	–
Halliday Tom	35	–	2	–
Bowen Sam	34	–	2	–
Warnes Billy	32	10	1	1
Manders Frank	31	8	2	1
Proctor Harry	31	–	2	–
Russell Cecil	31	14	1	–
Dukes Harry	24	–	2	–
Burditt Ken	22	4	1	–
Burke Peter	20	–		
Hall Fred	18	–		
Worton Alfred	18	–		
Friar John	12	2	2	–
Goffey Herbert	12	2	1	–
Houghton Harold	10	–		
Burley Ben	8	2		
Thorpe Albert	8	–		
Woodford George	6	–		
Lochhead Doug	5	1		
Ansell George	4	–		
Flack Len	4	–		
Williams Rod	4	–		
Scott Jack	3	–	2	–
Hewitt John	2	–		
Cole Norman	1	–		
Edwards George	1	–		
Roy John	1	–		
Smith Sam	1	–		
Own Goals		1		

DIVISION 2

1935–36	P	W	D	L	F	A	PTS
Manchester United	42	22	12	8	85	43	56
Charlton Athletic	42	22	11	9	85	58	55
Sheffield United	42	20	12	10	79	50	52
West Ham United	42	22	8	12	90	68	52
Tottenham Hotspur	42	18	13	11	91	55	49
Leicester City	42	19	10	13	79	57	48
Plymouth Argyle	42	20	8	14	71	57	48
Newcastle United	42	20	6	16	88	79	46
Fulham	42	15	14	13	76	52	44
Blackpool	42	18	7	17	93	72	43
Norwich City	**42**	**17**	**9**	**16**	**72**	**65**	**43**
Bradford City	42	15	13	14	55	65	43
Swansea Town	42	15	9	18	67	76	39
Bury	42	13	12	17	66	84	38
Burnley	42	12	13	17	50	59	37
Bradford Park Avenue	42	14	9	19	62	84	37
Southampton	42	14	9	19	47	65	37
Doncaster Rovers	42	14	9	19	51	71	37
Nottingham Forest	42	12	11	19	69	76	35
Barnsley	42	12	9	21	54	80	33
Port Vale	42	12	8	22	56	106	32
Hull City	42	5	10	27	47	111	20

1936–37 DIVISION 2

NO.		DATE	OPPONENTS	V.	H-T	F-T	Hall Fred	Halliday Tom	Bowen Sam	Robinson Bernard	Burke Peter	Proctor Harry	Warnes Billy	Manders Frank	Vinall Jack	Madden Owen	Clare Joseph	O'Reilly Jack	Goffey Herbert	Flack Len	Morris Robert	Edwards George	Burley Ben	Friar John	Scott Jack	Woodford George	Coleman Tim	Mackrell James	Worton Alfred	Dukes Harry	ATTD.
1	S	28 Aug 1936	Sheffield United	H	1-1	1-1	1	2	3	4	5	6	7	8	9^1	10	11														22,884
2	M	31 " 1936	Chesterfield	A	1-1	1-3	1	2	3	4	5	6	7	8	9	10	11^1														14,749
3	S	5 Sept 1936	Tottenham Hotspur	A	1-0	3-2	1	2	3	4	5	6		10	9^1		11	7^2	8												32,767
4	W	9 " 1936	Chesterfield	H	0-0	2-0	1	2	3	4	5			10^2	9		11	7	8	6											18,806
5	S	12 " 1936	Blackpool	H	1-1	1-2	1	2	3	4	5			10^1	9		11	7	8	6											22,631
6	M	14 " 1936	Barnsley	A	0-1	1-2	1	2	3	4	5			10	9		11^1		8		6	7									7,388
7	S	19 " 1936	Blackburn Rovers	A	0-0	0-1	1	2	3	4	5			10	9		11		8		6		7								13,284
8	S	26 " 1936	Bury	H	0-0	0-0	1	2	3	4	5		7	10	9		11		8		6										18,207
9	S	3 Oct 1936	Leicester City	A	1-1	2-2	1	2	3	4	5		7^2	8	9	10					6		11								9,736
10	S	10 " 1936	West Ham United	H	2-1	3-3	1	2	3	4	5		7	8	10^1		11^1		9^1		6										16,350
11	S	17 " 1936	Nottingham Forest	H	2-0	4-0	1	2	3	4	5		7^1	8	10		11^1		9^2		6										13,417
12	S	24 " 1936	Plymouth Argyle	A	0-0	0-2	1	2	3	4	5		7	8	10		11		9		6										17,941
13	S	31 " 1936	Coventry City	H	0-3	0-3	1	2	3	4	5		7	8	10				9		6		11								12,140
14	S	7 Nov 1936	Doncaster Rovers	A	0-0	2-1	1	2	3	4^1	5			10^1	9		11	7	8		6										11,235
15	S	14 " 1936	Fulham	H	0-0	3-0	1	2	3	4	5		7	10^1	9		11		8^2		6										12,941
16	S	21 " 1936	Burnley	A	0-2	0-3	1	2	3	4	5		7	10	9		11		8		6										9,352
17	S	28 " 1936	Southampton	H	1-2	4-2	1	2	3	4	5		7^1	10	9^2		11		8^1		6										11,287
18	S	5 Dec 1936	Swansea Town	A	1-0	1-2	1	2	3	4	5		7^1	10	9		11		8		6										7,850
19	S	12 " 1936	Bradford City	H	0-0	0-0	1	2	3	4	5		7	10	9		11		8		6										9,389
20	S	19 " 1936	Aston Villa	A	0-2	0-3	1	2	3	4	5		7	10	9		11		8		6										23,763
21	F	25 " 1936	Newcastle United	A	0-0	1-0	1	2	3	4	5		8	10	9		11^1	7			6										38,372
22	S	26 " 1936	Sheffield United	A	0-1	0-2	1	2	3	4	5		8	10	9		11	7			6										35,458
23	M	28 " 1936	Newcastle United	H	0-1	1-5	1	2	3	4	5		8	10	9		11				6			7^1							19,244
24	S	2 Jan 1937	Tottenham Hotspur	H	2-1	2-3	1	2	3	4	5	6	8	10	9^2		11	7													13,131
25	S	9 " 1937	Blackpool	A	2-0	2-0	1	2	3	8	4	6			9	11^1		7^1					10		5						12,999
26	S	23 " 1937	Blackburn Rovers	H	0-0	0-0	1	2	3		4	6		8	9	11		7					10		5						15,229
27	S	6 Feb 1937	Leicester City	H	1-2	1-2	1	2	3	4	6		11	9		10		7	8^1						5						13,488
28	W	10 " 1937	Bury	A	1-2	2-3	1		3	4	6			9^1		11		7^1	8				10		5	2					4,955
29	S	13 " 1937	West Ham United	A	0-3	1-4	1		3	6	4			9		11		7^1					10		5	2	8				23,796
30	S	20 " 1937	Nottingham Forest	A	3-1	4-3	1		3	4	5	6		11^2	9								10	7		2	8^2				11,102
31	S	27 " 1937	Plymouth Argyle	H	1-1	1-2	1		3	4	5	6		11^1	9								10	7		2	8				17,740
32	S	6 Mar 1937	Coventry City	A	0-1	1-1	1		2	4	5	6		11	9^1								10	7			8	3			15,791
33	S	13 " 1937	Doncaster Rovers	H	1-1	2-1	1		2	4		6		11^1				9^1					10	7	5		8	3			14,621
34	S	20 " 1937	Fulham	A	0-2	3-2	1		2	4		6		11^2	9						5		10	7			8^1	3			18,546
35	S	27 " 1937	Burnley	H	2-1	2-2	1		2	4	5	6		11^1	9								10	7			8^1	3			15,792
36	M	29 " 1937	Bradford Park Avenue	H	2-0	3-1	1		2	4	5	6		11^1	9^1								10	7			8^1	3			25,267
37	Tu	30 " 1937	Bradford Park Avenue	A	0-0	0-1	1		2	4	5	6		11	9								10	7			8		3		9,681
38	S	3 Apr 1937	Southampton	A	1-1	1-3	1		2^1	4	5	6		11	9			7					10				8	3			12,599
39	S	10 " 1937	Swansea Town	H	0-0	3-0	1		2	4	5	6		11^1	9^1								10	7			8^1	3			11,336
40	S	17 " 1937	Bradford City	A	0-2	0-2		5	2	4		6		11	9								10	7			8	3		1	6,471
41	S	24 " 1937	Aston Villa	H	3-0	5-1		5	2	4^1		6		11^1	10			9^1						7^2			8	3		1	25,052
42	S	1 May 1937	Barnsley	H	0-0	0-1		2	3	4	5	6		11	10				9					7			8			1	7,305

F.A. CUP

NO.		DATE	OPPONENTS		V.	H-T	F-T	Hall Fred	Halliday Tom	Bowen Sam	Robinson Bernard	Burke Peter	Proctor Harry	Warnes Billy	Manders Frank	Vinall Jack	Madden Owen	Clare Joseph	O'Reilly Jack	Goffey Herbert	Flack Len	Morris Robert	Edwards George	Burley Ben	Friar John	Scott Jack	Woodford George	Coleman Tim	Mackrell James	Worton Alfred	Dukes Harry	ATTD.
1	S	16 Jan 1937	Liverpool	(3rd Round)	H	2-0	3-0	1	2	3		4	6		8	9^2	11		7					10		5^1						26,856
2	S	30 " 1937	Bolton Wanderers	(4th Round)	A	0-0	1-1	1	2	3	4	5	6		9		11		7^1	8				10								24,791
3	Th	4 Feb 1937	Bolton Wanderers	AET (Replay)	H	0-0	1-2	1	2	3		4	6		10^1	9	11		7	8						5						30,108

1936–37 APPEARANCES & GOALS

	FOOTBALL LGE APPR.	FOOTBALL LGE GLS	F.A. CUP APPR.	F.A. CUP GLS
Bowen Sam	42	1	3	–
Manders Frank	41	16	3	1
Robinson Bernard	41	2	1	–
Hall Fred	39	–	3	–
Burke Peter	38	–	3	–
Vinall Jack	38	10	2	2
Halliday Tom	30	–	3	–
Clare Joseph	22	5		
Goffey Herbert	20	7	2	–
Morris Robert	19	–		
Proctor Harry	19	–	3	–
Warnes Billy	19	5		
Burley Ben	18	–	2	–
O'Reilly Jack	15	7	3	1
Coleman Tim	14	6		
Friar John	13	3		
Mackrell James	9	–		
Madden Owen	8	1	3	–
Scott Jack	6	–	2	1
Woodford George	4	–		
Dukes Harry	3	–		
Flack Len	2	–		
Edwards George	1	–		
Worton Alfred	1	–		

DIVISION 2

1936–37	P	W	D	L	F	A	PTS
Leicester City	42	24	8	10	89	57	56
Blackpool	42	24	7	11	88	53	55
Bury	42	22	8	12	74	55	52
Newcastle United	42	22	5	15	80	56	49
Plymouth Argyle	42	18	13	11	71	53	49
West Ham United	42	19	11	12	73	55	49
Sheffield United	42	18	10	14	66	54	46
Coventry City	42	17	11	14	66	54	45
Aston Villa	42	16	12	14	82	70	44
Tottenham Hotspur	42	17	9	16	88	66	43
Fulham	42	15	13	14	71	61	43
Blackburn Rovers	42	16	10	16	70	62	42
Burnley	42	16	10	16	57	61	42
Barnsley	42	16	9	17	50	64	41
Chesterfield	42	16	8	18	84	89	40
Swansea Town	42	15	7	20	50	65	37
Norwich City	**42**	**14**	**8**	**20**	**63**	**71**	**36**
Nottingham Forest	42	12	10	20	68	90	34
Southampton	42	11	12	19	53	77	34
Bradford Park Avenue	42	12	9	21	52	88	33
Bradford City	42	9	12	21	54	94	30
Doncaster Rovers	42	7	10	25	30	84	24

1937–38 DIVISION 2

NO.		DATE	OPPONENTS	V.	H-T	F-T	Dukes Harry	Halliday Tom	Mackrell James	Robinson Bernard	Burke Peter	Proctor Harry	Friar John	Coleman Tim	Vinall Jack	Furness Billy	Manders Frank	Bowen Sam	Worton Alfred	Madden Owen	Edwards George	Morris Robert	Cassidy Francis	Edwards Jim	Middleton John	Ware Harry	Burley Ben	Reilly Len	Hall Fred	Maskell Les	Flack Len	Church John	Law George	ATTD.
1	S	28 Aug 1937	Southampton	H	2-3	4-3	1	2	3	4	5	6	7	8^1	9^1	10^2	11																	23,407
2	Th	2 Sept 1937	Bradford Park Avenue	H	1-1	1-1	1	2	3	4	5	6	7	8^1	9	10	11																	17,491
3	S	4 " 1937	Blackburn Rovers	A	1-2	3-5	1	2	3	4	5	6	7^1	8^1	9	10	11^1																	16,259
4	M	6 " 1937	Bradford Park Avenue	A	0-3	0-3	1	5		4		6	7	8	9	10	11	2	3															7,678
5	S	11 " 1937	Sheffield Wednesday	H	2-1	3-1	1		3	4	5	6	7^2	8^1		10	9	2		11														19,548
6	Th	16 " 1937	Aston Villa	H	0-0	1-0	1	2		4	5	6		8^1		10	9	3		11	7													23,039
7	S	18 " 1937	Fulham	A	2-2	4-3	1	2		4		6		8^2		10^1	9^1	3		11	7	5												17,010
8	S	25 " 1937	Plymouth Argyle	H	1-0	4-0	1	2		4		6		8^1		10^2	9	3		11	7^1	5												20,394
9	S	2 Oct 1937	Chesterfield	A	1-4	2-6	1	2		4		6	7^1	8		10^1	9	3		11		5												15,245
10	S	9 " 1937	Swansea Town	H	0-1	1-1	1	2		4	5	6	7	8		10	9^1	3		11														17,510
11	S	16 " 1937	Nottingham Forest	H	1-0	2-0	1	2			5	6	7	8		10^2	9	3		11		4												16,102
12	S	23 " 1937	Coventry City	A	0-1	0-2	1	2			5	6	7	8		10	11	3				4	9											23,564
13	S	30 " 1937	Bury	H	0-0	1-2	1	2			5	6	7	8		10	9^1	3		11		4												15,190
14	S	6 Nov 1937	Burnley	A	0-1	0-3	1	5	3		4		7	9		10		2		11				6	8									11,073
15	S	13 " 1937	Tottenham Hotspur	H	1-1	2-1	1	2		4	5		7^1	8		10	11	3						6		9^1								19,019
16	S	20 " 1937	Stockport County	A	1-0	1-1	1	2		4	5	6	7	8		10	11	3								9^1								11,021
17	S	27 " 1937	Manchester United	H	0-2	2-3	1		3	4	5	6	7	8^2		10	11	2								9								17,397
18	S	4 Dec 1937	Sheffield United	A	1-0	1-4	1			4	5	6	7	8			11^1	2	3							9	10							10,698
19	S	11 " 1937	Barnsley	H	0-0	1-0	1			4	5		7	8			10	2	3	11		6				9^1								8,243
20	S	18 " 1937	Luton Town	A	1-1	1-1	1	2		4			7	8^1			10	3		11		6				9		5						14,492
21	M	27 " 1937	West Ham United	H	2-2	2-2	1	2		4	5		7^1	8^1		10		3		11		6				9								27,475
22	Tu	28 " 1937	West Ham United	A	0-2	3-3	1	2		4	5		7^1	8^2		10		3		11		6				9								17,087
23	S	1 Jan 1938	Southampton	A	1-3	1-3	1	2		4	5		7	8		10		3		11		6				9^1								14,217
24	S	15 " 1938	Blackburn Rovers	H	0-2	3-2		2		4			7	8^1		10	11^1	3				6				9^1		5	1					10,073
25	S	22 " 1938	Sheffield Wednesday	A	0-1	0-1		2	3	4			7	8		10	11					6				9		5	1					12,690
26	S	29 " 1938	Fulham	H	0-1	1-2		2	3	4			7	8		10	11^1					6				9		5	1					10,075
27	S	5 Feb 1938	Plymouth Argyle	A	1-0	1-1	1	2	3	4		6	7			10									8		11^1	5		9				14,050
28	S	19 " 1938	Swansea Town	A	0-0	0-1		2	3			6	7			10									8	4	11	5	1	9				9,404
29	Th	24 " 1938	Chesterfield	H	1-0	2-1		2	3	4		6	7^1			10										8	11	5	1	9^1				7,481
30	S	26 " 1938	Nottingham Forest	A	1-0	2-1		2	3		4	6				10^1					7					8	11^1	5	1	9				13,551
31	S	5 Mar 1938	Coventry City	H	0-2	0-2	1	2	3		4	6				10	9				7					8	11	5						16,051
32	S	12 " 1938	Bury	A	0-0	1-3	1	2	3		4	6	7^1			10	11									8		5		9				9,171
33	S	19 " 1938	Burnley	H	1-0	1-0		2	3		4	6	7^1			10	9									8	11	5	1					10,072
34	S	26 " 1938	Tottenham Hotspur	A	0-1	0-4		2	3		5	6	7	8		10	9									4	11		1					18,431
35	S	2 Apr 1938	Stockport County	H	0-0	1-0			3	2	5	6	7	8		10	11					4				9^1			1					10,142
36	S	9 " 1938	Manchester United	A	0-0	0-0		2	3	4	5	6	7	8		10	11												1	9				25,879
37	F	15 " 1938	Newcastle United	A	0-0	1-0		2	3	4	5	6^1	7	8		10	11									9			1					20,336
38	S	16 " 1938	Sheffield United	H	1-2	2-2		2		4	5	6	7	8		10^1	11^1									9			1		3			16,447
39	M	18 " 1938	Newcastle United	H	1-0	1-1		2		4	5	6	7	8		10^1	11									9			1		3			22,576
40	S	23 " 1938	Barnsley	A	0-0	0-0		2		4	5	6		8		10										9	11		1		3	7		9,350
41	S	30 " 1938	Luton Town	H	0-1	0-4		2		4	5	6		8		10					7					9			1		3	11		10,071
42	S	7 May 1938	Aston Villa	A	0-0	0-2			2	4	5	6		8		10	11				7								1		3		9	42,021

F.A. CUP

NO.		DATE	OPPONENTS	V.	H-T	F-T	Dukes Harry	Halliday Tom	Mackrell James	Robinson Bernard	Burke Peter	Proctor Harry	Friar John	Coleman Tim	Vinall Jack	Furness Billy	Manders Frank	Bowen Sam	Worton Alfred	Madden Owen	Edwards George	Morris Robert	Cassidy Francis	Edwards Jim	Middleton John	Ware Harry	Burley Ben	Reilly Len	Hall Fred	Maskell Les	Flack Len	Church John	Law George	ATTD.
1	S	8 Jan 1938	Aston Villa (3rd Round)	H	1-2	2-3	1	2		4	5		7	8^1		10	11^1	3				6				9								33,346

1937–38 APPEARANCES & GOALS

	FOOTBALL LGE APPR.	FOOTBALL LGE GLS	F.A. CUP APPR.	F.A. CUP GLS
Furness Billy	39	11	1	–
Halliday Tom	36	–	1	–
Coleman Tim	35	15	1	1
Friar John	34	10	1	–
Manders Frank	32	8	1	1
Proctor Harry	32	1	–	–
Robinson Bernard	32	–	1	–
Burke Peter	31	–	1	–
Dukes Harry	26	–	1	–
Ware Harry	25	6	1	–
Bowen Sam	21	–	1	–
Mackrell James	20	–		
Hall Fred	16	–		
Morris Robert	15	–	1	–
Madden Owen	14	–		
Reilly Len	11	–		
Burley Ben	9	2		
Edwards George	7	1		
Maskell Les	6	1		
Flack Len	5	–		
Vinall Jack	4	1		
Middleton John	3	–		
Worton Alfred	3	–		
Church John	2	–		
Edward Jim	2	–		
Cassidy Francis	1	–		
Law George	1	–		

DIVISION 2

1937–38	P	W	D	L	F	A	PTS
Aston Villa	42	25	7	10	73	35	57
Manchester United	42	22	9	11	82	50	53
Sheffield United	42	22	9	11	73	56	53
Coventry City	42	20	12	10	66	45	52
Tottenham Hotspur	42	19	6	17	76	54	44
Burnley	42	17	10	15	54	54	44
Bradford Park Avenue	42	17	9	16	69	56	43
Fulham	42	16	11	15	61	57	43
West Ham United	42	14	14	14	53	52	42
Bury	42	18	5	19	63	60	41
Chesterfield	42	16	9	17	63	63	41
Luton Town	42	15	10	17	89	86	40
Plymouth Argyle	42	14	12	16	57	65	40
Norwich City	**42**	**14**	**11**	**17**	**56**	**75**	**39**
Southampton	42	15	9	18	55	77	39
Blackburn Rovers	42	14	10	18	71	80	38
Sheffield Wednesday	42	14	10	18	49	56	38
Swansea Town	42	13	12	17	45	73	38
Newcastle United	42	14	8	20	51	58	36
Nottingham Forest	42	14	8	20	47	60	36
Barnsley	42	11	14	17	50	64	36
Stockport County	42	11	9	22	43	70	31

1938–39 DIVISION 2

No.		Date		Opponents	V.	H-T	F-T	Hall Fred	Halliday Tom	Flack Len	Robinson Bernard	Burke Peter	Smalley Tom	O'Reilly Jack	Coleman Tim	Law George	Furness Billy	Manders Frank	Friar John	Russell James	Dukes Harry	Maskell Les	Church John	Johnson Alex	Mackrell James	Proctor Harry	Taylor Jack	Ware Harry	Plunkett Sid	Reilly Len	Acquroff Jack	Graham Bill	Milburn John	Own Goals	ATTD.
1	S	27 Aug	1938	Bradford Park Avenue	H	1-1	1-3	1	2	3	4	5	6	7¹	8	9	10	11																	16,443
2	Th	1 Sept	1938	West Bromwich Albion	H	2-2	2-3	1	2	3	4	5	6	9			10	11¹	7¹	8															19,993
3	S	3 "	1938	Luton Town	A	1-2	1-2		2	3	4	5	6				10	11	7	8	1	9¹	11												16,547
4	W	7 "	1938	Nottingham Forest	A	0-1	0-1				4	5	8	9			10		7		1		11	2	3	6									11,077
5	S	10 "	1938	Plymouth Argyle	H	1-0	2-1				4	5	6			9¹	10	11¹	7	8	1			2	3										15,806
6	S	17 "	1938	Sheffield United	A	0-2	0-4				4	5	6			9	10	11	7	8	1			2	3										20,994
7	S	24 "	1938	Burnley	H	2-0	4-0			2	4	5	6	7¹		9¹	10¹	11¹		8	1						3								13,345
8	S	1 Oct	1938	Tottenham Hotspur	A	1-1	1-4			2	4	5	6	7		9	10¹	11		8	1						3								30,055
9	S	8 "	1938	Southampton	H	0-0	2-1			2	4	5	8				10	11¹	7		1					6	3	9¹							12,206
10	S	15 "	1938	Swansea Town	H	2-0	3-0			2	4	5	8¹				10	11	7		1					6	3	9²							10,721
11	S	22 "	1938	Chesterfield	A	0-2	0-2			2	4	5	8				10	11	7		1					6	3	9							11,452
12	S	29 "	1938	Milwall	H	0-2	0-2			2	4	5	8				10	11	7		1					6	3	9							21,593
13	S	5 Nov	1938	West Ham United	A	0-2	0-2			2	4	5	6				10	11	7		1						3	9	8						22,038
14	S	12 "	1938	Bury	H	2-0	3-1			2	4	5	6	9¹			10	11¹			1		7				3	8¹							9,049
15	S	19 "	1938	Sheffield Wednesday	A	0-4	0-7			2	4	5	6	9			10	11			1		7				3	8							16,958
16	S	26 "	1938	Fulham	H	1-2	3-3		2		4		6				10	11¹			1					8	3	9²	7	5					10,228
17	S	3 Dec	1938	Blackburn Rovers	A	0-1	0-6		2		4	5	6				10	11			1					8	3	9	7						12,584
18	S	10 "	1938	Tranmere Rovers	H	1-0	2-0	1	2			4	6				10	8¹	7				11¹				3	9		5					8,132
19	S	17 "	1938	Manchester City	A	0-3	1-4	1	2			5	6				10¹	8	7				11			4	3	9							19,500
20	S	24 "	1938	Bradford Park Avenue	A	0-2	0-3	1	2			5	6				10	8	7				11		3	4		9							8,766
21	Tu	27 "	1938	Newcastle United	A	0-2	0-4	1	2			5	6	9			10	11	7						3	4		8							26,156
22	S	31 "	1938	Luton Town	H	1-0	2-1	1				5	6	9¹			10	11	7	8					3	4¹	2								9,336
23	S	28 Jan	1939	Burnley	A	0-2	0-3	1			4	5	6	9			10	11	7	8					3		2								10,345
24	Th	2 Feb	1939	Sheffield United	H	1-0	1-2				4	5	6				8	11¹	7		1				3		2				9	10			8,156
25	S	4 "	1939	Tottenham Hotspur	H	1-0	1-2				4	5	6	7			8	11			1			3			2				9¹	10			15,347
26	S	11 "	1939	Southampton	A	1-0	1-3				4		6	7			11				1			3			2	8		5	9	10¹			11,880
27	S	18 "	1939	Swansea Town	A	0-0	1-0				4		6	7			8	11			1				3		2			5	9	10		–¹	11,645
28	S	25 "	1939	Chesterfield	H	1-0	2-0				4		6	7			8¹	11			1						2			5	9¹	10	3		11,483
29	S	4 Mar	1939	Millwall	A	0-2	0-6				4	5	6	7			8	11			1						2				9	10	3		18,413
30	S	11 "	1939	West Ham United	H	0-3	2-6	1			4		6		8		11		7¹								2			5	9¹	10	3		15,027
31	Th	16 "	1939	Newcastle United	H	1-0	1-1				4		6		8		11¹		7		1						2			5	9	10	3		7,764
32	S	18 "	1939	Bury	A	0-1	3-2				4		6		8¹		11¹		7		1						2			5	9	10¹	3		7,929
33	S	25 "	1939	Sheffield Wednesday	H	1-1	2-2				4		6		8		11¹		7¹		1						2	9		5		10	3		13,309
34	S	1 Apr	1939	Fulham	A	0-0	0-2				4		6		8		11		7		1						2	9		5		10	3		12,673
35	S	8 "	1939	Blackburn Rovers	H	2-0	4-0				4		6	7	8²		11				1						2			5	9²	10	3		18,547
36	M	10 "	1939	Coventry City	H	0-0	1-1				4		6	7	8		11				1						2			5	9	10¹	3		28,865
37	Tu	11 "	1939	Coventry City	A	0-2	0-2				4		6	7	8		11				1						2			5	9	10	3		18,708
38	S	15 "	1939	Tranmere Rovers	A	1-0	1-0	1			4		6		8		11		7								2			5	9¹	10	3		4,898
39	S	22 "	1939	Manchester City	H	0-0	0-0	1			4		6		8		11						7				2			5	9	10	3		14,340
40	S	29 "	1939	West Bromwich Albion	A	1-2	2-4	1			4		6		8¹		11						7				2			5	9	10¹	3		13,106
41	W	3 May	1939	Plymouth Argyle	A	0-1	0-1	1			4		6		8		10						11				2	9		5	7		3		7,747
42	S	6 "	1939	Nottingham Forest	H	0-0	1-0	1			4		6		8		11						7				2	9¹		5	10		3		19,715

F.A. CUP

No.		Date		Opponents		V.	H-T	F-T	Hall Fred	Halliday Tom	Flack Len	Robinson Bernard	Burke Peter	Smalley Tom	O'Reilly Jack	Coleman Tim	Law George	Furness Billy	Manders Frank	Friar John	Russell James	Dukes Harry	Maskell Les	Church John	Johnson Alex	Mackrell James	Proctor Harry	Taylor Jack	Ware Harry	Plunkett Sid	Reilly Len	Acquroff Jack	Graham Bill	Milburn John	Own Goals	ATTD.
1	Th	12 Jan	1939	Manchester City	(3rd Round)	H	0-2	0-5	1				5	6	9			10	11	7	8					3	4	2								21,061

1938–39 APPEARANCES & GOALS

	FOOTBALL LGE APPR.	FOOTBALL LGE GLS	F.A. CUP APPR.	F.A. CUP GLS
Furness Billy	42	7	1	–
Smalley Tom	42	1	1	–
Robinson Bernard	37	–		
Taylor Jack	34	–	1	–
Dukes Harry	28	–		
Manders Frank	26	8	1	–
Burke Peter	25	–	1	–
Friar John	23	3	1	–
O'Reilly Jack	18	4	1	–
Reilly Len	18	–		
Ware Harry	18	7		
Acquroff Jack	17	6		
Graham Bill	17	4		
Milburn John	15	–		
Coleman Tim	14	4		
Hall Fred	14	–	1	–
Flack Len	12	–		
Church John	11	1		
Proctor Harry	11	1	1	–
Halliday Tom	9	–		
Mackrell James	9	–	1	–
Russell James	8	–	1	–
Johnson Alex	5	–		
Law George	5	2		
Plunkett Sid	3	–		
Maskell Les	1	1		
Own Goals		1		

DIVISION 2

1938–39	P	W	D	L	F	A	PTS
Blackburn Rovers	42	25	5	12	94	60	55
Sheffield United	42	20	14	8	69	41	54
Sheffield Wednesday	42	21	11	10	88	59	53
Coventry City	42	21	8	13	62	45	50
Manchester City	42	21	7	14	96	72	49
Chesterfield	42	20	9	13	69	52	49
Luton Town	42	22	5	15	82	66	49
Tottenham Hotspur	42	19	9	14	67	62	47
Newcastle United	42	18	10	14	61	48	46
West Bromwich Albion	42	18	9	15	89	72	45
West Ham United	42	17	10	15	70	52	44
Fulham	42	17	10	15	61	55	44
Millwall	42	14	14	14	64	53	42
Burnley	42	15	9	18	50	56	39
Plymouth Argyle	42	15	8	19	49	55	38
Bury	42	12	13	17	65	74	37
Bradford Park Avenue	42	12	11	19	61	82	35
Southampton	42	13	9	20	56	82	35
Swansea Town	42	11	12	19	50	83	34
Nottingham Forest	42	10	11	21	49	82	31
Norwich City	**42**	**13**	**5**	**24**	**50**	**91**	**31**
Tranmere Rovers	42	6	5	31	39	99	17

1946–47 DIVISION 3 SOUTH

No.	Day	Date	Opponents	V.	H-T	F-T	Hall Fred	Reid Ernie	Taylor Jack	Flack Len	Robinson Bernard	Robinson Joe	Plunkett Sid	Walker Cyril	Guy James	Furness Billy	Church John	Tobin Maurice	Williams Grenville	Johnson Ralph	Davis Derek	Dutton Len	Ryder Terry	Taylor Geoff	Proctor Harry	Russell James	Jones Sid	Dukes Harry	Eyre Les	Reilly Len	Morgan Denis	Low Norman	Wiseman George	Darmody Aubrey	Spinks Henry	Morgan George	Pembery Gordon	Williams Alan	Mansfield Fred	Joy Harold	Hold Oscar	Gallego Antonio	Armes Ivan	ATTD.
1	S	31 Aug 1946	Cardiff City	H	0-0	2-1	1	2	3	4	5	6	7	8^1	9	10^1	11																																				20,678
2	W	4 Sept 1946	Bristol City	A	1-0	1-2	1	2	3	4	5	6	7	8	9^1	10	11																																				12,033
3	S	7 " 1946	Ipswich Town	A	0-1	0-5	1		3	4	5		7		8	10	9	2	6	11																															19,521
4	Th	12 " 1946	Swindon Town	H	0-1	1-5		4	3		5		7	8^1		11		2	6	9	1	10																													15,488
5	S	14 " 1946	Notts. County	A	0-3	0-3		4		2			7		8			3	6	9	1		10	11	5																											18,210
6	W	18 " 1946	Bristol City	H	1-0	2-2			3	2	4		7			10^1			6	9	1				5	8	11^1																			11,038
7	S	21 " 1946	Northampton Town	H	1-1	2-3			3	2	4					10	9		6	7					5	8^1	11^1	1																		16,215
8	Th	26 " 1946	Crystal Palace	H	1-3	2-3		2			5		7			10^1	9^1	3	6			4				8		1	11																	12,264
9	S	28 " 1946	Aldershot	A	0-2	1-3					2		7			10	9	3	6		1	4				8^1			11	5																5,734
10	S	5 Oct 1946	Brighton & Hove Albion	H	2-1	2-3			3	2			7		10				6	9^1		8^1			5		11	1			4														15,416
11	S	12 " 1946	Exeter City	A	0-1	0-3			3	2	4		7			9			6			8					11	1	10			5														9,160
12	S	19 " 1946	Leyton Orient	H	3-0	5-0			3	2	4		7^2						6	9^2		8					11^1	1	10			5														15,948
13	S	26 " 1946	Queens Park Rangers	A	1-1	1-1			3	2	4		7						6	9^1		8					11	1	10			5														15,581
14	S	2 Nov 1946	Southend United	H	0-0	1-5			3	2	4^1		7						6	9		8					11	1	10			5														19,836
15	S	9 " 1946	Bristol Rovers	A	2-0	2-1			3	2	4		7^1						6	9		8					11	1	10^1			5														8,963
16	S	16 " 1946	Mansfield Town	H	1-1	3-1			3	2	4		7						6	9		8^2					11	1	10^1			5														16,561
17	S	23 " 1946	Torquay United	A	1-1	1-2			3	2	4		7			11			6	9^1		8						1	10			5														3,194
18	S	7 Dec 1946	Reading	A	1-2	3-4			3	2	4		7						6	9^2		8					11	1	10^1			5														10,556
19	S	21 " 1946	Watford	A	0-3	1-4			3	2	4		7						6	9							11	1	10		8^1	5														3,078
20	W	25 " 1946	Bournemouth	A	0-0	1-0				2			4			9			6			8	7				11^1		10			5	1	3												10,071
21	Th	26 " 1946	Bournemouth	H	1-3	1-6				2	4		7^1			9			6			8					11		10			5	1	3												23,404
22	S	28 " 1946	Cardiff City	A	1-2	1-6				2									3	6			8			4		11	1	10			5			9^1	7								36.285
23	S	4 Jan 1947	Ipswich Town	H	0-1	0-1				2	4								3	6			8						11		10		7	5	1		9									23,030
24	S	18 " 1947	Notts. County	H	1-0	2-2				2			4						3	6	9^1		8					11		10^1			5	1			7								16,834
25	S	25 " 1947	Northampton Town	A	0-1	0-1				2			4						3	6	9		8							10			5	1			7	11							6,023
26	S	1 Feb 1947	Aldershot	H	1-2	2-3				2			4^1					11	3	6	9		8							10^1			5	1			7								12,125
27	S	8 " 1947	Brighton & Hove Albion	A	2-2	3-3				2			8^1		6		9	3				10	7^2						11			5	1						4						4,668
28	S	15 " 1947	Exeter City	H	1-1	1-3							8^1		6		9	3				10	7						11			5	1							2	4				12,696
29	S	22 " 1947	Leyton Orient	A	0-3	0-3				6	4		9				11	3			1	8	7						10			5							2					7,509
30	S	1 Mar 1947	Queens Park Rangers	H	0-1	0-1					4		8				11	3			1	6	7						10			5							2		9			15,233
31	S	8 " 1947	Southend United	A	0-1	0-3					4						11	3	6	9	1		7						10			5							2		8			6,810
32	S	15 " 1947	Bristol Rovers	H	1-3	3-3					4											6	7				11^1		10^1		3	5							2	9	8^1	1		18,047
33	S	22 " 1947	Mansfield Town	A	2-2	4-4					4										1	6	7				11		10^1		3	5							2	9^3	8			5,141
34	S	29 " 1947	Torquay United	H	1-0	2-0					4										1		7				11^1		10^1		3	5							2	9	8		6	14,512
35	F	4 April 1947	Port Vale	A	0-1	3-1					4										1		7^2				11		10^1		3	5							2	9	8		6	13,978
36	S	5 " 1947	Crystal Palace	A	1-0	1-0					4							3			1		7				11		10			5							2	9	8^1		6	13,315
37	M	7 " 1947	Port Vale	H	3-0	3-0					4							3			1		7				11^1		10^1			5							2	9^1	8		6	29,985
38	S	12 " 1947	Reading	H	0-1	0-2					4							3			1	8	7				11		10			5							2	9			6	19,519
39	S	19 " 1947	Walsall	A	0-1	2-2					4		11				9^1	3			1								10			5				7^1			2		8		6	10,258
40	S	26 " 1947	Watford	H	3-0	4-2					4						9^1				1		7^1						10^1		3	5				11			2		8^1		6	15,077
41	S	3 May 1947	Swindon Town	A	0-1	1-1					4						9				1		7						10		3	5				11			2		8^1		6	13,570
42	S	17 " 1947	Walsall	H	0-2	0-2					4						9				1		7						10		3	5				11			2		8		6	16,002

F.A. CUP

No.	Day	Date	Opponents	V.	H-T	F-T	Hall Fred	Reid Ernie	Taylor Jack	Flack Len	Robinson Bernard	Robinson Joe	Plunkett Sid	Walker Cyril	Guy James	Furness Billy	Church John	Tobin Maurice	Williams Grenville	Johnson Ralph	Davis Derek	Dutton Len	Ryder Terry	Taylor Geoff	Proctor Harry	Russell James	Jones Sid	Dukes Harry	Eyre Les	Reilly Len	Morgan Denis	Low Norman	Wiseman George	Darmody Aubrey	Spinks Henry	Morgan George	Pembery Gordon	Williams Alan	Mansfield Fred	Joy Harold	Hold Oscar	Gallego Antonio	Armes Ivan	ATTD.
1	S	30 Nov 1946	Brighton & Hove Albion (1st Round)	H	1-2	7-2			3	2	4^1		7						6	9^1		8					11	1	10^5			5														19,264
2	S	14 Dec 1946	Queens Park Rangers (2nd Round)	H	2-0	4-4			3	2	4		7						6	9^1		8					11^1	1	10^2			5														26,317
3	W	18 " 1946	Queens Park Rangers (Replay)	A	0-0	0-2			3	2	4		7						6	9		8					11	1	10			5														14,100

1946–47 APPEARANCES & GOALS

	FOOTBALL LGE APPR.	FOOTBALL LGE GLS	F.A. CUP APPR.	F.A. CUP GLS
Eyre Les	34	11	3	7
Robinson Bernard	33	1	3	1
Low Norman	32	–	3	–
Plunkett Sid	28	7	3	–
Dutton Len	26	3	3	–
Flack Len	25	–	3	–
Williams Grenville	25	–	3	–
Jones Sid	23	7	3	1
Tobin Maurice	19	–		
Johnson Ralph	18	8	3	2
Davis Derek	17	–		
Ryder Terry	17	5		
Church John	16	3		
Taylor Jack	16	–	3	–
Mansfield Fred	15	–		
Dukes Harry	13	–	3	–
Furness Billy	12	3		
Hold Oscar	12	4		
Morgan Denis	10	1		
Armes Ivan	9	–		
Joy Harold	8	4		
Morgan George	8	1		
Wiseman George	8	–		
Guy James	7	1		
Proctor Harry	5	–		
Reid Ernie	5	–		
Russell James	4	2		
Hall Fred	3	–		
Walker Cyril	3	2		
Darmody Aubrey	2	–		
Robinson Joe	2	–		
Spinks Henry	2	1		
Gallego Antonio	1	–		
Pembery Gordon	1	–		
Reilly Len	1	–		
Taylor Geoff	1	–		
Williams Alan	1	–		

DIVISION 3 SOUTH

1946–47	P	W	D	L	F	A	PTS
Cardiff City	42	30	6	6	93	30	66
Queens Park Rangers	42	23	11	8	74	40	57
Bristol City	42	20	11	11	94	56	51
Swindon Town	42	19	11	12	84	73	49
Walsall	42	17	12	13	74	59	46
Ipswich Town	42	16	14	12	61	53	46
Bournemouth	42	18	8	16	72	54	44
Southend United	42	17	10	15	71	60	44
Reading	42	16	11	15	83	74	43
Port Vale	42	17	9	16	68	63	43
Torquay United	42	15	12	15	52	61	42
Notts. County	42	15	10	17	63	63	40
Northampton Town	42	15	10	17	72	75	40
Bristol Rovers	42	16	8	18	59	69	40
Exeter City	42	15	9	18	60	69	39
Watford	42	17	5	20	61	76	39
Brighton & Hove Albion	42	13	12	17	54	72	38
Crystal Palace	42	13	11	18	49	62	37
Leyton Orient	42	12	8	22	54	75	32
Aldershot	42	10	12	20	48	78	32
Norwich City	**42**	**10**	**8**	**24**	**64**	**100**	**28**
Mansfield Town	42	9	10	23	48	96	28

1947–48 DIVISION 3 SOUTH

NO.		DATE	OPPONENTS	V.	H-T	F-T	Davis Derek	Mansfield Fred	Morgan Denis	Robinson Bernard	Williams Grenville	Armes Ivan	Ryder Terry	Dutton Len	Hold Oscar	Eyre Les	Jones Sid	Tobin Maurice	Low Norman	Kinsey Noel	Pickwick Don	Foan Albert	Rowlands Trevor	Church John	Guy James	Edwards Don	Nethercott Ken	Morgan George	Arnold Eric	Ashman Ron	Driver Allenby	Hollis Roy	Own Goals	ATTD.
1	S	23 Aug 1947	Queens Park Rangers	A	0-1	1-3	1	2	3	4	5	6	7	8	9^1	10	11																	18,704
2	W	27 " 1947	Port Vale	H	0-1	1-2	1	2	3	4	5	6	7	8^1	9	10	11																	22,024
3	S	30 " 1947	Watford	H	1-0	1-0	1		3		6		7	4		11		2	5	8	9	10^1												20,146
4	M	1 Sept 1947	Port Vale	A	0-0	0-2	1		3	8	6		7	4		11		2		9		10	5											11,688
5	S	6 " 1947	Brighton & Hove Albion	A	0-1	0-2	1		3		6		7	4	9	11		2	5	8		10												9,132
6	W	10 " 1947	Torquay United	H	1-1	1-1	1	2	3		5	6	7	4	8	10	11							9^1										14,248
7	S	13 " 1947	Ipswich Town	H	0-4	1-5	1	2	3		5			4		10	11			7		8		9^1	6									23,374
8	W	17 " 1947	Torquay United	A	0-0	1-1			3	4	6	2		8		10			5	7				11	9	1							$-^1$	6,720
9	S	20 " 1947	Bristol Rovers	H	0-2	1-5			3	4^1	6	2		8					5	7		10		11	9	1								15,438
10	S	27 " 1947	Northampton Town	A	0-1	0-1			3		6	4		8		10		2	5		7		9				1	11						9,757
11	S	4 Oct 1947	Aldershot	H	0-1	0-1			3	4	6				8	10	11		5								1	7	2	9				15,247
12	S	11 " 1947	Bristol City	A	0-2	0-6			3	4	6		7		8	10		2	5					11			1			9				27,896
13	S	18 " 1947	Reading	H	1-0	2-1		2			6		7	8		10^1	11	3	5	4				9^1			1							14,283
14	S	25 " 1947	Walsall	A	0-2	2-3		2			6			8		10^1	11	3	5	4				9			1	7^1						15,934
15	S	1 Nov 1947	Leyton Orient	H	2-0	3-0		2			6			8^1		10	11^1	3	5	4	7			9^1			1							17,896
16	S	8 " 1947	Exeter City	A	0-2	0-2		2						8		10	11	3	5	4				9	6		1	7						9,603
17	S	15 " 1947	Newport County	H	1-0	1-2	1	2	3					8^1		10	11	6	5	4	7			9										16,072
18	S	22 " 1947	Southend United	A	0-0	0-0		2	3					8	9	10	11	6	5	4				7			1							10,231
19	S	6 Dec 1947	Swansea Town	A	2-1	2-3		2	3					8^1	9	10^1	11	6	5	4	7						1							17,343
20	F	26 " 1947	Swindon Town	A	1-1	2-3		2	3					8	9	10^2	11	6	5	4				7			1							19,021
21	S	27 " 1947	Swindon Town	H	0-1	2-2		2	3					8	9^1	10^1	11	6	5	4				7			1							19,855
22	S	3 Jan 1948	Watford	A	0-1	2-2		2						6	9	10^1	11	3	5	4				7			1				8^1			7,400
23	S	17 " 1948	Brighton & Hove Albion	H	1-0	2-2		2						6		10^1	11^1	3	5	4	7			9			1				8			19,154
24	S	24 " 1948	Bournemouth	H	0-1	0-1		2		4				6		10	11	3	5	8				7			1				9			18,581
25	S	31 " 1948	Ipswich Town	A	1-0	2-1		2		4^1				6		10		3	5	8				7			1	11			9^1			19,689
26	S	7 Feb 1948	Bristol Rovers	A	3-0	3-2		2		4				6		10^2		3	5	8				7			1	11			9^1			11,655
27	S	14 " 1948	Northampton Town	H	0-2	2-3		2		4				6		10^1		3	4	8^1				7			1	11			9			23,470
28	S	28 " 1948	Bristol City	H	1-0	2-3	1			2				6	9^1	10		3	5	4				7				11^1			8			22,275
29	S	6 Mar 1948	Reading	A	4-1	4-2				2				6	9^1	10^1		3	5	4				7			1	11^1			8^1			12,419
30	S	13 " 1948	Walsall	H	1-0	1-0				2				6	9	10^1		3	5	4				7			1	11			8			22,751
31	S	20 " 1948	Leyton Orient	A	1-1	1-2				2				10	9			3	5	4				7^1	6		1	11			8			18,220
32	F	26 " 1948	Crystal Palace	H	1-0	3-1				2^1				6	9^1	10^1		3	5	4				7			1	11			8			24,802
33	S	27 " 1948	Exeter City	H	1-0	3-0				2				6	9^1	10		3	5	4				7			1	11^1			8^1			24,634
34	M	29 " 1948	Crystal Palace	A	0-1	0-2				2				6	9	10		3	5	4				7			1	11			8			20,724
35	S	3 Apr 1948	Newport County	A	1-1	1-1				2				6	9^1	10		3	5	4				7			1	11			8			8,929
36	W	7 " 1948	Aldershot	A	2-2	2-2				2				6	9^1	10		3	5	4	7						1	11^1		8				5,092
37	S	10 " 1948	Southend United	H	1-0	1-0				2				6	9^1	11		3	5	4							1	7		8	10			22,734
38	S	17 " 1948	Notts. County	A	1-1	2-1				2		6				10		3	5	4				7			1	11		9^1	8		$-^1$	19,183
39	W	21 " 1948	Queens Park Rangers	H	4-2	5-2				2				6		10		3	5	4				7			1	11^1			8^1	9^3		30,052
40	S	24 " 1948	Swansea Town	H	0-2	1-2				2				6		10		3		4			5	7			1	11			8	9^1		25,435
41	W	28 " 1948	Notts. County	H	0-1	0-1				2				6	11	10		3	5	4				7			1				8	9		37,863
42	S	1 May 1948	Bournemouth	A	1-1	3-1				2		6			9^2	10^1		3	5	4				7			1	11			8			12,216

F.A. CUP

NO.		DATE	OPPONENTS		V.	H-T	F-T	Davis Derek	Mansfield Fred	Morgan Denis	Robinson Bernard	Williams Grenville	Armes Ivan	Ryder Terry	Dutton Len	Hold Oscar	Eyre Les	Jones Sid	Tobin Maurice	Low Norman	Kinsey Noel	Pickwick Don	Foan Albert	Rowlands Trevor	Church John	Guy James	Edwards Don	Nethercott Ken	Morgan George	Arnold Eric	Ashman Ron	Driver Allenby	Hollis Roy	Own Goals	ATTD.
1	S	29 Nov 1947	Merthyr Town	(1st Round)	H	2-0	3-0		2	3					8^1	9	10^1	11	6	5	4^1	7						1							17,153
2	S	13 Dec 1947	Walsall	(2nd Round)	H	2-0	2-2		2	3					8	9^1	10	11	6	5	4^1	7						1							24,343
3	S	20 " 1947	Walsall	(Replay)	A	0-0	2-3		2	3					8^1	9^1	10	11	6	5	4				7			1							13,466

1947–48 APPEARANCES & GOALS

	FOOTBALL LGE APPR.	FOOTBALL LGE GLS	F.A. CUP APPR.	F.A. CUP GLS
Eyre Les	40	15	3	1
Dutton Len	38	4	3	2
Kinsey Noel	36	1	3	2
Low Norman	36	–	3	–
Tobin Maurice	35	–	3	–
Church John	32	5	1	–
Nethercott Ken	31	–	3	–
Robinson Bernard	26	3		
Hold Oscar	23	11	3	2
Morgan George	21	6		
Driver Allenby	20	6		
Mansfield Fred	19	–	3	–
Jones Sid	17	2	3	–
Morgan Denis	17	–	3	–
Williams Grenville	15	–		
Davis Derek	9	–		
Armes Ivan	8	–		
Ryder Terry	8	–		
Pickwick Don	7	–	2	–
Ashman Ron	5	1		
Foan Albert	5	1		
Guy James	5	–		
Hollis Roy	3	4		
Rowlands Trevor	3	–		
Edwards Don	2	–		
Arnold Eric	1	–		
Own Goals		2		

DIVISION 3 SOUTH

1947–48	P	W	D	L	F	A	PTS
Queens Park Rangers	42	26	9	7	74	37	61
Bournemouth	42	24	9	9	76	35	57
Walsall	42	21	9	12	70	40	51
Ipswich Town	42	23	3	16	67	61	49
Swansea Town	42	18	12	12	70	52	48
Notts. County	42	19	8	15	68	59	46
Bristol City	42	18	7	17	77	65	43
Port Vale	42	16	11	15	63	54	43
Southend United	42	15	13	14	51	58	43
Reading	42	15	11	16	56	58	41
Exeter City	42	15	11	16	55	63	41
Newport County	42	14	13	15	61	73	41
Crystal Palace	42	13	13	16	49	49	39
Northampton Town	42	14	11	17	58	72	39
Watford	42	14	10	18	57	79	38
Swindon Town	42	10	16	16	41	46	36
Leyton Orient	42	13	10	19	51	73	36
Torquay United	42	11	13	18	63	62	35
Aldershot	42	10	15	17	45	67	35
Bristol Rovers	42	13	8	21	71	75	34
Norwich City	**42**	**13**	**8**	**21**	**61**	**76**	**34**
Brighton & Hove Albion	42	11	12	19	43	73	34

1948–49 DIVISION 3 SOUTH

NO.		DATE	OPPONENTS	V.	H-T	F-T	Nethercott Ken	Morgan Denis	Tobin Maurice	Kinsey Noel	Low Norman	Armes Ivan	Dolding Len	Driver Allenby	Hold Oscar	Eyre Les	Chruch John	Ryder Terry	Hollis Roy	Robinson Bernard	Pickwick Don	Foan Albert	Ashman Ron	Morgan George	Ephgrave George	Dutton Len	Arnold Eric	McCoy Peter	Holmes Bert	Gavin Johnny	ATTD.
1	S	21 Aug 1948	Walsall	H	1-2	1-2	1	2	3	4	5	6[1]	7	8	9	10	11														27,655
2	W	25 " 1948	Northampton Town	H	1-0	2-1	1	2	3	4	5	6		8		10	11	7	9[2]												22,517
3	S	28 " 1948	Exeter City	A	1-2	1-4	1	2	3	4	5	6		8		10	11	7[1]	9												11,325
4	Th	2 Sept 1948	Northampton Town	A	0-1	0-1	1		3		5	6	7	8		10	11		9	2	4										7,127
5	S	4 " 1948	Bristol City	H	2-0	4-0	1		3		5	6		8[1]	10		11	7	9[2]	2[1]	4										22,667
6	W	8 " 1948	Brighton & Hove Albion	A	0-1	0-1	1		3		5	6			10		11	7		2	4	8	9								17,559
7	S	11 " 1948	Swindon Town	A	1-1	3-3	1		3		5	6		8[1]	10[1]	11		7	9[1]	2	4										18,222
8	W	15 " 1948	Brighton & Hove Albion	H	1-1	2-1	1		3		5	6		8	10	11		7[1]	9	2[1]	4										22,277
9	S	18 " 1948	Leyton Orient	H	0-0	0-0	1		3		5	6		8	10	11		7	9	2	4										24,355
10	S	25 " 1948	Port Vale	A	0-0	0-0	1		3		5	6		8	10		11	7	9	2	4										15,361
11	S	2 Oct 1948	Millwall	H	1-1	1-2	1		3		5	6		8	10[1]		11	7	9	2	4										24,202
12	S	9 " 1948	Notts. County	H	2-0	3-0	1		3	8[1]	5	6			9[1]	10[1]	11			2	4			7							29,998
13	S	16 " 1948	Ipswich Town	A	1-1	2-1			3	8	5	6				10	11			2	4		9[2]	7	1						24,569
14	S	23 " 1948	Swansea Town	H	1-0	1-0	1		3	8	5	6				10	11			2	4		9[1]	7							29,610
15	S	30 " 1948	Newport County	A	0-1	3-4	1		3	8	5	6				10[1]	11			2	4		9	7[2]							11,068
16	S	6 Nov 1948	Crystal Palace	H	2-0	3-0	1		3	8	5	6				10	11[1]			2	4		9[1]	7[1]							23,890
17	S	13 " 1948	Reading	A	0-2	1-2	1		3	8	5	6				10	11[1]			2	4		9	7							17,283
18	S	20 " 1948	Bournemouth	H	0-1	1-1	1		3	8	5	6				10	11			2	4		9[1]	7							28,349
19	S	4 Dec 1948	Bristol Rovers	H	3-0	3-0	1	3		8[2]	5	6				10	11			2	4		9[1]	7							20,246
20	S	18 " 1948	Walsall	A	1-3	1-4	1	3		8	5	6				10	11			2	4		9[1]	7							9,604
21	S	25 " 1948	Southend United	H	1-0	3-0	1	3		8[1]	5	6				10	11[1]			2	4		9[1]	7							22,168
22	M	27 " 1948	Southend United	A	0-2	2-2	1	3		8[1]	5	6	11			10				2	4		9	7[1]							9,019
23	S	1 Jan 1949	Exeter City	H	2-0	3-0	1	3		8	5	6				11[1]				2[1]	4		9	7		10[1]					18,766
24	S	15 " 1949	Bristol City	A	1-0	6-1	1	3		8[3]	5					10[1]	11			2	4		9[1]	7[1]		6					10,969
25	S	22 " 1949	Swindon Town	H	0-0	0-0	1	3		8	5					10	11			2	4		9	7		6					28,154
26	S	29 " 1949	Watford	A	1-1	1-1	1			8	5					10	11			2	4		9[1]	7		6	3				10,129
27	S	5 Feb 1949	Leyton Orient	A	1-0	3-0	1			8[1]	5					10	11		9	2	4[1]			7[1]		6	3				12,389
28	S	12 " 1949	Torquay United	A	1-2	1-2	1			8	5					10	11		9[1]	2	4			7		6	3				6,524
29	S	19 " 1949	Port Vale	H	2-0	2-0	1			9[1]	5			8[1]		10	11			2	4			7		6	3				28,323
30	S	26 " 1949	Millwall	A	1-1	3-1	1			8[1]	5			9[2]		10	11			2	4			7		6	3				25,114
31	S	5 Mar 1949	Notts. County	A	1-0	1-2	1				5			8		10	11			2	4		9	7[1]		6	3				34,285
32	S	12 " 1949	Ipswich Town	H	1-0	2-0	1		3		5	6		8		11[1]				2	4		9[1]	7		10					35,361
33	S	19 " 1949	Swansea Town	A	0-1	1-2	1		3		5	6		8		11[1]					4		9	7		10		2			23,676
34	S	26 " 1949	Newport County	H	0-0	0-0	1		3		5	6		8			11				4		9	7		10		2			23,214
35	S	2 Apr 1949	Crystal Palace	A	0-1	1-1	1		3		5	6		8			11[1]				4		9	7		10		2			16,501
36	S	9 " 1949	Reading	H	1-2	1-2	1		3		5	6	7			10			9[1]		4		8	11				2			21,969
37	F	15 " 1949	Aldershot	A	1-1	1-4	1		3		5	6	7			10	9					8		11[1]		4		2			7,483
38	S	16 " 1949	Bournemouth	A	2-0	2-1	1		3		5		7[1]			10[1]	9				4	8		11		6		2			13,044
39	M	18 " 1949	Aldershot	H	0-0	0-0	1	2	3		5		7			10	9				4	8		11		6					26,948
40	S	23 " 1949	Watford	H	0-0	0-1	1	2	3		5		7			10					4	8	9	11		6					16,509
41	S	30 " 1949	Bristol Rovers	A	0-2	2-2	1	2	3							10	11				4	8	9[1]			6[1]			5	7	12,755
42	S	7 May 1949	Torquay United	H	0-0	0-0	1	2	3							10	11				4	8	9			6			5	7	15,837

F.A. CUP

NO.		DATE	OPPONENTS		V.	H-T	F-T	Nethercott Ken	Morgan Denis	Tobin Maurice	Kinsey Noel	Low Norman	Armes Ivan	Dolding Len	Driver Allenby	Hold Oscar	Eyre Les	Chruch John	Ryder Terry	Hollis Roy	Robinson Bernard	Pickwick Don	Foan Albert	Ashman Ron	Morgan George	ATTD.
1	S	27 Nov 1948	Wellington Town	(1st Round)	H	0-0	1-0	1	3		8	5	6				10	11			2	4		9[1]	7	16,874
2	S	11 Dec 1948	Torquay United	(2nd Round)	H	0-1	1-3	1	3		8[1]	5	6				10	11			2	4		9	7	6,000

1948–49 APPEARANCES & GOALS

	FOOTBALL LGE APPR.	FOOTBALL LGE GLS	F.A. CUP APPR.	F.A. CUP GLS
Nethercott Ken	41	–	2	–
Low Norman	40	–	2	–
Pickwick Don	38	1	2	–
Eyre Les	36	7	2	–
Church John	33	4	2	–
Armes Ivan	29	1	2	–
Morgan George	29	8	2	–
Robinson Bernard	29	3	2	–
Tobin Maurice	29	–		
Ashman Ron	24	12	2	1
Kinsey Noel	22	11	2	1
Dutton Len	19	2		
Driver Allenby	17	5		
Morgan Denis	14	–	2	–
Hollis Roy	12	7		
Hold Oscar	9	3		
Ryder Terry	9	2		
Dolding Len	8	1		
Foan Albert	7	–		
Arnold Eric	6	–		
McCoy Peter	6	–		
Gavin Johnny	2	–		
Holmes Bert	2	–		
Ephgrave George	1	–		

DIVISION 3 SOUTH

1948–49	P	W	D	L	F	A	PTS
Swansea Town	42	27	8	7	87	34	62
Reading	42	25	5	12	77	50	55
Bournemouth	42	22	8	12	69	48	52
Swindon Town	42	18	15	9	64	56	51
Bristol Rovers	42	19	10	13	61	51	48
Brighton & Hove Albion	42	15	18	9	55	55	48
Ipswich Town	42	18	9	15	78	77	45
Millwall	42	17	11	14	63	64	45
Torquay United	42	17	11	14	65	70	45
Norwich City	**42**	**16**	**12**	**14**	**67**	**49**	**44**
Notts. County	42	19	5	18	102	68	43
Exeter City	42	15	10	17	63	76	40
Port Vale	42	14	11	17	51	54	39
Walsall	42	15	8	19	56	64	38
Newport County	42	14	9	19	68	92	37
Bristol City	42	11	14	17	44	62	36
Watford	42	10	15	17	41	54	35
Southend United	42	9	16	17	41	46	34
Leyton Orient	42	11	12	19	58	80	34
Northampton Town	42	12	9	21	51	62	33
Aldershot	42	11	11	20	48	59	33
Crystal Palace	42	8	11	23	38	76	27

1949–50 DIVISION 3 SOUTH

No.	Day	Date	Opponents	V.	H-T	F-T	Nethercott Ken	Morgan Denis	Tobin Maurice	Pickwick Don	Low Norman	Dutton Len	Gavin Johnny	Kinsey Noel	Driver Allenby	Jones Bryn	Eyre Les	Armes Ivan	Ephgrave George	Morgan George	Ashman Ron	Foan Albert	Church John	Rowlands Trevor	Dolding Len	Ryder Terry	Lewis Bill	Hollis Roy	Duffy John	Birch Cliff	Owens Les	Attd.
1	S	20 Aug 1949	Newport County	A	2-3	2-3	1	2	3	4	5	6	7	8^2	9	10	11															16,238
2	W	24 " 1949	Notts. County	H	2-1	4-3	1	2	3	4	5	6^1	7^1	8	9^1	10	11^1															32,131
3	S	27 " 1949	Bristol City	H	2-0	3-0	1	2	3	4	5	6	7	8^1	9	10	11^2															25,870
4	Th	1 Sept 1949	Notts. County	A	0-2	0-5	1	2	3	4	5		7	8	9	10	11	6														25,304
5	S	3 " 1949	Brighton & Hove Albion	A	2-1	3-1		2	3	4	5		7	8^1	9^2	10	11	6	1													18,716
6	W	7 " 1949	Aldershot	H	3-0	4-0		2	3	4	5			8^2	9^2	10	11	6	1	7												24,651
7	S	10 " 1949	Walsall	H	1-2	3-2		2	3	4	5			8^2	9	10	11^1	6	1	7												25,408
8	W	14 " 1949	Aldershot	A	0-2	0-2	1	2	3	4	5		7	8	9	10	11	6														5,862
9	S	17 " 1949	Millwall	A	1-1	2-1	1	2	3	4	5		7	8			11	6			9^1	10^1										26,670
10	S	24 " 1949	Swindon Town	H	1-0	4-0	1	2	3	4	5		7	8			11^1	6			9^1	10^2										27,448
11	S	1 Oct 1949	Torquay United	A	1-1	1-1	1	2	3	4^1	5		7	8			11	6			9	10										9,200
12	S	8 " 1949	Port Vale	H	0-1	0-1	1	2	3	4	5			8				6		7	9	10	11									26,831
13	S	15 " 1949	Ipswich Town	A	0-1	0-3	1	2	3	4	5	6	7	8			11				9	10										26,298
14	S	22 " 1949	Exeter City	H	1-1	1-2	1	2	3	4	5	6	7	8	9^1	10	11															22,734
15	S	29 " 1949	Leyton Orient	A	2-1	2-1	1	2	3	4	5				9^1	10	11							6	7	8^1						13,210
16	S	5 Nov 1949	Reading	H	0-1	1-1	1	2	3	4	5				9^1		10						11	6	7	8						17,836
17	S	12 " 1949	Watford	A	0-0	0-0	1	2		4	5				9	10	11							6	7	8	3					16,065
18	S	19 " 1949	Crystal Palace	H	0-0	2-0	1	2		4	5			8		10	11							6^2		7	3	9				25,558
19	S	3 Dec 1949	Bristol Rovers	H	2-0	4-0	1	2		4	5			8^1		10	11^2							6		7^1	3	9				19,205
20	S	17 " 1949	Newport County	H	1-0	4-0	1	2		4	5	6		8^2		10	11									7^1	3	9^1				17,895
21	S	24 " 1949	Bristol City	A	1-0	2-1	1	2		4	5			8^1		10	11^1							6		7	3	9				23,728
22	M	26 " 1949	Nottingham Forest	H	0-0	1-1	1	2		4	5			8^1		10	11							6		7	3	9				35,933
23	Tu	27 " 1949	Nottingham Forest	A	0-0	1-0	1	2		4	5		7	8			11	6								10^1	3	9				31,932
24	S	31 " 1949	Brighton & Hove Albion	H	0-1	1-2	1			4	5			8		10^1	11	6					7				3	9	2			22,871
25	S	14 Jan 1950	Walsall	A	1-1	1-1	1			4	5		7	8		10		6			9^1		11				3		2			9,960
26	S	21 " 1950	Millwall	H	0-2	0-2	1			4	5		7	8		10	11	6			9						3		2			21,114
27	S	4 Feb 1950	Swindon Town	A	1-0	1-1	1			4	5			8		10		6		11							3	9	2	7^1		13,238
28	S	11 " 1950	Southend United	A	0-0	0-1	1			4	5			8		10		6		11							3	9	2	7		10,478
29	S	18 " 1950	Torquay United	H	2-2	3-3	1			4	5			8		6	10^1						11				3	9^2	2	7		23,034
30	S	25 " 1950	Port Vale	A	0-0	2-2	1			4	5			8		6	10						11				3	9	2	7^2		11,204
31	S	4 Mar 1950	Ipswich Town	H	1-0	1-1	1			4	5			8			10			7	6		11^1				3		2	9		32,357
32	S	11 " 1950	Exeter City	A	0-2	1-3	1			4^1	5			8			10			7	6		11				3	9	2			9,935
33	S	18 " 1950	Leyton Orient	H	1-0	4-0	1			4	5			8			10				6		11^2				3	7	2		9^2	20,025
34	S	25 " 1950	Reading	A	1-1	1-4	1			4	5			8			10				6		11				3	7	2		9^1	13,093
35	S	1 Apr 1950	Watford	H	2-1	2-1	1			4	5			8			10^1				6		11				3	7	2		9^1	20,014
36	S	8 " 1950	Crystal Palace	A	0-1	0-2	1			4	5			8			10				6		11				3	7	2		9	18,064
37	M	10 " 1950	Northampton Town	H	1-1	2-1	1			4	5			8^1			10				6		11				3	7^1	2		9	21,015
38	Tu	11 " 1950	Northampton Town	A	1-1	1-3	1			4	5	10		8							6				11		3	7^1	2		9	11,167
39	S	15 " 1950	Bournemouth	H	0-0	0-1	1			4	5			8							6	10	11				3	7	2		9	18,355
40	S	22 " 1950	Bristol Rovers	A	0-3	1-5	1			4	5						10				6		11			8^1	3	7			9	12,546
41	S	29 " 1950	Southend United	H	0-0	0-0	1	2		4	5						10				6		11			8	3	7			9	10,252
42	S	6 May 1950	Bournemouth	A	0-1	0-2	1	2		4	5		7	8			11				6					10	3				9	10,748

F.A. CUP

No.	Day	Date	Opponents	V.	H-T	F-T	Nethercott Ken	Morgan Denis	Tobin Maurice	Pickwick Don	Low Norman	Dutton Len	Gavin Johnny	Kinsey Noel	Driver Allenby	Jones Bryn	Eyre Les	Armes Ivan	Ephgrave George	Morgan George	Ashman Ron	Foan Albert	Church John	Rowlands Trevor	Dolding Len	Ryder Terry	Lewis Bill	Hollis Roy	Duffy John	Birch Cliff	Owens Les	Attd.
1	S	26 Nov 1949	Gloucester City (1st Round)	A	0-1	3-2	1	2		4	5			8^1		10^1	11							6		7	3	9^1				9,500
2	S	10 Dec 1949	Hartlepools United (2nd Round)	A	1-1	1-1	1	2		4^1	5	6		8		10	11									7	3	9				11,144
3	Th	15 " 1949	Hartlepools United (Replay)	H	1-0	5-1	1	2		4	5	6		8^1		10	11^1									7	3	9^3				18,064
4	S	7 Jan 1950	Portsmouth (3rd Round)	A	1-0	1-1	1			4	5		7	8^1			11	6			9					10	3		2			42,059
5	Th	12 " 1950	Portsmouth (Replay)	H	0-0	0-2	1			4	5		7	8				6			9		11			10	3		2			43,129

1949–50 APPEARANCES & GOALS

	Football Lge Appr.	Football Lge Gls	F.A. Cup Appr.	F.A. Cup Gls
Low Norman	42	–	5	–
Pickwick Don	42	2	5	1
Nethercott Ken	39	–	5	–
Kinsey Noel	37	14	5	3
Eyre Les	36	10	4	1
Lewis Bill	26	–	5	–
Morgan Denis	25	–	3	–
Jones Bryn	23	1	3	1
Hollis Roy	21	5	3	4
Ashman Ron	19	3	2	–
Duffy John	17	–	2	–
Church John	16	3	1	–
Tobin Maurice	16	–		
Armes Ivan	15	–	2	–
Gavin Johnny	15	1	2	–
Driver Allenby	12	8		
Ryder Terry	12	5	5	–
Owens Les	10	4		
Dutton Len	7	1	2	–
Morgan George	7	–		
Rowlands Trevor	7	2	1	–
Foan Albert	6	3		
Birch Cliff	5	3		
Dolding Len	4	–		
Ephgrave George	3	–		

DIVISION 3 SOUTH

1949–50	P	W	D	L	F	A	PTS
Notts. County	42	25	8	9	95	50	58
Northampton Town	42	20	11	11	72	50	51
Southend United	42	19	13	10	66	48	51
Nottingham Forest	42	20	9	13	67	39	49
Torquay United	42	19	10	13	66	63	48
Watford	42	16	13	13	45	35	45
Crystal Palace	42	15	14	13	55	54	44
Brighton & Hove Albion	42	16	12	14	57	69	44
Bristol Rovers	42	19	5	18	51	51	43
Reading	42	17	8	17	70	64	42
Norwich City	**42**	**16**	**10**	**16**	**65**	**63**	**42**
Bournemouth	42	16	10	16	57	56	42
Port Vale	42	15	11	16	47	42	41
Swindon Town	42	15	11	16	59	62	41
Bristol City	42	15	10	17	60	61	40
Exeter City	42	14	11	17	63	75	39
Ipswich Town	42	12	11	19	57	86	35
Leyton Orient	42	12	11	19	53	85	35
Walsall	42	9	16	17	61	62	34
Aldershot	42	13	8	21	48	60	34
Newport County	42	13	8	21	67	98	34
Millwall	42	14	4	24	55	63	32

1950–51 DIVISION 3 SOUTH

NO.	DATE	OPPONENTS	V.	H-T	F-T	Nethercott Ken	Morgan Denis	Lewis Bill	Pickwick Don	Foulkes Reg	Ashman Ron	Gavin Johnny	Kinsey Noel	Owens Les	Eyre Les	Docherty Tom	Tobin Maurice	Duffy John	Hollis Roy	Dutton Len	Arnold Eric	Bradley Jack	Summers Johnny	Ephgrave George	Holmes Bert	ATTD.
1	S 19 Aug 1950	Port Vale	H	1-0	2-0	1	2	3	4	5	6	7^{1}	8	9^{1}	10	11										27,288
2	W 23 " 1950	Northampton Town	H	0-0	0-0	1	2	3	4	5	6	7	8	9	10	11										27,300
3	S 26 " 1950	Nottingham Forest	A	0-1	2-4	1	2	3	4	5	6	7	8^{1}	9	10^{1}	11										28,250
4	Th 31 " 1950	Northampton Town	A	0-0	2-1	1	2	3	4	5	6	7	8	9^{1}	10^{1}	11										17,696
5	S 2 Sept 1950	Torquay United	H	1-0	1-1	1	2	3	4	5	6	7	8	9^{1}	10	11										25,447
6	Th 7 " 1950	Walsall	A	1-0	1-0	1		3	4	5	6	7	8	9	10^{1}	11	2									10,831
7	S 9 " 1950	Aldershot	A	0-0	1-1	1		3	4	5	6	7	8	9	10^{1}	11	2									8,238
8	W 13 " 1950	Walsall	H	0-0	1-0	1		3	4	5	6	7	8	9	10^{1}	11	2									22,090
9	S 16 " 1950	Swindon Town	H	1-0	2-0	1		3	4	5	6	7^{1}	8^{1}		10	11		2	9							23,289
10	S 23 " 1950	Colchester United	A	1-1	3-2	1		3	4	5	6	7^{2}	8		10	11		2	9^{1}							13,843
11	S 30 " 1950	Bristol Rovers	H	1-0	2-0	1		3	4	5	6	7	8		10^{1}	11^{1}		2	9							23,965
12	S 7 Oct 1950	Watford	H	2-0	3-1	1		3	4	5	6	7^{1}	8^{1}		10^{1}	11		2	9							24,507
13	S 14 " 1950	Millwall	A	1-1	1-1	1		3	4	5	6	7	8		10	11		2	9^{1}							34,780
14	S 21 " 1950	Bristol City	H	0-0	0-0	1		3	4	5	6	7	8		10	11		2	9							27,130
15	S 28 " 1950	Gillingham	A	1-1	2-2	1		3	4	5	6	7	8		10	11		2	9^{2}							14,348
16	S 4 Nov 1950	Bournemouth	H	3-0	3-0	1		3	4	5	6	7^{1}	8^{1}		10	11		2	9^{1}							23,160
17	S 11 " 1950	Exeter City	A	1-0	2-1	1		3	4	5	6	7	8		10^{1}	11		2	9^{1}							12,595
18	S 18 " 1950	Southend United	H	3-0	3-0	1		3	4	5	6	7	8		10	11		2	9^{3}							24,783
19	S 2 Dec 1950	Plymouth Argyle	H	0-0	1-0	1		3	4	5	6	7^{1}	8		10	11		2	9							26,891
20	S 23 " 1950	Nottingham Forest	H	1-0	2-0	1		3	4	5	6	7^{1}	8^{1}		10	11		2	9							29,818
21	Tu 26 " 1950	Brighton & Hove Albion	A	0-0	1-1	1		3	4	5	6	7	8		10	11		2	9^{1}							14,134
22	W 27 " 1950	Brighton & Hove Albion	H	0-0	1-1	1		3	4	5	6	7^{1}	8		10	11		2	9							22,893
23	S 30 " 1950	Torquay United	A	3-0	5-1	1		3	4	5	6	7^{2}	8^{2}		10^{1}	11		2	9							5,948
24	Th 11 Jan 1951	Leyton Orient	A	1-2	1-3	1		3	4	5^{1}	6	7	8		10	11		2	9							4,475
25	S 13 " 1951	Aldershot	H	2-2	2-2	1		3	4	5	6^{1}	7	8		10	11		2	9^{1}							18,552
26	S 20 " 1951	Swindon Town	A	0-1	0-1	1		3	4	5	6	7	8		10	11		2	9							13,140
27	Th 1 Feb 1951	Leyton Orient	H	2-0	3-1	1		3	4^{1}	5	6	7^{1}	8^{1}			11		2	9	10						12,500
28	S 3 " 1951	Colchester United	H	1-0	1-1	1		3	4	5	6	7	8			11		2	9^{1}	10						25,110
29	W 14 " 1951	Reading	A	0-0	1-3	1		3	4	5^{1}	6	7	8		10	11		2	9							11,426
30	S 24 " 1951	Watford	A	1-0	2-0	1			4^{1}	5	6	7	8			11		2	9	10^{1}	3					13,293
31	S 3 Mar 1951	Millwall	H	2-0	2-1	1			4	5	6	7	8^{2}			11		2	9		3	10				26,959
32	S 10 " 1951	Bristol City	A	2-1	2-2	1			4	5	6	7^{1}	8^{1}			11		2	9		3	10				22,079
33	S 17 " 1951	Gillingham	H	0-0	2-0				4	5	6	7^{1}	8		10	11		2			3		9^{1}	1		19,010
34	S 24 " 1951	Bournemouth	A	0-0	0-0	1		3	4	5	6	7	8			11		2	9	10						8,742
35	M 26 " 1951	Newport County	H	0-1	2-1	1		3	4	5^{1}	6	7	8^{1}			11		2	9	10						35,267
36	S 31 " 1951	Exeter City	H	2-0	3-0	1		3	4	5	6	7^{2}	8^{1}			11		2	9	10						21,705
37	M 2 Apr 1951	Port Vale	A	0-0	1-2	1		3	4	5^{1}	6	7	8			11		2	9				10			10,247
38	S 7 " 1951	Southend United	A	0-0	2-0	1		3	4	5	6	7	8			11		2		10			9^{2}			12,836
39	W 11 " 1951	Ipswich Town	A	0-0	1-0	1		3	4	5^{1}	6	7	8			11		2		10			9			24,289
40	S 14 " 1951	Reading	H	1-1	2-1	1		3	4^{1}	5	6	7	8					2	9	10			11^{1}			30,003
41	W 18 " 1951	Crystal Palace	A	2-0	5-0	1		3		5	6	7	8		10^{2}	11		2	9^{3}	4						14,782
42	S 21 " 1951	Plymouth Argyle	A	0-2	1-2	1		3		5^{1}	6	7	8		10	11		2	9	4						20,451
43	W 25 " 1951	Newport County	A	0-1	1-1	1		3	4	5	6	7	8		10^{1}	11		2	9							13,862
44	S 28 " 1951	Ipswich Town	H	0-0	1-3	1		3		5	6	7	8		10	11		2	9^{1}	4						30,210
45	M 30 " 1951	Bristol Rovers	A	2-1	3-3	1		3			6	7^{1}	8	9^{1}	10^{1}	11		2		4					5	12,957
46	S 5 May 1951	Crystal Palace	H	3-0	3-1	1		3			6^{2}	7	8	9	10^{1}	11		2		4					5	15,693

F.A. CUP

NO.	DATE	OPPONENTS		V.	H-T	F-T	Nethercott Ken	Morgan Denis	Lewis Bill	Pickwick Don	Foulkes Reg	Ashman Ron	Gavin Johnny	Kinsey Noel	Owens Les	Eyre Les	Docherty Tom	Tobin Maurice	Duffy John	Hollis Roy	Dutton Len	ATTD.
1	S 25 Nov 1950	Watford	(1st Round)	H	0-0	2-0	1		3	4	5	6	7	8		10^{1}	11		2	9^{1}		22,045
2	S 9 Dec 1950	Rhyl	(2nd Round)	A	0-0	1-0	1		3	4	5	6	7	8^{1}		10	11		2	9		7,448
3	S 6 Jan 1951	Liverpool	(3rd Round)	H	1-0	3-1	1		3	4	5	6	7	8		10^{1}	11^{2}		2	9		34,693
4	S 27 " 1951	Newport County	(4th Round)	A	0-0	2-0	1		3	4	5	6	7	8			11^{1}		2	9	10^{1}	20,293
5	S 10 Feb 1951	Sunderland	(5th Round)	A	0-1	1-3	1		3	4	5	6	7^{1}	8		10	11		2	9		65,125

1950–51 APPEARANCES & GOALS

	FOOTBALL LGE APPR.	FOOTBALL LGE GLS	F.A. CUP APPR.	F.A. CUP GLS
Ashman Ron	46	3	5	–
Gavin Johnny	46	17	5	1
Kinsey Noel	46	13	5	1
Docherty Tom	45	1	5	3
Nethercott Ken	45	–	5	–
Foulkes Reg	44	6	5	–
Lewis Bill	42	–	5	–
Pickwick Don	41	3	5	–
Duffy John	38	–	5	–
Eyre Les	34	14	4	2
Hollis Roy	33	16	5	1
Dutton Len	14	1	1	1
Ownes Les	10	4		
Morgan Denis	5	–		
Summers Johnny	5	4		
Arnold Eric	4	–		
Tobin Maurice	3	–		
Bradley Jack	2	–		
Holmes Bert	2	–		
Ephgrave George	1	–		

DIVISION 3 SOUTH

1950–51	P	W	D	L	F	A	PTS
Nottingham Forest	46	30	10	6	110	40	70
Norwich City	**46**	**25**	**14**	**7**	**82**	**45**	**64**
Reading	46	21	15	10	88	53	57
Plymouth Argyle	46	24	9	13	85	55	57
Millwall	46	23	10	13	80	57	56
Bristol Rovers	46	20	15	11	64	42	55
Southend United	46	21	10	15	92	69	52
Ipswich Town	46	23	6	17	69	58	52
Bournemouth	46	22	7	17	65	57	51
Bristol City	46	20	11	15	64	59	51
Newport County	46	19	9	18	77	70	47
Port Vale	46	16	13	17	60	65	45
Brighton & Hove Albion	46	13	17	16	71	79	43
Exeter City	46	18	6	22	62	85	42
Walsall	46	15	10	21	52	62	40
Colchester United	46	14	12	20	63	76	40
Swindon Town	46	18	4	24	55	67	40
Aldershot	46	15	10	21	56	88	40
Leyton Orient	46	15	8	23	53	75	38
Torquay United	46	14	9	23	64	81	37
Northampton Town	46	10	16	20	55	67	36
Gillingham	46	13	9	24	69	101	35
Watford	46	9	11	26	54	88	29
Crystal Palace	46	8	11	27	33	84	27

1951–52 DIVISION 3 SOUTH

NO.		DATE	OPPONENTS	V.	H-T	F-T	Nethercott Ken	Duffy John	Lewis Bill	Pickwick Don	Foulkes Reg	Ashman Ron	Gavin Johnny	Kinsey Noel	Ackerman Alf	Eyre Les	Docherty Tom	Morgan Denis	Summers Johnny	Holmes Bert	Hollis Roy	Dutton Len	McCrohan Roy	Bradley Jack	Rackham Derrick	Jones Denys	Arnold Eric	Sloan Paddy	Atkinson Walter	Own Goals	ATTD.
1	S	18 Aug 1951	Swindon Town	A	0-1	1-1	1	2	3	4	5	6	7	8	9[1]	10	11														14,617
2	Th	23 " 1951	Colchester United	A	1-0	1-1	1	2	3	4	5	6	7	8[1]	9	10	11														14,085
3	S	25 " 1951	Leyton Orient	H	0-0	1-0	1		3	4	5	6	7	8	9		11	2	10[1]												28,117
4	W	29 " 1951	Colchester United	H	2-0	5-2	1		3	4	5	6[1]	7[1]	8	9[1]		11	2	10[2]												24,760
5	S	1 Sept 1951	Walsall	A	0-1	0-4	1		3	4	5	6	7	8	9		11	2	10												10,600
6	W	5 " 1951	Exeter City	A	2-1	4-2	1		3	4		6	7[1]	8		10[1]		2	11	5	9[2]										8,485
7	S	8 " 1951	Shrewsbury Town	H	1-1	3-2	1		3	4		6	7[1]	8[1]		10	11	2		5	9[1]	4									25,380
8	W	12 " 1951	Exeter City	H	0-1	1-1	1	2	3	4	5	6	7	10[1]			11				9		8								24,263
9	S	15 " 1951	Aldershot	A	0-2	0-2	1	2	3	4	5	6	7	8		11			10		9										7,083
10	W	19 " 1951	Torquay United	A	1-0	2-1	1	2	3	4	5	10	7[1]	8			11				9[1]	6									7,484
11	S	22 " 1951	Watford	H	1-0	3-0	1	2	3	4	5	10	7	8[1]			11[1]				9	6								–[1]	25,040
12	S	29 " 1951	Bristol Rovers	A	1-1	1-1	1	2	3	4	5	10	7	8			11[1]				9	6									26,131
13	S	6 Oct 1951	Bristol City	H	1-0	1-0	1	2	3	4	5	10	7	8			11				9[1]	6									28,302
14	S	13 " 1951	Port Vale	A	0-0	0-0	1	2	3	4	5	10	7	8			11				9	6									10,576
15	S	20 " 1951	Northampton Town	H	2-0	2-1	1	2	3	4	5	6	7		8		11[1]				9[1]			10							28,078
16	S	27 " 1951	Reading	A	0-0	1-1	1	2	3	4	5	6	7	8[1]	9		11							10							17,780
17	S	3 Nov 1951	Newport County	H	1-2	1-2	1	2	3	4	5	6	7[1]	8			11				9			10							25,854
18	S	10 " 1951	Southend United	A	1-0	1-2	1	2	3	4	5	6		8	9		11				7[1]			10							11,641
19	S	17 " 1951	Bournemouth	H	1-0	2-0	1		3	4	5	6	7[1]	8	10		11	2			9[1]										20,902
20	S	1 Dec 1951	Brighton & Hove Albion	H	0-0	0-1	1		3	4	5	6	7	8	10		11	2			9										23,021
21	S	8 " 1951	Gillingham	A	1-1	2-1	1		3	4	5	6	7	8	10			2			9[1]				11[1]						10,499
22	S	22 " 1951	Leyton Orient	A	2-2	3-3	1		3	4	5	6	7	8[1]	10			2			9[2]				11						10,424
23	Tu	25 " 1951	Ipswich Town	A	2-0	2-0	1		3	4	5	6	7	8[1]	10[1]			2			9				11						16,821
24	W	26 " 1951	Ipswich Town	H	2-0	2-0	1		3	4	5	6	7	8	10[1]			2			9[1]				11						32,008
25	S	29 " 1951	Walsall	H	4-0	8-0	1		3		5	6		8[1]	10			2			9[5]	4			11[1]	7[1]					18,537
26	S	5 Jan 1952	Shrewsbury Town	A	1-0	2-0	1		3		5	6		8[1]	10			2			9	4			11	7[1]					8,464
27	W	16 " 1952	Plymouth Argyle	A	0-1	1-3	1				5	6	7	8				2			9[1]	4			11		3	10			15,889
28	S	19 " 1952	Aldershot	H	0-1	1-2	1				5	6	7[1]	8				2			9	4			11		3	10			16,684
29	S	26 " 1952	Watford	A	1-1	1-1	1		3	4		6		8			11	2	10	5	9[1]					7					10,040
30	S	2 Feb 1952	Crystal Palace	H	1-0	1-0	1		3	4	9	6	7[1]	8			11	2	10	5											18,277
31	S	9 " 1952	Bristol Rovers	H	1-0	1-0	1	2	3	4	9	6	7	10	11					5			8[1]								16,463
32	S	16 " 1952	Bristol City	A	3-1	5-2	1		3	4		6	7[3]	10				2	11	5	9		8[1]							–[1]	19,825
33	S	23 " 1952	Crystal Palace	A	0-0	0-2	1		3	4		6	7	10				2	11	5	9		8								19,491
34	S	1 Mar 1952	Port Vale	H	2-0	2-3	1		3	4		6[1]	7	10				2	11[1]	5	9		8								17,642
35	S	8 " 1952	Northampton Town	A	1-1	2-1	1		3	4	5	10[1]	7					2	11		9[1]	6	8								14,625
36	S	15 " 1952	Reading	H	2-1	2-1	1		3	4	5	6	7[1]	8	10		11	2	9[1]												23,772
37	S	22 " 1952	Newport County	A	0-1	2-2	1		3	4	5	6[2]	7	8	11			2	9				10								10,350
38	W	2 Apr 1952	Southend United	H	1-0	1-0	1		3		5	6[1]	7	8	10		11	2	9										4		10,830
39	S	5 " 1952	Bournemouth	A	2-1	2-1	1		3	4	5	6[1]	7[1]	8	11			2	9									10			7,108
40	S	12 " 1952	Millwall	H	0-0	1-0	1		3		5	6[1]	7	8	11			2	9			4						10			21,182
41	M	14 " 1952	Torquay United	H	2-0	7-0	1		3		5	6	7[3]	8[1]	11			2	9[2]			4						10		–[1]	24,155
42	S	19 " 1952	Brighton & Hove Albion	A	0-1	0-2	1		3		5	6	7	8	11			2	9			4						10			19,410
43	W	23 " 1952	Millwall	A	1-1	1-2	1		3		5	6	7	8	11			2	9[1]			4	10								11,925
44	S	26 " 1952	Gillingham	H	2-0	5-0	1		3		5	6[1]	7[3]	8	11[1]			2	9			4	10								14,370
45	W	30 " 1952	Plymouth Argyle	H	0-0	3-0	1		3		5	6[2]	7	8	11			2	9[1]			4	10								20,490
46	S	3 May 1952	Swindon Town	H	1-0	2-0	1		3		5	6	7	8[1]	11[1]			2	9			4	10								13,988

F.A. CUP

NO.		DATE	OPPONENTS		V.	H-T	F-T	Nethercott Ken	Duffy John	Lewis Bill	Pickwick Don	Foulkes Reg	Ashman Ron	Gavin Johnny	Kinsey Noel	Ackerman Alf	Eyre Les	Docherty Tom	Morgan Denis	Summers Johnny	Holmes Bert	Hollis Roy	Dutton Len	McCrohan Roy	Bradley Jack	Rackham Derrick	Jones Denys	ATTD.
1	S	24 Nov 1951	Northampton Town	(1st Round)	H	2-1	3-2	1		3	4		6	7	8[1]	11[1]		11	2		5	9[1]						27,120
2	S	15 Dec 1951	Chesterfield	(2nd Round)	H	1-0	3-1	1		3	4	5	6	7[1]	8	10[1]			2			9[1]				11		26,089
3	S	12 Jan 1952	Arsenal	(3rd Round)	H	0-3	0-5	1		3		5	6		8	10			2			9	4			11	7	38,930

1951–52 APPEARANCES & GOALS

	FOOTBALL LGE APPR.	FOOTBALL LGE GLS	F.A. CUP APPR.	F.A. CUP GLS
Ashman Ron	46	11	3	–
Nethercott Ken	46	–	3	–
Kinsey Noel	44	11	3	1
Lewis Bill	44	–	3	–
Gavin Johnny	42	19	2	1
Foulkes Reg	40	–	2	–
Pickwick Don	33	–	2	–
Morgan Denis	32	–	3	–
Ackerman Alf	28	6	3	2
Hollis Roy	27	20	3	2
Docherty Tom	22	3	1	–
Summers Johnny	22	9		
Dutton Len	18	–	1	–
Duffy John	14	–		
McCrohan Roy	11	2		
Holmes Bert	8	–	1	–
Rackham Derrick	8	2	2	–
Sloan Paddy	6	–		
Eyre Les	5	1		
Bradley Jack	4	–		
Jones Denys	3	2	1	–
Arnold Eric	2	–		
Atkinson Walter	1	–		
Own Goals		3		

DIVISION 3 SOUTH

1951–52	P	W	D	L	F	A	PTS
Plymouth Argyle	46	29	8	9	107	53	66
Reading	46	29	3	14	112	60	61
Norwich City	**46**	**26**	**9**	**11**	**89**	**50**	**61**
Millwall	46	23	12	11	74	53	58
Brighton & Hove Albion	46	24	10	12	87	63	58
Newport County	46	21	12	13	77	76	54
Bristol Rovers	46	20	12	14	89	53	52
Northampton Town	46	22	5	19	93	74	49
Southend United	46	19	10	17	75	66	48
Colchester United	46	17	12	17	56	77	46
Torquay United	46	17	10	19	86	98	44
Aldershot	46	18	8	20	78	89	44
Port Vale	46	14	15	17	50	66	43
Bournemouth	46	16	10	20	69	75	42
Bristol City	46	15	12	19	58	69	42
Swindon Town	46	14	14	18	51	68	42
Ipswich Town	46	16	9	21	63	74	41
Leyton Orient	46	16	9	21	55	68	41
Crystal Palace	46	15	9	22	61	80	39
Shrewsbury Town	46	13	10	23	62	86	36
Watford	46	13	10	23	57	81	36
Gillingham	46	11	13	22	71	81	35
Exeter City	46	13	9	24	65	86	35
Walsall	46	13	5	28	55	94	31

1952–53 DIVISION 3 SOUTH

NO.		DATE		OPPONENTS	V.	H-T	F-T	Nethercott Ken	Morgan Denis	Lewis Bill	Pickwick Don	Foulkes Reg	Ashman Ron	Gavin Johnny	Kinsey Noel	Johnston Tom	Rattray Peter	Ackerman Alf	Summers Johnny	Duffy John	Holmes Bert	Dutton Len	McCrohan Roy	Docherty Tom	Jones Denys	Adams Chris	Coxon Billy	Proctor David	Own Goals	ATTD.
1	S	23 Aug	1952	Aldershot	H	3-0	5-0	1	2	3	4	5	6	7	8^2	9^1	10^1	11^1												27,243
2	W	27 "	1952	Ipswich Town	A	0-1	1-2	1	2	3	4	5	6	7	8	9	10	11^1												21,033
3	S	30 "	1952	Swindon Town	A	0-1	1-2	1	2	3	4	5	6	7	8	9^1	10	11												14,701
4	W	3 Sept	1952	Ipswich Town	H	1-0	1-0	1	2	3	4	5	6	7	8	9^1	10	11												28,528
5	S	6 "	1952	Queens Park Rangers	H	1-0	2-0	1	2	3	4	5	6	7	8	9^1	10		11^1											26,449
6	W	10 "	1952	Exeter City	A	0-0	0-1	1		3	4	5	6	7	8	9	10		11	2										15,720
7	S	13 "	1952	Shrewsbury Town	A	4-1	8-1	1		3	4		6	7^1	8	9^4	10^1		11^1	2	5								$–^1$	11,890
8	W	17 "	1952	Exeter City	H	0-0	2-0	1		3			6	7	8	9^1	10^1		11	2	5	4								18,695
9	S	20 "	1952	Walsall	H	1-0	3-0	1		3		5	6	7^1	8^1	9^1	10		11	2		4								24,694
10	W	24 "	1952	Crystal Palace	A	1-1	1-1	1		3		5	6	7	8	9	10		11^1	2		4								7,544
11	S	27 "	1952	Gillingham	A	3-0	3-0	1	2	3		5	6	7^1	8			9^2	11			4	10							14,384
12	M	29 "	1952	Bristol Rovers	A	1-2	1-3	1	2	3		5	6	7	8			9	11			4	10^1							22,958
13	S	4 Oct	1952	Millwall	H	1-2	2-2	1		3		5	6^1	7	8		10	9	11^1	2		4								27,377
14	S	11 "	1952	Reading	A	0-0	1-0	1	2	3		4	6	7^1	8		10	9	11		5									19,891
15	S	18 "	1952	Bournemouth	H	0-1	1-1	1	2	3			6	7	8	9^1	10		11		5	4								26,071
16	S	25 "	1952	Southend United	A	0-1	2-1	1	2	3		5	6	7^1	8	9	10	11^1				4								12,618
17	S	1 Nov	1952	Watford	H	3-1	5-2	1	2	3		5	6^1	7^2	4	8	10^1	9^1						11						23,937
18	S	8 "	1952	Brighton & Hove Albion	A	2-1	3-2	1	2	3		5	6	7^1		8	10	9^2				4		11						20,091
19	S	15 "	1952	Newport County	H	2-0	2-0	1	2	3		5	6			8^1	10	9^1				4		11	7					23,899
20	S	29 "	1952	Bristol City	H	0-0	0-0	1	2	3		5	6	7	8	9	10		11			4								20,020
21	S	13 Dec	1952	Northampton Town	H	1-1	1-2	1	2	3		5	6	7	10	8^1		9				4				11				21,093
22	S	20 "	1952	Aldershot	A	2-1	2-1	1	2	3		5	6	7		9	10					4				11^1	8^1			4,871
23	F	26 "	1952	Colchester United	H	2-0	3-0	1	2	3		5	6	7			10^1		9^2			4				11	8			19,563
24	S	3 Jan	1953	Swindon Town	H	0-0	1-1	1	2	3		5	6	7			10		9^1			4				11	8			18,124
25	Th	15 "	1953	Coventry City	A	0-1	1-2	1	2	3		5	6	7^1	8		10	9				4				11				6,869
26	S	17 "	1953	Queens Park Rangers	A	1-1	1-3	1	2	3		5	6^1	7		8		10	9			4				11				13,084
27	S	24 "	1953	Shrewsbury Town	H	1-1	2-1	1	2	3		5	4^1		8		10		9^1					6	7	11				15,256
28	S	31 "	1953	Coventry City	H	1-1	1-1	1		3		5	6	7^1	4			10	9							11	8	2		16,391
29	S	7 Feb	1953	Walsall	A	0-1	2-3	1	2	3		5	6	7	4	8		9^1					10^1			11				6,850
30	S	14 "	1953	Gillingham	H	1-1	3-2	1	2	3		5	6	7	4				9^2				8	10		11^1				12,221
31	S	21 "	1953	Millwall	A	3-1	3-2	1	2	3			4	7^1	8^1				9		5		10^1	6		11				21,974
32	S	28 "	1953	Reading	H	2-0	3-0	1	2	3			4	7^3	8				9		5		10	6		11				18,576
33	S	7 Mar	1953	Bournemouth	A	0-0	0-0	1	2	3			4	7	8				9		5		10	6		11				11,154
34	S	14 "	1953	Southend United	H	1-1	3-1	1	2	3			4^1	7^1	8^1				9		5		10	6		11				16,890
35	S	21 "	1953	Watford	A	2-1	2-3	1	2	3			4^2	7	8			9			5		10	6		11				15,697
36	S	28 "	1953	Brighton & Hove Albion	H	0-2	3-2	1	2	3			4	7^1	8			9^1			5		10^1	6		11				14,226
37	F	3 Apr	1953	Leyton Orient	A	0-1	1-3	1	2	3			4	7	8			9^1			5		10	6		11				18,650
38	S	4 "	1953	Newport County	A	1-1	1-1	1		3		4	6^1	7	8	10		9			5			11				2		8,375
39	M	6 "	1953	Leyton Orient	H	2-0	5-1	1		3		4	6	7^1	8			9^2			5		10^2	11				2		23,350
40	S	11 "	1953	Crystal Palace	H	3-0	5-1	1		3		4	6	7^1	8^1			9^2			5		10^1	11				2		16,270
41	W	15 "	1953	Torquay United	A	1-2	1-4	1		3		4	6	7^1	8			9			5		10	11				2		6,741
42	S	18 "	1953	Bristol City	A	0-0	1-0	1		3		4	6	7^1	8			9			5		10	11				2		17,650
43	W	22 "	1953	Bristol Rovers	H	0-0	0-0	1		3		4	6	7	8			9			5		10	11				2		30,575
44	S	25 "	1953	Torquay United	H	1-0	3-0	1		3		4	6	7		8^1		9^1			5					11	10^1	2		16,345
45	Th	30 "	1953	Northampton Town	A	0-1	3-3	1		3		4	6^1	7		8^1		9^1			5					11	10	2		9,555
46	S	2 May	1953	Colchester United	A	2-0	4-0	1		3		4	6	7	10^1	8		9^2			5					11^1		2		10,029

F.A. CUP

NO.		DATE		OPPONENTS		V.	H-T	F-T	Nethercott Ken	Morgan Denis	Lewis Bill	Pickwick Don	Foulkes Reg	Ashman Ron	Gavin Johnny	Kinsey Noel	Johnston Tom	Rattray Peter	Ackerman Alf	Summers Johnny	Duffy John	Holmes Bert	Dutton Len	McCrohan Roy	Docherty Tom	ATTD.
1	S	22 Nov	1952	Tonbridge	(1st Round)	A	0-0	2-2	1	2	3		5	6	7		8	10	9^2	11			4			5,700
2	Th	27 "	1952	Tonbridge	(Replay)	H	0-0	1-0	1		3		5		7	8	9	10		11^1	2		4		6	9,603
3	S	6 Dec	1952	Brighton & Hove Albion	(2nd Round)	A	0-0	0-2	1	2	3		5	6	7	8	9	10		11			4			21,265

1952–53 APPEARANCES & GOALS

	FOOTBALL LGE APPR.	FOOTBALL LGE GLS	F.A. CUP APPR.	F.A. CUP GLS
Ashman Ron	46	9	2	–
Lewis Bill	46	–	3	–
Nethercott Ken	46	–	3	–
Gavin Johnny	44	20	3	–
Kinsey Noel	38	7	2	–
Foulkes Reg	36	–	3	–
Morgan Denis	30	–	2	–
Ackerman Alf	29	20	1	2
Johnston Tom	24	15	3	–
Rattray Peter	23	5	3	–
Summers Johnny	22	10	3	1
Adams Chris	20	3		
Holmes Bert	20	–		
Docherty Tom	18	–	1	–
Dutton Len	17	–	3	–
McCrohan Roy	16	7		
Proctor David	10	–		
Pickwick Don	7	–		
Coxon Billy	6	2		
Duffy John	6	–	1	–
Jones Denys	2	–		
Own Goals		1		

DIVISION 3 SOUTH

1952–53	P	W	D	L	F	A	PTS
Bristol Rovers	46	26	12	8	92	46	64
Millwall	46	24	14	8	82	44	62
Northampton Town	46	26	10	10	109	70	62
Norwich City	**46**	**25**	**10**	**11**	**99**	**55**	**60**
Bristol City	46	22	15	9	95	61	59
Coventry City	46	19	12	15	77	62	50
Brighton & Hove Albion	46	19	12	15	81	75	50
Southend United	46	18	13	15	69	74	49
Bournemouth	46	19	9	18	74	69	47
Watford	46	15	17	14	62	63	47
Reading	46	19	8	19	69	64	46
Torquay United	46	18	9	19	87	88	45
Crystal Palace	46	15	13	18	66	82	43
Leyton Orient	46	16	10	20	68	73	42
Newport Country	46	16	10	20	70	82	42
Ipswich Town	46	13	15	18	60	69	41
Exeter City	46	13	14	19	61	71	40
Swindon Town	46	14	12	20	64	79	40
Aldershot	46	12	15	19	61	77	39
Gillingham	46	12	15	19	55	74	39
Queens Park Rangers	46	12	15	19	61	82	39
Colchester United	46	12	14	20	59	76	38
Shrewsbury	46	12	12	22	68	91	36
Walsall	46	7	10	29	56	118	24

1953–54 DIVISION 3 SOUTH

NO.	DATE	OPPONENTS	V.	H-T	F-T	Nethercott Ken	Proctor David	Lewis Bill	Foulkes Reg	Holmes Bert	Ashman Ron	Gavin Johnny	Johnston Tom	Ackerman Alf	Brennan Bobby	Collins Tony	Morgan Denis	McCrohan Roy	Summers Johnny	Coxon Billy	Pickwick Don	Adams Chris	Rattray Peter	Duffy John	Carberry Bert	Hansell Ron	Gordon Peter	Cleary Bill	Oxford Ken	Wilson John	Woan Alan	ATTD.
1	W 19 Aug 1953	Southend United	H	1-0	1-0	1	2	3	4	5	6	7	8	9	10^1	11																27,523
2	S 22 " 1953	Aldershot	A	0-0	0-0	1	2		4	5	6	7	8	9	10	11	3															8,776
3	W 26 " 1953	Queens Park Rangers	H	2-1	2-2	1		3	4	5	6	7^2			10	11	2	8	9													23,432
4	S 29 " 1953	Swindon Town	H	1-1	2-2	1		3	4^1	5	6	7			10	11^1	2		9	8												15,474
5	M 31 " 1953	Queens Park Rangers	A	2-0	2-0	1		3		5	6	7^1	9^1		8	11	2		10		4											11,742
6	S 5 Sept 1953	Walsall	A	1-0	4-1	1		3		5	6	7	9^1		8	11^1	2		10^2		4											11,048
7	W 9 " 1953	Colchester United	H	2-1	2-1	1		3		5	6	7	9		8	11	2		10^2		4											22,228
8	S 12 " 1953	Shrewsbury Town	H	0-0	1-0	1		3		5	6	7	9^1		8	11	2		10		4											21,757
9	Th 17 " 1953	Colchester United	A	0-0	1-0	1		3		5	6	7		9^1	8	11	2		10		4											10,218
10	S 19 " 1953	Exeter City	A	1-0	2-0	1		3		5	6			9^2	8	11	2		10		4	7										10,412
11	W 23 " 1953	Bristol City	H	0-1	1-1	1		3		5	6			9	8^1	11	2		10		4	7										20,776
12	S 26 " 1953	Newport County	H	0-0	2-0	1		3		5	6	7		9^1	8^1	11	2		10		4											23,840
13	W 30 " 1953	Bristol City	A	1-1	1-3	1		3		5	6	7		9^1	8	11	2		10		4											18,706
14	S 3 Oct 1953	Gillingham	A	0-1	1-3	1		3		5	6^1	7		9	10	11	2				4		8									11,092
15	S 10 " 1953	Torquay United	H	0-0	0-1	1		3		5	6	7		8	10	11	2		9		4											20,355
16	S 17 " 1953	Watford	A	1-1	3-1	1		3		5	6	7^1			10		2	8	9^2		4	11										15,116
17	S 24 " 1953	Brighton & Hove Albion	H	1-0	1-0	1		3		5	6	7^1			10		2	8	9		4	11										23,697
18	S 31 " 1953	Southend United	A	2-4	2-5	1		3		5	6	7	9		10^1		2	8			4^1	11										8,852
19	S 7 Nov 1953	Reading	H	2-1	2-3	1		3		5	6	7^1			10		2	8	9		4	11										17,620
20	S 14 " 1953	Leyton Orient	A	1-1	1-3	1			5		4	7			10		2		9			11		3	6	8^1						15,694
21	S 28 " 1953	Ipswich Town	A	1-1	1-1	1		3	5		6	7			10^1		2		9		4	11				8						26,183
22	S 5 Dec 1953	Bournemouth	H	1-2	1-3	1		3	5		6	7	9		8^1		2			10	4	11										16,246
23	S 19 " 1953	Aldershot	H	1-1	3-3	1			5		6	11^1	9		8^1	10	2							3			7^1	4				11,798
24	F 25 " 1953	Crystal Palace	A	0-1	0-1				5		6	11	9		8	10	3										7	4	1	2		11,742
25	S 26 " 1953	Crystal Palace	H	2-1	2-1				5		6	7	8^1		10	11	3		9^1									4	1	2		21,293
26	S 2 Jan 1954	Swindon Town	A	0-0	0-0			3	5		6	11	9		10		2									8	7	4	1			7,990
27	S 16 " 1954	Walsall	H	2-0	3-0			3	5		6^1	11	9^1				2	4		10^1						8	7		1			14,133
28	S 23 " 1954	Shrewsbury Town	A	0-3	0-4			3	5		6	11	9		10		2	4								8	7		1			7,694
29	S 6 Feb 1954	Exeter City	H	1-1	1-2			3	5		6	11^1	9		10		2	4								8	7		1			24,722
30	S 13 " 1954	Newport County	A	1-3	1-4			3	5		6	11	9		10		2	4								8^1	7		1			11,968
31	W 24 " 1954	Gillingham	H	0-0	0-0		2	3	5		10	11	9					4			6					8	7		1			6,697
32	S 27 " 1954	Torquay United	A	1-1	4-2		2	3	5	9^1	6	10^2	8			11		4									7^1		1			7,780
33	S 6 Mar 1954	Watford	H	0-0	4-1		2	3	5		6^1		9^1		10^1	11	8^1	4									7		1			14,365
34	S 13 " 1954	Millwall	A	1-1	3-1		2	3	5		6	10^1	9			11	8^1	4									7^1		1			11,947
35	S 20 " 1954	Ipswich Town	H	1-2	1-2		2	3	5		6	10			9	11	8	4									7^1		1			27,061
36	W 24 " 1954	Southampton	A	0-0	0-0			3	5		6	10	9		8	11	2	4									7		1			11,263
37	S 27 " 1954	Reading	A	1-0	4-4			3	5		6^1	10^1	9^2		8	11	2	4									7		1			13,413
38	S 3 Apr 1954	Leyton Orient	H	1-1	3-1	1		3	5		6	10	9^2		8^1	11	2	4									7					14,466
39	S 10 " 1954	Bournemouth	A	0-0	0-2	1		3	5		6	10	9		8	11	2	4									7					8,524
40	S 17 " 1954	Coventry City	H	0-0	2-1			3	5		6	10	9		8^1	11	2	4^1									7		1			16,006
41	M 19 " 1954	Northampton Town	H	3-1	4-1			3	5		6^1	7^1			8^1		2	4	9								11		1		10^1	22,961
42	Tu 20 " 1954	Northampton Town	A	0-2	0-2			3	5		6	7			8		2	4	9								11		1		10	8,906
43	S 24 " 1954	Brighton & Hove Albion	A	0-0	0-0			3	5			7	9		8		2	4							6		11		1		10	23,790
44	M 26 " 1954	Coventry City	A	0-1	0-1			3	5			7	9		8		2	4							6		11		1		10	6,925
45	W 28 " 1954	Millwall	H	3-1	4-3			3	5			7	8^1		10^2		2	4	9^1						6		11		1			9,160
46	S 1 May 1954	Southampton	H	0-0	1-0			3	5		6	7	8					4	9^1					2			11		1		10	11,731

F.A. CUP

NO.	DATE	OPPONENTS	V.	H-T	F-T	Nethercott Ken	Proctor David	Lewis Bill	Foulkes Reg	Holmes Bert	Ashman Ron	Gavin Johnny	Johnston Tom	Ackerman Alf	Brennan Bobby	Collins Tony	Morgan Denis	McCrohan Roy	Summers Johnny	Coxon Billy	Pickwick Don	Adams Chris	Rattray Peter	Duffy John	Carberry Bert	Hansell Ron	Gordon Peter	Cleary Bill	Oxford Ken	Wilson John	Woan Alan	ATTD.
1	S 21 Nov 1953	Yeovil Town (1st Round)	A	0-0	2-0	1		3	5		6	7			10		2		9^2		4	11				8						11,760
2	S 12 Dec 1953	Barnsley (2nd Round)	H	0-1	2-1	1			5		6	8	9^2		10	11	2				4			3			7					20,633
3	S 9 Jan 1954	Hastings United (3rd Round)	A	2-1	3-3			3	5		6	11^1			10^1		2		9							8^1	7	4	1			12,727
4	W 13 " 1954	Hastings United (Replay)	H	1-0	3-0			3	5		6	11	9^1		10		2	4								8^2	7		1			17,059
5	S 30 " 1954	Arsenal (4th Round)	A	0-0	2-1			3	5		6	11	9^2		10		2	4								8	7		1			55,767
6	S 20 Feb 1954	Leicester City (5th Round)	H	1-0	1-2			3	5		6	11	9		10^1		2	4								8	7		1			39,973

1953–54 APPEARANCES & GOALS

	FOOTBALL LGE APPR.	FOOTBALL LGE GLS	F.A. CUP APPR.	F.A. CUP GLS
Ashman Ron	43	5	6	–
Gavin Johnny	43	13	6	1
Morgan Denis	42	2	6	–
Brennan Bobby	41	13	6	2
Lewis Bill	41	–	5	–
Foulkes Reg	31	1	6	–
Johnston Tom	29	11	4	5
Collins Tony	27	2	1	–
McCrohan Roy	25	1	3	–
Nethercott Ken	25	–	2	–
Gordon Peter	23	4	5	–
Summers Johnny	22	10	2	2
Oxford Ken	21	–	4	–
Holmes Bert	20	1		
Pickwick Don	18	1	2	–
Ackerman Alf	9	5		
Adams Chris	9	–	1	–
Hansell Ron	8	2	5	3
Proctor David	7	–		
Woan Alan	5	1		
Carberry Bert	4	–		
Cleary Bill	4	–	1	–
Coxon Billy	3	1		
Duffy John	3	–	1	–
Wilson John	2	–		
Rattray Peter	1	–		

DIVISION 3 SOUTH

1953–54	P	W	D	L	F	A	PTS
Ipswich Town	46	27	10	9	82	51	64
Brighton & Hove Albion	46	26	9	11	86	61	61
Bristol City	46	25	6	15	88	66	56
Watford	46	21	10	15	85	69	52
Northampton Town	46	20	11	15	82	55	51
Southampton	46	22	7	17	76	63	51
Norwich City	**46**	**20**	**11**	**15**	**73**	**66**	**51**
Reading	46	20	9	17	86	73	49
Exeter City	46	20	8	18	68	58	48
Gillingham	46	19	10	17	61	66	48
Leyton Orient	46	18	11	17	79	73	47
Millwall	46	19	9	18	74	77	47
Torquay United	46	17	12	17	81	88	46
Coventry City	46	18	9	19	61	56	45
Newport Country	46	19	6	21	61	81	44
Southend United	46	18	7	21	69	71	43
Aldershot	46	17	9	20	74	86	43
Queens Park Rangers	46	16	10	20	60	68	42
Bournemouth	46	16	8	22	67	70	40
Swindon Town	46	15	10	21	67	70	40
Shrewsbury Town	46	14	12	20	65	76	40
Crystal Palace	46	14	12	20	60	86	40
Colchester United	46	10	10	26	50	78	30
Walsall	46	9	8	29	40	87	26

1954–55 DIVISION 3 SOUTH

NO.		DATE	OPPONENTS	V.	H-T	F-T	Nethercott Ken	Morgan Denis	Hepple Gordon	McCrohan Roy	Foulkes Reg	Pickwick Don	Gordon Peter	Hansell Ron	Johnston Tom	Brennan Bobby	Reagan Martin	Kearns Fred	Gavin Johnny	McMillan Tom	Lewis Bill	Woan Alan	Ashman Ron	Kell Len	Baxter Larry	Holmes Bert	Chung Sammy	Norman Maurice	Oxford Ken	Wilson John	Carberry Bert	Cleary Bill	Collins Tony	ATTD.
1	S	21 Aug 1954	Aldershot	H	1-0	4-3	1	2	3	4^{1}	5	6	7	8^{2}	9	10	11^{1}																	23,596
2	Th	26 " 1954	Newport County	A	0-1	1-1	1	2	3	4	5	6	7	8		10	11	9^{1}																13,318
3	S	28 " 1954	Swindon Town	A	0-0	0-1	1	2	3	4	5	6	7	8		10	11	9																13,348
4	W	1 Sept 1954	Newport County	H	1-0	2-0	1	2	3	4	5	6		8		10		9^{1}	7^{1}	11														16,382
5	S	4 " 1954	Crystal Palace	H	1-0	2-0	1	2		4	5	6		8^{1}	9	10^{1}			7	11	3													14,542
6	W	8 " 1954	Exeter City	A	1-0	1-0	1	2		4	5	6		8	9	10			7^{1}	11	3													9,767
7	S	11 " 1954	Northampton Town	A	0-1	1-1	1	2		4	5	6		8	9	10			7	11	3^{1}													9,560
8	W	15 " 1954	Exeter City	H	1-0	3-0	1	2		4	5	6		8	9^{2}	10^{1}			7	11	3													15,989
9	S	18 " 1954	Watford	H	1-1	3-1	1	2		4	5	6			9	10^{1}			7^{2}	11	3	8												20,962
10	Th	23 " 1954	Colchester United	A	0-1	0-1	1	2		4	5	6			9	10			7	11	3	8												8,506
11	S	25 " 1954	Bournemouth	A	0-0	3-1	1	2		4	5	6				10			7^{1}	11^{2}	3		9	8										16,389
12	W	29 " 1954	Colchester United	H	0-2	0-2	1	2		4	5	6				10		9	7	11	3			8										15,724
13	S	2 Oct 1954	Queens Park Rangers	H	0-0	1-1	1	2		4	5	6	7	8^{1}		10			9	11	3													20,353
14	S	9 " 1954	Torquay United	H	2-0	5-1	1	2		9	5	4		8			11^{1}		7^{1}		3	10^{2}	6^{1}											18,075
15	S	16 " 1954	Brighton & Hove Albion	A	1-0	1-0	1	2		9	5	4^{1}	7	8			11				3	10	6											18,016
16	S	23 " 1954	Brentford	H	1-0	1-0	1	2		9	5	4	7	8^{1}		10	11				3		6											20,148
17	S	30 " 1954	Shrewsbury Town	A	0-2	1-2	1	2		9	5	4	7	8		10^{1}	11				3		6											8,280
18	S	6 Nov 1954	Southampton	H	1-0	2-0	1	2		8	5	4^{1}	7			10	11^{1}	9			3		6											17,372
19	S	13 " 1954	Millwall	A	0-0	0-0	1	2		8	5	4	7			10	11	9			3		6											19,371
20	S	27 " 1954	Gillingham	A	0-0	1-2	1	2		4	5					10^{1}	11	9		7	3		6		8									8,484
21	S	4 Dec 1954	Reading	H	0-1	0-1	1	2		4	5					9	11			7	3	10	6		8									14,790
22	S	18 " 1954	Aldershot	A	0-2	1-4	1	2		4	5^{1}		7			8	11	9			3		6		10									4,669
23	S	25 " 1954	Southend United	A	1-2	1-4	1	4			5		7			8	11	9^{1}			3		6		10	2								9,195
24	M	27 " 1954	Southend United	H	1-1	3-3	1	3		4	5		7			8^{1}	11	9^{2}				10	6			2								21,971
25	S	1 Jan 1955	Swindon Town	H	1-1	2-1	1	3		4	5		7	10		8^{1}	11	9^{1}					6			2								11,307
26	S	8 " 1955	Bristol City	A	0-0	1-0	1			4	5		7			8	11	9			3		6			2	10^{1}							16,332
27	S	22 " 1955	Northampton Town	H	1-0	3-2	1			4	5		7^{1}			8	11	9^{2}			3		6			2	10							11,159
28	S	29 " 1955	Bristol City	H	0-1	0-1	1			4	5		7			8	11	9			3		6			2	10							24,189
29	S	5 Feb 1955	Watford	A	1-1	2-2	1	2			4		7			10^{1}	11	9			3		6				8^{1}	5						10,456
30	S	12 " 1955	Bournemouth	H	0-1	0-1		2		7	4					10	11	9			3		6				8	5	1					11,432
31	S	19 " 1955	Queens Park Rangers	A	0-1	1-2		3		7						10^{1}	11	9					6				8	5	1	2	4			6,530
32	S	26 " 1955	Torquay United	A	0-1	0-2		3		7		4		10		9				11			6				8	5	1	2				5,197
33	S	5 Mar 1955	Brighton & Hove Albion	H	0-0	0-0		3		7		4		8				9		11			6				10	5	1	2				9,412
34	S	12 " 1955	Brentford	A	0-0	0-1		3		7		4		8		9				11			6				10	5	1	2				11,155
35	S	19 " 1955	Shrewsbury Town	H	0-0	2-0		3		7		4		8		9^{1}				11			6				10^{1}	5	1	2				10,700
36	S	26 " 1955	Southampton	A	1-1	1-3		3		7		4				8	11					10^{1}	6				9	5	1	2				10,780
37	S	2 Apr 1955	Millwall	H	1-0	2-1		3		9^{1}			7				11					10	6				8^{1}	5	1	2		4		11,606
38	S	9 " 1955	Leyton Orient	A	0-1	2-1		3		9			7				11					10^{1}	6				8^{1}	5	1	2		4		15,203
39	M	11 " 1955	Walsall	H	1-0	2-1		3		9^{1}			7				11					10^{1}	6				8	5	1	2		4		19,034
40	Tu	12 " 1955	Walsall	A	0-2	1-2				9			7^{1}				11	3					6		10		8	5	1	2		4		17,173
41	S	16 " 1955	Gillingham	H	0-1	1-2				9		6	7				11	3				10^{1}					8	5	1	2		4		11,006
42	M	18 " 1955	Coventry City	A	0-3	0-4						6	7	8		10		3									9	5	1	2		4	11	9.127
43	S	23 " 1955	Reading	A	0-1	1-1				9			7			10		3		11			6				8^{1}	5	1	2		4		7,382
44	W	27 " 1955	Leyton Orient	H	0-1	1-1				9			7			10		3		11			6^{1}				8	5	1	2		4		9,288
45	S	30 " 1955	Coventry City	H	0-1	1-1				9			7			8^{1}		3		11		10	6					5	1	2		4		10,251
46	W	4 May 1955	Crystal Palace	A	0-1	0-2			3	4			7	8		10							6				9	5	1	2			11	7,379

F.A. CUP

NO.		DATE	OPPONENTS		V.	H-T	F-T	Nethercott Ken	Morgan Denis	Hepple Gordon	McCrohan Roy	Foulkes Reg	Pickwick Don	Gordon Peter	Hansell Ron	Johnston Tom	Brennan Bobby	Reagan Martin	Kearns Fred	Gavin Johnny	McMillan Tom	Lewis Bill	Woan Alan	Ashman Ron	Kell Len	Baxter Larry	Holmes Bert	Chung Sammy	Norman Maurice	Oxford Ken	Wilson John	Carberry Bert	Cleary Bill	Collins Tony	ATTD.
1	S	20 Nov 1954	Headington United	(1st Round)	H	1-1	4-2	1	2		8	5	4^{1}	7			10	11	9^{3}			3		6											18,948
2	S	11 Dec 1954	Brighton & Hove Albion	(2nd Round)	H	0-0	0-0	1	2		9	5		7	8							3	10	6									4	11	17,583
3	W	15 " 1954	Brighton & Hove Albion	(Replay)	A	0-1	1-5	1	2			5		7	8			11	9			3	10^{1}	6									4		10,374

1954–55 APPEARANCES & GOALS

	FOOTBALL LGE APPR.	FOOTBALL LGE GLS	F.A. CUP APPR.	F.A. CUP GLS
McCrohan Roy	43	3	2	–
Brennan Bobby	38	11	1	–
Morgan Denis	36	–	3	–
Ashman Ron	32	2	3	–
Foulkes Reg	30	1	3	–
Nethercott Ken	29	–	3	–
Gordon Peter	27	2	3	–
Reagan Martin	27	3	2	–
Pickwick Don	26	2	1	1
Kearns Fred	24	8	2	3
Lewis Bill	24	1	3	–
Chung Sammy	20	6		
Hansell Ron	20	5	2	–
McMillan Tom	19	2		
Norman Maurice	18	–		
Oxford Ken	17	–		
Wilson John	16	–		
Woan Alan	12	6	2	1
Gavin Johnny	11	6		
Cleary Bill	9	–	2	–
Johnston Tom	7	2		
Holmes Bert	6	–		
Baxter Larry	5	–		
Hepple Gordon	5	–		
Collins Tony	2	–	1	–
Kell Len	2	–		
Carberry Bert	1	–		

DIVISION 3 SOUTH

1954–55	P	W	D	L	F	A	PTS
Bristol City	46	30	10	6	101	47	70
Leyton Orient	46	26	9	11	89	47	61
Southampton	46	24	11	11	75	51	59
Gillingham	46	20	15	11	77	66	55
Millwall	46	20	11	15	72	68	51
Brighton & Hove Albion	46	20	10	16	76	63	50
Watford	46	18	14	14	71	62	50
Torquay United	46	18	12	16	82	82	48
Coventry City	46	18	11	17	67	59	47
Southend United	46	17	12	17	83	80	46
Brentford	46	16	14	16	82	82	46
Norwich City	**46**	**18**	**10**	**18**	**60**	**60**	**46**
Northampton Town	46	19	8	19	73	81	46
Aldershot	46	16	13	17	75	71	45
Queens Park Rangers	46	15	14	17	69	75	44
Shrewsbury Town	46	16	10	20	70	78	42
Bournemouth & B.A.	46	12	18	16	57	65	42
Reading	46	13	15	18	65	73	41
Newport Country	46	11	16	19	60	73	38
Crystal Palace	46	11	16	19	52	80	38
Swindon Town	46	11	15	20	46	64	37
Exeter City	46	11	15	20	47	73	37
Walsall	46	10	14	22	75	86	34
Colchester United	46	9	13	24	53	91	31

1955–56 DIVISION 3 SOUTH

NO.		DATE	OPPONENTS	V.	H-T	F-T	Nethercott Ken	Norman Maurice	Lewis Bill	McCrohan Roy	Foulkes Reg	Ashman Ron	Gordon Peter	Chung Sammy	Hunt Ralph	Brennan Bobby	Reagan Martin	Cleary Bill	Woan Alan	Oxford Ken	Coxon Billy	Pickwick Don	Hansell Ron	Morgan Denis	Kearns Fred	Gavin Johnny	Wilson John	Bacon Ron	Thurlow Bryan	Smith Ken	Billington Charlie	Lockwood Roy	McNeil Matt	Cole Mike	Englefield Grahame	Gilbert Noel	ATTD.
1	S	20 Aug 1955	Southend United	A	0-1	1-3	1	2	3	4	5	6	7	8	9	10	11^{1}																				12,190
2	W	24 " 1955	Shrewsbury Town	H	0-1	3-1	1	2	3	7^{1}	5	6		8	9^{1}	10^{1}	11	4																			12,694
3	S	27 " 1955	Coventry City	H	0-0	1-0	1	2	3	7	5	6			9	10^{1}	11	4	8																		17,322
4	M	29 " 1955	Shrewsbury Town	A	0-1	0-6	1	2	3	7	5	6		8	9	10	11	4																			8,853
5	S	3 Sept 1955	Brentford	A	1-1	2-1		2	3	4	5	6^{1}	7	8	9^{1}	10				1	11																12,565
6	W	7 " 1955	Exeter City	H	0-1	2-1		2	3	4	5	6	7^{1}	8	9^{1}	10				1	11																14,001
7	S	10 " 1955	Watford	H	0-1	4-1		2	3	4	5	6	7	8^{1}	9^{2}	10				1	11^{1}																16,432
8	W	14 " 1955	Exeter City	A	1-1	1-1		2	3	4	5	6	7	8	9	10				1	11^{1}																8,443
9	S	17 " 1955	Reading	A	1-1	2-2		5	3	2		6	8^{1}	7	9	10^{1}				1	11	4															10,078
10	W	21 " 1955	Colchester United	H	1-1	1-1		3		2	5	6	8	7	9					1	11^{1}	4	10														13,632
11	S	24 " 1955	Millwall	H	2-0	4-1		3		2	5	6	8^{1}	7	9^{3}	10				1	11	4															18,602
12	W	28 " 1955	Bournemouth	A	1-0	1-0		3		2	5	6	8^{1}	7	9	10				1	11	4															6,233
13	S	1 Oct 1955	Gillingham	A	1-1	1-3		3		2	5	6	8^{1}		9	10	7			1	11	4															13,022
14	S	8 " 1955	Walsall	A	0-1	0-2		3		2	5	6	8	7	9	10				1	11	4															12,784
15	S	15 " 1955	Torquay United	H	0-0	0-0		3		2	5	6	8	7	9	10				1	11	4															14,404
16	S	22 " 1955	Newport County	A	1-0	2-2		5		2		6	7		10^{1}	8				1	11	4		3	9^{1}												5,977
17	S	29 " 1955	Swindon Town	H	2-0	4-1		5		2		6	7		10^{2}	8^{1}				1	11^{1}	4		3	9												12,885
18	S	5 Nov 1955	Queens Park Rangers	A	0-2	3-2				2	5	6		4	10^{1}	8				1	11^{1}			3	9^{1}	7											10,162
19	S	12 " 1955	Northampton Town	H	0-1	4-1				2	5	6	8	4	9^{2}	10				1	11^{1}			3		7^{1}											21,845
20	S	26 " 1955	Crystal Place	H	2-0	3-1	1			2	5	6	8	4		10					11^{2}			3	9^{1}	7											14,556
21	S	3 Dec 1955	Brighton & Hove Albion	A	0-2	0-6				2	5	6	8		9	10		4		1	11			3		7											22,364
22	S	17 " 1955	Southend United	H	4-2	7-2				4	5	6	8^{1}		9^{1}	10				1	11^{1}			3		7^{4}	2										11,219
23	S	24 " 1955	Coventry City	A	2-3	3-5				4	5	6	8^{1}		9^{1}	10				1	11			3			2	7^{1}									19,812
24	M	26 " 1955	Leyton Orient	A	2-1	2-2	1			4	5	6	8		9^{1}	10^{1}					11			3			2	7									15,977
25	Tu	27 " 1955	Leyton Orient	H	0-2	2-2	1			4	5	6	8^{1}		9	10					11			3			2	7^{1}									30,889
26	S	31 " 1955	Brentford	H	1-0	1-0				4	5	6	8		9^{1}	10				1	11			3		7			2								18,542
27	S	14 Jan 1956	Watford	A	0-1	1-1				2		6	8		9^{1}	10				1	11	4		3				7		5							6,522
28	S	21 " 1956	Reading	H	0-1	2-1				2	5	6	8		9^{2}	10				1	11	4		3				7									15,610
29	S	28 " 1956	Southampton	H	0-2	1-4				2		6	8		9	10				1	11	4		3		7^{1}					5						17,069
30	S	11 Feb 1956	Gillingham	H	2-1	5-1				4		6			9^{1}	10				1	11^{1}					8^{2}		7^{1}	2		5	3					7,586
31	S	25 " 1956	Torquay United	A	0-0	1-1				4		6			9^{1}	10	11			1						8		7	2		5	3					4,970
32	S	3 Mar 1956	Newport County	H	2-0	2-3				4		6	8		9^{1}	10^{1}	11			1								7	2		5	3					14,139
33	S	10 " 1956	Swindon Town	A	1-0	1-1				2	5	6			9	10		4		1	11					7^{1}		8				3					9,716
34	S	17 " 1956	Queens Park Rangers	H	1-0	1-0				2	5	6			9	10				1	11					7^{1}		8				3	4				13,355
35	S	24 " 1956	Northampton Town	A	0-0	1-1				2	5	6			9	8			10	1	11^{1}					7						3	4				9,387
36	F	30 " 1956	Ipswich Town	A	0-3	1-4				2	5	6			9^{1}	8			10	1	11					7						3	4				22,984
37	S	31 " 1956	Aldershot	H	0-0	0-1				2	5	6			9	8			10	1	11					7						3	4				10,791
38	M	2 Apr 1956	Ipswich Town	H	2-0	3-2				2	5	6	8^{2}		9^{1}	10				1						11	3	7					4				31,054
39	S	7 " 1956	Crystal Palace	A	0-0	0-2				2		6	8		9	10				1						11	3	7			5		4				9,446
40	Th	12 " 1956	Walsall	H	1-1	3-2				2	5	6	10		9^{2}					1	11^{1}					8	3	7					4				6,981
41	S	14 " 1956	Brighton & Hove Albion	H	1-2	3-3				2	5	6	8^{1}		9					1	11^{1}					10	3	7^{1}					4				12,304
42	W	18 " 1956	Aldershot	A	0-0	0-0				2	5	6	8		9					1	11					10	3	7					4				3,738
43	S	21 " 1956	Southampton	A	2-1	5-2				2	5	6	8^{1}		9^{2}					1	11					10^{2}	3	7					4				9,762
44	W	25 " 1956	Bournemouth	H	0-1	0-2				2	5	6	8		9					1	11					10	3	7					4				12,769
45	S	28 " 1956	Colchester United	A	0-2	2-3				2		6	8		9^{1}					1	11					10^{1}					5			3	4	7	8,004
46	F	4 May 1956	Millwall	A	0-0	0-1				2		6	8		9					1	11					10		7			5	3	4				10,808

F.A. CUP

NO.		DATE	OPPONENTS		V.	H-T	F-T	Nethercott Ken	Norman Maurice	Lewis Bill	McCrohan Roy	Foulkes Reg	Ashman Ron	Gordon Peter	Chung Sammy	Hunt Ralph	Brennan Bobby	Reagan Martin	Cleary Bill	Woan Alan	Oxford Ken	Coxon Billy	Pickwick Don	Hansell Ron	Morgan Denis	Kearns Fred	Gavin Johnny	Wilson John	ATTD.
1	S	19 Nov 1955	Dorchester Town	(1st Round)	H	1-0	4-0				2	5	6	8^{2}	4	9^{1}	10				1	11			3		7^{1}		16,207
2	S	10 Dec 1955	Brighton & Hove Albion	(2nd Round)	A	0-0	2-1				4	5	6	8		9^{1}	10				1	11			3		7^{1}	2	24,450
3	S	7 Jan 1956	Sunderland	(3rd Round)	A	2-1	2-4				2^{1}	5	6	8^{1}		9	10				1	11	4		3		7		46,380

1955–56 APPEARANCES & GOALS

	FOOTBALL LGE APPR.	FOOTBALL LGE GLS	F.A. CUP APPR.	F.A. CUP GLS
Ashman Ron	46	1	3	–
McCrohan Roy	46	1	3	1
Hunt Ralph	45	31	3	2
Oxford Ken	39	–	3	–
Brennan Bobby	38	6	3	–
Coxon Billy	38	13	3	–
Foulkes Reg	35	–	3	–
Gordon Peter	35	12	3	3
Gavin Johnny	23	13	3	2
Bacon Ron	18	4		
Norman Maurice	17	–		
Chung Sammy	16	1	1	–
Morgan Denis	14	–	3	–
McNeil Matt	12	–		
Pickwick Don	12	–	1	–
Wilson John	11	–	1	–
Lewis Bill	9	–		
Lockwood Roy	9	–		
Billington Charlie	7	–		
Nethercott Ken	7	–		
Reagan Martin	7	1		
Cleary Bill	5	–		
Kearns Fred	4	3		
Thurlow Bryan	4	–		
Woan Alan	4	–		
Cole Mike	1	–		
Englefield Grahame	1	–		
Gilbert Noel	1	–		
Hansell Ron	1	–		
Smith Ken	1	–		

DIVISION 3 SOUTH

1955–56	P	W	D	L	F	A	PTS
Leyton Orient	46	29	8	9	106	49	66
Brighton & Hove Albion	46	29	7	10	112	50	65
Ipswich Town	46	25	14	7	106	60	64
Southend United	46	21	11	14	88	80	53
Torquay United	46	20	12	14	86	63	52
Brentford	46	19	14	13	69	66	52
Norwich City	**46**	**19**	**13**	**14**	**86**	**82**	**51**
Coventry City	46	20	9	17	73	60	49
Bournemouth	46	19	10	17	63	51	48
Gillingham	46	19	10	17	69	71	48
Northampton Town	46	20	7	19	67	71	47
Colchester United	46	18	11	17	76	81	47
Shrewsbury Town	46	17	12	17	69	66	46
Southampton	46	18	8	20	91	81	44
Aldershot	46	12	16	18	70	90	40
Exeter City	46	15	10	21	58	77	40
Reading	46	15	9	22	70	79	39
Queens Park Rangers	46	14	11	21	64	86	39
Newport County	46	15	9	22	58	79	39
Walsall	46	15	8	23	68	84	38
Watford	46	13	11	22	52	85	37
Millwall	46	15	6	25	83	100	36
Crystal Palace	46	12	10	24	54	83	34
Swindon Town	46	8	14	24	34	78	30

1956–57 DIVISION 3 SOUTH

NO.		DATE	OPPONENTS	V.	H-T	F-T	Oxford Ken	McCrohan Roy	Lockwood Roy	McNeil Matt	Billington Charlie	Englefield Grahame	Bacon Ron	Gordon Peter	Bly Terry	Gavin Johnny	Stenner Arthur	Hunt Ralph	Kitchener Ray	Pointer Reg	Ashman Ron	Chung Sammy	Rule Alan	Coxon Billy	Buchanan Cameron	Nethercott Ken	Heffer Bob	Wilson John	Bannister Keith	Laskey Russell	Smith Ken	Cole Mike	Savino Ray	Bullimore Alan	Thurlow Bryan	Brennan Bobby	ATTD.
1	S	18 Aug 1956	Crystal Palace	H	1-0	1-0	1	2	3	4	5	6	7	8	9	10[1]	11																				16,057
2	W	22 " 1956	Exeter City	A	0-0	0-0	1	2	3	4	5	6	8	8		10	11	9																			9,591
3	S	25 " 1956	Southend United	A	0-0	0-0	1	2	3	4	5	6	7	8	9	11		10																			10,022
4	W	29 " 1956	Exeter City	H	0-0	1-0	1	2	3	4[1]	5	6	7	8		10	11	9																			12,054
5	S	1 Sept 1956	Northampton Town	H	1-1	2-1	1	2	3	4	5	6	7	8[1]		10[1]	11	9																			15,246
6	W	5 " 1956	Coventry City	H	2-0	3-0	1	2	3	4	5	6	7[1]	8[1]		10[1]	11	9																			17,335
7	S	8 " 1956	Queens Park Rangers	A	0-1	1-3	1	2	3	4	5	6		8		7	11	9[1]	10																		12,631
8	M	10 " 1956	Coventry City	A	2-0	2-3	1	2	3	4		6	7	8		10[2]		9	11	5																	18,394
9	S	15 " 1956	Plymouth Argyle	H	1-0	3-0	1	2	3	4		6	7	8		10[1]		9[2]	11	5																	15,880
10	S	22 " 1956	Reading	A	0-1	1-2	1	2	3	4		6	7[1]	8		10		9	11	5																	9,897
11	S	29 " 1956	Newport County	H	1-1	1-1	1	2	3	4		6	7	8		10[1]		9	11	5																	16,920
12	W	3 Oct 1956	Southampton	A	0-0	0-2	1	2	3	4			7	10				9	11	5	6	8															18,986
13	S	6 " 1956	Bournemouth	A	0-0	1-1	1	2	3	4			7	9[1]		10		8	11	5	6																12,032
14	S	13 " 1956	Torquay United	H	1-0	1-2	1	2	3	4			7	8		10		9[1]	11	5	6																14,819
15	S	20 " 1956	Millwall	A	1-2	1-5	1	2	3	5			7			8		9[1]	11		6		4	10													14,191
16	S	27 " 1956	Brighton & Hove Albion	H	1-0	1-1	1	2	3	5			7	8[1]		10		9			6		4	11													11,526
17	S	3 Nov 1956	Gillingham	A	1-0	1-1	1	2	3	5			11	10[1]		7		9			6		4		8												8,253
18	S	10 " 1956	Swindon Town	H	0-3	2-4	1	2	3		5			10		7		9[2]	11		6		4		8												10,966
19	S	24 " 1956	Aldershot	H	1-0	1-1		2	3					10		7		9[1]	11	5	6		4		8	1											7,437
20	W	28 " 1956	Southampton	H	0-3	0-3		2	3			4	7			8		9	10	5	6					1	11										8,095
21	S	1 Dec 1956	Watford	A	0-3	3-3	1	2	3	4[1]		6	7			8		9[2]		5	10			11													9,538
22	S	15 " 1956	Crystal Palace	A	1-1	1-4	1	2	3	5		6		7		8[1]		10			9		4	11													8,361
23	S	22 " 1956	Southend United	H	0-2	1-2		2		5				7	9	8		10[1]			6		4	11		1		3									8,948
24	Tu	25 " 1956	Colchester United	A	1-1	1-1		2		5				7	9[1]	8		10			6			11		1		3	4								6,376
25	W	26 " 1956	Colchester United	H	0-0	1-2		2		5				7	9	8[1]		10			6			11		1		3	4								8,481
26	S	29 " 1956	Northampton Town	A	0-0	1-1		2		5			7		9	8		10[1]			6			11		1		3	4								7,603
27	S	5 Jan 1957	Walsall	H	1-1	2-2		2	3	5			7		9[1]	8		10[1]			6			11		1			4								9,789
28	S	12 " 1957	Queens Park Rangers	H	0-1	1-2		2			5					7		9[1]	11	3	6			10		1			4	8							11,722
29	S	19 " 1957	Plymouth Argyle	A	1-2	2-3		2	3		5					7		9[1]	11		6			10[1]		1			4	8							12,054
30	S	26 " 1957	Walsall	A	1-3	3-6		2	3		5					7[1]		9	11		6			10		1			4	8[2]							16,169
31	S	2 Feb 1957	Reading	H	0-4	2-5				4	5	3				7		9[2]	11		6			10		1				8	2						12,344
32	S	9 " 1957	Newport County	A	1-2	1-3		4			5			10		7[1]		9			6	8		11		1					2	3					7,088
33	W	20 " 1957	Bournemouth	H	1-0	1-3		4		5		6				7		9			3	10		11[1]		1					2		8				14,079
34	S	23 " 1957	Torquay United	A	0-4	1-7				5				10	9	7[1]					3		4	11		1					2		8	6			6,375
35	S	2 Mar 1957	Millwall	H	1-0	2-0	1	4		5		6		10[1]		7		9			3	8		11[1]											2		11,921
36	S	9 " 1957	Shrewsbury Town	A	2-4	5-4	1	4		5		6		10[1]		7[1]		9			3	8[2]		11[1]											2		7,206
37	S	16 " 1957	Gillingham	H	0-2	1-3	1	4		5		6		10		7		9[1]			3	8		11											2		13,764
38	S	23 " 1957	Swindon Town	A	1-1	1-1	1	4		5		6		10		7		9			3			11											2[1]	8	7,713
39	S	30 " 1957	Brentford	H	0-0	1-1	1	4		5		6		8		7[1]		9			3			11											2	10	11,685
40	S	4 Apr 1957	Aldershot	A	0-0	0-0	1	4						6		7		9			3	8		11							5				2	10	4,530
41	S	13 " 1957	Watford	H	0-2	1-2	1	4						6	9	7					3			11							5		8		2	10[1]	10,207
42	F	19 " 1957	Ipswich Town	H	1-1	1-2	1	4						6		7		9[1]			3			11							5		8		2	10	28,783
43	S	20 " 1957	Brighton & Hove Albion	A	0-1	0-3	1	4						6		7		9			3	8		11							5				2	10	12,807
44	M	22 " 1957	Ipswich Town	A	1-2	1-3	1	4			5			6		7[1]		9	11		3	8													2	10	21,755
45	S	27 " 1957	Brentford	A	0-1	1-1	1	4						6		7		9[1]	11		3	8									5				2	10	8,764
46	W	1 May 1957	Shrewsbury Town	H	0-0	3-0	1	4			5			6		7[1]		9			3[1]	8					11[1]								2	10	7,620

F.A. CUP

NO.		DATE	OPPONENTS	V.	H-T	F-T	Oxford Ken	McCrohan Roy	Lockwood Roy	McNeil Matt	Billington Charlie	Englefield Grahame	Bacon Ron	Gordon Peter	Bly Terry	Gavin Johnny	Stenner Arthur	Hunt Ralph	Kitchener Ray	Pointer Reg	Ashman Ron	Chung Sammy	Rule Alan	Coxon Billy	Buchanan Cameron	Nethercott Ken	Heffer Bob	Wilson John	Bannister Keith	Laskey Russell	Smith Ken	Cole Mike	Savino Ray	Bullimore Alan	Thurlow Bryan	Brennan Bobby	ATTD.
1	S	17 Nov 1956	Bedford Town (1st Round)	H	2-2	2-4	1	4	3					8		7		9[1]	11	5	6			10[1]											2		14,472

1956–57 APPEARANCES & GOALS

	FOOTBALL LGE APPR.	FOOTBALL LGE GLS	F.A. CUP APPR.	F.A. CUP GLS
Gavin Johnny	45	16	1	–
McCrohan Roy	44	–	1	–
Hunt Ralph	43	20	1	1
Gordon Peter	36	7	1	–
Ashman Ron	35	1	1	–
Oxford Ken	32	–	1	–
McNeil Matt	32	2		
Coxon Billy	25	4	1	1
Lockwood Roy	25	–	1	–
Englefield Grahame	21	–		
Bacon Ron	20	2		
Kitchener Ray	18	–	1	–
Billington Charlie	15	–		
Nethercott Ken	14	–		
Thurlow Bryan	12	1	1	–
Chung Sammy	11	2		
Pointer Reg	11	–	1	–
Bly Terry	9	2		
Brennan Bobby	9	1		
Smith Ken	9	–		
Rule Alan	8	–		
Bannister Keith	7	–		
Stenner Arthur	6	–		
Laskey Russell	4	2		
Savino Ray	4	–		
Wilson John	4	–		
Buchanan Cameron	3	–		
Heffer Bob	2	1		
Bullimore Alan	1	–		
Cole Mike	1	–		

DIVISION 3 SOUTH

1956–57	P	W	D	L	F	A	PTS
Ipswich Town	46	25	9	12	101	54	59
Torquay United	46	24	11	11	89	64	59
Colchester United	46	22	14	10	84	56	58
Southampton	46	22	10	14	76	52	54
Bournemouth	46	19	14	13	88	62	52
Brighton & Hove Albion	46	19	14	13	86	65	52
Southend United	46	18	12	16	73	65	48
Brentford	46	16	16	14	78	76	48
Shrewsbury Town	46	15	18	13	72	79	48
Queens Park Rangers	46	18	11	17	61	60	47
Watford	46	18	10	18	72	75	46
Newport County	46	16	13	17	65	62	45
Reading	46	18	9	19	80	81	45
Northampton Town	46	18	9	19	66	73	45
Walsall	46	16	12	18	80	74	44
Coventry City	46	16	12	18	74	84	44
Millwall	46	16	12	18	64	84	44
Plymouth Argyle	46	16	11	19	68	73	43
Aldershot	46	15	12	19	79	92	42
Crystal Palace	46	11	18	17	62	75	40
Exeter City	46	12	13	21	61	79	37
Gillingham	46	12	13	21	54	85	37
Swindon Town	46	15	6	25	66	96	36
Norwich City	**46**	**8**	**15**	**23**	**61**	**94**	**31**

1957–58 DIVISION 3 SOUTH

NO.		DATE	OPPONENTS	V.	H-T	F-T	Oxford Ken	McCrohan Roy	Ashman Ron	Wilson Robert	Butler Barry	Stewart Eddie	Gavin Johnny	Gordon Peter	Hunt Ralph	Brennan Bobby	Milne Maurice	Wilson John	Lockwood Roy	Coxon Billy	Crowe Matt	Bacon Ron	Nethercott Ken	Moran James	Allcock Terry	Lythgoe Derrick	Cole Mike	Spelman Ron	Greatrex John	ATTD.
1	S	24 Aug 1957	Crystal Palace	H	0-0	3-2	1	2	3	4	5	6	7[2]	8[1]	9	10	11													21,583
2	W	28 " 1957	Southend United	A	1-4	2-5	1	4	5			6	7[1]	8[1]	9	10	11	2	3											13,743
3	S	31 " 1957	Torquay United	A	1-0	1-1	1	2	3	4	5	6	7	8	9[1]	10				11										8,542
4	W	4 Sept 1957	Southend United	H	0-1	0-2	1	3	5	4		6	7	8	9	10		2		11										21,775
5	S	7 " 1957	Brentford	H	1-1	3-2	1	2	3	4	5	6	7[1]	8	9[1]	10[1]				11										19,150
6	M	9 " 1957	Shrewsbury Town	A	0-0	0-0	1	2	3	4	5	6	7	8	9	10				11										8,728
7	S	14 " 1957	Colchester United	A	2-0	2-1	1	2	3	4	5	6	7[1]	8	9	10[1]				11										11,077
8	W	18 " 1957	Shrewsbury Town	H	1-0	2-0	1	3	5	4		6	7	8	9[1]	10		2		11[1]										17,383
9	S	21 " 1957	Brighton & Hove Albion	A	0-0	1-0	1	2	3	4	5	6	7	8	9	10				11[1]										16,888
10	S	28 " 1957	Bournemouth	H	1-2	2-2	1	2	3[1]	4	5	6	7	8	9[1]	10	11													22,221
11	W	2 Oct 1957	Reading	A	1-0	2-1	1	2	3	4	5	6	11	7	9[1]	10					8[1]									12,882
12	S	5 " 1957	Walsall	A	0-2	1-2	1	2	3	4	5	6	7	8	9[1]	10				11										9,276
13	W	9 " 1957	Northampton Town	H	2-2	2-2	1	4	3	6	5		11[2]	7	9	10		2			8									22,850
14	S	12 " 1957	Queens Park Rangers	H	0-0	2-0	1	2	3	4	5		7	8[1]	9[1]	10				11	6									19,460
15	S	19 " 1957	Exeter City	A	1-1	2-2	1	2	3[1]	4	5	6		8	9					11[1]	10	7								7,412
16	W	23 " 1957	Reading	H	1-2	2-2	1		3	4	5		9[1]	8[1]		10		2		11	6	7								22,164
17	S	26 " 1957	Gillingham	H	0-0	2-0	1		3	4	5		9[2]	8		10		2		11	6	7								17,999
18	S	2 Nov 1957	Millwall	A	0-0	2-2	1		3	4	5		9	7	10[2]	8		2		11	6									16,476
19	S	9 " 1957	Swindon Town	H	0-0	1-1	1	2	3	4	5		9	7	10[1]	8				11	6									22,578
20	S	23 " 1957	Plymouth Argyle	H	1-0	1-0		6	3	4	5		9	7[1]	8			2		11			1	10						20,758
21	S	30 " 1957	Port Vale	A	0-1	2-2		2	3	4	5		9	7[1]	10[2]					11	6		1	8						13,816
22	S	14 Dec 1957	Southampton	A	2-4	3-7		2	3	4	5		11[1]	7	9	10					6		1	8[2]						11,342
23	S	21 " 1957	Crystal Palace	A	2-0	3-0		2	3	4	5		11[1]	7[2]	9	10					6		1	8						11,478
24	Th	26 " 1957	Northampton Town	A	0-0	1-0		2	3	4	5		11	7[1]	9	10					6		1	8						11,125
25	S	28 " 1957	Torquay United	H	2-0	3-1		6	3	4	5		11	7	9	10[1]		2					1	8[2]						24,706
26	S	11 Jan 1958	Brentford	A	0-5	1-7		2	3	4	5		9	7		10				11	6[1]		1	8						11,850
27	S	18 " 1958	Colchester United	H	1-1	1-1		2	3	4	5		7	8	9[1]	10				11	6		1							17,459
28	S	25 " 1958	Aldershot	A	1-2	1-2		2	3	4	5			7	9[1]	10				11	6	8	1							5,065
29	S	1 Feb 1958	Brighton & Hove Albion	H	0-0	0-0		2	3	4	5		7	8	9	10				11	6		1							20,698
30	S	8 " 1958	Bournemouth	A	1-1	1-3		2	3	4	5		7	8	9[1]	10				11	6		1							11,419
31	S	15 " 1958	Walsall	H	2-1	2-1		2	3	4	5		9[1]	7	10	8[1]				11	6		1							16,804
32	S	22 " 1958	Queens Park Rangers	A	1-1	1-1		2	3	4	5		9	7[1]	10	8				11	6		1							7,935
33	S	1 Mar 1958	Exeter City	H	3-0	3-2		2	3	4	5		9[2]	7	10	8				11[1]	6		1							16,748
34	W	5 " 1958	Coventry City	H	0-1	1-1		2	3	4	5		9	7	10[1]	8				11	6		1							18,461
35	S	8 " 1958	Gillingham	A	0-0	0-1		2	3	4	5		9	7	10	8				11	6		1							6,519
36	S	15 " 1958	Millwall	H	1-1	1-1		2	3	4	5		11	7	10	8					6[1]		1		9					21,163
37	S	22 " 1958	Plymouth Argyle	A	0-0	1-0		2	3	4	5			7		10	11				6		1		9	8[1]				17,818
38	S	29 " 1958	Southampton	H	0-1	0-2		2	3	4	5			7		10	11				6		1		9	8				21,784
39	F	4 Apr 1958	Watford	A	2-1	4-1		2	3	4	5		7[1]		11						6		1	8[1]	9	10[2]				10,931
40	S	5 " 1958	Swindon Town	A	1-0	2-1		2	3	4	5		7[1]		11						6		1	8	9[1]	10				10,145
41	M	7 " 1958	Watford	H	1-0	1-1		2	3	4	5		7		11						6		1	8	9	10[1]				29,782
42	S	12 " 1958	Port Vale	H	0-0	3-0		2	3[1]	4	5		7			11					6[1]		1	8[1]	9	10				17,843
43	W	16 " 1958	Newport County	A	3-1	5-2		3		4	5		7			11		2			6		1	8[3]	9[2]	10				19,486
44	S	19 " 1958	Newport County	A	0-0	0-1		3		4	5		7			11		2			6		1	8	9	10				6,081
45	M	21 " 1958	Coventry City	A	1-1	1-2		2		4	5		7			11			3		6		1	8[1]	9	10				7,606
46	S	26 " 1958	Aldershot	H	1-1	1-3		2		4	5			8		11					6				9	10[1]	3	7	1	13,857

F.A. CUP

NO.		DATE	OPPONENTS		V.	H-T	F-T	Oxford Ken	McCrohan Roy	Ashman Ron	Wilson Robert	Butler Barry	Stewart Eddie	Gavin Johnny	Gordon Peter	Hunt Ralph	Brennan Bobby	Milne Maurice	Wilson John	Lockwood Roy	Coxon Billy	Crowe Matt	Bacon Ron	Nethercott Ken	Moran James	Allcock Terry	Lythgoe Derrick	Cole Mike	Spelman Ron	Greatrex John	ATTD.
1	S	16 Nov 1957	Redhill	(1st Round)	H	3-0	6-1		2	3	4	5		9[2]	7	10[1]	8[2]				11[1]	6		1							16,675
2	S	7 Dec 1957	Brighton & Hove Albion	(2nd Round)	H	0-1	1-1		2	3	4	5		7[1]	8	9	10				11	6		1							19,713
3	W	11 " 1957	Brighton & Hove Albion	(Replay)	A	1-0	2-1		2	3	4	5		7[1]	8	9[1]	10				11	6		1							9,052
4	S	4 Jan 1958	Darlington	(3rd Round)	H	0-1	1-2		2	3	4	5		11[1]	7	9	10					6		1	8						24,348

1957–58 APPEARANCES & GOALS

	FOOTBALL LGE APPR.	FOOTBALL LGE GLS	F.A. CUP APPR.	F.A. CUP GLS
Wilson Robert	45	–	4	–
Butler Barry	43	–	4	–
McCrohan Roy	43	–	4	–
Ashman Ron	42	3	4	–
Gavin Johnny	41	17	4	5
Brennan Bobby	40	4	4	2
Gordon Peter	39	9	4	–
Hunt Ralph	36	16	4	2
Crowe Matt	33	4	4	–
Coxon Billy	26	4	3	1
Nethercott Ken	26	–	4	–
Oxford Ken	19	–		
Moran James	14	10	1	–
Stewart Eddie	13	–		
Allcock Terry	11	3		
Wilson John	11	–		
Lythgoe Derrick	10	5		
Milne Maurice	5	–		
Bacon Ron	4	–		
Lockwood Roy	2	–		
Cole Mike	1	–		
Greatrex John	1	–		
Spelman Ron	1	–		

DIVISION 3 SOUTH

1957–58	P	W	D	L	F	A	PTS
Brighton & Hove Albion	46	24	12	10	88	64	60
Brentford	46	24	10	12	82	56	58
Plymouth Argyle	46	25	8	13	67	48	58
Swindon Town	46	21	15	10	79	50	57
Reading	46	21	13	12	79	51	55
Southampton	46	22	10	14	112	72	54
Southend United	46	21	12	13	90	58	54
Norwich City	**46**	**19**	**15**	**12**	**75**	**70**	**53**
Bournemouth	46	21	9	16	81	74	51
Queens Park Rangers	46	18	14	14	64	65	50
Newport County	46	17	14	15	73	67	48
Colchester United	46	17	13	16	77	79	47
Northampton Town	46	19	6	21	87	79	44
Crystal Palace	46	15	13	18	70	72	43
Port Vale	46	16	10	20	67	58	42
Watford	46	13	16	17	59	77	42
Shrewsbury Town	46	15	10	21	49	71	40
Aldershot	46	12	16	18	59	89	40
Coventry City	46	13	13	20	61	81	39
Walsall	46	14	9	23	61	75	37
Torquay United	46	11	13	22	49	74	35
Gillingham	46	13	9	24	52	81	35
Millwall	46	11	9	26	63	91	31
Exeter City	46	11	9	26	57	99	31

1958–59 DIVISION 3

NO.		DATE		OPPONENTS	V.	H-T	F-T	Nethercott Ken	McCrohan Roy	Ashman Ron	Wilson Robert	Butler Barry	Crowe Matt	Hill Jimmy	Moran James	Allcock Terry	Lythgoe Derrick	Brennan Bobby	Hunt Morgan	Wilson John	Thurlow Bryan	Ripley Keith	Williamson Ian	Crossan Errol	Bly Terry	Creland Peter	Kennon Sandy	Mullett Joe	Own Goals	ATTD.
1	S	23 Aug	1958	Newport County	H	3-0	3-0	1	2	3	4	5	6	7	8	9^{1}	10	11^{2}												25,873
2	M	25 "	1958	Colchester United	A	1-1	1-2	1	2		4	5	6	7	8	9^{1}	10	11	3											9,379
3	S	30 "	1958	Southend United	A	0-0	0-1	1	3		4	5	6	7	8	9	10	11		2										15,661
4	W	3 Sept	1958	Colchester United	H	1-1	1-2	1	2		4	5	10	7	8	9^{1}					3	6	11							24,115
5	S	6 "	1958	Bury	H	2-2	3-2	1	2		4	5	6	7		8^{1}	10	11^{1}			3	9^{1}								20,477
6	M	8 "	1958	Stockport County	A	2-1	3-2	1	2		4	5	6	7^{1}		8	10^{1}	11			3	9^{1}								9,613
7	S	13 "	1958	Queens Park Rangers	A	0-1	1-2	1	2		4	5	6	7	10	8		11^{1}			3	9								10,498
8	W	17 "	1958	Stockport County	H	0-1	1-3	1	3			5	6		10	8^{1}		7	4	2		9	11							22,717
9	S	20 "	1958	Rochdale	H	2-0	2-1	1	2		4	5	8	7		9^{1}	10	11			3	6^{1}								16,422
10	W	24 "	1958	Bournemouth	A	0-1	0-2	1	2		4	5	8	7		9	10	11			3	6								8,407
11	S	27 "	1958	Doncaster Rovers	A	0-0	1-0	1	2	3	4	5	6			9		10				8^{1}	11	7						8,988
12	W	1 Oct	1958	Bournemouth	H	2-2	2-2	1	2	3	4	5	6			9^{1}		10				8	11	7^{1}						18,161
13	S	4 "	1958	Plymouth Argyle	H	1-1	1-1	1	2	3	4	5	6			9	10^{1}					8	11	7						22,221
14	M	6 "	1958	Tranmere Rovers	A	1-0	1-0	1	2	3	4	5	6			9	10					8^{1}	11	7						12,891
15	S	11 "	1958	Accrington Stanley	H	0-3	2-4	1	2	3	4	5	6			9	10^{1}	11				8^{1}		7						18,560
16	S	18 "	1958	Southampton	A	1-1	1-1	1	2	3		5	6		8	9^{1}	10		4				11	7						15,744
17	S	25 "	1958	Wrexham	H	1-1	2-2	1	2	3		5	6		8	9	10^{2}		4				11	7						17,176
18	S	1 Nov	1958	Bradford City	A	1-1	2-2	1	2	3		5	6		8^{1}	9^{1}	10	11	4					7						8,916
19	S	8 "	1958	Hull City	H	0-1	0-1	1	2			5	6		8	9	10	11	4		3			7						15,929
20	S	22 "	1958	Notts County	H	1-1	3-3	1	2		6	5	8	10				11^{1}	4		3			7^{2}	9					13,637
21	S	13 Dec	1958	Chesterfield	A	0-0	1-1	1	4	3		5	6	10				11			2			7		9				7,815
22	S	20 "	1958	Newport County	A	2-1	2-2	1	4	3		5	6		10^{1}	8		11			2			7		9			$–^{1}$	4,538
23	F	26 "	1958	Reading	H	1-0	1-0	1	4^{1}	3		5	6	10		8		11			2			7		9				13,281
24	S	27 "	1958	Reading	A	0-2	1-3	1	4	3		5	6	10	8	9		11			2			7^{1}						15,568
25	S	3 Jan	1959	Southend United	H	4-0	4-0	1	4	3		5	6	10		8^{2}		11			2			7^{1}	9^{1}					19,073
26	S	31 "	1959	Queens Park Rangers	H	1-0	5-1	1	4^{1}	3		5	6	10		8		11			2			7^{1}	9^{3}					16,781
27	W	4 Feb	1959	Doncaster Rovers	H	3-0	3-0	1	4	3		5	6	10		8		11			2			7^{1}	9^{2}					18,056
28	S	7 "	1959	Rochdale	A	0-1	2-1	1	4	3		5	6	10	8					2			11	7^{1}	9^{1}					4,608
29	S	21 "	1959	Plymouth Argyle	A	1-0	1-0	1	4	3	6	5		10		8^{1}		11			2			7	9					24,636
30	S	7 Mar	1959	Southampton	H	1-0	3-1		4			5	6	10	8						2		11^{1}	7^{1}	9^{1}		1	3		23,910
31	S	21 "	1959	Bradford City	H	3-1	4-2		4	3		5	6	10^{2}		8		11			2			7	9^{2}		1			23,554
32	M	23 "	1959	Accrington Stanley	A	0-0	2-0		4	3		5	6	10		8		11			2			7^{1}	9^{1}		1			7,848
33	S	28 "	1959	Hull City	A	1-2	3-3		4	3		5	6	10^{2}		8		11			2			7	9^{1}		1			24,156
34	M	30 "	1959	Halifax Town	H	1-0	3-1		4^{1}	3		5	6^{1}	10		8^{1}		11			2			7	9		1			29,976
35	Tu	31 "	1959	Halifax Town	A	1-1	1-1		4	3		5	6	10		8		11			2			7^{1}	9		1			11,938
36	S	4 Apr	1959	Brentford	H	2-0	4-1		4	3		5	6	10^{2}		8		11			2			7^{1}	9^{1}		1			27,870
37	M	6 "	1959	Mansfield Town	A	0-0	1-1		4	3		5	6	10^{1}		8		11			2			7	9		1			7,729
38	W	8 "	1959	Swindon Town	H	0-0	1-1			3	4	5	6	10		8		11			2			7	9^{1}		1			29,146
39	S	11 "	1959	Notts County	A	1-0	3-1		4	3		5	6	10		8^{2}		11			2			7	9^{1}		1			13,289
40	M	13 "	1959	Wrexham	A	0-1	2-1		4	3		5^{1}	6	10^{1}		8		11			2			7	9		1			12,946
41	Tu	14 "	1959	Bury	A	0-0	2-3		4	3		5	6	10		8^{1}		11			2			7	9^{1}		1			10,360
42	S	18 "	1959	Mansfield Town	H	0-0	1-0		4	3		5	6		10	8		11			2			7	9^{1}		1			21,228
43	W	22 "	1959	Tranmere Rovers	H	0-0	0-0		4	3		5	6		10	8		11			2			7	9		1			26,594
44	S	25 "	1959	Swindon Town	A	1-2	3-4		4	3		5	6	10		8^{1}		11						7	9^{2}		1	2		14,775
45	W	29 "	1959	Chesterfield	H	2-0	2-1		4	3		5	6	10^{1}		8		11						7	9^{1}		1	2		20,505
46	Th	30 "	1959	Brentford	A	2-0	4-0		4	3		5	6	10^{1}		8^{1}		11						7	9^{2}		1	2		19,035

F.A. CUP

NO.		DATE		OPPONENTS		V.	H-T	F-T	Nethercott Ken	McCrohan Roy	Ashman Ron	Wilson Robert	Butler Barry	Crowe Matt	Hill Jimmy	Moran James	Allcock Terry	Lythgoe Derrick	Brennan Bobby	Hunt Morgan	Wilson John	Thurlow Bryan	Ripley Keith	Williamson Ian	Crossan Errol	Bly Terry	Creland Peter	Kennon Sandy	Mullett Joe	Own Goals	ATTD.
1	S	15 Nov	1958	Ilford	(1st Round)	H	0-1	3-1	1	2			5	6	10^{1}	8	9		11^{2}	4		3			7						14,084
2	S	6 Dec	1958	Swindon Town	(2nd Round)	A	1-1	1-1	1	4	3		5	6	10^{1}		8		11			2			7	9					14,758
3	Th	11 "	1958	Swindon Town	(Replay)	H	0-0	1-0	1	4	3		5	6	10		8		11			2			7^{1}		9				11,724
4	S	10 Jan	1959	Manchester United	(3rd Round)	H	1-0	3-0	1	4	3		5	6	10		8		11			2			7^{1}	9^{2}					38,000
5	S	24 "	1959	Cardiff City	(4th Round)	H	0-1	3-2	1	4	3		5	6	10		8		11			2			7^{1}	9^{2}					38,000
6	S	14 Feb	1959	Tottenham Hotspur	(5th Round)	A	0-0	1-1	1	4	3		5	6	10		8^{1}		11			2			7	9					67,633
7	W	18 "	1959	Tottenham Hotspur	(Replay)	H	0-0	1-0	1	4	3		5	6	10		8		11			2			7	9^{1}					38,000
8	S	28 "	1959	Sheffield United	(6th Round)	A	0-1	1-1	1	4	3		5	6	10		8		11			2			7^{1}	9					57,000
9	W	4 Mar	1959	Sheffield United	(Replay)	H	2-1	3-2		4	3		5	6	10		8		11^{1}			2			7	9^{2}		1			38,000
10	S	14 "	1959	Luton Town	(Semi-Final)	W	0-1	1-1		4	3		5	6	10		8		11^{1}			2			7	9		1			63,500
11	W	18 "	1959	Luton Town	(Replay)	S	0-0	0-1		4	3		5	6	10		8		11			2			7	9		1			49,500

W – AT WHITE HART LANE S – AT ST. ANDREWS, BIRMINGHAM

1958–59 APPEARANCES & GOALS

	FOOTBALL LGE APPR.	FOOTBALL LGE GLS	F.A. CUP APPR.	F.A. CUP GLS
Butler Barry	46	1	11	–
Crowe Matt	45	1	11	–
McCrohan Roy	45	3	11	–
Allcock Terry	43	19	11	1
Brennan Bobby	39	5	11	4
Crossan Errol	36	12	11	4
Ashman Ron	34	–	10	–
Hill Jimmy	33	11	11	2
Thurlow Bryan	30	–	11	–
Nethercott Ken	29	–	8	–
Bly Terry	23	22	9	7
Kennon Sandy	17	–	3	–
Wilson Robert	17	–		
Moran James	16	2	1	–
Lythgoe Derrick	14	5		
Ripley Keith	12	6		
Williamson Ian	10	1		
Hunt Morgan	7	–	1	–
Mullett Joe	4	–		
Cleland Peter	3	–	1	–
Wilson John	3	–		
Own Goals		1		

DIVISION 3

1958–59	P	W	D	L	F	A	PTS
Plymouth Argyle	46	23	16	7	89	59	62
Hull City	46	26	9	11	90	55	61
Brentford	46	21	15	10	76	49	57
Norwich City	**46**	**22**	**13**	**11**	**89**	**62**	**57**
Colchester United	46	21	10	15	71	67	52
Reading	46	21	8	17	78	63	50
Tranmere Rovers	46	21	8	17	82	67	50
Southend United	46	21	8	17	85	80	50
Halifax Town	46	21	8	17	80	77	50
Bury	46	17	14	15	69	58	48
Bradford City	46	18	11	17	84	76	47
Bournemouth	46	17	12	17	69	69	46
Queens Park Rangers	46	19	8	19	74	77	46
Southampton	46	17	11	18	88	80	45
Swindon Town	46	16	13	17	59	57	45
Chesterfield	46	17	10	19	67	64	44
Newport County	46	17	9	20	69	68	43
Wrexham	46	14	14	18	63	77	42
Accrington Stanley	46	15	12	19	71	87	42
Mansfield Town	46	14	13	19	73	98	41
Stockport County	46	13	10	23	65	78	36
Doncaster Rovers	46	14	5	27	50	90	33
Notts County	46	8	13	25	55	96	29
Rochdale	46	8	12	26	37	79	28

1959–60 DIVISION 3

NO.		DATE	OPPONENTS	V.	H-T	F-T	Kennon Sandy	Thurlow Bryan	Ashman Ron	McCrohan Roy	Butler Barry	Crowe Matt	Crossan Errol	Allcock Terry	Bly Terry	Hill Jimmy	Brennan Bobby	Punton Bill	Moran James	Mullett Joe	Ronson Brian	Richards John	Edwards Bob	Whitehouse Brian	Larkin Bunny	Savino Ray	ATTD.
1	S	22 Aug 1959	Southampton	A	1-1	2-2	1	2	3	4	5	6	7	8	9^{1}	10^{1}	11										22,585
2	W	26 " 1959	Tranmere Rovers	H	0-0	3-0	1	2	3	4	5	6	7^{2}	8^{1}	9	10	11										31,527
3	S	29 " 1959	Reading	H	1-1	4-2	1	2	3	4	5	6	7^{1}	8^{1}	9	10^{1}	11										29,454
4	M	31 " 1959	Tranmere Rovers	A	0-0	0-0	1	2	3	4	5	6	7	8	9	10		11									17,580
5	S	5 Sept 1959	Shrewsbury Town	A	1-1	3-1	1	2	3	4	5	6^{1}	7	8	9^{1}	10^{1}	11										13,804
6	W	9 " 1959	Barnsley	H	0-0	0-0	1	2	3	4	5	6	7	8	9	10	11										36,479
7	S	12 " 1959	Port Vale	H	3-1	5-1	1	2	3	4	5	6^{1}	7	8^{1}	9	10^{2}	11^{1}										27,041
8	W	16 " 1959	Barnsley	A	0-0	0-2	1	2	3	4	5	6	7	8	9	10	11										9,155
9	S	19 " 1959	Wrexham	A	2-1	2-1	1	2	3	4	5	6	7	8	9	10^{1}	11^{1}										13,497
10	W	23 " 1959	Bury	H	0-0	2-0	1	2	3	4	5	6	7	8	9	10^{1}	11^{1}										32,243
11	S	26 " 1959	Brentford	A	1-2	4-3	1	2	3	4	5	6	7^{1}	8^{2}	9	10^{1}	11										21,634
12	Tu	29 " 1959	Bury	A	0-0	0-1	1	2	3	4	5	6	7	8	9	10	11										15,190
13	S	3 Oct 1959	Colchester United	H	1-0	3-2	1	2	3	4	5	6	7	8	9^{1}	10^{2}	11										27,759
14	M	5 " 1959	Southend United	A	0-1	0-1	1	2	3	4	5	6	7	8	9	10	11										16,568
15	S	10 " 1959	Bournemouth	H	1-2	2-3	1	2	3	4	5	6	7^{1}	8^{1}	9	10	11										25,163
16	S	17 " 1959	Accrington Stanley	A	2-1	4-3	1	2	3	4	5	6	7	9^{2}		10^{1}		11	8^{1}								4,780
17	S	24 " 1959	Newport County	H	0-0	1-0	1	2	3	4	5		7^{1}	9		10		11	8	6							24,138
18	S	31 " 1959	Grimsby Town	A	1-1	1-1	1	2	3	4	5	6	7	9		10		11	8^{1}								15,298
19	S	7 Nov 1959	Swindon Town	H	2-1	3-2		2	3	4	5	6	7	9^{1}		10	11		8^{2}		1						22,494
20	S	21 " 1959	Coventry City	H	0-1	1-4	1	2	3	4	5	6		8	9	10	7	11^{1}									21,089
21	S	28 " 1959	Bradford City	A	1-0	1-1	1	2	3^{1}	4	5	6	7	8	9			11	10								10,944
22	S	12 Dec 1959	Chesterfield	A	0-2	1-2	1	2	3	4	5	6	7					11	8^{1}			9	10				5,370
23	S	19 " 1959	Southampton	H	0-0	1-2	1	2	3	4	5	6	7	8		10		11^{1}				9					13,740
24	S	26 " 1959	Mansfield Town	A	0-2	2-3	1	2	3	4	5	6	7	8	9^{1}	10^{1}		11									7,554
25	M	28 " 1959	Mansfield Town	H	4-1	5-1	1	2	3	4	5^{1}	6	7^{2}	8^{1}	9	10^{1}		11									22,161
26	S	2 Jan 1960	Reading	A	2-0	2-0	1	2	3	4	5	6	7	8	9^{2}	10		11									11,065
27	S	9 " 1960	Halifax Town	A	1-0	1-0	1	2	3	4	5	6	7^{1}	8	9	10		11									5,008
28	S	23 " 1960	Port Vale	A	1-2	1-2	1	2	3	4	5	6	7	8^{1}	9	10		11									11,040
29	S	30 " 1960	Queens Park Rangers	H	0-0	1-0	1	2	3	4	5	6	7	8^{1}		10		11				9					17,053
30	S	6 Feb 1960	Wrexham	H	0-0	3-1	1	2	3	4	5	6	7	8^{1}		10^{2}		11				9					20,307
31	S	13 " 1960	Brentford	H	0-0	2-1	1	2	3	4	5	6^{1}	7^{1}	8	9	10	11										22,387
32	S	20 " 1960	Colchester United	A	0-2	0-3	1	2	3	4	5	6	7	8	9	10	11										13,053
33	S	27 " 1960	Bournemouth	A	0-0	0-0	1	2	3	4	5	6	7	8	9	10		11									12,806
34	S	5 Mar 1960	Accrington Stanley	H	2-0	4-0	1	2	3	4	5	6	7	8		10^{1}		11^{1}				9^{2}					21,127
35	S	12 " 1960	Newport County	A	1-1	1-1	1	2	3^{1}	4	5	6	7	8		10		11						9			6,106
36	W	16 " 1960	York City	A	2-1	2-1	1	2	3	4	5	6	7	8				11						9	10^{2}		6,510
37	S	19 " 1960	Bradford City	H	0-0	0-0	1	2	3	4	5	6	7	8				11						9	10		29,012
38	S	26 " 1960	Swindon Town	A	1-0	1-0	1	2	3	4	5	6	7	8^{1}				11						9	10		9,786
39	W	30 " 1960	Shrewsbury Town	H	0-0	1-1	1	2	3	4	5	6		8				11						9^{1}	10	7	29,029
40	S	2 Apr 1960	York City	H	1-0	1-0	1	2	3	4	5	6^{1}		8		10		11						9		7	26,952
41	S	9 " 1960	Coventry City	A	1-0	1-2	1	2	3	4	5	6	7	8				11						9^{1}	10		28,122
42	S	16 " 1960	Grimsby Town	H	0-0	1-1	1	2	3	4^{1}	5	6	7			8		11						9	10		33,723
43	M	18 " 1960	Halifax Town	H	1-0	3-0	1	2	3	4	5	6	7	9^{2}		8	11^{1}								10		33,232
44	S	23 " 1960	Queens Park Rangers	A	0-0	0-0	1	2	3	4	5	6	7	9		8	11								10		15,319
45	W	27 " 1960	Southend United	H	3-2	4-3	1	2	3	4	5	6	7^{2}	9		10		11^{1}						8^{1}			34,905
46	S	30 " 1960	Chesterfield	H	2-0	3-0	1	2	3	4	5	6	7^{1}	9				11						8^{1}	10^{1}		27,238

F.A. CUP

NO.		DATE	OPPONENTS		V.	H-T	F-T	Kennon Sandy	Thurlow Bryan	Ashman Ron	McCrohan Roy	Butler Barry	Crowe Matt	Crossan Errol	Allcock Terry	Bly Terry	Hill Jimmy	Brennan Bobby	Punton Bill	Moran James	ATTD.
1	S	14 Nov 1959	Reading	(1st Round)	H	1-1	1-1	1	2	3	4	5	6	7	9		10		11	8^{1}	25,076
2	W	18 " 1959	Reading	(Replay)	A	0-1	1-2	1	2	3	4	5	6^{1}		8	9	7		11	10	22,161

1959–60 APPEARANCES & GOALS

	FOOTBALL LGE		F.A. CUP	
	APPR.	GLS	APPR.	GLS
Ashman Ron	46	2	2	–
Butler Barry	46	1	2	–
McCrohan Roy	46	1	2	–
Thurlow Bryan	46	–	2	–
Crowe Matt	45	4	2	1
Kennon Sandy	45	–	2	–
Allcock Terry	44	16	2	–
Crossan Errol	43	13	1	–
Hill Jimmy	38	16	2	–
Punton Bill	27	4	2	–
Bly Terry	25	7	1	–
Brennan Bobby	20	4		
Whitehouse Brian	10	4		
Larkin Bunny	9	3		
Moran James	6	5	2	1
Richards John	5	2		
Savino Ray	2	–		
Edwards Bob	1	–		
Mullett Joe	1	–		
Ronson Brian	1	–		

DIVISION 3

1959–60	P	W	D	L	F	A	PTS
Southampton	46	26	9	11	106	75	61
Norwich City	**46**	**24**	**11**	**11**	**82**	**54**	**59**
Shrewsbury Town	46	18	16	12	97	75	52
Coventry City	46	21	10	15	78	63	52
Grimsby Town	46	18	16	12	87	70	52
Bury	46	21	9	16	64	51	51
Brentford	46	21	9	16	78	61	51
Queens Park Ranges	46	18	13	15	73	54	49
Colchester United	46	18	11	17	83	74	47
Bournemouth	46	17	13	16	72	72	47
Reading	46	18	10	18	84	77	46
Southend United	46	19	8	19	76	74	46
Newport County	46	20	6	20	80	79	46
Port Vale	46	19	8	19	80	79	46
Halifax Town	46	18	10	18	70	72	46
Swindon Town	46	19	8	19	69	78	46
Barnsley	46	15	14	17	65	66	44
Chesterfield	46	18	7	21	71	84	43
Bradford City	46	15	12	19	66	74	42
Tranmere Rovers	46	14	13	19	72	75	41
York City	46	13	12	21	57	73	38
Mansfield Town	46	15	6	25	81	112	36
Wrexham	46	14	8	24	68	101	36
Accrington Stanley	46	11	5	30	57	123	27

1960–61 DIVISION 2

NO.	DATE	OPPONENTS	V.	H-T	F-T	Kennon Sandy	Thurlow Bryan	Ashman Ron	McCrohan Roy	Butler Barry	Crowe Matt	Crossan Errol	Hill Jimmy	Allcock Terry	Larkin Bunny	Punton Bill	Whitehouse Brian	Lythgoe Derrick	Spelman Ron	Waites George	Burton Ollie	Scott Dick	Savino Ray	Own Goals	ATTD.
1	S 20 Aug 1960	Sheffield United	H	0-1	1-1	1	2	3	4	5	6	7	8	9^1	10	11									31,972
2	W 24 " 1960	Charlton Athletic	H	0-0	4-0	1	2	3	4	5	6	7	8^2	9^1	10^1	11									32.619
3	S 27 " 1960	Stoke City	A	0-1	1-1	1	2	3	4	5	6	7	10	9	8^1	11									11,716
4	W 31 " 1960	Charlton Athletic	A	0-0	1-0	1	2	3	4	5	6	7^1	10	9	8^1	11									9,874
5	S 3 Sept 1960	Swansea Town	H	0-0	0-0	1	2	3	4	5	6	7	10	9	8	11									26,077
6	W 7 " 1960	Plymouth Argyle	H	0-0	1-0	1	2	3	4	5	6	7	10	8		11	9							$-^1$	32,232
7	S 10 " 1960	Luton Town	A	1-0	2-0	1	2	3	4^1	5	6	7	10		8	11^1	9								22,252
8	W 14 " 1960	Plymouth Argyle	A	0-3	0-3	1	2	3	4	5	6	7	10		8	11	9								23,147
9	S 17 " 1960	Lincoln City	H	2-1	5-1	1	2	3	4	5	6	7^1	10^2		8^1	11^1	9								24.956
10	S 24 " 1960	Portsmouth	A	0-1	0-3	1	2	3	4	5	6	7	10		8	11	9								17,946
11	S 1 Oct 1960	Huddersfield Town	H	0-0	2-0	1	2	3	4	5	6	7	10			11^1	9	8^1							25,304
12	S 8 " 1960	Brighton & Hove Albion	H	1-0	2-2	1	2	3	4	5	6	7	10^1			11	9^1	8							22,922
13	S 15 " 1960	Middlesbrough	A	0-1	0-2	1	2	3	4	5	6	7	10			11	9	8							14,737
14	S 22 " 1960	Leeds United	H	2-1	3-2	1	2	3	4	5	6	7	10			11	9^1	8^2							18,970
15	S 29 " 1960	Southampton	A	1-1	2-2	1	2	3	4	5	6	7			10^1	11	9	8							21,979
16	S 5 Nov 1960	Rotherham United	H	1-0	3-1	1	2	3	4	5	6	7^1			10^1	11	9^1	8							22,504
17	S 12 " 1960	Liverpool	A	1-1	1-2	1	2	3	4	5	6	7			10	11^1	9	8							32,473
18	S 19 " 1960	Bristol Rovers	H	0-1	2-1	1	2	3	4	5	6^1				10	11	9	8	7					$-^1$	22,582
19	S 26 " 1960	Derby County	A	0-0	0-0	1	2	3	4	5	6	7			10	11	9	8							16,874
20	S 3 Dec 1960	Leyton Orient	H	2-0	3-2	1	2	3	4	5	6	7			10	11	9^1	8^1						$-^1$	19,464
21	S 10 " 1960	Scunthorpe United	A	1-1	1-2	1	2	3	4	5	6	7			10	11	9	8^1							8,444
22	S 17 " 1960	Sheffield United	A	0-1	1-1	1	2	3	4	5	6	7	10	9^1		11		8							16,904
23	M 26 " 1960	Ipswich Town	H	0-2	0-3	1	2	3	4	5	6	7	10	9		11		8							30,884
24	Tu 27 " 1960	Ipswich Town	A	1-2	1-4	1	2	3	4	5	6		8^1	9	10	11	7								23,321
25	S 31 " 1960	Stoke City	H	0-0	1-0	1	2	3	4	5	6	7	10	8		11	9^1								20,681
26	S 14 Jan 1961	Swansea Town	A	0-3	1-4	1	2	3	4	5	6		10		9^1	11		8		7					12,164
27	S 21 " 1961	Luton Town	H	0-1	2-1	1	2	3	4	5	6		10	8^1	9	11				7^1					21,290
28	S 4 Feb 1961	Lincoln City	A	1-0	4-1	1	2	3	4	5	6^1			8^1	9^1	11	10			7^1					8,276
29	S 11 " 1961	Portsmouth	H	1-1	3-1	1	2	3	4	5	6^1		10	8^2	9	11				7					30,160
30	Tu 21 " 1961	Huddersfield Town	A	1-1	1-1	1	2	3	4	5	6		10	8^1	9	11				7					16,984
31	S 25 " 1961	Brighton & Hove Albion	A	2-2	2-2	1	2	3	4	5	6		10^1	8^1		11	9			7					13,410
32	S 4 Mar 1961	Middlesbrough	H	1-0	4-1	1	2	3	4	5	6		10^1	9^2		11^1				7	8				25,610
33	S 11 " 1961	Leeds United	A	0-1	0-1	1	2	3	4	5	6		10	9		11				7	8				11,294
34	S 18 " 1961	Scunthorpe United	H	0-1	0-1	1	2	3	4	5	6		10	8	9	11				7					20,598
35	S 25 " 1961	Rotherham United	A	1-0	2-0	1	2	3	4	5	6			9	10^1	11		8^1		7					7,352
36	F 31 " 1961	Sunderland	A	1-0	3-0	1	2	3	4	5	6			9^1	10^1	11		8		7^1					33,690
37	S 1 Apr 1961	Derby County	H	0-1	0-2	1	2	3	4	5	6			9	10	11		8		7					22,315
38	M 3 " 1961	Sunderland	H	2-0	3-0	1	2	3		5	6		10	9^1		11	8^2			7		4			22,574
39	S 8 " 1961	Bristol Rovers	A	0-2	1-3	1	2	3	4	5	6		10^1	9^1		11	8			7					18,234
40	S 15 " 1961	Liverpool	H	1-0	2-1	1	2	3	4	5	6		10^1	9		11	8^1			7					21,205
41	S 22 " 1961	Leyton Orient	A	0-1	0-1	1	2	3	4	5	6		10	9		11	8			7					12,106
42	S 29 " 1961	Southampton	H	3-0	5-0	1	2	3^1		5	6^1		10	9^2		11^1	8			7					18,756

F.A. CUP

NO.	DATE	OPPONENTS		V.	H-T	F-T	Kennon Sandy	Thurlow Bryan	Ashman Ron	McCrohan Roy	Butler Barry	Crowe Matt	Crossan Errol	Hill Jimmy	Allcock Terry	Larkin Bunny	Punton Bill	Whitehouse Brian	Lythgoe Derrick	Spelman Ron	Waites George	Burton Ollie	Scott Dick	Savino Ray	Own Goals	ATTD.
1	S 7 Jan 1961	York City	(3rd Round)	A	0-0	1-1	1	2	3	4	5	6		8	9	10^1	11	7								9,463
2	W 11 " 1961	York City	(Replay)	H	0-0	1-0	1	2	3	4	5	6^1		10		9	11	8					7			27,464
3	S 28 " 1961	Scunthorpe	(4th Round)	A	2-1	4-1	1	2	3	4^1	5	6		10^1	8	9^1	11^1				7					15,485
4	S 18 Feb 1961	Sunderland	(5th Round)	H	0-0	0-1	1	2	3	4	5	6		10	8	9	11				7					41,949

FOOTBALL LEAGUE CUP

NO.	DATE	OPPONENTS		V.	H-T	F-T	Kennon Sandy	Thurlow Bryan	Ashman Ron	McCrohan Roy	Butler Barry	Crowe Matt	Crossan Errol	Hill Jimmy	Allcock Terry	Larkin Bunny	Punton Bill	Whitehouse Brian	Lythgoe Derrick	Spelman Ron	Waites George	Burton Ollie	Scott Dick	Savino Ray	Own Goals	ATTD.
1	W 26 Oct 1960	Oldham Athletic	(2nd Round)	H	3-0	6-2	1	2	3	4	5	6^1	7			10^2	11	9^2	8^1							13,080
2	M 14 Nov 1960	Derby County	(3rd Round)	A	1-1	4-1	1	2	3	4	5	6^1				10	11	9^1	8^1	7^1						21,864
3	W 14 Dec 1960	Shrewsbury Town	(4th Round)	A	0-1	0-1	1	2	3	4	5	6	7			10	11	9	8							7,627

1960–61 APPEARANCES & GOALS

	FOOTBALL LGE APPR.	GLS	F.A. CUP APPR.	GLS	LEAGUE CUP APPR.	GLS
Ashman Ron	42	1	4	–	3	–
Butler Barry	42	–	4	–	3	–
Crowe Matt	42	5	4	1	3	2
Kennon Sandy	42	–	4	–	3	–
Punton Bill	42	6	4	1	3	–
Thurlow Bryan	42	–	4	–	3	–
McCrohan Roy	40	1	4	1	3	–
Hill Jimmy	31	9	4	1		
Allcock Terry	26	16	3	–		
Larkin Bunny	26	9	4	2	3	2
Whitehouse Brian	25	8	2	–	3	3
Crossan Errol	23	3			2	–
Lythgoe Derrick	17	6			3	2
Waites George	17	3	2	–		
Burton Ollie	3	–				
Scott Dick	1	–				
Spelman Ron	1	–			1	1
Savino Ray			1	–		
Own Goals		3				

DIVISION 2

1960–61	P	W	D	L	F	A	PTS
Ipswich Town	42	26	7	9	100	55	59
Sheffield United	42	26	6	10	81	51	58
Liverpool	42	21	10	11	87	58	52
Norwich City	**42**	**20**	**9**	**13**	**70**	**53**	**49**
Middlesbrough	42	18	12	12	83	74	48
Sunderland	42	17	13	12	75	60	47
Swansea Town	42	18	11	13	77	73	47
Southampton	42	18	8	16	84	81	44
Scunthorpe United	42	14	15	13	69	64	43
Charlton Athletic	42	16	11	15	97	91	43
Plymouth Argyle	42	17	8	17	81	82	42
Derby County	42	15	10	17	80	80	40
Luton Town	42	15	9	18	71	79	39
Leeds United	42	14	10	18	75	83	38
Rotherham United	42	12	13	17	65	64	37
Brighton & Hove Albion	42	14	9	19	61	75	37
Bristol Rovers	42	15	7	20	73	92	37
Stoke City	42	12	12	18	51	59	36
Leyton Orient	42	14	8	20	55	78	36
Huddersfield Town	42	13	9	20	62	71	35
Portsmouth	42	11	11	20	64	91	33
Lincoln City	42	8	8	26	48	95	24

1961–62 DIVISION 2

NO.	DATE	OPPONENTS	V.	H-T	F-T	Kennon Sandy	Thurlow Bryan	Ashman Roy	McCrohan Roy	Butler Barry	Crowe Matt	Waites George	Allcock Terry	Conway Jim	Hill Jimmy	Punton Bill	Whitehouse Brian	Parnell Denis	Lythgoe Derrick	Larkin Bunny	Mannion Gerry	Savino Ray	Scott Dick	Barnsley Geoff	Mullett Joe	Burton Ollie	Nixon Bill	Own Goals	ATTD.
1	W 19 Aug 1961	Bury	H	1-1	3-1	1	2	3	4	5	6	7	8^{3}	9	10	11													23,604
2	W 23 " 1961	Scunthorpe United	H	0-2	2-2	1	2	3	4	5	6	7^{1}	10	9		11	8											$-^{1}$	27,407
3	S 26 " 1961	Charlton Athletic	A	0-1	2-2	1	2	3	4^{1}	5	6	7	10	9^{1}			8	11											13,940
4	Tu 29 " 1961	Scunthorpe United	A	0-1	0-2	1	2	3	4	5	6	7		9				11	8	10									8,923
5	S 2 Sept 1961	Liverpool	H	1-0	1-2	1	2	3	4	5	6	11	8	9^{1}						10	7								28,049
6	W 6 " 1961	Leeds United	H	0-0	2-0	1	2	3	4	5		8^{1}		9^{1}	10	11				6	7								26,860
7	S 9 " 1961	Rotherham United	A	0-2	1-3	1	2	3	4	5		8		9	10	11^{1}				6	7								8,622
8	S 16 " 1961	Sunderland	H	0-0	3-1	1	2	3	4	5	6		8	9^{1}	10^{1}	11						7^{1}							21,910
9	W 20 " 1961	Leeds United	A	1-0	1-0	1	2	3	4	5			8	9	10	11^{1}				6		7							10,948
10	S 23 " 1961	Stoke City	A	0-0	1-3	1	2	3	4	5			8	9^{1}	10	11				6		7							8,684
11	S 30 " 1961	Bristol Rovers	H	0-1	2-2	1	2	3	4	5		8^{2}		9	10	11						7	6						18,881
12	S 7 Oct 1961	Huddersfield Town	A	1-1	1-1	1	2	3	4	5		10^{1}	8	9		11					7		6						14,910
13	S 14 " 1961	Swansea Town	H	0-1	2-1	1	2	3	4	5		10^{2}	8	9		11					7		6						20,697
14	S 21 " 1961	Southampton	A	0-2	2-2	1	2	3	4	5		10	8^{1}	9		11^{1}					7		6						15,567
15	S 28 " 1961	Luton Town	H	0-3	0-4	1	2	3	4	5		10	8	9		11					7		6						18,845
16	S 4 Nov 1961	Newcastle United	A	0-0	0-0	1	2	3		5	6	11	8	9	10						7		4						25,895
17	S 11 " 1961	Preston North End	H	0-0	2-0	1	2	3		5	6	11	8^{1}	9^{1}	10						7		4						15,494
18	S 18 " 1961	Walsall	A	0-1	0-5	1	2	3		5	6		8	9	10	11					7		4						10,951
19	S 25 " 1961	Derby County	H	1-2	3-2	1		3	2	5	6	7	8^{1}	9	10^{2}	11							4						16,334
20	S 2 Dec 1961	Leyton Orient	A	0-1	0-2			3	2	5	6	7	8	9	10	11						4	4	1					12,847
21	S 9 " 1961	Middlebrough	H	0-2	5-4		2	3		5	6		8^{1}	9	10^{1}				11^{2}		7^{1}		4	1					14,928
22	S 16 " 1961	Bury	A	2-1	3-2		2	3		5	6		8	9^{1}	10				11^{2}		7		4	1					4,908
23	S 23 " 1961	Charlton Athletic	H	0-1	2-2			3	2	5	6		8^{2}	9	10				11			7	4	1					15,864
24	Tu 26 " 1961	Plymouth Argyle	H	0-1	0-2			3	2	5	6		8	9	10	7			11				4	1					18,364
25	S 30 " 1961	Plymouth Argyle	A	0-0	1-3			3	2	5	6		8^{1}		10		9		11			7	4	1					15,924
26	S 13 Jan 1962	Liverpool	A	1-2	4-5			3	2	5	6	7	8^{3}	9^{1}	10				11				4	1					35,576
27	S 20 " 1962	Rotherham United	H	0-1	0-1				2	5	6		8	9			10		11			7	4	1	3				24,269
28	S 3 Feb 1962	Sunderland	A	0-1	0-2	1	2	3	4	5			8	9	10				11		7				6				26,643
29	S 10 " 1962	Stoke City	H	0-0	1-0	1	2	3	4	5			8^{1}		10				11		7				6	9			31,304
30	S 24 " 1962	Huddersfield Town	H	0-0	1-2	1	2	3	4	5			8	9	10	11					7^{1}				6				16,112
31	Tu 27 " 1962	Bristol Rovers	A	0-1	1-2	1	2	3^{1}		5				9	10	11					7				6	4	8		9,205
32	S 3 Mar 1962	Swansea Town	A	3-0	3-0	1	2	3		5			9		10		8^{2}		11			7^{1}			6	4			6,945
33	S 10 " 1962	Southampton	H	0-0	1-1	1	2	3		5			9		10		8		11			7^{1}			6	4			17,294
34	S 17 " 1962	Luton Town	A	1-0	2-1	1	2	3		5		8^{1}	9^{1}		10				11			7			6	4			9,736
35	S 24 " 1962	Newcastle United	H	0-0	0-0	1	2	3		5		8		9	10				11			7			6	4			18,022
36	F 30 " 1962	Preston North End	A	0-0	0-2	1	2	3		5	8				10				11			7	9		6	4			11,015
37	S 7 Apr 1962	Walsall	H	0-0	3-1	1	2	3		5					10^{1}	11			8^{2}			7	9		6	4			14,206
38	S 14 " 1962	Derby Country	A	0-0	1-1	1	2	3		5^{1}	10					11			8			7	9		6	4			8,989
39	F 20 " 1962	Brighton & Hove Albion	A	1-2	1-2	1	2	3		5	10					11			8			7	9		6^{1}	4			13,398
40	S 21 " 1962	Leyton Orient	H	0-0	0-0	1	2	3		5					10	11			8		7		9		6	4			20,454
41	M 23 " 1962	Brighton & Hove Albion	H	0-0	3-0	1	2	3		5					10	11^{1}			8		7^{2}		9		6	4			16,162
42	S 28 " 1962	Middlesbrough	A	0-1	1-2	1		3	2	5					10^{1}				8		7	11	9		6	4			12,704

F.A. CUP

NO.	DATE	OPPONENTS	V.	H-T	F-T	Kennon Sandy	Thurlow Bryan	Ashman Roy	McCrohan Roy	Butler Barry	Crowe Matt	Waites George	Allcock Terry	Conway Jim	Hill Jimmy	Punton Bill	Whitehouse Brian	Parnell Denis	Lythgoe Derrick	Larkin Bunny	Mannion Gerry	Savino Ray	Scott Dick	Barnsley Geoff	Mullett Joe	Burton Ollie	Nixon Bill	Own Goals	ATTD.
1	W 10 Jan 1962	Wrexham (3rd Round)	H	0-1	3-1	1		3	2	5	6		8^{1}	10			9^{1}		11^{1}			7	4						27,676
2	S 27 " 1962	Ipswich Town (4th Round)	H	0-0	1-1	1	2	3	4	5			8^{1}	9	10				11		7				6				39,890
3	Tu 30 " 1962	Ipswich Town (Replay)	A	1-0	2-1	1	2	3	4	5			8^{2}	9	10				11		7				6				29,796
4	S 17 Feb 1962	Sheffield United (5th Round)	A	0-2	1-3	1	2	3	4	5			8		10^{1}				11		7				6	9			49,304

FOOTBALL LEAGUE CUP

NO.	DATE	OPPONENTS	V.	H-T	F-T	Kennon Sandy	Thurlow Bryan	Ashman Roy	McCrohan Roy	Butler Barry	Crowe Matt	Waites George	Allcock Terry	Conway Jim	Hill Jimmy	Punton Bill	Whitehouse Brian	Parnell Denis	Lythgoe Derrick	Larkin Bunny	Mannion Gerry	Savino Ray	Scott Dick	Barnsley Geoff	Mullett Joe	Burton Ollie	Nixon Bill	Own Goals	ATTD.
1	W 13 Sep 1961	Chesterfield (1st Round)	A	2-1	3-2	1	2	3		5	6		8	9	10^{1}	11	4					7^{1}							4,822
2	W 4 Oct 1961	Lincoln City (2nd Round)	H	0-1	3-2	1	2	3	4			8	10	9		11	5				7		6^{1}						15,552
3	W 15 Nov 1961	Middlesbrough (3rd Round)	H	1-1	3-2	1	2	3		5	6	11	8	9^{1}	10						7^{1}		4					$-^{1}$	15,242
4	W 7 Feb 1962	Sunderland (5th Round)	A	1-0	4-1	1	2	3	4^{1}	5			8		10				11^{1}		7				6	9^{1}			17,813
5	W 11 Apr 1962	Blackpool (Semi-Final)	H	1-0	4-1	1	2	3		5					10	11^{1}			8			7	9^{1}		6	4			19,296
6	M 16 " 1962	Blackpool (Semi-Final)	A	0-1	0-2	1	2	3		5	10					11			8			7	9		6	4			9,142
7	Th 26 " 1962	Rochdale (Final 1st Leg)	A	2-0	3-1	1		3	2	5					10	11^{1}			8^{2}			7	9		6	4			11,123
8	Th 1 May 1962	Rochdale (Final 2nd Leg)	H	0-0	1-0	1		3	2	5					10^{1}	11			8			7	9		6	4			19,800

1961–62 APPEARANCES & GOALS

	FOOTBALL LGE APPR.	FOOTBALL LGE GLS	F.A. CUP APPR.	F.A. CUP GLS	LEAGUE CUP APPR.	LEAGUE CUP GLS
Butler Barry	42	1	4	–	7	–
Ashman Ron	41	1	4	–	8	–
Kennon Sandy	34	–	4	–	8	–
Thurlow Bryan	34	–	3	–	6	–
Hill Jimmy	31	6	3	1	6	4
Conway Jim	30	8	3	–	3	1
Allcock Terry	29	15	4	4	4	2
McCrohan Roy	26	1	4	–	4	1
Scott Dick	24	–	1	–	6	2
Punton Bill	23	4			6	2
Crowe Matt	21	–	1	–	3	–
Lythgoe Derrick	21	6	4	1	5	4
Mannion Gerry	19	4	3	–	5	2
Waites George	19	8			2	–
Mullett Joe	16	1	3	–	5	–
Savino Ray	16	3	1	–	3	1
Burton Ollie	13	–	1	–	5	1
Barnsley Geoff	8	–				
Larkin Bunny	6	–				
Whitehouse Brian	6	2	1	1	2	–
Parnell Denis	2	–				
Nixon Bill	1	–				
Own Goals		1				1

DIVISION 2

1961–62	P	W	D	L	F	A	PTS
Liverpool	42	27	8	7	99	43	62
Leyton Orient	42	22	10	10	69	40	54
Sunderland	42	22	9	11	85	50	53
Scunthorpe United	42	21	7	14	86	71	49
Plymouth Argyle	42	19	8	15	75	75	46
Southampton	42	18	9	15	77	62	45
Huddersfield Town	42	16	12	14	67	59	44
Stoke City	42	17	8	17	55	57	42
Rotherham United	42	16	9	17	70	76	41
Preston North End	42	15	10	17	55	57	40
Newcastle United	42	15	9	18	64	58	39
Middlebrough	42	16	7	19	76	72	39
Luton Town	42	17	5	20	69	71	39
Walsall	42	14	11	17	70	75	39
Charlton Athletic	42	15	9	18	69	75	39
Derby County	42	14	11	17	68	75	39
Norwich City	**42**	**14**	**11**	**17**	**61**	**70**	**39**
Bury	42	17	5	20	52	76	39
Leeds United	42	12	12	18	50	61	36
Swansea Town	42	12	12	18	61	83	36
Bristol Rovers	42	13	7	22	53	81	33
Brighton & Hove Albion	42	10	11	21	42	86	31

1962–63 DIVISION 2

NO.		DATE	OPPONENTS	V.	H-T	F-T	Kennon Sandy	Ashman Ron	Staton Barry	Burton Ollie	Butler Barry	Bell Jackie	Mannion Gerry	Allcock Terry	Hill Jimmy	Oliver Jim	Miller Alistair	Punton Bill	Mullett Joe	Metcalf Colin	Kelly Phil	Conway Jim	Bryceland Tommy	Worrell Colin	Thurlow Bryan	Scott Dick	Jones Alan	Sutton Mike	Own Goals	ATTD.
1	S	18 Aug 1962	Preston North End	A	0-1	2-2	1	2	3	4[1]	5	6	7[1]	8	9	10	11													13,363
2	W	22 " 1962	Cardiff City	H	0-0	0-0	1	2	3	4	5	6	7	8	9	10		11												25,360
3	S	25 " 1962	Plymouth Argyle	H	0-1	2-1	1	2	3	4	5	6	7	8[1]	9	10		11[1]												21,043
4	W	29 " 1962	Cardiff City	A	0-1	4-2	1	2	3	4	5	8[2]	7	9[2]		10		11	6											26,103
5	S	1 Sept 1962	Grimsby Town	A	2-0	2-0	1	2	3	4	5	8[1]	7	9[1]		10		11	6											12,873
6	W	5 " 1962	Huddersfield Town	H	2-3	2-3	1	2	3	4		8	7	9[2]		10		11	6	5										28,794
7	S	8 " 1962	Bury	H	0-1	1-1	1	2	3	4		8	7	9		10	11		6	5									–[1]	19,271
8	W	12 " 1962	Huddersfield Town	A	0-0	0-0	1	5	3	4		8	7	9		10	11		6		2									13,285
9	S	15 " 1962	Walsall	H	0-0	2-1	1		3	4[1]	5	8	7	9		10[1]	11		6		2									17,818
10	S	22 " 1962	Newcastle United	A	0-2	1-2	1		3	4	5	6	7	8		10	11				2	9[1]								36,345
11	S	29 " 1962	Derby County	H	0-0	2-0	1		3	4[1]	5	6		9[1]	10	7	11				2		8							22,972
12	F	5 Oct 1962	Rotherham United	A	2-0	3-0	1	5	3	4		6		10[1]		7[1]	11				2	9	8[1]							12,561
13	S	13 " 1962	Charlton Athletic	H	1-1	1-4	1	5	3	4		6		10		7	11				2	9	8						–[1]	24,023
14	S	20 " 1962	Stoke City	A	0-1	0-3	1		3	4	5	6	7	8		9		11			2		10							24,201
15	S	27 " 1962	Sunderland	H	1-2	4-2	1		3	5		4		9	10[3]	7[1]		11	6		2		8							23,439
16	S	3 Nov 1962	Leeds United	A	0-2	0-3	1			5		4		9	10	7	11		6		2		8	3						16,019
17	S	10 " 1962	Swansea Town	H	3-0	5-0	1	5		4[1]				9[1]	10[1]	7		11	6		2[1]		8[1]	3						16,108
18	S	17 " 1962	Chelsea	A	0-1	0-2	1	5		4				9	10	7		11	6		2		8	3						28,816
19	S	24 " 1962	Luton Town	H	0-2	3-3	1	5		4[1]				9[2]	10	7		11	6		2		8	3						16,376
20	S	1 Dec 1962	Southampton	A	0-1	1-3	1	5		4				9	10	7		11[1]	6		2		8		3					15,312
21	S	8 " 1962	Scunthorpe United	H	1-2	3-3	1	5		4				10[1]		7		11[1]	6		2		8		3	9[1]				12,708
22	S	15 " 1962	Preston North End	H	1-0	1-1		5		4				10[1]		7		11	6		2		8		3	9	1			11,566
23	S	22 " 1962	Plymouth Argyle	A	0-1	0-1		5		4			7	9	10			11	6		2		8		3		1			15,663
24	S	29 " 1962	Middlesbrough	H	1-1	3-4		5		4			7	9	10[1]			11	6		2		8[1]		3		1			13,039
25	S	19 Jan 1963	Bury	A	1-0	3-0		5	3	4			7	9[3]	10			11	6		2		8				1			10,879
26	S	23 Feb 1963	Rotherham United	H	3-1	4-2		5	3	4[1]			7	9[2]	10			11	6		2		8[1]				1			15,212
27	S	2 Mar 1963	Charlton Athletic	A	1-0	2-0	1	5	3	4			7	9	10[1]			11	6		2		8[1]							14,856
28	S	9 " 1963	Stoke City	H	3-0	6-0	1	5	3	4			7[1]	9[1]		10[3]	11		6		2	8[1]								25,707
29	W	20 " 1963	Sunderland	A	0-3	1-7	1	5	3				7	9	10[1]			11	6		2		8			4				42,393
30	S	23 " 1963	Leeds United	H	3-0	3-2	1	5		4				9[1]	10[1]	7[1]		11	6		2		8		3					26,145
31	S	6 Apr 1963	Chelsea	H	3-1	4-1	1	5		4			7	9[1]	10[2]		11[1]		6		2		8		3					20,205
32	Tu	9 " 1963	Swansea Town	A	0-1	0-2	1	5		4			7	9	10		11		6		2		8		3					8,460
33	S	13 " 1963	Luton Town	A	2-2	2-4	1	5		4			7	9	10[2]		11		6		2		8		3					9,536
34	M	15 " 1963	Portsmouth	A	1-0	2-0	1	5		4				9[2]	10	7	11		6		2		8		3					13,349
35	Tu	16 " 1963	Portsmouth	H	5-2	5-3	1	5		4[1]			7	9[2]	10		11		6		2		8[1]		3				–[1]	18,722
36	S	20 " 1963	Southampton	H	1-0	1-0	1	5	3	4		6	7	9	10		11[1]				2		8							18,254
37	F	26 " 1963	Scunthorpe United	A	1-2	1-3	1	5	3	4				9	10[1]	7	11		6		2		8							6,012
38	S	4 May 1963	Newcastle United	H	0-1	1-2	1		3[1]	4				9	10	7	11		6	5	2		8							15,980
39	M	6 " 1963	Derby County	A	0-1	0-3		3		4				9	10		7	11	6	5	2		8				1			9,701
40	S	11 " 1963	Grimsby Town	H	0-0	0-0		3		4			7	9	10		11		6	5	2		8				1			10,395
41	Tu	14 " 1963	Walsall	A	1-1	1-3		3		4				9[1]	10		11		6	5	2		8				1	7		13,414
42	Tu	21 " 1963	Middlesbrough	A	0-3	2-6		3		4[1]			7	9				11	6	5	2		8				1	10[1]		7,626

F.A. CUP

NO.		DATE	OPPONENTS		V.	H-T	F-T	Kennon Sandy	Ashman Ron	Staton Barry	Burton Ollie	Butler Barry	Bell Jackie	Mannion Gerry	Allcock Terry	Hill Jimmy	Oliver Jim	Miller Alistair	Punton Bill	Mullett Joe	Metcalf Colin	Kelly Phil	Conway Jim	Bryceland Tommy	Worrell Colin	Thurlow Bryan	Scott Dick	Jones Alan	Sutton Mike	Own Goals	ATTD.
1	M	4 Mar 1963	Blackpool	(3rd Round)	H	0-1	1-1	1	5	3	4			7	9	10			11	6		2		8[1]							26,22
2	W	6 " 1963	Blackpool	A.E.T. (Replay)	A	0-0	3-1	1	5	3	4			7[1]	9	10[1]			11[1]	6		2		8							15,55
3	W	13 " 1963	Newcastle United	(4th Round)	H	2-0	5-0	1	5	3	4			7	9[4]	10			11	6[1]		2		8							34,82
4	S	16 " 1963	Manchester City	(5th Round)	A	1-0	2-1	1	5	3	4			7	9[2]	10			11	6		2		8							31,21
5	S	30 " 1963	Leicester City	(6th Round)	H	0-0	0-2	1	5	3	4			7	9	10			11	6		2		8							43,98

FOOTBALL LEAGUE CUP

NO.		DATE	OPPONENTS		V.	H-T	F-T	Kennon Sandy	Ashman Ron	Staton Barry	Burton Ollie	Butler Barry	Bell Jackie	Mannion Gerry	Allcock Terry	Hill Jimmy	Oliver Jim	Miller Alistair	Punton Bill	Mullett Joe	Metcalf Colin	Kelly Phil	Conway Jim	Bryceland Tommy	Worrell Colin	Thurlow Bryan	Scott Dick	Jones Alan	Sutton Mike	Own Goals	ATTD.
1	W	26 Sept 1962	Bolton Wanderers	(2nd Round)	H	1-0	4-0	1		3	4	5	6		8[1]	10	7[2]	11				2	9[1]								19,29
2	Th	16 Oct 1962	Carlisle United	(3rd Round)	A	1-1	1-1	1		3	4	5	6		10		7[1]	11				2	9	8							8,10
3	W	24 " 1962	Carlisle United	(Replay)	H	4-0	5-0	1		3	4		4		9[3]	10[2]	7		11	6		2		8							14,24
4	W	14 Nov 1962	Fulham	(4th Round)	H	0-0	1-0	1	5		4		8		9[1]	10	7		11	6		2			3						17,54
5	M	3 Dec 1962	Aston Villa	(5th Round)	A	1-1	1-4	1	5		4				10		7		11	6		2		8[1]		3	9				14,84

1962–63 APPEARANCES & GOALS

	FOOTBALL LGE APPR.	FOOTBALL LGE GLS	F.A. CUP APPR.	F.A. CUP GLS	LEAGUE CUP APPR.	LEAGUE CUP GLS		
Allcock Terry	42	26	5	6	5	5		
Burton Ollie	41	8	5	–	5	–		
Ashman Ron	35	–	5	–	2	–		
Kelly Phil	35	1	5	–	5	–		
Kennon Sandy	33	–	5	–	5	–		
Mullett Joe	33	–	5	1	3	–		
Bryceland Tommy	31	6	5	1	3	1		
Hill Jimmy	28	13	5	1	3	2		
Oliver Jim	27	7			5	3		
Mannion Gerry	25	3	5	1				
Staton Barry	23	1	5	–	3	–		
Punton Bill	22	3	5	1	3	–		
Miller Alistair	21	2			2	–		
Bell Jackie	17	3			4	–		
Thurlow Bryan	11	–			1	–		
Butler Barry	9	–			2	–		
Jones Alan	9	–						
Metcalf Colin	7	–						
Conway Jim	4	2			2	1		
Worrell Colin	4	–			1	–		
Scott Dick	3	1		1	1	–		
Sutton Mike	2	1						
Own Goals		3						

DIVISION 2

1962–63	P	W	D	L	F	A	PTS
Stoke City	42	20	13	9	73	50	53
Chelsea	42	24	4	14	81	42	52
Sunderland	42	20	12	10	84	55	52
Middlesbrough	42	20	9	13	86	85	49
Leeds United	42	19	10	13	79	53	48
Huddersfield Town	42	17	14	11	63	50	48
Newcastle United	42	18	11	13	79	59	47
Bury	42	18	11	13	51	47	47
Scunthorpe United	42	16	12	14	57	59	44
Cardiff City	42	18	7	17	83	73	43
Norwich City	**42**	**17**	**8**	**17**	**80**	**79**	**42**
Plymouth Argyle	42	15	12	15	76	73	42
Southampton	42	17	8	17	72	67	42
Rotherham United	42	17	6	19	67	74	40
Swansea Town	42	15	9	18	51	72	39
Portsmouth	42	13	11	18	63	79	37
Preston North End	42	13	11	18	59	74	37
Derby County	42	12	12	18	61	72	36
Grimsby Town	42	11	13	18	55	66	35
Charlton Athletic	42	13	5	24	62	94	31
Walsall	42	11	9	22	53	89	31
Luton Town	42	11	7	24	61	84	29

1963–64 DIVISION 2

NO.		DATE	OPPONENTS	V.	H-T	F-T	Keelan Kevin	Kelly Phil	Thurlow Bryan	Sharpe Freddie	Butler Barry	Mullett Joe	Miller Alistair	Bryceland Tommy	Allcock Terry	Conway Jim	Punton Bill	Mannion Gerry	Barnes Ron	Ashman Ron	Hill Ken	Davies Ron	Bell Jackie	Metcalf Colin	Kennon Sandy	Oliver Jim	Sutton Mike	Price Ray	Bolland Gordon	Shaw Colin	Worrell Colin	Own Goals	ATTD.
1	S	24 Aug 1963	Cardiff City	A	1-2	1-3	1	2	3	4	5	6	7	8	9	10[1]	11																21,977
2	W	28 " 1963	Bury	H	0-1	0-1	1	2	3	4	5	6		8	9	10	11	7															18,089
3	S	31 " 1963	Leyton Orient	H	0-1	1-2	1	2	3	4	5	6		8	9	10[1]	11		7														17,356
4	Tu	3 Sept 1963	Bury	A	0-3	2-4	1	2	3	6				8[1]	9	10[1]	11		7	5	4												10,037
5	S	7 " 1963	Scunthorpe United	H	0-1	2-1	1	2	3	6				8[1]		10	11		7	5	4	9[1]											16,222
6	W	11 " 1963	Northampton Town	H	1-2	3-3	1	2[1]	3	4				8		10	11[1]	7		5		9[1]	6										19,669
7	S	14 " 1963	Portsmouth	A	1-1	1-1	1	2	3	4				8		10	11	7		5		9[1]	6										13,996
8	M	16 " 1963	Northampton Town	A	2-1	2-3	1		2	4		3		8		10	11	7[1]		5		9[1]	6										14,928
9	S	21 " 1963	Rotherham United	H	0-0	2-2	1	2	3	4	5			8[1]	10		11[1]	7				9	6										16,465
10	S	28 " 1963	Leeds United	A	0-2	2-4	1	2	3			4		8	10		11	7		5		9[2]	6										22,795
11	W	2 Oct 1963	Preston North End	H	2-1	2-1		2				3		8	10		11[1]	7		5		9	6	4[1]	1								16,887
12	S	5 " 1963	Sunderland	H	0-0	2-3		2				3		8			11	7[1]		5		9	6	4	1	10[1]							19,694
13	Tu	15 " 1963	Swansea Town	A	0-0	1-3		2				3		8			11	7		5		9	6	4	1	10[1]							7,127
14	S	19 " 1963	Southampton	H	0-1	1-1		2				3		8			11	7		5		9[1]	6	4	1	10							15,695
15	S	26 " 1963	Grimsby Town	A	1-1	1-3		2			5	3		8	10[1]		11		7		4	9	6		1								8,981
16	S	2 Nov 1963	Newcastle United	H	2-1	3-1		2			5	3		8[2]	10[1]		11	7			4	9	6		1								17,200
17	S	9 " 1963	Huddersfield Town	A	0-0	1-1		2			5	3		8	10		11	7			4	9[1]	6		1								7,923
18	S	16 " 1963	Derby County	H	0-0	3-0		2			5	3		8	10[1]		11	7			4	9[1]	6		1							–[1]	16,079
19	S	23 " 1963	Plymouth Argyle	A	2-1	2-1		2			5	3		8[1]	10		11	7			4	9[1]	6		1								11,235
20	S	30 " 1963	Charlton Athletic	H	1-1	1-3		2			5	3		8			11		7		4	9[1]	6		1		10						16,869
21	S	7 Dec 1963	Middlesbrough	A	1-0	1-0		2			5	3		8			11[1]		7		4	9	6		1		10						15,592
22	S	14 " 1963	Cardiff City	H	4-0	5-1		2			5	3		8[1]			11[1]		7		4	9[3]	6		1		10						14,130
23	S	21 " 1963	Leyton Orient	A	0-0	1-1		2			5	3		8			11		7		4	9	6		1	10[1]							6,821
24	Th	26 " 1963	Swindon Town	H	0-2	3-2		2			5	3		8[1]			11		7		4	9[1]	6		1	10[1]							20,879
25	S	28 " 1963	Swindon Town	A	1-1	2-2		2			5	3		8			11		7		4	9[2]	6		1	10							17,718
26	S	11 Jan 1964	Scunthorpe United	A	2-0	2-2		2			5	3		8			11		7		4	9[1]	6		1		10[1]						5,235
27	S	18 " 1964	Portsmouth	H	1-1	3-1		2			5	3		8			11		7		4	9[2]	6		1		10						15,654
28	S	1 Feb 1964	Rotherham United	A	0-4	0-4		2			5	3	11	8					7		4	9	6		1		10						7,289
29	S	8 " 1964	Leeds United	H	0-0	2-2		2			5	3		8			11		7		4	9[2]	6		1		10						20,450
30	W	19 " 1964	Sunderland	A	0-0	0-0		2			5	3		8			11		7		4	9	6		1		10						44,514
31	S	22 " 1964	Swansea Town	H	0-0	3-0		2			5	3		8[2]			11		7		4	9	6		1		10[1]						15,631
32	S	29 " 1964	Derby County	A	0-0	1-2		2			5			8			11		7		4	9[1]	6		1		10	3					8,800
33	S	7 Mar 1964	Grimsby Town	H	2-0	2-0		2	3		5			8[1]			11		7		4	9[1]	6		1		10						11,461
34	Tu	17 " 1964	Preston North End	A	0-1	0-3		2			5	3		8			11		7		4	9	6		1				10				20,803
35	S	21 " 1964	Huddersfield Town	H	1-0	2-2		2	3		5	6		8					11[1]		4	9			1	7			10[1]				14,458
36	F	27 " 1964	Manchester City	A	0-3	0-5		2	3			6		8			11		7		4	9		5	1	10							20,212
37	S	28 " 1964	Southampton	A	0-2	0-3	1	2		5		3		8	10		11				4	9	6			7							13,151
38	M	30 " 1964	Manchester City	H	1-1	1-2	1	2		5		4		8			11	7				9[1]	6							10	3		16,737
39	S	4 Apr 1964	Plymouth Argyle	H	0-1	1-1	1	2		5		6		8	10		11	7			4	9[1]									3		9,420
40	S	11 " 1964	Charlton Athletic	A	0-1	1-3	1	2		6		5		8	10		11	7			4	9									3	–[1]	14,994
41	S	18 " 1964	Middlesbrough	H	1-0	1-1	1	2	3	6		5		8			11	7[1]			4	9							10				13,135
42	S	25 " 1964	Newcastle United	A	0-1	0-2	1	2		6	5	3		8			11	7			4	9							10				12,256

F.A. CUP

NO.		DATE	OPPONENTS		V.	H-T	F-T	Keelan Kevin	Kelly Phil	Thurlow Bryan	Sharpe Freddie	Butler Barry	Mullett Joe	Miller Alistair	Bryceland Tommy	Allcock Terry	Conway Jim	Punton Bill	Mannion Gerry	Barnes Ron	Ashman Ron	Hill Ken	Davies Ron	Bell Jackie	Metcalf Colin	Kennon Sandy	Oliver Jim	Sutton Mike	Price Ray	Bolland Gordon	Shaw Colin	Worrell Colin	Own Goals	ATTD.
1	S	4 Jan 1964	Bristol Rovers	(3nd Round)	A	0-1	1-2		2			5	3		8			11		7		4	9[1]	6		1	10							17,779

FOOTBALL LEAGUE CUP

NO.		DATE	OPPONENTS		V.	H-T	F-T	Keelan Kevin	Kelly Phil	Thurlow Bryan	Sharpe Freddie	Butler Barry	Mullett Joe	Miller Alistair	Bryceland Tommy	Allcock Terry	Conway Jim	Punton Bill	Mannion Gerry	Barnes Ron	Ashman Ron	Hill Ken	Davies Ron	Bell Jackie	Metcalf Colin	Kennon Sandy	Oliver Jim	Sutton Mike	Price Ray	Bolland Gordon	Shaw Colin	Worrell Colin	Own Goals	ATTD.
1	W	25 Sept 1963	Birmingham City	(2nd Round)	H	0-1	2-0	1	2				3			8[1]		11	7[1]		5		9[1]	6	4			10						16,781
2	W	30 Oct 1963	Blackpool	(3rd Round)	H	0-0	1-0		2			5	3		8	10		11	7			4	9	6[1]		1								15,422
3	W	27 Nov 1963	Halifax Town	(4th Round)	A	2-1	7-1		2[1]			5	3		8[1]	10[1]		11[1]		7		4	9[2]	6[1]		1								4,822
4	W	18 Dec 1963	Leicester City	(5th Round)	H	1-0	1-1		2			5	3		8			11		7		4	9[1]	6		1		10						20,122
5	W	15 Jan 1964	Leicester City	A.E.T. (Replay)	A	1-1	1-2		2			5	3		8	10		11		7		4	9	6		1							–[1]	10,645

1963–64 APPEARANCES & GOALS

	FOOTBALL LGE APPR.	GLS	F.A. CUP APPR.	GLS	LEAGUE CUP APPR.	GLS
Bryceland Tommy	42	12	1	–	4	1
Kelly Phil	41	1	1	–	5	1
Punton Bill	40	5	1	–	5	1
Davies Ron	38	26	1	1	5	3
Mullett Joe	35	–	1	–	5	–
Bell Jackie	31	–	1	–	5	2
Hill Ken	29	–	1	–	4	–
Butler Barry	26	–	1	–	4	–
Kennon Sandy	26	–	1	–	4	–
Barnes Ron	21	1	1	–	3	–
Mannion Gerry	19	3			2	1
Keelan Kevin	16	–			1	–
Allcock Terry	15	3			4	2
Sharpe Freddie	15	–				
Thurlow Bryan	14	–				
Sutton Mike	11	2			2	–
Ashman Ron	10	–			1	–
Oliver Jim	9	4	1	–		
Conway Jim	8	3				
Metcalf Colin	5	1			1	–
Bolland Gordon	4	1				
Worrell Colin	3	–				
Miller Alistair	2	–				
Price Ray	1	–				
Shaw Colin	1	–				
Own Goals		2				1

DIVISION 2

1963–64	P	W	D	L	F	A	PTS
Leeds United	42	24	15	3	71	34	63
Sunderland	42	25	11	6	81	37	61
Preston North End	42	23	10	9	79	54	56
Charlton Athletic	42	19	10	13	76	70	48
Southampton	42	19	9	14	100	73	47
Manchester City	42	18	10	14	84	66	46
Rotherham United	42	19	7	16	90	78	45
Newcastle United	42	20	5	17	74	69	45
Portsmouth	42	16	11	15	79	70	43
Middlesbrough	42	15	11	16	67	52	41
Northampton Town	42	16	9	17	58	60	41
Huddersfield Town	42	15	10	17	57	64	40
Derby County	42	14	11	17	56	67	39
Swindon Town	42	14	10	18	57	69	38
Cardiff City	42	14	10	18	56	81	38
Leyton Orient	42	13	10	19	54	72	36
Norwich City	**42**	**11**	**13**	**18**	**64**	**80**	**35**
Bury	42	13	9	20	57	73	35
Swansea Town	42	12	9	21	63	74	33
Plymouth Argyle	42	8	16	18	45	67	32
Grimsby Town	42	9	14	19	47	75	32
Scunthorpe United	42	10	10	22	52	82	30

1964–65 DIVISION 2

NO.		DATE	OPPONENTS	V.	H-T	F-T	Kennon Sandy	Kelly Phil	Mullett Joe	Sutton Mike	Butler Barry	Allcock Terry	Heath Don	Bolland Gordon	Davies Ron	Bryceland Tommy	Punton Bill	Worrell Colin	Hill Ken	Mannion Gerry	Lucas Mal	Oliver Jim	Sharpe Freddie	Shaw Colin	Keelan Kevin	Bradley Ron	Anderson Terry	Barnard Geoff	Stringer Dave	Willis Graham	Own Goals	ATTD.
1	S	22 Aug 1964	Swansea Town	H	2-0	2-1	1	2	3	4	5	6	7	8^1	9^1	10	11															16,824
2	W	26 " 1964	Derby County	A	0-0	1-0	1	2	3	4	5	6	7	8	9^1	10	11															13,719
3	S	29 " 1964	Rotherham United	A	0-1	0-4	1	2		4	5	6	7	8	9	10	11	3														9,659
4	W	2 Sept 1964	Derby County	H	4-0	5-2	1	2			5	6^1	7^1	8^2	9	10	11	3	4												$-^1$	18,418
5	S	5 " 1964	Ipswich Town	H	0-1	2-1	1	2	3		5	6	7	8^1	9^1	10			4	11												25,087
6	W	9 " 1964	Manchester City	A	1-0	2-0	1	2	3		5	6	7	8^2	9	10	11		4													16,191
7	S	12 " 1964	Crystal Palace	H	0-2	1-2	1	2	3		5	6	7^1	8	9	10			4	11												20,944
8	W	16 " 1964	Manchester City	H	3-1	4-1	1	2	3^1		5	6	7^1	8	9^1	10				11^1	4											22,443
9	S	19 " 1964	Bury	A	0-0	0-1	1	2	3		5	6	7	8	9	10				11	4											6,830
10	S	26 " 1964	Leyton Orient	H	0-0	2-0	1	2	3		5	6	7	8^1	9	10				11^1	4											20,081
11	S	3 Oct 1964	Charlton Athletic	A	0-2	1-2	1	2	3		5	6	7	8^1	9	10				11	4											16,496
12	W	7 " 1964	Preston North End	H	1-2	4-2	1	2	3		5	6	7^2	8^1	9^1	10				11	4											21,822
13	S	10 " 1964	Plymouth Argyle	A	0-0	0-1	1	2	3	7	5	6		8	9	10	11				4											17,367
14	S	17 " 1964	Bolton Wanderers	H	3-1	3-2	1	2	3		5	6	7	9^2		8^1	11				4	10										18,065
15	S	24 " 1964	Middlesbrough	A	0-0	0-2	1	2	3	6	5	8	7	9		10	11				4											10,061
16	S	31 " 1964	Newcastle United	H	0-1	1-1	1	2	3			6	7	9		8^1	11				4		5	10								19,075
17	S	7 Nov 1964	Northampton Town	A	0-0	0-0		2	3					8	9	10	11		6		4		5	7	1							16,774
18	S	14 " 1964	Southampton	H	0-1	2-2		2	3				7	8	9^2	10			6	11	4		5		1							17,844
19	S	21 " 1964	Huddersfield Town	A	0-0	0-0		2	3		5		7	8	9	10			6	11	4				1							6,536
20	S	28 " 1964	Coventry City	H	0-0	1-0		2	3		5	6	7	8	9	10				11^1	4				1							17,634
21	S	5 Dec 1964	Cardiff City	A	2-0	3-1		2	3		5	6	7	8^1	9^1	10				11^1	4				1							9,877
22	S	12 " 1964	Swansea Town	A	0-0	0-0		2	3		5	6	7	8	9	10				11	4				1							9,142
23	S	19 " 1964	Rotherham United	H	1-0	3-0		2	3	6	5		7^1	8^1	9^1	10				11	4				1							14,986
24	S	26 " 1964	Swindon Town	A	0-0	1-0		2	3	10	5		7	8^1	9					11	4				1	6						18,224
25	S	2 Jan 1965	Ipswich Town	A	0-2	0-3		2	3		5	6	7	8	9	10				11	4				1							25,863
26	S	16 " 1965	Crystal Palace	A	0-1	0-2		2	3	10	5	6	7	8	9		11				4				1							17,103
27	S	23 " 1965	Bury	H	0-1	1-1		2	3	10	5	6	7	8	9^1		11				4				1							16,731
28	S	30 " 1965	Swindon Town	H	1-1	3-1		2	3		5	9^2	7	8	10^1					11	4				1	6						15,459
29	S	6 Feb 1965	Leyton Orient	A	2-1	3-2		2	3	6	5	9		8^1			11			7	4	10^2			1							7,417
30	S	13 " 1965	Charlton Athletic	H	0-0	2-0		2	3	6	5	9	7^1			8				11	4	10^1			1							17,002
31	S	20 " 1965	Plymouth Argyle	H	1-0	3-0		2	3	6	5	9^1				8^1				11^1	4	10			1		7					19,163
32	S	27 " 1965	Bolton Wanderers	A	1-2	2-5		2	3	6	5	9		8^1		10				11	4				1		7^1					14,130
33	S	6 Mar 1965	Cardiff City	H	1-1	2-1		2	3		5	6		9	10^1	8^1				11	4				1		7					18,036
34	S	13 " 1965	Newcastle United	A	0-2	0-2		2	3		5	6		9	10	8				11	4				1		7					41,441
35	S	20 " 1965	Northampton Town	H	1-1	1-1		2	3	6	5	9^1	7		10	8	11				4				1							25,199
36	S	27 " 1965	Southampton	A	0-1	0-1		2	3	6	5	9	7		10	8	11				4				1							14,340
37	S	3 Apr 1965	Huddersfield Town	H	0-1	0-2		2	3		5	6	7	8	9	10				11	4				1							14,465
38	S	10 " 1965	Coventry City	A	0-2	0-3			3	6	5	9	7		10	8	11				4							1	2			22,624
39	S	17 " 1965	Middlesbrough	H	1-0	2-0			3	6	5	9			10	8^1	11^1				4						7	1	2			12,228
40	M	19 " 1965	Portsmouth	A	0-2	0-4				6	5	9			10	8	11				4						7	1	3	2		15,701
41	Tu	20 " 1965	Portsmouth	H	2-1	3-1				6	5	9^1			10^2	8	11		4	7	2		3		1							10,847
42	S	24 " 1965	Preston North End	A	0-3	1-3				6	5	9			10	8	11		4	7^1	2		3		1							11,900

F.A. CUP

NO.		DATE	OPPONENTS	V.	H-T	F-T	Kennon Sandy	Kelly Phil	Mullett Joe	Sutton Mike	Butler Barry	Allcock Terry	Heath Don	Bolland Gordon	Davies Ron	Bryceland Tommy	Punton Bill	Worrell Colin	Hill Ken	Mannion Gerry	Lucas Mal	Oliver Jim	Sharpe Freddie	Shaw Colin	Keelan Kevin	ATTD.
1	S	9 Jan 1965	Nottingham Forest (3rd Round)	A	0-1	0-1		2	3	10	5	6	7	8	9					11	4				1	28,594

FOOTBALL LEAGUE CUP

NO.		DATE	OPPONENTS	V.	H-T	F-T	Kennon Sandy	Kelly Phil	Mullett Joe	Sutton Mike	Butler Barry	Allcock Terry	Heath Don	Bolland Gordon	Davies Ron	Bryceland Tommy	Punton Bill	Worrell Colin	Hill Ken	Mannion Gerry	Lucas Mal	Oliver Jim	Sharpe Freddie	Shaw Colin	ATTD.
1	W	23 Sept 1964	Millwall (2nd Round)	A	0-0	2-1	1	2	3		5	6	7	8^1	9^1	10				11	4				8,458
2	W	21 Oct 1964	Chester (3rd Round)	H	2-2	5-3	1	2	3^1		5	6	7	9^3		8	11				4^1	10			9,439
3	W	4 Nov 1964	Workington (4th Round)	A	0-2	0-3	1	2	3					9		8	11		6	7	4		5	10	11,377

1964–65 APPEARANCES & GOALS

	FOOTBALL LGE APPR.	LGE GLS	F.A. CUP APPR.	F.A. CUP GLS	LEAGUE CUP APPR.	LEAGUE CUP GLS
Butler Barry	39	–	1	–	2	–
Allcock Terry	37	6	1	–	2	–
Bryceland Tommy	37	5			3	–
Kelly Phil	37	–	1	–	3	–
Mullett Joe	37	1	1	–	3	1
Davies Ron	35	14	1	–	1	1
Lucas Mal	35	–	1	–	3	1
Bolland Gordon	33	16	1	–	3	4
Heath Don	31	7	1	–	2	–
Mannion Gerry	25	6	1	–	2	–
Keelan Kevin	23	–	1	–		
Punton Bill	20	1			2	–
Sutton Mike	20	–	1	–		
Kennon Sandy	16	–			3	–
Hill Ken	9	–			1	–
Anderson Terry	6	1				
Sharpe Freddie	5	–			1	–
Oliver Jim	4	3			1	–
Barnard Geoff	3	–				
Stringer Dave	3	–				
Bradley Ron	2	–				
Shaw Colin	2	–			1	–
Worrell Colin	2	–				
Willis Graham	1	–				
Own Goals		1				

DIVISION 2

1964–65	P	W	D	L	F	A	PTS
Newcastle United	42	24	9	9	81	45	57
Northampton Town	42	20	16	6	66	50	56
Bolton Wanderers	42	20	10	12	80	58	50
Southampton	42	17	14	11	83	63	48
Ipswich Town	42	15	17	10	74	67	47
Norwich City	**42**	**20**	**7**	**15**	**61**	**57**	**47**
Crystal Palace	42	16	13	13	55	51	45
Huddersfield Town	42	17	10	15	53	51	44
Derby County	42	16	11	15	84	79	43
Coventry City	42	17	9	16	72	70	43
Manchester City	42	16	9	17	63	62	41
Preston North End	42	14	13	15	76	81	41
Cardiff City	42	13	14	15	64	57	40
Rotherham United	42	14	12	16	70	69	40
Plymouth Argyle	42	16	8	18	63	79	40
Bury	42	14	10	18	60	66	38
Middlesbrough	42	13	9	20	70	76	35
Charlton Athletic	42	13	9	20	64	75	35
Leyton Orient	42	12	11	19	50	72	35
Portsmouth	42	12	10	20	56	77	34
Swindon Town	42	14	5	23	63	81	33
Swansea Town	42	11	10	21	62	84	32

1965–66 DIVISION 2

NO.	DATE			OPPONENTS	V.	H-T	F-T	Keelan Kevin	Sharpe Freddie	Mullett Joe	Lucas Mal	Butler Barry	Hill Ken	Heath Don	Bryceland Tommy	Davies Ron	Bolland Gordon	Punton Bill	Allcock Terry	Anderson Terry	Stringer Dave	Sutton Mike	Mannion Gerry	Curran Hugh	Bradley Ron	Gladwin Robin	Own Goals	ATTD.
1	S	21 Aug	1965	Carlisle United	A	0-3	1-4	1	2	3	4	5	6	7	8¹	9	10	11										11,954
2	W	25 "	1965	Bristol City	H	0-0	0-0	1	2	3	4	5			10	9	8	11	6	7								16,616
3	S	28 "	1965	Cardiff City	H	2-1	3-2	1		3	4¹	5			8	9¹	10¹	11	6	7	2							13,437
4	Tu	31 "	1965	Bristol City	A	0-0	0-0	1		3	4	5			8	9	12	11	6	⑦	2	10						15,737
5	S	4 Sept	1965	Derby County	A	0-1	1-3	1		3	4	5		7	10¹	9		11	6		2	8						8,065
6	S	11 "	1965	Southampton	H	1-2	3-4	1	5		4¹		3	7	8	9	10²	11	6		2							13,870
7	W	15 "	1965	Mancester City	H	1-1	3-3	1	3		4¹	5			8	9	10	11	6		2		7					15,622
8	S	18 "	1965	Bury	A	1-1	5-2	1	3		4	5			8¹	9²	10¹	11	6		2		7¹					5,683
9	S	25 "	1965	Ipswich Town	H	0-0	1-0	1		3	4	5			8¹	9	10	11	6		2		7					26,407
10	S	2 Oct	1965	Wolverhampton Wanderers	H	0-3	0-3	1		3	4	5			⑧	9	10	11	6		2	12	7					20,548
11	S	9 "	1965	Birmingham City	A	0-1	0-1	1		3	4	5			8	9	⑩	11	6		2	12	7					11,626
12	S	16 "	1965	Leyton Orient	H	0-1	2-1	1	5	3	4				8	10¹	9	11	6		2		7				–¹	12,782
13	F	22 "	1965	Middlesbrough	A	1-0	1-0	1	5	3			4		8	10¹		11	6		2	9	7					10,897
14	W	27 "	1965	Manchester City	A	0-0	0-0	1	5	3	4				8	10		11	6		2	9	7					34,091
15	S	30 "	1965	Huddersfield Town	H	0-0	1-1	1	5	3	4				8	10¹		11	6		2	9	7					16,442
16	S	6 Nov	1965	Crystal Palace	A	0-0	0-0	1	5	3	4				8	9		11	6	7	2	10						15,906
17	S	13 "	1965	Preston North End	H	1-1	1-1	1	5	3	4¹				8	9	10	11	6		2		7					15,024
18	S	27 "	1965	Plymouth Argyle	H	0-0	0-0	1	5	3	4			10	8	9		11	6	7	2							10,630
19	S	4 Dec	1965	Portsmouth	A	2-0	3-0	1	5	3	4			8	10	9³		11	6	7	2							8,540
20	S	11 "	1965	Bolton Wanderers	H	2-0	3-0	1	5	3	4			8¹	10¹	9¹		11	6	7	2							14,363
21	M	27 "	1965	Coventry City	H	0-0	1-1	1	5	3				8	10	9¹		11	6	7	2	4						27,203
22	Tu	28 "	1965	Coventry City	A	0-0	0-2	1	5	3			4	8	10	9		11	6	7	2							24,888
23	S	1 Jan	1966	Birmingham City	H	1-1	2-2	1	5	3			4	8¹	10	9¹		11	6	7	2							15,297
24	S	8 "	1966	Preston North End	A	0-0	0-0	1	5	3			4	8	10	9		11	6	7	2							12,346
25	S	29 "	1966	Carlisle United	H	0-0	2-0	1	5	3	4				8	9¹		11	6	7	2			10¹				15,835
26	S	19 Feb	1966	Derby County	H	0-0	0-1	1	5	3	4				10	9		11	6	7	2			8				19,483
27	S	26 "	1966	Southampton	A	0-2	2-2	1	5	3	4			7	8¹	9	10	11¹	6		2							15,864
28	S	12 Mar	1966	Bury	H	3-0	4-0	1	5	3	4			7¹	8¹	10¹	9¹	11	6		2							10,834
29	S	19 "	1966	Ipswich Town	A	0-0	0-2	1	5	3	4			7	8	10	9	11	6		2							22,690
30	S	26 "	1966	Wolverhampton Wanderers	A	1-1	1-2	1	5	3	4			12	8¹	10	7	⑪	6		2			9				14,963
31	M	28 "	1966	Leyton Orient	A	0-0	0-0	1	5	3				7		9			6	11	2	4		10	8			4,740
32	S	2 Apr	1966	Crystal Palace	H	0-0	2-1	1	5	3				7¹		9	8		6	11¹	2			10	4			10,367
33	S	9 "	1966	Huddersfield Town	A	0-0	0-0	1	5	3	4			7	8	9		11	6		2			10				13,942
34	M	11 "	1966	Rotherham United	H	1-0	1-2	1	5	3	4			7	8	9¹	10	11	6		2							14,707
35	Tu	12 "	1966	Rotherham United	A	1-2	1-2	1		5	4¹			7	8	9		11	6		2			10		3		11,202
36	S	16 "	1966	Charlton Athletic	H	1-0	2-0	1		5	4			7¹	8	9		11	6		2			10¹		3		9,589
37	S	23 "	1966	Plymouth Argyle	A	0-0	0-2	1	5		4			7	8	9		11	6		2			10		3		9,540
38	W	27 "	1966	Middlesbrough	H	0-0	1-2	1	5	4				7	8	9¹			6	11	2			10		3		7,849
39	S	30 "	1966	Portsmouth	H	0-0	1-3	1	5		4			7	8	9			6	11	2			10¹		3		7,884
40	S	7 May	1966	Bolton Wanderers	A	0-1	1-1	1	5		4			7	8	9			6	11	2			10¹		3		7,420
41	Tu	10 "	1966	Cardiff City	A	0-0	2-0	1	5		④			7	8		9		6	11	2	12		10²		3		5,934
42	W	18 "	1966	Charlton Athletic	A	0-2	1-2	1	5		4¹			10	8			11	6	7	2			9		3		7,813

F.A. CUP

NO.	DATE			OPPONENTS		V.	H-T	F-T	Keelan Kevin	Sharpe Freddie	Mullett Joe	Lucas Mal	Butler Barry	Hill Ken	Heath Don	Bryceland Tommy	Davies Ron	Bolland Gordon	Punton Bill	Allcock Terry	Anderson Terry	Stringer Dave	Own Goals	ATTD.
1	S	22 Jan	1966	Leyton Orient	(3rd Round)	A	1-0	3-1	1	5	3	4			8¹	10	9		11	6	7¹	2	–¹	9,494
2	S	12 Feb	1966	Walsall	(4th Round)	H	0-0	3-2	1	5	3¹	4			8¹	10	9		11	6¹	7	2		28,754
3	S	5 Mar	1966	Blackburn Rovers	(5th Round)	H	0-2	2-2	1	5	3	4			7	8	9²	10	11	6		2		30,751
4	W	9 "	1966	Blackburn Rovers	(Replay)	A	1-1	2-3	1	5	3	4			7	8¹	10¹	9	11	6		2		33,135

FOOTBALL LEAGUE CUP

NO.	DATE			OPPONENTS		V.	H-T	F-T	Keelan Kevin	Sharpe Freddie	Mullett Joe	Lucas Mal	Butler Barry	Hill Ken	Heath Don	Bryceland Tommy	Davies Ron	Bolland Gordon	Punton Bill	Allcock Terry	Anderson Terry	Stringer Dave	Sutton Mike	Mannion Gerry	ATTD.
1	W	22 Sept	1965	Stoke City	(2nd Round)	A	1-0	1-2	1	3		4	5			8	9	10¹	11	6		2		7	12,896

1965–66 APPEARANCES & GOALS

	FOOTBALL LGE APPR.	S	GLS	F.A. CUP APPR.	S	GLS	LEAGUE CUP APPR.	S	GLS
Keelan Kevin	42	–	–	4	–	–	1	–	–
Allcock Terry	41	–	–	4	–	1	1	–	–
Bryceland Tommy	40	–	8	4	–	1	1	–	–
Davies Ron	40	–	18	4	–	3	1	–	–
Stringer Dave	40	–	–	4	–	–	1	–	–
Punton Bill	36	–	1	4	–	–	1	–	–
Lucas Mal	34	–	6	4	–	–	1	–	–
Mullett Joe	34	–	–	4	–	1			
Sharpe Freddie	34	–	–	4	–	–	1	–	–
Heath Don	25	1	5	4	–	2			
Anderson Terry	20	–	1	2	–	1			
Bolland Gordon	18	1	5	2	–	–	1	–	1
Curran Hugh	14	–	6						
Butler Barry	10	–	–				1	–	–
Mannion Gerry	10	–	1				1	–	–
Gladwin Robin	8	–	–						
Sutton Mike	8	3	–						
Hill Ken	6	–	–						
Bradley Ron	2	–	–						
Own Goals			1			1			

DIVISION 2

1965–66	P	W	D	L	F	A	PTS
Manchester City	42	22	15	5	76	44	59
Southampton	42	22	10	10	85	56	54
Coventry City	42	20	13	9	73	53	53
Huddersfield Town	42	19	13	10	62	36	51
Bristol City	42	17	17	8	63	48	51
Wolverhampton Wanderers	42	20	10	12	87	61	50
Rotherham United	42	16	14	12	75	74	46
Derby County	42	16	11	15	71	68	43
Bolton Wanderers	42	16	9	17	62	59	41
Birmingham City	42	16	9	17	70	75	41
Crystal Palace	42	14	13	15	47	52	41
Portsmouth	42	16	8	18	74	78	40
Norwich City	**42**	**12**	**15**	**15**	**52**	**52**	**39**
Carlisle United	42	17	5	20	60	63	39
Ipswich Town	42	15	9	18	58	66	39
Charlton Athletic	42	12	14	16	61	70	38
Preston North End	42	11	15	16	62	70	37
Plymouth Argyle	42	12	13	17	54	63	37
Bury	42	14	7	21	62	76	35
Cardiff City	42	12	10	20	71	91	34
Middlesbrough	42	10	13	19	58	86	33
Leyton Orient	42	5	13	24	38	80	23

1966–67 DIVISION 2

NO.		DATE		OPPONENTS	V.	H-T	F-T	Keelan Kevin	Stringer Dave	Gladwin Robin	Lucas Mal	Sharpe Freddie	Allcock Terry	Heath Don	Bryceland Tommy	Bolland Gordon	Curran Hugh	Punton Bill	Anderson Terry	Black Alan	Mullett Joe	Sutton Mike	Brown Laurie	Kelly Phil	Woolmer Tony	Barnard Geoff	Sheffield Laurie	Kenning Mike	Own Goals	ATTD.
1	S	20 Aug	1966	Portsmouth	H	0-0	0-0	1	2	3	4	5	6	7	8	9	10	11												9,256
2	S	27 "	1966	Birmingham City	A	0-2	1-2	1	2	3	4	5	6	7	8	9	10^{1}	11												26,846
3	W	31 "	1966	Hull City	H	0-2	0-2	1	2	3	4	5	6	7	8	9	10	11												14.215
4	S	3 Sept	1966	Ipswich Town	H	1-1	1-2	1	2	3	4	5	⑥	12	8	9^{1}	10	11	7											19,129
5	Tu	6 "	1966	Northampton Town	A	1-1	2-1	1	2		4	5			8	9^{1}	10	11	7^{1}	3	6									14.767
6	S	10 "	1966	Coventry City	H	0-0	1-1	1	2		4	5			8	9	10^{1}	11	7	③	6	12								12.771
7	S	17 "	1966	Bury	A	0-1	0-2	1	2		4	5		8		9	10	11	7	3	6									5.761
8	Tu	20 "	1966	Hull City	A	0-2	0-5	1	2		4				8	9	10	11	7	3	5	6								24.871
9	S	24 "	1966	Preston North End	H	0-1	1-1	1	2			5		12	8	9	10	⑪	7^{1}	3	6	4								9,280
10	Tu	27 "	1966	Carlisle United	A	0-1	0-1	1	2		12			7	8	9	10		11	3	⑥	4	5							10,329
11	S	1 Oct	1966	Rotherham United	A	1-1	1-2	1	2		6	4		7	8	9^{1}	10		11	3			5							9,222
12	S	8 "	1966	Bristol City	A	0-1	0-1	1	2		④	6	9	7		8	10		11	3			5	12						11,008
13	S	15 "	1966	Carlisle United	H	1-0	2-0	1	2		4		6	7	8^{1}	9^{1}	10		11		3		5							10,910
14	S	22 "	1966	Blackburn Rovers	A	0-0	0-0	1	②		4		6	7	8	9	10		11		3	12	5							12,029
15	S	29 "	1966	Bolton Wanderers	H	0-0	1-0	1	2		4		6	11	8^{1}	⑨	10				3	7	5		12					12,593
16	S	5 Nov	1966	Charlton Athletic	A	0-0	0-0	1	2		4		6		8	9	10		11		3	7	5							8,870
17	S	12 "	1966	Derby County	H	1-0	4-1		2		4		6		8^{1}	7	10		11		3		5			1	9^{3}			13,893
18	S	19 "	1966	Crystal Palace	A	0-0	0-0	1	2		4		6		8	7	10		11		3		5				9			17,114
19	S	26 "	1966	Huddersfield Town	H	0-0	0-0	1	2		4		6		8	7	10		11		3		5				9			14,854
20	S	3 Dec	1966	Cardiff City	A	0-1	0-2	1	2		4		6		8	7	10		11		3		5				9			5,647
21	S	10 "	1966	Wolverhampton Wanderers	H	1-1	1-2	1	2				6		8	7^{1}	10		11		3		5	4			9			14,899
22	S	17 "	1966	Portsmouth	A	2-0	3-3	1	2		4		6		8	7	10^{1}		11		3		5				9^{2}			12,431
23	M	26 "	1966	Millwall	A	0-2	1-2	1	2		4		6			8	10		11		3		5				9^{1}	7		19,571
24	Tu	27 "	1966	Millwall	H	1-1	1-1	1	2				6		4	8	10		11		3		5			1	9^{1}	7		24,153
25	S	31 "	1966	Birmingham City	H	2-2	3-3		2				6		4	8	10^{2}		11		3		5			1	9^{1}	7		15,260
26	S	14 Jan	1967	Coventry City	A	0-0	1-2	1	2		4		6			8	10		11		3		5				9^{1}	7		27,724
27	S	21 "	1967	Bury	H	1-0	2-0	1	2		4		6			8^{1}	10^{1}		11		3		5				9	7		14,488
28	S	4 Feb	1967	Preston North End	A	1-2	1-3	1	2		4		6		12	8	10^{1}		11		3		5				9	⑦		12,807
29	S	11 "	1967	Rotherham United	H	0-0	1-0	1	2		4		6	7	9^{1}	8	⑩		11	12	3		5							14,167
30	S	25 "	1967	Bristol City	H	0-0	1-0	1	2		4		6		10	8			11		3		5				9^{1}	7		28,147
31	S	4 Mar	1967	Bolton Wanderers	A	0-0	1-1	1	2		4		6		10^{1}	8			11		3		5				9	7		12,299
32	S	18 "	1967	Blackburn Rovers	H	0-0	0-1	1	2		4		6	10	8				11		3		5				9	7		13,015
33	F	24 "	1967	Plymouth Argyle	A	0-1	2-2	1	2		4		6		8	10			11		3		5				9^{2}	7		15,533
34	M	27 "	1967	Plymouth Argyle	H	1-1	3-1	1	2		4		6^{1}		8^{1}	10^{1}			11		3		5				9	7		16,253
35	S	1 Apr	1967	Charlton Athletic	H	0-0	1-1	1	2		4		6		8	10			11^{1}		3		5				9	7		15,040
36	S	8 "	1967	Derby County	A	0-0	1-1	1	2		④	6		11	8	10			12		3		5				9^{1}	7		12,519
37	S	15 "	1967	Crystal Palace	H	1-1	4-3	1	2		4	6		7	8^{2}	10					3		5^{1}				9	11^{1}		13,714
38	Tu	18 "	1967	Ipswich Town	A	1-0	2-0	1	2		4	6		7	8	10					3		5				9^{1}	11	$-^{1}$	28,047
39	S	22 "	1967	Hudersfield Town	A	0-0	1-0	1	2		4	6		7^{1}	⑧	10				12	3		5				9	11		10,041
40	S	29 "	1967	Cardiff City	H	1-1	3-2	1	2		④	6		7^{1}		10			12		3		5		8		9^{2}	11		14,264
41	S	6 May	1967	Wolverhampton Wanderers	A	0-3	1-4	1	2		4	6	12	7		10					3		5		8^{1}		⑨	11		27,901
42	S	13 "	1967	Northampton Town	H	1-0	1-0	1	2		4	12	6	⑦^{1}	8	10					3		5				9	11		13,544

F.A. CUP

NO.		DATE		OPPONENTS		V.	H-T	F-T	Keelan Kevin	Stringer Dave	Gladwin Robin	Lucas Mal	Sharpe Freddie	Allcock Terry	Heath Don	Bryceland Tommy	Bolland Gordon	Curran Hugh	Punton Bill	Anderson Terry	Black Alan	Mullett Joe	Sutton Mike	Brown Laurie	Kelly Phil	Woolmer Tony	Barnard Geoff	Sheffield Laurie	Kenning Mike	Own Goals	ATTD.
1	S	28 Jan	1967	Derby County	(3rd Round)	H	2-0	3-0	1	2		4		6		12	8	10		11^{1}		3		5				9	⑦^{2}		21,311
2	S	18 Feb	1967	Manchester United	(4th Round)	A	1-1	2-1	1	2		4		6	8^{1}	9	10^{1}			11		3		5					7		63,405
3	S	11 Mar	1967	Sheffield Wednesday	(5th Round)	H	0-2	1-3	1	2		4		6		8^{1}	10			11		3		5				9	7		41,000

FOOTBALL LEAGUE CUP

NO.		DATE		OPPONENTS		V.	H-T	F-T	Keelan Kevin	Stringer Dave	Gladwin Robin	Lucas Mal	Sharpe Freddie	Allcock Terry	Heath Don	Bryceland Tommy	Bolland Gordon	Curran Hugh	Punton Bill	Anderson Terry	Black Alan	Mullett Joe	Sutton Mike	Brown Laurie	Kelly Phil	Woolmer Tony	Barnard Geoff	Sheffield Laurie	Kenning Mike	Own Goals	ATTD.
1	W	14 Sept	1966	Brighton & Hove Albion	(2nd Round)	H	0-0	0-1	1	2	3	4	5		10		9	8	11	7		6									7,36

1966–67 APPEARANCES & GOALS

	FOOTBALL LGE APPR.	S	GLS	F.A. CUP APPR.	S	GLS	LEAGUE CUP APPR.	S	GLS
Stringer Dave	42	–	–	3	–	–	1	–	–
Bolland Gordon	41	–	7	3	–	1	1	–	–
Keelan Kevin	39	–	–	3	–	–	1	–	–
Lucas Mal	37	1	–	3	–	–	1	–	–
Mullett Joe	36	–	–	3	–	–	1	–	–
Bryceland Tommy	34	1	8	2	1	1			
Anderson Terry	31	2	3	3	–	1	1	–	–
Brown Laurie	33	–	1	3	–	–			
Allcock Terry	29	1	1	3	–	–			
Curran Hugh	29	–	7	1	–	–	1	–	–
Sheffield Laurie	25	–	16	2	–	–			
Heath Don	19	2	3	1	–	1	1	–	–
Kenning Mike	19	–	1	3	–	2			
Sharpe Freddie	16	1	–				1	–	–
Punton Bill	9	–	–				1	–	–
Black Alan	8	2	–						
Sutton Mike	5	2	–						
Gladwin Robin	4	–	–				1	–	–
Barnard Geoff	3	–	–						
Woolmer Tony	2	1	1						
Kelly Phil	1	1	–						
Own Goals			1						

DIVISION 2

1966–67	P	W	D	L	F	A	PTS
Coventry City	42	23	13	6	74	43	59
Wolverhampton Wanderers	42	25	8	9	88	48	58
Carlisle United	42	23	6	13	71	54	52
Blackburn Rovers	42	19	13	10	56	46	51
Ipswich Town	42	17	16	9	70	54	50
Huddersfield Town	42	20	9	13	58	46	49
Crystal Palace	42	19	10	13	61	55	48
Millwall	42	18	9	15	49	58	45
Bolton Wanderers	42	14	14	14	64	58	42
Birmingham City	42	16	8	18	70	66	40
Norwich City	**42**	**13**	**14**	**15**	**49**	**55**	**40**
Hull City	42	16	7	19	77	72	39
Preston North End	42	16	7	19	65	67	39
Portsmouth	42	13	13	16	59	70	39
Bristol City	42	12	14	16	56	62	38
Plymouth Argyle	42	14	9	19	59	58	37
Derby County	42	12	12	18	68	72	36
Rotherham United	42	13	10	19	61	70	36
Charlton Athletic	42	13	9	20	49	53	35
Cardiff City	42	12	9	21	61	87	33
Northampton Town	42	12	6	24	47	84	30
Bury	42	11	6	25	49	83	28

1967–68 DIVISION 2

No.		Date	Opponents	V.	H-T	F-T	Keelan Kevin	Stringer Dave	Mullett Joe	Lucas Mal	Brown Laurie	Bolland Gordon	Heath Don	Bryceland Tommy	Sheffield Laurie	Curran Hugh	Kenning Mike	Gladwin Robin	Allcock Terry	Sharpe Freddie	Mannion Gerry	Anderson Terry	Black Alan	Manning John	Foggo Ken	Painter Trevor	O'Donnell Neil	Howshall Gerry	Crickmore Charlie	Howard Trevor	Vasper Peter	Woolmer Tony	McDonald Colin	Cassidy Nigel	Own Goals	Attd.
1	S	19 Aug 1967	Aston Villa	H	1-0	1-0	1	2	3	4	5	6	7	8	9	10^1	11																			19,408
2	W	23 " 1967	Preston North End	H	0-1	1-3	1	2	3	4	5	6	7	8	9	10	11^1																			18,231
3	S	26 " 1967	Queens Park Rangers	A	0-0	0-2	1	2		4	5	9	7	8		10	11	3	6																	14,526
4	M	28 " 1967	Preston North End	A	0-1	0-1	1	2		4	5	9	7	8		10	11	3	6																	15,036
5	S	2 Sept 1967	Plymouth Argyle	H	1-0	2-0	1	2		4	5	9		8		10^1	11	3		6	7														$-^1$	13,791
6	W	6 " 1967	Derby County	H	0-0	3-2	1	2		4	5^1	9		8		10^1	11^1	3		6	⑦	12														14,933
7	S	9 " 1967	Cardiff City	A	0-2	1-3	1	2		4	5	9		8		10	11			6		7^1	3													14,863
8	S	16 " 1967	Portsmouth	H	0-2	1-3	1	2		4	5	9		8		10	11^1		6			7	3													11,802
9	S	23 " 1967	Ipswich Town	A	0-0	0-0	1	2		4	5			8		10	11			6		7	3	9												24,873
10	S	30 " 1967	Rotherham United	A	1-0	3-1	1	2		4	5			8		10^1	11			6		7	3	9^1											$-^1$	5,987
11	S	7 Oct 1967	Blackburn Rovers	H	1-0	1-0	1	2		4	5			8^1		10	11			6			3	9	7											18,080
12	S	14 " 1967	Bolton Wanderers	A	0-0	0-2	1	2	③	4	5			8		10	11		12	6				9	7											8,303
13	S	21 " 1967	Birmingham City	H	4-0	4-2	1	2	3	4	5			8		10^3	11			6				9	7^1											16,490
14	S	4 Nov 1967	Middlesbrough	H	1-0	2-1	1	2	3	4	5			8		10^1	11			6		7^1		9												11,658
15	S	11 " 1967	Hull City	A	1-0	2-0	1	2	3	4	5			8		10	11			6				9^1	7^1											14,720
16	S	18 " 1967	Huddersfield Town	H	0-0	0-1	1	2	3	4	5			⑧		10	11			6		12		9	7											17,573
17	S	25 " 1967	Blackpool	A	0-0	2-0	1	2	3					8^1		10	11		4	6				9^1	7	5										12,554
18	S	2 Dec 1967	Millwall	H	2-2	5-2	1	2	3	4				8		10	11^2		12	6				9^1	7^2	⑤										17,505
19	Tu	5 " 1967	Bristol City	A	1-0	2-0	1	2	3	4	5			8^1		10^1	11			6				9	7											13,444
20	S	9 " 1967	Carlisle United	A	2-0	2-2	1	2	3	4^1	5			8		10	11^1			6				9	7											8,076
21	S	16 " 1967	Aston Villa	A	2-2	2-4	1	②	3	4	5			8^1		10	11		12	6				9^1	7											16,493
22	S	23 " 1967	Queens Park Rangers	H	0-0	0-0	1	2	3	4	5			8		10	11		6	6				9	7											23,593
23	Tu	26 " 1967	Charlton Athletic	A	2-0	3-3	1		2	4	5			⑧		10	11^1		6	12			3	9^2	7											14,574
24	S	30 " 1967	Charlton Athletic	H	0-0	1-1	1	2	3	4	5					10^1	11		6					9	7		8									18,427
25	W	10 Jan 1968	Plymouth Argyle	A	1-1	2-2	1	2	12	4	5					10^1	11^1		⑥				3	9^1	7		8									7,946
26	S	20 " 1968	Portsmouth	A	0-1	0-3	1	2		4	5					10				6		12	3	9	7			⑧	11							24,028
27	S	3 Feb 1968	Ipswich Town	H	2-1	3-4	1	2	12	4	5					10^2				6		8	3	9	7				$⑪^1$							29,937
28	S	10 " 1968	Rotherham United	H	1-0	2-2	1	2		4	5			8		$⑩^1$				6		11	3	9	7^1					12						15,380
29	S	24 " 1968	Blackburn Rovers	A	0-0	0-0	1	2		4	5			8		10							3	9	7			6	11							12,803
30	S	2 Mar 1968	Bolton Wanderers	H	3-0	3-1		2		4	⑤			8		10^1			12				3	9^1	7			6	11		1				$-^1$	14,694
31	S	9 " 1968	Derby County	A	0-1	1-1		2		4	5			8^1		10							3	9	7			6	11		1					18,644
32	S	16 " 1968	Birmingham City	A	0-0	0-0		2		4	5					10						8	3	9	7			⑥	11	12	1					28,951
33	S	23 " 1968	Bristol City	H	1-1	3-2		2		4	5					10			6			8	3	9^2	7				11^1		1					13,634
34	S	30 " 1968	Middlesbrough	A	0-1	0-2		2		4	5					10			6			8	3	9	7				11		1					10,181
35	S	6 Apr 1968	Hull City	H	2-1	2-2		2		4	5			8^1		10^1			6				3	9	7				11		1					14,055
36	S	13 " 1968	Huddersfield Town	A	0-0	0-2		2		4	5			8		10				6			3	9	7				11		1					9,727
37	M	15 " 1968	Crystal Palace	H	1-1	2-1		2		4	5			8^2		10				6		12	3	9	7				⑪		1					15,352
38	Tu	16 " 1968	Crystal Palace	A	0-4	0-6		2		4	5			8		10				6		11	3	9	7						1	9				7,745
39	S	20 " 1968	Blackpool	H	0-2	1-2		2		6	5					10^1							3		7		8			4	1	9	11			15,852
40	S	27 " 1968	Millwall	A	0-0	0-1		2		4	5					10				6		8	3	9	7						1		11			11,347
41	S	4 May 1968	Carlisle United	H	1-0	2-1		2		4	5					10				6		8^1	3	9	7						1		11		$-^1$	11,429
42	S	8 " 1968	Cardiff City	H	1-0	1-0	1	2		4	5					10				6		8	3		7^1								11	9		10,177

F.A. CUP

No.		Date	Opponents		V.	H-T	F-T	Keelan Kevin	Stringer Dave	Mullett Joe	Lucas Mal	Brown Laurie	Bolland Gordon	Heath Don	Bryceland Tommy	Sheffield Laurie	Curran Hugh	Kenning Mike	Gladwin Robin	Allcock Terry	Sharpe Freddie	Mannion Gerry	Anderson Terry	Black Alan	Manning John	Foggo Ken	Painter Trevor	O'Donnell Neil	Howshall Gerry	Crickmore Charlie	Attd.
1	S	27 Jan 1968	Sunderland	(3rd Round)	H	0-0	1-1	1	2		4	5					10^1				6		8	3	9	7				11	26,389
2	W	31 Jan 1968	Sunderland	(Replay)	A	0-0	1-0	1	2		4	5					10				6		8	3	9^1	7				11	32,923
3	W	17 Feb 1968	Chelsea	(4th Round)	A	0-1	0-1	1	2		4	5			8		10				6			3	9	7				11	57,987

FOOTBALL LEAGUE CUP

No.		Date	Opponents		V.	H-T	F-T	Keelan Kevin	Stringer Dave	Mullett Joe	Lucas Mal	Brown Laurie	Bolland Gordon	Heath Don	Bryceland Tommy	Sheffield Laurie	Curran Hugh	Kenning Mike	Gladwin Robin	Allcock Terry	Sharpe Freddie	Mannion Gerry	Anderson Terry	Black Alan	Manning John	Foggo Ken	Painter Trevor	O'Donnell Neil	Attd.
1	W	13 Sept 1967	Rotherham United	(2nd Round)	H	1-1	1-1	1	2		4	5	9		8^1		10	11		6			7	3					12,935
2	Tu	19 " 1967	Rotherham United	(Replay)	A	0-0	2-0	1	2		4^1	5			8		9^1	11			6		7	3				10	7,054
3	W	11 Oct 1967	Huddersfield Town	(3rd Round)	H	0-0	0-1	1	2	3	4	5	9		8		10	11			6		7						12,278

1967–68 APPEARANCES & GOALS

	FOOTBALL LGE APPR.	S	GLS	F.A. CUP APPR.	S	GLS	LEAGUE CUP APPR.	S	GLS
Curran Hugh	42	–	16	3	–	1	3	–	1
Lucas Mal	41	–	1	3	–	–	3	–	1
Stringer Dave	41	–	–	3	–	–	3	–	–
Brown Laurie	40	–	1	3	–	–	3	–	–
Bryceland Tommy	31	–	8	1	–	–	3	–	1
Foggo Ken	31	–	6	3	–	–			
Manning John	31	–	11	3	–	1			
Keelan Kevin	30	–	–	3	–	–	3	–	–
Sharpe Freddie	25	1	–	3	–	–	2	–	–
Kenning Mike	25	–	8				3	–	–
Black Alan	24	–	–	3	–	–	2	–	–
Mullett Joe	15	2	–				1	–	–
Anderson Terry	14	4	3	2	–	–	3	–	–
Vasper Peter	12	–	–						
Allcock Terry	11	4	–				1	–	–
Crickmore Charlie	11	–	2	3	–	–			
Bolland Gordon	8	–	–				2	–	–
Howshall Gerry	5	–	–						
Gladwin Robin	4	–	–						
Heath Don	4	–	–						
McDonald Colin	4	–	–						
O'Donnell Neil	3	–	–				1	–	–
Mannion Gerry	2	–	–						
Painter Trevor	2	–	–						
Sheffield Laurie	2	–	–						
Woolmer Tony	2	–	–						
Cassidy Nigel	1	–	–						
Howard Trevor	1	2	–						
Own Goals			4						

DIVISION 2

1967–68	P	W	D	L	F	A	PTS
Ipswich Town	42	22	15	5	79	44	59
Queens Park Rangers	42	25	8	9	67	36	58
Blackpool	42	24	10	8	71	43	58
Birmingham City	42	19	14	9	83	51	52
Portsmouth	42	18	13	11	68	55	49
Middlesbrough	42	17	12	13	60	54	46
Millwall	42	14	17	11	62	50	45
Blackburn Rovers	42	16	11	15	56	49	43
Norwich City	**42**	**16**	**11**	**15**	**60**	**65**	**43**
Carlisle United	42	14	13	15	58	52	41
Crystal Palace	42	14	11	17	56	56	39
Bolton Wanderers	42	13	13	16	60	63	39
Cardiff City	42	13	12	17	60	66	38
Huddersfied Town	42	13	12	17	46	61	38
Charlton Athletic	42	12	13	17	63	68	37
Aston Villa	42	15	7	20	54	64	37
Hull City	42	12	13	17	58	73	37
Derby County	42	13	10	19	71	78	36
Bristol City	42	13	10	19	48	62	36
Preston North End	42	12	11	19	43	65	35
Rotherham United	42	10	11	21	42	76	31
Plymouth Argyle	42	9	9	24	38	72	27

1968–69 DIVISION 2

NO.		DATE	OPPONENTS	V.	H-T	F-T	Keelan Kevin	Stringer Dave	Black Alan	Sharpe Freddie	Brown Laurie	Anderson Terry	Foggo Ken	Bryceland Tommy	Manning John	Curran Hugh	Crickmore Charlie	Howshall Gerry	Lucas Mal	O'Donnell Neil	Briggs Max	Payne Clive	Howard Trevor	Forbes Duncan	Butler Geoff	Mallender Ken	Cassidy Nigel	Conlon Bryan	Bennett Albert	Vasper Peter	Allcock Terry	Own Goals	ATTD.
1	S	10 Aug 1968	Birmingham City	A	0-1	2-1	1	2	3	4	5	6	7	8	9^1	10^1	11																27,715
2	W	14 " 1968	Middlesbrough	H	0-1	0-2	1	2	3	4	5		7	8	9	10	11	6															19,431
3	S	17 " 1968	Cardiff City	H	1-1	3-1	1	2	3		5		7	8	9^1	10^2	11	6	4														14.476
4	Tu	20 " 1968	Huddersfield Town	A	1-1	2-2	1	2	3	12	5	7		8	9^1	10^1	11	⑥	4														9,167
5	S	24 " 1968	Charlton Athletic	A	0-0	1-2	1	2	3	12	5	7		8	9	10^1	11	⑥	4														14,861
6	W	28 " 1968	Crystal Palace	A	0-1	0-2	1	2	3	6	5	7		8	9	10	11		④	12													12,857
7	S	31 " 1968	Bury	H	2-1	2-2	1	2	3	6	5	4		8	9	10^2	11				7												12,757
8	S	7 Sept 1968	Sheffield United	H	2-0	2-0	1	5	3	6	5	4			9	10^2	11			8	7	2											16,246
9	S	14 " 1968	Carlisle United	A	3-0	4-0	1	5	3	6		4			9^1	10^2	11^1			8	7	2											7,348
10	S	21 " 1968	Portsmouth	H	0-1	0-1	1	5	3	6		4			9	10	11			8	7	2											18,440
11	S	28 " 1968	Preston North End	A	1-1	3-1	1	5	3	6	12	4	11^1		9^1	10^1				8	⑦	2											14,778
12	S	5 Oct 1968	Hull City	H	1-1	1-2	1	⑤	3	6		4	11		9	10^1				8	7	2	12										17,985
13	W	9 " 1968	Crystal Palace	H	0-0	0-1	1	3	4		6	7		9	10	11			8		2			5									18,119
14	S	12 " 1968	Fulham	A	1-0	3-1	1		3	4		6	7^1		9^1	10^1	11			8		2		5									17,443
15	S	19 " 1968	Aston Villa	H	1-1	1-1	1	2	3			6	7		9	10^1	11	4		8				5									14,579
16	S	26 " 1968	Blackburn Rovers	A	0-1	0-3	1	2		4			7		9	10	11	6		8		3		5									11,516
17	S	2 Nov 1968	Millwall	H	0-2	0-3	1	2				6	7	⑪	9	10		4		8				12	3	5							19,048
18	S	16 " 1968	Oxford United	H	1-1	1-1	1	2				11	7^1		9	10		4		⑧				6	3	5	12						11,213
19	S	23 " 1968	Bristol City	A	1-0	1-0	1	2				6	7		9	10	11	4		8^1					3	5							13,822
20	S	30 " 1968	Blackpool	H	0-0	0-1	1	2				6	7			10	11	4		8					3	5	9						14,608
21	W	4 Dec 1968	Bolton Wanderers	A	1-1	1-1	1					6	7		9	10^1		4		8		2			3	5							9,633
22	S	7 " 1968	Derby County	A	1-0	1-1	1	2				6^1	7		9	10		4		8				11	3	5							24,719
23	S	14 " 1968	Fullham	H	0-0	2-0	1	2				6	7		9^1	10	11^1	4		8					3	5							12,231
24	S	21 " 1968	Aston Villa	A	0-1	1-2	1	2				6	7		⑨	10		4		8			12	11^1	3	5							19,923
25	Th	26 " 1968	Hull City	A	1-0	1-0	1	2				6	7		9	10				8			12^1	11	3	5		④					20,312
26	S	11 Jan 1969	Millwall	A	1-0	1-3	1	2	3			4^1	7	8	9	10	⑪			12				6		5							14,765
27	S	18 " 1969	Bolton Wanderers	H	1-0	2-0	1	2	3			6	7^1	8	9	10^1		11						4		5							11,997
28	S	1 Feb 1969	Oxford United	A	1-0	2-0	1					6		8	9^1		10	11			7^1	2		4	3	5							9,305
29	S	1 Mar 1969	Birmingham City	H	0-0	1-1	1	2				6	7	8	9^1			4							3	5		11	10				15,894
30	F	7 " 1969	Cardiff City	A	0-2	1-3	1	②				6		8	9^1		7	4						12	3	5		11	10				21,415
31	S	15 " 1969	Charlton Athletic	H	0-0	0-1	1	2				6	7	8			11	4							3	5		9	10				13,293
32	W	19 " 1969	Blackpool	A	0-1	1-2		2					7				11^1	4	8					6	3	5		9	10	1			9,530
33	S	22 " 1969	Bury	A	0-1	2-1						2	7^1				11	4	8					6	3	5^1		9	10	1			4,648
34	W	26 " 1969	Bristol City	H	0-0	1-1		2				12	7^1				⑪	4	10					6	3	5		9	8	1			8,682
35	S	29 " 1969	Sheffield United	A	0-0	0-1		2					7	11				4	10				12	6	3	5		⑨	8	1			11,587
36	S	5 Apr 1969	Preston North End	H	1-1	1-1		2					7	8				④	6	10			11	12	3	5			9	1		–^{1}	10,515
37	M	7 " 1969	Huddersfield Town	H	0-0	1-0		2				10	7					4	6				11		3	5			8	1	9^1		9,26
38	Tu	8 " 1969	Middlesbrough	A	0-0	0-0		2	12			④	7						6	10			11		3	5			8	1	9		19,36
39	S	12 " 1969	Portsmouth	A	0-2	2-5		2					7^1					4	6	10			11	12	3	⑤			8^1	1	9		16,25
40	W	16 " 1969	Derby County	H	0-3	1-4		2				6	7^1	8					4	10		3	11	5						1	9		13,80
41	S	19 " 1969	Carlisle United	H	2-1	2-1		5	3			6	7	10^1			11					2	12	4					⑧	1	9	–^{1}	8,31
42	W	23 " 1969	Blackburn Rovers	H	3-0	3-1	1	②				6	7^1	10			11^1		12			3	8^1	4		5					9		7,86

F.A. CUP

NO.		DATE	OPPONENTS		V.	H-T	F-T	Keelan Kevin	Stringer Dave	Black Alan	Sharpe Freddie	Brown Laurie	Anderson Terry	Foggo Ken	Bryceland Tommy	Manning John	Curran Hugh	Crickmore Charlie	Howshall Gerry	Lucas Mal	O'Donnell Neil	Briggs Max	Payne Clive	Howard Trevor	Forbes Duncan	Butler Geoff	Mallender Ken	ATTD.
1	S	4 Jan 1969	West Bromwich Albion	(3rd Round)	A	0-2	0-3	1	2				4	7	12	9	10	11			8				⑥	3	5	30,10

FOOTBALL LEAGUE CUP

NO.		DATE	OPPONENTS		V.	H-T	F-T	Keelan Kevin	Stringer Dave	Black Alan	Sharpe Freddie	Brown Laurie	Anderson Terry	Foggo Ken	Bryceland Tommy	Manning John	Curran Hugh	Crickmore Charlie	Howshall Gerry	Lucas Mal	O'Donnell Neil	Briggs Max	Payne Clive	ATTD.
1	Tu	3 Sept 1968	Ipswich Town	(2nd Round)	A	2-0	4-2	1	5	3	6		4			9	10^3	11^1			8	7	2	23,08
2	Tu	24 " 1968	Brentford	(3rd Round)	A	2-0	2-0	1	⑤	3	6	12	4			9	10^2	11			8	7	2	17,42
3	W	16 Oct 1968	Southampton	(4th Round)	H	0-2	0-4	1	5	3	④		6	7		9	10	11	12		8		2	25,30

1968–69 APPEARANCES & GOALS

	FOOTBALL LGE APPR.	S	GLS	F.A. CUP APPR.	S	GLS	LEAGUE CUP APPR.	S	GLS
Stringer Dave	37	–	–	1	–	–	3	–	–
Anderson Terry	34	1	2	1	–	–	3	–	–
Foggo Ken	33	–	9	1	–	–	1	–	–
Keelan Kevin	32	–	–	1	–	–	3	–	–
Manning John	29	–	10	1	–	–	3	–	–
Crickmore Charlie	27	–	4	1	–	–	3	–	1
Curran Hugh	27	–	17	1	–	–	3	–	5
Howshall Gerry	26	–	–				–	1	–
Mallender Ken	24	–	1	1	–	–			
O'Donnel Neil	22	2	1	1	–	–	3	–	–
Butler Geoff	21	–	–	1	–	–			
Bryceland Tommy	19	–	1	–	1	–			
Black Alan	18	1	–				3	–	–
Forbes Duncan	18	4	1	1	–	–			
Lucas Mal	13	1	–						
Payne Clive	13	–	–				3	–	–
Bennett Albert	12	–	1						
Sharpe Freddie	12	2	–				3	–	–
Vasper Peter	10	–	–						
Conlon Bryan	8	–	–						
Briggs Max	7	–	1				2	–	–
Brown Laurie	7	1	–				–	1	–
Allcock Terry	6	–	1						
Howard Trevor	6	5	2						
Cassidy Nigel	1	1	–						
Own Goals			2						

DIVISION 2

1968–69	P	W	D	L	F	A	PTS
Derby County	42	26	11	5	65	32	63
Crystal Palace	42	22	12	8	70	47	56
Charlton Athletic	42	18	14	10	61	52	50
Middlesbrough	42	19	11	12	58	49	49
Cardiff City	42	20	7	15	67	54	47
Huddersfield Town	42	17	12	13	53	46	46
Birmingham City	42	18	8	16	73	59	44
Blackpool	42	14	15	13	51	41	43
Sheffield United	42	16	11	15	61	50	43
Millwall	42	17	9	16	57	49	43
Hull City	42	13	16	13	59	52	42
Carlisle United	42	16	10	16	46	49	42
Norwich City	**42**	**15**	**10**	**17**	**53**	**56**	**40**
Preston North End	42	12	15	15	38	44	39
Portsmouth	42	12	14	16	58	58	38
Bristol City	42	11	16	15	46	53	38
Bolton Wanderers	42	12	14	16	55	67	38
Aston Villa	42	12	14	16	37	48	38
Blackburn Rovers	42	13	11	18	52	63	37
Oxford United	42	12	9	21	34	55	33
Bury	42	11	8	23	51	80	30
Fulham	42	7	11	24	40	81	25

1969–70 DIVISION 2

O.		DATE		OPPONENTS	V.	H-T	F-T	Keelan Kevin	Stringer Dave	Butler Geoff	Mallender Ken	Forbes Duncan	Anderson Terry	Foggo Ken	Bryceland Tommy	Conlon Bryan	Bennett Albert	Crickmore Charlie	Payne Clive	Lucas Mal	O'Donnell Neil	Black Alan	Silvester Peter	Howshall Gerry	Howard Trevor	Paddon Graham	Briggs Max	Vasper Peter	Own Goals	ATTD.
1	S	9 Aug	1969	Aston Villa	A	0-0	1-0	1	2	3	4	5	6	7^1	8	9	10	11												32,663
2	W	13 "	1969	Hull City	A	0-0	0-1	1	2	3	4	5	6	7	8	9	10	11												11,791
3	S	16 "	1969	Blackpool	H	2-0	3-1	1	2	3	4	5	6	7^1	8	9	10	11^2												16,577
4	W	20 "	1969	Hull City	H	1-0	2-1	1	2		4	5	6	7	8	9^2	10	11	3											18,158
5	S	23 "	1969	Leicester City	A	0-1	0-3	1	2	③	4	5	6	7	8	9	10	11	12											26,716
6	W	27 "	1969	Portsmouth	H	0-0	0-0	1	2	3	4	5	⑥	7	8	9		11		12	10									17,792
7	S	30 "	1969	Carlisle United	H	1-0	1-0	1	2	3	4	5	6	7	8	9	10^1	11												14,054
8	S	6 Sept	1969	Sheffield United	A	0-0	0-1	1	2		4	5	6	7	8	9	10	11				3								16,007
9	S	13 "	1969	Charlton Athletic	H	0-0	1-1	1	2		4	5	6	7	8		10	11			9^1	3								13,401
0	Tu	16 "	1969	Birmingham City	A	0-1	1-3	1	2	3	4	5^1	6	7	8		10	11					9							26,408
1	S	20 "	1969	Bristol City	A	0-1	0-4	1	2	3	4	5	6	7	8		10	12					9	⑪						11,879
2	S	27 "	1969	Oxford United	H	1-0	2-0	1	2		4	5	6	7	8	⑩^1		11				3	9^1		12					11,454
3	S	4 Oct	1969	Blackburn Rovers	A	0-2	1-3	1	2		4	5		7^1	8	6	⑩	12				3	9			11				12,139
4	M	6 "	1969	Blackpool	A	0-0	0-0	1	2		4	5		7	8			11		6		3	9			10				12,485
5	S	11 "	1969	Queens Park Rangers	H	0-0	1-0	1	②		4	5^1		7	8			11		6		3	9		12	10				20,040
6	S	18 "	1969	Cardiff City	A	1-0	1-0	1	2		4	5		7	8			11^1		6		3	9			10				23,618
7	S	25 "	1969	Preston North End	H	1-2	1-2	1	2		4	5		7	8			11		6		3	9			10^1				15,273
8	S	1 Nov	1969	Swindon Town	A	0-0	0-2	1	2		4	5		7	8			11		6		3	9			10				17,736
9	S	8 "	1969	Huddersfield Town	H	0-2	1-2	1	2		4	5		7	⑧^1		10			6		3	9	12		11				13,646
0	S	15 "	1969	Millwall	A	0-0	0-1	1	4	2		5				9	10			6		3	8			11	7			9,617
1	S	22 "	1969	Bolton Wanderers	H	1-0	1-0	1	4			5	6	8		10^1			2	7		3	9			11				10,809
2	S	13 Dec	1969	Charlton Athletic	A	0-1	0-3	①	4			5		8		10			2	6	12	3	9			11	7			8,038
3	S	20 "	1969	Sheffield United	H	0-1	1-1		4			5	12	8^1		⑩			2	6		3	9			11	7	1		7,409
4	F	26 "	1969	Leicester City	H	0-0	3-0		4	2		5		8		10^2				6		3	9^1			11	7	1		14,905
5	S	27 "	1969	Carlisle United	A	0-0	1-2		4			5	12	8		10			2	6^1		3	9			11	⑦	1		9,668
6	S	10 Jan	1970	Bristol City	A	1-0	4-1		4	2		5		11		8^2				6		3	9^2			10	7	1		6,523
7	S	17 "	1970	Oxford United	A	0-0	0-1		4	2		5		11		⑧				6		3	9	12		10	7	1		10,353
8	S	31 "	1970	Blackburn Rovers	H	0-0	0-1		4	2		5		11		⑧				6		3	9	12		10	7	1		9,661
9	S	14 Feb	1970	Aston Villa	H	1-1	3-1		4	2		5		11^1			8			6		3	9^2			10	7	1		10,080
0	Tu	17 "	1970	Queens Park Rangers	A	0-1	0-4		4	2		5		11			8			6		3	9			10	7	1		17,270
1	S	21 "	1970	Huddersfield Town	A	0-1	1-1		4^1	2		5		11			8			6		3	9			10	7	1		16,060
2	S	28 "	1970	Cardiff City	H	1-0	1-1	1	4	2		5		11^1						6	12	3	9		⑧	10	7			11,290
3	W	11 Mar	1970	Middlesbrough	H	1-0	2-0	1	4	2		5		11			8^1			6		3	9^1			10	7			10,390
4	S	21 "	1970	Middlesbrough	A	0-0	0-0	1	4	2		5		11			⑧				12	3	9	6		10	7			24,514
5	S	28 "	1970	Millwall	H	2-1	2-1	1	4	2		5		11^1			8					3	9^1		6	10	7			11,403
6	M	30 "	1970	Swindon Town	H	1-0	1-0	1	4	2		5		11			8^1					3	9		6	10	7			16,309
7	Tu	31 "	1970	Preston North End	A	0-0	1-1	1	4	2		5		11^1			8					3	9		6	10	7			13,084
8	S	4 Apr	1970	Portsmouth	A	1-1	4-1	1	4	2		5		11^1		9	8^3					3			6	10	7			10,750
9	Tu	7 "	1970	Wafford	A	0-1	1-1	1	4	2		5		11		9	8^1					3			6	10	7			15,789
0	Th	9 "	1970	Bolton Wanderers	A	0-0	0-0	1	4	2		5		11			8					3	9		6	10	7			6,878
1	W	15 "	1970	Birmingham City	H	2-0	6-0	1	4	2		5		11^2			8^1					3	9^1		6	10^1	7		$–^1$	12,134
2	S	18 "	1970	Watford	H	1-0	1-1	1	4	2		5		11			8					3	9^1		6	10	7			16,202

F.A. CUP

O.		DATE		OPPONENTS	V.	H-T	F-T	Keelan Kevin	Stringer Dave	Butler Geoff	Mallender Ken	Forbes Duncan	Anderson Terry	Foggo Ken	Bryceland Tommy	Conlon Bryan	Bennett Albert	Crickmore Charlie	Payne Clive	Lucas Mal	O'Donnell Neil	Black Alan	Silvester Peter	Howshall Gerry	Howard Trevor	Paddon Graham	Briggs Max	Vasper Peter	Own Goals	ATTD.
1	S	3 Jan	1970	Wrexham (3rd Round)	H	0-2	1-2		4	2		5		8		9				6		3			10^1	11	7	1		13,162

FOOTBALL LEAGUE CUP

O.		DATE		OPPONENTS	V.	H-T	F-T	Keelan Kevin	Stringer Dave	Butler Geoff	Mallender Ken	Forbes Duncan	Anderson Terry	Foggo Ken	Bryceland Tommy	Conlon Bryan	Bennett Albert	Crickmore Charlie	Payne Clive	Lucas Mal	O'Donnell Neil	Black Alan	Silvester Peter	Howshall Gerry	Howard Trevor	Paddon Graham	Briggs Max	Vasper Peter	Own Goals	ATTD.
1	W	3 Sept	1969	Hull City (2rd Round)	A	0-0	0-1	1	2	12	5		6	7	8	9	10	11	③	4										10,824

1969–70 APPEARANCES & GOALS

	FOOTBALL LGE APPR.	S	GLS	F.A. CUP APPR.	S	GLS	LEAGUE CUP APPR.	S	GLS
Forbes Duncan	42	–	2	1	–	–			
Stringer Dave	42	–	1	1	–	–	1	–	–
Foggo Ken	41	–	11	1	–	–	1	–	–
Black Alan	33	–	–	1	–	–			
Keelan Kevin	33	–	–				1	–	–
Silvester Peter	31	–	10						
Paddon Graham	30	–	2	1	–	–			
Butler Geoff	27	–	–	1	–	–	–	1	–
Bennett Albert	26	–	8				1	–	–
Briggs Max	22	–	–	1	–	–			
Conlon Bryan	21	–	8	1	–	–	1	–	–
Lucas Mal	20	1	1	1	–	–	1	–	–
Bryceland Tommy	19	–	1				1	–	–
Mallender Ken	19	–	–				1	–	–
Crickmore Charlie	16	2	3				1	–	-
Anderson Terry	13	2	–				1	–	–
Howard Trevor	9	2	–	1	–	1			
Vasper Peter	9	–	–	1	–	–			
Payne Clive	5	1	–				1	–	–
Howshall Gerry	2	3	–						
O'Donnell Neil	2	3	1						
Own Goals			1						

DIVISION 2

1969–70	P	W	D	L	F	A	PTS
Huddersfield Town	42	24	12	6	68	37	60
Blackpool	42	20	13	9	56	45	53
Leicester City	42	19	13	10	64	50	51
Middlesbrough	42	20	10	12	55	45	50
Swindon Town	42	17	16	9	57	47	50
Sheffield United	42	22	5	15	73	38	49
Cardiff City	42	18	13	11	61	41	49
Blackburn Rovers	42	20	7	15	54	50	47
Queens Park Rangers	42	17	11	14	66	57	45
Millwall	42	15	14	13	56	56	44
Norwich City	**42**	**16**	**11**	**15**	**49**	**46**	**43**
Carlisle United	42	14	13	15	58	56	41
Hull City	42	15	11	16	72	70	41
Bristol City	42	13	13	16	54	50	39
Oxford United	42	12	15	15	35	42	39
Bolton Wanderers	42	12	12	18	54	61	36
Portsmouth	42	13	9	20	66	80	35
Birmingham City	42	11	11	20	51	78	33
Watford	42	9	13	20	44	57	31
Charlton Athletic	42	7	17	18	35	76	31
Aston Villa	42	8	13	21	36	62	29
Preston North End	42	8	12	22	43	63	28

1970–71 DIVISION 2

NO.		DATE	OPPONENTS	V.	H-T	F-T	Keelan Kevin	Butler Geoff	Black Alan	Mallender Ken	Forbes Duncan	Howard Trevor	Briggs Max	Bennett Albert	Silvester Peter	Paddon Graham	Foggo Ken	Stringer Dave	Darling Malcolm	Anderson Terry	Howshall Gerry	Payne Clive	Self Glenn	O'Donnell Neil	Livermore Doug	Cawston Mervyn	Govier Steve	Grapes Steve	Goodwin Steve	Own Goals	ATTD.
1	S	15 Aug 1970	Portsmouth	H	0-0	1-1	1	2	3	4	5	6	7	8	9	10	11														14,470
2	S	22 " 1970	Luton Town	A	0-0	0-0	1	2	3		5	6	7	8	9	10	11	4													16,110
3	S	29 " 1970	Sheffield United	H	1-0	1-0	1	2	3		5	6	7	8^1	9	10	11	4													13,159
4	W	2 Sept 1970	Millwall	H	1-0	1-0	1	2	3		5	6	7	8^1	9	10	11	4													14,748
5	S	5 " 1970	Sunderland	A	0-0	1-2	1	2	3		5	⑥	7		9^1	10	11	4	8	12											16,682
6	S	12 " 1970	Charlton Athletic	H	1-0	2-0	1	2	3		5	⑥	7	8^1	9^1	10	11	4		12											9,687
7	S	19 " 1970	Cardiff City	A	0-1	1-1	1	2	3		5	6	7	8^1	9	10	11	4													23,768
8	S	26 " 1970	Hull City	H	0-1	0-2	1	2	3		5	6	7	8	9	10	11	4													16,258
9	W	30 " 1970	Watford	A	0-1	0-2	1	2	3		5	6	7	8	9	10	11	4													14,163
10	S	3 Oct 1970	Oxford United	A	1-1	1-1	1	2	3		5	6	7	$⑧^1$	9	10	11	4		12											13,002
11	S	10 " 1970	Carlisle United	H	0-0	1-1	1		3		5	12^1	⑦	8	9	10		4	11		6	2									10,883
12	S	17 " 1970	Portsmouth	A	2-0	2-0	1		3	4	5	7^1		8		10				11	6	2	9^1								15,064
13	W	21 " 1970	Swindon Town	H	1-0	1-0	1		3	4	5	7	⑪	8		10				6	12	2	9^1								10,104
14	S	24 " 1970	Blackburn Rovers	A	0-2	1-2	1		3		5	6	7	8	9^1	10		4		11		2									7,161
15	S	31 " 1970	Orient	H	3-0	4-2	1	2			5	6	7		9^2	8	11^2	4				3	10								11,269
16	S	7 Nov 1970	Bolton Wanderers	A	0-0	1-0	1	2			5	6	7		8	10	11^1	4		12		3	⑨								6,908
17	S	14 " 1970	Sheffield Wednesday	H	0-0	0-0	1		3		5	6	7		9	10	11	4		8		2									12,950
18	S	21 " 1970	Leicester City	H	1-1	2-2	1		3		5	10	7		9^1		11^1	4		8	⑥	2		12							16,342
19	S	28 " 1970	Birmingham City	A	1-0	2-2	1		3		5	9			8^2	10	11	4		6		2			7						13,630
20	S	5 Dec 1970	Middlesbrough	H	1-1	1-1	1		3		5	9			8	10	11^1	4		6		2			7						13,073
21	S	12 " 1970	Bristol City	A	1-0	1-0	1		3		5	6	7		9^1	10	11	4				2			8						10,637
22	S	19 " 1970	Luton Town	H	0-1	1-1	1		3		5	6	⑦		9	10	11^1	4		12		2			8						16,596
23	S	9 Jan 1971	Watford	H	1-0	2-1			3		5	⑨		12	8	10	11	4^1		6		2			7	1				$–^1$	12,216
24	S	16 " 1971	Swindon Town	A	0-1	2-3	1		3			9			8	10	11	4		6^1		2			7^1		5				14.97
25	S	23 " 1971	Millwall	A	1-1	2-2	1		3			4	12	⑨	8	10	11^1			6		2			7^1		5				9,842
26	S	30 " 1971	Birmingham City	H	2-1	2-2	1		3		5	9^1			8	10	11^1	4		6		2			7						11,41
27	S	6 Feb 1971	Middlesbrough	A	0-3	0-5	1		3		5	⑨	12		8	10	11	4		6		2			7						19,106
28	S	13 " 1971	Bristol City	H	0-2	3-2	1		3		5			9^1	8^1	10	11	4		6^1		2			7						10,51
29	S	20 " 1971	Leicester City	A	1-0	1-2	1		3		5	12		⑨	8	10	11^1	4		6		2			7						24,86
30	S	26 " 1971	Orient	A	0-1	0-1	1		3		5	12			8	⑩	11	4	9	6		2			7						8,11
31	S	6 Mar 1971	Blackburn Rovers	H	1-0	2-1	1		3		5	10			8		11^1	4	9^1	6		2			7						9,01
32	S	13 " 1971	Sheffield Wednesday	A	0-1	1-2	1		3		5	12			9^1	⑩	11	4		8		2			7		6				13,13
33	S	20 " 1971	Bolton Wanderers	H	2-1	2-1	1		3		5				10	6	11	4	9^1	8		2			7^1						9,05
34	Tu	23 " 1971	Queens Park Rangers	A	1-0	1-0	1		3		5				8	10^1	11	4	⑦	6		2			9			12			9,92
35	S	27 " 1971	Sunderland	H	0-0	3-0	1		3		5	12			10^2	8	11^1	4	⑨	6		2			7						10,72
36	S	3 Apr 1971	Sheffield United	A	0-0	0-0	1		3		5	12			8	10	11	4	⑦	6		2			9						21,43
37	S	9 " 1971	Charlton Athletic	A	0-0	1-2	1		3		5	12			⑧	10	11^1	4	7	6		2			9						13,03
38	S	10 " 1971	Queens Park Rangers	H	2-0	3-0		3			5				8	10	11^1	4^1	7^1	6		2			9	1					14,97
39	M	12 " 1971	Oxford United	H	0-1	1-1		3			5	7			8	10	11^1	4		6		2			9	1					14,16
40	S	17 " 1971	Carlisle United	A	0-2	2-4	1		3		12				8	10	11^1	4	$⑦^1$	6		2			9		5				8,77
41	S	24 " 1971	Cardiff City	H	0-2	1-2	1		3		5				10^1	8	11	4	7	6		2			9						15,08
42	S	1 May 1971	Hull City	A	0-1	0-1					5	6			8	10	11	4		3		2			9	1		⑦	12		11,30

F.A. CUP

NO.		DATE	OPPONENTS	V.	H-T	F-T	Keelan Kevin	Butler Geoff	Black Alan	Mallender Ken	Forbes Duncan	Howard Trevor	Briggs Max	Bennett Albert	Silvester Peter	Paddon Graham	Foggo Ken	Stringer Dave	Darling Malcolm	Anderson Terry	Howshall Gerry	Payne Clive	Self Glenn	O'Donnell Neil	Livermore Doug	Cawston Mervyn	Govier Steve	Grapes Steve	Goodwin Steve	Own Goals	ATTD.
1	S	2 Jan 1971	Wolverhampton Wanderers (3rd Round)	A	1-1	1-5	1		3		5	9			8	10	11^1	4		6		2			7						29,22

FOOTBALL LEAGUE CUP

NO.		DATE	OPPONENTS	V.	H-T	F-T	Keelan Kevin	Butler Geoff	Black Alan	Mallender Ken	Forbes Duncan	Howard Trevor	Briggs Max	Bennett Albert	Silvester Peter	Paddon Graham	Foggo Ken	Stringer Dave	Darling Malcolm	Anderson Terry	Howshall Gerry	Payne Clive	Self Glenn	O'Donnell Neil	Livermore Doug	Cawston Mervyn	Govier Steve	Grapes Steve	Goodwin Steve	Own Goals	ATTD.
1	W	9 Sept 1970	Chester (2nd Round)	H	0-0	0-0	1	2	3		5	6	7	8	9	10	11	4													11,74
2	W	16 " 1970	Chester (Replay)	A	2-1	2-1	1	2	3		5	6	7	8	9^1	10	11^1	4													7,47
3	W	7 Oct 1970	Bristol Rovers (3rd Round)	H	1-0	1-1	1	2	3		5	6	7	⑧	9	10		4^1	11		12										11,51
4	Tu	13 " 1970	Bristol Rovers *(Replay)	A	1-0	1-3	1	12	3		5	7		8^1		10		④		11	6	2	9								19,12

*-After extra time

1970–71 APPEARANCES & GOALS

	FOOTBALL LGE APPR.	S	GLS	F.A. CUP APPR.	S	GLS	LEAGUE CUP APPR.	S	GLS
Paddon Graham	40	–	1	1	–	–	4	–	–
Silvester Peter	40	–	15	1	–	–	3	–	1
Forbes Duncan	39	1	–	1	–	–	4	–	–
Foggo Ken	38	–	15	1	–	1	2	–	1
Keelan Kevin	38	–	–	1	–	–	4	–	–
Stringer Dave	38	–	2	1	–	–	4	–	1
Black Alan	37	–	–	1	–	–	4	–	–
Payne Clive	32	–	–	1	–	–	1	–	–
Howard Trevor	29	7	3	1	–	–	4	–	–
Anderson Terry	27	5	2	1	–	–	1	–	–
Livermore Doug	24	–	3	1	–	–			
Briggs Max	19	2	–				3	–	–
Bennett Albert	16	1	6				4	–	1
Butler Geoff	14	–	–				3	1	–
Darling Malcolm	12	–	4				1	–	–
Cawston Mervyn	4	–	–						
Govier Steve	4	–	–						
Self Glenn	4	–	2				1	–	–
Howshall Gerry	3	1	–				1	1	–
Mallender Ken	3	–	–						
Grapes Steve	1	1	–						
Goodwin Steve	–	1	–						
O'Donnell Neil	–	1	–						
Own Goals			1						

DIVISION 2

1970–71	P	W	D	L	F	A	PTS
Leicester City	42	23	13	6	57	30	59
Sheffield United	42	21	14	7	73	39	56
Cardiff City	42	20	13	9	64	41	53
Carlisle United	42	20	13	9	65	43	53
Hull City	42	19	13	10	54	41	51
Luton Town	42	18	13	11	62	43	49
Middlesbrough	42	17	14	11	60	43	48
Millwall	42	19	9	14	59	42	47
Birmingham City	42	17	12	13	58	48	46
Norwich City	**42**	**15**	**14**	**13**	**54**	**52**	**44**
Queens Park Rangers	42	16	11	15	58	53	43
Swindon Town	42	15	12	15	61	51	42
Sunderland	42	15	12	15	52	54	42
Oxford United	42	14	14	14	41	48	42
Sheffield Wednesday	42	12	12	18	51	69	36
Portsmouth	42	10	14	18	46	61	34
Orient	42	9	16	17	29	51	34
Watford	42	10	13	19	38	60	33
Bristol City	42	10	11	21	46	64	31
Charlton Athletic	42	8	14	20	41	65	30
Blackburn Rovers	42	6	15	21	37	69	27
Bolton Wanderers	42	7	10	25	35	74	24

1971–72 DIVISION 2

NO.		DATE		OPPONENTS	V.	H-T	F-T	Keelan Kevin	Payne Clive	Butler Geoff	Stringer Dave	Forbes Duncan	Anderson Terry	Livermore Doug	Paddon Graham	Howard Trevor	Silvester Peter	Foggo Ken	Darling Malcolm	Sargent Gary	O'Donnell Neil	Briggs Max	Cross David	Black Alan	Govier Steve	Hubbard Phil	Grapes Steve	Bell Bobby	Bone Jimmy	Cheesley Paul	Own Goals	ATTD.
1	S	14 Aug	1971	Luton Town	A	0-0	1-1	1	2	3	4	5	6	7	8[1]	9	10	11														12,428
2	S	21 "	1971	Portsmouth	H	3-1	3-1	1	2	3	4	5	6	9	(10)	12	8[1]	11[1]	7[1]													13,080
3	S	28 "	1971	Fulham	A	0-0	0-0	1	2	3	4	5	6	8		9	10	11	(7)	12												10,668
4	W	1 Sept	1971	Orient	H	0-0	0-0	1	2	3	4	5	6	9		10	8	11	(7)		12											13,314
5	S	4 "	1971	Carlisle United	H	1-0	1-0	1	2	3	4	5	6	8	10	12	9[1]	11	(7)													10,967
6	S	11 "	1971	Blackpool	A	2-0	2-1	1	2	3	4	5	6	8	10	7[1]	9	(11)[1]			12											15,960
7	S	18 "	1971	Oxford United	H	2-1	3-2	1	2	3	4	5	6	9	10	(7)	8[2]	11				12										13,839
8	S	25 "	1971	Bristol City	A	0-0	1-0	1	2	3	4[1]	5	6	7	8	10	9	(11)				12										18,528
9	Tu	28 "	1971	Preston North End	A	0-0	2-0	1	2	3	4	5	6	9	10	7	8[1]	11[1]				12										15,644
10	S	2 Oct	1971	Queens Park Rangers	H	0-0	0-0	1	2	3	4	5	6	9	10	7	8	11				12										22,695
11	S	9 "	1971	Sunderland	A	0-1	1-1	1	2	3	4	5	6	7	10[1]		8	11					9									25,951
12	W	13 "	1971	Burnley	H	2-0	3-0	1	2	3	4[1]	5	6	7	10		8[1]	11[1]					9									24,356
13	S	16 "	1971	Luton Town	H	0-1	3-1	1	2	3	4	5	6	(7)	10	12[1]	8	11[2]					9									22,337
14	S	23 "	1971	Millwall	A	1-1	1-2	1	2	3	4	5	6	7	10		8[1]	11					(9)									22,763
15	S	30 "	1971	Cardiff City	H	1-0	2-1	1	2	3	4[1]	(5)	6	7	10		8	11					9[1]	12								20,546
16	S	6 Nov	1971	Hull City	A	2-0	2-1	1	2	3	4		6	7	8		10[1]	(11)				12	9[1]		5							11,878
17	S	13 "	1971	Birmingham City	H	1-2	2-2	1	2	3	4		6	7	8	12	10[1]	11					9		(5)[1]							24,094
18	S	20 "	1971	Sheffield Wednesday	A	0-0	1-1	1	2	3	4		5	7	10		8	11				6	9[1]									19,902
19	S	27 "	1971	Middlesbrough	H	0-0	2-0	1	2	3	4		5	7	10		8[1]	11[1]				6	9									21,303
20	S	4 Dec	1971	Swindon Town	A	1-0	1-0	1	2	3	4		5	7	10	12	8[1]	(11)				6	9									14,167
21	S	11 "	1971	Watford	H	1-0	1-1	1	2	3	4		5	7	10[1]		8	11				6	9									20,227
22	S	18 "	1971	Carlisle United	A	0-2	0-3	1	2	3	4		5	7	10	12	8	11				(6)	9									9,081
23	M	27 "	1971	Charlton Athletic	H	1-0	3-0	1	2		4		5	7	10		8[1]	11[2]				12	9	3		(6)						30,788
24	S	1 Jan	1972	Oxford United	A	1-0	2-0	1	2		4			6	8[1]		(10)	11				12	9[1]	3	5	7						11,808
25	S	8 "	1972	Fulham	H	1-1	2-1	1	2		4		5	7	10		8	11[1]				12	(9)	3		6[1]						21,878
26	S	22 "	1972	Preston North End	H	1-1	1-1	1	2		4		5	7	8[1]	12	(10)					11	9	3		6						20,948
27	S	29 "	1972	Burnley	A	0-0	0-1	1	2		4		5	7	10			(11)				6	9	3		8	12					13,572
28	S	12 Feb	1972	Millwall	H	1-0	2-2	1	2		4		6	7	10			11				8	9[1]	3				5			–[1]	33,999
29	S	19 "	1972	Cardiff City	A	0-0	0-0	1	2		4		6	8	10			11				7	(9)	3		12		5				17,706
30	S	4 Mar	1972	Birmingham City	A	0-2	0-4	1	2		4		(6)	7	10			12				11	9	3				5	8			40,899
31	S	11 "	1972	Sunderland	H	0-0	1-1	1	2		4	5	(6)	7	10			12				11	9	3					8[1]			21,815
32	W	15 "	1972	Hull City	H	0-0	2-0	1	2		4	5	6		10	12[1]		11[1]				7	(9)	3					8			30,342
33	S	18 "	1972	Portsmouth	A	0-2	1-2	1	2		4	5	6	7	10	12[1]		11					(9)	3					8			13,902
34	S	25 "	1972	Blackpool	H	4-1	5-1	1	2	3	4	5		7	10[2]			11[1]				6	9[1]						8[1]			23,540
35	S	1 Apr	1972	Charlton Athletic	A	1-0	2-0	1	2		4	5		7	10			11				6	9[1]	3					8[1]			12,567
36	M	3 "	1972	Queens Park Rangers	A	0-0	0-0	1	2		4	5	12	7	10			(11)				6	9	3					8			25,257
37	Tu	4 "	1972	Bristol City	H	1-0	2-2	1	2		4	5		7	10			11				6	9[1]	3					8[1]			34,914
38	S	8 "	1972	Sheffield Wednesday	H	0-0	1-0	1	2		4	5[1]		7	10	12		(11)				6	9	3					8			27,067
39	S	15 "	1972	Middlesbrough	A	0-0	0-0	1	2		4	5		7	10	12						6	(9)	3		11			8			14,279
40	S	22 "	1972	Swindon Town	H	1-0	1-0	1	2		4	5[1]		7	10			11				6	9	3					8			31,634
41	M	24 "	1972	Orient	A	0-0	2-1	1	2		4	5		7	10[1]			11[1]				6	9	(3)		12			8			15,530
42	S	29 "	1972	Watford	A	1-0	1-1	1	2		4[1]	5	12	7	10			11				6	9	(3)					8			22,421

F.A. CUP

NO.		DATE		OPPONENTS		V.	H-T	F-T	Keelan	Payne	Butler	Stringer	Forbes	Anderson	Livermore	Paddon	Howard	Silvester	Foggo	Darling	Sargent	O'Donnell	Briggs	Cross	Black	Govier	Hubbard	Grapes	Bell	Bone	Cheesley	Own Goals	ATTD.
1	S	15 Jan	1972	Hull City	(3rd Round)	H	0-2	0-3	1	2	3	4		6	7	10		(8)	11				12	9		5							22,044

FOOTBALL LEAGUE CUP

NO.		DATE		OPPONENTS		V.	H-T	F-T	Keelan	Payne	Butler	Stringer	Forbes	Anderson	Livermore	Paddon	Howard	Silvester	Foggo	Darling	Sargent	O'Donnell	Briggs	Cross	Black	Govier	Hubbard	Grapes	Bell	Bone	Cheesley	Own Goals	ATTD.
1	W	8 Sept	1971	Brighton & Hove Albion	(2nd Round)	H	1-0	2-0	1	2	3	4	5	6	9[1]	10	7	8	11[1]														11,810
2	W	6 Oct	1971	Carlisle United	(3rd Round)	H	1-0	4-1	1	2[1]	3	4	5	6	9	10[1]	7[2]	8	11														17,726
3	Tu	26 "	1971	Grimsby Town	(4th Round)	A	1-0	1-1	1	2	3	4	5	6	7	10[1]	9	8	11														22,408
4	W	3 Nov	1971	Grimsby Town	(Replay)	H	2-1	3-1	1	2[1]	3	4[1]		6	7	10	9[1]	8	11							5							27,531
5	W	17 "	1971	Chelsea	(5th Round)	H	0-0	0-1	1	2	3	4		5	7	10	9	8	11				(6)								12		35,927

1971–72 APPEARANCES & GOALS

	FOOTBALL LGE APPR.	S	GLS	F.A. CUP APPR.	S	GLS	LEAGUE CUP APPR.	S	GLS
Keelan Kevin	42	–	–	1	–	–	5	–	–
Payne Clive	42	–	–	1	–	–	5	–	2
Stringer Dave	42	–	4	1	–	–	5	–	1
Livermore Doug	41	–	–	1	–	–	5	–	1
Paddon Graham	40	–	8	1	–	–	5	–	2
Foggo Ken	38	2	13	1	–	–	5	–	1
Anderson Terry	32	2	–	1	–	–	5	–	–
Cross David	32	–	8	1	–	–			
Forbes Duncan	27	–	2				3	–	–
Silvester Peter	26	–	12	1	–	–	5	–	–
Butler Geoff	23	–	–	1	–	–	5	–	–
Briggs Max	21	6	–	–	1	–	1	–	–
Black Alan	19	1	–						
Bone Jimmy	13	–	4						
Howard Trevor	8	12	5				5	–	3
Hubbard Phil	6	2	1						
Darling Malcolm	4	–	1						
Bell Bobby	3	–	–						
Govier Steve	3	–	1	1	–	–	1	–	–
O'Donnell Neil	–	2	–						
Grapes Steve	–	1	–						
Sargent Gary	–	1	–						
Cheesley Paul							–	1	–
Own Goals			1						

DIVISION 2

1971–72	P	W	D	L	F	A	PTS
Norwich City	**42**	**21**	**15**	**6**	**60**	**36**	**57**
Birmingham City	42	19	18	5	60	31	56
Millwall	42	19	17	6	64	46	55
Queens Park Rangers	42	20	14	8	57	28	54
Sunderland	42	17	16	9	67	57	50
Blackpool	42	20	7	15	70	50	47
Burnley	42	20	6	16	70	55	46
Bristol City	42	18	10	14	61	49	46
Middlesbrough	42	19	8	15	50	48	46
Carlisle United	42	17	9	16	61	57	43
Swindon Town	42	15	12	15	47	47	42
Hull City	42	14	10	18	49	53	38
Luton Town	42	10	18	14	43	48	38
Sheffield Wednesday	42	13	12	17	51	58	38
Oxford United	42	12	14	16	43	55	38
Portsmouth	42	12	13	17	59	68	37
Orient	42	14	9	19	50	61	37
Preston North End	42	12	12	18	52	58	36
Cardiff City	42	10	14	18	56	69	34
Fulham	42	12	10	20	45	68	34
Charlton Athletic	42	12	9	21	55	77	33
Watford	42	5	9	28	24	75	19

1972–73 DIVISION 1

NO.		DATE		OPPONENTS	V.	H-T	F-T	Keelan Kevin	Payne Clive	Butler Geoff	Stringer Dave	Forbes Duncan	Briggs Max	Livermore Doug	Bone Jimmy	Cross David	Paddon Graham	Anderson Terry	O'Donnell Neil	Hubbard Phil	Foggo Ken	Self Glenn	Govier Steve	Blair Jim	Black Alan	Howard Trevor	Cheesley Paul	Hockey Trevor	Suggett Colin	Mellor Ian	Cawston Mervyn	Rollings Andy	Goodwin Steve	Own Goals	ATTD.
1	S	12 Aug	1972	Everton	H	1-0	1-1	1	2	3	4	5	6	⑦	8^1	9	10	11	12																25,851
2	Tu	15 "	1972	Ipswich Town	A	1-1	2-1	1	2	3	4	5	6	7	8^1	9	10	11^1																	29,828
3	S	19 "	1972	Manchester City	A	0-1	0-3	1	2	3	4	5	6	7	8	9	10	⑪		12															30,920
4	W	23 "	1972	Southampton	H	0-0	0-0	1	2	3	4	5	6	⑦	8	9	10	11			12														25,434
5	S	26 "	1972	Derby County	H	0-0	1-0	1	2	3	④	5	6	7	8	9	10^1	11				12													29,847
6	W	30 "	1972	Stoke City	H	2-0	2-0	1	2	3	4^1	5	6	7	8	9	10^1	11																	30,032
7	S	2 Sept	1972	Leeds United	A	0-2	0-2	1	2	3	4	5	6	7	8	9	10	⑪		12															34,261
8	S	9 "	1972	Sheffield United	H	0-0	1-1	1	2	3	4	5	6	7	8	9	10	⑪	12															$-^1$	22,228
9	S	16 "	1972	West Ham United	A	0-3	0-4	1	2	3		5	6	7	8	9	10	4	11																27,780
10	S	23 "	1972	Arsenal	H	2-1	3-2	1	2	3		5	6	7	8	⑨^1	10	11^2	12				4												32,170
11	S	30 "	1972	Crystal Palace	A	2-0	2-0	1	2	3		5	6	7	⑧^1	9	10^1	11					4	12											21,255
12	S	7 Oct	1972	Newcastle United	A	1-1	1-3	1	2	③		5	6	7	8	9^1	10	11					4	12											18,080
13	S	14 "	1972	Tottenham Hotspur	H	1-1	2-1	1	2		4	5	6	7	10	8^2	9	11							3										34,445
14	S	21 "	1972	Leicester City	A	0-0	2-1	1	2		4	5	6	7	8	9^1	10^1	11							3										19,787
15	S	28 "	1972	Liverpool	H	0-1	1-1	1	②	3	4	5	6	7	8	9	10	11^1								12									36,500
16	S	4 Nov	1972	Southampton	A	0-1	0-1	1	②	3	4	5	6	7	8	9	10	11								12									17,775
17	S	11 "	1972	Ipswich Town	H	0-0	0-0	1		2	4	5	6	7	8	9	10	11							3										34,640
18	S	18 "	1972	West Bromwich Albion	H	1-0	2-0	1		2	4^1	5	6	7	8	9	10^1	11							3										21,607
19	S	25 "	1972	Birmingham City	A	1-1	1-4	1		2	④		6	7	8	9	10	11	12				5		3^1										32,890
20	S	2 Dec	1972	Manchester United	H	0-1	0-2	1		2	4		6	7		9	10	⑪					5		3	12	8								35,770
21	S	9 "	1972	Chelsea	A	0-0	1-3	1		2	4		⑥	7	8^1	9	10	11					5		3	12									29,998
22	S	16 "	1972	Coventry City	A	0-1	1-3	1		2	4		6	7	8	9	10	⑪					5		3	12^1									19,819
23	S	23 "	1972	Wolverhampton Wanderers	H	1-0	1-1	1		2	4		6	7	8^1	9	10	11					5		3										19,320
24	Tu	26 "	1972	Arsenal	A	0-0	0-2	1		2	4		⑥	7	8		10	11					5		3	12	9								39,038
25	S	30 "	1972	Manchester City	H	1-0	1-1	1		2	④		6	7	8		10^1	11			12		5		3		9								23,900
26	S	6 Jan	1973	Derby County	A	0-1	0-1	1		2	4		6	7		9	10	11	12				5		3		⑧								27,850
27	S	20 "	1973	Leeds United	H	0-2	1-2	1	2	3	4	5	⑥	7		9^1	10	11	12							8									27,236
28	S	27 "	1973	Sheffield United	A	0-2	0-2	1	2	3	4	5	⑥	7	8	9	10	11								12									20,459
29	S	10 Feb	1973	West Ham United	H	0-1	0-1	1	2	3	4		6	7	⑧	9	10	5	12							11									32,286
30	S	24 "	1973	Newcastle United	H	0-1	0-1	1	2	3	4			7		9	10	12					⑤	8				6	11						26,41
31	W	7 Mar	1973	Coventry City	H	1-0	1-1	1	2	3	4	5		7		9^1		11						8		10		6							28,829
32	S	10 "	1973	Tottenham Hotspur	A	0-1	0-3	1	2	3	4	5		7		9	10							12		⑧		6		11					25,08
33	S	17 "	1973	Leicester City	H	1-1	1-1	1		2	4	5					10^1								3	7	9	6	8	11					25,299
34	S	24 "	1973	Liverpool	A	0-0	1-3	1		2	4	5	9				10								3	⑦	12	6	8	11^1					42,995
35	S	31 "	1973	Birmingham City	H	0-2	1-2	1		2	4^1	5	⑥			12	10	8							3			7	9	11					23,899
36	Tu	3 Apr	1973	Everton	A	2-0	2-2	1		2	4	5				9^2	10	7	12						3			⑥	8	11					21,806
37	S	7 "	1973	Manchester United	A	0-0	0-1	1		2	4	5				9	10	7							3			6	8	11					48,593
38	S	14 "	1973	Chelsea	H	1-0	1-0	1	2		4	5		7		9^1	10								3		12	6	⑧	11					24,42
39	S	21 "	1973	West Bromwich Albion	A	0-0	1-0	1	2		4	5		7		9^1	⑩								3		12	6	8	11					23,43
40	M	23 "	1973	Wolverhampton Wanderers	A	0-0	0-3	1	2		4	5	10	7											3	12	9	⑥	8	11					20,222
41	Tu	24 "	1973	Crystal Palace	H	1-1	2-1	1	2		4^1	5	10	7		9									3			6	8^1	11					36,68
42	S	28 "	1973	Stoke City	A	0-1	0-2	1	2		4	5	10	7		9									3			6	8	11					19,350

F.A. CUP

NO.		DATE		OPPONENTS	V.	H-T	F-T	Keelan Kevin	Payne Clive	Butler Geoff	Stringer Dave	Forbes Duncan	Briggs Max	Livermore Doug	Bone Jimmy	Cross David	Paddon Graham	Anderson Terry	O'Donnell Neil	Hubbard Phil	Foggo Ken	Self Glenn	Govier Steve	Blair Jim	Black Alan	Howard Trevor	Cheesley Paul	Hockey Trevor	Suggett Colin	Mellor Ian	Cawston Mervyn	Rollings Andy	Goodwin Steve	Own Goals	ATTD.
1	S	13 Jan	1973	Leeds United (3rd Round)	H	1-1	1-1	1		2	4	5	6		8	9^1	10	11							3	7									32,31
2	W	17 "	1973	Leeds United (Replay)	A	1-0	1-1	1		2	4	5	6		⑧	9^1	10	11							3	7	12								36,08
3	M	29 "	1973	Leeds United (2nd Replay)	V	0-4	0-5	1	2	3	4	5		7	8	9	10	11								6									33,27

V – PLAYED AT VILLA PARK

FOOTBALL LEAGUE CUP

NO.		DATE		OPPONENTS	V.	H-T	F-T	Keelan Kevin	Payne Clive	Butler Geoff	Stringer Dave	Forbes Duncan	Briggs Max	Livermore Doug	Bone Jimmy	Cross David	Paddon Graham	Anderson Terry	O'Donnell Neil	Hubbard Phil	Foggo Ken	Self Glenn	Govier Steve	Blair Jim	Black Alan	Howard Trevor	Cheesley Paul	Hockey Trevor	Suggett Colin	Mellor Ian	Cawston Mervyn	Rollings Andy	Goodwin Steve	Own Goals	ATTD.
1	W	6 Sept	1972	Leicester City (2nd Round)	H	1-0	2-1	1	2	3	4	5	6	7	8^2	9	10	11																	22,49
2	W	3 Oct	1972	Hull City (3rd Round)	A	1-0	2-1	1	2	3		5	6	7	⑧	9	10^2	11					4	12											11,52
3	W	1 Nov	1972	Stockport County (4th Round)	A	2-0	5-1	1	2	3	4^1	5	6		8^1	9^2	10	11								7^1									16,53
4	W	21 "	1972	Arsenal (5th Round)	A	2-0	3-0	1		2	4	⑤	6	7	8	9	10^3	11							3	12									37,67
5	W	13 Dec	1972	Chelsea (Semi-Final, 1st Leg)	A	2-0	2-0	1		2	4		6	7	8^1	9^1	10	⑪					5		3	12									31,77
6	W	3 Jan	1973	Chelsea (Semi-Final, 2nd Leg)	H	0-0	1-0	1		2	4		6	7		9	10	11					5^1		3		8								34,26
7	S	3 Mar	1973	Tottenham Hotspur (Wembley) (Final)	W	0-0	0-1	1	2	3	4	5	6	7		9	10	11						⑧		12									100,00

TEXACO CUP

NO.		DATE		OPPONENTS	V.	H-T	F-T	Keelan Kevin	Payne Clive	Butler Geoff	Stringer Dave	Forbes Duncan	Briggs Max	Livermore Doug	Bone Jimmy	Cross David	Paddon Graham	Anderson Terry	O'Donnell Neil	Hubbard Phil	Foggo Ken	Self Glenn	Govier Steve	Blair Jim	Black Alan	Howard Trevor	Cheesley Paul	Hockey Trevor	Suggett Colin	Mellor Ian	Cawston Mervyn	Rollings Andy	Goodwin Steve	Own Goals	ATTD.
1	W	13 Sept	1972	Dundee (1st Round, 1st Leg)	A	0-0	1-2			2			6		8^1		10	11	7				5		3		9				1	4			8,00
2	W	27 "	1972	Dundee (1st Round, 2nd Leg)	H	1-0	2-0	1	2	3		5	6	7	8^1	9		11	10				4											$-^1$	18,33
3	Tu	24 Oct	1972	Leicester City (2nd Round, 1st Leg)	A	0-2	0-2	1	2		④	5	6	7	8	9	10	11						12	3										9,37
4	W	8 Nov	1972	Leicester City * (2nd Round, 2nd Leg)	H	2-0	2-0	1		2	4	5^1	6	7	8	9	10	⑪^1							3		12								18,51
5	W	14 Mar	1973	Motherwell (Semi-Final, 1st Leg)	H	2-0	2-0	1		2	4	5	7				10								3	8	9			11^2			6		18,82
6	W	21 "	1973	Motherwell (Semi-Final, 2nd Leg)	A	2-2	2-3	1		2	4	5	12			8	10								3	7	⑨			11^1			6	$-^1$	9,81
7	F	4 May	1973	Ipswich Town (Final, 1st Leg)	A	0-1	1-2	1	2^1		4	5	6	7		9	10								3	⑧	12			11					29,69
8	M	7 May	1973	Ipswich Town (Final, 2nd Leg)	H	0-1	1-2	1	2		4	5	6	7		9^1		⑩						8	3		12			11					35,79

* MATCH FINISHED 2–2, NORWICH CITY WON ON PENALTIES AFTER EXTRA TIME

1972–73 APPEARANCES & GOALS

	FOOTBALL LGE			F.A. CUP			LEAGUE CUP			TEXACO CUP		
	APPR.	S	GLS	APPR.	S	GLS	APPR.	S	GLS	APPR.	S	GLS
Keelan Kevin	42	–	–	3	–	–	7	–	–	7	–	–
Paddon Graham	38	–	7	3	–	–	7	–	5	6	–	–
Stringer Dave	38	–	4	3	–	–	6	–	1	6	–	–
Livermore Doug	37	–	–	1	–	–	6	–	–	5	–	–
Cross David	36	1	11	3	–	2	7	–	3	6	–	1
Butler Geoff	35	–	–	3	–	–	7	–	–	5	–	–
Briggs Max	34	–	–	2	–	–	7	–	–	7	1	–
Anderson Terry	33	1	4	3	–	–	7	–	–	5	–	1
Forbes Duncan	32	–	–	3	–	–	5	–	–	7	–	1
Payne Clive	27	–	–	1	–	–	4	–	–	4	–	1
Bone Jimmy	26	–	5	3	–	–	5	–	4	4	–	2
Black Alan	22	–	1	2	–	–	3	–	–	7	–	–
Hockey Trevor	13	–	–									
Govier Steve	12	–	–				3	–	1	2	–	–
Mellor Ian	11	–	1							4	–	3
Suggett Colin	11	–	1									
Cheesley Paul	6	3	–	–	1	–	1	–	–	3	3	–
Howard Trevor	6	8	1	3	–	–	1	3	1	3	–	–
Blair Jim	2	3	–				1	1	–	1	1	–
O'Donnell Neil	1	8	–							2	–	–
Foggo Ken	–	2	–									
Hubbard Phil	–	2	–									
Self Glenn	–	1	–									
Goodwin Steve										2	–	–
Cawston Mervyn										1	–	–
Rollings Andy										1	–	–
Own Goals			1									2

DIVISION 1

1972–73	P	W	D	L	F	A	PTS
Liverpool	42	25	10	7	72	42	60
Arsenal	42	23	11	8	57	43	57
Leeds United	42	21	11	10	71	45	53
Ipswich Town	42	17	14	11	55	45	48
Wolverhampton Wanderers	42	18	11	13	66	54	47
West Ham United	42	17	12	13	67	53	46
Derby County	42	19	8	15	56	54	46
Tottenham Hotspur	42	16	13	13	58	48	45
Newcastle United	42	16	13	13	60	51	45
Birmingham City	42	15	12	15	53	54	42
Manchester City	42	15	11	16	57	60	41
Chelsea	42	13	14	15	49	51	40
Southampton	42	11	18	13	47	52	40
Sheffield United	42	15	10	17	51	59	40
Stoke City	42	14	10	18	61	56	38
Leicester City	42	10	17	15	40	46	37
Everton	42	13	11	18	41	49	37
Manchester United	42	12	13	17	44	60	37
Coventry City	42	13	9	20	40	55	35
Norwich City	**42**	**11**	**10**	**21**	**36**	**63**	**32**
Crystal Palace	42	9	12	21	41	58	30
West Bromwich Albion	42	9	10	23	38	62	28

1973–74 DIVISION 1

NO.		DATE			OPPONENTS	V.	H-T	F-T	Keelan Kevin	Prophett Colin	Black Alan	Stringer Dave	Govier Steve	Briggs Max	Anderson Terry	Suggett Colin	Cross David	Paddon Graham	Mellor Ian	Rollings Andy	O'Donnell Neil	Kellock Billy	Forbes Duncan	Grapes Steve	Howard Trevor	Livermore Doug	Wilson Les	Payne Clive	Cheesley Paul	Butler Geoff	MacDougall Ted	Machin Mel	Benson John	Steele Billy	Blair Jim	Silvester Peter	Sissons John	Boyer Phil	Kent Paul	Davies Ian	Cawston Mervyn	Goodwin Steve	Own Goals	ATTD.
1	S	25	Aug	1973	Wolverhampton Wanderers	A	1-1	1-3	1	2	3	4	5	6	7	8[1]	9	10	11																									22,744
2	W	29	"	1973	Queens Park Rangers	H	0-0	0-0	1	2	3	4		6	(7)	8	9	10	11	5	12																							24,285
3	S	1	Sept	1973	West Ham United	H	1-1	2-2	1	2	3	4		6	7	8	9	10[1]	11[1]	5																								25,378
4	Tu	4	"	1973	Southampton	A	2-1	2-2	1	2	3	4		6	7	8	9[1]	(10)	11	5		12																					–[1]	17,658
5	S	8	"	1973	Manchester City	A	0-2	1-2	1	2	3	4		6	7	8[1]	9		11				5	(10)	12																			31,209
6	W	12	"	1973	Southampton	H	0-0	2-0	1	2	3	4[1]		6	7	8	9[1]		11				5		10																			24,747
7	S	15	"	1973	Arsenal	H	0-3	0-4	1	(2)	3	4		6	10	8	9		11				5		12	7																		29,076
8	S	22	"	1973	Sheffield United	A	0-1	0-1	1		3	4		(6)		8	9	10	11		12		5			7	2																	19,974
9	S	29	"	1973	Leeds United	H	0-1	0-1	1	2		4		6		8	9	10	11				5			7	(3)	12																31,798
10	S	6	Oct	1973	Derby County	A	1-1	1-1	1	2		4		6		8[1]	9	10	11				5			7		3																25,984
11	S	13	"	1973	Coventry City	H	0-0	0-0	1	2		4		6		8	9	10	11				5			7		3																22,575
12	S	20	"	1973	Tottenham Hotspur	H	0-1	1-1	1	2	3	4		6		12	9	10	11				5			7[1]			(8)															24,819
13	F	26	"	1973	Chelsea	A	0-2	0-3	1	2	3	4		6		8	9	10	11				5		12	(7)																		21,953
14	S	3	Nov	1973	Leicester City	H	1-0	1-0	1			4		6	12	8	9	10			11		5		7		3	(2)															–[1]	20,565
15	S	10	"	1973	Stoke City	A	0-1	0-2	1	2	3	4		(6)		8	9	10	12				5		11	7																		15,563
16	S	17	"	1973	Everton	H	0-0	1-3	1	2		4				8		10	11				5		6	7	3	12	(9)														–[1]	19,825
17	S	24	"	1973	Manchester United	A	0-0	0-0	1			4		6		8		10	9		11		5		7		3			2														36,338
18	S	8	Dec	1973	Burnley	A	0-0	0-1	1	6		4		7		10			(11)		8		5		12		3			2	9													13,231
19	S	15	"	1973	Liverpool	H	1-1	1-1	1	6		4		11	7	9							5		12				10[1]		8	2	(3)											20,184
20	S	22	"	1973	Leeds United	A	0-0	0-1	1	3		4		11		9					12		5	7	6				(10)		8	2												34,747
21	W	26	"	1973	Ipswich Town	H	1-0	1-2	1	3		4		10		9							5	7	11					2	8[1]			6										29,637
22	S	29	"	1973	Manchester City	H	1-1	1-1	1	2		4	5	6		9								7	12						(8)[1]		3	11	10									23,978
23	Tu	1	Jan	1974	West Ham United	A	0-2	2-4	1	(6)		4	3	10		9				5				7	2						8[2]					12	11							32,259
24	S	12	"	1974	Arsenal	A	0-1	0-2	1			4		6		9			10				5	7							8	2	3				11							22,084
25	S	19	"	1974	Wolverhampton Wanderers	H	1-0	1-1	1	12		4				9							5	7	(6)						8[1]	2	3			10	11							19,404
26	S	2	Feb	1974	Liverpool	A	0-0	0-1	1	5		4				9									6						8	2	3	7		10	11							31,742
27	Tu	5	"	1974	Queens Park Rangers	A	2-0	2-1	1	5		4		10		9									6[1]						8	2	3[1]	7			11							12,427
28	S	9	"	1974	Sheffield United	H	2-0	2-1	1	5		4[1]				9								11	6						8[1]	2	3	7				10						21,651
29	S	23	"	1974	Derby County	H	1-3	2-4	1	5		4[1]				9									6[1]						8	2	3	7			11	10						25,175
30	Tu	26	"	1974	Coventry City	A	0-1	0-1	1	7		4				9							5		6						8	2	3				11	10						16,420
31	S	2	Mar	1974	Ipswich Town	A	0-0	1-1	1	7		4				9						12	5		6						8	2	(3)				11	10[1]						25,004
32	S	9	"	1974	Chelsea	H	0-1	2-2	1	7		4[1]				9							5		6						8[1]	2	3				11	10						19,357
33	S	16	"	1974	Tottenham Hotspur	A	0-0	0-0	1	7		4				9							5		6						8	2	3				11	10						18,466
34	W	20	"	1974	Birmingham City	H	1-0	2-1	1	6		4				9[1]							5		7						8	2	3				11	10[1]						18,309
35	S	23	"	1974	Stoke City	H	0-0	4-0	1	7		4				9[1]							5	12	(6)						8[1]	2	3				11[2]	10						19,365
36	S	6	Apr	1974	Manchester United	H	0-0	0-2	1	3		4				9							5	7	6						8	(2)					11	10	12					27,899
37	S	13	"	1974	Everton	A	0-0	1-4	1	2		4				9						11	5	7	6						8[1]		3					10						27,967
38	M	15	"	1974	Newcastle United	A	0-0	0-0	1			4				9							5	12	(6)					2	8		3	7				10	11					29,202
39	W	17	"	1974	Newcastle United	H	0-0	1-1	1	3		4				(9)							5	7							8[1]		2	6			11	10	12					17,673
40	S	20	"	1974	Burnley	H	1-0	1-0	1			4				9							5	6						2	8[1]		3	7			11	10						17,782
41	S	27	"	1974	Birmingham City	A	1-2	1-2	1			4[1]				9							5	(6)						2	8		3	7			11	10		12				44,182
42	M	29	"	1974	Leicester City	A	0-0	0-3	1	2		4				9							5	7							8		3	6			11	10						16,786

F.A. CUP

NO.		DATE			OPPONENTS	V.	H-T	F-T	Keelan Kevin	Prophett Colin	Black Alan	Stringer Dave	Govier Steve	Briggs Max	Anderson Terry	Suggett Colin	Cross David	Paddon Graham	Mellor Ian	Rollings Andy	O'Donnell Neil	Kellock Billy	Forbes Duncan	Grapes Steve	Howard Trevor	Livermore Doug	Wilson Les	Payne Clive	Cheesley Paul	Butler Geoff	MacDougall Ted	Machin Mel	Benson John	Steele Billy	Blair Jim	Silvester Peter	Sissons John	Boyer Phil	Kent Paul	Davies Ian	Cawston Mervyn	Goodwin Steve	Own Goals	ATTD.
1	S	5	Jan	1974	Arsenal (3rd Round)	H	0-1	0-1	1	3		4		6		9			11				5	7	10					2	8													12,500

FOOTBALL LEAGUE CUP

NO.		DATE			OPPONENTS	V.	H-T	F-T	Keelan Kevin	Prophett Colin	Black Alan	Stringer Dave	Govier Steve	Briggs Max	Anderson Terry	Suggett Colin	Cross David	Paddon Graham	Mellor Ian	Rollings Andy	O'Donnell Neil	Kellock Billy	Forbes Duncan	Grapes Steve	Howard Trevor	Livermore Doug	Wilson Les	Payne Clive	Cheesley Paul	Butler Geoff	MacDougall Ted	Machin Mel	Benson John	Steele Billy	Blair Jim	Silvester Peter	Sissons John	Boyer Phil	Kent Paul	Davies Ian	Cawston Mervyn	Goodwin Steve	Own Goals	ATTD.
1	W	10	Oct	1973	Wrexham (2nd Round)	H	3-0	6-2	1	2		4		6			9[2]	10	11[2]			8[1]	5			7[1]		3																10,937
2	Tu	30	"	1973	Everton (3rd Round)	A	1-0	1-0	1			4		(6)		8	9[1]	10	12		11		5		7		3	2																22,046
3	W	21	Nov	1973	Southampton (4th Round)	A	1-0	2-0	1			4		6	12	8[1]			9[1]		11		5		7	(10)	3			2														14,415
4	W	19	Dec	1973	Millwall (5th Round)	A	1-0	1-1	1	(3)		4		10	12	8					6		5	7	11[1]				9	2														10,708
5	W	16	Jan	1974	Millwall (Replay)	H	1-0	2-1	1	3		4				9[1]			10		6		5	7						2						8	11[1]							7,737
6	W	23	"	1974	Wolverhampton Wanderers (S.F. 1st Leg)	H	0-0	1-1	1	3		4				9			10[1]				5		6					2				7		8	11							20,517
7	S	26	"	1974	Wolverhampton Wanderers (S.F. 2nd Leg)	A	0-0	0-1	1	3		4				9			10				5		6					2				7		8	11							32,605

TEXACO CUP

NO.		DATE			OPPONENTS	V.	H-T	F-T	Keelan Kevin	Prophett Colin	Black Alan	Stringer Dave	Govier Steve	Briggs Max	Anderson Terry	Suggett Colin	Cross David	Paddon Graham	Mellor Ian	Rollings Andy	O'Donnell Neil	Kellock Billy	Forbes Duncan	Grapes Steve	Howard Trevor	Livermore Doug	Wilson Les	Payne Clive	Cheesley Paul	Butler Geoff	MacDougall Ted	Machin Mel	Benson John	Steele Billy	Blair Jim	Silvester Peter	Sissons John	Boyer Phil	Kent Paul	Davies Ian	Cawston Mervyn	Goodwin Steve	Own Goals	ATTD.
1	W	19	Sept	1973	St. Johnstone (1st Round, 1st Leg)	A	1-0	2-0					4					10		5	11[1]				9	7	2	3							8[1]						1	6		3,700
2	W	3	Oct	1973	St. Johnstone (1st Round, 2nd Leg)	H	0-0	1-0		2		4		6		8[1]	9	10	11				5			7		3													1			11,028
3	Tu	23	"	1973	Motherwell (2nd Round, 1st Leg)	H	0-0	2-0	1	2	3	4		6		8	9	10[1]	11				5[1]			7																		10,670
4	Tu	6	Nov	1973	Motherwell (2nd Round, 2nd Leg)	A	1-0	1-0	1	2		4		6	12	8	9	10[1]			(11)		5		7		3																	7,018
5	Tu	27	"	1973	Burnley (Semi-Final, 1st Leg)	A	0-1	0-2	1	3		4		6		8		10	9		11		5		7					2														4,848
6	W	12	Dec	1973	Burnley (Semi-Final, 2nd Leg)	H	1-0	2-3	1	6		4		11	7	9				5							3		10	2	8[2]													11,791

1973–74 APPEARANCES & GOALS

	FOOTBALL LGE APPR.	S	GLS	F.A. CUP APPR.	S	GLS	LEAGUE CUP APPR.	S	GLS	TEXACO CUP APPR.	S	GLS
Keelan Kevin	42	–	–	1	–	–	7	–	–	4	–	–
Stringer Dave	42	–	5	1	–	–	7	–	–	5	–	–
Suggett Colin	41	1	5	1	–	–	6	–	2	5	–	1
Prophett Colin	34	1	–	1	–	–	5	–	–	5	–	–
Forbes Duncan	32	–	–	1	–	–	7	–	–	4	–	1
MacDougall Ted	25	–	11	1	–	–				1	–	2
Briggs Max	24	–	–	1	–	–	4	–	–	5	–	–
Howard Trevor	22	6	2	1	–	–	5	–	1	3	–	–
Benson John	20	–	1									
Mellor Ian	17	1	1	1	–	–	5	1	4	3	–	–
Sissons John	17	–	2				3	–	1			
Boyer Phil	15	–	2									
Cross David	15	–	2				2	–	3	3	–	–
Machin Mel	15	–	–									
Grapes Steve	14	2	–	1	–	–	2	–	–			
Paddon Graham	14	–	1				2	–	–	5	–	2
Black Alan	11	–	–							1	–	–
Steele Billy	11	–	–				2	–	–			
Livermore Doug	9	–	1				2	–	1	3	–	–
Anderson Terry	8	1	–				–	2	–	1	1	–
Butler Geoff	6	–	–	1	–	–	5	–	–	2	–	–
Wilson Les	6	–	–				2	–	–	3	–	–
Cheesley Paul	4	–	1				1	–	–	1	–	–
Rollings Andy	4	–	–							2	–	–
Govier Steve	3	–	–							1	–	–
O'Donnell Neil	3	3	–				4	–	–	3	–	1
Payne Clive	3	2	–				2	–	–	2	–	–
Silvester Peter	2	1	–				3	–	–			
Kellock Billy	1	2	–				1	–	1			
Kent Paul	1	2	–									
Blair Jim	1	–	–							1	–	1
Davies Ian	–	1	–									
Cawston Mervyn										2	–	–
Goodwin Steve										1	–	–
Own Goals			3									

DIVISION 1

1973–74	P	W	D	L	F	A	PTS
Leeds United	42	24	14	4	66	31	62
Liverpool	42	22	13	7	52	31	57
Derby County	42	17	14	11	52	42	48
Ipswich Town	42	18	11	13	67	58	47
Stoke City	42	15	16	11	54	42	46
Burnley	42	16	14	12	56	53	46
Everton	42	16	12	14	50	48	44
Queens Park Rangers	42	13	17	12	56	52	43
Leicester City	42	13	16	13	51	41	42
Arsenal	42	14	14	14	49	51	42
Tottenham Hotspur	42	14	14	14	45	50	42
Wolverhampton Wanderers	42	13	15	14	49	49	41
Sheffield United	42	14	12	16	44	49	40
Manchester City	42	14	12	16	39	46	40
Newcastle United	42	13	12	17	49	48	38
Coventry City	42	14	10	18	43	54	38
Chelsea	42	12	13	17	56	60	37
West Ham United	42	11	15	16	55	60	37
Birmingham City	42	12	13	17	52	64	37
Southampton	42	11	14	17	47	68	36
Manchester United	42	10	12	20	38	48	32
Norwich City	**42**	**7**	**15**	**20**	**37**	**62**	**29**

1974–75 DIVISION 2

NO.		DATE	OPPONENTS	V.	H-T	F-T	Keelan Kevin	Machin Mel	Sullivan Colin	Morris Peter	Forbes Duncan	Stringer Dave	Grapes Steve	MacDougall Ted	Boyer Phil	Suggett Colin	Powell Tony	Benson John	Hansbury Roger	Butler Geoff	Steele Billy	Livermore Doug	Miller John	Goodwin Steve	McGuire Mick	Peters Martin	Howard Trevor	Prophett Colin	Sissons John	Kent Paul	ATTD.
1	S	17 Aug 1974	Blackpool	H	0-0	2-1	1	2	3	4	5	6	7	8^1	9	10	11^1														17,841
2	W	21 " 1974	Southampton	H	0-0	1-0	1	2	3	4	5	6	(7)^1	8	9	10	11	12													21,650
3	S	24 " 1974	Aston Villa	A	0-0	1-1	1	2	3	4	5	6	7	8	9	10^1	11														23,297
4	Tu	27 " 1974	Southampton	A	0-0	1-1	1	2	3	4	5	6	7	8	9	10^1	11														16,367
5	S	31 " 1974	Sheffield Wednesday	H	0-1	1-1	1	2	3	4	5	6	7^1	8	9	10	11														20,262
6	S	7 Sept 1974	Hull City	A	0-0	0-0	1	2	3	4	5	6		8	9	10	11	7													5,436
7	S	14 " 1974	Notts County	H	1-0	3-0	1	7	3^1	4	5	6		8^1	9^1	10	11	2													17,362
8	S	21 " 1974	Fulham	A	0-2	0-4			3	4	5	6	7	8	9	10	11	2	1												9,414
9	S	24 " 1974	Sunderland	A	0-0	0-0	1		3	4	5	6		8	9	10	11	2		(7)	12										27,737
10	W	28 " 1974	Manchester United	H	1-0	2-0	1	7	3	4	5	6		8^2	9	10	11			2											24,586
11	S	5 Oct 1974	Millwall	H	1-0	2-0	1	(7)	3	4		6		8^1	9	10	11^1	5		2		12									18,920
12	S	12 " 1974	Nottingham Forest	A	0-1	3-1	1	7^3	3	4	5	6		8	9	10	11			2											13,613
13	S	19 " 1974	Portsmouth	H	1-0	2-0	1	7	3	4	5	6^1		8	9^1	10	11			2											20,543
14	S	26 " 1974	Orient	A	3-0	3-0	1		3	4	5	6		8^1	9^2	10	11			2			7								8,708
15	S	2 Nov 1974	West Bromwich Albion	A	0-1	1-1	1		3	4	5	6		8^1	9	10	11	2					7								12,177
16	S	9 " 1974	Bristol Rovers	H	0-1	0-1	1		3	4	5	6		8	9	10	11	2					7								20,858
17	S	16 " 1974	Oldham Athletic	A	1-0	2-2	1	2	3	4	5	(6)		8	9^2	10	11			12			7								12,004
18	S	23 " 1974	Bolton Wanderers	H	1-0	2-0		2	3	4	5	6		8		10	11		1				7^2	9							18,268
19	S	30 " 1974	York City	A	0-1	0-1		11	3	4	5	6		8		10		2	1				7	9							7,456
20	S	7 Dec 1974	Cardiff City	H	1-0	1-1		2	3	4	5	6	12	8	9	10	(11)		1				7^1								17,337
21	S	14 " 1974	Blackpool	A	0-2	1-2	1	2	3	4	5	6		8	9^1	10	11						7								6,683
22	S	21 " 1974	Bristol City	H	1-2	3-2	1	2	3	4	5	6		8	9^2	10^1	(11)				12		7								16,981
23	Th	26 " 1974	Notts County	A	0-0	1-1	1	2	3	4	5	6		8^1	9	10					11		7								13,977
24	S	28 " 1974	Oxford United	H	1-0	1-0	1	2	3	4	5	6		8	9^1	10	11						7								23,252
25	S	11 Jan 1975	Cardiff City	A	0-2	1-2	1	7	3	4	5	6		8^1	9	10	11	2													11,637
26	S	18 " 1975	York City	H	0-2	2-3	1	2	3	4	5	6^1		8	9	10^1	11								7						22,053
27	S	25 " 1975	Oxford United	A	1-1	1-2	1	2	3	4	5	6		8^1	9		11						7		10						8,410
28	S	1 Feb 1975	Bristol Rovers	A	1-0	2-0	1	2	3			6	12	8^1	9	(11)^1	5				7	4			10						12,730
29	S	8 " 1975	West Bromwich Albion	H	1-1	3-2	1	2	3			6		8^2	9	10	5				12	(4)	7		11^1						34,160
30	S	15 " 1975	Bolton Wanderers	A	0-0	0-0	1		3	2	5	6		8	9	10	11				7				4						15,506
31	S	22 " 1975	Oldham Athletic	H	0-0	1-0	1		3	2	5	6		8	9^1	10	11				12		(7)		4						20,528
32	S	8 Mar 1975	Sunderland	H	0-0	0-0	1			4	5	6		8	9	10	3			2	7				11						29,026
33	S	15 " 1975	Manchester United	A	0-0	1-1	1			4	5	6		8^1	9	10	3			2					7	11					56,202
34	S	22 " 1975	Hull City	H	0-0	1-0	1			4	5	6		8^1	9	10	3			2					7	11					20,724
35	S	29 " 1975	Bristol City	A	1-0	1-0	1			4	5	6		8	9	10^1	3			2					7	11					22,204
36	M	31 " 1975	Fulham	H	1-1	1-2	1			4	5^1	6		8	9	10	3			(2)	12				7	11					29,512
37	S	5 Apr 1975	Orient	H	1-0	2-0	1			4	5	6		8^1	9^1	10	3			2					7	11					17,559
38	Tu	8 " 1975	Sheffield Wednesday	A	0-0	1-0	1		12	4	5	6		8^1	9	10	(3)			2					7	11					7,483
39	S	12 " 1975	Millwall	A	0-1	1-1	1		3	4	5	6		8	9	10	7			2^1						11					10,565
40	S	19 " 1975	Nottingham Forest	H	1-0	3-0	1		3	4	5			8	9^2	10	6			2					7	11^1					24,302
41	S	26 " 1975	Portsmouth	A	1-0	3-0	1		3	4	5			8	9^1	10	6			2					7^1	11^1					18,977
42	S	30 " 1975	Aston Villa	H	1-2	1-4	1		3	4	5			8	9^1	10	6			2					7	11					35,943

F.A. CUP

NO.		DATE	OPPONENTS	V.	H-T	F-T	Keelan Kevin	Machin Mel	Sullivan Colin	Morris Peter	Forbes Duncan	Stringer Dave	Grapes Steve	MacDougall Ted	Boyer Phil	Suggett Colin	Powell Tony	Benson John	Hansbury Roger	Butler Geoff	Steele Billy	Livermore Doug	Miller John	Goodwin Steve	McGuire Mick	Peters Martin	Howard Trevor	Prophett Colin	Sissons John	Kent Paul	ATTD.
1	S	4 Jan 1975	Coventry City (3rd Round)	A	0-2	0-2	1	2	3	4	5	6		8	9	10		7				11									19,252

FOOTBALL LEAGUE CUP

NO.		DATE	OPPONENTS	V.	H-T	F-T	Keelan Kevin	Machin Mel	Sullivan Colin	Morris Peter	Forbes Duncan	Stringer Dave	Grapes Steve	MacDougall Ted	Boyer Phil	Suggett Colin	Powell Tony	Benson John	Hansbury Roger	Butler Geoff	Steele Billy	Livermore Doug	Miller John	Goodwin Steve	McGuire Mick	Peters Martin	Howard Trevor	Prophett Colin	Sissons John	Kent Paul	ATTD.
1	Tu	10 Sept 1974	Bolton Wanderers (2nd Round)	A	0-0	0-0	1	2	3	4	5	6		8	9	10	11	7													11,205
2	Tu	17 " 1974	Bolton Wanderers (Replay)	H	1-1	3-1		(2)	3	4	5	6^1	12	8^1	9^1	10	11	7	1												14,376
3	W	9 Oct 1974	West Bromwich Albion (3rd Round)	A	1-1	1-1	1		3	4		6	7	8	9^1	10	11	5		2											11,63
4	W	16 " 1974	West Bromwich Albion (Replay*)	H	0-0	2-0	1	7	3	4	5	6		8^1	9^1	10	11			2											18,21
5	Tu	12 Nov 1974	Sheffield United (4th Round)	A	1-1	2-2	1	12	3	4	5	6		8^2	9	10	11			(2)			7								17,09
6	W	27 " 1974	Sheffield United (Replay)	H	0-0	2-1		11	3	4	5	6		8		10		12	1	(2)			7	9^2							19,509
7	W	4 Dec 1974	Ipswich Town (5th Round)	H	1-1	1-1	1	2	3	4	5	6	12	8	9	10^1	11						(7)								34,73
8	Tu	10 " 1974	Ipswich Town (Replay)	A	1-1	2-1	1	2	3	4	5	6		8	9	10	11						7^2								29,24
9	W	15 Jan 1975	Manchester United (Semi-Final, 1st Leg)	A	1-0	2-2	1	2	3	4	5	6		8^1	9	10	11^1	7													58,010
10	W	22 " 1975	Manchester United (Semi-Final, 2nd Leg)	H	0-0	1-0	1	2	3	4	5	6		8	9	10^1	11						7								31,62
11	S	1 Mar 1975	Aston Villa (Final)	W	0-0	0-1	1	2	3	4	5	6		8	9	10	11						7								100,000

W – PLAYED AT WEMBLEY   * – AFTER EXTRA TIME

TEXACO CUP

NO.		DATE	OPPONENTS	V.	H-T	F-T	Keelan Kevin	Machin Mel	Sullivan Colin	Morris Peter	Forbes Duncan	Stringer Dave	Grapes Steve	MacDougall Ted	Boyer Phil	Suggett Colin	Powell Tony	Benson John	Hansbury Roger	Butler Geoff	Steele Billy	Livermore Doug	Miller John	Goodwin Steve	McGuire Mick	Peters Martin	Howard Trevor	Prophett Colin	Sissons John	Kent Paul	ATTD.
1	S	3 Aug 1974	Peterborough United (Group Match)	A	0-0	2-1	1	2	3	6	5	4	7	8^2	10	9											11				12,16
2	Tu	6 " 1974	West Bromwich Albion (Group Match)	A	1-2	1-5	1			6		4	7	8	10^1	9		(3)			11						2	5	12		5,39
3	S	10 " 1974	Birmingham City (Group Match)	A	0-2	1-3	1			4	5	6	7	(8)	9^1						12			11			10	2		3	14,84

1974–75 APPEARANCES & GOALS

	FOOTBALL LGE			F.A. CUP			LEAGUE CUP			TEXACO CUP		
	APPR.	S	GLS	APPR.	S	GLS	APPR.	S	GLS	APPR.	S	GLS
MacDougall Ted	42	–	17	1	–	–	11	–	5	3	–	2
Suggett Colin	41	–	6	1	–	–	11	–	2	2	–	–
Boyer Phil	40	–	16	1	–	–	10	–	3	3	–	2
Morris Peter	40	–	–	1	–	–	11	–	–	3	–	–
Powell Tony	40	–	2				10	–	1			
Forbes Duncan	39	–	1	1	–	–	10	–	–	2	–	–
Stringer Dave	39	–	2	1	–	–	11	–	1	3	–	–
Keelan Kevin	38	–	–	1	–	–	9	–	–	3	–	–
Sullivan Colin	35	1	1	1	–	–	11	–	–	1	–	–
Machin Mel	24	–	3	1	–	–	9	1	–	1	–	–
Butler Geoff	17	1	1				4	–	–			
McGuire Mick	16	–	2									
Miller John	14	–	3				6	–	2			
Peters Martin	10	–	2									
Benson John	9	1	–	1	–	–	4	1	–	1	–	–
Grapes Steve	6	2	2				1	2	–	3	–	–
Hansbury Roger	4	–	–				2	–	–			
Steele Billy	4	5	–							1	1	–
Livermore Doug	2	1	–	1	–	–						
Goodwin Steve	2	–	–				1	–	2	1	–	–
Howard Trevor										3	–	–
Prophett Colin										2	–	–
Kent Paul										1	–	–
Sissons John										–	1	–

DIVISION 2

1974–75	P	W	D	L	F	A	PTS
Manchester United	42	26	9	7	66	30	61
Aston Villa	42	25	8	9	79	32	58
Norwich City	**42**	**20**	**13**	**9**	**58**	**37**	**53**
Sunderland	42	19	13	10	65	35	51
Bristol City	42	21	8	13	47	33	50
West Bromwich Albion	42	18	9	15	54	42	45
Blackpool	42	14	17	11	38	33	45
Hull City	42	15	14	13	40	53	44
Fulham	42	13	16	13	44	39	42
Bolton Wanderers	42	15	12	15	45	41	42
Oxford United	42	15	12	15	41	51	42
Orient	42	11	20	11	28	39	42
Southampton	42	15	11	16	53	54	41
Notts County	42	12	16	14	49	59	40
York City	42	14	10	18	51	55	38
Nottingham Forest	42	12	14	16	43	55	38
Portsmouth	42	12	13	17	44	54	37
Oldham Athletic	42	10	15	17	40	48	35
Bristol Rovers	42	12	11	19	42	64	35
Millwall	42	10	12	20	44	56	32
Cardiff City	42	9	14	19	36	62	32
Sheffield Wednesday	42	5	11	26	29	64	21

1975–76 DIVISION 1

NO.	DATE			OPPONENTS	V.	H-T	F-T	Keelan Kevin	Machin Mel	Sullivan Colin	Morris Peter	Forbes Duncan	Powell Tony	Grapes Steve	MacDougall Ted	Peters Martin	Suggett Colin	McGuire Mick	Boyer Phil	Butler Geoff	Stringer Dave	Steele Billy	Miller John	Jones David	Wilson Paul	Davids Neil	Bond Kevin	Own Goals	ATTD.
1	S	16 Aug	1975	Manchester City	A	0-0	0-3	1	2	3	4	5	6	7	8	9	10	11											29,103
2	W	20 "	1975	Leeds United	H	0-0	1-1	1	2	3	4	5	6	7	8	9	10	11										$–^{1}$	24,709
3	S	23 "	1975	Aston Villa	H	4-1	5-3	1	2	3	4	5^{1}	6	7^{1}	8^{3}	9	10	11											21,195
4	Tu	26 "	1975	Arsenal	A	1-1	1-2	1	2	3	4	5	6	7	8	9^{1}	10		11										22,613
5	S	30 "	1975	Tottenham Hotspur	A	0-1	2-2	1	2	3	4	5	6	7	8^{1}	11	10		9^{1}										23,145
6	S	6 Sept	1975	Everton	H	2-0	4-2	1	2	3	4	5	6	7	10^{3}	11	8^{1}		9										19,672
7	S	13 "	1975	Burnley	A	1-3	4-4	1	2		4	5	6		8^{2}	11^{1}	⑩	7	9^{1}	3	12								15,496
8	S	20 "	1975	Leicester City	H	1-0	2-0	1	2		4	5	6		8^{2}	11	10	7	9	3									22,266
9	Tu	23 "	1975	Ipswich Town	A	0-0	0-2	1	2		4	5	6		⑧	11	10	7	9	3	12								34,825
10	S	27 "	1975	Sheffield United	A	0-0	1-0	1	2		4	5	6		8^{1}	11	10	12	9	3		⑦							20,624
11	S	4 Oct	1975	Stoke City	H	0-0	0-1	1	2	3		5	6		8	11	10	4	9			12	⑦						21,784
12	S	11 "	1975	Derby County	H	0-0	0-0	1	2			5	6	7	8	11		4	9	3		10							22,537
13	S	18 "	1975	Newcastle United	A	1-1	2-5	1	2			5	6	7	8^{1}	11	⑩	4^{1}	9	12				3					31,868
14	S	25 "	1975	Birmingham City	H	1-0	1-0	1	10	3		5	6	7	8	11		4	9^{1}	2									19,605
15	S	1 Nov	1975	Manchester United	A	0-0	0-1	1	10	3		5	6		8	11		4	9	2		7							50,587
16	S	8 "	1975	Middlesbrough	H	0-0	0-1	1	4	3		5	6	7	8	11		10	9	②		12							19,286
17	S	15 "	1975	Coventry City	A	0-1	0-1	1		3	4	5	6		8	11	10		9				7	2					14,897
18	S	22 "	1975	Newcastle United	H	1-0	1-2	1		3^{1}	4	5	⑥		8	11	10		9				7	2	12				19,036
19	S	29 "	1975	Liverpool	A	0-0	3-1	1	7	3	4	5			8^{1}	11^{1}	10^{1}		9		6			2					34,780
20	S	6 Dec	1975	West Ham United	H	0-0	1-0	1	7	3	4	5			8^{1}	11	10		9		6			2					26,581
21	S	13 "	1975	Aston Villa	A	1-2	2-3	1	7	3	4	5			8^{1}	11^{1}	10		9		6			2					30,478
22	S	20 "	1975	Manchester City	H	0-2	2-2	1	7	3	4	5			8	11	10		9^{2}		6			2					19,100
23	F	26 "	1975	Queens Park Rangers	A	0-1	0-2	1	7	3	4	5			8	11	10		9		6			2					21,774
24	S	27 "	1975	Wolverhampton Wanderers	H	0-1	1-1	1	7	3	4	5			8	11^{1}	10		9		6			2					24,451
25	S	10 Jan	1976	Burnley	H	2-0	3-1	1	7	3	4	5^{1}			8	11^{1}	10		9^{1}		6			2					17,473
26	S	17 "	1976	Everton	A	0-0	1-1	1	7	3		5			8	11	10	4	9^{1}		6			2					23,164
27	S	31 "	1976	Leeds United	A	1-0	3-0	1	7	3		5			8^{2}	11	10	4^{1}	9		6			2					27,254
28	S	7 Feb	1976	Arsenal	H	2-1	3-1	1	7	3		5			8^{1}	11^{2}	10	4	9		6			2					22,375
29	S	21 "	1976	Coventry City	H	0-1	0-3	1	7	3		5			8	11	10	4	9		6			2					20,207
30	S	28 "	1976	Birmingham City	A	0-1	1-1	1		3		5	2		8	11^{1}	10	4	9		6	7							22,359
31	S	6 Mar	1976	Tottenham Hotspur	H	0-0	3-1	1		3		5	6		8^{1}	11	10^{1}	4	9^{1}			7		2					20,460
32	S	13 "	1976	Derby County	A	1-0	1-3	1		3		5^{1}	6		8	11	10	4	9			7		2					27,005
33	W	17 "	1976	Manchester United	H	0-1	1-1	1		3		5	6		8	11	10	4	9^{1}			⑦	12	2					27,782
34	S	20 "	1976	Liverpool	H	0-0	0-1	1		3		5	6		8	11	10	4	9				7	2					28,728
35	S	27 "	1976	West Ham United	A	1-0	1-0	1		3		5	6		8^{1}	11	10	4	9				7	2					20,628
36	W	31 "	1976	Ipswich Town	H	1-0	1-0	1		3	2		6		⑧	11^{1}	10	4	9			12	7			5			30,592
37	S	3 Apr	1976	Sheffield United	H	1-3	1-3	1		3	2		6		8	11	10	4	9^{1}				7			5			19,218
38	Tu	6 "	1976	Middlesbrough	A	0-0	1-0	1			2		6		8	11	10	4	9			3^{1}	7	5					16,000
39	S	10 "	1976	Leicester City	A	0-0	0-0	1			3	5	6		8	11	10	4	9			⑦		2			12		19,856
40	S	17 "	1976	Queens Park Rangers	H	1-1	3-2	1			4^{1}	5	6		8^{1}	11	10	7	9^{1}			3		2					30,895
41	M	19 "	1976	Wolverhampton Wanderers	A	0-1	0-1	1	2		3	5	6	12	8	11	10	4	9			⑦							16,168
42	S	24 "	1976	Stoke City	A	0-0	2-0	1			3	5	6		8^{1}	11	10^{1}	4	9			7		2					15,598

F.A. CUP

NO.	DATE			OPPONENTS		V.	H-T	F-T	Keelan Kevin	Machin Mel	Sullivan Colin	Morris Peter	Forbes Duncan	Powell Tony	Grapes Steve	MacDougall Ted	Peters Martin	Suggett Colin	McGuire Mick	Boyer Phil	Butler Geoff	Stringer Dave	Steele Billy	Miller John	Jones David	ATTD.
1	S	3 Jan	1976	Rochdale	(3rd Round)	H	1-1	1-1	1	7		4	5	3		8^{1}	11	10		9		6			2	14,187
2	Tu	6 "	1976	Rochdale	(Replay*)	A	0-0	0-0	1	7	3	4	5	2		8	11	10		9		6				8,284
3	Tu	13 "	1976	Rochdale	(2nd Replay)	H	1-0	2-1	1	7	3		5			8^{1}	11	10^{1}	4	9		6			2	18,868
4	S	24 "	1976	Luton Town	(4th Round)	H	1-0	2-0	1		3		5	7		8	11^{1}	10	4	9		6			2^{1}	24,328
5	M	23 Feb	1976	Bradford City	(5th Round)	H	1-1	1-2	1	7	3		5			8	11^{1}	10	4	9		6			2	27,047

* – AFTER EXTRA TIME

FOOTBALL LEAGUE CUP

NO.	DATE			OPPONENTS		V.	H-T	F-T	Keelan Kevin	Machin Mel	Sullivan Colin	Morris Peter	Forbes Duncan	Powell Tony	Grapes Steve	MacDougall Ted	Peters Martin	Suggett Colin	McGuire Mick	Boyer Phil	Butler Geoff	Stringer Dave	Steele Billy	ATTD.
1	W	10 Sept	1975	Manchester City	(2nd Round)	H	0-0	1-1	1	2		4	5	6	7	8^{1}	11	10		9	3			18,328
2	W	17 "	1975	Manchester City	(Replay*)	A	1-2	2-2	1	2		4	5	6		8^{2}	11	10	7	9	3			29,667
3	M	29 "	1975	Manchester City	(2nd Replay)	N	1-3	1-6	1	2		4	5	6		8	11^{1}	10		9	3		7	6,238

* – AFTER EXTRA TIME N – STAMFORD BRIDGE

1975–76 APPEARANCES & GOALS

	FOOTBALL LGE			F.A. CUP			LEAGUE CUP		
	APPR.	S	GLS	APPR.	S	GLS	APPR.	S	GLS
Keelan Kevin	42	–	–	5	–	–	3	–	–
MacDougall Ted	42	–	23	5	–	2	3	–	3
Peters Martin	42	–	10	5	–	2	3	–	1
Boyer Phil	39	–	11	5	–	–	3	–	–
Forbes Duncan	39	–	3	5	–	–	3	–	–
Suggett Colin	38	–	4	5	–	1	3	–	–
Powell Tony	31	–	–	3	–	–	3	–	–
Sullivan Colin	31	–	1	4	–	–			
McGuire Mick	29	1	2	3	–	–	1	–	–
Machin Mel	28	–	–	4	–	–	3	–	–
Morris Peter	26	–	1	2	–	–	3	–	–
Jones David	23	–	–	4	–	1			
Steele Billy	12	3	1				1	–	–
Stringer Dave	12	2	–	5	–	–			
Grapes Steve	10	1	1				1	–	–
Butler Geoff	8	1	–				3	–	–
Miller John	8	1	–						
Davids Neil	2	–	–						
Bond Kevin	–	1	–						
Wilson Paul	–	1	–						
Own Goals			1						

DIVISION 1

1975–76	P	W	D	L	F	A	PTS
Liverpool	42	23	14	5	66	31	60
Queens Park Rangers	42	24	11	7	67	33	59
Manchester United	42	23	10	9	68	42	56
Derby County	42	21	11	10	75	58	43
Leeds United	42	21	9	12	65	46	51
Ipswich Town	42	16	14	12	54	48	51
Leicester City	42	13	19	10	48	51	45
Manchester City	42	16	11	15	64	46	43
Tottenham Hotspur	42	14	15	13	63	63	43
Norwich City	**42**	**16**	**10**	**16**	**58**	**58**	**42**
Everton	42	15	12	15	60	66	42
Stoke City	42	15	11	16	48	50	41
Middlesbrough	42	15	10	17	46	45	40
Coventry City	42	13	14	15	47	57	40
Newcastle United	42	15	9	18	71	62	39
Aston Villa	42	11	17	14	51	59	39
Arsenal	42	13	10	19	47	53	36
West Ham United	42	13	10	19	48	71	36
Birmingham City	42	13	7	22	57	75	33
Wolverhampton Wanderers	42	10	10	22	51	68	30
Burnley	42	9	10	23	43	66	28
Sheffield United	42	6	10	26	33	82	22

1976–77 DIVISION 1

NO.		DATE	OPPONENTS	V.	H-T	F-T	Keelan Kevin	Ryan John	Stringer Dave	Jones David	Forbes Duncan	Powell Tony	Machin Mel	Steele Billy	Boyer Phil	Suggett Colin	Peters Martin	Gibbins Roger	Sullivan Colin	Davies Ian	MacDougall Ted	Grapes Steve	Busby Viv	Proudlove Andy	Neighbour Jimmy	Osgood Peter	Paddon Graham	Reeves Kevin	Evans Doug	Bond Kevin	Fleeting Jim	Hansbury Roger	Own Goals	ATTD.
1	S	21 Aug 1976	Liverpool	A	0-0	0-1	1	2	3	4	5	6	7	8	9	10	11																	49,753
2	W	25 " 1976	Arsenal	H	0-1	1-3	1	2		3	5	6	④	7	9	10	11[1]	8	12															26,224
3	S	28 " 1976	West Bromwich Albion	A	0-1	0-2	1	2		3	5	6		7	9	10	11			4	8													17,045
4	S	4 Sept 1976	Birmingham City	H	1-0	1-0	1	2			5	4		6	9[1]	10	11		3		8	7												18,506
5	S	11 " 1976	Coventry City	A	0-1	0-2	1	2			5	4		6	9	10	11		3		8	7												12,948
6	S	18 " 1976	Derby County	H	0-0	0-0	1	②		5		4	12	6	9	10	11		3			7	8											22,375
7	S	25 " 1976	Tottenham Hotspur	A	0-1	1-1	1	2		5		6	⑦	4	9	10	11		3				8	12									–[1]	22,440
8	S	2 Oct 1976	Newcastle United	H	3-0	3-2	1			5		6	2	4	9	10	11[2]		3				8[1]		7									20,873
9	Tu	5 " 1976	Queens Park Rangers	A	1-1	3-2	1			5		6	2	4	9	10	11[1]		3[1]				8[1]		7									16,086
10	S	9 " 1976	Middlesbrough	A	0-0	0-1	1			5		6	2	4	9	10	11	8	3						7									22,000
11	S	16 " 1976	Leeds United	H	0-0	1-2	1			5		6	2	4	9	10	11	8[1]	3						7									24,804
12	S	23 " 1976	Manchester United	A	0-2	2-2	1	12[1]		5		6	2	④	9[1]	10	11	8	3						7									54,356
13	S	30 " 1976	Manchester City	H	0-0	0-2	1	2		5		6		4	9	10	11	8	3						7									22,586
14	S	6 Nov 1976	Leicester City	A	0-0	1-1	1	2		5		6	4	8	9[1]	10	11		3						7									17,781
15	W	10 " 1976	West Ham United	H	1-0	1-0	1	2		5		6	12	④	9	10	11[1]		3						7	8								24,092
16	S	20 " 1976	Bristol City	A	0-2	1-3	1	2		5		6			9[1]	10	11		3						7	8	4							19,641
17	S	27 " 1976	Aston Villa	H	1-1	1-1	1	2		5		6			9[1]	4	11		3						7	8	10							22,110
18	S	18 Dec 1976	Sunderland	A	1-0	1-0	1	2		5		6	12		9	④	11		3				8[1]		7		10							23,468
19	M	27 " 1976	Queens Park Rangers	H	1-0	2-0	1	2		5		6	4[1]	10	9		11		3				8[1]		7									26,652
20	S	1 Jan 1977	Leicester City	H	2-2	3-2	1	2		5		6	4	⑩	9	12	11		3				8[3]		7									21,531
21	S	15 " 1977	Arsenal	A	0-1	0-1	1	2		5		6	4	12		10	11		3				8		7			⑨						30,537
22	S	22 " 1977	Liverpool	H	1-0	2-1	1	2		5		6	4	12		10	11[1]	8	3				⑨		7[1]									25,617
23	S	29 " 1977	Stoke City	H	1-0	1-1	1	2			5	6	4			10	11	9	3						7			8[1]						17,896
24	S	5 Feb 1977	West Bromwich Albion	H	1-0	1-0	1	2		5		6	4	12		⑩	11	9[1]	3						7			8						19,094
25	S	12 " 1977	Birmingham City	A	2-1	2-3	1	2		5		6		4[1]			11	9	3						7			8[1]	10					21,809
26	Tu	15 " 1977	Ipswich Town	A	0-2	0-5	1	2			5	6	④	10			11	9	3						7			8	12					34,735
27	S	19 " 1977	Coventry City	H	2-0	3-0	1	2		5		6	④	10			11		3				9[2]		7			8[1]	12					17,129
28	Tu	1 Mar 1977	Manchester City	A	0-0	0-2	1	2		5		6		10			11		3				9		7			8	④	12				36,021
29	S	5 " 1977	Tottenham Hotspur	H	1-0	1-3	1	2		5		6		10			11		3	4			9		7[1]			8						22,949
30	W	9 " 1977	Middlesbrough	H	0-0	1-0	1	2[1]		5	4	6				10	11		3				9		7			8						16,625
31	S	12 " 1977	Newcastle United	A	1-2	1-5	1	2		5	4	6				10	11		3				9		⑦			8[1]			12			26,216
32	W	23 " 1977	Leeds United	A	2-1	2-3	1	2		5		6	④	10			11	9[1]	3						7[1]			8	12					18,700
33	S	2 Apr 1977	Manchester United	H	2-0	2-1	1	2		5		6	4	12		⑩[1]	11	9	3						7			8[1]						24,161
34	W	6 " 1977	Derby County	A	2-1	2-2	1	2		5		6	4	10			11	9[2]							7			8	3					21,342
35	S	9 " 1977	Ipswich Town	H	0-1	0-1	1	2		5		6	④	10	12		11	9	3						7			8						30,993
36	M	11 " 1977	West Ham United	A	0-0	0-1	1	2		5		6	4	10	9		11		3						7			8						27,084
37	S	16 " 1977	Bristol City	H	1-1	2-1	1	2		5		6		10		4	11[1]	9	3						⑦			8[1]	12					17,839
38	Tu	19 " 1977	Everton	A	0-1	1-3	1	2		5		6		10[1]		4	11	9	3									8	7					26,644
39	S	23 " 1977	Aston Villa	A	0-1	0-1				12	5	6	7	⑩		4	11	9	3									8		2		1		35,899
40	S	30 " 1977	Everton	H	2-0	2-1		2		⑤		6				4	11	9	3				10[1]		7			8[1]		12		1		19,091
41	S	7 May 1977	Stoke City	A	0-0	0-0		2			5	6				4	11	9	3				10		7			8				1		13,202
42	S	14 " 1977	Sunderland	H	0-0	2-2		2		12	5	6				④	11	9	3				10[1]		7			8[1]				1		27,253

F.A. CUP

NO.		DATE	OPPONENTS	V.	H-T	F-T	Keelan Kevin	Ryan John	Stringer Dave	Jones David	Forbes Duncan	Powell Tony	Machin Mel	Steele Billy	Boyer Phil	Suggett Colin	Peters Martin	Gibbins Roger	Sullivan Colin	Davies Ian	MacDougall Ted	Grapes Steve	Busby Viv	Proudlove Andy	Neighbour Jimmy	Osgood Peter	Paddon Graham	Reeves Kevin	Evans Doug	Bond Kevin	Fleeting Jim	Hansbury Roger	Own Goals	ATTD.
1	S	8 Jan 1977	Leeds United (3rd Round)	A	1-5	2-5	1	2		5		6	4	9		10[1]	11[1]		3				8		7									28,130

FOOTBALL LEAGUE CUP

NO.		DATE	OPPONENTS	V.	H-T	F-T	Keelan Kevin	Ryan John	Stringer Dave	Jones David	Forbes Duncan	Powell Tony	Machin Mel	Steele Billy	Boyer Phil	Suggett Colin	Peters Martin	Gibbins Roger	Sullivan Colin	Davies Ian	MacDougall Ted	Grapes Steve	Busby Viv	Proudlove Andy	Neighbour Jimmy	Osgood Peter	Paddon Graham	Reeves Kevin	Evans Doug	Bond Kevin	Fleeting Jim	Hansbury Roger	Own Goals	ATTD.
1	Tu	31 Aug 1976	Exeter City (2nd Round)	A	2-1	3-1	1	2			5	4		6	9[1]	10	11	8	3		8[1]	7[1]												9,449
2	Tu	21 Sept 1976	Aston Villa (3rd Round)	A	0-1	1-2	1	2		5		6	7	4	9	⑩[1]	11		3					12										31,295

1976–77 APPEARANCES & GOALS

	FOOTBALL LGE			F.A. CUP			LEAGUE CUP		
	APPR.	S	GLS	APPR.	S	GLS	APPR.	S	GLS
Peters Martin	42	–	7	1	–	1	2	–	–
Powell Tony	42	–	–	1	–	–	2	–	–
Keelan Kevin	38	–	–	1	–	–	2	–	–
Sullivan Colin	38	1	1	1	–	–	2	–	–
Ryan John	36	1	2	1	–	–	2	–	–
Jones Dvaid	35	2	–	1	–	–	1	–	–
Neighbour Jimmy	33	–	3	1	–	–			
Suggett Colin	31	1	1	1	–	1	2	–	1
Steele Billy	29	4	2	1	–	–	2	–	–
Machin Mel	23	3	1	1	–	–	1	–	–
Boyer Phil	21	1	5				2	–	1
Reeves Kevin	21	–	8						
Gibbins Roger	20	–	5				1	–	–
Busby Viv	17	–	11	1	–	–			
Forbes Duncan	12	–	–				1	–	–
Evans Doug	4	4	–						
Hansbury Roger	4	–	–						
Grapes Steve	3	–	–				1	–	1
MacDougall Ted	3	–	–				1	–	1
Osgood Peter	3	–	–						
Paddon Graham	3	–	–						
Davies Ian	2	–	–						
Bond Kevin	1	2	–						
Stringer Dave	1	–	–						
Fleeting Jim	–	1	–						
Proudlove Andy	–	1	–				–	1	–
Own Goals			1						

DIVISION 1

1976–77	P	W	D	L	F	A	PTS
Liverpool	42	23	11	8	62	33	57
Manchester City	42	21	14	7	60	34	56
Ipswich Town	42	22	8	12	66	39	52
Aston Villa	42	22	7	13	76	50	51
Newcastle United	42	18	13	11	64	49	49
Manchester United	42	18	11	13	71	62	47
West Bromwich Albion	42	16	13	13	62	56	45
Arsenal	42	16	11	15	64	59	43
Everton	42	14	14	14	62	64	42
Leeds United	42	15	12	15	48	51	42
Leicester City	42	12	18	12	47	60	42
Middlesbrough	42	14	13	15	40	45	41
Birmingham City	42	13	12	17	63	61	38
Queens Park Rangers	42	13	12	17	47	52	38
Derby County	42	9	19	14	50	55	37
Norwich City	**42**	**14**	**9**	**19**	**47**	**64**	**37**
West Ham United	42	11	14	17	46	65	36
Bristol City	42	11	13	18	38	48	35
Coventry City	42	10	15	17	48	59	35
Sunderland	42	11	12	19	46	54	34
Stoke City	42	10	14	18	28	51	34
Tottenham Hotspur	42	12	9	21	48	72	33

1977–78 DIVISION 1

NO.		DATE	OPPONENTS	V.	H-T	F-T	Keelan Kevin	Ryan John	Sullivan Colin	Evans Doug	Jones David	Powell Tony	Neighbour Jimmy	Busby Viv	Reeves Kevin	Suggett Colin	Gibbins Roger	Davies Ian	Forbes Duncan	Machin Mel	Hansbury Roger	Bond Kevin	Peters Martin	Nightingale Mark	McGuire Mick	Paddon Graham	Lythgoe Phil	Robson Keith	Downs Greg	Baker Clive	Halsey Mark	Fleeting Jim	Own Goals	ATTD.
1	S	20 Aug 1977	West Ham United	A	1-0	3-1	1	2[1]	3	4	5[2]	6	7	8	9	10	11																	28,178
2	W	24 " 1977	Middlesbrough	H	1-1	1-1	1	2	3	4	5	6	7	9	8	10	11[1]																	14,245
3	S	27 " 1977	Queens Park Rangers	H	1-0	1-1	1	2	3	4	5	6	7	9	⑧	10	11[1]	12																17,249
4	S	3 Sept 1977	Manchester City	A	0-2	0-4	1	2	12	④	5	6	7	8		10	9		3	11														41,269
5	S	10 " 1977	Bristol City	H	0-0	1-0	1	2	3		5	6	7	⑧	9	10	12[1]	11		4														12,836
6	S	17 " 1977	Everton	A	0-1	0-3		2	3		5	6	7		8	10	9			④	1	12	11											34,405
7	S	24 " 1977	Arsenal	H	1-0	1-0	1	4[1]	3		5	6	7		8	10	9					2	11											18,718
8	S	1 Oct 1977	Nottingham Forest	A	0-0	1-1	1	4	3		5	6	7		8	10	9					2	11[1]											23,741
9	W	5 " 1977	Newcastle United	H	1-1	2-1	1	4	3		5	6	7		8[1]	10	9					2	11[1]											15,819
10	S	8 " 1977	Wolverhampton Wanderers	H	1-0	2-1	1	4	3		5	6	7		8	⑩	9					2	11[2]	12										17,890
11	S	15 " 1977	Aston Villa	A	0-1	0-3	1	4	3	10	5	6	7		8		9					2	11											32,978
12	S	22 " 1977	Leicester City	H	1-0	2-0	1	④[1]	3		5	6	7		8	10	9[1]					2	11		12									17,684
13	S	29 " 1977	Derby County	A	0-2	2-2	1	4	3		5	6	7		8[2]	10	⑨					2	11		12									21,957
14	S	5 Nov 1977	Leeds United	A	2-1	2-2	1	4[1]	3		5	6	7		8	10	9[1]					2	11											24,345
15	S	12 " 1977	Chelsea	H	0-0	0-0	1	4	3		5	6	7		8	10	9					2	11											18,957
16	S	19 " 1977	Manchester United	A	0-0	0-1	1	4	3		5	6	7		8	10	9					2	11											48,129
17	S	26 " 1977	Birmingham City	H	0-0	1-0	1	4	3		5	6	7		8		9[1]					2	11			10								16,800
18	S	3 Dec 1977	West Bromwich Albion	A	0-0	0-0	1	4	3		5	6	7			8	9					2	11			10								19,264
19	S	10 " 1977	Liverpool	H	1-0	2-1	1	4	3		5	6	7			8[1]	9					2	11[1]			10								24,715
20	S	17 " 1977	Chelsea	A	0-1	1-1	1	4	3		5	6	7			8[1]	9					2	11			10								22,751
21	M	26 " 1977	Ipswich Town	H	1-0	1-0	1	4[1]	3		5	6	7		12	8	9					2	11			⑩								27,340
22	Tu	27 " 1977	Coventry City	A	3-2	4-5	1	4[1]	3		5	6	7		10[2]	8	9					2	11[1]											21,578
23	S	31 " 1977	Middlesbrough	A	1-1	2-2	1	4[1]	3		5	6	7		8	10[1]	9					2	11											15,646
24	M	2 Jan 1978	West Ham United	H	0-1	2-2	1	4[1]	3		5	6	7		10	8	9					2	11[1]											29,168
25	S	14 " 1978	Queens Park Rangers	A	0-2	1-2	1	4	3			6	7		8[1]	10	9		5			2	11											14,247
26	S	21 " 1978	Manchester City	H	0-1	1-3	1	4	3		5	6			10	8	9[1]					2	11				7							20,009
27	S	4 Feb 1978	Bristol City	A	0-3	0-3	1	4	3		5	6	12		⑩	8	9					2	11		7									16,929
28	S	25 " 1978	Nottingham Forest	H	1-3	3-3		2[1]	3		5	6				10[1]	9				1		11		4	8		7[1]						25,705
29	Tu	28 " 1978	Arsenal	A	0-0	0-0		2	3		5	6			10	8					1		11		4	9		7						23,506
30	S	4 Mar 1978	Wolverhampton Wanderers	A	2-2	3-3		2[1]	3		5	6			10[2]	7					1		11		4	9		8						16,813
31	S	11 " 1978	Aston Villa	H	1-0	2-1		2[1]	3		5	6			9[1]	8					1		11		4	10		7						18,575
32	W	15 " 1978	Everton	H	0-0	0-0		2	3		5	6			9	8					1		11		4	10		7						18,905
33	S	18 " 1978	Leicester City	A	1-1	2-2		2[2]	3		5	6			9	8					1		11		4	10		7						13,077
34	S	25 " 1978	Coventry City	H	1-0	1-2		2	3		5	6			8[1]	10					1	12	⑪		4	7		9						20,346
35	M	27 " 1978	Ipswich Town	A	0-2	0-4		2	3		5	6	7		10	12					1				④	9		11	8					29,930
36	W	29 " 1978	Derby County	H	0-0	0-0		4	3		5	6	7		10	8					1	2				9	11							15,523
37	S	1 Apr 1978	Leeds United	H	1-0	3-0		4[1]	3		5[1]	6	7		10	8					1	2				9	11						–[1]	19,123
38	S	8 " 1978	Birmingham City	A	0-0	1-2		4	3		5	6	7		10[1]	8					1		2			9	11							20,858
39	S	15 " 1978	Manchester United	H	1-0	1-3		4	3		5	6	7		10	8					1		2			9	11[1]							19,778
40	S	22 " 1978	Liverpool	A	0-2	0-3		3			5	6	7		8	10					1	2	11			4	9							44,857
41	W	26 " 1978	Newcastle United	A	0-1	2-2		10[1]	3		5	6	7		8[1]							2	11				12	⑨		1	4			7,600
42	S	29 " 1978	West Bromwich Albion	H	0-1	1-1		4	3			⑥	7		8	10			5[1]			2	11				12	9		1				17,302

F.A. CUP

NO.		DATE	OPPONENTS	V.	H-T	F-T	Keelan Kevin	Ryan John	Sullivan Colin	Evans Doug	Jones David	Powell Tony	Neighbour Jimmy	Busby Viv	Reeves Kevin	Suggett Colin	Gibbins Roger	Davies Ian	Forbes Duncan	Machin Mel	Hansbury Roger	Bond Kevin	Peters Martin	Nightingale Mark	McGuire Mick	Paddon Graham	Lythgoe Phil	Robson Keith	Downs Greg	Baker Clive	Halsey Mark	Fleeting Jim	Own Goals	ATTD.
1	F	6 Jan 1978	Orient (3rd Round)	A	0-1	1-1	1	4	3		5	6	7		10	8	9[1]					2	11											14,538
2	M	16 " 1978	Orient (Replay)	H	0-0	0-1	1	4	3			6	7		10	8	9					2	11									5		20,421

FOOTBALL LEAGUE CUP

NO.		DATE	OPPONENTS	V.	H-T	F-T	Keelan Kevin	Ryan John	Sullivan Colin	Evans Doug	Jones David	Powell Tony	Neighbour Jimmy	Busby Viv	Reeves Kevin	Suggett Colin	Gibbins Roger	Davies Ian	Forbes Duncan	Machin Mel	Hansbury Roger	Bond Kevin	Peters Martin	Nightingale Mark	McGuire Mick	Paddon Graham	Lythgoe Phil	Robson Keith	Downs Greg	Baker Clive	Halsey Mark	Fleeting Jim	Own Goals	ATTD.
1	Tu	30 Aug 1977	Burnley (2nd Round)	A	0-2	1-3	1	2[1]	3	4	6	7			10	11		12						⑧					9					6,477

1977–78 APPEARANCES & GOALS

	FOOTBALL LGE			F.A. CUP			LEAGUE CUP		
	APPR.	S	GLS	APPR.	S	GLS	APPR.	S	GLS
Powell Tony	42	–	–	2	–	–	1	–	–
Ryan John	42	–	15	2	–	–	1	–	1
Sullivan Colin	40	1	–	2	–	–	1	–	–
Jones David	40	–	3	1	–	–	1	–	–
Suggett Colin	38	1	4	2	–	–	1	–	–
Reeves Kevin	36	1	12	2	–	–			
Peters Martin	34	–	7	2	–	–			
Neighbour Jimmy	33	1	–	2	–	–	1	–	–
Gibbins Roger	27	1	7	2	–	1	1	–	–
Bond Kevin	26	2	–	2	–	–			
Keelan Kevin	26	–	–	2	–	–	1	–	–
Paddon Grahan	18	–	–						
Hansbury Roger	14	–	–						
Robson Keith	10	–	1						
McGuire Mick	9	2	–						
Lythgoe Phil	6	2	1						
Busby Viv	5	–	–						
Evans Doug	5	–	–				1	–	–
Forbes Duncan	3	–	1				–	1	–
Machin Mel	3	–	–						
Baker Clive	2	–	–						
Davies Ian	1	1	–						
Downs Greg	1	–	–				1	–	–
Halsey Mark	1	–	–						
Nightingale Mark	–	1	–						
Fleeting Jim				1	–	–			
Own Goals			1						

DIVISION 1

1977–78	P	W	D	L	F	A	PTS
Nottingham Forest	42	25	14	3	69	24	64
Liverpool	42	24	9	9	65	34	57
Everton	42	22	11	9	76	45	55
Manchester City	42	20	12	10	74	51	52
Arsenal	42	21	10	11	60	37	52
West Bromwich Albion	42	18	14	10	62	53	50
Coventry City	42	18	12	12	75	62	48
Aston Villa	42	18	10	14	57	42	46
Leeds United	42	18	10	14	63	53	46
Manchester United	42	16	10	16	67	63	42
Birmingham City	42	16	9	17	55	60	41
Derby County	42	14	13	15	54	59	41
Norwich City	**42**	**11**	**18**	**13**	**52**	**66**	**40**
Middlesbrough	42	12	15	15	42	54	39
Wolverhampton Wanderers	42	12	12	18	51	64	36
Chelsea	42	11	14	17	46	69	36
Bristol City	42	11	13	18	49	53	35
Ipswich Town	42	11	13	18	47	61	35
Queens Park Rangers	42	9	15	18	47	64	33
West Ham United	42	12	8	22	52	69	32
Newcastle United	42	6	10	26	42	78	22
Leicester City	42	5	12	25	26	70	22

1978–79 DIVISION 1

No.	Date	Opponents	V.	H-T	F-T	Keelan Kevin	Bond Kevin	Sullivan Colin	Ryan John	Hoadley Phil	Powell Tony	Neighbour Jimmy	Reeves Kevin	Chivers Martin	Robson Keith	Peters Martin	McGuire Mick	Baker Clive	Paddon Graham	Robb David	Mendham Peter	Davies Ian	Downs Greg	Symonds Richard	Fashanu Justin	Lythgoe Phil	Forbes Duncan	Bennett Dave	Hansbury Roger	Evans Doug	Own Goals	Attd.
1	S 19 Aug 1978	Southampton	H	1-0	3-1	1	2	3	4[1]	5	6	7	8[1]	9[1]	10	11																20,295
2	Tu 22 " 1978	Bristol City	A	1-0	1-1	1	2	3	4[1]	5	6	7	8	9	10	11																19,274
3	S 26 " 1978	Coventry City	A	0-2	1-4	1	2	3	4	5	6	7	8	9	10	11[1]																20,452
4	S 2 Sept 1978	Manchester City	H	1-0	1-1	1	2	3	4	5	6	7	8	9[1]	10	11																18,069
5	S 9 " 1978	West Bromwich Albion	A	2-1	2-2	1	2	3	4[1]	5	6	7	8	9[1]	(10)	11	12															21,947
6	S 16 " 1978	Birmingham City	H	1-0	4-0		2	3	4[1]	5	6	7	8[1]	9[1]	10[1]	11		1														15,701
7	S 23 " 1978	Bolton Wanderers	A	2-1	2-3		2	3	4	5	(6)	7	8[1]	9	10[1]	11		1	12													19,901
8	S 30 " 1978	Derby County	H	2-0	3-0	1	2	3	4[1]	5	6	7	8[1]		(10)	11				9[1]	12											15,930
9	S 7 Oct 1978	Liverpool	H	0-3	1-4	1	2	3	4[1]	5	6	7	8		10	11				(9)		12										26,661
10	S 14 " 1978	Middlesbrough	A	0-1	0-2	1	2	3	4	5	6	7	8			11			10	(9)			12									18,203
11	S 21 " 1978	Leeds United	H	0-1	2-2	1	2		4[1]	5	6	7	8			11[1]					10	3	9									19,353
12	S 28 " 1978	Chelsea	A	0-1	3-3	1	2		4[1]	5	6	7	8			11[2]					10	3		9								23,941
13	S 4 Nov 1978	Tottenham Hotspur	H	1-2	2-2	1	2		4[1]	5	6	7	8			11[1]					(10)	3	12	9								27,031
14	S 11 " 1978	Southampton	A	1-1	2-2	1	2		4	5	6[1]	7[1]	8			11					10	3		9								21,183
15	S 18 " 1978	Coventry City	H	0-0	1-0	1	2[1]		4	5	6	7	9			8					11	3		10								17,270
16	S 25 " 1978	Everton	H	0-0	0-1	1	2		4	5	6	7	8		12	11					10	(3)		9								18,930
17	S 9 Dec 1978	Arsenal	H	0-0	0-0	1	2		4	5	6	7	8	(9)	12	11						3		10								19,742
18	S 16 " 1978	Aston Villa	A	0-0	1-1	1	2		4	5	6		8[1]	9	10	11	7					3										26,228
19	Tu 26 " 1978	Ipswich Town	A	1-0	1-1	1	2		4	5	6	12	8	(9)	10		7					3[1]		11								26,336
20	S 13 Jan 1979	West Bromwich Albion	H	0-1	1-1	1	2			5	6	7	8			11[1]	4					3		10	9							20,081
21	W 31 " 1979	Queens Park Rangers	H	1-0	1-1	1	2			5	6	7	8			11	4					3[1]		10	9							12,401
22	S 3 Feb 1979	Bolton Wanderers	H	0-0	0-0	1	2		4	5	6		8			11	10			12		3			(9)	7						14,690
23	S 10 " 1978	Derby County	A	0-0	1-1	1	2		4		6	7	(8)		10	11[1]				9		3					5	12				20,837
24	W 21 " 1979	Liverpool	A	0-1	0-6	1	2		4	5	6	7		9		11								8		10	3					35,754
25	S 24 " 1979	Middlesbrough	H	0-0	1-0		2		4		6	(7)			8	11[1]	12		10			3			9		5		1			12,914
26	Tu 27 " 1979	Manchester City	A	1-1	2-2		2		4	5	6				9[1]	11[1]	7		10					3	8				1			30,012
27	S 3 Mar 1979	Leeds United	A	0-1	2-2		2[1]		4	5	6				9	11	7		10					3	8[1]				1			23,038
28	W 7 " 1979	Wolverhampton Wanderers	H	0-0	0-0		2				6	7	5		9	11	4		10					3	8				1			14,201
29	S 10 " 1979	Chelsea	H	1-0	2-0		2			5	6	7	8		12	11[1]	4		(10)					3	9[1]				1			18,467
30	W 14 " 1979	Nottingham Forest	A	0-0	1-2		2			5	6	7	8		10	11	4								9[1]				1	3		24,046
31	S 17 " 1979	Tottenham Hotspur	A	0-0	0-0		2			5	6	7	8		9	(11)	4					3					12		1	10		24,982
32	S 24 " 1979	Bristol City	H	3-0	3-0		2			5	6	7[1]	8[1]		9		4		10			(3)		12					1	11[1]		13,238
33	Tu 27 " 1979	Birmingham City	A	0-0	0-1		2			5	6	(7)	8		9	12	4		10			3							1	11		12,168
34	F 30 " 1979	Everton	A	1-0	2-2		4			5	6	7	8[2]		9		11		10			3		2					1			28,825
35	S 7 Apr 1979	Manchester United	H	0-0	2-2		2			5	6	(7)	8		9[1]	11	4		10[1]			3		12					1			19,382
36	F 13 " 1979	Queens Park Rangers	A	0-0	0-0		2			5	6		8		9	11	(4)		10			3		7	12				1			14,654
37	S 14 " 1979	Ipswich Town	H	0-0	0-1		(2)			5	6		8		7	11	4		10			3		9	12				1			20,971
38	M 16 " 1979	Wolverhampton Wanderers	A	0-1	0-1		2			5	6		8		9	11	4		10			3			12	(7)			1			18,457
39	S 21 " 1979	Aston Villa	H	1-1	1-2		2			5	6		8			11	4		10		7	3			9[1]				1			13,421
40	W 25 " 1979	Manchester United	A	0-0	0-1		2			5	6	7	8		9	11	4					3			10				1			33,678
41	S 28 " 1979	Arsenal	A	0-0	1-1		2			5	6	7	8			11	4		10			3			9[1]				1			28,885
42	S 5 May 1979	Nottingham Forest	H	1-0	1-1		2			5	6	7	8[1]			11	4		10			3			9				1			16,616

F.A. CUP

No.	Date	Opponents	Round	V.	H-T	F-T	Keelan Kevin	Bond Kevin	Sullivan Colin	Ryan John	Hoadley Phil	Powell Tony	Neighbour Jimmy	Reeves Kevin	Chivers Martin	Robson Keith	Peters Martin	McGuire Mick	Baker Clive	Paddon Graham	Robb David	Mendham Peter	Davies Ian	Downs Greg	Symonds Richard	Fashanu Justin	Lythgoe Phil	Forbes Duncan	Bennett Dave	Hansbury Roger	Evans Doug	Own Goals	Attd.
1	S 6 Jan 1979	Leicester City	(3rd Round)	A	0-2	0-3	1	2		4	5	6	7	8	9		11	10					3										19,680

FOOTBALL LEAGUE CUP

No.	Date	Opponents	Round	V.	H-T	F-T	Keelan Kevin	Bond Kevin	Sullivan Colin	Ryan John	Hoadley Phil	Powell Tony	Neighbour Jimmy	Reeves Kevin	Chivers Martin	Robson Keith	Peters Martin	McGuire Mick	Baker Clive	Paddon Graham	Robb David	Mendham Peter	Davies Ian	Downs Greg	Symonds Richard	Fashanu Justin	Lythgoe Phil	Forbes Duncan	Bennett Dave	Hansbury Roger	Evans Doug	Own Goals	Attd.
1	Tu 29 Aug 1978	Wrexham	(2nd Round)	A	2-1	3-1	1	2	3	4[2]	5	6	7	8	9	10	11															–[1]	12,428
2	W 4 Oct 1978	Chester	(3rd Round)	A	0-0	2-0	1	2	3	4	5	6	7	8[1]		10	11[1]				9												8,749
3	W 8 Nov 1978	Manchester City	(4th Round)	H	1-0	1-3	1	2		4	5	6	7	8			11[1]					10	3		9								19,423

1978–79 APPEARANCES & GOALS

	FOOTBALL LGE APPR.	S	GLS	F.A. CUP APPR.	S	GLS	LEAGUE CUP APPR.	S	GLS
Bond Kevin	42	–	2	1	–	–	3	–	–
Powell Tony	42	–	1	1	–	–	3	–	–
Hoadley Phil	39	–	–	1	–	–	3	–	–
Peters Martin	38	1	10	1	–	–	3	–	2
Reeves Kevin	38	–	9	1	–	–	3	–	1
Neighbour Jimmy	33	1	2	1	–	–	3	–	–
Robson Keith	26	3	4				2	–	–
Davies Ian	26	1	2	1	–	–	1	–	–
Ryan John	25	–	9	1	–	–	3	–	2
McGuire Mick	22	2	–	1	–	–			
Keelan Kevin	22	–	–	1	–	–	3	–	–
Hansbury Roger	18	–	–						
Symonds Richard	17	2	–				1	–	–
Paddon Graham	16	1	1						
Fashanu Justin	13	3	5						
Chivers Martin	11	–	4	1	–	–	1	–	–
Sullivan Colin	10	–	–				2	–	–
Mendham Peter	7	1	–				1	–	–
Robb David	4	1	1				1	–	–
Evans Doug	4	–	1						
Forbes Duncan	3	1	–						
Lythgoe Phil	3	–	–						
Baker Clive	2	–	–						
Downs Greg	1	2	–						
Bennett Dave	–	1	–						
Own Goals									1

DIVISION 1

1978–79	P	W	D	L	F	A	PTS
Liverpool	42	30	8	4	85	16	68
Nottingham Forest	42	21	18	3	61	26	60
West Bromwich Albion	42	24	11	7	72	35	59
Everton	42	17	17	8	52	40	51
Leeds United	42	18	14	10	70	52	50
Ipswich Town	42	20	9	13	63	49	49
Arsenal	42	17	14	11	61	48	48
Aston Villa	42	15	16	11	59	49	46
Manchester United	42	15	15	12	60	63	45
Coventry City	42	14	16	12	58	68	44
Tottenham Hotspur	42	13	15	14	48	61	41
Middlesbrough	42	15	10	17	57	50	40
Bristol City	42	15	10	17	47	51	40
Southampton	42	12	16	14	47	53	40
Manchester City	42	13	13	16	58	56	39
Norwich City	**42**	**7**	**23**	**12**	**51**	**57**	**37**
Bolton Wanderers	42	12	11	19	54	75	35
Wolverhampton Wanderers	42	13	8	21	44	68	34
Derby County	42	10	11	21	44	71	31
Queens Park Rangers	42	6	13	23	45	73	25
Birmingham City	42	6	10	26	37	64	22
Chelsea	42	5	10	27	44	92	20

1979–80 DIVISION 1

NO.		DATE	OPPONENTS	V.	H-T	F-T	Keelan Kevin	Bond Kevin	McDowell John	McGuire Mick	Hoadley Phil	Powell Tony	Neighbour Jimmy	Reeves Kevin	Fashanu Justin	Paddon Graham	Peters Martin	Taylor Alan	Nightingale Mark	Ryan John	Brown Roger	Symonds Richard	Robson Keith	Bennett Dave	Goble Steve	Downs Greg	Evans Doug	Jones David	Barham Mark	Mendham Peter	Lythgoe Phil	Hansbury Roger	Halsey Mark	Woods Clive	Shepherd Greig			Own Goals	ATTD.
1	S	18 Aug 1979	Everton	A	3-2	4-2	1	2	3	4[1]	5	6	7	8	⑨[2]	10	11[1]	12																					26,539
2	W	22 " 1979	Tottenham Hotspur	H	0-0	4-0	1	2	3	4	5		7	8[2]	9[1]	10	11[1]		6																				16,647
3	S	25 " 1979	Leeds United	H	2-1	2-1	1	2[2]	3	4	5	6	7	8	⑨	10	11	12																					17,174
4	S	1 Sept 1979	Coventry City	A	0-0	0-2	1	2	③	4	5		7	8	9	10	11			12	6																		18,181
5	S	8 " 1979	Middlesbrough	A	0-1	0-1	1	2			5	6	7	8	9	10		11	④	12		3																	19,575
6	S	15 " 1979	Nottingham Forest	H	2-0	3-1	1	2	4		5	6		8[1]	9[1]	10		7				3	11[1]																18,056
7	S	22 " 1979	Liverpool	H	0-0	0-0	1	2	3		5	6		8	9	10	11	④				12	7																44,120
8	S	29 " 1979	Bolton Wanderers	H	0-0	2-1	1	2			5	6		8	9[1]	10	11[1]			3			7	4															16,528
9	S	6 Oct 1979	Stoke City	H	0-1	2-2	1	2[1]	3	12	5	6		8[1]	9	10	11						⑦	4															16,644
10	W	10 " 1979	Tottenham Hotspur	A	2-2	2-3	1	2	3	4	5	6		8[1]	9		11[1]						7	10															26,488
11	S	13 " 1979	Wolverhampton Wanderers	A	0-1	0-1	1	2	3	8	5	6			9		11	7				4		10															28,060
12	S	20 " 1979	Manchester City	H	0-1	2-2	1	2[1]	3	12	5	6		8	⑨	10	11[1]	4							7														18,200
13	S	27 " 1979	Brighton & Hove Albion	A	1-1	4-2	1	2				6		8[1]	9	10[1]	11	4[1]			5				7[1]	3													23,180
14	S	3 Nov 1979	Everton	H	0-0	0-0	1	2		4		6			9	10	11		12		5				7	3	⑧												18,025
15	S	10 " 1979	West Bromwich Albion	A	1-1	1-2	1	2		7		6		8	⑨	10	11[1]			4	5					3		12											19,341
16	S	17 " 1979	Southampton	H	0-1	2-1	1	2		4[1]		6		8	9[1]	10	11				5				7	3													17,915
17	S	24 " 1979	Manchester United	A	0-3	0-5	1	2		7		6		8	⑨	10	11	4			5					3			12										46,540
18	S	1 Dec 1979	Aston Villa	H	0-1	1-1	1	2[1]				6		8	9	10	11				5		7			3				4									15,257
19	S	8 " 1979	Derby County	A	0-0	0-0	1			12				⑧	9	10	11			2	5		7			3		6		4									15,381
20	S	15 " 1979	Bristol City	H	1-0	2-0	1	2								10	11	8[1]		4	5		9[1]			3		6		⑦	12								11,657
21	S	22 " 1979	Arsenal	A	0-0	1-1	1	2[1]								10	11	8		4	5		9			3		6		7									18,869
22	W	26 " 1979	Ipswich Town	H	2-1	3-3	1	2							12	10	11	8[1]		4	⑤		9[1]			3		6		7[1]									23,767
23	S	29 " 1979	Leeds United	A	1-2	2-2	1	2							9	10	11	8[1]	12	7	5					3		6		④[1]									23,493
24	Tu	1 Jan 1980	Crystal Palace	A	0-0	0-0	1	2				6			9	10	11	⑦	12	4	5					3				8									30,254
25	S	12 " 1980	Coventry City	H	1-0	1-0	1	2				6		8	12	10	11			4	5		⑨[1]			3				7									15,414
26	S	9 Feb 1980	Liverpool	H	2-2	3-5	1	2		12				8[1]	9[1]	10	11[1]			4	5					3		6		⑦									25,418
27	S	23 " 1980	Wolverhampton Wanderers	H	0-2	0-4		2						8	9	10	11				5				7	3		6		4		1							16,763
28	W	27 " 1980	Middlesbrough	H	0-0	0-0		2	6	12				8	⑨	10	11					3						5		4		1	7						13,666
29	S	1 Mar 1980	Manchester City	A	0-0	0-0		2	6					8	12	10	11	⑨				3						5		4		1	7						32,248
30	S	8 " 1980	Brighton & Hove Albion	H	2-0	2-2		2	6	7				8[1]		10	11	9[1]				3						5		4		1							15,232
31	Tu	11 " 1980	Bolton Wanderers	A	0-0	0-1		2	12	4		6				⑩	11	8				3	9					5		7		1							10,442
32	S	15 " 1980	Stoke City	A	0-2	1-2		3[1]		④		6				10	11	8	2				9					5		12		1		7					14,123
33	S	22 " 1980	West Bromwich Albion	H	0-1	1-1		2[1]				⑥			8	10	11	4	3				9					5		12		1		7					14,303
34	W	26 " 1980	Aston Villa	A	0-0	0-2		2			6				8	12	11	9	④				10			3		5				1		7					17,956
35	S	29 " 1980	Southampton	A	0-0	0-2		2		4						10	11	9					8			3		6		5		1		7					18,921
36	W	2 Apr 1980	Arsenal	H	1-1	2-1		2	④		5				8[1]	10	11					3	9			12		6[1]				1		7					15,999
37	S	5 " 1980	Ipswich Town	A	0-1	2-4		2[1]	4		5					10	11	9				3	8[1]					6				1		7					28,968
38	M	7 " 1980	Crystal Palace	H	1-1	2-1		2	5						8[2]	10	11	12				3	⑨					6		4		1		7					16,621
39	S	19 " 1980	Manchester United	H	0-0	0-2			3						8	10	11	12	⑤			2	9					6		4		1		7					23,274
40	S	26 " 1980	Bristol City	A	1-0	3-2		2	5						8	10	11[1]					3	9[2]					6	4			1		7					16,123
41	W	30 " 1980	Nottingham Forest	A	0-1	0-2		2	3							10	11					6	9					5	4	12		1		⑦	8				21,242
42	S	3 May 1980	Derby County	H	1-0	4-2		2	6						8[1]	10[1]	11					3	9[1]					5	4			1		7[1]					15,173

F.A. CUP

NO.		DATE	OPPONENTS	V.	H-T	F-T	Keelan Kevin	Bond Kevin	McDowell John	McGuire Mick	Hoadley Phil	Powell Tony	Neighbour Jimmy	Reeves Kevin	Fashanu Justin	Paddon Graham	Peters Martin	Taylor Alan	Nightingale Mark	Ryan John	Brown Roger	Symonds Richard	Robson Keith	Bennett Dave	Goble Steve	Downs Greg	Evans Doug	Jones David	Barham Mark	Mendham Peter	Lythgoe Phil	Hansbury Roger	Halsey Mark	Woods Clive	Shepherd Greig			Own Goals	ATTD.
1	S	5 Jan 1980	Yeovil Town (3rd Round)	A	1-0	3-0	1	2				6			9[1]	8[1]	11			4	5		10[1]			3				7									8,523
2	S	26 " 1980	Wolverhampton Wanderers (4th Round)	A	1-0	1-1	1	2[1]				6		8	⑨	10	11			4	5					3				7					12				25,516
3	W	30 " 1980	Wolverhampton Wanderers (Replay)	H	1-3	2-3	1	2[1]				6		8	9	10	11			4	5					3				7[1]									23,101

FOOTBALL LEAGUE CUP

NO.		DATE	OPPONENTS	V.	H-T	F-T	Keelan Kevin	Bond Kevin	McDowell John	McGuire Mick	Hoadley Phil	Powell Tony	Neighbour Jimmy	Reeves Kevin	Fashanu Justin	Paddon Graham	Peters Martin	Taylor Alan	Nightingale Mark	Ryan John	Brown Roger	Symonds Richard	Robson Keith	Bennett Dave	Goble Steve	Downs Greg	Evans Doug	Jones David	Barham Mark	Mendham Peter	Lythgoe Phil	Hansbury Roger	Halsey Mark	Woods Clive	Shepherd Greig			Own Goals	ATTD.
1	Tu	28 Aug 1979	Gillingham (2nd Round, 1st Leg)	A	0-1	1-1	1	2	3	4	5		7	8		10	11	9[1]	6																				10,594
2	W	5 Sept 1979	Gillingham (2nd Round, 2nd Leg)	H	1-2	4-2	1	2		4	5			8[1]	9	10[2]		11[1]	6	7		3																	10,406
3	W	26 " 1979	Manchester United (3rd Round)	H	2-1	4-1	1	2	③		5[1]	6		8	9[1]	10	11			12			7	4[1]														–[1]	18,312
4	W	31 Oct 1979	West Bromwich Albion (4th Round)	A	0-0	0-0	1	2				6		8	9	10	11	④			5				7	3		12											24,062
5	W	7 Nov 1979	West Bromwich Albion (Replay)	H	2-0	3-0	1			4[1]		6		8[2]	9	10	11			2	5				7	3													19,676
6	W	5 Dec 1979	Liverpool (5th Round)	H	1-3	1-3	1	2		⑦	5	6		8[1]		10	11	12					9			3				4									23,278

1979–80 APPEARANCES & GOALS

	FOOTBALL LGE APPR.	S	GLS	F.A. CUP APPR.	S	GLS	LEAGUE CUP APPR.	S	GLS
Bond Kevin	40	–	9	3	–	2	5	–	–
Peters Martin	40	–	8	3	–	–	5	–	–
Paddon Graham	39	1	2	3	–	1	6	–	2
Fashanu Justin	31	3	11	3	–	1	4	–	1
Keelan Kevin	26	–	–	3	–	–	6	–	–
Reeves Kevin	23	–	8	2	–	–	6	–	4
Robson Keith	23	–	8	1	–	1	2	–	–
Jones David	22	1	1				–	1	–
Powell Tony	21	–	–	3	–	–	4	–	–
McDowell John	20	1	–				2	–	–
Taylor Alan	20	4	5				3	1	2
Mendham Peter	17	3	2	3	–	1	1	–	–
Downs Greg	17	1	–	3	–	–	3	–	–
Brown Roger	16	–	–	3	–	–	2	–	–
Hansbury Roger	16	–	–						
Hoadley Phil	15	–	–				4	–	1
McGuire Mick	14	5	2				4	–	1
Symonds Richard	14	1	–				1	–	–
Woods Clive	11	–	1						
Ryan John	10	2	–	3	–	–	2	1	–
Nightingale Mark	6	3	–				2	–	–
Goble Steve	5	–	1				2	–	–
Neighbour Jimmy	5	–	–				1	–	–
Bennett Dave	4	–	–				1	–	1
Barham Mark	3	1	–						
Halsey Mark	2	–	–						
Evans Doug	1	–	–						
Shepherd Greig	1	–	–	–	1	–			
Lythgoe Phil	–	1	–						
Own Goals									1

DIVISION 1

1979–80	P	W	D	L	F	A	PTS
Liverpool	42	25	10	7	81	30	60
Manchester United	42	24	10	8	65	35	58
Ipswich Town	42	22	9	11	68	39	53
Arsenal	42	18	16	8	52	36	52
Nottingham Forest	42	20	8	14	63	43	48
Wolverhampton Wanderers	42	19	9	14	58	47	47
Aston Villa	42	16	14	12	51	50	46
Southampton	42	18	9	15	65	53	45
Middlesbrough	42	16	12	14	50	44	44
West Bromwich Albion	42	11	19	12	54	50	41
Leeds United	42	13	14	15	46	50	40
Norwich City	**42**	**13**	**14**	**15**	**58**	**66**	**40**
Crystal Palace	42	12	16	14	41	50	40
Tottenham Hotspur	42	15	10	17	52	62	40
Coventry City	42	16	7	19	56	66	39
Brighton & Hove Albion	42	11	15	16	47	57	37
Manchester City	42	12	13	17	43	66	37
Stoke City	42	13	10	19	44	58	36
Everton	42	9	17	16	43	51	35
Bristol City	42	9	13	20	37	66	31
Derby County	42	11	8	23	47	67	30
Bolton Wanderers	42	5	15	22	38	73	25

1980–81 DIVISION 1

NO.		DATE	OPPONENTS	V.	H-T	F-T	Hansbury Roger	McDowell John	Downs Greg	Mendham Peter	Bond Kevin	Powell Tony	Woods Clive	Fashanu Justin	Royle Joe	Paddon Graham	Goble Steve	Nightingale Mark	Barham Mark	Forbes Duncan	Bennett Dave	Symonds Richard	Hoadley Phil	Muzinic Drazen	Jack Ross	McGuire Mick	Baker Clive	Watson Dave	Robson Keith	O'Neill Martin	Woods Chris	Walford Steve	Own Goals	ATTD.
1	S	16 Aug 1980	Stoke City	H	4-1	5-1	1	2	3^1	4	5	6	7^1	8^3	9	10	11																	13,526
2	W	20 " 1980	Aston Villa	A	0-0	0-1	1	2	3	4	5	6	7	8	9	10	⑪	12																25,970
3	S	23 " 1980	Leeds United	H	0-1	2-3	1	②	3	4	5	6	7^1	8^1	9	10	11		12															16,965
4	S	30 " 1980	Liverpool	A	0-1	1-4	1		3		2	6	7	8	9	10			4	5	11^1													35,315
5	S	6 Sept 1980	West Bromwich Albion	A	0-0	0-3	1		12		2	6	7	8	9	10			4	⑤	11	3												15,414
6	S	13 " 1980	Southampton	H	1-0	1-0	1			12	2	6	7	8^1		10	11	3	④				5	9										17,892
7	S	20 " 1980	Brighton & Hove Albion	A	0-0	0-2	1				2	6	7	8	12	10	11	③	4				5	9										14,877
8	S	27 " 1980	Birmingham City	H	2-1	2-2	1		3		2	6	⑦	8^1		10^1	11		4				12	9	5									13,561
9	S	4 Oct 1980	Middlesbrough	A	0-2	1-6	1				2	6	7	8^1	12	10	11		4			3		9	⑤									12,837
10	S	11 " 1980	Wolverhampton Wanderers	H	0-1	1-1	1		③	12	2			8^1	9	10	11	6	4	5				7										12,680
11	S	18 " 1980	Coventry City	A	1-0	1-0	1		3^1		2			8	9	10	11	6	7				5			4								12,235
12	Tu	21 " 1980	Arsenal	A	0-1	1-3	1		3		2			8	9	10	11	6	7^1				5			4								21,839
13	S	25 " 1980	Nottingham Forest	H	0-0	1-1	1		3		2			8	9^1	10	11	6	7				5			4								17,792
14	W	29 " 1980	Crystal Palace	H	1-1	1-1	1		3		2			8^1	9	10	11	6	7				5			4								15,001
15	S	1 Nov 1980	Manchester City	A	0-0	0-1	1		3		2	12		8	9	10	11	6	7				⑤			4								33,056
16	S	8 " 1980	Everton	H	0-0	2-1	1		3		2			8^1	9^1	10	11	6	7				5			4								13,868
17	W	12 " 1980	Aston Villa	H	0-1	1-3	1	5	3		2			8	9	10^1	⑪	6	7						12	4								16,388
18	S	15 " 1980	Stoke City	A	0-1	1-3	1	5	3		2		⑪	8	9^1	10		6	7		12					4								11,207
19	S	22 " 1980	Sunderland	H	1-0	1-0			3		2	6		8	9	10	11^1		7				5		12	④	1							14,406
20	S	29 " 1980	Leicester City	A	2-1	2-1					2	3		8^1	9^1	10	11	6	⑦				5	12		4	1							13,958
21	S	6 Dec 1980	Manchester United	H	0-2	2-2					3	6		8^1	9	10	11	2	7				5	12		④	1						$–^1$	18,780
22	S	13 " 1980	Crystal Palace	A	1-3	1-4			3		2	5		8	9^1	10	11	6	7					4			1							15,257
23	S	20 " 1980	Coventry City	H	2-0	2-0		6		7	2	12		8	9^1	10^1	11						5	③		4	1							11,528
24	F	26 " 1980	Ipswich Town	A	0-1	0-2				7	2	3	12	8	9	10	11						5			④	1	6						27,890
25	S	27 " 1980	Tottenham Hotspur	H	1-1	2-2		6	③	7	2^1		12	8^1	9	10	11						5			4	1							23,145
26	S	10 Jan 1981	Sunderland	A	0-2	0-3		2		7				8	9	10					12	3	⑤		11	4	1	6						17,749
27	S	17 " 1981	Liverpool	H	0-1	0-1		5		11	2				8	9			3		10				12	④	1	6	7					23,268
28	S	31 " 1981	Leeds United	A	0-0	0-1				7	2	5		8	9	10			3		11				4		1	6						15,836
29	S	7 Feb 1981	Southampton	A	0-0	1-2	1	2		7		③		8	9	10	11		4				5	12				6^1						20,454
30	S	14 " 1981	West Bromwich Albion	H	0-1	0-2	1	2				3	12		⑨	10	11		4					5	7			6	8					14,590
31	F	20 " 1981	Birmingham City	A	0-0	0-4	1			5	2			8	9	10	11		7					③	12	4		6						14,686
32	S	28 " 1981	Brighton & Hove Albion	H	2-0	3-1	1	2	3					8^1	9	10			11				5			4^1		6^1		7				15,789
33	S	14 Mar 1981	Wolverhampton Wanderers	A	0-1	0-3		②	3					8	9	10			11		12					4		6		7	1	5		21,605
34	Tu	17 " 1981	Middlesbrough	H	2-0	2-0		2	3					8	9^2	10			11							4		6		7	1	5		13,561
35	S	21 " 1981	Arsenal	H	1-0	1-1		2	3					8^1	⑨	10			11							4		6	12	7	1	5		19,207
36	S	28 " 1981	Nottingham Forest	A	1-0	1-2		2	3					8^1	9	10			11			12				4		6		⑦	1	5		22,353
37	S	4 Apr 1981	Manchester City	H	2-0	2-0		2^1	3					8	9	10			11		12					4^1		6		⑦	1	5		17,685
38	S	11 " 1981	Everton	A	1-0	2-0		2	3					8^1	9^1	10			11							4		6		7	1	5		16,254
39	S	18 " 1981	Tottenham Hotspur	A	2-2	3-2		②	3					8	9	10			11				12			4		6^1		7^1	1	5	$–^1$	34,413
40	M	20 " 1981	Ipswich Town	H	0-0	1-0			3					8^1	9	10			⑪			2			12	4		6		7	1	5		25,636
41	S	25 " 1981	Manchester United	A	0-0	0-1			3					⑧	9	10		12			11	2				4		6		7	1	5		40,164
42	S	2 May 1981	Leicester City	H	1-2	2-3		②	3					8^1	9	10			11						12	4^1		6		7	1	5		24,675

F.A. CUP

NO.		DATE	OPPONENTS	V.	H-T	F-T	Hansbury Roger	McDowell John	Downs Greg	Mendham Peter	Bond Kevin	Powell Tony	Woods Clive	Fashanu Justin	Royle Joe	Paddon Graham	Goble Steve	Nightingale Mark	Barham Mark	Forbes Duncan	Bennett Dave	Symonds Richard	Hoadley Phil	Muzinic Drazen	Jack Ross	McGuire Mick	Baker Clive	Watson Dave	Robson Keith	O'Neill Martin	Woods Chris	Walford Steve	Own Goals	ATTD.
1	S	3 Jan 1981	Cambridge United (3rd Round)	H	0-0	1-0		2	3^1	7				8	9	10	11						5			4	1	6						18,420
2	S	24 " 1981	Manchester City (4th Round)	A	0-2	0-6		5		⑦	2	4		8	9	10			3		11						1	6	12					38,919

FOOTBALL LEAGUE CUP

NO.		DATE	OPPONENTS	V.	H-T	F-T	Hansbury Roger	McDowell John	Downs Greg	Mendham Peter	Bond Kevin	Powell Tony	Woods Clive	Fashanu Justin	Royle Joe	Paddon Graham	Goble Steve	Nightingale Mark	Barham Mark	Forbes Duncan	Bennett Dave	Symonds Richard	Hoadley Phil	Muzinic Drazen	Jack Ross	McGuire Mick	Baker Clive	Watson Dave	Robson Keith	O'Neill Martin	Woods Chris	Walford Steve	Own Goals	ATTD.
1	Tu	26 Aug 1980	Shrewsbury Town (2nd Round, 1st Leg)	A	1-0	1-1	1		3		2	6	7	8^1	9	10			4	5	11													5,536
2	W	3 Sept 1980	Shrewsbury Town (2nd Round, 2nd Leg)	H	0-0	2-0	1		3		2	6	7	8^1	9^1	10			4	5	11													9,185
3	Tu	23 " 1980	Ipswich Town (3rd Round)	A	0-1	1-1	1				2	6	7	8^1	12	10	11		4				5	3	⑨									26,462
4	W	8 Oct 1980	Ipswich Town (Replay)	H	0-1	1-3	1				2	6^1	7	8		10	11		4			12	3	9	⑤									24,523

1980–81 APPEARANCES & GOALS

	FOOTBALL LGE APPR.	S	GLS	F.A. CUP APPR.	S	GLS	LEAGUE CUP APPR.	S	GLS
Paddon Graham	42	–	3	2	–	–	4	–	–
Fashanu Justin	40	–	19	2	–	–	4	–	3
Royle Joe	38	2	9	2	–	–	2	1	1
Barham Mark	34	1	1	1	–	–	4	–	–
Downs Greg	28	1	2	1	–	1	2	–	–
Bond Kevin	28	–	1	1	–	–	4	–	–
McGuire Mick	28	–	3	1	–	–			
Goble Steve	25	–	1	1	–	–	2	–	–
Hansbury Roger	22	–	–				4	–	–
McDowell John	20	–	1	2	–	–			
Watson Dave	18	–	3	2	–	–			
Hoadley Phil	17	2	–	1	–	–	2	–	–
Powell Tony	17	2	–	1	–	–	4	–	1
Nightingale Mark	14	2	–						
Mendham Peter	11	2	–	2	–	–			
O'Neill Martin	11	–	1						
Woods Clive	10	3	2				4	–	–
Baker Clive	10	–	–	2	–	–			
Walford Steve	10	–	–						
Woods Chris	10	–	–						
Muzinic Drazen	9	3	–				2	–	–
Bennett Dave	5	4	1	1	–	–	2	–	–
Jack Ross	5	6	–				2	–	–
Symonds Richard	5	1	–				–	1	–
Forbes Duncan	3	–	–				2	–	–
Robson Keith	2	1	–	–	1	–			
Own Goals			2						

DIVISION 1

1980–81	P	W	D	L	F	A	PTS
Aston Villa	42	26	8	8	72	40	60
Ipswich Town	42	23	10	9	77	43	56
Arsenal	42	19	15	8	61	45	53
West Bromwich Albion	42	20	12	10	60	42	52
Liverpool	42	17	17	8	62	42	51
Southampton	42	20	10	12	76	56	50
Nottingham Forest	42	19	12	11	62	44	50
Manchester United	42	15	18	9	51	36	48
Leeds United	42	17	10	15	39	47	44
Tottenham Hotspur	42	14	15	13	70	68	43
Stoke City	42	12	18	12	51	60	42
Manchester City	42	14	11	17	56	59	39
Birmingham City	42	13	12	17	50	61	38
Middlesbrough	42	16	5	21	53	61	37
Everton	42	13	10	19	55	58	36
Coventry City	42	13	10	19	48	68	36
Sunderland	42	14	7	21	52	53	35
Wolverhampton Wanderers	42	13	9	20	43	55	35
Brighton & Hove Albion	42	14	7	21	54	67	35
Norwich City	**42**	**13**	**7**	**22**	**49**	**73**	**33**
Leicester City	42	13	6	23	40	67	32
Crystal Palace	42	6	7	29	47	83	19

1981–82 DIVISION 2

NO.		DATE		OPPONENTS	V.	H-T	F-T	Woods Chris	Barham Mark	Muzinic Drazen	McGuire Mick	Walford Steve	Watson Dave	Mendham Peter	Shepherd Greig	Bertschin Keith	Paddon Graham	Bennett Dave	Nightingale Mark	Downs Greg	Jack Ross	Symonds Richard	Woods Clive	Hoadley Phil	Hart Andrew	Donachie Willie	Fashanu John	Haylock Paul	Royle Joe	Deehan John	O'Neill Martin	Mountford Peter	Own Goals	ATTD.
1	S	29 Aug	1981	Rotherham United	A	1-2	1-4	1	2	③	4	5	6	7	8[1]	9	10	11	12															8,919
2	W	2 Sept	1981	Crystal Palace	H	1-0	1-0	1	7		4	5	6	12	8	9	⑩		2	3	11												–[1]	13,146
3	S	5 "	1981	Barnsley	H	1-1	1-1	1	7		4	5	6	12	8	9	⑩		2	3	11[1]													12,911
4	S	12 "	1981	Wrexham	A	1-0	3-2	1	7[1]		4	5	6		8[1]		10		2		⑪[1]	3	9	12										4,007
5	S	19 "	1981	Newcastle United	H	1-1	2-1	1	7		4	5	6[1]		8		10		②	3	11[1]		9		12									13,834
6	Tu	22 "	1981	Grimsby Town	A	2-0	2-1	1	7		4	5	6		8		10		2	3	11[1]		9[1]											10,185
7	S	26 "	1981	Chelsea	A	1-1	1-2	1	7		4	5	⑥		8	12	10		2	3	11[1]		9											14,509
8	S	3 Oct	1981	Oldham Athletic	H	1-1	1-2	1	7		4	5			12	9	⑩		2		8[1]		11	6		3								13,248
9	S	10 "	1981	Queens Park Rangers	A	0-0	0-2	1	7	12		5	6	4	10	9			2		8		⑪			3								11,806
10	S	17 "	1981	Shrewsbury Town	H	1-1	2-1	1	7		4	5		10[1]		9[1]					8	2	⑪	6		3	12							11,776
11	S	24 "	1981	Watford	A	0-2	0-3	1	7		4	5		10		⑨					12	2	11	6		3	8							14,463
12	S	31 "	1981	Bolton Wanderers	H	0-0	0-0	1	⑦		4	5	6	10	12			11			9	2				3		8						12,346
13	S	7 Nov	1981	Cardiff City	A	0-0	0-1	1			4	5	6	10	7			11			9	2				3		8						5,704
14	S	14 "	1981	Cambridge United	H	1-0	2-1	1		8	4[1]	5[1]	6		12			⑪			9	7				3		2	10					13,839
15	S	21 "	1981	Derby County	H	2-0	4-1	1	⑦[1]	8	4	5	6	11[1]		9[1]					12	2				3	10[1]							13,175
16	Tu	24 "	1981	Crystal Palace	A	0-0	1-2	1	7	8	4	5	6	⑪[1]		9					12	2				3	10							9,010
17	S	28 "	1981	Blackburn Rovers	A	0-1	0-3	1			4	5	6	11		9		8			12	2				3	10	⑦						8,153
18	S	5 Dec	1981	Leicester City	H	0-0	0-0	1		8	4	5	6	12		10		11			7	2				3			⑨					12,768
19	M	28 "	1981	Luton Town	H	1-3	1-3	1	7	⑧	4	5	6	12		10		11		3		2								9[1]				18,458
20	W	30 "	1981	Charlton Athletic	A	0-0	0-0	1			4	5	6	7		10		11		3	8	2								9				6,277
21	S	16 Jan	1982	Rotherham United	H	1-0	2-0	1			4	5	6	7		10[1]		11		3	8	2								9[1]				11,792
22	S	20 "	1982	Newcastle United	A	0-0	1-2	1	11		4	5	6	7		10				3[1]	8	2								9				14,447
23	W	3 Feb	1982	Sheffield Wednesday	H	1-1	2-3	1	12[1]		4	5	6	⑦		10		11		3		2								9	8[1]			14,746
24	S	6 "	1982	Wrexham	H	2-0	4-0	1	7		4	5	6[1]			10[1]		11[1]		③	12	2								9	8[1]			11,626
25	Tu	16 "	1982	Oldham Athletic	A	0-1	0-2	1			4	5	6	11		10				3	7	2								9	8			5,283
26	S	20 "	1982	Chelsea	H	2-1	2-1	1			4	5	6	11[1]	⑨	10				3	7[1]							2			8	12		15,766
27	W	24 "	1982	Barnsley	A	1-0	1-0	1			4	5	6	11	9	10[1]				3	7							2			8			15,360
28	S	27 "	1982	Queens Park Rangers	H	0-1	0-1	1			4	5	6	⑪		10				3	7							2		9	8	12		15,216
29	S	13 Mar	1982	Watford	H	1-2	4-2	1			4	5	6[1]	11		10[1]				3	7							2		9[1]	8[1]			15,125
30	Tu	16 "	1982	Orient	A	1-1	1-1	1			4	5	6	11		10		12		3	7[1]							②		9	8			2,933
31	S	20 "	1982	Bolton Wanderers	A	0-0	1-0	1				5	6		4	10		11		3	7							2		9	8[1]			6,199
32	S	27 "	1982	Cardiff City	H	0-0	2-1	1			4	5	6	11		10[1]				3	7[1]							2		9	8			11,923
33	S	3 Apr	1982	Cambridge United	A	0-0	2-1	1			4	5	6	11[1]		10		7		3								2		9[1]	8			7,035
34	S	10 "	1982	Charlton Athletic	H	2-0	5-0	1	4			5	6	11		10		⑦		3	12[1]							2		9[3]	8[1]			14,097
35	M	12 "	1982	Luton Town	A	0-0	0-2	1	7		4	5	6	11		10				3	12							②		9	8			15,601
36	S	17 "	1982	Derby County	A	1-0	2-0	1	7		4	5		11		10		6[1]		3								2		9	8[1]			12,508
37	Tu	20 "	1982	Shrewsbury Town	A	2-0	2-0	1	12		4	5	6	⑪[1]		10		7		3								2		9[1]	8			3,590
38	S	24 "	1982	Blackburn Rovers	H	2-0	2-0	1	7		4[1]	5	6			⑩[1]		11		3	12							2		9	8			15,430
39	S	1 May	1982	Leicester City	A	1-0	4-1	1	7[1]		4	5	6			10[1]		11				3						2		9[1]	8		–[1]	19,630
40	W	5 "	1982	Grimsby Town	H	0-0	2-1	1	7		4	5	6			10[1]		11		3	12							2		⑨[1]	8			17,795
41	S	8 "	1982	Orient	H	0-0	2-0	1	7		4	5	6			10[1]		11[1]		3	12							2		⑨	8			18,827
42	S	15 "	1982	Sheffield Wednesday	A	0-0	1-2	1	⑦		4	5	6			10[1]		11		3	12							2		9	8			24,687

F.A. CUP

NO.		DATE		OPPONENTS		V.	H-T	F-T	Woods Chris	Barham Mark	Muzinic Drazen	McGuire Mick	Walford Steve	Watson Dave	Mendham Peter	Shepherd Greig	Bertschin Keith	Paddon Graham	Bennett Dave	Nightingale Mark	Downs Greg	Jack Ross	Symonds Richard	Woods Clive	Hoadley Phil	Hart Andrew	Donachie Willie	Fashanu John	Haylock Paul	Royle Joe	Deehan John	O'Neill Martin	Mountford Peter	Own Goals	ATTD.
1	S	2 Jan	1982	Stoke City	(3rd Round)	A	1-0	1-0	1			4	5	6	7		10		11		3	8[1]	2								9				12,805
2	S	23 "	1982	Doncaster Rovers	(4th Round)	H	1-1	2-1	1	11		4	5	6[1]	7		10				3	8[1]	2								9				17,311
3	S	13 Feb	1982	West Bromwich Albion	(5th Round)	A	0-1	0-1	1	⑦		4	5	6	11		10				3	12	2								9	8			18,867

FOOTBALL LEAGUE CUP

NO.		DATE		OPPONENTS		V.	H-T	F-T	Woods Chris	Barham Mark	Muzinic Drazen	McGuire Mick	Walford Steve	Watson Dave	Mendham Peter	Shepherd Greig	Bertschin Keith	Paddon Graham	Bennett Dave	Nightingale Mark	Downs Greg	Jack Ross	Symonds Richard	Woods Clive	Hoadley Phil	Hart Andrew	Donachie Willie	Fashanu John	Haylock Paul	Royle Joe	Deehan John	O'Neill Martin	Mountford Peter	Own Goals	ATTD.
1	W	7 Oct	1981	Charlton Athletic	(2nd Round, 1st Leg)	H	1-0	1-0	1	7	12	4	5			⑩	9			2		8[1]		11	6		3								9,729
2	W	28 "	1981	Charlton Athletic	(2nd Round, 2nd Leg)	A	0-0	1-0	1	7		4	5	6	10				11			9[1]	2				3		8						7,366
3	Tu	10 Nov	1981	Arsenal	(3rd Round)	A	0-1	0-1	1		12	4	5	6	10	7			11			9	2				③		8						19,899

1981–82 APPEARANCES & GOALS

	FOOTBALL LGE			F.A. CUP			LEAGUE CUP		
	APPR.	S	GLS	APPR.	S	GLS	APPR.	S	GLS
Walford Steve	42	–	1	3	–	–	3	–	–
Woods Chris	42	–	–	3	–	–	3	–	–
McGuire Mick	39	–	2	3	–	–	3	–	–
Watson Dave	38	–	3	3	–	1	2	–	–
Bertschin Keith	35	1	12	3	–	–	1	–	–
Downs Greg	28	–	1	3	–	–			
Mendham Peter	25	4	6	3	–	–	2	–	–
Barham Mark	25	2	4	2	–	–	2	–	–
Jack Ross	24	11	10	2	1	2	3	–	2
Deehan John	22	–	10	3	–	–			
Bennett Dave	21	1	3	1	–	–	2	–	–
Haylock Paul	21	–	–				2	–	–
O'Neill Martin	20	–	6	1	–	–			
Symonds Richard	18	–	–	3	–	–	2	–	–
Shepherd Greig	12	3	2				2	–	–
Donachie Willie	11	–	–				3	–	–
Nightingale Mark	8	1	–				1	–	–
Paddon Graham	8	–	–						
Woods Clive	8	–	1				1	–	–
Muzinic Drazen	6	1	–				–	2	–
Fashanu John	4	1	1						
Hoadley Phil	3	1	–				1	–	–
Royle Joe	2	–	–						
Mountford Peter	–	2	–						
Hart Andrew	–	1	–						
Own Goals			2						

DIVISION 2

1981–82	P	W	D	L	F	A	PTS
Luton Town	42	25	13	4	86	46	88
Watford	42	23	11	8	76	42	80
Norwich City	**42**	**22**	**5**	**15**	**64**	**50**	**71**
Sheffield Wednesday	42	20	10	12	55	51	70
Queens Park Rangers	42	21	6	15	65	43	69
Barnsley	42	19	10	13	59	41	67
Rotherham United	42	20	7	15	66	54	67
Leicester City	42	18	12	12	56	48	66
Newcastle United	42	18	8	16	52	50	62
Blackburn Rovers	42	16	11	15	47	43	59
Oldham Athletic	42	15	14	13	50	51	59
Chelsea	42	15	12	15	60	60	57
Charlton Athletic	42	13	12	17	50	65	51
Cambridge United	42	13	9	20	48	53	48
Crystal Palace	42	13	9	20	34	45	48
Derby County	42	12	12	18	53	68	48
Grimsby Town	42	11	13	18	53	65	46
Shrewsbury Town	42	11	13	18	37	57	46
Bolton Wanderers	42	13	7	22	39	61	46
Cardiff City	42	12	8	22	45	61	44
Wrexham	42	11	11	20	40	56	44
Orient	42	10	9	23	36	61	39

1982–83 DIVISION 1

NO.	DATE		OPPONENTS	V.	H-T	F-T	Woods Chris	Haylock Paul	Downs Greg	McGuire Mick	Walford Steve	Watson Dave	Barham Mark	O'Neill Martin	Deehan John	Bertschin Keith	Mendham Peter	Jack Ross	Smith Colin	Mountford Peter	Fashanu John	Van Wijk Dennis	Alexander Phil	Walsh Mick	Bennett Dave	Hareide Aage	Metcalf Mark	Crowe Mark	Donowa Louie	Channon Mike	Symonds Richard	Own Goals	ATTD.
1	S	28 Aug 1982	Manchester City	H	0-2	1-2	1	2	3	4	5	6	7	8	9^{1}	10	(11)	12															21,781
2	Tu	31 " 1982	Arsenal	A	0-0	1-1	1	2		4	5	6	7	8	9^{1}	10	(11)		3	12													22,652
3	S	4 Sept 1982	Swansea City	A	0-3	0-4	1	2		4	5	6	7	8	9	10	11		3														11,694
4	W	8 " 1982	Birmingham City	H	3-1	5-1	1	2	3	4	5	6	7^{1}	8^{2}	9	$(10)^{2}$	11		12														13,007
5	S	11 " 1982	Southampton	H	0-0	1-1	1	2	3	4	5	6	7	8	9^{1}	(10)	11		12														15,849
6	S	18 " 1982	Everton	A	0-0	1-1	1	2^{1}	3	4	5	(6)	7	8	9		11				10	12											20,281
7	S	25 " 1982	West Bromwich Albion	H	1-1	1-3	1	2	3	4	5		7	8	6^{1}	10	11				(9)		12										14,404
8	S	2 Oct 1982	Sunderland	A	0-0	1-4	1	2	3	4	5		7	8	9	10								6	11^{1}								13,144
9	S	9 " 1982	Watford	A	1-2	2-2	1	2		4	5		7	8	9^{1}	10^{1}						3		6	11^{1}								18,597
10	S	16 " 1982	Tottenham Hotspur	H	0-0	0-0	1	3		4	5		7	8	9	10						2		6	11								21,668
11	S	23 " 1982	Aston Villa	H	0-0	1-0	1	2		4	5	6		8	9^{1}	10						7		3	11								14,968
12	S	30 " 1982	Coventry City	A	0-0	0-2	1	2			5	6	4	8	9	10						7		3	11								8,305
13	S	6 Nov 1982	Notts. County	H	0-0	1-2	1	2		(4)	5	6	7	8	9^{1}		12					10			11	3							12,591
14	S	13 " 1982	West Ham United	A	0-0	0-1	1	2			5	6	(7)	8	9	10						4			11	3	12						22,463
15	S	20 " 1982	Stoke City	H	0-1	4-2	1	2			5	6	7^{1}	8	9^{2}	10^{1}		12				4			11	(3)							12,813
16	S	27 " 1982	Manchester United	A	0-2	0-3	1	2			5	6	7	8	9	10		12				4			(11)	3							34,579
17	S	4 Dec 1982	Liverpool	H	0-0	1-0	1	2		4	5	6	(7)	8	9^{1}	10		12				11				3							22,826
18	S	11 " 1982	Brighton & Hove Albion	A	0-1	0-3	1	2		6	(5)			8	9	10		7		11		4				3		12					9,994
19	S	18 " 1982	Nottingham Forest	H	0-1	0-1	1	2		4	5	6		8	9	10		(7)				11				3			12				13,334
20	M	27 " 1982	Ipswich Town	A	1-1	3-2	1	2			5	6	7	8^{1}		10	4^{2}					11				3				9			29,596
21	Tu	28 " 1982	Luton Town	H	1-0	1-0	1	2	3		5	6	7	8		10	4					11								9^{1}			20,415
22	S	1 Jan 1983	Stoke City	A	0-1	0-1	1	2	12		5	6	7	8	3	10	4					(11)								9			15,669
23	M	3 " 1983	Swansea City	H	0-0	1-0	1	2	3		5	6	7	8	11	10	4													9^{1}			15,388
24	S	15 " 1983	Manchester City	A	1-3	1-4	1	(2)	3		5		7	8^{1}	9	10	4					11				6				12			22,000
25	S	22 " 1983	Everton	H	0-1	0-1	1	2	3		5		7	8	9	12	4					(11)				6				10			13,568
26	S	5 Feb 1983	Southampton	A	0-1	0-4	1	2	12		5	(6)	7		9	8	4					11				3				10			17,244
27	S	26 " 1983	Tottenham Hotspur	A	0-0	0-0	1	2	11		5	6	7		9	10	4					8				3							23,342
28	W	2 Mar 1983	Watford	H	1-0	3-0	1	2	3		5	6^{1}	7		9^{1}	10	4					11^{1}			8								15,660
29	S	5 " 1983	Aston Villa	A	1-1	2-3	1	2	3			6	7^{1}		9	10	4					11^{1}			(8)					12	5		18,624
30	S	19 " 1983	Notts. County	A	2-1	2-2	1	2	3		5	6	7		9^{1}	10^{1}	4	12				(11)			8								8,064
31	W	23 " 1983	Coventry City	H	0-0	1-1	1	2	3		5^{1}	6	7	(8)	9	10	4								11					12			12,633
32	S	26 " 1983	West Ham United	H	0-1	1-1	1	2	3		5	6	7	8	9^{1}	(10)	4	12												11			17,639
33	S	2 Apr 1983	Luton Town	A	1-0	1-0	1	2	3		5	6		8	9	10	4	12							7^{1}					(11)			11,211
34	M	4 " 1983	Ipswich Town	H	0-0	0-0	1	2	3		5	6	12	8	9	10	4					(11)								7			22,688
35	S	9 " 1983	Birmingham City	A	2-0	4-0	1	2	3		5	6	7		9^{2}	10^{2}	4								11					8			11,733
36	S	16 " 1983	Sunderland	H	0-0	2-0	1	2	3		5	6	7		9^{2}	10	4								11					8			14,844
37	W	20 " 1983	Arsenal	H	1-1	3-1	1	2	3		5	6	7	12	9^{2}	10^{1}	(4)								11					8			15,822
38	S	23 " 1983	Liverpool	A	0-0	2-0	1	2	3		5	6	7	4^{1}	9	10									11					8		$-^{1}$	37,022
39	S	30 " 1983	Manchester United	H	0-0	1-1	1	2	3		5	6	7^{1}	4	9	10									11					8			22,233
40	M	2 May 1983	West Bromwich Albion	A	0-1	0-1	1	2	3		5	(6)	7	4	9	10		12							11					8			9,221
41	S	7 " 1983	Nottingham Forest	A	2-1	2-2	1	2	3		5	6	7	4	9	10									11^{2}					8			16,308
42	S	14 " 1983	Brighton & Hove Albion	H	1-0	2-1	1	2	3		5	6	7	4	9^{1}	10									11					8^{1}			19,955

F.A. CUP

NO.	DATE		OPPONENTS		V.	H-T	F-T	Woods Chris	Haylock Paul	Downs Greg	McGuire Mick	Walford Steve	Watson Dave	Barham Mark	O'Neill Martin	Deehan John	Bertschin Keith	Mendham Peter	Jack Ross	Smith Colin	Mountford Peter	Fashanu John	Van Wijk Dennis	Alexander Phil	Walsh Mick	Bennett Dave	Hareide Aage	Metcalf Mark	Crowe Mark	Donowa Louie	Channon Mike	Symonds Richard	Own Goals	ATTD.
1	S	8 Jan 1983	Swansea City	(3rd Round)	H	2-1	2-1	1	2	3		5	6	7	8	9	10^{2}	4					11											13,222
2	S	29 " 1983	Coventry City	(4th Round)	A	0-1	2-2	1		3		5	6	7^{1}	8	9	10	4					11				2^{1}							13,073
3	W	2 Feb 1983	Coventry City *	(Replay)	H	0-1	2-1	1	12	3		5	6	7	(8)	9	10^{1}	4					11				2						$-^{1}$	18,625
4	S	19 " 1983	Ipswich Town	(5th Round)	H	1-0	1-0	1	2	11		5	6	7		9	10^{1}	4					8				3							28,001
5	S	12 Mar 1983	Brighton & Hove Albion	(6th Round)	A	0-0	0-1	1	2	3	12		6	7		9	10	4					(11)			8						5		28,800

* – AFTER EXTRA TIME

MILK CUP

NO.	DATE		OPPONENTS		V.	H-T	F-T	Woods Chris	Haylock Paul	Downs Greg	McGuire Mick	Walford Steve	Watson Dave	Barham Mark	O'Neill Martin	Deehan John	Bertschin Keith	Mendham Peter	Jack Ross	Smith Colin	Mountford Peter	Fashanu John	Van Wijk Dennis	Alexander Phil	Walsh Mick	Bennett Dave	Hareide Aage	Metcalf Mark	Crowe Mark	Donowa Louie	Channon Mike	Symonds Richard	Own Goals	ATTD.
1	W	6 Oct 1982	Preston North End	(2nd Round, 1st Leg)	H	1-1	2-1	1	2	3	(4)	5		7	8^{1}	9	10^{1}	12		6						11								7,273
2	Tu	26 " 1982	Preston North End	(2nd Round, 2nd Leg)	A	1-0	2-1	1	2			5	6	7	8	9	10^{1}	(4)	12				3			11^{1}								6,082
3	W	10 Nov 1982	Sunderland	(3rd Round)	A	0-0	0-0	1	2		4	5	6	7	8	9							10			11	3							10,934
4	W	24 " 1982	Sunderland	(Replay)	H	1-1	3-1	1	2		4	5	6^{2}	7	8	9^{1}	(10)		11				3							12				19,776
5	Tu	30 " 1982	Liverpool	(4th Round)	A	0-1	0-2	1	(2)		4	5	6	7	8	9	10		12				3				11							13,235

1982–83 APPEARANCES & GOALS

	FOOTBALL LGE			F.A. CUP			LEAGUE CUP		
	APPR.	S	GLS	APPR.	S	GLS	APPR.	S	GLS
Haylock Paul	42	–	1	3	1	–	5	–	–
Woods Chris	42	–	–	5	–	–	5	–	–
Walford Steve	41	–	1	4	–	–	5	–	–
Deehan John	40	–	20	5	–	–	5	–	1
Bertschin Keith	39	1	8	5	–	4	4	–	2
Barham Mark	37	1	4	5	–	1	5	–	–
Watson Dave	35	–	1	5	–	–	4	–	2
O'Neill Martin	34	1	5	3	–	–	5	–	1
Downs Greg	26	2	–	5	–	–	1	–	–
Mendham Peter	25	1	2	5	–	–	1	1	–
Van Wijk Dennis	22	1	2	5	–	–	4	–	–
Bennett Dave	22	–	4	1	–	–	3	–	1
Channon Mike	17	3	3						
McGuire Mick	15	–	–	–	1	–	4	–	–
Hareide Aage	12	–	–	3	–	1	2	–	–
Walsh Mick	5	–	–						
Jack Ross	2	8	–				1	2	–
Smith Colin	2	2	–				1	–	–
Fashanu John	2	–	–						
Mountford Peter	1	1	–						
Symonds Richard	1	–	–	1	–	–			
Alexander Phil	–	1	–						
Crowe Mark	–	1	–						
Donowa Louie	–	1	–				–	1	–
Metcalf Mark	–	1	–						
Own Goals			1			1			

DIVISION 1

1982–83	P	W	D	L	F	A	PTS
Liverpool	42	24	10	8	87	37	82
Watford	42	22	5	15	74	57	71
Manchester United	42	19	13	10	56	38	70
Tottenham Hotspur	42	20	9	13	65	50	69
Nottingham Forest	42	20	9	13	62	50	69
Aston Villa	42	21	5	16	62	50	68
Everton	42	18	10	14	66	48	64
West Ham United	42	20	4	18	68	62	64
Ipswich Town	42	15	13	14	64	50	58
Arsenal	42	16	10	16	58	56	58
West Bromwich Albion	42	15	12	15	51	49	57
Southampton	42	15	12	15	54	58	57
Stoke City	42	16	9	17	53	64	57
Norwich City	**42**	**14**	**12**	**16**	**52**	**58**	**54**
Notts. County	42	15	7	20	55	71	52
Sunderland	42	12	14	16	48	61	50
Birmingham City	42	12	14	16	40	55	50
Luton Town	42	12	13	17	65	84	49
Coventry City	42	13	9	20	48	59	48
Manchester City	42	13	8	21	47	70	47
Swansea City	42	10	11	21	51	69	41
Brighton & Hove Albion	42	9	13	20	38	68	40

1983–84 DIVISION 1

NO.	DATE	OPPONENTS	V.	H-T	F-T	Woods Chris	Devine John	Downs Greg	Mendham Peter	Young Willie	Watson Dave	Barham Mark	Van Wijk Dennis	Deehan John	Bertschin Keith	Bennett Dave	Haylock Paul	Channon Mike	Hareide Aage	Donowa Louie	Pickering Mike	Godbold Daryl	Clayton Paul	Rigby Jon	Rosario Robert	Spearing Tony	Goss Jeremy	Farrington Mark	Own Goals	ATTD.
1	S 27 Aug 1983	Sunderland	A	0-0	1-1	1	2	3	4	5	6	7	8	9	10^1	11														17,057
2	W 31 " 1983	Liverpool	H	0-1	0-1	1		3	4	5	6	7		9	10	11	2	8												23,271
3	S 3 Sept 1983	Wolverhampton Wanderers	H	2-0	3-0	1		3	4	5	6	7	11	9^2	10^1		2	8												12,997
4	Tu 6 " 1983	Luton Town	A	2-0	2-2	1		3	4^1	5	6	7	11	9	10		2	8^1												11,095
5	S 10 " 1983	Aston Villa	A	0-1	0-1	1	12	3	4	5	6	7	11	9	10		(2)	8												18,887
6	S 17 " 1983	Nottingham Forest	H	2-2	2-3	1	7	3	4		6		11	9^1	10^1		(2)	8	5	12										14,605
7	S 24 " 1983	Arsenal	A	0-1	0-3	1	2	3	4	12	6		(11)	9	10	7		8	5											24,438
8	S 1 Oct 1983	Manchester United	H	0-1	3-3	1	7	3	4		(6)				10	11^1	2	8^1	5	9^1	12									19,290
9	S 15 " 1983	Watford	A	0-0	3-1	1	9^1	3	4		6				10	11	2	8	5	7^1									–^{1}	12,745
10	W 19 " 1983	Leicester City	H	1-1	3-1	1	9	3	4		6				10^1	11	2	8^1	5	7^1										13,780
11	S 22 " 1983	West Ham United	A	0-0	0-0	1	9	3	4		6				10	11	2	8	5	7										18,958
12	S 29 " 1983	Queens Park Rangers	H	0-2	0-3	1	9	3	4		6	12			10	(11)	2	8	5	7										15,960
13	S 5 Nov 1983	Southampton	H	0-0	1-0	1	9	3	4		6	11	12		10^1		2	(8)	5	7										13,637
14	S 12 " 1983	Notts. County	A	1-1	1-1	1	9	3	4		6	11^1		8	10		2		5	7										7,882
15	S 19 " 1983	West Bromwich Albion	H	0-0	2-0	1	9	3^1	4		6	11^1	12	8	10		2		(5)	7										13,045
16	S 26 " 1983	Everton	A	0-0	2-0	1		3	4		6	11	9	5	10		2	8		7^1									–^{1}	14,106
17	S 3 Dec 1983	Tottenham Hotspur	H	1-1	2-1	1	2	3	4		6	(11)	9	5	10^1			8^1		7		12								21,987
18	S 10 " 1983	Birmingham City	A	1-0	1-0	1		3^1	4		6		9	5	10		2	8	11	7										9,971
19	S 17 " 1983	Coventry City	H	0-0	0-0	1		3	4		6		11	5	10		2	8	(9)	7			12							15,901
20	M 26 " 1983	Stoke City	A	0-1	0-2	1	9	3	4		6		11	5	10		2	8		7										12,049
21	Tu 27 " 1983	Ipswich Town	H	0-0	0-0	1	9	3	(4)		6		11	5	10		2	8	12	7										24,812
22	S 31 " 1983	Wolverhampton Wanderers	A	0-0	0-2	1	9	3	4		6		11	5	10		2	(8)	12	7										10,725
23	M 2 Jan 1984	Arsenal	H	0-0	1-1	1		3	4		6		11	9^1	10		2	8	5	(7)			12							19,788
24	S 14 " 1984	Sunderland	H	3-0	3-0	1	7	3^1	4		6		11		10^1		2	(8)	5^1	9			12							12,195
25	S 21 " 1984	Nottingham Forest	A	0-3	0-3	1	7	3	4				(11)	6	10		2	8	5			12	9							13,993
26	S 4 Feb 1984	Manchester United	A	0-0	0-0	1	7	3	4		6		11	9	10		2	8	5											36,851
27	S 11 " 1984	Aston Villa	H	0-0	3-1	1	5	3	4		6		11	9^2	10	12	2	8^1					(7)							13,658
28	Tu 14 " 1984	Queens Park Rangers	A	0-0	0-2	1	5	3	4		6		11	9	10		2	(8)					7	12						12,901
29	S 25 " 1984	West Ham United	H	0-0	1-0	1	7	3	4		6		11	9^1	10		2	8	5											15,937
30	S 3 Mar 1984	Southampton	A	0-1	1-2	1		3	4		6		11	9^1		7	2	8	5					10						17,456
31	W 14 " 1984	Notts. County	H	0-0	0-1	1		(3)	4		6		11	9		7	2	8	5	12				10						12,116
32	S 17 " 1984	Luton Town	H	0-0	0-0	1		3	4		6		11	9		7	2	8	5					10						13,112
33	S 31 " 1984	Leicester City	A	0-2	1-2	1	7	3	4		6			9^1		(10)	2	8	5	11				12						11,278
34	S 7 Apr 1984	Watford	H	3-1	6-1	1	7^1	3^1	4		6			9^4			2	8	5	11					10					13,391
35	S 14 " 1984	West Bromwich Albion	A	0-0	0-0	1	7	3	4		6		9				2	8	5	11					10					11,572
36	S 21 " 1984	Stoke City	H	0-1	2-2	1	2	3	4		6		10	9^1			12	8	(5)	11					7^1					14,709
37	M 23 " 1984	Ipswich Town	A	0-1	0-2	1	7	3			6		(4)	9	8		2		5	11			12		10					22,135
38	S 28 " 1984	Everton	H	0-1	1-1	1	7	3	4		6		11	9	(10)		2	8	5^1						12					12,533
39	S 5 May 1984	Tottenham Hotspur	A	0-1	0-2	1	7	5	4		6		(11)	9	10		2	8							12	3				18,874
40	M 7 " 1984	Birmingham City	H	0-0	1-1	1	7	5	4		6^1		11	9			2	8							10	3				12,111
41	S 12 " 1984	Coventry City	A	1-1	1-2	1	7	5	4		6		11	(9)^1			2								10	3	12	8		14,007
42	Tu 15 " 1984	Liverpool	A	1-1	1-1	1	6^1	5	4				11	9	10		2	8		7						(3)		12		38,837

F.A. CUP

NO.	DATE	OPPONENTS	V.	H-T	F-T	Woods Chris	Devine John	Downs Greg	Mendham Peter	Young Willie	Watson Dave	Barham Mark	Van Wijk Dennis	Deehan John	Bertschin Keith	Bennett Dave	Haylock Paul	Channon Mike	Hareide Aage	Donowa Louie	ATTD.
1	S 7 Jan 1984	Aston Villa (3rd Round)	A	1-1	1-1	1	7	3	4		6		11	9^1	10		2	8	5		21,454
2	W 11 " 1984	Aston Villa (Replay)	H	1-0	3-0	1	7	3	4^1		6		11	9	10^1		2	(8)^1	5	12	16,420
3	S 28 " 1984	Tottenham Hotspur (4th Round)	A	0-0	0-0	1	7	3	4		6		11	9	10		2	8	5		37,792
4	W 1 Feb 1984	Tottenham Hotspur (Replay)	H	2-0	2-1	1	7	3	4		6		11^1	9	10		2	8^1	5		26,811
5	S 18 " 1984	Derby County (5th Round)	A	0-0	1-2	1	7	(3)	4		6		11	9^1	10	12	2	8	5		25,793

MILK CUP

NO.	DATE	OPPONENTS	V.	H-T	F-T	Woods Chris	Devine John	Downs Greg	Mendham Peter	Young Willie	Watson Dave	Barham Mark	Van Wijk Dennis	Deehan John	Bertschin Keith	Bennett Dave	Haylock Paul	Channon Mike	Hareide Aage	Donowa Louie	ATTD.
1	Tu 4 Oct 1983	Cardiff City (2nd Round, 1st Leg)	A	0-0	0-0	1	7	3	4	6					11	10	2	8	5	9	4,425
2	W 26 " 1983	Cardiff City (2nd Round, 2nd Leg)	H	1-0	3-0	1	9	3	4		6	12			10	(11)	2	8^3	5	7	9,887
3	W 9 Nov 1983	Sunderland (3rd Round)	H	0-0	0-0	1	9	3	4			11		6	10		2	8	5	7	12,406
4	Tu 22 " 1983	Sunderland (Replay)	A	1-0	2-1	1		3	4		6	11	10	5	9^2		2	8		7	14,149
5	W 30 " 1983	Ipswich Town (4th Round)	A	0-0	1-0	1		3	4		6	11	9	5	10		2	8^1		7	25,570
6	Tu 17 Jan 1984	Aston Villa (5th Round)	H	0-2	0-2	1	7	3	4		(6)		11	9	10		2	8	5	12	21,568

1983–84 APPEARANCES & GOALS

	FOOTBALL LGE			F.A. CUP			LEAGUE CUP		
	APPR.	S	GLS	APPR.	S	GLS	APPR.	S	GLS
Downs Greg	42	–	4	5	–	–	6	–	–
Woods Chris	42	–	–	5	–	–	6	–	–
Mendham Peter	41	–	1	5	–	1	6	–	–
Watson Dave	40	–	1	5	–	–	4	–	–
Haylock Paul	38	1	–	5	–	–	6	–	–
Channon Mike	37	–	5	5	–	2	6	–	4
Deehan John	34	–	15	5	–	2	4	–	–
Bertschin Keith	33	–	7	5	–	1	6	–	2
Van Wijk Dennis	31	2	–	5	–	1	3	–	–
Devine John	31	1	3	5	–	–	4	–	–
Hareide Aage	26	2	2	5	–	–	4	–	–
Donowa Louie	23	2	4	–	1	–	5	1	–
Bennett Dave	12	1	1	–	1	–	2	–	–
Barham Mark	10	1	2				3	1	–
Rosario Robert	6	2	1						
Young Willie	5	1	–				1	–	–
Spearing Tony	4	–	–						
Clayton Paul	3	4	–						
Rigby Jon	3	2	–						
Farrington Mark	1	1	–						
Godbold Daryl	–	2	–						
Goss Jeremy	–	1	–						
Pickering Mike	–	1	–						
Own Goals			2						

DIVISION 1

1983–84	P	W	D	L	F	A	PTS
Liverpool	42	22	14	6	73	32	80
Southampton	42	22	11	9	66	38	77
Nottingham Forest	42	22	8	12	76	45	74
Manchester United	42	20	14	8	71	41	74
Queens Park Rangers	42	22	7	13	67	37	73
Arsenal	42	18	9	15	74	60	63
Everton	42	16	14	12	44	42	62
Tottenham Hotspur	42	17	10	15	64	65	61
West Ham United	42	17	9	16	60	55	60
Aston Villa	42	17	9	16	59	61	60
Watford	42	16	9	17	68	77	57
Ipswich Town	42	15	8	19	55	57	53
Sunderland	42	13	13	16	42	53	52
Norwich City	**42**	**12**	**15**	**15**	**48**	**49**	**51**
Leicester City	42	13	12	17	65	68	51
Luton Town	42	14	9	19	53	66	51
West Bromwich Albion	42	14	9	19	48	62	51
Stoke City	42	13	11	18	44	63	50
Coventry City	42	13	11	18	57	77	50
Birmingham City	42	12	12	18	39	50	48
Notts. County	42	10	11	21	50	72	41
Wolverhampton Wanderers	42	6	11	25	27	80	29

1984–85 DIVISION 1

No.	Date	Opponents	V.	H-T	F-T	Woods Chris	Haylock Paul	Van Wijk Dennis	Mendham Peter	Bruce Steve	Watson Dave	Devine John	Channon Mike	Deehan John	Bertschin Keith	Gordon Dale	Goss Jeremy	Farrington Mark	Donowa Louie	Corrigan Joe	Hartford Asa	Downs Greg	Barham Mark	Clayton Paul	Rowell Gary	Benstead Graham	Fairclough David	Rigby Jon	Rosario Robert	Spearing Tony	Own Goals	Attd.
1	S 25 Aug 1984	Liverpool	H	1-2	3-3	1	2	3	4[1]	5	6	7	8[1]	9	10[1]	11															21,560
2	Tu 28 " 1984	Coventry City	A	0-0	0-0	1	2	3	4	5	6	7	8	9	10	11															10,632
3	S 1 Sept 1984	Tottenham Hotspur	A	0-1	1-3	1	2	3	4	5	5	(7)	8	9	10[1]	11	12														24,947
4	W 5 " 1984	West Bromwich Albion	H	0-0	2-1	1	2	11	4[1]	5	6	3		9	10	(7)	12	8[1]													13,070
5	S 15 " 1984	Southampton	A	0-1	1-2	1	2	11	4	6	5	(3)		9	10	7		8	12[1]												16,431
6	W 19 " 1984	Stoke City	H	0-0	0-0	1	2	3	(4)	6	5	10		9		7	12	8	11												12,261
7	S 22 " 1984	Watford	H	1-1	3-2	1	2	3	4	6	5	10		9[3]		7		8	11												13,876
8	S 29 " 1984	Nottingham Forest	A	0-1	1-3		2	3	4[1]	6	5	10		9		7		8	11	1											15,166
9	S 6 Oct 1984	Chelsea	H	0-0	0-0		2	(3)	5	4	6	10	12	9		7		8	11	1											16,881
10	S 13 " 1984	Sunderland	A	0-1	1-2		2		5	4	6	(3)	8[1]	9		7		12	11	1	10										15,155
11	S 20 " 1984	Aston Villa	A	2-1	2-2	1	2		5	4	6	7	8	9[1]					11[1]		10	3									14,149
12	S 27 " 1984	Queens Park Rangers	H	1-0	2-0	1	2		5	4	6	7	8[1]	9[1]					11		10	3									13,817
13	S 3 Nov 1984	Sheffield Wednesday	A	1-0	2-1	1	2	12	5	4	6	(7)	8	9[1]					11[1]		10	3									21,847
14	S 10 " 1984	Luton Town	H	2-0	3-0	1	2	12	(5)[1]	4	6		8	9		11[1]			7		10[1]	3									13,610
15	S 17 " 1984	Leicester City	A	0-1	0-2	1	2		5	4	6		8	9		11			7		10	3									9,693
16	S 24 " 1984	Everton	H	3-1	4-2	1	2		5	4	6		8	9[2]		11[1]			7[1]		10	3									16,477
17	S 1 Dec 1984	Manchester United	A	0-2	0-2	1	2		5	4	6		8	(9)		11	12		7		10	3									36,635
18	S 8 " 1984	West Ham United	H	1-0	1-0	1	2		5	4	6		8			11		9[1]	7		10	3									13,485
19	S 15 " 1984	Newcastle United	A	1-0	1-1	1	2	12	5	4	6		8	9		(11)			7[1]		10	3									20,030
20	S 22 " 1984	Tottenham Hotspur	H	0-1	1-2	1	2	12	5	4	6		8	9[1]		11			7		10	(3)									16,954
21	W 26 " 1984	Arsenal	H	1-0	1-0	1	2	3	5	4	6		8	9[1]		11			7		10										16,668
22	S 29 " 1984	West Bromwich Albion	A	1-0	1-0	1	2	(3)	5	4	6	7	8[1]	9		12		10	11												13,403
23	Tu 1 Jan 1985	Ipswich Town	A	0-1	0-2	1	2		5	4	6	7	8	9		12		(10)	11			3									21,710
24	S 12 " 1985	Southampton	H	0-0	1-0	1	2		5	4	(6)		8	9[1]			10	12	11			3	7								12,629
25	S 19 " 1985	Liverpool	A	0-1	0-4	1	2	6	5	4		12	8	9					(11)		10	3	7								30,627
26	S 2 Feb 1985	Nottingham Forest	H	0-0	0-1	1	2	3	5	4	6	11		9				8			10		7								13,753
27	S 2 Mar 1985	Queens Park Rangers	A	0-2	2-2	1	2	6	5	4			8[1]	9[1]					11		10	3	7								12,975
28	S 9 " 1985	Aston Villa	H	0-0	2-2	1	2[1]	3	5	4	6		8						(11)		10		7	9	12[1]						21,120
29	S 16 " 1985	Sunderland	H	1-2	1-3	1	2	4	5		6		8	9[1]					(11)		10	3	7		12						12,130
30	S 30 " 1985	Coventry City	H	2-1	2-1	1	2	3	5	4	6		8[2]	9					11		10		7								12,897
31	W 3 Apr 1985	Sheffield Wednesday	H	1-1	1-1	1	2	3	(5)	4	6		8	9					11		10		7[1]		12						13,862
32	S 6 " 1985	Arsenal	A	0-0	0-2		2	3		4	6	5		9							10		7	11		1	8				19,597
33	M 8 " 1985	Ipswich Town	H	0-1	0-2	1	2	3		4	6	5	8	9					11		10		7								16,884
34	S 13 " 1985	Watford	A	0-0	0-2	1	2	3		4	6	5	8	9							10		(7)		11		12				15,372
35	Tu 16 " 1985	Luton Town	A	1-0	1-3	1	2	3		4	6	5	8[1]	9					7		10				11						8,794
36	S 20 " 1985	Leicester City	H	1-1	1-3	1	2	3	5	4	6		8	9		11			7[1]		(10)				12						12,634
37	W 24 " 1985	Stoke City	A	2-1	3-2	1	2	3	5					9		11[1]			7[1]			6		10				4	8[1]			4,597
38	S 27 " 1985	Everton	A	0-1	0-3	1	2	3		4	6			9		11			7			(5)		12				10	8			32,085
39	S 4 May 1985	Manchester United	H	0-1	0-1	1		3	5		6		8	9					7		10	4		11				2				15,502
40	M 6 " 1985	West Ham United	A	0-0	0-1	1	2	3		4	6		(8)	9					11		10	12	7					5				16,233
41	S 11 " 1985	Newcastle United	H	0-0	0-0	1	2	3	5	4	6			9					11		(10)		7					12	8			17,020
42	Tu 14 " 1985	Chelsea	A	1-1	2-1	1	2	3	5	4[1]	6			9							10[1]	11	7						8			22,882

F.A. CUP

No.	Date	Opponents	V.	H-T	F-T	Woods Chris	Haylock Paul	Van Wijk Dennis	Mendham Peter	Bruce Steve	Watson Dave	Devine John	Channon Mike	Deehan John	Bertschin Keith	Gordon Dale	Goss Jeremy	Farrington Mark	Donowa Louie	Corrigan Joe	Hartford Asa	Downs Greg	Barham Mark	Clayton Paul	Rowell Gary	Benstead Graham	Fairclough David	Rigby Jon	Rosario Robert	Spearing Tony	Own Goals	Attd.
1	S 5 Jan 1985	Birmingham City (3rd Round)	A	0-0	0-0	1	2		5	4	6		8	9			11	10				3	7								12,941
2	W 23 " 1985	Birmingham City * (Replay)	H	0-0	1-1	1	2[1]	6	5	4		11	8	9							10		7							3		11,724
3	S 26 " 1985	Birmingham City * (2nd Replay)	A	0-0	1-1	1	2	6	5[1]	4		11	8					(9)	12		10	3	7								11,755
4	M 28 " 1985	Birmingham City (3rd Replay)	H	1-0	1-0	1	2	6	5	4[1]		11	8					9			10	3	7								12,396
5	M 4 Feb 1985	West Ham United (4th Round)	A	1-0	1-2	1	2	3	5	4	6		8	9					11[1]		10		7								20,098

MILK CUP

No.	Date	Opponents	V.	H-T	F-T	Woods Chris	Haylock Paul	Van Wijk Dennis	Mendham Peter	Bruce Steve	Watson Dave	Devine John	Channon Mike	Deehan John	Bertschin Keith	Gordon Dale	Goss Jeremy	Farrington Mark	Donowa Louie	Corrigan Joe	Hartford Asa	Downs Greg	Barham Mark	Clayton Paul	Rowell Gary	Benstead Graham	Fairclough David	Rigby Jon	Rosario Robert	Spearing Tony	Own Goals	Attd.
1	Tu 25 Sept 1984	Preston North End (2nd Round, 1st Leg)	A	2-1	3-3	1	2	3	6	4[1]	5[1]	10		9[1]		7		8	11												5,265
2	W 10 Oct 1984	Preston North End (2nd Round, 2nd Leg)	H	2-0	6-1		2		5	4[1]	6	3	8[1]	9		7			11[2]	1	10[2]										13,454
3	W 31 " 1984	Aldershot (3rd Round)	H	0-0	0-0	1	(2)	12	5	4	6	7	8	9					11		10	3									11,783
4	Tu 6 Nov 1984	Aldershot (Replay)	A	2-0	4-0	1	2	12	5[1]	4	6		8[1]	9[1]		(7)			11		10	3								–[1]	9,773
5	W 21 " 1984	Notts. County (4th Round)	H	1-0	3-0	1	2		5	4	6		8[1]	9[1]		11			7[1]		10	3									14,471
6	W 16 Jan 1985	Grimsby Town (5th Round)	H	1-0	1-0	1	2	6	5	4			8	9[1]					11		10	3	7								15,050
7	S 23 Feb 1985	Ipswich Town (Semi-Final, 1st Leg)	A	0-1	0-1	1		3	5	4	6	2	8	9							10		7	11							27,404
8	W 6 Mar 1985	Ipswich Town (Semi-Final, 2nd Leg)	H	1-0	2-0	1	2	3	5	4[1]	6		8	9[1]					11		10		7								23,545
9	Su 24 Mar 1985	Sunderland (Final)	W	0-0	1-0	1	2	3	5	4	6		8	9					11		10[1]		7								100,000

W – PLAYED AT WEMBLEY * AFTER EXTRA TIME

1984–85 APPEARANCES & GOALS

	FOOTBALL LGE APPR.	S	GLS	F.A. CUP APPR.	S	GLS	LEAGUE CUP APPR.	S	GLS
Haylock Paul	41	–	1	5	–	1	8	–	–
Deehan John	40	–	13	3	–	–	9	–	5
Bruce Steve	39	–	1	5	–	1	9	–	3
Watson Dave	39	–	–	2	–	–	8	–	1
Woods Chris	38	–	–	5	–	–	8	–	–
Mendham Peter	36	–	4	5	–	1	9	–	1
Donowa Louie	33	1	7	1	1	1	8	–	3
Channon Mike	30	1	8	5	–	–	8	–	3
Van Wijk Dennis	29	4	–	4	–	–	5	1	–
Hartford Asa	28	–	2	4	–	–	8	–	3
Gordon Dale	21	2	3				4	–	–
Devine John	20	1	–	3	–	–	4	–	–
Downs Greg	19	1	–	3	–	–	4	–	–
Barham Mark	14	–	1	5	–	–	4	–	–
Farrington Mark	10	2	2	3	–	–	1	–	–
Bertschin Keith	5	–	2						
Clayton Paul	4	1	–				1	–	–
Rigby Jon	4	1	–						
Rosario Robert	4	–	1						
Corrigan Joe	3	–	–				1	–	–
Rowell Gary	2	4	1						
Goss Jeremy	1	4	–	1	–	–			
Fairclough Dave	1	1	–						
Benstead Graham	1	–	–						
Spearing Tony				1	–	–			
Own Goals									1

DIVISION 1

1984–85	P	W	D	L	F	A	PTS
Everton	42	28	6	8	88	43	90
Liverpool	42	22	11	9	68	35	77
Tottenham Hotspur	42	23	8	11	78	51	77
Manchester United	42	22	10	10	77	47	76
Southampton	42	19	11	12	56	47	68
Chelsea	42	18	12	12	63	48	66
Arsenal	42	19	9	14	61	49	66
Sheffield Wednesday	42	17	14	11	58	45	65
Nottingham Forest	42	19	7	16	56	48	64
Aston Villa	42	15	11	16	60	60	56
Watford	42	14	13	15	81	71	55
West Bromwich Albion	42	16	7	19	58	62	55
Luton Town	42	15	9	18	57	61	54
Newcastle United	42	13	13	16	55	70	52
Leicester City	42	15	6	21	65	73	51
West Ham United	42	13	12	17	51	68	51
Ipswich Town	42	13	11	18	46	57	50
Coventry City	42	15	5	22	47	64	50
Queens Park Rangers	42	13	11	18	53	72	50
Norwich City	**42**	**13**	**10**	**19**	**46**	**64**	**49**
Sunderland	42	10	10	22	40	62	40
Stoke City	42	3	8	31	24	91	17

1985–86 DIVISION 2

NO.		DATE	OPPONENTS	V.	H-T	F-T	Woods Chris	Haylock Paul	Van Wijk Dennis	Bruce Steve	Phelan Mick	Watson Dave	Mendham Peter	Drinkell Kevin	Deehan John	Brooke Garry	Williams David	Donowa Louie	Barham Mark	Spearing Tony	Rosario Robert	Culverhouse Ian	Biggins Wayne	Gordon Dale	Clayton Paul	Own Goals	ATTD.
1	S	17 Aug 1985	Oldham Athletic	H	1-0	1-0	1	2	3	4	5	6	7^1	8	9	10	11										11,752
2	Tu	20 " 1985	Blackburn Rovers	A	1-0	1-2	1	2	3	4^1	5	6	7	8	9	10	11										6,567
3	S	24 " 1985	Millwall	A	1-1	2-4	1	2	3	4	5	6	7	8	9^1	10^1	⑪	12									7,100
4	M	26 " 1985	Barnsley	H	0-0	1-1	1	2	③	4^1	5	6	10	8	9	11	12		7								12,376
5	S	31 " 1985	Portsmouth	A	0-1	0-2	1	②		4	5	6	10	8	9		11	12	7	3							15,504
6	S	7 Sept 1985	Sheffield United	H	1-0	4-0	1	2^1		4^1	5	6	10	8^2	9		11		7	3							11,956
7	S	14 " 1985	Middlesbrough	A	0-1	1-1	1	2	12	4	5	6	10	8^1			11		7	3	⑨						5,475
8	W	18 " 1985	Crystal Palace	H	2-2	4-3	1	2		4	5^1	6^1	10	8^1			11		7^1	3	9						12,541
9	S	21 " 1985	Huddersfield Town	A	0-0	0-0	1	2		4	5	6	10	8			11		7	3	9						7,225
10	S	28 " 1985	Hull City	H	1-0	2-0	1	2		4	5	6	10^1	8			11		7	3	9^1						11,945
11	S	5 Oct 1985	Wimbledon	H	1-2	1-2	1	2	11	4	5	6	10	8^1		12			7	③	9						12,028
12	S	12 " 1985	Carlisle United	A	1-0	4-0	1		3	4	5^1	6	10	8^1		11^1			7		9^1	2					2,907
13	S	19 " 1985	Shrewsbury Town	H	2-1	3-1	1		3	4	5	6	10^1	8^1		11	12		7^1		⑨	2					11,148
14	S	26 " 1985	Sunderland	A	0-0	2-0	1		3	4	5	6	10^1	8			11^1		7			2	9				17,908
15	S	2 Nov 1985	Brighton & Hove Albion	A	0-0	1-1	1		3	4	5	6	10				11		7		8	2	9^1				10,423
16	S	9 " 1985	Bradford City	H	0-0	0-0	1		3	4	5	6	10	8		12	⑪		7			2	9				12,749
17	S	16 " 1985	Stoke City	A	0-0	1-1	1		3	4	5	6	10	8^1			⑪		7			2	9	12			6,469
18	S	23 " 1985	Grimsby Town	H	1-0	3-2	1		3	4	5	6^1	10	8			11		7			2	9^1			$-^1$	12,108
19	S	30 " 1985	Leeds United	A	1-0	2-0	1		3	4^1	5	6	10	8^1		12	11		⑦			2	9				11,425
20	S	7 Dec 1985	Blackburn Rovers	H	2-0	3-0	1		3^1	4^1	5	6	10	8			11		7^1			2	⑨	12			12,156
21	S	14 " 1985	Oldham Athletic	A	0-0	3-1	1		3	4	5	6^1	10	8^1	12		11		7			2	⑨			$-^1$	3,949
22	S	21 " 1985	Millwall	H	4-0	6-1	1		3	4	5^1	⑥	10^1	8^1	12		11^2		7^1			2	9				11,939
23	Th	26 " 1985	Charlton Athletic	H	0-0	3-1	1		3	4	5	6	10	8^2	12^1		⑪		7			2	9				16,965
24	W	1 Jan 1986	Fulham	A	0-0	1-0	1		3	4	5	6	10	8^1	12		11		7			2	⑨				7,463
25	S	11 " 1986	Middlesbrough	H	1-0	2-0	1		3	4^1	5	6	10	8			11^1		7			2	9				13,050
26	S	18 " 1986	Portsmouth	H	0-0	2-0	1		3	4	5	6	10	8^1			11		7^1			2	9				18,956
27	S	25 " 1986	Crystal Palace	A	2-0	2-1	1			4	5	6	10^1	8	3		11		7			2	9^1				8,369
28	S	1 Feb 1986	Barnsley	A	2-1	2-2	1			4	5	6	10^1	8	3^1		11		7			2	9				5,608
29	S	8 " 1986	Shrewsbury Town	A	2-0	3-0	1			4	5	6	10	8^2	3		11		7^1			2	9				5,157
30	S	8 Mar 1986	Wimbledon	A	1-0	1-2	1			4	5	6	10	8	3		1		7^1			2	9				5,827
31	W	12 " 1986	Huddersfield Town	H	1-1	4-1	1			4^1	5	6	10	8^1	3		11		7			2	9^2				11,477
32	S	15 " 1986	Carlisle United	H	1-0	2-1	1			4	5	6	10	8	3		11^2		7			2	9				13,030
33	S	22 " 1986	Sheffield United	A	2-1	5-2	1			4	5	6	10^1	8^1	3		11		7^1			2	9^1			$-^1$	11,894
34	S	29 " 1986	Fulham	H	2-1	2-1	1			4	5	6	10	8	3^1		11		7^1			2	9				16,848
35	M	31 " 1986	Charlton Athletic	A	0-0	0-1	1		12	4	5	6	10	8	3		11		7			2	⑨				8,458
36	S	5 Apr 1986	Brighton & Hove Albion	H	0-0	3-0	1		3	4	5	6		8^1	10		11^1		⑦			2	9	12		$-^1$	14,318
37	W	9 " 1986	Sunderland	H	0-0	0-0	1		3	4	5	6		8	10				7			2	9	11			17,021
38	S	12 " 1986	Bradford City	A	1-0	2-0	1		3	4	5	6		8^1	10		11		7			2	9^1				7,190
39	S	19 " 1986	Stoke City	H	0-0	1-1	1		3	4	5	6		8	10	12	11					2	⑨	7^1			17,404
40	S	26 " 1986	Grimsby Town	A	0-0	0-1	1		3	4	5	6		8	10	12	11					2	9	⑦			8,090
41	Tu	29 " 1986	Hull City	A	0-0	0-1	1	2	3	4	5	6		8	10	7	11			12			⑨				6,146
42	S	3 May 1986	Leeds United	H	1-0	4-0	1		3	4^1	5	6		8^1	9	7	11^1					2			10	$-^1$	17,078

F.A. CUP

NO.		DATE	OPPONENTS	V.	H-T	F-T	Woods Chris	Haylock Paul	Van Wijk Dennis	Bruce Steve	Phelan Mick	Watson Dave	Mendham Peter	Drinkell Kevin	Deehan John	Brooke Garry	Williams David	Donowa Louie	Barham Mark	Spearing Tony	Rosario Robert	Culverhouse Ian	Biggins Wayne	Gordon Dale	Clayton Paul	Own Goals	ATTD.
1	S	4 Jan 1986	Liverpool	A	0-2	0-5	1		3	4	5	6	10	8	12		⑪		7			2	9				29,802

MILK CUP

NO.		DATE	OPPONENTS	V.	H-T	F-T	Woods Chris	Haylock Paul	Van Wijk Dennis	Bruce Steve	Phelan Mick	Watson Dave	Mendham Peter	Drinkell Kevin	Deehan John	Brooke Garry	Williams David	Donowa Louie	Barham Mark	Spearing Tony	Rosario Robert	Culverhouse Ian	Biggins Wayne	Gordon Dale	Clayton Paul	Own Goals	ATTD.
1	M	30 Sept 1985	Preston North End (2nd Round, 1st Leg)	A	1-1	1-1	1	2	6	4^1	5		10	8			11		7	3	9						4,330
2	W	9 Oct 1985	Preston North End (2nd Round, 2nd Leg)	H	0-1	2-1	1		3	4	5	6	10	8		11^1			7		9^1	2					10,262
3	Tu	29 " 1985	Luton Town (3rd Round)	A	2-0	2-0	1		3	4^1	5	6	10^1	8			11		7		9	2					8,202
4	W	20 Nov 1985	Oxford United (4th Round)	A	1-1	1-3	1		3	4	5	6	10	8^1		12	⑪		7		9	2					7,851

SCREEN SPORT SUPER CUP

NO.		DATE	OPPONENTS	V.	H-T	F-T	Woods Chris	Haylock Paul	Van Wijk Dennis	Bruce Steve	Phelan Mick	Watson Dave	Mendham Peter	Drinkell Kevin	Deehan John	Brooke Garry	Williams David	Donowa Louie	Barham Mark	Spearing Tony	Rosario Robert	Culverhouse Ian	Biggins Wayne	Gordon Dale	Clayton Paul	Own Goals	ATTD.
1	W	2 Oct 1985	Everton (Group Match)	A	0-0	0-1	1	2	6	4	5		10	8		12	11		⑦	3	9						10,329
2	W	23 " 1985	Everton (Group Match)	H	0-0	1-0	1		3	4	5	6	$⑩^1$	8		12	11		7			2	9				12,021
3	W	6 Nov 1985	Manchester United (Group Match)	A	1-0	1-1	1		3	4	5	6	10	8			11		7			2	9^1				20,130
4	W	11 Dec 1985	Manchester United (Group Match)	H	1-0	1-1	1		3	4	5	6	10	8			11^1		7			2	9				15,110
5	W	5 Feb 1986	Liverpool (Semi-Final, 1st Leg)	H	0-0	1-1	1			4	5	6	10	8^1	③		11		7			2	9	12			15,313
6	Tu	6 May 1986	Liverpool (Semi-Final, 2nd Leg)	A	1-1	1-3	1	12	3	4	⑤	6		8	9	7^1	11					2			10		26,696

1985–86 APPEARANCES & GOALS

	FOOTBALL LGE			F.A. CUP			LEAGUE CUP			SUPER CUP		
	APPR.	S	GLS	APPR.	S	GLS	APPR.	S	GLS	APPR.	S	GLS
Bruce Steve	42	–	8	1	–	–	4	–	2	6	–	–
Phelan Mick	42	–	3	1	–	–	4	–	–	6	–	–
Watson Dave	42	–	3	1	–	–	3	–	–	5	–	–
Woods Chris	42	–	–	1	–	–	4	–	–	6	–	–
Drinkell Kevin	41	–	22	1	–	–	4	–	1	6	–	1
Williams David	37	2	8	1	–	–	3	–	–	6	–	1
Barham Mark	35	–	9	1	–	–	4	–	–	5	–	–
Mendham Peter	35	–	8	1	–	–	4	–	1	5	–	1
Culverhouse Ian	30	–	–	1	–	–	3	–	–	5	–	–
Biggins Wayne	28	–	7	1	–	–				4	–	1
Van Wijk Dennis	27	2	1	1	–	–	4	–	–	5	–	–
Deehan John	22	4	4	–	1	–				2	–	–
Haylock Paul	12	–	1				1	–	–	1	1	–
Brooke Garry	8	5	2				1	1	1	1	2	1
Rosario Robert	8	–	2				4	–	1	1	–	–
Spearing Tony	7	1	–				1	–	–	1	–	–
Gordon Dale	3	3	1							–	1	–
Clayton Paul	1	–	–							1	–	–
Donowa Louie	–	2	–									
Own Goals			5									

DIVISION 2

1985–86	P	W	D	L	F	A	PTS
Norwich City	**42**	**25**	**9**	**8**	**84**	**37**	**84**
Charlton Athletic	42	22	11	9	78	45	77
Wimbledon	42	21	13	8	58	37	76
Portsmouth	42	22	7	13	69	41	73
Crystal Palace	42	19	9	14	57	52	66
Hull City	42	17	13	12	65	55	64
Sheffield United	42	17	11	14	64	63	62
Oldham Athletic	42	17	9	16	62	61	60
Millwall	42	17	8	17	64	65	59
Stoke City	42	14	15	13	48	50	57
Brighton & Hove Albion	42	16	8	18	64	64	56
Barnsley	42	14	14	14	47	50	56
Bradford City	42	16	6	20	51	63	54
Leeds United	42	15	8	19	56	72	53
Grimsby Town	42	14	10	18	58	62	52
Huddersfield Town	42	14	10	18	51	67	52
Shrewsbury Town	42	14	9	19	52	64	51
Sunderland	42	13	11	18	47	61	50
Blackburn Rovers	42	12	13	17	53	62	49
Carlisle United	42	13	7	22	47	71	46
Middlesbrough	42	12	9	21	44	53	45
Fulham	42	10	6	26	45	69	36

1986-87 DIVISION 1

NO.		DATE		OPPONENTS	V.	H-T	F-T	Benstead Graham	Culverhouse Ian	Spearing Tony	Bruce Steve	Phelan Mick	Elliott Shaun	Williams David	Drinkell Kevin	Biggins Wayne	Crook Ian	Putney Trevor	Gordon Dale	Barham Mark	Brooke Gary	Hodgson David	Butterworth Ian	Mendham Peter	Gunn Bryan	Seagraves Mark	Fox Ruel	Brown Kenny	Goss Jeremy	Rosario Robert	Own Goals	ATTD.
1	S	23 Aug	1986	Chelsea	A	0-0	0-0	1	2	3	4	5	6	7	8	9	10	⑪	12													19,887
2	S	30 "	1986	Southampton	H	0-2	4-3	1	2	3	4^{1}	5	6	7^{1}	8^{1}	9	10		11^{1}													15,205
3	W	3 Sept	1986	Manchester City	A	1-2	2-2	1	2	3	4	5	6^{1}	7	8	9			11	10^{1}	12											19,122
4	S	6 "	1986	Charlton Athletic	A	1-1	2-1	1	2	3	4	5	6	7^{1}	8^{1}	9			11	10												5,312
5	S	13 "	1986	Watford	H	1-0	1-3	1	2	3	4	5	6	7^{1}	8	9			11	⑩		12										15,487
6	W	17 "	1986	Leicester City	H	1-1	2-1	1	2	3	4	5	⑥	7	8	9^{1}			11	10^{1}		12										14,814
7	S	20 "	1986	Aston Villa	A	2-0	4-1	1	2	3	4^{1}	5^{1}		7	8	9^{1}	12		11^{1}	⑩			6									12,304
8	S	27 "	1986	Newcastle United	H	1-0	2-0	1	2	3	4	5		7	8^{2}	9			11	10			6									15,735
9	S	4 Oct	1986	Queens Park Rangers	H	0-0	1-0	1	2	3	4	5		7	8	9			11^{1}	10			6									15,894
10	S	11 "	1986	Luton Town	A	0-0	0-0	1	2	3	4	5		⑦	8	9	12		11	10			6									10,022
11	S	18 "	1986	West Ham United	H	0-0	1-1	1	2	3	4	5	6		8^{1}	9	7		⑪	10		12										22,884
12	S	25 "	1986	Wimbledon	A	0-2	0-2	1	2	3	4	5	6		8	⑨	7	12	11	10												6,172
13	S	1 Nov	1986	Liverpool	A	0-2	2-6	1	2	3	4	5^{1}	6		8		⑦	12	11			9^{1}		10								36,915
14	S	8 "	1986	Tottenham Hotspur	H	0-0	2-1		2	3	4	5	6^{1}		8		7^{1}		11			9		10	1							22,139
15	S	15 "	1986	Manchester United	H	0-0	0-0		②	3	4	5	6		8	12		7	11			9		10	1							22,684
16	S	22 "	1986	Coventry City	A	1-1	1-2		2		4	⑤	6		8	9^{1}	7	10	11	12					1	3						10,993
17	S	29 "	1986	Oxford United	H	2-1	2-1		2		4		6		8^{1}	⑨	5	10	11^{1}						1	3	7	12				13,610
18	S	6 Dec	1986	Everton	A	0-2	0-4		2		4				8		5	10	11				6		1	3			7	9		26,746
19	S	13 "	1986	Arsenal	H	0-0	1-1		2	3	4	5			8^{1}	9	7		11				6		1					10		21,409
20	F	19 "	1986	Watford	A	1-1	1-1		2	3	4	5			8	9	7		11				6		1					10	$–^{1}$	12,900
21	F	26 "	1986	Nottingham Forest	H	0-0	2-1		2	3	4	5			8	9	7^{1}		11				6		1					10^{1}		22,131
22	S	27 "	1986	Manchester United	A	0-0	1-0		2	3	4	5			8^{1}	9	7		11				6		1					10		44,610
23	Th	1 Jan	1987	Sheffield Wednesday	A	0-0	1-1		2	3	4	5			8^{1}	9	7		11				6		1					10		20,956
24	S	3 "	1987	Charlton Athletic	H	0-1	1-1		2	3	4	5			8	9^{1}	7	12	11				6		1					⑩		16,827
25	S	24 "	1987	Chelsea	H	1-1	2-2		2	3	4	5	6		8^{1}	9	7		11						1					10^{1}		16,562
26	S	7 Feb	1987	Southampton	A	0-0	2-1			3	4	5^{1}			8^{1}		7	10	⑪	12			6		1			2		9		12,754
27	S	14 "	1987	Manchester City	H	1-1	1-1			3	4	5			8		7^{1}	10		⑪			6		1		12	2		9		16,094
28	S	21 "	1987	Leicester City	A	1-0	2-0			3	4	5			8		7^{1}	10^{1}	11				6		1			2		9		8,742
29	S	28 "	1987	Aston Villa	H	0-1	1-1			③	4	5^{1}			8	12	7	10	11				6		1			2		9		15,070
30	S	7 Mar	1987	Wimbledon	H	0-0	0-0			3	4	5			8	12	7	10	⑪				6		1			2		9		14,293
31	S	14 "	1987	West Ham United	A	1-0	2-0			3	4^{1}	5			8^{1}		7	10	11				6		1			2		9		21,531
32	S	21 "	1987	Luton Town	H	0-0	0-0			3	④	5			8	12	7	10	11				6		1			2		9		16,440
33	S	28 "	1987	Queens Park Rangers	A	1-1	1-1			3	4	5			8^{1}	12	7	10	⑪				6		1			2		9		9,834
34	S	4 Apr	1987	Tottenham Hotspur	A	0-0	0-3			3	4	5			8	12	7	⑩	11				6		1			2		9		22,400
35	W	8 "	1987	Newcastle United	A	1-1	1-4			3	4	5			8^{1}	10	7		11				6		1			2		9		24,534
36	S	11 "	1987	Liverpool	H	0-1	2-1			3	④	5			8^{1}	12	7	10^{1}	11				6		1			2		9		22,879
37	S	18 "	1987	Sheffield Wednesday	H	1-0	1-0			3		5	4		8		7	10^{1}	11				6		1			2		9		17,924
38	M	20 "	1987	Nottingham Forest	A	0-0	1-1			3	4	5			8		7	10	11				6		1			2		9^{1}		14,446
39	S	25 "	1987	Coventry City	H	1-0	1-1			3	4	5			8^{1}	12	⑦	10	11				6		1			2		9		14,610
40	S	2 May	1987	Oxford United	A	1-0	1-0			3	4	5		7	8			10	11^{1}				6		1			2		9		8,394
41	M	4 "	1987	Everton	H	0-1	0-1			3	4	5		7	8	⑩			11				6		1		12	2		9		23,489
42	S	9 "	1987	Arsenal	A	1-0	2-1			3	4	5			8		7^{1}	10^{1}	11				6		1			2		9		24,001

F.A. CUP

NO.		DATE		OPPONENTS	V.	H-T	F-T	Benstead Graham	Culverhouse Ian	Spearing Tony	Bruce Steve	Phelan Mick	Elliott Shaun	Williams David	Drinkell Kevin	Biggins Wayne	Crook Ian	Putney Trevor	Gordon Dale	Barham Mark	Brooke Gary	Hodgson David	Butterworth Ian	Mendham Peter	Gunn Bryan	Seagraves Mark	Fox Ruel	Brown Kenny	Goss Jeremy	Rosario Robert	Own Goals	ATTD.
1	S	10 Jan	1987	Huddersfield Town (3rd Round)	H	0-0	1-1		2	3	4	5			8^{1}	10	7		11			9	6		1							11,524
2	W	21 "	1987	Huddersfield Town (3rd Round Replay)	A	2-1	4-2		2	3	4	5^{1}			8^{1}	10	7		11				6		1					9^{1}		8,970
3	S	31 "	1987	Wigan Athletic (4th Rd)	A	0-0	0-1		2	3	4	5			8	10	7		11				6		1					9		8,095

LITTLEWOODS CUP

NO.		DATE		OPPONENTS	V.	H-T	F-T	Benstead Graham	Culverhouse Ian	Spearing Tony	Bruce Steve	Phelan Mick	Elliott Shaun	Williams David	Drinkell Kevin	Biggins Wayne	Crook Ian	Putney Trevor	Gordon Dale	Barham Mark	Brooke Gary	Hodgson David	Butterworth Ian	Mendham Peter	Gunn Bryan	Seagraves Mark	Fox Ruel	Brown Kenny	Goss Jeremy	Rosario Robert	Own Goals	ATTD.
1	W	24 Sept	1986	Peterborough United (2nd Rd 1st leg)	A	0-0	0-0	1	2	3	4	5		7	8	9	12		11	10										⑥		6,956
2	W	8 Oct	1986	Peterborough United (2nd Rd 2nd leg)	H	0-0	1-0	1	2	3	4	5		7	8	9^{1}	6		11	10												10,027
3	W	29 "	1986	Millwall (3rd Rd)	H	2-1	4-1	1	2	3	4	5	6		8^{1}		7		11	⑩		9^{3}		12								10,277
4	W	19 Nov	1986	Everton (4th Rd)	H	1-2	1-4		2	③	4	5	6		8	9		7	11	12^{1}				10	1							17,988

FULL MEMBERS CUP

NO.		DATE		OPPONENTS	V.	H-T	F-T	Benstead Graham	Culverhouse Ian	Spearing Tony	Bruce Steve	Phelan Mick	Elliott Shaun	Williams David	Drinkell Kevin	Biggins Wayne	Crook Ian	Putney Trevor	Gordon Dale	Barham Mark	Brooke Gary	Hodgson David	Butterworth Ian	Mendham Peter	Gunn Bryan	Seagraves Mark	Fox Ruel	Brown Kenny	Goss Jeremy	Rosario Robert	Own Goals	ATTD.
1	W	4 Nov	1986	Coventry City (2nd Rd)	H	1-1	2-1		2	3	4	5	6		8^{2}		10	11				9			1		7					6,236
2	Tu	9 Dec	1986	Southampton (3rd Rd)	A	0-0	*2-1		3		4				8	⑨^{1}	5		11		12		6		1			2	7	10^{1}		5,745
3	W	25 Feb	1987	Portsmouth (QF)	H	1-0	3-1			3	4	5			8	12^{1}	7	10	⑪^{1}		12		6		1			2		9^{1}		9,204
4	Tu	10 Mar	1987	Charlton Athletic (SF)	A	0-0	*1-2			3	4	⑤•	13•		8	12••	7	10	11				6		1			②••		9^{1}		5,431

* AFTER EXTRA TIME

1986-87 APPEARANCES & GOALS

	FOOTBALL LGE			F.A. CUP			LEAGUE CUP			FULL MEMBERS CUP		
	APPR.	S	GLS	APPR.	S	GLS	APPR.	S	GLS	APPR.	S	GLS
Kevin Drinkell	42	–	16	3	–	2	4	–	1	4	–	2
Steve Bruce	41	–	3	3	–	–	4	–	–	4	–	–
Dale Gordon	40	1	5	3	–	1	4	–	–	3	–	1
Mick Phelan	40	–	4	3	–	1	4	–	–	3	–	–
Tony Spearing	39	–	–	3	–	–	4	–	–	3	–	–
Ian Crook	31	2	5	3	–	–	2	1	–	4	–	–
Bryan Gunn	29	–	–	3	–	–	1	–	–	4	–	–
Ian Butterworth	28	–	–	3	–	–	–	–	–	3	–	–
Ian Culverhouse	25	–	–	3	–	–	4	–	–	2	–	–
Robert Rosario	25	–	3	2	–	1	1	–	–	3	–	3
Wayne Biggins	23	8	4	3	–	–	3	–	1	1	2	2
Trevor Putney	20	3	4	–	–	–	1	–	–	3	–	–
Kenny Brown	17	1	–	–	–	–	–	–	–	3	–	–
Shaun Elliott	15	–	2	–	–	–	2	–	–	1	1	–
Graham Benstead	13	–	–	–	–	–	3	–	–	–	–	–
David Williams	12	–	3	–	–	–	2	–	–	–	–	–
Mark Barham	11	2	2	–	–	–	3	1	1	–	–	–
David Hodgson	3	3	1	1	–	–	1	–	3	1	–	–
Peter Mendham	3	–	–	–	–	–	1	1	–	–	–	–
Mark Seagraves	3	–	–	–	–	–	–	–	–	–	–	–
Ruel Fox	1	2	–	–	–	–	–	–	–	1	–	–
Jeremy Goss	1	–	–	–	–	–	–	–	–	1	–	–
Garry Brooke	–	1	–	–	–	–	–	–	–	–	1	–
own goals	–	–	1	–	–	–	–	–	–	–	–	–

BARCLAYS LEAGUE DIVISION 1

1986-87	P	W	D	L	F	A	PTS
Everton	42	26	8	8	76	31	86
Liverpool	42	23	8	11	72	42	77
Tottenham Hotspur	42	21	8	13	68	43	71
Arsenal	42	20	10	12	58	35	70
Norwich City	**42**	**17**	**17**	**8**	**53**	**51**	**68**
Wimbledon	42	19	9	14	57	50	66
Luton Town	42	18	12	12	47	45	66
Nottingham Forest	42	18	11	13	64	51	65
Watford	42	18	9	15	67	54	63
Coventry City	42	17	12	13	50	45	63
Manchester United	42	14	14	14	52	45	56
Southampton	42	14	10	18	69	68	52
Sheffield Wednesday	42	13	13	16	58	59	52
Chelsea	42	13	13	16	53	64	52
West Ham United	42	14	10	18	52	67	52
Queens Park Rangers	42	13	11	18	48	64	50
Newcastle United	42	12	11	19	47	65	47
Oxford United	42	11	13	18	44	69	46
Charlton Athletic	42	11	11	20	45	55	44
Leicester City	42	11	9	22	54	76	42
Manchester City	42	8	15	19	36	57	39
Aston Villa	42	8	12	22	45	79	36

1987-88 DIVISION 1

NO.	DATE	OPPONENTS	V.	H-T	F-T	Gunn Bryan	Brown Kenny	Spearing Tony	Bruce Steve	Phelan Mick	Butterworth Ian	Williams David	Drinkell Kevin	Biggins Wayne	Putney Trevor	Gordon Dale	Crook Ian	Culverhouse Ian	Fox Ruel	Bowen Mark	Rosario Robert	Ratcliffe Simon	Elliott Shaun	Goss Jeremy	O'Neill John	Fleck Robert	Benstead Graham	Linighan Andy	Own Goals	ATTD.
1	S 15 Aug 1987	Everton	A	0-1	0-1	1	(2)	3	4	5	6	10	8	9	11	7	14													31,728
2	W 19 " 1987	Southampton	H	0-0	0-1	1		3	4	5	6		8	9			10	2	7	(11)	12									14,429
3	S 22 " 1987	Coventry City	H	1-0	3-1	1		3	4^1	5	6		8^2	9			10	2	7	11										13,726
4	S 29 " 1987	West Ham United	A	0-0	0-2	1		3	4	5	6		8	9		12	10	2	7	(11)										16,394
5	Tu 1 Sept 1987	Newcastle United	H	0-0	1-1	1		3	4	5	(6)		8	9^1			10	2	7	11		12								16,636
6	S 5 " 1987	Watford	A	0-0	1-0	1		3	4^1	5	6		8	9			10	2	7	11										11,724
7	S 12 " 1987	Derby County	H	0-0	1-2	1		3	4	5	6		8	9			10	2	7	(11)	12^1									14,402
8	S 19 " 1987	Chelsea	A	0-1	0-1	1		(3)••	4	5	6		8	9			10	2	(7)•	11	12•	14••								15,242
9	S 26 " 1987	Nottingham Forest	H	0-2	0-2	1			4	5		14••	8		(11)•	12•	(10)••	2	7		9	6	3							13,755
10	S 3 Oct 1987	Oxford United	A	0-1	0-3	1	2		4	5		10	8		11	7					9	6	3							6,847
11	S 10 " 1987	Tottenham Hotspur	H	1-1	2-1	1			4	5		(10)	8^1	9^1			14	2	7	11		6	3							18,669
12	S 17 " 1987	Manchester United	A	1-0	1-2	1			4	5		(10)	8	9^1			14	2	7	11		6	3							39,345
13	S 24 " 1987	Sheffield Wednesday	A	0-1	0-1	1			(4)••	5	12••	10	8	9			14•	2	7	11		(6)•	3							15,861
14	S 31 " 1987	Queens Park Rangers	H	0-0	1-1	1	2	3	4	5	6		8	9^1	10		11		7											14,522
15	S 7 Nov 1987	Charlton Athletic	A	0-2	0-2	1	2	(3)•	4	5	6	12•	8	9			11		7		14••	(10)••								5,044
16	S 14 " 1987	Arsenal	H	1-0	2-4	1	2		4	5	6		8^2	12		11	(7)				9		3	10						20,558
17	S 21 " 1987	Liverpool	A	0-0	0-0	1	2		4	5	6		8		10	11	7				9		3							37,446
18	S 28 " 1987	Portsmouth	H	0-1	0-1	1	(2)		4	5	6		8		10	11	7			14	9		3							13,099
19	S 5 Dec 1987	Luton Town	A	0-1	2-1	1			4	5	6		8		10	(11)^1	7^1	2	12		9		3							7,002
20	F 18 " 1987	Wimbledon	A	0-1	0-1	1				5	6		8		10	11	7	2			12••		(3)••	14•	(4)•	9				4,026
21	S 26 " 1987	Derby County	A	1-0	2-1	1				5	6		8			11^1		2	7	3			4	10		9^1				15,452
22	M 28 " 1987	Chelsea	H	0-0	3-0	1				5	6		8^1		14	11		2	7^1	4	9		(3)	10^1						19,668
23	F 1 Jan 1988	West Ham United	H	0-1	4-1	1				5	6		8^1		4	11^1		2	7	3^1	9^1			10						20,059
24	S 16 " 1988	Everton	H	0-1	0-3	1				5	6		8		4	11		2	(7)	3			12	10		9				15,750
25	S 23 " 1988	Southampton	A	0-0	0-0					5	6		8		4	11		2	7	3				10		9	1			12,002
26	S 6 Feb 1988	Watford	H	0-0	0-0					5	6		8		4	(11)		2	7	3			12	10		9	1			13,316
27	S 13 " 1988	Newcastle United	A	1-1	3-1	1				5	6		8^1		(4)	11		2	7	3			10	12		9^2				21,068
28	S 20 " 1988	Coventry City	A	0-0	0-0	1				5	6		8			11	12	2	(7)	3			10	4		9				15,577
29	S 5 Mar 1988	Manchester United	H	0-0	1-0	1				5			8		6	(11)	12	2	7	3				10		9^1		4		19,129
30	S 12 " 1988	Tottenham Hotspur	A	1-0	3-1	1				5	6		8^1		11			2	7	3				10^1		9^1		4		19,322
31	W 16 " 1988	Oxford United	H	1-1	4-2	1				5	6		8^1		11			2	7	3				10		9^2		4^1		12,260
32	S 19 " 1988	Queens Park Rangers	A	0-1	0-3	1				(5)•	6		8	14••	11		12•	2	7	(3)••				10		9		4		9,033
33	S 26 " 1988	Sheffield Wednesday	H	0-1	0-3	1		12			6		8		11		(5)	2	7	3				10		9		4		13,280
34	S 2 Apr 1988	Charlton Athletic	H	0-0	2-0	1		3			6	5	8^1		11			2	7^1					10		9		4		15,015
35	M 4 " 1988	Arsenal	A	0-1	0-2	1		3			6	(5)	8	14	11			2	7					10		9		4		19,341
36	W 20 " 1988	Liverpool	H	0-0	0-0	1		3		5	6		8		11			2	7					10		9		4		22,509
37	S 23 " 1988	Portsmouth	A	1-0	2-2	1		3		5	6			12•^{1}	11	14••		2	7		8			10		(9)•		4^1		12,762
38	S 30 " 1988	Luton Town	H	0-0	2-2	1		3		5	6		(8)•^{1}	12	11^1			2	(7)••					10		9		4		12,700
39	W 4 May 1988	Nottingham Forest	A	0-2	0-2	1		3		5	6			8	11	12•		2	7			14••		(10)•		(9)••		4		11,610
40	S 7 " 1988	Wimbledon	H	0-0	0-1	1		3		5	6		8	9	11	12		2	7					(10)				4		11,782

F.A. CUP

NO.	DATE	OPPONENTS	V.	H-T	F-T	Gunn Bryan	Brown Kenny	Spearing Tony	Bruce Steve	Phelan Mick	Butterworth Ian	Williams David	Drinkell Kevin	Biggins Wayne	Putney Trevor	Gordon Dale	Crook Ian	Culverhouse Ian	Fox Ruel	Bowen Mark	Rosario Robert	Ratcliffe Simon	Elliott Shaun	Goss Jeremy	O'Neill John	Fleck Robert	Benstead Graham	Linighan Andy	Own Goals	ATTD.
1	S 9 Jan 1988	Swindon Town (3rd Rd)	A	0-0	0-0	1				5	6		8		4	11		2	7	3	9			10						12,807
2	W 13 " 1988	Swindon Town (3rd Rd Replay)	H	0-0	0-2	1				5	6		8		4	11		2	7	3	(9)			10		12				12,501

LITTLEWOODS CUP

NO.	DATE	OPPONENTS	V.	H-T	F-T	Gunn Bryan	Brown Kenny	Spearing Tony	Bruce Steve	Phelan Mick	Butterworth Ian	Williams David	Drinkell Kevin	Biggins Wayne	Putney Trevor	Gordon Dale	Crook Ian	Culverhouse Ian	Fox Ruel	Bowen Mark	Rosario Robert	Ratcliffe Simon	Elliott Shaun	Goss Jeremy	O'Neill John	Fleck Robert	Benstead Graham	Linighan Andy	Own Goals	ATTD.
1	Tu 22 Sept 1987	Burnley (2nd Rd 1st leg)	A	1-1	1-1	1			4	5	6		8	9^1		7	10	2		11			3							7,926
2	W 7 Oct 1987	Burnley (2nd Rd 2nd leg)	H	0-0	1-0	1			4	5		10	8	9				2	7	11^1		6	3							6,168
3	Tu 27 " 1987	Stoke City (3rd Rd)	A	0-2	1-2	1			4^1	5	12••	(10)•	8	9			14•	2	7	(11)••		6	3							8,603

SIMOD CUP

NO.	DATE	OPPONENTS	V.	H-T	F-T	Gunn Bryan	Brown Kenny	Spearing Tony	Bruce Steve	Phelan Mick	Butterworth Ian	Williams David	Drinkell Kevin	Biggins Wayne	Putney Trevor	Gordon Dale	Crook Ian	Culverhouse Ian	Fox Ruel	Bowen Mark	Rosario Robert	Ratcliffe Simon	Elliott Shaun	Goss Jeremy	O'Neill John	Fleck Robert	Benstead Graham	Linighan Andy	Own Goals	ATTD.
1	Tu 19 Jan 1988	Millwall (3rd Rd)	A	2-1	3-2	(1)				5	6		8		4	11		2	7	3	14			10^1		9^2				4,654
2	Tu 23 Feb 1988	Swindon Town (QF)	A	0-0	0-2	1				5	6		8	11			12	2	7	(3)			10	4		9				10,491

1987-88 APPEARANCES & GOALS

	FOOTBALL LGE			F.A. CUP			LEAGUE CUP			SIMOD CUP		
	APPR.	S	GLS	APPR.	S	GLS	APPR.	S	GLS	APPR.	S	GLS
Kevin Drinkell	38	–	12	2	–	–	3	–	–	2	–	–
Bryan Gunn	38	–	–	2	–	–	3	–	–	2	–	–
Mick Phelan	37	–	–	2	–	–	3	–	–	2	–	–
Ian Butterworth	34	1	–	2	–	–	1	1	–	2	–	–
Ruel Fox	33	1	2	2	–	–	2	–	–	2	–	–
Ian Culverhouse	33			2	–	–	3	–	–	2	–	–
Trevor Putney	25	1	1	2	–	–	–	–	–	1	–	–
Mark Bowen	23	1	1	2	–	–	3	–	1	2	–	–
Jeremy Goss	20	2	2	2	–	–	–	–	–	2	–	1
Steve Bruce	19	–	2	–	–	–	3	–	1	–	–	–
Robert Fleck	18	–	7	–	1	–	–	–	–	2	–	2
Tony Spearing	17	1	–	–	–	–	–	–	–	–	–	–
Ian Crook	16	7	1	–	–	–	1	1	–	–	1	–
Dale Gordon	16	5	3	2	–	–	1	–	–	1	–	–
Wayne Biggins	15	5	5	–	–	–	3	–	1	1	–	–
Shaun Elliott	14	2	–	–	–	–	3	–	–	1	–	–
Andy Linighan	12	–	2	–	–	–	–	–	–	–	–	–
Robert Rosario	9	5	2	2	–	–	–	–	–	–	1	–
David Williams	7	2	–	–	–	–	2	–	–	–	–	–
Kenny Brown	7	–	–	–	–	–	–	–	–	–	–	–
Simon Ratcliffe	6	3	–	–	–	–	2	–	–	–	–	–
Graham Benstead	2	–	–	–	–	–	–	–	–	–	–	–
John O'Neill	1	–	–	–	–	–	–	–	–	–	–	–
own goals	–	–	–	–	–	–	–	–	–	–	–	–

BARCLAYS LEAGUE DIVISION 1

1987-88	P	W	D	L	F	A	PTS
Liverpool	40	26	12	2	87	24	90
Manchester United	40	23	12	5	71	38	81
Nottingham Forest	40	20	13	7	67	39	73
Everton	40	19	13	8	53	27	70
Queens Park Rangers	40	19	10	11	48	38	67
Arsenal	40	18	12	10	58	39	66
Wimbledon	40	14	15	11	58	47	57
Newcastle United	40	14	14	12	55	53	56
Luton Town	40	14	11	15	57	58	53
Coventry City	40	13	14	13	46	53	53
Sheffield Wednesday	40	15	8	17	52	66	53
Southampton	40	12	14	14	49	53	50
Tottenham Hotspur	40	12	11	17	38	48	47
Norwich City	**40**	**12**	**9**	**19**	**40**	**52**	**45**
Derby County	40	10	13	17	35	45	43
West Ham United	40	9	15	16	40	52	42
Charlton Athletic	40	9	15	16	38	52	42
Chelsea	40	9	15	16	50	68	42
Portsmouth	40	7	14	19	36	66	35
Watford	40	7	11	22	27	51	32
Oxford United	40	6	13	21	44	80	31

1988-89 DIVISION 1

NO.		DATE		OPPONENTS	V.	H-T	F-T	Gunn Bryan	Culverhouse Ian	Bowen Mark	Butterworth Ian	Linighan Andy	Crook Ian	Gordon Dale	Fleck Robert	Rosario Robert	Phelan Mick	Putney Trevor	Allen Malcolm	Townsend Andy	Fox Ruel	Taylor Alan	Coney Dean	Cook Paul	Sheffield Jon	Goss Jeremy	Own Goals	ATTD.
1	S	27 Aug	1988	Nottingham Forest	H	2-0	2-1	1	2	3^{1}	4	5	6	7	⑧^{1}	9	10	11	14									13,488
2	S	3 Sept	1988	Middlesbrough	A	2-1	3-2	1	2	3	4	5	6	⑦•	⑧••^{2}	9^{1}	10	11	14••	12•								18,259
3	S	10 "	1988	Queens Park Rangers	H	0-0	1-0	1	2	3	4	5	⑥	7	8	9	10^{1}	11		14								11,174
4	S	17 "	1988	Newcastle United	A	1-0	2-0	1	2	3	4	5	6	7^{1}	8^{1}	⑨	10	11	12									22,801
5	S	24 "	1988	Millwall	H	0-0	2-2	1	2	3	4	5	6^{1}	7	8	9^{1}	10	⑪		14								16,616
6	S	1 Oct	1988	Charlton Athletic	H	1-1	1-3	1	2	③•	4	5^{1}	6	7	⑧••	9	10	11	12••	14•								11,470
7	S	8 "	1988	Derby County	A	0-0	1-0	1	2	3	4	5	⑥••	7	⑧•	9	10	11	12•	14••							$-^{1}$	14,117
8	S	22 "	1988	Tottenham Hotspur	H	2-0	3-1	1	2	3	4	5^{1}	6	7	8^{1}	9^{1}	10			11								20,330
9	W	26 "	1988	Manchester United	A	0-0	2-1	1	2	3	4	5	⑥	7	8	9	10^{1}			11^{1}	12							36,998
10	S	29 "	1988	Southampton	H	0-0	1-1	1	2	3	4	5	6	7	8^{1}	9	10			⑪	14							14,808
11	S	5 Nov	1988	Wimbledon	A	1-0	2-0	1	2	3	4	5^{1}		7	⑧	9	10	11	12^{1}	6								5,853
12	S	12 "	1988	Sheffield Wednesday	H	1-0	1-1	1	2	3	4	5		7	⑧		10	11^{1}	9	6		14						14,353
13	S	19 "	1988	Everton	A	0-0	1-1	1	2	3	4	5		7	⑧		10	11	9^{1}	6		14						28,118
14	S	26 "	1988	Luton Town	H	1-1	2-2	1	2	3	4	5		7^{1}	8	14	10	11	⑨	6							$-^{1}$	13,541
15	S	3 Dec	1988	Aston Villa	A	1-1	1-3	1	2	3	4	5	12••	⑦••	⑧•	14•	10	11^{1}	9	6								19,653
16	S	10 "	1988	Arsenal	H	0-0	0-0	1	2	3	4	5		7	⑧	9	10	11	14	6								23,069
17	S	17 "	1988	Liverpool	A	0-0	1-0	1	2	3		5	4	7	8	9	10	11		6^{1}								34,325
18	Tu	27 "	1988	West Ham United	H	0-0	2-1	1	2	3	12	5	4	7^{1}	8	9	10	11		⑥^{1}								17,491
19	S	31 "	1988	Middlesbrough	H	0-0	0-0	1	2	3	12••	5	4	7	⑧•	9	10	⑪••		6		14•						16,021
20	M	2 Jan	1989	Queens Park Rangers	A	0-0	1-1	1	2	3	4	⑤•	6	7	12••	⑨••	10	14•		11		8^{1}						12,410
21	S	14 "	1989	Coventry City	H	0-0	1-2	1	2	3	4	5		7^{1}	8	9	10	11		6								14,399
22	Su	22 "	1989	Millwall	A	2-2	3-2	1	2	3^{1}	4^{1}	5		7	8^{1}	9	10	11		6								13,687
23	S	4 Feb	1989	Charlton Athletic	A	0-0	2-1	1	2	3	4	5		7	8		10	11	9^{1}	6^{1}								7,518
24	S	11 "	1989	Derby County	H	0-0	1-0	1	2	③	4	5	12	7	8^{1}		10	11	9	6								17,227
25	Tu	21 "	1989	Tottenham Hotspur	A	0-1	1-2	1	2	3	④	5	12	7		8	10	11^{1}	9	6								19,120
26	S	25 "	1989	Manchester United	H	2-0	2-1	1	2	3	4^{1}	5		7		8	10	11	9^{1}	6								23,155
27	S	11 Mar	1989	Wimbledon	H	0-0	1-0	1	2	3	4	5		7		8	10	11^{1}	9	6								15,159
28	S	25 "	1989	Newcastle United	H	0-1	0-2	1	②•	3	4	5	12•	7	14••	⑧••	10	11	9	6								22,440
29	M	27 "	1989	West Ham United	A	0-0	2-0	1	2	3	4	5^{1}	12••	7	⑧•		⑩••	11	9^{1}	6			14•					27,265
30	S	1 Apr	1989	Liverpool	H	0-1	0-1	1	2	3	4	5		7	14		10	11	⑨	6			8					26,338
31	W	5 "	1989	Nottingham Forest	A	0-2	0-2	1	②••	3	'4	5	12••	7	14•		10	11	⑨•	6			8					19,872
32	S	8 "	1989	Coventry City	A	1-1	1-2	1	2	3	4	5	12	7	9^{1}		⑩	11		6			8					12,740
33	W	19 "	1989	Southampton	A	0-0	0-0	1	2		4	5	10	7			12•	③•	8	6	⑪••		9	14••				14,403
34	S	22 "	1989	Aston Villa	H	0-0	2-2		2	3	4	5	10	⑦•			11		9	6^{1}	12		8^{1}		1			14,550
35	M	1 May	1989	Arsenal	A	0-2	0-5	1	2	3	4	5		7	8		10	11		6			9					28,449
36	S	6 "	1989	Everton	H	0-0	1-0	1	2		4	⑤	3	7^{1}	8	9	10	12		6				11				13,239
37	S	13 "	1989	Luton Town	A	0-0	0-1	1	2		4		3	⑦••	8	9	⑩•	5	14••	6			12•	11				10,862
38	W	17 "	1989	Sheffield Wednesday	A	0-0	2-2	1	2	3	4	5	10	7	8^{1}	9^{1}				6				11				16,238

F.A. CUP

NO.		DATE		OPPONENTS		V.	H-T	F-T	Gunn Bryan	Culverhouse Ian	Bowen Mark	Butterworth Ian	Linighan Andy	Crook Ian	Gordon Dale	Fleck Robert	Rosario Robert	Phelan Mick	Putney Trevor	Allen Malcolm	Townsend Andy	Fox Ruel	Taylor Alan	Coney Dean	Cook Paul	Sheffield Jon	Goss Jeremy	Own Goals	ATTD.
1	Su	8 Jan	1989	Port Vale	(3rd Rd)	A	0-1	3-1	1	2	3	4	5	14••	7	12•^{1}	9	10	11		⑥••^{2}		⑧•						15,697
2	S	28 "	1989	Sutton United	(4th Rd)	H	3-0	8-0	1	2	3	4	5	12	7	8^{3}		10	11^{1}	9^{4}	⑥								23,073
3	S	18 Feb	1989	Sheffield United	(5th Rd)	H	1-1	3-2	1	2	3	4	5		7^{1}	⑧	12	10	11	9^{1}	6							$-^{1}$	24,139
4	S	18 Mar	1989	West Ham United	(6th Rd)	A	0-0	0-0	1	2	3	4	5		7		8	10	11	⑨	6	14							29,119
5	W	22 "	1989	West Ham United	(6th Rd Replay)	H	2-0	3-1	1	2	3	4	5	12	7^{1}		8	10	11	9^{2}	⑥								25,785
6	S	15 Apr	1989	Everton	(Semi-Final)	N*	0-1	0-1	1	2	3	4	5	10	7		9		11	⑧	6	14							46,553

* PLAYED AT VILLA PARK

LITTLEWOODS CUP

NO.		DATE		OPPONENTS		V.	H-T	F-T	Gunn Bryan	Culverhouse Ian	Bowen Mark	Butterworth Ian	Linighan Andy	Crook Ian	Gordon Dale	Fleck Robert	Rosario Robert	Phelan Mick	Putney Trevor	Allen Malcolm	Townsend Andy	Fox Ruel	Taylor Alan	Coney Dean	Cook Paul	Sheffield Jon	Goss Jeremy	Own Goals	ATTD.
1	W	28 Sept	1988	Preston North End	(2nd Rd 1st leg)	H	1-0	2-0	1	2	3	4	5	⑥••^{1}	7	⑧•	9^{1}	10	11	12•	14••								7,484
2	Tu	11 Oct	1988	Preston North End	(2nd Rd 2nd leg)	A	1-0	3-0	1	2	3	4	5	6	7^{1}	8^{1}	9^{1}	10	11										7,002
3	W	2 Nov	1988	Leicester City	(3rd Rd)	A	0-1	0-2	1	2	③•	4	5	⑥••	7	8	9	10	11	12•		14••							14,856

SIMOD CUP

NO.		DATE		OPPONENTS		V.	H-T	F-T	Gunn Bryan	Culverhouse Ian	Bowen Mark	Butterworth Ian	Linighan Andy	Crook Ian	Gordon Dale	Fleck Robert	Rosario Robert	Phelan Mick	Putney Trevor	Allen Malcolm	Townsend Andy	Fox Ruel	Taylor Alan	Coney Dean	Cook Paul	Sheffield Jon	Goss Jeremy	Own Goals	ATTD.
1	W	9 Nov	1988	Swindon Town	(1st Rd)	H	0-0	2-1	1	2^{1}		4	5		7			10	3	8		⑨	14		11		6^{1}		5,014
2	Tu	20 Dec	1988	Ipswich	(2nd Rd)	A	0-0	*0-1	1	2	3		5	4	7		⑨••	10	⑪•	8	6	14••			12•				18,024

* AFTER EXTRA TIME

1988-89 APPEARANCES & GOALS

	FOOTBALL LGE			F.A. CUP			LEAGUE CUP			SIMOD CUP		
	APPR.	S	GLS	APPR.	S	GLS	APPR.	S	GLS	APPR.	S	GLS
Ian Culverhouse	38	–	–	6	–	–	3	–	–	2	–	1
Dale Gordon	38	–	5	6	–	2	3	–	1	2	–	–
Bryan Gunn	37	–	–	6	–	–	3	–	–	2	–	–
Andy Linighan	37	–	4	6	–	–	3	–	–	2	–	–
Mick Phelan	36	1	2	5	–	–	3	–	–	2	–	–
Ian Butterworth	35	2	2	6	–	–	3	–	–	1	–	–
Mark Bowen	35	–	2	6	–	–	3	–	–	1	–	–
Andy Townsend	31	5	5	6	–	2	–	1	–	1	–	–
Trevor Putney	31	2	4	6	–	1	3	–	–	2	–	–
Robert Fleck	29	4	10	2	1	4	3	–	1	–	–	–
Robert Rosario	25	2	4	4	1	–	3	–	2	1	–	–
Ian Crook	19	7	1	1	3	–	3	–	1	1	–	–
Malcolm Allen	15	8	5	5	–	7	–	2	–	2	–	–
Dean Coney	6	2	1	–	–	–	–	–	–	–	–	–
Paul Cook	3	1	–	–	–	–	–	–	–	1	1	–
Ruel Fox	1	3	–	–	2	–	–	1	–	1	1	–
Alan Taylor	1	3	1	1	–	–	–	–	–	–	1	–
Jon Sheffield	1	–	–	–	–	–	–	–	–	–	–	–
Jeremy Goss	–	–	–	–	–	–	–	–	–	1	–	1
own goals	–	–	2	–	–	1	–	–	–	–	–	–

BARCLAYS LEAGUE DIVISION 1

1988-89	P	W	D	L	F	A	PTS
Arsenal	38	22	10	6	73	36	76
Liverpool	38	22	10	6	65	28	76
Nottingham Forest	38	17	13	8	64	43	64
Norwich City	**38**	**17**	**11**	**10**	**48**	**45**	**62**
Derby County	38	17	7	14	40	38	58
Tottenham Hotspur	38	15	12	11	60	46	57
Coventry City	38	14	13	11	47	42	55
Everton	38	14	12	12	50	45	54
Queens Park Rangers	38	14	11	13	43	37	53
Millwall	38	14	11	13	47	52	53
Manchester United	38	13	12	13	45	35	51
Wimbledon	38	14	9	15	50	46	51
Southampton	38	10	15	13	52	66	45
Charlton Athletic	38	10	12	16	44	58	42
Sheffield Wednesday	38	10	12	16	34	51	42
Luton Town	38	10	11	17	42	52	41
Aston Villa	38	9	13	16	45	56	40
Middlesbrough	38	9	12	17	44	61	39
West Ham United	38	10	8	20	37	62	38
Newcastle United	38	7	10	21	32	63	31

1989-90 DIVISION 1

NO.		DATE		OPPONENTS	V.	H-T	F-T	Gunn Bryan	Culverhouse Ian	Bowen Mark	Butterworth Ian	Linighan Andy	Townsend Andy	Gordon Dale	Fleck Robert	Coney Dean	Crook Ian	Phillips David	Cook Paul	Sherwood Tim	Rosario Robert	Fox Ruel	Allen Malcolm	Goss Jeremy	Mortensen Henrik	Pennock Adrian	Tanner Nick	Smith David	Walton Mark	Power Lee	Own Goals	ATTD.
1	S	19 Aug	1989	Sheffield Wednesday	A	1-0	2-0	1	2	3	4	5	6	7	8¹	9	10	11¹														19,142
2	W	23 "	1989	Nottingham Forest	H	1-0	1-1	1	2	3	(4)	5	6	7¹	8	9	10	11	14													18,267
3	S	26 "	1989	Queens Park Rangers	H	0-0	0-0	1	2	3		5	6	7	8	9	10	11		4												14,021
4	W	30 "	1989	Manchester United	A	1-0	2-0	1	(2)	3	4	5	6	7¹	8¹		10	11		14	9											39,610
5	S	9 Sept	1989	Southampton	H	1-2	4-4	1		3	4	5	6	7	8¹		10	11	14	(2)¹	9²											14,259
6	S	16 "	1989	Liverpool	A	0-0	0-0	1		3	4	5	6	7	8		10	11		2	9											36,885
7	S	23 "	1989	Tottenham Hotspur	H	0-2	2-2	1		3¹	4	5	6	7	8		10	11¹		2	9											20,095
8	S	30 "	1989	Millwall	A	0-0	1-0	1		3¹	4	5	6	7	8		10	11		2	9											13,295
9	S	14 Oct	1989	Chelsea	H	1-0	2-0	1		3¹	4	5	6	7	8¹		10	11		2	9											19,042
10	S	21 "	1989	Luton Town	A	0-1	1-4	1		3	4	5		7	(8)•		10	11		2	9	(6)••	12•¹	14••								9,038
11	S	28 "	1989	Everton	H	1-0	1-1	1	2	3	4	5¹	(6)•	7	8		(10)••	11		14••	9		12•									18,637
12	S	4 Nov	1989	Arsenal	A	2-0	3-4	1	2	3	4	5		7				11¹		6¹	9		8¹	10								35,338
13	S	11 "	1989	Aston Villa	H	0-0	2-0	1	2	3	4	5¹	6	7		9		11		10			8								–¹	18,186
14	S	18 "	1989	Charlton Athletic	H	0-0	0-0	1	2	3	4	5	(6)••	7		(9)•	12••	11		10	14•		8									16,084
15	S	25 "	1989	Coventry City	A	0-0	0-1	1	2	3	4	5	6	7				11		10	9		8									11,999
16	S	2 Dec	1989	Sheffield Wednesday	H	2-1	2-1	1	14•	3	4	5	6¹	7		12••	10	11		(2)•	(9)••				8						–¹	15,341
17	S	9 "	1989	Nottingham Forest	A	1-0	1-0	1	2	3¹	4	5	6	7			10	11			9				8							18,939
18	S	16 "	1989	Derby County	H	1-0	1-0	1	2	3	4	5	6	7			10	11			9¹				8							16,184
19	Tu	26 "	1989	Manchester City	A	0-0	0-1	1	2	3	4	5	6	7			10	11		12	9				(8)							29,534
20	S	30 "	1989	Crystal Palace	A	0-0	0-1	1	2	3	4	5	6	7	14•		(10)•	11		12••	9				(8)••							14,250
21	M	1 Jan	1990	Wimbledon	H	0-0	0-1	1	2	3	4	5	6	7	8		10	11			9											16,680
22	S	13 "	1990	Queens Park Rangers	A	0-0	1-2	1	2	(3)	4	5	6	7¹	8		10	11		12	9											11,439
23	Su	21 "	1990	Manchester United	H	0-0	2-0	1	2	3	4	5	6	7	8²		10	11			9											17,370
24	Su	4 Feb	1990	Tottenham Hotspur	A	0-2	0-4	1	2	3		5	6	7	8	12•	10	(11)••		4	(9)•			14••								19,599
25	S	10 "	1990	Liverpool	H	0-0	0-0	1	2	3		5	6	7	8	(9)	10	11		4			14									20,210
26	S	17 "	1990	Southampton	A	1-0	1-4	1	2	3		(5)••	6	(7)•	8		10	11					9¹	14••	12•	4						13,668
27	S	3 Mar	1990	Charlton Athletic	A	1-0	1-0	1	2	3			6		8¹		10	11			5		9		7		4					7,918
28	S	10 "	1990	Chelsea	A	0-0	0-0	1	2	3		5	6		8		10	11			12		9		(7)		4					18,796
29	W	14 "	1990	Coventry City	H	0-0	0-0	1	2	3		5	6		8		10	11			(9)		7		12		4					13,673
30	S	17 "	1990	Millwall	H	0-0	1-1	1	2	3		5	6¹		8		10	11					7		9		4					14,699
31	S	24 "	1990	Everton	A	1-0	1-3	1	?	3		5	6		8		10	11¹		7	9						4					21,707
32	S	31 "	1990	Luton Town	H	1-0	2-0	1	2	3¹		5	6¹			14••	10	11		7	(9)••	12•			(8)•		4					14,451
33	W	4 Apr	1990	Crystal Palace	H	2-0	2-0	1	2	3		5	6				10	11		4¹	9	7			8						–¹	12,640
34	S	14 "	1990	Wimbledon	A	1-0	1-1	1	2	3¹		5	6				10	11		4	9	(7)		14	8							4,638
35	M	16 "	1990	Manchester City	H	0-1	0-1	1	2	3		5	6		14		10	11		4	9			7	(8)							18,914
36	S	21 "	1990	Derby County	A	1-0	2-0	1	2	3		5	6		(8)••		10	11		4	(9)•¹	7¹			12••			14•				13,758
37	S	28 "	1990	Aston Villa	A	1-0	3-3		2	3		5	6		(8)		10	11		4	9¹	7¹							1	14	–¹	28,998
38	S	5 May	1990	Arsenal	H	2-1	2-2	1	2	3¹		5			8		10	11		4	9	7¹		6								19,256

F.A. CUP

NO.		DATE		OPPONENTS		V.	H-T	F-T	Gunn Bryan	Culverhouse Ian	Bowen Mark	Butterworth Ian	Linighan Andy	Townsend Andy	Gordon Dale	Fleck Robert	Coney Dean	Crook Ian	Phillips David	Cook Paul	Sherwood Tim	Rosario Robert	Fox Ruel	Allen Malcolm	Goss Jeremy	Mortensen Henrik	Own Goals	ATTD.
1	S	6 Jan	1990	Exeter City	(3rd Rd)	A	0-0	1-1	1	2	3	4	5	6	7	8¹		10	11			9						9,061
2	W	10 "	1990	Exeter City	(3rd Rd Replay)	H	1-0	2-0	1	2	3	4	5	6	7¹	8		10	11			9¹						18,202
3	Su	28 "	1990	Liverpool	(4th Rd)	H	0-0	0-0	1	2	3	4	5	6	7	8		10	11			9						23,152
4	Tu	31 "	1990	Liverpool	(4th Rd Replay)	A	1-1	1-3	1	2	3	4	5	6	7	8¹		10	11			9						29,339

LITTLEWOODS CUP

NO.		DATE		OPPONENTS		V.	H-T	F-T	Gunn Bryan	Culverhouse Ian	Bowen Mark	Butterworth Ian	Linighan Andy	Townsend Andy	Gordon Dale	Fleck Robert	Coney Dean	Crook Ian	Phillips David	Cook Paul	Sherwood Tim	Rosario Robert	Fox Ruel	Allen Malcolm	Goss Jeremy	Mortensen Henrik	Own Goals	ATTD.
1	W	20 Sept	1989	Rotherham United	(2nd Rd 1st leg)	H	1-1	1-1	1		3	4	5	6	7	8¹		10	11		2	9						9,531
2	Tu	3 Oct	1989	Rotherham United	(2nd Rd 2nd leg)	A	2-0	2-0	1		3	4	5	6	7¹	8¹		10	11		2	9						9,064
3	W	25 "	1989	Manchester City	(3rd Rd)	A	0-1	1-3	1		3	4	5	6	7	8¹		10	11		(2)	9		14				20,126

ZENITH DATA SYSTEMS CUP

NO.		DATE		OPPONENTS		V.	H-T	F-T	Gunn Bryan	Culverhouse Ian	Bowen Mark	Butterworth Ian	Linighan Andy	Townsend Andy	Gordon Dale	Fleck Robert	Coney Dean	Crook Ian	Phillips David	Cook Paul	Sherwood Tim	Rosario Robert	Fox Ruel	Allen Malcolm	Goss Jeremy	Mortensen Henrik	Own Goals	ATTD.
1	W	29 Nov	1989	Brighton & Hove Albion	(2nd Rd)	H	2-0	5-0	1		3	4	5	6	7¹			10¹	11		2¹	9¹				8¹		5,704
2	W	24 Jan	1990	Swindon Town	(3rd Rd)	A	1-2	1-4	1	2	3	4	5	6	7	8		10	(11)•¹		12•	(9)••		14••				5,314

1989-90 APPEARANCES & GOALS

	FOOTBALL LGE			F.A. CUP			LEAGUE CUP			ZDS CUP		
	APPR.	S	GLS	APPR.	S	GLS	APPR.	S	GLS	APPR.	S	GLS
Mark Bowen	38	–	7	4	–	–	3	–	–	2	–	–
David Phillips	38	–	4	4	–	–	3	–	–	2	–	1
Bryan Gunn	37	–	–	4	–	–	3	–	–	2	–	–
Andy Linighan	37	–	2	4	–	–	3	–	–	2	–	–
Andy Townsend	35	–	3	4	–	–	3	–	–	2	–	–
Ian Crook	34	1	–	4	–	–	3	–	–	2	–	1
Ian Culverhouse	31	1	–	4	–	–	–	–	–	1	–	–
Robert Rosario	29	2	5	4	–	1	3	–	–	2	–	1
Robert Fleck	25	2	7	4	–	2	3	–	3	1	–	–
Tim Sherwood	22	5	3	–	–	–	3	–	–	1	1	1
Dale Gordon	26	–	3	4	–	1	3	–	1	2	–	1
Ian Butterworth	22	–	–	4	–	–	3	–	–	2	–	–
Henrik Mortensen	12	3	–	–	–	–	–	–	–	1	–	1
Malcolm Allen	9	3	3	–	–	–	–	1	–	–	1	–
Dean Coney	6	3	–	–	–	–	–	–	–	–	–	–
Ruel Fox	6	1	3	–	–	–	–	–	–	–	–	–
Jeremy Goss	3	4	–	–	–	–	–	–	–	–	–	–
Nick Tanner	6	–	–	–	–	–	–	–	–	–	–	–
Paul Cook	–	2	–	–	–	–	–	–	–	–	–	–
Adrian Pennock	1	–	–	–	–	–	–	–	–	–	–	–
Mark Walton	1	–	–	–	–	–	–	–	–	–	–	–
Lee Power	–	1	–	–	–	–	–	–	–	–	–	–
David Smith	–	1	–	–	–	–	–	–	–	–	–	–
own goals	–	–	4	–	–	–	–	–	–	–	–	–

BARCLAYS LEAGUE DIVISION 1

1989-90	P	W	D	L	F	A	PTS
Liverpool	38	23	10	5	78	37	79
Aston Villa	38	21	7	10	57	38	70
Tottenham Hotspur	38	19	6	13	59	47	63
Arsenal	38	18	8	12	54	38	62
Chelsea	38	16	12	10	58	50	60
Everton	38	17	8	13	57	46	59
Southampton	38	15	10	13	71	63	55
Wimbledon	38	13	16	9	47	40	55
Nottingham Forest	38	15	9	14	55	47	54
Norwich City	**38**	**13**	**14**	**11**	**44**	**42**	**53**
Queens Park Rangers	38	13	11	14	45	44	50
Coventry City	38	14	7	17	39	59	49
Manchester United	38	13	9	16	46	47	48
Manchester City	38	12	12	14	43	52	48
Crystal Palace	38	13	9	16	42	66	48
Derby County	38	13	7	18	43	40	46
Luton Town	38	10	13	15	43	57	43
Sheffield Wednesday	38	11	10	17	35	51	43
Charlton Athletic	38	7	9	22	31	57	30
Millwall	38	5	11	22	39	65	26

1990-91 DIVISION 1

No.	Day	Date	Opponents	V.	H-T	F-T	Gunn Bryan	Blades Paul	Bowen Mark	Butterworth Ian	Polston John	Sherwood Tim	Gordon Dale	Fox Ruel	Crook Ian	Rosario Robert	Phillips David	Fleck Robert	Goss Jeremy	Minett Jason	Culverhouse Ian	Power Lee	Sutch Daryl	Smith David	Mortensen Henrik	Walton Mark	Ullathorne Robert	Sutton Chris	Woodthorpe Colin	Own Goals	ATTD.
1	S	25 Aug 1990	Sunderland	H	2-0	3-2	1	2	3	4	5	6[1]	7[1]	8[1]	9	10	11														17,247
2	Tu	28 " 1990	Southampton	A	0-0	0-1	1	2	3	4	5	6	7	⑧•	⑨••	10	11	12•	14••												17,206
3	S	1 Sept 1990	Leeds United	A	0-2	0-3	1	2	③••	4	5	6	7	⑧•		10	11	12•	9	14••											25,684
4	S	8 " 1990	Crystal Palace	H	0-2	0-3	1	2	3	4	5	⑥••	7	12•		⑩•	11	8	9	14••											15,306
5	S	15 " 1990	Manchester City	A	0-2	1-2	1	5	3	4		6	7	10	9		11	8[1]			2										26,247
6	S	22 " 1990	Derby County	H	0-0	2-1	1	5	3	4		9	7	10[1]	6		11[1]	8			2										13,258
7	S	29 " 1990	Luton Town	H	1-0	1-3	1	⑤•	3	4		9	⑦••[1]	10	6		11	8	12•		2	14••									12,794
8	S	6 Oct 1990	Arsenal	A	0-2	0-2	1	5	3	4		9	7	10	6		11	⑧			2	14									36,048
9	S	20 " 1990	Liverpool	H	1-1	1-1	1	5	3	4		9	7	10[1]	6		11				2	8									21,275
10	S	27 " 1990	Queens Park Rangers	A	2-0	3-1	1	5	3	4		9	7	⑩	6		11[1]		14		2	8[2]									11,103
11	S	3 Nov 1990	Sheffield United	H	1-0	3-0	1	5	3	4		9[1]	7	10	6		11[1]				2	8								–[1]	14,806
12	S	10 " 1990	Chelsea	A	1-1	1-1	1	5	3	4		9	7[1]	10	6		⑪	12			2	8									16,925
13	S	17 " 1990	Aston Villa	H	1-0	2-0	1	5	3	4		9	7	10[1]	6[1]		11	12			2	⑧									17,243
14	S	24 " 1990	Tottenham Hotspur	A	1-1	1-2	1	5	3	4		9	7	10	6[1]		11	12			2	⑧									33,942
15	S	1 Dec 1990	Wimbledon	H	0-4	0-4	1	5	3	4		9	7	10	⑥••		11	12•	14••		2	⑧•									12,324
16	S	8 " 1990	Southampton	H	1-1	3-1	1		3[1]	4	5	9	7	⑩	6	8	11[1]				2	14								–[1]	11,705
17	S	15 " 1990	Sunderland	A	0-1	2-1	1		3	4	5	9[1]	7[1]		6	10	11				2	8									18,693
18	S	22 " 1990	Everton	H	1-0	1-0	1		3	4	5[1]	9	7		6	10	11		12		2	⑧									14,294
19	W	26 " 1990	Manchester United	A	0-0	0-3	1		3	4	5	9	7	10	6		11				2	⑧	14								39,801
20	S	29 " 1990	Coventry City	A	0-0	0-2	1		3	4	5	9	7	⑩	6	8	11				2		14								12,039
21	W	2 Jan 1991	Nottingham Forest	H	1-2	2-6	1		3	4	5	9[1]	7		6	10	11	8[1]			2										17,043
22	S	12 " 1991	Leeds United	H	1-0	2-0	1		3	4	5	9[1]	7[1]		6		11	8	10		2										17,786
23	S	19 " 1991	Crystal Palace	A	1-0	3-1	1		3	4	5	9	7		6		11	8[2]	10[1]		2										17,201
24	S	2 Feb 1991	Manchester City	H	0-2	1-2	1		3	4	5[1]	⑨	7		6		11	8			2			10	12						15,194
25	S	23 " 1991	Derby County	A	0-0	0-0	1	4	3		5	9	7	12	⑥		11	8	10		2										14,102
26	S	2 Mar 1991	Wimbledon	A	0-0	0-0	1	4	3		5	9	7				11	8	10		2			6							4,541
27	S	16 " 1991	Luton Town	A	1-0	1-0	1	4	3		5	9[1]	7		6		11	8	10		2										8,604
28	S	23 " 1991	Arsenal	H	0-0	0-0	1	4	3		5	9	7	10	6		11	8			2										20,131
29	S	30 " 1991	Manchester United	H	0-2	0-3	1	4	3		5	9	7	10	6		11	8			2										18,282
30	M	1 Apr 1991	Everton	A	0-0	0-1	1	4	3		5	⑨		10	6		11	8	7		2				12						20,485
31	S	6 " 1991	Coventry City	H	1-1	2-2	1		3	4	5	9[1]	7	12			11	8[1]	6		2	⑩									11,550
32	W	10 " 1991	Tottenham Hotspur	H	1-1	2-1	1		3	4	5	9	⑦	12	6[1]		11	8			2	10[1]									19,014
33	W	17 " 1991	Chelsea	H	0-2	1-3	1		3	4	5[1]	9	7	12	6		11	8			2	⑩									12,301
34	S	20 " 1991	Liverpool	A	0-2	0-3	1		3	4	5	9		10			11	8	6		2		7								37,065
35	W	24 " 1991	Nottingham Forest	A	0-2	0-5				4	5	⑨••	12•	10	14••		11	⑧•	6		2		7			1	3				17,641
36	S	4 May 1991	Queens Park Rangers	H	0-0	1-0			3	4	5	9	7[1]	10			11	⑧	6		2					1		14			13,469
37	W	8 " 1991	Aston Villa	A	1-1	1-2			3	4	5	9	7[1]		⑩		11	8	6		2					1		12			16,697
38	S	11 " 1991	Sheffield United	A	1-2	1-2			3		5[1]		7		6		11	8	⑩••		2			14••	12•	1	⑨•		4		21,019

F.A. CUP

No.	Day	Date	Opponents	Round	V.	H-T	F-T	Gunn	Blades	Bowen	Butterworth	Polston	Sherwood	Gordon	Fox	Crook	Rosario	Phillips	Fleck	Goss	Minett	Culverhouse	Power	Sutch	Smith	Mortensen	ATTD.
1	S	5 Jan 1991	Bristol City	(3rd Rd)	H	1-1	2-1	1		3	④	5	9	7		6	10[1]	11	8[1]	12		2					12,630
2	S	26 " 1991	Swindon Town	(4th Rd)	H	0-0	3-1	1		3	4	5	9	7[1]		6		11	8[1]			2			⑩	12[1]	14,408
3	M	18 Feb 1991	Manchester United	(5th Rd)	H	1-1	2-1	1		3	4	5	9	7[1]	14	6		11	8[1]			2			⑩		23,058
4	S	9 Mar 1991	Nottingham Forest	(6th Rd)	H	0-0	0-1	1	4	3		5	9	7	12	⑥		11	8	10		2					24,018

RUMBLELOWS LEAGUE CUP

No.	Day	Date	Opponents	Round	V.	H-T	F-T	Gunn	Blades	Bowen	Butterworth	Polston	Sherwood	Gordon	Fox	Crook	Rosario	Phillips	Fleck	Goss	Minett	Culverhouse	Power	Sutch	ATTD.
1	W	26 Sept 1990	Watford	(2nd Rd 1st leg)	H	1-0	2-0	1	5	3	4		9[1]	7	10	6[1]		11	8			2			7,720
2	Tu	9 Oct 1990	Watford	(2nd Rd 2nd leg)	A	1-0	3-0	1	5		4		9	⑦	10	6		11	8[1]	3[2]		2		14	6,148
3	Tu	30 " 1990	Middlesbrough	(3rd Rd)	A	0-2	0-2	1	5	3	4		9	7	10	6		11				2	8		17,024

ZENITH DATA SYSTEMS CUP

No.	Day	Date	Opponents	Round	V.	H-T	F-T	Gunn	Blades	Bowen	Butterworth	Polston	Sherwood	Gordon	Fox	Crook	Rosario	Phillips	Fleck	Goss	Minett	Culverhouse	Power	Sutch	Smith	Mortensen	ATTD.
1	W	19 Dec 1990	Millwall	(2nd Rd)	H	0-0	*1-1	1		3	4	5	9	7		⑥••	10[1]	11				2		⑧•	14••	12•	4,741
2	W	20 Feb 1991	Southampton	(3rd Rd)	H	2-1	2-1	1	4	3		5		7	10	6		11	⑧[1]	9[1]		2				12	5,920
3	W	27 " 1991	Ipswich Town	(Area S-F)	H	0-0	2-0	1	4	3		5	9	7[1]	14	⑥		11	8[1]	10		2					16,225
4	Tu	5 Mar 1991	Crystal Palace	(Area Final 1st leg)	H	1-1	1-1	1	4	3		5	9[1]	7	12			11	8	10		2			⑥		7,554
5	Tu	19 Mar 1991	Crystal Palace	(Area Final 2nd leg)	A	0-1	0-2	1	④•	3	14•	5	9	7	12••	6		11	8	⑩••		2					13,857

* NORWICH WON 6-5 ON PENALTIES AFTER EXTRA TIME

1990-91 APPEARANCES & GOALS

	FOOTBALL LGE			F.A. CUP			LEAGUE CUP			ZDS CUP		
	APPR.	S	GLS	APPR.	S	GLS	APPR.	S	GLS	APPR.	S	GLS
David Phillips	38	–	4	4	–	–	3	–	–	5	–	–
Mark Bowen	37	–	1	4	–	–	2	–	–	5	–	–
Tim Sherwood	37	–	7	4	–	–	3	–	1	4	–	1
Dale Gordon	35	1	7	4	–	2	3	–	–	5	–	1
Ian Culverhouse	34	–	–	4	–	–	3	–	–	5	–	–
Bryan Gunn	34	–	–	4	–	–	3	–	–	5	–	–
Ian Crook	31	1	3	4	–	–	3	–	1	4	–	–
Ian Butterworth	31	–	–	3	–	–	3	–	–	1	1	–
Robert Fleck	23	6	5	4	–	3	2	–	1	4	–	2
Ruel Fox	23	5	4	–	2	–	3	–	–	1	3	–
John Polston	27	–	4	4	–	–	–	–	–	5	–	–
Paul Blades	21	–	–	1	–	–	3	–	–	4	–	–
Jeremy Goss	14	5	1	1	1	–	1	–	2	4	–	1
Lee Power	13	3	3	–	–	–	1	–	–	–	–	–
Robert Rosario	9	–	–	1	–	1	–	–	–	1	–	1
Mark Walton	4	–	–	–	–	–	–	–	–	–	–	–
Daryl Sutch	2	2	–	–	–	–	–	1	–	1	–	–
David Smith	2	1	–	2	–	–	–	–	–	1	1	–
Henrik Mortensen	–	3	–	–	1	1	–	–	–	–	2	–
Robert Ullathorne	2	–	–	–	–	–	–	–	–	–	–	–
Jason Minett	–	2	–	–	–	–	–	–	–	–	–	–
Chris Sutton	–	2	–	–	–	–	–	–	–	–	–	–
Colin Woodthorpe	1	–	–	–	–	–	–	–	–	–	–	–
own goals	–	–	2	–	–	–	–	–	–	–	–	–

BARCLAYS LEAGUE DIVISION 1

1990-91	P	W	D	L	F	A	PTS
Arsenal	38	24	13	1	74	18	83*
Liverpool	38	23	7	8	77	40	76
Crystal Palace	38	20	9	9	50	41	69
Leeds United	38	19	7	12	65	47	64
Manchester City	38	17	11	10	64	53	62
Manchester United	38	16	12	10	58	45	59†
Wimbledon	38	14	14	10	53	46	56
Nottingham Forest	38	14	12	12	65	50	54
Everton	38	13	12	13	50	46	51
Tottenham Hotspur	38	11	16	11	51	50	49
Chelsea	38	13	10	15	58	69	49
Queens Park Rangers	38	12	10	16	44	53	46
Sheffield United	38	13	7	18	36	55	46
Southampton	38	12	9	17	59	69	45
Norwich City	**38**	**13**	**6**	**19**	**41**	**64**	**45**
Coventry City	38	11	11	16	42	49	44
Aston Villa	38	9	14	15	46	58	41
Luton Town	38	10	7	21	42	61	37
Sunderland	38	8	10	20	38	60	34
Derby County	38	5	9	24	37	75	24

* Arsenal 2 pts deducted
† Manchester United 1 pt deducted

1991-92 DIVISION 1

NO.		DATE	OPPONENTS	V.	H-T	F-T	Gunn Bryan	Culverhouse Ian	Bowen Mark	Butterworth Ian	Blades Paul	Crook Ian	Gordon Dale	Fleck Robert	Newman Rob	Beckford Darren	Phillips David	Fox Ruel	Goss Jeremy	Ullathorne Robert	Ball Steve	Sherwood Tim	Sutton Chris	Polston John	Woodthorpe Colin	Sutch Daryl	Walton Mark	Power Lee	Smith David	Johnson Andy	Mortensen Henrik	Own Goals	ATTD.
1	S	17 Aug 1991	Sheffield United	H	0-1	2-2	1	2	3	4	5	6	7	8^{2}	9	⑩	11	12															16,380
2	W	21 " 1991	Queens Park Rangers	A	1-0	2-0	1	2	3	4	5	6	7^{1}	8	9^{1}	⑩	11	12															10,726
3	S	24 " 1991	Oldham Athletic	A	1-2	2-2	1	2	3	4	5	6^{1}	7	8	9^{1}	10	11																13,548
4	W	28 " 1991	Manchester City	H	0-0	0-0	1	2	3	4	5	6	7	8	9	⑩	11	12															15,376
5	S	31 " 1991	Tottenham Hotspur	H	0-1	0-1	1	②	3	4	5	6	7	8	9	10	11	12															19,460
6	Tu	3 Sept 1991	Everton	A	0-0	1-1	1	2	3	4	5	6	7	8	9	⑩	11^{1}	12															19,197
7	S	7 " 1991	Manchester United	A	0-3	0-3	1	2	3	4	5	6	7	8	9	⑩•	⑪••	12•	14••														44,946
8	S	14 " 1991	West Ham United	H	2-1	2-1	1	2	3	4	5	6	7^{1}	8	9			10^{1}	14	⑪													15,348
9	W	18 " 1991	Sheffield Wednesday	H	1-0	1-0	1		3	4	5	6	7	8^{1}	9		2	10	14	⑪													12,503
10	S	21 " 1991	Notts. County	A	0-1	2-2	1		3^{1}	4	5	6	⑦••	8	9	12••	2	10		⑪•^{1}	14•												9,488
11	S	28 " 1991	Leeds United	H	0-0	2-2	1		3	4	5	6	7^{2}	8	9		2	10		11													15,828
12	S	5 Oct 1991	Wimbledon	A	0-1	1-3	1		3	4	5	⑥	7		9	8^{1}	2	10	12	11													3,531
13	S	19 " 1991	Southampton	A	0-0	0-0	1		3	4	5		⑦	8	9	12	2	10	6	11													12,516
14	S	26 " 1991	Luton Town	H	1-0	1-0	1		3	4	5		7	8	9^{1}	12	2	10	6	⑪													10,514
15	S	2 Nov 1991	Nottingham Forest	H	0-0	0-0	1		3	4	5		7	8	9	11	2	10	6														13,014
16	S	16 " 1991	Chelsea	A	2-0	3-0	1		3^{1}	4	5			8^{2}	9	11	2		6	7		10											15,755
17	S	23 " 1991	Coventry City	H	0-1	3-2	1		3^{1}	4	5	12•		8^{1}	9	⑪••	2		6	7		⑩•	14••^{1}										12,056
18	S	30 " 1991	Liverpool	A	1-2	1-2	1		3	④	5			8	9	11^{1}	2		6	7		10	14										34,881
19	S	7 Dec 1991	Crystal Palace	H	1-1	3-3	1		3			5		8	9^{1}	11^{1}	2	12	6	⑦		10	4									–^{1}	12,667
20	S	21 " 1991	Queens Park Rangers	H	0-0	0-1	1		3		5			8	9	11	2	12	6	7		⑩	4										11,436
21	Th	26 " 1991	Manchester City	A	1-2	1-2	1		3		5			8	9^{1}	⑪••	2	12••	6	⑦•		10	4	14•									28,164
22	S	28 " 1991	Tottenham Hotspur	A	0-1	0-3	1		3		5			8	9	12	2	11	6			10	4		⑦								27,969
23	W	1 Jan 1992	Aston Villa	H	0-0	2-1	1		3		5			8^{1}	9	10	2	7	6	11^{1}			④	12									15,318
24	S	11 " 1992	Oldham Athletic	A	1-1	1-2	1		3		5	6		8	9	⑩^{1}	2	7		11			4			14							10,986
25	S	18 " 1992	Sheffield United	A	0-0	0-1	①		3			10		8	9	12			6	11			4	5	2	7							17,549
26	S	1 Feb 1992	Southampton	H	0-0	2-1			3			⑩		8^{1}	9	7	2	12	6	11^{1}			4	5			1						10,660
27	S	8 " 1992	Luton Town	A	0-0	0-2		2	3	4		10		8		⑨	11	7	6					5		14	1						8,554
28	Tu	11 " 1992	Arsenal	A	0-0	1-1		2		4				8	9		11	7^{1}	6				10	5	3		1						22,352
29	S	22 " 1992	Liverpool	H	0-0	3-0		2		4				8^{2}	9		11	7	6				10	5	3^{1}		1						20,411
30	S	29 " 1992	Crystal Palace	A	4-2	4-3		2		4				8	9^{1}		11	7	6^{1}				10^{1}	5^{1}	3		1						14,021
31	W	4 Mar 1992	Coventry City	A	0-0	0-0		2		4				12•	9		11	⑦•	6		14••		⑩••	5	3	8	1						8,459
32	W	11 " 1992	Chelsea	H	0-0	0-1		2		4				8	9		11	7	6				12	5	3	⑩	1						13,430
33	S	14 " 1992	Nottingham Forest	A	0-2	0-2		2	12	4				8	9		⑪	7	6				10	5	3		1						20,721
34	S	21 " 1992	Everton	H	1-2	4-3		2	③•	4		11			9^{1}	8^{3}		7	6				10	⑤••	12••	14•	1						11,900
35	S	28 " 1992	Aston Villa	A	0-0	0-1		2	3	4		11			9			7	6				10		5	8	1						16,985
36	Tu	31 " 1992	Manchester United	H	0-1	1-3		2	3	4		⑪••			9		⑧•	7	6				10	12••	5		1	14•^{1}					17,489
37	W	8 Apr 1992	Arsenal	H	0-1	1-3		2	3	4^{1}					9	10		7	6	11			14	5			1	⑧					12,971
38	S	11 " 1992	West Ham United	A	0-2	0-4			2	4					9	10		7	6	3			⑭••	5		12••	1	⑧•	11				16,896
39	S	18 " 1992	Notts. County	H	0-0	0-1			2	4				8	9	10		7	6					5	3	11	1						12,100
40	M	20 " 1992	Sheffield Wednesday	A	0-2	0-2			2		4			8	9	⑩		7	6					5	3		1	12		11			27,362
41	S	25 " 1992	Wimbledon	H	1-0	1-1		2	3		4			8^{1}	9	⑩	11	7	6					5	12		1						11,061
42	S	2 May 1992	Leeds United	A	0-1	0-1		2			4			8	9		11	7	6	③				5	12		1			10			32,673

F.A. CUP

NO.		DATE	OPPONENTS	V.	H-T	F-T	Gunn Bryan	Culverhouse Ian	Bowen Mark	Butterworth Ian	Blades Paul	Crook Ian	Gordon Dale	Fleck Robert	Newman Rob	Beckford Darren	Phillips David	Fox Ruel	Goss Jeremy	Ullathorne Robert	Ball Steve	Sherwood Tim	Sutton Chris	Polston John	Woodthorpe Colin	Sutch Daryl	Walton Mark	Power Lee	Smith David	Johnson Andy	Mortensen Henrik	Own Goals	ATTD.
1	S	4 Jan 1992	Barnsely (3rd Rd)	H	0-0	1-0	1		3		⑤•	14••		8^{1}	9	⑩••	2	7	6	11			4	12•									12,189
2	W	5 Feb 1992	Millwall (4th Rd)	H	1-0	2-1			3^{1}			10		8^{1}	9	7	2		6	11			4	5			1						17,010
3	S	15 " 1992	Notts. County (5th Rd)	H	2-0	3-0		2		4				8	9		11^{1}	7	6				10^{2}	5	3		1						14,511
4	S	7 Mar 1992	Southampton (6th Rd)	A	0-0	0-0		2		4				8	9		11	7	6				10	5	3		1						20,088
5	W	18 " 1992	Southampton (6th Rd Replay)	H	0-1	2-1**		2	11	4		12•		⑧••	9^{1}	14••		7	6				10^{1}	5	③•		1						21,017
6	Su	5 Apr 1992	Sunderland (S-Final)	*N	0-1	0-1		2	11	4				8	9			7	6				⑩	5	3	12	1						40,462

* PLAYED AT HILLSBOROUGH

** AFTER EXTRA TIME

RUMBELOWS LEAGUE CUP

NO.		DATE	OPPONENTS	V.	H-T	F-T	Gunn Bryan	Culverhouse Ian	Bowen Mark	Butterworth Ian	Blades Paul	Crook Ian	Gordon Dale	Fleck Robert	Newman Rob	Beckford Darren	Phillips David	Fox Ruel	Goss Jeremy	Ullathorne Robert	Ball Steve	Sherwood Tim	Sutton Chris	Polston John	Woodthorpe Colin	Sutch Daryl	Walton Mark	Power Lee	Smith David	Johnson Andy	Mortensen Henrik	Own Goals	ATTD.
1	W	25 Sept 1991	Charlton Athletic (2nd Rd 1st leg)	A	1-0	2-0	1		3	4	5	6	7^{1}	⑧••	9^{1}	12••	②•	10		11					14•								2,886
2	W	9 Oct 1991	Charlton Athletic (2nd Rd 2nd leg)	H	2-0	3-0	1		③•	4	5		7	⑥••^{2}	9	8^{1}		10	2	11	14••				12•								5,507
3	W	30 " 1991	Brentford (3rd Rd)	H	0-0	4-1	1		3	4	⑤•		7	8^{1}	9	11^{2}	2	10^{1}	⑥••		14••			12•									7,394
4	W	4 Dec 1991	West Ham United (4th Rd)	H	0-0	2-1	1		3		⑤•	12•		8^{2}	9	⑪••	2	14••	6	7		10	4										16,325
5	W	8 Jan 1992	Tottenham Hotspur (5th Rd)	A	1-0	1-2	1		3		5	⑩		8^{1}	9	14	2	7	6	11			4										29,471

ZENITH DATA SYSTEMS CUP

NO.		DATE	OPPONENTS	V.	H-T	F-T	Gunn Bryan	Culverhouse Ian	Bowen Mark	Butterworth Ian	Blades Paul	Crook Ian	Gordon Dale	Fleck Robert	Newman Rob	Beckford Darren	Phillips David	Fox Ruel	Goss Jeremy	Ullathorne Robert	Ball Steve	Sherwood Tim	Sutton Chris	Polston John	Woodthorpe Colin	Sutch Daryl	Walton Mark	Power Lee	Smith David	Johnson Andy	Mortensen Henrik	Own Goals	ATTD.
1	W	23 Oct 1991	Queens Park Rangers (2nd Rd)	H	1-1	1-2	1		3	4	⑤		7		9	8^{1}	2	10	6						14						11		4,436

1991-92 APPEARANCES & GOALS

	FOOTBALL LGE			F.A. CUP			LEAGUE CUP			ZDS CUP		
	APPR.	S	GLS	APPR.	S	GLS	APPR.	S	GLS	APPR.	S	GLS
Rob Newman	41	–	7	6	–	1	5	–	1	1	–	–
Ruel Fox	27	10	2	5	–	–	4	1	1	1	–	–
Robert Fleck	35	1	11	6	–	2	5	–	6	–	–	–
Mark Bowen	35	1	3	4	–	1	5	–	–	1	–	–
David Phillips	34	–	1	4	–	1	4	–	–	1	–	–
Jeremy Goss	29	4	1	6	–	–	4	–	–	1	–	–
Ian Butterworth	31	–	1	4	–	–	3	–	–	1	–	–
Darren Beckford	25	5	7	2	1	–	3	2	3	1	–	1
Paul Blades	26	–	–	1	–	–	5	–	–	1	–	–
Bryan Gunn	25	–	–	1	–	–	5	–	–	1	–	–
Ian Culverhouse	21	–	–	4	–	–	–	–	–	–	–	–
Ian Crook	20	1	1	1	2	–	2	1	–	–	–	–
Chris Sutton	16	5	2	6	–	3	2	–	–	–	–	–
Robert Ullathorne	20	–	3	2	–	–	4	–	–	–	–	–
John Polston	16	3	1	5	1	–	–	1	–	–	–	–
Mark Walton	17	–	–	5	–	–	–	–	–	–	–	–
Dale Gordon	15	–	4	–	–	–	3	–	1	1	–	–
Colin Woodthorpe	12	3	1	4	–	–	–	2	–	–	1	–
Daryl Sutch	5	4	–	–	1	–	–	–	–	–	–	–
Tim Sherwood	7	–	–	–	–	–	1	–	–	–	–	–
Lee Power	2	2	1	–	–	–	–	–	–	–	–	–
Andy Johnson	2	–	–	–	–	–	–	–	–	–	–	–
Steve Ball	–	2	–	–	–	–	–	2	–	–	–	–
David Smith	1	–	–	–	–	–	–	–	–	–	–	–
Henrik Mortensen	–	–	–	–	–	–	–	–	–	1	–	–
own goals	–	–	1	–	–	–	–	–	–	–	–	–

BARCLAYS LEAGUE DIVISION 1

1991-92	P	W	D	L	F	A	PTS
Leeds United	42	22	16	4	74	37	82
Manchester United	42	21	15	6	63	33	78
Sheffield Wednesday	42	21	12	9	62	49	75
Arsenal	42	19	15	8	81	46	72
Manchester City	42	20	10	12	61	48	70
Liverpool	42	16	16	10	47	40	64
Aston Villa	42	17	9	16	48	44	60
Nottingham Forest	42	16	11	15	60	58	59
Sheffield United	42	16	9	17	65	63	57
Crystal Palace	42	14	15	13	53	61	57
Queens Park Rangers	42	12	18	12	48	47	54
Everton	42	13	14	15	52	51	53
Wimbledon	42	13	14	15	53	53	53
Chelsea	42	13	14	15	50	60	53
Tottenham Hotspur	42	15	7	20	58	63	52
Southampton	42	14	10	18	39	55	52
Oldham Athletic	42	14	9	19	63	67	51
Norwich City	**42**	**11**	**12**	**19**	**47**	**63**	**45**
Coventry City	42	11	11	20	35	44	44
Luton Town	42	10	12	20	38	71	42
Notts. County	42	10	10	22	40	62	40
West Ham United	42	9	11	22	37	59	38

1992-93 FA PREMIER LEAGUE

NO.		DATE		OPPONENTS	V.	H-T	F-T	Gunn Bryan	Culverhouse Ian	Bowen Mark	Butterworth Ian	Polston John	Megson Gary	Fox Ruel	Newman Rob	Sutton Chris	Goss Jeremy	Phillips David	Robins Mark	Crook Ian	Power Lee	Woodthorpe Colin	Sutch Daryl	Beckford Darren	Johnson Andy	Smith David	Minett Jason	Ekoku Efan	Walton Mark	Own Goals	ATTD.
1	S	15 Aug	1992	Arsenal	A	0-2	4-2	1	2	3	4	5	(6)••	7[1]	8	(9)•	10	11[1]	12•[2]	14••											24,030
2	W	19 "	1992	Chelsea	H	0-1	2-1	1	2	3	4	(5)	6	7	8	12	10	11[1]	9[1]												15,164
3	S	22 "	1992	Everton	H	0-0	1-1	1	2	3	4		(6)•	7[1]	(8)••	5	10	11	9	12••	14•										14,150
4	W	26 "	1992	Manchester City	A	0-1	1-3	1	2	3	4		6[1]	(7)•	12•	5	8	11	(9)••	10		14••									23,182
5	S	29 "	1992	Crystal Palace	A	1-1	2-1	1	2	3	4		6		8	5	(10)	11[1]		7	9[1]		14								12,033
6	M	31 "	1992	Nottingham Forest	H	1-1	3-1	1	2	3	4		6		8	5	10	11[1]		7[1]	9[1]										14,104
7	S	5 Sept	1992	Southampton	H	0-0	1-0	1	2	3	(4)		6		8	5	10	11	12[1]	7	9										12,452
8	S	12 "	1992	Chelsea	A	0-2	3-2	1	2	3		4	6		8	5	10	11[1]	9[2]	(7)			12								16,880
9	S	19 "	1992	Sheffield Wednesday	H	1-0	1-0	1	2	3	4		6		8[1]	5	10	11	9	7											14,367
10	S	26 "	1992	Coventry City	A	1-1	1-1	1	2	3		4			8	5	10	11	9	7[1]			6								16,436
11	S	3 Oct	1992	Blackburn Rovers	A	1-4	1-7	1	2	3	4				8[1]	5	10	(11)	9	7	14		6								16,312
12	S	17 "	1992	Queens Park Rangers	H	0-0	2-1	1	2	3[1]	4	5				11[1]	10	8	(9)	7	14		6								16,009
13	Su	25 "	1992	Liverpool	A	1-2	1-4	1	2	3	4[1]	5		14••	6	11	(10)••	8	(9)•	7			12•								36,318
14	S	31 "	1992	Middlesbrough	H	0-0	1-1	1		3	4	(5)••		12•	8	(2)•	10	11	9	7			6[1]	14••							14,499
15	M	9 Nov	1992	Oldham Athletic	A	2-2	3-2	1	2	3	4	5		10		14•		11	9[3]	7			6	(8)							11,018
16	S	21 "	1992	Sheffield United	H	0-0	2-1	1	2	3	4	5		10				11	9[1]	7			6	8						-[1]	14,874
17	S	28 "	1992	Aston Villa	A	2-1	3-2	1	2	3	4	5		10		12		11[1]	9	7			6[1]	(8)[1]							28,837
18	S	5 Dec	1992	Wimbledon	H	0-0	2-1	1	2	3	4	5	14••	10		12•		11[1]	9[1]	7			(6)••	(8)•							14,161
19	S	12 "	1992	Manchester United	A	0-0	0-1	1	2	3	4	5	14••	10		12•		11	9	(7)••			6	(8)•							34,580
20	M	21 "	1992	Ipswich Town	H	0-0	0-2	1	2	3	(4)••	5	7	10	14••	12•		11	9				6	(8)•							20,032
21	S	26 "	1992	Tottenham Hotspur	H	0-0	0-0	1	2	3		5	6	10	4	8		11	9	7											19,413
22	M	28 "	1992	Leeds United	A	0-0	0-0	1	2	3		5	6	10	(4)	8		11	9	7			12								30,282
23	Su	10 Jan	1993	Sheffield Wednesday	A	0-1	0-1	1	2	3	4	5	6	10				11	(9)	7	8		12								23,360
24	S	16 "	1993	Coventry City	H	1-0	1-1	1	2	3	4	(5)••		10		9[1]	6	11		(7)•		14••	12•	8							13,613
25	W	27 "	1993	Crystal Palace	H	2-2	4-2	1	2	3	4	5	6	10		9[1]	7[1]	11			8[2]										13,543
26	S	30 "	1993	Everton	A	1-0	1-0	1	2	3	4	5	6	10		9[1]	7	11	12		(8)										20,301
27	W	10 Feb	1993	Southampton	A	0-2	0-3	1	2	3	4	5	6	10			7	11	(9)		8		12								12,969
28	S	20 "	1993	Manchester City	H	2-0	2-1	1	2	3	4	5	6	10			(7)•	11	9[1]		(8)••[1]		12•		14••						16,386
29	Su	28 "	1993	Blackburn Rovers	H	0-0	0-0	1	2	3		5		10		4		11	9		8		7			6					15,821
30	W	3 Mar	1993	Arsenal	H	1-0	1-1	1	2	3		5		10[1]		4		11	9		8		7			6					14,820
31	S	6 "	1993	Queens Park Rangers	A	1-2	1-3	1	2	3				10		4		11	9[1]	7	(8)	5	6				14				13,892
32	W	10 "	1993	Sheffield United	A	0-0	1-0	1	2	3		5		10[1]		4		11	9	7		8	(6)			12					15,583
33	S	13 "	1993	Oldham Athletic	H	1-0	1-0	1	2	3		5		10		4		11	(9)	7	12	8				6				-[1]	19,597
34	W	17 "	1993	Nottingham Forest	A	1-0	3-0	1	2	3		5		10		4		11	(9)[1]	7[1]	12[1]	8				6					20,799
35	S	20 "	1993	Wimbledon	A	0-2	0-3	1	2	3		5		10		4		11	9	7	14	(8)				6					10,875
36	W	24 "	1993	Aston Villa	H	0-0	1-0	1	2	3		5[1]	6	10		4	8	11	(9)	7	12										19,528
37	M	5 Apr	1993	Manchester United	H	0-3	1-3	1	2	3		5	(6)	10		4	8	11	9[1]	7								14			20,582
38	F	9 "	1993	Tottenham Hotspur	A	0-2	1-5	1	2	3		5	6	10		4	8	(11)	9	7								12[1]			31,425
39	W	14 "	1993	Leeds United	H	3-1	4-2	1	2	3	4	5		10		8[3]	6	11[1]	9	7											18,613
40	M	19 "	1993	Ipswich Town	A	1-1	1-3	1	2	3	4	5		10		8[1]	6	11	9	7											21,087
41	S	1 May	1993	Liverpool	H	0-0	1-0	1	2	3		5	14••	10	4	8	(6)••	11[1]	(9)•	7								12•			20,610
42	S	8 "	1993	Middlesbrough	A	1-1	3-3	1	2	3		5		10	4	8		11		7					6[1]			9[2]			15,155

F.A. CUP

NO.		DATE		OPPONENTS	V.	H-T	F-T	Gunn Bryan	Culverhouse Ian	Bowen Mark	Butterworth Ian	Polston John	Megson Gary	Fox Ruel	Newman Rob	Sutton Chris	Goss Jeremy	Phillips David	Robins Mark	Crook Ian	Power Lee	Woodthorpe Colin	Sutch Daryl	Beckford Darren	Johnson Andy	Smith David	Minett Jason	Ekoku Efan	Walton Mark	Own Goals	ATTD.
1	W	13 Jan	1993	Coventry City (3rd Rd)	H	0-0	1-0	1	2	3	4	5	(6)	10		9	12	11		7				8[1]							15,301
2	Su	24 "	1993	Tottenham Hotspur (4th Rd)	H	0-1	0-2	1	2	3	4	5	6	10		9	(7)	11			12			8							15,003

COCA-COLA LEAGUE CUP

NO.		DATE		OPPONENTS	V.	H-T	F-T	Gunn Bryan	Culverhouse Ian	Bowen Mark	Butterworth Ian	Polston John	Megson Gary	Fox Ruel	Newman Rob	Sutton Chris	Goss Jeremy	Phillips David	Robins Mark	Crook Ian	Power Lee	Woodthorpe Colin	Sutch Daryl	Beckford Darren	Johnson Andy	Smith David	Minett Jason	Ekoku Efan	Walton Mark	Own Goals	ATTD.
1	Tu	22 Sept	1992	Carlisle United (2nd Rd 1st leg)	A	0-1	2-2	1	2	3		4			8	5	10[1]	11	9[1]	7			6								10,328
2	W	7 Oct	1992	Carlisle United (2nd Rd 2nd leg)	H	0-0	2-0		2	3	4	5			8	11[2]	10		9	7			6						1		8,489
3	W	28 "	1992	Blackburn Rovers (3rd Rd)	A	0-1	0-2	1	(2)•	3	4	5		12•	9	11	(10)••	8	13••	7			6								14,216

1992-93 APPEARANCES & GOALS

	PREMIER LGE			F.A. CUP			LEAGUE CUP		
	APPR.	S	GLS	APPR.	S	GLS	APPR.	S	GLS
Mark Bowen	42	–	1	2	–	–	3	–	–
Bryan Gunn	42	–	–	2	–	–	2	–	–
David Phillips	42	–	9	2	–	–	2	–	–
Ian Culverhouse	41	–	–	2	–	–	3	–	–
Mark Robins	34	3	15	–	–	–	2	1	1
Chris Sutton	32	5	8	2	–	–	3	–	2
John Polston	34	–	1	2	–	–	3	–	–
Ruel Fox	32	2	4	2	–	–	–	1	–
Ian Crook	32	2	3	1	–	–	3	–	–
Ian Butterworth	26	–	1	2	–	–	2	–	–
Jeremy Goss	25	–	1	1	1	–	3	–	1
Gary Megson	20	3	1	2	–	–	–	–	–
Daryl Sutch	14	8	2	–	–	–	3	–	–
Rob Newman	16	2	2	–	–	–	3	–	–
Lee Power	11	7	6	–	1	–	–	–	–
Darren Beckford	7	1	1	2	–	1	–	–	–
Colin Woodthorpe	5	2	–	–	–	–	–	–	–
David Smith	5	1	–	–	–	–	–	–	–
Efan Ekoku	1	3	3	–	–	–	–	–	–
Andy Johnson	1	1	1	–	–	–	–	–	–
Jason Minett	–	1	–	–	–	–	–	–	–
Mark Walton	–	–	–	–	–	–	1	–	–
own goals	–	–	2	–	–	–	–	–	–

F.A. PREMIER LEAGUE

1992-93	P	W	D	L	F	A	PTS
Manchester United	42	24	12	6	67	31	84
Aston Villa	42	21	11	10	57	40	74
Norwich City	**42**	**21**	**9**	**12**	**61**	**65**	**72**
Blackburn Rovers	42	20	11	11	68	46	71
Queens Park Rangers	42	17	12	13	63	55	63
Liverpool	42	16	11	15	62	55	59
Sheffield Wednesday	42	15	14	13	55	51	59
Tottenham Hotspur	42	16	11	15	60	66	59
Manchester City	42	15	12	15	56	51	57
Arsenal	42	15	11	16	40	38	56
Chelsea	42	14	14	14	51	54	56
Wimbledon	42	14	12	16	56	55	54
Everton	42	15	8	19	53	55	53
Sheffield United	42	14	10	18	54	53	52
Coventry City	42	13	13	16	52	57	52
Ipswich Town	42	12	16	14	50	55	52
Leeds United	42	12	15	15	57	62	51
Southampton	42	13	11	18	54	61	50
Oldham Athletic	42	13	10	19	63	74	49
Crystal Palace	42	11	16	15	48	61	49
Middlesbrough	42	11	11	20	54	75	44
Nottingham Forest	42	10	10	22	41	62	40

1993-94 FA CARLING PREMIERSHIP

NO.		DATE	OPPONENTS	V.	H-T	F-T	Gunn Bryan	Culverhouse Ian	Polston John	Butterworth Ian	Newman Rob	Fox Ruel	Goss Jeremy	Crook Ian	Bowen Mark	Sutton Chris	Robins Mark	Ekoku Efan	Megson Gary	Prior Spencer	Eadie Darren	Sutch Daryl	Ullathorne Robert	Power Lee	Woodthorpe Colin	Smith David	Johnson Andy	Howie Scott	Adams Neil	Akinbiyi Ade	Own Goals	ATTD.
1	Su	15 Aug 1993	Manchester United	H	0-1	0-2	1	5	10	17■	3	14	11	4	2	22	(12)•	7•														19,705
2	W	18 " 1993	Blackburn Rovers	A	1-1	3-2	1	5	10	17■	3[1]	14	11	4	2	22[2]	12															14,236
3	S	21 " 1993	Leeds United	A	2-0	4-0	1	5	10	17■	3	14[2]	11[1]	4	2	(22)•[1]	12	7•														32,008
4	W	25 " 1993	Ipswich Town	H	1-0	1-0	1	5	10	17■	3	14	11[1]	4	2	22	12															18,976
5	S	28 " 1993	Swindon Town	H	0-0	0-0	1	5	10	(17)•■	3	14	11	4	2	22	(12)••	7••	9•													17,614
6	W	1 Sept 1993	Sheffield Wednesday	A	0-0	3-3	1	5	10■		3	14	11	4	2[1]	22[1]	(12)•	7•[1]		27												25,175
7	S	11 " 1993	Wimbledon	H	0-0	0-1	1	5	10■		3	14	11	4	2	22	12•	7		(27)•												14,851
8	S	18 " 1993	Queens Park Rangers	A	2-1	2-2	1	5	10■		3	14	11	4	2	22		7			20[1]										–[1]	13,359
9	S	25 " 1993	Everton	A	1-1	5-1	1	5	10	17■	3	14	11	4	2	22[1]		7[4]														20,531
10	S	2 Oct 1993	Coventry City	H	1-0	1-0	1	5	10■		3	14[1]	11	4	2	22		7	9													16,239
11	S	16 " 1993	Chelsea	A	1-0	2-1	1	5		17■	3	14[1]	11	4	2	22[1]	12			27												16,923
12	S	23 " 1993	West Ham United	H	0-0	0-0	1	5		17■	3	14	11	4	2	22			9		20•	(15)•										20,175
13	S	30 " 1993	Arsenal	A	0-0	0-0	1	5		17■	3	14		4	2	22			9	27	20											30,506
14	S	6 Nov 1993	Sheffield United	A	1-1	2-1	1	5	10	17■	3	14	11[1]	4		22					20[1]		18									18,254
15	S	20 " 1993	Manchester City	H	0-0	1-1	1	5	10	17■	3	(14)•[1]	11	4	2	22			9			15•										16,626
16	S	27 " 1993	Oldham Athletic	A	0-0	1-2	1	5	10	17■	(3)•	14	11	4	2	22[1]							18•	16								10,198
17	S	4 Dec 1993	Manchester United	A	1-2	2-2	1	5		(17)•■	3	(14)••[1]	11		2	22[1]			9		20••	15•		16	8							44,694
18	M	13 " 1993	Leeds United	H	1-0	2-1	1	5			3■	14			2	22[1]		(7)••[1]	9	(27)•			18•	16••	8	21						16,586
19	S	18 " 1993	Ipswich Town	A	1-1	1-2	1	5		17■	3	14			2[1]	22		(7)•	9					16•	8	21						19,498
20	M	27 " 1993	Tottenham Hotspur	A	2-0	3-1	1	5		17■	3	(14)•		4	2	22[2]		7[1]	9				18•		8							33,130
21	W	29 " 1993	Aston Villa	H	1-0	1-2	1	5		(17)••■	3	14		4	2	22[1]		7					18•		8	(21)•	19••					20,650
22	S	1 Jan 1994	Southampton	A	1-0	1-0	1	5		17■	3	14		4	2	22[1]		7	9						8							16,556
23	W	4 " 1994	Newcastle United	H	1-1	1-2	1	5		17■	3	14		4	2[1]	22		7	9						8							19,564
24	S	15 " 1994	Chelsea	H	0-1	1-1	1	5		17■	3	14		4	2	22		7[1]	(9)•						8		19•					19,472
25	M	24 " 1994	West Ham United	A	1-1	3-3	1	5		17■	3	14[1]	11	4	2	22[2]		7•	(9)•						8							20,738
26	S	5 Feb 1994	Liverpool	H	1-0	2-2	1	5	10■		3		11	4	2	22[2]		7	(9)•		(20)••				8			13••				19,746
27	Su	13 " 1994	Arsenal	H	0-1	1-1	1	5	10■		3		11	4	2	22		7[1]	(9)••		20•			16••	(8)•							17,667
28	S	19 " 1994	Swindon Town	A	2-2	3-3		5	10■		3[1]		11[1]	4	2	22[1]		7			20•				(8)•			13	6			15,405
29	Tu	22 " 1994	Blackburn Rovers	H	1-1	2-2	1	5	10■	17•	3		11	4	2	22[2]		(7)••			20••		18						(6)•			15,124
30	S	26 " 1994	Sheffield Wednesday	H	0-0	1-1	1	5	10■	17•	3		11	4	(2)•	22[1]		7					18						6			18,311
31	S	5 Mar 1994	Wimbledon	A	1-1	1-3	1	5		17■	3		11	4	2	22		7[1]					18						6			7,206
32	S	12 " 1994	Queens Park Rangers	H	1-0	3-4	1	5			(3)•		(11)••	4■	2[1]	22		7[2]					18••		8	21			6	26•		16,499
33	M	21 " 1994	Everton	H	1-0	3-0	1	5[1]	10	17■			11	4	2[1]	22[1]			(9)•		20					21•			6			16,432
34	S	26 " 1994	Coventry City	A	0-1	1-2	1	5	(10)•	17■			11	4	2	22			9		20[1]				8•				6			13,514
35	Tu	29 " 1994	Newcastle United	A	0-1	0-3	1	5					11	4■	2				9	27	20		18		8				(6)•	26•		32,216
36	S	2 Apr 1994	Tottenham Hotspur	H	0-0	1-2	1	5					(11)•	4■	2	22[1]	12•		9	27	20				8				6			21,181
37	M	4 " 1994	Aston Villa	A	0-0	0-0	1	5					11	4■	2	22			(9)•	27	(20)••		18		8	21•			6••			25,416
38	S	9 " 1994	Southampton	H	1-1	4-5	1	5					11[1]	4■	2	22[2]	12•[1]		(9)•	27	(20)••		18		8••				6			17,150
39	S	16 " 1994	Manchester City	A	1-0	1-1	1	5	10■				11	4	2	22	(12)••	7••		27			18[1]			(21)•			6•			28,020
40	S	23 " 1994	Sheffield United	H	0-1	0-1	1	5	10■				11	4	2	22	12	7•		27			18						(6)•			18,474
41	S	30 " 1994	Liverpool	A	1-0	1-0	1	5	10■				11[1]	4	2	22		7		27			18		8							44,339
42	S	7 May 1994	Oldham Athletic	H	0-1	1-1	1	5	10■				11		2	22	12••	7	(9)••	(27)•			18[1]		8				6•			20,434

F.A. CUP

NO.		DATE	OPPONENTS	V.	H-T	F-T	Gunn Bryan	Culverhouse Ian	Polston John	Butterworth Ian	Newman Rob	Fox Ruel	Goss Jeremy	Crook Ian	Bowen Mark	Sutton Chris	Robins Mark	Ekoku Efan	Megson Gary	Prior Spencer	Eadie Darren	Sutch Daryl	Ullathorne Robert	Power Lee	Woodthorpe Colin	Smith David	Johnson Andy	Howie Scott	Adams Neil	Akinbiyi Ade	Own Goals	ATTD.
1	S	8 Jan 1994	Wycombe Wanderers (3rd Rd)	A	1-0	2-0	1	5		17■	3	14		4	2	22[2]		(7)••	(9)•				18••		8	21•						7,802
2	Su	30 " 1994	Manchester United (4th Rd)	H	0-1	0-2	1	5	10■		3	14	11	(4)•	2	22		7•	9						8							21,060

COCA-COLA CUP

NO.		DATE	OPPONENTS	V.	H-T	F-T	Gunn Bryan	Culverhouse Ian	Polston John	Butterworth Ian	Newman Rob	Fox Ruel	Goss Jeremy	Crook Ian	Bowen Mark	Sutton Chris	Robins Mark	Ekoku Efan	Megson Gary	Prior Spencer	Eadie Darren	Sutch Daryl	Ullathorne Robert	Power Lee	Woodthorpe Colin	Smith David	Johnson Andy	Howie Scott	Adams Neil	Akinbiyi Ade	Own Goals	ATTD.
1	W	22 Sept 1993	Bradford City (2nd Rd 1st leg)	A	0-1	1-2	1	2	5■		6	10[1]		4	3	12•	9	(7)•			11						8					8,988
2	W	6 Oct 1993	Bradford City (2nd Rd 2nd leg)	H	0-0	3-0	1	2	5■		6	10[1]	11	4	3	9[1]	12•	(7)•[1]	8													12,787
3	Tu	26 " 1993	Arsenal (3rd Rd)	A	1-0	1-1	1	2		4■	6	10	11	4[1]	3	9				5	8											24,539
4	W	10 Nov 1993	Arsenal (3rd Rd Replay)	H	0-2	0-3	1	2	5	4■	6	10	11	4	3	9					(8)•	15•										16,319

UEFA CUP

NO.		DATE	OPPONENTS	V.	H-T	F-T	Gunn Bryan	Culverhouse Ian	Polston John	Butterworth Ian	Newman Rob	Fox Ruel	Goss Jeremy	Crook Ian	Bowen Mark	Sutton Chris	Robins Mark	Ekoku Efan	Megson Gary	Prior Spencer	Eadie Darren	Sutch Daryl	Ullathorne Robert	Power Lee	Woodthorpe Colin	Smith David	Johnson Andy	Howie Scott	Adams Neil	Akinbiyi Ade	Own Goals	ATTD.
1	W	15 Sept 1993	Vitesse Arnhem (1st Rd 1st leg)	H	0-0	3-0	1	2	5[1]■		4	10	11[1]	8	3	(9)•	12•	7[1]	(6)••		16••											16,818
2	W	29 " 1993	Vitesse Arnhem (1st Rd 2nd leg)	A	0-0	0-0	1	2	5	4■	6	10	11	8	3	9		(7)•	12•													9,133
3	Tu	20 Oct 1993	Bayern Munich (2nd Rd 1st leg)	A	2-1	2-1	1	2		4■	6	10	11[1]	8	3[1]	9	(7)•			5		14•										28,500
4	W	3 Nov 1993	Bayern Munich (2nd Rd 2nd leg)	H	0-1	1-1	1	2	5	4■	6	(10)••	11[1]	8	3	9					7	14•								16••		20,829
5	W	24 " 1993	Inter Milan (3rd Rd 1st leg)	H	0-0	0-1	1	2	5	4■	6	10	11	8	3	9						(7)•		16•								20,805
6	W	8 Dec 1993	Inter Milan (3rd Rd 2nd leg)	A	0-0	0-1	1				6■	10	11		3	9		(7)•	4	(5)••		12•	2	16•	8							30,000

1993-94 APPEARANCES & GOALS

	PREMIERSHIP APPR.	S	GLS	F.A. CUP APPR.	S	GLS	LEAGUE CUP APPR.	S	GLS	UEFA CUP APPR.	S	GLS
Ian Culverhouse	42	–	1	2	–	–	4	–	–	5	–	–
Mark Bowen	41	–	5	2	–	–	4	–	–	6	–	1
Bryan Gunn	41	–	–	2	–	–	4	–	–	6	–	–
Chris Sutton	41	–	25	2	–	2	3	1	1	6	–	–
Ian Crook	38	–	–	2	–	–	4	–	1	5	–	–
Jeremy Goss	34	–	6	1	–	–	3	–	–	6	–	3
Rob Newman	32	–	2	2	–	–	4	–	–	6	–	–
Efan Ekoku	20	7	12	1	1	–	2	–	1	3	–	1
Ruel Fox	25	–	7	2	–	–	4	–	2	6	–	–
Ian Butterworth	23	2	–	1	–	–	2	–	–	4	–	–
John Polston	24	–	–	1	–	–	3	–	–	4	–	1
Gary Megson	21	1	–	2	–	–	1	–	–	2	1	–
Colin Woodthorpe	18	2	–	2	–	–	–	–	–	1	–	–
Robert Ullathorne	11	5	2	–	1	–	–	–	–	1	–	–
Darren Eadie	9	6	3	–	–	–	3	–	–	1	1	–
Neil Adams	11	3	–	–	–	–	–	–	–	–	–	–
Spencer Prior	13	–	–	–	–	–	1	–	–	2	–	–
Mark Robins	9	4	1	–	–	–	1	1	–	1	1	–
David Smith	5	2	–	–	1	–	–	–	–	–	–	–
Lee Power	2	3	–	–	–	–	–	–	–	–	2	–
Daryl Sutch	1	2	–	–	–	–	–	1	–	1	3	–
Scott Howie	1	1	–	–	–	–	–	–	–	–	–	–
Andy Johnson	–	2	–	–	–	–	1	–	–	–	–	–
Ade Akinbiyi	–	2	–	–	–	–	–	–	–	–	1	–
own goals	–	–	1	–	–	–	–	–	–	–	–	–

FA CARLING PREMIERSHIP

1993-94	P	W	D	L	F	A	PTS
Manchester United	42	27	11	4	80	38	92
Blackburn Rovers	42	25	9	8	63	36	84
Newcastle United	42	23	8	11	82	41	77
Arsenal	42	18	17	7	53	28	71
Leeds United	42	18	16	8	65	39	70
Wimbledon	42	18	11	13	56	53	65
Sheffield Wednesday	42	16	16	10	76	54	64
Liverpool	42	17	9	16	59	53	60
Queens Park Rangers	42	16	12	14	62	61	60
Aston Villa	42	15	12	15	46	50	57
Coventry City	42	14	14	14	43	45	56
Norwich City	**42**	**12**	**17**	**13**	**65**	**61**	**53**
West Ham United	42	13	13	16	47	58	52
Chelsea	42	13	12	17	49	53	51
Tottenham Hotspur	42	11	12	19	54	59	45
Manchester City	42	9	18	15	38	49	45
Everton	42	12	8	22	42	63	44
Southampton	42	12	7	23	47	66	43
Ipswich Town	42	9	16	17	35	58	43
Sheffield United	42	8	18	16	42	60	42
Oldham Athletic	42	9	13	20	42	68	40
Swindon Town	42	5	15	22	47	100	30

1994-95 FA CARLING PREMIERSHIP

NO.		DATE	OPPONENTS	V.	H-T	F-T	Gunn Bryan	Bradshaw Carl	Bowen Mark	Polston John	Newsome Jon	Goss Jeremy	Newman Rob	Crook Ian	Ullathorne Robert	Ekoku Efan	Robins Mark	Adams Neil	Sutch Daryl	Eadie Darren	Akinbiyi Ade	Sheron Mike	Milligan Mike	Prior Spencer	Wright Johnny	O'Neill Keith	Cureton Jamie	Ward Ashley	Marshall Andy	Tracey Simon	Johnson Andy	Megson Gary	Own Goals	ATTD.
1	S	20 Aug 1994	Chelsea	A	0-1	0-2	1	16	2	10	5	11	(3)•	4	18	(7)••	9	6•	15••															23,098
2	W	24 " 1994	Crystal Palace	H	0-0	0-0	1	16	2	10	5	11		4	18	7	(9)•	6		20•														19,015
3	S	27 " 1994	West Ham United	H	0-0	1-0	1	16	2	10	5	11	3••	4	18	(7)•	(9)••[1]	6			26•													19,110
4	W	31 " 1994	Sheffield Wednesday	A	0-0	0-0	1	16	2	10	5	11	3••	4	18		(9)••	6			(26)•	22•												25,072
5	S	10 Sept 1994	Arsenal	H	0-0	0-0	1	16	2	10	5	11	3	4	18	(7)••	9••	(6)•	15•															17,768
6	M	19 " 1994	Ipswich Town	A	1-1	2-1	1	16[1]	2	10	5	11	3[1]	(4)•		7••		6		20•		(22)••	8											17,447
7	S	24 " 1994	Manchester City	A	0-0	0-2	1	16	2	10	5	11	3	4	(18)••		9•	(6)•				22	8••											21,031
8	S	1 Oct 1994	Blackburn Rovers	H	1-1	2-1	1	16	2[1]	10	5[1]	11•	3	4		(7)••	9••	(6)•		20			8											18,146
9	S	8 " 1994	Leeds United	H	0-0	2-1	1	16	2		(5)•	11••	3	4			9[1]	6[1]		20		22	(8)••	14•										17,390
10	S	15 " 1994	Aston Villa	A	0-0	1-1	1	(16)•	2				3	4			(9)••	6		20	26••	22	8[1]	14	32•									22,468
11	S	22 " 1994	Queens Park Rangers	H	0-1	4-2	1		2[1]	10	5	11••	3•	4			9[1]	(6)••		20		22[1]	8		(32)•								–1	19,431
12	Su	30 " 1994	Wimbledon	A	0-0	0-1	1		2	10		11	3	4•	(18)•			6••	15		(26)••	22	8	14										8,242
13	W	2 Nov 1994	Southampton	A	0-0	1-1	1		2	10		11	(3)•	4			9[1]	6	15•		(26)••		8	14		21••								12,976
14	S	5 " 1994	Everton	H	0-0	0-0	1		2	10		11	3	4			(9)•	6	15				8	14			25•							18,377
15	S	19 " 1994	Coventry City	A	0-0	0-1	1		2	10	5	11••	3	4			(9)••	(6)•	15•	20			8	14										11,855
16	S	26 " 1994	Leicester City	H	0-1	2-1	1		2	10	5[1]	11•	3	4				6	15[1]	20		(22)••	(8)•				25••							20,657
17	S	3 Dec 1994	Manchester United	A	0-1	0-1	1	16	2	10	5	11	(3)•	4	18		9		15								25•							43,789
18	S	10 " 1994	Chelsea	H	2-0	3-0	1	16		10	5		3••	(4)••	18		(9)•		15	20			8				25•[1]	7[2]						18,246
19	S	17 " 1994	Crystal Palace	A	0-0	1-0	1	(16)•	2•	10	5		3••	(4)••	18		9		15	20			8					7[1]						12,252
20	M	26 " 1994	Tottenham Hotspur	H	0-1	0-2	1		(2)•	10	5	11	3•	4	18		9	6••	(15)••	20								7						21,814
21	Tu	27 " 1994	Nottingham Forest	A	0-0	0-1	(1)•			10	5	11	3	4	18			6••	15			22					(25)••	7	24•					21,010
22	S	31 " 1994	Newcastle United	H	2-1	2-1				10	5	11	3•	(4)•	18			6[1]	15			(22)••	8				25••	7[1]	24					21,172
23	M	2 Jan 1995	Liverpool	A	0-2	0-4				10		(11)••	(3)•	4	18			6•	15	20••		22	8	14				7	24					34,709
24	S	14 " 1995	Wimbledon	H	1-1	1-2			2	10	5	11[1]		(4)•	18			(6)••	15		26•	22		14••				7	24					18,261
25	W	25 " 1995	Coventry City	H	1-1	2-2			2	10	5		3					6[1]	(15)•	20•		22	8	14				7[1]		34				14,024
26	S	4 Feb 1995	Everton	A	0-1	1-2			2	10	5	11••		4	18			6•	(15)•	20		(22)••	8[1]					7	24					23,293
27	S	11 " 1995	Southampton	H	1-2	2-2		16	2		5[1]	11		4	(18)••			6•	15••	20		22		(14)•				7[1]	24					18,361
28	W	22 " 1995	Manchester United	H	0-2	0-2		16	2	10	5							6		20		22	8					7	24		19			21,824
29	S	25 " 1995	Blackburn Rovers	A	0-0	0-0		16	2	10	5							(6)••	15••	20		22	(8)•				25•	7	24		19			25,579
30	S	4 Mar 1995	Manchester City	H	0-0	1-1		16	(2)•	10			3					6		20		22••	(8)••	14•			25[1]	7	24		19			16,266
31	W	8 " 1995	Sheffield Wednesday	H	0-0	0-0		(16)•	2	10	5		3•	(4)••	18				15	20							25	7	24		19••			13,530
32	S	11 " 1995	West Ham United	A	1-0	2-2				10	5		3		18[1]			6•	15	(20)•[1]	26••			14			(25)••	7	24		19			21,464
33	W	15 " 1995	Queens Park Rangers	A	0-0	0-2				10			3		18			6•	15	20	26••		8	14			(25)••	7	24		(19)•			10,519
34	M	20 " 1995	Ipswich Town	H	0-0	3-0			2	10	5		3••	4	18			(6)•	15•	20[1]			8				(25)••[1]	7[1]	24					17,510
35	S	1 Apr 1995	Arsenal	A	1-3	1-5		16	2		5		3		(18)•			6	15•	20							25[1]	7	24		19			36,942
36	W	5 " 1995	Leicester City	A	0-0	0-1		16	2•	10	5		3		(18)••				15	20				14••			25	7	24			(9)•		15,992
37	S	8 " 1995	Newcastle United	A	0-2	0-3		16	2	(10)••	5			4	(18)•				15•	20			8	14			25••	7	24					35,518
38	W	12 " 1995	Nottingham Forest	H	0-0	0-1		16	2	10	5			4				6		(20)•	26••		8	14•			(25)••	7	24					19,005
39	M	17 " 1995	Tottenham Hotspur	A	0-1	0-1		16	2	10	5		3	4					15•		26••	(22)••	(8)•	14				7	24					32,304
40	S	29 " 1995	Liverpool	H	1-1	1-2		(16)•	2	10	5			4	(18)••[1]			6••	15		26		8				25•	7	24					21,843
41	S	6 May 1995	Leeds United	A	1-0	1-2		16•	2	10	5	11	3	(4)•	18				15		(26)••	22••						7[1]	24					31,982
42	Su	14 " 1995	Aston Villa	H	0-1	1-1		16	2	10	5	11[1]		4	18				15		(26)•	22•						7	24					19,374

F.A. CUP

NO.		DATE	OPPONENTS		V.	H-T	F-T	Gunn Bryan	Bradshaw Carl	Bowen Mark	Polston John	Newsome Jon	Goss Jeremy	Newman Rob	Crook Ian	Ullathorne Robert	Ekoku Efan	Robins Mark	Adams Neil	Sutch Daryl	Eadie Darren	Akinbiyi Ade	Sheron Mike	Milligan Mike	Prior Spencer	Wright Johnny	O'Neill Keith	Cureton Jamie	Ward Ashley	Marshall Andy	Tracey Simon	Johnson Andy	Megson Gary	Own Goals	ATTD.
1	S	7 Jan 1995	Grimsby Town	(3rd Rd)	A	0-0	1-0				10	5	11•	3	4[1]	18			(6)•	15	20		(22)••	8				25••		24					11,198
2	S	28 " 1995	Coventry City	(4th Rd)	A	0-0	0-0			2	10	5		(3)••		18			6	15	20	26••	(22)•••	8				25•••		24•	(34)•				15,101
3	W	8 Feb 1995	Coventry City	(4th Rd Replay)	H	1-1	*3-1			2	10	5	11••		(4)••	18			(6)•	15	20[1]	26•	22[2]	8						24					14,673
4	S	18 " 1995	Everton	(5th Rd)	A	0-2	0-5		16	2		5	11	3		(18)•				15	20		22		14•						34	19			31,616

* AFTER EXTRA TIME

COCA-COLA CUP

NO.		DATE	OPPONENTS		V.	H-T	F-T	Gunn Bryan	Bradshaw Carl	Bowen Mark	Polston John	Newsome Jon	Goss Jeremy	Newman Rob	Crook Ian	Ullathorne Robert	Ekoku Efan	Robins Mark	Adams Neil	Sutch Daryl	Eadie Darren	Akinbiyi Ade	Sheron Mike	Milligan Mike	Prior Spencer	Wright Johnny	O'Neill Keith	Cureton Jamie	Ward Ashley	Marshall Andy	Tracey Simon	Johnson Andy	Megson Gary	Own Goals	ATTD.
1	W	21 Sept 1994	Swansea City	(2nd Rd 1st leg)	H	1-0	3-0	1	16[1]		(10)•	5	11	3•	4••	18		9	6[1]		20		22[1]									(19)••			8,053
2	Tu	4 Oct 1994	Swansea City	(2nd Rd 2nd leg)	A	0-0	0-1	1	16	2		5	11	3	4••		(7)•	9•	6		20			(8)••	14										3,568
3	W	26 " 1994	Tranmere Rovers	(3rd Rd)	A	1-0	1-1	1		2	10[1]		11••	3	4			9	(6)•	15•	(20)••		22	8	14										10,232
4	W	9 Nov 1994	Tranmere Rovers	(3rd Rd Replay)	H	0-1	4-2	1		2	10[1]		11•	3[1]	(4)•			9	6	15	20			8	14[1]									–1	13,311
5	W	30 " 1994	Notts. County	(4th Rd)	H	1-0	1-0	1		2	10	5	11••	3	4				6	15	(20)••[1]		(22)•	8				25•							14,030
6	W	11 Jan 1995	Bolton Wanderers	(5th Rd)	A	0-0	0-1			2	10	5	11	3	4	18••			(6)••	15	(20)•	26•	22							24					17,029

1994-95 APPEARANCES & GOALS

	PREMIERSHIP APPR.	S	GLS	F.A. CUP APPR.	S	GLS	LEAGUE CUP APPR.	S	GLS
John Polston	38	–	–	3	–	–	5	–	2
Mark Bowen	34	2	2	3	–	–	5	–	–
Jon Newsome	35	–	3	4	–	–	4	–	–
Ian Crook	33	1	–	2	–	1	4	2	–
Neil Adams	23	10	3	3	–	–	6	–	1
Rob Newman	23	9	1	3	–	–	5	1	1
Daryl Sutch	20	10	1	4	–	–	3	1	–
Robert Ullathorne	27	–	2	4	–	–	1	1	–
Mike Milligan	25	1	2	3	–	–	4	–	–
Carl Bradshaw	25	1	1	1	–	–	2	–	1
Darren Eadie	22	4	2	4	–	1	6	–	1
Ashley Ward	25	–	8	–	–	–	–	–	–
Jeremy Goss	19	6	2	1	2	–	3	3	–
Bryan Gunn	21	–	–	–	–	–	5	–	–
Andy Marshall	20	1	–	2	1	–	1	–	–
Mike Sheron	17	4	1	4	–	2	4	–	1
Mark Robins	14	3	4	–	–	–	3	1	–
Spencer Prior	12	5	–	–	1	–	3	–	1
Jamie Cureton	9	8	4	–	2	–	–	1	–
Ade Akinbiyi	6	7	–	–	2	–	–	1	–
Andy Johnson	6	1	–	1	–	–	1	–	–
Efan Ekoku	5	1	–	–	–	–	1	–	–
Johnny Wright	1	1	–	–	–	–	–	–	–
Simon Tracey	1	–	–	2	–	–	–	–	–
Gary Megson	1	–	–	–	–	–	–	–	–
Keith O'Neill	–	1	–	–	–	–	–	–	–
own goals	–	–	1	–	–	–	–	–	1

FA CARLING PREMIERSHIP

1994-95	P	W	D	L	F	A	PTS
Blackburn Rovers	42	27	8	7	80	39	89
Manchester United	42	26	10	6	77	28	88
Nottingham Forest	42	22	11	9	72	43	77
Liverpool	42	21	11	10	65	37	74
Leeds United	42	20	13	9	59	38	73
Newcastle United	42	20	12	10	67	47	72
Tottenham Hotspur	42	16	14	12	66	58	62
Queens Park Rangers	42	17	9	16	61	59	60
Wimbledon	42	15	11	16	48	65	56
Southampton	42	12	18	12	61	63	54
Chelsea	42	13	15	14	50	55	54
Arsenal	42	13	12	17	52	49	51
Sheffield Wednesday	42	13	12	17	49	57	51
West Ham United	42	13	11	18	44	48	50
Everton	42	11	17	14	44	51	50
Coventry City	42	12	14	16	44	62	50
Manchester City	42	12	13	17	53	64	49
Aston Villa	42	11	15	16	51	56	48
Crystal Palace	42	11	12	19	34	49	45
Norwich City	**42**	**10**	**13**	**19**	**37**	**54**	**43**
Leicester City	42	6	11	25	45	80	29
Ipswich Town	42	7	6	29	36	93	27

1995-96 DIVISION 1

NO.		DATE	OPPONENTS	V.	H-T	F-T	Gunn Bryan	Mills Danny	Bowen Mark	Milligan Mike	Newsome Jon	Prior Spencer	Adams Neil	Akinbiyi Ade	Ward Ashley	Johnson Andy	Eadie Darren	Polston John	Ullathorne Robert	Sutch Daryl	Sheron Mike	Newman Rob	Rush Matthew	Cureton Jamie	Fleck Robert	Crook Ian	Marshall Andy	O'Neill Keith	Simpson Karl	Bradshaw Carl	Scott Keith	Carey Shaun	Goss Jeremy	Molby Jan	Wright Johnny			Own Goals	ATTD.
1	Su	13 Aug 1995	Luton Town	A	1-0	3-1	1	2	3	(4)•	5[2]	6	7[1]	8	9	(10)••	11	12•••	13•	14•••																			7,848
2	S	19 " 1995	Sunderland	H	0-0	0-0	1	2	3	4	5	6	7	8		(10)•	11				(9)••	13•	14••																16,739
3	S	26 " 1995	Birmingham City	A	0-1	1-3	1	2	3	(4)•	5	6	7	9		(10)••	11			13•	8[1]			14••															19,267
4	W	30 " 1995	Oldham Athletic	H	0-0	2-1	1		3[1]		5		7	9		10[1]	11	6	4	2	12				(8)														14,816
5	S	2 Sept 1995	Port Vale	H	2-1	2-1	1		3		5	13•	7		9	(10)••[1]	11	(6)•	4	2	12••				8[1]														13,908
6	S	9 " 1995	Sheffield United	A	1-1	1-2	1	2	3	13•	5	6	7	14•••	9[1]	(10)•••	11					12••			(8)••	(4)•													11,205
7	W	13 " 1995	Wolverhampton Wanderers	A	0-0	2-0	1	2	3	14	5	6	7		9[1]	10[1]	11								8	(4)													27,064
8	S	16 " 1995	Millwall	H	0-0	0-0	1	2	3	14•	5	6	7	12••	(9)••	10	11								8	(4)•													15,962
9	S	23 " 1995	Grimsby Town	A	1-2	2-2			3		5	6	(7)•••	9[1]		10	11		14•	(2)•	13•••	12••			(8)••[1]	4	1												5,901
10	S	30 " 1995	Leicester City	H	0-0	0-1			3		5	6	(7)•	9		10	11		2		14••				(8)••	4	1	13•											18,435
11	S	7 Oct 1995	Stoke City	A	1-0	1-1	1		3	13•	5	6	(7)•	9[1]		10		12•••	2		14••				(8)••	4		(11)•••											12,106
12	S	14 " 1995	Barnsley	H	0-1	3-1	1		3	12•	5[1]	6			9	10[1]			2						8[1]	4		11	(7)										14,002
13	S	21 " 1995	Charlton Athletic	A	0-0	1-1	1		3[1]	7	5	6			9	10			2						8	4		11											13,369
14	Su	29 " 1995	Tranmere Rovers	H	1-0	1-1	1		(3)•	14••	5	6		13•••	9	10[1]	7	12•	2						(8)•••	(4)••		11											15,513
15	S	4 Nov 1995	Huddersfield Town	A	0-1	2-3	1	7			5	6		(8)	9[2]	10	11	3	2						12	4													13,747
16	S	11 " 1995	Crystal Palace	H	1-0	1-0	1		7		5	6	12•	14••	9	(10)••[1]	11		3						8	(4)•				2									14,156
17	Su	19 " 1995	Ipswich Town	H	1-0	2-1	1		7	(10)••	5[1]	6	4	12••	9				3	13•					8[1]			11		(2)•									17,862
18	Tu	21 " 1995	West Bromwich Albion	A	1-1	4-1	1		(7)•		5	6	11[1]	12••	9[1]			4	3	2					(8)••[1]						10[1]	14•							13,680
19	Su	26 " 1995	Watford	A	1-0	2-0	1		7		5	6	(11)•••		9[1]		12••	4	3	(2)•					(8)••	13•••				14•	10[1]								7,798
20	S	2 Dec 1995	Stoke City	H	0-0	0-1	1		7		5	6	4	12	9		11		3	(2)					8						10								15,707
21	S	9 " 1995	Grimsby Town	H	1-1	2-2	1		7		5	6	4		9[1]		11[1]	2	3						(8)						12	10							13,283
22	Su	17 " 1995	Leicester City	A	2-1	2-3	1		7	4	5	6	12••		9		(11)••[1]	2	3						(8)•[1]						14•	10							14,251
23	S	23 " 1995	Portsmouth	A	0-0	0-1	1		3		5	6	7		9	(10)••		2	11	14••					(8)•						12•	4							9,960
24	Tu	26 " 1995	Southend United	H	0-0	0-1	1		2	(4)•	5	6	7		9	10			3			13•••			(8)••			(11)•••			14••		12•						17,029
25	S	30 " 1995	Reading	H	1-1	3-3	1		2		5	6	7		9[1]	(10)••[1]			3			13•			8[1]			11					12••	(4)•					13,556
26	M	1 Jan 1996	Derby County	A	0-1	1-2	1		3	13•••		(6)••	7		9			5	10	2		12••			14•[1]			(11)•••				(4)•	8						16,714
27	Su	14 " 1996	Sunderland	A	1-0	1-0	1		3			6	7		9[1]		10	5	13••						(8)•			(11)••		2	12•			4					14,983
28	S	20 " 1996	Luton Town	H	0-1	0-1	1		(3)••			6	7		9		(10)•••	5				13•			8			11		(2)•	14•		12•••	4					12,474
29	Su	4 Feb 1996	Birmingham City	H	0-0	1-1	1		(3)•			6	7	(11)•••	9[1]	(10)••		5				13•			8	4				2	14••		12••						12,612
30	S	10 " 1996	Oldham Athletic	A	0-1	0-2	1	13•				6	7	(11)•••	9	10		5				3		12•••	(8)••	(4)•				2			14••						5,604
31	S	17 " 1996	Wolverhampton Wanderers	H	2-2	2-3	1		3			6	7		9	10	11[1]	5						13••	(8)••	(4)•[1]				2		14•							14,691
32	S	24 " 1996	Millwall	A	0-0	1-2	1		3	10[1]		6	7	12••	(9)••		11	5				2				(4)•		8					13•						8,218
33	W	28 " 1996	Sheffield United	H	0-0	0-0	1			8		6	(7)•	(9)••		10	11	5				3			12••	4		14•		2									10,945
34	S	2 Mar 1996	Southend United	A	0-1	1-1	1				12	6	7	9			11	5				3				4				2[1]		(10)	8						6,208
35	S	9 " 1996	Portsmouth	H	1-1	1-1	1			10[1]	5	6	7		9		11					3			14	4				2			(8)						13,004
36	S	16 " 1996	Reading	A	1-0	3-0	1	14•		10		6[1]	7				(11)••[1]	5				3			8	(4)•		12••[1]		2			9						8,501
37	W	20 " 1996	Port Vale	A	0-1	0-1	1	13•••		10		6	7			14•		5				3		12••	(8)••	(4)•		11		2			(9)•••						6,085
38	S	23 " 1996	Derby County	H	0-0	1-0	1	14•		10		6	7	13•••				5				3		(9)•••	(8)••	(4)•		12••		2			11[1]						15,348
39	S	30 " 1996	Charlton Athletic	H	0-0	0-1	1		14•	10		6	7				13••	5				3		(9)•	8	4				2			(11)••						13,434
40	Tu	2 Apr 1996	Barnsley	A	1-1	2-2	1	14•••		10		6	7				(11)•••	5	3			4[1]		12•	(8)•[1]			13••		2			(9)••						6,375
41	S	6 " 1996	Tranmere Rovers	A	1-0	1-1	1			10		6	(7)•				11[1]		3			5			8	4		13••		2	(9)••		12•						6,613
42	M	8 " 1996	Huddersfield Town	H	0-0	2-0	1	12•••		10			7	(9)••[1]			(11)•••	5	3	14•		6		13••	8[1]	(4)•				2									13,021
43	Su	14 " 1996	Ipswich Town	A	0-1	1-2	1			(10)•••		12•	7	(9)••		14•••	11	(5)•	3			6		13••[1]	8	4				2									20,355
44	S	20 " 1996	West Bromwich Albion	H	0-1	2-2	1			(10)•••		2	7			14•••	11[1]	(5)•	3			6		13••[1]		4				12•	(9)••								14,667
45	S	27 " 1996	Watford	H	0-1	1-2	1			10		2	7					5	3			6		(9)••	8	(4)•[1]		14•••		12••		13•	(11)•••						14,188
46	Su	5 May 1996	Crystal Palace	A	1-0	1-0		4		10		5	7					6	3	13				9	8		1					11			(2)			–[1]	19,354

F.A. CUP

NO.		DATE	OPPONENTS		V.	H-T	F-T	Gunn Bryan	Mills Danny	Bowen Mark	Milligan Mike	Newsome Jon	Prior Spencer	Adams Neil	Akinbiyi Ade	Ward Ashley	Johnson Andy	Eadie Darren	Polston John	Ullathorne Robert	Sutch Daryl	Sheron Mike	Newman Rob	Rush Matthew	Cureton Jamie	Fleck Robert	Crook Ian	Marshall Andy	O'Neill Keith	Simpson Karl	Bradshaw Carl	Scott Keith	Carey Shaun	Goss Jeremy	Molby Jan	Wright Johnny			Own Goals	ATTD.
1	S	6 Jan 1996	Brentford	(3rd Rd)	H	0-1	1-2	1		(3)••		5[1]	12•	7		9		14•••	6	4	13••					(8)•••			11		(2)•			10						10,082

COCA-COLA CUP

NO.		DATE	OPPONENTS		V.	H-T	F-T	Gunn Bryan	Mills Danny	Bowen Mark	Milligan Mike	Newsome Jon	Prior Spencer	Adams Neil	Akinbiyi Ade	Ward Ashley	Johnson Andy	Eadie Darren	Polston John	Ullathorne Robert	Sutch Daryl	Sheron Mike	Newman Rob	Rush Matthew	Cureton Jamie	Fleck Robert	Crook Ian	Marshall Andy	O'Neill Keith	Simpson Karl	Bradshaw Carl	Scott Keith	Carey Shaun	Goss Jeremy	Molby Jan	Wright Johnny			Own Goals	ATTD.
1	W	20 Sept 1995	Torquay United	(2nd Rd 1st leg)	H	3-0	6-1		12••	3		5	6		9[2]		(10)••	(11)•••			2	8[2]					(4)•[1]	1	13•••	7			14•						–[1]	7,542
2	W	4 Oct 1995	Torquay United	(2nd Rd 2nd leg)	A	0-0	3-2	1	2[1]		10			7	(9)••			14••[1]	6	3[1]		(8)•	5			12•			11				4							1,790
3	W	25 " 1995	Bradford City	(3rd Rd)	H	0-0	0-0	1		3	(7)	5	6			9	10	8		2						14	4		11											11,649
4	Tu	7 Nov 1995	Bradford City	(3rd Rd Replay)	A	2-1	5-3*	1	14••		7		(6)••		12•	9[3]	10[1]	11		3			(5)•			8[1]	4				2									8,665
5	W	29 " 1995	Bolton Wanderers	(4th Rd)	H	0-0	0-0	1		7		5	6	11		9		10	4	3						8	(2)					14								13,820
6	W	20 Dec 1995	Bolton Wanderers	(4th Rd Replay)	A	0-0	0-0**	1		7	4	5	6	12		9			2	3	11					(8)							10							8,736
7	W	10 Jan 1996	Birmingham City	(5th Rd)	H	0-0	1-1	1		3		(5)•	14•	7		(9)••		10	6	13•••						8[1]			(11)•••		2	12••			4					13,028
8	W	24 " 1996	Birmingham City	(5th Rd Replay)	A	0-0	1-2	1		3			6	7		9	12	(10)	5							8			11		2				4[1]					21,097

* AFTER EXTRA TIME

** AFTER EXTRA TIME WON 3-2 ON PENALTIES

1995-96 APPEARANCES & GOALS

	FOOTBALL LGE			F.A. CUP			LEAGUE CUP		
	APPR.	S	GLS	APPR.	S	GLS	APPR.	S	GLS
Spencer Prior	42	2	1	–	1	–	6	1	–
Bryan Gunn	43	–	–	1	–	–	7	–	–
Neil Adams	40	2	2	1	–	–	4	1	–
Robert Fleck	37	4	10	1	–	–	5	2	2
Mark Bowen	30	1	2	1	–	–	6	–	–
Darren Eadie	29	2	6	–	1	–	6	1	1
John Polston	27	3	–	1	–	–	5	–	–
Robert Ullathorne	26	3	–	1	–	–	5	1	1
Ashley Ward	28	–	10	1	–	–	6	–	3
Ian Crook	27	1	2	–	–	–	4	–	1
Mike Milligan	21	7	2	–	–	–	4	–	–
Jon Newsome	26	1	4	1	–	1	5	–	–
Andy Johnson	23	3	7	–	–	–	3	1	1
Rob Newman	15	8	1	–	–	–	2	–	–
Ade Akinbiyi	13	9	3	–	–	–	2	1	2
Carl Bradshaw	18	3	1	1	–	–	3	–	–
Keith O'Neill	12	7	1	1	–	–	4	1	–
Jeremy Goss	9	7	1	1	–	–	–	–	–
Danny Mills	8	6	–	–	–	–	1	2	1
Daryl Sutch	7	6	–	–	1	–	2	–	–
Keith Scott	5	7	2	–	–	–	–	2	–
Jamie Cureton	4	8	2	–	–	–	–	–	–
Shaun Carey	6	3	–	–	–	–	2	1	–
Mike Sheron	2	5	1	–	–	–	2	–	2
Jan Molby	3	–	–	–	–	–	2	–	1
Andy Marshall	3	–	–	–	–	–	1	–	–
Karl Simpson	1	–	–	–	–	–	1	–	–
Johnny Wright	1	–	–	–	–	–	–	–	–
Matthew Rush	–	1	–	–	–	–	–	–	–
own goals	–	–	1	–	–	–	–	–	1

ENDSLEIGH LEAGUE DIVISION 1

1995-96	P	W	D	L	F	A	PTS
Sunderland	46	22	17	7	59	33	83
Derby County	46	21	16	9	71	51	79
Crystal Palace	46	20	15	11	67	48	75
Stoke City	46	20	13	13	60	49	73
Leicester City	46	19	14	13	66	60	71
Charlton Athletic	46	17	20	9	57	45	71
Ipswich Town	46	19	12	15	79	69	69
Huddersfield Town	46	17	12	17	61	58	63
Sheffield United	46	16	14	16	57	54	62
Barnsley	46	14	18	14	60	66	60
West Bromwich Albion	46	16	12	18	60	68	60
Port Vale	46	15	15	16	59	66	60
Tranmere Rovers	46	14	17	15	64	60	59
Southend United	46	15	14	17	52	61	59
Birmingham City	46	15	13	18	61	64	58
Norwich City	**46**	**14**	**15**	**17**	**59**	**55**	**57**
Grimsby Town	46	14	14	18	55	69	56
Oldham Athletic	46	14	14	18	54	50	56
Reading	46	13	17	16	54	63	56
Wolverhampton Wanderers	46	13	16	17	56	62	55
Portsmouth	46	13	13	20	61	69	52
Millwall	46	13	13	20	43	63	52
Watford	46	10	18	18	62	70	48
Luton Town	46	11	12	23	40	64	45

1996-97 DIVISION 1

NO.	DATE		OPPONENTS	V.	H-T	F-T	Gunn Bryan	Mills Danny	Newman Rob	Eadie Darren	Polston John	Crook Ian	Adams Neil	Fleck Robert	Milligan Mike	Johnson Andy	O'Neill Keith	Akinbiyi Ade	Sutch Daryl	Bradshaw Carl	Carey Shaun	Forbes Adrian	Wright Johnny	Rush Matthew	Scott Keith	Jackson Matt	Rocastle David	Ottosson Ulf	Scott Kevin	Marshall Andy	Broughton Drewe	Bellamy Craig	Simpson Karl	Moore Neil	Own Goals	ATTD.
1	S	17 Aug 1996	Swindon Town	H	2-0	2-0	1	2	3	4	5	6	7	⑧•[1]	⑨••	10[1]	11	13•	14••																	15,165
2	S	24 " 1996	Bolton Wanderers	A	0-1	1-3	1	2	3	4[1]	5	6	7	⑧	9	10	11	14																		13,507
3	Tu	27 " 1996	Oxford United	A	1-0	1-0	1	3	2	11	5	6	7[1]	⑧	9	10		14		4																7,436
4	S	31 " 1996	Wolverhampton Wanderers	H	1-0	1-0	1	3	2		5	6	7[1]	⑧•	9	⑩••		14•	⑪•••	4	12••	13•••														14,456
5	S	7 Sept 1996	Bradford City	A	2-0	2-0	1	3	2	4[1]	5	6	7	⑧•	9		⑪••	14•	10[1]		12••															10,054
6	W	11 " 1996	Queens Park Rangers	H	1-0	1-1	1	3	2	11	5	6	7[1]		10			9	8		4															14,000
7	S	14 " 1996	Southend United	H	0-0	0-0	1	3	2	11	5	6	7		10			9	8		4															12,461
8	S	21 " 1996	Portsmouth	A	1-0	1-0	1	3	2	4	5	⑥[1]	7		10		11	9	8		14															7,511
9	S	28 " 1996	Tranmere Rovers	H	0-1	1-1	1		2	4	5		7	8[1]	10	12	11		9		⑥		3													14,511
10	Tu	1 Oct 1996	Grimsby Town	A	3-1	4-1	1	3	②•	④••[2]	5		7	⑧•••	9	10	11[1]	14•••	6				12•	13••											–[1]	5,266
11	F	11 " 1996	Ipswich Town	H	2-0	3-1	1	3	2	4	5[1]	12••	7	⑧•	9	⑩••[1]	11	13•	6																	20,256
12	W	16 " 1996	Oldham Athletic	H	0-0	2-0	1	3	2	4[1]	5	10	7	⑧	9		11		6						14											12,271
13	S	19 " 1996	Manchester City	A	0-1	1-2	1	③•	2	4	5	10	7	⑧••	9	13••	11		6						14•[1]											28,269
14	S	26 " 1996	Birmingham City	A	1-1	3-2	1	3	2	11	5	⑥	7[1]		9	8[1]	14		4						10[1]											18,869
15	W	30 " 1996	Sheffield United	H	0-1	1-1	1	3	2	4	5	12•	7[1]	14••	9	⑧•	11		6						⑩••											14,534
16	S	2 Nov 1996	Charlton Athletic	H	0-0	1-2	1	3	2	11	5	6	7	⑧•	9[1]			13•	4			⑩••			14••											14,145
17	Tu	12 " 1996	Barnsley	A	0-0	1-3	1	3	2[1]	11	5	⑥•	7	8	9	⑩••			4	12••		13•														9,697
18	S	16 " 1996	Reading	H	0-0	1-1	1		2	4	5		7	8	9	10	11		6	③					14[1]											14,412
19	S	30 " 1996	Birmingham City	H	0-0	0-1	1	13•	2	4	5	12•••	⑦••	8	9	⑩•••	11		6	③•					14••											12,764
20	S	7 Dec 1996	Huddersfield Town	A	0-1	0-2	1	3	2	4	5		7	8	9	10	⑪		6						14											10,749
21	S	14 " 1996	Crystal Palace	H	0-1	1-1	1	3	2	11	5	6	7[1]	⑧		10	14		4						9											16,395
22	W	18 " 1996	West Bromwich Albion	A	0-2	1-5	1	5	2	11		9	7	8		10	12••[1]		4		14•		③•		⑥••											12,620
23	S	21 " 1996	Port Vale	A	0-2	1-6	1	3	2	11		6	7	12[1]		10	9		4		⑧		5													6,278
24	Th	26 " 1996	Queens Park Rangers	A	1-2	2-3	1		2	9[1]	5	6[1]	7		8	10	11		4							3										15,699
25	S	28 " 1996	Bradford City	H	1-0	2-0	1	12•••	2	④•	5		7[1]	⑧••	9	⑩•••	11[1]		6			13•			14••	3										13,473
26	W	1 Jan 1997	Portsmouth	H	0-0	1-0	1		2	4	5		7	⑧	9	10	11	12	6							3[1]										11,946
27	S	18 " 1997	Grimsby Town	H	2-1	2-1	1	7	2	4	⑤[1]	8					11		6[1]		10					3	9	12•								16,687
28	W	22 " 1997	Stoke City	A	2-1	2-1	1		2	4[1]		⑧•	7				⑪••[1]		6		10				14••	3	9	13•	5							10,179
29	Tu	28 " 1997	Tranmere Rovers	A	1-2	1-3	1		2	4[1]			7	⑧•	11				6		⑩••	13•				3	9	14••	5							5,891
30	S	1 Feb 1997	Barnsley	H	0-1	1-1	1		2	11[1]		4	7	8	10	12			6							3	⑨		5							17,001
31	Su	9 " 1997	Sheffield United	A	0-0	3-2	1	2				4	7	8	11	10[1]			3	12							6	⑨•[1]	5						–[1]	15,301
32	S	15 " 1997	West Bromwich Albion	H	0-1	2-4	1	2		11		4	7[1]		8	10			3[1]	12••		14•					⑥•	⑨••	5							14,845
33	S	22 " 1997	Charlton Athletic	A	2-2	4-4	1	5	②	4[2]		8	7[2]		11	10			3	12							6	9								12,405
34	Tu	25 " 1997	Southend United	A	0-0	1-1	1		2	4			7	14••[1]	11	10			6	12•						3	⑧•	⑨••	5							5,169
35	S	1 Mar 1997	Huddersfield Town	H	1-0	2-0			2	4[2]			7	8	11	10			6							3	9		5	1						13,001
36	Tu	4 " 1997	Reading	A	1-1	1-2			2	4		12	7[1]	8	11	⑩			6							3	9		5	1						8,174
37	S	8 " 1997	Port Vale	H	1-1	1-1			2	4		⑩••	7	8	11				6	12••	14•					3[1]	⑨•		5	1						16,101
38	S	15 " 1997	Crystal Palace	A	0-2	0-2	1		2			④•	7	8					6	5	⑨••	11		13•	⑩•••	3					12•••	14••				17,378
39	S	22 " 1997	Bolton Wanderers	H	0-1	0-1	1		2	10		④•	7	8	9		⑪••		6	5		14••				3					12•					17,585
40	S	29 " 1997	Swindon Town	A	1-0	3-0	1	12•••	2	10[2]	14••	④•	7	8	9		⑪•••[1]		6	⑤••						3					13•					10,249
41	M	31 " 1997	Oxford United	H	1-1	1-1	1		2	11[1]	14••	4	7	8	10				6	⑤••		13•				3					⑨•					14,644
42	S	5 Apr 1997	Wolverhampton Wanderers	A	2-2	2-3	1	12•	2	11		④•	7[1]	⑧••	10				6	5	13••					3					9[1]					26,938
43	S	12 " 1997	Stoke City	H	1-0	2-0		13••	2	10[1]	14•	4	7	⑧•	⑨••		⑪•••[1]		6	5						3				1	12•••					13,805
44	F	18 " 1997	Ipswich Town	A	0-2	0-2		10	2	9	12•	4	7	8			⑪••		6	⑤•						3				1			13••			22,397
45	F	25 " 1997	Manchester City	H	0-0	0-0		10	2		6	4	7						3			⑪								1	9	12	8	5		14,080
46	Su	4 May 1997	Oldham Athletic	A	0-2	0-3		10	2	11	⑥••	④•	7	⑧•••					9							3				1	13••	14•	12•••	5		5,562

F.A. CUP

NO.	DATE		OPPONENTS		V.	H-T	F-T	Gunn Bryan	Mills Danny	Newman Rob	Eadie Darren	Polston John	Crook Ian	Adams Neil	Fleck Robert	Milligan Mike	Johnson Andy	O'Neill Keith	Akinbiyi Ade	Sutch Daryl	Bradshaw Carl	Carey Shaun	Forbes Adrian	Wright Johnny	Rush Matthew	Scott Keith	Jackson Matt	Rocastle David	Ottosson Ulf	ATTD.
1	S	4 Jan 1997	Sheffield United	(3rd Rd)	H	1-0	1-0	1		2	4	5[1]	8	7		⑨•	⑩••	11		6		12••				14•	3			12,356
2	S	25 " 1997	Leicester City	(4th Rd)	A	1-1	1-2	1	5	2	11			7[1]	⑧••	10				6		④•	9			14•	3		12••	16,703

COCA-COLA CUP

NO.	DATE		OPPONENTS		V.	H-T	F-T	Gunn Bryan	Mills Danny	Newman Rob	Eadie Darren	Polston John	Crook Ian	Adams Neil	Fleck Robert	Milligan Mike	Johnson Andy	O'Neill Keith	Akinbiyi Ade	Sutch Daryl	Bradshaw Carl	Carey Shaun	ATTD.
1	Tu	20 Aug 1996	Oxford United	(1st Rd 1st leg)	A	1-1	1-1	1	2	3	4	5	6	7	⑧•	9	⑩••[1]	11	14•		12••		6,062
2	W	4 Sept 1996	Oxford United	(1st Rd 2nd leg)	H	1-0	*2-3	1	3	2	4	5	⑥•	7[2]	8	9		⑪••	14••	10		12•	7,301

* AFTER EXTRA TIME

1996-97 APPEARANCES & GOALS

	FOOTBALL LGE			F.A. CUP			LEAGUE CUP		
	APPR.	S	GLS	APPR.	S	GLS	APPR.	S	GLS
Neil Adams	45	–	13	2	–	1	2	–	2
Rob Newman	44	–	1	2	–	–	2	–	–
Daryl Sutch	43	1	3	2	–	–	1	–	–
Darren Eadie	42	–	17	2	–	–	2	–	–
Bryan Gunn	39	–	–	2	–	–	2	–	–
Mike Milligan	37	–	1	2	–	–	2	–	–
Ian Crook	33	4	2	1	–	–	2	–	–
Robert Fleck	33	3	4	1	–	–	2	–	–
Danny Mills	27	5	–	1	–	–	2	–	–
John Polston	27	4	2	1	–	1	2	–	–
Andy Johnson	24	3	5	1	–	–	1	–	1
Keith O'Neill	23	3	6	1	–	–	2	–	–
Matt Jackson	19	–	2	2	–	–	–	–	–
Carl Bradshaw	11	6	–	–	–	–	–	1	–
Shaun Carey	8	6	–	1	1	–	–	1	–
Keith Scott	5	8	3	–	2	–	–	–	–
Ade Akinbiyi	3	9	–	–	–	–	–	2	–
David Rocastle	11	–	–	–	–	–	–	–	–
Adrian Forbes	3	7	–	1	–	–	–	–	–
Kevin Scott	9	–	–	–	–	–	–	–	–
Drewe Broughton	3	5	1	–	–	–	–	–	–
Andy Marshall	7	–	–	–	–	–	–	–	–
Ulf Ottosson	4	3	1	–	1	–	–	–	–
Johnny Wright	3	1	–	–	–	–	–	–	–
Karl Simpson	1	2	–	–	–	–	–	–	–
Craig Bellamy	–	3	–	–	–	–	–	–	–
Neil Moore	2	–	–	–	–	–	–	–	–
Matthew Rush	–	2	–	–	–	–	–	–	–
own goals	–	–	2	–	–	–	–	–	–

NATIONWIDE LEAGUE DIVISION 1

1996-97	P	W	D	L	F	A	PTS
Bolton Wanderers	46	28	14	4	100	53	98
Barnsley	46	22	14	10	76	55	80
Wolverhampton Wanderers	46	22	10	14	68	51	76
Ipswich Town	46	20	14	12	68	50	74
Sheffield United	46	20	13	13	75	52	73
Crystal Palace	46	19	14	13	78	48	71
Portsmouth	46	20	8	18	59	53	68
Port Vale	46	17	16	13	58	55	67
Queens Park Rangers	46	18	12	16	64	60	66
Birmingham City	46	17	15	14	52	48	66
Tranmere Rovers	46	17	14	15	63	56	65
Stoke City	46	18	10	18	51	57	64
Norwich City	**46**	**17**	**12**	**17**	**63**	**68**	**63**
Manchester City	46	17	10	19	59	60	61
Charlton Athletic	46	16	11	19	52	66	59
West Bromwich Albion	46	14	15	17	68	72	57
Oxford United	46	16	9	21	64	68	57
Reading	46	15	12	19	58	67	57
Swindon Town	46	15	9	22	52	71	54
Huddersfield Town	46	13	15	18	48	61	54
Bradford City	46	12	12	22	47	72	48
Grimsby Town	46	11	13	22	60	81	46
Oldham Athletic	46	10	13	23	51	66	43
Southend United	46	8	15	23	42	86	39

1997-98 DIVISION 1

NO.		DATE		OPPONENTS	V.	H-T	F-T	Marshall Andy	Fleming Craig	Newman Rob	Sutch Daryl	Segura Victor	Polston John	Adams Neil	Mills Danny	Roberts Iwan	Eadie Darren	O'Neill Keith	Bellamy Craig	Fleck Robert	Scott Kevin	Bradshaw Carl	Grant Peter	Milligan Mike	Forbes Adrian	Jackson Matt	Coote Adrian	Kenton Darren	Simpson Karl	Marshall Lee	Broughton Drewe	Fuglestad Erik	Carey Shaun	Gunn Bryan	Llewellyn Chris	Fenn Neale	Russell Darel		Own Goals	ATTD.
1	S	9 Aug	1997	Wolverhampton Wanderers	H	0-1	0-2	1	2	(3)*	4	5	6	7	8	(9)**	10	11	13*	14**																				17,230
2	F	15 "	1997	Nottingham Forest	A	1-1	1-4	1		2	8	5	6	7	12*	9	10	11[1]	13**		(3)*	(4)**																		16,524
3	S	23 "	1997	Crewe Alexandra	H	0-1	0-2	1		3	5	14*	6	7	(2)*	9	11			8			(4)**	10	13**															11,821
4	S	30 "	1997	Sunderland	A	0-0	1-0	1		3	5[1]	2	6	7		9	11	14*		(8)*			4	(10)**		13**														29,204
5	Tu	2 Sept	1997	Portsmouth	A	0-0	1-1	1		3	5	(2)*	6	7[1]		9	11	(14)**		(8)**	12***		4	10		13*														10,577
6	S	13 "	1997	Port Vale	H	0-0	1-0	1		3	5		6	7		(9)**			14*	(8)*[1]			4	10	11	2	13**													11,269
7	W	17 "	1997	Charlton Athletic	H	0-3	0-4	1	12*	3	5		(6)*	7					14**	8			4	(10)**	11	2	9													10,157
8	S	20 "	1997	Manchester City	A	1-1	2-1	1	2	14*	3		12**	7[1]	13***				(10)***	(8)*	5		4		11	6	(9)**[1]													27,258
9	F	26 "	1997	Ipswich Town	H	1-0	2-1	1	2		3			7			9[1]		14*	8	5		4	(10)*	(11)**	6	13**												–[1]	18,911
10	S	4 Oct	1997	Tranmere Rovers	A	0-1	0-2	1		5	3			7	2		9			(8)*			4	10	(11)**	6	13*	12**												6,674
11	S	18 "	1997	Stockport County	H	0-1	1-1	1	(2)**		3			7	12*		(9)*[1]		10	8	5		4		(11)***	6	13***		14**											12,689
12	Tu	21 "	1997	Reading	H	0-0	0-0	1		14**	3			7					10	(8)**	5		4	9	11	6	13*		(2)*											17,781
13	S	25 "	1997	Swindon Town	A	0-0	0-1	1		14*	3			7	12***				10	(8)**	5		4	9	(11)***	6	13**		(2)*											9,256
14	S	1 Nov	1997	Bury	H	2-1	2-2	1			3			7[1]					10[1]		5		4	9	(11)**	6	(8)*		13**	2	14*									14,419
15	Tu	4 "	1997	West Bromwich Albion	A	0-0	0-1	1		12**	3			7		14***			10		5		4	9	11	(6)**	(8)***		13*	(2)*										13,949
16	S	8 "	1997	Birmingham City	A	2-1	2-1	1		6	3	(2)		7	4	9				8	5			10	11[2]				12											16,464
17	S	15 "	1997	Middlesbrough	H	1-1	1-3	1		6	3	2		7	(12)**	9[1]			14***	(8)***	5		(4)*	10	11							13**								16,011
18	S	22 "	1997	Oxford United	H	1-0	2-1	1				2		7		9			4[1]	8[1]	5			10	11	6						3								11,241
19	S	29 "	1997	Bradford City	A	0-1	1-2	1			3	2		(7)		9			4[1]	8	5			10	14	6						11								16,637
20	W	3 Dec	1997	Queens Park Rangers	A	0-0	1-1	1		12**	(3)*	2		7		9			4	8	5			(10)**	14*[1]	6						11								10,141
21	S	6 "	1997	Sheffield United	H	0-0	2-1	1				2		7	3	9			4	8	5				10	6						11[1]							–[1]	11,745
22	S	13 "	1997	Huddersfield Town	A	2-0	3-1	1				2		7	3	9			4[1]	(8)*	5		12*[1]		(10)**[1]	6						11	14**							11,436
23	S	20 "	1997	Stoke City	H	0-0	0-0	1				2			3	9		14	10		5		4		7	6						11	(8)							12,265
24	F	26 "	1997	Charlton Athletic	A	0-0	1-2	1				2			3	(9)		14	10[1]		5		4	11	7	6						8								14,472
25	Tu	30 "	1997	Portsmouth	H	1-0	2-0	1				2			3			11	10[1]	14	5		4	9	(7)	6[1]						8								16,441
26	S	10 Jan	1998	Wolverhampton Wanderers	A	0-4	0-5		12*		7				3	9		11	10		(5)*		4			6						2	(8)**	1	14**					23,703
27	S	17 "	1998	Nottingham Forest	H	0-0	1-0		5		2					9[1]	10	11					4		7	6	8					3		1						17,059
28	W	28 "	1998	Sunderland	H	1-0	2-1		5		2	12**			13*	9	11[1]						4	(10)**	(7)*	6	8					3		1					–[1]	15,940
29	S	31 "	1998	Crewe Alexandra	A	0-0	0-1		5		2					9	11		10				4		7	6	8					3		1						5,559
30	S	7 Feb	1998	Manchester City	H	0-0	0-0	1			2	5			13*	9	(11)**		10				4		12**	6	8	7				(3)*								15,274
31	S	14 "	1998	Port Vale	A	0-1	2-2	1	3		2	5				(9)**			10	14**			4[1]			6[1]	8	(7)*				11			13*					6,664
32	W	18 "	1998	Tranmere Rovers	H	0-0	0-2	1	5		2	3			(7)**		11		10	(8)***			(4)*			6	9	12**					14*		13***					12,105
33	S	21 "	1998	Ipswich Town	A	0-3	0-5	1	5		2	(3)***			12**		11			(8)**			4		(7)*	6	9	14***					10		13*					21,858
34	Tu	24 "	1998	Stockport County	A	0-1	2-2	1	5		2	3					11						4[1]		(7)	6	14*[1]	8					10		9					7,471
35	S	28 "	1998	Queens Park Rangers	H	0-0	0-0	1	5		2	3					(11)**			14*			4		(7)*	6	12**	8					10		9					12,730
36	W	4 Mar	1998	Birmingham City	H	0-2	3-3	1	5		2	(3)*							11[2]	(8)**			4		7	6	14**	12*					10		9[1]					9,819
37	S	7 "	1998	Bury	A	0-0	0-1	1	5		2				12***				11	(8)***			(4)*		(7)**	6	13*	3		14**			10		9					5,154
38	S	14 "	1998	West Bromwich Albion	H	1-0	1-1	1	5		2					14**			9[1]	(8)**			4		(7)*	6		3		12*		(11)***	10		13***					19,069
39	Su	22 "	1998	Middlesbrough	A	0-1	0-3	1	5		2			7		9			8				4		13	6		(3)				11	10							30,040
40	S	28 "	1998	Oxford United	A	0-0	0-2	1	5		2		12**	7		9			8				4		(11)**	6						3	(10)*			14*				7,869
41	S	4 Apr	1998	Bradford City	H	0-1	2-3	1	5		2			7		9	14		8[1]				(4)			6						3			11[1]	10				13,260
42	S	11 "	1998	Sheffield United	A	0-2	2-2	1	5		2			7		9	4		8[1]							6						3			11[1]	10				16,915
43	M	13 "	1998	Huddersfield Town	H	2-0	5-0	1	(5)**[1]		2	12*		7[1]		9[2]	(4)*		8		14**					6						3[1]			11	10				16,550
44	S	18 "	1998	Stoke City	A	0-1	0-2	1			2	(4)**	12*	7		9			8		5		14***			6	13**					(3)*			11	(10)***				13,098
45	S	25 "	1998	Swindon Town	H	2-0	5-0	1			2		12***	7		9[1]			(8)**[1]		5			(4)*		6[1]	14**					3	13*		(11)***[1]	10[1]				18,443
46	Su	3 May	1998	Reading	A	0-0	1-0	1			2		12*	7		(9)*			8[1]		5					6						3	4		11	(10)**	14**			14,817

F.A. CUP

NO.		DATE		OPPONENTS		V.	H-T	F-T	Marshall Andy	Fleming Craig	Newman Rob	Sutch Daryl	Segura Victor	Polston John	Adams Neil	Mills Danny	Roberts Iwan	Eadie Darren	O'Neill Keith	Bellamy Craig	Fleck Robert	Scott Kevin	Bradshaw Carl	Grant Peter	Milligan Mike	Forbes Adrian	Jackson Matt	Coote Adrian	Kenton Darren	Simpson Karl	Marshall Lee	Broughton Drewe	Fuglestad Erik	Carey Shaun	Gunn Bryan	Llewellyn Chris	Fenn Neale	Russell Darel		Own Goals	ATTD.
1	S	3 Jan	1998	Grimsby Town	(3rd Rd)	A	0-1	0-3	1	6		12*	(2)*			3			11	7	(8)**	5		4	10								9			15**					8,161

COCA-COLA CUP

NO.		DATE		OPPONENTS		V.	H-T	F-T	Marshall Andy	Fleming Craig	Newman Rob	Sutch Daryl	Segura Victor	Polston John	Adams Neil	Mills Danny	Roberts Iwan	Eadie Darren	O'Neill Keith	Bellamy Craig	Fleck Robert	Scott Kevin	Bradshaw Carl	Grant Peter	Milligan Mike	Forbes Adrian	Jackson Matt	Coote Adrian	Kenton Darren	Simpson Karl	Marshall Lee	Broughton Drewe	Fuglestad Erik	Carey Shaun	Gunn Bryan	Llewellyn Chris	Fenn Neale	Russell Darel		Own Goals	ATTD.
1	Tu	12 Aug	1997	Barnet	1st Rd 1st leg)	H	2-1	2-1	1	(2)	12	4	5	6	7[1]		9[1]			10	8	3	11																		5,429
2	Tu	26 "	1997	Barnet	(1st Rd 2nd leg)	A	0-0	1-3	1		3	5	2	6	7		9[1]	11	14		(8)			4	10																2,846

1997-98 APPEARANCES & GOALS

	FOOTBALL LGE APPR.	S	GLS	F.A. CUP APPR.	S	GLS	LEAGUE CUP APPR.	S	GLS		
Andy Marshall	42	–	–	1	–	–	2	–	–		
Matt Jackson	39	2	3	–	–	–	–	–	–		
Daryl Sutch	40	–	1	–	1	–	2	–	–		
Craig Bellamy	30	6	13	1	–	–	1	–	–		
Peter Grant	33	2	3	1	–	–	1	–	–		
Adrian Forbes	28	5	4	–	–	–	–	–	–		
Iwan Roberts	29	2	5	–	–	–	2	–	2		
Neil Adams	30	–	4	–	–	–	2	–	1		
Robert Fleck	23	4	2	1	–	–	2	–	–		
Victor Segura	22	3	–	1	–	–	2	–	–		
Erik Fuglestad	23	1	2	1	–	–	–	–	–		
Kevin Scott	22	2	–	1	–	–	1	–	–		
Adrian Coote	11	12	2	–	–	–	–	–	–		
Craig Fleming	20	2	1	1	–	–	1	–	–		
Mike Milligan	20	–	–	1	–	–	1	–	–		
Danny Mills	11	9	–	1	–	–	–	–	–		
Darren Eadie	18	1	3	–	–	–	1	–	–		
Rob Newman	10	5	–	–	–	–	1	1	–		
Chris Llewellyn	10	5	4	–	1	–	–	–	–		
Shaun Carey	11	3	–	–	–	–	–	–	–		
John Polston	7	5	–	–	–	–	2	–	–		
Darren Kenton	7	4	–	–	–	–	–	–	–		
Keith O'Neill	5	4	1	1	–	–	–	1	–		
Neale Fenn	6	1	1	–	–	–	–	–	–		
Karl Simpson	2	4	–	–	–	–	–	–	–		
Bryan Gunn	4	–	–	–	–	–	–	–	–		
Lee Marshall	2	2	–	–	–	–	–	–	–		
Carl Bradshaw	1	–	–	–	–	–	1	–	–		
Drewe Broughton	–	1	–	–	–	–	–	–	–		
Darel Russell	–	1	–	–	–	–	–	–	–		
own goals	–	–	3	–	–	–	–	–	–		

NATIONWIDE LEAGUE DIVISION 1

1997-98	P	W	D	L	F	A	PTS
Nottingham Forest	46	28	10	8	82	42	94
Middlesbrough	46	27	10	9	77	41	91
Sunderland	46	26	12	8	86	50	90
Charlton Athletic	46	26	10	10	80	49	88
Ipswich Town	46	23	14	9	77	43	83
Sheffield United	46	19	17	10	69	54	74
Birmingham City	46	19	17	10	60	35	74
Stockport County	46	19	8	19	71	69	65
Wolverhampton Wanderers	46	18	11	17	57	53	65
West Bromwich Albion	46	16	13	17	50	56	61
Crewe Alexandra	46	18	5	23	58	65	59
Oxford United	46	16	10	20	60	64	58
Bradford City	46	14	15	17	46	59	57
Tranmere Rovers	46	14	14	18	54	57	56
Norwich City	**46**	**14**	**13**	**19**	**52**	**69**	**55**
Huddersfield Town	46	14	11	21	50	72	53
Bury	46	11	19	16	42	58	52
Swindon Town	46	14	10	22	42	73	52
Port Vale	46	13	10	23	56	66	49
Portsmouth	46	13	10	23	51	63	49
Queens Park Rangers	46	10	19	17	51	63	49
Manchester City	46	12	12	22	56	57	48
Stoke City	46	11	13	22	44	74	46
Reading	46	11	9	26	39	78	42

1998-99 DIVISION 1

NO.		DATE		OPPONENTS	V.	H-T	F-T	Marshall Andy	Sutch Daryl	Kenton Darren	Grant Peter	Fleming Craig	Jackson Matt	Adams Neil	Bellamy Craig	Carey Shaun	Eadie Darren	O'Neill Keith	Marshall Lee	Llewellyn Chris	Brannan Ged	Roberts Iwan	Milligan Mike	Fuglestad Erik	Segura Victor	Mackay Malky	Watt Michael	Forbes Adrian	Coote Adrian	Russell Darel	Wilson Che	Hughes Paul	Green Robert	Dalglish Paul	Mulryne Philip	Anselin Cedric	Scott Kevin		Own Goals	ATTD.
1	S	8 Aug	1998	Crewe Alexandra	H	2-1	2-1	1	2	3[1]	4	5	6	7	8[1]	9	10	11																							15,016
2	S	15 "	1998	Stockport County	A	1-0	2-0	1	2	3	4	5	6		8[1]	(9)*	10	(11)**	7	13***		12**	(14)***																–[1]	6,538
3	S	22 "	1998	Queens Park Rangers	H	3-2	4-2	1	2	3	4	5	6[1]		8[3]		(10)**	11	7	(9)*	13*	12**																		16,317
4	S	29 "	1998	West Bromwich Albion	A	0-0	0-2	1	2	3	4	5	6		8		(10)	11	7		9	12																		17,401
5	Tu	8 Sept	1998	Barnsley	A	0-1	3-1	(1)*	2	(3)**	4	5	6		8[1]		10		7[1]	12**	11	9[1]					13*													15,695
6	Su	13 "	1998	Bury	H	0-0	0-0	1	2		4	5	(6)*		8		10		7	3	(11)**	9			12*			14**												16,919
7	S	19 "	1998	Sheffield United	A	0-1	1-2	1	(2)*		4	5			8		10		7	14***	11[1]	(9)***		3	(6)**	12**		13*												16,155
8	S	26 "	1998	Birmingham City	H	0-0	2-0	1	2	3	4	5			8[1]		10		7		(11)	9[1]				6		14												16,584
9	Tu	29 "	1998	Sunderland	H	2-1	2-2	1	2	(3)**	4	5			8		(10)*[1]		7		11	9		12**		6[1]		14*												17,504
10	S	3 Oct	1998	Port Vale	A	0-0	0-1	1	2	(3)*	4	5			8		10		7		(11)**	9		12*		6			14**											5,580
11	S	17 "	1998	Crystal Palace	A	1-2	1-5	1	2	3	(4)*	5		12*	(8)**		10		7	13**	11	9[1]		6																18,100
12	Tu	20 "	1998	Ipswich Town	A	0-0	1-0	1	12*	3		5		14**	8[1]		10		7		11	9		2	(6)**			(4)*												22,079
13	S	24 "	1998	Huddersfield Town	H	3-0	4-1	1	(4)*	3		5	6	12*	(8)**[2]		10	14**	7		11	9[2]		2																15,403
14	Tu	3 Nov	1998	Watford	A	1-1	1-1	1	11		4	5	6		8		10[1]		7			9		3		2														10,011
15	W	7 "	1998	Bradford City	H	0-1	2-2	1	2		(4)	5	6	11[1]	8		10	12	7			9		3															–[1]	14,722
16	Tu	10 "	1998	Portsmouth	A	0-1	2-1	1	(2)*		12**	5	6	4	(8)**		10[1]	11	7	14*		9[1]				3														9,335
17	S	14 "	1998	Wolverhampton Wanderers	H	0-0	0-0	1			4	5	6	11	(8)		10	12	7	2		9				3														17,275
18	S	21 "	1998	Tranmere Rovers	A	2-0	3-1	1		2	4	5	6	11	8[1]			10[1]	7			9[1]				3														6,319
19	Su	29 "	1998	Oxford United	H	1-2	1-3	1		2	(4)*	5	6	11	8[1]			10	(7)**			9				3		14**		12*										17,851
20	W	2 Dec	1998	Grimsby Town	H	1-0	3-1			2	4	5	6	11[1]	8[1]			10	7			9[1]				3	1													12,024
21	S	5 "	1998	Swindon Town	A	1-1	1-1			2	4		6		8				7	11		9[1]				3	1			10	5									9,262
22	S	12 "	1998	Wolverhampton Wanderers	A	1-0	2-2			2	4		6	7[1]	(8)**		14**		13*	(11)***		9[1]			12***	3	1			10	(5)*									21,014
23	S	19 "	1998	Bristol City	H	2-1	2-1		13*	2	4		6	(7)*			8		12**	11		9[2]				3	1			(10)**	5									17,022
24	S	26 "	1998	Queens Park Rangers	A	0-2	0-2			(2)*	4	12***	6	7					(8)**	11		9				3	1	13*	(10)***	14**	5									15,251
25	Tu	29 "	1998	Watford	H	0-0	1-1		2		4		6	7			10		8	11		9[1]		3		5	1													19,255
26	S	9 Jan	1999	Crewe Alexandra	A	2-0	2-3		2		4		6	7			10		8[1]	(11)[1]		9		3		5	1		14											4,782
27	S	16 "	1999	West Bromwich Albion	H	0-0	1-1	1	2			5	6	7			10		8[1]	11		9		3							4									15,411
28	S	30 "	1999	Bolton Wanderers	A	0-1	0-2	1	4	3	13**	5	6	7	14*			11	(8)**	(10)*		9									2									17,269
29	S	6 Feb	1999	Stockport County	H	0-2	0-2	1	10	(3)*	(4)**	5	6	(7)***	8			11	13***	14**		9				12*					2									14,675
30	Tu	16 "	1999	Barnsley	H	0-0	0-0	1	2		4	5	6		8				7	10		9		3				11												13,232
31	S	20 "	1999	Bury	A	1-0	2-0	1	2		(4)**	5[1]	6		8[1]				7	10		9		(3)*		14**		(11)***		12***	13*									4,285
32	S	27 "	1999	Sheffield United	H	1-0	1-1	1	2		4	5	6		8			12	7	(10)[1]		9		3				11												14,224
33	Tu	2 Mar	1999	Birmingham City	A	0-0	0-0	1	2		4	5	6		8			10	7	12*		9		(3)*				(11)**			13**									20,749
34	S	6 "	1999	Sunderland	A	0-1	0-1	1	2		(4)*	5	6		(8)**			11	7	12**		9		3						13*	10									39,004
35	Tu	9 "	1999	Port Vale	H	1-2	3-4	1	2		4	5[1]	6		8[1]			11	7	12		9[1]		(3)							10									12,960
36	S	13 "	1999	Bradford City	A	0-4	1-4	1	2		(4)**	5			8			(11)*	7	13*		9[1]	10			6		12**			3									13,331
37	S	20 "	1999	Portsmouth	H	0-0	0-0	1	2			5	6		8				10	11		(9)						7	12	4	3									16,662
38	W	24 "	1999	Huddersfield Town	A	1-0	1-1	1	2			5	6		8	13**			10	(11)**		9						(7)*		4[1]	3	12*								9,717
39	S	3 Apr	1999	Crystal Palace	H	0-1	0-1	1	2				6		8				(7)*	(11)***		9				5		14*		4	3	(10)**		12***	13**					16,754
40	M	5 "	1999	Grimsby Town	A	1-0	1-0	1	2				6		8	11						12		3		5				4				(9)	10[1]	7				6,302
41	Su	11 "	1999	Ipswich Town	H	0-0	0-0		2			5	(6)*		8	9			14*			12**		3		4							1	(11)**	10	7				19,511
42	S	17 "	1999	Tranmere Rovers	H	1-1	2-2		2						8[1]	13*			5			9		3		4				11		(6)*	1	12**	10[1]	(7)**				14,735
43	Tu	20 "	1999	Bolton Wanderers	H	2-0	2-2	1	2			14*	(6)*		12**	8			4	(11)***		9[2]		3		5				13***				(10)**		7				11,137
44	S	24 "	1999	Oxford United	A	1-1	4-2	1		(2)*		6[1]			8[1]	4			13**	11		(9)***[1]		3		5			12***		14*				10	(7)**[1]				7,345
45	S	1 May	1999	Swindon Town	H	0-0	2-1	1				6	12**			(4)***			13***	10		9[1]		(3)**		5			8		(2)*	14*[1]			11	7				17,306
46	Su	9 "	1999	Bristol City	A	0-1	0-1	1		2			6		8	12			4	11		9		3		5									10	(7)				11,362

F.A. CUP

NO.		DATE		OPPONENTS		V.	H-T	F-T	Marshall Andy	Sutch Daryl	Kenton Darren	Grant Peter	Fleming Craig	Jackson Matt	Adams Neil	Bellamy Craig	Carey Shaun	Eadie Darren	O'Neill Keith	Marshall Lee	Llewellyn Chris	Brannan Ged	Roberts Iwan	Milligan Mike	Fuglestad Erik	Segura Victor	Mackay Malky	Watt Michael	Forbes Adrian	Coote Adrian	Russell Darel	Wilson Che	Hughes Paul	Green Robert	Dalglish Paul	Mulryne Philip	Anselin Cedric	Scott Kevin		Own Goals	ATTD.
1	Su	3 Jan	1999	Sheffield Wednesday	(3rd Rd)	A	1-3	1-4		2		4	12*	6	7			10		(8)**	11		9[1]		3		(5)*	1	14**												18,737

WORTHINGTON CUP

NO.		DATE		OPPONENTS		V.	H-T	F-T	Marshall Andy	Sutch Daryl	Kenton Darren	Grant Peter	Fleming Craig	Jackson Matt	Adams Neil	Bellamy Craig	Carey Shaun	Eadie Darren	O'Neill Keith	Marshall Lee	Llewellyn Chris	Brannan Ged	Roberts Iwan	Milligan Mike	Fuglestad Erik	Segura Victor	Mackay Malky	Watt Michael	Forbes Adrian	Coote Adrian	Russell Darel	Wilson Che	Hughes Paul	Green Robert	Dalglish Paul	Mulryne Philip	Anselin Cedric	Scott Kevin		Own Goals	ATTD.
1	Tu	11 Aug	1998	Swansea City	(1st Rd 1st leg)	A	0-0	1-1	1		3	4	(5)*	6	(7)**	8[1]	9	(10)***	11	2	13**		12***															14*			3,803
2	Tu	18 "	1998	Swansea City	(1st Rd 2nd leg)	H	0-0	*1-0	1	2	3	4	5	6		8		10	(11)	7	9		12[1]																		13,146
3	W	16 Sept	1998	Wigan Athletic	(2nd Rd 1st leg)	H	1-0	1-0	1	2	3	4	5			8		10		7	(11)**		(9)*			6			12**	14*										–[1]	11,426
4	Tu	22 "	1998	Wigan Athletic	(2nd Rd 2nd leg)	A	2-0	3-2	1	2	3	4	5			8[1]		10		(7)*		11	9[2]				6		14												3,402
5	Tu	27 Oct	1998	Bolton Wanderers	(3rd Rd)	H	0-0	**1-1	1	4	3		5	(6)*	(11)***	8		(10)**	13***[1]	7			9	14**	2		12*														14,189

* AFTER EXTRA TIME

** AFTER EXTRA TIME BOLTON WON 3-1 ON PENALTIES

1998-99 APPEARANCES & GOALS

	FOOTBALL LGE			F.A. CUP			LEAGUE CUP		
	APPR.	S	GLS	APPR.	S	GLS	APPR.	S	GLS
Iwan Roberts	40	5	19	1	–	1	3	2	3
Lee Marshall	38	6	3	1	–	–	5	–	–
Craig Bellamy	38	2	17	–	–	–	5	–	2
Andy Marshall	37	–	–	–	–	–	5	–	–
Matt Jackson	36	1	1	1	–	–	3	–	–
Craig Fleming	35	2	3	–	1	–	5	–	–
Daryl Sutch	34	2	–	1	–	–	4	–	–
Peter Grant	31	2	–	1	–	–	4	–	–
Chris Llewellyn	21	10	2	1	–	–	2	1	–
Malky Mackay	24	4	1	1	–	–	1	1	–
Erik Fuglestad	22	2	–	1	–	–	1	–	–
Darren Kenton	22	–	1	–	–	–	5	–	–
Darren Eadie	21	1	3	1	–	–	5	–	–
Neil Adams	15	3	3	1	–	–	2	–	–
Keith O'Neill	14	4	1	–	–	–	2	1	1
Che Wilson	14	3	–	–	–	–	–	–	–
Adrian Forbes	7	8	–	–	1	–	–	2	–
Darel Russell	8	5	1	–	–	–	–	–	–
Ged Brannan	10	1	1	–	–	–	1	–	–
Shaun Carey	7	2	–	–	–	–	1	–	–
Michael Watt	7	1	–	1	–	–	–	–	–
Cedric Anselin	7	–	1	–	–	–	–	–	–
Philip Mulryne	6	1	2	–	–	–	–	–	–
Adrian Coote	2	4	–	–	–	–	–	1	–
Paul Dalglish	3	2	–	–	–	–	–	–	–
Victor Segura	2	2	–	–	–	–	1	–	–
Paul Hughes	2	2	1	–	–	–	–	–	–
Robert Green	2	–	–	–	–	–	–	–	–
Mike Milligan	1	1	–	–	–	–	–	1	–
Kevin Scott	–	–	–	–	–	–	–	1	–
own goals	–	–	2	–	–	–	–	–	1

NATIONWIDE LEAGUE DIVISION 1

1998-99	P	W	D	L	F	A	PTS
Sunderland	46	31	12	3	91	28	105
Bradford City	46	26	9	11	82	47	87
Ipswich Town	46	26	8	12	69	32	86
Birmingham City	46	23	12	11	66	37	81
Watford	46	21	14	11	65	56	77
Bolton Wanderers	46	20	16	10	78	59	76
Wolverhampton Wanderers	46	19	16	11	64	43	73
Sheffield United	46	18	13	15	71	66	67
Norwich City	**46**	**15**	**17**	**14**	**62**	**61**	**62**
Huddersfield Town	46	15	16	15	62	71	61
Grimsby Town	46	17	10	19	40	52	61
West Bromwich Albion	46	16	11	19	69	76	59
Barnsley	46	14	17	15	59	56	59
Crystal Palace	46	14	16	16	58	71	58
Tranmere Rovers	46	12	20	14	63	61	56
Stockport County	46	12	17	17	49	60	53
Swindon Town	46	13	11	22	59	81	50
Crewe Alexandra	46	12	12	22	54	78	48
Portsmouth	46	11	14	21	57	73	47
Queens Park Rangers	46	12	11	23	52	61	47
Port Vale	46	13	8	25	45	75	47
Bury	46	10	17	19	35	60	47
Oxford United	46	10	14	22	48	71	44
Bristol City	46	9	15	22	57	80	42

1999-2000 DIVISION 1

NO.		DATE	OPPONENTS	V.	H-T	F-T	Marshall Andy	Sutch Daryl	Fuglestad Erik	Fleming Craig	Jackson Matt	Mulryne Philip	De Blasis Jean Yves	Llewellyn Chris	Roberts Iwan	Dalglish Paul	Anselin Cedric	Marshall Lee	Mackay Malky	Diop Pape	Coote Adrian	Carey Shaun	Wilson Che	Eadie Darren	Russell Darel	Kenton Darren	Forbes Adrian	Milligan Mike	Green Robert	Hamilton Des	Brady Garry	De Waard Raymond	Derveld Fernando	Giallanza Gaetano	Bellamy Craig	McVeigh Paul		Own Goals	ATTD.
1	S	7 Aug 1999	West Bromwich Albion	A	0-0	1-1	1	2	3	5	6■	10	25	(20)*	9	14[1]	7	4*																					16,196
2	S	14 " 1999	Birmingham City	H	0-1	0-1	1	2	(3)**	5	(6)*■	10	25	(20)***	9	14	7	4***	21*	26**																			15,261
3	S	21 " 1999	Charlton Athletic	A	0-0	0-1	1	2	3	5■		(10)***	25	(20)**	9	14	(7)*	4***	21	26*	16**																		19,623
4	S	28 " 1999	Blackburn Rovers	H	0-1	0-2	1	2	3	5■		(10)*	(25)***	(20)**	9	14	7	4*	21		16**	15***																	15,407
5	M	30 " 1999	Walsall	A	1-1	2-2	1	(2)*	(3)**	5■				20**	(9)***	14***	7	4[1]	21	26*	16[1]	15	23																6,187
6	S	11 Sept 1999	Crewe Alexandra	H	1-1	2-1	1	2	3	5■					9[1]	(14)*	(7)**	(4)**	21	26***	16**	15	23	11*[1]															13,172
7	S	18 " 1999	Huddersfield Town	A	0-0	0-1	1	2	(3)**	5■				20**	9	14*		4	21		(16)*	15		11	12														12,823
8	S	25 " 1999	Stockport County	A	1-1	2-2	1	2		5	6■			20	9[1]	14[1]		4				15			12	19													7,603
9	Tu	28 " 1999	Manchester City	H	1-0	1-0	1	2		5	6■			20*	9[1]	(14)*		4				15		11	12	19													15,130
10	S	2 Oct 1999	Fulham	H	1-0	1-2	1	2**		5	6■			20*	9	14		(4)**				15		11	12	19	(17)*[1]												16,332
11	S	16 " 1999	Port Vale	A	0-0	1-0	1			5[1]	6■		25		9			4				15		11	12	19	17												5,790
12	Tu	19 " 1999	Sheffield United	A	0-0	0-0	1	2		5	6■		25	20**	9	14*						15		(11)*	12	19	(17)**												11,907
13	Su	24 " 1999	Bolton Wanderers	H	0-0	2-1	1	2		5	6■		25		9	14*						15		11	12[2]	19	(17)*												12,468
14	Tu	26 " 1999	Stockport County	H	1-0	2-0	1	2		5	6■		25		9[1]							15		11	12	19	17											–[1]	16,880
15	S	30 " 1999	Fulham	A	0-1	1-1	1	2		(5)**	6■		25		9[1]		7***		21**			(15)*		11	12	19	17	(22)***											13,552
16	S	6 Nov 1999	Nottingham Forest	H	1-0	1-0	1	2[1]			6■		25		9	14*		4	21					11		19	(17)*	22											15,818
17	F	12 " 1999	Swindon Town	A	0-0	0-0	1	2			6■		25	20**	9			4*	21					(11)**	12	19	(17)*	22											7,405
18	Su	21 " 1999	Ipswich Town	H	0-0	0-0	1	2		5	6■		25	(20)*		14*	7**	(4)**							12	19	17	22											19,948
19	Tu	23 " 1999	Crystal Palace	A	0-0	0-1	1	2		5	6■		25	20**	9	(14)*						15			12	19	17*	(22)**											12,110
20	Su	28 " 1999	Grimsby Town	A	1-1	1-2	1	2		5	6■		25		9	14*			21**					11	12	(19)**[1]	(17)*	22											5,333
21	S	4 Dec 1999	West Bromwich Albion	H	1-1	2-1	1	2	3	5	6■		25		9[1]	(14)*	7							11	12[1]		17*												15,183
22	F	17 " 1999	Tranmere Rovers	A	0-1	2-1	1	2	3	5	6■		25	20	9[2]		7			26*					12		(17)*												5,863
23	Su	26 " 1999	Queens Park Rangers	H	1-1	2-1	1	2	3	5	6■		25	20[1]	9		7			26					12													–[1]	17,823
24	Tu	28 " 1999	Wolverhampton Wanderers	A	0-0	0-1	1	2	3	5	6■		(25)**	20	9		(7)*	4*		26		15**			12														25,072
25	Tu	3 Jan 2000	Portsmouth	H	2-0	2-1	1	2	3	5[1]	6■		(25)***	20	9[1]		(7)*	4**					23***		(12)**	19	17*												16,637
26	S	8 " 2000	Barnsley	H	1-0	2-2	1	2	(3)*	5	6■		25	20	9[2]		(7)**	4**			16*				12	19													14,039
27	S	15 " 2000	Birmingham City	A	0-2	0-2	1	2			6■		(25)*		9	14**	(7)**	4	21		16	15				19			13*										21,007
28	S	22 " 2000	Charlton Athletic	H	0-1	0-3	1	2	(3)*		6■			20	9	14*		4**	21			(15)**			12	19	17												15,642
29	S	5 Feb 2000	Walsall	H	1-1	1-1		2	3		6■			20[1]	9	(14)*		4	21		16*	15	23**				(17)**		13										16,837
30	S	12 " 2000	Manchester City	A	1-1	1-3		2	3		6■		25**	20	9[1]	14		4*	21			(15)**			(12)***		17***	(22)*	13										32,681
31	S	19 " 2000	Grimsby Town	H	1-0	3-0	1	2	3		6■		(25)**	20[1]	9	14			21			15	23*		12**[1]	(19)*												–[1]	13,533
32	S	26 " 2000	Huddersfield Town	H	0-0	1-1	1	2	3	5**	(6)**■		25***	(20)*	9[1]	14			21			(15)***			12	19	17*												16,464
33	Tu	29 " 2000	Blackburn Rovers	A	1-0	1-1	1	2[1]	3	5■			25	20	9	(14)*			21						12	19	17*												15,671
34	S	4 Mar 2000	Crewe Alexandra	A	0-1	0-1	1	(2)*	3	5■			25	20	9	14			21						12	19	17*												5,450
35	W	8 " 2000	Nottingham Forest	A	1-1	1-1	1	2	3	5	6■		25	20	9[1]	(14)**		4**							12	(19)*		22*											15,640
36	S	11 " 2000	Crystal Palace	H	0-0	0-1	1	2	3	5	6■		(25)*	20	9	(14)**		4**							12		17*	22											15,064
37	Su	19 " 2000	Ipswich Town	A	2-0	2-0	1	2	3	5	6■			20	(9)**[2]	(14)*	7*	4			16**				12			22											21,760
38	W	22 " 2000	Swindon Town	H	0-0	0-2	1	2	3	5	6■			(20)**		14	7*	4			16				12		17**	(22)*											13,662
39	S	25 " 2000	Queens Park Rangers	A	1-0	2-2	1	2	3	5	6■			20**	9	(14)*		4[2]				15*								11	18	(26)**							11,918
40	S	1 Apr 2000	Tranmere Rovers	H	1-1	1-1	1	2	3	5	(6)***■			(20)**	9			4[1]	21***		16**					19*				11	(18)*	26							13,734
41	S	8 " 2000	Portsmouth	A	1-0	1-2	1	2		5	6■	(10)***		20*	9			4[1]	21**						12***	19				11	(18)**	(26)*							14,003
42	S	15 " 2000	Wolverhampton Wanderers	H	0-0	1-0	1	2		5	6■	10**		(20)***	9[1]			4								19*	17			(11)**	18		(31)*	32***					15,910
43	S	22 " 2000	Port Vale	H	0-0	0-0	1	2		5	6■	10**			9		(7)***	4									17***			(11)**	18		31	(32)*	8*				15,526
44	M	24 " 2000	Barnsley	A	0-2	1-2	1	2		5■				20**	9	14		4	21						12***		(17)*			(11)***	(18)**		31		8*[1]				15,253
45	S	29 " 2000	Sheffield United	H	2-0	2-1	1	2		5[1]	6■	10		20**	9			4							12***	19*				(11)***		(26)**	(31)*		8[1]				16,921
46	Su	7 May 2000	Bolton Wanderers	A	0-0	0-1	1	2		5	6■	10		20***	9		(7)**	4							(12)***								31	(32)*	8	33*			17,987

AXA F.A. CUP

NO.		DATE	OPPONENTS	V.	H-T	F-T	Marshall Andy	Sutch Daryl	Fuglestad Erik	Fleming Craig	Jackson Matt	Mulryne Philip	De Blasis Jean Yves	Llewellyn Chris	Roberts Iwan	Dalglish Paul	Anselin Cedric	Marshall Lee	Mackay Malky	Diop Pape	Coote Adrian	Carey Shaun	Wilson Che	Eadie Darren	Russell Darel	Kenton Darren	Forbes Adrian	Milligan Mike	Green Robert	Hamilton Des	Brady Garry	De Waard Raymond	Derveld Fernando	Giallanza Gaetano	Bellamy Craig	McVeigh Paul		Own Goals	ATTD.
1	S	11 Dec 1999	Coventry City	H	0-0	1-3	1	2	3	5	6■		25	20[1]	9	(14)**	(7)*								12	19*	17**												15,702

WORTHINGTON CUP

NO.		DATE	OPPONENTS	V.	H-T	F-T	Marshall Andy	Sutch Daryl	Fuglestad Erik	Fleming Craig	Jackson Matt	Mulryne Philip	De Blasis Jean Yves	Llewellyn Chris	Roberts Iwan	Dalglish Paul	Anselin Cedric	Marshall Lee	Mackay Malky	Diop Pape	Coote Adrian	Carey Shaun	Wilson Che	Eadie Darren	Russell Darel	Kenton Darren	Forbes Adrian	Milligan Mike	Green Robert	Hamilton Des	Brady Garry	De Waard Raymond	Derveld Fernando	Giallanza Gaetano	Bellamy Craig	McVeigh Paul		Own Goals	ATTD.
1	Tu	10 Aug 1999	Cheltenham Town (1st Rd 1st leg)	H	2-0	2-0	1	2	3	5	6■	10	25	(20)***	9[2]	(14)**	(7)*	4***		26*	16**																		12,276
2	Tu	24 " 1999	Cheltenham Town (1st Rd 2nd leg)	A	0-0	*1-2	1	2		5■		10	25**	20	9	(14)*	(7)**	4[1]	21	26*			23																4,203
3	Tu	14 Sept 1999	Fulham (2nd Rd 1st leg)	H	0-1	0-4	1	2	3*	5■					9				21	26	16	15	(23)*	11	12														11,760
4	Tu	21 " 1999	Fulham (2nd Rd 2nd leg)	A	0-1	0-2	1	2		5	6■			20**	(9)***	14***		4	21			15	(23)*	(11)**	12	19*													5,246

*after extra time

1999-2000 APPEARANCES & GOALS

	FOOTBALL LGE APPR.	S	GLS	F.A. CUP APPR.	S	GLS	LEAGUE CUP APPR.	S	GLS
Daryl Sutch	44	1	2	1	–	–	4	–	–
Andy Marshall	44	–	–	1	–	–	4	–	–
Iwan Roberts	44	–	17	1	–	–	4	–	2
Craig Fleming	38	1	3	1	–	–	4	–	–
Matt Jackson	38	–	–	1	–	–	2	–	–
Darel Russell	28	5	4	1	–	–	2	–	–
Jean Yves De Blasiis	26	2	–	1	–	–	1	1	–
Erik Fugelstad	26	–	–	1	–	–	1	1	–
Chris Llewellyn	24	12	3	1	–	1	2	1	–
Darren Kenton	23	3	1	–	1	–	–	1	–
Paul Dalglish	22	9	2	1	–	–	2	1	–
Lee Marshall	21	12	5	–	–	–	2	1	1
Shaun Carey	18	3	–	–	–	–	2	–	–
Malky Mackay	16	5	–	–	–	–	3	–	–
Adrian Forbes	15	10	1	–	1	–	–	–	–
Cedric Anselin	15	4	–	1	–	–	2	–	–
Darren Eadie	12	1	1	–	–	–	2	–	–
Mike Milligan	9	2	–	–	–	–	–	–	–
Phillip Mulryne	7	2	–	–	–	–	2	–	–
Des Hamilton	7	–	–	–	–	–	–	–	–
Garry Brady	6	–	–	–	–	–	–	–	–
Fernando Derveld	5	–	–	–	–	–	–	–	–
Raymond De Waard	4	–	–	–	–	–	–	–	–
Adrian Coote	4	7	1	–	–	–	1	1	–
Pape Diop	2	5	–	–	–	–	1	2	–
Che Wilson	2	3	–	–	–	–	3	–	–
Craig Bellamy	2	2	2	–	–	–	–	–	–
Robert Green	2	1	–	–	–	–	–	–	–
Gaetano Giallanza	2	1	–	–	–	–	–	–	–
Paul McVeigh	–	1	–	–	–	–	–	–	–
own goals	–	–	3	–	–	–	–	–	–

NATIONWIDE LEAGUE DIVISION 1

1999-2000	P	W	D	L	F	A	PTS
Charlton Athletic	46	27	10	9	79	45	91
Manchester City	46	26	11	9	78	40	89
Ipswich Town	46	25	12	9	71	42	87
Barnsley	46	24	10	12	88	67	82
Birmingham City	46	22	11	13	65	44	77
Bolton Wanderers	46	21	13	12	69	50	76
Wolverhampton Wanderers	46	21	11	14	64	48	74
Huddersfield Town	46	21	11	14	62	49	74
Fulham	46	17	16	13	49	41	67
Queens Park Rangers	46	16	18	12	62	53	66
Blackburn Rovers	46	15	17	14	55	51	62
Norwich City	**46**	**14**	**15**	**17**	**45**	**50**	**57**
Tranmere Rovers	46	15	12	19	57	68	57
Nottingham Forest	46	14	14	18	53	55	56
Crystal Palace	46	13	15	18	57	67	54
Sheffield United	46	13	15	18	59	71	54
Stockport County	46	13	15	18	55	67	54
Portsmouth	46	13	12	21	55	66	51
Crewe Alexandra	46	14	9	23	46	67	51
Grimsby Town	46	13	12	21	41	67	51
West Bromwich Albion	46	10	19	17	43	60	49
Walsall	46	11	13	22	52	77	46
Port Vale	46	7	15	24	47	69	36
Swindon Town	46	8	12	26	38	77	36

2000-2001 DIVISION 1

NO.	DAY	DATE	OPPONENTS	V.	H-T	F-T	Marshall Andy	Sutch Daryl	Derveld Fernando	Marshall Lee	Fleming Craig	Bellamy Craig	Roberts Iwan	Mulryne Philip	Russell Darel	Kenton Darren	Llewellyn Chris	De Waard Raymond	Forbes Adrian	Giallanza Gaetano	Jackson Matt	McGovern Brian	Whitley Jim	McVeigh Paul	Brady Garry	Nedergaard Steen	Cottee Tony	Mackay Malky	Walsh Steve	Dalglish Paul	Granville Danny	Parker Scott	Coote Adrian	Notman Alex	De Blasiis Jean Yves	Abbey Zema	Drury Adam	Holt Gary	Peschisolido Paul	Green Robert	Own Goals
1	S	12 Aug 2000	Barnsley	A	0-0	0-1	1	2	3	4	5	8	9	10	(12)***	(19)*	(20)**	11*	17**	18***																					
2	S	19 " 2000	Nottingham Forest	H	0-0	0-0	1	2	(3)*	4	5		9	10	12	19	20	11*		18																					
3	S	26 " 2000	Blackburn Rovers	A	0-1	2-3	1	2	3	4	5		9[1]	(10)*	12	(19)**	20		17**	18*[1]	(6)***	24***																			
4	M	28 " 2000	Fulham	H	0-0	0-1	1	2	3	4	5		9		12	19	(20)*	11**	(17)*[1]	(18)***			25	22***																	
5	S	9 Sept 2000	Crewe Alexandra	A	0-0	0-0	1	2	3	4	5		9		12				17***	(18)***	(6)*	24*	25		(26)**	23**															
6	Tu	12 " 2000	Stockport County	A	2-0	3-1	1	2	3	4	5		9[2]		12				17*			(24)**	25[1]			(23)*	8	21**													
7	S	16 " 2000	Crystal Palace	H	0-0	0-0	1	2	3	4	5		9		12			11**	17*	18***		24	(25)**			(23)*	(8)***														
8	Su	24 " 2000	Wolverhampton Wanderers	A	0-3	0-4	1	2	3	4	5		9		12			11**	17	18*			(25)**				(8)*	21***	(30)***												
9	S	30 " 2000	Huddersfield Town	H	0-0	1-1	1	2	3	(4)**	5		9		12	19	20**			18*[1]			25		(26)***		(8)*		30***												
10	S	14 Oct 2000	West Bromwich Albion	A	2-1	3-2	1	2	3[1]	4	5		9	(10)**	(12)***	19[1]	20[1]			18*			25***			(23)*		21**													
11	Tu	17 " 2000	Preston North End	A	0-0	0-1	1	2	3	4	5		9	10		(19)*	(20)***		17***	18			(25)**				8**	21*													
12	S	21 " 2000	Sheffield United	H	2-2	4-2	1	2	3	4	5		9[1]	10[1]		19	20[1]			(18)*							8*[1]	21													
13	Tu	24 " 2000	Portsmouth	H	0-0	0-0	1	2	(3)**	4	5		9	10	12**	(19)***	20					24***					(8)*	21		14*											
14	S	4 Nov 2000	Tranmere Rovers	H	0-0	1-0	1	2		4	5		9[1]	10	12*		20		(17)**									21	30**		31	(25)*									
15	Tu	7 " 2000	Birmingham City	H	1-0	1-0	1	2		4	5		9	10	12*		20		(17)*[1]									21			31	(25)*	16**								
16	S	11 " 2000	Sheffield Wednesday	A	1-1	2-3	1	2	3**	4[1]	5		9	10	12***		(20)**		(17)*									21			31	(25)***[1]	16*								
17	S	18 " 2000	Bolton Wanderers	H	0-0	0-2	1	2	3**	(4)***	5		9	10	12*		(20)**		17									21			31	(25)*	16***								
18	Tu	21 " 2000	Burnley	A	0-0	0-2	1	2		(4)*	5		9	10	12*		(20)**	11**	(17)***									21			31	25	16***								
19	S	25 " 2000	Wimbledon	H	1-1	1-2	1	2	(3)**	4**	5		9[1]	10			(20)*		17									21			31	25	16*								
20	S	2 Dec 2000	Portsmouth	A	0-1	0-2	1	2	(3)***	4*	5		9	(10)**	12		20		(17)*									21					16***	8	15**						
21	S	9 " 2000	Gillingham	H	0-0	1-0	1	2		4	5		9		12	19*	20[1]				6							21						8	(15)*						
22	S	16 " 2000	Grimsby Town	A	0-1	0-2	1	(2)***		4	5		9	10	(12)*	19***	20		17**		6							21						(8)**		32*					
23	S	23 " 2000	Barnsley	H	0-0	0-0	1	2		(4)**	5		9	10	12		20				6							21		14**				(8)*		32*					
24	Tu	26 " 2000	Queens Park Rangers	A	1-2	3-2	1	2		4[1]	5		9[2]	10	(12)**	19**	20				6							21					16***	(8)*		(32)***					
25	S	30 " 2000	Nottingham Forest	A	0-0	0-0	1	2		4	5		(9)*	(10)**	12	19**	20				6							21		14***			16*			32***					
26	M	1 Jan 2001	Blackburn Rovers	H	1-0	1-1	1	2		4	5			10*	12		20		(17)***[1]		6							21		14***			(16)**	8**		(32)*					
27	S	13 " 2001	Fulham	A	0-1	0-2	1	2		4	5		9	(10)***	12	19	20				(6)*	24*												(8)**	15***	32**					
28	S	20 " 2001	Queens Park Rangers	H	1-0	1-0	1	(2)***		4			9		12	19	20				6							21	30***				(16)*	8**	15*	(32)**[1]					
29	S	27 " 2001	Watford	H	0-0	2-1	1	(2)**		4[1]			9			19	20				6			22**		23*[1]		21		14***			(16)***		(15)*	32					
30	S	3 Feb 2001	Birmingham City	A	0-1	1-2	1	2		(4)*			9		12	(19)**	20[1]				6					(23)***		21		14***			16*		15**	32					
31	S	10 " 2001	Crewe Alexandra	H	0-0	1-1	1	2		4					12	19	20[1]		17*		6			(22)*		23		21					16**			(32)**					
32	S	17 " 2001	Crystal Palace	A	0-1	1-1	1	2		4			9		12[1]	19	20		17*		6					(23)*		21								32					
33	Tu	20 " 2001	Stockport County	H	3-0	4-0	1	2		4			9[3]		(12)*	19	20[1]		17***		6			(22)**		23*		21		14**						(32)***					
34	S	24 " 2001	Wolverhampton Wanderers	H	1-0	1-0	1	2			5		9		12	(19)**	20		17***		6	24**		(22)***[1]		23*		21								(32)*					
35	S	3 Mar 2001	Huddersfield Town	A	0-1	0-2	1	2			5		9		12		20		17*		6			22		23		21								(32)*					
36	Tu	6 " 2001	West Bromwich Albion	H	0-1	0-1	1				5		9		12	(19)***	20		17*		(6)**	24***		22		23		21					16**			(32)*					
37	S	10 " 2001	Watford	A	1-1	1-4	1	2		(4)***	5		9		12		20		(17)*[1]		6			22*		(23)**		21							15***	32**					
38	S	17 " 2001	Preston North End	H	1-1	1-2	1	(2)**		4	5		9[1]		12		20		(17)***		6			(22)*		23**		21						8*		32***					
39	S	31 " 2001	Grimsby Town	H	1-1	2-1	1	2			(5)*		9[1]	10		19*	20[1]		17									21								32**	4	11	(31)**		
40	S	7 Apr 2001	Gillingham	A	0-2	3-4		2					9[1]	10	12*[1]		20[1]		(17)*		6							21						8**			4	11	(31)**	13	
41	Tu	10 " 2001	Sheffield United	A	0-1	1-1					5		9	10	12	19[1]	20				6							21						(8)*			4		31*	13	
42	S	14 " 2001	Tranmere Rovers	A	0-0	1-0					5		(9)***	10	12	19	20		17***		6	24*[1]						21						8**			(4)*		(31)**	13	
43	M	16 " 2001	Burnley	H	2-1	2-3					5		9[1]	10	12	(19)*	20		17*		(6)***	24***						21						(8)**[1]			4		31**	13	
44	S	21 " 2001	Bolton Wanderers	A	0-0	0-1					5		9	(10)*	12	(19)**	20				6	24**						21						(8)***		32***	4	11*		13	
45	S	28 " 2001	Sheffield Wednesday	H	1-0	1-0	1				5		9	10	12	19	(20)*				6			22*		23		21[1]						8							
46	Su	6 May 2001	Wimbledon	A	0-0	0-0	1	2***			5		(9)*	10	12	(19)***	(20)**					24		22**		23		21								32*		11			

F.A. CUP

NO.	DAY	DATE	OPPONENTS	V.	H-T	F-T	Marshall Andy	Sutch Daryl	Derveld Fernando	Marshall Lee	Fleming Craig	Bellamy Craig	Roberts Iwan	Mulryne Philip	Russell Darel	Kenton Darren	Llewellyn Chris	De Waard Raymond	Forbes Adrian	Giallanza Gaetano	Jackson Matt	McGovern Brian	Whitley Jim	McVeigh Paul	Brady Garry	Nedergaard Steen	Cottee Tony	Mackay Malky	Walsh Steve	Dalglish Paul	Granville Danny	Parker Scott	Coote Adrian	Notman Alex	De Blasiis Jean Yves	Abbey Zema	Drury Adam	Holt Gary	Peschisolido Paul	Green Robert	Own Goals
1	S	6 Jan 2001	Sheffield Wednesday (3rd Rd)	A	0-1	1-2	1	(2)***		4	5		9	(10)*	12	19***	20		(17)**		6							21[1]					16*	8**							

WORTHINGTON CUP

NO.	DAY	DATE	OPPONENTS	V.	H-T	F-T	Marshall Andy	Sutch Daryl	Derveld Fernando	Marshall Lee	Fleming Craig	Bellamy Craig	Roberts Iwan	Mulryne Philip	Russell Darel	Kenton Darren	Llewellyn Chris	De Waard Raymond	Forbes Adrian	Giallanza Gaetano	Jackson Matt	McGovern Brian	Whitley Jim	McVeigh Paul	Brady Garry	Nedergaard Steen	Cottee Tony	Mackay Malky	Walsh Steve	Dalglish Paul	Granville Danny	Parker Scott	Coote Adrian	Notman Alex	De Blasiis Jean Yves	Abbey Zema	Drury Adam	Holt Gary	Peschisolido Paul	Green Robert	Own Goals
1	Tu	22 Aug 2000	AFC Bournemouth (1st Rd 1st leg)	H	0-0	0-0	1	2		4	5		9	(10)**	12	19	20	(11)***	17*	(18)*		24**											16***								
2	Tu	5 Sept 2000	AFC Bournemouth (1st Rd 2nd leg)	A	0-1	2-1	1	2	3	4	5		9		12[1]					(18)**[1]	6	24			(26)*	23*							16**								
3	Tu	19 " 2000	Blackpool (2nd Rd 1st leg)	H	3-2	3-3	1	2	3	4[1]	5		9[1]		12			11***	17*	18**		24				(23)***	(8)**[1]		(30)*												
4	M	2 Oct 2000	Blackpool (2nd Rd 2nd leg)	A	2-0	5-0	1	2	3	4	5		9[2]		(12)**[1]	19	(20)*			18[2]					26	23*	8**														
5	W	1 Nov 2000	Derby County (3rd Rd)	A	0-3	0-3	1	2			5		9	10	12	(19)**	20	11**	(17)***					22***				21		(14)*			16*								

2000-2001 APPEARANCES & GOALS

	FOOTBALL LGE APPR.	S	GLS	F.A. CUP APPR.	S	GLS	LEAGUE CUP APPR.	S	GLS
Iwan Roberts	44	–	15	1	–	–	5	–	3
Chris Llewellyn	41	1	8	1	–	–	3	–	–
Andy Marshall	41	–	–	1	–	–	5	–	–
Daryl Sutch	39	1	–	1	–	–	5	–	–
Craig Fleming	39	–	–	1	–	–	5	–	–
Darel Russell	34	7	2	1	–	–	5	–	2
Malky Mackay	34	4	1	1	–	1	1	–	–
Lee Marshall	34	2	3	1	–	–	4	–	1
Philip Mulryne	27	1	1	1	–	–	2	–	–
Matt Jackson	26	–	–	1	–	–	1	–	–
Darren Kenton	24	5	2	–	1	–	3	–	–
Fernando Derveld	15	2	1	–	–	–	3	–	–
Adrian Forbes	13	16	3	1	–	–	1	2	–
Zema Abbey	11	9	1	–	–	–	–	–	–
Steen Nedergaard	10	5	1	–	–	–	1	2	–
Alex Notman	10	5	1	–	1	–	–	–	–
Jim Whitley	7	1	1	–	–	–	–	–	–
Paul McVeigh	6	5	1	–	–	–	–	1	–
Scott Parker	6	–	1	–	–	–	–	–	–
Adam Drury	6	–	–	–	–	–	–	–	–
Danny Granville	6	–	–	–	–	–	–	–	–
Gaetano Giallanza	5	6	2	–	–	–	3	1	3
Tony Cottee	5	2	1	–	–	–	1	1	1
Robert Green	5	–	–	–	–	–	–	–	–
Adrian Coote	3	11	–	–	1	–	–	3	–
Brian McGovern	3	9	1	–	–	–	2	1	–
Paul Peschisolido	3	2	–	–	–	–	–	–	–
Gary Holt	3	1	–	–	–	–	–	–	–
Jean Yves De Blasiis	2	5	–	–	–	–	–	–	–
Garry Brady	2	–	–	–	–	–	2	–	–
Steve Walsh	1	3	–	–	–	–	1	–	–
Craig Bellamy	1	–	–	–	–	–	–	–	–
Paul Dalglish	–	7	–	–	–	–	1	–	–
Raymond De Waard	–	6	–	–	–	–	1	2	–
own goals	–	–	–	–	–	–	–	–	–

NATIONWIDE LEAGUE DIVISION 1

2000-2001	P	W	D	L	F	A	PTS
Fulham	46	30	11	5	90	32	101
Blackburn Rovers	46	26	13	7	76	39	91
Bolton Wanderers	46	24	15	7	76	45	87
Preston North End	46	23	9	14	64	52	78
Birmingham City	46	23	9	14	59	48	78
West Bromwich Albion	46	21	11	14	60	52	74
Burnley	46	21	9	16	50	54	72
Wimbledon	46	17	18	11	71	50	69
Watford	46	20	9	17	76	67	69
Sheffield United	46	19	11	16	52	49	68
Nottingham Forest	46	20	8	18	55	53	68
Wolverhampton Wanderers	46	14	13	19	45	45	55
Gillingham	46	13	16	17	61	66	55
Crewe Alexandra	46	15	10	21	47	62	55
Norwich City	**46**	**14**	**12**	**20**	**46**	**58**	**54**
Barnsley	46	15	9	22	49	62	54
Sheffield Wednesday	46	15	8	23	52	71	53
Grimsby Town	46	14	10	22	43	62	52
Stockport County	46	11	18	17	58	65	51
Portsmouth	46	10	19	17	47	59	49
Crystal Palace	46	12	13	21	57	70	49
Huddersfield Town	46	11	15	20	48	57	48
Queens Park Rangers	46	7	19	20	45	75	40
Tranmere Rovers	46	9	11	26	46	77	38

APPEARANCES AND GOALSCORERS IN COMPETITIVE GAMES BETWEEN 1902–03 AND 1919–20

	SOUTHERN LEAGUE		UNITED LEAGUE		N & S LEAGUE		FA CUP		AMATEUR CUP		NORFOLK SENIOR CUP		SOUTHERN CHARITY CUP	
	APPRS.	GOALS	APPRS.	GOALS	APPRS.	GOALS	APPRS.	GOALS	APPRS.	GOALS	APPRS.	GOALS	APPRS.	GOALS
ABBS CHARLES WILLIAM CHRISTMAS	1	–												
ALLEN JOHN HENRY	29	–					5	–					1	–
ALLSOPP THOMAS CHARLESWORTH	115	18	8	4			9	5						
ARCHER ARTHUR	67	10	11	–			5	1						
ASKEW LESLIE WILLIAM	10	–					2	–						
ASTILL WILLIAM HENRY	1	–												
BACON ARTHUR EVERITT	1	–												
BACON SAMUEL THOMAS	17	5	3	2										
BAKER LANGFORD	2	–			11	5	4	3	7	3	1	–		
BAKER ROBERT WILLIAM	1	–			14	2	2	1						
*BARCLAY WILLIAM ALEXANDER	4	–												
BARDWELL GEORGE FREDERICK					14	–	1	–	2	–	1	–		
BARNFATHER PERCY	32	4					2	–						
BATEY THOMAS	13	2												
BAUCHOP JAMES RAE	22	11					2	1						
BAUCHOP WILLIAM FOTHERINGHAM	32	1					4	–						
BEALE ROBERT HUGHES	105	–	3	–			3	–						
BEEVERS THOMAS JOSEPH	1	–												
BELL GEORGE	34	1					2	–					3	–
*BELL WALTER CHARLES	7	2												
BELLAMY JAMES FRANCIS	6	3												
BEMMENT FREDERICK CHARLES	67	2	12	–			6	–						
BIBBY RALPH WATSON	43	–					2	–						
BIRCHALL RICHARD	30	7					1	1						
BIRNIE ALEXANDER KELMAR	6	–	6	1										
BOWMAN JOHN WILLIAM	7	–					1	–						
BRINDLEY HORACE	24	–	4	–			4	1						
BROADHEAD JAMES EDWARD	30	8					1	–						
BROOKS ARTHUR FREDERICK			1	1										
BROWN A.							1	–						
BROWN THOMAS HENRY STAUNTON	2	–												
BROWN GEORGE GRAVER	19	1												
BUCKLEY FRANKLIN CHARLES	1	–												
BUGG WALTER JAMES	2	–	3	–										
BUSHELL WILLIAM	132	2	12	1			10	1						
BUTCHER HERBERT WALKER					1	–								
BYRNE JOHN	1	–	3	–										
CAMPLING ERNEST HENRY					3	–								
CANNON JOHN WILSON			1	–										
CHALMERS JAMES	14	2	10	2			1	–						
CHAMBERLIN EDMUND GEORGE					25	1	6	–	7	–	1	–		
CHAMBERS HORACE FRANK	9	–	1	–			1	–						
CHICK JOHN WILLIAM	47	1					2	–						
CHILDS WILLIAM HENRY EDWARD	2	–					1	–						
CHURCH WALTER HERBERT	4	–	4	–										
CLARKE ALFRED					3	2								
COLLINS ARTHUR	28	1					1	–						
COLLINSON ROBERT WHITELEY					29	16	7	5	9	7	1	–		
COOCH GEORGE	12	–					2	–						
COOKS WILLIAM ARTHUR HOWARD CLAUDE					28	–	6	–	7	–	1	–		
COXHEAD ERNEST ALFRED BENJAMIN	38	4	2	–			2	–						
CRACKNELL WILLIAM					10	–	1	–	2	–	1	–		
CRAIG CHARLES THOMSON	48	1	3	–			7	–						
CROME WALTER VALENTINE					1	–	1	–						
CROSSLEY ARTHUR	4	2												
CULLUM CHARLES	3	–												
CUMMINGS WILLIAM JAMES	6	–												
CURTIN CHARLES	22	4					2	–					1	–
CUTMORE JOHN	6	–	1	–	9	–	2	–						
DENOON JOHN	8	–												
DESBOROUGH REGINALD ALBERT BERTRAM					10	1	1	–						
DEXTER GEORGE	1	–												
DIVINE ALEX FLETCHER	5	1												
DIX HARRY ALBAN	3	1												
DONNELLY GEORGE	10	–												
DORAN JOHN FRANCIS	25	18					1	–						
DRUCE WILLIAM ROBERT	18	–	4	–										
DUNNING CYRIL EDWARD	43	25	5	2	1	–	1	–						
ELLIS HORACE HILTON					4	–								
FIELDING ARTHUR	2	–												
FISKE WILLIAM			1	–										
FITCHIE THOMAS TINDAL			1	–										
FLANAGAN JOHN	34	2	4	1			5	1						
FRENCH CHARLES WILLIAM	25	2	3	–			5	–						
*FROSDICK ALBERT WALTER	13	–					1	–						
*GADSDEN ERNEST	2	–												
GLAZEBROOK HAROLD	1	–												

	SOUTHERN LEAGUE		UNITED LEAGUE		N & S LEAGUE		FA CUP		AMATEUR CUP		NORFOLK SENIOR CUP		SOUTHERN CHARITY CUP	
	APPRS.	GOALS	APPRS.	GOALS	APPRS.	GOALS	APPRS.	GOALS	APPRS.	GOALS	APPRS.	GOALS	APPRS.	GOALS
GOOCH PERCY GEORGE	23	13	2	1	25	12	7	4	7	5	1	1		
GRAHAM SAMUEL	24	6					4	2						
*GRAY GEORGE WILLIAM	41	–					1	–						
GREEN A					3	–					1	–		
GROVES JACK WILLIAM	6	–					1	–						
GUNTON SAMUEL ARTHUR	6	1	5	5			1	–						
HALL FRETWELL	30	–					1	–						
HALL WILLIAM HORACE	4	–												
HAMPSON WILLIAM	134	8					6	2					1	–
HARRIS EDWARD					34	–	4	–	2	–				
HAWES ARTHUR ROBERT	36	8					1	–						
HEMNELL RUSSELL JOHNSON	4	–												
HERBERT JOSEPH HENRY	17	3					1	–						
HILL FRANK	5	–												
HOLT HENRY	2	–												
HOOK JAMES HENRY MILLER					3	–								
*HOPE PHILIP	9	–												
HORTON WILLIAM HENRY					6	1			1	–				
HOUGHTON JOHN	43	–					8	–					3	–
HUBBARD ARCHIBALD	28	6					1	–						
HUGHES WILLIAM JOHN	25	5					4	1						
HUMPHREYS PERCY	3	1												
HUNT ERNIE			2	1										
HUTCHISON HAROLD	28	–					1	–						
INGHAM WILLIAM	128	31					3	1					3	1
JEFFRIES WILLIAM HENRY					1	–								
JENNINGS SAMUEL	26	15					1	–						
JENNINGS WILLIAM	38	2					1	–						
JEX WILLIAM	10	3					1	–						
JOBLING LEONARD	60	3					2	–						
JONES ALBERT THOMAS	6	–												
KAY ALEXANDER					1	1								
KELF JOSEPH WILLIAM					3	–								
KENNEDY JAMES JOHN	4	–											1	–
*KING ALFRED PAGE	2	–												
KING CHARLES	1	–												
KING HORACE HERBERT	16	1	4	3	26	12	5	–	2	1	1	1		
KIRK WALTER EDWARD	5	1												
KIRKMAN ALBERT	2	–					2	–						
LACEY WILLIAM BERNARD	2	–												
LAMBERTON GEORGE	37	11	9	3			1	–						
LAMBERTON JAMES	1	–	5	–										
LAMING RICHARD	1	–												
*LANSDALE JOSEPH	62	–					5	–					3	–
LATHAN THOMAS					1	–								
*LAXTON EDWARD GEORGE	22	1												
LEVI HAROLD JOSEPH	22	2												
LIDDELL ALEXANDER HADDOW	7	–	5	–										
LINWARD WILLIAM HENRY	3	–												
LIVINGSTONE ARCHIBALD	109	1	16	1			9	–						
LONG SIDNEY THOMAS	5	–	6	1			2	–						
McCALL JOHN BAINBRIDGE	4	–					1	–						
McEWEN JAMES	103	–	10	–			8	–						
McINTYRE ROBERT					1	–								
McLARNEY PATRICK	3	–	1	–										
McQUEEN HUGH			1	–										
MACDONALD GEORGE	33	4					3	1					2	–
MACKENZIE JOHN	186	2					15	–					3	–
MAKIN THOMAS	11	1												
MARTIN GEORGE HARLOW	8	3	1	–										
*MARTIN ISAAC GEORGE	83	–					8	–					3	–
MELLOR WILLIAM	65	–					7	–					1	–
MILLER GEORGE LANE					2	–								
MILNES FREDERICK HOUGHTON			2	–										
MITCHELL LOYD					2	–								
MOLYNEUX WILLIAM	22	–											1	–
MOSLEY FRED	9	5												
MUIR ROBERT BRUCE	64	5	2	–			5	–						
NEWELL THOMAS HENRY					25	5	4	–	8	1	2	–		
NEWLANDS GERRY	96	1	6	–			9	–						
*O'BRIEN MICHAEL TERRENCE	10	1												
OSBORNE ALFRED MOSS	9	5					4	1						
PALMER JAMES MARSH					11	3			4	1				
PALMER ROWLAND MARK					7	–			1	1				
PALING GEORGE LESLIE	1	–												
PEACOCK JAMES WILLIAM	4	–												
PEARSON JAMES HENRY	28	1					1	–						
PEGG JOSEPH COOPER	12	–	4	1										
PILCH ROBERT GEORGE	2	–												
PLAYFORD BERTIE					18	10	4	–	3	–	1	–		
POINTER ROBERT GEORGE					30	–	5	–	6	–	1	–		
POOLE WILLIAM	1	1												

	SOUTHERN LEAGUE		UNITED LEAGUE		N & S LEAGUE		FA CUP		AMATEUR CUP		NORFOLK SENIOR CUP		SOUTHERN CHARITY CUP	
	APPRS.	GOALS	APPRS.	GOALS	APPRS.	GOALS	APPRS.	GOALS	APPRS.	GOALS	APPRS.	GOALS	APPRS.	GOALS
POPHAM REGINALD FRANCIS	5	–												
PORTER GEORGE	9	–												
POTTER CECIL BERTRAM	121	27					10	4					2	2
POTTS JOHN WILLIAM	2	–												
RACKHAM FRANCIS HENRY					18	1	3	–	7	2	1	–		
RANDALL THOMAS THEODORE LAURENCE	2	–	1	–										
RAYNER WALTER JESSE	12	–	4	–										
RAYNER WILLIAM THOMAS	35	17												
REYNOLDS WALTER JAMES	22	–	6	–										
RIDDELL FREDERICK	8	1												
RITCHIE GEORGE WIGHT	35	11					5	1					1	–
RONALDSON DUNCAN McKAY	89	15	12	11			8	1						
RONEY PETER	53	–	9	–			7	–						
ROSE FREDERICK GEORGE	2	–												
ROSS DAVID	57	36	8	7			6	6						
ROYAL HENRY JAMES					15	1	2	–						
SAYER HENRY JAMES					3	–								
SCHMIDT ERNEST FREDERICK					3	–								
SHIELDS JAMES PRATT ADDISON					1	2	1	–						
SIDWELL WALTER THOMAS					9	3	3	–	7	–	1	–		
SILOR WILLIAM	27	7	9	4										
SIMPSON VIVIAN SUMNER	1	–												
SIMS GEORGE			1	–										
*SKERMER HERBERT EDWARD	22	–												
*SMITH BENJAMIN GEORGE	28	–					1	–						
SMITH JOHN	29	14	7	9			5	1						
SMITH WALTER ALFRED	11	3												
SNELLING CHARLES					5	–								
SPARKS WILLIAM					2	–	1	–	2	–				
STEELE THOMAS RICHARD					8	–			2	–	1	–		
STRINGFELLOW ARTHUR	19	3					1	–						
SUTCLIFFE PERCY	51	3					7	1					3	–
SUTHERLAND ALEXANDER THOMAS					11	2	4	–	7	–	1	–		
SWANN CHARLES FREDERICK	7	–	2	1										
*TAYLOR WALTER JOSEPH	46	5	2	1			6	2					1	–
THOMPSON FREDERICK	53	–	12	–			2	–						
THOMPSON GEORGE WILFRED	5	–												
TIDMAN ALFRED JAMES					2	–								
TOMLINSON JAMES	26	6	5	1			5	2						
TRAVIS AARON	8	2					2	–						
TURNER ARTHUR	18	3											1	2
TURNER WALTER WILLIAM	2	–												
VALENTINE THOMAS	16	3												
VALIANT JAMES	17	1					2	–						
VIGAR HERBERT EVELYN	1	–			12	12	2	–						
WAGSTAFFE EDWARD	25	–	3	–			5	–						
WALLACE WILLIAM GEORGE RICHARD JAMES					7	–					1	–		
WHITEMAN ROBERT	56	1	7	–			6	–						
WHITESIDE EDWARD	36	6					2	1						
WILCOX THOMAS WALTER	7	–					2	–						
WILKINSON FRED	66	5					2	–						
WILKINSON FREDDY	2	1												
*WILKINSON REGINALD GEORGE	6	–												
WILLIAMS CHARLES ALBERT	27	–					2	–						
WILSON DANIEL LAMBERT	58	16					7	4					4	1
WITHAM ALFRED					14	6	2	–	2	4	2	–		
WOLSTENHOLME ARTHUR	32	13					2	2					2	–
WOLSTENHOLME SAMUEL	138	7					7	1						
WOOD WILLIAM	44	15	11	2			2	–						
WOODLAND ARTHUR	79	1					10	1					1	–
WOODS HAROLD	136	30					12	5					3	2
YALLOP GEORGE THOMAS					5	–	1	–	2	–	1	–		
YALLOP JOHN FREDERICK					7	–	1	–	2	–	1	–		
YOUNG JAMES	24	6					2	–						
OWN GOALS	–	8	–	1	–	1			–	1	–	1		

PLAYED ON INTO THE FOOTBALL LEAGUE

APPEARANCES AND GOALSCORERS IN COMPETITIVE GAMES BETWEEN 1920–21 AND 2000–01 (up to and including 31.08.01)

	FOOTBALL LEAGUE			FA CUP			LEAGUE CUP			TEXACO CUP			FMC/OTHER			DIV. 3 SOUTH CUP		TOTAL		
	APPRS.	SUBS.	GOALS	APPRS.	SUBS.	GOALS	APPRS.	SUBS.	GOALS	APPRS.	SUBS.	GOALS	APPRS.	SUBS.	GOALS	APPRS.	GOALS	APPRS.	SUBS.	GOALS
ABASCAL VICTOR SEGURA	24	5	–	1	–	–	3	–	–									28	5	–
ABBEY ZEMA	15	9	1															16	9	1
ACKERMAN ALF	66	–	31	4	–	4												70	–	35
ACQUROFF JACK	17	–	6															17	–	6
ADAMS CHRIS	29	–	3	1	–	–												30	–	3
ADAMS NEIL	164	18	25	7	–	1	16	1	4									187	19	30
ADDY GEORGE	31	–	6	2	–	–												33	–	6
AITKEN JOHN	42	–	8	4	–	–												46	–	8
AITKEN WILLIAM	14	–	–															14	–	–
AKINBIYI ADE	22	27	3	–	2	–	2	4	2				–	1	–			24	34	5
ALEXANDER PHIL	–	1	–															–	1	–
ALLCOCK TERRY	334	5	106	33	–	12	17	–	9									384	5	127
ALLEN MALCOLM	24	11	8	5	–	7	–	3	–				2	1	–			31	15	15
ALLMAN LESLIE	15	–	–															15	–	–
ANDERSON GEORGE	28	–	12	2	–	–												30	–	12
ANDERSON TERRY	218	18	16	13	–	2	21	2	–	6	1	1						258	21	19
ANSELIN CEDRIC	22	4	1	1	–	–	2	–	–									25	4	1
ANSELL GEORGE	4	–	–															4	–	–
ARMES IVAN	61	–	1	4	–	–												65	–	1
ARMSTRONG JOSEPH	18	–	7	4	–	1												22	–	8
ARNOLD ERIC	13	–	–															13	–	–
ASHMAN RON	592	–	55	56	–	1	14	–	–									662	–	56
ATKINSON WALTER	1	–	–															1	–	–
AUSTIN SAM	152	–	35	12	–	4												164	–	39
BACON RON	42	–	6															42	–	6
BAKER CLIVE	14	–	–	2	–	–												16	–	–
BALL STEPHEN	–	2	–				–	2	–									–	4	–
BANKS JAMES	124	–	22	12	–	4												136	–	26
BANNISTER KEITH	7	–	–															7	–	–
BARHAM MARK	169	8	23	14	–	1	25	2	1				5	–	–			213	10	25
BARKAS EDWARD	1	–	–															1	–	–
BARNARD GEOFF	6	–	–															6	–	–
BARNES RON	21	–	1	1	–	–	3	–	–									25	–	1
BARNSLEY GEOFF	8	–	–															8	–	–
BAXTER LARRY	5	–	–															5	–	–
BECKFORD DARREN	32	6	8	4	1	1	3	2	3				1	–	1			40	9	13
BELL JACKIE	48	–	3	1	–	–	9	–	2									58	–	5
BELL BOBBY	3	–	–															3	–	–
BELL SAM	76	–	26	1	–	–										2	1	79	–	27
BELL WALTER	3	–	2															3	–	2
BELLAMY CRAIG	71	13	32	1	–	–	6	–	2									78	13	34
BENNETT ALBERT	54	1	15				5	–	1									59	1	16
BENNETT DAVE	64	7	9	3	1	–	10	–	2									77	8	11
BENNETT EDWARD	11	–	–															11	–	–
BENSON JOHN	29	1	1	1	–	–	4	1	–	1	–	–						35	2	1
BENSTEAD GRAHAM	16	–	–				3	–	–									19	–	–
BERTRAM WILLIAM	25	–	2	5	–	1												30	–	3
BERTSCHIN KEITH	112	2	29	13	–	5	11	–	4									136	2	38
BIGGINS WAYNE	66	13	16	4	–	–	6	–	2				6	2	3			82	15	21
BILLINGTON CHARLIE	22	–	–															22	–	–
BIRCH CLIFF	5	–	3															5	–	3
BLACK ALAN	172	4	1	7	–	–	12	–	–	8	–	–						199	4	1
BLADES PAUL	47	–	–	2	–	–	8	–	–				5	–	–			62	–	–
BLAIR JIM	3	3	–				1	1	–	2	1	1						6	5	1
BLAKEMORE CECIL	70	–	29															70	–	29
de BLASIIS JEAN YVES	28	7	–	1	–	–	1	1	–									30	8	–
BLY TERRY	57	–	31	10	–	7												67	–	38
BOLLAND GORDON	104	1	29	6	–	1	7	–	5									117	1	35
BOND KEVIN	137	5	12	7	–	2	12	–	–									156	5	14
BONE JIMMY	39	–	9	3	–	–	5	–	4	4	–	2						51	–	15
BOOTH CURTIS	62	–	11	3	–	2												65	–	13
BOTTO LEWIS	2	–	–															2	–	–
BOWEN MARK	315	5	25	28	–	1	34	–	1				17	–	1			394	5	27
BOWEN SAM	129	–	2	10	–	–												139	–	2
BOYER PHIL	115	1	34	6	–	–	15	–	4	3	–	2						139	1	40
BRADBROOK CHARLES	96	–	1	10	–	–												106	–	1
BRADLEY CECIL	4	–	1															4	–	1
BRADLEY JACK	6	–	–															6	–	–
BRADLEY RON	4	–	–															4	–	–
BRADSHAW CARL	55	10	2	2	–	–	6	1	1									63	11	3
BRADY GARRY	8	–	–				2	–	–									10	–	–
BRAIN JOE	13	–	5															13	–	5
BRANNAN GERARD	10	1	1				1	–	–									11	1	1
BRENNAN BOBBY	225	–	44	25	–	8												250	–	52
BRIGGS MAX	127	8	1	4	1	–	17	–	1	12	1	–						160	10	2
BROOKE GARRY	8	6	2				1	1	1				1	3	1			10	10	4
BROUGHTON DREWE	3	6	1															3	6	1

	FOOTBALL LEAGUE			FA CUP			LEAGUE CUP			TEXACO CUP			FMC/OTHER			DIV. 3 SOUTH CUP		TOTAL		
	APPRS.	SUBS.	GOALS	APPRS.	SUBS.	GOALS	APPRS.	SUBS.	GOALS	APPRS.	SUBS.	GOALS	APPRS.	SUBS.	GOALS	APPRS.	GOALS	APPRS.	SUBS.	GOALS
BROWN KENNY	24	1	–										3	–	–			27	1	–
BROWN LAURIE	80	1	2	6	–	–	3	1	–									89	2	2
BROWN OLIVER	51	–	33															51	–	33
BROWN ROGER	16	–	–	3	–	–	2	–	–									21	–	–
BROWN WILLIAM	50	–	2	3	–	–												53	–	2
BRUCE STEVE	141	–	14	9	–	1	20	–	6				10	–	–			180		20
BRYCELAND TOMMY	253	1	49	13	2	3	15	–	3									281	3	55
BUCHANAN CAMERON	3	–	–															3	–	–
BULLIMORE ALAN	1	–	–															1	–	–
BURDITT KEN	162	–	58	7	–	3										4	–	173	–	61
BURKE PETER	114	–	–	5	–	–												119	–	–
BURLEY BEN	35	–	4	2	–	–												37	–	4
BURTON OLLIE	57	–	8	6	–	–	10	–	1									73	–	9
BUSBY VIV	22	–	11	1	–	–												23	–	11
BUTLER BARRY	303	–	3	27	–	–	19	–	–									349	–	3
BUTLER GEOFF	151	2	1	7	–	–	27	2	–	7	–	–						192	4	1
BUTTERWORTH IAN	230	5	4	25	–	–	17	1	–				14	1	–			286	7	4
CAMPBELL ARCHIE	87	–	–	10	–	–												97	–	–
CARBERRY BERT	5	–	–															5	–	–
CAREY SHAUN	50	17	–	1	1	–	5	2	–									56	20	–
CASSIDY FRANCIS	1	–	–															1	–	–
CASSIDY NIGEL	2	1	–															2	1	–
CAWSTON MERVYN	4	–	–							3	–	–						7	–	–
CHANNON MIKE	84	4	16	10	–	2	14	–	7									108	4	25
CHAPPELL ARCHIE	10	–	2															10	–	2
CHEESLEY PAUL	10	3	1	–	1	–	2	1	–	4	3	–						16	8	1
CHIVERS MARTIN	11	–	4	1	–	–	1	–	–									13	–	4
CHRISTIE ALEX	5	–	–															5	–	–
CHUNG SAMMY	47	–	9	1	–	–												48	–	9
CHURCH JOHN	110	–	16	4	–	–												114	–	16
CLARE JOSEPH	22	–	5															22	–	5
CLAYTON PAUL	8	5	–				1	–	–				1	–	–			10	5	–
CLEARY BILL	18	–	–	3	–	–												21	–	–
CLELAND PETER	3	–	–	1	–	–												4	–	–
COLE MIKE	3	–	–															3	–	–
COLE NORMAN	1	–	–															1	–	–
COLEMAN TIM	63	–	25	1	–	1												64	–	26
COLLINS TONY	29	–	2	2	–	–												31	–	2
CONEY DEAN	12	5	1															12	5	1
CONLON BRYAN	29	–	8	1	–	–	1	–	–									31	–	8
CONWAY JIM	42	–	13	3	–	–	5	–	2									50	–	15
COOK PAUL	3	3	–										1	1	–			4	4	–
COOKE GEORGE	4	–	–	2	–	–												6	–	–
COOTE ADRIAN	20	34	3	–	1	–	1	5	–									21	40	3
CORNWELL RALPH	2	–	–															2	–	–
CORRIGAN JOE	3	–	–				1	–	–									4	–	–
COTTEE TONY	5	2	1				1	1	1									6	3	2
COULTHARD TOM	40	–	1	2	–	–												42	–	1
COUSINS WILLIAM	26	–	–															26	–	–
COXON BILLY	98	–	24	7	–	2												105	–	26
CRICKMORE CHARLIE	54	2	9	4	–	–	4	–	1									62	2	10
CROCKFORD HAROLD	2	–	–															2	–	–
CROOK IAN	314	27	18	19	5	1	31	5	4				16	1	1			380	38	24
CROPPER ARTHUR	23	–	3															23	–	3
CROPPER REG	49	–	16	4	–	2												53	–	18
CROSS DAVID	83	1	21	4	–	2	9	–	6	9	–	1						105	1	30
CROSSAN ERROL	102	–	28	12	–	4	2	–	–									116	–	32
CROWE MARK	–	1	–															–	1	–
CROWE MATT	186	–	14	22	–	2	6	–	2									214	–	18
CULVERHOUSE IAN	295	1	1	28	–	–	23	–	–				22	–	1			368	1	2
CURETON JAMIE	13	16	6	–	2	–	–	1	–									13	19	6
CURRAN HUGH	112	–	46	5	–	1	7	–	6									124	–	53
DALGLISH PAUL	25	18	2	1	–	–	3	1	–									29	19	2
DARLING MALCOLM	16	–	5				1	–	–									17	–	5
DARMODY AUBREY	2	–	–															2	–	–
DAVIDS NEIL	2	–	–															2	–	–
DAVIES GLYN	3	–	–															3	–	–
DAVIES GORDON	1	–	–															1	–	–
DAVIES IAN	29	3	2	1	–	–	1	–	–									31	3	2
DAVIES RON	113	–	58	6	–	4	7	–	4									126	–	66
DAVIS DEREK	26	–	–	2	–	–												28	–	–
DEEHAN JOHN	158	4	62	16	1	2	18	–	6				2	–	–			194	5	70
DEMPSEY WILLIAM	8	–	–															8	–	–
DENNINGTON CHARLIE	195	–	–	14	–	–												209	–	–
DENNIS GEORGE	1	–	–															1	–	–
DENNISON ROBERT	117	–	35	9	–	4												126	–	39
DENT FRED	24	–	12															24	–	12
DERVELD FERNANDO	20	2	1				3	–	–									23	2	1
DEVINE JOHN	51	2	3	8	–	–	8	–	–									67	2	3
DICKINSON JAMES	16	–	–															16	–	–
DIOP PAPE	2	5	–				1	2	–									3	7	–
DOBSON GEORGE	27	–	1	1	–	–												28	–	1

	FOOTBALL LEAGUE			FA CUP			LEAGUE CUP			TEXACO CUP			FMC/OTHER			DIV. 3 SOUTH CUP		TOTAL		
	APPRS.	SUBS.	GOALS	APPRS.	SUBS.	GOALS	APPRS.	SUBS.	GOALS	APPRS.	SUBS.	GOALS	APPRS.	SUBS.	GOALS	APPRS.	GOALS	APPRS.	SUBS.	GOALS
DOCHERTY TOM	85	–	4	7	–	3												92	–	7
DOLDING LEN	12	–	1															12	–	1
DONACHIE WILLIE	11	–	–				3	–	–									14	–	–
DONOWA LOUIE	56	6	11	1	2	1	13	2	3									70	10	15
DOWNS GREG	162	7	7	20	–	1	17	–	–									199	7	8
DRINKELL KEVIN	121	–	50	6	–	2	11	–	2				12	–	3			150	–	57
DRIVER ALLENBY	49	–	19															49	–	19
DRURY ADAM	10	–	–				1	–	–									11	–	–
DUFFUS JACK	77	–	4	3	–	–												80	–	4
DUFFY JOHN	78	–	–	9	–	–												87	–	–
DUKES HARRY	118	–	–	6	–	–												124	–	–
DUNCAN JOHN	4	–	–															4	–	–
DUNCAN WILLIAM	2	–	–															2	–	–
DUTHIE JOHN	27	–	4															27	–	4
DUTTON LEN	139	–	11	13	–	3												152	–	14
EADIE DARREN	153	15	35	7	1	1	25	1	2				1	1	–			186	18	38
EARL SIDNEY	29	–	1	1	–	–												30	–	1
EASTON CLINT JUDE	–	1	–															–	1	–
EDWARDS BOB	1	–	–															1	–	–
EDWARDS DON	2	–	–															2	–	–
EDWARDS GEORGE	9	–	1															9	–	1
EDWARDS JIM	2	–	–															2	–	–
EKOKU EFAN	26	11	15	1	1	–	3	–	1				3	–	1			33	12	17
ELLIOTT SHAUN	29	2	2				5	–	–				2	1	–			36	3	2
EMBLEN NEIL ROBERT	1	–	–															1	–	–
ENGLEFIELD GRAHAME	22	–	–															22	–	–
EPHGRAVE GEORGE	5	–	–															5	–	–
EVANS DOUG	14	4	1				1	–	–									15	4	1
EYRE LES	185	–	58	16	–	11												201	–	69
FAIRCLOUGH DAVID	1	1	–															1	1	–
FARRINGTON MARK	11	3	2	3	–	–	1	–	–									15	3	2
FASHANU JOHN	6	1	1															6	1	1
FASHANU JUSTIN	84	6	35	5	–	1	8	–	4									97	6	40
FEATHERBY LEN	26	–	3															26	–	3
FENN NEALE	6	1	1															6	1	1
FERRARI FRED	4	–	–															4	–	–
FIELD RICHARD	28	–	–	1	–	–												29	–	–
FLACK LEN	49	–	–	5	–	–												54	–	–
FLECK ROBERT	223	24	56	19	2	11	22	2	13				7	–	4			271	28	84
FLEETING JIM	–	1	–	1	–	–												1	1	–
FLEMING CRAIG	136	5	7	3	1	–	16	–	–									155	6	7
FOAN ALBERT	18	–	4															18	–	4
FOGGO KEN	181	4	54	7	–	1	9	–	2									197	4	57
FORBES ADRIAN	66	46	8	2	2	–	1	4	–									69	52	8
FORBES DUNCAN	289	6	10	13	–	–	35	1	–	13	–	2						350	7	12
FORD ALF	1	–	–															1	–	–
FOULKES REG	216	–	8	22	–	–												238	–	8
FOX RUEL	148	24	22	11	4	–	13	3	3				12	4	–			184	35	25
FRIAR JOHN	82	–	18	4	–	–												86	–	18
FROSDICK ALBERT	5	–	–															5	–	–
FUGLESTAD ERIK	71	3	2	3	–	–	2	1	–									76	4	2
FULTON JOHN	1	–	–															1	–	–
FURNESS BILLY	93	–	21	3	–	–												96	–	21
GADSDEN ERNIE	19	–	–															19	–	–
GALLEGO ANTONIO	1	–	–															1	–	–
GARDINER JOHN	1	–	–															1	–	–
GAVIN JOHNNY	312	–	122	26	–	10												338	–	132
GIALLANZA GAETANO	7	7	2				3	1	3									10	8	5
GIBBINS ROGER	47	1	12	2	–	1	2	–	–									51	1	13
GILBERT NOEL	1	–	–															1	–	–
GILGUN PATRICK	12	–	4															12	–	4
GLADWIN ROBIN	16	–	–				1	–	–									17	–	–
GOBLE STEVE	30	–	2	1	–	–	4	–	–									35	–	2
GODBOLD DARYL	–	2	–															–	2	–
GOFFEY HERBERT	32	–	9	3	–	–												35	–	9
GOODWIN STEVE	2	1	–				1	–	2	4	–	–						7	1	2
GORDON DALE	194	12	31	19	–	6	21	–	3				14	1	3			248	13	43
GORDON PETER	160	–	34	16	–	3												176	–	37
GOSS JEREMY	155	33	14	14	4	–	14	3	3				15	–	6			198	40	23
GOVIER STEVE	22	–	1	1	–	–	4	–	1	3	–	–						30	–	2
GRAHAM BILL	17	–	4	1	–	1												18	–	5
GRAHAM ROBERT	50	–	–	2	–	–												52	–	–
GRANT PETER	64	4	3	2	–	–	5	–	–									71	4	3
GRANVILLE DANNY	6	–	–															6	–	–
GRAPES STEVE	34	7	3	1	–	–	5	2	1	3	–	–						43	9	4
GRAY GEORGE	50	–	–	1	–	–												51	–	–
GREATREX JOHN	1	–	–															1	–	–
GREEN ROBERT	13	1	–				1	–	–									14	1	–
GREENWELL WILF	47	–	2	5	–	1												52	–	3
GUNN BRYAN	390	–	–	27	–	–	38	–	–				22	–	–			477	–	–
GURKIN JOHN	10	–	–															10	–	–
GUY JAMES	12	–	1															12	–	1

	FOOTBALL LEAGUE			FA CUP			LEAGUE CUP			TEXACO CUP			FMC/OTHER			DIV. 3 SOUTH CUP		TOTAL		
	APPRS.	SUBS.	GOALS	APPRS.	SUBS.	GOALS	APPRS.	SUBS.	GOALS	APPRS.	SUBS.	GOALS	APPRS.	SUBS.	GOALS	APPRS.	GOALS	APPRS.	SUBS.	GOALS
HALL BERTIE	2	–	–															2	–	–
HALL FRED	90	–	–	4	–	–												94	–	–
HALLIDAY TOM	191	–	–	11	–	–										1	–	203	–	–
HALSEY MARK	3	–	–															3	–	–
HAMILTON DES	7	–	–															7	–	–
HANNAH JOE	398	–	19	25	–	3										4	–	427	–	22
HANSBURY ROGER	78	–	–				6	–	–									84	–	–
HANSELL RON	29	–	7	7	–	3												36	–	10
HAREIDE AAGE	38	2	2	8	–	1	6	–	–									52	2	3
HARLEY ALEX	1	–	–															1	–	–
HARRIS ARTHUR	1	–	–															1	–	–
HART ANDREW	–	1	–															–	1	–
HARTFORD ASA	28	–	2	4	–	–	8	–	3									40	–	5
HAYLOCK PAUL	154	1	3	13	1	1	22	–	–				1	1	–			190	3	4
HEATH DON	79	3	15	6	–	3	3	–	–									88	3	18
HEFFER BOB	2	–	1															2	–	1
HEPPLE GORDON	5	–	–															5	–	–
HETHERINGTON JOE	1	–	–															1	–	–
HEWITT JOHN	13	–	2	2	–	–												15	–	2
HIGGINS ALEX	7	–	2															7	–	2
HILL JIMMY	161	–	55	25	–	5	9	–	6									195	–	66
HILL KEN	44	–	–	1	–	–	5	–	–									50	–	–
HINTON WILLIAM	3	–	–															3	–	–
HOADLEY PHIL	74	3	–	2	–	–	10	–	1									86	3	1
HOCKEY TREVOR	13	–	–															13	–	–
HODGE JAMES	51	–	1	4	–	–												55	–	1
HODGSON DAVID	3	3	1	1	–	–	1	–	3				1	–	–			6	3	4
HOLD OSCAR	44	–	18	3	–	2												47	–	20
HOLLIS ROY	96	–	52	11	–	7												107	–	59
HOLMES BERT	58	–	1	1	–	–												59	–	1
HOLT GARY	7	1	–				1	–	–									8	1	–
HOOPER CHARLIE	3	–	–	1	–	1												4	–	1
HOPE PHILIP	98	–	1	11	–	–												109	–	1
HOPEWELL HARRY	27	–	–															27	–	–
HOUGHTON HAROLD	52	–	10	4	–	–												56	–	10
HOWARD TREVOR	81	42	13	6	–	1	15	3	5	9	–	–						111	45	19
HOWELL HENRY	4	–	–															4	–	–
HOWIE SCOTT	1	1	–															1	1	–
HOWSHALL GERRY	36	4	–				1	2	–									37	6	–
HUBBARD PHIL	6	4	1															6	4	1
HUGHES PAUL	2	2	1															2	2	1
HUNT MORGAN	7	–	–	1	–	–												8	–	–
HUNT RALPH	124	–	67	8	–	5												132	–	72
HUNT THOMAS	50	–	33	1	–	–												51	–	33
JACK ROSS	31	25	10	2	1	2	6	2	2									39	28	14
JACKSON JAMES	111	–	54	8	–	3												119	–	57
JACKSON MATT	158	3	6	5	–	–	6	–	–									169	3	6
JARVIE JOHN	42	–	–	2	–	–												44	–	–
JOBLING JOE	72	–	1	4	–	–												76	–	1
JOHNSON ALEX	5	–	–															5	–	–
JOHNSON ANDY	56	10	13	2	–	–	6	1	2									64	11	15
JOHNSON RALPH	18	–	8	5	–	2												23	–	10
JOHNSTON TOM	60	–	28	7	–	5												67	–	33
JONES ALLAN	9	–	–															9	–	–
JONES BRYN	23	–	1	3	–	1												26	–	2
JONES DAVID	120	3	4	6	–	1	2	1	–									128	4	5
JONES DENYS	5	–	2	1	–	–												6	–	2
JONES ORMOND	9	–	–	1	–	–												10	–	–
JONES SID	40	–	9	8	–	1												48	–	10
JORDAN HUGH	18	–	3	2	–	–												20	–	3
JOY HAROLD	8	–	4															8	–	4
KEARNS FRED	28	–	11	2	–	3												30	–	14
KEATING REG	2	–	–	1	–	–												3	–	–
KEELAN KEVIN	571	–	–	31	–	–	57	–	–	14	–	–						673	–	–
KEELING HARRY	5	–	1															5	–	1
KELL LEN	2	–	–															2	–	–
KELLOCK BILLY	1	2	–				1	–	1									2	2	1
KELLY PHIL	114	1	2	7	–	–	13	–	1									134	1	3
KENNING MIKE	44	–	9	3	–	2	3	–	–									50	–	1
KENNON SANDY	213	–	–	19	–	–	23	–	–									255	–	–
KENT PAUL	1	2	–							1	–	–						2	2	–
KENTON DARREN	80	12	4	–	2	–	9	1	–									89	15	4
KIDGER EDMUND	4	–	–															4	–	–
KING ALFRED	3	–	–															3	–	–
KINSEY NOEL	223	–	57	20	–	8												243	–	65
KIRCHEN ALF	14	–	7	4	–	3												18	–	10
KITCHENER RAY	18	–	–	1	–	–												19	–	–
KNOX WILLIAM	3	–	–															3	–	–
LAMB JOSEPH	80	–	2	6	–	–												86	–	2
LARKIN BUNNY	41	–	12	4	–	2	3	–	2									48	–	16
LASKEY RUSSELL	4	–	2															4	–	2
LAW GEORGE	6	–	2															6	–	2

	FOOTBALL LEAGUE			FA CUP			LEAGUE CUP			TEXACO CUP			FMC/OTHER			DIV. 3 SOUTH CUP		TOTAL		
	APPRS.	SUBS.	GOALS	APPRS.	SUBS.	GOALS	APPRS.	SUBS.	GOALS	APPRS.	SUBS.	GOALS	APPRS.	SUBS.	GOALS	APPRS.	GOALS	APPRS.	SUBS.	GOALS
LAXTON EDWARD	16	–	–															16	–	–
LEWIS BILL	232	–	1	24	–	–												256	–	1
LIBBRA MARC SYLVAIN-RENE	–	3	2				1	–	–									1	3	2
LINIGHAN ANDY	86	–	8	10	–	–	6	–	–				4	–	–			108	–	8
LIVERMORE DOUG	113	1	4	4	–	–	13	–	2	8	–	–						138	1	6
LLEWELLYN CHRIS	98	28	17	3	1	1	7	2	–									108	31	18
LOCHHEAD DOUG	209	–	5	11	–	–												220	–	5
LOCKWOOD ROY	36	–	–	1	–	–												37	–	–
LONGDON SAM	3	–	–															3	–	–
LOW NORMAN	150	–	–	13	–	–												163	–	–
LUCAS MAL	180	3	8	12	–	–	9	–	2									201	3	10
LUMLEY WILLIAM	24	–	6	5	–	–												29	–	6
LYTHGOE DERRICK	62	–	22	4	–	1	8	–	6									74	–	29
LYTHGOE JOHN	14	–	3	1	–	–												15	–	3
LYTHGOE PHIL	9	3	1															9	3	1
McCOY PETER	6	–	–															6	–	–
McCROHAN ROY	385	–	20	34	–	2	7	–	1									426	–	23
McCUDDEN FRANK	38	–	14	3	–	–												41	–	14
McDONALD COLIN	4	–	–															4	–	–
McDOWELL JOHN	40	1	1	2	–	–	2	–	–									44	1	1
McGOVERN BRIAN	3	12	1				2	1	–									5	13	1
McGRAE JOE	114	–	3	10	–	–												124	–	3
McGUIRE MICK	172	10	11	8	1	–	12	–	1									192	11	12
McKENNA FRANK	41	–	18	3	–	–												44	–	18
McKINNEY DANIEL	48	–	4	4	–	–												52	–	4
McLAVERTY BERNARD	55	–	4	1	–	–												56	–	4
McMILLAN TOM	19	–	2															19	–	2
McNEIL MATT	44	–	2															44	–	2
McVEIGH PAUL	8	6	2				1	1	–									9	7	2
McWHIRR JAMES	1	–	1	3	–	1												4	–	2
MACDOUGALL TED	112	–	51	7	–	2	15	–	9	4	–	4						138	–	66
MACHIN MEL	93	3	4	6	–	–	13	1	–	1	–	–						113	4	4
MACKAY MALKY	78	13	2	2	–	1	6	1	–									86	14	3
MACKRELL JAMES	38	–	–	1	–	–												39	–	–
MADDEN OWEN	22	–	1	3	–	–												25	–	1
MALLENDER KEN	46	–	1	1	–	–	1	–	–									48	–	1
MANDERS FRANK	130	–	40	7	–	3												137	–	43
MANNING JOHN	60	–	21	4	–	1	3	–	–									67	–	22
MANNION GERRY	100	–	17	9	–	1	10	–	3									119	–	21
MANSFIELD FRED	34	–	–	3	–	–												37	–	–
MARSHALL ANDY	194	1	–	5	1	–	18	–	–									217	2	–
MARSHALL LEE	95	22	11	2	–	–	11	1	2									108	23	13
MARTIN GEORGE	223	–	1	20	–	–												243	–	1
MASKELL LES	7	–	2															7	–	2
MASON ARTHUR	7	–	–	1	–	–												8	–	–
MEGSON GARY	42	4	1	4	–	–	1	–	–				2	1	–			49	5	1
MELLON DAVID	1	–	–															1	–	–
MELLOR IAN	28	1	2	1	–	–	5	1	4	7	–	3						41	2	
MENDHAM PETER	200	11	23	24	–	3	25	2	2				5	–	1			254	13	29
METCALF ARTHUR	2	–	–															2	–	–
METCALF COLIN	12	–	1				1	–	–									13	–	1
METCALF MARK	–	1	–															–	1	–
MIDDLETON JOHN	3	–	–															3	–	–
MILBURN JOHN	15	–	–															15	–	–
MILLER ALISTAIR	23	–	2				2	–	–									25	–	2
MILLER JOHN	22	1	3				6	–	2									28	1	5
MILLIGAN MIKE	113	11	5	6	–	–	11	1	–									130	12	5
MILLS DANNY	46	20	–	2	–	–	3	2	1									51	22	1
MILLS JAMES	6	–	3															6	–	3
MILNE MAURICE	5	–	–															5	–	–
MINETT JASON	–	3	–															–	3	–
MOLBY JAN	3	–	–				2	–	1									5	–	1
MOORE NEIL	2	–	–															2	–	–
MORAN JAMES	36	–	17	4	–	1												40	–	18
MORGAN DENIS	225	–	3	25	–	–												250	–	3
MORGAN GEORGE	65	–	15	2	–	–												67	–	15
MORRIS PETER	66	–	1	3	–	–	14	–	–	3	–	–						86	–	1
MORRIS ROBERT	41	–	–	1	–	–										4	–	46	–	–
MORTENSEN HENRIK	12	6	–	–	1	1							2	2	1			14	9	2
MOULE ALF	32	–	11	3	–	1												35	–	12
MOUNTFORD PETER	1	3	–															1	3	–
MULLETT JOE	211	2	2	17	–	2	18	–	1									246	2	5
MULRYNE PHIL	44	4	3	1	–	–	5	–	–									50	4	3
MURPHY JOHN	35	–	–	1	–	–												36	–	–
MURPHY LIONEL	128	–	24	4	–	1												132	–	25
MUZINIC DRAZEN	15	4	–				2	2	–									17	6	–
NEDERGAARD STEEN	11	7	1				1	2	–									12	9	1
NEIGHBOUR JIMMY	104	2	5	4	–	–	5	–	–									113	2	5
NETHERCOTT KEN	378	–	–	38	–	–												416	–	–
NEWMAN ROB	181	24	14	13	–	1	22	2	2				7	–	–			223	26	17
NEWSOME JON	61	1	7	5	–	1	9	–	–									75	1	8
NIGHTINGALE MARK	28	7	–				4	–	–									32	7	–

	FOOTBALL LEAGUE			FA CUP			LEAGUE CUP			TEXACO CUP			FMC/OTHER			DIV. 3 SOUTH CUP		TOTAL		
	APPRS.	SUBS.	GOALS	APPRS.	SUBS.	GOALS	APPRS.	SUBS.	GOALS	APPRS.	SUBS.	GOALS	APPRS.	SUBS.	GOALS	APPRS.	GOALS	APPRS.	SUBS.	GOALS
NIXON BILL	1	–	–															1	–	–
NOBLE ARTHUR	1	–	–															1	7	–
NORMAN MAURICE	35	–	–															35	–	–
NORTH ERNEST	56	–	19	4	–	1												60	–	20
NOTMAN ALEX	10	6	1	–	1	–												10	7	1
O'BRIEN MICK	64	–	5	1	–	1												65	–	5
O'DONNELL NEIL	31	19	2	1	–	–	8	–	–	5	–	1						45	19	3
O'NEILL JOHN	1	–	–															1	–	–
O'NEILL KEITH	54	19	9	3	–	–	8	3	1									65	22	10
OGLE ROGER	1	–	–															1	–	–
O'HAGAN WILLIAM	53	–	–	4	–	–												57	–	–
OLIVER JIM	40	–	14	1	–	–	6	–	3									47	–	17
O'NEILL MARTIN	65	1	12	4	–	–	5	–	1									74	1	13
O'REILLY JOHN	33	–	11	4	–	1												37	–	12
OSBORNE HAROLD	1	–	–															1	–	–
OSGOOD PETER	3	–	–															3	–	–
OTTOSSON ULF	4	3	1	–	1	–												4	4	1
OWENS LES	20	–	8															20	–	8
OXFORD KEN	128	–	–	8	–	–												136	–	–
PADDON GRAHAM	288	2	25	11	–	1	28	–	9	11	–	2						338	2	37
PAINTER TREVOR	2	–	–															2	–	–
PARKER JOHN	11	–	2	1	–	–												12	–	2
PARKER SCOTT	6	–	1															6	–	1
PARNELL DENIS	2	–	–															2	–	–
PAYNE CLIVE	122	3	–	3	–	–	16	–	2	6	–	1						147	3	3
PEARCE WILLIAM	19	–	2	2	–	–												21	–	2
PEARSON JAMES	19	–	3	1	–	–												20	–	3
PEART JACK	21	–	6	3	–	2												24	–	8
PEED FRANK	17	–	4	2	–	2												19	–	6
PEGG FRANK	6	–	2															6	–	2
PEMBERY GORDON	1	–	–															1	–	–
PEMBLETON ARTHUR	18	–	–	3	–	–												21	–	–
PENNOCK ADRIAN	1	–	–															1	–	–
PERFECT FRANK	1	–	–															1	–	–
PESCHISOLIDO PAUL	3	2	–															3	2	–
PETERS MARTIN	206	1	44	12	–	3	13	–	3									231	1	50
PHELAN MIKE	155	1	9	11	–	1	14	–	–				13	–	–			193	1	10
PHILIPSON JOHN	1	–	–															1	–	–
PHILLIPS ALAN	4	–	3															4	–	3
PHILLIPS DAVE	152	–	9	14	–	1	12	–	–				8	–	1			186	–	20
PICKERING MIKE	–	1	–															–	1	–
PICKWICK DON	224	–	9	20	–	2												244	–	11
PIGGIN ALBERT	2	–	–															2	–	–
PIKE THEO	20	–	7													1	–	21	–	7
PLUNKETT SID	31	–	7	5	–	–												36	–	7
POINTER REG	11	–	–	1	–	–												12	–	–
POLSTON JOHN	200	15	8	17	1	1	20	1	2				9	–	1			246	17	12
PORTER ERNEST	130	–	30	9	–	1												139	–	31
POWELL TONY	235	2	3	11	–	–	27	–	2									273	2	5
POWER LEE	28	16	10	–	1	–	1	–	–				–	2	–			29	19	10
PRICE ERIC	16	–	6															16	–	6
PRICE RAY	1	–	–															1	–	–
PRIOR SPENCER	67	7	1	–	2	–	10	1	1				2	–	–			79	10	2
PROCTOR DAVID	17	–	–															17	–	–
PROCTOR HARRY	108	–	3	8	–	–												116	–	3
PROPHETT COLIN	34	1	–	1	–	–	5	–	–	7	–	–						47	1	–
PROUDLOVE ANDY	–	1	–				–	1	–									–	2	–
PUNTON BILL	219	–	24	16	–	2	21	–	3									256	–	29
PURDY ARTHUR	11	–	–	1	–	–												12	–	–
PUTNEY TREVOR	76	6	9	8	–	1	4	–	–				6	–	–			94	6	10
RACKHAM DERRICK	8	–	2	2	–	–												10	–	2
RAMSAY STAN	79	–	1	2	–	–										2	–	83	–	1
RATCLIFFE SIMON	6	3	–				2	–	–									8	3	–
RATTRAY PETER	24	–	5	3	–	–												27	–	5
REAGAN MARTIN	34	–	4	2	–	–												36	–	4
REAY ARCHIE	2	–	–															2	–	–
REEVES KEVIN	118	1	37	5	–	–	9	–	5									132	1	42
REID ERNIE	5	–	–	2	–	–												7	–	–
REILLY LEN	30	–	–															30	–	–
RICHARDS JOHN	5	–	2															5	–	2
RICHMOND JOE	124	–	9	6	–	–												130	–	9
RIGBY JON	7	3	–															7	3	–
RIPLEY KEITH	12	–	6															12	–	6
ROBB DAVID	4	1	1				1	–	–									5	1	1
ROBERTS IWAN	161	7	57	3	–	1	14	3	10									178	10	68
ROBINS MARK	57	10	20				6	3	1				1	1	–			64	14	21
ROBINSON BERNARD	360	–	13	17	–	1										3	–	380	–	14
ROBINSON JOE	2	–	–															2	–	–
ROBINSON LES	31	–	10	3	–	2												34	–	12
ROBINSON ROBERT	34	–	–	1	–	–										2	–	37	–	–
ROBSON KEITH	61	4	13	1	1	1	4	–	–									66	5	14
ROCASTLE DAVID	11	–	–															11	–	–

	FOOTBALL LEAGUE			FA CUP			LEAGUE CUP			TEXACO CUP			FMC/OTHER			DIV. 3 SOUTH CUP		TOTAL		
	APPRS.	SUBS.	GOALS	APPRS.	SUBS.	GOALS	APPRS.	SUBS.	GOALS	APPRS.	SUBS.	GOALS	APPRS.	SUBS.	GOALS	APPRS.	GOALS	APPRS.	SUBS.	GOALS
ROGERS JOHN	12	–	4	1	–	–												13	–	4
ROLLINGS ANDY	4	–	–							3	–	–						7	–	–
RONSON BRIAN	1	–	–															1	–	–
ROSARIO ROBERT	115	12	18	13	1	3	11	–	3				8	1	5			147	14	29
ROWE GEORGE	3	–	–															3	–	–
ROWELL GARY	2	4	1															2	4	1
ROWELL JOE	1	–	–															1	–	–
ROWLANDS TREVOR	10	–	2	1	–	–												11	–	2
ROY JOHN	6	–	–													4	1	10	–	1
ROYLE JOE	40	2	9	2	–	–	2	1	1									44	3	10
RULE ALAN	8	–	–															8	–	–
RUSH MATTHEW	–	3	–															–	3	–
RUSSELL CECIL	56	–	23	5	–	–												61	–	23
RUSSELL DAREL	72	20	7	2	–	–	8	–	2									82	20	9
RUSSELL JAMES	12	–	2	2	–	–												14	–	2
RYAN JOHN	113	3	26	7	–	–	8	1	3									128	4	29
RYDER TERRY (senior)	3	–	–															3	–	–
RYDER TERRY (junior)	46	–	12	5	–	–												51	–	12
SARGEANT CHARLES	13	–	1															13	–	1
SARGENT GARY	–	1	–															–	1	–
SAVINO RAY	22	–	3	2	–	–	3	–	1									27	–	4
SCOTT DICK	28	–	1	1	–	–	7	–	2									36	–	3
SCOTT JACK	33	–	–	8	–	1										4	–	45	–	1
SCOTT JOHN	10	–	4															10	–	4
SCOTT KEITH	10	15	5	–	2	–	–	2	–									10	19	5
SCOTT KEVIN	31	2	–	1	–	–	1	1	–									33	3	–
SCOTT SIDNEY	21	–	–	5	–	1												26	–	1
SCOTT THOMAS	53	–	26	2	–	–												55	–	26
SEAGRAVES MARK	3	–	–															3	–	–
SELF GLENN	4	1	2				1	–	–									5	1	2
SHARPE FREDDIE	107	4	–	7	–	–	8	–	–									122	4	–
SHAW COLIN	3	–	–				1	–	–									4	–	–
SHEFFIELD JON	1	–	–															1	–	–
SHEFFIELD LAURIE	27	–	16	2	–	–												29	–	16
SHEPHERD GREIG	13	3	2	–	1	–	2	–	–									15	4	2
SHERON MIKE	19	9	2	4	–	2	6	–	3									29	9	7
SHERWOOD TIM	66	5	10	4	–	–	7	–	1				5	1	2			82	6	13
SHORT JAMES	11	–	3															11	–	3
SILVERTHORNE JAMES	20	–	7	2	–	1												22	–	8
SILVESTER PETER	99	1	37	2			11	–	–									112	1	37
SIMONS HENRY	3	–	–															3	–	–
SIMPSON KARL	4	6	–				1	–	–									5	6	–
SISSONS JOHN	17	–	2				3	–	1	–	1	–						20	1	3
SKERMER HERBERT	67	–	–	6	–	–												73	–	–
SLACK WILLIAM	29	–	2	2	–	–												31	–	2
SLICER JACKY	125	–	12	8	–	2												133	–	14
SLOAN PADDY	6	–	–															6	–	–
SMALLEY TOM	42	–	1	1	–	–												43	–	1
SMITH BEN	73	–	–	8	–	–												81	–	–
SMITH COLIN	2	2	–				1	–	–									3	2	–
SMITH DAVID	13	5	–	2	1	–	1	1	–									16	7	–
SMITH JAMES	31	–	–	1	–	–												32	–	–
SMITH KEN	10	–	–															10	–	–
SMITH SAM	1	–	–															1	–	–
SMITH SYDNEY	3	–	–															3	–	–
SMITH TOM	1	–	–															1	–	–
SMITH WILLIAM	98	–	1	3	–	–										1	–	102	–	1
SPEARING TONY	67	2	–	4	–	–	5	–	–				4	–	–			80	2	–
SPELMAN RON	2	–	–				1	–	1									3	–	1
SPINKS HENRY	2	–	1															2	–	1
STATON BARRY	23	–	1	5	–	–	3	–	–									31	–	1
STEELE BILLY	56	12	3	1	–	–	5	–	–	1	1	–						63	13	3
STENNER ARTHUR	6	–	–															6	–	–
STEPHENSON JOHN	19	–	2	2	–	–												21	–	2
STEWART EDDIE	13	–	–															13	–	–
STEWART ROBERT	15	–	–															15	–	–
STOAKES JAMES	140	–	5	10	–	1												150	–	6
STRINGER DAVE	417	2	18	24	–	–	42	–	4	14	–	–						497	2	22
STURGESS ALBERT	47	–	–	5	–	–												52	–	–
SUGGETT COLIN	200	3	21	10	–	2	23	–	5	7	–	1						240	3	29
SULLIVAN COLIN	154	3	3	8	–	–	16	–	–	1	–	–						179	3	3
SUMMERS JOHNNY	71	–	33	5	–	3												76	–	36
SUTCH DARYL	249	37	9	9	3	–	24	3	–				2	3	–			284	46	9
SUTTON CHRIS	89	12	35	10	–	5	8	1	3				6	–	–			113	13	43
SUTTON MIKE	46	5	3	1	–	–	2	–	–									49	5	3
SYMONDS RICHARD	55	4	–	4	–	–	4	1	–									63	5	–
TANNER NICK	6	–	–															6	–	–
TAYLOR ALAN	21	7	6	1	–	–	3	1	2				–	1	–			25	9	8
TAYLOR GEOFF	1	–	–															1	–	–
TAYLOR JACK	50	–	–	6	–	–												56	–	–
TAYLOR WALTER	2	–	–															2	–	–

	FOOTBALL LEAGUE			FA CUP			LEAGUE CUP			TEXACO CUP			FMC/OTHER			DIV. 3 SOUTH CUP		TOTAL		
	APPRS.	SUBS.	GOALS	APPRS.	SUBS.	GOALS	APPRS.	SUBS.	GOALS	APPRS.	SUBS.	GOALS	APPRS.	SUBS.	GOALS	APPRS.	GOALS	APPRS.	SUBS.	GOALS
TAYLOR WILLIAM	13	–	2	1	–	–												14	–	2
TENNANT WILLIAM	10	–	1	2	–	–												12	–	1
THOMPSON ANDREW	12	–	2	2	–	1												14	–	3
THOMPSON JAMES	28	–	17	2	–	–												30	–	17
THOMSON NORMAN	16	–	–															16	–	–
THORPE ALBERT	61	–	–	1	–	–												62	–	–
THURLOW BRYAN	193	–	1	21	–	–	10	–	–									224	–	1
TOBIN MAURICE	102	–	–	3	–	–												105	–	–
TOWNSEND ANDY	66	5	8	10	–	2	3	1	–				3	–	–			82	6	10
TRACEY SIMON	1	–	–	2	–	–												3	–	–
TRAVERS GEORGE	29	–	14	1	–	–												30	–	14
TURNER DAVID	3	–	–															3	–	–
ULLATHORNE ROBERT	86	8	7	7	1	–	10	2	1				1	–	–			104	11	8
VAN WIJK DENNIS	109	9	3	15	–	1	16	1	–				5	–	–			145	10	4
VARCO PERCY	57	–	37	8	–	10												65	–	47
VASPER PETER	31	–	–	1	–	–												32	–	–
VINALL JACK	168	–	72	9	–	5										4	3	181	–	80
de WAARD RAYMOND	4	6	–				1	2	–									5	8	–
WAITES GEORGE	36	–	11	2	–	–	2	–	–									40	–	11
WALFORD STEVE	93	–	2	7	–	–	8	–	–									108	–	2
WALKER CYRIL	3	–	2															3	–	2
WALLS NICK	30	–	2	1	–	–												31	–	2
WALLBANKS JAMES	3	–	–															3	–	–
WALSH MICK	5	–	–															5	–	–
WALSH STEVE	1	3	–				1	–	–									2	3	–
WALTON MARK	22	–	–	5	–	–	1	–	–									28	–	–
WARD ASHLEY	53	–	18	1	–	–	6	–	3									60	–	21
WARE HARRY	43	–	13	2	–	1												45	–	14
WARNES BILLY	112	–	45	2	–	1										4	3	118	–	49
WATSON DAVE	212	–	11	18	–	1	21	–	3				5	–	–			256	–	15
WATT MICHAEL	7	1	–	1	–	–												8	1	–
WEIR JAMES	9	–	–															9	–	–
WHARTON NORMAN	101	–	–	6	–	–										2	–	109	–	–
WHING JOHN	7	–	–															7	–	–
WHITEHOUSE BRIAN	41	–	14	3	–	1	5	–	3									49	–	18
WHITHAM VIC	9	–	3	1	–	–												10	–	3
WHITLEY JIM	7	1	1															7	1	1
WIGG PERCY	9	–	3															9	–	3
WILKINSON REG	102	–	7	5	–	2												107	–	9
WILLIAMS ALAN	1	–	–															1	–	–
WILLIAMS DAVID	56	4	11	1	–	–	7	–	–				6	–	1			70	4	12
WILLIAMS GRENVILLE	40	–	–	3	–	–												43	–	–
WILLIAMS ROD	19	–	9													1	3	20	–	12
WILLIAMS THOMAS	27	–	13	1	–	–												28	–	13
WILLIAMSON ERNEST	43	–	–	4	–	–												47	–	–
WILLIAMSON IAN	10	–	1															10	–	1
WILLIAMSON TOM	82	–	4	3	–	–												85	–	4
WILLIS GRAHAM	1	–	–															1	–	–
WILSON CHE	16	6	–				3	–	–									19	6	–
WILSON GORDON	2	–	–													1	–	3	–	–
WILSON JOHN	47	–	–	1	–	–												48	–	–
WILSON JOSEPH	41	–	4															41	–	4
WILSON LES	6	–	–				2	–	–	3	–	–						11	–	–
WILSON PAUL	–	1	–															–	1	–
WILSON ROBERT	62	–	–	4	–	–												66	–	–
WINGHAM HARRY	43	–	1	1	–	–												44	–	1
WISEMAN GEORGE	8	–	–															8	–	–
WOAN ALAN	21	–	7	2	–	1												23	–	8
WOODFORD GEORGE	10	–	–															10	–	–
WOODHOUSE CHRIS	13	–	3	5	–	2												18	–	5
WOODS CHRIS	216	–	–	19	–	–	26	–	–				6	–	–			267	–	–
WOODS CLIVE	29	3	4				5	–	–									34	3	4
WOODTHORPE COLIN	36	7	1	6	–	–	–	2	–				1	1	–			43	10	1
WOOLLEY ROBERT	3	–	–															3	–	–
WOOLMER TONY	4	1	1															4	1	1
WORRELL COLIN	9	–	–				1	–	–									10	–	–
WORTON ALFRED	23	–	–															23	–	–
WREN THOMAS	2	–	–															2	–	–
WRIGHT JONNY	5	2	–															5	2	–
WRIGHT STEPHEN	36	–	1	4	–	–												40	–	1
YOUNG WILLIE	5	1	–				1	–	–									6	1	–
OWN GOALS			64			4			5			2								75

TOP 50 APPEARANCES COMPETITIVE GAMES
1902–03 TO 2000–01 (up to and including 31.08.01)

1	KEVIN KEELAN	673
2	RON ASHMAN	662
3	DAVE STRINGER	499
4	BRYAN GUNN	477
5	JOE HANNAH	427
6	ROY McCROHAN	426
7	IAN CROOK	418T
8	KEN NETHERCOTT	416
9	MARK BOWEN	399
10	TERRY ALLCOCK	389
11	BERNARD ROBINSON	380
12	IAN CULVERHOUSE	369
13	DUNCAN FORBES	357
14	BARRY BUTLER	349
15	GRAHAM PADDON	340
16	JOHNNY GAVIN	338
17	GEORGE MARTIN	337
18	*DARYL SUTCH	330
19	ROBERT FLECK	299
20	IAN BUTTERWORTH	293
21	TOMMY BRYCELAND	284
22	TERRY ANDERSON	279
23	TONY POWELL	275
24	PETER MENDHAM	267
	CHRIS WOODS	267
26	JOHN POLSTON	263
27	DALE GORDON	261
28	BILL LEWIS	256
	BILL PUNTON	256
	DAVE WATSON	256
31	SANDY KENNON	255
32	BOBBY BRENNAN	250
	DENIS MORGAN	250
34	ROBERT NEWMAN	249
35	JOE MULLETT	248
36	DON PICKWICK	244
37	NOEL KINSEY	243
	COLIN SUGGETT	243
39	REG FOULKES	238
	JERRY GOSS	238
41	MARTIN PETERS	232
42	BRYAN THURLOW	224
43	MARK BARHAM	223
44	DOUG LOCHHEAD	220
45	RUEL FOX	219
	ANDY MARSHALL	219
47	MATT CROWE	214
48	CHARLIE DENNINGTON	209
49	NEIL ADAMS	206
	GREG DOWNS	206

NB – The above totals include substitute appearances.
* – Denotes current player.

TOP 20 GOALSCORERS COMPETITIVE GAMES
1902–03 TO 2000–01 (up to and including 31.08.01)

1	JOHNNY GAVIN	132
2	TERRY ALLCOCK	127
3	ROBERT FLECK	84
4	JACK VINALL	80
5	RALPH HUNT	72
6	JOHN DEEHAN	70
7	LES EYRE	69
8	*IWAN ROBERTS	68
9	RON DAVIES	66
	JIMMY HILL	66
	TED MACDOUGALL	66
12	NOEL KINSEY	65
13	KEN BURDITT	61
14	ROY HOLLIS	59
15	KEVIN DRINKELL	57
	KEN FOGGO	57
	JAMES JACKSON	57
18	RON ASHMAN	56
19	TOMMY BRYCELAND	55
20	HUGH CURRAN	53

* – Denotes current player.

NORWICH CITY PLAYER OF THE YEAR
BARRY BUTLER MEMORIAL TROPHY

1966/67	TERRY ALLCOCK
1967/68	HUGH CURRAN
1968/69	KEN FOGGO
1969/70	DUNCAN FORBES
1970/71	KEN FOGGO
1971/72	DAVE STRINGER
1972/73	KEVIN KEELAN
1973/74	KEVIN KEELAN
1974/75	COLIN SUGGETT
1975/76	MARTIN PETERS
1976/77	MARTIN PETERS
1977/78	JOHN RYAN
1978/79	TONY POWELL
1979/80	KEVIN BOND
1980/81	JOE ROYLE
1981/82	GREG DOWNS
1982/83	DAVE WATSON
1983/84	CHRIS WOODS
1984/85	STEVE BRUCE
1985/86	KEVIN DRINKELL
1986/87	KEVIN DRINKELL
1987/88	BRYAN GUNN
1988/89	DALE GORDON
1989/90	MARK BOWEN
1990/91	IAN CULVERHOUSE
1991/92	ROBERT FLECK
1992/93	BRYAN GUNN
1993/94	CHRIS SUTTON
1994/95	JON NEWSOME
1995/96	SPENCER PRIOR
1996/97	DARREN EADIE
1997/98	MATT JACKSON
1998/99	IWAN ROBERTS
1999/00	IWAN ROBERTS
2000/01	ANDY MARSHALL

THE NORWICH CITY RECORD IN THE FOOTBALL LEAGUE
1920–21 TO 2000–01 (up to and including 31.08.01)

The 2000–01 season was City's 75th in the Football League. During the season City will play their 1000th game in Division 1. The full record in each division of the football league is as follows:

PREMIER

3 Seasons **P** 126 **W** 43 **D** 39 **L** 44 **F** 163 **A** 180

DIVISION 1

24 Seasons **P** 976 **W** 302 **D** 296 **L** 378 **F** 1134 **A** 1358

DIVISION 2

20 Seasons **P** 840 **W** 329 **D** 209 **L** 302 **F** 1231 **A** 1208

DIVISION 3 & 3 (SOUTH)

28 Seasons **P** 1216 **W** 469 **D** 315 **L** 432 **F** 1950 **A** 1831

Norwich City have played 90 teams in the Football League and among this total are six that are no longer members, namely – Aberdare Athletic, Accrington Stanley, Bradford Park Avenue, Doncaster Rovers, Merthyr Town and Thames. City have yet to play a league match against 11 of the current members – Cheltenham, Chester, Darlington, Hartlepool, Hereford, Kidderminster, Macclesfield, Peterborough, Rushden, Wigan, Wycombe. City need to win 14 games more than they lose to have an overall winning record and the club fully expect to score their 4,500th league goal.

DIVISION	YEAR	P	W	D	L	F	A	PTS	POS
3	1920–21	42	10	16	16	44	53	36	16
3 (s)	1921–22	42	12	13	17	50	62	37	15
3 (s)	1922–23	42	13	10	19	51	71	36	18
3 (s)	1923–24	42	16	8	18	60	59	40	11
3 (s)	1924–25	42	14	13	15	53	51	41	12
3 (s)	1925–26	42	15	9	18	58	73	39	16
3 (s)	1926–27	42	12	11	19	59	71	35	16
3 (s)	1927–28	42	10	16	16	66	70	36	17
3 (s)	1928–29	42	14	6	22	69	81	34	17
3 (s)	1929–30	42	18	10	14	88	77	46	8
3 (s)	1930–31	42	10	8	24	47	76	28	22
3 (s)	1931–32	42	17	12	13	76	67	46	10
3 (s)	1932–33	42	22	13	7	88	55	57	3
3 (3)	1933–34	42	25	11	6	88	49	61	1
2	1934–35	42	14	11	17	71	61	39	14
2	1935–36	42	17	9	16	72	65	43	11
2	1936–37	42	14	8	20	63	71	36	17
2	1937–38	42	14	11	17	56	74	39	14
2	1938–39	42	13	5	24	50	91	31	21
3 (s)	1946–47	42	10	8	24	64	100	28	21
3 (s)	1947–48	42	13	8	21	61	76	34	21
3 (s)	1948–49	42	16	12	14	67	49	44	10
3 (s)	1949–50	42	16	10	16	65	63	42	11
3 (s)	1950–51	46	25	14	7	82	45	64	2
3 (s)	1951–52	46	26	9	11	89	50	61	3
3 (s)	1952–53	46	25	10	11	99	55	60	4
3 (s)	1953–54	46	20	11	15	73	66	51	7
3 (s)	1954–55	46	18	10	18	60	60	46	12
3 (s)	1955–56	46	19	13	14	86	82	51	7
3 (s)	1956–57	46	8	15	23	61	94	31	24
3 (s)	1957–58	46	19	15	12	75	70	53	8
3	1958–59	46	22	13	11	89	62	57	4
3	1959–60	46	24	11	11	82	54	59	2
2	1960–61	42	20	9	13	70	53	49	4
2	1961–62	42	14	11	17	61	70	39	17
2	1962–63	42	17	8	17	80	79	42	11
2	1963–64	42	11	13	18	64	80	35	17
2	1964–65	42	20	7	15	61	57	47	6

DIVISION	YEAR	P	W	D	L	F	A	PTS	POS
2	1965–66	42	12	15	15	52	52	39	13
2	1966–67	42	13	14	15	49	55	40	11
2	1967–68	42	16	11	15	60	65	43	9
2	1968–69	42	15	10	17	53	66	40	13
2	1969–70	42	16	11	15	49	46	43	11
2	1970–71	42	15	14	13	54	52	44	10
2	1971–72	42	21	15	6	60	36	57	1
1	1972–73	42	11	10	21	36	63	32	20
1	1973–74	42	7	15	20	37	62	29	22
2	1974–75	42	20	13	9	58	37	53	3
1	1975–76	42	16	10	16	58	58	42	10
1	1976–77	42	14	9	19	47	64	37	16
1	1977–78	42	11	18	13	52	66	40	13
1	1978–79	42	7	23	12	51	57	37	16
1	1979–80	42	13	14	15	58	66	40	12
1	1980–81	42	13	7	22	49	73	33	20
2	1981–82	42	22	5	15	64	50	71	3
1	1982–83	42	14	12	16	52	58	54	14
1	1983–84	42	12	15	15	48	49	51	14
1	1984–85	42	13	10	19	46	64	49	20
2	1985–86	42	25	9	8	84	37	84	1
1	1986–87	42	17	17	8	53	51	68	5
1	1987–88	40	12	9	19	40	52	45	14
1	1988–89	38	17	11	10	48	45	62	4
1	1989–90	38	13	14	11	44	42	53	10
1	1990–91	38	13	6	19	59	64	45	15
1	1991–92	42	11	12	19	47	63	45	18
PREM	1992–93	42	21	9	12	61	65	72	3
PREM	1993–94	42	12	17	13	65	61	53	12
PREM	1994–95	42	10	13	19	37	54	43	20
1	1995–96	46	14	15	17	59	55	57	16
1	1996–97	46	17	12	17	63	68	63	13
1	1997–98	46	14	13	19	52	69	55	15
1	1998–99	46	15	17	14	62	61	62	9
1	1999–00	46	14	15	17	45	50	57	12
1	2000–01	46	14	12	20	46	58	54	15
1	2001–02	4	3	0	1	5	4	9	N/A
		3162	**1146**	**859**	**1157**	**4483**	**4581**		

LEAGUE RECORD CLUB BY CLUB
1920–21 TO 2000–01 (up to and including 31.08.01)

The last win over Q.P.R. was the 100th league fixture between the sides. The coming season affords us the chance of scoring our 100th goal against Coventry and there is another chance to improve our record against Wimbledon and Wolves

	ALL IN					
	P	W	D	L	F	A
Aberdare Athletic	12	4	4	4	20	17
Accrington Stanley	4	3	0	1	12	7
Aldershot	28	6	10	12	41	47
Arsenal	40	8	16	16	40	66
Aston Villa	46	15	13	18	66	70
Barnsley	24	6	10	8	27	28
Birmingham City	44	15	13	16	69	65
Blackburn Rovers	30	9	8	13	36	50
Blackpool	16	6	2	8	23	19
Bolton Wanderers	32	12	8	12	35	39
Bournemouth	50	20	13	17	83	71
Bradford City	12	4	7	1	18	10
Bradford Park Avenue	10	3	2	5	13	14
Brentford	40	17	8	15	60	67
Brighton & Hove Albion	64	21	21	22	86	96
Bristol City	56	28	15	13	88	67
Bristol Rovers	48	17	14	17	73	77
Burnley	18	6	3	9	25	28
Bury	32	15	6	11	59	43
Cambridge United	2	2	0	0	4	2
Cardiff City	32	18	5	9	55	43
Carlisle United	16	9	2	5	27	20
Charlton Athletic	64	19	16	29	87	95
Chelsea	30	12	10	8	42	34
Chesterfield	10	5	1	4	16	16
Colchester United	20	8	5	7	29	28
Coventry City	82	20	23	39	99	127
Crewe Alexandra	8	2	2	4	7	10
Crystal Palace	84	38	12	34	119	122
Derby County	44	19	14	11	63	49
Doncaster Rovers	6	5	0	1	10	6
Everton	40	13	13	14	54	57
Exeter City	52	20	12	20	79	68
Fulham	30	10	9	11	41	48
Gillingham	46	19	10	17	69	64
Grimsby Town	22	11	7	4	37	23
Halifax Town	4	3	1	0	8	2
Huddersfield Town	34	9	15	10	42	35
Hull Cty	22	9	4	9	24	23
Ipswich Town	68	24	11	33	69	108
Leeds United	36	14	8	14	59	51
Leicester City	32	12	8	12	46	44
Lincoln City	2	2	0	0	9	2
Liverpool	44	11	11	22	46	79
Luton Town	64	24	18	22	89	94

	ALL IN					
	P	W	D	L	F	A
Manchester City	47	7	18	22	45	76
Manchester United	48	9	12	27	41	82
Mansfield Town	8	3	3	2	19	16
Merthyr Town	20	11	6	3	39	18
Middlesbrough	42	14	11	17	48	63
Millwall	61	22	16	23	90	102
Newcastle United	42	12	12	18	44	67
Newport County	52	19	20	13	89	71
Northampton Town	58	20	18	20	92	92
Nottingham Forest	52	18	14	20	74	78
Notts. County	22	6	7	9	37	40
Oldham Athletic	18	7	4	7	23	26
Orient	48	25	12	11	85	51
Oxford United	20	11	4	5	30	23
Plymouth Argyle	56	18	13	25	63	84
Portsmouth	48	20	11	17	68	65
Port Vale	30	10	9	11	44	40
Preston North End	22	5	8	9	26	32
Queens Park Rangers	100	38	29	33	137	133
Reading	52	19	13	20	82	85
Rochdale	2	2	0	0	4	2
Rotherham United	18	8	2	8	30	30
Scunthorpe United	8	1	3	4	11	16
Sheffield United	46	15	15	16	60	59
Sheffield Wednesday	33	11	12	10	36	41
Shrewsbury Town	20	15	2	3	46	25
Southampton	76	25	23	28	115	123
Southend United	60	19	17	24	80	91
Stockport County	12	6	4	2	22	15
Stoke City	32	11	10	11	44	37
Sunderland	32	13	10	9	43	38
Swansea City	36	13	7	16	51	53
Swindon Town	76	30	23	23	126	116
Thames	4	1	1	2	7	3
Torquay United	38	16	11	11	75	52
Tottenham Hotspur	46	14	11	21	59	80
Tranmere Rovers	18	8	7	3	21	15
Walsall	38	16	7	15	69	73
Watford	76	31	27	18	138	101
West Bromwich Albion	34	10	11	13	42	51
West Ham United	38	13	11	14	52	62
Wimbledon	23	4	5	14	14	31
Wolverhampton Wanderers	32	6	8	18	27	57
Wrexham	6	5	1	0	16	7
York City	4	2	0	2	5	5

SOUTHERN LEAGUE

City were elected to the Southern League on Tuesday 30 May 1905. They remained in the Southern League until the Football League decided to extend its activity in the 1920–21 season. City achieved their highest position in this competition in their first season i.e. 1905–06. Later years saw them mostly in the lower half of the table. The full record is as follows:

YEAR	P	W	D	L	F	A	PTS.	POS.
1905–06	34	13	10	11	46	38	36	7
1906–07	38	15	12	11	57	48	42	8
1907–08	38	12	9	17	46	49	33	16
1908–09	40	12	11	17	59	75	35	19
1909–10	42	13	9	20	59	78	35	17
1910–11	38	15	8	15	46	48	38	10
1911–12	38	10	14	14	40	60	34	12
1912–13	38	10	9	19	39	50	29	18
1913–14	38	9	17	12	49	51	35	14
1914–15	38	11	14	13	53	56	36	13
1919–20	42	15	11	16	64	57	41	12
	424	135	124	165	558	610		

UNITED LEAGUE

The United League was constituted as a midweek competition. City only took part during the 1906–07 and 1908–09 seasons and although City were quite successful gates were small and uneconomic.

YEAR	P	W	D	L	F	A	PTS.	POS.
1906–07	14	6	4	4	34	22	16	4
1908–09	12	7	2	3	33	19	16	3
	26	13	6	7	67	41		

NORFOLK & SUFFOLK LEAGUE

This League was formed in the summer of 1897 and provided Norwich City with their first taste of competitive League football. The League was of course an amateur concern and City dropped out after they turned professional in 1905.

YEAR	P	W	D	L	F	A	PTS.	POS.
1902–03	14	8	0	6	34	33	16	3
1903–04	14	5	5	4	32	20	15	3
1904–05	16	10	4	2	33	16	24	1
	44	23	9	12	99	69		

F.A. CHALLENGE CUP

City first entered the competition in 1902–03 and have with the exception of the war years when the competition was suspended, taken part every season. One cup-tie was abondoned and has been included as an away draw. 101 different clubs have been met and the full record between 1902–03 and 2000–01 is as follows:

HOME						NEUTRAL						AWAY					
P	W	D	L	F	A	P	W	D	L	F	A	P	W	D	L	F	A
123	70	23	30	244	140	9	1	2	6	4	14	117	32	32	53	138	208

The draw for venue has been none too kind for City for they have had to travel away on 99 occasions while they have been dealt only 92 home draws. To City fans young and not so young the highlights will always be the magnificent cup run during the 1958–59 campaign. City pushed Luton Town to a semi-final replay and so nearly became the first Division 3 side to play in a Wembley Final. The record against all opponents in the competition is as follows:

	P	W	D	L	F	A
ARSENAL	3	1	0	2	2	7
ASTON VILLA	3	1	1	1	6	4
BARNSLEY	4	2	1	1	5	4
BATH CITY	1	1	0	0	2	0
BEDFORD TOWN	1	0	0	1	2	4
BIRMINGHAM CITY	4	1	3	0	3	2
BLACKBURN ROVERS	3	0	1	2	5	9
BLACKPOOL	2	1	1	0	4	2
BOLTON WANDERERS	3	0	1	2	2	5
BRADFORD CITY	5	0	2	3	3	7
BRENTFORD	3	0	0	3	2	7
BRIGHTON & HOVE ALBION	10	3	2	5	15	19
BRISTOL CITY	3	1	0	2	2	4
BRISTOL ROVERS	4	0	2	2	4	6
CAMBRIDGE UNITED	1	1	0	0	1	0
CARDIFF CITY	1	1	0	0	3	2
CHATHAM TOWN	2	2	0	0	11	1
CHELSEA	3	0	1	2	2	5
CHESTERFIELD	1	1	0	0	3	1
CLAPTON	1	0	0	1	1	3
CORINTHIANS	1	0	0	1	0	5
COVENTRY CITY	9	3	3	3	12	14
CRYSTAL PALACE	4	1	1	2	2	5
DARLINGTON	2	0	0	2	1	7
DERBY COUNTY	2	1	0	1	4	2
DONCASTER ROVERS	2	2	0	0	4	2
DORCHESTER TOWN	1	1	0	0	4	0
EVERTON	2	0	0	2	0	6
EXETER CITY	2	1	1	0	3	1
FOLKESTONE	3	2	0	1	5	3
FULHAM	1	0	0	1	1	2
GLOUCESTER CITY	1	1	0	0	3	2
GRAYS UNITED	2	0	1	1	2	3
GRIMSBY TOWN	3	1	0	2	1	4
HALIFAX TOWN	1	1	0	0	2	0
HARTLEPOOL UNITED	2	1	1	0	6	2
HARWICH & PARKESTON	1	1	0	0	4	2
HASTINGS & ST. LEONARDS	1	1	0	0	3	1
HASTINGS UNITED	2	1	1	0	6	3
HEADINGTON UNITED	1	1	0	0	4	2
HUDDERSFIELD TOWN	2	1	1	0	5	3
HULL CITY	1	0	0	1	0	3
ILFORD	2	2	0	0	8	2
IPSWICH TOWN	3	2	1	0	4	2
LEEDS UNITED	6	1	3	2	9	16
LEICESTER CITY	6	1	1	4	6	10
LEYTON ORIENT	3	1	1	1	4	3
LIVERPOOL	6	3	1	2	10	11
LOWESTOFT TOWN	2	1	0	1	4	6
LUTON	4	1	1	2	3	8
MANCHESTER CITY	3	1	0	2	2	12
MANCHESTER UNITED	5	3	0	2	7	7
MERTHYR TYDFIL	1	1	0	0	3	0
METROGAS	1	1	0	0	2	1
MILLWALL	1	1	0	0	2	1
NEWCASTLE UNITED	1	1	0	0	5	0
NEWPORT COUNTY	2	2	0	0	8	0
NORTHAMPTON TOWN	1	1	0	0	3	2
NOTTINGHAM FOREST	3	1	0	2	4	3
NOTTS. COUNTY	2	1	0	1	3	4
OXFORD CITY	2	1	1	0	4	1
POOLE TOWN	2	1	1	0	6	1
PORT VALE	1	1	0	0	3	1
PORTSMOUTH	2	0	1	1	1	3
QUEENS PARK RANGERS	4	0	2	2	4	9
READING	5	1	3	1	6	6
REDHILL	1	1	0	0	6	1
RHYL UNITED	1	1	0	0	1	0
ROCHDALE	4	2	2	0	4	2
SCUNTHORPE UNITED	1	1	0	0	4	1
SHEFFIELD UNITED	5	3	1	1	9	8
SHEFFIELD WEDNESDAY	5	1	0	4	5	10
SHEPPEY UNITED	1	1	0	0	2	0
SOUTHAMPTON	3	1	1	1	2	4
SOUTHEND UNITED	2	1	1	0	4	3
STOCKPORT COUNTY	1	1	0	0	2	0
STOKE CITY	1	1	0	0	1	0
SUNDERLAND	7	2	1	4	8	11
SUTTON UNITED	1	1	0	0	8	0
SWANSEA CITY	1	1	0	0	2	1
SWINDON TOWN	6	3	2	1	7	4
TONBRIDGE	2	1	1	0	3	2
TORQUAY UNITED	1	0	0	1	1	3
TOTTENHAM HOTSPUR	6	3	2	1	7	6
TUNBRIDGE WELLS	2	1	1	0	6	1
WALSALL	3	1	1	1	7	7
WALTHAMSTOWE GRANGE	1	1	0	0	6	0
WATFORD	1	1	0	0	2	0
WEST BROMWICH ALBION	3	0	0	3	0	5
WEST HAM UNITED	3	1	1	1	4	3
WEST NORWOOD	1	0	1	0	1	1
WELLINGTON TOWN	1	1	0	0	1	0
WIGAN	1	0	0	1	0	1
WIMBLEDON	1	1	0	0	3	1
WOLVERHAMPTON WANDERERS	3	0	1	2	4	9
WREXHAM	2	1	0	1	4	3
WYCOMBE WANDERERS	\1	1	0	0	2	0
YARMOUTH TOWN	1	1	0	0	2	1
YEOVIL TOWN	2	2	0	0	5	0
YORK CITY	2	1	1	0	2	1

LEAGUE CUP

(INCORPORATES ALL THE SPONSORED NAMES OF THE COMPETITION IN SUBSEQUENT SEASONS)

This competition has been very rewarding for Norwich City. Since its inauguration in the 1960–61 season, City have twice been winners and have twice been beaten in the Final. 63 different sides have been met. The draw has again been unkind, 46 home draws against 56 away. The full record is as follows up to and including 31.08.01:

HOME						NEUTRAL						AWAY					
P	W	D	L	F	A	P	W	D	L	F	A	P	W	D	L	F	A
81	53	16	12	162	77	4	1	0	3	2	8	93	37	25	31	141	113

	P	W	D	L	F	A
ALDERSHOT	2	1	1	0	4	0
ARSENAL	4	1	1	2	4	5
ASTON VILLA	4	0	0	4	2	9
BARNET	2	1	0	1	3	4
BIRMINGHAM CITY	3	1	1	1	4	3
BLACKBURN ROVERS	1	0	0	1	0	2
BLACKPOOL	5	3	1	1	13	6
BOLTON WANDERERS	7	2	4	1	8	3
BOURNEMOUTH	2	1	1	0	2	1
BRADFORD CITY	4	2	1	1	9	5
BRENTFORD	3	2	0	1	6	2
BRIGHTON & HOVE ALBION	2	1	0	1	2	1
BRISTOL ROVERS	2	0	1	1	2	4
BURNLEY	3	1	1	1	3	4
CARDIFF CITY	2	1	1	0	3	0
CARLISLE UNITED	5	3	2	0	14	4
CHARLTON ATHLETIC	4	4	0	0	7	0
CHELSEA	3	2	0	1	3	1
CHELTENHAM	2	1	0	1	3	2
CHESTER	4	3	1	0	9	4
CHESTERFIELD	1	1	0	0	3	2
DERBY COUNTY	2	1	0	1	4	4
EVERTON	2	1	0	1	2	4
EXETER CITY	1	1	0	0	3	1
FULHAM	3	1	0	2	1	6
GILLINGHAM	2	1	1	0	5	3
GRIMSBY TOWN	3	2	1	0	5	2
HALIFAX TOWN	1	1	0	0	7	1
HUDDERSFIELD TOWN	1	0	0	1	0	1
HULL CITY	2	1	0	1	2	2
IPSWICH TOWN	8	4	2	2	12	9
LEICESTER CITY	4	1	1	2	4	6

	P	W	D	L	F	A
LINCOLN CITY	1	1	0	0	3	2
LIVERPOOL	2	0	0	2	1	5
LUTON TOWN	1	1	0	0	2	0
MANCHESTER CITY	5	0	2	3	6	15
MANCHESTER UNITED	3	2	1	0	7	3
MIDDLESBROUGH	2	1	0	1	3	4
MILLWALL	4	3	1	0	9	4
NOTTS. COUNTY	2	2	0	0	4	0
OLDHAM ATHLETIC	1	1	0	0	6	2
OXFORD UNITED	3	0	1	2	4	7
PETERBOROUGH UNITED	2	1	1	0	1	0
PRESTON NORTH END	8	6	2	0	21	8
ROCHDALE	2	2	0	0	4	0
ROTHERHAM UNITED	4	2	2	0	6	2
SHEFFIELD UNITED	2	1	1	0	4	3
SHREWSBURY TOWN	3	1	1	1	3	2
SOUTHAMPTON	2	1	0	1	2	4
STOCKPORT COUNTY	1	1	0	0	5	1
STOKE CITY	2	0	0	2	1	4
SUNDERLAND	6	4	2	0	10	3
SWANSEA CITY	4	2	1	1	5	2
TORQUAY UNITED	2	2	0	0	9	3
TOTTENHAM HOTSPUR	2	0	0	2	1	3
TRANMERE ROVERS	2	1	1	0	5	3
WATFORD	2	2	0	0	5	0
WEST BROMWICH ALBION	4	2	2	0	6	1
WEST HAM UNITED	1	1	0	0	2	1
WIGAN	2	2	0	0	4	2
WOLVERHAMPTON WANDERERS	2	0	1	1	1	2
WORKINGTON	1	0	0	1	0	3
WREXHAM	2	2	0	0	9	3

SCREEN SPORT SUPER CUP

Played during the 1985–86 season as a substitute for European competition. As winner of the Milk Cup in 1984–85 City should have qualified for the UEFA Cup but because of the ban on Football League clubs they had to be content with domestic competition. Full record:

P	W	D	L	F	A
6	1	3	2	5	7

F.A. AMATEUR CUP

City took part in the F.A. Amateur Cup only twice (they were excluded in 1904–05 by an F.A. commission). In 1903–04 they preferred to continue in the Amateur Cup rather than continue in the F.A. Cup (see text for season). Full record:

YEAR	P	W	D	L	F	A
1902–03	2	1	0	1	7	4
1903–04	7	5	1	1	19	5

DIVISION 3 SOUTH CUP

This competition was competed for by Division 3 South clubs between 1933–34 and 1938–39. City only played in the 1933–34 competition as this was the year they won promotion to Division 2. They reached the semi-final before being eliminated by Torquay United. See season line-ups.

SOUTHERN CHARITY CUP

City competed in 1913–14 and 1914–15. The latter competition was abandoned with City being undefeated. See season line-ups.

TEXACO CUP

Another short lived competition that was squeezed out by a congestion of fixtures. Norwich City reached the final in 1972–73 and the semi-final in 1973–74. The following year the competition became a pre-season affair with City being eliminated in the group matches.

YEAR	P	W	D	L	F	A
1972–73	8	3	0	5	11	11
1973–74	6	4	0	2	8	5
1974–75	3	1	0	2	4	9

NORFOLK SENIOR CUP

City's first team only took part in this competition on two occasions (1902–03 & 1903–04). They were eliminated at the first hurdle in both seasons. See season line-ups.

UEFA CUP

P	W	D	L	F	A
6	2	2	2	6	4

SIMOD CUP

P	W	D	L	F	A
2	1	0	1	3	4

FULL MEMBERS CUP

P	W	D	L	F	A
16	8	2	6	26	23

PENALTIES SCORED IN COMPETITIVE MATCHES 1902–03 TO 2000–01 (up to and including 31.08.01)

Norwich City have scored 270 penalties in competitive games in the period under review. 181 have been scored at home and 89 away. 134 of the home penalties were scored at Carrow Road, 36 at The Nest and 11 at Newmarket Road. In all, 197 have been scored in the Football League, 21 in the FA Cup, 13 in the Milk/League Cup etc., 3 in the Texaco Cup, 26 in the Southern League, 4 in the United League, 5 in the Norfolk & Suffolk League Cup, and 1 in the Amateur Cup. Penalties have been scored by 71 different players and the leading scorers are Ron Ashman with 17, Ted MacDougall with 15, John Deehan 14, Matt Crowe 13, Neil Adams 12, and Joe Hannah with 11. The full list of all penalties scored is as follows:

26.12.02	Bob Collinson	Norwich CEYMS	N & S League
26.12.02	Bob Collinson	Norwich CEYMS	N & S League
10.10.03	Langford Baker	Cromer	N & S League
21.11.03	Langford Baker	Leiston	FA Amateur Cup
26.11.04	Bob Collinson	Cromer	N & S League
17.12.04	Bob Collinson	Lowestoft Town	N & S League
14.10.05	David Ross	Fulham	Southern League
02.12.05	Arthur Archer	Luton Town	Southern League
23.12.05	Arthur Archer	Northampton Town	Southern League
06.01.06	Arthur Archer	Southampton	Southern League
31.03.06	Arthur Archer	Millwall	Southern League
14.04.06	Arthur Archer	Tottenham Hotspur	Southern League
15.09.06	Arthur Archer	West Ham United	Southern League
26.12.06	Arthur Archer	Queens Park Rangers	Southern League
12.01.07	Arthur Archer	Hastings & St. Leonards	FA Cup
07.03.07	Arthur Archer	Bristol Rovers	Southern League
09.09.08	John Smith	Lincoln City	United League
10.12.08	Tommy Allsopp	Rotherham Town	United League
12.12.08	Tommy Allsopp	West Ham United	Southern League
20.01.09	Tommy Allsopp	Reading	FA Cup
21.01.09	Ernie Hunt	Walsall	United League
06.02.09	Tommy Allsopp	Liverpool	FA Cup
13.02.09	Tommy Allsopp	Millwall	Southern League
15.03.09	John Smith	Rotherham Town	United League
12.04.09	John Smith	Queens Park Rangers	Southern League
23.10.09	Percy Gooch	Reading	Southern League
29.03.10	Tommy Allsopp	Swindon Town	Southern League
26.12.10	Sam Wolstenholme	Swindon Town	Southern League
28.01.11	Billy Hampson	Queens Park Rangers	Southern League
04.03.11	Jock MacKenzie	Watford	Southern League
18.04.11	Jock MacKenzie	Brentford	Southern League
30.09.11	Fred Wilkinson	Stoke	Southern League
02.12.11	Billy Hampson	New Brompton	Southern League
24.02.12	Billy Hampson	Luton Town	Southern League
24.03.13	Billy Hampson	Northampton Town	Southern League
11.10.13	Billy Hampson	Exeter City	Southern League
28.03.14	Percy Sutcliffe	Plymouth Argyle	Southern League
13.02.15	Danny Wilson	Southend United	Southern League
17.04.15	Cecil Potter	Plymouth Argyle	Southern League
27.11.20	George Addy	Luton Town	Football League
26.03.21	George Addy	Watford	Football League
12.01.22	Sam Austin	Barnsley	FA Cup
14.10.22	Sam Austin	Northampton Town	Football League
03.03.23	Reg Wilkinson	Newport County	Football League
10.03.23	Reg Wilkinson	Newport County	Football League
17.03.23	Reg Wilkinson	Bristol City	Football League
30.03.23	Reg Wilkinson	Watford	Football League
01.09.23	Sam Austin	Millwall	Football League
10.11.23	Sam Austin	Newport County	Football League
04.10.24	Joe Hannah	Brentford	Football League
09.10.24	Joe Hannah	Bournemouth	Football League
13.12.24	Joe Hannah	Rochdale	FA Cup
23.03.25	Joe Hannah	Merthyr Town	Football League
26.09.25	James Jackson	Millwall	Football League
27.02.26	Harry Wingham	Charlton Athletic	Football League
27.08.27	Joe Hannah	Crystal Palace	Football League
05.11.27	Joe Hannah	Merthyr Town	Football League
14.01.28	Joe Hannah	Newport County	Football League
10.03.28	Joe Hannah	Plymouth Argyle	Football League
24.11.28	Joe Hannah	Chatham Town	FA Cup
08.12.28	Joe Hannah	Newport County	FA Cup
11.01.30	Joe Hannah	Torquay United	Football League
18.01.30	Mick O'Brien	Crystal Palace	Football League
18.04.31	Mick O'Brien	Newport County	Football League
08.10.32	Ken Burditt	Aldershot	Football League
14.01.33	Ken Burditt	Torquay United	Football League
11.11.33	Jack Vinall	Bournemouth	Football League
07.04.34	Jack Vinall	Watford	Football League
23.11.35	Cecil Russell	Manchester United	Football League
25.12.35	Cecil Russell	Bury	Football League
26.12.35	Cecil Russell	Bury	Football League
04.04.36	Cecil Russell	Bradford City	Football League
13.04.36	Cecil Russell	Nottingham Forest	Football League
29.08.36	Jack Vinall	Sheffield United	Football League
28.11.36	Jack Vinall	Southampton	Football League
03.04.37	Sam Bowen	Southampton	Football League
28.08.37	Billy Furness	Southampton	Football League
16.10.37	Billy Furness	Nottingham Forest	Football League
24.02.38	John Friar	Chesterfield	Football League
17.12.38	Billy Furness	Manchester City	Football League
30.11.46	Bernard Robinson	Brighton & Hove Albion	FA Cup
20.09.47	Bernard Robinson	Bristol Rovers	Football League
06.12.47	Len Dutton	Swansea Town	Football League
26.03.48	Bernard Robinson	Crystal Palace	Football League
04.09.48	Bernard Robinson	Bristrol City	Football League
15.09.48	Bernard Robinson	Brighton & Hove Albion	Football League
30.04.49	Len Dutton	Bristol Rovers	Football League
24.08.49	Len Dutton	Notts County	Football League
26.11.49	Noel Kinsey	Gloucester City	FA Cup
17.12.49	Noel Kinsey	Newport County	Football League
30.12.50	Noel Kinsey	Torquay United	Football League
11.01.51	Reg Foulkes	Leyton Orient	Football League
14.02.51	Reg Foulkes	Reading	Football League
02.04.51	Reg Foulkes	Port Vale	Football League
21.04.51	Reg Foulkes	Plymouth Argyle	Football League
05.05.51	Ron Ashman	Crystal Palace	Football League
08.09.51	Noel Kinsey	Shrewsbury Town	Football League
24.11.51	Noel Kinsey	Northampton Town	FA Cup
25.12.51	Noel Kinsey	Ipswich Town	Football League
01.03.52	Ron Ashman	Port Vale	Football League
02.04.52	Ron Ashman	Southend United	Football League
05.04.52	Ron Ashman	Bournemouth	Football League
26.04.52	Ron Ashman	Gillingham	Football League
30.04.52	Bon Ashman	Plymouth Argyle	Football League
30.04.52	Ron Ashman	Plymouth Argyle	Football League
03.05.52	Noel Kinsey	Swindon Town	Football League
04.10.52	Ron Ashman	Millwall	Football League
01.11.52	Ron Ashman	Watford	Football League
17.01.53	Ron Ashman	Queens Park Rangers	Football League
21.03.53	Ron Ashman	Watford	Football League
21.03.53	Ron Ashman	Watford	Football League
04.04.53	Ron Ashman	Newport County	Football League
16.01.54	Ron Ashman	Walsall	Football League
06.03.54	Ron Ashman	Watford	Football League
27.03.54	Ron Ashman	Reading	Football League
19.04.54	Ron Ashman	Northampton Town	Football League
15.09.54	Bobby Brennan	Exeter City	Football League
30.10.54	Bobby Brennan	Shrewsbury Town	Football League
05.02.55	Bobby Brennan	Watford	Football League
19.03.55	Bobby Brennan	Shrewsbury Town	Football League
11.04.55	Alan Woan	Walsall	Football League
17.09.55	Bobby Brennan	Reading	Football League
21.09.55	Billy Coxon	Colchester United	Football League
05.11.55	Billy Coxon	Queens Park Rangers	Football League
11.02.56	Billy Coxon	Gillingham	Football League
24.03.56	Billy Coxon	Northampton Town	Football League
10.09.56	Johnny Gavin	Conventry City	Football League
26.01.57	Johnny Gavin	Walsall	Football League
26.10.57	Johnny Gavin	Gillingham	Football League
16.11.57	Johnny Gavin	Redhill	FA Cup
16.11.57	Johnny Gavin	Redhill	FA Cup
11.12.57	Johnny Gavin	Brighton & Hove Albion	FA Cup
01.03.58	Johnny Gavin	Exeter City	Football League
05.04.58	Johnny Gavin	Swindon Town	Football League
20.09.58	Keith Ripley	Rochdale	Football League
30.03.59	Matt Crowe	Halifax Town	Football League
05.09.59	Matt Crowe	Shrewsbury Town	Football League
12.09.59	Matt Crowe	Port Vale	Football League
13.02.60	Matt Crowe	Brentford	Football League
02.04.60	Matt Crowe	York City	Football League
26.10.60	Matt Crowe	Oldham Athletic	League Cup
29.10.60	Matt Crowe	Southampton	Football League
14.11.60	Matt Crowe	Derby County	League Cup
19.11.60	Matt Crowe	Bristol Rovers	Football League
11.01.61	Matt Crowe	York City	FA Cup
04.02.61	Matt Crowe	Lincoln City	Football League
11.02.61	Matt Crowe	Portsmouth	Football League
29.04.61	Matt Crowe	Southampton	Football League

20.04.62	Joe Mullett	Brighton & Hove Albion	Football League
13.03.63	Terry Allcock	Newcastle United	FA Cup
21.09.63	Tommy Bryceland	Rotherham United	Football League
02.09.64	Terry Allcock	Derby County	Football League
16.09.64	Joe Mullett	Manchester City	Football League
21.10.64	Joe Mullett	Chester	League Cup
22.10.65	Ron Davies	Middlesbrough	Football League
05.03.66	Ron Davies	Blackburn Rovers	FA Cup
23.08.67	Mike Kenning	Preston North End	Football League
16.09.67	Mike Kenning	Portsmouth	Football League
03.09.68	Charlie Crickmore	Ipswich Town	League Cup
14.12.68	Charlie Crickmore	Fulham	Football League
12.04.69	Ken Foggo	Portsmouth	Football League
16.04.69	Ken Foggo	Derby County	Football League
16.08.69	Charlie Crickmore	Blackpool	Football League
18.10.69	Charlie Crickmore	Cardiff City	Football League
19.12.70	Ken Foggo	Luton Town	Football League
06.03.71	Ken Foggo	Blackburn Rovers	Football League
14.08.71	Graham Paddon	Luton Town	Football League
26.10.71	Graham Paddon	Grimsby Town	League Cup
22.01.72	Graham Paddon	Preston North End	Football League
25.03.72	Graham Paddon	Blackpool	Football League
24.04.72	Graham Paddon	Orient	Football League
17.03.73	Graham Paddon	Leicester City	Football League
01.09.73	Graham Paddon	West Ham United	Football League
23.10.73	Graham Paddon	Motherwell	Texaco Cup
06.11.73	Graham Paddon	Motherwell	Texaco Cup
12.12.73	Ted MacDougall	Burnley	Texaco Cup
16.01.74	John Sissons	Millwall	League Cup
24.04.74	Ted MacDougall	Burnley	Football League
28.09.74	Ted MacDougall	Manchester United	Football League
05.10.74	Ted MacDougall	Millwall	Football League
26.10.74	Ted MacDougall	Orient	Football League
08.02.75	Ted MacDougall	West Bromwich Albion	Football League
22.03.75	Ted MacDougall	Hull City	Football League
05.04.75	Ted MacDougall	Orient	Football League
23.08.75	Ted MacDougall	Aston Villa	Football League
13.09.75	Ted MacDougall	Burnley	Football League
20.09.75	Ted MacDougall	Leicester City	Football League
03.01.76	Ted MacDougall	Rochdale	FA Cup
13.01.76	Ted MacDougall	Rochdale	FA Cup
06.03.76	Ted MacDougall	Tottenham Hotspur	Football League
31.08.76	Ted MacDougall	Exeter City	League Cup
02.10.76	Martin Peters	Newcastle United	Football League
05.10.76	Martin Peters	Queens Park Rangers	Football League
22.01.77	Martin Peters	Liverpool	Football League
30.08.77	John Ryan	Burnley	League Cup
22.10.77	John Ryan	Leicester City	Football League
27.12.77	John Ryan	Coventry City	Football League
02.01.78	John Ryan	West Ham United	Football League
25.02.78	John Ryan	Nottingham Forest	Football League
11.03.78	John Ryan	Aston Villa	Football League
22.08.78	John Ryan	Bristol City	Football League
16.09.78	John Ryan	Birmingham City	Football League
07.10.78	John Ryan	Liverpool	Football League
04.11.78	John Ryan	Tottenham Hotspur	Football League
25.08.79	Kevin Bond	Leeds United	Football League
06.10.79	Kevin Bond	Stoke City	Football League
20.10.79	Kevin Bond	Manchester City	Football League
01.12.79	Kevin Bond	Aston Villa	Football League
15.03.80	Kevin Bond	Stoke City	Football League
22.03.80	Kevin Bond	West Bromwich Albion	Football League
27.12.80	Kevin Bond	Tottenham Hotspur	Football League
04.04.81	John McDowell	Manchester City	Football League
22.09.81	Ross Jack	Grimsby Town	Football League
03.10.81	Ross Jack	Oldham Athletic	Football League
13.03.82	John Deehan	Watford	Football League
08.05.82	Keith Bertschin	Orient	Football League
11.09.82	John Deehan	Southampton	Football League
23.10.82	John Deehan	Aston Villa	Football League
20.11.82	John Deehan	Stoke City	Football League
20.11.82	John Deehan	Stoke City	Football League
19.03.83	John Deehan	Notts County	Football League
26.03.83	John Deehan	West Ham United	Football League
17.09.83	John Deehan	Nottingham Forest	Football League
19.10.83	Mike Channon	Leicester City	Football League
07.04.84	John Deehan	Watford	Football League
07.04.84	John Deehan	Watford	Football League
12.05.84	John Deehan	Coventry City	Football League
25.08.84	Mike Channon	Liverpool	Football League
22.09.84	John Deehan	Watford	Football League
22.12.84	John Deehan	Tottenham Hotspur	Football League
24.08.85	John Deehan	Millwall	Football League
11.01.86	David Williams	Middlesbrough	Football League
15.03.86	David Williams	Carlisle United	Football League
05.04.86	David Williams	Brighton & Hove Albion	Football League
29.10.86	Kevin Drinkell	Millwall	Littlewoods Cup
29.12.87	Kevin Drinkell	Chelsea	Football League
23.04.88	Wayne Biggins	Portsmouth	Football League
18.02.89	Malcolm Allen	Sheffield United	FA Cup
30.08.89	Robert Fleck	Manchester United	Football League
14.10.89	Robert Fleck	Chelsea	Football League
21.10.89	Malcolm Allen	Luton Town	Football League
02.12.89	Andy Townsend	Sheffield Wednesday	Football League
31.03.90	Andy Townsend	Luton Town	Football League
18.09.91	Robert Fleck	Sheffield Wednesday	Football League
21.09.91	Mark Bowen	Notts. County	Football League
04.12.91	Robert Fleck	West Ham United	Rumbelows Cup
01.01.92	Robert Fleck	Aston Villa	Football League
04.01.92	Robert Fleck	Barnsley	FA Cup
01.05.93	Dave Phillips	Liverpool	Football League
04.12.93	Ruel Fox	Manchester United	Football League
22.02.94	Chris Sutton	Blackburn Rovers	Football League
21.09.94	Carl Bradshaw	Swansea City	Coca Cola Cup
25.01.95	Neil Adams	Coventry City	Football League
31.08.96	Neil Adams	Wolverhampton Wanderers	Football League
04.09.96	Neil Adams	Oxford United	Coca Cola Cup
26.10.96	Neil Adams	Birmingham City	Football League
28.12.96	Neil Adams	Bradford City	Football League
25.01.97	Neil Adams	Leicester City	FA Cup
15.02.97	Neil Adams	West Bromwich Albion	Football League
22.02.97	Neil Adams	Charlton Athletic	Football League
04.03.97	Neil Adams	Reading	Football League
05.04.97	Neil Adams	Wolverhampton Wanderers	Football League
22.08.98	Craig Bellamy	Queens Park Rangers	Football League
22.08.98	Craig Bellamy	Queens Park Rangers	Football League
07.11.98	Neil Adams	Bradford City	Football League
12.12.98	Neil Adams	Wolverhampton Wanderers	Football League
03.01.00	Iwan Roberts	Portsmouth	Football League
12.09.00	Iwan Roberts	Stockport County	Football League
19.09.00	Iwan Roberts	Blackpool	Worthington Cup
16.04.01	Iwan Roberts	Burnley	Football League

INDIVIDUAL PENALTY SCORERS IN COMPETITIVE MATCHES

ASHMAN RON	17
MacDOUGALL TED	15
DEEHAN JOHN	14
CROWE MATT	13
ADAMS NEIL	12
HANNAH JOE	11
RYAN JOHN	10
ARCHER ARTHUR	9
PADDON GRAHAM	9
GAVIN JOHNNY	8
BOND KEVIN	7
KINSEY NOEL	7
FLECK ROBERT	6
ALLSOPP TOMMY	6
BRENNAN BOBBY	5
HAMPSON BILLY	5
ROBINSON BERNARD	5
RUSSELL CECIL	5
AUSTIN SAM	4
COLLINSON BOB	4
COXON BILLY	4
CRICKMORE CHARLIE	4
FOGGO KEN	4
FOULKES REG	4
ROBERTS IWAN	4
VINALL JACK	4
WILKINSON REG	4
DUTTON LEN	3
FURNESS BILLY	3
MULLETT JOE	3
PETERS MARTIN	3
SMITH JOHN	3
WILLIAMS DAVID	3
ADDY GEORGE	2
ALLCOCK TERRY	2
ALLEN MALCOLM	2
BAKER LANGFORD	2
BELLAMY CRAIG	2
BURDITT KEN	2
CHANNON MICK	2
DAVIES RON	2
DRINKELL KEVIN	2
JACK ROSS	2
KENNING MIKE	2
MacKENZIE 'JOCK'	2
O'BRIEN MICK	2
TOWNSEND ANDY	2
BERTSCHIN KEITH	1
BIGGINS WAYNE	1
BOWEN MARK	1
BOWEN SAM	1
BRADSHAW CARL	1
BRYCELAND TOMMY	1
FOX RUEL	1
FRIAR JOHN	1
GOOCH PERCY	1
HUNT ERNIE	1
JACKSON JAMES	1
McDOWELL JOHN	1
PHILLIPS DAVID	1
POTTER CECIL	1
RIPLEY KEITH	1
ROSS DAVID	1
SISSONS JOHN	1
SUTCLIFFE PERCY	1
SUTTON CHRIS	1
WILKINSON FREDDY	1
WILSON DANNY	1
WINGHAM HARRY	1
WOAN ALAN	1
WOLSTENHOLME SAM	1

ABANDONED MATCHES 1902–2001

1	29.11.02	H	KIRKLEY	NORFOLK & SUFFOLK LEAGUE	78 MINS.	BAD LIGHT	1–1
2	11.01.13	A	LEICESTER FOSSE	FA CUP	65 MINS.	SNOW	0–0
3	14.01.39	A	PLYMOUTH ARGYLE	FOOTBALL LEAGUE	66 MINS.	SNOW	0–1
4	17.02.51	A	BRISTOL ROVERS	FOOTBALL LEAGUE	45 MINS.	WATERLOGGED PITCH	1–2
5	23.03.51	A	NEWPORT COUNTY	FOOTBALL LEAGUE	70 MINS.	WATERLOGGED PITCH	1–5
6	29.11.58	A	MANSFIELD TOWN	FOOTBALL LEAGUE	33 MINS.	FOG	1–0
7	08.09.65	A	MANCHESTER CITY	FOOTBALL LEAGUE	45 MINS.	WATERLOGGED PITCH	1–1
8	20.12.72	H	CHELSEA	LEAGUE CUP	85 MINS.	FOG	3–2

SIX OLDEST PLAYERS TO MAKE AN APPEARANCE FOR NORWICH CITY IN A COMPETITIVE MATCH

ALBERT STURGESS	42 YEARS 249 DAYS	LIONEL MURPHY	39 YEARS	7 DAYS
DUNCAN SCOTT FORBES	39 YEARS 114 DAYS	BRYNMOR JONES	38 YEARS	11 DAYS
KEVIN DAMIEN KEELAN	39 YEARS 35 DAYS	ISAAC GEORGE 'POMPEY' MARTIN	37 YEARS	347 DAYS

SIX YOUNGEST DEBUTANTS FOR NORWICH CITY IN A COMPETITIVE MATCH

IAN CLAUDE DAVIES	17 YEARS 29 DAYS	STEPHEN ALAN GOODWIN	17 YEARS	67 DAYS
DONALD EDWARDS	17 YEARS 46 DAYS	MARK FRANCIS BARHAM	17 YEARS	135 DAYS
MARK PETER METCALF	17 YEARS 49 DAYS	DALE ANDREW GORDON	17 YEARS	229 DAYS

TOP ATTENDANCES AT THE VARIOUS GROUNDS

NEWMARKET ROAD					
	1	11,500	14.04.06	TOTTENHAM HOTSPUR	SOUTHERN LEAGUE
	2	10,366	11.01.08	SHEFFIELD WEDNESDAY	FA CUP
	3	10,245	25.12.05	SWINDON TOWN	SOUTHERN LEAGUE
	4	10,000	25.12.06	NORTHAMPTON TOWN	SOUTHERN LEAGUE
THE NEST					
	1	25,037	16.02.35	SHEFFIELD WEDNESDAY	FA CUP
	2	22,433	02.04.34	NEWPORT COUNTY	FOOTBALL LEAGUE
	3	20,566	01.12.34	BOLTON WANDERERS	FOOTBALL LEAGUE
	4	20,540	17.04.33	CRYSTAL PALACE	FOOTBALL LEAGUE
CARROW ROAD					
	1	43,984	30.03.63	LEICESTER CITY	FA CUP
	2	43,129	12.01.50	PORTSMOUTH	FA CUP
	3	41,949	18.02.61	SUNDERLAND	FA CUP
	4	41,000	11.03.67	SHEFFIELD WEDNESDAY	FA CUP

NORWICH CITY UNUSED SUBSTITUTES IN THE FOOTBALL LEAGUE

(Shown figure indicates number of appearances in above category)

82 R. Green

38 J. Goss

33 M. Mackay

26 I. Crook

21 M. Allen; S. Carey

20 J. Polston

18 W. Biggins; A. Coote; T. Howard; N. O'Donnell

17 D. Mills; C. Woodthorpe

16 F. Sharpe; D. Sutch; C. Wilson

15 T. Anderson

14 A. Forbes; M. Jackson; A. Marshall; D. Russell; W. Steele

13 M. Briggs; D. Smith

12 G. Brooke; D. Forbes; M. McGuire; M. Sutton; R. Ullathorne; D. Van Wijk

11 I. Butterworth; P. Dalglish; R. Fox; B. McGovern; R. Newman; R. Rosario; M. Watt

10 D. Coney; D. Heath; G. Megson

9 A. Akinbiyi; J. Benson; P. Cook; G. Downs; S. Elliott; R. Fleck; C. Llewellyn; M. Milligan; Kth. Scott

8 C. Anselin; G. Butler; C. Fleming; S. Grapes; K. Hill; G. Howshall; L. Marshall; H. Mortensen; M. Nightingale

7 T. Allcock; D. Beckford; K. Bond; D. Evans; D. Gordon; R. Jack; A. Johnson; M. Robins; K. Robson; V. Segura; J. Wright

6 P. Blades; T. Bryceland; I. Davies; D. Gay; J. Miller; T. Putney

5 M. Barham; J. Blair; C. Bradshaw; N. Cassidy; L. Donowa; E. Fuglestad; M. Lucas; P. McVeigh; M. Machin; M. O'Neill; A. Powell; J. Rigby; Kvn. Scott

4 D. Bennett; A. Black; G. Bolland; R. Bradley; B. Conlon; P. Crichton; J. Cureton; J. Devine; E. Ekoku; M. Farrington; J. Fleeting; D. Hilton; G. Holt; P. Mountford; S. Nedergaard; J. Neighbour; C. Payne; M. Rush; J. Ryan; T. Sherwood; D. Stringer; C. Sutton; A. Taylor

3 J.Y de Blasiis; M. Channon; H Curran; A Fensome; A Hareide; P. Hubbard; W. Kellock; D. Livermore; P. Lythgoe; P. Mendham; J. Mullett; G. Paddon; L. Power; S. Prior; U. Ottosson; K. Reeves; C. Sullivan; R. Symonds; R. de Waard; S. Walsh; D. Williams.

2 Z. Abbey; N. Adams; P. Clayton; I. Culverhouse; M. Bowen; F. Derveld; W. Donachie; D. Eadie; G. Giallanza; R. Gladwin; S Goodwin; P. Grant; P. Hoadley; P. Hughes; P. Kelly; D. Kenton; B. McGovern; P. Morris; D. Muzinic; C. Prophett; S. Ratcliffe; G. Shepherd; A. Woolmer

1 P. Alexander; K. Ball; L. Barber; C. Bellamy; K. Bertschin; G. Brady; D. Broughton; K. Brown; R. Brown; A. Brownrigg; P. Cheesley; A. Cottee; C. Crickmore; D. Cross; M.A. Crowe; N. Davids; P. Diop; D. Dunthorne; C. Easton; J.S. Fashanu; R. Gibbins; S. Govier; P. Haylock; D. Jones; J. Minett; T. Painter; M. Peters; G. Peyton; G. Reeve; I. Roberts; K. Robson; G. Rowell; G. Self; P. Silvester; A. Spearing; A. Townsend; D. Way; E. Way; J. Whitley; G. Willis; R. Wright; W. Young

NORWICH CITY UNUSED SUBSTITUTES IN CUP MATCHES

F.A. CUP

5 S. Elliott

4 I. Crook; T. Sherwood

3 I. Butterworth; L. Donowa; T. Putney; D. Sutch

2 M. Allen; P. Blades; S. Carey; P. Clayton; R. Fleck; R. Fox; R. Green;R. Jack; D. Jones; A. Marshall; H. Mortensen; J. Mullett; N. O'Donnell; A. Powell; R. Ullathorne

1 N. Adams; T. Anderson; M. Barham; C. Bellamy; D. Bennett; A. Black; M. Briggs; I. Davies; J. Devine; D. Evans; D. Gordon; J. Goss; P. Haylock; D. Heath; G. Howshall; W. Kellock; D. Kenton; M. Machin; M. Mackay; J. Miller; P. Mountford; M. Nightingale; G. Paddon; G. Shepherd; W. Steele; A. Taylor; S. Walsh; C. Wilson; C. Woodthorpe

LEAGUE CUP (incorporates all sponsored names of the competition in subsequent years)

9 R. Green

7 A. Marshall

5 J. Goss

4 N. O' Donnell; J. Polston

3 M. Allen; K. Brown; A. Coote; M.A. Crowe; M. Farrington; R. Newman; R. Rosario; M. Watt

2 M. Briggs; G. Brooke; I. Davies; G. Downs; A. Forbes; S. Govier; T. Howard; D. Livermore; M. Mackay; M. McGuire; G. Megson; M. Nightingale; T. Painter; W. Steele; D. Sutch

1 A. Akinbiyi; T. Anderson; D. Beckford; J. Benson; P. Clayton; P. Crichton; I. Crook; J. Cureton; P. Dalglish; M. Darling; J. Devine; P. Diop; D. Eadie; D. Evans; R. Fox; E. Fuglestad; S. Goble; S. Goodwin; B. Gunn; P. Haylock; D. Hodgson; C. Llewellyn; L. Marshall; P. McVeigh; J. Miller; S. Nedergaard; A. Notman; C. Payne; S. Ratcliffe; D. Robb; K. Robson; Kth. Scott; V. Segura; F. Sharpe; G. Shepherd; A. Spearing; D. Stringer; M. Sutton; R. Symonds; A. Townsend; R. de Waard; S. Walsh; D. Van Wijk; C. Woodthorpe; A. Woolmer

SCREEN SPORT SUPER CUP

2 D. Gordon; P. Haylock; R. Rosario

1 G. Brooke; J. Deehan

TEXACO CUP

12 M. Cawston

2 R. Hansbury; K. Keelan

1 T. Anderson; J. Blair; W. Kellock; N. O'Donnell; C. Payne; C. Prophett; G. Self; P. Silvester; L. Wilson

SIMOD CUP/ZENITH DATA SYSTEMS CUP

2 T. Sherwood

1 S. Ball; I. Butterworth; D. Coney; S. Elliott; S. Ratcliffe; D. Smith; D. Williams

FULL MEMBERS CUP

1 P. Chapple; S. Elliott; D. Gordon; S. Westley

UEFA CUP

2 D. Eadie

1 R. Rosario

NORFOLK & NORWICH HOSPITAL CUP

The Norfolk & Norwich Hospital Cup was founded by public subscription in 1903. The Cup was a handsome trophy which stood 2ft 8ins high including plinth. Some of the most famous teams of the day contested the trophy which sadly was lost in the fire in the early hours of Thursday 25 October 1985. The full list of matches is as follows :

DATE	OPPONENTS	RESULT	ATTENDANCE	AMOUNT PAID TO CHARITY	SCORERS
14.04.04	C.E.Y.M.S.	0-0	3,500	£88	
28.04.04	C.E.Y.M.S. (replay)	2-0	3,000		KING (2)
15.04.05	C.E.Y.M.S.	1-1	5,240	£130	COLLINSON
26.04.05	C.E.Y.M.S. (replay)	3-2	4,900		COLLINSON (2), VIGAR
19.04.06	C.E.Y.M.S.	5-0	3,000	£52-10-0	WILKINSON (2), KING (2), LINWARD
30.04.07	Everton	1-1 *	9,500	£210	G. LAMBERTON
30.04.08	Chelsea	3-3 *	6,150	£120	G. LAMBERTON, FLANAGAN, DUNNING
19.04.09	Hull City	0-0 *	6,700	£130	
25.04.10	Hull City	0-1 (AET)	7,700	£150	
19.09.10	Newcastle United	1-1	13,473	£330	KIRKMAN (pen)
23.11.10	Newcastle United (replay)	0-3	5,944		
22.04.12	Newcastle United	0-0 *	8,307	£140	
28.04.13	Middlesbrough	1-1	7,679	£150	HAMPSON (pen)
30.04.14	Woolwich Arsenal	0-3	6,683	£143-14-9	
1914–15	NO MATCH				
06.05.16	Argyll & Sutherland Highlanders	4-1	3,123	£42	THOMPSON (2), POTTER (pen), WOODS
28.04.17	East Anglian Munitions League	4-1	1,260	£36-1-8	SCOTT (3), HAWES
01.04.18	193rd Infantry Brigade	2-1	3,959	***not known	HAWES, COLLINS (og)
17.05.19	Boulton & Paul	2-1	3,145	£53	DORAN, S. JENNINGS (2)
08.05.20	Tottenham Hotspur	0-4	11,902	£735	
25.04.21	South Shields	0-0 *	13,010	£700	
24.04.22	Notts County	0-2	8,885	£417-10-3	
16.04.23	Huddersfield Town	0-3	10,148	£525	
05.05.24	West Ham United	3-4	8,956	£420	JACKSON (2), AUSTIN
30.04.25	West Ham United	6-1	9,150	£440	McCUDDEN (3), JACKSON (3)
26.04.26	Leicester City	1-2	8,202	£380	WILSON
02.05.27	Leicester City	1-4	7,901	£380	RICHMOND
26.04.28	Stoke City	4-4 *	6,347	£200	ROBINSON (2), VARCO, SLICER
29.04.29	Stoke City	3-2	3,510	£150	SLICER (2), McKENNA
1929–30	NO MATCH				
20.04.31	Liverpool	0-6	10,293	£475	
02.05.32	Liverpool	1-2	10,323	£445	MURPHY
08.05.33	Liverpool	1-1 *	9,345	£228-6-5	J. SCOTT
07.05.34	Grimsby Town	7-2	13,219	£680	VINALL (5), KIRCHEN (2)
06.05.35	Arsenal	0-1	15,550	£806	
04.05.36	Middlesbrough	1-3	14,006	£614	EDWARDS
03.05.37	Middlesbrough	0-0 *	8,625	£310	
09.05.38	Leeds United	2-1	7,721	£265	FURNESS, LAW
08.05.39	Middlesbrough	3-0	4,160	£23	ACQUROFF (2), CHURCH
1940–46	NO MATCHES				
12.05.47	Tottenham Hotspur	0-2	18,687	£1,245	
1947–48	NO MATCH				
09.05.49	Bolton Wanderers	0-2	12,484	£630	
08.05.50	Tottenham Hotspur	2-2 *	13,929	£1,002	GAVIN, KINSEY
07.05.51	Bolton Wanderers	3-2	10,253	£483	HOLLIS (2), EYRE
05.05.52	Cardiff City	4-3	9,357	£504	GAVIN, ACKERMAN, SUMMERS, McCROHAN
06.05.53	Fulham	2-3	7,689	£398	ASHMAN, GAVIN
05.05.54	Manchester United	2-1	9,066	£627	WOAN (2)
1954–55	NO MATCH				
07.05.56	Leeds United	4-3	14,381	£1,148	HUNT, COXON, GAVIN, BLY
08.05.57	Nottingham Forest	2-7	6,533	£385	GORDON, HUNT
05.05.58	Leicester City	3-2	6,486	£435	ASHMAN, GAVIN, HALLIDAY
04.05.59	Ipswich Town	2-4	20,958	not known	CROWE (pen), HILL
02.05.60	Southampton	0-0 **	12,592	not known	
12.08.89	Ipswich Town	0-4			
10.08.91	Ipswich Town	3-0			BECKFORD, FLECK, PHILLIPS

* no replay ** Norwich won on the toss of a coin *** proceeds of gate absorbed in compensation for accident on the ground during the match

CITY AT WAR

FIRST WORLD WAR

City played a full season in the Southern League in 1914–15 but then all competition was abandoned until the 1919–20 season. Some friendly matches were played and these are included with the rest of the friendlies. The story of the near extinction of the club is included in the text.

SECOND WORLD WAR

1939–40

War was declared on Sunday 3 September 1939. Up to this time only three Division 3 (South) matches had been completed. The City side in all three games was Harry Dukes, Jack Taylor, John Milburn, Bernard Robinson, Len Reilly, Tom Smalley, Frank Manders, Billy Furness, Jack Acquroff, Bill Graham and John Church. The League Programme was soon abandoned after 3 September and the appearances do not count in the career records of the players. Details of the three matches are as follows:

DATE	OPPONENTS	VENUE	RESULT	SCORERS	ATTENDANCE
26.08.39	Cardiff City	H	1 – 2	Furness	13,453
30.08.39	Bristol City	A	2 – 1	Acquroff, Church	11,544
02.09.39	Ipswich Town	A	1 – 1	Furness	10,729

After discussions with the government the Football League set up a series of regional competitions. Norwich City played first in Section A and later in Section D. Guest players, mainly locally based servicemen and men from neighbouring Ipswich Town, were allowed to take part in these regional leagues. Details of both sections are as follows:

REGIONAL LEAGUE – SECTION A

DATE	OPPONENTS	VENUE	RESULT	SCORERS	ATTENDANCE
21.10.39	Millwall	A	1 – 1	Furness	7,363
28.10.39	West Ham United	H	5 – 3	Robinson, Acquroff, Ware, Plunkett, Manders	1,500
04.11.39	Watford	A	1 – 4	Plunkett	2,700
11.11.39	Arsenal	H	1 – 1	Plunkett	11,200
18.11.39	Charlton Athletic	A	1 – 1	Plunkett	2,500
25.11.39	Clapton Orient	H	4 – 0	Chadwick 2, Acquroff, Plunkett	3,500
02.12.39	Crystal Palace	A	0 – 1		5,400
09.12.39	Southend United	A	4 – 2	Robinson, Furness, Proctor, Manders	3,000
16.12.39	Tottenham Hotspur	H	5 – 2	Chadwick 4, Furness (pen)	4,100
25.12.39	West Ham United	A	1 – 4	Acquroff	6,200
26.12.39	Watford	H	3 – 2	Chadwick, Brain, Furness	4,350
30.12.39	Arsenal	*N	2 – 2	Chadwick, Furness	3,000
13.01.40	Clapton Orient	A	1 – 1	Chadwick	3,000
29.02.40	Charlton Athletic	H	1 – 3	Chadwick	1,350
07.03.40	Millwall	H	1 – 3	Acquroff	1,018
13.04.40	Crystal Palace	H	5 – 2	Taylor (pen) Chadwick, Plunkett 2, Acquroff	3,500
13.05.40	Southend United	H	3 – 2	Furness 2, Chadwick	1,400
27.05.40	Tottenham Hotspur	A	2 – 2	Plunkett, Chadwick	1,000

* – Played at White Hart Lane

REGIONAL LEAGUE – SECTION D

DATE	OPPONENTS	VENUE	RESULT	SCORERS	ATTENDANCE
10.02.40	Clapton Orient	H	2 – 2	Plunkett, Manders	2,100
17.02.40	Southend United	A	0 – 3		500
24.02.40	Bournemouth	H	4 – 3	Acquroff, Plunkett, Hall, Chadwick	2,816
02.03.40	Crystal Palace	A	0 – 2		4,500
90.03.40	Reading	H	5 – 2	Chadwick, Manders, Furness 3 (1 pen)	2,500

16.03.40	Queens Park Rangers	A	0 – 0		4,205
22.03.40	Brighton & Hove Albion	A	3 – 3	Acquroff 2, Manders	3,300
23.03.40	Watford	H	2 – 0	Chadwick 2	4,270
25.03.40	Brighton & Hove Albion	H	3 – 0	Proctor, Plunkett, Manders	8,500
30.03.40	Aldershot	A	1 – 4	Acquroff	3,500
04.04.40	Aldershot	H	3 – 2	Furness, Chadwick, Manders	901
06.04.40	Clapton Orient	A	3 – 4	Plunkett, Chadwick, Hall	1,500
18.05.40	Watford	A	0 – 0		1,200
25.05.40	Queens Park Rangers	H	3 – 1	Brain, Chadwick, Little	2,020
29.05.40	Reading	A	1 – 2	Plunkett	500
01.06.40	Southend United	H	1 – 3	Little	1,222
08.06.40	Crystal Palace	H	1 – 3	Taylor (pen)	1,024
	Bournemouth	A	Not Played		

SECTION A

	P	W	D	L	F	A	Pts
Arsenal	18	13	4	1	62	22	30
West Ham	18	12	1	5	57	33	25
Millwall	18	8	5	5	46	38	21
Watford	18	9	3	6	44	38	21
Norwich City	**18**	**7**	**6**	**5**	**41**	**36**	**20**
Charlton Athletic	18	8	1	9	61	58	17
Crystal Palace	18	5	3	10	39	56	13
Clapton Orient	18	5	3	10	28	60	13
Tottenham Hotspur	18	5	2	11	37	43	12
Southend United	18	4	0	14	30	61	8

SECTION D

	P	W	D	L	F	A	Pts
Crystal Palace	18	13	1	4	64	30	27
Queens Park Rangers	18	10	3	5	38	28	23
Watford	18	7	7	4	41	29	21
Southend United	18	8	3	7	41	37	19
Aldershot	18	7	3	8	38	36	17
Clapton Orient	18	7	3	8	33	45	17
Bournemouth	17	7	2	8	38	40	16
Norwich City	**17**	**6**	**4**	**7**	**32**	**34**	**16**
Reading	18	6	2	10	31	42	14
Brighton & Hove Albion	18	2	4	12	30	65	8

In addition Norwich City also took part in the League War Cup – Southern Section A. Each round was fought on a two leg basis. Results as follows:

DATE	OPPONENTS	VENUE	RESULT	SCORERS	ATTENDANCE
20.04.40	Millwall (Rd 1 – 1st Leg)	H	2 – 1	Manders, Acquroff	5,973
27.04.40	Millwall (Rd 1 – 2nd Leg)	A	1 – 1	Furness	12,000
04.05.40	Fulham (Rd 2 – 1st Leg)	H	1 – 1	Chadwick	7,583
11.05.40	Fulham (Rd 2 – 2nd Leg)	A	0 – 1		8,220

1940–41

During this season the League competition was divided into two parts – a Northern and Southern Section. 34 clubs comprised the Southern Section and it was not expected that each club would meet every other side. Accordingly the league was not contested on points but by taking an average of points per game. City eventually finished in 7th Position playing in all 19 games. Full details as follows:

DATE	OPPONENTS	VENUE	RESULT	SCORERS	ATTENDANCE
31.08.40	Mansfield Town	A	0 – 4		1,500
07.09.40	Luton town	H	2 – 2	Whittingham, Brooks	1,447
21.09.40	Crystal Palace	A	1 – 7	Brooks	1,040
28.09.40	Southend United	* A	0 – 3		800
05.10.40	Crystal Palace	H	3 – 1	Brooks 2, Joyner	1,191
19.10.40	Southend United	H	8 – 4	Joyner 3, Furness 2, Ware 2, Westwood	1,175
26.10.40	Luton Town	A	2 – 3	Joyner 2	1,176
16.11.40	Southend United	* A	3 – 3	Chadwick 2, McLuckie	600
07.12.40	Aldershot	A	4 – 5	Maskell 2, Housego, Plunkett	2,170
14.12.40	Aldershot	H	10 – 1	Chadwick 4, Roberts 2, Hurst 2, Howe, Sinclair	700
21.12.40	Southend United	H	3 – 0	Sinclair, Curtis, Roberts (pen)	624
25.12.40	Brighton & Hove Albion	H	18 – 0	Chadwick 6, Marshall 3, Roberts 3, Plunkett 3, Howe 2, 1 o.g. (Ithell)	1,419

08.03.41	Fulham	H	2 – 0	Brain, Plunkett	1,380
15.03.41	Luton Town	A	0 – 4		1,050
29.03.41	Southend United	* A	2 – 3	Maskell, Lello	800
12.04.41	Watford	A	1 – 7	Furness	1,800
14.04.41	Luton Town	H	4 – 1	Ashmore, Plunkett, Brain, Furness (pen)	2,134
19.04.41	Watford	H	5 – 4	Proctor 2, Ashmore, Plunkett, Needs	1,289
03.05.41	Southend United	H	5 – 3	Maskell 2, Furness, Ashmore, Plunkett	1,126

* Played at New Writtle Street, Chelmsford.

FOOTBALL LEAGUE WAR CUP

DATE	OPPONENTS	VENUE	RESULT	SCORERS	ATTENDANCE
15.02.41	West Ham United	H	2 – 1	Roberts 2	4,555
22.02.41	West Ham United	A	1 – 4	Plunkett	5,500

1941–42

Before the 1941–42 season began the London based clubs plus Aldershot, Brighton & Hove Albion, Partsmouth and Reading decided to form their own league – the London War League. The rest of the Southern Regional League clubs continued as in the previous season with placings again being decided on average points rather than total points. City eventually finished in 4th place playing a total of 8 games. We list them below.

DATE	OPPONENTS	VENUE	RESULT	SCORERS	ATTENDANCE
30.08.41	Leicester City	A	1 – 1	Plunkett	2,750
06.09.41	Leicester City	H	0 – 0		3,972
13.09.41	Luton Town	H	8 – 1	Mulraney 3, Manley 2, Scrimshaw 2, Plunkett	2,795
20.09.41	Luton Town	A	4 – 1	Maskell 2, Furness, Mulraney	2,157
27.09.41	Northampton Town	A	1 – 3	Maskell	3,820
04.10.41	Northampton Town	H	3 – 1	Maskell, Manley, (pen) Scrimshaw	4,099
08.11.41	Nottingham Forest	A	2 – 0	Proctor 2	1,958
06.12.41	Leicester City	A	1 – 6	Maskell	3,000

The Football League War Cup in 1941–42 was first organised on a qualifying basis. Successful clubs later going forward to the competition proper.

DATE	OPPONENTS	VENUE	RESULT	SCORERS	ATTENDANCE
27.12.41	Northampton Town	A	2 – 3	Flowers, Maskell	4,000
03.01.42	Northampton Town	H	4 – 1	Howe 2, Maskell, Sinclair	3,459
24.01.42	Luton Town	H	2 – 0	Plunkett, Maskell	1,138
31.01.42	Luton Town	A	2 – 3	Howe, Roberts	1,000
21.02.42	Leicester City	A	1 – 1	Howe	2,000
28.02.42	Leicester City	H	6 – 3	Maskell 3, Thornton, Howe, Furness (pen)	5,653

COMPETITION PROPER

DATE	OPPONENTS	VENUE	RESULT	SCORERS	ATTENDANCE
04.04.42	Leicester City (Rd 1-1st Leg)	A	0 – 2		8,500
06.04.42	Leicester City (Rd 1-2nd Leg)	H	*3 – 0	Thornton 2, Roberts	8,769
11.04.42	Northampton Town (Rd 2-1st Leg)	A	4 – 3	Roberts 2, Maskell, Thornton	7,000 7,000
18.04.42	Northampton Town (Rd 2 - 2nd Leg)	H	3 – 1	Howe, Roberts, 1 o.g. (Shepherdson)	9,871
25.04.42	Grimsby Town (Rd 3-1st Leg)	H	1 – 0	Furness	11,888
02.05.42	Grimsby Town (Rd 3-2nd Leg)	A†	0 – 2		8,000

* After Extra Time † Played at Old Show Ground, Scunthorpe

1942–43, 1943–44 & 1944–45

Norwich City only played friendlies during these seasons and results can be found in the friendlies section.

1945–46 TRANSITIONAL SEASON

The Second World War ended in May 1945 but it took some time for life to get back to normal. Food, clothes & fuel were short and were rationed, many servicemen were still involved in the clearing up operation. Football then was deprived of many of its resources and players, many of whom of course were now too old to continue playing. The Football League decided to continue to organise football on a regional basis and Norwich City took part in Division 3 South – North Region and Division 3 South – North Region Cup competition. Neither of these two competitions count towards the career figures of the players who took part. Guest players were still allowed to participate.

FOOTBALL LEAGUE DIVISION 3 SOUTH-NORTH REGION

DATE	OPPONENTS	VENUE	RESULT	SCORERS	ATTENDANCE
25.08.45	Watford	H	8 – 1	Newsome 4, Plunkett, Johnson, Moore, Taylor (pen)	8,157
30.08.45	Port Vale	H	3 – 4	Plunkett 2, Antonio	7,507
01.09.45	Watford	A	1 – 2	Antonio	4,842
03.09.45	Port Vale	A	2 – 2	Graham, Coleman	7,157
13.09.45	Clapton Orient	H	3 – 0	Newsome 2 (1 pen), Johnson	7,206
22.09.45	Notts County	A	2 – 2	Newsome, Johnson	11,692
29.09.45	Notts County	H	5 – 1	Moore 3, Johnson, Jones	11,179
06.10.45	Mansfield Town	H	5 – 1	Plunkett 3, Furness, Jones	11,007
13.10.45	Mansfield Town	A	1 – 4	Coleman	5,000
20.10.45	Southend United	A	4 – 1	Johnson 3, Plunkett	7,000
27.10.45	Southend United	H	6 – 1	Johnson 2, Jones 2, Plunkett, Newsome	11,178
03.11.45	Walsall	H	2 – 1	Russell, Jones	11,171
10.11.45	Walsall	A	2 – 1	Newsome, Jones	4,000
01.12.45	Ipswich Town	H	4 – 0	Newsome 2, Plunkett, Jones	16,301
19.12.45	Ipswich Town	A	0 – 0		5,040
22.12.45	Northampton Town	H	2 – 1	Furness, Robinson	8,418
25.12.45	Queens Park Rangers	H	1 – 1	Graham	20,082
26.12.45	Queens Park Rangers	A	2 – 1	Jones, Robinson (pen)	19,069
29.12.45	Clapton Orient	A	0 – 3		5,000
01.01.46	Northampton Town	A	1 – 4	Duffield	2,000

FOOTBALL LEAGUE DIVISION 3 SOUTH-NORTH REGION CUP

DATE	OPPONENTS	VENUE	RESULT	SCORERS	ATTENDANCE
12.01.46	Clapton Orient	A	1 – 2	Liddell	7,746
19.01.46	Clapton Orient	H	3 – 4	Furness 3	7,842
26.01.46	Northampton Town	H	2 – 1	Jones, Furness	7,881
02.02.46	Northampton Town	A	1 – 1	Furness	4,000
09.02.46	Ipswich Town	H	1 – 0	Johnson	10,821
16.02.46	Ipswich Town	A	0 – 4		14,980
23.02.46	Southend United	A	0 – 1		4,000
02.03.46	Southend United	H	0 – 1		4,317
09.03.46	Crystal Palace	A	3 – 2	Furness, Russell, Jones	12,000
16.03.46	Crystal Palace	H	6 – 1	Church 4, Furness 2	10,892
23.03.46	Watford	A	1 – 2	Church	5,289
30.03.46	Watford	H	3 – 0	Plunkett 2, Jones	10,924
06.04.46	Walsall	A	2 – 4	Church, Jones	9,000
13.04.46	Walsall	H	1 – 1	Plunkett	12,497
19.04.46	Notts County	A	1 – 0	Maskell	10,000
22.04.46	Notts County	H	2 – 1	Furness, Plunkett	16,122

DIVISION 3 (SOUTH) – NORTH REGION

	P	W	D	L	F	A	Pts
Queens Park Rangers	20	14	4	2	50	15	32
Norwich City	**20**	**11**	**4**	**5**	**54**	**31**	**26**
Port Vale	20	9	6	5	34	25	24
Watford	20	10	2	8	42	47	22
Ipswich Town	20	8	4	8	33	36	20
Notts County	20	8	4	8	39	47	20
Northampton Town	20	8	3	9	37	34	19
Clapton Orient	20	5	6	9	28	42	16
Walsall	20	6	3	11	31	42	15
Southend United	20	5	5	10	33	49	15
Mansfield Town	20	3	5	12	29	42	11

DIVISION 3 (SOUTH) – NORTH REGION CUP

	P	W	D	L	F	A	Pts
Queens Park Rangers	16	11	3	2	38	11	25
Walsall	16	10	4	2	34	18	24
Mansfield	16	8	4	4	24	15	20
Southend United	16	7	5	4	22	21	19
Norwich City	**16**	**7**	**2**	**7**	**27**	**25**	**16**
Ipswich Town	16	7	1	8	19	24	15
Clapton Orient	16	6	3	7	22	31	15
Port Vale	16	5	4	7	21	25	14
Northampton Town	16	5	2	9	27	28	12
Watford	16	5	1	10	23	35	11
Notts County	16	5	0	11	17	31	10

FA CUP

Each round up to and including the Sixth Round was played on a two leg basis. This was the first FA Cup competition since the 1938–39 season and City did not join the competition until the Third Round. These matches do count to players career totals.

Saturday 5 January 1946 (3rd Rd-1st Leg) BRIGHTON & HOVE ALBION H 1-2
City Team – DAVIS Derek, REID Ernie, TAYLOR Jack (Capt), FLACK Len, ROBINSON Bernard, PROCTOR Harry, PLUNKETT Sid, FURNESS Billy, JOHNSON Ralph, GRAHAM Bill & JONES Sid. Scorer – Bill Graham.

Wednesday 9 January 1946 (3rd Rd-2nd Leg) BRIGHTON & HOVE ALBION A 1-4
City team – DAVIS Derek, REID Ernie, TAYLOR Jack (Capt), FLACK Len, ROBINSON Bernard, PROCTOR Harry, JOHNSON Ralph, RUSSELL James, WARE Harry, PLUNKETT Sid & JONES Sid. Scorer – Harry Ware.

FRIENDLY MATCHES

1902–03

S	06.09.02	HARWICH & PARKESTON (FIRST EVER MATCH)	H	1-1
S	13.09.02	YARMOUTH TOWN	H	2-3
S	04.10.02	YARMOUTH TOWN	A	1-2
S	18.10.02	NORWICH CEYMS	A	2-1
S	01.11.02	KIRKLEY	H	2-1
S	22.11.02	SELWYN COLLEGE (HOSPITAL CHARITY)	H	1-1
S	20.12.02	LYNN SWIFTS (ABANDONED 84 MINS.)	H	4-0
S	27.12.02	HENDON	H	3-1
S	21.02.03	CROYDON WANDERERS	H	4-0
S	07.03.03	HARWICH & PARKESTON	A	3-3
S	21.03.03	WEST HAM GARFIELD	H	5-0
S	28.03.03	NORWICH CEYMS (LYNN HOSPITAL CUP)*	N	1-3
S	04.04.03	YARMOUTH TOWN (YARMOUTH HOSPITAL CUP)	A	0-1
S	11.04.03	BURNLEY BELVEDERE	H	1-0
S	25.04.03	NORWICH CEYMS	H	0-2

* – PLAYED AT 'THE WALKS', KING'S LYNN

1903–04

S	05.09.03	HARWICH & PARKESTON	H	6-1
S	12.09.03	YARMOUTH TOWN	H	3-2
Tu	15.09.03	YARMOUTH TOWN ('NEW SKYLARK' BENEFIT FUND)	A	0-2
S	26.09.03	LYNN SWIFTS	H	7-0
S	24.10.03	LYNN TOWN (NORFOLK CHARITY CUP)	H	5-2
M	28.12.03	SHEFFIELD WYCLIFFE	H	0-1
S	16.01.04	SELWYN COLLEGE, CAMBS	H	2-1
F	01.04.04	WOODFORD	H	3-4
S	02.04.04	UPTON PARK	H	1-0
Th	07.04.04	NORWICH CEYMS (NORFOLK CHARITY CUP)	H	1-0
S	09.04.04	LYNN TOWN (LYNN HOSPITAL CUP)	A	0-1
S	30.04.04	YARMOUTH TOWN (YARMOUTH HOSPITAL CUP)	A	0-1

1904–05

S	03.09.04	HITCHIN	H	2-0
S	10.09.04	YARMOUTH TOWN	H	7-1
S	17.09.04	WAR OFFICE	H	1-0
S	01.10.04	WEST NORWOOD	H	1-0
S	08.10.04	LONDON CALEDONIANS	H	5-2
S	22.10.04	NORWICH CEYMS (NORFOLK CHARITY CUP)	A	3-1
S	05.11.04	CLARE COLLEGE, CAMBRIDGE	H	3-1
S	03.12.04	SELWYN COLLEGE, CAMBRIDGE	H	3-1
S	10.12.04	ROYAL SCOTS GREYS	H	3-0
S	24.12.04	SHEFFIELD WYCLIFFE	H	2-3
Tu	27.12.04	COLDSTREAM GUARDS	H	2-0
S	07.01.05	HARWICH & PARKESTON	H	11-1
S	21.01.05	NOTTINGHAM FOREST II	H	3-3
S	28.01.05	CHESHAM TOWN	H	5-1
S	04.02.05	WELLINGBOROUGH	H	1-1
S	18.02.05	NORTHAMPTON TOWN	H	3-4
S	11.03.05	YARMOUTH TOWN (YARMOUTH HOSPITAL CUP)	A	0-1
S	22.04.05	WAR OFFICE	H	7-0
Th	25.04.05	DERBY COUNTY	H	0-6
S	27.04.05	WOOLWICH ARSENAL	H	2-1
S	29.04.05	LUTON TOWN	H	0-0

1905–06

Th	07.09.05	YARMOUTH TOWN	A	8-0
Th	14.09.05	CLAPTON	H	3-0
Th	21.09.05	QUEEN'S PARK RANGERS	H	2-3
Th	28.09.05	CLUB ATHLETIQUE PROFESSIONEL PARISIEN	H	11-0
Th	05.10.05	SWINDON TOWN	H	4-4
W	01.11.05	IPSWICH TOWN	A	5-0
W	08.11.05	LYNN TOWN	A	2-1
Th	16.11.05	NORWICH CEYMS	A	6-1
Th	30.11.05	CRYSTAL PALACE	H	0-2
Tu	26.12.05	GREENOCK MORTON	H	3-1
M	01.01.06	CLAPTON	A	4-0
F	21.03.06	KIRKLEY	A	7-0
F	13.04.06	STOCKTON	H	7-1
W	18.04.06	NEW CRUSADERS	H	1-1
M	23.04.06	LEICESTER FOSSE	H	3-3
Th	26.04.06	COLCHESTER TOWN	A	3-1

1906–07

Th	07.02.07	NORFOLK COUNTY (BENEFIT NCFA FUNDS)	H	6-2
M	01.04.07	BIRMINGHAM CITY (GOOCH TRANSFER MATCH)	H	5-2
Tu	02.04.07	MANCHESTER CITY (ROSS TRANSFER MATCH)	H	2-2

1907–08

M	16.09.07	NOTTS. COUNTY	H	2-2
Th	26.09.07	CROMER (3 CLUB BENEFIT AT LOWESTOFT)	N	5-1
Th	26.09.07	LOWESTOFT/KIRKLEY XI	N	3-3
F	17.04.08	CRYSTAL PALACE	H	3-0

1908–09

Tu	01.09.08	FULHAM (FIRST MATCH AT THE NEST)	H	2-1
M	26.10.08	LEYTON	A	6-1
Th	19.11.08	LEYTON	H	3-2
Th	03.12.08	NORWICH CITY PAST XI (T) ROBERT MUIR	H	5-4

1909–10

Th	25.11.09	NORFOLK COUNTY	H	6-1
S	19.02.10	BRIGHTON & HOVE ALBION (T) WIDOW OF HONRIE JAMES REED	A	0-6

1910–11

M	05.09.10	MERTHYR TOWN	A	0-0
Th	22.09.10	NORWICH CEYMS	H	2-2

1911–12

M	18.11.11	HULL CITY (HULL CHARITY CUP)	A	0-3
M	11.12.11	PONTYPRIDD	A	1-3

1915–16

Th	16.09.15	LIVERPOOL SCOTTISH	H	3-1
S	18.09.15	CHESHIRE REGIMENT	H	6-3
S	25.09.15	NEW EXPLOSIVES	H	6-0
S	02.10.15	ROYAL WELSH FUSILIERS	H	2-1
S	09.10.15	SOUTH LANCASHIRES	H	7-0
S	16.10.15	ROYAL FIELD ARTILLERY	H	3-1
S	23.10.15	6th NORFOLK CYCLISTS	H	3-1
S	30.10.15	AIRCRAFT	H	9-0
S	06.11.15	PROVISIONAL BATTALION	H	3-1
Th	11.11.15	1/16th NORFOLK REGIMENT	A	3-4
S	13.11.15	48th PROVISIONAL BATTALION	H	12-0
S	20.11.15	65th PROVISIONAL BATTALION	H	3-2
S	27.11.15	ROYAL WELSH FUSILIERS	H	3-1
Th	02.12.15	9th HAMPSHIRES	H	13-1
S	04.12.15	FIFE & FORFAR YEOMANRY	H	4-0
S	11.12.15	CARROW	H	6-1
S	18.12.15	PROVISIONAL ASC	H	12-0
S	25.12.15	DERBYSHIRE RFA	H	14-0
M	27.12.15	ROYAL WELSH FUSILIERS	H	2-0
S	01.01.16	6th NORFOLKS (AT N. WALSHAM)	A	6-3
S	08.01.16	1st ARMY SIGNALS TROOPS	H	11-0
S	15.01.16	LOVAT SCOUTS	H	12-1
Th	20.01.16	3rd NORFOLKS	H	2-0
S	22.01.16	SHROPSHIRE YEOMANRY	H	0-1
S	29.01.16	INVERNESS RHA	H	6-0
Th	03.02.16	HEREFORD RAMC	H	1-0
S	05.12.16	62nd PROVISIONALS	H	8-2
Th	10.02.16	SHROPSHIRE YEOMANRY (AT GORLESTON)	A	3-2
S	12.02.16	COUNTY OF LONDON YEOMANRY	H	3-0
S	19.02.16	ROYAL FLYING CORPS	H	13-1
S	04.03.16	GLOUCESTER HUSSARS	H	7-0
S	11.03.16	SHROPSHIRE ROYAL ARTILLERY	H	1-4
S	18.03.16	EAST ANGLIAN FIELD AMBULANCE	H	7-0
S	25.03.16	HIGHLAND BRIGADE	H	7-2
S	01.04.16	MILITARY LEAGUE	H	2-2
S	08.04.16	2/6TH BLACKWATCH	H	4-3
S	15.04.16	ARGYLL & SUTHERLAND HIGHLANDERS	H	2-0
S	22.04.16	64th HIGHLAND DIV. R.F.	H	6-0
S	29.04.16	2/4th CAMERONS	H	1-0

1916–17

S	02.09.16	ROYAL NAVY AIR SERVICE	H	4-1
S	09.09.16	NORTHERN SIGNAL CO.	H	4-2
S	16.09.16	ROYAL FLYING CORPS	H	5-4
S	23.09.16	ROYAL NAVY AIR SERVICE	H	4-3
S	30.09.16	YORKSHIRE LIGHT INFANTRY	H	4-0
S	16.10.16	ROYAL GARRISON ARTILLERY	H	1-2
S	23.10.16	R.A.M.E.	H	13-2
S	30.10.16	R.E. SIGNALLERS	H	1-0
S	04.11.16	R.N.A.S.	H	4-2
S	11.11.16	ROYAL FLYING CORP	H	2-0
S	18.11.16	R.E. SIGNALLERS (LONDON)	H	1-0
S	25.11.16	2/7th BLACKWATCH	H	1-1
S	02.12.16	ROYAL FIELD ARTILLERY	H	0-1
S	09.12.16	MONMOUTHS (AT CROWN MEADOW, LOWESTOFT)	A	9-0
S	16.12.16	ARGYLE & SUTHERLAND HIGHLANDERS	H	2-1
S	23.12.16	BLACK WATCH	H	5-0
M	25.12.16	BLACK WATCH	H	3-1
Tu	26.12.16	ARGYLE & SUTHERLAND HIGHLANDERS	H	6-5
S	30.12.16	ROYAL FLYING CORPS	H	4-0
S	06.01.17	ARGYLE & SUTHERLAND HIGHLANDERS	H	2-1
S	13.01.17	MONMOUTH & HEREFORDS	H	14-1
S	20.01.17	ARGYLE & SUTHERLAND HIGHLANDERS	H	0-0
S	27.01.17	ROYAL FIELD ARTILLERY	H	6-0

S	03.02.17	FIELD ARTILLERY	H	6-0
S	10.02.17	GORDON HIGHLANDERS	H	3-2
S	17.02.17	ROYAL FIELD ARTILLERY	H	4-0
S	24.02.17	ARGYLE & SUTHERLAND HIGHLANDERS	H	3-1
S	03.03.17	BOULTON & PAUL	H	4-1
S	10.03.17	R.F.A. (STAFFORDS)	H	7-0
S	17.03.17	GORDON HIGHLANDERS	H	3-1
S	24.03.17	BOULTON & PAUL (AT NEWMARKET RD.)	A	3-1
	06.04.17	ARGYLE & SUTHERLAND HIGHLANDERS	H	2-3
S	07.04.17	GORDON HIGHLANDERS	H	6-2
M	09.04.17	BLACKWATCH	H	3-2

917–18

Th	27.10.17	CAPT. R.F. POPHAMS XI (BENEFIT BRITISH RED CROSS SOCIETY)	H	3-2

918–19

S	11.01.19	51st BEDFORDS	H	5-0
S	18.01.19	R.A.F. (YARMOUTH)	H	1-5
S	25.01.19	51st BEDFORDS	H	3-2
S	01.02.19	193rd BRIGADE	H	3-2
S	08.02.19	R.A.F. (THETFORD)	H	5-0
S	15.02.19	52nd MIDDLESEX	H	5-3
S	22.02.19	R.A.F.	H	12-0
S	08.03.19	R.A.F. (PULHAM)	H	7-0
S	15.03.19	YARMOUTH	A	1-1
S	22.03.19	LOWESTOFT CASUALS	H	14.0
S	29.03.19	NORFOLK COUNTY	A	7-1
S	05.04.19	YARMOUTH (DEREHAM CHARITY CUP)	H	4-0
S	12.04.19	MAJOR BUCKLEY'S XI	H	5-0
W	23.04.19	NORFOLK COUNTY	H	6-1
S	26.04.19	LOWESTOFT TOWN	A	6-0
S	03.05.19	BIRMINGHAM	H	2-1
S	10.05.19	DURHAM CITY	H	3-1

919–20

S	10.01.20	BRIGHTON	A	3-3
Th	15.01.20	SUFFOLK COUNTY	A	3-1
Th	29.01.20	VICTORY CUP XI	H	3-2
Th	05.02.20	CAMBRIDGE UNIV.	H	1-1
M	01.03.20	MID RHONDDA	A	0-3

920–21

Th	11.11.20	CAMBRIDGE UNIVERSITY	A	3-3
S	18.12.20	WATFORD	H	4-2
Tu	28.12.20	NORFOLK COUNTY	H	3-2
Su	16.01.21	FOOT GUARDS	H	9-0
Th	03.03.21	LOWESTOFT TOWN (MAYOR'S UNEMPLOYMENT FUND)	A	1-1
W	13.04.21	SHERINGHAM	H	3-0

921–22

Th	22.09.21	COLCHESTER TOWN	A	4-4
M	03.10.21	BRIDGEND	A	3-3
W	19.10.21	SHERINGHAM	A	4-0
Th	03.11.21	CAMBRIDGE UNIVERSITY	H	2-1
Th	16.02.22	YARMOUTH & GORLESTON	H	4-0

922–23

Th	02.11.22	CAMBRIDGE UNIVERSITY	A	4-1
Th	08.03.23	YARMOUTH & GORLESTON (T) A.W. POSTLE	A	3-1

924–25

M	22.09.24	MANCHESTER CITY	H	1-2

925–26

Th	22.10.25	TOTTENHAM HOTSPUR (AT BURY ST. EDMUNDS)	N	3-2
M	19.04.26	HULL CITY (T) 'POMPEY' MARTIN	H	2-5

927–28

Th	13.10.27	TOTTENHAM HOTSPUR (AT BURY ST. EDMUNDS)	N	1-1
M	23.04.28	TOTTENHAM HOTSPUR (T) CHARLIE DENNINGTON	H	3-0

929–30

S	14.12.29	BRENTFORD	H	5-2

931–32

M	25.04.32	DERBY COUNTY (T) JOE HANNAH	H	2-2

932–33

S	10.12.32	YORK CITY	H	7-0

933–34

S	09.12.33	CORINTHIANS	H	0-0
Tu	01.05.34	GRIMSBY TOWN (GRIMSBY HOSPITAL CUP)	A	0-3

936–37

M	26.04.37	IPSWICH TOWN (IPSWICH HOSPITAL CUP)	A	2-3
W	28.04.37	IPSWICH TOWN (T) ROBINSON/SCOTT	H	3-1

937–38

S	12.02.38	WOLVERHAMPTON WANDERERS	H	1-7

1938–39

S	20.08.38	IPSWICH TOWN (LEAGUE JUBILEE FUND)	H	1-1

1939–40

S	19.08.39	IPSWICH TOWN (LEAGUE JUBILEE FUND)	A	1-2
S	16.09.39	SOUTHEND UNITED	A	2-6
S	14.10.39	NORTHAMPTON TOWN	H	6-1
S	06.01.40	CHARLTON ATHLETIC (ABANDONED 15 MINS.)	H	1-0

1940–41

S	12.10.40	ARMY XI (AT HELLESDON)	A	5-3
M	04.11.40	ARMY XI (AT WYMONDHAM)	A	4-3
S	23.11.40	R.A.F. XI	H	1-1
S	30.11.40	FIELD ARTILLERY	H	5-2
S	22.03.41	CZECH ARMY XI	H	6-0
S	05.04.41	DUTCH ARMY XI	H	7-0
S	10.05.41	UNITED SERVICES	H	1-4
S	17.05.41	POLICE & SPECIAL CONSTABLES	H	9-0
S	24.05.41	R.A.F. XI (R.A.F. WELFARE FUND)	H	0-4
M	02.06.41	JIMMY McLUCKIE XI (AT IPSWICH)	A	4-4

1941–42

S	22.11.41	R.A.F. XI	H	9-2
S	29.11.41	NAVY XI (AT IPSWICH)	A	3-2
M	15.12.41	ARMY XI	H	4-3
Th	25.12.41	GUNNERS XI	H	4-2
W	10.01.42	ARMY XI	H	6-3
S	07.03.42	ARMY XI	H	0-2
S	14.03.42	ARMY XI (AT CAMBRIDGE)	A	13-0
M	16.05.42	ARMY XI	A	1-8

1942–43

S	12.09.42	SUFFOLK NAVY XI (AT IPSWICH)	A	8-1
S	19.09.42	NAVY XI	H	3-0
S	26.09.42	CHELMSFORD	A	1-5
S	03.10.42	CHELMSFORD	H	4-3
S	10.10.42	ARMY XI	H	7-2
S	17.10.42	ARMY XI	H	6-4
S	24.10.42	R.A.F. XI (AT COLCHESTER)	A	6-1
S	31.10.42	R.A.F. XI (AT YARMOUTH)	A	1-2
S	07.11.42	R.A.F. XI	H	0-0
S	14.11.42	ARMY XI	H	5-3
S	21.11.42	ARMY XI	H	6-1
S	28.11.42	EASTERN COMMAND (AT IPSWICH)	A	4-1
S	05.12.42	R.A.F. XI	H	8-2
S	12.12.42	SUFFOLK LEAGUE XI	H	3-4
S	19.12.42	ARMY XI	H	3-1
S	26.12.42	NORWICH FITNESS LEAGUE XI	H	5-6
S	02.01.43	ARMY XI	H	8-4
S	09.01.43	NORWICH FITNESS LEAGUE XI	H	7-1
S	16.01.43	CAMBRIDGE UNIVERSITY	H	3-2
S	23.01.43	ARMY XI	H	3-2
S	30.01.43	ARMY XI	H	8-1
S	06.02.43	ARMY XI (BECCLES NURSING HOME FUND)	A	3-8
S	13.02.43	SERVICE LEAGUE	A	2-1
S	06.03.43	ARMY XI	H	5-4
S	13.03.43	KINGS OWN SCOTTISH BORDERERS	H	2-4
S	20.03.43	R.A. XI	H	4-2
S	27.03.43	KINGS OWN SCOTTISH BORDERERS	H	3-1
S	03.04.43	ARMY XI	H	2-0
S	24.04.43	EASTERN COMMAND	H	3-1
S	01.05.43	ARMY XI	H	4-3
S	08.05.43	ARMY XI	H	5-2

1943–44

S	04.09.43	FORCES XI (AT WYMONDHAM)	A	6-3
S	11.09.43	NAVY XI	H	3-3
S	18.09.43	ARMY XI	H	10-1
S	25.09.43	SUFFOLK NAVY (AT IPSWICH)	A	1-0
S	09.10.43	R.A. XI	H	3-0
S	16.10.43	R.A. XI	H	5-0
S	23.10.43	R.A.F. XI	H	3-4
S	30.10.43	CAMBRIDGE UNIVERSITY	H	7-3
S	06.11.43	NAVY XI	H	5-2
S	13.11.43	KINGS OWN RIFLES	H	2-2
S	20.11.43	R.A. XI	H	9-1
S	27.11.43	UNITED SERVICES XI	H	3-4
S	04.12.43	R.A. XI	H	2-3
S	11.12.43	BECCLES UNITED	A	2-3
S	18.12.43	EASTERN COMMAND	H	6-3
M	27.12.43	EASTERN COMMAND	H	3-2
S	08.01.44	R.A.F. XI	H	9-3
S	15.01.44	R.A.F. XI	H	5-1
S	22.01.44	R.A. XI	H	2-0
S	05.02.44	KINGS OWN RIGLES	H	3-0
S	12.02.44	R.A. XI	H	3-4
S	19.02.44	RECONNAISSANCE CORPS XI	H	9-4
S	26.02.44	EAST LANCS. REGIMENT	H	5-2

S	11.03.44	FITNESS LEAGUE XI	H	6-2
S	18.03.44	ROYAL ARTILLERY XI	H	2-2
S	25.03.44	R.A.F. XI	H	2-1
S	01.04.44	R.A. XI (AT YARMOUTH)	A	3-0
S	08.04.44	R.A.F. XI	H	7-3
M	10.04.44	ANTI-AIRCRAFT XI	H	2-5
S	15.04.44	ARMY XI	H	4-4
S	22.04.44	ROYAL ARTILLERY XI	H	4-0
S	29.04.44	ARMY XI	H	9-0
S	06.05.44	R.A.S.C. XI		

1944–45

S	16.09.44	R.A.F. XI	H	9-1
S	23.09.44	R.E.M.E. XI	H	5-0
S	30.09.44	R.A.F. XI	H	10-1
S	14.10.44	R.A.F. XI	H	8-1
S	21.10.44	CAMBRIDGE UNIVERSITY	H	6-2
S	28.10.44	R.A.C. XI	H	3-5
S	04.11.44	R.A.C. XI	H	5-1
S	11.11.44	FITNESS LEAGUE XI	H	8-1
S	18.11.44	R.A.F. XI	H	8-2
S	02.12.44	R.A.F. XI	H	7-2
S	09.12.44	UNITED SERVICES XI	H	3-4
S	16.12.44	R.A.F. XI	H	2-2
S	23.12.44	R.A.F. XI	H	1-5
Tu	26.12.44	R.A.F. XI	H	3-3
S	30.12.44	R.E.M.E. XI	H	7-0
S	06.01.45	R.E.M.E. XI	H	8-1
S	20.01.45	ROYAL CORP SIGNAL	H	3-3
S	03.02.45	ELY & DISTRICT XI	H	4-1
S	10.02.45	UNITED SERVICES XI (AT LOWESTOFT)	A	2-2
S	17.02.45	MINESWEEPERS	H	5-0
S	24.02.45	ROYAL NAVY XI	H	4-1
S	03.03.45	MET. POLICE	H	0-1
S	10.03.45	ARMY XI	H	0-4
S	17.03.45	ROYAL ARTILLERY XI	H	7-2
S	24.03.45	R.E.M.E. XI	H	11-1
S	31.03.45	YARMOUTH NAVY XI	A	7-3
M	02.04.45	ROYAL CORPS SIGNALS	H	2-3
S	07.04.45	LOWESTOFT NAVY XI	H	3-4
S	21.04.45	ARMY XI	H	4-2
S	28.04.45	ROYAL ARTILLERY	H	3-1

1945–46

S	08.09.45	GILLINGHAM	H	7-4
S	15.09.45	GILLINGHAM	A	3-3
S	17.11.45	CRYSTAL PALACE	H	2-5
S	24.11.45	CRYSTAL PALACE	A	0-4
S	15.12.45	SOUTHEND UNITED	H	4-2
S	27.04.46	IPSWICH TOWN (NORFOLK JUBILEE CUP)	H	1-2
S	04.05.46	IPSWICH TOWN (NORFOLK JUBILEE CUP)	A	2-3

1946–47

S	24.05.47	IPSWICH TOWN (NORFOLK JUBILEE CUP)	H	2-1

1947–48

S	10.01.48	ARSENAL XI	H	3-1
W	05.05.48	IPSWICH TOWN (NORFOLK JUBILEE CUP)	H	2-1

1948–49

M	25.04.49	LUTON TOWN (T) BERNARD ROBINSON	H	1-2
M	02.05.49	WISBECH TOWN (T) BERT BLACKSHAW	A	6-2
S	14.05.49	IPSWICH TOWN (NORFOLK JUBILEE CUP)	H	1-0

1949–50

S	28.01.59	FULHAM	H	1-1
W	10.05.50	IPSWICH TOWN (NORFOLK JUBILEE CUP)	A	1-2

1950–51

S	12.05.51	SERVETTE SWITZERLAND (FESTIVAL OF BRITAIN)	H	5-1

1951–52

S	18.05.52	ENSCHEDE XI (TOUR OF HOLLAND)	A	1-0
W	21.05.52	HAGUE COMBINED XI (TOUR OF HOLLAND)	A	2-1
Su	25.05.52	SITTARDIA (TOUR OF HOLLAND)	A	3-0
W	28.05.52	HAARLEM COMBINED XI (TOUR OF HOLLAND)	A	3-1

1952–53

Th	19.02.53	CAMBRIDGE UNIVERSITY	A	5-1

1953–54

W	20.01.54	ALL STAR XI (T) HARRY PROCTOR	H	2-4

1956–57

W	17.10.56	SUNDERLAND (OPENING OF FLOODLIGHTS)	H	0-3
W	31.10.56	THE ARMY	H	5-2
S	08.12.56	BRADFORD CITY	H	0-2
W	27.02.57	KING'S LYNN (CITY APPEAL FUND)	H	5-1
M	01.04.57	SHEFFIELD WEDNESDAY	H	0-2
M	08.04.57	ST. MIRREN	H	0-2

1957–58

W	30.10.57	HEART OF MIDLOTHIAN	H	3-4
W	06.11.57	ABERDEEN	H	1-0
W	18.12.57	THE ARMY	H	3-1
W	19.03.58	IPSWICH TOWN	H	2-2
M	28.04.58	IPSWICH TOWN (T) A. SCOTT DUNCAN	A	1-2

1958–59

W	29.10.58	WEST HAM UNITED	H	2-4
W	17.12.58	ROUEN (FRANCE)	H	3-2
M	20.04.59	SPALDING UNITED (T) DON PICKWICK	A	4-1
W	06.05.59	CRUSADERS	A	1-1
F	08.05.59	SHAMROCK ROVERS (T) MACKEY/AMBROSE	A	4-1
Th	14.05.59	ROUEN (FRANCE)	A	2-2

1959–60

M	12.10.59	HEART OF MIDLOTHIAN	A	0-0
W	21.10.59	NOTTINGHAM FOREST	H	3-1
W	04.11.59	FULHAM	H	4-3
S	05.12.59	NORTHAMPTON TOWN	H	0-2
W	23.03.60	KING'S LYNN	H	4-2
W	04.05.60	IPSWICH TOWN (IPSWICH HOSPITAL CUP)	A	0-1
M	09.05.60	SOUTHAMPTON	A	1-1

1960–61

M	03.10.60	CHELMSFORD CITY (FLOODLIGHTS OPENING)	A	3-2
W	19.10.60	ARSENAL	H	3-2
Tu	14.03.61	NORTHAMPTON TOWN	A	3-1
M	17.04.61	MOTHERWELL	H	2-0
F	12.05.61	DRUMCONDRA (DUBLIN)	A	1-2
Su	14.05.61	CORK CELTIC	A	5-3

1961–62

W	25.10.61	PETERBOROUGH UNITED	H	1-3
W	29.11.61	BELGRADE SPORTS CLUB	H	2-1
M	26.03.62	PETERBOROUGH UNITED	A	6-0
Th	03.05.62	PETERBOROUGH UNITED (NORFOLK INVITATION CUP)	H	2-4

1962–63

S	04.08.62	ST. MIRREN (PAISLEY CHARITY CUP)	A	1-1

1963–64

W	09.10.63	SLIEMA WANDERERS (MALTA)	H	5-0
Tu	21.01.64	SHEFFIELD WEDNESDAY	H	2-1
S	15.02.64	IPSWICH TOWN	A	1-2
W	26.02.64	INTERNATIONAL XI (T) BARRY STATON	H	1-3
M	09.03.64	PETERBOROUGH UNITED (NORFOLK INVITATION CUP)	A	1-3
W	22.04.64	IPSWICH TOWN (T) RON ASHMAN	H	0-0
Th	07.05.64	SLIEMA WANDERERS (TOUR OF MALTA)	A	4-3
S	09.05.64	COMBINED SERVICES XI (TOUR OF MALTA)	A	4-1
Su	10.05.64	VALLETTA CITY (TOUR OF MALTA)	A	1-1

1964–65

S	01.08.64	ST. MIRREN (PAISLEY CHARITY CUP)	A	0-0
Tu	11.08.64	CAMBRIDGE CITY	A	4-4
S	15.08.64	COLCHESTER UNITED	H	5-1
Tu	18.08.64	COLCHESTER UNITED	A	2-1
W	17.03.65	NYKOBING BOLDKLUB (DENMARK)	H	6-1
M	12.04.65	ST. MIRREN	H	1-1
M	26.04.65	E.C.L. PRESIDENT XI (AT LOWESTOFT)	A	5-1
Th	29.04.65	WISBECH TOWN (BANCROFT CUP)	A	4-2
S	08.05.65	S.C. TELSTAR (THE HAGUE)	A	4-3
Tu	11.05.65	ADO (THE HAGUE)	A	1-5
Th	13.05.65	DOS (UTRECHT)	A	2-1
Su	16.05.65	AJAX (AMSTERDAM)	A	1-5

1965–66

Tu	10.08.65	CAMBRIDGE CITY	A	5-1
W	11.08.65	MILLWALL	H	4-1
S	14.08.65	MILLWALL	A	0-1
M	16.08.65	SOUTHEND UNITED	A	2-2
W	10.11.65	ADO (THE HAGUE)	H	4-1
W	04.05.66	S.C. TELSTAR (THE HAGUE)	H	2-1
F	13.05.66	CHELMSFORD CITY	A	3-0
M	16.05.66	WISBECH TOWN (BANCROFT CUP)	A	2-3
W	25.05.66	IPSWICH TOWN (T) BARRY BUTLER	H	3-1
F	27.05.66	LOWESTOFT TOWN (FISHERMEN'S CHARITY – A.E.T.)	A	3-2
F	10.06.66	AKRANES (TOUR OF ICELAND)	A	6-1
Su	12.06.66	COMBINED XI (TOUR OF ICELAND)	A	2-1
W	15.06.66	KEFLAVIK (TOUR OF ICELAND)	A	3-2

1966–67

Tu	09.08.66	QUEEN'S PARK RANGERS	A	0-1
S	13.08.66	QUEEN'S PARK RANGERS	H	0-2
Su	14.05.67	DUNDALK (EIRE)	A	1-0

1967–68

Tu	08.08.67	WATFORD	A	2-1
Th	10.08.67	CAMBRIDGE UNITED	A	2-1
S	12.08.67	SHEFFIELD UNITED	H	3-1

W	04.10.67	SELECT XI (T) PHIL KELLY	H	6-3
M	13.11.67	DARLINGTON (T) GEORGE McGEACHIE	A	7-4
W	28.02.68	BRATISLAVA SLOVNAFT (CZECH)	H	1-0
F	17.05.68	LINCOLN CITY (T) JIM GRUMMITT	A	3-3

1968–69

S	27.07.68	DERRY CITY	A	1-0
Th	01.08.68	PETERBOROUGH UNITED	A	2-2
S	03.08.68	LUTON TOWN	H	2-2
S	25.01.69	NOTTINGHAM FOREST	H	1-1
W	30.04.69	IPSWICH TOWN (T) TERRY ALLCOCK	H	3-1
F	09.05.69	BENIDORM (SPAIN)	A	1-0

1969–70

F	01.08.69	FULHAM	A	3-1
M	04.08.69	ROTHERHAM UNITED	H	2-0
F	06.02.70	STOCKPORT COUNTY	A	2-0
S	14.03.70	STOKE CITY	H	2-1
Th	30.04.70	ROUEN (FRANCE)	A	4-1
S	24.07.70	RADNICKI (TOUR OF YUGOSLAVIA)	A	0-2
M	26.07.70	VOJVODINA (TOUR OF YUGOSLAVIA)	A	1-1
Th	29.07.70	BOR (TOUR OF YUGOSLAVIA)	A	2-1
F	07.08.70	COLCHESTER UNITED	A	1-1
M	03.05.71	SELECT XI (T) BILLY FURNESS	A	6-1
Th	06.05.71	ATLETICO LISBON (BATISTA TOURNAMENT)	A	2-1
S	08.05.71	DUNDEE (BATISTA TOURNAMENT)	A	5-3
Tu	11.05.71	SPORTING LISBON (BATISTA TOURNAMENT)	A	*1-1
Su	16.05.71	UNIANO PORTUGAL	A	1-1

* – CITY WON 4-2 ON PENALTIES AND WON THE TOURNAMENT

1971–72

W	04.08.71	IPSWICH TOWN	H	4-3
S	07.08.71	PETERBOROUGH UNITED	A	1-0
S	26.02.72	COVENTRY CITY	H	2-1
M	01.05.72	LOWESTOFT TOWN (FISHERMEN'S FUND)	H	6-0
W	03.05.72	ALL STAR XI (T) ALBERT BENNETT	H	0-1

1972–73

S	29.07.72	CAMBRIDGE UNITED	A	3-0
Tu	01.08.72	GRIMSBY TOWN	A	1-0
S	05.08.72	ST. MIRREN	H	4-1
Th	10.05.73	S.K. BRANN (NORWAY)	A	1-0

1973–74

S	11.08.73	COLCHESTER UNITED	A	4-2
Tu	14.08.73	FULHAM	A	1-3
S	18.08.73	SHELBOURNE (EIRE)	H	0-0
F	03.05.74	IPSWICH TOWN (T) KEVIN KEELAN	H	1-3
Tu	07.05.74	COLCHESTER UNITED	A	3-3
Th	09.05.74	LOWESTOFT TOWN (FISHERMEN'S FUND)	A	6-1

1974–75

M	12.08.74	TORQUAY UNITED	A	0-1
W	20.11.74	YEOVIL TOWN (T) HOUSLEY/CLANCY/CLARK	A	2-2
F	02.05.75	ALL STAR XI (T) JIMMY THOMPSON	A	4-2
W	07.05.75	COLCHESTER UNITED (T) PAUL AIMSON	A	2-3
F	09.05.75	WEST HAM UNITED (T) DAVE STRINGER	H	1-1
M	12.05.75	LOWESTOFT TOWN (FISHERMEN'S FUND)	A	0-1
F	23.05.75	GILLINGHAM	A	1-1
S	31.05.75	GORMAHIA (NAIROBI) (TOUR OF KENYA)	A	4-1
Su	01.06.75	ABALUHYA (NAIROBI) (TOUR OF KENYA)	A	6-1
S	07.06.75	CHAMPION KENYA (TOUR OF KENYA)	A	8-0
Su	08.06.75	MWENGE (MOMBASA) (TOUR OF KENYA)	A	3-1
Tu	10.06.75	YOUNG AFRICANS (TOUR OF KENYA)	A	2-1

1975–76

S	02.08.75	FULHAM (ANGLO SCOTTISH CUP)	H	1-2
W	06.08.75	CHELSEA (ANGLO SCOTTISH CUP)	A	1-1
S	09.08.75	BRISTOL CITY (ANGLO SCOTTISH CUP)	A	1-4
M	11.08.75	PETERBOROUGH UNITED	A	3-2
Tu	14.10.75	ALDERSHOT	A	2-1
M	19.01.76	BOURNEMOUTH (T) ARTHUR CUNLIFFE	A	3-0
M	09.02.76	RED STAR BELGRADE	H	0-1
Tu	27.04.76	BRIGHTON & HOVE ALBION	A	2-2
M	03.05.76	LARVIK TURN (TOUR OF NORWAY)	A	5-3
W	05.05.76	VARD (HAVGESUND) (TOUR OF NORWAY)	A	0-1
Th	06.05.76	SKEID (OSLO) (TOUR OF NORWAY)	A	2-0
M	10.05.76	PRESIDENT'S XI (TOUR OF TRINIDAD)	A	0-2
F	14.05.76	COMBINED CLUBS XI (TOUR OF TRINIDAD)	A	3-0

1976–77

S	07.08.76	ORIENT (ANGLO SCOTTISH CUP)	H	0-0
W	11.08.76	CHELSEA (ANGLO SCOTTISH CUP)	A	1-1
S	14.08.76	FULHAM (ANGLO SCOTTISH CUP)	A	1-1
Tu	16.11.76	TORQUAY UNITED	A	4-3
M	21.02.77	SHEFFIELD WEDNESDAY (T) NEIL O'DONNELL	A	0-2
M	09.05.77	IPSWICH TOWN (T) COLIN VILJOEN	A	1-2
M	16.05.77	BRIGHTON & HOVE ALBION	A	2-1
W	18.05.77	MANSFIELD TOWN	A	2-3
M	23.05.77	OXFORD UNITED (T) COLIN CLARKE	A	2-2

1977–78

S	30.07.77	EXETER CITY	A	0-5
M	01.08.77	PLYMOUTH ARGYLE	A	0-3
W	03.08.77	TORQUAY UNITED	A	1-1
S	06.08.77	ORIENT (ANGLO SCOTTISH CUP)	H	1-1
W	10.08.77	FULHAM (ANGLO SCOTTISH CUP)	H	0-1
S	13.08.77	CHELSEA (ANGLO SCOTTISH CUP)	A	2-2
M	26.09.77	LAVAL (FRANCE – PONT L'ABBE FESTIVAL)	A	2-2
M	24.10.77	BEDFORD TOWN (T) SKINN/COOLEY	A	4-0
F	17.02.78	CHARLTON ATHLETIC	A	2-3
Tu	11.04.78	NORWICH CITY 71/72 SIDE (T) DUNCAN FORBES	H	0-3
W	03.05.78	TAMPA BAY ROWDIES (TOUR OF U.S.A.)	*A	11-10
S	13.05.78	U.S.A. NATIONAL UNDER 21 XI (TOUR OF U.S.A.)	**A	1-0

* – PLAYED INDOORS AT BAYFRONT CENTRE, ST. PETERSBURG
** – PLAYED AT TAMPA STADIUM

1978–79

S	29.07.78	CAMBRIDGE UNITED (WILLHIRE CUP)	A	3-1
Tu	01.08.78	COLCHESTER UNITED (WILLHIRE CUP)	A	2-1
S	05.08.78	NOTTS. COUNTY (ANGLO SCOTTISH CUP)	A	1-2
Tu	08.08.78	IPSWICH TOWN (WILLHIRE CUP)	A	1-2
W	09.08.78	MANSFIELD TOWN (ANGLO SCOTTISH CUP)	H	1-1
S	12.08.78	ORIENT (ANGLO SCOTTISH CUP)	H	0-0
M	14.08.78	HILLINGDON BOROUGH (T) 'NOBBY' CLARK	A	0-0
M	11.09.78	BEDFORD TOWN (T) FOLDS/GOULD	A	4-3
Tu	26.09.78	WINTERTHUR (SWITZERLAND)	A	3-1
W	18.10.78	ENGLAND 1966 WORLD CUP XI (T) MARTIN PETERS	H	4-2
W	15.11.78	IFK GOTHENBURG (SWEDEN)	H	3-0
M	27.11.78	BRISTOL CITY (T) PAUL CHEESLEY	A	6-3
M	05.02.79	IPSWICH TOWN (T) TREVOR WHYMARK	A	1-2
M	23.04.79	SKEGNESS TOWN (T) CHRIS DANIELS	A	6-3
M	30.04.79	DISS TOWN (NOBBS CUP)	A	7-2
F	11.05.79	NEW ZEALAND XI – (AUCKLAND)	A	4-1
Su	13.05.79	WESTERN AUSTRALIA – (PERTH)	A	2-1
W	16.05.79	SOUTH AUSTRALIA – (ADELAIDE)	A	4-0
Su	20.05.79	VICTORIA – (MELBOURNE)	A	4-2
Tu	22.05.79	QUEENSLAND – (BRISBANE)	A	1-0
Th	24.05.79	NEWCASTLE KB UTD. – (NEWCASTLE)	A	3-0
Su	27.05.79	NEW SOUTH WALES – (SYDNEY)	A	1-4

1979–80

S	28.07.79	CAMBRIDGE UNITED (WILLHIRE CUP)	A	0-2
Th	02.08.79	COLCHESTER UNITED (WILLHIRE CUP)	A	2-2
M	06.08.79	GILLINGHAM	A	3-3
Th	09.08.79	LOWESTOFT TOWN	A	2-0
Tu	14.08.79	IPSWICH TOWN (WILLHIRE CUP)	H	2-0
Tu	16.10.79	SAFFRON WALDEN (OPENING FLOODLIGHTS)	A	10-1
M	22.10.79	NEW ZEALAND XI	H	5-0
Su	04.11.79	DOWNHAM TOWN (T) ALAN HEMMINGS	A	9-1
Tu	11.12.79	ENGLAND XI (T) BILLY STEELE	H	0-5
Tu	18.03.80	CHELSEA (NORFOLK INVITATION CUP)	H	2-0
M	21.04.80	OXFORD UNITED (T) ROY BURTON	A	1-1
Tu	06.05.80	MAIDSTONE UNITED (T) PETER SILVESTER	A	4-0
Th	15.05.80	CHINA NATIONAL XI – (PEKING)	A	2-0
Su	18.05.80	HEBEI PROVINCE – (HEBEI)	A	2-0
W	21.05.80	AUGUST 1st ARMY XI – (PEKING)	A	0-0
Su	25.05.80	BULOVA – (HONG KING)	A	2-1

1980–81

Tu	29.07.80	CAMBRIDGE UNITED (WILLHIRE CUP)	H	4-0
Th	31.07.80	COLCHESTER UNITED (WILLHIRE CUP)	H	1-1
M	04.08.80	GILLINGHAM	A	2-2
W	06.08.80	SUDBURY TOWN (T) BILL BOWEN	A	5-1
F	08.08.80	CHELSEA	H	1-1
Tu	12.08.80	IPSWICH TOWN (WILLHIRE CUP)	A	2-2
M	15.09.80	SPALDING UNITED (FLOODLIGHTS OPENING)	A	4-0
M	13.10.80	WEST BROMWICH ALBION (T) PAUL KENT	N	*2-3
Tu	25.11.80	ALL STAR XI (KEVIN KEELAN FAREWELL)	H	4-3
S	07.03.81	BIRMINGHAM CITY (AT BOSTON)	A	0-2
S	09.05.81	FLORIDA UNIVERSITY (TOUR OF U.S.A.)	A	6-0
M	11.05.81	ATLANTA CHIEFS (TOUR OF U.S.A.)	A	1-2
Tu	12.05.81	FORT LAUDERDALE STRIKERS (TOUR OF U.S.A.)	A	0-4

* – PLAYED AT SPALDING

1981–82

W	05.08.81	GLENTORAN (TOUR OF NORTHERN IRELAND)	A	2-0
Th	06.08.81	GLENAVON (TOUR OF NORTHERN IRELAND)	A	3-0
M	10.08.81	SOUTHEND UNITED	A	1-1
W	12.08.81	TOTTENHAM HOTSPUR	H	2-2
S	15.08.81	PETERBOROUGH UNITED (GROUP CUP)	H	2-2
W	19.08.81	LINCOLN CITY (GROUP CUP)	A	1-0
S	22.08.81	NOTTS. COUNTY (GROUP CUP)	H	3-0
W	30.09.81	FORT LAUDERDALE STRIKERS	H	2-2
Tu	22.12.81	IPSWICH TOWN – (AT GREAT YARMOUTH)	N	5-1
W	06.01.82	ABERDEEN	H	1-4
F	05.03.82	NOTTINGHAM FOREST	H	1-1
Tu	30.03.82	WOKINGHAM TOWN	A	1-1
W	26.05.82	JAMAICA NATIONSL XI – (AT KINGSTON)	A	1-0

1982–83

F	06.08.82	CORBY TOWN – (ABAN. HALF-TIME RAIN)	A	1-0
M	09.08.82	SOUTHEND UNITED	A	0-4
W	11.08.82	BOURNEMOUTH	A	1-3
S	14.08.82	NORTHAMPTON TOWN (F. LEAGUE TROPHY)	H	3-0
W	18.08.82	PETERBOROUGH UNITED (F. LEAGUE TROPHY)	H	6-2
S	21.08.82	MANSFIELD TOWN (F. LEAGUE TROPHY)	A	3-1
W	15.09.82	KING'S LYNN	A	2-0
Tu	19.10.82	WOODFORD TOWN	A	2-2
Tu	16.11.82	ALL STAR XI (T) DAVID JONES	H	3-2
W	08.12.82	LINCOLN CITY (F. LEAGUE TROPHY)	A	1-3
Tu	18.01.83	GORLESTON (FLOODLIGHTS OPENING)	A	3-1
M	16.05.83	KARNES (TOUR OF NORWAY)	A	17-1
Tu	17.05.83	TROMSO (TOUR OF NORWAY)	A	1-0
Th	19.05.83	SORTLAND (TOUR OF NORWAY)	A	11-2
F	20.05.83	F.C. MOLDE (TOUR OF NORWAY)	A	5-2

1983–84

S	16.07.83	A.F.C. LEOPARDS NAIROBI (TOUR OF KENYA)	A	0-1
Su	17.07.83	GOR MAHIA NAIROBI (TOUR OF KENYA)	A	2-4
F	22.07.83	CARGO F.C. MOMBASA (TOUR OF KENYA)	A	3-0
Su	24.07.83	KENYA BREWERIES MOMBASA (TOUR OF KENYA)	A	2-2
Tu	02.08.83	LILLEHAMMER (TOUR OF NORWAY)	A	7-0
Th	04.08.83	DRAMMEN (TOUR OF NORWAY)	A	5-3
S	06.08.83	DROBAK/FROGN (TOUR OF NORWAY)	A	6-0
S	13.08.83	WOKINGHAM TOWN	A	7-0
Tu	16.08.83	GRIMSBY TOWN	A	1-2
S	20.08.83	CAMBRIDGE UNITED (CAMB. PRO. CUP)	A	*1-1
M	10.10.83	KING'S LYNN (DAIRY CREST CUP)	A	1-0
Tu	28.02.84	HAMRUN SPARTANS (MALTA)	A	1-0
Tu	06.03.84	LOWESTOFT TOWN	A	2-1
F	23.03.84	DUNDEE	H	3-2
M	09.04.84	KING'S LYNN (T) FREDDIE EASTHALL	A	2-2
Th	17.05.84	TROMSO (TOUR OF NORWAY)	A	1-0
F	18.05.84	BARDUFOSS & OMEGN (TOUR OF NORWAY)	A	0-0
S	19.05.84	SORTLAND (TOUR OF NORWAY)	A	7-2

* – CAMBRIDGE WON ON PENALTIES

1984–85

Su	29.07.84	BRUMUNDDAL (TOUR OF NORWAY)	A	1-2
M	30.07.84	JEVNAKER (TOUR OF NORWAY)	A	2-0
Tu	31.07.84	RAUFOSS (TOUR OF NORWAY)	A	5-1
W	01.08.84	FREDRIKSTAD (TOUR OF NORWAY)	A	0-4
F	03.08.84	ULLERN (TOUR OF NORWAY)	A	3-1
Su	05.08.84	SAFFLE-ALLIANSEN (TOUR OF SWEDEN)	A	2-1
Tu	07.08.84	IFK VELENS VARMLANDS (TOUR OF SWEDEN)	A	5-0
Th	09.08.84	WARGONS (TOUR OF SWEDEN)	A	3-2
S	11.08.84	AHLAFORS (TOUR OF SWEDEN)	A	2-2
Su	12.08.84	FILIPSTADS (TOUR OF SWEDEN)	A	3-0
S	18.08.84	CAMBRIDGE UNITED (CAMB. PRO. CUP)	A	3-0
Su	30.09.84	CHATHAM TOWN	A	5-0
M	22.10.84	KING'S LYNN (DAIRY CREST CUP)	A	5-2
M	03.12.84	STOWMARKET (OPENING FLOODLIGHTS)	A	6-4
Tu	26.03.85	NORWICH CITY 1974/75 SIDE (T) GREG DOWNS	H	7-6

1985–86

Tu	30.07.85	GILLINGHAM	A	2-1
Th	01.08.85	READING	A	2-0
S	03.08.85	SLOUGH TOWN	A	1-0
W	07.08.85	CAMBRIDGE UNITED (CAMB. PRO. CUP)	A	4-1
S	10.08.85	TOTTENHAM HOTSPUR	H	1-1
M	14.10.85	TRIMTOC (TRINIDAD) (AT PORT OF SPAIN)	N	1-1
Tu	15.10.85	LUTON TOWN (AT SAN FERNANDO)	N	2-3
S	01.03.86	CAMBRIDGE UNITED	H	1-0
W	19.03.86	KING'S LYNN (DAIRY CREST CUP)	H	3-0
W	26.03.86	IPSWICH TOWN (T) PAUL COOPER	A	1-0

1986–87

Su	27.07.86	LYCKSELE IF (TOUR OF SWEDEN)	A	1-
Tu	29.07.86	MORO-BERGSBY (TOUR OF SWEDEN)	A	2-
Th	31.07.86	HARNOSAND (TOUR OF SWEDEN)	A	9-
M	04.08.86	TEGS SK (TOUR OF SWEDEN)	A	1-
Tu	05.08.86	FRISKA VILJOR (TOUR OF SWEDEN)	A	5-
S	09.08.86	SOUTHEND UNITED	A	0-
Tu	12.08.86	CAMBRIDGE UNITED	A	3-
S	16.08.86	COLCHESTER UNITED	A	2-
Tu	19.08.86	LOWESTOFT TOWN	A	4-
M	01.12.86	RAJA (CASABLANCA)	A	1-
W	01.04.87	MINEHEAD	A	4-
Tu	12.05.87	SOUTHEND UNITED	A	1-
M	18.05.87	BOURNEMOUTH	A	2-
S	30.05.87	BRAVERT CO SELECT XI (TOUR OF USA)	A	7-
Su	31.05.87	ORLANDO LIONS (TOUR OF USA)	A	2-
F	05.06.87	SEATTLE STORM (TOUR OF USA)	A	0-
Su	07.06.87	CALIFORNIA KICKERS (TOUR OF USA)	A	4-

1987–88

Th	23.07.87	HARADS IF (TOUR OF SWEDEN)	A	9-
Su	26.07.87	MJOLNER FK (TOUR OF NORWAY)	A	2-
Tu	28.07.87	OTP (TOUR OF FINLAND)	A	1-
Th	30.07.87	KEPS (TOUR OF FINLAND)	A	0-
Su	02.08.87	BURTRASKS IF (TOUR OF SWEDEN)	A	4-
M	03.08.87	LULEA (TOUR OF SWEDEN)	A	3-
S	08.08.87	REAL SOCIEDAD (T) PETER MENDHAM	H	2-
Tu	29.09.87	FAKENHAM TOWN	A	9-
F	26.02.88	OLDHAM ATHLETIC	H	1-
W	13.04.88	SOUTHEND UNITED	A	3-
Tu	17.05.88	GIBRALTA SELECT XI	A	0-

1988–89

Su	07.08.88	CLEVEDON TOWN	A	5-
Mo	08.08.88	BATH CITY	A	2-
We	10.08.88	MANGOTSFIELD	A	8-
Th	11.08.88	GLOUCESTER CITY	A	3-
S	13.08.88	HEREFORD UNITED	A	0-
Tu	16.08.88	MANSFIELD TOWN	A	1-
F	19.08.88	IPSWICH TOWN (IPSWICH H.C.)	A	1-
W	01.03.89	DYNAMO MOSCOW	H	0-
M	15.05.89	JOHN O'NEILL XI (T)	H	2-
W	24.05.89	ARIS SALONIKA (GREECE)	A	1-

1989–90

M	24.07.89	EDSBRO IF (TOUR OF SWEDEN)	A	4-
W	26.07.89	VASTERAS TOWN (TOUR OF SWEDEN)	A	2-
S	29.07.89	VASTRA NYLANDS (TOUR OF FINLAND)	A	7-
Su	30.07.89	STARBLACKA NOFFKOPING (TOUR OF SWEDEN)	A	7-
T	01.08.89	IK BRAGE (TOUR OF SWEDEN)	A	0-
S	07.08.89	CAMBRIDGE UNITED (T) A. CHAPMAN	A	2-
W	09.08.89	ARIS SALONIKA (GREECE)	H	1-
F	16.02.90	FERENCVAROS (HUNGARY) NRFK FA INV. CUP	H	2-
Tu	20.02.90	SUTTON UNITED (T) A. RAINS/M. STEPHENS	A	7-
Th	10.05.90	GUANCHOW (CHINA)	A	1-
S	12.05.90	CHINESE NAT XI (CHINA)	A	0-

1990–91

M	30.07.90	ORKANGER/ORDAL (NORWAY TOUR)	A	3-
W	01.08.90	MOLDE (NORWAY TOUR)	A	2-
Th	02.08.90	STRINDHEIM (NORWAY TOUR)	A	1-
M	06.08.90	STJ ORDALS/BRINK (NORWAY TOUR)	A	5-
Tu	07.08.90	NESSEGUTTEN (NORWAY TOUR)	A	2-
S	11.08.90	WATFORD	A	1-
Tu	14.08.90	HEYBRIDGE SWIFTS	A	0-
F	17.08.90	IPSWICH TOWN (IPSWICH H.C.)	A	1-

1992-93

† denotes games of 60 minutes duration

Tu	21.07.92	OK ODDEVOLD	A	1-2	SWEDISH TOUR TRIANGULAR TOURNAMENT
W	22.07.92	ALVENA-MARDAKLEVS IK	A	5-0	SWEDISH TOUR TRIANGULAR TOURNAMENT
F	24.07.92	OSCERLEN SELECT XI	A	4-0†	SWEDISH TOUR TRIANGULAR TOURNAMENT
F	24.07.92	SVENTORPS IF.MALMO FF	A	0-1†	SWEDISH TOUR TRIANGULAR TOURNAMENT
Su	26.07.92	G.A.I.S. (GOTHENBURG)	A	2-1	SWEDISH TOUR TRIANGULAR TOURNAMENT
M	27.07.92	MARKARYDS IF	A	1-3	SWEDISH TOUR TRIANGULAR TOURNAMENT
W	29.07.92	TRELLEBORG FF	A	1-2	SWEDISH TOUR TRIANGULAR TOURNAMENT
S	01.08.92	COLCHESTER UTD	A	3-1	
Tu	04.08.92	SOUTHEND UTD	A	1-1	
S	08.08.92	OXFORD UTD	A	2-1	OXFORDSHIRE BENEVOLENT CUP
M	10.8.92	ZENIT ST. PETERSBURG	H	1-1	
Tu	25.8.92	KUWAIT	H	1-2	
S	10.10.92	OTELUL GALATI (ROMANIA)	A	2-3	
Tu	05.01.93	MONTPELIER HERAULT SC (FRANCE)	A	1-3	
W	12.05.93	JAMAICA	A	1-2	CARIBBEAN TOUR
Su	16.05.93	CAYMAN ISLANDS	A	0-1	CARIBBEAN TOUR

1993-94

* PLAYED AT MILE HIGH STADIUM, DENVER

F	16.07.93	FC COPENHAGEN	N*	3-3	FOUR NATIONS CUP SEMI-FINAL, COPENHAGEN WON 4-3 ON PENALTIES
S	17.07.93	COLORADO FOXES	N*	2-3	3RD PLACE PLAY-OFF
Su	25.07.93	NACKA FF	A	3-1	SWEDISH TOUR
M	26.07.93	IFK VASTERAS	A	1-1	SWEDISH TOUR
W	28.07.93	BKV NORRTALJE	A	6-2	SWEDISH TOUR
S	31.07.93	KRYLBO IF	A	15-0	SWEDISH TOUR
W	04.08.93	SCUNTHORPE UTD	A	2-0	
S	07.08.93	BIRMINGHAM CITY	A	3-2	BIRMINGHAM-E. ANGLIA REGIONAL CHALLENGE TROPHY
M	09.05.94	GENOA (ITALY) (T) J. GOSS	H	4-5	

1994-95

S	23.07.94	CORBY TOWN	A	4-1	CITY FIELDED TEAMS OF MIXED 1ST-2ND TEAM PLAYERS
S	23.07.94	RUSHDEN & DIAMONDS	A	0-0	CITY FIELDED TEAMS OF MIXED 1ST-2ND TEAM PLAYERS
F	29.07.94	VITESSE ARNHEM	A	0-2	DUTCH TOUR
Su	31.07.94	DEN BOSCH	A	2-1	DUTCH TOUR
W	03.08.94	ROYAL ANTWERP	A	2-0	BELGIAN TOUR
S	06.08.94	MECHELEN	A	0-0	BELGIAN TOUR
M	08.08.94	PETERBOROUGH UTD	A	2-1	
S	13.08.94	PROGRESUL BUCHAREST (ROMANIA)	A	0-1	PLAYED AT NATIONAL STADIUM

1995-96

W	19.07.95	COLERAINE	A	2-1	IRISH TOUR
S	22.07.95	GLANAVON	A	1-0	IRISH TOUR
M	24.07.95	ARDS	A	5-0	IRISH TOUR
W	26.07.95	GLENTORAN	A	2-1	IRISH TOUR
S	29.07.95	DERBY CITY	A	1-0	IRISH TOUR
W	02.08.95	SWINDON TOWN	A	2-1	
S	05.08.95	BRISTOL ROVERS	N	0-3	PLAYED AT YEOVIL
M	07.08.95	AFC BOURNEMOUTH	A	4-2	

1996-97

Su	21.07.96	KILKENNY CITY	A	4-2	IRISH TOUR
M	22.07.96	HOME FARM EVERTON	A	2-1	IRISH TOUR
W	24.07.96	BRAY WANDERERS	A	2-0	IRISH TOUR
S	27.07.96	LINCOLN CITY	A	1-1	
W	31.07.96	MANSFIELD TOWN	A	2-1	
S	03.08.96	NORTHAMPTON TOWN	A	0-0	
W	07.08.96	LUTON TOWN	A	0-2	
S	10.08.96	SPARTA ROTTERDAM (HOLLAND) (T) I. CROOK	H	0-0	
M	04.11.96	MANCHESTER UTD XI (T) B. GUNN	H	0-3	

1997-98

W	16.07.97	HIBERNIAN	A	2-0	SCOTTISH TOUR
S	19.07.97	ST. MIRREN	A	2-2	SCOTTISH TOUR
M	21.07.97	DUMBARTON	A	2-3	SCOTTISH TOUR
W	23.07.97	DISS TOWN (T) W. PUNTON	A	2-1	
F	25.07.97	BOLTON WANDERERS	H	0-1	
Tu	29.07.97	CAMBRIDGE UTD	A	1-1	
F	01.08.97	PETERBOROUGH UTD	A	0-1	
M	04.08.97	ARSENAL	H	2-6	

1998-99

Th	16.07.98	BRAY WANDERERS	A	2-1	IRISH TOUR
S	18.07.98	ST. PATRICK'S ATHLETIC	A	0-1	IRISH TOUR
M	20.07.98	LONGFORD TOWN	A	4-0	IRISH TOUR
W	22.07.98	HOME FARM EVERTON	A	2-2	
S	25.07.98	ENFIELD	A	3-0	
W	29.07.98	TOTTENHAM HOTSPUR	H	1-3	
M	03.08.98	LEICESTER CITY	H	0-1	

1999-2000

W	14.07.99	COLCHESTER UTD	A	1-1	SWEDISH TOUR
F	16.07.99	SOUTHEND UTD	A	1-2	SWEDISH TOUR
Tu	20.07.99	HELSINGBORG IF	A	1-0	SWEDISH TOUR
S	24.07.99	NORDOST	A	2-1	SWEDISH TOUR
Tu	27.07.99	ORGRYTE	A	1-4	SWEDISH TOUR
F	30.07.99	AZ ALKMAAR (HOLLAND) (T) D. SUTCH	H	0-0	

2000-01

Tu	11.07.00	LOWESTOFT TOWN	A	4-0	
W	12.07.00	DEREHAM TOWN	A	9-0	
S	15.07.00	ST. JOHNSTONE	A	1-2	SCOTTISH TOUR
W	19.07.00	QUEEN'S PARK	A	4-0	SCOTTISH TOUR
S	22.07.00	DUNFERMLINE ATHLETIC	A	0-1	SCOTTISH TOUR
S	29.07.00	HEERENVEEN (HOLLAND)	H	1-1	
Tu	01.08.00	CAMBRIDGE UTD	A	2-1	
S	05.08.00	MILLWALL	A	1-1	
M	22.01.01	GLASGOW CELTIC (T) T. SHEPPARD	H	2-4	

2001-02

Tu	10.07.01	DEREHAM TOWN	A	3-0	
W	11.07.01	FAKENHAM TOWN	A	8-1	
S	14.07.01	ST. MIRREN	A	3-2	SCOTTISH TOUR
Tu	17.07.01	QUEENS PARK	A	1-0	SCOTTISH TOUR
S	21.07.01	MOTHERWELL	A	0-0	SCOTTISH TOUR
W	25.07.01	COLCHESTER UTD	A	3-2	
S	28.07.01	LEICESTER CITY	H	2-2	
Tu	31.07.01	CAMBRIDGE UTD	A	0-0	
S	04.08.01	LUTON TOWN	A	3-1	
Tu	07.08.01	ARSENAL	H	2-4